THE MODERN LIBRARY

of the World's Best Books

SIXTEEN FAMOUS AMERICAN PLAYS

>>

>>

SIXTEEN FAMOUS AMERICAN PLAYS

EDITED BY
BENNETT A. CERF
AND
VAN H. CARTMELL

With an Introduction by
Brooks Atkinson

THE MODERN LIBRARY
NEW YORK

THE MODERN LIBRARY

IS PUBLISHED BY

RANDOM HOUSE, INC.

BENNETT A. CERF • DONALD S. KLOPFER • ROBERT K. HAAS

Manufactured in the United States of America
By H. Wolff

ACKNOWLEDGMENTS

For permission to include the following plays, acknowledgment is here made to the authors of the plays and the publishers under whose imprint they were originally issued:

Ah, Wilderness!, *Boy Meets Girl*, *Dead End*, *"Having Wonderful Time,"* *The Little Foxes*, *The Man Who Came to Dinner*, *The Women* and *Waiting for Lefty* reprinted by permission of Random House, Inc.

Biography reprinted by permission of Brandt and Brandt, Inc., and Random House, Inc.

Life with Father reprinted from Clarence Day's *Life with Father*, made into a play by Howard Lindsay and Russel Crouse, by permission of and special arrangement with Alfred A. Knopf, Inc., authorized publishers.

Our Town reprinted by permission of Coward, McCann, Inc.

The Front Page reprinted by permission of Covici, Friede, Inc.

The Green Pastures reprinted by permission of Farrar and Rinehart, Inc.

The Petrified Forest reprinted by permission of Charles Scribner's Sons.

The Time of Your Life reprinted by permission of Harcourt, Brace and Company, Inc.

They Knew What They Wanted reprinted by permission of the Theatre Guild, Inc., and Samuel French.

FOREWORD

The selection of sixteen modern American plays for an anthology must necessarily be arbitrary. Limitation of space prevented the inclusion of a score of plays that had as obvious claims for recognition as those that were chosen. Granted the fact that we could include only sixteen, we exercised our personal preferences. Fortunately, we secured permission to reprint every play that we wanted, and owe a debt of genuine gratitude to the playwrights and publishers for their courtesy—particularly to those concerned with resounding successes that are still playing to capacity audiences on Broadway and on tour.

The sixteen plays in this collection have many things in common. All of them are products of the past two fruitful decades in the American theatre. All of them are by native playwrights and are concerned with native themes. All of them were outstanding commercial successes, and most of them will continue to be played by professional and amateur groups for many years to come. Three of them are Pulitzer Prize winners.

The plays are arranged chronologically, in the order of their original presentation on the Broadway stage. The texts in every case are complete and unabridged. No two plays are by the same author. And the selection was purposely made to cover as wide a variety of themes as possible—the open spaces, Hollywood, Park Avenue, the small towns and the big ones, rich people and poor. The moods range from the nostalgia of *Ah, Wilderness!* and *Life with Father* to the bitterness of *Waiting for Lefty* and *The Little Foxes* and the fantasy of *The Green Pastures* and *The Time of Your Life*. If there is a preponderance of comedy, it is because the American theatre has reached its greatest form of development in that medium—and, we repeat, because the editors have exercised their personal prerogatives in the selection.

The contents of this volume had been decided upon before

Brooks Atkinson was asked to contribute an introduction to it. What brickbats may be hurled at it, therefore, what indignant protests at the exclusion of plays that other editors might have fought and bled for, should be aimed directly at the heads of the undersigned.

BENNETT A. CERF
and
VAN H. CARTMELL

New York
January, 1941

CONTENTS

		PAGE
INTRODUCTION	Brooks Atkinson	xi
THEY KNEW WHAT THEY WANTED	Sidney Howard	5
THE FRONT PAGE	Ben Hecht and Charles MacArthur	59
THE GREEN PASTURES	Marc Connelly	147
BIOGRAPHY	S. N. Behrman	207
AH, WILDERNESS!	Eugene O'Neill	279
THE PETRIFIED FOREST	Robert Sherwood	361
WAITING FOR LEFTY	Clifford Odets	423
DEAD END	Sidney Kingsley	453
BOY MEETS GIRL	Bella and Samuel Spewack	537
THE WOMEN	Clare Boothe	603
"HAVING WONDERFUL TIME"	Arthur Kober	681
OUR TOWN	Thornton Wilder	751
THE LITTLE FOXES	Lillian Hellman	799
THE MAN WHO CAME TO DINNER	Moss Hart and George S. Kaufman	857
THE TIME OF YOUR LIFE	William Saroyan	921
LIFE WITH FATHER	Howard Lindsay and Russel Crouse	983

INTRODUCTION

BY BROOKS ATKINSON

During the past two or three days I have been having a good time. I have been reading the sixteen plays that constitute this volume. As a professional theatregoer of mellowing vintage I have met all but one of them in line of duty and might reasonably be expected to remember their salient characteristics. But to refresh my mind about Sidney Howard's *They Knew What They Wanted,* which was produced the year before my term as drama critic began, I started the other day to read the printed text. Since it made good reading and revived good memories, I ventured on to *The Front Page,* which is a volcano. In short, I have just emerged from the glow of reading all sixteen. Although they are only part of the fifty or seventy-five excellent plays written in the period between 1924 and 1939, I can honestly endorse them as lively reading and as evidence of the continuous vitality of the American theatre.

In the years before his harrowing death in 1939, Sidney Howard wrote at least two other major dramas—*The Silver Cord,* which brought the theatre up to date in the science of human behavior, and *Yellow Jack,* which taught the theatre how to tell a heroic story in experimental medicine. Both those plays pushed the theatre a little further ahead as a mature form of popular art and might logically find a place in a book like this one. But I think I have an affection for *They Knew What They Wanted* that goes a little deeper than my admiration for his two best works of later years. For his romantic and savory story of love and magnanimity in a California vineyard was his first popular success. It also presented with warmth and sympathy some of the best characters he ever created. Those of us who saw the Theatre Guild's production of *They Knew What They Wanted* in 1924 will never be able to read the racy dialogue of Mr. Howard's drama without hearing the voices of Pauline Lord, Richard Bennett and Glenn Anders rising and falling over the crises of the story. Those voices, all distinct and individual with remarkable contrast in tone and inflection, still haunt the text of the play.

On a sticky August evening in 1928, *The Front Page* swept into town and bowled over the public with the excitement and sting of a callous newspaper story. Up to that time there had never been a newspaper drama that newspaper people could recognize as authentic; since 1928 there has never been another. For Ben Hecht and Charles MacArthur, hardened from leg-work on Chicago newspapers, still had a relish for the alertness, cynicism, shrewdness, penury and exuberance of the working newspaper man and they missed none of it in the characterizations of their drama. *The Front Page* is to journalism what *What Price Glory?* is to the marines—rudely realistic in style but romantic in its loyalties, and also audaciously profane. I cannot pretend that I still hear any individual voices above the resonant hubbub of that melodrama, but I can still see Lee Tracy nervously racing through the plot and Osgood Perkins, an extraordinarily skillful actor—now dead, alas—cutting through the uproar like a bright, sharp penknife, and peeling off the layers of the plot as he went along.

Probably there was a little rejoicing in heaven, in addition to the usual jubilation on Broadway, on the night of February 26, 1930. For Marc Connelly's classic, *The Green Pastures*, opened then; and as Rollo Ogden, venerable editor of the New York *Times*, remarked to me the next morning, Broadway "got religion" immediately. Using some of Roark Bradford's Negro stories as his source book, Mr. Connelly was telling the story of the Bible as a Negro Sunday School might imagine it, and his play has become a genuine part of American dramatic culture. I had gone to the theatre that evening with no particular knowledge of what was to take place. When the curtain rose the quiet scene laid in a Negro Sunday School was disarming enough. Then, while the scene was being changed, the Hall Johnson choir sang, "Rise, Shine, Give God the Glory," which was profoundly moving, and the ensuing scene representing a festival in heaven was both humorous and tender. Then came the greatest entrance cue in modern drama. "Gangway!" the Angel Gabriel called, "Gangway for de Lawd God Jehovah!" On to the stage walked a kindly, broad-shouldered man of many years, in a parson's coat. At that moment *The Green Pastures* became a classic. The man was Richard B. Harrison, a Negro reader, lecturer and teacher, who had never been on the stage before. As a person of genuine devotion, he had feared that *The Green Pastures* might be irreverent or sacrilegious. It turned out to be quite the contrary, and partly because of Harrison's playing. For he was a man of broadness of soul. After he had been playing the part a few weeks it was hard not to believe that a special divinity surrounded him. He was treated with great respect backstage. On two occasions I had the honor of meeting him socially, and I confess that I stood considerably in awe of him, for he was a thoughtful conversationalist, slow and sincere, anxious not to give any false impressions. When he died about five years later it became impossible to keep *The Green Pastures* on the stage. For those who had seen Mr. Harrison, no substitution in the part was possible. He had left an indelible imprint on the play.

Ever since *The Second Man* was produced by the Theatre Guild in 1927, S. N. Behrman has been America's nimblest author of high comedy. His characters have a worldly air; his dialogue is lightly humorous; his plots are usually insubstantial. What he writes might be dismissed as drawing-room comedy if Mr. Behrman were not interested in serious themes like politics, ethics and cross-currents of thought. Having a singularly scrupulous mind he writes his comedies impartially—pitting reactionary against radical; and since he is a listener to other people's thoughts he seldom takes sides. Although he is amused by pompousness he respects both points of view in any intelligent discussion. *Biography* was produced by the Theatre Guild in 1932, with Ina Claire irradiating the central part and Earle Larimore acting the part of the bristling insurgent. Although Mr. Behrman continues from season to season to look into the hearts and under the motives of modern people who are caught in the web of circumstance, he has never improved on the characterizations in *Biography,* and he has never managed to make a more buoyant play from his observations.

Ah, Wilderness! represents Eugene O'Neill's only holiday from somber thoughts about mankind. In 1933, when the Theatre Guild mounted his comedy of recollection, Mr. O'Neill was known as the author of heroic tragedies like *Desire Under the Elms, Strange Interlude* and *Mourning Becomes Electra*—black, passionate, dour studies of man's struggle with fate. The idea for a sentimental comedy popped into his mind while he was working on *Days Without End,* a turgid drama of religious mysticism. He wrote *Ah, Wilderness!* for the fun of it, rapidly and easily. Although the comedy is not autobiographical, many of the ideas come out of his youth and his recollections of New London, Conn., where his father and the family spent the summers. It was a stroke of good fortune to get George M. Cohan to play the part of the father. This was the first time Mr. Cohan had appeared in a play he had not written or helped to write. Gene Lockhart played the part of the bibulous and remorseful uncle, and Elisha Cook, Jr., played the boy. *Ah, Wilderness!* had a long run in New York and throughout the country. Full of humorous nostalgia, it helped a great deal to round out the elusive character of the one great dramatist America has contributed to the world.

When *The Petrified Forest* turned up in 1935, Robert Sherwood was already widely celebrated as the author of *Reunion in Vienna, The Queen's Husband* and *The Road to Rome.* Although the last two plays were popular, I confess that I thought their humor sophomoric and dull, and *Reunion in Vienna,* with the Lunts on a skylark, seemed to me no better than smart comedy. But *The Petrified Forest,* with the lucent Leslie Howard in the chief part, delighted me enormously as gusty melodrama and strongly appealed to me as just the sort of play a liberal with a sense of humor ought to write. Mr. Sherwood likes to mull things over; he also likes the roar and rumble of a good show. In *The Petrified Forest* he succeeded in making a plausible comment on the state of the world, simultaneously ripping off a good story of shooting. Humphrey Bogart, who had not then made much impression on stage or screen, emerged in *The Petrified Forest* unshaven, with two guns and a professional career. And to me Mr. Sherwood's career as a working dramatist also began with this robust shooting show. Now his career rises high against the skyline of modern drama. Out of his brooding mind, out of his courage and integrity have come *Abe Lincoln in Illinois* and *There Shall Be No Night,* which have made an impression on the morals of the country. Although Mr. Sherwood is not a creative dramatic poet, like Eugene O'Neill, he is, I think, our greatest contemporary. I have never known another man so completely fulfilled.

About the same time a minor actor in the Group Theatre was chafing at the tugs. Clifford Odets was submitting the script of a dynamic play about labor problems to a prize-play contest. *Waiting for Lefty,* he called it. Produced at a series of special Sunday performances, it awakened general interest in a fresh talent in playwriting. Not being able to find a good script by any other author, the Group Theatre then decided to risk a production of Mr. Odets's first full-length play, *Awake and Sing,* which had been kicking around for some time. It is now recognized as one of the truly creative dramas in our literature. After it was produced Mr. Odets became the white-haired boy of the season and he plunged with enthusiasm and confidence into a career. Although he has not fulfilled the entire promise of that cyclonic first year, he is a writer with great talent for the theatre. He feels in theatre terms and his emotion is fiery and centrifugal. *Waiting for Lefty* is a case in point. It is not so much a "well-made play" as the score for a whirling experience in the theatre. By the technical device of using the stage as a speaker's platform it draws the audience well inside the play. Actors rise from all parts of the house, race down the aisles and destroy the usual barrier between stage and auditorium. A small play, *Waiting for Lefty* has the natural form of a theatrical inspiration, and

I shall never forget the hot excitement of the first performance I saw on a Sunday afternoon in the battered, dog-eared Civic Repertory Theatre in Fourteenth Street.

Sidney Kingsley's *Dead End,* which appeared the next autumn, is another play difficult to read without considering the stage setting. Some of the text looks like gibberish on the printed page. But it was played against one of Norman Bel Geddes's most extraordinary settings, representing an East River slum street where a luxurious apartment house butted against a decrepit tenement rookery. The pier-head of the street dropped straight into the orchestra pit. Some of the most scabrous street urchins ever assembled on a stage dove off the end of the pier and tore shrieking up and down the street to a sound track of accompanying river noises. Against this shocking background Mr. Kingsley's street scene with melodramatic devices was translated into a raucous tone poem of the modern city. It enlarged the experience of New York theatregoers; it also vividly directed attention to one of New York's most urgent social problems.

There is no problem involved in *Boy Meets Girl,* by Bella and Samuel Spewack, who are legally married and can therefore be as funny as they like on any topic. After giving their all for a fortune in Hollywood, they came back to Broadway in 1935 with a remarkably hilarious comedy about the hocus-pocus of screen writing. Since Hart and Kaufman's *Once in a Lifetime,* acted in 1930, there had not been a really successful cartoon of Hollywood antics, and there has never been such a good one since. Mr. and Mrs. Spewack were not writing at random. The two scribbling pranksters who turn comic handsprings through the play were suggested by the fantastic Hollywood behavior of Ben Hecht and Charles MacArthur, represented in this volume as authors of *The Front Page.* Mr. Hecht and Mr. MacArthur are not easily impressed by big industry, and they do not take Hollywood seriously. No one goes so far as to suggest that the plot of *Boy Meets Girl* is a literal record of their escapades. The Spewacks' play is a free improvisation on a practical joker's theme, and George Abbott's racy stage direction accounted for a good deal of the boisterous fun of *Boy Meets Girl* on Broadway. It had 669 performances in New York.

Clare Boothe, *la belle dame sans merci,* conquered Broadway on the night after Christmas in 1936. She had already written one drama about the pangs of married life, *Abide with Me,* which failed. But in *The Women* she succeeded by spraying vitriol over the members of her own sex with cutting wit and remarkable knowledge of her subject. In the foreword to the published script she says that "*The Women* is a satirical play about a numerically small group of ladies native to the Park Avenues of America," and that the title was chosen from several others she had considered—*Park Avenue, The Girls, The Ladies,* etc. On Broadway *The Women* was luxuriously produced with a sharp-clawed cast of "speaking cats," as Dr. Johnson might have called them, and with scenery that amounted to a Park Avenue sight-seeing tour—from cardroom to beauty parlor and bathroom. To keep this record straight, *The Women* is the only play in this volume that I did not applaud. "This reviewer disliked it," I wrote laconically at the end of my first-night notice. Miss Boothe's calculated and spiteful writing was too poisonous for my taste. But who are you and I against so many? *The Women* had 657 performances on Broadway. Since 1936 Miss Boothe has written *Kiss the Boys Goodbye* and *Margin for Error,* both of them successes, and more recently she has written a book about the first enigmatic year of the European war with a suggestion that the United States take warning.

Arthur Kober's "*Having Wonderful Time*" is a tender comedy about a Jewish summer resort in the Berkshires. Mr. Kober is a humorous and sympathetic writer with considerable affection for the little people who are trying to find a place for themselves in a cold world. As a young man he knew at first hand these summer colonies where Jewish young people devote a brief fortnight vacation to as much social and cultural achievement as they can manage. According to standards of assured society, Mr. Kober's portrait is comic. But it is never insensible, for Mr. Kober respects the dreams and hopes of desperate vacationers who are driven by an inarticulate desire to improve themselves. When *"Having Wonderful Time"* was produced in 1937, Katherine Locke and Jules (now John) Garfield made quite a stir on Broadway. For all practical purposes that was the beginning of two wonderful times on stage and screen.

Like *The Green Pastures, Our Town,* produced in 1938, is a classic by reason of its humanity. The novelty of Thornton Wilder's stagecraft has overshadowed the artistic—or shall we say, the spiritual—qualities of the drama. It was played virtually without scenery and props. Much of the acting was in pantomime. The curtain was always kept rolled up; and Frank Craven, who played the composite rôle of manager, commentator and occasional dramatic character, stood informally over the footlights and personally guided the performance. The novelty of the bare stage production, however, was an integral part of the drama. For Mr. Wilder offers Grover's Corners, N. H., as a living fragment of the universe, indigenous not merely to New Hampshire, but to the life of man, and his point of view is not detached but compassionate. The story is the simple idyll of a neighborhood —talk about people, love and marriage, death and immortality. In style it is familiar, suffused in wonder. Mr. Wilder is a modest writer with no taste for passionate affirmation. But in one speech, spoken meditatively in the moonlight by a young country girl to her brother, he draws a deeply moving and imaginative connection between his gentle village and the profound riddle of the universe—

REBECCA. I never told you about that letter Jane Crofut got from her minister when she was sick. The minister of her church in the town she was in before she came here. He wrote Jane a letter and on the envelope the address was like this: It said: Jane Crofut, The Crofut Farm; Grover's Corners; Sutton County; New Hampshire; United States of America.

GEORGE. What's funny about that?

REBECCA. But listen, it's not finished: the United States of America; Continent of North America; Western Hemisphere; the Earth; the Solar System; the Universe; the Mind of God—that's what it said on the envelope.

GEORGE. What do you know!

REBECCA. And the postman brought it just the same.

GEORGE. What do you know!

Martha Scott had her first conspicuous success in *Our Town* in the part of Emily Webb; and John Craven, son of Frank Craven, made something memorable out of the part of George Gibbs.

The Little Foxes, produced in the fertile year of 1939, is Lillian Hellman's second successful drama. Her first, *The Children's Hour,* was produced in the autumn of 1934. It was an excoriating record of the mischief caused by idle gossip. Her second play, *Days to Come,* was not a success two years later, but it better represented Miss Hellman's dominant interest in matters of social importance. *The Little Foxes,* which indulges that interest, is the story of greedy brothers and a greedy sister who coldly devour the earth, scheming, twisting, driving their way to material success. As a craftsman, Miss Hellman is the chief representative of the "well-made play." She has a clear, organized mind; she can plan a plot that yields excitement, and her literary style is dramatic. What she has to say in *The Little Foxes* she says concretely, with great decision, and her portrait of voracity is a bitter one. On a night in February, 1939, it also gave Tallulah Bankhead her first popular success in this country. After shuffling through a number of inconsequential plays, Miss Bankhead strode through the part of Regina Giddens with great singleness of purpose like an actress awakened by a well-written part. Patricia Collinge also gave a notable performance as the humiliated Birdie Hubbard.

The Man Who Came to Dinner reveals George S. Kaufman and Moss Hart at the top of their bent. After collaborating for the first time in 1930 on *Once in a Lifetime,* they have worked together on several plays—including *You Can't Take It with You* and *The American Way. The Man Who Came to Dinner* is a merciless cartoon of Alexander Woollcott's bad manners, shameless egoism, bountiful mischief and widely assorted friendships; it is written with destructive wit. It is an example of loud, swift, blistering American comedy at its best. If Mr. Kaufman, Mr. Hart and Mr. Woollcott were not chums, *The Man Who Came to Dinner* might reasonably call for a cessation of familiarities—particularly since Mr. Kaufman and Mr. Hart, with the instinct of friendship, have concentrated on the most vulnerable aspects of Mr. Woollcott's character. But he has been sufficiently delighted with the malicious virtuosity of their play to act the central rôle himself in other parts of the country. In New York the part is played with superb relish and authority by Monty Woolley, a former Yale savant, with wit and a beard. At this writing Mr. Woollcott is girding his mountainous loins for another tour in a wheelchair.

Nine days after *The Man Who Came to Dinner* shot into town, William Saroyan's *The Time of Your Life* took up residence across the street, and eventually captured both the Critic's Circle and the Pulitzer prizes. Mr. Saroyan, the ebullient Armenian, is the imp of the modern drama. He has an instinct for characters and themes, but no artistic discipline. To Mr. Saroyan the lack of discipline is an essential part of his genius; but a good many theatregoers, accustomed to orderly drama, merely regard him as a pain in the neck. The truth lies somewhere between these two points of view. Since Mr. Saroyan lacks discipline, since he uses material impulsively just as it pops into his head and lives exclusively off the top of his emotion, he is an erratic writer, and any contact he makes with the mind of the theatregoer is chiefly accidental. His happiest accident was *My Heart's in the Highlands,* a one-act lyric in celebration of friendship and good will, played with imaginative beauty by the Group Theatre. The three-act form is a harder test of Mr. Saroyan's endurance, but *The Time of Your Life* passed the test with the assistance of Eddie Dowling, who helped to direct and also played the part of Joe with sweetness and understanding. Mr. Saroyan's liking for undistinguished people, his enthusiasm for the minor crotchets of living, and his comradely sense of humor are original, innocent and enjoyable. I liked *The Time of Your Life* the first time I saw it. I was enthusiastic the second time I saw it and I enjoy reading it now. Some time, I hope, the stars in their course may be propitious again, and, working under their influence, Mr. Saroyan may dash off another friendly drama to the surprise of Broadway and himself.

While *The Time of Your Life* was breaking up old friendships in that rushing autumn of 1939, *Life with Father* settled into the Empire Theatre, apparently forever. For this is the perfect American comedy with popular appeal. The joke on which it is based is the fundamental one of the "papa love mama?" comic strip. But there is nothing cheap or commonplace about *Life with Father*. Although the basic joke is an old one, father is a man worth respecting. He is logical, industrious, unselfish, fond of his sons, devoted to his wife, the backbone of America. He lacks humor and imagination, but he has in abundance the enduring virtues of the head of a family. As a matter of fact, he was the father of the late Clarence Day, who wrote sketches about him with humorous independence in *The New Yorker*. After Clarence Day's death, Howard Lindsay and Russel Crouse, who had previously collaborated on musical comedies, made a play out of the sketches and managed with great skill to preserve the good taste and mettlesome humor of the source material. Father is comic, but a real person. His anxiety over his wife's health is genuinely touching, which illustrates Bernard Shaw's thesis that no comedy is a good one unless it is also moving. After trying in vain to persuade a star actor to play the part of the monumental parent, Mr. Lindsay decided to act the part himself and he engaged his wife, Dorothy Stickney, to play the part of Vinnie. His choice in actors has turned out to be excellent. *Life with Father* has restored the era of good feelings to the stage.

New York
January, 1941

They Knew What They Wanted

BY SIDNEY HOWARD

They Knew What They Wanted was first produced at the Garrick Theatre, New York City, by the Theatre Guild, on November 24, 1924, and closed on November 14, 1925. Following is the original cast:

Joe	Glenn Anders
Father McKee	Charles Kennedy
Ah Gee	Allen Atwell
Tony	Richard Bennett
The R.F.D.	Robert Cook
Amy	Pauline Lord
Angelo	Hardwick Nevin
Giorgio	Jacob Zollinger
The Doctor	Charles Tazewell
First Italian Mother	Frances Hyde
Her Daughter	Antoinette Bizzoco
Second Italian Mother	Peggy Conway
Her Son	Edward Rosenfeld

Production directed by Philip Moeller

Settings and costumes by Carolyn Hancock

SCENE

Tony's farmhouse in the Napa Valley, California

ACT ONE

Morning, in early summer

ACT TWO

Evening. Same day

ACT THREE

Three months later

THEY KNEW WHAT THEY WANTED

SCENE

The scene of the play is the home of an Italian winegrower in the Napa Valley in California. All of the action takes place in the main downstairs room which serves as general living and dining room.

It is necessary to understand that the house is not in the least Spanish in its architecture. As a matter of fact, it would serve any respectable Middle-Western farmer as a fitting and inconspicuous residence. It was built in the 'nineties of wood, is painted white on its exterior, and has only one story.

A door at the back, the main one to the outer world, gives on the porch. Another door, to the right of the audience, gives on the kitchen. The kitchen is three steps above the level of the room and so placed that the audience can see into it. It is completely furnished. A third door, to the left of the audience, gives on a flight of steps which leads to the cellar of the house. A fourth door, also on the left and farther down stage, gives on the bedroom.

The back wall should also be broken by windows; on the right of the central door, a bay window, on the left, a double flat window.

The view from the house is over a valley and toward brown Californian hills. The landscape is checkered with cultivation. Some of the checkers are orchards. Most of them are vineyards. The foreground is all vines. Vines twine about the pillars of the porch. In the beginning of the play—it begins in summer—the grapes on the porch vines are small and green. In the last act—three months having elapsed—they are large and purple.

The back stage must be so arranged that people who approach the house from the highroad appear to mount the porch steps from a much lower level. At other times, however, it is required that the characters be able to go and come on the level of the house itself where the farmyard is.

Inside the room the wallpaper and the carpet are new and garish. The cheapest variety of lace curtains hangs in the windows. The furniture is new and includes a golden-oak dining table with chairs to match, a morris chair, another easy chair, a chest of drawers, a sideboard, a hat rack.

On one wall hangs a picture of Garibaldi. A picture of George Washington hangs over the central door. Other mural decorations include a poster of the Navigazione Generale Italiana, a still-life chromo, a religious chromo, and a small mirror.

On the hat rack hangs a double-barrelled shotgun draped with a loaded cartridge belt.

The whole impression must be one of gaiety and simple good living.

ACT ONE

The red, white and green of Italy combine with the red, white and blue of these United States in bunting, garlands of fluted paper, pompons and plumes of shredded tissue, to make up a scheme of decoration which is, to say the least, violent. The picture of Garibaldi is draped with an American flag, the picture of Washington with an Italian flag. The full glare of the early morning sun streams in through door and windows.

The room is fairly littered with boxes. Atop one of these, from which it has just been extracted, stands a handsome wedding cake, surmounted by statuary representing the ideal bride and groom in full regalia under a bell. The boxes are all addressed to

Tony Patucci,
R. F. D., Napa, Calif.

AH GEE *stands on a ladder on the porch outside the open entrance door, hanging Chinese lanterns. He is a silent, spare Chinaman, of age maturely indeterminate. He wears blue overalls and a black chambray shirt.*

JOE—*dark, sloppy, beautiful, and young—is busy opening a packing case in the center of the stage. His back is turned upon the door.*

JOE (*as he works, he half sings, half mutters to himself the words of "Remember," an I. W. W. song, to the tune of "Hold the Fort"*).

"We speak to you from jail to-day,
Two hundred union men,
We're here because the bosses' laws
Bring slavery again."

(*Through this the curtain rises and* FATHER MC KEE *is seen climbing the porch steps. He wears the sober garb of a Catholic priest, not over clean, what with dust, spots, and all. He nods to* AH GEE *and comes into the doorway. He stands a moment to mop his large, pale face with a red bandana. Then he lowers lugubrious disapproval upon everything in sight. Then he yawns.*

He is one of those clerics who can never mention anything except to denounce it. And his technique of denunciation is quite special to himself. It consists in a long, throaty abstention from inflection of any kind which culminates in a vocal explosion when he reaches the accented syllable of a word upon which his emphasis depends. This word always seems to wake him up for an instant. Once it is spoken, however, he relapses into semi-somnolence for the remainder of his remarks. At heart, he is genial and kindly enough, quite the American counterpart of the French village curé.)

FATHER MC KEE. Hello, Joe.

JOE. Hello there, Padre. What do you think?

FATHER MC KEE. Looks to me like a bawdy house.

JOE. It's goin to be *some* festa. . . . Lily Cups! What do you know about that for style?

FATHER MC KEE. Where's Tony?

JOE (*nods toward the door of the bedroom*). In there gettin' dolled up. . . . Hey, there, bridegroom! The Padre's out here.

FATHER MC KEE. I come up to have a serious talk with Tony.

JOE. Well, for God's sake, don't get him upset no more'n what he is already. He's been stallin' around all mornin', afraid to go down and meet the bride. You better leave him alone.

FATHER MC KEE. I'm always glad to have your advice, Joe. I didn't look to find you still hangin' 'round.

JOE. Oh, didn't you, Padre?

FATHER MC KEE. Tony told me you'd decided to go away.

JOE. Well, Padre, I'll tell you how it is. (*He grins impudently*) I don't believe in stayin' any one place too long. 'Tain't fair for me not to give the rest of California a chance at my society. But I ain't goin' before I seen all the fun, got Tony safely married, an' kissed the bride. (*He turns to the door and* AH GEE) That's fine, Ah Gee. Better take these here Lily Cups in the kitchen when you get through.

(*Magnificently* TONY *enters from the bedroom. He is stout, floridly bronzed, sixty years old, vigorous, jovial, simple, and excitable. His great gift is for gesture. To-day we meet him in his Sunday best, a very brilliant purple suit with a more than oriental waistcoat which serves to display a stupendous gold watch chain. He wears a boiled shirt, an emerald-green tie, and a derby hat. He carries his new patent-leather shoes in his hand. He seems to be perspiring rather freely.*)

TONY. Looka me! I'm da most stylish fella in da world.

FATHER MC KEE. I come up to talk tc you, Tony.

TONY. I'm glad you come, Padre. How you like my clothes, eh? Costa playnta good money! (*Attention is called to the shoes*) For da feet. . . .

JOE (*a motion to the wedding cake*). How's it strike you, Tony?

TONY. Madonna! (*He throws his shoes into the morris chair. His hat assumes a terrific angle. He cannot keep his hands off that cake*) Look, Padre! From Frisco! Special! Twelve dollar' an' two bits! Look! (*The miniature bride and groom particularly please him*) Ees Tony an' his Amy!

JOE. Them lanterns is Ah Gee's personal donation.

TONY. Thank you, Ah Gee! Ees verra fine. Ah Gee, you go an' bring vino, now, for Padre, eh? (AH GEE *obeys the order, taking the Lily Cups with him into his kitchen.*)

JOE. Show some speed now, Tony. It's past nine. 'Tain't hardly pretty to keep the bride waitin'.

TONY (*as he sits down to the struggle with his shoes*). I'm goin' verra quick.

FATHER MC KEE. I got to have a word with you, Tony, before you go to the station.

JOE. The Padre's been tryin' to tell me you're scared to have me around where I can kiss the bride. (*He picks up a couple of flags and goes outside.*)

TONY (*in undisguised terror*). You ain't goin' be kissin' no bride, Joe. You hear dat?

JOE (*off stage he is heard singing*).

"We laugh and sing, we have no fear
  Our hearts are always light,
We know that every Wobbly true
  Will carry on the fight."

TONY. He's too goddam fresh, dat fella, with kissin' my Amy an' all dose goddam Wobbly songs. Don' you think so, Padre?

FATHER MC KEE. I didn't come up here to talk about Joe, Tony. I come up to talk about this here weddin'.

TONY. I'm glad you come, Padre. I'm verra bad scare'.

FATHER MC KEE. You got good reason for bein' scared, if you want to know what *I* think.

TONY. I got verra special reason.

FATHER MC KEE. What reason?

TONY. Don' you never mind! Da's my secret dat I don' tell nobody. You tell Joe he go away quick, Padre. Den, maybe, ees all right.

FATHER MC KEE. So that's it! Well, I don't blame you for that.

TONY (*deeply indignant at the implication*). Oh! . . . No, by God! You don' ondrastan', Padre. Joe is like my own son to me! Ees som'-thing verra different. Madonna mia! Ees som'thing I been doin' myself! Ees som'thing Tony's been doin' w'at's goin' mak' verra bad trouble for Tony.

FATHER MC KEE. I'll tell Joe nothin'. You've made your own bed and if you won't get off it while there's time, you got to lie on it. But I want you to understand that I don't like nothin' 'bout this here weddin'. It ain't got my approval.

TONY (*the first shoe slips on and he sits up in amazement*). You don' like weddin', Padre?

FATHER MC KEE. No, I don't. An' that's just what I come up here to tell you. I don't like nothin' about it, an' if you persist in goin' ahead in spite of my advice, I don't want you sayin' afterwards that you wasn't warned.

TONY. Dio mio! (*He amplifies this with the sign of the cross. Then his confidence rather returns to him*) Aw . . . tak' a pinch-a snuff! You mak' me tire', Padre! You think festa is no good for people. You padre fellas don' know nothing. Work! Work! Work evra day! Den, by-an'-by, is comin' festa. After festa workin' is more easy. (*He resumes the shoe problem.*)

FATHER MC KEE. Tony, you know perfectly well that I ain't got no more objection to no festa than I have to any other pomp of the flesh. But I'm your spirichool adviser an' I been mullin' this weddin' over in my mind an' I come to the conclusion that I'm agin it. I don't like it at all. I got my reasons for what I say.

TONY (*does the Padre guess his secret?*). W'at reason you got?

FATHER MC KEE. In the first place, you ain't got no business marryin' no woman who ain't a good Cath'lic.

TONY (*immeasurable relief*). Ees no matter.

FATHER MC KEE. A mixed marriage ain't no better'n plain livin' in sin.

TONY. Ain' we got you for keep' sin away, Padre?

FATHER MC KEE. Why ain't you marryin' a woman out of your own parish instead of trapesin' all the way to Frisco to pick out a heretic?

TONY. Is no good womans in dees parish.

FATHER MC KEE. What's wrong with 'em?

TONY. Joe is sleepin' with evra one.

FATHER MCKEE. That ain't the point.

TONY (*enlisting the shoe to help his gesticulation*). Oh, ees point all right, Padre. Joe is told me 'bout evrathing. I been lookin' all 'round here at all da womans in dees parish. I been lookin' evra place for twent' mile. Ees no good womans for wife here. Joe is told me 'bout evra one. Den I'm gone to Napa for look all 'round dere an' in Napa ees no better . . . ees just da same like here. So den I go down all da way to Frisco for look after wife an' I find my Amy. She is like a rose, all wilt'. You puttin' water on her an' she come out most beautiful. I'm goin' marry with my Amy, Padre, an' I don' marry with nobody else. She's been tellin' me she is no Cath'lic. I say, w'at I care? By an' by, maybe, if we bein' patient, we bringin' her in da church, an' showin' her da candles and da Madonna, all fix up good with flowers and da big tin heart, an' evrathing smellin' so prett' an' you preachin' verra loud an' da music an' evrathing, maybe . . . by an' by . . . (*He turns again to his shoe*) But now ees no mater. W'at I care?

FATHER MCKEE. It don't look good to me.

TONY. Ees all right. . . . If you don' want my Amy an' me gettin' married with good Cath'lic priest like you, den, by God—

FATHER MC KEE. I ain't said I wouldn't marry you.

TONY. Eh bene!

FATHER MC KEE. I'm only tryin' to tell you. . .

TONY. Ahi! Dio mio. . . . (*The shoes goes on, producing intense pain*) He look much better as he feel!

FATHER MC KEE. There ain't no good in no old man marryin' with no young woman.

TONY. You think anybody marry with old woman? Tak' a pinch-a snuff!

FATHER MCKEE. I know one old man who married a young woman an' she carried on with a stage driver!

TONY. Dio mio!

FATHER MCKEE. He had knowed her all her life, too, an' you ain't knowed your Amy more'n 'bout five minutes.

TONY. Ees no matter.

FATHER MCKEE. An' I know another fellow who married one of them city girls like your Amy without bein' properly acquainted an' she turned out to be a scarlet woman.

TONY. My Amy don' do dat.
(AH GEE *enters from kitchen with two glasses and a bottle of wine.*)

FATHER MC KEE. Ain't you just now been tellin' me you're scared of her seein' Joe?

TONY. No, by God!

FATHER MC KEE. Joe ain't the only young fellow around, either!

TONY. Young fellas is no matter. Only Joe. An' I ain' scare' over Joe excep' for special reason. You tell Joe, Padre . . . (*He is returning to his old subject, but the wine distracts him*) Ah-h-h!

FATHER MCKEE. Why didn't you get married forty years ago?

TONY. I think you know verra good w'y. Ees because I'm no dam' fool. . . . W'en I'm young, I got nothing. I'm broke all da time, you remember? I got no money for havin' wife. I don' want no wife for mak' her work all da time. Da's no good, dat. Da's mak' her no more young, no more prett'. Evrabody say Tony is crazy for no' havin' wife. I say Tony is no dam' fool. W'at is happen? Pro'ibish' is com'. Salute! (*A glass of wine.* AH GEE *has returned to his kitchen*) An' wat I say? I say, "Ees dam' fool law. Ees dam' fool fellas for bein' scare' an' pullin' up da grape' for tryin' growin' som'-thing different.' W'at I'm doin'? I'm keep the grape, eh? I say, "I come in dees country for growin' da grape! God mak' dees country for growin' da grape! Ees not for pro'ibish' God mak' dees country. Ees for growin' da grape!" Ees true? Sure ees true! (*Another glass of wine*) An' w'at happen? Before pro'ibish' I sell my grape' for ten, maybe twelve dollar' da ton. Now I sell my grape' some'-time one hundra dollar' da ton. Pro-'bish' is mak' me verra rich. (*Another glass of wine*) I got my fine house. I got Joe for bein' foreman. I got two men for helpin' Joe. I got one Chink for cook. I got one Ford car. I got all I want, evrathing, excep' only wife. Now I'm goin' have wife. Verra nice an' young an' fat. Not for work. No! For sit an' holdin' da hands and havin' kids. Three kids. (*He demonstrates the altitude of each*) Antonio . . . Giuseppe . . . Anna . . . Da's like trees an' cows an' all good people. Da's fine for God an' evrabody! I tell you, Padre, Tony know w'at he want!

FATHER MCKEE. Whatever made you think a man of your age could have children? (*This staggers* TONY) I tell you, Tony, it ain't possible.

TONY. Eh? Tony is too old for havin' kids? I tell you, Tony can have twent' kids if he want! I tell you Tony can have kids w'en he is one hundra year' old. Dio mio! From da sole of his feet to da top of his hat, Tony is big, strong man! I think I ondrastan' you verra good, Padre. Tony is not too old for havin' kids. He's too rich, eh? (*This rather strikes home*) Yah! Tony is rich an', if he don' have no kids, den da church is gettin' all Tony's money an da Padre is gettin Tony's fine house all fix' up good for livin' in, eh?

FATHER MCKEE (*a very severe shepherd*). Tony!

TONY (*the horns of the devil with his fingers*). Don' you go for puttin' no evil eye on Tony an' his Amy!

FATHER MCKEE. You're givin' way to ignorant superstition, which ain't right in no good Cath'lic.

TONY (*on his feet in a panic*). Dio mio! My Amy is comin' on dat train an' here you keep me, sittin', talkin'. . . .

FATHER MC KEE. You irreverent old lunatic, you, if you're bent on marryin', I'll marry you. (JOE *reappears in the doorway*) But I don't want you comin' around afterwards squawkin' about it.

TONY. Eh, Joe! Da Padre don' want me gettin' marry with my Amy because he's scare' da church don' never get my money!

JOE. For cripe's sake, Tony, ain't you heard that whistle?

TONY. I go! I go!

JOE. Train's in now.

TONY. Porco Dio! Ah Gee!

JOE. Fix your tie.

TONY. I fix. . . . (AH GEE *comes from the kitchen for his master's order*) Un altro fiasco. (AH GEE *returns to the kitchen.*)

JOE. You won't make no hit if you're drunk, Tony.

TONY. Not drunk, Joe. Only scare'. Verra bad scare'.

JOE. Bridegrooms is always scared.

TONY. Jes' Chris', maybe I'm sick!

JOE. No!

TONY. Santa Maria, I *am* sick!

JOE. What's wrong with you?

TONY. I don' know! I'm sick! I'm sick! I'm sick!
(AH GEE *returns with the wine bottle refilled.* TONY *seeks prompt solace.* AH GEE *goes back to his kitchen.*)

JOE. You'll be a helluva sight sicker if you don't lay off that stuff.

TONY. I canno' go for get my Amy, Joe. I canno' go. . . .

JOE. All right. I'll go . . .

TONY. Oh, by God! No! NO!

JOE. Tony, if you drive the Ford down the hill in this state of mind you'll break your dam' neck.

TONY (*more solace*). I feel good now. I drive fine. I don' want nobody for go for my Amy but only me. . . . (*Then he weakens again*) Joe, I'm scare', I'm scare', I'm scare'!

JOE. What you scared of, Tony?

TONY. Maybe my Amy . . .

JOE. Come on, beat it!

TONY. I feel good now an' I don' want nobody for go for my Amy but only me. You bet! (*He starts.*)

JOE. That's the boy!

TONY (*another relapse*). Joe, you don't get mad if I ask you som'thing? I got verra good reason, Joe . . . Joe . . . how soon you goin' away, Joe?

JOE. You don't *want* me to go, do you?

TONY. I think ees much better.

JOE. What's the idea, Tony?

TONY. Joe . . . som'thing is happen', da's all. . . . You go, Joe. I been tryin' for three days for ask you dees, Joe, an' I been scare' you get mad. I pay you double extra for goin' to-day, for goin' now, eh? Joe? Verra quick?

JOE. An' miss the festa? Like hell!

TONY. Joe, you don' ondrastan'. . . .

JOE. Forget it, Tony.

TONY. Joe . . .

JOE. If you keep her waitin', she'll go back to Frisco.

TONY. Dio Mio! (*He goes to the door and turns yet once again*) Joe . . . ? (*He catches* FATHER MC KEE'S *eye*) Som'thing verra bad is goin' happen with Tony. . . . Clean evrathing clean before my Amy come. (*He is really gone.* JOE *follows him out and stands on the porch looking after him. A Ford motor roars and dies away into high speed.*)

FATHER MC KEE (*at the window*). Look at him!

JOE. He could drive that Ford in his sleep.

FATHER MCKEE. I don't hold with no old man gallivantin'.

JOE. Don't you fret, Padre. Didn't I tell you not to get him all worked up? (*This ruffles the good priest who makes to follow* TONY. JOE *intercepts him and forces him back into the room.*)

FATHER MC KEE. Well?

JOE. Sit down a minute. You been tellin' Tony what you think. Now I got some tellin' to do.

FATHER MC KEE. Have you, indeed? Well, I don't see no good—

JOE. Maybe *I* don't see much good, but what the hell!

FATHER MC KEE. Young man! That's the pernicious doctrine of Lacey Fairey.

JOE. What's that?

FATHER MC KEE. A French expression meanin' "Sufficient unto the day."

JOE. What of it? If folks is bent on makin' mistakes, an' you can't stop 'em, let 'em go ahead, that's what I say. I don't want nobody hatin' my guts for bein too dam' right all the time, see? Not bein' a priest, I aim to get along with folks. That way, when they're in wrong, I can be some use.

FATHER MC KEE. That ain't in accord with the teachin's of Jesus!

JOE. A helluva lot you an' me know about the teachin's of Jesus.

FATHER MC KEE. Joe, if you ain't goin' to be rev'rent . . .

JOE. I'm talkin' now.

FATHER MC KEE. Oh, are you?

JOE. Yeah. I wouldn't have no harm come to Tony, not for anything in the world, see? An' I been agitatin' against this weddin' a lot longer'n you have an' I know what it's all about, see? I'm here goin' on five months, now, an' that's longer'n I ever stayed any one place.

FATHER MC KEE. Is it?

JOE. Excep' once in jail, it is. An' I been lookin' after Tony all the time since I come here. I come in to bum a meal an' I stayed five months. Five months I been workin' for Tony an' lookin' after him and he's treated me dam' good an' that's God's truth. I wouldn't have worked that long for him if he hadn't treated me dam' good, either. I ain't none too strong for stayin' put, you know. I like to move an' now I'm goin' to move. I'm what the papers call a "unskilled migratory" an' I got to migrate, see? Tony wants me to go an' I want to go. But, what I want to know is: who's goin' to look after Tony when I'm gone?

FATHER MCKEE. Ain't that his wife's place?

JOE. Sure it's his wife's place. But suppose this weddin' don't turn out so good? Are you goin' to look out for him?

FATHER MC KEE. Ain't Tony my spirachool charge an' responsibility?

JOE. All *right!* An' I ain't so sure you're goin' to have much trouble, either. Amy looks to me like a fair to middlin' smart kid an' she knows what she's in for, too.

FATHER MCKEE. You seem to be well informed, Joe! Do you happen to know the lady?

JOE. I ain't never laid eyes on her. (*Then the implication percolates*) Oh, I may go chasin' women plenty, but I don't chase Tony's wife, see? An' I ain't fixin' to, neither. Just get that straight.

FATHER MC KEE. I'm glad to hear it, Joe.

JOE. But I happen to know about her. Didn't I have to write all Tony's letters for him? You wouldn't expect Tony to be writin' to no lady with *his* education, would you?

FATHER MC KEE. No, I can't say that I would.

JOE. Why, I even had to read him the letters she wrote back. That's how I got my dope. An' what I say is: she's got plenty of sense. Don't you fool yourself she hasn't. I'll show you. (*He goes to the chest of drawers for some letters and photographs. He brings them back to the* PADRE) You can see for yourself. (*And he submits Exhibit A—a letter*) Tony goes to Frisco lookin' for a wife, see? The nut! An' he finds Amy waitin' on table in a spaghetti joint. Joint's called "Il Trovatore." Can you beat it? He ain't even got the nerve to speak to her. He don't even go back to see her again. He just falls for her, gets her name from the boss an' comes home an' makes me write her a letter proposin' marriage. That's her answer.

FATHER MC KEE. It's good clear writin'. It's a good letter. It looks like she's got more character'n what I thought. But, just the same, it ain't no way to conduct a courtship.

JOE. There's worse ways.

FATHER MC KEE. She says she likes the letter you wrote.

JOE. The second time I wrote, I told her all about the farm an' just how she was goin' to be fixed. Oh, I was careful not to say nothin' about Tony's money. Only the Ford. I thought she ought to know about the Ford. (*He hands the second letter over*) An' she wrote this one back.

FATHER MC KEE. She likes the country, does she? She wants Tony's photo.

JOE. Say, you ought to have seen Tony gettin' his face shot! By God! It took me a whole week to talk him into it. An' when I did get him down there—you know that place across from the depot?—dam' if he wasn't scared right out of his pants!

FATHER MC KEE. By what?

JOE. By the camera! Would you believe it? We had to clamp him into the chair, both of us, the photographer an' me! You ought to have seen that wop sweat! And when we try to point the machine at him, he gives a yell you could hear a block an' runs right out in the street!

FATHER MC KEE. No!

JOE. I couldn't get him back, only I promised to let the guy shoot me first. They was some pictures! Tony's (*he hands a specimen to the* PADRE) sure looks like him, but she must have seen somethin' in it, because she sent hers right back. (*He studies* AMY's *photograph for a moment before submitting it*) Here. Not bad, huh?

FATHER MC KEE (*a long and very pleased contemplation*). There ain't no explainin' women! (*He returns the photograph*) Do you think she's straight, Joe?

JOE. What the hell! If she ain't, she wants to be. That's the main thing.

FATHER MC KEE. Maybe it won't turn out so bad, after all. There's always this about life: no man don't never get everything he sets out to get, but half the time he don't never find out he ain't got it.

JOE. Oh, if you're goin' off on that tack!

FATHER MC KEE. It's the tack life travels on, with the help of Almighty God.

JOE. What the hell! Life ain't so bad.

FATHER MC KEE. I'm delighted to hear you say so!

JOE (*he has returned the exhibits to the drawer*). I never put over anything half so good myself!

FATHER MC KEE. Do you think Tony's goin' to put it over?

JOE. Wait and see.

FATHER MC KEE. Well, I don't know how I can approve of this weddin', but I'm willin' to give it the benefit of my sanction an' to do all I can to help it along an' look out for Tony. Does that satisfy you? . . . Just the same, I don't believe in unnecessary chances, Joe. Pull along out of here 'ike Tony asked you to.

JOE. Say, you make me sore! Why, anybody 'ud think, to hear you talk, that I'm all set to . . .
(*The* R. F. D. *has appeared on the porch. He carries a dusty coat on his arm, and wipes the sweat from his brow with his blue handkerchief. He wears a gray flannel shirt, old trousers hitched to suspenders that are none too secure. His badge is his only sign of office. He is an eager, tobacco-chewing old countryman.*)

THE R. F. D. Hey, Tony! Tony! (*As he reaches the door*) Where's Tony? 'Mornin', Padre.

JOE. Tony's gone to town. You're early.

THE R. F. D. That's more'n Tony is. I got to get his signature on a piece of registered mail.

JOE. What is it?

THE R. F. D. It's his wife. (JOE *and the* PRIEST *rise astonished*) Sure! I got her outside in the buckboard an' she's madder'n hell because Tony didn't meet her. She's some girl, too. I never heard the beat! Lands a girl like that an' don't even take the trouble to— (*The other two are already at the windows.*)

JOE. Where'd *you* find her?

THE R. F. D. I finds her pacin' up and down the platform an' I gives her a lift. I sure do hate to see a good-lookin' girl cry—an' she sure was cryin'. I reckoned Tony couldn't get the Ford started so—

FATHER MC KEE. He went down all right. I wonder what happened to him?

JOE. He must have took the short cut.

FATHER MC KEE. Didn't you pass him?

JOE. I knew I ought to have went instead.

FATHER MC KEE. He wasn't in no condition.

THE R. F. D. I'll have a look on my way back.

JOE. What are *we* goin' to do with her?

THE R. F. D. Ask her in.

JOE. Ah Gee! (*He goes out, calling*) Giorgio! Angelo! (THE R. F. D. *follows him.* AH GEE *comes from his kitchen and evinces some confusion, but does not hold back from the summons.* FATHER MC KEE *arranges his costume and goes out last. The stage remains empty for a moment. A babble of voices is heard, voices that speak both English and Italian.* JOE *is heard shouting*) Lend a hand with that trunk!

AMY'S VOICE. How do you do? I'm pleased to meet you. I certainly had some time getting here. I certainly expected somebody would meet me at the station.

FATHER MC KEE'S VOICE. The old man left all right.

JOE'S VOICE. He started a little too late.

THE R. F. D.'S VOICE. I'll have a look for him. (*The rest is lost in a babble of Italian as* AMY *comes on to the porch and the others follow her, not the least among them being the two Italian hands,* GIORGIO *and* ANGELO *whose volubility subsides only as* AMY *enters the room. As for* AMY, *she is all that* TONY *said of her and much more. She wears a pretty dress, new, ready-made, and inexpensive, and a charming and equally cheap hat. Her shoes are bright coloured and her handbag matches them. But her own loveliness is quite beyond belief. She is small and plump and vivid and her golden hair shimmers about her face like morning sunshine. She herself shines with an inner, constitutional energy. Her look is, to be sure, just a little tired. She probably is not more than twenty-two or -three, but she seems older. Her great quality is definiteness. It lends pathos to her whole personality. At the moment, her vanity is piqued by* TONY'S *remissness and she carries matters with a hand a little too high to be entirely convincing. She is embarrassed, of course, but she won't admit it.*)

AMY (*as she enters*). I must say it ain't my idea of the way a gentleman ought to welcome his blooming bride. I don't get it. I don't get it at all. What was the matter?

JOE. Why, nothin'.

FATHER MC KEE. He was scared.

AMY. Scared of me? Why didn't you come yourself?

JOE. I wanted to, but . . .

AMY (*the decorations have caught her eye*). Say, did you folks go and do all this for the wedding?

JOE. Sure we did.

AMY. Well, if that ain't the cutest ever! A regular wop wedding! Excuse me. I meant Italian. (*The "I" is long.*)

JOE. That's all right.

AMY. And here's the priest, too, all set and ready. Say! I can see right now I'm going to like it here.

JOE. I don't guess nobody's goin' to kick at that.

AMY. All right, then, I'll forgive you. That's the way I am. Forgive and forget! I always believe in letting bygones be bygones. And down at the station I was thinking: Well, if they ain't got enough sense of politeness to come after the bride, I'm going to hop the very next train back to Frisco. I'd have done it, too, only—would you believe it?—I didn't have the price of a ticket! I spent the last cent I had on this hat. Say, when I remembered that, maybe I didn't cry! That's what I was crying over when you come up. (*This to the* R. F. D.; *otherwise her eyes have scarcely left* JOE'S *face.*)

THE R. F. D. Pleased to have been of service, ma'am.

AMY. Well, you certainly was of service. But here I am alive and well, as they say, so I guess we don't need to fuss about that any more. I guess I'll sit down. (*She does so.*)

JOE. Here's the cook an' the hands to pay their respects.

ANGELO (*a deep obeisance to* AMY). Eh, la nostra padrona! Tanti auguri, cara Signora, e buona festa! Come sta? Ha fatto buon viaggio? (*Here* GIORGIO *adds his voice.*)

ANGELO (*together*)	GIORGIO
Siamo tanto contenti di vedevla. Speriamo che si troverà sempre bene e felice nella casa ospitale del nostro generoso padrone.	Sia la benvenuta, egregia Signora. Auguriamo la buona fortuna a lei, e al suo stimatissimo sposo. Che la Santa Madonna le dia la sua benedizione e che tutti i santi l'accompagnino nel matrimonio!

JOE. Hey, that's enough!

AMY. Now, that was very nice of them. I liked every word they said. I guess I better study up on the lingo. All I know is words like spaghetti and raviole. . . .

ANGELO *and* GIORGIO (*sotto voce*). Ah! La Signora parla Italiano!

AMY. . . . I guess you got plenty of that around. Well, you can't make me mad. I just love it. (*Then she sees* AH GEE's *ceremonious obeisance*) How do you do? Are you the cook?

AH GEE. Yes, missy. Velly good cook.

AMY. Say! I didn't know I drew a chef. You didn't tell me. (AH GEE *takes himself off*) Say, my baggage is out there.

JOE. All right boys, lend a hand. (ANGELO *and* GIORGIO *go down the steps.*)

AMY. If you don't mind I'll just keep an eye on them. My wedding dress is in that trunk. I bet you didn't expect me to bring a wedding dress. Well, I didn't expect to, myself. And I don't know why I did. But I did! I just blew myself. I said: "You only get married once" and—I got a veil, too. I got the whole works. (*She hears her trunk en route*) Go easy there! (*She is out on the porch.*)

THE R. F. D. Well, that's her.

JOE (*as he goes to help*). She ain't bad.

FATHER MC KEE. No, she ain't half bad.

AMY (*calling down*). Not upside down! Be careful, can't you?

THE R. F. D. I don't hold much with city girls myself, but—

JOE (*calling down*). Careful boys! Look out for that vine! Gimme the grip.

FATHER MC KEE. Oh, she's above the average.

THE R. F. D. (*nudging him*). Do you think she . . . ?

FATHER MC KEE. I wouldn't hardly like to say off-hand, but . . .

THE F. D. R. I wouldn't think so.

FATHER MC KEE. Joe, do you think she . . . ?

JOE. No. Not her. Not on your life. (*He puts grip down inside the bedroom door. At the same time* ANGELO *and* GIORGIO *carry in* AMY's *pathetic little trunk, which they take into the bedroom.)*

THE R. F D. Well, I got my deliveries.

FATHER MCKEE. I'll come along with you. You stay here an' keep things conversational, Joe.

JOE. No! I'll come, too.

THE R. F. D. Till the groom turns up, Joe. You don't want her to get all upset again, do you?

FATHER MCKEE *(as* AMY *comes along the porch to the door).* Shh! Don't get her worryin'.

AMY *(in the doorway, finishing the feminine touch of powder to the nose).* I thought a little of this wouldn't make me any harder to look at.

THE R. F. D. We'll have to be movin' on, ma'am.

FATHER MCKEE. Yes.

AMY *(shaking hands with him).* I'm pleased to have made your acquaintance.

THE R. F. D. I hope to have the pleasure soon again.

AMY. Why, ain't you coming to the wedding?

THE R. F. D. Sure I am, if I'm invited.

AMY. I'll never forgive you, if you don't. And I certainly want to thank you for the lift. *(A handshake to him)* Thank you. . . . Good-bye. . . . Good-bye. . . .

THE F. D. R. Good-bye, ma'am. *(He shuffles out.* JOE *starts to follow.)*

AMY. You ain't going, too?

JOE. Well, I—

THE R. F. D. *(through the window).* Just the Padre an' me.

FATHER MC KEE *(as he goes, to* JOE*).* We'll send him right up.

THE R. F. D. *(as they disappear).* Good-bye, ma'am.

AMY. Good-bye. See you later. *(Awkward silence)* I ain't sorry they went. I think they ought to have done it sooner and left us to get acquainted. They got me all fussed up staring that way. I just couldn't think of what to say next. A girl gets kind of fussed, coming off like this to marry a man she ain't never seen. I was a mile up in the air. I—I guess I must have sounded kind of fresh. I wouldn't want you to think I was fresh.

JOE. I didn't.

AMY. I'm glad you didn't. You know, I like it up here already. You got it fixed up so cute and— *(She discovers the cake)* and that. . . . It was awful nice of you to think of that. And the view! Is them all vines?

JOE. Yeah. . . . *(An awkward pause.)*

AMY. It certainly is a pretty sight. Coming up I could taste the wind way down inside me. It made me think of where I used to live.

JOE. Where was that?

AMY. In the Santa Clara. You know, I wrote you.

JOE. Oh, yeah. In the Santa Clara. I forgot.

AMY. We had a big place in the Santa Clara. Prunes and apricots. Ninety acres in prunes and fifty in apricots. . . . (*Again an awkward silence*) I guess I'll sit down. (*She does so*) There ought to have been good money in prunes and apricots. But the prunes didn't do so good and the apricots got the leaf curl.

JOE. You're quite a farmer.

AMY. My old man was, but he got to drinking.

JOE. That's bad.

AMY. So we lost it after my mother died. But I used to love it there. In the spring, when the blossoms was out, I used to climb up on the windmill at night, when there was a moon. You never saw such a pretty sight as them blossoms in the moonlight. You could see for miles and miles all round—for miles and miles.

JOE. It must have been pretty. (*Awkward pause.*)

AMY. Ever been in the Santa Clara?

JOE. Sure. I worked there before I come here.

AMY. Where did you work?

JOE. Near Mountain View. I forget the guy's name.

AMY. I went to school in Mountain View. Our place was near there. Ever know Father O'Donnell?

JOE. No.

AMY. Thought you might have, being a Catholic and all.

JOE. I was organizer for the Wobblies.

AMY. The Wobblies?

JOE. I. W. W.

AMY. Say! You ain't one of them?

JOE. I used to be.

AMY. I sure am glad you gave that up. You don't talk one bit like an Italian.

JOE. I ain't. Only by descent. I was born in Frisco.

AMY. Oh, in Frisco? I see. . . . I'm Swiss by descent myself. My father was born in Switzerland and my grandfather, on my mother's side, he was born there, too. I don't know what that makes me—Swiss cheese, I guess. . . . (*She laughs.* JOE *does not. This crushes her and there is another awkward gap*) Our old house in the Santa Clara was bigger than this one, but it wasn't near so pretty. I must say you keep this house nice and clean for having no woman around. Our house got awful dirty toward the end. You see, my mother got to drinking, too. Hard stuff, you know. I got nothing against beer or vino, but the hard stuff don't do nobody any good. . . . That how you stand on prohibition?

JOE. Sure, I guess so.

AMY. I'm glad to hear that. I sure am. I don't want no more experience with the hard stuff. . . . That certainly is some view. Got the Santa Clara beat a mile. The Santa Clara's so flat. You couldn't get no view at all unless you climbed up on that windmill like I told you about. . . . Our old house had a cellar. Has this house got a cellar?

JOE. Sure, it has. Underneath the whole house. (*She goes to the cellar door to see.*)

AMY. I used to hide in our cellar when things got too rough upstairs. You could hear the feet running around over your head, but they never come down in the cellar after me because there was a ladder, and when you're that way you don't care much for ladders. . . . They always took it out on me.

JOE. Did they?

AMY. Yeah. I always had the cellar though. I used to play down there hot days. It smelt like apricots.

JOE. Our cellar smells like hell. It's full of vino.

AMY. That's a nice clean smell. It's sour, but it's healthy.

JOE. You're a regular wop, ain't you?

AMY. Well, after two years in a spaghetti joint! I like Italians. They always left me alone. Guess it wouldn't have done 'em much good getting fresh with me, at that. . . . Say, I'm getting pretty confidential.

JOE. Go right ahead.

AMY. All right. . . . I guess I ain't got much reason for being shy with you, at that. I wouldn't never have said I was going to marry an Italian, though. But I guess I just jumped at the chance. I got so tired of things. Oh, everything! I used to think I just couldn't keep on any longer.

JOE. Poor kid!

AMY. Oh, I usually know which side my bread's buttered on. I just said to myself: "He looks all right and I like the country and anyway it can't be no worse than this." And I said: "Why shouldn't I take a chance? He's taking just as much of a chance on me as I am on him."

JOE. That's fair enough.

AMY. Sure it is. And—maybe I hadn't ought to say it—but when I come in here and seen all you done, fixing things up for the wedding and all, and looked out the window, and smelt that wind, I said to myself, I said: "Amy, old kid, you're in gravy." Now, what do you think of that for an admission?

JOE. You're dead right. That's just what I said when I come here. I only intended to stay a few days. I'm that way, see? I been here goin' on five months now.

AMY. Is *that* all?

JOE. That's the longest I ever stayed any one place since I was old enough to dress myself.

AMY. You *have* been a rover!

JOE. I been all over—with the Wobblies, you see. Before I come here, that is.

AMY. What did you used to do?

JOE. Cherries an' hops—melons down in the Imperial an' oranges down South an' the railroad an' the oilfields. . . . Before I come here. When I come here I just stayed. Maybe I was gettin' tired of bummin'. Now I'm tired of this. But I don't mind.

AMY. Well, don't get too tired of it. I'm not a bit strong for moving myself. I had all I want of that in my time.

JOE. I guess you have.

AMY. I wonder what you think of me coming all the way up here like I did, all by myself, to marry a man I ain't never seen, only his photograph.

JOE. You couldn't have picked a better man.

AMY. Say! Don't get a swelled head, will you?

JOE. Who, me?

AMY. Oh, no, nobody! (AH GEE *passes along the porch*) I hope you're right that's all. And I guess you are, at that. And believe me, if I thought this wasn't a permanent offer, I wouldn't be here. I mean business. I hope you do.

JOE. Me?

AMY. Well, I certainly ain't referring to the Chink.

JOE. Say, who do you think . . . ?

AMY (*touching his sleeve with a kind gentle diffidence which is her first attempt at intimacy*). Don't get sore. The minute I came in I knew I was all right. I am. Why, I feel just as comfortable as if we was old friends. There don't seem to be anything strange in me being here like I am. Not now, anyhow. It just goes to show you: you never can tell how things is going to turn out. Why, if a fortune-teller had told me that I would come up here like I did, do you know what I would have said to her? I'd have said, "You're no fortune-teller." Life sure is funny, though. It's lucky for me I can say that now and laugh when I say it. I ain't always been so good at laughing. I guess we'll get used to each other in time. Don't you think we will, Tony?

JOE. Tony? Say, I ain't . . . ! Oh, Jesus! (*His words are lost in the roar of a Ford motor as it approaches, and the motor, in turn, is drowned in wild cries of dismay from* GIORGIO *and* ANGELO. (*The tension between the two in the room is broken by the excited entrance of* AH GEE, *who has evidently seen, from his kitchen window, the cause of disturbance.*)

FATHER MC KEE (*calling from off stage*). Joe! Joe!

JOE (*following* AH GEE *toward the door*). What is it? (*From the porch he sees what it is*) What—Is he dead? . . . Take that bench! (*He disappears in the direction of the disturbance which continues in both English and Italian.*)

AMY. What's the matter? Is somebody hurt?

(*The* DOCTOR, *with his fedora hat and his little black satchel, appears. He is the perfect young rural medico, just out of medical school and full of learned importance.*)

THE DOCTOR. I'll get the ambulance.

JOE (*following him in*). Is he bad, Doc?

THE DOCTOR (*as he goes into the bedroom*). Both legs above the knee—compound fractures.

JOE. Why didn't you take him to the hospital?

THE R. F. D. (*as he enters*). The Ford went right off the bridge.

FATHER MC KEE (*as he enters*). Not two hundred yards from here, Joe.

THE R. F. D. Must have fell twenty feet!

FATHER MC KEE. Never seen such a wreck! (*To* AMY) We found him lyin' in two feet of water. The car was turned right upside down.

AMY. But who is it? I don't get it. I don't know what's happened.

FATHER MC KEE. Two broken legs, that's what's happened.

THE DOCTOR (*he reappears in his shirt sleeves*) Better lend a hand, Joe! (*He vanishes again.* GIORGIO *and* ANGELO *appear, carrying the bench and apostrophizing the deity in Italian.* TONY *is recumbent and unconscious on this improvised stretcher. Much "Steady" from* JOE. *Much "There now, Tony" from the* R. F. D. *Much and prolonged groaning from* TONY.)

JOE (*as the bench is set down*). All right now, Tony.

TONY (*reviving*). AH-h-h! . . . Ees you, Joe?

JOE. Yeah. It's me. Amy's here.

TONY. Amy? Ees all right, Joe? You been makin' evrathing all right?

JOE. Sure. Everything's fine.

TONY. Where is my Amy? (*He sees her where she stands dumbfounded against the wall*) Ah-h-h, Amy! . . . Amy, don' be standin' way off dere! Come over here for shake hands. (AMY *shakes her head*) You ain' mad with me, Amy? . . . (AMY *shakes her head again.*) Amy ain' mad with me, Joe?

JOE. Nobody's mad. . . . Don't you worry.

TONY. Den we have da weddin' just da same? We have da weddin' just da same? (*The* DOCTOR *appears in the bedroom doorway, holding a hypodermic.*)

JOE. Sure, we will.

THE DOCTOR. All right, boys, bring him in. I want to give him another one of these and clean up his cuts.

JOE. Come on now, boys! Avanti! Careful there!

TONY. Amy! . . . Amy! . . . (*The jar of movement hurts him. He breaks down into groans and is carried into the bedroom. All others go with him except* JOE *and* AMY.)

JOE (*as he starts to go, a strangled sound from* AMY *arrests him. He turns and meets her gaze. He closes the door*) This is tough on you.

AMY (*almost voiceless with her terrible surmise*). Who—who is that old guy?

JOE. That? That's Tony. . . .

AMY. Tony?

JOE. It's too bad he never got to meet you. It's too bad he wasn't here when you come. (AMY *sways desperately a moment, then, with a choked cry, makes for the bedroom*) You can't go in there.

AMY. I want my trunk.

JOE. Now, listen! It ain't Tony's fault he's had an accident. . . .

AMY. Of all the dirty, low-down tricks that was ever played on a girl!

JOE. An' it ain't his fault you made a little mistake.

AMY. What do you think you are—a bunch of Houdinis? (*She tears open her handbag which she put down on the table at her first entrance and produces a photograph*) Is this your photo or isn't it?

JOE (*in amazement*). Where did you get it?

AMY. Where do you think I got it?

JOE. Good God, Tony didn't send you this, did he? For God's sake, tell me! Did Tony send you this?

AMY. Ain't I just told you?

JOE. By God, he must have been plumb crazy! By God, he was so dead gone on you he was afraid you wouldn't have nothin' to do with an old man like him. . . . He didn't have the nerve. . . . An' he just went an' sent you my photo instead of his. . . . Tony's like that, Amy. He ain't nothing but a kid. He's like a puppy, Tony is. Honest, Amy, it's God's truth I'm telling you. . . . I wouldn't have had nothin' to do with no such thing. Honest I wouldn't. I did write the letters for him, but that was only because he don't write good English like I do.

AMY. That ain't no excuse.

JOE. But there wasn't one word in them letters that wasn't God's own truth. I never knew nothin' about this photo, though. Honest to God, I never! An' Tony never meant no harm neither, Amy. Honest he never. An' he's been after me to beat it, too. Every day he has. . . . Sure it was a dirty trick an' he was crazy to think he could get away with it. I ain't denyin' it's the dirtiest trick I ever heard of. . . . Only he didn't mean no harm.

AMY. Oh, didn't he? Well, how about *my* feelings? How about *me*?

JOE. I'll do everything I can to square it. I'll drive you right down to the station now, and you can hop the first train back.

AMY. Oh, *can* I? And what do you expect me to do when I get there? Ain't I thrown up my job there? Do you think jobs is easy for a girl to get? And ain't I spent every cent I had on my trousseau?

JOE. I'll make Tony square it.

AMY. Oh, my God! Oh, my God! I got to go back and wait on table! What'll all those girls say when they see me? And I ain't even got the price of my ticket!

JOE. We can fix that.

AMY. I'll get a lawyer, I will! I wish to God I hadn't never heard of no wops!

JOE. Don't start cryin'. (*He tries to comfort her.*)

AMY. You take your hands off me and get my things.

JOE. All right. . . . (*He looks at her a moment, his distress quite evident. Then he gives it up and goes into the bedroom. As he opens the door, the* DOCTOR *and* TONY *are audible. He closes the door after him.*)

(AMY *picks up the few belongings she has left about the room. She stands a moment holding them, looking about her, at the four walls, at the country outside. Then her eye falls upon* JOE'S *photograph which still lies, face-up, on the table. She takes it in her hand and looks at it. Mechanically she makes as though to put it into the bosom of her dress. She changes her mind, drops it on the table and looks around her again. She seems to reach a decision. Her face sets and she pushes the photograph vigorously away from her.* JOE *returns with her satchel.*)

JOE. The doc's give him something to make him sleep. They're goin' to get an ambulance an' take him to the hospital. We can take the doc's Ford an' . . . It's a shame, but . . .

AMY. I ain't going.

JOE. What?

AMY. No. I ain't going. Why should I go? I like the country. This place suits me all right. It's just what I was looking for. I'm here and I might as well stick. I guess he ain't so bad, at that. I guess I could have done a lot worse. If he wants to marry me, I'm game. I'm game to see it through. It's nice up here. (*She pulls off her hat and sits, exhausted.* JOE *stares in mute admiration as the curtain falls.*)

ACT TWO

The scene remains unchanged. It is late evening of the same day. The lanterns out-of-doors have been burning so long that some of them have already guttered out. The room is lighted by two oil lamps.

TONY *lies groaning faintly on a cot, his legs encased in a plaster cast, his eternal wine bottle by his side. The* DOCTOR *sits beside him.*

Outside, the festa is in full swing. A desperate Italian tenor is singing "La Donna è Mobile" from "Rigoletto" as the curtain rises. His tones ring frantically out.

A short pause follows the song. The hiss of a skyrocket is audible. The light from the rocket flares through the windows and a long "Ah" rises from the crowd out-of-doors.

TONY. Fireworks!

THE DOCTOR. Lie quiet.

TONY. Someone verra sick in bed. Povereto! Povereto! Tony miss festa. (*Gay voices outside call to children and children answer. The* DOCTOR *rises impatiently and goes to the door.* TONY *turns his head ever so slightly*) Eh, Doc! W'ere you go?

THE DOCTOR. It's high time those coyotes went home.
(*Applause rings from the crowd. The tenor is again vigorously repeating the last phrase and cadenza of "La Donna è Mobile."*)

TONY. Dat fella is no coyot'! He is music artiste.

THE DOCTOR. It's a marvel to me the man has any lungs left. He's been howling for five hours.

TONY. You don' ondrastan' such music. Come è bella! Ees "Rigoletto!"

THE DOCTOR. Look here now, Tony! I let you out of the hospital to get married.

TONY. You bet your life! You think any goddam doc is stoppin' me from gettin married?

THE DOCTOR. I'm talking medicine, not love.

TONY. You talkin' too goddam much. You been spoil evrathing.

THE DOCTOR. Now, be reasonable, Tony. I let them bring you in here where you could see your friends.

TONY. An' den you mak' all my friends go outside.

THE DOCTOR. You're a sick man.

TONY. Ahi! Tony is verra sick . . . verra sick!

THE DOCTOR. Enough's enough. Why, half of what you have been through to-day would have killed a white man! You wops are crazy.

TONY. I don't let nobody stop no festa in my house. You go outside an' have a good time.

THE DOCTOR. I don't sing and I don't dance and I don't talk Italian and I don't drink.

TONY. I'm surprise' how much you don' know, Doc. (*He laughs. The jar is painful. He groans. The* DOCTOR *comes over to his bedside*) W'ere is my Amy?

THE DOCTOR. She's all right. Keep quiet.

TONY. You goin' look for my Amy, Doc? You goin' see if she is havin' fine time?
(*Mandolins, a guitar, and an accordion strike up a sentimental waltz outside.*)

THE DOCTOR. If you'll be quiet. (*Humoring him, he goes to the door*) I can see her from here and she's having a splendid time. Does that satisfy you?

TONY. Now evrabody goin' for dance!
(*A brief silence filled by the dance music to which* TONY, *the incorrigible, beats time. Then* JOE *and* AH GEE *come along the porch pushing a wheelbarrow, a little flurry of the crowd in their wake. The* DOCTOR *shoos out the crowd.* JOE *and* AH GEE *come in.*)

JOE. How you makin' out, Tony?

TONY. Verra sick, Joe. Is festa goin' good?

JOE. Festa's goin' fine, Tony. Me and Ah Gee's after more vino.

TONY. Da's good! Da's good!

JOE. Sure it's good. But it's a wonder everybody ain't drownded already.

TONY. Italian fellas don' get drownded in vino. Is my Amy havin' good fun, Joe?

JOE. Sure, she is! She's playin' with the kids.

TONY. Ah! . . . You go in da cellar with Ah Gee, Joe, and bring back playnta vino. Den you come back here and mak' little talk with Tony.

JOE. That's the idea. . . . (*He goes into the cellar, followed by* AH GEE.)

THE DOCTOR (*in the door, a fractious eye on the festa*). Those mothers ought to be reported for keeping youngsters up this time of night. (*A pause filled with voices and laughter.*)

TONY (*crescendo*). Doc! Doc! Doc! (*The* DOCTOR *turns.*) You think I am well next week, Doc?

THE DOCTOR. I sincerely hope, Tony, that you may be well in six months.

TONY. Six month'?

THE DOCTOR. You don't seem to realize what a bad smash you had. (*As he sits down to his professional manner*) Both tibia and fibula are fractured in the right leg. The femur is crushed in the left, and the ischium damaged as well. Now, if no systemic complications develop . . .

TONY. Oh, my God!

THE DOCTOR. . . . six months. . . .

TONY (*crescendo again*). Six month'! Six month'! Six month'!

THE DOCTOR. You won't make it any shorter by exciting yourself.

TONY. Da's right, Doc. Ees no good get excit'. I ondrastan'. But six month' . . . (*A pause*) Doc, I'm goin' ask you som'thing an' you goin' tell me just da truth, eh?

THE DOCTOR. I know what's on your mind, Tony. If you keep quiet and take care of yourself, you'll have all the kids you want.

TONY. How many?

THE DOCTOR. Ten, anyway!

TONY. Three is playnta.
(*The music is loud again as* JOE *and* AH GEE *come back from the cellar with the new barrel of wine. They load it on the wheelbarrow and* AH GEE *takes it off to the thirsty populace.* JOE *remains behind.*)

THE DOCTOR. In the meanwhile Amy's going to have her hands full, taking care of you.

TONY (*violently*). I don' marry with no woman for mak' her work. I don't want my Amy do nothing but only be happy an' fat.

JOE. There ain't nothin' too good for Tony. He marries a fine wife to play the piano for him an' he's goin' to rent a trained nurse to take care of him.
(AH GEE *is greeted with shouts of*

"Vino! Vino!" from the men and "Viva Antonio" from the girls.)

TONY. You bet your life!

THE DOCTOR. Renting trained nurses is expensive, Tony.

TONY. I got playnta money.
(*The concertina and the mandolin begin playing the chorus of "Funiculi, Funicula!" The music is continued throughout the following scene.*)

JOE (*cigarette business*). You old son of a gun! Give us a light, doc.

THE DOCTOR. Not in here, Joe!
(JOE *takes his cigarette outside. He sits with a wave to the crowd, who answer, "Joe! Joe!"*)

TONY. Is my Amy havin' good fun, Joe?

JOE. Sure. She's dancin' with the postman.

TONY. Da's good! Ees verra funny weddin' for me, Joe, but my Amy must have good time.

THE DOCTOR. Tony's got it bad.

JOE. Don't blame him. She's some girl.

TONY. I got to talk verra secret with Joe, Doc. You go outside for talk with my Amy. You better get good acquaint' with my Amy, Doc.
(*Applause outside for the dancers.*)

JOE. You could do worse, an' that's a fact.

THE DOCTOR. Tony's got to go to sleep.
(*The crowd outside shouts vociferously.*)

JOE. I won't keep him up.

TONY. Just a little w'ile, Doc? Fifteen minute'?

THE DOCTOR. Well, don't make it any longer. I want some sleep myself. Anybody would think I haven't a thing to do but take care of Tony.

JOE. We know you're a busy baby, Doc.

THE DOCTOR. Busy is right. (*Very expansive*) To-morrow, now, I've got two confinements I'm watching and an appendicitis, all up on the St. Helena road. Then, just the other side of town, I've got the most beautiful tumor you could hope to see. And the sheriff's wife! Operated her yesterday. Gallstones. Gallstones? They were cobblestones. I never saw such a case! And then, with my regular practice and my own scientific researches to keep up with things.

TONY. Corpo Dio, goddam, Doc; don' be tellin' me no more 'bout who is sick and w'at he's sick for! I'm sick playnta myself, an' I got playnta trouble here. You go outside an' leave me for talk with Joe.

THE DOCTOR. All right, but I won't have any more nonsense when I come back. (*He goes; to* JOE *on the porch*) I cannot be responsible unless the patient enjoys complete quiet, after a shock like this to his nervous system.

JOE. Has Tony got a nervous system?

THE DOCTOR. Of course he has! (*He disappears. A shout welcomes him.*)

TONY. W'at is nervous system, Joe?

JOE. It's what make things hurt, Tony.

TONY. I got playnta.
(JOE *comes in and stands over* TONY *for a moment with a look of half-tender amusement on his face.* TONY *hums distractedly keeping time with one hand to the music of "Funiculi, Funicula." With the end of the music he drops his hands with a sigh.*)

JOE. What's on your mind, Tony?

TONY. Oh, Joe! . . . Joe!! . . . Joe!!

JOE. What's the matter, Tony. Ain't you feelin' good?

TONY. Ees Amy! . . .
(JOE *sits in the* DOCTOR'S *chair, hitching it closer to the bed.*)

JOE. What do you want for a nickel? She married you, didn't she?

TONY. I'm scare', Joe. I'm scare' verra bad. I love my Amy, but my Amy don' love me.

JOE. Give her time, can't you? She wouldn't have married you if she wasn't all set to go through on the level.

TONY. You think?

JOE. Hell, I *know*.

TONY. W'at Amy say w'en she see me dees morning?

JOE. Oh, forget it, I tell you.

TONY. I got to know, Joe. You got to tell me. She's pretty goddam mad, eh?

JOE. Well, if she was, she got over it.

TONY. W'at I'm goin' to do for mak' evrathing all right, Joe? Da's w'at I want to know.

JOE. I tell you everythin' *is* all right, Tony. Oh, I ain't sayin' you ain't got to keep things movin' along easy an' friendly an' all. But that ain't goin' to be so hard. Just be good to her and take care of her. That's what Amy needs. She's tired, poor kid!

TONY. I'm all ready for tak' care like hell.

JOE. From what Amy was tellin' me this mornin', she's been a-havin' a helluva hard life for a girl, an' if she come through straight like she did, well, there ain't no credit due nobody but just only herself, and that's a fact.

TONY. You're a goddam smart fella, Joe.

JOE. I dunno how smart I am, Tony, but you can't tell me much. Not about women, you can't. Believe me, a girl gets a lousy deal any way you look at it. (*He reflects upon this for an instant before he illustrates*) Take a fella, now, a young fella like me, see? It's goin' to do him good to knock around an' have his troubles an' all. (*A solemn shake of the head.*) But knockin' around just raises hell with a girl. She can't stand it. She can't stand it, because it ain't in her nature to get away with the whole show like a fella can. (TONY *is much impressed and signifies approval with a grunt.*) If a fella wants a meal, he swipes it, don't he? A girl can't be swipin' things. It 'ud make her feel bad. She'd think she was doin' somethin' wrong. (*This surprises* TONY, *but he is willing to take* JOE's *word for it.*) Gee, I sure would hate to be a woman!

TONY (*nodding agreement*). Nobody is wantin' to be woman, Joe . . . But ees playnta good womans like my Amy!

JOE. Sure, there's good ones an' bad ones. But that ain't exactly what I mean, Tony. What I mean is, as far as I can see, it don't make a helluva lot of difference what a woman is: good or bad, young or old . . .

TONY. I lik' best fat!

JOE. . . . all women is up against it, and it's a dirty shame, too, because women ain't so bad. They ain't much use, maybe, but they ain't so bad.

TONY. My Amy is goin' have evrathing she want.

JOE. Ever heard anythin' about this dam' women's rights stuff? You know. Equality of the sexes. Woman doin' a man's work an' all that bunk?

TONY. Da's crazy idea!

JOE. The idea ain't so bad.

TONY. Ees crazy idea! Looka me! You think any woman is goin' be doin' my work? No, by God! I tell you, Joe, woman is best for sit in da house an' love da husband.

JOE. The trouble with women is, there's too goddam many of 'em. Why, I was readin' in the paper only the other day about England havin' three and a half women to every man.

TONY. W'at you mean?—half a womans!

JOE. I'm only tellin' you what the paper said.

TONY. Ees crazy idea! Half a womans! I tell you, Joe . . .

JOE. I been lookin' women over from San Diego to Seattle an' what most of 'em is after is a home. A good safe home, whether they get any rights with it or not. You take my advice an' make everythin' nice an' comfortable for Amy an' you won't have no trouble. Amy's satisfied here. Don't you kid yourself she ain't.
(*Outside the crowd is off again, the tenors leading them in "Maria Mari."*)

TONY. You're a good boy, Joe, you're pretty smart.

JOE. I'm just tellin' you the truth. You're dam' lucky you picked a girl like Amy.

TONY (*a moment of comfort; then despair again*). Ees no good, Joe—ees no good.

JOE. Oh, for cripe's sake, Tony!

TONY. I'm tellin' you, Joe, ees no good. I'm the most unhappy fella in the world. W'y? Because I been verra bad sinner an' God is goin' get me for sure! He's broke both my legs already an' he's not finish' with me yet! God is no cheap fella, Joe. God is lookin' out at Tony right now, and you know what he's sayin'? He's sayin': "Tony, you been one goddam sonuvabitch for playin' goddam dirty trick on Amy!" Da's w'at God is sayin', Joe, an' I know verra good wat God is goin' do more. Just for playin' goddam dirty trick like dat on Amy, Tony don' never have no kids, never! W'at you think is mak' me do such a thing, Joe?

JOE. Oh, hell, you always was crazy.

TONY. Ees no good, for such a bad fella like me gettin' married. God is goin' fix me playnta, all right.

JOE. I seen God let worse guys'n you get by.

TONY. You think?

JOE. If you want to square things, you better make Amy glad you done what you done.

TONY. You think? . . . Yes. . . . (*Pause*) Look, Joe. . . . (*He draws a plush box from under his blanket.*) Ees present for Amy. You open him.

JOE (*obeying*). Say! Them's what I call regular earrings!

TONY. You bet your life! He's cost four hundra dollar'!

JOE. Are them real diamonds?

TONY (*nodding*). I guess Amy like 'em pretty good, eh?

JOE. She'll be crazy about 'em. You're a pretty wise old wop, Tony, ain't you? (*He hands the box back to* TONY, *who laughs delightedly.* JOE *looks at him for a moment then goes to door and calls out*) Amy!

TONY. Eh, Joe!

JOE. You're goin' to make the presentation right away now. That'll settle your worries for you. . . . Amy, come here! Tony wants to see you!

TONY. You think is good time now?

JOE. *I know.* . . . Amy!

(AMY *appears in doorway. She wears her wedding dress and veil. The dress is undeniably pretty and only wrong in one or two places. The veil has been pulled rather askew. The whole picture is at once charming and pathetic.*)

AMY. What's the idea? (*Her voice is a little tired. She does not look at* JOE.)

JOE. Tony wants you.

AMY (*she comes in stolidly and takes the chair farthest from* TONY'S *cot. She sits there stiffly*) Well, here I am.

TONY (*ultra-tenderly*). My Amy is tire'!

AMY. You don't blame me, do you? I've had quite a day. Gee, them kids out there have been climbing all over me.

TONY. Da's good.

AMY. Oh, I don't mind kids if they go to bed when they ought to and know how to behave. Believe me, if I ever have any kids, they're going to behave.

TONY. You hear dat, Joe?

AMY. I said "if." (*A silence.*) I wouldn't object.

TONY (*amorously*). Amy . . . Come over here.

AMY (*rising quickly*). I guess I ain't so tired. I guess I better go back or they'll be wondering what's become of the blooming bride. Some bloom, huh? (*The fireworks hiss and flare again and* AMY, *very like a little girl, is out on the porch for the delight of seeing them. The enthusiasm of the crowd fairly rattles the windows.*) They sure do yell out there! When you get enough wops together and put enough vino in 'em, they sure can speak up! . . . I think I'll take off my veil. (*She does*) Phew! That thing don't look like no weight at all, but it feels like a ton of bricks.

TONY. Amy, come over here.

AMY. I'm all right where I am.

TONY. Amy!

AMY. What?

TONY. You like earrings, Amy?

AMY. Earrings? I'm human, ain't I?

JOE. That's the idea.

AMY (*a real snarl*). I didn't speak to you. I was addressing Tony.

TONY. Ah, you call me Tony for da first time!

AMY. Expect me to call my husband mister? That'd sound swell, wouldn't it? Tony. Short for Antonio. Antonio and Cleopatra, huh? Can you beat it? You'll have to call me Cleo.

TONY. I like better Amy.

AMY. There ain't no short for Amy. It's French and it means beloved. Beloved! Can you beat it? The boss in the spaghetti palace told me that the night he tried to give me a twelve-dollar pearl necklace. Twelve dollars! He was some sport. When he seen I couldn't see it that way, he give it to Blanche. She was the other girl that worked there. He had a wife and three kids too. (TONY *beckons again and* AMY *takes further refuge in conversation*) I like that name Blanche. I used to wish my name was Blanche instead of Amy. Blanche got in trouble. Poor Blanche! Gee, I was sorry for that girl!

TONY. Come over here, Amy. (*He holds out the box.*)

AMY. What's that?

TONY. Ees my present for my Amy.

AMY. What you got there, Tony?

TONY. For you.

AMY. Something for me? (*By this time, she has got over to the cot. She takes the box*) Honest? Well, now, if that isn't sweet of you, Tony. (*She opens it.*) Oh! . . . Oh!! . . . Oh!!!

TONY. Ees for mak' Amy happy.

JOE. They're real! Real diamonds!

TONY. You bet our life! Four hundra dollar'.

AMY. I . . . I . . . (*Tears come*) Real diamonds. . . . (*She sits in the* DOCTOR's *chair and cries and cries.*)

TONY. Don' cry, Amy! Don' cry! Ees no' for cry, earrings! Ees for festa! Ees for marryin' with Tony!

AMY. I don't know what to say! I don't know what to do!

JOE. Put 'em on. (*He gets the mirror, brings it over to where* AMY *sits, and holds it for her while she begins to put the earrings on. Her sobs gradually subside.*)

AMY. I had another pair once, so I got my ears pierced already. Ma pierced my ears herself with a needle and thread. Only these kind screw on! Say, ain't they beautiful! My others were turquoises and gold. Real turquoises and real gold. But these here cost four hundred dollars! Oh, I never dreamed of anything so gorgeous! (*She takes the mirror from* JOE.)

TONY. Amy . . . Amy . . .

AMY. Can I wear 'em whenever I want?

TONY. You can wear 'em in da bed if you want!

AMY. Oh, thank you, Tony! (*She is just about to kiss him.*)

JOE. Now, everything's fine!

AMY (*furiously*). Say what's the idea? What have you got to do with this? You're always buttin' in. Say . . . (*Suddenly she remembers the momentous photograph which still lies on the table*) Wait a minute. (*She picks it up and hands it quite violently to* JOE) Here's your picture.

TONY (*watching in terror*). Santa Maria!

AMY. *Here!* You better take it! Take it, I tell you! I don't want it.
(JOE *looks first at the photograph, then at the lady.*)

JOE. I guess you ain't far wrong. Amy I hope there ain't no hard feelin's.

AMY. Why should there be any hard feelings?

TONY. Benissimo!

JOE. All right. Only I didn't want you to think. . . . (*A long pause.*)

AMY (*very steadily*). You ain't got much of a swelled head, have you, Mr. Joe?
(JOE'S *face falls. The tension is snapped by a gesture from* TONY.)

TONY. Tear him up, Joe! Tear him up!
(JOE *obeys.*)

AMY. Now we don't ever have to think of that again.

TONY. Madonna! . . . Da's verra good.

AMY. You see, that's the only way to do. There ain't no use of keeping things around to remind you of what you want to forget. Start in all over again new and fresh. That's my way. Burn up everything you want to put behind you. No reminders and no souvenirs. I been doing that regular about once a month ever since I was a kid. No memories for me. No hard feelings. It's a great life, if you don't weaken. I guess, if I keep at it long enough, I may get somewhere, some day. (*She turns and deliberately kisses* TONY *on the brow.*)

JOE (*to* TONY). Will that hold you? I guess you don't need to worry no more after that. I guess that fixes your troubles for good. I guess you better admit I was pretty near right.

TONY. Now you know for w'y I been wantin' you go away, Joe. Dat goddam picture photograph! But evra thing is fix' now. Evrathing is fine. You don' need go away now, Joe.

JOE. You don't need me now. I guess I can migrate now. You got Amy to take care of you.

TONY. No! No! I need you here for tak' care of my vineyard. I don' let you go away now. Amy don' let you go away now.

AMY. Is he thinking of going away, Tony?

TONY. He don't go now, Dio mio! Ees no good Joe goin' away and leavin' Tony sick in da bed with nobody for runnin' vineyard!

JOE. You'll get somebody.

AMY. When's he going?

TONY. He say to-morrow. You don't let him go, Amy?

AMY. I got nothing to say about it.

TONY. You hear dat, Joe. Amy is askin' you for stay here.

AMY (*scorn*). *Yes,* I am!

JOE. I got to go, Tony. I just plain got to go.

AMY. If he won't stay for you, Tony, he won't stay for me. It ain't the place of a lady to be coaxing him, anyhow. . . . (*She again turns malevolent attention upon* JOE) Where you headed for?

JOE. The next place.

AMY. What's the idea?

JOE. I just got to be on my way, an' that's all there is to it.

TONY. Ees all dose goddam Wobblies, Amy. You tell him stay here, w'ile Tony is so sick in da bed like dees. You don' go to-morrow, Joe. You and me is talkin' more by-an'-by, in da mornin'.

JOE. Oh, what's the use? I'm goin', I tell you.

AMY (*smiling darkly*). It must be pretty swell, being free and independent and beating it around the country just however you feel like, sleeping any place the notion hits you, no ties, work a day and bum a week, here and there, you and the—what do you call 'em? Wobblies? Huh! I never could see much in it myself. Calling in at farmhouses for a plate of cold stew and a slab of last Sunday's pie. Down in the Santa Clara we used to keep a dog for those boys. I guess it's a fine life if you like it. Only I never had much use for hoboes myself.

TONY. Joe ain' no hobo, Amy!

AMY. Ain't he?

JOE (*completely discomfited*). I guess I'll say good-night.

FATHER MC KEE (*furiously shouting off stage*). You got no business callin' it sacramental, because it ain't got no sanction from the Church!
(TONY *looks at the pair of them in unbelieving horror.* JOE *starts to go.* AMY *smiles triumphantly. Then the situation is saved by a tumult of voices and the porch is suddenly packed with the guests of the festa: men, women, and children, old and young, fat and lean. They follow* THE DOCTOR *and* FATHER MC KEE, *who are engaged in a furious argument.*)

THE DOCTOR. Is the Church opposed to the law or is it not?

FATHER MC KEE. The Church is opposed to interfering with the divine gifts of Providence.

THE DOCTOR (*as he enters*). It's the greatest reform since the abolition of slavery.

FATHER MC KEE (*as he enters*). "The ruler of the feast calleth the bridegroom and sayeth unto him: 'Every man setteth on first the good wine'."

THE DOCTOR. Oh, hell!

FATHER MC KEE. You're a godless heretic, young man, or you wouldn't be talkin' such blasphemy! I ain't got no sympathy with drunkenness, but there's plenty of worse things. How about chamberin'? Ain't chamberin' a worse sin than drunkenness? You think you can put a stop to drunkenness by pullin' up all the grapes. I suppose you can put a stop to chamberin' by pulling up all the women!

JOE. There's an argument for you, Doc.

THE DOCTOR. Alcohol is a poison to the entire alimentary system whether you make it in a still or in a wine barrel. It's poison, and poison's no good for any man. As for the Church . . .

FATHER MC KEE (*beside himself*). It ain't poison if you don't get drunk on it, an' you don't get drunk if you're a good Cath'lic!

THE DOCTOR. I suppose that drunkenness is confined to such scientific heretics as myself?

AMY. You certainly was lappin it up outside, Doc.

TONY. Don' fight!

FATHER MC KEE You'll have to pardon me, Tony, but when I hear these heretics gettin' full on bootleg liquor and callin' it sacramental! (*The rest of the argument is drowned in the pandemonium of the crowd. At first* THE DOCTOR *tries to keep them out.*)

THE GUESTS. Buona notte! Buon riposo! Evviva Antonio! Tanti auguri! Felice notte! Tante grazie!

JOE. Festa's over.

THE GUESTS. Come sta Antonio? Come vas Voglio veder la padrona! Grazie, Antonio! Buona notte! Tanti auguri! A rivederci!

THE DOCTOR (*to* JOE). Tell them to cut the row!

THE GUESTS. Grazie, Antonio! Mille grazie, Antonio! Buona notte, Antonio! Tanti auguri! A rivederci!

THE DOCTOR. Keep those wops out of here! There's been enough noise already with this bigoted old soak.

FATHER MC KEE. You heretical, blasphemin' . . .

TONY. Padre, Madonna mia, don' fight no more! (To the crowd) Eh!

THE DOCTOR (*still holding the crowd back in the doorway*). No, you can't come in here!

THE GUESTS. Si, si, dottore! Si, si dottore! Prego, dottore!

THE DOCTOR. No! Tony's too sick!

TONY. Tak' a pinch-a snuff, Doc, an sit down. (*The guests surge in as*

TONY *calls to them*) Vieni! Vieni qui! Venite tutti! Venite tutti!

THE GUESTS. Come va? Sta bene? Sta meglio, Antonio? Ha tanto sofferto, poveretto! Poveretto!

TONY (*picking out a small boy*). Ecco il mio Giovannino! Ah, com' è grande e bello e forte! Quanto pesa?

GIOVANNINO'S MOTHER. Ah, si, è grande, non è vero? Pesa sessanta cinque libbre.

TONY. Sessanta cinque! (*To* AMY) Amy, looka him! He weigh' sixty-five pound', an' he's only . . . (*To the mother*) Quant' anni?

GIOVANNINO'S MOTHER. Soltanto nove.

TONY. He's only nine year' old an' he weigh sixty-five pound'!

ANOTHER MOTHER. Antonio, ecco la mia.
(*A little girl runs to throw her arms around* TONY'S *neck and kiss him. Exclamations of delight.*)

TONY (*to the mother*). Ah! Come so chiama?

THE SECOND MOTHER. Maria Maddalena Rosina Vittoria Emanuela.

TONY. Maria Maddalena Rosina Vit— (*To* AMY) Looka Maria Maddalena! Ah, Maria Maddalena is goin' grow up an' be a fine, beautiful lady like my Amy.

GIOVANNINO'S MOTHER. E il mio Giovannino! (*To* MARIA'S MOTHER) Santa Madonna! Ella non è più bella che il mio Giovannino!

MARIA'S MOTHER (*furious*). Si, è più bella! E molto più bella che un ragazzone come questo.

GIOVANNINO'S MOTHER. Non è ragazzone, senti!

MARIA'S MOTHER. Si! Ma, la mia carina.

THE MEN (*hilariously*). Giovannino! Giovannino!

THE WOMEN (*at the same time*). Maria Maddalena! Maria Maddalena!

THE DOCTOR. Come on, now, get out! We've had enough of this!

ANGELO *and* GIORGIO (*facing the howling mob*). Basta! Basta! Via! Via! Fuori! Avanti! Al diavolo!
(*Uproar and retreat.*)

AMY (*on the porch, she stops them*). No, wait a minute! I want to tell 'em all good-night. Good-night! Good-night! Thank you. I've had the very best wedding that ever was and I'm the happiest girl in the world because you've been so good to me. Come back to-morrow and see Tony and tell him all the news. Good-night and God bless you.

VOICES. Siamo molto contenti! Com' è gentile! Com' è bella! Com' è simpatica! Grazie tanto, Amy!

JOE. They say thank you and God bless you. . . . Beat it, now. Buona notte! Run along. Come back to-morrow.
(*As they go down the hill, tenor, concertina, and chorus strike into song.*)

TONY. Oh, Amy, I w'isper in your ear, Amy. You ain' goin' be mad with Tony for bein' so crazy-wild with love? You come in da house like da spring come in da winter. You come in da house like da pink flower dat sit on da window sill. W'en you come da whole world is like da inside da wine cup. You ondrastan', Amy? I canno' help talkin' dees way. I got for tell you, Amy, an' I ain't got no English language for tell you. My Amy is so good, so prett!' My Amy. . . . (*He fairly breaks down.* AMY *pats his hand.*)

JOE (*to* FATHER MC KEE). Look at the poor wop. (*He is just going.*)

THE DOCTOR. Don't go, Joe. I want a hand with Tony.

FATHER MC KEE. Listen. . . .(*He holds up his hand for them to attend to the music. He pours wine into a cup*) Here's to the bridal couple!

JOE (*same business*). Doc?

THE DOCTOR. No, thanks.

AMY. Oh, Doctor!

TONY. Doc, you no drink Tony's health?

THE DOCTOR. Oh, all right! (*He drinks with the others*) Nasty stuff. (*He drains his glass. They laugh, all of them*) Off to bed with you now, Tony!

TONY. My leg is hurt too much. I canno' sleep.

THE DOCTOR. I've got something that'll make you sleep. (*He mixes a powder in water and presents it to* TONY *for consumption.*)

TONY. Jes' Chris'! I canno' drink water, Doc! (*With the* DOCTOR'S *consent he adds wine to the draught.*)

THE DOCTOR. That's right. . . . Drink up. . . . (*The potion is downed.*)

TONY. Amy, you lookin' sad!

JOE. Do you blame her? She's had some day. (*A pat on her shoulder. She shrinks angrily.*)

AMY. I ain't sad. . . . It was a swell wedding and everybody had a swell time. Hear that? They're still singing. Ain't it pretty? And I don't want to hear no more of what the Doc was telling me outside about bringing a trained nurse up here from Napa. I'm all the nurse Tony needs, and don't nobody be afraid of my working, because there's nothing I like better. And when Tony's good and strong and don't have to be in bed all the time, we'll have Giorgio and Angelo carry him out in the sun and I'll sit beside him and read the paper out loud and we'll look at the view and feel that nice wind and we'll just enjoy ourselves. And the doc'll come up and see us. And the Padre, too, if they can keep from fighting. And if Joe goes away—why—he goes away, that's all. Don't nobody fret about little Amy. She's going to be all right. (*The* DOCTOR *and the* PRIEST *exchange approving glances.*)

FATHER MC KEE. Amy, you're a credit to the parish.

THE DOCTOR (*at the head of the cot*). Joe, take that end!

TONY (*still spellbound*). My Amy. . . .

AMY. Yes, Tony?

TONY. I'm sleepy.

THE DOCTOR. (*as* JOE *and he lift the cot.*) Not too high.

TONY (*groaning, he can still reach to take his bottle along*). Wait!

JOE. Steady! You hold the door, Padre.

THE DOCTOR. Easy now! Not too fast.

AMY. Watch out for his hand!

THE DOCTOR. Take shorter steps, Joe. Every man ought to be taught how to carry a stretcher. Why, when I was in France . . . (*He backs through the door*) Lower your end, Joe! You'll give him apoplexy.

TONY. Oh! . . .

JOE. I got him. . . . (*He follows through the door with the foot of the cot. Another groan from* TONY. AMY *takes a step toward door.*)

FATHER MC KEE. Better give 'em a minute. (*He goes into the bedroom.* AMY *is left alone. She stands quite still for a moment; then, giddily, drops into a chair.* FATHER MC KEE *returns.*)

FATHER MC KEE. You're a fine brave girl.

AMY. Thanks.

FATHER MC KEE. We have our trials, all of us.

AMY. Sure, I know that.

FATHER MC KEE. If ever you need a word of comfort, call on me, my daughter.

AMY. Thanks.

FATHER MC KEE. You may not be a Cath'lic, but I'll do my best by you. (AMY *smiles wanly*) I had my doubts of this here marriage, but God knows who's meant for who in this world. He ain't done a bad turn by either you or Tony.

AMY. I got no kick.
(*The* DOCTOR *enters, quietly closing the bedroom door after him.*)

FATHER MC KEE. Be patient with him. He's old enough to be your father, and no man ain't got no business marryin' at his age, but he's a good fella.

AMY. I guess I better go in there now.

THE DOCTOR. (*wiping his hands medically on his spotless handkerchief*). He's asleep. I've never known the like. Never in all my years of practice. It's a case that ought to be written up for the whole, entire medical profession. Both legs broken in the morning. Tibia, fibula, femur, and ischium. X-rayed and set inside of an hour after the accident. Patient married at noon and survives ten hours of whooping Dago celebration with no apparent ill effects.

AMY (*grim*). Yeah! What do you want me to do, Doctor?

THE DOCTOR. Let me send up a nurse in the morning.

AMY. No.

THE DOCTOR. A man in a cast's a handful. It's going to be a long siege.

AMY. I can manage. (*Suddenly desperate*) God! I got to have something to do!

THE DOCTOR. Well. . . . (*He shrugs his shoulders.*) If he wakes up tonight, give him another one of those powders in a little wine. Wine won't harm the drug and the water might kill the patient. Eh, Padre?

AMY. Is that all, Doctor?

THE DOCTOR. That's all. I'll come up early in the morning.

AMY. Thanks.

THE DOCTOR. Sure about the nurse? (*She nods*) You take it pretty calmly.

AMY. Ain't much else I can do, is there?

THE DOCTOR. Good-night. Joe's fixing you up a bed. He'll be here if you want him.

FATHER MC KEE (*going with the* DOCTOR). I ain't kissed the bride.

THE DOCTOR. Come on! (*He pushes* FATHER MC KEE *in front of him and they go off. Their voices die away.*) (AMY *goes to the table and mechanically removes her earrings.* AH GEE *enters by the outer door with a tray of glasses.* JOE *enters from the bedroom, closing the door carefully after him.*.

JOE. You turn in, Ah Gee. I'm going to sleep in here. (AH GEE *goes to his kitchen.* JOE *watches* AMY *with the same puzzled frown he has worn since she first turned upon him.*) Amy . . . (*She stiffens*) I got you fixed up in Tony's big bed. I'm goin' to sleep in here in case you want any help.

AMY. All right.

JOE. Well, good-night. (*He goes about making himself comfortable for the night.*)

AMY. Good-night, Joe.

JOE. Keep a stiff upper lip. Everything's going to turn out O. K. Good-night.

AMY. You certainly do think you're God Almighty, don't you?

JOE. I don't get you.

AMY. Oh, well, let it go. I guess I don't feel so good.

JOE (*still busy with his bed*). Maybe it's the vino. It don't agree with some folks.
(*A slight pause.*)

AMY. I guess I'm just nervous.

JOE. I'd be nervous myself if I'd just been married.

AMY. Would you?

JOE. If I was a girl, I would.

AMY. Maybe that's why I'm nervous

JOE. Sure it is. I often think how it must be for a girl takin' a big, important step like gettin' married. Everything new an' diff'rent an' all that.

AMY. Yeah.

JOE. But I wouldn't let it worry me if I was you.

AMY. I won't, Mister Joe. (*She takes up one of the lamps.*)

JOE. That's the idea. Good-night.

AMY. Good-night. (*She turns and looks desperately at him.*)

JOE. Say, look here, Amy . . .

AMY. I don't remember of giving you leave to use my Christian name.

JOE. Excuse me . . . only . . . there's something I just got to say to you before I go away. Because I am going. I'm going in the morning just as soon as Tony wakes up so's I can tell him good-by. But there's something I just got to ask you.

AMY. What is it?

JOE. You like Tony all right, don't you?

AMY. I married him, didn't I? And I let him give me jewelry, too, didn't I? A nice, self-respecting girl don't accept jewelry from a man she don't like. Not real jewelry.

JOE. I know that . . . only . . it ain't just what I mean. Because, Tony—oh, he's a nut an' a wop an' all that, but he's just the best old fella I ever knew. Regular salt of the earth, Tony is. I wouldn't like to see Tony in trouble or unhappy or gettin' his feelings hurt or anything in that line. . . .

AMY (*dangerously*). Oh, wouldn't you?

JOE. No. An' it's all up to you now. . . . An' . . . well, you see what a fine old fella he is, don't you?

AMY. I ain't been complaining about him that I remember. When I start in complaining there'll be plenty of time then for outsiders to butt in and make remarks.

JOE. Don't get sore.

AMY (*fury again*). Who's sore? Say, listen to me. I know what I'm about, see? I married for a home, see? Well, I got a home, ain't I? I wanted to get away from working in the city. Well, I got away, didn't I? I'm in the country, ain't I? And I ain't working so very hard, either, that I can notice. Oh, I know what's expected of me and I ain't going to lay down on my job. Don't you fret. You be on your way, and mind your own business.

JOE. Oh, all right!

AMY. I got all I bargained for and then some. I'm fixed. I'm satisfied. I didn't come up here . . . like I did . . . looking for love. . . or . . . or anything like that.

JOE. All I got to say is it's a good thing you got so dam' much sense.

AMY. I'll thank you not to swear about me, too. . . .

JOE. You got me wrong, Amy. I apologize. Maybe I was only seein' Tony's side of the question. Some girls would have been sorer'n you was over what old Tony done to get you here. But you're a real sport, that's what you are. You're a great girl an' I'm all for you. (*He emphasizes his approval with another patronizing pat on her shoulder.*)

AMY. Oh, for God's sake, leave me alone, can't you?

JOE (*who can grow angry himself*). Sure, I can! Good-night!

AMY. Good-night! (*She stands quite still, so does he. Far, far away the irrepressible tenor resumes "Maria Mari."*)

JOE. I'm sleeping in here in case . . .

AMY. There won't be any need of you putting yourself out.

JOE. How do you know but what Tony . . .

AMY. I can take care of Tony and the further off *you* keep yourself the better I'll be pleased. (*Their eyes blaze.*)

JOE. Well, if you feel that way, I'll go back to my own shack. (*He grabs his coat and makes for the door*) That wop'll be singing all night. (*He is out on the porch.*)

AMY. Joe!

JOE. What? (*He returns.*)

AMY. Would you mind waiting just a minute? There's something *I* got to ask *you.*

JOE. Shoot. . . .

AMY. You got to tell *me* the truth this time. You just got to tell me the truth. . . . You really and honestly didn't know nothing about his sending me that photo of you instead of his own, did you? You didn't know nothing at all about that?

JOE. Honest to God, I didn't. . . . Honest to God. . . .

AMY. On your sacred word of honor?

JOE. Honest.

AMY. I'm glad. And I want to apologize to you for what I said just now . . . and for that other thing I said about your being a common hobo and all. . . . I'm sorry, Joe. Will you forgive me?

JOE. Oh, that's all right.

AMY. I wouldn't want to have you go away to-morrow thinking what a mean character I got.

JOE. Nothing like that.

AMY. You mean it?

JOE. Shake. (*They shake hands, standing in the doorway*) You're cryin'! . . . What's the matter, kid?

AMY. Oh, I don't know. . . . Nothing. . . . I'm all right. . . .

JOE. Come on! Don't get upset. Just make the best of things.

AMY. It ain't that.

JOE. Well, just make the best of things, anyway.

AMY. I'm trying to! I'm trying to!

JOE (*his hands on her shoulders*). You're married to a good man. I know the weddin' was kind of funny with Tony all smashed up an' all. But you just hold on a while an' everythin'll be O. K. You'll see!

AMY. I bet all those people are laughing at me.

JOE. No, they ain't.

AMY. I bet you're laughing at me.

JOE. I ain't, Amy. I'm sorry. . . .

AMY (*moving back from him*). Leave me alone, can't you?

JOE (*his voice very low*). Say, you're all right, Amy. . . . You're plumb all right.

AMY. I always was all right till I come up here. Now I wish I was dead! I wish I was dead!

JOE. Don' talk that way. You're all right. . . . (*Clumsily, he takes her arm. She stumbles. He catches her. There is a moment of silence broken only by their deep breathing as the physical being of one is communicated to the physical being of the other. Suddenly and irresistibly he clutches her to his breast and kisses her. She struggles a moment, then abandons herself.*)

TONY (*calling out in the bedroom*). Amy! (*She breaks loose, sobbing hysterically.*)

JOE (*a whisper*). Jesus! (*She stifles a little cry and turns for the bedroom door*) No, you don't. . . . (*He catches her.*)

AMY (*struggling*). Let me go!

TONY. Amy!

(*She breaks free, terrified, and runs out of the house.* JOE *stands listening a moment, then runs after her as the curtain falls.*)

ACT THREE

The scene is unchanged, but the woman's presence has made itself felt. Handsome, though inexpensive, cretonne curtains grace the windows. A garish jardinière of porcelain holds a geranium plant and stands upon a colored oriental tabouret. The lamps have acquired art shades: one of some light-colored silk on a wire form and adorned with roses of the same material in a lighter shade, the other of parchment painted with windmills and Dutch kiddies. New pictures selected from the stock-in-trade of almost any provincial "art department" hang upon the walls; one of them, perhaps, a portrait of a well-known lady screen star. These have replaced Washington and Garibaldi and the Italian Steamship Company's poster. Painted and elaborately befringed leather sofa cushions fill the large chairs. It is hoped that one of the variety showing the head of Hiawatha can be secured for this, as they say, "touch." A brilliantly embroidered centerpiece covers the dining-room table and the flowers in the middle are palpably artificial. A white waste-paper basket is girt by a cerise ribbon which makes some corner of the room splendid. A victrola graces another corner.

Three months have passed. It is mid-afternoon.

An invalid chair has been made by laying a board between the seat of the morris chair and the top of a box. In this TONY *reclines, his crutches lying on the floor by his side.* FATHER MC KEE *nods drowsily in another chair.* JOE *sits on the porch rail outside the window perusing the scareheads of an I. W. W. paper.*

FATHER MC KEE (*continuing the discussion*). Now, Joe, don't be tryin' to tell me that things is goin' to be any better for havin' a revolution, because they ain't. Gover'ment's always gover'ment no matter what you call it, an' no particular kind of gover'ment ain't no more'n a label anyway. You don't change nothin' by givin' it a new name. Stick a "peppermint" label on a bottle of castor oil an' then drink it an' see what happens to you. Castor oil happens!

TONY. I am work' just as much like Joe an' I don' want changin' nothing.

JOE. I suppose you both come over here in the first place because you was satisfied with everythin' just like it was in the old country?

FATHER MC KEE. Human nature ain't nothin' but human nature an' the only way you ever could make a gov-er'ment is by obedience. Scalliwag-gin' around about grievances an' labels don't accomplish nothin'. An' the only way you can make a revolu-tion anythin' but a mess to no pur-pose is to change the people's ideas an' thank goodness there ain't no-body can accomplish that. It can't be done.

JOE. They're changin' already, Padre.

FATHER MC KEE. I'm talkin' to you with the cassock off, Joe. I'm lettin' you in on the secrets of the Mother Church. She knows the stock of ideas the world over an' she knows they don't never change. The Mother Church just keeps hammerin' an' hammerin' the same old nails because she knows there ain't no new ones worth hammerin'.

TONY. People come in da Unita State' because ees good place. I been comin' for mak' money.

JOE. You certainly succeeded.

TONY. You don' ondrastan', Joe. You got crazy idea. I'm comin' here for mak' money an' you want tak' my money all away.

JOE. What's your idea of progress, Padre?

FATHER MC KEE. Improvin' yourself! Now, Joe, it comes to my notice that you been 'round here talkin' pretty uppity 'bout the U. S. gover'ment. 'Tain't no good just makin' slurrin' remarks 'bout the gover'ment when you ain't got the ability nor the power to do nothin' toward improvin' it. You have got the power to do somethin' toward improvin' yourself, but I don't see you doin' it.

TONY. W'at I care for gover'ment? Peoples is tellin' me king is no good an' freedom is verra fine. W'at I care for king? W'at I care for freedom? Evrabody say dees gover'ment is bad for havin' pro'ibish'. I say pro'ibish' mak' me dam' rich. Evra man got his own idea w'at is good for evrabody else.

JOE. You're a bloomin' capitalist, that's what you are!

TONY. You mak' me tire', Joe. Evra minute talkin' 'bout Russia. . . . Russia. . . . Tak' a pinch-a snuff an' shut up!

JOE. Russia's got the right idea.

FATHER MC KEE. Now, listen to me, young man. If you had the energy an' the reverence for authority and the continence that Tony has, you wouldn't be carryin' on 'bout no revo-lutions in Russia. 'Tain't sense. I've read a-plenty of your radical litera-ture an' if you ask me, it's just plain stupid. I may be a priest an' I may be a celibate, but that don't make me no less of a man. An' no real man ain't never got no use for carryin's on. You radicals, Joe, you're always an' forever hollerin' an' carryin' on 'bout your rights. How 'bout your duties? There ain't no one to prevent your doin' your duties but you ain't never done 'em in your life.

JOE. I'm savin' my duties for the brotherhood of man.

TONY. Dio mio!

FATHER MC KEE. You're talkin' a lot of balderdash. Mind your own business an' leave the brotherhood of man to me. Brothers is *my* job.

TONY. You think evrabody's goin' be brother like dat an' don' scrap no more? Ees crazy idea! You ain' got no good sense, Joe, you an' does goddam Wobblies.

FATHER MC KEE. I been mullin' this over in my mind, Joe, ever since Tony asked me to come up an' talk to you. An' I come to the conclusion that capital an' labor'll go on scrappin' to the end of time and they'll always be a certain number of people that'll stand up for the underdog. I been standin' up for the underdog all my life . . .

JOE (*indignant, he comes into the room*). Yes, you have! A helluva lot of standin' up you ever done for anybody but yourself!

TONY (*talking at the same time*). Now, Joe, don' you be gettin' fresh! You listen to w'at da Padre's sayin'!

FATHER MC KEE (*talking at the same time*). . . . but I learned a long time ago that the dog on top needs just as much standin' up for as the other kind and I ain't got much use for either of 'em because both of 'em's always complainin' an' carryin' on.

TONY. I been 'Merican citizen for twent' year'. I been vote evra year—some times two times. Ees fine thing, vote! I like. He mak' me feel like I am good man an' patriotic fella. But w'at I know 'bout vote? I don't know nothing. I don' care nothing. You think you know so much, eh? You want for change evrathing an' w'en you got evrathing change' like you want, some other fella is comin' for changin' you. Ees no good. (*A defiant look about him*) You look-a me an' do like I done. You marry with good wife like my Amy an' live quiet in a fine house an' gettin' rich like me an' . . . an' . . . an' raisin' playnta kids like I am goin' do. Da's w'at is for life. Not for runnin' evra place, goddam to hell gover'ment with goddam Wobblies!

JOE. Now you got Tony goin' on kids again. I sure am catchin' all that's comin' my way. But, just the same, I'm goin' to take my trip to Frisco an' see what's what.

FATHER MC KEE. Well, Joe, I can understand your wantin' to shake the dust of this place off'n your feet. But I got to tell you that the adventures of the spirit is a great deal more interestin' than the adventures of the flesh. No man can't do no more'n 'bout six things with his flesh. But he can have a heap of fun with his immortal soul.

TONY. Joe is dam' lucky havin' good job here. Last time he talk 'bout goin' away, he tak' my advice an' stay here for runnin' da vineyard. Dees time he better tak' my advice some more.

(FATHER MC KEE *is fingering* JOE'S *papers ominously.*)

JOE. I'll just trouble you for them papers, Padre.

FATHER MC KEE. If you take my advice you'll burn 'em.

TONY. Joe don' mean no harm.

JOE. Maybe I don't mean nothin' at all. Maybe I'm just restless an' rarin' to go. I read these things an' they make me think. A man ought to think if he can. Oh, not tall talk. Just what he could be doin' himself. I think how I could get into the scrap. I ought to have been in on the dock strike at San Pedro, but I wasn't. I don't want to miss another big fight like that, do I? You fellows don't understand, but that's the way it is. An' maybe you're right an' I'm wrong. I can't help that. Maybe when I get down to Frisco I'll hear the same old bull from the same old loud-mouths, just like it used to be. Maybe I'll get disgusted and beat it south for the orange pickin's, or maybe go back on the railroad, or maybe in the oilfields. But, what the hell! I been hangin' around here on the point of goin' for three months now. I might just as well pick up and clear out to-morrow or the day after. I'll come back some day, Tony. Anyway, there ain't no use of expectin' anythin' out of a guy like me. Don't get sore. What the hell!

TONY. You goin' in da jail, sure!

JOE. I could go worse places. A guy went to jail up in Quincy, in Plumas County, awhile back, for carryin' a Wobbly card—like this one, see? (*He displays the famous bit of red cardboard*) His lawyer pleads with the judge to go easy on the sentence. "Your honor," he says, "this chap served in France an' won the Croy de Gaire an' the Distinguished Service Cross." An' right there the guy jumps up an' says: "Don't you pay no attention to that stuff," he says. "I don't want no credit for no services I ever performed for no gover'ment that tells me I got to go to jail to stand up for my rights."

FATHER MC KEE. Do you want to go to jail?

JOE. There's worse places, I tell you. I been there before, too. That guy in Quincy got the limit an' I'd like to shake hands with him, I would. Tony says this is a free country. Well, Tony ought to know. He's a bootlegger.

TONY (*indignantly*). Hah!

JOE. What I say is: about the only freedom we got left is the freedom to choose which one of our rights we'll go to jail for.

FATHER MC KEE (*super-sententiously*). Joe.

TONY. Shhh! Here's Amy!

AMY (*off stage*). Ah Gee!

(JOE *rises;* FATHER MC KEE *pauses in his harangue;* TONY *beams;* AMY *enters. She wears a bright dress and a red straw hat which pushes her hair down about her face. A duster swings dashingly from her shoulders. Her market basket hangs from her arm. She has stuffed some late lupin in the top of it.*)

AMY. Scrapping again, are you? What's the matter, this time? Has

Joe got another attack of the foot-itch? (*She sets the basket down on the table, doffs hat and duster, and, as she does so, sees* JOE'S *papers*) Oho! So that's it. (*Patiently* JOE *folds the papers up*) See them, Tony? (*She exhibits the lupin and begins to stuff it into the vase with the artificial flowers*) Ain't they sweet? They're so pretty they might be artificial.

FATHER MC KEE. We been talkin' 'bout reformin' the social system.

AMY. Well, you got a fine day for it. (*She hugs* TONY'S *head and lets him pat her hand*) Ain't the doctor come yet?

TONY. Doc don' come to-day.

AMY. Sure he does.

JOE. He comes on Thursday.

FATHER MC KEE. To-day's Wednesday.

AMY. Well, I never! Here they are reforming the world and they don't even know what day of the week it is. Ain't men the limit?

TONY. Nobody is so smart like my Amy. (*With a toss of her head she swirls off into the kitchen.*)

AMY. Don't let me stop you! Go right ahead. (*In the kitchen*) Ah Gee . . . Oh, there you are. . . .

FATHER MC KEE. Thursday! It's my day to talk to the boys down at the parish school.

JOE. Hand 'em what you just been handin' me, Padre.

FATHER MC KEE. What I told you was confidential, Joe. I'm sorry you won't listen to it.

AMY (*she returns, carrying a dish with apples and a knife*). See them, Tony?

TONY. Apples!

AMY. Guess what for?

TONY. Apples pie?

AMY (*she sits beside* TONY *and falls to on the apples*). Well, the world may need reforming but I got no kick. The grapes is near ripe and ready for picking. The nights is getting longer, the mornings is getting colder, and Tony's getting better. Down town they're putting up the posters for the circus and I hear the show's going into winter quarters just the other side of Napa. I guess that's all the remarks I got to make now.

JOE. Here's the doc, now. . . .
(*A Ford motor.*)

THE DOCTOR (*off stage*). Hello!

AMY. Yoo hoo!
(*The* DOCTOR *appears, shakes hands with* AMY, *nods to* JOE *and the* PADRE, *and then he comes in to* TONY.)

THE DOCTOR. Well, how do the crutches go?

AMY. Just fine.

TONY. You want see me walkin', Doc?

THE DOCTOR. Perhaps, I do. Let's see. . . . (*He feels the injured legs*)

Tibia . . . Fibula . . . Feels all right.

TONY (*with a proud, anatomical gesture*). Ischium?

THE DOCTOR (*he rises and nods approvingly*). All right, Tony, show us what you can do. No jumping, mind! Lend him a hand, Joe.
(*He stands aside to watch.* JOE *assists* TONY. *Grunting,* TONY *stands on his crutches and grins proudly.*)

TONY. Ees hurtin' here. (*Indicating arm pits*) But ees goin' fine! (*A few tottering steps.*)

THE DOCTOR. Steady! Whoa! (*Laughter as* TONY *barely makes a chair*) You ought to be put on exhibition. If anyone had told me that day when I had you on the table that I should see you on crutches in three months! Well, all I can say is, it pays to know how to set a fracture.

AMY. I guess it makes you realize what a good doctor you are.

THE DOCTOR. He owes something to your nursing, ma'am.

FATHER MC KEE. It's like the layin' on of hands, her nursin' is.

AMY. Funny you're saying that, Padre. I once had my fortune told down in Frisco. Out of a palmistry book one of my friends had. Everything in your hand means something, you know. See those bumps? Ain't they funny? Well, the book said that those bumps mean you're a good nurse and can take care of anybody no matter how sick he is. That's why I wouldn't let you send for no trained nurse, Doc. I was afraid she wouldn't have my bumps. . . . Gee, I got funny hands! . . .

THE DOCTOR. I'm not sure that medical science pays much attention to the nursing bump, ma'am, but you have certainly got it. I'll admit that.

TONY. My Amy is da best nurse I ever see.

AMY. Oh, Tony!

THE DOCTOR. I'm going to put your patient outside in the sun. Is there a good level place?

AMY. Under the arbor! . . . Oh Tony!

TONY. After three month' in dees goddam house!

THE DOCTOR. Fix him up right with a big easy chair.

AMY. And plenty of pillows.

TONY. Amy, you ain' forgot how you promise' 'bout readin' da paper outside in da sun?

AMY. You bet I ain't forgot.

THE DOCTOR. Go on, now. I want to see you fixed.

TONY (*hobbles to the door and calls out*). Giorgio . . . Angelo . . . Eccomi!
(GIORGIO *and* ANGELO *arrive in a whirlwind of Italian.* TONY *hobbles out of sight.* AMY *follows with two pillows, looking back at the* DOCTOR *and laughing.* FATHER MC KEE *carries the board and box. The* DOCTOR *goes to the door as though he intended following them. He stands looking out and speaks without turning.*)

THE DOCTOR. Joe . . .

JOE. What is it?

THE DOCTOR. I hear you're going away.

JOE. Yeah. I'm really goin' this time.

THE DOCTOR. Where to?

JOE. Search me. Frisco first.

THE DOCTOR. Hadn't you better take Amy with you? (*He turns then and looks sternly into* JOE's *startled eyes.*)

JOE. What?

THE DOCTOR. You heard me.

JOE. I don't get you.

THE DOCTOR. Amy came to see me last week. I didn't tell her what the trouble was. I didn't have the heart. I put her off. . . . Oh, it's easy to fool a woman. But you can't fool a doctor, Joe. (*A step nearer* JOE *and eyes hard on his face*) Tony isn't the father. . . . He couldn't be. (*A long pause.*)

JOE (*under his breath*). Oh, Christ!

THE DOCTOR. I thought so. (*Another long pause*) I've been trying to figure out how to make things easiest for Tony. It upset me a good deal. Doctors get shocked more often than you'd think. . . . And a girl like Amy, too. . . . I didn't know what to do. I guess it's up to you.

JOE. Poor old Tony!

THE DOCTOR. You might have thought of him sooner—and of Amy, too, for that matter.

JOE. It wasn't on purpose. It was only once! But—honest to God, we wouldn't either of us have put anything like that over on old Tony. Not for a million dollars!

THE DOCTOR. You couldn't have wasted much time about it.

JOE. It was the first night.

THE DOCTOR. Good Lord!

JOE. It just happened. There was a reason you don't know about. I'm a swell guy, ain't I? To do a thing like that to a fellow like Tony.

THE DOCTOR. Shall I tell Tony? Or Amy?

JOE. No. . . . Gimme time to think.

THE DOCTOR. There's no concealing this. Don't try anything of that sort. I won't have it.

JOE. No.

THE DOCTOR. This is going to come near killing him.
(JOE *nods fearsomely. The* DOCTOR *turns and is going when* AMY *appears, marshalling* ANGELO *and* GIORGIO.)

AMY. Just cut out the welcome to our city stuff and carry this chair down there under the arbor where the boss is. (*As they pick it up, she turns to the* DOCTOR) Say! You'd think to hear 'em that Tony'd just been raised from the dead. (*She turns back to the two Italians*) Put it in the shade. . . . Mind that varnish, you club-footed wops. . . . There. . . . (*She has seen the chair safely along the porch. She returns and makes for the bedroom, saying, as she goes*) He wants a cover and everything you can think of. . . .

THE DOCTOR (*to* JOE). Let me know if I can do anything.

(AMY *returns carrying a great, thick quilt. She cuts for the door, muttering happily to herself. On the porch she stops to call through the window to the stricken* JOE.)

AMY. Joe—just hand me them newspapers, will you?

JOE (*obeying*). Here.

AMY (*in the doorway, her arms filled with papers and comforter, she sees his face*). Gee—you look something fierce.

JOE (*in a strangled voice*). Amy . . .

AMY. What is it?

JOE. I got to see you by an' by. . . . I got to see you alone . . . (*She starts to speak. He sees that he has frightened her*) God damn . . . oh, God damn. . . .

AMY. What's the matter with you? What you scaring me this way for?

JOE. Amy. . . . Just a minute ago . . .

AMY. Make it snappy. . . . I don't like this being alone with you. . . . It makes me think . . . I want to forget all that.

JOE. Yeah . . . An' me . . . that's what I mean.

AMY. What?

JOE (*after an awful pause*). You're goin' to have a kid. (*She stares incredulously at him without making a sound*) Yeah. . . . It's so, Amy. . . . I'm awfully sorry. . . . The doc just told me. . . . He found out when you was sick last week. . . . He knows all about it . . .

AMY (*she stands a moment without moving at all. Suddenly she lets quilt and papers slip to the floor and her hands clasp themselves over her abdomen*). Oh, my God! (*She picks the quilt and papers up very carefully and puts them on the table. She drops weakly into one of the chairs as though her knees had failed her, her face rigid with terror.*)

JOE. I know how it is. . . . Just keep your head, now. . . .

AMY. What am I going to do?

JOE. I got to think. . . .

AMY. If you go wrong, you're sure to get it sooner or later. I got it sooner.

JOE. That kind of talk won't help any.

AMY. I'm glad of it. It serves me right. . . .

JOE. There's ways, you know . . . there's doctor. . . .

AMY (*shakes her head vigorously*). Them kind of doctors is no good.

JOE. But maybe . . .

AMY. They're no good. I'm too far gone anyway . . . I know . . . and anyway . . . doing that . . . It's worse than the other.

JOE. I'm sorry, Amy. . . .

AMY. You being sorry ain't got nothing to do with it, either. I'm thinking of Tony.

JOE. So'm I.

AMY. Tony's a white guy if he *is* a wop.

JOE. Yeah. . . .

AMY (*desperately loud*). What am I going to do? What am I going to do?

JOE. Hey! . . . Not so loud!

AMY. But I ain't got no money . . . only my earrings. . . .

JOE. I got money enough.

AMY. You?

JOE. Tony made me save it. It's in the bank. More'n two hundred bucks. That'll see you through.

AMY. Tony'll be crazy. . . . Tony'll be just crazy.

JOE. The doc said for me to take you away with me.

AMY. You?

JOE. Yeah. . . . An' believe me, Amy, I'll do anything . . .

AMY. Going away with you won't help things any.

JOE. I'll treat you right, Amy.

AMY. Poor Tony!

JOE. I'll do the right thing if it kills me.

AMY. I must have been crazy that night.

JOE. We both was . . . but there's no use sayin' that now.

AMY. No. . . . Tony'll be crazy. (*She lifts her head, recognizing the inevitable*) I guess the doc's right. I guess I'll have to go with you. . . . Somebody's got to help me out. . . . There ain't nobody but you.

JOE. That's all right. . . . I'm willing. . . .

AMY. And afterwards . . . Oh, my God! . . . And Tony'll be thinking that all the time . . . you and me . . . Oh! (*This is an exclamation of unutterable disgust*) Poor Tony! You don't know how good he's been to me. And all the time he was so crazy for a kid. . . . Oh, I can't stick around here now! I got to go. I got to go quick.

JOE. I'm ready, if you are.

AMY. I'll just pack my grip.

JOE. Don't take it too hard, Amy. (*He tries to take her hand.*)

AMY (*shaking him off*). None of that! I don't want no sympathy.

JOE. Excuse me.

AMY. You better get your own things.

JOE. All right. . . . I'll be back in a minute.

AMY. I'll get a move on, too.
(AH GEE *comes in with the dishes for dinner and begins to lay the table. Apparently* JOE *thinks of something more to say, but is deterred by* AH GEE'*s presence. He goes quickly*

AMY *hears* AH GEE *and watches him for a moment as though she were unable to understand what he is doing.*)

AH GEE (*as he puts down dishes*). Velly good dinner tonight, Missy. Beans an' roas' veal an' apple pie!

TONY (*calling from off stage*). Eh, Joe! Eh, JOE! W'ere you go like dat? Amy! W'ere are you, Amy? (*He comes up on to the porch*) Ah! Here you are!

AH GEE. Oh, Bossy! Velly good dinner tonight. Apple pie!

TONY (*pleased*). Ah! Apples pie! (AH GEE *goes into his kitchen.* TONY *leans against door*) Amy! W'y you no' come back?

AMY (*who has been clinging desperately to the back of a chair*). I don't know!

TONY. You leave me alone so long.

AMY. I just come in for the papers and . . .

TONY. . . . An' Joe is runnin' crazy wild an' don' say nothing w'en I'm askin' him, "Joe, w'ere you goin' like dat?"

AMY. Joe's going away.

TONY. He's no' goin' without sayin' goo'-by?

AMY. I dunno. . . . Maybe he is. . . .

TONY. That boy mak' me verra unhappy. I been lovin' Joe like he was my own son an' he's goin' away like dat. He's no good.

AMY. People who ain't no good ain't worth worrying about. The thing to do is let 'em go and forget 'em.

TONY. Da's no' so easy like you think, Amy. I been lovin' Joe like my own son.

AMY. Joe ain't no worse than other people I could mention.

TONY. I love Joe but he don' love me.

AMY. I love you, Tony! I love you!

TONY. I know, Amy, I know.

AMY. And you ain't never going to believe that I do again.

TONY. W'at you talkin' 'bout, Amy?

AMY. Something's happened, Tony!

TONY. Eh?

AMY. It's going to make you terrible mad.

TONY. Amy!

AMY (*nerving herself*). It's going to make you just crazy, but I'm going to tell you just exactly what it is, Tony, because I ain't going to have you thinking afterwards that I wasn't grateful or that I ain't been happy here . . . happier than I ever been in my whole life. . . .

TONY. Amy!

AMY. Wait a minute. . . . I got to confess, Tony. I got to tell you the whole business so's you won't be thinking I been any worse than just what I have. . . .

TONY Amy!

AMY. Yeah. . . . And I don't want you blaming Joe no more'n what you blame me and anyway you're a-bound to find out sooner or later, an' it'll hurt you a lot less in the long run if I tell you the truth right now, and I got to tell you the truth anyway. I simply got to. Wait a minute, Tony! I'm going to tell you the truth and after I go away and you don't see me no more you can say: "Well, she wasn't no good but it wasn't my fault." Because it wasn't your fault, Tony. Not one bit, it wasn't. You didn't have nothing to do with it. And I wouldn't be going away, neither, not for a million dollars I wouldn't, only for what's happened. . . .

TONY. Amy, w'at you talkin' 'bout goin' away?

AMY. That's what I'm trying to tell you, Tony, only you got to give me a chance because it ain't easy to tell you no more'n it's easy to go away. And I got to go. But it ain't because I don't love you. I do. And it ain't because I don't appreciate all you done for me. I ain't never going to forget none of it, nor you, nor this place. . . .

TONY. Amy!

AMY. Listen to me, Tony! You're going to kick me out when you hear what I got to say, but I don't care if you do. I'm going to have a baby, Tony . . . and it's . . . God help me! . . . it's Joe's baby.

TONY (*raising his crutch with a great cry of anger*). Ah!

AMY. Didn't I tell you you'd kick me out?

TONY (*faltering*). Dio mio! Dio mio! No! Amy, you fool with me? Eh?

AMY. No, I'm not fooling. It's so. And that's why I'm going away, Tony.

TONY (*pursuing her as she retreats*). You been Joe's woman!

AMY. I was crazy!

TONY. You been Joe's woman!

AMY. I was crazy!

TONY. You been lovin' Joe!

AMY. No . . . I ain't . . . I ain't . . . I never loved Joe. Honest, I never. I was crazy.

TONY. You been just like da Padre say you was. . . . You been a whore. . . .

AMY. I ain't! . . . I ain't! I been straight all my life! Only that one night. . . .

TONY. W'at night?

AMY. The first night I come here.

TONY. Da night you marry with me!

AMY. I ain't even spoke to Joe alone since that night.

TONY. You lyin'!

AMY. I swear to God I ain't! Not once! Not till to-day after the doc told him what was going to happen.

TONY. You lyin' to me! You been Joe's woman!

AMY. I ain't, Tony! That's what I'm trying to tell you. It's the truth I'm trying to tell you and now I'm going away.

TONY. You goin' away with Joe?

AMY. My God, what else can I do?

TONY (*furiously he forces her back into the corner where the shotgun is hanging, spluttering all the time with slobbering, half-intelligible rage*). I don' let you go! I don' let you go! By God, I'm goin' kill dat Joe! Questo bastardo, Joe! I'm goin' kill him an' keep you here for see me kill him! Goddam you! You goddam dirty . . . (*He has got the gun down, broken it, and is loading it.*)

AMY (*speaking at the same time*). No, you won't, Tony! Don't do anything like that, now, Tony! You'll be sorry if you do! You know what'll happen to you if you do that! You know what'll happen to you, Tony! That ain't no way to act! You'll see what you get! You'll see!

TONY. Goddam! . . . You wait, you dirty . . . (*He flourishes the broken gun. She covers her eyes with her hands.* JOE *arrives, sees what* TONY *is doing, gives a cry, springs on him, wrenches the gun away. The struggle upsets* TONY'S *balance and he topples headlong off his crutches.* AMY *screams.*)

AMY. Oh, his leg! (JOE *drops the gun and bends over him.*)

JOE. I tried to catch him. . . . (TONY'S *bellows are terrifying to hear*) Did you hurt yourself, Tony? (TONY'S *answer is untranslatable into speech.*)

AMY (*as she pulls a chair over*). For God's sake, pick him up, can't you?

JOE (TONY *fights him, trying to choke him, and sinks into the chair, howling with pain and fury*). All right now, Tony! Steady!

AMY. Tony. . . . Tony. . . . (*She kneels down by him.* TONY'S *roars subside into moans*) I had to tell him! Oh, my God! I just had to tell him!

JOE. He didn't hurt himself much. (TONY'S *moans break into sobs.*)

AMY. This is awful.

JOE. Get your things. Let's pull out of here. We can send the Padre up to look after him.

AMY. I'm only taking my little grip, Tony. I'm leaving the earrings on the dresser. (*She goes quickly into the bedroom.* TONY'S *sobs keep up wretchedly and terribly.*)

JOE. Tony, I . . . (*Again* TONY *springs madly at* JOE'S *throat.* JOE *wrenches away and runs quickly to the table where he gets a glass of wine which he brings back to* TONY. TONY *pushes it away, spilling the wine over his shirt.* JOE *drops the glass.*)

TONY. Amy! Amy! Amy! Amy!

AMY (*she comes back, with her hat on and her coat over her arm. She has her yellow grip half open with clothes sticking out.* JOE *takes it from her*). Here I am, Tony. Here I am.

TONY. W'ere you goin' Amy? W'ere you goin' away from here?

AMY. I dunno. . . . Frisco, I guess. . . .

TONY (*bitter sobs*). You goin' be livin' with Joe?

AMY (*vague misery*). I dunno. . . . No, I ain't going to live with Joe. . . . No matter what happens, I ain't.

TONY. Who is goin' be lookin' after you, Amy?

JOE. I am, Tony. I'll do the right thing if it kills me.

TONY. You? . . . You? . . . Oh, Dio mio! Dio mio! No! No!

JOE. Come on, Amy, for the love of Pete!

AMY. I'm coming.

TONY (*a hand out to stop her*). You ain' got no money, Amy.

AMY. It don't matter.

TONY. Yes!

JOE. I got plenty.

TONY. No! . . . No! . . . No! . . . Joe is no good for lookin' after womans an' baby!

AMY. Don't take on, Tony. . . . Please don't take on! Let me go, and forget all about me. There ain't no use in talking any more.

TONY. You goin' have baby!

AMY. God, I know I am!

TONY. How you goin' mak' money for keep him? Before you go, you tell me dat!

AMY. God knows. . . . I don't.

TONY. Pretty quick Joe is leavin' you desert, and den w'at is goin' happen?

JOE. I swear I'll stick, Tony!

TONY. No! *No!* NO!! Ees no good! My Amy havin' baby in da street. Ees no good.

AMY. Don't say that for God's sake, Tony, don't say that . . .

TONY. W'at is goin' happen, Amy? W'at's goin' happen with you?

AMY. Joe . . . I can't stand no more of this.

TONY (*frenzied*). No! *No!* NO!! NO!!!

AMY. Let go, Tony! Let go of my skirt!

TONY. You ain' goin', Amy! I don't let you go! You stayin' here with Tony!

AMY. Don't talk that way, Tony! It ain't no good.

TONY. No! No! You goin' listen to w'at Tony say now. You goin' listen, Amy. You don' love Joe. You love Tony. You been good wife, Amy. . . .

AMY. Good wife!

TONY. W'at is Tony goin' do without you?

JOE. Come on!

TONY. Amy, I get excite' just now, Amy. Excuse! Excuse! I think verra good once more. You ain' goin' with Joe. You stayin' here with Tony just like nothin' is happen', an' by an' by da little fella is come. . . .

AMY. Don't talk that way, Tony!

TONY. W'y not?

AMY. Because it ain't no way to talk!

TONY. Yes . . . yes . . . ees good sense! Ees w'at is evrabody wantin' here! You an' Joe an' me! . . . Looka Joe. Joe is wantin' go with Wobblies, eh? With goddam Wobblies. All right . . . Looka Amy . . . Amy is wantin' stay here nice an' safe in dees fine house with Tony. Is not true, eh? (AMY *nods through her tears*) Sure is true. Look Tony, Dio mio, an' ask him w'at he want? Don' he want baby?

AMY. But not this baby, Tony?

TONY. W'at I care?

AMY. But, think of what people would say!

TONY. W'at I care w'at evrabody say? We tellin' evrabody he's Tony's baby. Den evrabody say Tony is so goddam young an' strong he's break both his leg' an' havin' baby just da same! . . . Eees good, eh? You don' go with Joe now, Amy? . . . Oh, Amy! . . .

AMY (*he has swayed her, but she looks at him as at a madman*). No. . . . It wouldn't work, Tony. . . . You wouldn't mean it afterward. . . . You're crazy. . . .

TONY (*a last frantic appeal*). No! No! No! (*Leaning back in his chair and looking around the room*) W'at's good for me havin' dees fine house? W'at's good for me havin' all dis money w'at I got? I got nobody for give my house an' my money w'en I die. Ees for dat I want dis baby, Amy. Joe don' want him. Ees Tony want him. Amy, . . . Amy, . . . for God's sake don' go away an' leave Tony!

AMY. But, Tony! Think of what I done?

TONY. What you done was mistake in da head, not in da heart. . . . Mistake in da head is no matter.

AMY. You—you ain't kiddin' me, are you? . . . You're serious, ain't you—Tony? You'll stick to this afterwards, won't you, Tony? (*She walks slowly over to him. She throws her arms around his neck and presses his head against her breast. A prolonged pause*) Well, Joe, I guess you better be going.

JOE. You mean?

AMY. I guess you'd better be going. (JOE *straightens in great relief.*)

JOE. All right. (*He picks up his knapsack which he dropped when he came in*) I guess you're right. (*He pulls on his cap and stands a moment in the doorway, a broad grin spreading over his face*) I guess there ain't none of us got any kick comin', at that. No real kick. (*He goes out slowly.*)

AMY (*lifting her face*). No. (TONY *clutches her even closer as the curtain falls.*)

The Front Page

BY BEN HECHT AND
CHARLES MAC ARTHUR

TO
MADISON AND CLARK STREETS

The Front Page was first produced at the Times Square Theatre, New York City, by Jed Harris, on August 14, 1928, and closed on April 13, 1929. Following is the original cast:

WILSON, *American*	Vincent York
ENDICOTT, *Post*	Allen Jenkins
MURPHY, *Journal*	Willard Robertson
MCCUE, *City Press*	William Foran
SCHWARTZ, *Daily News*	Tammany Young
KRUGER, *Journal of Commerce*	Joseph Spurin-Calleia
BENSINGER, *Tribune*	Walter Baldwin
MRS. SCHLOSSER	Violet Barney
WOODENSHOES EICHORN	Jay Wilson
DIAMOND LOUIS	Eduardo Cianelli
HILDY JOHNSON, *Herald-Examiner*	Lee Tracy
JENNIE	Carrie Weller
MOLLY MALLOY	Dorothy Stickney
SHERIFF HARTMAN	Claude Cooper
PEGGY GRANT	Frances Fuller
MRS. GRANT	Jessie Cromette
THE MAYOR	George Barbier
MR. PINCUS	Frank Conlan
EARL WILLIAMS	George Leach
WALTER BURNS	Osgood Perkins
CARL, A DEPUTY	Mathew Cromley
FRANK, A DEPUTY	Gene West
A POLICEMAN	Larry Doyle
A POLICEMAN	George T. Fleming

Staged by George S. Kaufman

Setting by Raymond Sovey

SCENE

The scene is the Press Room in the Criminal Courts Building, Chicago

ACT ONE

Eight-thirty o'clock on a Friday night

ACT TWO

Shortly afterward

ACT THREE

A few minutes later

THE FRONT PAGE

ACT ONE

This is the press room in the Criminal Courts Building, Chicago; a chamber set aside by the City Fathers for the use of journalists and their friends.

It is a bare, disordered room, peopled by newspapermen in need of shaves, pants pressing and small change. Hither reporters are drawn by an irresistible lure, the privilege of telephoning free.

There are seven telephones in the place, communicating with the seven newspapers of Chicago.

All are free.

An equally important lure is the continuous poker game that has been going on now for a generation, presumably with the same pack of cards.

Here is the rendezvous of some of the most able and amiable bums in the newspaper business; here they meet to gossip, play cards, sleep off jags and date up waitresses between such murders, fires, riots and other public events as concern them.

The furniture is the simplest; two tables, an assortment of chairs, spittoons and waste baskets, a water cooler, etc.—two dollars worth of dubious firewood, all told.

There is one elegant item, however; a huge, ornate black walnut desk, the former property of Mayor Fred A. Busse, deceased about 1904. It now belongs to ROY BENSINGER, *feature writer for the Chicago Tribune and a fanatic on the subject of hygiene.*

Despite MR. BENSINGER*'s views, his desk is the repository for soiled linen, old sandwiches, empty bottles and other items shed by his colleagues.*

The two tables serve as telephone desks, gaming boards and (in a pinch) as lits d'amour.

The electric lights are naked of shades.

The walls, unpainted since the building was erected in 1885, sport a frieze of lithographs, hand painted studies, rotogravure cuttings and heroic pencil sketches, all on the same theme: Woman. The political unrest of the journalists is represented by an unfavorable picture of Kaiser Wilhelm II hand drawn.

At the stage left is a door, labelled "Gents."

At the back is a double door, opening on the main corridor of the building.

At the stage right are two high, old-fashioned windows overlooking the Cook County jail.

It is eight-thirty at night.

Four men are playing poker at the main table in the center of the room. They are MURPHY *of the Journal,* ENDICOTT *of the Post,* SCHWARTZ *of the News and* WILSON *of the American; four braves known to their kind as police reporters. Katatonic, seedy Paul Reveres, full of strange oaths and a touch of childhood.*

Off by himself in a chair sits ERNIE KRUGER, *a somnolent reporter for the*

Journal of Commerce. ERNIE *is gifted beyond his comrades. He plays the banjo and sings. He is dreamily rendering his favorite piece, "By the Light of the Silvery Moon," as the poker game progresses.*

MC CUE *of the City News Bureau is telephoning at* BENSINGER'S *desk through the gamblers' chatter. He is calling all the police stations, hospitals, etc. on behalf of his companions, in a never-ending quest for news. His reiterations, whined in a manner intended to be ingratiating, have in them the monotonous bally-hoo wail of the Press.*

And so:

THE CARD PLAYERS. Crack it for a dime. . . . By me. . . . I stay. . . . Me too. . . . I'm behind again. . . . I was even a couple of minutes ago. . . . Papers? . . . Three. . . . Two. . . . Three to the dealer.

MC CUE (*into phone*). Kenwood three four hundred. . . . (*Another telephone rings*) Hey, take that, one of you guys. Ernie, you're not doing anything. (*They pay no attention. With a sigh,* MC CUE *props one telephone receiver against his ear; reaches over and answers the other phone*) What's the matter with you guys? Are you all crippled or something? (*Into second phone*) Press room! (*Suddenly he gives attention to the first phone*) Hello, Sarge . . . McCue. Hold the line a minute. (*Back to second phone*) No, I told you it was the press room. (*Hangs up; takes first phone again*) Anything doing, Sarge? . . . All right. Thank you, Sarge. (*Hangs up.*)

THE CARD PLAYERS. What are you waiting for? How'd I know you were out? Two Johns. Ladies, *etc.*

MC CUE. Robey four five hundred.

MURPHY. Ernie! Take that mouth organ in the can and play it!
(*The music swells a little in reply.*)

ENDICOTT. These cards are like washrags.

WILSON. Let's chip in for a new deck.

SCHWARTZ. These are good enough—I'm eighty cents out already!

MC CUE (*into phone*). Is this the home of Mrs. F. D. Margolies?

MURPHY. I'd like a deck with some aces in it.

MC CUE (*cordially, into phone*). This is Mr. McCue of the City News Bureau. . . . Is it true, Madame, that you were the victim of a Peeping Tom?

KRUGER. Ask her if she's worth peeping at.

WILSON. Has she got a friend?

MC CUE (*into phone*). Now, that ain't the right attitude to take, Madame. All we want is the facts. . . . Well, what did this Peeping Tom look like? I mean, for instance, would you say he looked like a college professor?

ENDICOTT. Tell her I can run up for an hour.

KRUGER. I'll accommodate her if she'll come down here.

SCHWARTZ. By me.

MC CUE (*into phone*). Just a minute, Madame. Is it true, Mrs. Margolies, that you took the part of Pocahontas in the Elks' Pageant seven years ago? . . . Hello. (*To the others*) She hung up.

MURPHY. The hell with her! A dime. (*The fire-alarm box, over the door, begins to ring.*)

ENDICOTT. Where's that fire?

WILSON. Three-two-one!

SCHWARTZ. Clark and Erie.

KRUGER (*wearily as he strums*). Too far.

MC CUE (*into phone*). Harrison four thousand.

SCHWARTZ (*rises, stretching; ambles over and looks out the window*). Oh, Christ!—what time is it, anyway?

WILSON. Half past eight. (*Rises; goes to the water cooler.*)

MURPHY (*drawing cards*). One off the top.

WILSON. How's the wife, Ed? Any better?

SCHWARTZ. Worse.

WILSON. That's tough.

SCHWARTZ. Sitting here all night, waiting for 'em to hang this bastard! (*A gesture toward the jail.*)

KRUGER. It's hard work, all right.

MC CUE (*into phone*). Hello, Sarge? McCue. Anything doing? . . . Yeah? That's swell. . . . (*The players pause*) A love triangle, huh? . . . Did he kill her? . . . Killed em *both!* Ah! . . . Was she good looking? . . . (*A pause. With vast disgust*) What? Oh, Niggers! (*The players relax.*)

KRUGER. That's a *break.*

MC CUE. No, never mind—thank you, Sarge. (*Jiggles receiver*) Englewood, six eight hundred. (*The Examiner phone rings. It is on the main table.* ENDICOTT *answers.*)

ENDICOTT (*into phone*). Criminal Courts press room. . . . No, Hildy Johnson ain't here. . . . Oh, hello, Mr. Burns. . . . No, he ain't here yet, Mr. Burns. (*Hangs up*) Walter Burns again. Something must have happened.

SCHWARTZ. I'm telling you what's happened. Hildy quit.

MURPHY. What do you mean, quit? He's a fixture on the Examiner.

KRUGER. Yeh! He goes with the woodwork.

SCHWARTZ. I got it from Bert Neeley. I'm *telling* you—he's gettin' married.

MURPHY. Walter wouldn't let him get married. He'd kidnap him at the altar.

MC CUE (*into phone*). Hello, Sarge. McCue. Anything doing?

ENDICOTT. Remember what he did to Bill Fenton, when he wanted to go to Hollywood? Had him thrown into jail for arson.

MURPHY. Forgery.

MC CUE. Shut up! . . . (*Into phone*) Anybody hurt? . . . Oh, fine! What's his name? . . . Spell it. . . . S. . . . C. . . . Z. . . . J. . . . Oh, the hell with it. (*Hangs up.*)

ENDICOTT. A guy ain't going to walk out on a job when he's drawing down seventy bucks a week.

SCHWARTZ. Yeah? Well, if he ain't quit, why ain't he here covering the hanging?

MC CUE (*into phone*). Give me re-write.

ENDICOTT. Walter sounded like he was having a hemorrhage.

MC CUE (*into phone*). Hello, Emil. Nothing new on the hanging. But here's a big scoop for you.

SCHWARTZ. I wish to God *I* could quit.

KRUGER. You'd think he'd come in and say goodbye.

MURPHY. That Swede bastard!

MC CUE. Shut up, fellas. (*Into phone*) Ready, Emil? (*He intones*) Dr. Irving Zobel—Z for Zebra—O for onion—B for baptize—E for anything and L for Lousy—

CARD PLAYERS. Pass. . . . By me. . . . Crack it for a dime. . . . Stay.

MC CUE (*into phone*). Yes, Zobel! That's right! With offices at sixteen-o-eight Cottage Grove Avenue. Well, this bird was arrested to-night on complaint of a lot of angry husbands. They claim he was treating their wives with electricity for a dollar a smack.

MURPHY. Is the Electric Teaser in again?

MC CUE (*intoning into phone*). He had a big following, a regular army of fat old dames that was being neglected by their husbands. So they was visiting this Dr. Zobel in their kimonos to get electricity.

ENDICOTT. I understand he massages them too.

MC CUE (*into phone*). Anyhow, the Doctor is being held for mal-practice and the station is full of his patients who claim he's innocent. But from what the husbands say it looks like he's a Lothario. All right. (*Hangs up; jiggles receiver.*)

MURPHY. Hey, Ernie, why don't you go in for electricity instead of the banjo?

(BENSINGER *enters. He is a studious and slightly neurotic fellow who stands out like a sore thumb owing to his tidy appearance.*)

KRUGER. It's got no future.

MC CUE (*into phone*). Sheridan two thousand.

BENSINGER (*with horror*). What the hell, Mac! Is that the only telephone in the place?

MC CUE. It's the only one with a mouthpiece on it. (*This is true.*)

MURPHY (*putting down his hand*). Read 'em and weep. (*Takes the pot. Prepares to deal.*)

BENSINGER (*howling*). How many times have I got to tell you fellows to leave my phone alone? If you've got to talk through a mouthpiece go *buy* one, like I did!

MURPHY. Aw, shut up, Listerine.

MC CUE (*at another phone*). Sheridan two thousand.

BENSINGER. My God, I'm trying to keep this phone clean and I'm not going to have you fellows coughing and spitting in it, either, or pawing it with your hands!

SCHWARTZ. What is this—a hospital or something?

ENDICOTT. How's that pimple coming along, Roy?

BENSINGER (*pulling a suit of dirty underwear from a drawer of his desk*). And you don't have to use this desk for a toilet!

MURPHY. Yeah? Well, suppose you quit stinking up this place with your God-damn antiseptics for a change! (*Removing a mouldy piece of pie from a desk drawer.*)

BENSINGER (*wailing*). Ain't you guys got any self-respect?

MC CUE (*into phone*). Hello, Sarge! . . . McCue. Congratulations on that Polack capture, Sarge. I hear you're going to be promoted. Anything doing?

THE CARD PLAYERS. Nickel. . . . Up a dime. . . . Drop. . . . Stay.

MC CUE (*into phone*). Yeah? . . . Just a second, Sarge. . . . (*To the players*). Nice little feature, fellas. Little kid, golden curls, everything, lost out near Grand Crossing. The cops are feeding her candy.

MURPHY. What else are they doing to her?

MC CUE. Don't you want it?

SCHWARTZ. No!

ENDICOTT. Stick it!

WILSON. All yours. (*Starts to deal a new hand.*)

MC CUE (*into phone*). Never mind, Sarge. Thank you, Sarge. (MC CUE *hangs up.*)

SCHWARTZ. Anything new on the hanging, Bensinger?

WILSON (*dealing*). My deal, ain't it?

MURPHY. Hey! Zonite!

BENSINGER. What is it?

MURPHY. Question before the house: Gentleman wants to know what's new on the hanging.

BENSINGER. Nothing special.

KRUGER (*with a yawn*). Did you see the sheriff?

BENSINGER (*bitterly*). Why don't you get your own news?

KRUGER (*philosophically*). Somebody ought to see the sheriff.

ENDICOTT. Anyhow, this looks like the last hanging we'll ever have to cover.

SCHWARTZ. Yeah. Can you imagine their putting in an electric chair? That's awful.

ENDICOTT. Going to toast them, like Lucky Strikes.

MURPHY. Who opened?

SCHWARTZ. What's the matter? Got a hand?

(MRS. SCHLOSSER *enters. She is the wife of* HERMAN SCHLOSSER, *of the Examiner.* MRS. S. *once used to go to dances, movies and ice cream parlors and she is still pretty, although shop-worn. If she is a bit acidulated, tight-lipped and sharp-spoken, no one can blame her, least of all these bravos of the press room, who have small respect for themselves or each other as husbands, fathers and lovers.*)

ENDICOTT (*as guiltily as if he were the errant* MR. SCHLOSSER). Hello, Mrs. Schlosser. Herman hasn't been in yet.

MC CUE. Hello, Mrs. Schlosser. Have you tried the Harrison Street Station? (*Helpfully*) He may be sleeping in the squad room.

SCHWARTZ (*bitterly*). What became of that rule about women coming into this press room?

MURPHY. Yeah—I don't let my *own* wife come in here.

MRS. SCHLOSSER (*inexorably*). Did he have any money left when you saw him?

MC CUE. Well, I didn't exactly see him. Did you, Mike?

ENDICOTT. No, I didn't really see him either.

MRS. SCHLOSSER (*like twenty wives*). Oh, you didn't? Well, was he still drinking?

MC CUE (*with unconvincing zeal*). I tell you what, I'll call up the grand jury room if you want. Sometimes he goes to sleep up there.

MRS. SCHLOSSER. Don't trouble yourself! I notice Hildy Johnson ain't here either. I suppose the two of them are out sopping it up together.

SCHWARTZ. Now, you oughn't to talk that way, Mrs. Schlosser. Hildy's reformed—he's gettin' married.

MRS. SCHLOSSER. Married? Well, all I can say is, God help his wife!

MURPHY. Come on—are we playing cards or aren't we?

MRS. SCHLOSSER. I suppose you've cleaned Herman out.

WILSON (*a nervous husband in his own right*). Honest, Mrs. Schlosser, we ain't seen him.

MRS. SCHLOSSER (*bitterly*). He can't come home. I kept dinner waiting till eleven o'clock last night and he never even called up.

ENDICOTT. Well, why pick on us?

KRUGER. Yeah—we're busy.
(*A phone rings.*)

ENDICOTT (*answering it*). Press room!

MRS. SCHLOSSER. You know where he is. You're covering up for him.

MC CUE. Honest to God, Mrs. Schlosser—

ENDICOTT (*into phone*). . . . No, Mr. Burns, Hildy ain't showed up yet.

MRS. SCHLOSSER. Is that Walter Burns? Let me talk to him!

ENDICOTT (*into phone*). Just a minute, Mr. Burns. Herman Schlosser's wife wants to talk to you.

MRS. SCHLOSSER (*taking the phone; honeyed and polite*). Hello, Mr. Burns.

MURPHY. Come on—who opened?

ENDICOTT. Check it.

MURPHY. A dime.

MRS. SCHLOSSER. This is Mrs. Schlosser. . . . Oh, I'm very well, thank you. . . . Mr. Burns, I was just wondering if you knew where Herman was. He didn't come home last night, and you know it was pay day. . . . (*Tearfully*) But it won't be all right. I'm just going crazy. . . . I've done that, but the cashier won't give it to me. . . . So I thought maybe if you gave me some sort of order—oh, will you, Mr. Burns? That's awfully nice of you. . . . I'm sorry to have to do a thing like that, but you know how Herman is about money. Thank you ever so much. (*Hangs up; turns on the reporters viciously*) You're all alike, every one of you! You ought to be ashamed of yourselves!

MURPHY. All right, we're ashamed. (*To* WILSON) A dime's bet.

MRS. SCHLOSSER. Sitting around like a lot of dirty, drunken tramps! Poker! (*She grabs* MURPHY'*s cards.*)

MURPHY (*leaping up in fury*). Here! Gimme those! What the hell!

MRS. SCHLOSSER. You know where he is, and I'm going to stay right here till I find out!

MURPHY. He's at Hockstetter's, that's where he is! Now give me those cards!

MRS. SCHLOSSER. Where?

WILSON. The Turkish Bath on Madison Street!

ENDICOTT. In the basement!

MURPHY. Give me those!

MRS. SCHLOSSER. So! You did know. (MURPHY *nervously awaits his cards*) Liars! (*She throws the cards face up on the table.*)

MURPHY (*as she throws them*). Hey! (*They spread out on the table.*)

MRS. SCHLOSSER. You're a bunch of gentlemen, I must say! Newspapermen! Bums! (*Exits.*)

MURPHY (*almost in tears*). Look! The second straight flush I ever held.

ENDICOTT. Jesus!

MURPHY. Eight, nine, ten, jack, and queen of spades. If I was married to that dame I'd kick her humpbacked.

BENSINGER (*having cleansed his telephone with a dab of absorbent cotton and a bottle of antiseptic: into phone*). City Desk!

ENDICOTT (*gathering the cards together*). I don't know what gets into women. I took Bob Brody home the other night and his wife broke his arm with a broom.

BENSINGER (*having collected his notes, and thoroughly protected himself from contagion by wrapping a piece of paper around the handle of his telephone*). Shut up, you fellows! (*Into phone*) This is Bensinger. Here's a new lead on the Earl Williams hanging. . . . Yeah, I just saw the sheriff. He won't move the hanging up a minute. . . . I don't care *who* he promised. . . . All right, I'll talk to him again, but it's no use. The execution is set for seven o'clock in the morning.

KRUGER (*to the tune of "Three O'Clock in the Morning"; sings*). Seven o'clock in the morning—

BENSINGER. Shut up Ernie. . . . (*Into phone*) Give me a rewrite man.

KRUGER (*morose*). Why can't they jerk these guys at a reasonable hour, so we can get some sleep?

BENSINGER (*to the room*). I asked the sheriff to move it up to five, so we could make the City Edition. Just because I asked him to, he wouldn't.

MURPHY. That guy wouldn't do anything for his mother.

KRUGER. He gives a damn if we stay up all night!

ENDICOTT. You've got no kick coming. I've had two dinners home in the last month.

BENSINGER (*into phone*). Hello. Jake? . . . New lead on the Williams hanging. And listen—don't put Hartman's name in it. Just say "the Sheriff." (*The* REPORTERS *listen*) Ready? . . . The condemned man ate a hearty dinner. . . . Yeah, mock turtle soup, chicken pot pie, hashed brown potatoes, combination salad, and pie a la mode.

KRUGER. Make mine the same.

BENSINGER (*into phone*). No—I don't know *what* kind of pie.

MURPHY. Eskimo!

MC CUE (*wistfully*). I wish I had a hamburger sandwich.

BENSINGER (*into phone*). And, Jake, get this in as a big favor. The whole dinner was furnished by Charlie Apfel. . . . Yeah—Apfel. A for adenoids, P for psychology, F for Frank. E for Eddie, and L for—ah—

MURPHY. Lay an egg.

BENSINGER. Proprietor of the Apfel—wants—to—see—you—restaurant.

WILSON. That means a new hat for *some*body. (*A soft cadenza from the banjo.*)

MURPHY. I better catch the fudge, fellas. (*Without dropping his cards,* MURPHY *picks up a telephone. He pantomimes for three cards.*)

BENSINGER (*into phone*). Now here's the situation on the eve of the hanging. The officials are prepared for a general uprising of radicals at the hour of execution, but the Sheriff still refuses to be intimidated by the Red menace.

MURPHY (*into his phone, while accepting three cards*). Give me a rewrite man, will you? . . . Yeah. Some more crap on the Earl Williams hanging.

BENSINGER (*into phone, as the reporters listen*). A double guard has just been thrown around the jail, the municipal buildings, railroad terminals, and elevated stations. Also, the Sheriff has just received four more letters threatening his life. He is going to answer these threats by a series of raids against the Friends of American Liberty and other Bolshevik organizations. Call you later. (*Hangs up.*)

SCHWARTZ. Bet a dime.

MURPHY (*into phone*). Ready? . . . Sheriff Hartman has just put two hundred more relatives on the payroll to protect the city against the Red army, which is leaving Moscow in a couple of minutes. (*Consults his hand*) Up a dime. (*Back to phone*) And to prove to the voters that the Red menace is on the square, he has just wrote himself four more letters threatening his life. I know he wrote them on account of the misspelling.

ENDICOTT. Drop.

MURPHY (*into phone*). That's all, except the doomed man ate a hearty dinner. As follows: Noodle soup, rustabiff, sweet a-potat', cranberry sauce, and pie-a-la mud.

SCHWARTZ. I raise another dime.

MURPHY (*consults his cards*). Wait a minute. Up again. (*Back to phone*) Statement from who? The Sheriff? . . . Quote him for anything you want—*he* can't read. (*Hangs up.* BENSINGER'S *phone rings.*)

THE CARD PLAYERS. Call. . . . Three bullets. . . . Pay at this window. . . . Shuffle that deck. . . . I get the same hand every time.

BENSINGER (*answering his phone*). What? (*To* MC CUE, *as* SCHWARTZ *starts to shuffle*) Didn't you send that in about the new alienist?

MC CUE (*flat on his back on the smaller table*). I got my hands full with the stations.

BENSINGER (*into phone*). All right, I'll give you what I got. Dr. Max J. Eglehofer. From Vienna. There's a dozen envelopes on him in the morgue. . . . Well, he's going to examine Williams at the request of — ah — wait a minute — (*Shuffles through his notes*)—the United Federation for World Betterment.

KRUGER. I'm for that.

BENSINGER. Sure—He's one of the biggest alienists in the world. He's the author of that book, "The Personality Gland."

MC CUE. And where to put it.

BENSINGER (*modestly into phone*). He just autographed it for me.

MURPHY. Did he bite his initials in your pants, too? . . . Nickel.

KRUGER (*into phone lazily*). Give me the City Desk!

BENSINGER (*into phone*). All right. He's going to examine him in about fifteen minutes. I'll let you know. (*He hangs up and resumes his study of "The Personality Gland."*)

KRUGER (*very tired*). Kruger calling! Nothing new on the hanging.

SCHWARTZ. Say, how about roodles on straights or better? I want to get some of my dough back.

WILSON. Hey, I thought we weren't going to give them alienists any more free advertising.

ENDICOTT. That's the fourteenth pair of whiskers they called in on this God-damned case.

MURPHY. Them alienists make me sick. All they do is goose you and send you a bill for five hundred bucks.

MC CUE (*into phone*). This is McCue. . . . Looks like the hanging's coming off at seven all right. . . . Yeah, the Governor's gone fishing and can't be found. . . . No, fishing. (*From the direction of the jail comes a sudden whirr and crash*) They're testing the gallows now. . . . Yeah —testing 'em, with sandbags. . . . Maybe you can hear 'em. (*He holds up phone towards window and laughs pleasantly. Then, bitterly*) What? The same to you! (*Hangs up. Another whirr and crash.*)

SCHWARTZ. I wish they'd quit practising. It makes me nervous.

WILSON. Up a dime.

KRUGER (*yelling out of window*). Hey, Jacobi! Quit playing with that gallus! How do you expect us to do any *work?*

VOICE FROM JAIL YARD. Cut that yelling, you God damned bums!

MC CUE. Ain't much respect for the press around here. (*The fire alarm sounds the same number as before.*)

MC CUE. That's a second alarm, ain't it?

MURPHY. Who cares?

KRUGER (*motionless*). Probably some orphanage.

MURPHY. Maybe it's another cathouse. Remember when Big Minnie's burned down, and the Mayor of Galesburg came running out? (*A phone rings.*)

THE CARD PLAYERS. Dime. . . . I call. . . . Two sixes, *etc.*

MC CUE (*answering phone*). What? The Mayor's office! (*To the rest*) Maybe a statement.

KRUGER. Tell 'em we're busy.

MC CUE (*into phone*). Hello. (*Then exuberantly*) Hello, you God-damn Swede! (*To the others*) It's Hildy.

MURPHY. What's he doing in the Mayor's office?

MC CUE (*into phone*). What? What's that? What? (*To the others*) He's stinko! (*Into phone*) What are you doing with the Mayor?

MURPHY. If he's got any left tell him to bring it over.

MC CUE (*into phone*). Huh? Kissing him good-bye?

ENDICOTT. Tell him to come over and kiss us.

MURPHY. I'm getting ready.

MC CUE (*into phone*). Well hurry up. (*To the room*) He's stepping high.

MURPHY. What did he say?

KRUGER. Is he coming over?

MC CUE. That's what he said.

THE CARD PLAYERS. Pass. . . . By me. . . . Take a deal, *etc.*

(WOODENSHOES EICHHORN *enters. He is a big, moon-faced, childish and incompetent German policeman.*)

BENSINGER. Hello, Woodenshoes. Got any news?

WOODENSHOES (*solemnly*). I just been over to the death house. Did you hear what Earl Williams said to the priest?

ENDICOTT. Aw, forget it!

MURPHY. The paper's full of the hanging now. We ain't got room for the ads.

BENSINGER (*looking up from his book*). What did he say, Woodenshoes?

WOODENSHOES (*awed*). He says to the priest that he was innocent.

MURPHY. Do you know any more jokes?

WOODENSHOES. Well, I'm just telling you what he says.

MURPHY. I suppose that copper committed suicide. Or maybe it was a love pact.

WOODENSHOES. Well, Williams has got a very good explanation for that.

ENDICOTT (*derisively, to the reporters*). He'll start crying in a minute. (*To* WOODENSHOES) Why don't you send him some roses, like Mollie Malloy?

SCHWARTZ. Yeah. She thinks he's innocent, too.

WOODENSHOES. You fellas don't understand. He admits killing the policeman, but he claims they're just using that as an excuse to hang him, on account he's a radical. But the thing that gets me—

MC CUE. Before you go on, Woodenshoes, would you mind running down to the corner and getting me a hamburger sandwich?

WOODENSHOES (*patiently*). Personally, my feeling is that Earl Williams is a dual personality type on account of the way his head is shaped. It's a typical case of psychology. (*The card game goes on*) Now you take the events leading up to the crime; his hanging a red flag out of the window on Washington's Birthday. That ain't normal, to begin with. The officer ought to have realized when he went up there that he was dealing with a lunatic. I'm against having colored policemen on the force, anyway. And I'll tell you why—

ENDICOTT (*suddenly*). Make that two hamburgers, will you, Woodenshoes, like a good fellow?

WOODENSHOES (*hurt*). I thought you fellas might be interested in the psychological end of it. None of the papers have touched that aspect.

MURPHY (*profound, but casual*). Listen, Woodenshoes, this guy Williams is just a bird that had the tough luck to kill a nigger policeman in a town where the nigger vote is important.

KRUGER. Sure! If he'd bumped him off down South they'd have given him a banquet and a trip to Europe.

MC CUE. Oh, the South ain't so bad. How about Russia, where they kill all the Jews and nobody says anything?

MURPHY. Williams was a bonanza for the City Hall. He gets hung—everybody gets elected on a law and order platform.

ENDICOTT. "Reform the Reds with a Rope."
(WILSON *makes an unprintable sound.*)

MURPHY. When that baby drops through the trap tomorrow, it's a million votes. He's just a divine accident. Bet a dime.

WOODENSHOES (*blinking through the above*). That's it—an accident. He didn't know it was a policeman, even. Why, when this officer woke him up—

MC CUE (*tolerantly*). Sure. You're right, Woodenshoes. And ask 'em to put a lot of ketchup on one of them sandwiches, will you?

WILSON (*sore*). I haven't filled a hand all night.
(DIAMOND LOUIE, *a ham gunman, enters. He is sleek, bejewelled and sinister to everybody but the caballeros of the press room, who knew him when he ran a fruit stand. He is greeted with unction.*)

LOUIE. Hello, fellows.

SCHWARTZ. Well, well, well! Diamond Louie!

MURPHY. If it ain't the Kid himself! Oooh! Look at the pop bottles!

MC CUE. Hurry up, Woodenshoes! I'm starving!

KRUGER. Get one for me, Woodenshoes!

BENSINGER. Make mine a plain lettuce—on gluten bread.

WOODENSHOES (*blinking*). Where am I gonna get the dough for all these eats?

MC CUE. Charge it.

MURPHY. You got a badge, ain't you? What's it good for?

WOODENSHOES (*shuffling out*). Four hamburgers and a lettuce.

DIAMOND LOUIE. Where's Hildy Johnson?

ENDICOTT (*rudely*). Up in Minnie's room.

MURPHY. Who wants to know?

KRUGER. Say Louie, I hear your old gang is going to bump off Kinky White.

DIAMOND LOUIE (*with sinister reticence*). Is that so?

MURPHY. Better wait till after election or you won't make the front page.

ENDICOTT. Yeah. We had to spike that Willie Mercer killing.

DIAMOND LOUIE. Well, I'll tell you. I'm off that racket. I don't even associate with them fellas, any more.

MURPHY. Go on! You gotta kill somebody every day or you don't get any supper.

DIAMOND LOUIE. No. No kiddin'. I'm practically retired, you know what I mean?

SCHWARTZ. Retired from what? You never carried anything but a bean blower!

DIAMOND LOUIE. All joking aside. Honest. I'm one of you fellas now. I'm in the newspaper game.

MURPHY (*with scorn*). You're what?

ENDICOTT. He's gettin' delusions of grandeur.

DIAMOND LOUIE. Yeah. That's right. I'm a newspaperman . . . working for Walter Burns.

WILSON. What!

ENDICOTT (*very politely*). What you doin' for Burns? A little pimping?

MURPHY. He's marble editor.

DIAMOND LOUIE (*with dignity*). I'm assistant circulation manager for de nort' side.

WILSON. Got a title and everything.

ENDICOTT. Burns'll be hiring animal acts next.

SCHWARTZ. What d'ye want Hildy for? Tailing him for Walter?

ENDICOTT. What do you know about that, Louie. We hear he's quit the Examiner.

MC CUE. Yeah. What's the dope, Louie?

DIAMOND LOUIE. Well, I don't think it's permanent, you know what I mean?

SCHWARTZ. What the hell happened?

ENDICOTT. They must of murdered each other, the way Walter sounded.

DIAMOND LOUIE. Naaaa! Just a little personal argument. Nothin' serious.

MC CUE. Come on . . . what's the dirt?

DIAMOND LOUIE. I don't know a single thing about it.

MC CUE. Should we tell Hildy you were lookin' for him?

DIAMOND LOUIE (*with affected nonchalance*). No. Never mind. (*Again the whirr and crash of the gallows.* LOUIE *looks*) What's that?

ENDICOTT. They're fixin' up a pain in the neck for somebody.

DIAMOND LOUIE (*with a genteel lift of his eyebrows*) Hah! Mr Weeliams!

MURPHY. They'll be doing that for you some day.

DIAMOND LOUIE (*very flattered*). Maybe. (*To the players*) Well—keep your eye on the dealer. (*He starts to leave.*)

MURPHY (*turning from the card game for the first time*). Wait a second, Louie. (DIAMOND LOUIE *pauses politely*) Come here. (*As* DIAMOND LOUIE *approaches*) Where do you keep your cap pistol? . . . Here? (*He gooses* DIAMOND LOUIE.)

DIAMOND LOUIE (*with a leap*). Hey! For God's sake! Look out, will you!

Jesus, that's a hell of a thing to do! . . . (*He exits angrily.*)

ENDICOTT (*calling after him*). Call again, Louie.

MURPHY. Any time you're in the building.

KRUGER. And don't bump off anybody before election day.

MURPHY (*sadly*). Louie hasn't got much self control.

ENDICOTT. What do you know about Hildy? Looks like he's quit, all right.

WILSON. Yeah. . . . What do you think of that?

ENDICOTT. There won't be any good reporters left after awhile.

MURPHY (*gently*). No. Mossie Enright getting stewed and falling down the elevator shaft. And poor old Larry Malm.

SCHWARTZ. And Carl Pancake that disappeared. (*A phone rings.*)

ENDICOTT (*answering it*). Hello . . . Oh hello, Mr. Burns. Why, he was in the mayor's office a few minutes ago . . .

(HILDY JOHNSON *enters. He is a happy-go-lucky Swede with a pants-kicking sense of humor. He is barbered and tailored like a normal citizen—a fact which at once excites the wonder and mirth of his colleagues.* HILDY *is of a vanishing type—the lusty, hoodlumesque half-drunken caballero that was the newspaperman of our youth. Schools of journalism and the advertising business have nearly extirpated the species. Now and then one of these boys still pops up in the profession and is hailed by his editor as a survival of a golden age. The newspapermen who have already appeared in this press room are in reality similar survivals. Their presence under one roof is due to the fact that Chicago is a sort of journalistic Yellowstone Park offering haven to a last herd of fantastic bravos that once roamed the newspaper offices of the country.* MR. JOHNSON *carries a new suitcase, two paper parcels and —a cane! A rowdy outburst follows his entrance.*)

MURPHY (*loudly*). Ooh! Lookit the cane! What are you doing? Turning fairy?

MC CUE. Yum, yum! Kiss me!

WILSON. Where the hell you been?

ENDICOTT. Walter Burns on the wire, Hildy.

HILDY. What's that?

MC CUE. What's the matter, Hildy? My God! He's got a shave!

SCHWARTZ. Jesus! Look at the crease in his pants!

ENDICOTT. It's Walter Burns, Hildy. Will you talk to him for God's sake?

HILDY. Tell that paranoiac bastard to take a sweet kiss for himself! . . . Come on Ernie! . . . (*Sings. "Goodbye, Forever . . ."*)

ENDICOTT. Say, listen, Hildy. Will you do me a personal favor and talk to Walter? He knows you're here.

MC CUE. He's calling up about nine million times.

KRUGER. All we do is answer that God-damn phone . . .

MURPHY. What's the matter? Scared of him?

HILDY. I'll talk to that maniac—with pleasure. (*Into phone, with mock formality*) Hello, Mr. Burns. . . . What's that, Mr. Burns? . . . Why, your language is shocking, Mr. Burns . . . Now, listen, you lousy baboon. Get a pencil and paper and take this down: Get this straight because this is important. It's the Hildy Johnson curse. The next time I see you—no matter where I am or what I'm doing —I'm going to walk right up to you and hammer on that monkey skull of yours until it rings like a Chinese gong. . . .

MC CUE. Oh, boy!

ENDICOTT. That's telling him!

HILDY (*holding sizzling receiver to the nearest reporter*). Listen to him! (*Into phone*) No, I ain't going to cover the hanging! I wouldn't cover the last supper for you! Not if they held it all over again in the middle of Clark Street. . . . Never mind the Vaseline, Jocko! It won't do you any good this time! Because I'm going to New York like I told you, and if you know what's good for you you'll stay west of Gary, Indiana! A Johnson never forgets! (*He hangs up*) And that, boys, is what is known as telling the managing editor. (*The reporters agree loudly.*)

BENSINGER. Can't you guys talk without yelling?

HILDY (*his song rising again. "Goodbye, Forever!"*)

VOICE (*from jail yard*). Hey, cut the yodeling! Where do you think you are!

HILDY (*moving toward the window, takes out his pocket flask*). Hey, Jacobi! Pickle-nose! (*He takes a final drink from the flask, then aims and throws it out the window. A scream of rage arises from the jail yard.*)

HILDY (*smiles and salutes his victim*). On the button! (*Turns to* ERNIE, *resumes his song.*)

BENSINGER (*pleading*). Oh, shut up!

WILSON. What did you quit for, Hildy?

SCHWARTZ. We hear you're going to get married?

HILDY. I'm getting married, all right. (*Shows tickets*) See that? Three tickets to New York! Eleven-eighteen tonight!

WILSON. Tonight!

MC CUE. Jesus, that's quick!

MURPHY. What do you mean three?

HILDY. Me and my girl and her God-damn ma!

ENDICOTT. Kinda sudden, ain't it?

SCHWARTZ. What the hell do you want to get married for?

HILDY. None of your business!

MURPHY. Ooooh! He's in love! Tootsie-wootsie!

MC CUE. Is she a white girl?

ENDICOTT. Has she got a good shape?

WILSON. Does Walter know you're getting married?

HILDY. Does he know I'm getting married? He congratulated me! Shook hands like a pal! Offered to throw me a farewell dinner even.

ENDICOTT. That's his favorite joke—farewell dinners.

MURPHY. He poisons people at them.

HILDY. He gets me up to Polack Mike's—fills me full of rotgut—I'd have been there yet if it hadn't been for the fire escape!

SCHWARTZ. That's what he done to the Chief of Police!

HILDY. Can you imagine? Trying to bust up my marriage! After shaking hands! . . . (*Anxiously*) Say, my girl didn't call up, did she, or come in looking for me? What time is it, anyway?

SCHWARTZ. Quarter past nine.

MC CUE. Eighteen minutes after.

HILDY (*starting to take off his coat*). I got to be at this house at seven.

ENDICOTT. What house?

HILDY. Somebody giving a farewell party to my girl.

WILSON. At seven tonight?

HILDY. Yeah?

MURPHY. You got to run like hell.

HILDY. Oh, that's all right. Fellow doesn't quit a job every day. Especially when its Walter Burns. The lousy baboon—

ENDICOTT. When's the wedding, Hildy?

HILDY. It's in New York, so you guys ain't going to have any fun with it. None of them fake warrants or kidnapping the bride, with me! (HILDY *folds his old shirt and puts it in* BENSINGER'S *drawer.*)

BENSINGER. Aw, for God's sake! Cut that out! (*Throws the shirt on the floor.*)

WILSON. Everybody's getting this New York bug. It's just a rube town for mine.

SCHWARTZ. I was on a New York paper once—the Times. You might as well work in a bank.

MURPHY. I hear all the reporters in New York are lizzies.

MC CUE. Remember that fellow from the New York World?

ENDICOTT. With the derby?

MURPHY (*presumably mimicking a New York journalist*). Could you please instruct me where the telegraph office is? (*Makes a rude noise*) You'll be talking like that, Hildy.

HILDY. Yeah?

ENDICOTT. Which one of them sissy journals are you going to work for?

HILDY. None of them! Who the hell wants to work on a newspaper? A lot of crumby hoboes, full of dandruff and bum gin they wheedle out of nigger Aldermen.

MURPHY. That's what comes of stealing a cane.

ENDICOTT. What are *you* going in for—the movies?

HILDY. I am not. Advertising business. One hundred and fifty smackers a week.

MC CUE. Yeah?

ENDICOTT. One hundred and fifty *what?*

SCHWARTZ (*a sneer*) A hundred and fifty!

HILDY. Here's the contract. (*Hands it to* MC CUE, *who starts to look through it. They crowd around this remarkable document*) I was just waiting to get it down in black and white before I walked in and told Walter I was through.

MC CUE (*with contract*). Jesus, it *is* a hundred and fifty!

WILSON. Was Walter sore?

HILDY. The lousy snake-brain! The God-damn ungrateful ape! Called me a traitor, after ten years of sweating my pants off for practically nothing. Traitor to what? What did he or anybody else in the newspaper business ever do for me except try to make a bum out of me! Says "You can't quit without notice!" What the hell does he think I am? A hired girl? Why, one more word and I'd have busted his whiskey snout for him!

KRUGER. Why didn't you?

MURPHY. Who's going to cover the hanging for the Examiner?

MC CUE. Why the hell didn't you tell a fellow?

WILSON. Yeah—instead of waiting till the last day?

HILDY. And have Walter hear about it? I've always wanted to walk in and quit just like that! (*A snap of the fingers*) I been planning this for two months—packed up everything yesterday, and so did my girl! Furniture and all. (*The fire signal has been sounding through the last few words.* HILDY *looks up*) Hey, fellows, that's Kedzie and Madison ain't it? The Washington Irving School's out there.

MURPHY. Who the hell's in school this time of night?

MC CUE. What do you care, anyhow? You've quit.

HILDY (*laughs, chagrined*). Just thought it might be a good fire, that's all. (*Again the whirr and crash of the gallows.*)

KRUGER. For Christ's sake! (*At the window*) Ain't you got anything else to do? Hey! You Jacobi!

BESSINGER. Hey, fellows. I'm trying to read.

WILSON (*also near window*). They're changing the guards down there. Look—they've got sixteen of them. (*Voices come from the courtyard—"Hey!" "Hurry up." "Get a move on, Carl!" etc.*)

MC CUE (*hands back the contract*). You're going to miss a swell hanging, Hildy.

HILDY. Yeah? You can stick it.

MURPHY. So you're going into the advertising business, eh? Writing poetry about Milady's drawers.

ENDICOTT. Going to wear an eye shade?

WILSON. I'll bet he has a desk with his name on it, and a stenographer.

MURPHY. You'll be like a firehorse tied to a milk wagon.

ENDICOTT (*to* MURPHY). I don't know what gets into these birds. Can you imagine punching a clock, and sitting around talking like a lot of stuffed shirts about statistics?

HILDY. Yeah—sour grapes, that's all it is. Sour grapes.

MURPHY. I got a dumb brother went in for business. He's got seven kids and a mortgage, and belongs to a country club. He gets worse every year. Just a fat-head.

HILDY. Listen to who's talking. Journalists! Peeking through keyholes! Running after fire engines like a lot of coach dogs! Waking people up in the middle of the night to ask them what they think of Mussolini. Stealing pictures off old ladies of their daughters that get raped in Oak Park. A lot of lousy, daffy buttinskis, swelling around with holes in their pants, borrowing nickels from office boys! And for what? So a million hired girls and motormen's wives'll know what's going on.

MURPHY. Your girl must have handed you that line.

HILDY. I don't need anybody to tell me about newspapers. I've been a newspaperman fifteen years. A cross between a bootlegger and a whore. And if you want to know something, you'll all end up on the copy desk—gray-headed, humpbacked slobs, dodging garnishees when you're ninety.

SCHWARTZ. Yeah, and what about you? How long do you think you'll last in that floosie job?

ENDICOTT. You'll get canned cold the minute your contract's up, and then you'll be out in the street.

KRUGER. Sure—that's what always happens.

HILDY. Well, it don't happen to me. And I'll tell you why, if you want to know. Because my girl's uncle owns the business, that's why.

WILSON. Has he got a lot of jack?

HILDY. It's choking him. You know what he sent us for a wedding present?

MURPHY. A dozen doilies.

HILDY. I wouldn't tell you bums, because it's up in high finance and you wouldn't understand it.

ENDICOTT. Probably gave you a lot of stock in the company, that you can't sell.

KRUGER. I know them uncles.

HILDY. The hell he did! He gave us five hundred in cash, that's what he gave us.

MC CUE. Go on!

SCHWARTZ. There *ain't* five hundred in cash.

HILDY. Yeah? (*Pulling out a roll*) Well, there it is—most of it, except what it costs to get to New York.

MC CUE. Jees, let's see.

HILDY. Oh, no!

MURPHY. How about a finif till to-morrow?

HILDY. (*mimicking an androgyne*): I won't be here tomorrow. And that reminds me. (*Takes out a little book*) It comes to— (*Consults book*) eight dollars and sixty-five cents altogether, Jimmie. Eight dollars and sixty-five cents.

MURPHY. What does?

HILDY. That includes the four bucks in front of the Planter's Hotel, when you were with that waitress from King's.

MURPHY. I thought I paid that.

HILDY. No. (*Reading from notes*). Herman Schlosser . . . altogether twenty dollars and . . .

MC CUE. Ha! Ha! Ha!

ENDICOTT. Ho! Ho! Ho!

HILDY. All right. I guess I might as well call it off, all around. I should have known better than to try to collect, anyhow. (*Tears out the page and throws it ct* MURPHY) You might say thanks.

MURPHY. Not after that waitress.

SCHWARTZ. About that fifty bucks, Hildy. If you want a note—

HILDY. What fifty bucks? Aw, forget it.

SCHWARTZ. You see, it wasn't only the wife taking sick, but then besides . . .

(JENNIE, *a slightly idiotic scrub-woman, enters. She receives an ovation. "Yea, Jennie!" "Jennie!" "Well, if it ain't Jennie," all delivered in various dialects with intended comedy effect.*)

KRUGER. I hear you just bought another apartment house, Jennie!

MURPHY. I hear you've fallen in love again, Jennie!

JENNIE (*giggling*). Can I wash up now, please?

BENSINGER. Yeah, for God's sake do! This place smells like a monkey cage.

HILDY. Go on! You don't want to wash up on a night like this! This is a holiday! I'm going away, Jennie! Give us a kiss! (*He embraces her.*)

JENNIE (*squealing*). Now you Hildy Johnson, you keep away from me! I'll hit you with this mop! I will!

HILDY (*tickling her*). What's the matter? Ain't I your fellow any more? I'll tell you what we'll do, Jennie! You and I'll go around and say good-bye! Everbody in the building!

MC CUE. Hey, the warden called you up! Wants to see you before you go!

HILDY. There you are, Jennie! We're *invited!* He invited Jennie, didn't he? You bet he did!

JENNIE. Now you know he didn't!

HILDY (*lifting pail of water*). Only we can't carry this all over! I know!

(*At window*) Hey! Jacobi! Look! (*Throws water out.* JENNIE *giggles hysterically.*)

VOICE (*off*). Who did that?

SCHWARTZ. Better shut off them lights. Somebody's liable to come up.

HILDY (*to* JENNIE). Come on, Jennie! We'll say good-bye to the warden! (*He embraces her again.*)

JENNIE (*struggling*). No, no! You let go of me! The warden'll be mad! He'll *do* something!

HILDY. To hell with him! *I* own this building! Come on! (*Pausing in the door*) If my girl calls up, tell her I'm on my way! (*Exits with* JENNIE, *singing "Waltz Me Around Again, Jennie." Coy screams from* JENNIE, and *the banging of a pail as it is kicked down the corridor.*)

BENSINGER. Thank God *that's* over!

KRUGER. What's the Examiner go ing to do with Hildy off the job?

WILSON. It must be great to walk into a place and quit.

MC CUE. Yeah. (*He moves sadly away and uses one of the phones on the long table*) Diversey three two hundred.

ENDICOTT (*sentimentally*). I got an offer from the publicity department of the stock yards last year. I shoulda took it.

SCHWARTZ. What I'd like would be a job on the side.

MC CUE (*a lump in his throat*). A desk and a stenographer. That wouldn't be so bad. I wouldn't mind a nice big blonde.

MURPHY (*outlining a voluptuous bust*). With a bozoom! (*Phone on small table rings.*)

MC CUE (*sighs, then into his own phone*). Hello, Sarge. McCue. Anything doing?

WILSON (*answering other phone*). What's that? (*His tone becomes slightly formal*) Yes, ma'am. . . . No, Hildy ain't here just now, madam. He left a message for you, though. . . . Why, he said he was on his way. . . . No, he didn't say where—just that he was on his way. . . . All right, I'll tell him, ma'am. (*Hangs up*) Oooh! Is *she* sore?

SCHWARTZ. Hildy oughtn't to do that. She's a swell kid.

MC CUE (*into phone*): All right! Thank you, Sarge! (*Hangs up*) A hundred and fifty bucks a week! Can you imagine?

KRUGER. Probably gets Saturdays and Sundays off, too.

WILSON (*sadly*). And Christmas.

MC CUE. I wonder who Walter'll send over here in Hildy's place. (MOLLIE MALLOY *enters. She is a North Clark Street tart, cheap black sateen dress, red hat and red slippers run over at the heels. She is a soiled and gaudy houri of the pavement. Despite a baleful glare on* MOLLIE'S *part, the boys brighten visibly. They are always glad to see whores.*)

MURPHY (*warmly*). Hello, Mollie!

ENDICOTT. Well, well! Nookie!

WILSON. Hello, kid! How's the old tomato-can?

MC CUE (*feeling himself to be a Chauncey Olcott*). Shure, and how are yez, Mollie?

MOLLIE (*in a tired, banjo voice*). I've been looking for you bastards!

MURPHY. Going to pay a call on Williams?

SCHWARTZ. He's just across the court-yard!

KRUGER. Better hurry up—he hasn't got all night.

MC CUE. Yes, he has!

ENDICOTT (*formally*). Say, Mollie, those were pretty roses you sent Earl. What do you want done with them tomorrow morning?

MOLLIE (*tensely*). A lot of wise guys, ain't you? Well, you know what I think of you—all of you.

MURPHY. Keep your pants on, Mollie.

MOLLIE (*to* MURPHY). If you was worth breaking my fingernails on, I'd tear your puss wide open.

MURPHY. What you sore about, sweetheart? Wasn't that a swell story we give you?

MOLLIE. You cheap crumbs have been making a fool out of me long enough!

ENDICOTT. Now what kind of language is that?

BENSINGER. She oughtn't to be allowed in here! I caught her using the drinking cup yesterday!

MOLLIE (*flaring*). I never said I loved Earl Williams and was willing to marry him on the gallows! You made that up! And all that other crap about my being his soul mate and having a love nest with him!

MC CUE. Well, didn't you?

ENDICOTT. You've been sucking around that cuckoo ever since he's been in the death house! Everybody knows you're his affinity!

MOLLIE (*blowing up*). That's a lie! I met Mr. Williams just once in my life, when he was wandering around in the rain without his hat and coat on like a sick dog. The day before the shooting. And I went up to him like any human being would and I asked what was the matter, and he told me about bein' fired after working at the same place twenty-two years and I brought him up to my room because it was warm there.

ENDICOTT. Did he have the two dollars?

MURPHY. Aw, put it on a Victrola.

MOLLIE. Just because you want to fill your lying papers with a lot of dirty scandal, you got to crucify him and make a bum out of me!

ENDICOTT. Got a match, Mollie?

MOLLIE (*heedless*). I tell you he just sat there talking to me . . . all night . . . just sat there talkin' to me . . . and never once laid a hand on me! In the morning he went away and I never saw him again till the day at the trial!

ENDICOTT. Tell us what you told the jury!
(*They laugh reminiscently.*)

MOLLIE. Go on, laugh! God damn your greasy souls! Sure I was his witness—the only one he had. Yes, me! Mollie Malloy! A Clark Street tart! I was the only one with guts enough to stand up for him! And that's why you're persecuting me! Because he treated me decent, and not like an animal, and I said so!

ENDICOTT. Why didn't you adopt him instead of letting him run around shooting policemen?

SCHWARTZ. Suppose that cop had been your own brother?

MOLLIE. I wish to God it had been one of you!

MURPHY (*finally irritated*). Say, what's the idea of this song and dance, anyhow? This is the press room. We're busy.

SCHWARTZ. Go on home!

MURPHY. Go and see your boy friend, why don't you?

MC CUE. Yeah—he's got a nice room.

ENDICOTT (*with a wink at the rest*). He won't have it long. He's left a call for seven A. M.

MOLLIE (*through her teeth*). It's a wonder a bolt of lightning don't come through the ceiling and strike you all dead! (*Again the sound of the gallows*) What's that? Oh, my God! (*She begins to cry.*)

BENSINGER (*rising*). Say, what's the idea?

MOLLIE. Talking that way about a fellow that's going to die.

ENDICOTT (*uncomfortable at this show of grief*). Don't get hysterical.

MOLLIE (*sobbing*). Shame on you! Shame on you!

MC CUE (*to the rest*). It wasn't my fault. *I* didn't say anything.

MOLLIE (*hysterically*). A poor little crazy fellow that never did any harm. Sitting there alone this minute, with the Angel of Death beside him, and you cracking jokes.

MURPHY (*getting up meaningly*). Listen, if you don't shut up, I'll give you something *good* to cry about!

MOLLIE (*savage*). Keep your dirty hands off me!

MURPHY (*in a short and bitter struggle with her*). Outside, *bum!*

MOLLIE (*shooting through the door*). You dirty punks! Heels! Bastards! (*Exit.*)

MURPHY (*slams the door. A pause*). The nervy bitch!

MC CUE. Whew!

MURPHY. You guys want to play some more poker?

ENDICOTT. What's the use? *I* can't win a pot.

MURPHY. I'm the big loser.

WILSON. Me too. I must be out three dollars, anyhow.

ENDICOTT. It's God-damn funny who's got it.

SCHWARTZ. Don't look at me. I started in with five bucks, and I got two-eighty left.

MC CUE (*who has taken up the phone again*). Michigan eight thousand. (SHERIFF HARTMAN *enters briskly, bitter words forming on his lips. He is a diabetic and overwrought little fellow, an incompetent fuss budget. He has come to raise hell, but an ovation checks him. "Ah, Sheriff!" "Hello, Pinky!" "How's the old statesman?"* BENSINGER *puts down his book;* MC CUE *abandons his telephoning.*)

ENDICOTT. Any news, Sheriff?

SHERIFF (*briefly*). Hello fellas. (*In another tone*) Now, who dumped that bucket of water out the window?

KRUGER. What bucket of water?

SHERIFF. Who threw it out the window is what I asked, and I want to know!

MURPHY. Judge Pam threw it out.

SHERIFF. I suppose Judge Pam threw that bottle!

ENDICOTT. Yeah. That was Judge Pam, too.

MURPHY. He was in here with his robes on, playing fireman.

SHERIFF. Come on now, fellas, I know who it was. (*Wheedling*) It was Hildy Johnson, wasn't it? Where is he?

MC CUE. Out with a lady.

ENDICOTT. Hildy's quit, Sheriff. Didn't you hear?

SHERIFF. Well, I'm glad of it. It's good riddance! Now personally, I don't give a God damn, but how do you suppose it looks to have a lot of hoodlums yelling and throwing things out of windows? (*In a subdued voice*) Besides there's somebody *in* that death house. How do you suppose he feels, listening to all this re-*vel*-ery?

MURPHY. A hell of a lot you care how he feels!

SCHWARTZ. Keep your shirt on, Pinky.

SHERIFF. Wait a minute, you! I don't want to hear any more of that Pinky stuff. I got a name, see? Peter B. Hartman.

MURPHY. What's the matter with Pinky?

MC CUE (*taking the cue*). He's all right.

THE REPORTERS (*lustily*). *Who's* all right?

SHERIFF (*desperate*). Now stop! (*Whining*) Honest, boys, what's the idea of hanging a name like that on me? Pinky Hartman! How's that look to the voters? Like I had sore eyes or something.

MURPHY. You never heard of Bathhouse John kicking, did you?

WILSON. Or Hinky Dink?

ENDICOTT. It's made you famous!

SHERIFF. I swear I don't know what to do about you fellows. You abuse every privilege you get. I got a damn good notion to take this press room away from you.

MURPHY. That would be a break.

ENDICOTT. Yeah. The place is so full of cockroaches you can't walk.

BENSINGER (*rising*). Wait a minute, fellows. Now listen, Pete, this is the last favor I'm ever going to ask you, and it ain't me that's asking it. Get me? *You* know who's asking it—a certain party is asking it. Once and for all, how about hanging this guy at five o'clock instead of seven? It ain't going to hurt you and we can make the City Edition.

SHERIFF (*sincerely*). Aw, now, Roy, that's kind of raw. You can't hang a fella in his sleep, just to please a newspaper.

MURPHY. No, but you can reprieve him twice so the hanging'll come three days before election! So you can run on a law-and-order ticket! You can do that all right!

SHERIFF. I had nothing whatsoever to do with those reprieves. That was entirely up to the Governor.

ENDICOTT. And who told the Governor what to do?

SCHWARTZ. How do we know there won't be another reprieve tonight? For all I know I'm hanging around here for nothing! When I've got a sick wife!

WILSON. Yeah, with another alienist getting called in!

MURPHY. This Wop gooser!

SCHWARTZ. Sure—what's all that about? Suppose he finds he's insane or something?

SHERIFF. He *won't* find he's insane. Because he isn't. This ruse of reading the Declaration of Independence day and night is pure fake. But I've got to let this doctor see him, on account of his being sent by these Personal Liberty people, or whatever they call themselves. You and I know they're nothing but a bunch of Bolsheviks, but a hanging is a serious business. At a time like this you want to please everybody.

ENDICOTT. Everybody that can vote, anyhow.

SHERIFF. Now he's going to look him over in my office in a couple of minutes, and then you'll know all about it. Besides, there's nothing he *can* find out. Williams is as sane as I am.

SCHWARTZ. Saner!

SHERIFF. The hanging's going to come off exactly per schedule. And when I say "per schedule" that means seven o'clock and not a minute earlier. There's such a thing as being humane, you know.

BENSINGER. Just wait till *you* want a favor.

SHERIFF (*to change the subject*). Now here are the tickets. Two for each paper.

MC CUE. What do you *mean*, two for each paper?

SHERIFF (*stung*). What do you want to do—take your family?

SCHWARTZ. Now listen, Pete. I promised a pair to Ernie Byfield. He's never seen a hanging.

WILSON. The boss wants a couple for the advertising department.

SHERIFF (*passing out tickets*). This ain't the "Follies," you know. I'm tired of your editors using these tickets to get advertising accounts.

ENDICOTT. You got a lot of nerve! Everybody knows what *you* use 'em for—to get in socially.

MURPHY. He had the whole Union League Club over here last time.

ENDICOTT. Trying to suck in with Chatfield-Taylor. I suppose you'll wear a monocle tomorrow morning.

SHERIFF (*melting*). Now that ain't no way to talk, boys. If any of you want a couple of extra tickets, why I'll be more than glad to take care of you. Only don't *kill* it.

SCHWARTZ. Now you're talking!

WILSON. That's more like it.

SHERIFF. Only you fellas got to lend a hand with us once in a while. We got a big job on our hands, smashing this Red menace—

ENDICOTT. We gave you four columns yesterday. What do you want?

SHERIFF (*always the boy for a speech*). That ain't it. The newspapers got to put their shoulders to the wheel. They've got to forcibly impress on the Bolsheviks that the death-warrant for Earl Williams is a death-warrant for every bomb-throwing un-American Red in this town. This hanging means more to the people of Chicago today— (*To* MURPHY, *who is reading a comic supplement*) This is a *statement*, Jimmie. What's the matter with you?

MURPHY. Aw, go home.

SHERIFF. All right, you'll just get scooped. Now we're going to reform these Reds with a rope. That's our slogan. Quote me if you want to: "Sheriff Hartman pledges that he is going to reform the Reds with a rope."

ENDICOTT. Oh, for Christ's sake, Pinky! We've been printing that chestnut for weeks! (*He goes into the can.*)

SHERIFF. Well, print it once more, as a favor to me.

WILSON. You don't have to worry about the election. You're as good as in now, with the nigger vote coming around.

SHERIFF (*Lafayette, at least*). I was never prejudiced against the Negro race in any shape, manner, or form.

MURPHY. Are *you* still talking?

SHERIFF (*suddenly querulous*). During the race riots I just had to do my duty, that's all. And of course I was misunderstood.

KRUGER. Go on! You're a Southern gentleman, and you know it. (*Phone rings.*)

SHERIFF. Now, boys!

MURPHY. Shoah! (*In bogus Negro dialect*) Massa Hartman, of the Vahginia Hartmans. (*Phone on small table rings.* MC CUE *heads for it.*)

ENDICOTT (*in the can, his voice rising above the plumbing*). I hear you used to own slaves.

SCHWARTZ (*answering phone*). Press room! (*Into phone*) Who? Yeah, he's here. . . . For you, Sheriff.

SHERIFF. Me? (*Into phone—very businesslike*) Sheriff Hartman talking. . . . (*An eagle falling out of the clouds*) Oh, hello, dear.

KRUGER. Sounds like the ball and chain.

SHERIFF. Why, no, I didn't figure on coming home at all. . . . Well, you see on account of the hanging being so early—

MURPHY. Tell her she's getting a break when you don't go home.

SHERIFF (*winningly*). But you see this is business, dear. You don't think a hanging's any fun for me!

ENDICOTT. Music for this, Ernie!

SHERIFF (*agitatedly motions for silence*). But I have a whole lot to do first—getting things ready.

MURPHY. Why don't you take him out to your house and hang him?

SHERIFF (*fishhooks in his pants*). I'll call you up later, Irma—I'm not in my own office, now. Besides, I've got to meet an alienist. . . . No—alienist. No. Not for me. For Williams.

(HILDY *re-enters, bringing back* JENNIE'S *mop.*)

HILDY (*throwing the mop across the room*). Boy, we cleaned up!

SHERIFF (*hurriedly*). I'll call you later, dear. (*He hangs up; turns on* HILDY) Now Johnson, what the hell do you mean? Throwing things out of windows. Who do you think you are?

(*During the quieter moments of the remainder of this act,* HILDY *is opening his parcels and putting the contents into his suitcase.*)

HILDY. Who wants to know?

SHERIFF. You think you and Walter Burns are running this town! Well, I'm going to send a bill to the Examiner tomorrow for all the wreckage that's been committed around here in the past year! How do you like that?

HILDY. I think that's swell! You know what else you can do?

SHERIFF (*belligerently*). What?

HILDY. Guess.

SHERIFF. You stick your nose in this building tomorrow and I'll have you arrested!

HILDY. It's damn near worth staying for!

SHERIFF. And I'll tell you another thing, and you can pass it on to Walter Burns! The Examiner don't get any tickets for this hanging after the lies they been printing! You can make up your story like you do everything else—out of whole cloth.

HILDY. Listen, you big pail of lard! If I wanted to go to your God-damn hanging I'd go! See? And sit in a box!

SHERIFF. The hell you would!

HILDY. And I'd only have to tell *half* of what I know, at that!

SHERIFF. You don't know *any*thing.

HILDY. No? Tell me, Mr. Hartman, where'd you spend the night before that last hanging! At the Planter's Hotel with that librarian. Room Six Hundred and Two. And I got two bell boys and a night manager to prove it!

SHERIFF. If I didn't have to go and see that alienist I'd tell *you* a few things. (*Exits.*)

HILDY (*calling after him*). And if I were you I'd get two tickets for the hanging over to Walter Burns pretty fast, or he's liable to come over here and stick a firecracker in your pants!

WILSON. Hey! Hildy! Your girl called up.

HILDY (*stricken*). My girl? When? (*Starts for the telephone.*)

WILSON. Just after you went out. And if you take my advice, you'll call her back.

HILDY. Jesus! Why didn't you tell a fellow!
(WOODENSHOES *re-enters with sandwiches and a bottle of ketchup.*)

MC CUE. *Yea!* Sandwiches.

HILDY (*at phone*). Edgewater two-one-six-four. (*To the rest*) Was she mad at me?

MC CUE. Did you bring the ketch-up?
(*They are crowding about* WOODENSHOES.)

BENSINGER. How about my plain lettuce?

ENDICOTT. A hamburger for me!

SCHWARTZ. I ordered one, didn't I?

KRUGER. You did not! This way, Woodenshoes!
(*They are taking their sandwiches from* WOODENSHOES — ENDICOTT *tosses one at* KRUGER.)

HILDY (*into phone*). Hello, Peggy? . . . Hello. . . . (*His voice becomes romantic.*)

MC CUE. Attaboy! God, I'm starved.

HILDY (*into phone*). Why, darling, what's the matter?

BENSINGER. For God's sake, I said gluten bread.

HILDY (*into phone*). But there isn't anything to cry about.

MURPHY. The service is getting terrible around here.

HILDY (*into phone*). But listen, darling! I had business to attend to. I'll tell you all about it the minute I see you . . . Aw, darling, I just dropped in here for one second. . . . Because I *had* to. I couldn't go away without saying good-bye to the fellows. (*To the others*) Will you guys talk or something? (*Back to phone*) But listen! Sweetheart! . . . Yes, I . . . Of *course* I handed in my resignation . . . Yes, I've got a taxi waiting . . . Right outside.

WOODENSHOES (*uneasily*). Go easy on that ketchup. I'm responsible for that.

HILDY (*into phone*). I've got them right in my pocket, honey . . . Three on the eleven-eighteen. I'm bringing 'em right out, mile a minute.

WOODENSHOES. She says you fellows have got to pay something soon.

HILDY (*into phone*). Aw, darling, if you talk like that I'm going to go right out and jump in the lake. I swear I will, because I can't stand it. Listen! (*He looks around to see if it is safe to continue.*)

KRUGER. We're listening.

HILDY (*trying to lower his voice. With his mouth pasted to the mouthpiece, the following speeches are gargled into phone*) Darling . . . I love you. (*Appropriate music by* KRUGER) I said . . . I love you. (*Music again.*)

SCHWARTZ. Aw, give him a break, Ernie.
(KRUGER *stops playing.*)

HILDY (*into phone*). That's more like it.

WOODENSHOES. Are you finished with this? (*Reaching for ketchup.*)

MC CUE (*operating the bottle*). No.

HILDY (*into phone*). Feel better now? . . . Well, smile. And say something . . . You know what I want to hear.

SCHWARTZ (*a Cinderella*). Give me a half a one, somebody!

ENDICOTT. Nothing doing.

HILDY (*into the phone*). That's the stuff. That's better . . . Are you all packed? . . . Oh, swell . . . I'll be right there.

WOODENSHOES. You fellas ought to pay her a little something on account. (*Exits.*)

WILSON (*answering Examiner phone*). What do you want?

HILDY. Listen, darling, will you wear that little blue straw hat?

WILSON (*into phone*). Wait a minute—I'll see.

HILDY (*into phone*). And are you all happy now? . . . I bet you're not as happy as I am. Oh, I'll bet you anything you want . . . All right . . . All right . . . I'm on my way . . . Not more than fifteen minutes. *Really* this time . . . Bye. (*Hangs up.*)

WILSON (*his hand over the mouthpiece*). Jesus Christ, Hildy—here's Walter again! Tell him to give us a rest, will you?

HILDY. Oh, bollacks! (*Into phone*) You're just making a God-damn nuisance of yourself! . . . What's the idea of calling up all the time! . . . *No!* I'm through with newspapers! I don't give a God damn what you think of me! I'm leaving for New York tonight! Right now! This minute! (*Hangs up. Phone rings again. He tears it from the wall and throws it out the window.*)

KRUGER (*calmly*). Wrong number.

MC CUE (*nervous*). For God's sake, Hildy!

SCHWARTZ (*putting out the lights*). You'll get us in a hell of a jam!

BENSINGER. Haven't you got any sense?

HILDY (*yelling out the window*). Tell Pinky to stick that among his souvenirs! (*To the rest*) If that lunatic calls up again tell him to put it in writing and mail it to Hildebrand Johnson, care of the Waterbury-Adams Corporation, Seven Thirty-five Fifth Avenue, New York City . . .

MURPHY. Put it on the wall, Mike.

ENDICOTT (*going to the rear wall*). Waterbury what?

MC CUE. Adams.

HILDY (*opening a parcel and showing a pale pair of gloves*). How do you like those onions? Marshall Field!

MC CUE. Very individual.

HILDY. Where's my cane?

ENDICOTT. What cane?

HILDY (*suddenly desperate*). Come now, fellas. That ain't funny, who's got my cane?

MURPHY (*in a Central Office manner*) Can you describe this cane?

HILDY (*frantic*). Aw, for God's sake! Now listen, fellas--

KRUGER (*solicitous*). Are you sure you had it with you when you came into the room?

WILSON. Was there any writing on it?

HILDY (*diving into* BENSINGER'S *desk*). Come on! Cut the clowning! Where is it?

BENSINGER. Keep out of my desk! Of all the God-damn kindergartens!

HILDY. Jesus! I only got fifteen minutes. Now, cut the kidding! My God, you fellows have got a sense of humor!

MURPHY. Aw, give him his fairy wand!

ENDICOTT (*a Uranian for the moment, he produces cane from trouser leg*). Here it is, Gladys.

HILDY. God! You had me worried. (*He picks up his suitcase. Bravura*). Well, good-bye, you lousy wage slaves! When you're crawling up fire escapes, and getting kicked out of front doors, and eating Christmas dinner in a one-armed joint, don't forget your old pal, Hildy Johnson!

ENDICOTT. Good-bye, Yonson.

MC CUE. So long, Hildy.

MURPHY. Send us a postcard, you big stewbum.

KRUGER. When'll we see you again, Hildy?

HILDY. The next time you see me I'll be riding in a Rolls-Royce, giving out interviews on success-y.

BENSINGER. Good-bye, Hildy.

WILSON. Good-bye.

SCHWARTZ. Take care of yourself.

HILDY. So long, fellows! (*He strikes a Sidney Carton pose in the door-*

way; starts on a bit of verse) "And as the road beyond unfolds—" *(He is interrupted by a terrific fusillade of shots from the courtyard. A roar of voices comes up from the jail yard. For a tense second everyone is motionless.)*

VOICES *(in the courtyard)*. Get the riot guns! Spread out, you guys! *(Another volley.)*

WILSON. There's a jail break!

MURPHY *(at window, simultaneously)*. Jacobi! What's the matter? What's happened?

VOICES *(in the jail yard)*. Watch the gate! He's probably trying the gate! *(A huge siren begins to wail.)*

SCHWARTZ *(out the window)*. Who got away? Who was it?

VOICE *(outside)*. Earl . . . Williams ! ! !

THE REPORTERS. Who? Who'd he say? Earl Williams! It was Earl Williams! He got away!

MC CUE. Holy God! Gimme that telephone! *(He works hook frantically)* Hurry! Hurry up! Will you? This is important. *(Others are springing for the telephones as searchlights sweep the windows from the direction of the jail.)*

SCHWARTZ. Jeez, this is gonna make a bum out of the Sheriff!

*(*HILDY *stands paralyzed, his suitcase in his hand. There is a second rifle volley. Two window panes crash within the room. Some plaster falls. Gongs sound above the siren.)*

MC CUE *(screaming)*. Look out!

MURPHY *(out of the window)*. Where you shooting, you God-damn fools? For Christ's sake! *(Another pane goes)* Look out where you're aiming, will you?

SCHWARTZ. There's some phones in the state's attorney's office!

KRUGER. Yeah!

(There is a general panic at the door. The REPORTERS *leave as if a bomb had broken in a trench.* HILDY *is left alone, still holding his suitcase. It falls. He moves back into the room, absently trailing a chair. Another shot.)*

HILDY. Ahh, Jesus Christ! *(He lets go of the chair and takes one of the telephones)* Examiner? Gimme Walter Burns! Quick! *(Very calmly he sits on one of the long tables, his back against the wall. Then, quietly)* Hello, Walter! Hildy Johnson! Forget that! Earl Williams just lammed out of the County Jail! Yep . . . yep . . . yep . . . don't worry! I'm on the job! *(There is a third volley.* HILDY *sails his hat and coat into a corner and is removing his overcoat as the curtain falls.)*

ACT TWO

The Scene is the same as Act I—It is twenty minutes later. Searchlights play outside the windows. JENNIE, *the scrubwoman, is on stage, sweeping up broken glass and doing a little miscellaneous cleaning.* WOODENSHOES *enters.*

WOODENSHOES. Where are all the reporters? Out looking for him?

JENNIE. They broke all the windows. and pulled off a telephone. Aiiy, those newspaper fellows! They're worse'n anything.

WOODENSHOES. There wasn't any excuse for his escaping. This sort of thing couldn't ever happen, if they listened to me.

JENNIE. Oooh, they'll catch him. Those big lights.

WOODENSHOES. What good will that do Society? The time to catch 'em is while they're little kids. That's the whole basis of my crime prevention theory. It's all going to be written up in the papers soon.

JENNIE. Ooooh, what they print in the papers! I never seen anything like it. (*She is sweeping.* ENDICOTT *enters and makes for a phone.* WOODENSHOES *watches him.*)

WOODENSHOES. Has anything happened, Mr. Endicott?

ENDICOTT (*into phone*). Endicott calling. Gimme a rewrite man.

WOODENSHOES. You know, this would be just the right time for you to print my theory of crime prevention, that you said you were going to. (*Pulling out a sheaf of documents.*)

ENDICOTT (*into phone, waving him off as if he were a horsefly*). Well, hurry it up.

WOODENSHOES. Now here I got the city split up in districts. I got them marked in red.

ENDICOTT. What? For God's sake, can't you see I'm— (*Into phone*) Hello! Gill?

WOODENSHOES. But you been promising me you'd—

ENDICOTT (*snatches papers*). All right—I'll take it home and study it. Now for God's sake stop annoying me—I got to work! I can't sit around listening to you! Get out of here and stop bothering me! (*Back to phone*) Ready, Gill? . . . Now, here's the situation so far.

WOODENSHOES (*to* JENNIE). He's going to take it home and study it. You'll see it in the paper before long. (*Exits.*)

ENDICOTT (*into phone*). Right! . . . At ten minutes after nine Williams was taken to the Sheriff's private office to be examined by this Professor

Eglehofer, and a few minutes later he shot his way out . . . No—nobody knows where he got the gun. Or if they do they won't tell . . . Yeah . . . Yeah . . . He run up eight flights of stairs to the infirmary, and got out through the skylight. He must have slid down the rainpipe to the street . . . Yeah . . . No, I tell you nobody knows where he got it. I got hold of Jacobi, but he won't talk. (MURPHY *enters.*)

MURPHY (*crossing to phone*). Outside, Jennie! Outside!

ENDICOTT. They're throwing a dragnet around the whole North Side. Watching the railroads and Red headquarters. The Chief of Police has ordered out every copper on the force and says they'll get Williams before morning.

MURPHY (*into phone*). Hello, sweetheart. Give me the desk, will you?

ENDICOTT (*into phone, after a final look at his notes*). The Crime Commission has offered a reward of ten thousand dollars for his capture . . . Yeah. I'm going to try to get hold of Eglehofer. He knows what's happened, if I can find him. Call you back. (*Hangs up and exits swiftly.*)

MURPHY. For Chris' sake, Jennie! Every time we turn our backs you start that God-damn sweeping.

JENNIE (*picking up her traps*). All right. Only it's dirty. I get scolded.

MURPHY (*into phone*). Murphy talking . . . No clue yet as to Earl Williams' whereabouts. Here's a little feature, though. . . . A tear bomb . . . *tear* bomb . . . criminals cry for it . . .

(SHERIFF HARTMAN *appears in the doorway. He has been running around, shouting a million orders, nervous, bewitched and sweating like a June bride. He is in his shirt sleeves, and his diamond-studded badge of office is visible.*)

MURPHY (*into phone*). Yeh! Tear bomb.

SHERIFF (*as he enters, speaking to someone in the corridor*). To hell with the Mayor! If he wants me he knows where I am.

MURPHY (*into phone*). A tear bomb went off unexpectedly in the hands of Sheriff Hartman's bombing squad.

SHERIFF (*stunned*). What went off?

MURPHY (*into phone*). The following deputy sheriffs were rushed to Passavant Hospital: . . .

SHERIFF. A fine fair-weather friend you are!

MURPHY (*remorselessly, into phone*). Philip Lustgarten . . .

SHERIFF. After all I've done for you!

MURPHY (*phoning*). Herman Waldstein . . .

SHERIFF. Putting stuff like that in the papers!

MURPHY (*phoning*). Sidney Matsburg . . .

SHERIFF. That's gratitude for you! (*He exits.*)

MURPHY (*phoning*). Henry Koo . . .

JENNIE (*going toward door*). Ain't that terrible?

(KRUGER *enters and goes to a phone.*)

MURPHY (*phoning*). Abe Lefkowitz . . .

JENNIE. All those fellows! (*Exits.*)

KRUGER (*at his phone*). Give me rewrite.

MURPHY (*phoning*). And William Gilhooly. Call you back. (*Hangs up and exits.*)

KRUGER (*into phone*). Ready? . . . A man corresponding to Earl Williams' description was seen boarding a southbound Cottage Grove Avenue car at Austen Avenue by Motorman Julius L. Roosevelt. (MC CUE *enters*) Yeah—Roosevelt. I thought it would make a good feature on account of the name.

MC CUE (*phoning*). McCue talking. Give me the desk.

KRUGER (*phoning*). All right, I'll go right after it. Call you back. (*Exits.*)

MC CUE (*into phone*). Hello. Is that you, Emil? Are you ready? . . . Sidelights on the man hunt . . . Mrs. Irma Schlogel, fifty-five, scrublady, was shot in the left leg while at work scrubbing the eighth floor of the Wrigley Building by one of Sheriff Hartman's special deputies. (*There is a fusillade of shots in the distance.* HILDY JOHNSON *enters.*)

HILDY. There goes another scrublady. (*Goes to phone, but starts arranging notes.*)

MC CUE (*phoning*). No, just a flesh wound. They took her to Passavant Hospital. (*Hangs up. To* HILDY) Any dope on how he got out?

HILDY. From all I can get they were playing leap frog.

MC CUE. How about Jacobi? Did he say anything to you?

HILDY. Not a word. (MC CUE *goes.*)

HILDY (*quickly picks up his receiver*). Gimme Walter Burns. (*He gets up and closes the door carefully; comes back to his phone*) Walter? Say, listen. I got the whole story from Jacobi and I got it exclusive . . . That's right, and it's a pip. Only listen. It cost me two hundred and sixty bucks, see? . . . Just a minute—I'll *give* you the story. I'm telling you first I had to give him all the money I had on me and it wasn't exactly mine. Two hundred and sixty bucks, and I want it back. (*Yells*) Well, did you hear what I said about the money? . . . All right, then here's your story. It's the jail break of your dreams . . . Dr. Max J. Eglehofer, a profound thinker from Vienna, was giving Williams a final sanity test in the Sheriff's office—you know, sticking a lot of pins in him to get his reflexes. Then he decided to re-enact the crime exactly as it had taken place, so as to study Williams' powers of co-ordination. . . . Well, I'm coming to it, God damn it. Will you shut up? . . . Of course he had to have a gun to reenact with. And who do you suppose supplied it? . . . Peter B. Hartman . . . "B" for brains. . . . I tell you, I'm *not* kidding. Hartman gave his gun to the Professor, the Professor gave it to Earl, and Earl shot the Professor right in the belly . . . Ain't it perfect? If the Sheriff had unrolled a red carpet like at a Polish wedding and loaned Williams an umbrella, it couldn't have been more ideal . . . Eglehofer? No, not bad. They spirited him away to Passavant Hospital . . . No, we got it exclusive. Now listen, Walter. It cost me two hundred and sixty bucks for this story, and I want it back . . . I had to give it to Jacobi before he'd cough up his guts. Two hundred and sixty dollars—the money I'm going to get married on . . . Never mind about fine work—I want the money . . . No, I tell you, I'm not going to cover anything else—I'm going away. (PEGGY *appears in the doorway. She is a pretty girl of twenty.* HILDY *has his back to the door.*) Listen, you lousy stiff. I just did this as a personal favor. Now I'm leaving town and I gave Jacobi every cent I got, and I want it back right away! . . . *When* will you send it over? . . . Well, see that you do or I can't get married! . . . All right, and tell him to run. I'll be waiting right here in the press— (*He hangs up and sees* PEGGY. *With a guilty start*) Hello, Peggy.

PEGGY. What was that, over the telephone?

HILDY. Nothing. I was just telling Walter Burns I was all through, that's all. Hello, darling.
(PEGGY, *despite her youth and simplicity, seems overwhelmingly mature in comparison to* HILDY. *As a matter of fact,* PEGGY *belongs to that division of womanhood which dedicates itself to suppressing in its lovers or husbands the spirit of D'Artagnan, Roland, Captain Kidd, Cyrano, Don Quixote, King Arthur or any other type of the male innocent and rampant. In her unconscious and highly noble efforts to make what the female world calls "a man" out of* HILDY, PEGGY *has neither the sympathy nor acclaim of the authors, yet —regarded superficially, she is a very sweet and satisfying heroine.*)

PEGGY. You haven't done something foolish with that money? Our money!

HILDY. No. No!

PEGGY. You still *have* got the rest of it?

HILDY. Of course. Gee, darling, you don't think for a minute—

PEGGY. I think I'd better take care of it from now on!

HILDY. Now listen, honey, I can look after a couple of hundred dollars all right. . . .

PEGGY. Hildy, if you've still got that money I want you to give it to me.

HILDY. Now, sweetheart, it's going to be perfectly all right. . . .

PEGGY (*she divines, alas, her lover's failing*). Then you haven't got it.

HILDY. Not—this minute, but I—

PEGGY. You *did* do something with it!

HILDY. No, no. He's sending it right over—Walter, I mean. It'll be here any minute.

PEGGY (*her vocabulary is reduced to a coal of fire*). Oh, Hildy!

HILDY (*a preposterous fellow*). Listen, darling, I wouldn't have had this happen for the world. But it's going to be all right. Now here's what happened: I was just starting out to the house to get you when this guy Williams broke out of jail.

You know, the fellow they were going to hang in the morning.

PEGGY (*intolerant of the antics of the Cyrano sex*). Yes, I know.

HILDY. Ah now, listen, sweetheart, I *had* to do what I did. And—and the same thing when it came to the money— (*She turns away*) Peggy! Now listen. I shouldn't tell you this, but I haven't got any secrets from you. Do you know how this guy escaped? He was down in the Sheriff's office when Hartman—that's the Sheriff—and Eglehofer—that's this fellow from Vienna—

PEGGY. Hildy!

HILDY. Aw, now I can't tell you if you won't listen. I *had* to give him the money so he wouldn't give the story to anybody else. Jacobi, I mean. That's the assistant warden. I got the story exclusive—the biggest scoop in years, I'll bet.

PEGGY. Do you know how long mother and I waited, out at that house?

HILDY. Aw, Peggy, listen. You ain't going to be mad at me for this. I couldn't help it. You'd have done the same thing yourself. I mean, the biggest story in the world busting, and nobody on the job.

PEGGY. I might have known it would happen again.

HILDY. Aw, listen—

PEGGY. Every time I've ever wanted you for something—on my birthday, and New Year's Eve, when I waited till five in the morning—

HILDY. But a big story broke; don't you remember.

PEGGY. It's always a big story—the biggest story in the world, and the next day everybody's forgotten it, even you!

HILDY. What do you mean forgotten? That was the Clara Hamon murder—on your birthday. Now for God's sake, Peggy, it won't hurt to wait five more minutes. The boy's on his way with the money now.

PEGGY. Mother's sitting downstairs waiting in a taxicab. I'm just ashamed to face her, the way you've been acting. If she knew about that money—it's all we've got in the world, Hildy. We haven't even got a place to sleep in, except the train, and—

HILDY. Aw, gee, I wouldn't do anything in the world to hurt you, Peggy. You make me feel like a criminal.

PEGGY. It's all that Walter Burns. Oh, I'll be so glad when I get you away from him.—You simply can't resist him.

HILDY. For God's sake, Peggy, I've told you what I think of him. I wouldn't raise a finger if he was dying. Honest to God.

PEGGY. Then why did you loan him the money?

HILDY. I didn't! You see, you won't listen to me, or you'd know I didn't. Now, listen. I had to give the money to Jacobi, the assistant—

(WOODENSHOES *ushers in* MRS. GRANT. MRS. GRANT *is a confused little widow who has tried her best to adjust her mind to* HILDY *as a son-in-law.*)

WOODENSHOES. Here they are, ma'am. (*Exits immediately.*)

HILDY. Oh, hello, Mrs. Grant—mother. I was just explaining to Peggy—

PEGGY. Mother, I thought you were going to wait in the cab.

MRS. GRANT (*a querulous yet practical soul*). Well, I just came up to tell you the meter's gone to two dollars.

HILDY. Yeah, sure. But that's all right. . . .

MRS. GRANT (*with the wandering egoism of age*). I had a terrible time finding you. First I went into a room where a lot of policemen were playing cards.

HILDY. Yeah—that was—now, I'll tell you what we'll do.

MRS. GRANT. Then I met that policeman and I asked him where Mr. Johnson's office was, and he brought me here.

PEGGY. Now listen, mother, I think you'd better go downstairs and we'll come as soon as we can.

MRS. GRANT (*inspecting*). You've got a big room, haven't you? Where do you sit?

HILDY. Now, I tell you what you do. You and Peggy go on over to the station and get the baggage checked . . . now here's the tickets.

PEGGY. Now, Hildy.

HILDY. I'll be along in fifteen minutes—maybe sooner.

MRS. GRANT. How do you mean—that you aren't going?

HILDY. Of course I am. Now, I'll meet you at the Information Booth—

PEGGY. Come, mother. Hildy has to wait here a few minutes. It's something to do with the office—he's getting some money.

MRS. GRANT (*on familiar ground*). Money?

HILDY. Yeah—they're sending over—it's my salary. They're sending over my salary.

MRS. GRANT (*the voice of womankind*). Your salary? At this hour?

HILDY. They were awful busy, and I couldn't disturb them very well.

MRS. GRANT. The trouble is you're too easy with people—letting them wait till this hour before paying you your salary. How do you know they'll give it to you at all?

PEGGY. Mother, we'll go on over. Hildy'll be along.

MRS. GRANT. Do you know what I'm beginning to think?

HILDY (*apprehensive*). What?

MRS. GRANT. I think you must be a sort of irresponsible type or you wouldn't do things this way. It's just occurred to me you didn't do one blessed thing to help our getting away.

PEGGY. Now you stop picking on my Hildy, mother.

MRS. GRANT. Why, I had to sublet the apartment, and pack all the wedding presents— (MC CUE *enters. Goes to phone, with side glances at the others*) Why, that's work a man ought to do. You weren't even there to put things in the taxi—I had to give the man fifty cents. And now here you are standing here with the train leaving any minute—

HILDY. Now, mother, I never missed a train in my life. You run along with Peggy—

MC CUE (*into phone*). Hello. McCue talking.

PEGGY. Come on, mother. We're disturbing people.

HILDY. This is my girl, Mac, and her mother. Mr. McCue.

MC CUE (*tipping his hat*). Pleased to meet you. (*Into phone*) Here's a hell of a swell feature on the man hunt. (*To the ladies*) Excuse my French! (*Into phone*) Mrs. Phoebe De Wolfe, eight-sixty-one and a half South State Street, colored, gave birth to a pickaninny in a patrol wagon, with Sheriff Hartman's special Rifle Squad acting as midwives.

MRS. GRANT. Mercy!

MC CUE (*pleased at having interested her*). You oughta have seen 'em, ma'am.

PEGGY. Come on, mother.

HILDY. Listen, mother, you better run along. I'll put my suitcase in the cab.

MC CUE (*phoning*). Well, Phoebe was walking along the street when all of a sudden she began having labor pains. No! Labor pains! Didn't you ever have labor pains? Righto! She was hollering for her husband, who's been missing for five months, when the police seen her. And Deputy Henry Shereson, who's a married man, saw what her condition was. So he coaxed her into the patrol wagon and they started a race with the stork for Passavant Hospital.

HILDY (*to* MC CUE, *as he goes out*) If a boy comes here for me hold him. I'll be right back! (*They are gone.*)

MC CUE (*into phone*). Listen—when the pickaninny was born the Rifle Squad examined him carefully to see if it was Earl Williams, who they knew was hiding somewhere. (*Laughs at his own joke*) They named him Peter Hartman De Wolfe in honor of the Sheriff, and they all chipped in a dollar apiece on account of it being the first baby ever born in a man hunt. (*The Mayor enters*) Wait a minute—here's the Mayor himself. Maybe there's a statement. (*Under ordinary circumstances the* MAYOR *is a bland, unruffled soul, full of ease and confidence; a bit stupid, walking as if he were on snowshoes and carrying an unlighted cigar with which he gestures as if it were a wand. The events of the last hour have unhinged him. He is eager for news—even the worst.*)

MAYOR. Don't pester me now, please I got a lot on my mind.

MC CUE (*into phone*). The Mayor won't say anything. (*He hangs up.*)

MAYOR. Have you seen Sheriff Hartman?

MC CUE. Been in and out all night your Honor . . .

(MURPHY *and* ENDICOTT *enter.*)

MURPHY. Now listen, your Honor. We've got to have a statement. . . .

ENDICOTT. We go to press in twenty minutes.

MAYOR. I can't help that, boys. I have nothing to say—not at this time.

MURPHY. What do you mean—"not at this time?" Who do you think you are, Abraham Lincoln?

ENDICOTT. Come on, cut the statesman stuff! What do you know about the escape? How'd he get out?

MURPHY. Where'd he get the gun?

MAYOR. Wait a minute, boys . . . Not so fast!

ENDICOTT. Well, give us a statement on the election, then.

MURPHY. What effect's all this going to have on the colored voters?

MAYOR. Not an iota. In what way can an unavoidable misfortune of this sort influence the duty of every citizen, colored or otherwise?

MURPHY. Baloney. . . .

ENDICOTT. Listen here, Mayor. *Is* there a Red Menace or ain't there? and how did he get out of that rubber jail of yours?

MC CUE. Are you going to stand the gaff, Mayor? Or have you picked out somebody that's responsible?

MURPHY (*innocently*). Any truth in the report that you're on Trotsky's payroll?

ENDICOTT. Yeah—the Senator claims you sleep in red underwear.

MAYOR. Never mind the jokes. Don't forget that I'm Mayor of this town and that the dignity of my office . . . (HARTMAN *enters—the* MAYOR *turns abruptly on him*) Hartman! I've been looking for you. . . .

ENDICOTT (*leaping at the* SHERIFF). What's the dope, Pinky? How did he get out?

MC CUE. What was he doing in your office?

MURPHY. What's this about somebody gettin' shot?

ENDICOTT. Where did he get the gun?

SHERIFF (*jotting notes on a piece of paper with the hope that he will seem busy*). Just a minute, fellas.

MURPHY. For God's sake, cut the stallin'! Who engineered the getaway?

ENDICOTT. Was it the Reds?

SHERIFF. Just a minute, I tell you. We've got him located!

MURPHY. Who? Williams!

ENDICOTT. Where?

MC CUE. Where is he?

SHERIFF. Out to the place where he used to live . . . on Clark Street . . . Just got the tip.

ENDICOTT. Holy God!

MC CUE. Why didn't you say so?

SHERIFF. The Rifle Squad is just going out.

ENDICOTT. Where are they?

SHERIFF. Downstairs. All the boys are with them.

MURPHY. For the love of God! (MURPHY, ENDICOTT *and* MC CUE *rush out.*)

ENDICOTT (*in the hall*). Hey, there, Charlie!

SHERIFF (*calling into the corridor*). Report to me, Charlie, the minute you get there! I'll be in the building!

MAYOR. Pete, I want to talk to you!

SHERIFF. I ain't got time, Fred—honest. I'll see you after.

MAYOR. Pete, there's one thing I've got to know. Did you yourself actually give Williams that gun?

SHERIFF (*wailing*). The Professor asked me for it. I didn't know what he wanted it for. I thought it was something scientific.

MAYOR. Now listen, Fred— (KRUGER *enters, whistling. Both statesmen become silent and self-conscious.*)

KRUGER (*heading for phone*). Hello, your Honor. Any statement on the Red uprising tomorrow?

MAYOR. What Red uprising?

SHERIFF. There'll be no Red uprising!

KRUGER. The Senator claims the situation calls for the militia.

MAYOR. You can quote me as saying that anything the Senator says is a tissue of lies.

KRUGER (*at phone*). Kruger calling.

SHERIFF. Why aren't you with the Rifle Squad? They've just gone out.

KRUGER. We've got a man with them. (*Into phone*) Here's a red-hot statement from the Senator. Ready? . . . He says the City Hall is another Augean Stables . . . Augean! . . . Oh, for God's sake! (*Turns*) He don't know what Augean means.

MAYOR. The Senator don't know either.

KRUGER. Well, take the rest, anyhow. (*Into phone*) The Senator claims that the Mayor and the Sheriff have shown themselves to be a couple of eight-year-olds playing with fire. Then this is quote: "It is a lucky thing for the city that next Tuesday is Election Day, as the citizens will thus be saved the expense of impeaching the Mayor and the Sheriff." That's all—call you back. (*Hangs up*) How are you, Mayor? (*Exits, whistling.*)

MAYOR (*closing the door*). I've got a mighty unpleasant task to perform, Pete—

SHERIFF (*beside himself*). Now listen, Fred, you're just gonna get me rattled.

MAYOR (*inexorably*). Two years ago we almost lost the colored vote on account of that coon story you told at the Dixie Marching Club . . . Mandy and the traveling salesman. . . .

SHERIFF. Why harp on that *now?* . . .

MAYOR. Now you come along with another one of your moron blunders. . . . The worst of your whole career.

SHERIFF (*frantic*). Listen, Fred. Stop worrying, will you? Just do me a favor and stop worrying! I'm doing everything on God's green earth! I've just sworn in four hundred deputies!

MAYOR. Four hundred! Do you want to bankrupt this administration?

SHERIFF (*pleadingly*). I'm getting them for twelve dollars a night.

MAYOR. Twelve dollars—! For those God damn uncles of yours? What do you think this is—Christmas Eve?

SHERIFF (*with dignity*). If you're talking about my brother-in-law, he's worked for the city fifteen years.

MAYOR (*bitterly*). I know. Getting up fake tag days! . . . Pete, you're through!

SHERIFF (*stunned*). What do you mean—through?

MAYOR. I mean I'm scratching your name off the ticket Tuesday and running Czernecki in your place. It's nothing personal. . . . And Pete —it's the only way out. It's a sacrifice we all ought to be glad to make.

SHERIFF (*David to Jonathan*). Fred!

MAYOR. Now, Pete! Please don't appeal to my sentimental side. . . .

SHERIFF. I don't know what to say. A thing like this almost destroys a man's faith in human nature. . . .

MAYOR. I wish you wouldn't talk like that, Pete. . . .

SHERIFF. Our families, Fred. My God, I've always looked on Bessie as my own sister.

MAYOR (*wavering and desperate*). If there was any way out . . .

SHERIFF (*as a phone rings*). There is a way out. I've got this Williams surrounded, haven't I? What more do you want? Now if you just give me a couple of hours— (*Into phone*) Hello. . . . Yes. . . . Hello! (*Wildly*) Four hundred suppers! Nothing doing! This is a man hunt—not a banquet! . . . The twelve dollars includes everything! . . . Well, the hell with them! Earl Williams ain't eating, is he? (*He hangs up*) That gives you an idea of what I'm up against!

MAYOR (*hotly*). We're up against a lot more than that with that nutty slogan you invented. "Reform the Reds with a rope." (SHERIFF winces) There ain't any God damn Reds and you know it!

SHERIFF. Yeah, but why go into that now, Fred?

MAYOR. The slogan I had was all we needed to win—"Keep King George Out of Chicago!"

SHERIFF. My God, I ain't had a bite to eat since this thing happened.

MAYOR. Pete, two hundred thousand colored votes are at stake! And we've got to hang Earl Williams to get them.

SHERIFF. But we're *going* to hang him, Fred. He can't get away. (*A knock on the door.*)

MAYOR. What do you mean he can't get away! He *got* away, didn't he? Now look here, Pete— (*Knocking louder*) Who's out there? . . .

A VOICE (*outside*). Is Sheriff Hartman in there?

SHERIFF (*starts for door; relieved*). Ah! It's for me! (*Opens the door. A small man named* PINCUS *stands there*) I'm Sheriff Hartman. Do you want me?

PINCUS (*a very colorless and uneffectual person*). Yes, *sir*. I've been looking all over for you, Sheriff. You're certainly a hard fellow to find.

MAYOR (*annoyed*). What do you want?

PINCUS (*taking a document from his pocket and proffering it to the* SHERIFF. *He smiles in a comradely fashion*). From the Governor.

MAYOR. What's from the Governor?

SHERIFF. Huh?

PINCUS. The reprieve for Earl Williams.

SHERIFF (*stunned*). For *who?*

PINCUS (*amiably*). Earl Williams. The reprieve. (*A ghastly pause*) I thought I'd never find you. First I had a helluva time getting a taxi—

MAYOR. Wait—a minute. (*Getting his bearings*) Is this a joke or something?

PINCUS. Huh?

SHERIFF (*bursting out*). It's a mistake—there must be a mistake! The Governor gave me his word of honor he wouldn't interfere! Two days ago!

MAYOR. And you fell for it! Holy God, Pete! It frightens me what I'd like to do to you! Wait a minute! Come here, you! Who else knows about this?

PINCUS. They were all standing around when he wrote it. It was after they got back from fishing.

MAYOR. Get the Governor on the phone, Hartman.

PINCUS. They ain't got a phone. They're duck-shooting now.

MAYOR. A lot of God-damn nimrods.

SHERIFF (*who has been reading the reprieve*). Can you beat that? Read it! (*Thrusts the paper into* MAYOR's *hands*) Insane, he says! (*Striding over to the messenger*) He knows God damn well that Earl Williams ain't insane!

PINCUS. Yeah! But I—

SHERIFF. This reprieve is pure politics and you know it! It's an attempt to ruin us!

MAYOR (*reading*). Dementia praecox! My God!

SHERIFF. We got to think fast before those lying reporters get hold of this. What'll we tell 'em?

MAYOR. What'll you tell 'em? I'll tell you what you can tell 'em! You can tell 'em your damn relatives were out there shooting everybody they see, for the hell of it!

SHERIFF. Now Fred, you're just excited. (*Phone rings;* SHERIFF *starts for the phone, talking as he goes*) We aren't going to get any place, rowing like this.

MAYOR. And you can tell 'em the Republican Party is through in this state on account of you.

SHERIFF (*into phone*). Hello! This is Hartman.

MAYOR (*apoplectic*). And you can add as an afterthought that I want your resignation now.

SHERIFF (*from the phone*). Sssh. Wait, Fred. (*Excitedly, into phone*) What? Where? . . . Where? My God!

MAYOR. What is it?

SHERIFF. They got him! (*Back to phone*) Wait a minute—hold the wire. (*To the* MAYOR) They got Earl Williams surrounded . . . the Rifle Squad has . . . in his house.

MAYOR. Tell 'em to hold the wire.

SHERIFF. I did. (*Into phone*) Hold the wire.

MAYOR. Cover up that transmitter! (SHERIFF *does so.* MAYOR *faces* PINCUS) Now listen! You never arrived here with this—whatever it is. Get that?

PINCUS (*blinking*). Yes, I did.

MAYOR. How much do you make a week?

PINCUS. Huh?

MAYOR (*impatiently*). How much do you make a week? What's your salary?

PINCUS (*reluctantly*). Forty dollars.

SHERIFF (*into phone*). No—don't cut me off.

MAYOR. How would you like to have a job for three hundred and fifty dollars a month? That's almost a hundred dollars a week!

PINCUS. Who? Me?

MAYOR. Who the hell do you think? (PINCUS *is a little startled; the* MAYOR *hastens to adopt a milder manner*) Now listen. There's a fine opening for a fellow like you in the City Sealer's office.

PINCUS. The what?

MAYOR. The City Sealer's office!

PINCUS. You mean here in Chicago?

MAYOR (*foaming*). Yes, yes.

SHERIFF (*at phone*). Well, wait a minute, will you? I'm in conference.

PINCUS (*a very deliberate intellect*). No, I couldn't do that.

MAYOR. Why not?

PINCUS. I couldn't work in Chicago. You see, I've got my family in Springfield.

MAYOR (*desperate*). But you could bring 'em to Chicago! We'll pay all your expenses.

PINCUS (*with vast thought*). No, I don't think so.

MAYOR. For God's sake, why not?

PINCUS. I got two kids going to high school there, and if I changed them from one town to another they'd probably lose a grade.

MAYOR. No, they wouldn't—they'd gain one! They could go into any class they want to. And I guarantee that they'll graduate with highest honors!

PINCUS (*lured*). Yeah?

MAYOR. And the Chicago school system is the best in the world. (*To* SHERIFF) Isn't it?

SHERIFF. Far and away! (*Into phone*) Hold your horses—will you, Mittelbaum. Hurry up, Fred!

MAYOR. Now what do you say?

PINCUS. What did you say this job was?

MAYOR. In the City Sealer's office!

PINCUS. What's he do?

MAYOR (*jumping*). Oh, for God's sake!

SHERIFF. He has charge of all the important documents. He puts the City seals on them.

MAYOR. That's about on a par with the rest of your knowledge! The City Sealer's duty, my friend, is to see that the people of Chicago are not mulcted by unscrupulous butchers and grocers.

SHERIFF. That's what I meant.

MAYOR. It's his duty to go around and test their scales.

PINCUS. Yeah?

MAYOR. But only twice a year.

PINCUS. This puts me in a hell of a hole.

MAYOR. No it doesn't. . . . (*Hands him the reprieve*) Now remember. You never delivered this, whatever it is. You got caught in the traffic or something. . . . Now get out of here and don't let anybody see you. . . .

PINCUS. But how do I know . . .

MAYOR. Come in and see me in my office tomorrow. What's your name?

PINCUS. Pincus.

MAYOR. All right, Mr. Pincus, all you've got to do is lay low and keep your mouth shut. Here! (*He hands him a card*) Go to this address. It's a nice homey little place, and you can get anything you want. (*He sees* PINCUS *through the door*) Just tell 'em Fred sent you. (PINCUS *goes.*)

SHERIFF (*into phone, desperately*). Will you wait, for God's sake? I'll tell you in a minute! (*He turns to the* MAYOR *with a gesture of appeal.*)

MAYOR (*huskily*). All right. Tell 'em to shoot to kill.

SHERIFF. What?

MAYOR. Shoot to kill, I said.

SHERIFF. I don't know, Fred. There's that reprieve if they ever find out.

MAYOR. Nobody reprieved that policeman he murdered. Now do as I tell you.

SHERIFF (*into phone*). Hello, Mittelbaum . . . Listen. (*His voice is weak*) Shoot to kill. . . . That's the orders—pass the word along. . . . No! We don't want him! And listen, Mittelbaum—five hundred bucks for the guy that does the job. . . . Yes, I'll be right out there. (*Hangs up*) Well, I hope that's the right thing to do. (*There is a great kicking on the door.*)

HILDY (*outside*). Hey! Who's in there? Open that door!

MAYOR (*en route to the door*). For God's sake take that guilty look off your face. And stop trembling like a horse. (*The* SHERIFF *starts whistling, "Ach, du Lieber Augustine" in what he imagines is a care-free manner. The* MAYOR *opens the door;* HILDY *enters.*)

HILDY. Oh, it's you two! Well, what's the idea of locking the door? Playing post-office? (*Going to phone.*)

SHERIFF (*with elaborate unconcern, as he walks toward the door*). Oh, hello, Hildy.

MAYOR. Come on, Hartman.

HILDY (*into the phone*). Gimme Walter Burns. (*To the others*) Was there a fellow in here asking for me?

SHERIFF. Did you hear we've got Williams surrounded?

HILDY. Yeah. I heard you only let him out so he could vote for you on Tuesday.

MAYOR. Hartman! (*He pulls* SHERIFF *out of the room.*)

HILDY (*into phone*). Hello, Duffy . . . this is Hildy. Listen, where's Walter? Well, where did he go? God damn it, Duffy, I'm waitin' here for the boy to bring over my money . . . the two hundred and sixty dollars he owes me. . . . Yeah . . . in the press room. He told me the boy was on his way. . . . What the hell are you laughin' about? . . . Listen, Duffy, has that maniac started the money over or not? . . . No, I ain't got time to come over to the office. I'll miss the train. . . . Oh, for God's sake! . . . that double-crossing louse! (*He hangs up.*)
(WOODENSHOES *enters.*)

WOODENSHOES. The trouble is, nobody's using the right psychology. Now you take this aspect of the situation: you got a man named Earl Williams who has escaped . . .

HILDY (*seizing at a straw*). Have you got two hundred and sixty dollars on you?

WOODENSHOES. What?

HILDY. Have you got two hundred and sixty dollars?

WOODENSHOES. No, but I got a way of making it, and more. I know how we can get ten thousand dollars, if you'll just listen. (*Pointing his finger at* HILDY *in the manner of a man letting the cat out of the bag*) Serchay la femme!

HILDY. What?

WOODENSHOES (*inexorably—for him*). Who is it that's been defendin' this feller Williams right along? Who is it that was hangin' around his room just before the escape happened?

HILDY. O, for God's sake! I ain't g[illegible] time, Woodenshoes. I got to get t[illegible] hundred and sixty dollars in the next five minutes!

WOODENSHOES. It's gonna take longer than five minutes. I know where Earl Williams is!

HILDY. He's out at Clark and Fullerton, getting his head blown off. But that don't get me any money.

WOODENSHOES. Earl Williams is with that girl, Mollie Malloy! *That's* where he is!

HILDY (*despairing*). Can you imagine—this time tomorrow I'd have been a gentleman. (DIAMOND LOUIE *enters.* HILDY *leaps for him*) Thank God! Have you got the dough?

LOUIE. Huh?

WOODENSHOES. She sent him a lot of roses, didn't she?

HILDY. God damn it—the hell with your roses. Gimme the dough. I'm in a hell of a hurry, Louie.

LOUIE. What are you talkin' about?

WOODENSHOES. I'll betcha I'm right. (*Exits.*)

HILDY. Listen, Louie! Do you mean to say Walter didn't give you the dough he owes me?

LOUIE. Walter's pretty sore. You better come over and see him.

HILDY. But that's all settled! Walter and I are like this! (*He illustrates with two twined fingers*) I just did a swell favor for him—scooped the whole town! We're pals again! I'm telling you.

LOUIE. He just told me be sure and get you, you know what I mean?

HILDY (*frantically*). I tell you that's fixed! By God, Louie, do you think I'd try to put something over on you?

LOUIE. What do you mean fixed? He wants to talk to you. I been looking all over—

HILDY. But I did talk to him! Everything's all right! I swear to you!

LOUIE (*weakening*). Jesus, Hildy, I don't know.

HILDY. Certainly! My God, he *wants* me to go! Now listen, Louie—you've always got a lot of money—will you help me out? This two hundred and sixty bucks—Walter's sending a boy with it, but I can't wait! I gotta catch a train, see? Now—

LOUIE. What two hundred and sixty bucks?

HILDY. The money I spent on the story! He's sending it over, but I want *you* to take *that* and give *me* the money *now!*

LOUIE. Oh! You want two hundred and sixty dollars—*now.*

HILDY. *YES!*

LOUIE. Well, that's a lot of money, you know what I mean?

HILDY. You can get it from Walter I'll give you my I. O. U.

LOUIE. Lis'en, Hildy, I'd like to help you out. But I've been stung on so many I. O. U.'s lately that I made myself a promise.

HILDY. But this ain't an I. O. U. . . . It's money comin' to me from the paper!

LOUIE. What have you got to show for it?

HILDY. Louie, listen! My whole future is dependent on this. My girl's waitin' at the train. I've just got fifteen minutes to get there. If you'll help me out, I swear . . . Honest to God . . .

LOUIE (*interrupting*). Two hundred and sixty dollars . . . that's a big gamble!

HILDY. It's no gamble at all. I'll write out a note to Walter sayin' for him to give you the money he owes me.

LOUIE. Well, I'll tell you what I'll do with you. I'll take a chance.

HILDY (*as he writes out note*). That's the stuff!—You're a white man, Louie, you're a real white man. God —I knew I could depend on you.

LOUIE. I tell you what I'll do. I'll give you a hundred and fifty dollars for the debt. (*Hildy stares at him.*)

HILDY. That's just takin' advantage, Louie.

LOUIE. That's the best I can do.

HILDY. Well, Christ! I lose almost a hundred bucks by that.

LOUIE. All right. (*Puts money back in his pocket*) Have it your own way.

HILDY. Make it two hundred.

LOUIE. One hundred and fifty!

HILDY. All right, give me the dough. (DIAMOND LOUIE *takes the paper that* HILDY *has written out and reads it very carefully, folds it, puts it in his pocket and then proceeds to count out the money, as* HILDY *is looking for his hat and coat.*)

LOUIE. Here you are. (HILDY *grabs the money and begins to count it*) Well, good-bye and good luck. I'll look you up in New York—if there's anything wrong with this. (LOUIE *exits.*)

HILDY (*counting the money*). Ten, twenty, thirty, thirty-five, forty-five — (*Gets confused; starts again*) Ten, twenty, thirty, forty, forty-five, fifty-five— (*In trouble again; he gives up*) The hell with it. Anyway, I get out of this lousy place. They can take their story now and— (HILDY *pockets the money and starts hurriedly to pick up his parcels, including his old felt hat in a paper bag. As he starts for the door he is arrested by a sound at the window. The sound is caused by* EARL WILLIAMS *falling through the window into the room.* MR. WILLIAMS *is a little harmless-looking man with a mustache. He is coatless and is shod with death-house sneakers. He carries a large gun. He is on the verge of collapse and holds on to a chair for support. He talks in an exhausted voice.* HILDY, *at the sight of him, drops his packages and stands riveted.*)

EARL. They're after me with search lights . . .

HILDY. Put—put down that gun!

EARL (*supporting himself*). It ain't loaded. I fired all the bullets already.

HILDY. Holy God Almighty! . . .

EARL (*weakly—handing* HILDY *the gun*). I surrender. . . . I couldn't hang off that roof any longer.

HILDY. Holy God!— Get away from that window. (EARL *obeys.* HILDY *strides to the door and locks it. He comes back and stands staring at* EARL *and scratches his head*) Well, for God's sake . . .

EARL. I'm not afraid to die. I was tellin' the fella that when he handed me the gun.

HILDY. Shut up a second! (*He locks the door.*)

EARL (*babbling on*). Wakin' me up in the middle of the night . . . talking to me about things they don't understand. Callin' me a Bolshevik. I ain't a Bolshevik. I'm an anarchist. (HILDY *is pulling down the blinds and putting out the lights*) It's got nothin' to do with bombs. It's the one philosophy that guarantees every man freedom. (*Weakly*) All those poor people being crushed by the System. And the boys that were killed in the war. And in the slums—all those slaves to a crust of bread—I can hear 'em cryin'—

HILDY. Be quiet! The hell with that. Shut up! . . . will you? (*He is hunting for a hiding place.*)

EARL. Go on . . . take me back and hang me . . . I done my best. . . . (*He crumples and falls to the floor.* HILDY *stands for a second, desperate. His eye falls on the toilet door. He considers, picks up* WILLIAMS *and hurriedly dumps him inside the toilet. He closes the door and springs for the telephone.*)

HILDY (*into phone*). Hello. . . . Gimme Walter Burns, *quick!* (*Second phone rings.* HILDY *hesitates, then answers it, propping first receiver between ear and shoulder*) Hello! . . . Hello! . . . Oh, hello, Peggy. . . . Listen, for God's sake have a heart, will you? Something terrific has happened! (*Into first phone*) Walter? Hildy . . . No, the hell with that. Listen—come right over here. . . . Come over here *right away*. . . . Wait a minute. (*Into second phone*) For God's sake, Peggy, quit bawling me out, will you? I'm in a hell of a jam! (*Back to* WALTER) Walter! Get this—I only want to say it once. . . . I got Earl Williams. . . . Yes! . . . Here in the press room! . . . Honest to God! . . . For God's sake, hurry! I need you. . . . I will. (*Hangs up. Into* PEGGY'S *phone again*) Listen, darling, this is the biggest thing that ever happened. . . . Now, wait! Don't cry. Wait till I tell you. (*Lowers his voice*) I just captured Earl Williams! (*In an intense whisper*) Earl Williams . . . the murderer! I got him. . . . For God's sake, don't tell anybody. . . . Aw, Peggy . . . Peggy . . . I can't. . . . I can't now! . . . Good Lord! Don't you realize . . . *I know*, but Peggy . . . (*She has hung up*) Hello, Peggy . . . Peggy! (HILDY *hangs up the phone dejectedly. During the last few speeches, there has been a knocking on the door.* HILDY *glares apprehensively and holds himself ready for fight. He moves to the door, and as he approaches it, cries*) Who is it? (*There is no answer.* HILDY *opens the door cautiously.* MOLLIE *bounds in like a wildcat. He seizes her and wrestles with her*) Wait a minute! What the hell do *you* want?

MOLLIE (*wildly*). Where they gone? You know where they are.

HILDY. Get outa here, Mollie!

MOLLIE. They got him surrounded. They're gonna shoot him—like a dog.

HILDY. Listen! They're lookin' for you, too! If you're smart, you'll get outa here.

MOLLIE. For God's sake, tell me where they've gone. I ain't afraid of them, the yella murderers . . .

HILDY. I'll tell you where they are. They're out at Clark Street! That's where they are! Clark and Fullerton!

MOLLIE. Where? Where? . . . (*The toilet door opens and* EARL WILLIAMS *appears, dazed and blinking.* MOLLIE *sees him*) Oh! (*A knock on the outer door is heard.*)

HILDY (*with a desperate look at the door*). Oh, for Christ's—! . . . Sh—! (*With a desperate gesture for silence, and tiptoeing towards door*) Who is it?

WOODENSHOES (*outside*). It's me.

HILDY. What do you want, Woodenshoes?

WOODENSHOES (*outside*). I got some important information for you . . . a clue . . .

HILDY. I'll be right with you. I'm making a personal call. . . . (*Turning to the two, tensely*) Get back in there! (*Indicating toilet.*)

MOLLIE. What's this . . . a double cross?

HILDY. Damn it! I'm trying to save him. . . .

WOODENSHOES (*outside*). This is very important.

MOLLIE (*to* EARL). What are *you* doing here?

HILDY (*to* MOLLIE). Keep him *quiet!* It's a cop! (*On his way to the door*) I'll get rid of him . . . (*He opens the door cautiously and steps quickly into the hall, leaving his arm behind him, his hand on the inside knob of the door. Loud and friendly*) Hello, Woodenshoes! What's on your mind? (*During the ensuing scene a hardly audible conversation takes place between* HILDY *and* WOODENSHOES. HILDY'S *shoulder is visible in the door.*)

EARL. Thank you for those roses . . .

MOLLIE. How did you get here? Does anybody know?

EARL. I came down the rainpipe. I didn't mean to shoot him. I don't know what happened.

MOLLIE. But what are you going to do? You can't stay here! They'll get you!

EARL. I don't care any more.

MOLLIE. You've got to hide! You've got to hide somewhere! The rats!

EARL. No. Don't do anything. I'm ready to go. I don't care. It's better to die for a cause than the way most people die—for no reason.

MOLLIE. You won't die. They'll never get you.

EARL. I ain't important. It's humanity that's important, like I told you. Humanity is a wonderful thing, Mollie.

MOLLIE. No, it ain't. They're just dirty murderers. Look what they done to you . . . and to me . . .

EARL. That's because they don't know any better.

MOLLIE. You're too good for 'em . . . that's why.

EARL. You're good, too.

MOLLIE (*with wonder*). Me?

EARL. Yeah, I think you're wonderful. . . . I wrote out a statement today and left it with Mr. Jacobi, so that when I was dead people would understand what I meant. There was a lot about you in it. I said you were the most beautiful character I ever met.

MOLLIE (*blinking and dazed*). Yeah?

HILDY (*entering, indicating toilet*). Get back in there! The fellows are coming down the hall now! (*He locks the door.*)

MOLLIE. They'll find him there!

HILDY. Well, there isn't any place else. (*He looks helplessly around the room; at that moment someone tries the door knob.*)

MOLLIE. There's somebody!

HILDY. Sssh!

ENDICOTT (*outside*). Who locked the door?

HILDY. Coming right away, Mike. (*Whispers to* MOLLIE) He's got to go in there!

ENDICOTT (*outside*). Well, for God's sake, hurry.

MOLLIE. Oh, my God!

HILDY. Wait a minute! I got an idea! (*Springs and opens the desk*) Can you get in this desk?

WILSON (*outside*). What the hell's going on in there? (*Starts to pound on door.*)

EARL. What good'll it do?

HILDY. We'll get you out in ten minutes.

WILSON (*outside*). *Open up* there, will you?

HILDY. All right, all right. God damn it!

EARL. Please, don't talk like that in front of her.

MOLLIE (*to* EARL). Go on! Please! Please!

EARL. They'll find me, anyhow. (*More pounding.*)

HILDY. All right, I'm coming! (*To* EARL) Keep dead quiet. Don't even breathe.

MOLLIE. I'll be right here. I won't leave you.

ENDICOTT (*outside, shouting*). Hey, what the God-damn hell?

HILDY. Keep your shirt on! (*He opens the door*) What are you trying to do! Kick down the building? (ENDICOTT *and* WILSON *enter. Head for phones at back.*)

ENDICOTT. Kind of exclusive, ain't you? (*Sees* MOLLIE) Oh! (*Elaborately*) I beg your pardon.

WILSON. City desk, please! What's the idea of locking the door?

HILDY. I was interviewing her.

ENDICOTT (*at phone*). Gimme the city desk. . . . What was he doing to her?

WILSON. With the blinds down. (MURPHY *enters.*)

MURPHY. Where the hell you been, Hildy? There's the damnedest Hallowe'en going on—the whole police force standing on its ear. (*At phone*) Murphy talking. Gimme the desk.

WILSON (*into phone*). Wilson speaking. No luck yet on Williams. Call you back!
(KRUGER *enters.*)

KRUGER. God, I never was so tired in my life.

HILDY. Any news?

MURPHY (*into phone*). This is Murphy. . . . Well, they surrounded the house, only Williams wasn't there.

KRUGER. Gimme a rewrite man.
(MC CUE *enters.*)

MC CUE (*entering*). Jesus, what a chase!

MURPHY (*into phone*). Wait a minute. They shot somebody, anyhow. Here you are! Ready? Herman Schulte, the Sheriff's brother-in-law. He was leading the squad through the house and was looking under a bed when Deputy John F. Watson came in the room and mistook him for Earl. Shot him right in the pants. Yeah. A bull's eye. Right. (*Hangs up.*)

HILDY (*on edge*). He always had lead in his pants.

MC CUE (*at his phone*). McCue talking. Gimme the desk.

KRUGER (*phoning*). This is Kruger, out with Hartman's deputies. . . . Yeah?. . . . I'm in the drug store at Clark and Fullerton. Well, call me back if you don't believe me. (*Hangs up.*)

MC CUE (*into phone*). That so? I'll check on it. (*Hangs up*) There's something doing at Harrison Street Station. (*Into phone*) Gimme Harrison 2500. Hurry it, will you please?

KRUGER (*to* MOLLIE, *who is in the swivel chair in front of the desk*). What's the idea, Mollie? Can't you flop somewhere else?

MURPHY. Yeah, parking her fanny in here like it was a cathouse. (*Takes a sniff of the air*) Fleur de Floosie, she's got on.

KRUGER (*neighing like a horse*). Makes me passionate!

MURPHY. Go on, Mollie, put it somewhere else. Go out and stink up Clark Street.

MOLLIE (*nervous and twitching*). You lay off me!

MC CUE. Look out—she'll start bawling again. (*Into phone*) I'll hold the wire. Only don't forget me.

HILDY. Let her alone, fellas. She's not doing anything.

MURPHY (*to* HILDY). What the hell are you two so chummy about?

ENDICOTT. Yeah, they were locked in here together when we come along.

WILSON. Wouldn't open the door.

MC CUE. You'll be out of training for your honeymoon—playing pinochle with this baby.

MURPHY. I thought you were going to catch a train.

KRUGER. He was running around here ten minutes ago with his pants on fire about going to New York.

ENDICOTT. Told us he was interviewing her.

MURPHY. What are you trying to do? Scoop us?

HILDY. I'm waiting here for Walter. He's coming over with some dough.

MC CUE (*phoning*). Hello, Sarge. McCue. I hear you got a tip on Williams.

WILSON. Look, she's got the shakes. What the hell you making faces about?

ENDICOTT (*singing childishly*). She's jealous because Hildy's going to be married.

HILDY. Go on— Show 'em you can smile through your tears. Relax.

MOLLIE. You let me alone—all of you. (SCHWARTZ *enters.*)

MC CUE (*into phone*). Yeah! What's the address!

SCHWARTZ. Hello, fellas. What the hell, Hildy? You still here?

ENDICOTT. Yeah, and trying to hang something on us, if you ask me What's the low-down, Hildy?

SCHWARTZ. Who the hell pulled these shades down?

MC CUE (*turning from phone*). Hey! this looks good. An old lady just called up the detective bureau and claims Williams is hiding under her piazza.

ENDICOTT. Tell her to stand up.

MURPHY. Who you got there?

MC CUE. The Captain.

MURPHY. Let me talk to him. (*Taking the phone*) Hello, Turkey. . . . How's your gussie mollie? . . . I hear this guy Williams is hiding in your mustache. . . . Yeah? Well, get your nose out of the way. (*Hangs up. Points to* MOLLIE'S *crossed and highly visible legs*) Oooh! Lookit! Pike's Peak!

MC CUE. Listen, fellows, that sounds like a pretty good tip. What do you say?

HILDY. If you boys want to get out I'll cover this end for you.

ENDICOTT. Aw, the hell with chasing around any more. I spent a dollar forty on taxis already.

KRUGER (*flat on his back*). Don't let's do any more going out.

SCHWARTZ (*who has gone to the window*). If you ask me, I got a hunch Williams ain't anywhere they been looking for him.

WILSON. How do you mean?

SCHWARTZ. Well, I just been talking to Jacobi about that roof he's supposed to have jumped off of. Look! Now there's that skylight he got out of.

ENDICOTT. Where?

MC CUE (*looking out*). Jesus, how could he get from there to the ground?

SCHWARTZ. That's just the point. Jacobi's gone up there with a couple of cops to look over the whole roof.

MC CUE (*leaning out*). I tell you what he could have done, though. Look! He could have jumped over to this roof. That's only about four feet.

ENDICOTT. Yeah, he could have done that, all right.

KRUGER (*wearily*). I'm pretending there ain't no Earl Williams.

SCHWARTZ. And that's why I'm telling you guys that I don't think this guy Williams is anywhere they been looking for him. I got a stinking hunch he's right in this building.

HILDY (*derisive*). Hanging around like a duck in a shootin' gallery, I suppose! You're a lot of bright guys. . . .

MC CUE (*still looking*). It'd be easy, once he got on this roof. . . .

HILDY (*with nervous hilarity*). Hey —Sherlock Holmes, what correspondence school did you graduate from?

SCHWARTZ. What's the matter with that? He could come down the rain-pipe and crawl into any one of these windows on this side. . . .

KRUGER. Well if the story's going to walk right in the window—!

HILDY. The master minds at work! Why don't you guys go home—he'll probably *call* on you. . . .
(BENSINGER *enters and approaches his desk.* MOLLIE, *sitting in his chair, is hidden from him at the moment by one or two of the* REPORTERS.)

BENSINGER. Hello, Hildy. Thought you were going to New York. (HILDY *has sprung into action with* BENSINGER'S *entrance.* BENSINGER *sees* MOLLIE) For God's sake, what's she doing in my chair? (MOLLIE *springs up*) Is that the only place you can sit? That's my property and I don't want anybody using it!

HILDY (*leaning against the closed desk*). Nobody's using it, Roy. Everything's all right.

BENSINGER (*anxiously*). Any of you fellows got some aspirin?

ENDICOTT. No, sweetheart, but I got some nice cyanide.

BENSINGER (*sitting down*). Cut the kidding, fellows. I tell you I'm sick.

SCHWARTZ. How about a good truss? I'll sell it to you cheap.

HILDY. What's the matter, Roy? Off your feed?

BENSINGER. If I haven't got a good case of grippe coming, I miss my guess. (*Reaching for desk cover*) Get out of the way, will you?

HILDY (*not moving*). I hope you didn't get it off me.

BENSINGER. I got it off somebody. Everybody using my phone all the time—it's a wonder I ain't caught anything worse. (*Pushing* HILDY *slightly*) Look out, I got to get my cup.

HILDY (*doubling up as if with a violent cramp*). Wait a minute, will you?

BENSINGER (*frightened*). What's the matter?

HILDY (*faintly*). I don't know, oh—

BENSINGER. Don't you feel all right?

HILDY. No. (*Coughs violently in* BENSINGER'S *face.*)

BENSINGER. Don't do that!

HILDY (*weakly*). Do what?

BENSINGER. Cough on a guy! Jesus!

HILDY. Well, I don't know what's the matter. I suddenly got a pain right— (*Vaguely indicates his throat*) and a kind of rash on my chest. (*Opening his shirt.*)

BENSINGER (*recoiling*). What? You've probably got some disease!

MURPHY. Sure! He's got the pazooza!

HILDY (*advancing on* BENSINGER, *tries to take his hand*). Feel! Ain't that fever?

BENSINGER (*retreating from the desk*). Hey, cut it out! It may be diphtheria!

HILDY. I woke up this morning, and had yellow spots all over my stomach.

BENSINGER. That ain't funny!

KRUGER. For God's sake, Roy, can't you see he's kidding you. (HILDY *following* BENSINGER, *seizes him.*)

BENSINGER. Let go of me! You may have something contagious! If you're sick go to a hospital! (HILDY *coughs in his face*) For the love of God!

MURPHY. It's no worse than a bad cold, Roy.

HILDY (*opening his mouth*). Can you see anything in there? Aaah!

BENSINGER. Listen, fellows! You ain't got any sense, letting him hang around here. We'll all catch it, whatever it is! (*They all laugh*) All right, laugh! But I'm going to get this place fumigated!

MURPHY. The hell you are!

BENSINGER (*furiously*). The hell I ain't. We got to breathe this air. I'm gonna get Doc Springer and clean this whole place up! You God-damn maniacs. (*Exits.* HILDY *leans weakly up against the desk and laughs hysterically.*)

ENDICOTT. What's the idea, Hildy? Now he'll be burning sulphur for a week like last time. . . .

MC CUE. Yeah, you're leavin', but we gotta work here, with all them stink pots. . . . What a sense of humor you got.

SCHWARTZ. Now look here. What about Williams? Let's get the cops and search the building. What do you say?

ENDICOTT. I could use that reward.

MURPHY. What the hell could you do with ten grand? . . .

ENDICOTT. You could have a girl in every room at the Sherman Hotel for that. . . .

MURPHY. You'd never get past the basement.

MC CUE. It would be funny if we found him right here in the building.

SCHWARTZ. What do you say? Should we get the cops?

MURPHY. Call up Lieut. Callahan, Mac. Tell him we got a hot tip.

HILDY. Wait! What do you want to call the cops for? Suppose he *is* in the building. They'll grab all the reward and you guys won't get a smell.

SCHWARTZ. Huh?

WILSON. That's right.

HILDY. Listen! Each of us take a floor and whoever finds him, we split it up. What do you say?

WILSON. That's not a bad idea.

KRUGER. I'll stay here.

HILDY. Two grand apiece! Why we could retire for life! You could pay off all those loan sharks, Jimmie, and have enough left to stay stinko forever!

MC CUE. I don't know, getting my can blown off.

HILDY. What else is it good for? . . . Besides, he can't hurt anybody. . . . What do you say? Do you want to try it?

MRS. GRANT (*enters, in a very righteous mood*). Well!

HILDY (*stricken*). Now—now, listen, mother—

MRS. GRANT. Don't you mother me! If you've got anything to say for yourself you come downstairs and say it to Peggy.

HILDY. Listen, mother, tell Peggy I'll be downstairs in five minutes, will you? Will you go down and tell her that?

MRS. GRANT. No, sir—I don't move out of here without you.

HILDY. Listen, mother, you don't understand. Now I told Peggy—

MRS. GRANT. I know what you told her! A lot of gibberish about a murderer!

HILDY. No—no!

MRS. GRANT. I don't care if you *did* catch him, you come with me this minute!

THE REPORTERS. I knew something stunk around here. Who says he caught him? What's going on. What do you mean caught a murderer? etc. (*In the midst of this babel,* WOODENSHOES *enters; stands listening.*)

HILDY. No, No! I don't know what she's talking about! I didn't tell her any such thing.

MRS. GRANT. Yes, you did!

MOLLIE. He never told her that!

HILDY. I said I was *trying* to catch one, that's all! You got it balled up, mother!

MURPHY (*to* MOLLIE). What do *you* know about it? How do you know he didn't?

MOLLIE. Let go of my arm!

ENDICOTT. Hildy and that tart were in here together!

WOODENSHOES. Yah! Yah! She's the one that knows! Ask *her!*

MURPHY (*wheeling on him*). What do you mean she knows?

WOODENSHOES. Serchay la femme! (*To* MOLLIE) Where's Earl Williams?

MOLLIE. How the hell should I know?

WOODENSHOES. Where have you got him hid?

MURPHY (*viciously*). Who you holding out on, Hildy? Come clean, or God damn it, we'll knock it out of you! (*The* REPORTERS *surround* HILDY *menacingly.*)

MC CUE. Yeah. What the hell! Sock him, Jimmie!

ENDICOTT. You dirty double-crosser.

MOLLIE (*wildly*). Wait! You God damn stool pigeons! He don't know where Earl Williams is. I'm the one that knows.

ENDICOTT. What do you mean you know? (*The* REPORTERS *turn on* MOLLIE.)

WOODENSHOES. Where is he?

MOLLIE. Go find out, you lousy heels You don't think I'm gonna tell!

WOODENSHOES. You'll tell all right! We'll make you . . .

MOLLIE (*slowly backing toward the door*). Yeah? . . . Yeah . . . the hell I will.

HILDY (*who has remained riveted to the desk*). Let her alone . . . she's goofy! (MOLLIE *lunges suddenly for the door.*)

THE REPORTERS. Look out! . . . Close that door . . . For Chris' sake! Don't let her get away. (*She is headed off at the door.*)

MC CUE. You ain't gettin' out o' here, Mollie.

ENDICOTT. Now where is he? In the building?

MC CUE. Where you hidin' him?

MOLLIE. I ain't gonna squeal! I ain't gonna squeal!

MURPHY (*approaching her slowly*). Come on, you lousy tart! Before we kick your teeth out!

ENDICOTT. D'ye want us to call the cops and give you the boots?

MURPHY. Go on, Woodenshoes. Slap it out of her!

WOODENSHOES (*reaching for her*). Come on now. Where is he before I hurt you?

MOLLIE (*tearing away from him, wild and blubbering*). Take your hands off me, you God-damn kidney foot! (*She snatches at a chair and swings it at the slowly advancing circle of men*) Let me alone or I'll knock your God-damn heads off. . . .

ENDICOTT. Put down that chair!

SCHWARTZ. Get around—get on the side of her.

MOLLIE (*backing away, swinging her chair*). No you don't! You bastards! Keep away from me!

KRUGER. Grab her.

MOLLIE (*with a last wild look at the circling foe*). You'll never get it out of me. . . . (*She hurls the chair at their heads and screams*) I'll never tell! Never! (*She leaps for the open window and disappears. Her scream of terror and exultation is heard as she drops through the darkness to the ground. The* REPORTERS *stand riveted for an instant, powerless before the tragedy. Then they rush forward. An assortment of awed and astonished oaths rise from them. They lean out of the window.* WOODENSHOES *the Theorist stands sick at heart. His body is doubled up with pain for a moment. Through the babble of cries his voice comes thickly.*)

WOODENSHOES. Oh! I never thought she'd do that! That's terrible. . . .

MRS. GRANT (*coming out of a trance*). Take me out of here! Take me out of here! Oh, my God! (*She collapses in a chair.*)

THE REPORTERS (*at the window*). She ain't killed. . . . No. . . . She's moving. . . . Get the cops, Woodenshoes. . . . Come on fellas. . . .

HILDY. Holy God—the poor kid . . . the poor kid. (*Voices come from the jail yard—"Hey Carl. . . . Get a doctor! What the hell! Who is it? What happened?" etc. The* REPORTERS *rush out to get to* MOLLIE. HILDY *stands dazed, looking out of the window.* MRS. GRANT *moans through her hands. As the vibrations subside a newcomer is standing in the door. This is* MR. WALTER BURNS, *the Managing Editor. Beneath a dapper and very citizen-like exterior lurks a hobgoblin, perhaps the Devil himself. But if* MR. BURNS *is the Devil he is a very naif one. He is a Devil with neither point nor purpose to him—an undignified Devil hatched for a bourgeois Hallowe'en. In less hyperbolic language* MR. BURNS *is that product of thoughtless, pointless, nerve-drumming unmorality that is the Boss Journalist—the licensed eavesdropper, trouble maker, bombinator and Town Snitch, misnamed The Press. At this moment* MR. BURNS, *in the discharge of his high calling, stands in the door, nerveless and meditative as a child, his mind open to such troubles as he can find or create.*)

HILDY (*seeing him*). Walter! My God—did you see that?

WALTER (*quietly*). Yes. Where is he?

HILDY. She jumped out of the window.

WALTER. I know. . . . Where is he, I said?

HILDY (*looking out of the window*). She's moving! Thank God she ain't killed herself!

WALTER. Come to, Hildy! Where have you got Williams?

HILDY (*still absorbed in the* MOLLIE *matter*). Huh? He's—he's in the desk. (*As* WALTER *goes to desk*) Thank God she ain't dead. (WALTER *opens desk a crack.*)

EARL (*muffled*). Let me out, I can't stand it!

WALTER. Keep quiet! You're sitting pretty.

MRS. GRANT (*staring at the Editor*). What's the matter?

WALTER (*he wheels*). Who the hell is that?

HILDY. It's my girl's mother.

MRS. GRANT. What are you doing? Oh, my God!

WALTER. Shut up!

MRS. GRANT. I won't shut up! That girl killed herself. Oh! You're doing something wrong. What's in there? (DIAMOND LOUIE *appears in the doorway.*)

HILDY. Now, mother, please!

WALTER. Take her out of here, will you?

MRS. GRANT. What did you say?

HILDY. Now look here, Walter—

WALTER. Louie, take this lady over to Polack Mike's, and lock her up. See that she don't talk to anyone on the way!

MRS. GRANT. What's that? What's that?

HILDY (*startled*). Aw, now, Walter, you can't do that!

LOUIE (*calls*). Hey, Tony!

MRS. GRANT. Don't you touch me!

WALTER. Tell 'em it's a case of delirium tremens.

LOUIE. Tony, give me a hand with this lady.

HILDY (*helplessly*). Listen, Walter, this'll get me in a hell of a jam. . . . (*To* MRS. GRANT *who, a hand over her mouth, is being dragged off, her heels trailing*) Now don't worry, mother, this is only temporary. . . . Honest to God, Walter . . .

MRS. GRANT (*vaguely heard*). Peggy, Peggy! Oh, my God! (*Exit* TONY, LOUIE *and* MRS. GRANT. HILDY *starts out.*)

WALTER (*grabs his arm*). Where the hell do you think you're going?

HILDY. Let go of me! I gotta get my girl! She's downstairs in a cab all alone.

WALTER. Your girl! Good God, what are you? Some puking college boy! Why, in time of war you could be shot for what you're doing—for less than you're doing!

HILDY. To hell with you—there's your story—locked up in that desk! Smear it all over the front page—Earl Williams caught by the Examiner—and take all the credit. . . . I covered your story and I covered it God damn right. . . . Now I'm gettin' out. . . .

WALTER. You drooling saphead . . . What do you mean—a story? You've got the whole city by the seat of the pants!

HILDY. I know all about that, but . . .

WALTER. You know hell—You got the brains of a pancake. . . . Listen, Hildy, if I didn't have your interests at heart would I be wastin' time now arguin' with you! You've done somethin' big—you've stepped into a new class . . .

HILDY (*D'Artagnan never gave Richelieu an ear more startled or more innocent*). Huh?

WALTER. Listen, we'll make such monkeys out of these ward heelers that *nobody* will vote for them—not even their *wives*.

HILDY. Expose 'em, huh . . .

WALTER. Expose 'em! Crucify 'em! We're gonna keep Williams under cover till morning so's the Examiner can break the story exclusive. . . . Then we'll let the Senator in on the capture—share the glory with him.

HILDY. I see—I see! (*Blinking and warming up.*)

WALTER. You've kicked over the whole City Hall like an applecart. You've got the Mayor and Hartman back against a wall. You've put one administration out and another in. . . . This ain't a newspaper story—it's a career. And you standin' there bellyachin' about some girl. . . .

HILDY. Jesus, I— I wasn't figuring it that way, I guess. We'll be the white-haired boys, won't we?

WALTER. Why, they'll be naming streets after you. Johnson Street! You and I and the Senator are going to *run* this town. . . . Do you understand that?

HILDY. Yeah. . . . Yeah! But—wait a minute—we can't leave Williams here. . . . One of those reporters'll . . .

WALTER. We're going to take him over to my private office right away. . . . Where's the Examiner phone?

HILDY. That one. The red one. How the hell you gonna do it? They'll see him!

WALTER. Not if he's inside the desk. We'll carry the desk over. (*Into phone*) Hello! Examiner. Give me Duffy. . . . I'd have had him there now if you hadn't give me such an argument.

HILDY. You can't take that out. It's crawling with cops outside.

WALTER. We'll lower it out of the window with pulleys. Quit stallin'. (*To* HILDY) Hildy! Get that machine and start pounding out a lead, will you. . . . Come on—snap into it. . . .

HILDY. How much you want on it? . . .

WALTER. All the words you got. . . .

HILDY. Where the hell is there some paper?

WALTER (*into phone*). Hello. . . Hello!

HILDY (*moving for* BENSINGER'S *desk*). Can I call the Mayor an animal at bay?

WALTER. Call him a nigger if you want to! Come on! Come on!

HILDY. How about that time he had his house painted by the fire department.

WALTER. Give him the works. . . . (*Into phone*) Hello, Duffy. Get set! We got the biggest story in the world. Earl Williams caught by the Examiner . . . exclusive. . . . (HILDY *has opened the drawers of* BENSINGER'S *desk and in a frantic search for paper is tossing play manuscripts, syringes, patent medicines and old socks in the air.*)

WALTER (*continuing into phone*). Duffy! Send down word to Butch McGuirk I want ten huskies from the circulation department to lam right over here—press room criminal courts building. That's what I said —Butch McGuirk. (*To* HILDY) He'll get that desk out—nothin' ever stopped those boys yet. (HILDY *has unearthed a full package of* BENSINGER'S *personal stationery. He now picks up the typewriter*) What if they start shootin'?

WALTER. Fine! (*Into phone*) Now listen, Duffy. I want you to tear out the whole front page. . . . That's what I said—the whole front page . . . out . . . (*Into phone*). Johnson's writing the lead. . . .
(PEGGY *enters—a desperate and strident antagonist.*)

PEGGY. Hildy!

WALTER. What the hell do you want?

PEGGY. Hildy!

HILDY (*holding the typewriter in his arms. Dazed*). What?

WALTER. Listen, Miss, you can't come in here! (*Into phone*) To hell with the Chinese earthquake! . . . What's that?

HILDY. Listen, darling—

PEGGY. Where's mother?

WALTER (*into phone*). I don't care if there's a *million* dead.

HILDY. Peggy, I got to ask you to do something! A big favor!

PEGGY. You're not coming!

WALTER (*into phone*). What? I don't hear you.

HILDY. Now don't get sore and fly off the handle, darling. What happened was—

PEGGY. You're *not! Are* you? Tell me, Hildy! Tell me the truth!

WALTER (*into phone*). Take all those Miss America pictures off Page 6. Wait a minute, Duffy. (*Turns*) Now look here, little girl—

PEGGY (*wheels on* WALTER). You're doing this to him! He was going and you stopped him!

HILDY. Something terrific's happened, Peggy! Wait till I tell you! I couldn't—

WALTER. You'll tell her nothing! She's a woman, you damn fool!

PEGGY. Well, I'm not going to let you do it! You're coming right now! With me!

WALTER. Holy God!

HILDY. But it's the biggest chance of my life. Now listen, darling—

WALTER (*frenzied*). Shut up, will you?

PEGGY. You don't *want* to marry me! That's all!

HILDY (*putting down the typewriter*). That ain't true! Just because you won't listen you're saying I don't love you when you know I'd cut off my hands for you! I'd do anything in the world for you! Anything!

WALTER (*into phone*). Hello, Duffy! What? . . . What's that? . . . To hell with the League of Nations! Spike it!

PEGGY. You never intended to be decent and live like a human being! You were lying all the time!

HILDY. Peggy, don't keep saying that!

WALTER (*into phone*). What's that? What?

PEGGY. Lying! That's what you were! Just lying!

HILDY (*his tortured male spirit takes refuge in hysteria*). All right! If that's what you think!

WALTER (*shouting at the lovers*). H. Sebastian God! I'm trying to concentrate!

PEGGY. I see what you are now! You're just a bum! Like him— (*Indicates* WALTER) and all the rest!

HILDY. Sure! That's what I am!

WALTER (*into phone*). No! Leave the rooster story alone—that's human interest!

PEGGY. You're just a heartless selfish animal without any feelings! (*To* WALTER) And you're worse! It's all your fault and if you think I'm going to put up with it—

WALTER. Shut up, will you? . . . (*Into phone*) Duffy, let me talk to Butch—

HILDY. Shut up, will you? Yeah! That's what I am! A bum! Without any feelings! And that's all I want to be!

WALTER (*into phone*). Get a hold o' Butch as fast as you can.

PEGGY. You never did love me or you couldn't talk to me like that! (*The desk top opens slowly and* EARL WILLIAMS *sticks his head out.*)

WALTER (*screaming across the room*). Get back in there—you God-damn turtle . . . (*The desk top falls, the fugitive disappears within and* PEGGY, *her heartbreak audible in her sobs, moves blindly toward the door.*)

HILDY (*sitting before his typewriter calls after her, his voice tormented but his egoism intact*). If you want me you'll have to take me as I am instead of trying to turn me into some lah de dah with a cane! I'm no stuffed shirt writing peanut ads. . . . God damn it—I'm a newspaper man. . . . (PEGGY *exits, her sobs filling the room and corridor.*)

WALTER. Shut up! (*Into phone as the curtain is falling*) Hello, Duffy!

The edition gone in yet? . . . Well don't. . . . Never mind the mail trains. . . . You ain't working for the advertising department. . . . The hell with Marshall Field's! ! Stick on this wire!

HILDY (*has started typing. The click of the keys stops suddenly and he rips the piece of copy paper from the machine. He is not quite himself—he has made an error in his lead*). . . . God damn it——

CURTAIN

ACT THREE

The same scene, five minutes later. HILDY *is typing furiously.* WALTER *is pacing up and down. He finally picks up the receiver, which has been standing on the table. Into phone, with moderate excitement.*

WALTER. Duffy. . . . Duffy! (*To* HILDY) God damn it! I told him to stay on that phone. If I had a few people who did what they were told I could get something accomplished. . . . I bet he never told 'em to take taxis. . . . Butch and the gang are probably *walking* over here. . . . (*Looking out of the window*) Oh, for Chris' sake . . . Now the *moon's* out! (HILDY *types on.* WALTER *skitters to the desk and taps three times.* EARL *taps back three times from within.*) Fine! Three taps is me! Don't forget! . . . You're sitting pretty now. Got enough air? (*He raises the roll top an inch or two and fans air in with his hand*) Is that better? (*Closing the desk and going to phone*) Lam into 'em, Hildy! Below the belt! Every punch! (*Into phone, with great sarcasm*) Hello! . . . Duffy! Where the hell you been? Well, the hell with your diabetes! You stick on this phone! Listen, did you impress it on Butch to take a taxi—that every minute counts? Who's he bringing with him? What do you mean, you don't know? But you told Butch it was life and death, huh? All right, stick on the wire! (*Putting down receiver*) Duffy's getting old. . . . Well, Butch is on the way, Hildy. All we got to do is hold out for fifteen minutes. . . .

HILDY (*over his typing*). The boys'll be back. They'll be coming in to phone.

WALTER. I'll handle them. It's that three-toed Sheriff I'm worrying about. If he starts sticking his snoot into this . . . (*Cudgeling his brain*) I wonder if we could arrest him for anything? (HILDY *has never ceased his typing*) Did you ever get the dope on that stenographer he seduced?

HILDY (*over his shoulder*). That was the coroner.

WALTER. Haven't we got *any*thing on him—besides graft?

HILDY (*thoughtfully*). He's got an idiot kid in the asylum.

WALTER (*depressed*). I don't see how we can use that against him. (*Brightening*) Wait a minute! Idiot kid. Idiot kid. . . . (*He meditates, then sighs*) No, that's impractical . . . (*Approaching* HILDY) What's your lead?

HILDY (*with authorly pride*). "While hundreds of Sheriff Hartman's paid gunmen stalked through Chicago shooting innocent bystanders, spreading their reign of terror, Earl Williams was lurking less than twenty yards from the Sheriff's office where . . .

WALTER. That's *lousy!* Aren't you going to mention the Examiner? Don't we take *any* credit?

HILDY. I'm putting that in the second paragraph. . . .

WALTER. Who the hell's going to read the second paragraph? Ten years I've been telling you how to write a newspaper story—My God, have I got to do everything? Get the story? Write the story? . . .

HILDY. Listen, you bastard! I can blow better newspaper stories out of my nose than you can write!

WALTER (*cackling*). "While hundreds of paid gunmen are out taking a walk . . ." God, that stinks! You ought to go back to chasing pictures!

HILDY. Yeah?

WALTER. You were *good* at that!

HILDY. You ungrateful bastard! Who wrote the Fitzgerald confession? Who wrote Ruth Randall's diary? How about the Dayton flood? Even the telegraph operator was crying!

WALTER. All right, make me cry now! (*Into phone*) Duffy! Listen, Duffy. What's the name of that religious editor of ours? The fellow with the dirty collar? Sipper what? Well, tell the Reverend Sipperly I want to see him right away! . . . (*To* HILDY) Do you know what I'm gonna do?

HILDY. Shut up, or I'll throw this typewriter at your head!

WALTER (*happily*). I'm going to get the Reverend Sipperly to make up a prayer for the City of Chicago—right across the top of the paper! . . . "Our Father Who art in Heaven—There were four hundred and twenty-one murders in Chicago last year!" All in religious lingo, see? Eight columns Old English Boldface! The God-damnedest prayer you ever heard. . . . (*Awed at his own resourcefulness*) Christ, what an idea!

HILDY. You better pray that this desk will float out of the window over to the paper.

WALTER. Wait a minute, Hildy. . . . (*The Pentecostal fire upon him*) Wait, wait! . . . I got an inspiration! Now take this down, just as I say it! (*He yanks a page from the typewriter.*)

HILDY (*leaping*). Some day you're going to do that, Walter, and I'm gonna belt you in the jaw . . . ! You God-damn Know-it-all!

WALTER (*chanting*). Here's your lead: "The Chicago Examiner again rode to the rescue of the city last night in the darkest hour of her history! (*Lowering his voice*) Earl Williams—Earl Williams, the Bolshevik Tiger, who leaped snarling from the gallows upon the flanks of the city, was captured . . .

HILDY. I got you! I got you! . . .

WALTER. Go on from *there!* (HILDY *is hurriedly putting another sheet into the machine as the door knob is rattled. A pause.*)

HILDY. What do you want to do?

BENSINGER'S VOICE (*outside*). What's the idea of locking that door?

HILDY. That's Bensinger. That's his desk.

WALTER. What's his name again? (*The door knob is rattled violently.*)

HILDY. Bensinger. Reporter for the Tribune. . . . Covers the building.

BENSINGER'S VOICE. Open this door, will you? Who's in there?

WALTER. I'll handle him! The Tribune, eh? Watch me. (*He opens the door. Bensinger appears.*)

BENSINGER (*entering*). Ain't you got any more sense than to . . . (*Sees* WALTER. *Is overcome at this visitation*) Oh, hello, Mr. Burns. . . . Why, quite an honor, having you come over here.

WALTER (*casually*). Hello, Bensinger.

BENSINGER. Excuse me. I just want to— (*Starts for the desk.*)

WALTER (*blocking his path*). Quite a coincidence, my running into you tonight. . . . Isn't it, Hildy?

HILDY. Yeah.

BENSINGER. How do you mean?

WALTER. I was having a little chat about you just this afternoon—with Mr. Duffy.

BENSINGER. Is that so? (*Essaying a pleasantry*) Nothing detrimental, I hope.

WALTER. I should say not! That was one swell story you had in the paper this morning.

BENSINGER (*deeply moved*). Well, I'm glad you think so, Mr. Burns. Did you care for the poem?

WALTER. The poem? . . . The poem was great! I got a big kick out of that.

BENSINGER (*blinking at these sweet words*). Did you like the ending? (*He recites*)

"... And all is well, outside his cell
But in his heart he hears
The hangman calling and the gallows
falling
And his white-haired mother's
tears . . ."

WALTER (*overcome*). Heartbreaking! Isn't it, Hildy? Bensinger, how would you like to work for me?

BENSINGER. What!

WALTER. I mean it. We need somebody like you. All we got now is a lot of lowbrows and legmen. Like Johnson, here. (*Pushing* BENSINGER *farther from the desk*) I tell you what you do. Go over and talk to Duffy now. I just had him on the phone. You'll catch him if you hurry.

BENSINGER. You mean seriously, Mr. Burns?

WALTER. I'll show you how serious I am. . . . (*Clinging to* BENSINGER'S *pants, he takes him to the phone. Into phone*) Duffy! I'm sending Bensinger over to see you. (*To* BENSINGER) Marvin, isn't it?

BENSINGER. No. Roy. Roy V.

WALTER. Funny I should forget that! (*Into phone*) Roy Bensinger, the poet. Put him right on the staff!

BENSINGER. Right away, you mean?

WALTER (*into phone*). Never mind what doing . . . He'll tell you. No, I'll talk salary with him right here. (*To* ROY) How much you getting on the Tribune, Roy?

BENSINGER. Seventy-five.

WALTER. Bensinger, I'll give you a hundred and a by-line. (*Into phone*) He's to get a hundred and a by-line, Duffy. Tell the cashier. Let him have everything he wants. He can use the big desk in the corner. (*To* BENSINGER, *dropping receiver*) Now hustle right over to the office and tell Duffy I've—I've assigned you to write the human interest side of the man hunt. I want it from the point of view of the escaped man. (*Acting it out*) He hides, cowering . . . afraid of every light, of every sound . . . hears footsteps . . . his heart going like that . . . And all the time they're closing in . . . get the sense of an animal at bay!

BENSINGER. Sort of a Jack London style?

WALTER. Exactly. Now you ain't got a minute to lose. Hop right over to the office.

BENSINGER. Well, I don't know about quitting the Tribune that way, Mr. Burns. It's not quite ethical. . . .

WALTER. What did they ever do for you? . . . They've never considered your interests—that is, from what I hear. . . .

BENSINGER. Well, between you and me they have given me a pretty rotten deal. The way they handle my copy's a shame—just butcher it.

WALTER. Your copy will be sacred on the Examiner. I guarantee that personally. . . . (*He edges* BENSINGER *toward the door.*)

BENSINGER (*the artist*). You can't lop off the end of a story and get the same effect. The whole *feeling* goes . . .

WALTER. Of course. Now I want a real Bensinger story tomorrow morning, with a crackerjack poem on the side. (*He has him nearly to the door.*)

BENSINGER (*indicating his desk*). I got my rhyming dictionary in . . .

WALTER. It don't have to rhyme! Now duck!

BENSINGER. Gee, I'm terribly grateful, Mr. Burns. (*Pausing in the doorway*) Do you suppose there might be an opening some time as foreign correspondent? I parlay a little French, you know.

WALTER (*shaking hands with him and pushing him out*). That'll all depend on your self. I'll keep you in mind.

BENSINGER (*on his way to Garcia*). Well, au revoir, mon capitaine!

WALTER (*never at a loss in any language*). Bon jour! (WALTER *closes the door and skips to the phone. Into phone*) Duffy! Listen. Now get this! A God damn Tribune sneak is coming over to get a job. Yeah, Bensinger, the fellow I told you about. Now listen, handle him with kid gloves and tell him to get busy writing poetry. No . . . no! We don't want him. But wait till he gets through. Then tell him his poetry stinks and kick him down the stairs. . . . (*Lays receiver down. To* HILDY) His white-haired mother's tears! (*Picks up* HILDY'S *copy*) Come on, Hildy, tear into it! Don't sit there like a frozen robin!

HILDY (*coming out of the ether*). You've just bitched up my whole life! That's what you've done!

WALTER (*oblivious to this mood*). Listen, Hildy. We ought to have our plans all set when Butch gets here. All we can look for out of that guy is pure, peasant strength . . . A mental blank. (*Sentimentally*) But he'd go through hell for me!

HILDY. What a fine horse's bustle I turned out to be!

WALTER (*as before*). The window's *out*. . . . We'll have him pick it up and walk right out of the building with it. With ten guys it'll be a cinch.

HILDY. She was the most wonderful girl I'll ever know . . . (WALTER *looks at him in horror and disgust*) She had spirit, brains, looks . . . everything!

WALTER. Who the hell you talking about?

HILDY. My girl! God damn it! Who do you think?

WALTER. What are you going to do? Start mumbling about your girl *now*? You got a story to write!

HILDY. I practically told her to go to hell—like she was some waitress!

WALTER. You acted like a man for the first time in your life! Now, don't start crawling now!

HILDY. I'll never love anybody else again! They don't come like that twice in a man's life.

WALTER. You'll sleep it off. Now listen, Hildy. I got enough on my mind!

HILDY. When she was sick in the hospital and you sent me on that wild goose chase all over Kentucky for three weeks she never even complained. . . .

WALTER. Ha, ha. Sick in the hospital!

HILDY. Damn it, she was! She nearly died!

WALTER. I see. She didn't complain, but she just nearly died! That's all!

HILDY (*almost to himself*). I would have been on the train now . . . I would have been . . .

WALTER (confidentially). Listen, Hildy. *I* was in love once—with my third wife. I treated her white—let her have a maid and everything! I was sweet to her!

HILDY. Who cares about your God damned wife?

WALTER. I trusted her. Then I let her meet a certain party on the Tribune and what happened? One night I came home unexpectedly—I let myself in through the bathroom window—and there they were! In bed.

HILDY. I don't want to hear about your troubles. I got enough. . . .

WALTER (*interrupting ecstatically*). The very next morning, what do I find in the Tribune, all over the front page? *My traction story*, I'd been saving for two months!

HILDY. You know a lot about women! You and your God-damn stable of tarts! You never met a decent woman! You wouldn't know what to *do* with a pure girl! . . .

WALTER (*owlishly*). Oh, yes I would!

HILDY. You take that back!

WALTER (*deciding to reason with his young friend*). What do you think women are? Flowers? Take that dame that shot the dentist! And Mrs. Vermilya! Husband comes home all worn out, hungry, takes a spoonful of soup and falls dead! Arsenic! And Mrs. Petras! Burning her husband up in a furnace! When you've been in this business as long as I have you'll know what women are! Murderers! Borgias!

HILDY. My God, I'm a sap! Falling for your line of crap . . . ! Naming streets after me!

WALTER. Now, listen, Hildy. You've had a good rest. Get back on the story. That's all you got to do. . . . (*Hands him a pocket flask*) Here. You're just nervous. . . .

HILDY. *I'll* take that! . . . (*Goes to the water cooler. Pouring*) I'll get stewed tonight, and I'm gonna stay stewed for the rest of my life! Yeah, I'll be a newspaperman! Right in your class! (*The door knob is tried.*)

WALTER (*whispering*). Shut up!

HILDY. On my pratt in a monkey cage!

WALTER. Shut up, you *fathead!* (HILDY *drinks. The knocking continues.* WALTER *approaches the door*) If that's Bensinger again, we'll crown him and throw him in the can for keeps! (*To the door*) Who is it?

DIAMOND LOUIE (*outside*). Hello, Boss. . . .

WALTER. It's Louie. . . . (*He opens* the door. DIAMOND LOUIE *appears, bearing some evidence of a mishap His hat is crushed, face bruised, clothes torn.* WALTER *sees this with alarm*) My God, what's the matter!

HILDY (*frantically*). Where's the old lady?

WALTER. What did you do with her?

HILDY. What the hell happened?

WALTER. You been in a fight?

LOUIE (*still out of breath*). Down Wentworth Avenue. We were going sixty-five miles an hour, you know what I mean?

WALTER. Take the mush out of your mouth!

HILDY. Where's the old lady!

LOUIE. I'm *telling* you! We run smack into a police patrol. You know what I mean? We broke it in half!

HILDY. My God! Was she hurt?

WALTER. Where is she? Tell me! . . .

HILDY. For God's sake, Louie! . . .

LOUIE. I'm *telling* you. Can you imagine bumping into a load of cops? They come rolling out like oranges!

HILDY (*seizing him*). What did you *do* with her, God damn you!

WALTER. What became of her, I'm asking you!

LOUIE. Search me! When I come to I was running down Thirty-fifth Street! Get me?

HILDY. You were with her! You were in the *cab,* weren't you!

LOUIE (*exposing his bruised scalp*). *Was* I! Tony got knocked cold!

WALTER. You God-damn butter-fingers! I give you an old lady to take somewhere and you hand her over to the cops!

LOUIE. What do you mean, I hand her? The patrol wagon was on the wrong side of the street!

WALTER (*bitterly*). Oh, my God! She's probably squawking her head off in some police station! Now everything is *fine.*

LOUIE (*holding his head*). I don't think she's talking much, you know what I mean! (*He winks reassuringly.*)

HILDY. My God! Was she killed?

WALTER (*hopefully*). Was she? Did you notice?

LOUIE. Say, with that alky rap and the bank job and the big blow on my hip! I should stick around asking questions from a lot of cops!

HILDY (*overcome*). Oh, my God! Dead! That finishes me! . . .

WALTER. Listen, Hildy. That's Fate. What will be, will be!

HILDY (*wildly*). What am I going to say to Peggy, for God's sake! What'll I *tell* her? . . .

WALTER. You're never going to see her again. Snap out of it! Would you rather have the old dame dragging the whole police force in here? . . .

HILDY. I killed her! I did it! Oh, my God, what can I do *now*? How can I ever face her? . . .

WALTER (*becoming the entire Foreign Legion*). Listen, Hildy, if it was my own mother, I'd carry on, you know I would!

HILDY. You God-damn murdering bastard!

WALTER (*crescendo*). No matter how I felt! If my heart was breaking! I'd carry on! For the paper!

HILDY (*to* LOUIE). Where was it? I'll go out!

WALTER. You stay here! I'll find out everything! (*Into phone*) Duffy! . . . Just a minute. . . . (*To* LOUIE) Where was it?

LOUIE. Wentworth and Thirty-fourth . . . near the corner . . .

WALTER (*into phone*). Call up the Thirty-fifth Street station and ask Nick Gallagher if he's got a report on any old lady that was in a smash-up at Thirty-fourth and Wentworth. . . . (*To* HILDY) What's her name?

HILDY (*brokenly*). Mrs. Amelia Grant.

WALTER (*into phone*). Millie Grant. About . . . fifty-seven? (*With an enquiring look at* HILDY) Refined. White hair. Blue eyes. Black cotton stockings. She was wearing rubbers. (*To* HILDY, *pleased*) How's that for noticing?

HILDY (*grabbing a phone*). Gimme an outside wire.

WALTER. Never *mind*. We'll get the dope right here . . . in two minutes! (*Another phone rings.*)

HILDY (*into phone*). Gimme Wentworth, Four, five, five, seven! . . .

WALTER (*answering the other telephone in guarded tones*). Hello. Hello. Who? (*Wildly*) Hello, Butch! Where are you ! !

HILDY (*into phone*). Passavant Hospital? Gimme the Receiving Room, will you?

WALTER. Hotel? You mean *you're* in a hotel? What are you doing there! Ain't you even *started*? !

HILDY (*into phone*). Hello, Eddie, Hildy Johnson. Was there an old lady brought in from an auto smash-up? . . .

WALTER (*panic*). Oh, for . . . (*Screaming*) H. Sebastian God! Butch! Listen, it's a matter of life and death, Butch! *Listen!*

HILDY (*into phone*). Nobody? (*Jiggles hook*) Archer three one two four. . . .

WALTER (*into phone*). I can't hear you! You got who? Speak up! A what? ! ! ! . . . Holy God, you can't stop for a dame *now!*

HILDY (*into phone*). Is this the German Deaconess Hospital?

WALTER (*howling*). I don't care if you've been trying to make her for six *years!* Now, listen, Butch! Our whole lives are at stake! Are you going to let some blonde pushover ruin everything? . . . What do you mean —an hour? It'll be too late in an hour!

HILDY (*into phone*). Hello, Max. Hildy Johnson. Was there an old lady . . .

WALTER. *Butch! !* I'd put my arm in the fire for you up to here! (*Indicates up to where*) I'd go through hell for you! Now you ain't gonna double cross me. . . . She does? All right— put her on the wire. *I'll* talk to her. . . . *Hello!* . . . Oh, hello, Madam! Now listen here, you God-damn bum . . . You can't keep Butch away from his duty! . . . What! *What! !* . . . What kind of language is that! Hello, hello . . . (*Turning to* LOUIE *hanging up the telephone*) That tub of guts! Lousy whore-headed flannel mouth! (*Into phone*) Duffy! (*To* HILDY) I'll *kill* 'em—both of them! I'll butter this town with their brains! (*Into phone*) Duffy! (*To the world*) Mousing around with some big blonde Annie! *That's* co-operation! (*Screaming into Examiner phone*) Duffy! . . .

HILDY (*to* WALTER) Shut up, will you? (*Into phone*) You sure! Nobody?

WALTER (*a howl*). Duffy! (*Throwing the receiver to the desk*) I ought to know better than hire anybody with a disease! (*To* LOUIE, *panting*) Louie! It's up to you!

LOUIE (*loyally*). Anything you want, boss.

WALTER. Beat it out and get me hold of some guys, will you?

LOUIE. Who do you want?

WALTER (*trembling*). I want anybody with hair on their chests! Get them off the streets—anywhere! Offer them anything—only get them! (*Confidentially*) Listen, Louie. We got to get this desk out of here!

LOUIE (*surveys the desk calmly*). Is it important?

WALTER. Is it important!!! Louie, you're the best friend I got. I'd go through hell for you and I know you won't fail me. Get me enough people to move it! Do you understand that? Now, beat it! And remember, I'm relying on you!

LOUIE (*departing*). You know me. The shirt off my back.

WALTER (*yelling after him*). Don't bump into anything! (*He locks the door.*)

HILDY (*emotionally, into phone*). Calumet two one hundred . . .

WALTER. That lousy immigrant'll flop on me! I know it. (*Bitterly*) Can you imagine Butch laying up with some whisker at the Revere House! At a time like this! Listen, Hildy . . . (*Confidentially*) If Louie don't come back in five minutes, we'll get it out alone! There's millions of ways! We can start a fire and get the firemen to carry it out in the confusion! . . .

HILDY. Do anything you damn please! . . . (*Into phone*) Ring that number, will you?

WALTER (*very excited*). We don't even have to do that. We'll get the Chicago Historical Society to claim it as an antique. We can move it out in a decent normal manner ourselves! Just the two of us!

HILDY. I don't give a God damn what you do!

WALTER. Come on, Hildy! Come here and see if we can move it!

HILDY (*into phone*). Hello! Hello! Is this the Lying-in Hospital? Did you have an auto accident in the last hour?

WALTER. Will you come here?

HILDY (*into phone*). Oh, I see. I beg your pardon.

WALTER. Right when I'm surrounded, with my back against the wall, you ain't going to lie down on me!

HILDY (*jiggling the phone hook*). I'm going to lay down on you and spit in your eye, you murderer!

WALTER. Scared, huh? Yellow running out of your collar!

HILDY. I don't care what you think! I'm going to find my girl's mother! (*Madly jiggling the hook*) Oh, for God's sake!

WALTER. Your girl! You and Butch McGuirk! Woman lovers!

HILDY (*hangs up phone with a bang*). God damn it! I'm going to go *out* and find her! (*Starts for door. At that instant there comes a loud knock.*)

WALTER. Who's that? Don't open that!

HILDY. The hell I won't! I'm going to the morgue! To . . . look! . . . (*He flings the door open. The* SHERIFF, *accompanied by two Deputies—*CARL *and* FRANK*—surrounded by* MC CUE, KRUGER *and* MURPHY, *bar his exit.*)

THE REPORTERS. Oh, there he is! Say Hildy! Wait a second, *etc.* (HILDY *is struggling past them. The* SHERIFF *grabs him.*)

SHERIFF. Just a minute, Johnson!

HILDY. Let go of me! What the hell's the idea?

THE REPORTERS. What's your hurry? We want to see you! *etc.*

HILDY Take your God damn paws off me!

SHERIFF. Hold him, boys!

WALTER (*to the* SHERIFF). Who the hell do you think you are, breaking in here like this?

SHERIFF. You can't bluff me, Burns! I don't care who you are or what paper you're editor of!

HILDY. God damn it! Let me go! (*Hysterically*) Let me go, fellas! Something's happened to my girl's mother!

SHERIFF. Hang on to him!

THE REPORTERS. We know what you're up to! Going out to get Williams, probably! The door was locked! He and Mollie were talking! They know where he is! *etc.*

HILDY (*retreating back into the room before* HARTMAN *and his deputies*). Listen, guys! I don't know anything, I tell you! There's been an accident—I just been calling up the hospitals! I was just going out to the morgue to see if she was there! Now . . .

SHERIFF. Johnson, there's something very, very peculiar going on. . . .

HILDY. Listen, Pinky! You can send somebody *with* me if you want to! If you don't believe me!

SHERIFF. I wasn't born yesterday, Johnson. Now the boys tell me you and Mollie . . .

HILDY. Nobody's trying to put anything over on you! Now, I'm getting out of here and you can't stop me!

MURPHY. You're not going anywhere! He's got the story sewed up, Pete! He and his God damn boss. That's why he's here!

WALTER (*purring*). If you've got any accusations to make, Hartman, make them in the proper manner! Otherwise I'll have to ask you to get out!

SHERIFF (*pop-eyed*). You'll ask me to *what?*

WALTER. I'll ask you to get out.

SHERIFF (*to his deputies*). Close that door! Don't let anybody in or out!

MURPHY. Come on, Pinky! Give him a little third degree!

SHERIFF. Johnson, I'm going to the bottom of this! Now then, come clean! What do you know about Williams? Are you going to talk or aren't you?

HILDY. What the hell do *I* know about Williams?

SHERIFF. All right, boys! Take him along. I got ways of making him talk. (HILDY *struggles.*)

HILDY. Look out, you . . . !

MC CUE. What's the use of fighting, Hildy? (THE REPORTERS *swarm around* HILDY. *Shouts of "I got him." "No, you don't!" "Hey, what you doing?" "Paste him!" "Aw, Hildy! What the hell!" etc.* HILDY'S *voice rises out of the din.*)

HILDY. Say what the hell's the idea?

THE DEPUTIES. He's got a gun on him! Look out! He's got a gun! He's got a gun!

HILDY. No, you don't! Hey, Walter!

WALTER. What is it? Here!

SHERIFF. Gimme that! (*Takes the gun.*)

HILDY (*resisting*). That's mine! . . .

MURPHY. Jesse James, huh! The drug store cowboy!

MC CUE. He's been going to the movies. Two-gun Johnson!

KRUGER. The terror of Wilson Avenue beach!

SHERIFF (*frozen, looking at the gun*). Where did you get this?

HILDY. I got a right to carry a gun if I want to.

SHERIFF. Not *this* gun!

WALTER (*easily*). I can explain that, Hartman. He was having some trouble with the Durkin story and I gave it to him . . . to defend himself!

SHERIFF. Oh, you *did!* . . . Well, that's very, *very* interesting! This *happens* to be the gun that Earl Williams shot his way out with!

THE REPORTERS. What? What's that? *etc.*

WALTER (*to* HARTMAN). Are you trying to make me out a liar?

SHERIFF (*wildly*). I know my own gun, don't I?

MURPHY (*bitterly to* HILDY). Getting married, huh!

KRUGER. Maybe Williams was gonna be his best man.

SHERIFF (*trembling*). Where is he? Where you got him?

WALTER (*sympathetically*). You're barking up the wrong tree, Hartman.

SHERIFF. I'll give you three minutes to tell me where he is!

HILDY. He went over to the hospital to call on Professor Eglehofer!

SHERIFF. What! ! !

HILDY. With a bag of marshmallows.
(*The* SHERIFF *stands silent, a gypsy; then streaks wildly for the toilet and throws open the door.*)

WALTER. Take a magazine along.

THE REPORTERS. Come on, Hildy. Where is he? That's a hell of a trick, Hildy. I thought we were friends! *etc.*

SHERIFF (*rushing back from the toilet*). By God, I'll show you!

THE REPORTERS. Look here, Pete! What about Mr. Burns? Ask the Master Mind! Yeah. What's *he* doing over here? *etc.*

SHERIFF (*grabbing* WALTER's *arm*). Speak up, Burns! What do you know about this?

WALTER (*gently but firmly disengaging his arm*). Listen Hartman . . .

MURPHY. The hell with that! Where is he?

WALTER (*continuing*). The Examiner is not obstructing justice or aiding criminals. You ought to know that!

CARL (*pointing to the Examiner phone*). Look! Somebody was talking on there! The receiver is off! (MC CUE *jumps for the phone.*)

MC CUE. I'll find out who it is . . .

SHERIFF (*also jumping*). Leave that alone! *I'm* in charge here!

HILDY. Walter, listen! If I don't get out of here . . .

SHERIFF. Quiet, everybody! I'll handle this. It may be Earl Williams.

HILDY. Tell him to come on over.

SHERIFF. Sssh! (*Into phone, swallowing, then elaborately disguising his voice*) Hello, Earl!

WALTER (*smiling*). Scotland Yard.

SHERIFF (*to* MC CUE, *in a whisper*). Trace this call—quick! (MC CUE *jumps for another phone*) Yes, this is Walter.

MC CUE (*into another phone*). Trace the call on twenty-one! In a hurry!

SHERIFF (*into Examiner phone*). What? You gotta do what? Who is this? ! ! !

WALTER. You're talking to the Examiner, Hawkshaw!
(*The* SHERIFF *wheels.*)

MC CUE. That's right, Sheriff!

SHERIFF. Johnson, you're under arrest! You too, Burns!

WALTER (*calmly, without moving from his post at the desk*). Who's under arrest? . . . Listen, you pimple-headed German spy, do you realize what you're doing?

SHERIFF. We'll see about this. Get the Mayor, Carl! Ask him to come over here! (*As* CARL *goes to the telephone the door opens and* MRS. GRANT, *disheveled, with her hat over one ear, enters with two policemen.*)

FIRST POLICEMAN (*entering*). . . . In here, Madam?

HILDY (*leaping forward, happily*). Mother!

MRS. GRANT (*to* POLICEMAN). That man there! With the gray necktie! (*She points accusingly at* WALTER.)

HILDY (*hugging her*). Mother! Oh, my God, I'm glad to see you! Are you all right? Tell me! (MRS. GRANT *indignantly shakes* HILDY *off.*)

SHERIFF. What's the idea here?

POLICEMAN. This lady claims she was kidnapped!

SHERIFF. What? ! !

MRS. GRANT. They dragged me all the way down the stairs—I tried to get help and they began to pinch me —I'm black and blue all over! Then they ran into another automobile and I was nearly killed! . . .

SHERIFF. Just a minute! What did this man have to do with it, lady? (*He points at* WALTER.)

MRS. GRANT. He was the one in charge of everything! He told them to kidnap me!

WALTER (*amazed*). Are you referring to *me*, Madam?

MRS. GRANT (*to* WALTER). You know you did! You told them to take me out of here!

SHERIFF. What about this, Burns! Kidnapping, eh?

WALTER (*round-eyed*). It's beyond *me*. Who is this woman?

MRS. GRANT Oh! Oh, what a thing to say! I was standing right there . . . after the girl jumped out of that window!

SHERIFF. Did you get the Mayor? Was he in?

A DEPUTY. He's coming over.

WALTER (*to* MRS. GRANT). Now, Madam, be honest, if you were out joy-riding—drunk! . . . and got in some scrape . . . why don't you *admit* it instead of accusing innocent people!

MRS. GRANT (*beginning to doubt her senses*). You ruffian! You unprincipled man! How dare you say a thing like that!

HILDY. Please, mother! He's just crazy! Don't! . . .

MRS. GRANT. I'll tell you something more, officer! I'll tell you why they did it!

WALTER (*fidgeting*). Come on, Sheriff. We've got to get bail.

MRS. GRANT (*continuing crescendo*). I was in here and they had some kind of a murderer—hiding him! (*This is a bombshell. The room is electrified by the old lady's announcement.*)

SHERIFF. Hiding him! Hiding him! In here?

MURPHY. Hiding him where?

HILDY. Mother!

THE REPORTERS. Where was he? Where did they have him? *etc.*

WALTER (*with superb indignation*). Madam, you're a God-damn liar! (*To emphasize his righteousness* WALTER *pounds on the desk three times—and then stands horrified. He remembers, too late, the signal.*)

THE REPORTERS. For God's sake, tell us where he was! Did they tell you where? Tell us! *etc.*

SHERIFF. Shut up, everybody! Now! Where was he? Tell me, where he was!

MRS. GRANT. Well, I was sitting right in this chair.
(*Three answering knocks come from* WILLIAMS. *The* SHERIFF *leaps as if the desk had bitten him.*)

SHERIFF (*whispering*). What was that?

THE REPORTERS. My God, he's in the desk! For the love of Christ! Holy God, he's in there! *etc.*

SHERIFF. Aha! *I thought so!* Stand back, everybody!

DEPUTY. Look out, Sheriff! He may shoot!

SHERIFF. Get your guns out! (*The police all take out guns.*)

HILDY. He's harmless, for God's sake!

SHERIFF. Don't take any chances! Shoot through the desk!

HILDY. He can't hurt anybody! You got his gun!

MRS. GRANT (*panic-stricken*). Oh, dear! Oh, dear!

WALTER (*to* MRS. GRANT). You gray-haired old Judas!

MRS. GRANT. Let me out! Let me out of here! (*Streaks for the door; exits.* THE REPORTERS *are going for the telephones.*)

MURPHY (*into phone*). City desk! Quick!

SHERIFF (*to* POLICEMEN). Close the door. You stand there. You cover the windows. (*Indicates with his gun.*)

MURPHY. Look out where you're pointing that gun, Pinky!

MC CUE (*into phone*). Gimme Emil.

KRUGER (*into phone*). Gimme the city desk.

MURPHY. Hold the wire! I've got a flash for you.

WALTER (*to* HILDY). Call Duffy.

SHERIFF. No, you don't!

WALTER. Do you want us to get scooped?

MC CUE (*into phone*). Emil? Hang on for a second.

SHERIFF. Now then! Everybody aim right at the centre. And when I say three—

HILDY. God damn it! That's murder!

SHERIFF. Carl! Frank! One of you get on each side of the desk. Take hold of the cover. Now then! We got you covered, Williams—don't try to move. *Now!* Everybody quiet and ready for any emergency. I'm going to count three.

MURPHY (*phoning in the silence*). I'll have it in a minute . . .

SHERIFF. One! . . .

KRUGER. Right away now!

SHERIFF. Two! . . . (DIAMOND LOUIE *enters, accompanied by three people he has picked up in the street. One is a boy in short pants, the second is a sailor, the third is a seedy old man of the Trader Horn type.*)

POLICEMAN (*at the door, opposing them*). What do you want? (WALTER *waves violently,* LOUIE *and his assistants disappear.*)

SHERIFF (*wheeling*). Who was that?

WALTER (*white with rage*). Double crossing Sicilian!

SHERIFF. Shut up!

KRUGER (*into phone*). Keep holding it!

SHERIFF. Now then! Keep everybody out of here! I want quiet! . . . There's a dozen guns on you, Williams! You can't escape! Do you surrender or not?

WALTER (*into phone*). Duffy!

SHERIFF. Are you ready, boys?

CARL. Yah. . . .

SHERIFF. All right. Now everybody aim right at the centre. (*Looking around*) Are you all ready? (*To the men at the desk*) You boys? (*From the* DEPUTIES *comes a whispered "Yes."*) Ready back there? (*This to the men at the door and windows; they give quick nods in reply*) All right. Now then—up with it. (CARL *and* FRANK *raise the cover. The* SHERIFF *waits a discreet distance until he sees there is no danger.* WILLIAMS *is cowering in the desk, his hands over his face. The* SHERIFF *rushes on him, jabbing his gun into him.*)

WILLIAMS (*a wail*). Go on—shoot me!

SHERIFF. Got you, Williams!

THE POLICE AND DEPUTIES. Grab him there! That's him! That's him! Don't let him shoot! Stick 'em up, you! Clout him! Give him the boots! Hold his arm! (*Through this* THE REPORTERS *are telephoning in. As they talk, the police drag the screaming little anarchist out. The* SHERIFF *follows them.*)

MURPHY (*into phone*). Earl Williams was just captured in the press room o' the Criminal Courts Building hiding in a desk.

MC CUE (*into phone*). The Sheriff just caught Williams in a roll top right here in the room.

KRUGER (*into phone*). Just nabbed Williams hiding in a desk, Criminal Court press room.

MC CUE (*into phone*). Williams put up a desperate struggle but the police overpowered him.

MURPHY (*into phone*). Williams tried to shoot it out with the cops but his gun wouldn't work.

KRUGER (*into phone*). Williams was unconscious when they opened the desk . . .

WALTER (*into phone*). Duffy! The Examiner just turned Earl Williams over to the Sheriff . . .
(*The* SHERIFF *rushes back.*)

SHERIFF (*indicating* WALTER *and* HILDY). Just a minute! Put the cuffs on those two! (*The police obey*) Harboring a fugitive from justice!

MURPHY (*into phone*). A well dressed society woman tipped off the cops. Call you back in a minute . . .

KRUGER (*into phone*). An old sweetheart of Williams double crossed him . . . Call you back . . .

MC CUE (*into phone*). More in a minute.

THE REPORTERS. Where's that old lady? Hey madam! . . . Wait a minute! . . . Where's the old dame? (*They exit in a hurry.*)

SHERIFF (*into phone*). Hello, girlie! Gimme Jacobi! Quick! . . .

WALTER. Hartman . . . you're going to wish for the rest of your life you'd never been born!
(*The* MAYOR *enters.*)

MAYOR. Fine work, Pete! You certainly delivered the goods! I'm proud of you!

SHERIFF (*over his shoulder as he phones*). Look kind of natural, don't they, Fred? (*Referring to the handcuffs.*)

MAYOR (*happily*). A sight for sore eyes! Well, it looks like you boys stepped in something up to your neck!

HILDY (*to His Honor*). Go on! Laugh! You big tub of guts!

MAYOR. That's pretty, isn't it? Aiding an escaped criminal, huh?

SHERIFF (*rolling in catnip*). And a little charge of kidnapping I'm looking into! (*Into phone*) That's the jail! There must be *some*body over there!

MAYOR. Well! Looks like about ten years apiece for you birds.

WALTER. Does it? Well, whenever you think you've got the Examiner licked, that's a good time to get out of town.

HILDY. On a hand car.

MAYOR. Whistling in the dark, eh? Well, it isn't going to help you. You're through.

WALTER. Yeah? The last man that told me that was Barney Schmidt . . . a week before he cut his throat.

MAYOR. Is that so?

WALTER. And remember George T. Yorke, blowing his head off with a shot-gun? We've been in worse jams than this—haven't we, Hildy? But something seems to watch over the Examiner. (*He raises his eyebrows.*)

HILDY. Yeah. When that minister sued us—remember? False arrest?

WALTER. Oh, yes . . . (*Coolly to the* MAYOR) The Reverend J. B. Godolphin sued the Examiner once for . . . a hundred thousand dollars. It seems that we'd called him a fairy. Well, the day of the trial came and the Reverend was on his way to court . . .

HILDY. With all his lawyers and medical witnesses.

WALTER (*orgiastic*). Drowned by God! Drowned in the river! With their automobile, their affidavits and their God-damn law books! And I got the same feeling right now that I had five minutes before that accident!

MAYOR. Your luck ain't with you now.

SHERIFF (*into telephone*). Jacobi? . . . I caught him. Williams. Singlehanded. . . . Yeah. They're bringing him right over. Notify everybody. We're going to proceed with the hanging per schedule. (*Wiggles telephone for another call.*)

WALTER (*to the* MAYOR). You're going to be in office for exactly two days more and then we're pulling your big nose out of the feed bag and setting you out on your fat can!

SHERIFF. Give me the state's attorney's office.

HILDY. And when you're walking up and down North Avenue with blue eyeglasses selling lead pencils, we're not going to forget you, either!

SHERIFF (*merrily*). We're going to be selling lead pencils, eh?

MAYOR. Don't even answer him.

THE SHERIFF. Well, I'll tell you what you'll be doing. Making *brooms* in the state penitentiary. . . . (*Into phone*) Hello, Pyrstalski? This is Hartman. Come right over to my office, will you? I've just arrested a couple of important birds. I want you to take their confessions. (*Hangs up.*)

WALTER (*seizing the Examiner phone*). Duffy! Get Clarence Darrow! ! ! !

MAYOR. Get anybody you want! All the Darrows in the world aren't going to help you!

WALTER. Schmidt, Yorke, Godolphin. . . . You're next, Fred.

MAYOR. The power of the press, huh? Well, it don't scare me! Not an iota!

SHERIFF. It's a big windbag! That's all it is! Take 'em along, Carl!

WALTER. Bigger men than you have found out what it is! Presidents! Yes . . . and Kings!
(PINCUS, *the governor's messenger, reels in, stewed.*)

PINCUS (*woozy*). Here's your reprieve.

MAYOR (*seeing him, in panic*). Get out of here!

PINCUS. You can't bribe me!

SHERIFF. Get out of here, you!

PINCUS. I won't! Here's your reprieve!

HILDY. What's that?

PINCUS. I don't want to be City Sealer.

MAYOR. Who *is* this man?

SHERIFF (*frenzied*). Throw him out, Frank!

HILDY (*seizing* PINCUS *with his free hand*). Who was bribing you? (WALTER *also seizes* PINCUS, *already being pulled out of shape.*)

PINCUS. They wouldn't take it! . . .

MAYOR. You're insane!

WALTER. What did I tell you? An unseen power. What's your name?

PINCUS. Irving Pincus!

MAYOR. You drunken idiot! Arrest him! The idea of coming in here with a cock-and-bull story like that.

SHERIFF. It's a frameup! That's what it is! Some imposter!

HILDY. Wait a minute! (*To the* DEPUTIES) Let go there!

WALTER. Murder, huh?

HILDY. Hanging an innocent man to win an election!

SHERIFF. That's a lie!

MAYOR. I never saw him before in my life!

WALTER (*to* PINCUS). When did you deliver this first?

HILDY. Who did you talk to?

PINCUS. They started right in bribing me!

HILDY. Who's "they"?

PINCUS (*indicating the* MAYOR *and* SHERIFF). Them!

MAYOR. That's absurd on the face of it, Mr. Burns! He's talking like a child!

WALTER (*really impressed*). An unseen power.

MAYOR. Certainly! He's insane or drunk or something! Why, if this unfortunate man Williams has really been reprieved, I personally am tickled to death! Aren't you, Pete?

HILDY. Go on, you'd kill your mother to get elected!

MAYOR (*shocked*). That's a hell of a thing to say, Johnson, about anybody! Now, look here, Walter, you're an intelligent man . . .

WALTER (*stopping the* MAYOR). Just a minute. (*To* PINCUS) All right, Mr. Pincus. Let's have your story.

PINCUS. Well, I've been married for nineteen years . . .

WALTER. Skip all that.

MAYOR (*loudly*). Take those handcuffs off the boys, Pete. That wasn't at all necessary. . . .

SHERIFF (*springing to obey*). I was just going to. . . .

MAYOR. I can't tell you how badly I feel about this, Walter. There was no excuse for Hartman flying off the handle.

SHERIFF (*busy with the handcuffs*). I was only doing my duty. There wasn't anything personal intended.

HILDY. You guys had better quit politics and take in washing. (*They are set free.*)

MAYOR. Sheriff. . . . (*He is looking over the reprieve*) This document is authentic! Earl Williams, thank God, has been reprieved, and the commonwealth of Chicago has been spared the painful necessity of shedding blood.

WALTER. Save that for the Tribune.

MAYOR (*to* PINCUS). What did you say your name was—Pincus?

PINCUS. That's right. (*Shows a locket*) Here's a picture of the wife.

MAYOR (*trapped*). A very fine-looking woman.

PINCUS (*mysteriously angered*). She's good enough for me.
(PEGGY ENTERS.)

HILDY. I'll bet she is.

MAYOR. A real character.

PEGGY. Hildy, what's the matter? What are they going to do? Mother said—

HILDY (*seeing her*). Peggy, don't bawl me out now.

WALTER. Nobody's going to do anything to anybody.

MAYOR. Of course not. My good friend Walter Burns and I understand each other perfectly, I trust.

SHERIFF (*eager*). And so do I.

MAYOR. So do you *what,* you God damn hoodoo! And now, Mr. Pincus, if you'll come with us we'll take you over to the Warden's office and deliver that reprieve.

PEGGY. But Hildy, mother said that they'd arrested you . . .

PINCUS (*being escorted out by the* MAYOR). If I was to go home and tell my wife—

MAYOR. The hell with you wife!

PINCUS (*drunkenly loyal to his mate*). She *loves* me. (*Exit* PINCUS *and the* MAYOR.)

SHERIFF (*pauses. His eyes lower. He speaks winningly*). By the way, Walter . . . We were going to have a little feed after the hanging . . . a sort of buffet breakfast. . . .

MAYOR (*calling from the corridor*). Hartman!

SHERIFF (*nervously*). I'm coming, Fred. (*Coyly, as* WALTER *stares*) What do you say we eat it now? . . . Hmm? (*Still the dead pan from* WALTER) Delicious ham . . . and some of Mrs. Hartman's own preserves. . . .

MAYOR (*loudly from the hall*). Hartman! ! !
(*The* SHERIFF *sighs. A plaintive shrug indicates that he has a great deal to contend with. He leaves.*)

WALTER (*dreamily*). Wait till those two Greeks read the Examiner tomorrow! (*Back to life*) Hildy, I'll tell you what I want you to do.

HILDY. What?

WALTER. I want you to get this guy Pincus over to the office tomorrow—

HILDY. Nothing doing, Walter. I'm all washed up. I mean it this time, Walter.

PEGGY. Oh, Hildy, if I only thought you did.

HILDY. Listen, Peggy,—if I'm not telling you the absolute truth may God strike me dead right now. I'm going to New York with you to-night—if you give me this one last chance! I'll cut out drinking and swearing and everything connected with the God-damn newspaper business. I won't even *read* a newspaper.

WALTER. Listen, Hildy, I got an idea . . .

HILDY (*to* WALTER). There's nothing you can say can make me change my mind. This time I'm through, and I *mean* it. I know I don't deserve you, Peggy. I've done everything in the world to prove that, I guess.

PEGGY. Hildy, please! Don't say things like that.

HILDY. I've gotta hell of a nerve to ask you to marry me. I'm a prize package, all right. But if you'll take me, here I am.

PEGGY. Darling, don't talk that way. I want you just the way you are. (*Anyway* PEGGY *will always remember that she said this and always forget that she didn't mean it.*)

WALTER. God, Hildy, I didn't know it was anything like this. Why didn't you *say* something? I'd be the last person in the world to want to come between you and your happiness.

HILDY (*staggered*). What?

WALTER. You ought to know that . . . (*As* HILDY *continues to blink*) I love you, you crazy Swede! (*To* PEGGY) You're getting a great guy, Peggy.

HILDY. Never mind the Valentines. Goodbye, you lousy bohunk. (*They shake hands.*)

WALTER. You're a great newspaperman, Hildy. I'm sorry to see you go. Damn sorry.

HILDY. Well, if I ever come *back* to the business . . . (*To* PEGGY) Which I won't . . . (*To* WALTER, *his arm around* PEGGY) There's only one man I'd work for. You know that, don't you?

WALTER. I'd kill you if you ever worked for anybody else.

HILDY. Hear that, Peggy? That's my diploma. (*He hesitates*) Well, Walter . . . I don't know what to say . . . except I'm going to miss you like hell.

WALTER. Same here, son.

HILDY (*to* PEGGY). Twelve years we've been knocking around together . . . before you were born . . . (*To* WALTER, *his face lighting up*) Remember the time we hid the missing heiress in the sauerkraut factory?

WALTER. Do I! (*To* PEGGY) Get him to tell you some time about how we stole Old Lady Haggerty's stomach . . . off the coroner's physician. We *proved* she was poisoned. . . .

HILDY (*laughing*). We had to hide for a week!

PEGGY. Darling . . .

HILDY (*back to life*). What?

PEGGY. You don't want to go to New York . . . down deep.

HILDY. Aw . . . what do you mean? I was just talking. (*With a nervous laugh*) I'd feel worse if I stayed, I guess. . . .

PEGGY. Hildy, if I thought you were going to be unhappy—I mean, if you really wanted to— (*Firmly*) No. No. It's your chance to have a home and be a human being—and I'm going to make you take it.

WALTER (*to* PEGGY). Why, I wouldn't let him stay. . . . Go on, Hildy, before I make you city editor.

HILDY (*starting*). Hurry up, Peggy. He means it.

WALTER (*as* PEGGY *follows*). Any objection to my kissing the bride?

HILDY (*stopping*). It's O.K. with me. (*He looks at* PEGGY. *She smiles*) Go ahead, Mrs. Johnson.

WALTER (*removing his hat and kissing her chastely*). Thank you. . . . What time does your train go?

PEGGY. There's another one at twelve-forty. (*To* HILDY) We came awfully near going without you.

WALTER. New York Central, eh? (*To* HILDY) I wish there was time to get you a little wedding present . . . but it's awful short notice.

PEGGY (*straining to be gone*). Thank you, Mr. Burns, but Hildy's all the wedding present I want. . . . (*Laughing a little*) If I've really got him.

HILDY. Ah, forget it, Walter. (*He, too, is leaving.*)

WALTER. Hold on! I want you to have something to remember me by. You can't just leave like this. . . . (*Thoughtfully reaching for his watch*) And I know what it's going to be. . . . (*Produces the watch.*)

HILDY (*embarrassed*). Aw, Jesus, no, Walter! You make me feel like a fairy or something!

WALTER (*with affected brusqueness*). Shut up! You're going to take it, I tell you! It was a present from the Big Chief himself! And if you'll look inside . . . (*Opening the watch*) You'll find a little inscription: "To the Best Newspaperman I know." . . . When you get to New York, you can scratch out my name and put yours in its place, if you want to. . . .

HILDY. You know I wouldn't do that. . . .

WALTER. Here. . . . (*Giving him the watch.*)

HILDY. Aw, Walter! It's too good for me! I can't take it!

WALTER. You *got* to! (*To* PEGGY) *Make* him!

PEGGY. Go on, Hildy . . . if Mr. Burns wants you to. You don't want to hurt his feelings. . . .
(HILDY *takes it.* WALTER *pats him on the shoulder, his face averted.*)

HILDY (*a lump in his throat*). Well, this is the first and last thing I ever got from a newspaper. . . .

PEGGY. Goodbye, Mr. Burns. . . . I always had a queer opinion of you,

Mr. Burns. I *still* think you're a little peculiar, but you're all right . . . underneath. I mean I think you're a peach.

WALTER (*winningly*). So are you! You look just like a little flower!

HILDY (*ushering* PEGGY *out*). Goodbye, you big baboon. . . .

PEGGY. Goodbye. . . . (*They exit.*)

WALTER (*calling after, leaning against the door*). Goodbye, Johnson! Be good to yourself . . . and the little girl. . . .

HILDY'S VOICE. The same to you and many of them!

(WALTER *waits till* HILDY *and* PEGGY *are out of sight and earshot, then closes the door. He walks slowly to the telephone. The receiver is still off the hook, the obedient* DUFFY *still on the other end.* WALTER *hesitates sentimentally, the receiver in his hand. Then he heaves a huge sigh and speaks.*)

WALTER. Duffy! . . . (*He sounds a bit tired*) Listen. I want you to send a wire to the Chief of Police of La Porte, Indiana. . . . That's right. . . . Tell him to meet the twelve-forty out of Chicago . . . New York Central . . . and arrest Hildy Johnson and bring him back here. . . . Wire him a full description. . . . The son of a bitch stole my watch!

CURTAIN

This epilogue is one of apology.

When we applied ourselves to write a newspaper play we had in mind a piece of work which would reflect our intellectual disdain of and superiority to the Newspaper.

What we finally turned out, as the reader may verify if he will, is a romantic and rather doting tale of our old friends—the reporters of Chicago.

It developed in writing this play that our contempt for the institution of the Press was a bogus attitude; that we looked back on the Local Room where we had spent half our lives as a veritable fairyland—and that we were both full of a nostalgia for the bouncing days of our servitude.

The same uncontrollable sentimentality operated in our treatment of Chicago which, as much as any of our characters, is the hero of our play.

The iniquities, double dealings, chicaneries and immoralities which, as ex-Chicagoans, we knew so well, returned to us in a mist called the Good Old Days, and our delight in our memories would not be denied.

As a result The Front Page, *despite its oaths and realisms is a Valentine thrown to the past, a Ballad (to us) full of* Heimweh *and Love.*

So it remains for more stern and uncompromising intellects than ours to write of the true Significance of the Press. Therefore our apology to such bombinators, radicals, Utopians and Schoengeisten *who might read this work expecting intellectual mayhem.*

In writing it we found we were not so much dramatists or intellectuals as two reporters in exile.

—THE AUTHORS

The Green Pastures

BY MARC CONNELLY

TO

MY MOTHER

AUTHOR'S NOTE

The Green Pastures is an attempt to present certain aspects of a living religion in the terms of its believers. The religion is that of thousands of Negroes in the deep South. With terrific spiritual hunger and the greatest humility these untutored black Christians—many of whom cannot even read the book which is the treasure house of their faith—have adapted the contents of the Bible to the consistencies of their everyday lives.

Unburdened by the differences of more educated theologians, they accept the Old Testament as a chronicle of wonders which happened to people like themselves in vague but actual places, and of rules of conduct, true acceptance of which will lead them to a tangible, three-dimensional Heaven. In this Heaven, if one has been born in a district where fish frys are popular, the angels do have magnificent fish frys through an eternity somewhat resembling a series of earthly holidays. The Lord Jehovah will be the promised comforter, a just but compassionate patriarch, the summation of all the virtues His follower has observed in the human beings about him. The Lord may look like the Reverend Mr. Dubois, as our Sunday School teacher speculates in the play, or he may resemble another believer's own grandfather. In any event, His face will be familiar to the one who has come for his reward.

The author is indebted to Mr. Roark Bradford, whose retelling of several of the Old Testament stories in *Ol' Man Adam an' His Chillun* first stimulated his interest in this point of view.

One need not blame a hazy memory of the Bible for the failure to recall the characters of Hezdrel, Zeba and others in the play. They are the author's apocrypha, but he believes persons much like them have figured in the meditations of some of the old Negro preachers, whose simple faith he has tried to translate into a play.

The Green Pastures was first produced at the Mansfield Theatre, New York City, by Laurence Rivers, Inc., on February 26, 1930, and closed on August 29, 1931. Following is the original cast:

MR. DESHEE	Charles H. Moore
MYRTLE	Alicia Escamilla
FIRST BOY	Jazzlips Richardson, Jr.
SECOND BOY	Howard Washington
THIRD BOY	Reginald Blythwood
RANDOLPH	Joe Byrd
A COOK	Frances Smith
CUSTARD MAKER	Homer Tutt
FIRST MAMMY ANGEL	Anna Mae Fritz
A STOUT ANGEL	Josephine Byrd
A SLENDER ANGEL	Edna Thrower
ARCHANGEL	J. A. Shipp
GABRIEL	Wesley Hill
THE LORD	Richard B. Harrison
CHOIR LEADER	McKinley Reeves
ADAM	Daniel L. Haynes
EVE	Inez Richardson Wilson
CAIN	Lou Vernon
CAIN'S GIRL	Dorothy Randolph
ZEBA	Edna M. Harris
CAIN THE SIXTH	James Fuller
BOY GAMBLER	Louis Kelsey
FIRST GAMBLER	Collington Hayes
SECOND GAMBLER	Ivan Sharp
VOICE IN SHANTY	Josephine Byrd
NOAH	Tutt Whitney
NOAH'S WIFE	Susie Sutton
SHEM	Milton J. Williams
FIRST WOMAN	Dinks Thomas
SECOND WOMAN	Anna Mae Fritz
THIRD WOMAN	Geneva Blythwood
FIRST MAN	Emory Richardson

FLATFOOT	Freddie Archibald
HAM	J. Homer Tutt
JAPHETH	Stanleigh Morrell
FIRST CLEANER	Josephine Byrd
SECOND CLEANER	Florence Fields
ABRAHAM	J. A. Shipp
ISAAC	Charles H. Moore
JACOB	Edgar Burks
MOSES	Alonzo Fenderson
ZIPPORAH	Mercedes Gilbert
AARON	McKinley Reeves
A CANDIDATE MAGICIAN	Reginald Fenderson
PHARAOH	George Randol
THE GENERAL	Walt McClane
FIRST WIZARD	Emory Richardson
HEAD MAGICIAN	Arthur Porter
JOSHUA	Stanleigh Morrell
FIRST SCOUT	Ivan Sharp
MASTER OF CEREMONIES	Billy Cumby
KING OF BABYLON	Jay Mondaaye
PROPHET	Ivan Sharp
HIGH PRIEST	J. Homer Tutt
THE KING'S FAVORITES	Leona Winkler, Florence Lee, Constance Van Dyke, Mary Ella Hart, Inez Persand
OFFICER	Emory Richardson
HEZDREL	Daniel L. Haynes
ANOTHER OFFICER	Stanleigh Morrell

Production designed by Robert Edmond Jones
Music under the direction of Hall Johnson
Staged by Marc Connelly

SCENES

PART ONE

SCENE I
The Sunday School

SCENE II
A Fish Fry

SCENE III
A Garden

SCENE IV
Outside the Garden

SCENE V
A Roadside

SCENE VI
A Private Office

SCENE VII
Another Roadside and a House

SCENE VIII
A House

SCENE IX
A Hillside

SCENE X
A Mountain Top

PART TWO

SCENE I
The Private Office

SCENE II
The Mouth of a Cave

SCENE III
A Throne Room

SCENE IV
The Foot of a Mountain

SCENE V
A Cabaret

SCENE VI
The Private Office

SCENE VII
Outside a Temple

SCENE VIII
Another Fish Fry

THE GREEN PASTURES

PART ONE

SCENE I

A corner in a Negro church.

Ten children and an elderly preacher.

The costumes are those that might be seen in any lower Louisiana town at Sunday-School time. As the curtain rises, MR. DESHEE, *the preacher, is reading from a Bible. The* CHILDREN *are listening with varied degrees of interest. Three or four are wide-eyed in their attention. Two or three are obviously puzzled, but interested, and the smallest ones are engaged in more physical concerns. One is playing with a little doll, and another runs his finger on all the angles of his chair.*

DESHEE. "An' Adam lived a hundred and thirty years, an' begat a son in his own likeness, after his image; an' called his name Seth. An' de days of Adam, after he had begotten Seth, were eight hundred years; an' he begat sons an' daughters; an' all de days dat Adam lived were nine hundred an' thirty years; an' he died. An' Seth lived a hundred an' five years an' begat Enos; an' Seth lived after he begat Enos eight hundred an' seven years and begat sons and daughters. An' all de days of Seth were nine hundred and twelve years; an' he died." An' it go on like dat till we come to Enoch an' de book say: "An' Enoch lived sixty an' five years and begat Methuselah." Den it say: "An' all de days of Methuselah were nine hund'ed an' sixty an' nine years an' he died." An' dat was de oldest man dat ever was. Dat's why we call ol' Mr. Gurney's mammy ol' Mrs. Methuselah, caize she's so ol'. Den a little later it tell about another member of de fam'ly. His name was Noah. Maybe some of you know about him already. I'm gonter tell you all about him next Sunday. Anyway dat's de meat an' substance of de first five chapters of Genesis. Now, how you think you gonter like de Bible?

MYRTLE. I think it's jest wonderful, Mr. Deshee. I cain't understand any of it.

FIRST BOY. Why did dey live so long, Mr. Deshee?

DESHEE. Why? Caize dat was de way God felt.

SECOND BOY. Dat made Adam a way back.

DESHEE. Yes, he certainly 'way back by de time Noah come along. Want to ask me any mo' questions?

SECOND BOY. What de worl' look like when de Lawd begin, Mr. Deshee?

DESHEE. How yo' mean what it look like?

MYRTLE. Carlisle mean who was in N'Orleans den.

DESHEE. Dey wasn't nobody in N'Orleans on 'count dey wasn't any N'Orleans. Dat's de whole idea I tol' you at de end of de first Chapter. Yo' got to git yo' minds fixed. Dey wasn't any Rampart Street. Dey wasn't any Canal Street. Dey wasn't any Louisiana. Dey wasn't nothin' on de earth at all caize fo' de reason dey wasn't any earth.

MYRTLE. Yes, but what Carlisle wanter know is—

DESHEE (*interrupting and addressing little boy who has been playing with his chair and paying no attention*). Now Randolph, if you don't listen, how yo' gonter grow up and be a good man? Yo' wanter grow up an' be a transgressor?

LITTLE BOY (*frightened*). No.

DESHEE. You tell yo' mammy yo' sister got to come wid you next time. She kin git de things done in time to bring you to de school. You content yo'self. (*The* LITTLE BOY *straightens up in his chair*) Now, what do Carlisle want to know?

CARLISLE. How he decide he want de worl' to be right yere and how he git de idea he wanted it?

MYRTLE. Caize de Book say, don't it, Mr. Deshee?

DESHEE. De Book say, but at de same time dat's a good question. I remember when I was a little boy de same thing recurred to me. An' ol' Mr. Dubois, he was a wonderful preacher at New Hope Chapel over in East Gretna, he said: "De answer is dat de Book ain't got time to go into all de details." And he was right. You know sometimes I think de Lawd expects us to figure out a few things for ourselves. We know that at one time dey wasn't anything except Heaven, we don't know jest where it was but we know it was dere. Maybe it was everywhere. Den one day de Lawd got the idea he'd like to make some places. He made de sun and de moon, de stars. An' he made de earth.

MYRTLE. Who was aroun' den, nothin' but angels?

DESHEE. I suppose so.

FIRST BOY. What was de angels doin' up dere?

DESHEE. I suppose dey jest flew aroun' and had a good time. Dey wasn't no sin, so dey musta had a good time.

FIRST BOY. Did dey have picnics?

DESHEE. Sho, dey had the nicest kind of picnics. Dey probably had fish frys, wid b'iled custard and ten cent seegars for de adults. God gives us humans lotsa ideas about havin' good times. Maybe dey were things he'd seen de angels do. Yes, sir, I bet dey had a fish fry every week.

MYRTLE. Did dey have Sunday School, too?

DESHEE. Yes, dey musta had Sunday School for de cherubs.

MYRTLE. What did God look like, Mr. Deshee?

DESHEE. Well, nobody knows exactly what God looked like. But when I was a little boy I used to imagine dat he looked like de Reverend Dubois. He was de finest lookin' ol' man I ever knew. Yes, I used to bet de Lawd looked exactly like Mr. Dubois in de days when he walked de earth in de shape of a natchel man.

MYRTLE. When was dat, Mr. Deshee?

DESHEE. Why, when he was gettin' things started down heah. When He talked to Adam and Eve and Noah and Moses and all dem. He made mighty men in dem days. But aldo dey was awful mighty dey always knew dat He was beyond dem all. Pretty near one o'clock, time fo' you chillun to go home to dinner, but before I let you go I wan' you to go over wid me de main facts of de first lesson. What's de name of de book?

CHILDREN. Genesis.

DESHEE. Dat's right. And what's de other name?

CHILDREN. First Book of Moses.

DESHEE. Dat's right. And dis yere's Chapter One. (*The lights begin to dim*) "In de beginnin' God created de heaven an' de earth. An' de earth was widout form an' void. An' de darkness was upon de face of de deep."

SCENE II

In the darkness many voices are heard singing "Rise, Shine, Give God The Glory." They sing it gaily and rapidly. The lights go up as the second verse ends. The chorus is being sung diminuendo by a mixed company of angels. That is they are angels in that they wear brightly colored robes and have wings protruding from their backs. Otherwise they look and act like a company of happy Negroes at a fish fry. The scene itself is a pre-Creation Heaven with compromises. In the distance is an unbroken stretch of blue sky. Companionable varicolored clouds billow down to the floor of the stage and roll overhead to the branches of a live oak tree which is up left. The tree is leafy and dripping with Spanish moss, and with the clouds makes a frame for the scene. In the cool shade of the tree are the usual appurtenances of a fish fry: a large kettle of hot fat set on two small parallel logs, with a fire going underneath, and a large rustic table formed by driving four stakes into the ground and placing planks on top of the small connecting boards. On the table are piles of biscuits and corn bread and the cooked fish in dishpans. There are one or two fairly large cedar or crock "churns" containing boiled custard, which looks like milk. There is a gourd dipper beside the churns and several glasses and cups of various sizes and shapes from which the custard is drunk.

The principal singers are marching two by two in a small area at the right of the stage. Two MAMMY ANGELS *are attending to the frying beside the kettle. Behind the table a* MAN ANGEL *is skinning fish and passing them to the cooks. Another is ladling out the custard. A* MAMMY ANGEL *is putting fish on bread for a brood of cherubs, and during the first scene they seat themselves on a grassy bank upstage. Another* MAMMY ANGEL *is clapping her hands disapprovingly and beckoning a laughing* BOY CHERUB *down from a cloud a little out of her reach. Another* MAMMY ANGEL *is solicitously slapping the back of a girl cherub who has a large fish sandwich in her hand and a bone in her throat. There is much movement about the table, and during the first few minutes several individuals go up to the table to help themselves to the food and drink. Many of the women angels wear hats and a few of the men are smoking cigars. A large boxful is on the table. There is much laughter and chatter as the music softens, but continues, during the early part of the action. The following short scenes are played almost simultaneously.*

FIRST COOK (*at kettle; calling off*). Hurry up, Cajey. Dis yere fat's cryin' fo' mo' feesh.

A VOICE (*off stage*). We comin', fas' we kin. Dey got to be ketched, ain't dey? We cain't say, "C'm'on, little fish. C'm'on an' git fried," kin we?

SECOND COOK (*at table*). De trouble is de mens is all worm fishin'.

FIRST MAN ANGEL (*at table*). Whut dif'runce do it make? Yo' all de time got to make out like somebody's doin' somethin' de wrong way.

SECOND COOK (*near table*). I s'pose you got de perfec' way fo' makin' bait.

FIRST MAN ANGEL. I ain't sayin' dat. I is sayin' what's wrong wid worm fishin'.

SECOND COOK. Whut's wrong wid worm fishin'? Ever'thing, dat's all. Dey's only one good way fo' catfishin', an' dat's minny fishin'. Anybody know dat.

FIRST MAN ANGEL. Well, it jest so happen dat minny fishin' is de doggondest fool way of fishin' dey is. You kin try minny fishin' 'til de cows come home an' all you catch'll be de backache. De trouble wid you, sister, is you jest got minny fishin' on de brain.

SECOND COOK. Go right on, loud mouf. You tell me de news. My, my! You jest de wisest person in de worl'. First you, den de Lawd God.

FIRST MAN ANGEL (*to the custard ladler*). You cain't tell dem nothin'. (*Walks away to the custard churn*) Does you try to 'splain some simple fac' dey git man-deaf.

FIRST MAMMY ANGEL (*to* CHERUB *on the cloud*). Now, you heerd me. (*The* CHERUB *assumes several mocking poses, as she speaks*) You fly down yere. You wanter be put down in de sin book? (*She goes to the table, gets a drink for herself and points out the* CHERUB *to one of the men behind the table*) Dat baby must got imp blood in him he so vexin'. (*She returns to her position under the cloud*) You want me to fly up dere an' slap you down? Now, I tol' you (*The* CHERUB *starts to come down.*)

STOUT ANGEL (*to the* CHERUB *with a bone in her throat*). I tol' you you was too little fo' catfish. What you wanter git a bone in yo' froat fo'? (*She slaps the* CHERUB'*s back.*)

SLENDER ANGEL (*leisurely eating a sandwich as she watches the back-*

slapping). What de trouble wid Leonetta?

STOUT ANGEL. She got a catfish bone down her froat. (*To the* CHERUB) Doggone, I tol' you to eat grinnel instead.

SLENDER ANGEL. Ef'n she do git all dat et, she gonter have de bellyache.

STOUT ANGEL. Ain't I tol' her dat? (*To* CHERUB) Come on now; let go dat bone. (*She slaps* CHERUB's *back again. The bone is dislodged and the* CHERUB *grins her relief*) Dat's good.

SLENDER ANGEL (*comfortingly*). Now she all right.

STOUT ANGEL. Go on an' play wid yo' cousins. (*The* CHERUB *joins the* CHERUBS *sitting on the embankment. The concurrency of scenes ends here*) I ain't see you lately, Lily. How you been?

SLENDER ANGEL. Me, I'm fine. I been visitin' my mammy. She waitin' on de welcome table over by de throne of grace.

STOUT ANGEL. She always was pretty holy.

SLENDER ANGEL. Yes, ma'am. She like it dere. I guess de Lawd's took quite a fancy to her.

STOUT ANGEL. Well, dat's natural. I declare yo' mammy one of de finest lady angels I know.

SLENDER ANGEL. She claim you de best one she know.

STOUT ANGEL. Well, when you come right down to it, I suppose we is all pretty near perfec'.

SLENDER ANGEL. Yes, ma'am. Why is dat, Mis' Jenny?

STOUT ANGEL. I s'pose it's caize de Lawd he don' 'low us 'sociatin' wid de devil any mo' so dat dey cain' be no mo' sinnin'.

SLENDER ANGEL. Po' ol' Satan. Whutevah become of him?

STOUT ANGEL. De Lawd put him some place I s'pose.

SLENDER ANGEL. But dey ain't any place but Heaven, is dey?

STOUT ANGEL. De Lawd could make a place, couldn't he?

SLENDER ANGEL. Dat's de truth. Dey's one thing confuses me though.

STOUT ANGEL. What's dat?

SLENDER ANGEL. I do a great deal of travelin' an' I ain't never come across any place but Heaven anywhere. So if de Lawd kick Satan out of Heaven jest whereat did he go? Dat's my question.

STOUT ANGEL. You bettah let de Lawd keep his own secrets, Lily. De way things is goin' now dey ain't been no sinnin' since dey give dat scamp a kick in de pants. Nowadays Heaven's free of sin an' if a lady wants a little constitutional she kin fly till she wing-weary widout gittin' insulted.

SLENDER ANGEL. I was jest a baby when Satan lef'. I don't even 'member what he look like.

STOUT ANGEL. He was jest right fo' a devil. (*An* ARCHANGEL *enters. He is older than the others and wears a*

white beard. His clothing is much darker than that of the others and his wings a trifle more imposing) Good mo'nin', Archangel.
(Others say good morning.)

ARCHANGEL. Good mo'nin', folks. I wonder kin I interrup' de fish fry an' give out de Sunday-school cyards? *(Cries of "Suttingly!" "Mah goodness, yes"—etc. The marching* CHOIR *stops)* You kin keep singin' if you want to. Why don' you sing "When de Saints Come Marchin' In?" Seem to me I ain' heard dat lately. *(The* CHOIR *begins "When the Saints Come Marching In," rather softly, but does not resume marching. The* ARCHANGEL *looks off left)* All right, bring 'em yere. *(A prim-looking* WOMAN TEACHER-ANGEL *enters, shepherding ten* BOY *and* GIRL CHERUBS. *The* TEACHER *carries ten beribboned diplomas, which she gives to the* ARCHANGEL. *The* CHERUBS *are dressed in stiffly starched white suits and dresses, the little girls having enormous ribbons at the backs of their dresses and smaller ones in their hair and on the tips of their wings. They line up in front of the* ARCHANGEL *and receive the attention of the rest of the company. The* CHOIR *sings through the ceremony)* Now, den, cherubs, why is you yere?

CHILDREN. Because we so good.

ARCHANGEL. Dat's right. Now who de big boss?

CHILDREN. Our dear Lawd.

ARCHANGEL. Dat's right. When you all grow up what you gonter be?

CHILDREN. Holy angels at de throne of grace.

ARCHANGEL. Dat's right. Now, you passed yo' 'xaminations and it gives me great pleasure to hand out de cyards for de whole class. Gineeva Chaproe. *(The* FIRST GIRL CHERUB *goes to him and gets her diploma. The* CHOIR *sings loudly and resumes marching, as the* ARCHANGEL *calls out another name—and presents diplomas)* Corey Moulter. *(*SECOND GIRL CHERUB *gets her diploma)* Nootzie Winebush. *(*THIRD GIRL CHERUB*)* Harriet Prancy. *(*FOURTH GIRL CHERUB*)* I guess you is Brozain Stew't. *(He gives the* FIFTH GIRL CHERUB *the paper. Each of the presentations has been accompanied by hand-clapping from the bystanders)* Now you boys know yo' own names. Suppose you come yere and help me git dese 'sorted right?
*(*BOY CHERUBS *gather about him and receive their diplomas. The little* GIRLS *have scattered about the stage, joining groups of the adult angels. The angel* GABRIEL *enters. He is bigger and more elaborately winged than even the* ARCHANGEL, *but he is also much younger and beardless. His costume is less conventional than that of the other men, resembling more the Gabriel of the Doré drawings. His appearance causes a flutter among the others. They stop their chattering with the children. The* CHOIR *stops as three or four audible whispers of "Gabriel!" are heard. In a moment the heavenly company is all attention.)*

GABRIEL *(lifting his hand)*. Gangway! Gangway for de Lawd God Jehovah!
(There is a reverent hush as GOD *enters. He is the tallest and biggest of them all. He wears a white shirt with a white bow tie, a long Prince Albert coat of black alpaca, black trousers and congress gaiters. He*

looks at the assemblage. There is a pause. He speaks in a rich, bass voice.)

GOD. Is you been baptized?

OTHERS (*chanting*). Certainly, Lawd.

GOD. Is you been baptized?

OTHERS. Certainly, Lawd.

GOD (*with the beginning of musical notation*). Is you been baptized?

OTHERS (*now half singing*). Certainly, Lawd. Certainly, certainly, certainly, Lawd. (*They sing the last two verses with equivalent part division.)*

Is you been redeemed?
  Certainly, Lawd.
Is you been redeemed?
  Certainly, Lawd.
Is you been redeemed?
  Certainly, Lawd. Certainly, certainly, certainly, Lawd.

Do you bow mighty low?
  Certainly, Lawd.
Do you bow mighty low?
  Certainly, Lawd.
Do you bow mighty low?
  Certainly, Lawd. Certainly, certainly, certainly, Lawd.

(*As the last response ends all heads are bowed.* GOD *looks at them for a moment; then lifts His hand.)*

GOD. Let de fish fry proceed.
(EVERYONE *rises. The* ANGELS *relax and resume their inaudible conversations. The activity behind the table and about the cauldron is resumed. Some of the* CHOIR *members cross to the table and get sandwiches and cups of the boiled custard. Three or four of the* CHILDREN *in the Sunday School class and the* LITTLE GIRL *who had the bone in her throat affectionately group themselves about* GOD *as he speaks with the* ARCHANGEL. *He pats their heads, they hang to his coat-tails, etc.)*

ARCHANGEL. Good mo'nin', Lawd.

GOD. Good mo'nin', Deacon. You lookin' pretty spry.

ARCHANGEL. I cain' complain. We jest been givin' our cyards to de chillun.

GOD. Dat's good.
(*A small* CHERUB, *his feet braced against one of* GOD'S *shoes, is using* GOD'S *coat tail as a trapeze. One of the* COOKS *offers a fish sandwich which* GOD *politely declines.)*

FIRST MAMMY ANGEL. Now, you leave go de Lawd's coat, Herman. You heah me?

GOD. Dat's all right, sister. He jest playin'.

FIRST MAMMY ANGEL. He playin' too rough.
(GOD *picks up the* CHERUB *and spanks him good-naturedly. The* CHERUB *squeals with delight and runs to his mother.* GABRIEL *advances to* GOD *with a glass of the custard.)*

GABRIEL. Little b'iled custud, Lawd?

GOD. Thank you very kindly. Dis looks nice.

CUSTARD MAKER (*offering a box*). Ten cent seegar, Lawd?

GOD (*taking it*). Thank you, thank you. How de fish fry goin'? (*Ad lib. cries of "O. K. Lawd," "Fine an' dandy, Lawd," "De best one yit, Lawd," etc. To the* CHOIR) How you shouters gittin' on?

CHOIR LEADER. We been marchin' and singin' de whole mo'nin'.

GOD. I heerd you. You gettin' better all de time. You gittin' as good as de one at de throne. Why don' you give us one dem ol' time jump-ups?

CHOIR LEADER. Anythin' you say, Lawd. (*To the others*) "So High!" (*The* CHOIR *begins to sing "So High You Can't Get Over It." They sing softly, but do not march. An* ANGEL *offers his cigar to* GOD *from which He can light His own.*)

GOD. No, thanks. I'm gonter save dis a bit. (*He puts the cigar in his pocket and listens to the singers a moment. Then he sips his custard. After a second sip, a look of displeasure comes on his face.*)

GABRIEL. What's de matter, Lawd?

GOD (*sipping again*). I ain't jest sure, yit. Dey's somethin' 'bout dis custard. (*Takes another sip.*)

CUSTARD MAKER. Ain't it all right, Lawd?

GOD. It don't seem seasoned jest right. You make it?

CUSTARD MAKER. Yes, Lawd. I put everythin' in it like I allus do. It's supposed to be perfec'.

GOD. Yeah. I kin taste de eggs and de cream and de sugar. (*Suddenly*) I know what it is. It needs jest a little bit mo' firmament.

CUSTARD MAKER. Dey's firmament in it, Lawd.

GOD. Maybe, but it ain' enough.

CUSTARD MAKER. It's all we had, Lawd. Dey ain't a drap in de jug.

GOD. Dat's all right. I'll jest r'ar back an' pass a miracle. (CHOIR *stops singing*) Let it be some firmament! An' when I say let it be some firmament, I don't want jest a little bitty dab o' firmament caize I'm sick an' tired of runnin' out of it when we need it. Let it be a whole mess of firmament! (*The stage has become misty until* GOD *and the heavenly company are obscured. As he finishes the speech there is a burst of thunder. As the stage grows darker*) Dat's de way I like it.
(*Murmurs from the others: "Dat's a lot of firmament." "My, dat is firmament!" "Look to me like he's created rain," etc.*)

FIRST MAMMY ANGEL (*when the stage is dark*). Now, look Lawd, dat's too much firmament. De cherubs is gettin' all wet.

SECOND MAMMY ANGEL. Look at my Carlotta, Lawd. She's soaked to de skin. Dat's *plenty* too much firmament.

GOD. Well, 'co'se we don't want de chillun to ketch cold. Can't you dreen it off?

GABRIEL. Dey's no place to dreen it, Lawd.

FIRST MAMMY ANGEL. Why don't we jest take de babies home, Lawd?

GOD. No, I don' wanta bust up de fish fry. You angels keep quiet an' I'll pass another miracle. Dat's always de trouble wid miracles. When you pass one you always gotta r'ar back an' pass another. (*There is a hush*) Let dere be a place to dreen off dis firmament. Let dere be mountains an' valleys an' let dere be oceans an' lakes. An' let dere be rivers an' bayous to dreen it off in, too. As a matter of fac' let dere be de earth. An' when dat's done let dere be de sun, an' let it come out an' dry my cherubs' wings.

(*The lights go up until the stage is bathed in sunlight. On the embankment upstage there is now a waist-high wrought-iron railing such as one sees on the galleries of houses in the French quarter of New Orleans. The* CHERUBS *are being examined by their parents and there is an ad lib. murmur of, "You all right, honey?" "You feel better now, Albert?" "Now you all dry, Vangy?" until the* ARCHANGEL, *who has been gazing in awe at the railing, drowns them out.*)

ARCHANGEL. Look yere!

(*There is a rush to the embankment accompanied by exclamations, "My goodness!" "What's dis?" "I declah!" etc.* GABRIEL *towers above the group on the middle of the embankment.* GOD *is wrapped in thought, facing the audience. The* CHOIR *resumes singing "So High You Can't Get Over It" softly. The babbling at the balustrade dies away as the people lean over the railing.* GABRIEL *turns and faces* GOD *indicating the earth below the railing with his left hand.*)

GABRIEL. Do you see it, Lawd?

GOD (*quietly, without turning his head upstage*). Yes, Gabriel.

GABRIEL. Looks mighty nice, Lawd.

GOD. Yes.

(GABRIEL *turns and looks over the railing.*)

GABRIEL (*gazing down*). Yes, suh. Dat'd make mighty nice farming country. Jest look at dat South forty over dere. You ain't going to let dat go to waste, is you, Lawd? Dat would be a pity an' a shame.

GOD (*not turning*). It's a good earth. (GOD *turns, room is made for him beside* GABRIEL *on the embankment*) Yes. I ought to have somebody to enjoy it. (*He turns, facing the audience. The others, save for the* CHOIR *who are lined up in two rows of six on an angle up right, continue to look over the embankment*) Gabriel! (GOD *steps down from the embankment two paces.*)

GABRIEL (*joining him*). Yes, Lawd.

GOD. Gabriel, I'm goin' down dere.

GABRIEL. Yes, Lawd.

GOD. I want you to be my working boss yere while I'm gone.

GABRIEL. Yes, Lawd.

GOD. You know dat matter of dem two stars?

GABRIEL. Yes, Lawd.

GOD. Git dat fixed up! You know dat sparrow dat fell a little while ago? 'Tend to dat, too.

GABRIEL. Yes, Lawd.

GOD. I guess dat's about all. I'll be back Saddy. (*To the* CHOIR) Quiet, angels. (*The* CHOIR *stops singing. Those on the embankment circle down stage.* GOD *goes to embankment. Turns and faces the company*) I'm gonter pass one more miracle. You all gonter help me an' not make a soun' caize it's one of de most impo'tant miracles of all. (*Nobody moves.* GOD *turns, facing the sky and raises his arms above his head*) Let there be man.

(*There is growing roll of thunder as stage grows dark. The* CHOIR *bursts into "Hallelujah," and continues until the lights go up on the next scene.*)

SCENE III

Enclosing the stage is a heterogeneous cluster of cottonwood, camphor, live oak and sycamore trees, yaupon and turkey-berry bushes, with their purple and red berries, sprays of fern-like indigo fiera and splashes of various Louisiana flowers. In the middle of the stage, disclosed when the mistiness at rise grows into warm sunlight, stands ADAM. *He is a puzzled man of 30, of medium height, dressed in the clothing of the average field hand. He is bare-headed. In the distance can be heard the choir continuing "Bright Mansions Above." A bird begins to sing.* ADAM *smiles and turns to look at the source of this novel sound. He senses his strength and raises his forearms, his fists clenched. With his left hand he carefully touches the muscles of his upper right arm. He smiles again, realizing his power. He looks at his feet which are stretched wide apart. He stamps once or twice and now almost laughs in his enjoyment. Other birds begin trilling and* ADAM *glances up joyfully toward the foliage.* GOD *enters.*

GOD. Good mo'nin', Son.

ADAM (*with a little awe*). Good mo'nin', Lawd.

GOD. What's yo' name, Son?

ADAM. Adam.

GOD. Adam which?

ADAM (*frankly, after a moment's puzzled groping*). Jest Adam, Lawd.

GOD. Well, Adam, how dey treatin' you? How things goin'?

ADAM. Well, Lawd, you know it's kind of a new line of wukk.

GOD. You'll soon get de hang of it. You know yo' kind of a new style with me.

ADAM. Oh, I guess I'm gonter make out all right soon as I learn de ropes.

GOD. Yes, I guess you will. Yo' a nice job.

ADAM. Yes, Lawd.

GOD. Dey's jest one little thing de matter with you. Did you notice it?

ADAM. Well, now you mentioned it, Lawd, I kind of thought dey was somethin' wrong.

GOD. Yes suh, you ain't quite right. Adam, you need a family. De reason for dat is in yo' heart you is a family man. (*Flicking the ash off his cigar*) I'd say dat was de main trouble at de moment.

ADAM (*smiling*). Yes sir. (*His smile fades and he is puzzled again*) At de same time—dey's one thing puzzlin' me, Lawd. Could I ask you a question?

GOD. Why, certainly, Adam.

ADAM. Lawd, jest what *is* a family?

GOD. I'm gonter show you. (*Indicates a spot*) Jest lie down dere, Adam. Make out you was goin' to slumber.

ADAM (*gently*). Yes, Lawd. (*He lies down.* GOD *stands beside him and as he raises his arms above his head the lights go down. In the darkness* GOD *speaks.*)

GOD. Eve. (*Lights go up.* EVE *is standing beside* ADAM. *She is about twenty-six, and quite pretty. She is dressed like a country girl. Her gingham dress is quite new and clean.* GOD *is now at the other side of the stage, looking at them critically.* EVE *looks at* ADAM *in timid wonder and slowly turns her head until she meets the glance of* GOD. ADAM *stands beside* EVE. *They gaze at each other for a moment.* GOD *smiles*) Now you all right, Eve. (ADAM *and* EVE *face him*) Now I'll tell you what I'm gonter do. I'm gonter put you in charge here. I'm gonter give you de run of dis whole garden. Eve, you take care of dis man an' Adam you take care of dis woman. You belong to each other. I don' want you to try to do too much caize yo' both kind of experiment wid me an' I ain't sho' whether you could make it. You two jest enjoy yo'self. Drink de water from de little brooks an' de wine from de grapes an' de berries, an' eat de food dat's hangin' for you in de trees. (*He pauses, startled by a painful thought*) Dat is, in all but one tree. (*He pauses. Then, not looking at them*) You know what I mean, my children?

ADAM *and* EVE. Yes, Lawd. (*They slowly turn their heads left, toward the branches of an off-stage tree. Then they look back at* GOD.)

ADAM. Thank you, Lawd.

EVE. Thank you, Lawd.

GOD. I gotter be gittin' along now. I got a hund'ed thousan' things to do 'fo' you take you' nex' breath. Enjoy yo'selves— (GOD *exits.*)
(ADAM *and* EVE *stand looking after Him for a moment, then each looks down and watches their hands meet and clasp. After a moment they lift their heads slowly until they are again gazing at the tree.*)

EVE. Adam.

ADAM (*looking at the tree, almost in terror*). What?

EVE (*softly as she too continues to look at the tree*). Adam.
(*The* CHOIR *begins singing "Turn You Round" and as the lights go down the* CHOIR *continues until there is blackness. The* CHOIR *suddenly stops. The following scene is played in the darkness.*)

MR. DESHEE'S VOICE. Now, I s'pose you chillun know what happened after God made Adam 'n' Eve. Do you?

FIRST GIRL'S VOICE. I know, Mr. Deshee.

MR. DESHEE'S VOICE. Jest a minute, Randolph. Didn't I tell you you gotta tell yo' mammy let yo' sister bring you. Carlisle, take way dat truck he's eatin'. You sit by him, see kin you keep him quiet. Now, den, Myrtle, what happened?

FIRST GIRL'S VOICE. Why, den dey ate de fo'bidden fruit and den dey got driv' out de garden.

MR. DESHEE'S VOICE. An' den what happened?

FIRST GIRL'S VOICE. Den dey felt ver' bad.

MR. DESHEE'S VOICE. I don' mean how dey feel, I mean how dey do. Do dey have any children or anything like dat?

FIRST GIRL'S VOICE. Oh, yes, suh, dey have Cain 'n' Abel.

MR. DESHEE'S VOICE. Dat's right, dey have Cain an' Abel.

BOY'S VOICE. Dat was a long time after dey got married, wasn't it, Mr. Deshee? My mammy say it was a hund'ed years.

MR. DESHEE'S VOICE. Well, nobody kin be so sure. As I tol' you befo' dey was jest beginnin' to be able to tell de time an' nobody was any too sure 'bout anythin' even den. So de bes' thing to do is jest realize dat de thing happened an' don't bother 'bout how many years it was. Jest remember what I told you about it gittin' dark when you go to sleep an' it bein' light when you wake up. Dat's de way time went by in dem days. One thing we do know an' dat was dis boy Cain was a mean rascal.
(*The lights go up on the next scene.*)

SCENE IV

A roadside.

CAIN, *a husky young Negro, stands over the body of the dead* ABEL. *Both are dressed as laborers.* CAIN *is looking at the body in awe, a rock in his right hand.* GOD *enters.*

GOD. Cain, look what you done to Abel.

CAIN. Lawd, I was min'in' my own business and he come monkeyin' aroun' wit' me. I was wukkin' in de fiel' an' he was sittin' in de shade of de tree. He say "Me, I'd be skeered to git out in dis hot sun. I be 'fraid my brains git cooked. Co'se you ain't got no brains so you ain't in no danger." An' so I up and flang de rock. If it miss 'im all right, an' if it hit 'im, all right. Dat's de way I feel.

GOD. All right, but I'm yere to tell you dat's called a crime. When de new Judge is done talkin' to you

you'll be draggin' a ball and chain de rest of yo' life.

CAIN. Well, what'd he want to come monkeyin' aroun' me fo' den? I was jest plowin', min'in' my own business, and not payin' him no min', and yere he come makin' me de fool. I'd bust anybody what make me de fool.

GOD. Well, I ain't sayin' you right an' I ain't sayin' you wrong. But I do say was I you I'd jest git myself down de road 'til I was clean out of de county. An' you better take an' git married an' settle down an' raise some chillun. Dey ain't nothin' to make a man fo'git his troubles like raisin' a family. Now, you better git.

CAIN. Yessuh. (CAIN *walks off.*)
(GOD *watches him from the forestage and as the lights begin to dim looks off. The* CHOIR *begins "Run, Sinner, Run."*)

GOD. Adam an' Eve, you better try again. You better have Seth an' a lot mo' chillun.
(*There is darkness. The* CHOIR *continues until the lights go up on the next scene.*)

SCENE V

CAIN *is discovered walking on an unseen treadmill. A middle distance of trees, hillsides and shrubbery passes him on an upper treadmill. Behind is the blue sky. He stops under the branches of a tree to look at a sign on a fence railing. Only half the tree is visible on the stage. The sign reads,* "NOD PARISH, COUNTY LINE."

CAIN (*sitting down with a sigh of relief under the tree*). At las'! Phew! (*Wipes his forehead with a handkerchief*) Feels like I been walkin' fo'ty years. (*He looks back*) Well, dey cain' git me now. Now I kin raise a fam'ly. (*An idea occurs to him, and suddenly he begins looking right and left*) Well, I'll be hit by a mule! Knock me down for a trustin' baby! Where I gonter git dat fam'ly? Dat preacher fooled me. (*He is quite dejected*) Doggone!

CAIN'S GIRL (*off-stage*). Hello, Country Boy!
(CAIN *glances up to the off-stage branches of the tree.*)

CAIN. Hey-ho, Good lookin'! Which way is it to town?

CAIN'S GIRL (*off-stage*). What you tryin' to do? You tryin' to mash me? I be doggone if it ain't gittin' so a gal cain't hardly leave de house 'out some of dese fast men ain' passin' remarks at her.

CAIN. I ain' passin' remarks.

CAIN'S GIRL (*off-stage*). If I thought you was tryin' to mash me, I'd call de police an' git you tooken to de first precinct.

CAIN. Look yere, gal, I ast you a question, an' if you don' answer me

I'm gonter bend you 'cross my pants an' burn you up.

CAIN'S GIRL (*off-stage*). I'm comin' down.
(CAIN *takes his eyes from the tree.*)

CAIN. Yes, an' you better hurry.
(CAIN'S GIRL *enters. She is as large as* CAIN, *wickedly pretty, and somewhat flashily dressed. She smiles at* CAIN.)

CAIN'S GIRL. I bet you kin handle a gal mean wid dem big stout arms of your'n. I sho' would hate to git you mad at me, Country Boy.

CAIN (*smiling*). Come yere. (*She goes a little closer to him*) Don't be 'fraid, I ain' so mean.

CAIN'S GIRL. You got two bad-lookin' eyes. I bet yo' hot coffee 'mong de women folks.

CAIN. I ain' never find out. What was you doin' in dat tree?

CAIN'S GIRL. Jest coolin' myself in de element.

CAIN. Is you a Nod Parish gal?

CAIN'S GIRL. Bo'n an' bred.

CAIN. You know yo' kinda pretty.

CAIN'S GIRL. Who tol' you dat?

CAIN. Dese yere two bad eyes of mine.

CAIN'S GIRL. I bet you say dat to everybody all de way down de road.

CAIN. Comin' down dat road I didn't talk to nobody.

CAIN'S GIRL. Where you boun' for, Beautiful?

CAIN. I'm jest seein' de country. I thought I might settle down yere fo' a spell. You live wit' yo' people?

CAIN'S GIRL. Co'se I does.

CAIN. S'pose dey'd like to take in a boarder?

CAIN'S GIRL. Be nice if dey would, wouldn't it?

CAIN. I think so. You got a beau?

CAIN'S GIRL. Huh-uh!

CAIN (*smiling*). You has *now.*

CAIN'S GIRL. I guess—I guess if you wanted to kiss me an' I tried to stop you, you could pretty nearly crush me wit' dem stout arms.

CAIN. You wouldn't try too much, would you?

CAIN'S GIRL. Maybe for a little while.

CAIN. An' den what?

CAIN'S GIRL. Why don' we wait an' see?

CAIN. When would dat be?

CAIN'S GIRL. Tonight. After supper. Think you kin walk a little further now, City Boy?

CAIN. Yeh, I ain't so weary now.
(*She takes his hand.*)

CAIN'S GIRL. What yo' name? (*Takes his arm.*)

CAIN. Cain.

CAIN'S GIRL. Den I'm Cain's Gal. Come on, honey, an' meet de folks. (*They exit. The* CHOIR *is heard singing "You Better Mind," as* GOD *enters.* GOD *watches the vanished* CAIN *and his girl.*)

GOD (*after shaking his head*). Bad business. I don' like de way things is goin' atall.

(*The stage is darkened. The* CHOIR *continues singing until the lights go up on the next scene.*)

SCENE VI

GOD'S *private office in Heaven. It is a small room, framed by tableau curtains. A large window up center looks out on the sky. There is a battered roll-top desk. On the wall next to the window is a framed religious oleograph with a calendar attached to it underneath. A door is at the left. A hat rack is on the wall above the door. There are two or three cheap pine chairs beside the window, and beyond the door. In front of the desk is an old swivel armchair which creaks every time* GOD *leans back in it. The desk is open and various papers are stuck in the pigeonholes. Writing implements, etc. are on the desk. On a shelf above the desk is a row of law books. A cuspidor is near the desk, and a waste basket by it. The general atmosphere is that of the office of a Negro lawyer in a Louisiana town. As the lights go up* GOD *takes a fresh cigar from a box on the desk and begins puffing it without bothering to light it. There is no comment on this minor miracle from* GABRIEL *who is sitting in one of the chairs with a pencil and several papers in his hand. The singing becomes pianissimo.*

GABRIEL (*looking at the papers*). Well, I guess dat's about all de impo'tant business dis mornin', Lawd.

GOD. How 'bout dat cherub over to Archangel Montgomery's house?

GABRIEL. Where do dey live, Lawd? (*The singing stops.*)

GOD. Dat little two-story gold house, over by de pearly gates.

GABRIEL. Oh, *dat* Montgomery. I thought you was referrin' to de ol' gentleman. Oh, yeh. (*He sorts through the papers and finds one he is looking for*) Yere 'tis. (*Reads*) "Cherub Christina Montgomery; wings is moltin' out of season an' nobody knows what to do."

GOD. Well, now, take keer of dat. You gotter be more careful, Gabe.

GABRIEL. Yes, Lawd. (*Folds the papers and puts them in a pocket.* GOD *turns to his desk, takes another puff or two of the cigar, and with a pencil, begins checking off items on a sheet of paper before him. His back is turned toward* GABRIEL. GABRIEL *takes his trumpet from the hat rack and burnishes it with his robe. He then wets his lips and puts the mouthpiece to his mouth.*)

GOD (*without turning around*). Now, watch yo'self, Gabriel.

GABRIEL. I wasn't goin' to blow, Lawd. I jest do dat every now an' den so I can keep de feel of it. (*He leans trumpet against the wall.* GOD *picks up the papers and swings his chair around toward* GABRIEL.)

GOD. What's dis yere about de moon?

GABRIEL (*suddenly remembering*). Oh! De moon people say it's beginnin' to melt a little, on 'count caize de sun's so hot.

GOD. It's goin' 'roun' 'cordin' to schedule, ain't it?

GABRIEL. Yes, Lawd.

GOD. Well, tell 'em to stop groanin'. Dere's nothin' de matter wid dat moon. Trouble is so many angels is flyin' over dere on Saddy night. Dey git to beatin' dere wings when dey dancin' an' dat makes de heat. Tell dem dat from now on dancin' 'roun' de moon is sinnin'. Dey got to stop it. Dat'll cool off de moon. (*He swings back and puts the paper on the desk. He leans back in the chair comfortably, his hands clasped behind his head*) Is dere anythin' else you ought to remin' me of?

GABRIEL. De prayers, Lawd.

GOD (*puzzled, slowly swinging chair around again*). De prayers?

GABRIEL. From mankind. You know, down on de earth.

GOD. Oh, yeh, de poor little earth. Bless my soul, I almos' forgot about dat. Mus' be three or four hund'ed years since I been down dere. I wasn't any too pleased wid dat job.

GABRIEL (*laughing*). You know you don' make mistakes, Lawd.

GOD (*soberly, with introspective detachment*). So dey tell me. (*He looks at* GABRIEL, *then through the window again*) So dey tell me. I fin' I kin be displeased though, an' I was displeased wid de mankind I las' seen. Maybe I ought to go down dere again—I need a little holiday.

GABRIEL. Might do you good, Lawd.

GOD. I think I will. I'll go down an' walk de earth agin an' see how dem poor humans is makin' out. What time is it, by de sun an' de stars?

GABRIEL (*glancing out of the window*). Jest exactly half-past, Lawd. (GOD *is taking his hat and stick from the hat rack.*)

GOD (*opening the door*). Well, take keer o' yo'self. I'll be back Saddy. (*He exits.*)
(*The stage is darkened. The* CHOIR *begins "Dere's No Hidin' Place," and continues until the lights go up on the next scene.*)

SCENE VII

GOD *is walking along a country road. He stops to listen. Church bells are heard in the distance.*

GOD. Dat's nice. Nice an' quiet. Dat's de way I like Sunday to be. (*The sound is broken by a shrill voice of a girl. It is* ZEBA *singing a "blues."*) Now, dat ain't so good. (GOD *resumes his walk and the upper treadmill brings on a tree stump on which* ZEBA *is sitting. She is accompanying her song with a ukulele.* GOD *and the treadmill stop. When the stump reaches the center of the stage, it is seen that* ZEBA *is a rouged and extremely flashily dressed chippy of about eighteen*) Stop dat!

ZEBA. What's de matter wid you, Country Boy? Pull up yo' pants. (*She resumes singing.*)

GOD. Stop dat!

ZEBA (*stops again*). Say, listen to me, Banjo Eyes. What right you got to stop a lady enjoyin' herself?

GOD. Don't you know dis is de Sabbath? Da's no kin' o' song to sing on de Lawd's day.

ZEBA. Who care 'bout de Lawd's day, anymo'? People jest use Sunday now to git over Saddy.

GOD. You a awful sassy little girl.

ZEBA. I come fum sassy people! We even speak mean of de dead.

GOD. What's yo' name?

ZEBA (*flirtatiously*). "What's my name?" Ain't you de ol'-time gal hunter! Fust, "What's my name?" den I s'pose, what would it be like if you tried to kiss me? You preachers is de debbils.

GOD. I ain't aimin' to touch you, daughter. (*A sudden sternness frightens* ZEBA. *She looks at him sharply*) What is yo' name?

ZEBA. Zeba.

GOD. Who's yo' fam'ly?

ZEBA. I'm de great-great gran' daughter of Seth.

GOD. Of Seth? But Seth was a good man.

ZEBA. Yeh, he too good, he die of holiness.

GOD. An' yere's his little gran' daughter reekin' wid cologne. Ain't nobody ever tol' you yo' on de road to Hell?

ZEBA (*smiling*). Sho', dat's what de preacher say. Exceptin' of course, I happens to know dat I'm on de road to de picnic groun's, an' at de present time I'm waitin' to keep a engagement wid my sweet papa. He don' like people talkin' to me.
(CAIN THE SIXTH *enters. He is a young buck, wearing a "box" coat and the other flashy garments of a Rampart Street swell.*)

CAIN THE SIXTH. Hello, sugah! (*He crosses in front of* GOD *and faces* ZEBA) Hello, mamma! Sorry I'm late, baby, but de gals in de barrelhouse jest wouldn't let me go. Doggone, one little wirehead swore she'd tear me down.
(ZEBA *smiles and takes his hand.*)

GOD. What's yo' name, son?

CAIN THE SIXTH (*contemptuously; without turning*). Soap 'n' water, Country Boy.

GOD (*sternly*). What's yo' name, son? (CAIN *slowly turns and for a moment his manner is civil.*)

CAIN THE SIXTH. Cain the Sixth.

GOD. I was afraid so.

CAIN THE SIXTH (*his impudence returning*). You a new preacher?

GOD. Where you live?

CAIN THE SIXTH. Me, I live mos' any place.

GOD. Yes, an' you gonter see dem all. Is de udder young men all like you?

CAIN THE SIXTH (*smiling*). De gals don' think so. (*He turns towards* ZEBA *again, picks her up and sits on the stump with the laughing* ZEBA *on his lap.*)

ZEBA. Dey ain't nobody in de worl' like my honey-cake.
(CAIN *kisses her and she resumes her song.* GOD *watches them.* ZEBA *finishes a verse of the song and begins another softly.* CAIN THE SIXTH'*s eyes have been closed during the singing.*)

CAIN THE SIXTH (*his eyes closed*). Is de preacher gone?
(ZEBA *looks quickly at* GOD *without seeing him, and then looks off. She stops the song.*)

ZEBA. Yeh, I guess he walks fast.
(CAIN *pushes her off his lap and rises.*)

CAIN THE SIXTH (*with acid sweetness*). Dey tell me las' night you was talkin' to a creeper man, baby.

ZEBA. Why, you know dey ain't nobody in de world fo' me but you.

CAIN THE SIXTH (*smiling*). I know dey ain't. I even got dat guaranteed. (*Takes a revolver from his pocket*) See dat, baby?

ZEBA. Sho' I see it, honey.

CAIN THE SIXTH. Dat jest makes me positive. (*Puts the gun back.*)

ZEBA (*pushing him back on the stump*). You don' wanter believe dem stories, papa.

CAIN THE SIXTH (*with sinister lightness*). No, I didn't believe dem, baby. Co'se dat big gorilla, Flatfoot, from de other side of de river *is* in town ag'in.

ZEBA. Dat don' mean nothin'. Flatfoot ain't nothin' to me.

CAIN THE SIXTH (*sitting again*) Co'se he ain't. Go' head, sing some mo', baby.
(ZEBA *resumes singing.*)

GOD. Bad business. (*The treadmills start turning.* GOD *resumes his walk.* ZEBA, *still singing, and* CAIN THE SIXTH *recede with the landscape.* GOD *is again alone on the country road. There is a twitter of birds.* GOD *looks up and smiles*) De birds is goin' 'bout dere business, all right. (*A patch of flowers goes by, black-eyed Susans, conspicuously*) How you flowers makin' out? (CHILDREN'S *voices answer, "We O. K., Lawd."*) Yes, an' you looks very pretty. (CHILDREN'S *voices: "Thank you, Lawd." The flowers pass out of sight.*) It's only de human bein's makes me downhearted. Yere's as nice a Sunday as dey is turnin' out anywhere, an' nobody makin' de right use of it. (*Something ahead of him attracts his attention. His face brightens*) Well, now dis is mo' like it. Now dat's nice to see people prayin'. It's a wonder dey don' do it in de church. But I fin' I don' min' it if dey do it outdoors.

(*A group of five adult Negroes and a boy on their knees in a semicircle appears. The treadmills stop. The* BOY, *his head bent, swings his hands rhythmically up to his head three or four times. There is a hush.*)

GAMBLER. Oh, Lawd, de smoke-house is empty. Oh, Lawd, lemme git dem groceries. Oh, Lawd, lemme see dat little *six.* (*He casts the dice*) Wham! Dere she is, frien's.

(*Exclamations from the others: "Well damn my eyes!" "Doggone, dat's de eighth pass he make." "For God's sake, can't you ever crap?" etc. The* BOY *is picking up the money.*)

GOD. Gamblin'! (*Looks over the group's shoulders*) An' wid frozen dice!

BOY GAMBLER. Dey's a dolla' 'n' a half talkin' fo' me. How much you want of it, Riney?

FIRST GAMBLER. I take fo' bits. Wait a minute. Mebbe I take a little mo'. (*He counts some money in his hand.*)

SECOND GAMBLER (*glancing up at* GOD). Hello, Liver Lips. (*To the others*) Looka ol' Liver Lips.

(*The others look up and laugh good-naturedly, repeating "Liver Lips."*)

FIRST GAMBLER. Ain't his pockets high from de groun'? Ol' High-Pockets.

(*The others keep saying "Ol' Liver Lips." "Ol' Liver Lips don't like to see people dicin'." "Dat's a good name, 'High Pockets'."*)

BOY GAMBLER (*to others*). Come on, you gonter fade me or not?

(GOD *seizes the* BOY'*s ears and drags him to his feet. The others do not move, but watch amused.*)

GOD. Come yere, son. Why, yo' jest a little boy. Gamblin' an' sinnin'. (GOD *looks at the* BOY'*s face*) You been chewin' tobacco, too, like you was yo' daddy. (GOD *sniffs*) An' you been drinkin' sonny-kick-mammy-wine. You oughta be 'shamed. (*To the others*) An' you gamblers oughta be 'shamed, leadin' dis boy to sin.

FIRST GAMBLER. He de bes' crap shooter in town, mister.

GOD. I'm gonter tell his mammy. I bet she don' know 'bout dis.

FIRST GAMBLER. No, she don' know. (*The others laugh*) She don' know anythin'.

SECOND GAMBLER. Das de God's truth.

FIRST GAMBLER. See kin you beat 'im, High Pockets. Dey's a dolla' open yere.

GOD. I ain't gonter beat 'im. I'm gonter teach 'im. I may have to teach you all. (*He starts walking from them. The* BOY *sticks out his tongue the moment* GOD'*s back is turned.*)

BOY GAMBLER. If you fin' my mammy you do mo'n I kin. Come on, gamblers, see kin you gimme a little action. Who wants any part of dat dollar?

(*The treadmill carries them off. The* FIRST GAMBLER *is heard saying: "I'll take another two bits," and the others, "Gimme a dime's wo'th," "I ain't only got fifteen cents left," etc. as they disappear.*)

GOD (*walking*). Where's dat little boy's home? (*The front of a shanty appears and* GOD *stops in front of the door*) Yere's de place. It ain't any too clean, either. (*Knocks on the door with his cane.*)

VOICE IN SHANTY. Who dar?

GOD. Never you min' who's yere. Open de door.

VOICE IN SHANTY. You gotta search warrant?

GOD. I don' need one.

VOICE IN SHANTY. Who you wanter see?

GOD. I wanter see de mammy of de little gamblin' boy.

VOICE IN SHANTY. You mean little Johnny Rucker?

GOD. Dat may be his name.

VOICE IN SHANTY. Well, Mrs. Rucker ain't home.

GOD. Where's she at?

VOICE IN SHANTY. Who, Mrs. Rucker?

GOD. You heerd me.

VOICE IN SHANTY. Oh, she run away las' night wid a railroad man. She's eloped.

GOD. Where's Rucker?

VOICE IN SHANTY. He's flat under de table. He so drunk he cain't move.

GOD. Who are you?

VOICE IN SHANTY. I'se jest a fren' an' neighbor. I come in las' night to de party, an' everybody in yere's dead drunk but me. De only reason I kin talk is I drank some new white mule I made myself, an' it burn my throat so I cain't drink no mo'. You got any mo' questions?

GOD. Not for you.
(*The shanty begins to move off as* GOD *starts walking again.*)

VOICE IN SHANTY. Good riddance, I say.
(*Shanty disappears.*)

GOD. Dis ain't gittin' me nowheres. All I gotta say dis yere mankind I been peoplin' my earth wid sho' ain't much. (*He stops and looks back*) I got good min' to wipe 'em all off an' people de earth wid angels. No. Angels is all right, singin' an' playin' an' flyin' around, but dey ain't much on workin' de crops and buildin' de levees. No, suh, mankind's jest right for my earth, if he wasn't so doggone sinful. I'd rather have my earth peopled wit' a bunch of channel catfish, dan I would mankin' an' his sin. I jest can't stan' sin. (*He is about to resume his walk when* NOAH *enters.* NOAH *is dressed like a country preacher. His coat is of the "hammer-tail" variety. He carries a prayer book under his arm.*)

NOAH. Mo'nin', brother.

GOD. Mo'nin', brother. I declare you look like a good man.

NOAH. I try to be, brother. I'm de preacher yere. I don't think I seen you to de meetin'.
(*They resume walking.*)

GOD. I jest come to town a little while ago an' I been pretty busy.

NOAH. Yeh, mos' everybody say dey's pretty busy dese days. Dey so busy dey cain't come to meetin'. It seem like de mo' I preaches de mo' people ain't got time to come to church. I ain't hardly got enough members to fill up de choir. I gotta do de preachin' an' de bassin' too.

GOD. Is dat a fac'?

NOAH. Yes, suh, brother. Everybody is mighty busy, gamblin', good-timin', an' goin' on. You jest wait, though. When Gabriel blow de horn you gonter fin' dey got plenty of time to punch chunks down in Hell. Yes, suh.

GOD. Seems a pity. Dey all perfec'ly healthy?

NOAH. Oh, dey healthy, all right. Dey jest all lazy, and mean, and full of sin. You look like a preacher, too, brother.

GOD. Well, I am, in a way.

NOAH. You jest passin' through de neighborhood?

GOD. Yes. I wanted to see how things was goin' in yo' part of de country, an' I been feelin' jest 'bout de way you do. It's enough to discourage you.

NOAH. Yes, but I gotta keep wres'lin' wid 'em. Where you boun' for right now, brother?

GOD. I was jest walkin' along. I thought I might stroll on to de nex' town.

NOAH. Well, dat's a pretty good distance. I live right yere. (*He stops walking*) Why don' you stop an' give us de pleasure of yo' comp'ny for dinner? I believe my ol' woman has kilt a chicken.

GOD. Why, dat's mighty nice of you, brother. I don' believe I caught yo' name.

NOAH. Noah, jest brother Noah. Dis is my home, brother. Come right in. (GOD *and* NOAH *start walking towards* NOAH*'s house which is just coming into view on the treadmill. The stage darkens, the* CHOIR *sings "Feastin' Table," and when the lights go up again, the next scene is disclosed.*)

SCENE VIII

Interior of NOAH*'s house. The ensemble suggests the combination living-dining room in a fairly prosperous Negro's cabin. Clean white curtains hang at the window. A table and chairs are in the center of the room. There is a cheerful checked tablecloth on the table, and on the wall, a framed, highly colored picture reading "God Bless Our Home."*

NOAH'S WIFE, *an elderly Negress, simply and neatly dressed,* GOD *and* NOAH *are discovered grouped about the table.*

NOAH. Company, darlin'. (NOAH's WIFE *takes* NOAH's *and* GOD's *hats*) Dis gemman's a preacher, too. He's jest passin' through de country.

GOD. Good mo'nin', sister.

NOAH'S WIFE. Good mo'nin'. You jest ketch me when I'm gittin' dinner ready. You gonter stay with us?

GOD. If I ain't intrudin'. Brother Noah suggested—

NOAH'S WIFE. You set right down yere. I got a chicken in de pot an' it'll be ready in 'bout five minutes. I'll go out de back an' call Shem, Ham an' Japheth. (*To* GOD) Dey's our sons. Dey live right acrost de way but always have Sunday dinner wid us. You mens make yo'selves comf'table.

GOD. Thank you, thank you very kindly.

NOAH. You run along, we all right. (GOD *and* NOAH *seat themselves.* NOAH'S WIFE *exits.*)

GOD. You got a fine wife, Brother Noah.

NOAH. She pretty good woman.

GOD. Yes, suh, an' you got a nice little home. Have a ten cent seegar? (GOD *offers him one.*)

NOAH. Thank you, much obliged. (*Both men lean back restfully in their chairs.*)

GOD. Jest what seems to be de main trouble 'mong mankind, Noah?

NOAH. Well, it seems to me de main trouble is dat de whol' distric' is wide open. Now you know dat makes fo' loose livin'. Men folks spen's all dere time fightin', loafin' an' gamblin', an' makin' bad likker.

GOD. What about de women?

NOAH. De women is worse dan de men. If dey ain't makin' love powder dey out beg-borrow-an'-stealin' money for policy tickets. Doggone, I come in de church Sunday 'fo' las' 'bout an hour befo' de meetin' was to start, and dere was a woman stealin' de altar cloth. She was goin' to hock it. Dey ain't got no moral sense. Now you take dat case las' month, over in East Putney. Case of dat young Willy Roback.

GOD. What about him?

NOAH. Dere is a boy seventeen years old. Doggone, if he didn't elope with his aunt. Now, you know, dat kin' of goin' on is bad fo' a neighborhood.

GOD. Terrible, terrible.

NOAH. Yes, suh. Dis use' to be a nice, decent community. I been doin' my best to preach de Word, but seems like every time I preach de place jest goes a little mo' to de dogs. De good Lawd only knows what's gonter happen.

GOD. Dat is de truth.
(*There is a pause. Each puffs his cigar. Suddenly* NOAH *grasps his knee, as if it were paining him, and twists his foot.*)

NOAH. Huh!

GOD. What's de matter?

NOAH. I jest got a twitch. My buck-aguer I guess. Every now and den I gets a twitch in de knee. Might be a sign of rain.

GOD. That's just what it is. Noah, what's de mos' rain you ever had 'round dese parts?

NOAH. Well, de water come down fo' six days steady last April an' de ribber got so swole it bust down de levee up 'bove Freeport. Raise cain all de way down to de delta.

GOD. What would you say was it to rain for forty days and forty nights?

NOAH. I'd say dat was a *complete* rain!

GOD. Noah, you don't know who I is, do you?

NOAH (*puzzled*). Yo' face looks easy, but I don' think I recall de name. (GOD *rises slowly, and as he reaches his full height there is a crash of lightning, a moment's darkness, and a roll of thunder. It grows light again.* NOAH *is on his knees in front of* GOD) I should have known you. I should have seen de glory.

GOD. Dat's all right, Noah. You didn't know who I was.

NOAH. I'm jes' ol' preacher Noah, Lawd, an' I'm yo servant. I ain' very much, but I'se all I got.

GOD. Sit down, Noah. Don' let me hear you shamin' yo'se'f, caize yo' a good man. (*Timidly* NOAH *waits until* GOD *is seated, and then sits, himself*) I jest wanted to fin' out if you was good, Noah. Dat's why I'm walkin' de earth in de shape of a natchel man. I wish dey was mo' people like you. But, far as I kin see, you and yo' fam'ly is de only respectable people in de worl'.

NOAH. Dey jest all poor sinners, Lawd.

GOD. I know. I am your Lawd. I am a god of wrath and vengeance an' dat's why I'm gonter destroy dis worl'.

NOAH (*almost in a whisper; drawing back*). Jest as you say, Lawd.

GOD. I ain't gonter destroy you, Noah. You and yo' fam'ly, yo' sheep an' cattle, an' all de udder things dat ain't human I'm gonter preserve. But de rest is gotta go. (*Takes a pencil and a sheet of paper from his pocket*) Look yere, Noah. (NOAH *comes over and looks over his shoulder*) I want you to build me a boat. I want you to call it de "Ark," and I want it to look like dis. (*He is drawing on the paper. Continues to write as he speaks*) I want you to take two of every kind of animal and bird dat's in de country. I want you to take seeds an' sprouts an' everythin' like dat an' put dem on dat Ark, because dere is gonter be all dat rain. Dey's gonter be a deluge, Noah, an' dey's goin' to be a flood. De levees is gonter bust an' everything dat's fastened down is comin' loose, but it ain't gonter float long, caize I'm gonter make a storm dat'll sink everythin' from a hencoop to a barn. Dey ain't a ship on de sea dat'll be able to fight dat tempest. Dey all got to go. Everythin'. Everythin' in dis pretty worl' I made, except one thing, Noah. You an' yo' fam'ly an' de things I said are going to ride dat storm in de Ark. Yere's de way it's to be. (*He hands* NOAH *the paper.* NOAH *takes it and reads.*)

NOAH (*pause; looks at paper again*). Yes, suh, dis seems to be complete. Now 'bout the animals, Lawd, you say you want everythin'?

GOD. Two of everythin'.

NOAH. Dat would include jayraffes an' hippopotamusses?

GOD. Everythin' dat is.

NOAH. Dey was a circus in town las' week. I guess I kin fin' dem. Co'se I kin git all de rabbits an' possums an' wil' turkeys easy. I'll sen' de boys out. Hum, I'm jest wonderin'—

GOD. 'Bout what?

NOAH. 'Bout snakes. Think you'd like snakes, too?

GOD. Certainly, I want snakes.

NOAH. Oh, I kin git snakes, lots of 'em. Co'se, some of 'em's a little dangerous. Maybe I better take a kag of likker, too?

GOD. You kin have a kag of likker.

NOAH (*musingly*). Yes, suh, dey's a awful lot of differ'nt kin's of snakes, come to think about it. Dey's water moccasins, cotton-moufs, rattlers—mus' be a hund'ed kin's of other snakes down in de swamps. Maybe I better take two kags of likker.

GOD (*mildly*). I think de one kag's enough.

NOAH. No. I better take two kags. Besides I kin put one on each side of de boat, an' balance de ship wid dem as well as havin' dem fo' medicinal use.

GOD. You kin put one kag in de middle of de ship.

NOAH (*buoyantly*). Jest as easy to take de two kags, Lawd.

GOD. I think one kag's enough.

NOAH. Yes, Lawd, but you see, forty days an' forty nights—
(*There is a distant roll of thunder.*)

GOD (*firmly*). One kag, Noah.

NOAH. Yes, Lawd. One kag.
(*The door in the back opens and* NOAH'S WIFE *enters with a tray of dishes and food.*)

NOAH'S WIFE. Now, den, gen'lemen, if you'll jest draw up cheers.
(*The stage is darkened. The* CHOIR *is heard singing "I Want to Be Ready." They continue in the darkness until the lights go up on the next scene.*)

SCENE IX

In the middle of the stage is the Ark. On the hillside, below the Ark, a dozen or more men and women, townspeople, are watching NOAH. SHEM, HAM *and* JAPHETH *on the deck of the Ark. The three sons are busily nailing boards on the cabin.* NOAH *is smoking a pipe. He wears a silk hat, captain's uniform and a "slicker."*

NOAH (*to* SHEM). You, Shem, tote up some ol' rough lumber, don' bring up any planed-up lumber, caize dat ain't fo' de main deck.

SHEM. Pretty near supper time, daddy.

NOAH. Maybe 'tis, but I got de feelin' we ought to keep goin'.

FIRST WOMAN. You gonter work all night, Noah, maybe, huh?

NOAH (*without looking at her*). If de sperit move me.

SECOND WOMAN. Look yere, Noah, whyn't you give up all dis damn foolishness? Don' you know people sayin' yo' crazy? What you think you doin' anyway?

NOAH. I'se buildin' a Ark. (*Other men and women join those in the foreground*) Ham, you better stop for a while 'n' see whether dey bringin' de animals up all right. (*He looks at his watch*) Dey ought to be pretty near de foot o' de hill by dis time; if dey ain't you wait fo' dem and bring 'em yo'sef.

(HAM *goes down a ladder at the side of the ship and exits during the following scene. The newcomers in group have been speaking to some of the early arrivals.*)

SECOND WOMAN (*to* THIRD WOMAN, *one of the newcomers*). No, you don't mean it!

THIRD WOMAN. I do so. Dat's what de talk is in de town.

FIRST WOMAN. You hear dat, Noah? Dey say yo' ol' lady is tellin' everybody it's gonter rain fo' fo'ty days and fo'ty nights. You know people soon gonter git de idea you *all* crazy.

NOAH. Lot I keer what you think. (*To* JAPHETH) Straighten up dem boards down dere, Japheth. (*Indicates floor of deck.*)

FIRST WOMAN (*to* THIRD WOMAN). Was I you, I wouldn' go 'round with Mrs. Noah anymore, lady. Fust thing you know you'll be gittin' a hard name, too.

THIRD WOMAN. Don' I know?

SECOND WOMAN. A lady cain't be too partic'lar these days.

(ZEBA *and* FLATFOOT, *a tall, black. wicked-looking buck, enter, their arms around each other's waists.*)

ZEBA. Dere it is, baby. Was I lyin'?

FLATFOOT. Well, I'll be split in two!

FIRST MAN. What you think of it, Flatfoot?

FLATFOOT. I must say! Look like a house wit' a warpin' cellar.

NOAH. Dis yere vessel is a boat.

FLATFOOT. When I was a little boy dey used to build boats down near de ribber, where de water was.

(*The others laugh.*)

NOAH. Dis time it's been arranged to have de water come up to de boat. (JAPHETH *looks belligerently over the rail of the Ark at* FLATFOOT. *To* JAPHETH) Keep yo' shirt on, son.

SECOND WOMAN (*to* THIRD WOMAN). Now, you see de whole fam'ly's crazy.

THIRD WOMAN. Listen, dey ain't gonter 'taminate me. It was me dat started resolvin' dem both out o' de buryin' society.

ZEBA. When all dis water due up yere, Noah?

NOAH. You won't know when it gits yere, daughter.

ZEBA. Is she goin' to be a side-wheeler, like de Bessy-Belle?

FLATFOOT. No! If she was a side-wheeler she'd get her wheels all clogged wid sharks. She gonter have jus' one great big stern wheel, like de Commodore. Den if dey ain't 'nuf water why de big wheel kin stir some up.

(*General laughter. Two or three of the* GAMBLERS *enter and join the group, followed by* CAIN THE SIXTH.)

CAIN THE SIXTH. Dere's de fool an' his monument, jest like I said.

(*The* GAMBLERS *and* CAIN THE SIXTH *roar with laughter, slap their legs, etc., the members of the main group talk sotto voce to each other as* CAIN THE SIXTH *catches* ZEBA'S *eye.* FLATFOOT *is on her right and is not aware of* CAIN THE SIXTH'S *presence.*)

NOAH. See how dey makin' out inside, son. (*Stops hammering.* JAPHETH *exits into Ark.* NOAH *turns and gazes towards the east.*)

CAIN THE SIXTH. Hello, honey.

ZEBA (*frightened but smiling*). Hello, sugah.

CAIN THE SIXTH (*pleasantly*). Ain' dat my ol' frien' Flatfoot wid you?

ZEBA. Why, so 'tis! (FLATFOOT *is now listening. To* FLATFOOT) He's got a gun.

CAIN THE SIXTH. No, I ain't. (*He lifts his hands over his head.* ZEBA *quickly advances and runs her hands lightly over his pockets.*)

ZEBA (*relieved*). I guess he ain't.

CAIN THE SIXTH. No, I ain't got a gun for my ol' friend, Flatfoot. (*He walks up to him.*)

FLATFOOT (*smiling*). Hi, Cain. How's de boy?

(CAIN *quickly presses his chest against* FLATFOOT'S, *his downstage arm sweeps around* FLATFOOT'S *body and his hand goes up to the small of* FLATFOOT'S *back.*)

CAIN THE SIXTH (*quietly, but triumphantly*). I got a little *knife* fo' him.

(FLATFOOT *falls dead. The laughter of the others stops and they look at the scene.* ZEBA *for a moment is terrified, her clenched hand pressed to her mouth. She looks at* CAIN THE SIXTH, *who is smiling at her. He tosses the knife on the ground and holds his hands out to her. She goes to him, smiling.*)

ZEBA. You sho' take keer of me, honey.

CAIN THE SIXTH. Dat's caize I think yo' wo'th takin' keer of. (*To the others*) It's all right, folks. I jest had to do a little cleanin' up.

FIRST WOMAN (*smiling*). You is de quickes' scoundrel.

FIRST GAMBLER. It was a nice quick killin'. Who was he?

SECOND WOMAN (*casually*). Dey called him Flatfoot. From over de river. He wa'nt any good. He owed me for washin' for over a year.

THIRD WOMAN. Used to peddle muggles. Said it had a kick like reg'lar snow. Wasn't no good.

SECOND GAMBLER. Think we ought to bury him?

FIRST MAN. No, just leave him dere. Nobody comes up yere, 'cept ol' Manatee. (*Indicates* NOAH. *Cries of "Ol' Manatee! Ol' Manatee, dat's good!"*)

NOAH (*still looking off*). You bettah pray, you po' chillun.
(*They all laugh.*)

FIRST WOMAN. We bettah pray? You bettah pray, Ol' Manatee!

ZEBA. You bettah pray for rain.
(*Laughter again.*)

NOAH. Dat's what I ain't doin', sinners. Shem! Japheth! (*To others, as he points off. Patter of rain*) Listen!

CAIN THE SIXTH (*casually*). Doggone, I believe it *is* gonter shower a little.

FIRST GAMBLER. It do look like rain.

FIRST WOMAN. I think I'll git on home. I got a new dress on.

ZEBA. Me, too. I wants to keep lookin' nice fo' my sweet papa. (*She pats* CAIN THE SIXTH'S *cheek.* CAIN THE SIXTH *hugs her.*)

NOAH (*almost frantically*). Ham! Is de animals dere?

HAM (*offstage*). Yes, sir, dere yere. We're comin'.

NOAH. Den bring 'em on.
(SHEM *and* JAPHETH *come on deck with their hammers. The stage begins to darken.*)

THIRD WOMAN. I guess we all might go home 'til de shower's over. Come on, papa.

SECOND GAMBLER. See you after supper, Noah.
(*Crowd starts moving off, right.*)

NOAH. God's gittin' ready to start, my sons. Let's git dis plankin' done.

ZEBA. Put a big Texas on it, Noah, an' we'll use it fo' excursions.
(*There is a distant roll of thunder, there are cries of "Good night, Admiral." "See you later." "So long, Manatee," as the crowd goes off. The thunder rumbles again. There is the sound of increasing rain. The hammers of* SHEM *and* JAPHETH *sound louder and are joined by the sounds of other hammerers. There is a flash of lightning. The* CHOIR *begins "Dey Ol' Ark's a-Movering," the sounds on the Ark become faster and louder. The rush of rain grows heavier.*)

NOAH. Hurry! Hurry! Where are you, Ham?

HAM (*just off-stage*). Yere I am, father, wid de animals.

NOAH. God's give us his sign. Send 'em up de gangplank.
(*An inclined plank is thrown against the Ark from the side of the stage by* HAM, *who cracks a whip.*)

HAM. Get on, dere.
(*The heads of two elephants are seen.*)

NOAH. Bring 'em on board! De Lawd is strikin' down de worl'!
(*The singing and the noises reach fortissimo as* HAM *cracks his whip again, and the rain falls on the stage. The stage is completely darkened. The* CHOIR *continues singing in the darkness.*)

SCENE X

When the lights go up on scene, the Ark is at sea. Stationary waves run in front of it. The hillside has disappeared. The Ark is in the only lighted area.

SHEM *is smoking a pipe on the deck, leaning on the rail. A steamboat whistle blows three short and one long blast.* SHEM *is surprised. In a moment* HAM *appears, also with a pipe, and joins* SHEM *at the rail.*

SHEM. Who'd you think you was signallin'?

HAM. Dat wasn't me, dat was daddy.

SHEM. He think he gonter git a reply?

HAM. I don' know. He's been gittin' a heap of comfort out of dat likker.

SHEM. De kag's nearly empty, ain't it?

HAM. Pretty nearly almos'. (*They look over the rail. A pause*) Seen anythin'?

SHEM. Dis mornin' I seen somethin' over dere might' a' been a fish.

HAM. Dat's de big news of de week.

SHEM. How long you think dis trip's gonter las'?

HAM. I don' know! Rain fo'ty days 'n' fo'ty nights an' when dat stop' I thought sho' we'd come up ag'inst a san' bar o' somethin'. Looks now like all dat rain was jest a little incident of de trip. (*The whistle blows again*) Doggone! I wish he wouldn't do dat. Fust thing we know he'll wake up dem animals ag'in.
(JAPHETH *appears.*)

SHEM. What de matter wit' de ol' man, Jape?

JAPHETH. Doggone, he say he had a dream dat we're nearly dere. Dat's why he pullin' de whistle cord. See kin he git a' answer. (*He looks over the rail*) Look to me like de same ol' territory.
(MRS. NOAH *appears on deck.*)

NOAH'S WIFE. You boys go stop yo' paw pullin' dat cord. He so full of likker he think he's in a race.

JAPHETH. He claim he know what he's doin'.

NOAH'S WIFE. I claim he gittin' to be a perfec' nuisance. Me an' yo' wives cain't hardly heah ou'sel'es think. (NOAH *appears, his hat rakishly tilted on his head. He goes to the railing and looks out*) You 'spectin' company?

NOAH. Leave me be, woman. De watah don' look so rough today. De ol' boat's ridin' easier.

NOAH'S WIFE. Ridin' like a ol' mule!

NOAH. Yes, suh, de air don't feel so wet. Shem! 'Spose you sen' out 'nother dove. (SHEM *goes into the Ark*) Ham, go git de soundin' line. Jape, keep yo' eye on de East.
(JAPHETH *goes to the end of the boat.*)

NOAH'S WIFE. As fo' you, I s'pose you'll help things along by takin' a little drink.

NOAH. Look yere, who's de pilot of dis vessel?

NOAH'S WIFE. Ol' Mister Dumb Luck.

NOAH. Well, see, dat's where you don' know anythin'.

NOAH'S WIFE. I s'pose you ain't drunk as a fool?

NOAH (*cordially*). I feel congenial.

NOAH'S WIFE. An' you look it. You look jest wonderful. I wonder if you'd feel so congenial if de Lawd was to show up?

NOAH. De Lawd knows what I'm doin', don' you worry 'bout dat.

NOAH'S WIFE. I wouldn't say anythin' ag'inst de Lawd. He suttinly let us know dey'd be a change in de weather. But I bet even de Lawd wonders sometimes why he ever put you in charge.

NOAH. Well, you let de Lawd worry 'bout dat.
(SHEM *appears with the dove*).

SHEM. Will I leave her go, Paw?

NOAH. Leave 'er go. (*There is a chorus of "Good Luck, Dove," from the group as the dove flies off-stage.* HAM *appears with the sounding line.*) Throw 'er over, Boy.
(HAM *proceeds to do so.*)

NOAH'S WIFE. An' another thing—

HAM. Hey!

NOAH (*rushing to his side*). What is it?

HAM. Only 'bout a inch! Look!
(*They lean over.*)

JAPHETH. It's gettin' light in de East.
(*As* HAM *works the cord up and down,* NOAH *and* NOAH'S WIFE *turn toward* JAPHETH. *The* CHOIR *begins "My Soul Is a Witness for the Lord."*)

NOAH. Praise de Lawd, so it is.

NOAH'S WIFE. Oh, dat's pretty.

NOAH (*to* HAM). An' de boat's stopped. We've landed. Shem, go down 'n' drag de fires an' dreen de boiler. Yo' go help 'im, Ham.

JAPHETH. Look, Paw.
(*The dove wings back to the Ark with an olive branch in its mouth.*)

NOAH. 'N' yere's de little dove wid greenery in its mouth! Take 'er down, Jape, so she kin tell de animals. (JAPHETH *exits after* SHEM *and* HAM *carrying the dove. To* MRS. NOAH) Now, maybe you feel little different.

NOAH'S WIFE (*contritely*). It was jes' gittin' to be so tiresome. I'm sorry, Noah.

NOAH. Dat's all right, ol' woman. (NOAH'S WIFE *exits.* NOAH *looks about him. The lights have changed and the water piece is gone and the Ark is again on the hillside. Two mountains can be seen in the distance and a rainbow slowly appears over the Ark. The singing has grown louder*) Thank you, Lawd, thank you very much indeed. Amen.
(*The singing stops with the "Amen."* GOD *appears on the deck.*)

GOD. Yo' welcome, Noah.
(NOAH *turns and sees him.*)

NOAH. O, Lawd, it's wonderful.

GOD (*looking about him*). I sort of like it. I like de way you handled de ship, too, Noah.

NOAH. Was you watchin', Lawd?

GOD. Every minute. (*He smiles*) Didn't de ol' lady light into you?

NOAH (*apologetically*). She was kinda restless.

GOD. That's all right. I ain't blamin' nobody. I don' even min' you' cussin' an' drinkin'. I figure a steamboat cap'n on a long trip like you had has a right to a little redeye, jest so he don' go crazy.

NOAH. Thank you, Lawd. What's de orders now?

GOD. All de animals safe?

NOAH. Dey all fin'n' dandy, Lawd.

GOD. Den I want you to open dat starboard door, an' leave 'em all out. Let 'em go down de hill. Den you an' de family take all de seeds 'n' de sprouts an' begin plantin' ag'in. I'm startin' all over, Noah.
(NOAH *exits.* GOD *looks around.*)

GOD. Well, now we'll see what happens. (GOD *listens with a smile, as noises accompanying the debarking of the animals are heard. There are the cracks of whips, the voices of the men on the Ark, shouting: "Git along dere." "Whoa, take it easy." "Duck yo' head." "Keep in line dere," etc. Over the Ark there is a burst of centrifugal shadows, and the sound of a myriad of wings.* GOD *smiles at the shadows*) Dat's right, birds, fin' yo' new homes. (*Bird twitters are heard again.* GOD *listens a moment and rests an arm on the railing. He speaks softly*) Gabriel, kin you spare a minute?
(GABRIEL *appears.*)

GABRIEL. Yes, Lawd?
(*The sounds from the other side of the Ark are by now almost hushed.* GOD *indicates the new world with a wave of the hand.*)

GOD. Well, it's did.

GABRIEL (*respectfully, but with no enthusiasm*). So I take notice.

GOD. Yes, suh, startin' all over again.

GABRIEL. So I see.

GOD (*looking at him suddenly*). Don' seem to set you up much.

GABRIEL. Well, Lawd, you see— (*He hesitates*) 'Tain't none of my business.

GOD. What?

GABRIEL. I say, I don' know very much about it.

GOD. I know you don'. I jest wanted you to see it. (*A thought strikes him*) Co'se, it ain' yo' business, Gabe. It's my business. 'Twas my idea. De whole thing was my idea. An' every bit of it's my business 'n' nobody else's. De whole thing rests on my shoulders. I declare, I guess *dat's* why I feel so solemn an' serious, at dis particklar time. You know *dis* thing's turned into quite a proposition.

GABRIEL (*tenderly*). But, it's all right, Lawd. As you say, it's did.

GOD. Yes, suh, it's did. (*Sighs deeply. Looks slowly to the right and the left. Then softly*) I only hope it's goin' to work out all right.

CURTAIN

PART TWO

SCENE I

GOD'S *office again.*

Somewhere the CHOIR *is singing: "A City Called Heaven." In the office are two* WOMEN CLEANERS. *One is scrubbing the floor, the other dusting the furniture. The one dusting stops and looks out the window. There is a whirr and a distant faint Boom. The* CHOIR *stops.*

FIRST CLEANER. Dat was a long way off.

SECOND CLEANER (*at window*). Yes, ma'am. An' dat must a' been a big one. Doggone, de Lawd mus' be mad fo' sho', dis mo'nin'. Dat's de fo'ty-six' thunde'bolt since breakfast.

FIRST CLEANER. I wonder where at He's pitchin' dem.

SECOND CLEANER. My goodness, don' you know?

FIRST CLEANER (*a little hurt*). Did I know I wouldn't ask de question.

SECOND CLEANER. Every one of dem's bound fo' de earth.

FIRST CLEANER. De earth? You mean dat little ol' dreenin' place?

SECOND CLEANER. Dat's de planet. (*Another faint whirr and boom*) Dere goes another.

FIRST CLEANER. Well, bless me. I didn't know dey was thunde'bolts.

SECOND CLEANER. Wha'd you think dey was?

FIRST CLEANER (*above desk*). I wasn't sho', but I thought maybe He might be whittlin' a new star o' two, an' de noise was jest de chips fallin'.

SECOND CLEANER. Carrie, where you been? Don' you know de earth is de new scandal? Ever'body's talkin' about it.

FIRST CLEANER. Dey kep' it from me.

SECOND CLEANER. Ain't you noticed de Lawd's been unhappy lately?

FIRST CLEANER (*thoughtfully*). Yeah, He ain't been his old self.

SECOND CLEANER. What did you think was de matteh? Lumbago?

FIRST CLEANER (*petulantly*). I didn't know. I didn't think it was fo' me t'inquieh.

SECOND CLEANER. Well, it jest so happens dat de Lawd is riled as kin be by dat measly little earth. Or I should say de scum dat's on it.

FIRST CLEANER. Dat's mankind down dere.

SECOND CLEANER. Dey mus' be scum, too, to git de Lawd so wukked up.

FIRST CLEANER. I s'pose so. (*Another whirr and boom*) Looks like He's lettin' dem feel de wrath. Ain' dat a shame to plague de Lawd dat way?

SECOND CLEANER. From what I hear dey been beggin' fo' what dey're gittin'. My brother flew down to bring up a saint de other day and he say from what he see mos' of de population down dere has made de debbil king an' dey wukkin' in three shifts fo' him.

FIRST CLEANER. You cain't blame de Lawd.

SECOND CLEANER. Co'se you cain't. Dem human bein's 'd make anybody bile oveh. Ev'rytime de Lawd try to do sompin' fo' dem, doggone if dey don't staht some new ruckus.

FIRST CLEANER. I take notice He's been wukkin' in yere mo' dan usual.

SECOND CLEANER. I wish He'd let us ladies fix it up. Wouldn't take a minute to make dis desk gold-plated.

FIRST CLEANER. I s'pose He likes it dis way. De Lawd's kind o' ol' fashioned in some ways. I s'pose He keeps dis office plain an' simple on purpose.

SECOND CLEANER (*finishing her work*). I don' see why.

FIRST CLEANER (*looking off*). Well, it's kind of a nice place to come to when He's studyin' somethin' impo'tant. 'Most evahthin' else in heaven's so fine 'n' gran', maybe ev'ry now an' den He jest gits sick an' tired of de glory. (*She is also collecting her utensils.*)

SECOND CLEANER. Maybe so. Jest de same I'd like to have a free hand wid dis place for a while, so's I could gold it up.

(GOD *appears in the doorway.*)

GOD. Good mo'nin', daughters.

FIRST *and* SECOND CLEANERS. Good mo'nin', Lawd. We was jest finishin'.

GOD. Go ahead den, daughters. (*Goes to the window.*)

FIRST *and* SECOND CLEANERS. Yes, Lawd. (*They exeunt. Off-stage*) Good mo'nin', Gabriel.

(*Off-stage* GABRIEL *says, "Good mo'-*

nin', sisters," and enters immediately. He stands in the doorway for a moment watching GOD*—a notebook and pencil in his hand.*)

GOD. What's de total?

GABRIEL (*consulting the book*). Eighteen thousand nine hund'ed an' sixty for de mo'nin'. Dat's includin' de village wid de fo'tune tellers. Dey certainly kin breed fast.

GOD (*softly*). Dey displease me. Dey displease me greatly.

GABRIEL. Want some more bolts, Lawd?

GOD (*looking through window*). Look at 'em dere. Squirmin' an' fightin' an' bearin' false witness. Listen to dat liar, dere. He don' intend to marry dat little gal. He don' even love her. What did you say?

GABRIEL. Should I git mo' bolts?

GOD. Wait a minute. (*He carefully points his finger down through the window*) I'm goin' to git dat wicked man myself. (*From a great distance comes an agonized cry: "Oh, Lawd!"* GOD *turns from the window*) No use gittin' mo' thunde'bolts. Dey don' do de trick. (*He goes to the swivel chair and sits*) It's got to be somethin' else.

GABRIEL. How would it be if you was to doom 'em all ag'in, like dat time you sent down de flood? I bet dat would make dem mind.

GOD. You see how much good de flood did. Dere dey is, jest as bad as ever.

GABRIEL. How about cleanin' up de whole mess of 'em and sta'tin' all over ag'in wid some new kind of animal?

GOD. An' admit I'm licked?

GABRIEL (*ashamedly*). No, of co'se not, Lawd.

GOD. No, suh. No, suh. Man is a kind of pet of mine and it ain't right fo' me to give up tryin' to do somethin' wid him. Doggone, mankin' *mus'* be all right at de core or else why did I ever bother wid him in de first place? (*Sits at desk.*)

GABRIEL. It's jest dat I hates to see you worryin' about it, Lawd.

GOD. Gabe, dere ain't anythin' worth while anywheres dat didn't cause somebody some worryin'. I ain't never tol' you de trouble I had gittin' things started up yere. Dat's a story in itself. No, suh, de more I keep on bein' de Lawd de more I know I got to keep improvin' things. An' dat takes time and worry. De main trouble wid mankin' is he takes up so much of my time. He ought to be able to help hisself a little. (*He stops suddenly and cogitates*) Hey, dere! I think I got it!

GABRIEL (*eagerly*). What's de news?

GOD (*still cogitating*). Yes, suh, dat seems like an awful good idea.

GABRIEL. Tell me, Lawd.

GOD. Gabriel, have you noticed dat every now an' den, mankin' turns out some pretty good specimens?

GABRIEL. Dat's de truth.

GOD. Yes, suh. Dey's ol' Abraham and Isaac an' Jacob an' all dat family.

GABRIEL. Dat so, Lawd.

GOD. An' every one of dem boys was a hard wukker an' a good citizen. We got to admit dat.

GABRIEL. Dey wouldn't be up yere flyin' wid us if dey hadn't been.

GOD. No, suh. An' I don' know but what de answer to de whole trouble is right dere.

GABRIEL. How you mean, Lawd?

GOD. Why, doggone it, de good man is de man dat keeps busy. I mean I been goin' along on de principle dat he was something like you angels—dat you ought to be able to give him somethin' an' den jest let him sit back an' enjoy it. Dat ain't so. Now dat I recollec' I put de first one down dere to take keer o' dat garden an' den I let him go ahead an' do nothin' but git into mischief. (*He rises*) Sure, *dat's* it. He ain't *built* jest to fool 'roun' an' not do nothin'. Gabe, I'm gonter try a new scheme.

GABRIEL (*eagerly*). What's de scheme, Lawd?

GOD. I'll tell you later. Send in Abraham, Isaac an' Jacob. (*A voice outside calls: "Right away, Lawd."*) You go tell dem to put dem bolts back in de boxes. I ain' gonter use dem ag'in a while.

GABRIEL. O. K., Lawd.

GOD. Was you goin' anywhere near de Big Pit?

GABRIEL. I could go.

GOD. Lean over de brink and tell Satan he's jest a plain fool if he thinks he kin beat anybody as big as me.

GABRIEL. Yes, suh, Lawd. Den I'll spit right in his eye. (GABRIEL *exits.*) (GOD *looks down through the window again to the earth below.*)

GOD. Dat new polish on de sun makes it powerful hot. (*He "r'ars back"*) Let it be jest a little bit cooler. (*He feels the air*) Dat's nice. (*Goes to His desk. A knock on the door*) Come in. (ABRAHAM, ISAAC *and* JACOB *enter. All are very old men, but the beard of* ABRAHAM *is the longest and whitest, and they suggest their three generations. They have wings that are not quite so big as those of the native angels.*)

ISAAC. Sorry we so long comin', Lawd. But Pappy and me had to take de boy (*Pointing to* JACOB) over to git him a can of wing ointment.

GOD. What was de matter, son?

JACOB. Dey was chafin' me a little. Dey fine now, thank you, Lawd.

GOD. Dat's good. Sit down an' make yo'selves comf'table. (*The three sit.* MEN: *"Thank you, Lawd"*) Men, I'm goin' to talk about a little scheme I got. It's one dat's goin' to affec' yo' fam'lies an' dat's why I 'cided I'd talk it over wid you, 'fo' it goes into eefect. I don't know whether you boys know it or not, but you is about de three best men of one fam'ly dat's come up yere since I made little apples. Now I tell you what I'm gonter do. Seein' dat you human bein's cain't 'preciate anythin' lessen you fust wukk to git it and den keep strugglin' to hold it, why I'm gonter turn over a very valuable piece of property to yo' fam'ly, and den see what kin dey do with it. De rest of de worl' kin go jump in de river fo' all I keer. I'm gonter be lookin' out fo' yo' descendants only. Now den, seein' dat you boys know de country pretty tho'ly, where at does you think is de choice piece of property in de whole worl'? Think it over for a minute. I'm gonter let you make de s'lection.

ABRAHAM. If you was to ask me, Lawd, I don't think dey come any better dan de Land of Canaan.

GOD (*to* ISAAC *and* JACOB). What's yo' feelin' in de matter?

JACOB (*after a nod from* ISAAC). Pappy an' me think do we get a pick, dat would be it.

GOD (*goes to window again; looks out*). De Land of Canaan. Yes, I guess dat's a likely neighborhood. It's all run over wid Philistines and things right now, but we kin clean dat up. (*He turns from the window and resumes his seat*) All right. Now who do you boys think is de best of yo' men to put in charge down dere? You see I ain't been payin' much attention to anybody in partic'lar lately.

ISAAC. Does you want de brainiest or de holiest, Lawd?
(MEN *look up.*)

GOD. I want de holiest. I'll make him brainy.
(MEN *appreciate the miracle.*)

ISAAC (*as* ABRAHAM *and* JACOB *nod to him*). Well, if you want A Number One goodness, Lawd, I don't know where you'll git more satisfaction dan in a great-great-great-great grandson of mine.

GOD. Where's he at?

ISAAC. At de moment I b'lieve he's in de sheep business over in Midian County. He got in a little trouble down in Egypt, but t'wan't his doin'. He killed a man dat was abusin' one of our boys in de brick works. Of co'se you know old King Pharaoh's got all our people in bondage.

GOD. I heard of it. (*With some ire*) Who did you think put them dere? (*The visitors lower their heads*) It's all right, boys. (*All rise*) I'm gonter take dem out of it. An' I'm gonter turn over de whole Land of Canaan to dem. An' do you know whose gonter lead dem dere? Yo' great, great, great, great grandson. Moses, ain't it?

ISAAC. Yes, Lawd.

GOD (*smiling*). Yes. I been noticin' *him.*

ABRAHAM. It's quite a favor fo' de fam'ly, Lawd.

GOD. Dat's why I tol' you. You see, it so happens I love yo' fam'ly, an' I delight to honor it. Dat's all, gen'lemen. (*The three others rise and cross to the door, murmuring, "Yes, Lawd," "Thank you, Lawd," "Much obliged, Lawd," etc. The* CHOIR *begins, "My Lord's A-Writin' All De Time" pianissimo.* GOD *stands watching the men leave*) Enjoy yo'selves. (*He goes to the window. The singing grows softer. He speaks through the window to the earth*) I'm comin' down to see you, Moses, an' dis time my scheme's got to wukk.
(*The stage is darkened. The singing grows louder and continues until the lights go up on the next scene.*)

SCENE II

The tableau curtains frame the opening of a cave, which is dimly lighted. A large turkey-berry bush is somewhere near the foreground. MOSES *is seated on the grass eating his lunch from a basket in his lap.* ZIPPORAH, *his wife, stands watching him. He is about forty,* ZIPPORAH *somewhat younger. They are dressed inconspicuously.* MOSES *stutters slightly when he speaks. He looks up to see* ZIPPORAH *smiling.*

MOSES. What you smilin' at, Zipporah?

ZIPPORAH. Caize you enjoyin' yo'self.

MOSES. You is a good wife, Zipporah.

ZIPPORAH. You is a good husband, Moses. (MOSES *wipes his mouth with a handkerchief and begins putting into the basket the various implements of the meal which had been on the ground about him*) Why you suppose it's so dark yere today? Dey's no rain in de air.

MOSES. Seems like it's jest aroun' dis cave. Yo' father's house is got de sun on it. (*He looks in another direction*) Looks all clear down toward Egypt.

ZIPPORAH. Co'se it *would* be fine weather in Egypt. De sky looks all right. Maybe it's gonter rain jest right yere. Why don't you move de sheep over to de other pasture?

MOSES (*a bit puzzled*). I don' know. It got dark like dis befo' you come along wid de dinner an' I was gonter stop you on de top of de hill. Den somethin' kep' me vere.

ZIPPORAH. S'pose it could be de Lawd warnin' you dat dey's 'Gyptians hangin' 'roun'?

MOSES. Dey may have fo'gotten all about dat killin' by now. Dey got a new Pharaoh down dere.

ZIPPORAH. An' I hear he's jest as mean to yo' people as his pappy was. I wouldn't put it pas' him to send soljahs all the way up yere fo' you.

MOSES. Dat's all right. De Lawd's looked after me so far, I don't 'spect him to fall down on me now. You better be gittin' home.

ZIPPORAH (*taking the basket*). I'll be worryin' about you.

MOSES (*kissing her and then smiling*). 'Parently de Lawd ain't. He knows I'm safe as kin be. Lemme see you feel dat way.

ZIPPORAH. You is a good man, Moses.

MOSES. I'se a lucky man. (ZIPPORAH *exits with the basket.* MOSES *looks up at the sky*) Dat's funny. De sun seems to be shinin' everyplace but right yere. It's shinin' on de sheep. Why ain't dey no cloud dere?

GOD (*off-stage*). Caize I want it to be like dat, Moses.

MOSES (*looking about him*). Who's dat?

GOD (*off-stage again*). I'm de Lawd, Moses.

MOSES (*smiling*). Dat's what you say. Dis yere shadow may be de Lawd's wukk, but dat voice soun' pretty much to me like my ol' brother Aaron.

GOD (*off-stage*). Den keep yo' eyes open, son. (*The turkey-berry bush begins to glow and then turns completely red.* MOSES *looks at it fascinated*) Maybe you notice de bush ain't burnin' up.

MOSES. Dat's de truth. (MOSES *is full of awe but not frightened.*)

GOD (*off-stage*). Now you believe me?

MOSES. Co'se I does. It's wonderful. (*The light in the bush dies and* GOD *appears from behind it.*)

GOD. No, it ain't, Moses. It was jest a trick.

MOSES. 'Scuse me doubtin' you, Lawd. I always had de feelin' you wuz takin' keer of me, but I never 'spected you'd fin' de time to talk wid me pussunly. (*He laughs*) Dat was a good trick, Lawd. I'se seen some good ones, but dat was de beatenest.

GOD. Yo' gonter see lots bigger tricks dan dat, Moses. In fac', yo' gonter perfo'm dem.

MOSES (*incredulously*). Me? I'm gonter be a tricker?

GOD. Yes, suh.

MOSES. An' do magic? Lawd, my mouth ain't got de quick talk to go wid it.

GOD. It'll come to you now.

MOSES (*now cured of stuttering*). Is I goin' wid a circus?

GOD (*slowly and solemnly*). Yo' is goin' down into Egypt, Moses, and lead my people out of bondage. To do dat I'm gonter make you de bes' tricker in de worl'.

MOSES (*a little frightened*). Egypt! You know I killed a man dere, Lawd. Won't dey kill me?

GOD. Not when dey see yo' tricks. You ain't skeered, is you?

MOSES (*simply and bravely*). No, suh, Lawd.

GOD. Den yere's what I'm gonter do. Yo' people is my chillun, Moses. I'm sick and tired o' the way ol' King Pharaoh is treatin' dem, so I'se gonter take dem away, and yo' gonter lead dem. You gonter lead 'em out of Egypt an' across de river Jordan. It's gonter take a long time, and you ain't goin' on no excursion train. Yo' gonter wukk awful hard for somethin' yo' goin' to fin' when de trip's over.

MOSES. What's dat, Lawd?

GOD. It's de Land of Canaan. It's de bes' land I got. I've promised it to yo' people, an' I'm gonter give it to dem.

MOSES. Co'se, ol' King Pharaoh will do everything he kin to stop it.

GOD. Yes, an' dat's where de tricks come in. Dey tell me he's awful fond of tricks.

MOSES. I hear dat's *all* he's fon' of. Dey say if you can't take a rabbit out of a hat you cain't even git in to see him.

GOD. Wait'll you see de tricks you an' me's goin' to show him.

MOSES (*delightedly*). Doggone! Huh, Lawd?

GOD. Yes, suh. Now de first trick—(GOD *is lifting a stick which he carries.*)

MOSES. Jest a minute, Lawd. (GOD *halts the demonstration*) I'm gonter learn de tricks and do just like you tell me, but I *know* it's gonter take me a little time to learn all dat quick talkin'. Cain't I have my brother Aaron go wid me? He's a good man.

GOD. I was gonter have him help you wid de Exodus. I guess he can watch, too.

MOSES. I'll call 'im. (*He turns as if to shout.*)

GOD. Wait. (MOSES *turns and looks at* GOD) I'll *bring* him. (*Softly*) Aaron!

(AARON *appears between* GOD *and* MOSES *in the mouth of the cave. He is a little taller than* MOSES *and slightly older. He, too, is dressed like a field hand.*)

AARON (*blankly*). Hey!

(MOSES *goes to him, takes his hand and leads him, bewildered, down to where* MOSES *had been standing alone.* AARON *then sees* GOD.)

MOSES (*almost in a whisper*). It's all right.

GOD. Don't worry, son, I'm jest showin' some tricks. Bringin' you yere was one of dem. (AARON *stares at* GOD *as if hypnotized*) Now den, you see dis yere rod? Looks like a ordinary walking stick, don' it?

MOSES. Yes, Lawd.

GOD. Well, it ain't no ordinary walkin' stick, caize look. (MOSES *leans forward*) When I lays it down on de groun'—

(*The stage is darkened. The* CHOIR *begins, "Go Down, Moses," and continues until the lights go up on the next scene.*)

SCENE III

The throne room of PHARAOH. *It suggests a Negro lodge room. The plain board walls are covered by several large parade banners of varying sizes, colors and materials, bordered with gold fringe and tasseled. Some of the inscriptions on them read:*

SUBLIME ORDER OF PRINCES OF THE HOUSE OF PHARAOH
HOME CHAPTER

MYSTIC BROTHERS OF THE EGYPTIAN HOME GUARD
LADIES AUXILIARY, NO. 1

SUPREME MAGICIANS AND WIZARDS OF THE UNIVERSE

PRIVATE FLAG OF HIS HONOR OLD KING PHARAOH

ROYAL YOUNG PEOPLE'S PLEASURE CLUB

ENCHANTED AND INVISIBLE CADETS OF EGYPT BOYS' BRIGADE

There is one door up right and a window. The throne, an ordinary armchair with a drapery over its back, is on a dais. PHARAOH *is seated on the throne. His crown and garments might be those worn by a high officer in a Negro lodge during a ritual. About the throne itself are high officials, several of them with plumed hats, clothing that suggests military uniforms, and rather elaborate sword belts, swords and scabbards. A few soldiers carrying spears are also in his neighborhood and one or two bearded ancients in brightly colored robes with the word "Wizard" on their conical hats. In the general group of men and women scattered elsewhere in the room Sunday finery is noticeable everywhere. Most of the civilians have bright "parade" ribbons and wear medals. In a cleared space immediately before the throne a* CANDIDATE MAGICIAN *is performing a sleight-of-hand trick with cards.* PHARAOH *watches him apathetically. He is receiving earnest attention from a few of the others, but the majority of the men and women are talking quietly among themselves. Beside the* CANDIDATE MAGICIAN *are several paraphernalia of previously demonstrated tricks.*

CANDIDATE MAGICIAN (*holding up some cards*). Now den, ol' King Pharaoh, watch dis. (*He completes a trick. There is a murmur of "Not Bad," "Pretty Good," etc. from a few of the watchers.* PHARAOH *makes no comment*) Now, I believe de cyard I ast you to keep sittin' on was de trey of diamonds, wasn't it?

PHARAOH. Yeah.

CANDIDATE MAGICIAN. Den kin I trouble you to take a look at it now? (PHARAOH *half rises to pick up a card he has been sitting on, and looks at it*) I believe you'll now notice dat it's de King of Clubs? (PHARAOH *nods and shows the card to those nearest him. The* CANDIDATE MAGICIAN *waits for an audible approval and gets practically none*) An' dat, ol' King Pharaoh, completes de puffomance.

(*An elderly man in a uniform steps forward.*)

GENERAL. On behalf of my nephew I beg Yo' Honor to let him jine de ranks of de royal trickers and magicians.

PHARAOH (*to the two* WIZARDS). What do de committee think? (*The* WIZARDS *shake their heads*) Dat's what I thought. He ain't good enough. I'd like to help you out, General, but you know a man's got to be a awful good tricker to git in de royal society dese days. You better go back an' steddy some mo', son. (*He lifts his voice and directs two* SOLDIERS *guarding the door*) Is de head magician reached de royal waitin' room yit? (*One of the* SOLDIERS *opens the door to look out*) If he is, send him in.

(*The* SOLDIER *beckons to some one off-stage, throws the door open, and announces to the court.*)

SOLDIER. De Head Magician of de land of Egypt.

(*A very old and villainous man enters. His costume is covered with cabalistic and zodiacal signs. He advances to the King, the other magician and his uncle making way for him. He bows curtly to* PHARAOH.)

HEAD MAGICIAN. Good mo'nin', ol' King Pharaoh.

PHARAOH. Mo'nin', Professor. What's de news?

HEAD MAGICIAN. Evahthing's bein' carried out like you said.

PHARAOH. How's de killin' of de babies 'mongst de Hebrews comin' along?

HEAD MAGICIAN. Jes' like you ordered.

PHARAOH (*genially*). Dey killed all of 'em, huh?

HEAD MAGICIAN. Do dey see one, dey kill 'im. You teachin' 'em a great lesson. Dey don' like it a-tall.

PHARAOH (*smiling*). What do dey say?

HEAD MAGICIAN (*pawing the air inarticulately*). I hates to tell in front of de ladies.

PHARAOH. Dey feels pretty bad, huh?

HEAD MAGICIAN. Dat's jest de beginnin' of it. Betwixt de poleece and de soljahs we killed about a thousan' of 'em las' night. Dat's purty good.

PHARAOH (*thoughtfully*). Yeh, it's fair. I guess you boys is doin' all you kin. But I fin' I ain't satisfied, though.

HEAD MAGICIAN. How you mean, Yo' Honor?

PHARAOH. I mean I'd like to make dose Hebrew chillun realize dat I kin be even mo' of a pest. I mean I hates dem chillun. An' I'm gonter think of a way of makin' 'em even mo' mizzable.

HEAD MAGICIAN. But dey *ain't* anythin' meaner dan killin' de babies, King.

PHARAOH. Dey must be sump'n. Doggone, you is my head tricker, you put yo' brains on it. (*To the others*) Quiet, whilst de Head Magician go into de silence.

HEAD MAGICIAN (*after turning completely around twice, and a moment's cogitation*). I tell you what I kin do. All de Hebrews dat ain't out to de buryin' grounds or in the hospitals is laborin' in de brick wukks.

PHARAOH. Yeh?

HEAD MAGICIAN (*after a cackling laugh*). How would it be to take de straw away from 'em and tell 'em dey's got to turn out jest as many bricks as usual? Ain't dat nasty?

PHARAOH. Purty triflin', but I s'pose it'll have to do for de time bein'. Where's de extreme inner guard? (*One of the military attendants comes forward*) Go on out an' tell de sup'intendent to put dat into ee-ffect. (*The attendant bows and starts for he door. *He stops as* PHARAOH *calls o him*) Wait a minute! Tell 'im to :hop off de hands of anybody dat ay he cain't make de bricks dat way. *(The attendant salutes and exits, the loor being opened and closed by one of the* SOLDIERS) Now what's de iews in de magic line?

IEAD MAGICIAN. I ain't got very many novelties today, King, I bin wukkin' oo hard on de killin's. I'm so tired I don' believe I could lift a wand. *(There are murmurs of protest from the assemblage.)*

PHARAOH. Doggone, you was to 'a been de chief feature o' de meetin' dis mornin'. Look at de turn-out you got account of me tellin' 'em you was comin'.

HEAD MAGICIAN. Well, dat's de way it is, King. Why don' you git de wizards to do some spell castin'?

PHARAOH. Dey say it's in de cyards dat dey cain't wukk till high noon. *(He glances at the* WIZARDS) Think mebbe you kin cheat a little?

FIRST WIZARD. Oh dat cain't be done, King.

PHARAOH. Well, we might as well adjourn, den. Looks to me like de whole program's shot to pieces. *(He starts to rise, when there is a furious banging on the door)* What's de idea, dere? See who dat is. *(The* SOLDIERS *open the door.* MOSES *and* AARON *enter, pushing the two* SOLDIERS *aside and coming down in front of* PHARAOH. *The* SOLDIERS *are bewildered and* PHARAOH *is angry)* Say, who tol' you two baboons you could come in yere?

MOSES. Is you ol' King Pharaoh?

PHARAOH. Dat's me. Did you hear what I asked you?

MOSES. My name is Moses, and dis is my brother Aaron.
(Murmur of "Hebrews" spreads through the room.)

PHARAOH *(in a rage)*. Is you Hebrews?

MOSES. Yes, suh.

PHARAOH *(almost screaming)*. Put 'em to de sword!
(As the courtiers approach, AARON *suddenly discloses the rod, which he swings once over his head. The courtiers draw back as if their hands had been stung. Cries of "Hey!" "Look out," etc.)*

MOSES. Keep outside dat circle.
(The courtiers nearest MOSES *and* AARON *look at each other, exclaiming ad lib., "Did you feel dat?" "What is dat?" "What's goin' on heah?" "My hands is stingin'!" etc.)*

PHARAOH *(puzzled but threatening)*. What's de idea yere?

MOSES. We is magicians, ol' King Pharaoh.

PHARAOH *(to the* HEAD MAGICIAN*)*. Put a spell on 'em. *(The* HEAD MAGICIAN *stands looking at them bewildered. To* MOSES*)* I got some magicians, too. We'll see who's got de bes' magic. *(*MOSES *and* AARON *laugh. Most of the courtiers are cowering. To the* HEAD MAGICIAN*)* Go ahead, give 'em gri-gri.

MOSES. Sure, go ahead.

PHARAOH. Hurry up, dey's laughin' at you. What's de matter?

HEAD MAGICIAN. I cain't think of de right spell.

PHARAOH (*now frightened himself*). You mean dey got even *you* whupped?

HEAD MAGICIAN. Dey's got a new kind of magic.

PHARAOH (*gazes at* HEAD MAGICIAN *a moment, bewildered. To the* WIZARDS). I s'pose if de Professor cain't, you cain't.

FIRST WIZARD. Dat's a new trick, King.

HEAD MAGICIAN (*rubbing his fingers along his palms*). It's got 'lectricity in it!

PHARAOH. Hm, well, dat may make it a little diff'rent. So you boys is magicians, too?

MOSES. Yes, suh.

PHARAOH. Well, we's always glad to see some new trickers in de co't, dat is if dey is good. (*He glances about him*) You look like you is O. K.

MOSES. Dat's what we claims, ol' King Pharaoh. We think we's de best in de worl'.

PHARAOH. You certainly kin talk big. Jest what is it you boys would like?

MOSES. We came to show you some tricks. Den we's goin' to ask you to do somethin' for us.

PHARAOH. Well, I s'pose you know I'm a fool for conjurin'. If a man kin show me some tricks I ain't seen, I goes out of my way to do him a favor.

MOSES. Dat's good. Want to see de first trick?

PHARAOH. It ain't goin' to hurt nobody?

MOSES. Dis one won't.

PHARAOH. Go ahead.

MOSES. Dis yere rod my brother has looks jes' like a walkin' stick, don't it? (*The courtiers now join the King in interest.*)

PHARAOH. Uh huh. Le's see. (AARON *hands him the rod, which* PHARAOH *inspects and returns.*)

MOSES. Well, look what happens when he lays it on de groun'. (AARON *places the rod on the second step of the throne. It turns into a lifelike snake. There are exclamations from the assemblage.*)

PHARAOH. Dat's a good trick! Now turn it back into a walkin' stick again. (AARON *picks it up and it is again a rod. Exclamations of "Purty good!" "Dat's all right!" "What do you think of that!" etc.*) Say, you is good trickers!

MOSES. You ain't never seen de beat of us. Now I'm goin' to ask de favor.

PHARAOH. Sure, what is it?

MOSES (*solemnly*). Let de Hebrew chillun go!

PHARAOH (*rises and stares at them. There is a murmur of "Listen to 'im!" "He's got nerve!" "I never in my life!" "My goodness!" etc.)* What did you say?

MOSES. Let de Hebrew chillun go. (PHARAOH *seats himself again.)*

PHARAOH (*slowly*). Don' you know de Hebrews is my slaves?

MOSES. Yes, suh.

PHARAOH. Yes, suh, my slaves. (*There is a distant groaning*) Listen, and you kin hear 'em bein' treated like slaves. (*He calls toward the window*) What was dey doin' den?

MAN NEAR THE WINDOW. Dey's jest gettin' de news down in de brickyard.

PHARAOH. I won't let them go. (*He snorts contemptuously*) Let's see another trick.

MOSES. Yes, suh, yere's a better one. (*He lowers his head*) Let's have a plague of de flies.
(AARON *raises the rod. The room grows dark and a great buzzing of flies is heard. The courtiers break out in cries of "Get away fum me!" "Take 'em away!" "De place is filled with flies!" "Dis is terrible!" "Do sump'n, Pharaoh!")*

PHARAOH (*topping the others*). All right—stop de trick!

MOSES. Will you let de Hebrews go?

PHARAOH. Sho' I will. Go ahead stop it!

MOSES (*also above the others*). Begone!
(*The buzzing stops and the room is filled with light again, as* AARON *lowers the rod. All except* MOSES *and* AARON *are brushing the flies from their persons.)*

PHARAOH (*laughing*). Doggone, dat was a good trick! (*The others, seeing they are uninjured, join in the laughter, with exclamations of "Doggone!" "You all right?" "Sho' I'm all right." "Didn' hurt me," etc.)* You *is* good trickers.

MOSES. Will you let de Hebrew chillun go?

PHARAOH (*sitting down again*). Well, I'll tell you, boys. I'll tell you sump'n you didn' know. You take me, *I'm* a pretty good tricker, an' I jest outtricked you. So, bein' de bes' tricker, I don't think I will let 'em go. You got any mo' tricks yo'self?

MOSES. Yes, suh. Dis is a little harder one. (AARON *lifts the rod*) Gnats in de mill pon', gnats in de clover, gnats in de tater patch, stingin' all over.
(*The stage grows dark again. There is the humming of gnats and the slapping of hands against faces and arms, and the same protests as were heard with the flies, but with more feeling. "I'm gittin' stung to death!" "I'm all stung!" "Dey'r like hornets!" "Dey's on my face!" etc.)*

PHARAOH. Take 'em away, Moses!

MOSES (*his voice drowning the others*). If I do, will you let 'em go?

PHARAOH. Sho' I will, dis time.

MOSES. Do you mean it?

PHARAOH. Co'se I mean it! Doggone, one just stang me on de nose.

MOSES. Begone! (*Lights come up as* AARON *lowers the rod. There is a moment of general recovery again.* PHARAOH *rubs his nose, looks at his hands, etc., as do the others.*) Now, how about it?

PHARAOH (*smiling*). Well, I'll tell you, Moses. Now dat de trick's over—
(MOSES *takes a step toward* PHARAOH.)

MOSES. Listen, Pharaoh. You been lyin' to me, and I'm gittin' tired of it.

PHARAOH. I ain't lyin', I'm trickin', too. You been trickin' me and I been trickin' you.

MOSES. I see. Well, I got one mo' trick up my sleeve which I didn't aim to wukk unless I had to. Caize when I does it, I cain't undo it.

PHARAOH. Wukk it an' I'll trick you right back. I don' say you ain't a good tricker, Moses. You is one of de best I ever seen. But I kin outtrick you. Dat's all.

MOSES. It ain't only me dat's goin' to wukk dis trick. It's me an' de Lawd.

PHARAOH. Who?

MOSES. De Lawd God of Israel.

PHARAOH. I kin outtrick you an' de Lawd too!

MOSES (*angrily*). Now you done it, ol' King Pharaoh. You been mean to de Lawd's people, and de Lawd's been easy on you caize you didn't know no better. You been givin' me a lot of say-so and no do-so, and I didn' min' dat. But now you've got to braggin' dat you's better dan de Lawd, and dat's too many.

PHARAOH. You talk like a preacher, an' I never did like to hear preachers talk.

MOSES. You ain't goin' to like it any better, when I strikes down de oldes' boy in every one of yo' people's houses.

PHARAOH. Now you've given up trickin' and is jest lyin'. (*He rises*) Listen, I'm Pharaoh. I do de strikin' down yere. I strike down my enemies, and dere's no one in all Egypt kin kill who he wants to, 'ceptin' me.

MOSES I'm sorry, Pharaoh. Will you let de Hebrews go?

PHARAOH. You heard my word. (AARON *is lifting his rod again at a signal from* MOSES) Now, no more tricks or I'll—

MOSES. Oh, Lawd, you'll have to do it, I guess. Aaron, lift de rod.
(*There is a thunderclap, darkness and screams. The lights go up. Several of the younger men on the stage have fallen to the ground or are being held in the arms of the horrified elders.*)

PHARAOH. What have you done yere? Where's my boy?
(*Through the door come four* MEN *bearing a young man's body.*)

FIRST OF THE FOUR MEN. King Pharaoh.
(PHARAOH *drops into his chair, stunned, as the dead boy is brought to the throne.*)

PHARAOH (*grief-stricken*). Oh, my son, my fine son.
(*The courtiers look at him with mute appeal.*)

MOSES. I'm sorry, Pharaoh, but you cain't fight de Lawd. Will you let his people go?

PHARAOH. Let them go.

(The lights go out. The CHOIR *begins, "Mary Don't You Weep," and continues until it is broken by the strains of "I'm Noways Weary and I'm Noways Tired." The latter is sung by many more voices than the former, and the cacophony ends as the latter grows in volume and the lights go up on the next scene.)*

SCENE IV

The CHILDREN OF ISRAEL *are marching on the treadmill and now singing fortissimo. They are of all ages and most of them are ragged. The men have packs on their shoulders, one or two have hand carts. The line stretches across the stage. It is nearing twilight, and the faces of the assemblage are illumined by the rays of the late afternoon sun. The upper treadmill carries a gradually rising and falling middle distance past the marchers. The foot of a mountain appears; a trumpet call is heard as the foot of the mountain reaches stage center. The marchers halt. The picture now shows the mountain running up out of sight off right. The singing stops. A babel of "What's de matter?" "Why do we stop?" "'Tain't sundown yet!" "What's happened?" "What's goin' on?" "What are they blowin' for?" etc. Those looking ahead begin to murmur. "It's Moses," "Moses." "What's happened to him?" The others take up the repetition of "Moses," and* MOSES *enters, on the arm of* AARON. *He is now an old man, as is his brother, and he totters toward the center of the stage. Cries of "What's de matter, Moses?" "You ain't hurt, is you?" "Ain't that too bad?" etc. He slowly seats himself on the rock at the foot of the mountain.*

AARON. How you feelin' now, brother?

MOSES. I'm so weary, Aaron. Seems like I was took all of a sudden.

AARON. Do we camp yere?

MOSES *(pathetically)*. No, you got to keep goin'.

AARON. But you cain't go no further tonight, brother.

MOSES. Dis never happened to me befo'.

A YOUNG WOMAN. But you's a ol' man, now, Father Moses. You cain't expect to go as fas' as we kin.

MOSES. But de Lawd said I'd do it. He said I was to show you de Promised Land. Fo'ty years I bin leadin' you. I led you out o' Egypt. I led you past Sinai, and through de wilderness. Oh, I cain't fall down on you now!

AARON. Le's res' yere fo' de night. Den we'll see how you feel in de mo'nin'.

MOSES. We tol' de scouts we'd meet 'em three miles furder on. I hate fo' 'em to come back all dis way to report. 'Tis gettin' a little dark, ain't it?

AARON. It ain't dark, Brother.

MOSES. No, it's my eyes.

AARON. Maybe it's de dust.

MOSES. No, I jest cain't seem to see. Oh, Lawd, dey cain't have a blind man leadin' 'em! Where is you, Aaron?

AARON. I'se right yere, Moses.

MOSES. Do you think— (*Pause*) Oh! Do you think it's de time He said?

AARON. How you mean, Moses? (*Crowd look from one to another in wonder.*)

MOSES. He said I could lead 'em to de Jordan, dat I'd *see* de Promised Land, and dat's all de further I could go, on account I broke de laws. Little while back I thought *I did* see a river ahead, and a pretty land on de other side. (*Distant shouts "Hooray!" "Yere dey are!" "Dey travelled quick." etc.*) Where's de young leader of de troops? Where's Joshua? (*The call "Joshua" is taken up by those on the right of the stage, followed almost immediately by "Yere he is!" "Moses wants you!" etc.* JOSHUA *enters. He is a fine-looking Negro of about thirty.*)

JOSHUA (*going to* MOSES' *side*). Yes, suh.

MOSES. What's de shoutin' 'bout, Joshua?

JOSHUA. De scouts is back wid de news. De Jordan is right ahead of us, and Jericho is jest on de other side. Moses, we're dere! (*There are cries of "Hallelujah!" "De Lawd be praised!" "Hooray!" "De Kingdom's comin'!" etc. With a considerable stir among the marchers, several new arrivals crowd in from right, shouting, "Moses, we're dere!"* JOSHUA *seeing the newcomers*) Yere's de scouts!
(*Three very ragged and dusty young men advance to* MOSES.)

MOSES (*as the shouting dies*). So it's de River Jordan!

FIRST SCOUT. Yes, suh.

MOSES. All we got to take is de city of Jericho.

FIRST SCOUT. Yes, suh.

MOSES. Joshua, you got to take charge of de fightin' men, an' Aaron's gotta stay by de priests.

JOSHUA. What about you?

MOSES. You are leavin' me behind. Joshua, you gonter get de fightin' men together and take dat city befo' sundown.

JOSHUA. It's a big city, Moses, wid walls all 'round it. We ain't got enough men.

MOSES. You'll take it, Joshua.

JOSHUA. Yes, suh, but how?

MOSES. Move up to de walls wid our people. Tell de priests to go wid you with de rams' horns. You start marchin' 'roun' dem walls, and den—

JOSHUA. Yes, suh.

MOSES. De Lawd'll take charge, jest as he's took charge ev'y time I've led you against a city. He ain't never failed, has he?

SEVERAL VOICES. No, Moses. (*All raise their heads.*)

MOSES. And he ain't goin' to fail us now. (*He prays. All bow*) Oh, Lawd, I'm turnin' over our brave young men to you, caize I know you don' want me to lead 'em any further. (*Rises*) Jest like you said, I've got to de Jordan but I cain't git over it. An' yere dey goin' now to take de city of Jericho. In a little while dey'll be marchin' 'roun' it. An' would you please be so good as to tell 'em what to do? Amen. (*To* JOSHUA) Go ahead. Ev'ybody follows Joshua now. Give de signal to move on wid ev'ything. (*A trumpet is heard*) You camp fo' de night in de city of Jericho. (MOSES *seats himself on the rock.*)

JOSHUA. Cain't we help you, Moses?

MOSES. You go ahead. De Lawd's got his plans fo' me. Soun' de signal to march. (*Another trumpet call is heard. The company starts marching off.* AARON *lingers a moment*) Take care of de Ark of de Covenant, Aaron.

AARON. Yes, Brother. Good-bye.

MOSES. Good-bye, Aaron. (*The singing is resumed softly and dies away. The last of the marchers has disappeared*) Yere I is, Lawd. De chillun is goin' into de Promised Land. (GOD *enters from behind the hill. He walks to* MOSES, *puts his hands on his shoulders*) You's with me, ain't you, Lawd?

GOD. Co'se I is.

MOSES. Guess I'm through, Lawd. Jest like you said I'd be, when I broke de tablets of de law. De ol machine's broke down.

GOD. Jest what was it I said to you, Moses? Do you remember?

MOSES. You said I couldn't go into de Promised Land.

GOD. Dat's so. But dat ain't all dey was to it.

MOSES. How you mean, Lawd?

GOD. Moses, you been a good man. You been a good leader of my people. You got me angry once, dat's true. And when you anger me I'm a God of Wrath. But I never meant you wasn't gonter have what was comin' to you. An' I ain't goin' to do you out of it, Moses. It's jest de country acrost de River dat you ain't gonter enter. You gonter have a Promised Land. I been gettin' it ready fo' you, fo' a long time. Kin you stand up?

MOSES (*rising, with* GOD'S *help*). Yes, suh, Lawd.

GOD. Come on, I'm goin' to show it to you. We goin' up dis hill to see it. Moses, it's a million times nicer dan de Land of Canaan. (*They start up the hill.*)

MOSES. I cain't hardly see.

GOD. Don't worry. Dat's jest caize you so old. (*They take a step or two up the hill, when* MOSES *stops suddenly.*)

MOSES. Oh!

GOD. What's de matter?

MOSES. We cain't be doin' dis!

GOD. Co'se we kin!

MOSES. But I fo'got! I fo'got about Joshua and de fightin' men!

GOD. How about 'em?

MOSES. Dey're marchin' on Jericho. I tol' 'em to march aroun' de walls and den de Lawd would be dere to tell 'em what to do.

GOD. Dat's all right. He's dere.

MOSES. Den who's dis helpin' me up de hill?

GOD. Yo' faith, yo' God.

MOSES. And is you over dere helpin' them too, Lawd? Is you goin' to tell dem poor chillun what to do?

GOD. Co'se I is. Listen, Moses, I'll show you how I'm helpin' dem.

(From the distance comes the blas of the rams' horns, the sound o crumbling walls, a roar, and a mo ment's silence. The CHOIR *begin "Joshua Fit De Battle of Jericho and continues through the rest of the scene.)*

MOSES. You did it, Lawd! You've tooken it! Listen to de chillun—dey' in de Land of Canaan at last! You' de only God dey ever was, ain't you Lawd?

GOD *(quietly)*. Come on, ol' man.

(They continue up the hill. The stage is darkened.)

MR. DESHEE *(in the dark)*. But even dat scheme didn' work. Caize after dey got into the Land of Canaan dey went to de dogs again. And dey went into bondage again. Only dis time it was in de city of Babylon.

(The CHOIR, *which has been singing "Cain't Stay Away," stops as the next scene begins.)*

SCENE V

Under a low ceiling is a room vaguely resembling a Negro night club in New Orleans. Two or three long tables run across the room, and on the left is a table on a dais with a gaudy canopy above it. The table bears a card marked "Reserved for King and guests."

Flashy young men and women are seated at the tables. About a dozen couples are dancing in the foreground to the tune of a jazz orchestra. The costumes are what would be worn at a Negro masquerade to represent the debauchees of Babylon.

FIRST MAN. When did yuh git to Babylon?

SECOND MAN. I jes' got in yesterday.

THIRD MAN *(dancing)*. How do you like dis baby, Joe?

FOURTH MAN. Hot damn! She could be de King's pet!

A WOMAN. Anybody seen my papa?

THIRD MAN. Don' fo'git de dance at de High Priest's house tomorrow.
(*The dance stops as a bugle call is heard. Enter* MASTER OF CEREMONIES.)

MASTER OF CEREMONIES. Stop! To-night's guest of honor, de King of Babylon an' party of five.
(*Enter the* KING *and five* GIRLS. *The* KING *has on an imitation ermine cloak over his conventional evening clothes and wears a diamond tiara. All rise as the* KING *enters, and sing, "Hail, de King of Bab—Bab—Baby-lon."*)

KING. Wait till you see de swell table I got. (*He crosses the stage to his table. The* GIRLS *are jabbering*) Re-mind me to send you a peck of rubies in de mo'nin'.

MASTER OF CEREMONIES. Ev'nin', King!

KING. Good ev'nin'. How's de party goin'?

MASTER OF CEREMONIES. Bes' one we ever had in Babylon, King.

KING. Any Jew boys yere?

MASTER OF CEREMONIES (*indicating some of the others*). Lot o' dem yere. I kin go git mo' if you want 'em.

KING. I was really referrin' to de High Priest. He's a 'ticlar frien' o' mine an' he might drop in. You know what he look like?

MASTER OF CEREMONIES. No, suh, but I'll be on de look-out fo' him.

KING. O. K. Now le's have a li'l good time.

MASTER OF CEREMONIES. Yes, suh. (*To the orchestra*) Let 'er go, boys. (*The music begins, waiters appear with food and great urns painted gold and silver, from which they pour out wine for the guests. The* MASTER OF CEREMONIES *exits. The* KING'*s dancing-girls go to the middle of the floor, and start to dance. The* KING *puts his arms about the waists of two* GIRLS, *and draws them to him.*)

KING. Hot damn! Da's de way! Let de Jew boys see our gals kin dance better'n deres. (*There is an ad lib. babel of "Da's de truth, King!" "I don' know—we got some good gals, too!" etc.*) Dey ain' nobody in de worl' like de Babylon gals.
(*The dancing grows faster, the watchers keep time with hand-claps. The door at the left opens suddenly, and the* PROPHET, *a patriarchal, ragged figure, enters. He looks bel-ligerently about the room, and is followed almost immediately by the* MASTER OF CEREMONIES.)

PROPHET. Stop!
(*The music and the dancers halt.*)

KING. What's de idea, bustin' up my party?

MASTER OF CEREMONIES. He said he was expected, King. I thought meb-be he was de—

KING. Did you think he was de High Priest of de Hebrews? Why, he's jest an ol' bum! De High Priest is a fashion plate. T'row dis ole bum out o' yere!

PROPHET. Stop!
(*Those who have been advancing to seize him stop, somewhat amused.*)

KING. Wait a minute. Don't throw him out. Let's see what he has to say.

PROPHET. Listen to me, King of Babylon! I've been sent yere by de Lawd God Jehovah. Don't you dare lay a hand on de Prophet!

KING. Oh, you're a prophet, is yuh? Well, you know we don' keer much fo' prophets in dis part of de country.

PROPHET. Listen to me, sons and daughters of Babylon! Listen, you children of Israel dat's given yo'selves over to de evil ways of yo' oppressors! You're all wallowin' like hogs in sin, an' de wrath of Gawd ain' goin' to be held back much longer! I'm tellin' you, repent befo' it's too late. Repent befo' Jehovah casts down de same fire dat burned up Sodom and Gomorrah. Repent befo' de— (*During this scene yells increase as the* PROPHET *continues. The* HIGH PRIEST *enters left. He is a fat voluptuary, elaborately clothed in brightly-colored robes. He walks in hand in hand with a gaudily dressed "chippy."*)

HIGH PRIEST (*noise stops*). Whoa, dere! What you botherin' de King fo'?

PROPHET (*wheeling*). And you, de High Priest of all Israel, walkin' de town wid a dirty li'l tramp.

KING. Seems to be a frien' o' yours, Jake.

HIGH PRIEST (*crossing to the* KING *with his girl*). Aw, he's one of dem wild men, like Jeremiah and Isaiah. Don' let him bother you none. (*Pushes* PROPHET *aside and goes to* KING'*s table.*)

PROPHET. You consort with harlots, an' yo' pollution in the sight of de Lawd. De Lawd God's goin' to smite you down, jest as he's goin' to smite down all dis wicked world! (*Grab* HIGH PRIEST *and turns him around.*)

KING (*angrily against the last part of the preceding speech*). Wait a minute. I'm getting tired of dis. Don throw him out. Jest kill him!

(*There is the sound of a shot. The* PROPHET *falls.*)

PROPHET. Smite 'em down, Lawd like you said. Dey ain't a decent person left in de whole world. (*He dies* MASTER OF CEREMONIES, *revolver in hand, looks down at the* PROPHET.)

MASTER OF CEREMONIES. He's dead, King.

KING. Some of you boys take him out. (*A couple of young men come from the background and walk off with the body.*)

HIGH PRIEST. Don' know whether you should'a done that, King.

KING. Why not?

HIGH PRIEST. I don' know whether de Lawd would like it.

KING. Now, listen, Jake. You know yo' Lawd ain't payin' much attention to dis man's town. Except fo' you boys, it's tho'ly protected by de Gawds o' Babylon.

HIGH PRIEST. I know, but jest de same—

KING. Look yere, s'pose I give you a couple hund'ed pieces of silver. Don' you s'pose you kin arrange to persuade yo' Gawd to keep his hands off?

HIGH PRIEST (*oilily*). Well of co'se we could try. I dunno how well it would work. (*As the* HIGH PRIEST *speaks, the* KING *claps his hands.* MASTER OF CEREMONIES *enters with bag of money.)*

KING. Yere it is.

HIGH PRIEST (*smiling*). I guess we kin square things up. (*He prays—whiningly*) Oh Lawd, please forgive my po' frien' de King o' Babylon. He didn't know what he was doin' an—

(*There is a clap of thunder, darkness for a second. The lights go up and* GOD *is standing in the center of the room.*)

GOD (*in a voice of doom*). Dat's about enough. (*The guests are horrified*) I'se stood all I kin from you. I tried to make dis a good earth. I helped Adam, I helped Noah, I helped Moses, an' I helped David. What's de grain dat grew out of de seed? Sin! Nothin' but sin throughout de whole world. I've given you ev'y chance. I sent you warriors and prophets. I've given you laws and commandments, an' you betrayed my trust. Ev'ything I've given you, you've defiled. Ev'y time I've fo'given you, you've mocked me. An' now de High Priest of Israel tries to trifle wid my name. Listen, you chillun of darkness, yo' Lawd is tired. I'm tired of de struggle to make you worthy of de breath I gave you. I put you in bondage ag'in to cure you an' yo' worse dan you was amongst de flesh pots of Egypt. So I renounce you. Listen to the words of yo' Lawd God Jehovah, for dey is de last words yo' ever hear from me. I repent of dese people dat I have made and I will deliver dem no more.

(*There is darkness and cries of "Mercy!" "Have pity, Lawd!" "We didn' mean it, Lawd!" "Forgive us, Lawd!" etc. The* CHOIR *sings "Death's Gwineter Lay His Cold Icy Hands On Me" until the lights go up on the next scene.*)

SCENE VI

GOD *is writing at his desk. Outside, past the door, goes* HOSEA, *a dignified old man, with wings like* JACOB'S. GOD, *sensing his presence, looks up from the paper he is examining, and follows him out of the corner of his eye. Angrily he resumes his work as soon as* HOSEA *is out of sight. There is a knock on the door.*

GOD. Who is it?

(GABRIEL *enters.*)

GABRIEL. It's de delegation, Lawd.

GOD (*wearily*). Tell 'em to come in. (ABRAHAM, ISAAC, JACOB, *and* MOSES *enter*) Good mo'nin', gen'lemen.

THE VISITORS. Good mo'nin', Lawd.

GOD. What kin I do for you?

MOSES. You know, Lawd. Go back to our people.

GOD (*shaking his head*). Ev'ry day fo' hund'eds of years you boys have come in to ask dat same thing. De answer is still de same. I repented of de people I made. I said I would deliver dem no more. Good mo'nin', gen'lemen. (*The four* VISITORS *rise and exeunt.* GABRIEL *remains*) Gabe, why do dey do it?

GABRIEL. I 'spect dey think you gonter change yo' mind.

GOD (*sadly*). Dey don' know me. (HOSEA *again passes the door. His shadow shows on wall.* GABRIEL *is perplexed, as he watches.* GOD *again looks surreptitiously over His shoulder at the passing figure*) I don' like dat, either.

GABRIEL. What, Lawd?

GOD. Dat man.

GABRIEL. He's jest a prophet, Lawd. Dat's jest old Hosea. He jest come up the other day.

GOD. I know. He's one of de few dat's come up yere since I was on de earth last time.

GABRIEL. Ain' been annoyin' you, has he?

GOD. I don' like him walkin' past de door.

GABRIEL. All you got to do is tell him to stop, Lawd.

GOD. Yes, I know. I don' want to tell him. He's got a right up yere or he wouldn't be yere.

GABRIEL. You needn' be bothered by him hangin' aroun' de office all de time. I'll tell 'im. Who's he think he—

GOD. No, Gabe. I find it ain't in me to stop him. I sometimes jest wonder why he don' come in and say hello.

GABRIEL. You want him to do dat? (*He moves as if to go to the door.*)

GOD. He never has spoke to me, and if he don' wanta come in, I ain't gonter make him. But dat ain't de worst of it, Gabriel.

GABRIEL. What is, Lawd?

GOD. Ev'y time he goes past de door I hears a voice.

GABRIEL. One of de angels?

GOD (*shaking his head*). It's from de earth. It's a man.

GABRIEL. You mean he's prayin'?

GOD. No, he ain't exactly prayin'. He's jest talkin' in such a way dat I got to lissen. His name is Hezdrel.

GABRIEL. Is he on de books?

GOD. No, not yet. But ev'y time dat Hosea goes past I hear dat voice.

GABRIEL. Den tell *it* to stop.

GOD. I find I don' want to do that, either. Dey's gettin' ready to take Jerusalem down dere. Dat was my big fine city. Dis Hezdrel, he's jest one of de defenders. (*Suddenly and passionately, almost wildly*) I ain't comin' down. You hear me? I ain't comin' down. (*He looks at* GABRIEL) Go ahead, Gabriel. 'Tend to yo' chores. I'm gonter keep wukkin' yere.

GABRIEL. I hates to see you feelin' like dis, Lawd.

GOD. Dat's all right. Even bein' Gawd ain't a bed of roses. (GABRIEL *exits.* HOSEA'*s shadow is on the wall*

For a second HOSEA *hesitates.* GOD *looks at the wall. Goes to window)* I hear you. I know yo' fightin' bravely, but I ain't comin' down. Oh, why don' you leave me alone? You know you ain't talkin' to me. *Is* you talkin' to me? I cain't stand yo' talkin' dat way. I kin only hear part of what yo' sayin', and it puzzles me. Don' you know you cain't puzzle God? *(A pause. Then tenderly)* Do you want me to come down dere ve'y much? You know I said I wouldn't come down? *(Fiercely)* Why don' he answer me a little? *(With clenched fists, looks down through the window)* Listen! I'll tell you what I'll do. I ain't goin' to promise you anythin', and I ain't goin' to do nothin' to help you. I'm jest feelin' a little low, an' I'm only comin' down to make myself feel a little better, dat's all.
(The stage is darkened. CHOIR *begins "A Blind Man Stood In De Middle of De Road," and continues until the lights go up on the next scene.)*

SCENE VII

It is a shadowed corner beside the walls of the temple in Jerusalem. The light of campfires flickers on the figure of HEZDREL, *who was* ADAM *in Part I. He stands in the same position* ADAM *held when first discovered but in his right hand is a sword, and his left is in a sling. Around him are several prostrate bodies. Pistol and cannon shots, then a trumpet call. Six* YOUNG MEN *enter from left in command of a* CORPORAL. *They are all armed.*

CORPORAL. De fightin's stopped fo' de night, Hezdrel.

HEZDREL. Yes?

CORPORAL. Dey're goin' to begin ag'in at cockcrow. *(*MAN *enters, crosses the stage and exits)* Herod say he's goin' to take de temple tomorrow, burn de books and de Ark of de Covenant, and put us all to de sword.

HEZDREL. Yo' ready, ain't you?

EVERYBODY. Yes, Hezdrel.

HEZDREL. Did de food get in through de hole in de city wall?
(Two SOLDIERS *enter, cross the stage and exit.)*

CORPORAL. Yessuh, we's goin' back to pass it out now.

HEZDREL. Good. Any mo' of our people escape today?

CORPORAL. Ol' Herod's got de ol' hole covered up now, but fifteen of our people got out a new one we made.
(Other SOLDIERS *enter, cross the stage and exit.)*

HEZDREL. Good. Take dese yere wounded men back and git 'em took care of.

CORPORAL. Yes, suh.
(They pick up the bodies on the ground and carry them offstage as HEZDREL *speaks.)*

HEZDREL. So dey gonter take de temple in de mo'nin'? We'll be waitin' for 'em. Jest remember, boys, when dey kill us we leap out of our skins, right into de lap of God.

(The men disappear with the wounded; from the deep shadow upstage comes GOD.*)*

GOD. Hello, Hezdrel—Adam.

HEZDREL *(rubbing his forehead)*. Who is you?

GOD. Me? I'm jest an ol' preacher, from back in de hills.

HEZDREL. What you doin' yere?

GOD. I heard you boys was fightin'. I jest wanted to see how it was goin'.

HEZDREL. Well, it ain't goin' so well.

GOD. Dey got you skeered, huh?

HEZDREL. Look yere, who is you, a spy in my brain?

GOD. Cain't you see I'se one of yo' people?

HEZDREL. Listen, Preacher, we ain't skeered. We's gonter be killed, but we ain't skeered.

GOD. I'se glad to hear dat. Kin I ask you a question, Hezdrel?

HEZDREL. What is it?

GOD. How is it you is so brave?

HEZDREL. Caize we got faith, dat's why!

GOD. Faith? In who?

HEZDREL. In our dear Lawd God.

GOD. But God say he abandoned ev' one down yere.

HEZDREL. Who say dat? Who dare say dat of de Lawd God of Hosea?

GOD. De God of Hosea?

HEZDREL. You heard me. Look yere, you *is* a spy in my brain!

GOD. No, I ain't, Hezdrel. I'm jest puzzled. You ought to know dat.

HEZDREL. How come you so puzzled 'bout de God of Hosea?

GOD. I don' know. Maybe I jest don' hear things. You see, I live 'way back in de hills.

HEZDREL. What you wanter find out?

GOD. Ain't de God of Hosea de same Jehovah dat was de God of Moses?

HEZDREL *(contemptuously)*. No. Dat ol' God of wrath and vengeance? We have de God dat Hosea preached to us. He's de one God.

GOD. Who's he?

HEZDREL *(reverently)*. De God of mercy.

GOD. Hezdrel, don' you think dey must be de same God?

HEZDREL. I don' know. I ain't bothered to think much about it. Maybe dey is. Maybe our God is de same ol' God. I guess we jest got tired of his appearance dat ol' way.

GOD. What you mean, Hezdrel?

HEZDREL. Oh, dat ol' God dat walked de earth in de shape of a man. I ess he lived wid man so much dat he seen was de sins in man. Dat's hat made him de God of wrath and ngeance. Co'se he made Hosea. n' Hosea never would a found hat mercy was unless dere was a ttle of it in God, too. Anyway, he n't a fearsome God no mo'. Hosea owed us dat.

OD. How you s'pose Hosea found at mercy?

EZDREL. De only way he could find . De only way I found it. De only ay anyone kin find it.

OD. How's dat?

EZDREL. Through sufferin'.

OD (*after a pause*). What if dey ill you in de mo'nin', Hezdrel.

EZDREL. If dey do, dey do. Dat's ll.

OD. Herod say he's goin' to burn e temple—

EZDREL. So he say.

OD. And burn de Ark an' de books. Den dat's de end of de books, ain't ?

EZDREL (*buoyantly*). What you nean? If he burns dem things in ere? Naw. Dem's jest copies.

OD. Where is de others?

EZDREL (*tapping his head*). Dey's set in yere. Fifteen got out through le hole in the city wall today. A hunlred and fifty got out durin' de week. Each of 'em is a set of de books. Dey's scattered safe all over de counryside now, jest waitin' to git pen and paper fo' to put 'em down ag'in.

GOD (*proudly*). Dey cain't lick you, kin dey, Hezdrel?

HEZDREL (*smiling*). I know dey cain't. (*Trumpet*) You better get out o' yere, Preacher, if you wanter carry de news to yo' people. It'll soon be daylight.

GOD. I'm goin'. (*He takes a step upstage and stops*) Want me to take any message?

HEZDREL. Tell de people in de hills dey ain't nobody like de Lawd God of Hosea.

GOD. I will. If dey kill you tomorrow I'll bet dat God of Hosea'll be waitin' for you.

HEZDREL. I *know* he will.

GOD (*quietly*). Thank you, Hezdrel.

HEZDREL. Fo' what?

GOD. Fo' tellin' me so much. You see I been so far away, I guess I was jest way behin' de times. (*He exits. Pause, then trumpet sounds.*)

(HEZDREL *paces back and forth once or twice. Another young* SOLDIER *appears. Other men enter and stand grouped about* HEZDREL.)

SECOND OFFICER (*excitedly*). De cock's jest crowed, Hezdrel. Dey started de fightin' ag'in.

HEZDREL. We's ready fo' 'em. Come on, boys. (*From the darkness upstage comes another group of* SOLDIERS) Dis is de day dey say dey'll git us. Le's fight till de last man goes. What d'you say?

CORPORAL. Le's go, Hezdrel!

HEZDREL (*calling left*). Give 'em ev'ything, boys!

(*There is a movement toward the*

left, a bugle call and the sound of distant battle. The lights go out. The CHOIR *is heard singing, "March On," triumphantly. They continue to sin after the lights go up on the ne scene.)*

SCENE VIII

It is the same setting as the Fish Fry Scene in Part I. The same angels ar present but the CHOIR, *instead of marching, is standing in a double row o an angle upstage right.* GOD *is seated in an armchair near center. He faces th audience. As the* CHOIR *continues to sing,* GABRIEL *enters, unnoticed by th chattering angels. He looks at* GOD *who is staring thoughtfully toward th audience.*

GABRIEL. You look a little pensive, Lawd. (GOD *nods his head*) Have a seegar, Lawd?

GOD. No thanks, Gabriel.

(GABRIEL *goes to the table, accepts a cup of custard; chats with the angel behind the table for a moment as he sips, puts the cup down and returns to the side of* GOD.)

GABRIEL. You look awful pensive, Lawd. You been sittin' yere, lookin' dis way, an awful long time. Is it somethin' serious, Lawd?

GOD. Very serious, Gabriel.

GABRIEL (*awed by His tone*). Lawd, is de time come for me to blow?

GOD. Not yet, Gabriel. I'm just thinkin'.

GABRIEL. What about, Lawd? (*Puts up hand. Singing stops.*)

GOD. 'Bout somethin' de boy tol' me. Somethin' 'bout Hosea, and himself. How dey foun' somethin'.

GABRIEL. What, Lawd?

GOD. Mercy. (*A pause*) Throug *sufferin'*, he said.

GABRIEL. Yes, Lawd.

GOD. I'm tryin' to find it, too. I. awful impo'tant. It's awful impo'ta to all de people on my earth. Did h mean dat even God must suffe (GOD *continues to look out over th audience for a moment and then look of surprise comes into his fac He sighs. In the distance a voi cries.*)

THE VOICE. Oh, look at him! O look, dey goin' to make him carry up dat high hill! Dey goin' to na him to it! Oh, dat's a terrible burde for one man to carry!

(GOD *rises and murmurs "Yes!" as in recognition. The heavenly bein have been watching him closely, an now, seeing him smile gently, dra back, relieved. All the angels bur into "Hallelujah, King Jesus."* GO *continues to smile as the lights fad away. The singing becomes forti simo.*)

CURTAIN

Biography

BY S. N. BEHRMAN

FOR
SONYA AND CARL

Biography was first produced at the Guild Theatre, New York City, by the Theatre Guild, on December 12, 1932, and closed on July 29, 1933 Following is the original cast:

RICHARD KURT	Earle Larimore
MINNIE, *Marion Froude's maid*	Helen Salinger
MELCHIOR FEYDAK, *a Viennese composer*	Arnold Korff
MARION FROUDE	Ina Claire
LEANDER NOLAN	Jay Fassett
WARWICK WILSON	Alexander Clark
ORRIN KINNICOTT	Charles Richman
SLADE KINNICOTT, *his daughter*	Mary Arbenz

Production directed by Philip Moeller

Setting designed by Jo Mielziner

SCENES

The entire action takes place in Marion Froude's studio in New York City.
The time is 1932

ACT ONE

About five o'clock of an afternoon in November

ACT TWO

Afternoon, three weeks later

ACT THREE

Late afternoon, two weeks later

The curtain is lowered during the act to denote a lapse of time

BIOGRAPHY

ACT ONE

SCENE—*The studio apartment of* MARION FROUDE *in an old-fashioned studio building in West 57th St., New York. A great, cavernous room expressing in its polyglot furnishings the artistic patois of the various landlords who have sublet this apartment to wandering tenants like* MARION FROUDE. *The styles range from medieval Florence to contemporary Grand Rapids; on a movable raised platform in the center is a papal throne chair in red velvet and gold fringes. Not far from it is an ordinary American kitchen chair. The hanging lamp which sheds a mellow light over a French Empire sofa is filigreed copper Byzantine. Another and longer sofa across the room against the grand piano is in soft green velvet and has the gentility of a polite Park Avenue drawing room. Under the stairs, rear, which go up to* MARION'S *bedroom, are stacks of her canvases. There is a quite fine wood carving of a Madonna which seems to be centuries old and in the wall spaces looking at audience are great, dim canvases—copies by some former tenant left probably in lieu of rent—of Sargent's Lord Ribblesdale and Mme. X.*

Whether it is due to the amenable spirit of the present incumbent or because they are relaxed in the democracy of art, these oddments of the creative spirit do not suggest disharmony. The room is warm, musty, with restful shadows and limpid lights. The enormous leaded window on the right, though some of its members are patched and cracked, gleams in the descending twilight with an opalescent light; even the copper cylinder of the fire extinguisher and its attendant axe, visible in the hall, seem to be not so much implements against calamity, as amusing museum-bits cherished from an earlier time. Every school is represented here except the modern. The studio has the mellowness of anachronism.

There is a door upstage left leading to the kitchen and MINNIE'S *bedroom; a door, center, under the stairs leads into hallway. A door on the stair landing, center, leads to* MARION'S *bedroom.*

TIME—*About five o'clock of an afternoon in November.*

AT RISE—RICHARD KURT *is finishing a nervous cigarette. He has the essential audacity which comes from having seen the worst happen, from having endured the keenest pain. He has the hardness of one who knows that he can be devastated by pity, the bitterness which comes from having seen, in early youth, justice thwarted and tears unavailing, the self-reliance which comes from having seen everything go in a disordered world save one stubborn, unyielding core of belief—at everything else he laughs, in this alone he trusts. He has the intensity of the fanatic and the carelessness of the vagabond. He goes to the door from the hall and calls.*

KURT. Say, you, hello there—what's your name?

(MINNIE, MARION FROUDE's *inseparable maid, a German woman of about fifty, comes in. She is indignant at being thus summarily summoned, and by a stranger.*)

MINNIE (*with dignity*). My name iss Minnie, if you please.

KURT. What time did Miss Froude go out?

MINNIE. About two o'clock.

KURT. It's nearly five now. She should be home, shouldn't she?

MINNIE. She said she vas coming home to tea and that iss all I know.

KURT (*grimly*). I know. She invited me to tea. . . . Where did she go to lunch?

MINNIE (*acidly*). That I do not know.

KURT. Did someone call for her or did she go out alone? I have a reason for asking.

MINNIE. She went out alone. Any more questions?

KURT. No. I see there's no point in asking you questions.

MINNIE. Den vy do you ask dem? (*The doorbell rings.* MINNIE *throws up her hands in despair. She goes out muttering: "Ach Gott."* KURT *is rather amused at her. He lights another cigarette.*)

(*Sounds of vociferous greeting outside. "Ach mein lieber Herr Feydak . . ."* MELCHIOR FEYDAK, *the Austrian composer, comes in. He is forty-five, tall, hook-nosed, thin-faced, a humorist with a rather sad face.*)

FEYDAK. Nun, Minnie, und vo is die schlechte. . . . ? (MINNIE *makes a sign to him not to disclose their free-masonry in the presence of strangers. She is cautious. . . .*) Not home yet, eh, Minnie? Where is she? Well—well. How do they say—gallivanting—I love that word—gallivanting as usual. Well, I'll wait. It's humiliating—but I'll wait. Chilly! Brr! I don't mind so much being cold in London or Vienna. I expect it. But I can't stand it in New York. (*He warms himself before fire*) And who is this young man?

MINNIE (*shortly*). Ich weiss nicht! . . . Er hat alle fünf minuten gefragt wo sie ist— (*She goes out.*)

FEYDAK. You've offended Minnie, I can see that.

KURT. That's just too bad!

FEYDAK. We all tremble before Minnie. . . . Been waiting long?

KURT. Over half an hour!

FEYDAK. Extraordinary thing—ever since I've known Marion there's always been someone waiting for her. There are two kinds of people in one's life—people whom one keeps waiting—and the people for whom one waits. . . .

KURT. Is that an epigram?

FEYDAK. Do you object to epigrams?

KURT (*with some pride*). I despise epigrams.

FEYDAK (*tolerantly sizing* KURT *up*). Hm! Friend of Miss Froude's?

KURT. Not at all.

FEYDAK. That at least is no cause for pride.

KURT. I just don't happen to be, that's all.

FEYDAK. I commiserate you.

KURT. I despise gallantry also.

FEYDAK (*lightly*). And I thought Americans were so sentimental. . . .

KURT. And, together with other forms of glibness, I loathe generalization. . . .

FEYDAK (*drily*). Young man, we have a great deal in common.

KURT. Also, there is a faint flavor of condescension in the way you say "young man" for which I don't really care. . . .

FEYDAK (*delighted and encouraging him to go on*). What about me do you like? There must be something.

KURT. If I were that kind your question would embarrass me.

FEYDAK (*very pleased*). Good for Marion!

KURT. Why do you say that?

FEYDAK. She always had a knack for picking up originals!

KURT. You are under a misapprehension. Miss Froude did not pick me up. I picked her up. (FEYDAK *stares at him. This does shock him*) I wrote Miss Froude a letter—a business-letter. She answered and gave me an appointment for four-thirty. It is now after five. She has taken a half-hour out of my life. . . .

FEYDAK. I gather that fragment of time has great value. . . .

KURT. She has shortened my life by thirty minutes. God, how I hate Bohemians!

FEYDAK (*innocently*). Are you by any chance—an Evangelist?

KURT. I am—for the moment—a businessman. I'm not here to hold hands or drink tea. I'm here on business. My presence here is a favor to Miss Froude and likely to bring her a handsome profit. . . .

FEYDAK. Profit! Ah! That accounts for her being late. . . .

KURT (*sceptically*). You despise profit, I suppose! Are you—by any chance—old-world?

FEYDAK. Young man, your technique is entirely wasted on me. . . .

KURT. Technique! What are you talking about?

FEYDAK. When I was a young man—before I achieved any sort of success—I was rude on principle. Deliberately rude and extravagantly bitter in order to make impression. When it is no longer necessary for you to wait around for people in order to do them favors you'll mellow down, I assure you.

KURT (*fiercely, he has been touched*). You think so, do you! That's where you're mistaken! I'm rude now. When I'm successful I'll be murderous!

FEYDAK (*genially*). More power to you! But I've never seen it happen yet. Success is the great muffler! Not an epigram, I hope. If it is—forgive me.
(*A moment's pause.* KURT *studies him while* FEYDAK *crosses to stove and warms his hands.*)

KURT. I know you from somewhere. It's very tantalising.

FEYDAK. I don't think so. I have only just arrived in this country. . . .

KURT. Still I know you—I'm sure—I've seen you somewhere. . . .

FEYDAK (*understanding the familiarity*). Maybe you know Miss Froude's portrait of me. . . .

KURT (*doubtfully*). Yes—maybe that's it . . . may I ask. . . . ?

FEYDAK. Certainly. My name is Feydak.

KURT. The composer?

FEYDAK (*drily*). Yes. . . .

KURT. I thought he was dead. . . .

FEYDAK. That is true. But I hope you won't tell anyone—for I am his ghost. . . .

KURT (*putting this down for Continental humor and genuinely contrite*). Forgive me. . . .

FEYDAK. But why?

KURT. If you really are Feydak the composer—I have the most enormous admiration for you. I worship music above everything.

FEYDAK (*slightly bored*). Go on. . . .

KURT. I read in the paper—you're on your way to Hollywood. . . .

FEYDAK. Yes. I am on my way to Hollywood. . . .

KURT. In the new state men like you won't have to prostitute themselves in Hollywood. . . .

FEYDAK. Ah! A Utopian!

KURT. Yes. You use the word as a term of contempt. Why? Every artist is a Utopian. You must be very tired or you wouldn't be so contemptuous of Utopians.

FEYDAK (*with a charming smile*). I am rather tired. Old-world, you would call it.

KURT. You can be anything you like. . . .

FEYDAK (*satirically*). Thank you. . . .

KURT. You've written lovely music—I have a friend who plays every note of it. I didn't see your operetta when it was done here. . . . I didn't have the price . . . it was very badly done though, I heard. . . .

FEYDAK. I must explain to you—you are under a misapprehension. . . .

KURT. It was done here, wasn't it?

FEYDAK. Not about the operetta. You are under a misapprehension—about me. I am a composer—but I didn't write "Danubia." That was my brother, Victor Feydak. You are right. He is dead. You are the first person I have met in New York who even suspected it.

KURT. I'm sorry.

FEYDAK. Not at all. I am flattered. At home our identities were never confused. Is this the well-known American hospitality? It is, in some sort, compensation for his death. . . . (KURT *is embarrassed and uncomfortable. It is part of his essential insecurity; he is only really at home in protest. He wants to get out.*)

KURT. I'm sorry—I. . . .

FEYDAK (*easily*). But why?

KURT. I think I'll leave a note for Miss Froude—get that girl in here, will you?

FEYDAK. Let's have some tea—she's sure to be in any minute. . . .

KURT. No, thanks. And you might tell her for me that if she wants to see me about the matter I wrote her about she can come to my office. . . . (MARION FROUDE *comes in. She is one of those women the sight of whom on Fifth Ave., where she has just been walking, causes foreigners to exclaim enthusiastically that American women are the most radiant in the world. She is tall, lithe, indomitably alive. Unlike* KURT, *the tears in things have warmed without scalding her; she floats life like a dancer's scarf in perpetual enjoyment of its colors and contours.*)

MARION (*to* KURT). I'm *so* sorry!

FEYDAK (*coming toward her*). I don't believe a word of it!
(*She is overjoyed at seeing* FEYDAK. *She can't believe for a second that it is he. Then she flies into his arms.*)

MARION. Feydie! Oh, Feydie, I've been trying everywhere to reach you —I can't believe it. . . . Feydie darling!

FEYDAK (*severely*). Is this how you keep a business appointment, Miss Froude?

MARION. How long have you waited? If I'd only known. . . . (*Suddenly conscious that* KURT *had waited too*) Oh, I'm sorry, Mr.— Mr.— . . . ?

KURT. Kurt. Richard Kurt.

MARION. Oh, of course, Mr. Kurt. I say—could you possibly—would it be too much trouble—could you come back?

FEYDAK (*same tone*). This young man is here on business. It is more important. I can wait. I'll come back.

MARION. No, no, Feydie—no, no. I can't wait for that. I'm sure Mr. Kurt will understand. Mr. Feydak is an old friend whom I haven't seen in ever so long. It isn't as if Mr. Kurt were a regular businessman.

FEYDAK (*amused*). How do you know he isn't?

MARION (*breathless with excitement*). I can tell. He's not a bit like his letter. When I got your letter I was sure you were jowley and, you know— (*She makes a gesture*) convex. I'm sure, Feydie—whatever the business is— (*To* KURT) you did say you had some, didn't you?—I'm sure it can wait. A half-hour anyway. Can't it wait a half-hour? You see, Feydie and I haven't seen each other since. . . .

KURT. Vienna!

MARION (*astonished*). Yes. How did you know?

KURT. It's always since Vienna that Bohemians haven't seen each other, isn't it? I'll be back in thirty minutes. (*He goes.*)

MARION. What a singular young man!

FEYDAK. I've been having a very amusing talk with him. Professional rebel, I think. Well, my dear—you look marvelous! (*They take each other in.*)

MARION. Isn't it wonderful. . . .

FEYDAK. It is nice! (*They sit on sofa,* MARION *left of* FEYDAK.)

MARION. How long is it?

FEYDAK. Well, it's since. . . .

MARION (*firmly*). Since Vicki died.

FEYDAK. That's right. I haven't seen you since.

MARION. Since that day—we walked behind him.

FEYDAK. Yes.

MARION. I felt I couldn't bear to stay on. I left for London that night.

FEYDAK. Yes.

MARION. It's six years, isn't it?

FEYDAK. Yes. Six years last June. (*A pause.*)

MARION. What's happened since then? Nothing. . . .

FEYDAK. How long have you been here?

MARION. Two weeks.

FEYDAK. Busy?

MARION. Not professionally, I'm afraid. People are charming—they ask me to lunch and dinner and they're—"oh, so interested"—but no commissions so far. And God, how I need it. . . .

FEYDAK. I'm surprised. I gathered you'd been very successful.

MARION. It's always sounded like it, hasn't it? The impression, I believe, is due to the extreme notoriety of some of my sitters Oh, I've managed well enough up to now—if I'd been more provident I dare say I could have put a tidy bit by—but at the moment people don't seem in a mood to have their portraits done. Are they less vain than they used to be? Or just poorer?

FEYDAK. Both, I think. . . .

MARION. Last time I came here I was awfully busy. Had great réclame because I'd been in Russia doing leading Communists. Obeying some subtle paradox the big financiers flocked to me. Pittsburgh manufacturers wanted to be done by the same brush that had tackled Lenin. Now they seem less eager. Must be some reason, Feydie. But what about you? Let me hear about you. How's Kathie?

FEYDAK. Well. She's here with me.

MARION. And Sadye?

FEYDAK. Splendid.

MARION. She must be a big girl now.

FEYDAK. As tall as you are.

MARION. Kathie used to hate me, didn't she? Frightened to death of me. Was afraid I was after Vicki's money. . . .

FEYDAK. Yes. She was afraid you'd marry him and that we should have less from him. When we knew he was dying she was in a panic.

MARION. Poor dear—I could have spared her all that worry if she'd been halfway civil to me.

FEYDAK. Kathie is practical. And she is a good mother. Those are attributes which make women avaricious.

MARION. Did Vicki leave you very much?

FEYDAK. Not very much. Half to you.

MARION. Really? How sweet of him! How dear of him!

FEYDAK. We've spent it. . . .

MARION. Of course you should.

FEYDAK. But I'll soon be in position to repay you your share. I'm on my way to Hollywood.

MARION. Are you really? How wonderful for you, Feydie! I'm so glad.

FEYDAK. You've been there, haven't you?

MARION. Yes. Last time I was in America.

FEYDAK. Did you like it?

MARION. Well, it's the new Eldorado—art on the gold-rush.

FEYDAK (*with a kind of ironic bitterness*). Vicki left me an inheritance subject, it appears, to perpetual renewal.

MARION. How do you mean?

FEYDAK. Things have been going from bad to worse in Vienna—you haven't been there since '25 so you don't know. The theatre's pretty well dead—even the first-rate fellows have had a hard time making their way. I managed to get several scores to do—but they were not—except that they were failures—up to my usual standard. . . .

MARION (*laughing, reproachful*). Oh, Feydie . . . !

FEYDAK. If it weren't for the money Vicki left me—and you!—I don't know how we should have got through at all these six years. About a month ago we reached the end of our rope—we were hopelessly in debt—no means of getting out—when the miracle happened. . . .
(MARION *is excited, touches his knee with her hand.*)

MARION (*murmuring*). I can't bear it. . . .

FEYDAK. It was my dramatic agent on the phone. A great American film magnate was in town and wanted to see me. Ausgerechnet me and no other. Even my agent couldn't keep the surprise out of his voice. Why me? I asked. God knows, says the agent. Well, we went around to the Bristol to see the magnate. And, as we talked to him, it gradually became apparent. He thought I was Vicki. He didn't know Vicki was dead! He thought I had written "Danubia."

MARION. Did he say so?

FEYDAK. No—not at all. But as we shook hands at the end he said to me: "Any man that can write a tune like this is the kind of man we want." And he whistled, so out of tune that I could hardly recognize it myself, the waltz from Danubia. Do you remember it? (*He starts to hum the waltz and* MARION *joins him. They hum together, then* FEYDAK *continues to talk as* MARION *continues to hum a few more measures*) He was so innocent, so affable that I had an impulse to say to him: "Look here, old fellow, you don't want me, you want my brother and, in order to get him, you'll have to resurrect him!" But noble impulses are luxury impulses. You have to be well off to gratify them. I kept quiet. We shook hands and here I am. Tonight they're giving me a dinner at the Waldorf Astoria for the press to meet my brother! Irony if you like, eh, Marion? (*There is a pause.*)

MARION. Feydie . . . (*A moment. He does not answer*) Feydie—do you mind if I say something to you—very frankly?

FEYDAK. I doubt whether you can say anything to me more penetrating than the remarks I habitually address to myself.

MARION. You know Vicki was very fond of you. He used to say you put too high a valuation on genius.

FEYDAK. Because he had it he could afford to deprecate it.

MARION. Over and over again he used to say to me: "You know, Marion," he would say, "as a human being Feydie's far superior to me, more amiable, more witty, more talented, more patient. . . ."

FEYDAK. (*shakes his head*). Not true. I simply give the impression of these things. . . .

MARION. You underrate yourself, Feydie. . . . How this would have amused him—this incident with the Hollywood man!

FEYDAK (*smiling bitterly*). It would rather. . . .

MARION. Why do you grudge giving him a laugh somewhere? I never had a chance to tell you in Vienna—things were so—so close and terrible—at the end—but he had the greatest tenderness for you. He used to speak of you—I can't tell you how much. "Because of this sixth sense for making tunes which I have and he hasn't," he said to me one day—not a week before he died— "he thinks himself less than me." He used to tell me that everything he had he owed to you—to the sacrifices you made to send him to the Conservatory when he was a boy. . . . The extent to which he had outstripped you hurt him—hurt him. I felt he would have given anything to dip into the golden bowl of his genius and pour it over you. And do you know what was the terror of his life, the obsessing terror of his life?—his fear of your resenting him. . . .

FEYDAK (*moved, deeply ashamed*). Marion. . . .

MARION. Don't resent him now, Feydie. . . . Why, it's such fun—don't you see? It's such a curious, marginal survival for him—that a badly-remembered waltz-tune, five years after his death, should be the means of helping you at a moment when you need it so badly. . . . It's delicious, Feydie. It's such fun! The only awful thing is the possibility that he is unaware of it. It would have pleased him so, Feydie. Must you grudge him it?

FEYDAK. You make me horribly ashamed. . . .

MARION (*brightly*). Nonsense. . . .

FEYDAK. Because I did grudge him it—yes—I won't, though—I see now that it never occurred to me how . . . (*Bursts out laughing suddenly*) God, it is funny, isn't it. . . .

MARION (*joining in his laughter*). Of course—it's delightful. . . . (*They both laugh heartily and long.*)

MARION. And the funny thing is—you'll be much better for them out there than he would have been.

FEYDAK. Surely! They'll be able to whistle *my* tunes!

MARION. Don't you see!

FEYDAK. Oh, Lieber Schatzel, come out there with me.

MARION. Can't.

FEYDAK. I wish, Marion, you would come. I never feel life so warm and good as when you are in the neighborhood.

MARION. Dear Feydie, you're very comforting.

FEYDAK. Is there someone that keeps you here?

MARION. No, there's no one. I'm quite alone.

FEYDAK. Well then. . . !

MARION. No, this isn't the moment for me, Feydie. Besides, I can't afford the journey. I'm frightfully hard up at the moment.

FEYDAK. Well, look here, I . . .

MARION. No, that's sweet of you but I couldn't.

FEYDAK. I don't see why—it's too silly. . . .

MARION. Vanity. A kind of vanity.

FEYDAK. But I owe it to you!

MARION. I suppose it is foolish in a way—but I've a kind of pride in maneuvering on my own. I always have done it—in that way at least I've been genuinely independent. I'm a little proud of my ingenuity. And do you know, Feydie, no matter how hard up I've been at different times something's always turned up for me. I have a kind of curiosity to know what it will be this time. It would spoil the fun for me to take money from my friends. Nothing so much as that would make me doubtful of my own—shall we say—marketability?

FEYDAK. Paradoxical, isn't it?

MARION. Why not? Anyway, it's a pet idée of mine, so be a darling and let me indulge it, will you, Feydie, and don't offer me money. Anyway, I've a business proposition on. . . .

FEYDAK. Have you?

MARION. That young man who was just here. Do you suppose he'll come back? Now I think of it we were a

bit short with him, weren't we? I was so glad to see you I couldn't be bothered with him! (*Sound of door-bell*) Ah! You see! (*Calls outside*) Show him in, Minnie!
(MINNIE *comes in and exits hall-door to admit the visitor.*)

FEYDAK. What are you doing for dinner?

MARION. There's a young man who attached himself to me on the boat

FEYDAK. Oh, Marion!

MARION. I seem to attract youth, Feydie. What shall I do about it?

FEYDAK. Where are you dining?

MARION. I don't know. . . . Which speakeasy? Tell me which one and I'll . . .
(MINNIE *ushers in* MR. LEANDER NOLAN. *He is middle-aged, ample, handsome. Looks like the late Warren Gamaliel Harding. Soberly dressed and wears a waistcoat with white piping on it. The façade is impeccable but in* NOLAN'S *eye you may discern, at odd moments, an uncertainty, an almost boyish anxiety to please, to be right, that is rather engaging.* MARION, *who expected the young man, is rather startled.* MR. NOLAN *regards her with satisfaction.*)

NOLAN. Hello, Marion.

MARION (*doubtfully, feels she should remember him*). How do you do? Er—will you excuse me—just a second. . . ?

NOLAN (*genially*). Certainly. (*He moves right.* MARION *walks* FEYDIE *to the hall door.*)

FEYDAK (*under his breath to her*) Looks like a commission. (*She makes a gesture of silent prayer.*)

MARION (*out loud*). Telephone me in an hour, will you, Feydie, and let me know which speakeasy. . . .

FEYDAK (*once he has her in the hallway out of* NOLAN'S *hearing*). Also, du kommst ganz sicher?

MARION. Vielleicht später. 'Bye, Feydie dear.
(FEYDIE *goes out.* MARION *turns to face* NOLAN *who is standing with his arms behind his back rather enjoying the surprise he is about to give her.*)

NOLAN. How are you, Marion?

MARION (*delicately*). Er—do I know you?

NOLAN. Yes. You know me.

MARION. Oh, yes—of course!

NOLAN. About time!

MARION (*brightly insecure*). Lady Winchester's garden-party at Ascot—two summers ago. . . .

NOLAN. Guess again!

MARION. No—I know you perfectly well—it's just that—no, don't tell me. . . . (*She covers her eyes with her hand, trying to conjure him out of the past.*)

NOLAN. This is astonishing. If someone had said to me that I could walk into a room in front of Marion Froude and she not know me I'd have told 'em they were crazy . . .

MARION (*desperate*). I do know you. I know you perfectly well—it's just that . . .

NOLAN. You'll be awful sore at yourself—I warn you . . .

MARION. I can't forgive myself now—I know!

NOLAN. I don't believe it!

MARION. The American Embassy dinner in Rome on the Fourth of July—last year—you sat on my right.

NOLAN. I did not!

MARION (*miserably*). Well, you sat somewhere. Where did you sit?

NOLAN. I wasn't there.

MARION. Well, I think it's very unkind of you to keep me in suspense like this. I can't bear it another second!

NOLAN. I wouldn't have believed it!

MARION. Well, give me some hint, will you?

NOLAN. Think of home—think of Tennessee!

MARION. Oh . . . !

NOLAN. Little Mary Froude. . . .

MARION (*a light breaking in on her*). No! Oh, no!

NOLAN. Well, it's about time. . . .

MARION. But . . . ! You were . . .

NOLAN. Well, so were you!

MARION. But—Bunny—you aren't Bunny Nolan, are you? You're his brother!

NOLAN. I have no brother.

MARION. But Bunny—Bunny dear—how important you've become!

NOLAN. I haven't done badly—no.

MARION. Here, give me your coat and hat— (MARION, *taking his coat and hat, crosses upstage to piano, and leaves them there. Laughing, a little hysterical*) You should have warned me. It's not fair of you. Bunny! Of all people—I can scarcely believe it. . . . (*A moment's pause. He doesn't quite like her calling him Bunny but he doesn't know how to stop it. She sits on model stand looking up at him as she says:*) You look wonderful. You look like a—like a—Senator or something monumental like that.

NOLAN (*sits on sofa below piano*). That's a good omen. I'll have to tell Orrin.

MARION. What's a good omen? And who is Orrin?

NOLAN. Your saying I look like a Senator. Because—I don't want to be premature—but in a few months I may be one.

MARION. A Senator!

NOLAN (*smiling*). Senator. Washington. Not Nashville.

MARION. Do you want to be a Senator or can't you help it?

NOLAN (*to whom this point of view is incomprehensible*). What do you mean?

MARION. I'll paint you, Bunny. Toga. Ferrule. Tribune of the people.

NOLAN. Not a bad idea. Not a bad idea at all. I remember now—you were always sketching me. Sketching everything. Say, you've done pretty well yourself, haven't you?

MARION. Not as well as you have, Bunny. Imagine. Bunny Nolan—a Senator at Washington. Well, well! And tell me—how do I seem to you? You knew me at once, didn't you?

NOLAN. Sure I did. You haven't changed so much—a little, perhaps.

MARION (*delicately*). Ampler?

NOLAN (*inspecting her*). No . . . not that I can notice. . . .

MARION (*with a sigh of relief*). That's wonderful. . . .

NOLAN. You look just the same. You are just the same.

MARION. Oh, you don't know, Bunny. I'm artful. How long is it since we've seen each other? Twelve years anyway. More than that—fifteen . . .

NOLAN. Just about—hadn't even begun to practice law yet. . . .

MARION. We were just kids . . . children. . . . And now look at you! I can see how successful you are, Bunny.

NOLAN. How?

MARION. White piping on your vest. That suggests directorates to me. Multiple control. Vertical corporations. Are you vertical or horizontal, Bunny?

NOLAN. I'm both.

MARION. Good for you! Married?

NOLAN. Not yet . . .

MARION. How did you escape? You're going to be, though.

NOLAN. I'm engaged.

MARION. Who's the lucky girl?

NOLAN. Slade Kinnicott. Daughter of Orrin Kinnicott.

MARION. Orrin Kinnicott. The newspaper publisher?

NOLAN. Yes. He's backing me for the Senate.

MARION. Well, if he's backing you you ought to get in. All that circulation—not very good circulation, is it? Still, one vote's as good as another, I suppose. . . .

NOLAN (*hurt*). In my own State the Kinnicott papers are as good as any . . .

MARION. Well, I wish you luck. I'm sure you'll have it. My! Senator Nolan!

NOLAN. If I get in I'll be the youngest Senator . . .

MARION. And the best-looking too, Bunny . . .

NOLAN (*embarrassed*). Well . . .

MARION. You're fussed! How charming of you! (*She sits beside him*) Oh, Bunny, I'm very proud of you, really.

NOLAN. You see, Marion, I've been pretty successful in the law. Tremendously successful, I may say. I've organized some of the biggest mergers of recent years. I've made a fortune—a sizeable fortune. Well, one day I woke up and I said to myself: Look here, Nolan, you've got to take stock. You've got to ask yourself where you're heading. I'd been so busy I'd never had a chance to ask myself these fundamental questions before. And I decided to call a halt. You've got enough, more than enough for life, I said to myself. It's time you quit piling up money for yourself and began thinking about your fellow-man. I've always been ambitious, Marion. You know that. You shared all my early dreams . . .

MARION. Of course I did. . . .

NOLAN. Remember I always told you I didn't want money and power for their own sakes—I always wanted to be a big man in a real sense—to do something for my country and my time . . .

MARION. Yes. Sometimes you sounded like Daniel Webster, darling. I'm not a bit surprised you're going in the Senate.

NOLAN. I never thought—even in my wildest dreams. . . .

MARION. Well, you see you underestimated yourself. You may go even higher—the White House—why not?

NOLAN. I never let myself think of that.

MARION. Why not? It's no more wonderful that what's happened already, is it?

NOLAN (*Napoleon at Saint Helena*). Destiny!

MARION. Exactly. Destiny!

NOLAN (*kind, richly human, patronizing*). And you, my dear . . . ?

MARION. As you see. Obscure. Uncertain. Alone. Nowhere at all. Not the remotest chance of my getting into the Senate—unless I marry into it. Oh, Bunny, after you get to Washington will you introduce me to some Senators?

NOLAN. Well, that's premature . . . Naturally if the people should favor me I'd do what I could. I never forget a friend. Whatever faults I may have, disloyalty, I hope, is not one of them.

MARION. Of course it isn't. You're a dear. You always were. (*A moment's pause.*)

NOLAN. Who was that fellow I found you with when I came in?

MARION. An old friend of mine from Vienna—a composer.

NOLAN. You've been a lot with foreigners, haven't you?

MARION. A good deal . . .

NOLAN. Funny, I don't understand that.

MARION. Foreigners are people, you know, Bunny. Some of 'em are rather nice.

NOLAN. When I'm abroad a few weeks home begins to look pretty good to me.

MARION. I love New York but I can't say I feel an acute nostalgia for Tennessee. (*Another pause. He stares at her suddenly—still incredulous that he should be seeing her at all, and that, after all these years and quite without him, she should be radiant still.*)

NOLAN. Little Marion Froude! I can't believe it somehow. . . .

MARION. Oh, Bunny! You're sweet! You're so—ingenuous. That's what I always liked about you.

NOLAN. What do you mean?

MARION. The way you look at me, the incredulity, the surprise. What did you expect to see? A hulk, a remnant, a whitened sepulchre . . . what?

NOLAN (*uncomfortable at being caught*). Not—not at all. . . .

MARION. Tell me, Bunny, what . . . ? I won't be hurt . . .

NOLAN (*miserably, stumbling*). Well, naturally, after what I'd heard . . .

MARION. What have you heard? Oh, do tell me, Bunny.

NOLAN. Well, I mean—about your life. . . .

MARION. Racy, Bunny? Racy?

NOLAN. No use going into that. You chose your own way. Everybody has a right to live their own life, I guess.

MARION (*pats his arm*). That's very handsome of you Bunny. I hope you take that liberal point of view when you reach the Senate.

NOLAN. I came here, Marion, in a perfectly sincere mood, to say something to you, something that's been on my mind ever since we parted, but if you're going to be flippant I suppose there's no use my saying anything—I might as well go, in fact. (*But he makes no attempt to do so.*)

MARION (*seriously*). Do forgive me, Bunny. One gets into an idiom that passes for banter but really I'm not so changed. I'm not flippant. I'm awfully glad to see you, Bunny. (*An undertone of sadness creeps into her voice*) After all, one makes very few real friends in life—and you are part of my youth—we are part of each other's youth . . .

NOLAN. You didn't even know me!

MARION. Complete surprise! After all I've been in New York many times during these years and never once—never once have you come near me. You've dropped me all these years. (*With a sigh*) I'm afraid, Bunny, your career has been too much with you.

NOLAN (*grimly*). So has yours!

MARION. I detect an overtone—faint but unmistakable—of moral censure.

NOLAN (*same tone*). Well, I suppose it's impossible to live one's life in art without being sexually promiscuous! (*He looks at her accusingly.*)

MARION. Oh, dear me, Bunny! What shall I do? Shall I blush? Shall I hang my head in shame? What shall I do? How does one react in the face of an appalling accusation of this sort? I didn't know the news had got around so widely . . .

NOLAN. Well, so many of your lovers have been famous men. . . .

MARION. Well, you were obscure . . . But you're famous now, aren't you? I seem to be stimulating if nothing else . . .

NOLAN. If I had then some of the fame I have now you probably wouldn't have walked out on me at the last minute the way you did . . .

MARION. Dear, dear Bunny, that's not quite—

NOLAN (*irritated beyond control*). I wish you wouldn't call me Bunny. . . .

MARION. Well, I always did. What is your real name?

NOLAN. You know perfectly well . . .

MARION. I swear I don't. . . .

NOLAN. My name is Leander. . . .

MARION. Bunny, really. . . .

NOLAN. That is my name.

MARION. Really I'd forgotten that. Leander! Who was he—he did something in the Hellespont, didn't he? What did he do in the Hellespont?

NOLAN (*sharply*). Beside the point.

MARION. Sorry! You say you wanted to tell me something—

NOLAN (*grimly*). Yes!

MARION. I love to be told things.

NOLAN. That night you left me—

MARION. We'd quarrelled about something, hadn't we?

NOLAN. I realized after you left me how much I'd grown to depend on you—

MARION. Dear Bunny!

NOLAN. I plunged into work. I worked fiercely to forget you. I did forget you— (*He looks away from her*) And yet—

MARION. And yet—?

NOLAN. The way we'd separated and I never heard from you—it left something bitter in my mind--something— (*He hesitates for a word.*)

MARION (*supplying it*). Unresolved!

NOLAN (*Quickly—relieved that she understands so exactly*). Yes. All these years I've wanted to see you, to get it off my mind—

MARION. Did you want the last word, Bunny dear?

NOLAN (*fiercely*). I wanted to see you, to stand before you, to tell myself—"Here she is and—and what of it!"

MARION. Well, can you?

NOLAN (*heatedly, with transparent overemphasis*). Yes! Yes!

MARION. Good for you, Bunny. I know just how you feel—like having a tooth out, isn't it? (*Sincerely*) In justice to myself—I must tell you this—that the reason I walked out on you in the summary way I did was not, as you've just suggested, because I doubted your future—it was ob vious to me, even then, that you were destined for mighty things—but the reason was that I felt a disparity in our characters not conducive to matrimonial contentment. You see how right I was. I suspected in myself a—a tendency to explore, a spiritual and physical wanderlust—that I knew would horrify you once you found it out. It horrifies you now when we are no longer anything to each other. Imagine, Leander dear, if we were married how much more difficult it would be— If there is any one thing you have to be grateful to me for it is that instant's clear vision I had which made me see, which made me look ahead, which made me tear myself away from you. Why, everything you have now—your future, your prospects—even your fiancée, Leander dear—you owe to me—no, I won't say to me—to that instinct—to that premonition. . . .

NOLAN (*nostalgic*). We might have done it together. . . .

MARION. I wouldn't have stood for a fiancée, Bunny dear—not even I am as promiscuous as that. . . .

NOLAN. Don't use that word!

MARION. But, Leander! It's your own!

NOLAN. Do you think it hasn't been on my conscience ever since, do you think it hasn't tortured me . . . !

MARION. What, dear?

NOLAN. That thought!

MARION. Which thought?

NOLAN. Every time I heard about you—all the notoriety that's attended you in the American papers . . . painting pictures of Communist statesmen, running around California with movie comedians!

MARION. I have to practice my profession, Bunny. One must live, you know. Besides, I've done Capitalist statesmen too. And at Geneva. . . .

NOLAN (*darkly*). You know what I mean . . . !

MARION. You mean . . . (*She whispers through her cupped hand*) you mean promiscuous? Has that gotten around, Bunny? Is it whispered in the sewing-circles of Nashville? Will I be burned for a witch if I go back home? Will they have a trial over me? Will you defend me?

NOLAN (*quite literally, with sincere and disarming simplicity*). I should be forced, as an honest man, to stand before the multitude and say: In condemning this woman you are condemning me who am asking your suffrages to represent you. For it was I with whom this woman first sinned before God. As an honorable man that is what I should have to do.

MARION. And has this worried you—actually . . . !

NOLAN. It's tortured me . . . !

MARION. You're the holy man and I'm Thais! That gives me an idea for the portrait which I hope you will commission me to do. I'll do you in a hair-shirt. Savonarola. He was a Senator too, wasn't he? Or was he?

NOLAN (*gloomily contemplating her*). I can't forget that it was I who . . .

MARION. Did you think you were the first, Bunny? Was I so unscrupu-

lously coquettish as to lead you to believe that I—oh, I couldn't have been. It's not like me.
(*She crosses to right of model stand.*)

NOLAN (*fiercely*). Don't lie to me!

MARION (*sitting on stand*). Bunny, you frighten me!

NOLAN (*stands over her almost threateningly*). You're lying to me to salve my conscience but I won't have it! I know my guilt and I'm going to bear it!

MARION. Well, I don't want to deprive you of your little pleasures but . . .

NOLAN. You're evil, Marion. You haven't the face of evil but you're evil—evil!

MARION. Oh, Bunny darling, now you can't mean that surely. What's come over you? You never were like that—or were you? You know perfectly well I'm not evil. Casual—maybe—but not evil. Good Heavens, Bunny, I might as well say you're evil because you're intolerant. These are differences in temperament, that's all—charming differences in temperament.

NOLAN (*shakes his head, unconvinced*). Sophistry!

MARION. All right, Dean Inge. Sophistry. By the way I've met the Gloomy Dean and he's not gloomy at all—he's very jolly. (*Gets up from stand*) Let's have a cup of tea, shall we? Will your constituents care if you have a cup of tea with a promiscuous woman? Will they have to know?

NOLAN. I'm afraid I can't, Marion. I have to be getting on. . . .

MARION. Oh, stay and have some tea— (*Makes him sit down*) what do you have to do that can't wait for a cup of tea? . . . (*Calls off*) Minnie—Minnie. . . .

MINNIE (*appears in doorway*). Ja, Fraulein. . . .

MARION. Bitte—Thee. . . .

MINNIE. Ja, Fraulein. . . . (*She goes out.* MARION *smiles at* NOLAN *and sits beside him. He is quite uncomfortable.*)

NOLAN (*slightly embarrassed*). About the painting, Marion. . . .

MARION. Oh, I was only joking . . . don't let yourself be bullied into it . . .

NOLAN. I've never been painted in oils. It might do for campaign purposes. And, if I should be elected, it would be very helpful to you in Washington.

MARION. You're awfully kind, Bunny. I must tell you frankly though that the dignified Senatorial style isn't exactly my forte. However, I might try. Yes—I'll try . . . (*She gives him a long look*) I'll go the limit on you, Bunny—when I get through with you you'll be a symbol of Dignity. Solid man. No nonsense. Safe and sane. Holds the middle course —a slogan in a frock-coat. I'll make you look like Warren G. Harding—even handsomer— Get you the women's votes.

NOLAN. Well, that'll be very nice of you. . . .
(MARION *suddenly kisses him.*)

MARION. Thank you, darling! (*He is very uncomfortable, embarrassed and thrilled.*)

NOLAN. Marion . . . !

MARION. Just a rush of feeling, dear!

NOLAN. You understand that this—this commission . . .

MARION. Of course. Strictly business. Don't worry. I shan't kiss you again till it's finished.

NOLAN. I don't know whether I told you—I'm going to be married in a month.

MARION. I'll have the portrait ready for your wedding-day.

NOLAN. And I am devoted to Slade with every fibre of my being. . . .

MARION. Every fibre—how thorough!

NOLAN. I'm not a Bohemian, you know, Marion.

MARION. Don't tell me! You're a gypsy! (*She continues to study him, poses him, poses his hand.* MINNIE *enters from left with tea tray containing teapot, cups and saucers, spoons, sugar and cream, and a plate of cakes. She puts tray on model stand and exits left*) Oh, Bunny, what fun it'll be to do you. Thank you, Minnie. Tell me—how do you see yourself?

NOLAN. What do you mean?

MARION. In your heart of hearts—how do you see yourself? Napoleon, Scipio, Mussolini . . . ?

NOLAN. Nonsense! Do you think I'm an actor?

MARION. Of course. Everybody is. Everybody has some secret vision of himself. Do you know what mine is? Do you know how I see myself? (*The doorbell rings.*)

NOLAN (*ironically*). More visitors!

MARION (*calls to* MINNIE). See who it is, will you, Minnie? . . . Probably the young man I met on the boat coming to take me to dinner.

NOLAN. What's his name?

MARION. I've forgotten. He's just a boy I met on the boat.

NOLAN. How can anybody live the way you live?

MARION. It's a special talent, dear. (*Doorbell rings again*) Minnie, go to the door. (MINNIE *comes in and exits hallway*) This is my lucky day Bunny.

NOLAN. Would you mind, in front of strangers, not calling me Bunny?

MARION. Oh, of course, what is it?

NOLAN (*irritated*). Leander.

MARION. (*mnemonic*). Leander—Hellespont—Leander. . . . (MINNIE *comes downstage a few feet from the door.*)

MINNIE (*just inside the room*). It's the Junge who was here before—er sagt er ist ausgeschifft da—

MARION. Oh, show him in, Minnie, and bring a cup for him too.

MINNIE (*as she goes*). Ja.

NOLAN. And don't use these extravagant terms of endearment—anybody who didn't know you would misunderstand it. . . .

MARION (*very happy*). All right, darling. (MINNIE *ushers in* RICHARD KURT, *goes out, comes back again with more tea.* MARION *comes forward to greet him*) I'm so glad to see you again, Mr. ——. . . .

KURT. Kurt.

MARION. Oh. . . .

KURT. With a K.

MARION (*reassured*). Oh—I'll try to remember. This is Senator Nolan—Mr. Kurt. . . .

NOLAN (*glowering*). I am not Senator Nolan.

MARION. But you will be. (*She offers him a cup of tea, he takes it*) Can't I just call you that—between ourselves? It gives me such a sense of quiet power. And maybe it'll impress my visitor. Do have a cup of tea, Mr. Kurt. (*She gives him one.*)

KURT (*puts his hat on sofa left*). I am not impressed by politicians. And I didn't come to drink tea. I am here on business. (*Nevertheless he takes a hearty sip.*)

MARION. Well, you can do both. They do in England. American businessmen are so tense.

KURT. I'm not a businessman.

NOLAN. Well, whatever you are, you are very ill-mannered.

KURT (*pleased*). That's true!

MARION (*delighted*). Isn't it nice you agree? For a moment I thought you weren't going to hit it off. . . .

NOLAN. In my day if a boy came in and behaved like this before a lady he'd be horsewhipped.

KURT. Well, when you get into the Senate you can introduce a horsewhipping bill. Probably bring you great kudos.

NOLAN. You talk like a Bolshevik.

KURT. Thank you! You talk like a Senator!

(MARION *wants to laugh but thinks better of it. She looks at* KURT *with a new eye.*)

MARION (*quickly offering him more tea*). Another cup, Mr. Kurt. . . .

KURT (*taking it*). Thank you.

MARION. And one of these cakes—they're very nice . . . Minnie made them—almost as good as lebkuchen. Minnie spoils me.

KURT (*taking it*). Thank you. (*Eats cake*) Having said, from our respective points of view, the worst thing we could say about each other, having uttered the ultimate insult, there's no reason we can't be friends, Senator. Damn good cake. No lunch as a matter of fact.

MARION. That's what's the matter with him—he was hungry—hungry boy. . . .

NOLAN (*puts teacup on piano*). He probably wants to sell you some insurance. . . .

KURT. Not at all. I'm not here to sell I'm here to buy.

MARION. A picture!

KURT. Do I look like a picture-buyer?

MARION. As a matter of fact you don't . . . but I haven't anything to sell except pictures.

KURT (*confidently*). I think you have!

MARION (*to* NOLAN). This young man is very tantalizing.

NOLAN. Well, why don't you ask him to state his proposition and have done with it?

MARION (*turns to* KURT *and repeats mechanically*). State your proposition and have done with it.

KURT (*puts his cup down on table rear of sofa left*). What a nuisance women are!

NOLAN (*starting toward him*). Why, you insolent young whelp—I've half a mind to . . .

KURT (*pleasantly*). That's an impulse you'd better control. I wrote this lady a business letter asking for an appointment. She granted it to me at four o'clock. It is now six. In that interval I've climbed these five flights of stairs three times. I've lost over an hour of my life going away and coming back. An hour in which I might have read a first-class book or made love to a girl or had an idea—an irreparable hour. That's rudeness if you like. It's unbusinesslike. It's sloppy. (*To* MARION) Now will you see me alone or will you keep me here fencing with this inadequate antagonist?

MARION. You are unquestionably the most impossible young man I've ever met. Go away!

KURT. Right! (*He turns to go and means it and she knows that he means it. And she is consumed with curiosity. As he goes*) So long, Senator! Yours for the Revolution!

MARION (*as he reaches door, goes after him—pleads pitifully*). Young man! Mr. Nolan is an old friend of mine. I should consult him in any case about whatever business you may suggest. Can't you speak in front of him? (*At the same time she shakes her head to him not to go away.*)

KURT. I cannot!

MARION. Please wait a minute. . . .

KURT. All right—one. (*He picks up a magazine and leafs through it negligently.*)

MARION (*to* LEANDER). After all, Leander, I can't afford—it may be something. . . . (*She takes his arm and starts walking him to the door, whispering*) I'm just curious to hear what he's got to say for himself. . . .

NOLAN. I'm not sure it's safe to leave you alone with a character like that. . . .

MARION. Minnie's in her room . . . with a bow and arrow!

NOLAN (*going up to hall door*). I have to go in any case—I'm late now.

MARION. When will I see you, Bunny? (*She is at door with him.*)

NOLAN (*taking up his hat and coat*). I don't know. I'm very busy. I'll telephone you.

MARION. Do. Telephone me tonight. I'll tell you what he said. It'll probably be funny.

NOLAN (*out loud at* KURT). It pains me, Marion, that you are so unprotected that any hooligan—(KURT *turns page of magazine*) can write you and come to see you in your apartment. However, that is the way you have chosen. Good night.

MARION. Good night, dear. Are you in the book? I'll telephone you . . .

NOLAN (*hastily*). No—no—you'd better not. I shall communicate with you. Good-bye.

KURT. Good-bye, Sir Galahad.
(NOLAN *starts to retort, changes his mind and, in a very choleric mood, he goes out. There is a pause.*)

MARION. Well, I'm afraid you didn't make a very good impression on him!

KURT (*putting magazine away*). That's just too bad!

MARION. That's no way for a young man to get on in the world—he's a very important person.

KURT. That's what passes for importance. You're not taken in by him, are you? Stuffed shirt—flatulent and pompous—perfect legislator!

MARION. As a matter of fact he's a very nice man—simple and kindly. (*Gets cigarettes and offers one to* KURT *who takes it and lights it. She takes one too but he forgets to light hers.*)

KURT. I bet he isn't simple and he isn't kindly. I bet he's greedy and vicious. Anyway he's a hypocrite. When a man starts worrying out loud about unprotected women you may know he's a hypocritical sensualist.

MARION. You're a violent young man, aren't you? (*Not getting light from* KURT *she lights her own. Throwing match to floor.*)

KURT. Yes. The world is full of things and people that makes me see red. . . . Why do you keep calling me youth and young man? I'm twenty-five.

MARION. Well, you seem to have the lurid and uncorrected imagination of the adolescent.

KURT. Imagination! That's where you're wrong. I may tell you, Miss Froude, that I'm as realistic as anybody you've ever met.

MARION (*sitting on upstage arm of sofa, right*). Anybody who'd be so unreasonable over a nice fellow like Bunny Nolan . . . if you only knew—if only you'd been present at the interview I had with him just before you came. You'd have seen how wrong you are about him. Why, he was—he was awfully funny—but he was also touching.

KURT. You're one of those tolerant people, aren't you—see the best in people?

MARION. You say that as if tolerance were a crime.

KURT. Your kind is. It's criminal because it encourages dishonesty, incompetence, weakness and all kinds of knavery. What you call tolerance I call sloppy laziness. You're like those book-reviewers who find something to praise in every mediocre book.

MARION. You are a fanatical young man.

KURT. Having said that you think you dispose of me. Well, so be it. I'm disposed of. Now, let's get down to business. (*His manner plainly says: "Well, why should I bother to convince you? What importance can it possibly have what you think of me?" It is not wasted on* MARION.)

MARION. You are also a little patronizing . . .

KURT (*pleased*). Am I?

MARION. However, I don't mind being patronized. That's where my tolerance comes in. It even amuses me a little bit. (*Crossing to piano seat*) But as I have to change for dinner perhaps you'd better . . .

KURT. Exactly.

MARION. Please sit down . . . (*A moment . . . She sits on piano bench facing him.*)

KURT (*goes to piano and talks to her across it*). I am the editor of a magazine called Every Week. Do you know it?

MARION. It seems to me I've seen it on newsstands. . . .

KURT. You've never read it?

MARION. I'm afraid I haven't.

KURT. That is a tribute to your discrimination. We have an immense circulation. Three millions, I believe. With a circulation of that size you may imagine that the average of our readers' intelligence cannot be very high. Yet occasionally we flatter them by printing the highbrows—in discreet doses we give them, at intervals, Shaw and Wells and Chesterton. So you'll be in good company anyway. . . .

MARION (*amazed*). *I* will?

KURT. Yes. I want you to write your biography to run serially in Every Week. Later of course you can bring it out as a book.

MARION. My biography!

KURT. Yes. The story of your life.

MARION (*with dignity*). I know the meaning of the word.

KURT. The money is pretty good. I am prepared to give you an advance of two thousand dollars.

MARION. Good Heavens, am I as old as that—that people want my biography?

KURT. We proceed on the theory that nothing exciting happens to people after they are forty. . . .

MARION. What a cruel idea!

KURT. Why wait till you're eighty? Your impressions will be dimmed by time. Most autobiographies are written by corpses. Why not do yours while you are still young, vital, in the thick of life?

MARION. But I'm not a writer. I shouldn't know how to begin.

KURT. You were born, weren't you? Begin with that.

MARION. I write pleasant letters, my friends tell me. . . . But look here, why should you want this story from me—why should anybody be interested?—I'm not a first-rate artist you know—not by far—I'm just clever. . . .

KURT (*bluntly*). It's not you—it's the celebrity of your subjects. . . .

MARION (*amused*). You're a brutal young man—I rather like you . . .

KURT. Well, you've been courageous. You've been forthright. For an American woman you've had a rather extraordinary career—you've done pretty well what you wanted. . . .

MARION. The-Woman-Who-Dared sort of thing. . . . Isn't that passé?

KURT. I think your life will make good copy. You might have stayed here and settled down and done Pictorial Review covers of mothers hovering fondly over babies. Instead you went to Europe and managed to get the most inaccessible people to sit for you. How did you do it?

MARION. You'd be surprised how accessible some of these inaccessible people are!

KURT. Well, that's just what I want to get from your story. Just that. Tell what happened to you, that's all. The impulse that made you leave home, that made you go, for instance, to Russia, before the popular emigration set in, that's made you wander ever since, that's kept you from settling down in any of the places where you had a chance to get established.

MARION (*quite seriously*). But supposing I don't know that. . . .

KURT. Well, that's interesting. That enigma is interesting. Maybe, while writing, you can solve it. It's a form of clarification. The more I talk to you the more I feel there's a great story in you and that you'll have great fun telling it.

MARION. Young man, you make me feel like an institution!

KURT. Should do you a lot of good in your professional career too—we'll reprint the portraits you've made of Lenin, Mussolini, Shaw—anything you like. . . .
(*She begins to laugh, quietly at first, then heartily.*)

MARION. Forgive me. . . .

KURT (*unperturbed*). What's the matter?

MARION. Something I remembered—the funniest thing—isn't it funny how the oddest things pop into your mind?

KURT. What was it?

MARION. Something that happened years ago. . . .

KURT. What?

MARION. Oh, I couldn't possibly tell you. It wouldn't be fair!

KURT. In that case it'll probably be great for the magazine. Save it!

MARION (*frightened*). You won't do anything lurid, will you?

KURT. Just print the story—just as you write it—practically as you write it.

MARION. I'm scared! (*She puts out her cigarette in ash tray on the piano.*)

KURT. Nonsense. Here's your first check. Two thousand dollars. (*He puts the check down on the table in front of her.*)

MARION (*wretched suddenly, picks up check, rises, looks at check*). I can't tell you how old this makes me feel!

KURT. Suppose I asked you to write a novel! That wouldn't make you feel old, would it? Well, I'm simply asking you to write a novel of your life. The only lively reading these days is biography. People are bored with fiction. It's too tame. The fiction-writers haven't the audacity to put down what actually happens to people.

MARION. You may be disappointed, you know. You probably see headlines in your mind. The Woman of a Hundred Affairs, The Last of the Great Adventuresses, The Magda Who Wouldn't Go Home. I promise you—it won't be a bit like that.

KURT. We'll announce it next month—first installment the following month. O.K.?

MARION (*puts down check, paces down right*). Oh dear! I can't promise a thing like that—I really can't. . . .

KURT. Why not?

MARION. It'll worry me too much.

KURT. Well, don't promise. Just get to work.

MARION (*faces him*). But what'll I do first?

KURT (*getting up*). Well, if I were you I'd sit down. (*She does so helplessly on piano bench.* KURT *then gives her paper, one of his own pencils*) There now! You're all set!

MARION (*wailing*). How can I go out to dinner—how can I ever do anything—with a chapter to write?

KURT. After all you don't have to make up anything. Just tell what happened to you. (*He lights a fresh cigarette.*)

MARION. Can I use names?

KURT. When they're prominent, yes. The obscure ones you can fake if you want to. Nobody'll know 'em anyway.

MARION (*looks at him*). Oh . . . what's your name?

KURT (*looks at her*). I told you—my name's Kurt.

MARION. I know—with a K—I can't call you Kurt! What's your *name?*

KURT (*sulkily*). Richard.

MARION. That's better. I tell you, Dickie, when I think—when I think—of the funny men I've known . . . they're pretty nearly all brothers under the skin you know, Dickie.

KURT. Well, that, as they say in the office, is an angle.
(*Suddenly her fear vanishes and she is overcome with the marvelous possibilities.*)

MARION (*jumps up and leans toward him as if to kiss him, but quickly thinks better of it*). Dickie, I think it'll be marvelous! It'll be a knockout. And imagine— (*Picking up check*) I'm going to be paid for it! Dickie, you're an angel!

KURT (*sardonically*). That's me. Angel Kurt! Well, so long. I'll be seeing you. (*Starts upstage toward hall door.*)

MARION (*suddenly panicky*). Oh, don't go!

KURT. You don't think I'm going to sit here and hold your hand while you're remembering your conquests, do you?

MARION. Well, you can't go away and leave me like this—alone with my life. . . .

KURT. Perhaps it's time you got a good, straight, clear-eyed look at it—alone by yourself, without anybody around to hold your hand. . . .

MARION (*suddenly*). No. I don't want to. (*Shrugs her shoulders as if she were cold*) I think it would worry me. Besides, I feel superstitious about it.

KURT (*following her downstage*). Superstitious!

MARION. Yes. A kind of—ultimate act. After you've written your biography, what else could there possibly be left for you to do?

KURT. Collect material for another!

MARION. What could you do over again—that wouldn't be repetitious? (*Sits on right arm of sofa right.*)

KURT. It's repetitious to eat or to make love, isn't it? You keep on doing it.

MARION. You're cynical!

KURT (*almost spits it out*). You're sentimental.

MARION. I am—Sentimental Journey—no, that's been used, hasn't it?

KURT. Don't worry about a title—I'll get that from the story after you've finished it.

MARION. There's something about it—I don't know—

KURT. What?

MARION. Vulgar. *Everybody* spouting memoirs. Who cares?

KURT. Well, wrong hunch! Sorry to have taken your valuable time. Goodbye.

MARION (*the finality frightens her*). What do you mean?

KURT (*he is withering—crosses to her*). I'm prepared to admit I was mistaken—that's all. In your desire to escape vulgarity you would probably be—thin. You might even achieve refinement. I'm not interested. Padded episodes hovering on the edge of amour—

MARION (*turns on him*). Young man, you're insufferable!

KURT. And you're a false alarm!

MARION (*after a moment*). I congratulate you! You've brought me to the verge of losing my temper! But I tell you this—you're quite mistaken about the character of my life—and about my relations with my friends. My story won't be thin and episodic because my life hasn't been thin and episodic. And I won't have to pad—the problem will be to select. I'm going to write the damn thing just to show you. Come in tomorrow afternoon for a cocktail.

KURT. Whose memoirs are these going to be, yours or mine?

MARION. Well, you're an editor, aren't you? (*She smiles at him*) Come in and edit.

KURT. All right, I'll come. But if you aren't here I'll go away. I won't wait a minute.

(*He goes out quickly.* MARION *stands looking after him, inclined to laugh, and yet affected. This is a new type even for her.*)

MARION (*she speaks to herself*). What an extraordinary young man! (*In a moment* KURT *comes back in.* MARION *is very glad to see him, greets him as if there had been a long separation*) Oh, hello!

KURT (*embarrassed*). I forgot my hat! (*He can't see it at once.*)

MARION (*without moving nor looking away from him, she indicates the hat on the sofa left*). There it is! Right next to mine.

KURT (*crosses for it*). Oh yes. (*Picks up the hat*) Thanks. (*For a moment he stands uncertairly, hat in hand, looking at* MARION *who has not taken her eyes off him. He is embarrassed*) Well, so long!

MARION. So long. (KURT *leaves again. She stands as before looking after him. She turns toward the piano—sees the check—picks it up and reads it to make sure it's true. The whole thing has a slightly fantastic quality to her. She is very happy and excited. She waves the check in her hand like a pennant and humming she crosses to the piano seat and sits and plays the waltz from "Danubia." She sees the pad and pencil on the piano and stops playing and, picking up the pencil and the pad, she crosses to the small armchair in the upstage end of the window and sits with her feet on the window seat. She repeats the first words of the first chapter aloud to herself as she writes them down*) I am born . . . (MINNIE *enters from door left to get the tea things she had left on the model stand.* MARION *taps the pencil on the pad as she repeats the words*) I am born . . . (*The time seems remote to her*) I am born—I meet Richard Kurt—Well, Minnie, here's the outline—I am born . . . I meet Richard Kurt —now all I have to do is to fill in. . . . (MINNIE, *used to having irrelevancies addressed to her, takes this program rather stolidly.*)

MINNIE. Was, Marion?

MARION (*trying to get rid of her*). Fix something light, will you, Minnie . . . I'm not going out.

MINNIE. Aber der Junge kommt!

MARION. What Junge?

MINNIE. Der Junge dem sie . . .

MARION. Oh, yes! The Junge I met on the boat. You'll have to send him away. I can't go out tonight. From now on, Minnie, no more frivolous engagements!

MINNIE (*astonished*). Sie bleiben ganzen abend zu Hause?

MARION. Yes, Minnie. I'm spending the evening alone with my life . . . (*She remembers* KURT'*s words and repeats them as if, after all, they have made a profound impression on her*) . . . get a good, straight, clear-eyed look at it . . .

MINNIE (*picks up the tea tray and, bustling toward the kitchen, promising delights*). Ein fleisch brühe und pfannkuchen! . . . (MINNIE *exits door left.*)

MARION (*already brooding over her past*). I am born. . . .

(*Slowly the curtain falls.*)

ACT TWO

SCENE—*The same. About three weeks later. Afternoon.*

AT RISE—MARION *is putting some touches on the full-length portrait of* LEANDER NOLAN *which stands away from the audience. She is wearing her working costume, baggy red corduroy trousers, a sash and a worn blue smock over a kind of sweater-jacket. She is very happy. . . . On the piano nearby are her writing things. While touching up* LEANDER *she is struck by an idea for her book. Puts down her brush and palette and goes to the piano to jot down some notes. The idea pleases her. She giggles to herself. Then she returns to her easel.* MINNIE *comes in and stands watching her a moment before* MARION *sees her.*

MARION (*sees* MINNIE *at last*). Oh yes, Minnie—do you want anything?

MINNIE. You asked me to come right away, Marion.

MARION. Did I?

MINNIE. Ja. (*Sitting on sofa right*) Zo! You have left a note on the kitchen I should come in right away I am back from the market.

MARION (*studying the portrait*). Of course I did. That's right, Minnie.

MINNIE. Well, what did you want, Marion?

MARION (*washing paint brush in turpentine jar*). Did I tell you there'd be two for dinner?

MINNIE. Ja. Gewiss! Das ist vy I vent to the market.

MARION. Well, I've changed my plans. I'm dining out with Feydie after all.

MINNIE (*rising and looking at picture*). Ach, Gott! (*She studies the portrait.*)

MARION (*looks humorously at* MINNIE *and puts her arm about* MINNIE'S *shoulders.*) Gut?

MINNIE. Ziemlich gut—

MARION. Do you know who it is?

MINNIE. Oh, das sieht man ja gleich. Das ist Herr Nolan!

MARION (*shaking her hand in gratitude*). Thank you, Minnie. (*Door-*

bell rings) See who that is, will you, Minnie?

MINNIE. Fraulein ist zu hause?

MARION. Ich erwarte Herr Feydak. Für ihn bin ich immer zu hause.

MINNIE (*agreeing heartily as she crosses to the door*). Ja, Ja, der Herr Feydak. . . . (MINNIE *goes out.* MARION *jots down a note on the pad which is on the piano.* FEYDAK *enters.* MINNIE *closes the door and exits left.*)

MARION (*at piano*). Hello, Feydie! Sit down!

FEYDAK. Well, my dear, which career do I interrupt?

MARION (*laughing*). I don't know!

FEYDAK. One comes to see you with diffidence nowadays. (FEYDAK *removes coat and hat and places them on the upstage end of the sofa right, and sits on the left side of the sofa.*)

MARION. While I'm painting I think of funny things to say, funny phrases. It won't be a serious biography, thank God. I'm dedicating it to Vicki: "To Vicki—the gayest person I have ever known!" By the way, have you got any little snapshots of Vicki—all I've got are formal photographs with his orders. I'd like to get something a little more intimate.

FEYDAK. I'll hunt some up for you.

MARION. Have you heard from the Powers yet, when you are to leave?

FEYDAK. Tomorrow.

MARION (*stricken—sits right of him*). Feydie!

FEYDAK (*fatalistically*). Tomorrow. (*They sit*). I shall leave you with sorrow, Marion.

MARION. I'll have no one to laugh with.

FEYDAK. For me it's an exile.

MARION. You'll have a wonderful time. I shall miss you terribly.

FEYDAK. Perhaps you'll come out.

MARION. Perhaps I will. I've always wanted to go to China. If I have enough money left from all my labors I'll stop in on you—en route to China.

FEYDAK. That would be marvelous.

MARION. You know writing one's life has a sobering effect on one—you get it together and you think: "Well! look at the damn thing . . ."

FEYDAK. Do you want to be impressive?

MARION. Well, I don't wan't to be trivial . . .

FEYDAK. I think *you* escape that.

MARION. My friendships haven't been trivial. . . . (*She gives his hand a squeeze.*)

FEYDAK. Have you seen that bombastic young man?

MARION. Oh, yes. He comes in every once in a while to see how I'm getting on. He's quite insulting. Underneath his arrogance I suspect he's very uncertain.

FEYDAK. Oh, now, don't tell me he has an inferiority complex!

MARION. Well, I think he has!

FEYDAK. The new pyschology is very confusing. In my simple day you said: "That young man is bumptious and insufferable" and you dismissed him. Now you say: "He has an inferiority complex" and you encourage him to be more bumptious and more insufferable. It's very confusing.

MARION. There's a kind of honesty about him that I like.

FEYDAK (*instantly putting two and two together*). Oh!

MARION. Nothing like that, Feydie! As a matter of fact—I don't mind telling you . . . I like him very much—

FEYDAK. I think he is destined . . .

MARION. He's not interested. He's some kind of fanatic. Social, I think: I've met that kind in Russia—quite unassailable. But I'm optimistic. . . . (*They laugh*) Well, one must never despair, must one. Life is so much more resourceful and resilient than one is oneself. Three weeks ago when you came to see me I felt quite at the end of my rope. I didn't tell you quite but I actually didn't know which way to turn. I felt tired too—which troubled me. Well, now I find myself, quite suddenly, (*She indicates portrait*) doing Leander and—(*She indicates manuscript on piano*) doing myself. New Vista. Very exciting.

FEYDAK. All this enthusiasm for art alone?

MARION (*laughing*). Of course!—Feydie, what did you think?

FEYDAK. I don't believe it.

MARION. Come here and have a look at Leander!

FEYDAK (*he rises—walks to the canvas on the easel*). Hm! Formal!

MARION. It's to hang in the White House. (*She winks at him, he laughs, puts his arm around her shoulder.*)

FEYDAK. Marion, you're adorable! (*They walk downstage together, their arms around each other's shoulders, very affectionately.*)

MARION. Oh, Feydie, I'm having a wonderful time. Quiet too. Writing *enforces* silence and solitude on one. I've always lived in such a rush—a kind of interminable scherzo. . . .

FEYDAK. Good title! . . .

MARION. Think so? I'll put it down. . . . (*Writes on pad on piano.* FEYDAK *sits on right arm of sofa left, facing her*) Interminable scherzo. . . . How do you spell it? A little affected. Might do for a chapter heading maybe. . . . (*Returns to him—sitting on model stand—facing him*) But I realize now I haven't in years had time to stop and think. I sit here for hours, Feydie, and nothing comes to me. Then, suddenly, the past will come in on me with such a rush—odd, remote, semi-forgotten things of the past. Are they true? How much is true? One can never be sure, can one? I remember certain griefs and fears. I remember their existence without recalling at all their intensity—their special anguish. Why? What was the matter with me? What made them so acute? It is like recalling a landscape with out color, a kind of color-blindness of the memory. (*Doorbell rings. She calls out to her factotum*) Minnie! (MINNIE *enters left and crosses rapidly to hall door.* MARION *arranges the model stand on which stands the papal armchair in red and gold*) This is probably the Hon. Nolan. He's due for a sitting. He pretends he doesn't like to have his picture painted, but I know he does.

(MINNIE *enters from hallway. She is flustered and giggly.*)

MINNIE (*very high-pitched voice*). Herr Varvick Vilson!

MARION. Tympi Wilson!

MINNIE (*to* FEYDAK). Der *film star!*

FEYDAK. So?

MINNIE (*radiant*). Ja! Ja!

MARION. Oh, Feydie, you'll adore this. Ask him in, Minnie.

MINNIE (*as she goes out to admit* WILSON). Gott, ist er schön!

MARION. Warwick's public.

FEYDAK. And mine!

MARION (*in a quick whisper*). Whatever you do—outstay him!

(MINNIE *has opened the door and* WARWICK WILSON *enters. He is very handsome, explosively emotional, and given to cosmic generalization. He is in evening clothes, a red carnation in his buttonhole.*)

WILSON (*crossing to* MARION *and kissing her hand*). Marion!

MARION. Warwick!

WILSON. Darling! How are you?

MARION. I'm splendid. Been up all night?

WILSON. No, no! This is business.

(MINNIE *has crossed to kitchen door upper left, never taking her eyes from* WILSON.)

MARION. This is Mr. Feydak. Mr. Warwick Wilson, the famous film star.

WILSON (*crosses to sofa and shakes hands with* FEYDAK—*dramatically*). Feydak! *The* Mr. Feydak?

FEYDAK (*again mistaken for his brother*). Ja.

WILSON. I've heard of you indeed!

FEYDAK. Have you? Thanks.

MARION. Mr. Feydak is on his way to Hollywood. He is to write the music for . . .

WILSON (*sits on the model stand—facing front*). Of course! I am honored, Mr. Feydak—deeply honored. That unforgettable waltz—how does it go? . . . (*He starts to hum with a swaying gesture the waltz from the "Merry Widow"*) Music's my one passion!

MARION. Once you said it was me.

WILSON. A lot of good it did me!

MARION (*to* WILSON). Well, tell me . . . (*She sees* MINNIE, *who is still staring at* WILSON) Look at Minnie. The mere sight of you has upset her so that she's speechless.

MINNIE. Aber, Fraulein!

(WILSON *rises graciously and gives* MINNIE *a friendly wave of the hand.*

He's no snob. MINNIE, *speechless with delight, exits left.*)
(WILSON *returns to his position on the model stand.*)

MARION. All right, Minnie! Warwick, Warwick! You mustn't do things like that to Minnie, at her age!

WILSON (*tragically*). There you are! This face! This cursed face! I should go masked really. One has no private life!

MARION (*sits in throne chair on model stand*). What would you do with it if you had it, eh, Tympi?

WILSON (*delighted*). That nickname!

MARION. It just rolled off my tongue. Did I call you that?

WILSON. You did! You invented it. No one's called me that since you left Hollywood. And you promised to explain the significance to me, but you never did.

MARION. Did it have a significance?

FEYDAK. Marion has a knack for nicknames.

MARION. I love 'em. I'd like to do a chapter on nicknames.

WILSON (*highly pleased*). Tympi! Tympi! (*Very patronizing to* FEYDAK) You are an intuitive person, Mr. Feydak. I can see that. (FEYDAK *ad libs: "Danke schön"*) Can you imagine what she meant?

FEYDAK. Her vagaries are beyond me, Mr. Wilson.

WILSON (*leaning back toward* MARION). Speak, Oracle! No! Don't tell me now. Put it into that book you're writing.

MARION (MARION *and* FEYDAK *exchange glances*). How things get around.

WILSON. It's been in the back of my mind for years, Marion . . . to have you paint me. Now that we're both in town together . . .

MARION. Well, I'd *love* to . . .

WILSON. In the costume of the Dane. (MARION *and* FEYDAK *exchange a look. Strikes a pose*) I'd like to be done in *his* costume. I hope, Mr. Feydak, that they won't break your spirit in Hollywood as they've almost broken mine!

FEYDAK (*with a smile*). My spirit is indestructible!

WILSON (*rises and crosses to rear of sofa and pats* FEYDAK *on the back*). I'm glad to hear it. (*Returns to left of model stand and stands with his right foot on it*) You know, for years I've been begging them to do Shakespeare. (*Gesticulates.*)

MARION (*interrupting him*). Sit down and be comfortable.

WILSON. They simply won't listen. But I'm going to give up acting and produce!

MARION. Oh, good God! Don't do that!

WILSON. Why not?

MARION. What would Minnie do with her night off?

WILSON (*smiles*). My public, eh?

MARION. Yes!

WILSON. Quite so! (*Patronizingly*) You artists who work in media like painting or literature— (*To* FEYDAK) or music, that too is a beautiful art, Mr. Feydak—transcends speech—transcends everything; by saying nothing it says all.

FEYDAK. Ja!
(*The doorbell rings.*)

WILSON. You are certainly lucky compared to us poor actors. We— (MINNIE *enters and crosses to hall door upper center*) Wouldn't it be ironic if all that remained of me after I am gone were your painting of me? That is why I want it, perhaps—my poor grasp on immortality.

FEYDAK. You see, Marion, you confer immortality!

MARION. I think immortality is an overrated commodity. But tell me, Tympi, what are you doing away from Hollywood?

MINNIE (*comes in announcing*). Der Herr Nolan! (MINNIE *then looks at* WILSON. WILSON *stands—looks at* MINNIE.)

MARION. Show him in. Show him in. (*With a lingering look at* WILSON, MINNIE *goes back. To others, after watching* MINNIE *exit*) You see!

FEYDAK. The effect is instantaneous —like music . . .
(NOLAN *enters.* MINNIE *follows* NOLAN *in and exits into kitchen, murmuring ecstatically, "Gott! Ist er schön!", looking at* WILSON.)

MARION. Hello, Bunny. (*Introducing* NOLAN) You know Mr. Feydak. Mr. Nolan, this is Warwick Wilson, you've heard of him.
(FEYDAK *bows to* NOLAN, *who returns the bow.*)

WILSON. It's a pleasure, Mr. Nolan. I've heard of you indeed! (*They shake hands.*)

MARION. You're late for your sitting, Bunny. Will the presence of these gentlemen embarrass you? I don't mind if you don't.

NOLAN (*has entered rather worried and angry. He has a magazine rolled in his hand. He now speaks very irritatedly*). As a matter of fact, Marion . . .

MARION (*putting him in throne chair on model stand*). Oh, sit down, like a good fellow. The light is getting bad. (NOLAN *sits.* WILSON *sits on the right arm of the sofa left on which* FEYDAK *is sitting.* MARION *gets to work on* BUNNY) How did you find me, Tympi?

WILSON. I read in a magazine that you were barging into literature . . .

NOLAN (*half rising, showing magazine*). This is true then!

MARION. Don't get up, Bunny . . . (*Nevertheless she takes the magazine and looks at it*) Well, Dickie has gone and spread himself, hasn't he? (*She sits on sofa left between* WILSON *and* FEYDAK) Look here, Feydie! (*Shows him the full-page announcement of her book in magazine.*)

FEYDAK (*looking*). Do you think you can live up to this?

MARION. Why will they write this sort of thing? (*Rises and goes back*) Makes me out a kind of female Casanova. (*She drops the magazine on the stand at* NOLAN'S *feet*) Well, they'll be disappointed.

NOLAN (*bitterly*). Will they?

MARION. Bunny! (*But she thinks nothing of it—merely pushes him into a better light.*)

FEYDAK (*tactfully—he senses danger*). May I ask, Mr. Wilson—are you making a picture at the moment?

WILSON. No, I'm in New York making some personal appearances.

MARION. Personal appearances. I love that phrase. Has such an air of magnanimity about it. (*Crosses to painting.*)

WILSON. Pretty boring, I can tell you! I've got writer's cramp signing autograph books. It's a perfect martyrdom I assure you. It's no fun at all. (WILSON *crosses to stand—puts his right foot on it, leans on his knee with his right arm and studies* NOLAN, *his face not six inches away from* NOLAN'S. NOLAN *fidgets.*)

MARION. I can imagine! What's the matter, Bunny? You seem under a strain today . . . not relaxed.

NOLAN (*bursting out and glaring at all of them*). It's like being watched while you're taking a bath!

MARION. Oh, I'm so sorry, Bunny!

FEYDAK (*rising*). I quite sympathize with Mr. Nolan.

WILSON (*moves away*). Supposing I were so shy, eh, Mr. Nolan?

FEYDAK (*crosses to* MARION *who is above her easel, right*). I'm off, Marion. (*Kisses her hand*) Auf wiedersehen!

MARION (*meaningfully*). You'll have to go— (WILSON *sits again on arm of sofa left*) both of you . . .

WILSON (*rises*). I was just going myself. My next appearance is at 6:45. (*Speaks to others.*)

FEYDAK (*to help her*). Perhaps I can drop you, Mr. Wilson.

WILSON (*faces* FEYDAK). No, I'll drop you . . . (*Turns to* MARION.) I say, Marion . . .
(FEYDAK, *helpless, goes upstage putting on coat.*)

MARION. Yes, Tympi?

WILSON. If you started my portrait right away and it turns out—I am sure it will turn out—you might put it in your book, mightn't you? I'm frankly sick of just appearing in fan magazines.

MARION. We'll see. Why not?

WILSON. Splendid! *Don't fail to come tonight*. Good-bye, dearest Marion. Good-bye again, Mr. Nolan. (*He starts to shake* NOLAN'S *hand but is interrupted by* MARION, *almost screaming.*)

MARION. No, no, no! Don't do *that* —don't touch him.

WILSON. Most happy! See you later. . . . (*He waves himself off at last—* MARION *returns to her easel.*)

MARION (*to* FEYDAK). Don't forget —I'm dining with you.

FEYDAK (*like the player in "Hamlet" who burlesques Polonius*). Most happy—see you later. (FEYDAK *leaves.*)

MARION (*with relief*). Now then . . .

NOLAN (*muttering to himself*). Silly ass!

MARION (*working on painting*). That young man is one of the most famous people in the world, do you realize that, Bunny? His profile follows you all over Europe—*and* Asia. Ubiquitous profile. Have you ever seen him?

NOLAN (*unswerved*). He's a silly ass!

MARION. I admit he's somewhat on that side—but that other one—that Feydie—he's the darling of the world!

NOLAN (*very short—bitterly*). Evidently!

MARION (*surprised*). Bunny!

NOLAN (*savage now*). Who isn't a darling? Everyone's a darling as far as I can see! The world's full of darlings. Your world at any rate.

MARION. But, darling . . . (*She suddenly stops—sits at right end of sofa right*). Oh, Bunny, I remember now!

NOLAN. You remember what?

MARION. Tympi! Why I nicknamed him Tympi. Don't you see?

NOLAN. No, I don't see . . .

MARION. For tympanum—a large instrument in the orchestra producing a hollow sound. (*She beats an imaginary drum with her paint brush*) Boom! (*Suddenly* NOLAN *quits the pose*) What is it?

NOLAN. I can't sit today. I'm not in the mood.

MARION. I could tell there was something worrying you.

NOLAN. There is something worrying me!

MARION. Well, what is it?

NOLAN. This confounded story! Are you really writing it?

MARION. Well, yes—I am.

NOLAN. What do you intend to tell?

MARION. Well, that's a rather difficult question to answer—it's like asking me what I've been doing all my life.

NOLAN. When does this biography start?

MARION (*beginning to wonder about this questioning*). With my birth—coincidence, isn't it?

NOLAN. All the time back home—when you were a girl in Knoxville?

MARION. Yes, of course. I've had a wonderful time going back over it all.

NOLAN. Everything?

MARION. Everything I can remember.

NOLAN. Do I come into it?

MARION (*smiling to herself*). You do! You certainly do!

NOLAN. You must leave me out of that story!

MARION. But Bunny, how can I possibly leave you out?

NOLAN. You must, that's all!

MARION. But how can I? You were too important—think of the rôle you played in my life. By your own confession, Bunny darling, you—you started me. That's a good idea for a chapter heading, isn't it? "Bunny Starts Me." I must put that down.

NOLAN. This is no joke, Marion. (*With menace*) I warn you . . .

MARION. Warn me! Let me understand you. Are you seriously asking me to give up an opportunity like this just because . . .

NOLAN (*rises and gets down from the model stand. Speaks with brutal command*). Opportunity! Cheap exhibitionism! A chance to flaunt your affairs in a rag like this. (*Indicating magazine on piano*) I won't be drawn into it. I can tell you that! (*He is in a towering rage.*)

MARION (*after a pause*). I know that by your standards, Bunny, I'm a loose character. But there are other standards, there just are.

NOLAN (*crosses to center—drops magazine on model stand*). Not in Tennessee!

MARION (*rises*). I'm afraid you're provincial, Bunny.

NOLAN. I'm sorry.

MARION (*takes off her smock, crosses to small table down right, gets her notes, then crosses to desk upper right*). I don't care what the advertisements say about my story—I know what I'm writing . . .

NOLAN. I'm sorry.

MARION. That's all right. (*But this has gone pretty deep.*)

NOLAN (*after a pause*). If you're doing this for money— (*She turns and watches him*) I know you've been pretty hard up—I promise you I'll get you commissions enough to more than make up for this story. I was talking about you only the other day to my prospective father-in-law. He's a big man, you know. I am sure I can get him to sit for you . . .

MARION. The tip isn't big enough.

NOLAN (*scared now that he sees the extent to which he has hurt her*) Marion! . . .

MARION. It amuses me to write my life. I am pleasure-loving—you know that—I will therefore pass up the opportunity of painting your big father-in-law. I will even give up the pleasure of painting you. And we can part friends, then, can't we? (*She reaches out her hand to him*) Goodbye, Bunny.

NOLAN (*devastated*). Marion—you can't do this to me—you can't send me away like this . . .

MARION. I don't think I've ever in my life had a vulgar quarrel with anyone. This is the nearest I've come to it. I'm a little annoyed with you for that. I think it's better we part now while we can still do so with some—dignity. Shall we?

NOLAN. You don't realize what's involved—or you wouldn't talk like that . . .

MARION. What *is* involved?

NOLAN. My entire career. That's what's involved.

MARION. Oh!

NOLAN. This is the most critical moment of my life. My fiancée's father is the most powerful leader of opinion in my state. Frankly, I depend on him for support. To have this kind of thing bandied about now might cause a permanent rift between him and me—might seriously interfere, not only with my candidacy for the Senate, but with my marriage.

MARION. They are interlocking—I quite understand.

NOLAN. A revelation of this kind—coming at this moment—might be fatal . . .

MARION. Revelation! You make me feel like—I can't tell you what you make me feel like . . . (*She laughs—semihysterically.*)

NOLAN (*sepulchral*). You must give this up, Marion.

MARION. I've met distinguished men abroad — politicians, statesmen — a Prime Minister even—and this kind of "revelation"—as you so luridly call it—is no more to them than a theme for after-dinner banter. They take it in their stride. My God, Bunny, you take it so big!

NOLAN. These people I'm depending on to elect me aren't sophisticated like you or me. (MARION *looks at* NOLAN *with some surprise*) What I mean is—they're country people essentially—my future father-in-law is sympathetic to their point of view.

MARION. Tell me—your father-in-law, is he the man with the chest expansion?

NOLAN. He's a fine sturdy man—as you perhaps know, he makes a fetish of exercise.

MARION (*bubbling again*). You see his pictures in shorts in health magazines.

NOLAN. There's no disgrace in that.

MARION (*sits on right arm of sofa left*). It doesn't shock me, Bunny. I was just identifying him, that's all.

NOLAN. I owe everything to Kinnicott—I wouldn't be running for the Senate right now if not for him. I can't risk offending him.

MARION. What the devil's happened to you anyway? You used to be quite a nice boy—even fun occasionally . . .

NOLAN (*wistful—turns away*). Maybe—if you had stuck to me . . .

MARION. Ts! Ts! Ts! Poor Bunny. I'm sorry for you. Really I am. (*She strokes his arm.*)

NOLAN (*suddenly passionate—faces her*). Don't touch me!

MARION (*amazed*). Bunny!

NOLAN. Do you think I'm not human!

MARION. Well, if you aren't the most contradictory . .

NOLAN. I realized the moment I came in here the other day—the moment I saw you . . .

MARION (*interrupting*). But Bunny! You're engaged and you're going to be a Senator.

NOLAN (*walks away from her*). Forget it! Forget I ever said it. . . .

MARION. You bewilder me . . .

NOLAN (*bitterly*). I'm not surprised I bewilder you. You've spent your life among a lot of foreign counts. It's well known that foreigners are more immoral than we are.

MARION. I'm very touched. I am really. (*She kisses him in a friendly way.*)

NOLAN. Don't do that! I forbid you!

MARION. All right. I'll never attack you again, I promise.

NOLAN. I wish I had never come back into your life—it was a terrible mistake—you'd forgotten me.

MARION (*seriously*). Oh, you're wrong. First love—one doesn't forget that.

NOLAN (*passionately*). But you did! You forgot me! And if you got the chance again, you'd humiliate me again.

MARION. Humiliate! What queer notions you have— Is it a question of pride or vanity between us? We're old friends—friends.

NOLAN (*moves a step right*). Please forget this—I don't know what came over me—I . . .

MARION. Of course. There's nothing to forget. (*Moves a step toward him*) It's quite all right, dear . . . (*She pats him on his hand*) . . . Oh, excuse me . . .

NOLAN. I warn you, Marion—I solemnly warn you—if you persist in this—

MARION. Never in my life have I seen a man vacillate so between passion and threat . . .

NOLAN. I shall find ways to stop you. Mr. Kinnicott, my future father-in-law, is a powerful man.

MARION. I know. Extraordinary biceps.

NOLAN. I warn you, Marion. This matter is beyond flippancy.

MARION (*sits*). There'll be some very distinguished people in my biography. You needn't be ashamed.

NOLAN. That movie-actor!

MARION. Tympi in Hamlet costume—you in a toga. I'll print your portraits on opposite pages—my two men!

NOLAN. You are malicious!

MARION. I must admit, Bunny, that you provoke in me all my malicious impulses. You come here suddenly and you convey to me what I've missed in not marrying you. (*The back-door bell rings.* MINNIE *crosses to answer it during* MARION'*s speech*) You dangle before me the inventory of your felicities—a career, a fortune, a fabulous bride—and then, because I get a chance to chronicle my own adventures—you object—you tell me

I mustn't! I have a nice nature, Bunny, or I should be angry—I should be indignant.
(KURT *enters.*)

NOLAN (*sharply and with threat*). Now, Marion, I've warned you . . . You'll regret this.

MARION. Hello, Dickie, do talk to Bunny for a minute, will you? (*Crosses to the stairs and starts up them to her bedroom*) I've simply got to change. (MINNIE *enters up center and exits left*) Feydie's coming to take me out to dinner.

NOLAN. But, Marion . . .

MARION. I couldn't do anything about this in any case, Bunny dear, because I've promised Dickie. In fact, I signed something, didn't I, Dickie? Don't go away, either of you. . . . (MARION *blows them a kiss and exits into her bedroom. A pause between the two men.* KURT *crosses downstage to above the model stand. Suddenly,* NOLAN *goes to* KURT *and reaches out his hand to him.*)

NOLAN. How do you do, young man?

KURT (*very much surprised*). How do *you* do? (*He looks at him narrowly, his head a little on one side, a terrier appraising a mastiff.*)

NOLAN. I am very glad to see you.

KURT. Isn't that nice . . . ?

NOLAN. You may be surprised to learn that on the one occasion when we met you made quite an impression on me.

KURT. Did I?

NOLAN (*sits on sofa right*). You did. Sit down. In fact—I hope you don't mind—if you will allow me as a prerogative of seniority—to ask you a few questions. I have a purpose in mind and not—I trust—an idle purpose.

KURT. Shoot! (*Sits*) Anything to enlighten the professor! (*He knows he is going to be pumped and has decided to be casual, naive and even respectful.*)

NOLAN (*clearing his throat*). Now then—your present position on the magazine you represent—have you been on it long?

KURT. About two years.

NOLAN. And before that?

KURT. Newspaper work.

NOLAN. And before that?

KURT. Tramping around the world. Odd jobs. Quite a variety.

NOLAN. College?

KURT. Believe it or not—Yale—two years . . . worked my way through—washed dishes.

NOLAN. Very interesting preparation . . . very interesting . . . Tell me now—your present work—do you find it interesting? Is the remuneration satisfactory?

KURT. Two hundred smackers a week. That's twice what I've ever earned in my life before.

NOLAN. Now then—to come to the point—no doubt you've heard of my prospective father-in-law, Mr. Orrin Kinnicott?

KURT. Heard of him! We pay him the compliment of imitation. He is our model, our criterion, our guiding star!

NOLAN. As you know, Mr. Kinnicott's interests are varied. He owns some powerful newspapers in my state. The other day I heard him say that he wanted a new man in Washington.

KURT (*playing naively excited*). Now that's something to give one's eye-teeth for!

NOLAN (*pleased at the result*). I think it might be possible to swing it—very possible.

KURT. God, what a break!

NOLAN. As it happens, Mr. Kinnicott is at present in town. I shall arrange an appointment for you in the next few days. Naturally, I expect you to keep the matter entirely confidential.

KURT. Naturally! You needn't worry on that score, Senator, I assure you.

NOLAN. Thank you, Mr. Kurt. That is all I ask. (*A pause.*)

KURT. Mr. Nolan—do you mind if I ask *you* something?

NOLAN. Certainly not . . .

KURT. You won't consider me impertinent?

NOLAN (*with a smile*). I don't object to impertinence, Mr. Kurt. I was often considered impertinent myself when I was your age.

KURT. Why are you making me this offer?

NOLAN. I am not making you an offer. I shall merely attempt to expedite . . .

KURT. Why? The first time we met we didn't exactly hit it off, now, did we? Why then are you going to all this trouble?

NOLAN. I have discussed you with Miss Froude, who is an old friend of mine and whose opinion I greatly respect. She thinks very highly of you, Mr. Kurt. My own impression . . .

KURT (*inexorably*). Why? What, as they say, is the pay-off?

NOLAN. I'll tell you. I'll tell you quite frankly. I don't want Miss Froude's autobiography, which you have persuaded her to write, to appear in your magazine. I want it killed!

KURT. Oh! You want it killed?

NOLAN. Exactly.

KURT. Why?

NOLAN. Marion knows why. We needn't go into that.

KURT (*wounded by a sudden and devastating jealousy*). Good God! You! You too!

(MARION *enters from balcony. She is wearing a dove-colored evening dress—the gamine transformed into lady-of-the-world.*)

MARION. Well! How have you two boys been getting on? What do you think?

KURT (*seething. Crosses to foot of stairs*). I'll tell you what I think. . . .

MARION. About the dress I mean . . . (*She does a turn for them.*)

NOLAN (*without looking up at her or the dress. He is watching* KURT). It's charming.

MARION. Thank you, Bunny. With all his faults Bunny is much more satisfactory than you are, Dickie.

KURT (*at boiling point*). He's chivalrous, he is! His chivalry is so exquisite that he has just been attempting to bribe me to keep your story from being published. His gallantry is so delicate that he's terrified about being mentioned in it.

MARION (*comes down stairs during* KURT'S *speech*). Don't be so worked up about it, Dickie. You're another one who takes it big. It's catching!

KURT (*flaring at her*). You're not very sensitive. . . .

MARION. Why should I be? You misapprehend Bunny. If he doesn't want to be in the same story with me that's his business. And it's nothing to do with chivalry or gallantry or nonsense like that.

NOLAN. Marion—this young man . . .

KURT (*taunting him*). What about Washington, Mr. Nolan? Mr. Nolan, a prospective Senator, offers to bribe me with a post in Washington controlled by his prospective father-in-law. . . .

MARION. If it's a good job take it, Dickie, by all means. . . .

KURT. I am afraid, Marion, that your code is more relaxed than mine . . .

MARION. Code, nonsense! I gave up codes long ago. I'm a big laissez-faire girl!

NOLAN. If this young man is an example of the distinguished company you've come to associate with, Marion . . .

MARION. Don't quarrel, children—please. It distresses me.

NOLAN. He's extremely objectionable.

KURT. What about Washington, now, *Senator?* Are you still willing to expedite . . . ! (KURT *and* NOLAN *stand glaring at each other.* MARION *tries to calm the troubled waters. Crosses to* NOLAN.)

MARION. Really, Dickie, you're very naughty. Don't mind him, Bunny. He's very young.

KURT. And incorruptible!

NOLAN. Marion, I claim the privilege of a friendship that antedates Mr. Kurt's by some years, to beg you, very solemnly, not to prostitute your talents to his contemptible, sensation-mongering rag.

KURT (*faces them*). There's a Senatorial sentence!

MARION. Hush, Dickie, hush! Bunny darling, it's true that Dickie's magazine isn't the Edinburgh Review. On the other hand your assumption that my story will be vulgar and sensational is a little gratuitous, isn't it?

NOLAN. You *refuse* then?

MARION (*gently but with a serious overtone*). Yes. This—censorship before publication seems to me, shall we say, unfair. It is—even in an old friend—dictatorial.

NOLAN (*with an air of finality*). You leave me then no alternative. I am very sorry.

KURT. Don't let him frighten you, Marion, he can't do anything.

NOLAN. I can forgive you anything, Marion, but the fact that you value my wishes below those of this insolent young man.

MARION. But this insolent young man hasn't anything to do with it! Can't you see, Bunny—it's my own wish that is involved.

NOLAN. I have explained to you the special circumstances. If you would consent to delay publication till after election. . . .
(*She turns to* KURT *to ask him to make this concession but can't get a word in. She is wedged between both of them.*)

KURT. She has nothing to do with the publication date. That's my province. Gosh, what a chance for the circulation manager in Tennessee! (*He rubs his palms together in mock anticipation of profits.*)

NOLAN (*losing his temper at last*). You are tampering with more than you bargain for Mr.— Mr.— . . .

KURT. Kurt.

MARION. With a "K."

NOLAN. There are ways of dealing with a young man like this and you'll soon find out what they are!

KURT. Them's harsh words, Senator!

NOLAN. You wait and see.

MARION. Bunny!

NOLAN. Don't speak to me! I never want to see you again! (*He goes out.*)

MARION (*really distressed*). This is awful!

KURT (*highly elated*). It's wonderful!

MARION. But I'm very fond of Bunny. Oh dear! I'll telephone him tonight . . .

KURT (*grimly*). Over my dead body!

MARION. Can it be, Dickie, that I control the election of Senators from Tennessee? (*Sits at right end of sofa left.*)

KURT (*after a moment*). How could you ever have loved a stuffed shirt like that?

MARION. He wasn't a stuffed shirt. That's the funny part. He was charming. He was a charming boy. Rather thin. Rather reticent. He was much nicer than you, as a matter of fact. . . .

KURT. I'm sure he was!

MARION. He was much less violent!

KURT (*sits*). Hypocritical old buccaneer!

MARION. He used to work hard all day and at night he studied law. We used to walk the country lanes and dream about the future. He was scared—he was wistful. How did he emerge into this successful, ambitious, overcautious—mediocrity? How do we all emerge into what we are? How did I emerge into what I am? I've dug up some of my old diaries. I was a tremulous young girl. I was eager. I believe I was naive. Look at me now! Time, Dickie . . . What will you be at forty? A bondholder and a commuter . . . Oh, Dickie!

KURT (*tensely*). I'll never be forty!

MARION (*laughing*). How will you avoid it?

KURT (*same tone*). I'll use myself up before I'm forty.

MARION. Do you think so? I don't think so. (*Rises*) I sometimes wake up on certain mornings feeling absolutely — immortal! Indestructible! One is perpetually reborn, I think, Dickie. Everyone should write one's life, I think—but not for publication. For oneself. A kind of spiritual Spring-cleaning!

KURT. The Ego preening . . . !

MARION (*sitting on right arm of sofa left*). Well, why not? After all, one's ego is all one really has.

KURT. Reminiscence is easy. So is anticipation. It's the *present* that's difficult and most people are too lazy or too indifferent to cope with it.

MARION. It's natural for you to say that—at your age one has no past and no future either, because the intimation of the future comes only with the sense of the past . . .

KURT (*with sudden bitterness*). I see the past as an *evil thing*—to be extirpated.

MARION. How awful! (*Pause*) Why?

KURT. That's not important.

MARION (*rises*). You freeze up so whenever I try to find out anything about you. I'm not used to that. Usually people open up to me—I'm a born confidante. But not you. . . . I'm interested too, because in an odd way I've become very fond of you.

KURT. My life's very dull, I assure you. *My* past lacks completely what you would call *glamour*.

MARION. No, Dickie. I don't believe that. I don't believe that's true of anybody's life.

KURT. Well, it's true. Moreover it's true of most people's lives. It's easy for anyone who's lived as you have to make romantic generalizations. It's very pleasant for you to believe them. Well, I shan't disillusion you. (*Turns away from her*) Why should I? It's not important. (*She is sitting down, smoking a cigarette in a holder, watching him. He becomes conscious that she is studying him.*)

MARION. I had no idea you felt this way about me—you despise me, don't you? (*He doesn't answer*) Don't you?

KURT. Yes.

MARION. Why?

KURT (*rises. Walks away*). Why did we start this?

MARION. You're annoyed at having even momentarily revealed yourself, aren't you? I'll have your secret, Dickie—I'll pluck out the heart of your mystery.

KURT. Secret! Mystery! More romantic nonsense. I have no secret. Nobody has a secret. There are different kinds of greed, different kinds of ambition—that's all!

MARION. Oh, you simplify too much—really I'm afraid you do. Tell me—why do you disapprove of me? Is it—as Bunny does—on moral grounds?

KURT (*right end of sofa left—angrily*). You're superficial and casual and irresponsible. You take life, which is a tragic thing, as though it were a trivial bedroom farce. You're a second-rate artist who's acquired a reputation through vamping celebrities to sit for you.

MARION (*quietly, she continues smoking*). Go on . . .

KURT. As an unglamorous upstart who has been forced to make my way I resent parasitism, that's all!

MARION. Isn't there in biology something about benevolent parasites, Dickie? Many great men, I believe, owe a debt of gratitude to their parasites, as many plants do . . . there are varieties. Again, Dickie, you simplify unduly. It is a defect of the radical and the young.

KURT. To return to the Honorable Nolan . . .

MARION. I return to him with relief . . .

KURT. He may exert pressure on us, you know . . .

MARION. How? I'm very interested. . . .

KURT. Well, for one thing, his future father-in-law might get me fired.

MARION. Could he do that?

KURT. He might. He might easily. (MARION *sits upright and looks at him*) Some form of bribery. He might go to my chief and offer him a bigger job—anything.

MARION. All on account of my poor little biography— It seems incredible that anyone would take all this trouble. . . .

KURT. I'd just like to see them try—I'd just like to, that's all . . .

MARION. What would you do?

KURT. Do?! I'd make the Honorable Nolan the laughing stock of the country, and his athletic father-in-law too. I'd just plaster them, that's what I'd do.

MARION. You sound vindictive.

KURT. Baby, I am vindictive!

MARION. Funny, I'm just amused. . . .

KURT. Well, everything's a spectacle to you! (*Turns away from her*) God, how I hate detachment!

MARION. Your desire to break up Bunny is quite impersonal then.

KURT. Surgical. Just as impersonal as that.

MARION. You're a funny boy, Dickie.

KURT (*turns away from her*). I'm not funny and I'm not a boy. You've been around with dilettantes so long you don't recognize seriousness when you see it.

MARION. But it's the serious people who are funny, Dickie! Look at Bunny.

KURT (*faces her*). Yes, look at him! An epitome of the brainless muddle of contemporary life, of all the self-seeking second-raters who rise to power and wield power. That's why I'm going to do him in. (*The phone rings—for a moment they pay no attention to it*) It's the most beautiful chance anybody ever had and I'd just like to see them try and stop me. (*Phone keeps ringing.* MARION *answers it.*)

MARION. Yes . . . yes . . . certainly. (*To* KURT*—a bit surprised*) It's for you . . . (*She hands him hand-receiver.*)

KURT (*takes phone and talks from rear of sofa*). Yes. Hello . . . sure. Well, what about it? . . . Oh, you want to talk to me about it, do you? . . . I thought you would . . . I'll be around . . . sure . . . so long. (*He hangs up*) They've begun! (*He is almost gay with the heady scent of battle.*)

MARION. What do you mean?

KURT. That was my chief. He wants to talk to me about your story. Kinnicott's begun to put the screws on him. He's going to ask me to kill it. All right—I'll kill it!

MARION (*faintly*). I can't believe it. . . .

KURT. Neff's had a call from the father-in-law . . .

MARION. Did he say so?

KURT. No, but you can bet he has!

MARION. I must say this puts my back up . . .

KURT. I'll make a fight for it to keep my job. But if he's stubborn I'll tell him to go to hell—and go to a publisher with your manuscript. And if I don't get quick action that way I'll publish it myself—I'll put every penny I've saved into it . . .

MARION. But why should you? Why does it mean so much to you?

KURT. Do you think I'd miss a chance like this?— It'll test the calibre of our magazines, of our press, our Senators, our morality . . .

MARION. All on account of my poor little story—how Vicki would have laughed!

KURT (*a spasm of jealousy again*). Who's Vicki?

MARION (*aware of it*). An old friend to whom I'm dedicating the biography.

KURT. Yeah! (*Sits beside her then speaks*) Where is he now?

MARION. He's dead. (*A pause. She gets up and crosses to center*) I've always rather despised these contemporary women who publicize their emotions. (*Another moment. She walks upstage. She is thinking aloud*) And here I am doing it myself. Too much self-revelation these days. Loud speakers in the confessional. Why should I add to the noise? I think, as far as this story is concerned, I'll call it a day, Dickie

KURT. What!

MARION. Let's forget all about it, shall we?

KURT. If you let me down now, I'll hate you.

MARION. Will you? Why won't you take me into your confidence then? Why won't you tell me about yourself? What are you after?

KURT (*after a moment of inhibition decides to reveal his secret dream*). My ambition is to be critic-at-large of things-as-they-are. I want to find out everything there is to know about the intimate structure of things. I want to reduce the whole system to absurdity. I want to laugh the powers-that-be out of existence in a great winnowing gale of laughter.

MARION. That's an interesting research. Of course it strikes me it's vitiated by one thing—you have a preconceived idea of what you will find. In a research biased like that from the start you are apt to overlook much that is noble and generous and gentle.

KURT (*challenging and bitter*). Have you found generosity and gentleness and nobility?

MARION. A good deal—yes.

KURT. Well, I haven't!

MARION. I'm sorry for you.

KURT. You needn't be. Reserve your pity for weaklings. I don't need it!

MARION. Are you so strong? (*A pause.* KURT *doesn't answer*) How old are you, Dickie?

KURT (*turns away*). What difference does that make?

MARION. Who do you live with?

KURT. I live alone.

MARION. Are you in love with anybody?

KURT. No.

MARION. Where are your parents?

KURT. They're dead.

MARION. Long?

KURT. My mother is. I hardly remember her. Just barely remember her.

MARION. Your father? (*He doesn't answer*) Do you remember your father?

KURT (*in a strange voice*). Yes. I remember him all right.

MARION. What did your father do?

KURT. He was a coal miner.

MARION. Oh! Won't you tell me about him? I'd like to know.

KURT. I was a kid of fourteen. There was a strike. One day my father took me out for a walk. Sunny spring morning. We stopped to listen to an organizer. My father was a mild little man with kind of faded, tired blue eyes. We stood on the outskirts of the crowd. My father was holding me by the hand. Suddenly somebody shouted: "The militia!" There was a shot. Everybody scattered. My father was bewildered—he didn't know which way to turn. A second later he crumpled down beside me. He was bleeding. He was still holding my hand. He died like that. . . . (*A moment. He concludes harshly—coldly—like steel*) Are there any other glamorous facts of my existence you would like to know?

MARION (*stirred to her heart*). You poor boy . . . I knew there was something . . . I knew. . . . !

KURT (*hard and ironic*). It's trivial really. People exaggerate the importance of human life. One has to die. (*Turns to her*) The point is to have fun while you're alive, isn't it? Well, you've managed. I congratulate you!

MARION (*her heart full*). Dickie darling—why are you so bitter against me? Why against me . . . ?

KURT. Do you want to know that too? Well, it's because . . . (*His voice rises. She suddenly doesn't want him to speak.*)

MARION. Hush, dearest—hush—don't say any more—I understand—not any more . . .
(*His defenses vanish suddenly. He sinks to his knees beside her, his arms around her.*)

KURT. Marion, my angel!

MARION (*infinitely compassionate, stroking his hair*). Dickie—Dickie—Dickie . . . Why have you been afraid to love me?

CURTAIN

ACT THREE

SCENE—*The same.*

TIME—*Late afternoon. Two weeks later.*

The telephone is ringing as the curtain rises. There is a moment and MINNIE *enters and crosses to rear of the table, rear of the sofa left. She picks up the receiver.*

MINNIE (*speaking into the phone*). Hello.—No, Mr. Kurt, she's not yet back. Vot? You're not coming home to dinner?!—But I've made the pfannkuchen you like— Vot?— You're tired of my damn pfannkuchen—(*She shouts angrily*) Every night I make dinner and you and Marion go out!—I'm *not* yelling— Vot? Vot shall I tell Marion?— Vot?— (*Doorbell rings*) Vait—vait a minute.—Someone's ringing. (*She puts the receiver on the table and goes to the door.* MINNIE *shows in* LEANDER NOLAN, *who is followed by* ORRIN KINNICOTT, *who is a big, well-developed Southerner, about fifty-five, with a high-pitched voice. He is a superbly-*

built man with a magnificent chest development. He is aware that he is a fine figure of a man, impeccably dressed in formal afternoon clothes.)

NOLAN (*to* MINNIE, *who has preceded him into the room*). Did Miss Froude say she was expecting us for tea, Minnie?

MINNIE. No, Mr. Nolan. She didn't say nothing to me.

NOLAN. Not even when she'd be back?

MINNIE (*hangs up coats*). No. She just went out.

NOLAN. All right, Minnie. We'll wait.

MINNIE. Yes, Mr. Nolan. (*She is about to go out into kitchen when she remembers that* KURT *is on the telephone. She picks up the receiver and says*) Hello—Mr. Kurt—you dere?— Good-bye! (*She then hangs up the receiver and exits left.*)

KINNICOTT (*querulously. Sits on sofa right*). Did you tell her four o'clock?

NOLAN. Yes. I told her. (NOLAN'S *manner with his father-in-law-to-be in this scene conveys the beginnings of a secret irritation, an inner rebellion.*)

KINNICOTT. Does she know I'm a busy man?

NOLAN (*gloomily*). She's not impressed much by busy men.

KINNICOTT. I know these fly-by-night characters. I've dealt with 'em before . . . Bad— (*He sniffs the air of the room*) bad air. (*Rises—tries to open window, fails, sits on window seat*) Bet she's underexercised.

NOLAN. On the contrary—she's radiantly healthy!

KINNICOTT. Cosmetics, I bet! These fly-by-night characters. . . .

NOLAN (*very irritated*). Why do you keep calling her a fly-by-night character? She's nothing of the sort!

KINNICOTT (*crosses to* NOLAN). Look here, Leander. . . .

NOLAN. Well?

KINNICOTT. Have you been entirely frank with me, in this matter?

NOLAN. Of course I have. . . .

KINNICOTT (*cryptic*). About the past —yes. But I refer to the present.

NOLAN. I don't know what you mean.

KINNICOTT. I think you do know what I mean. Sometimes the way you talk I suspect—I suspect, Leander—that you are still in love with this woman.

NOLAN. Nonsense! I simply tell you that she's not a fly-by-night character. That doesn't mean I'm in love with her!

KINNICOTT. My daughter feels the same thing.

NOLAN. Slade! You've discussed this with Slade!

KINNICOTT. She's discussed it with me. She's no fool, that girl. She's noticed things lately.

NOLAN. What things?

KINNICOTT. She says she talks to you and that you're off somewhere else —dreaming. I tried to put her on another scent—but she was positive. She said: "Come on now, dad—don't stall me—come clean!" So I told her!

NOLAN. You did!

KINNICOTT. Yes.

NOLAN. When?

KINNICOTT. Yesterday. Told her it happened fifteen years ago, that you were a naive young feller, didn't know anything about women, were just naturally taken in . . .

NOLAN. That's not true though. I was not taken in.

KINNICOTT. There you go again—defending the woman that's endangering your entire career and using up my energies and yours when you ought to be home right now getting together with folks and thinking how to cinch this here election. Not going to be a walk-over, you know. (*Again trying the window*) How do you open this thing to get some air? (*Sits on window seat.*)

NOLAN. I don't know. What did Slade say when you told her?

KINNICOTT. Nothin'. You know Slade's not the talkin' kind.

NOLAN. Funny she didn't mention it to me last night.

KINNICOTT. Didn't want to worry yer probably . . . all wool and a yard wide that girl is. I warn you, Leander, don't tamper with the most precious and rare thing. . . .

NOLAN (*impatient of oratory*). I know—I know. The point is—what are we going to do?

KINNICOTT. 'Course I can get that young fellow—what's his name?

NOLAN. Kurt.

KINNICOTT. I can get him fired all right. From what you've told me, Leander, he's got something else up his sleeve. . . .

NOLAN. I'm afraid so.

KINNICOTT. That's what I want to find out from your lady friend. And I've got a pretty sure idea right now what it is.

NOLAN. What do you mean?

KINNICOTT. Money!

NOLAN (*still not understanding*). Money. . . . ?

KINNICOTT. Blackmail!

NOLAN. You're crazy!

KINNICOTT. You don't know much about women, Leander; when you know the sex as well as I do you'll know that every woman has blackmail up her sleeve.

NOLAN. Look here, Orrin. . . . !

KINNICOTT (*rises, confronts* NOLAN). Now, you listen to me for a moment, son. . . . This situation's gone about far enough right now. You'd better make up your mind whether you want this blackmailing female or whether you want my daughter . . . and you'd better make it up right quick.

NOLAN (*flaring up*). I resent your tone, Orrin, and I won't be ordered around as if I were a high-grade servant!

KINNICOTT. Now son, when you get control of your temper, and cool down a little bit, you'll see that my ordering hasn't been so bad for you. I'll acknowledge you were mighty successful as a lawyer, but in politics, you're nothing but a novice.

NOLAN (*resentful*). Am I?
(*Doorbell.*)

KINNICOTT. Just look back a bit, that's all—I've had to push and bolster you to get you where you are.

NOLAN (*desperately*). I know—I have every reason to be grateful to you—that's the worst of it.
(MINNIE *enters and crosses to hall door. Both men turn and watch to see who it is that is calling.*)

MINNIE (*speaking to someone at the door*). Ja, Fraulein?

SLADE (*off stage*). Is Miss Froude in?

MINNIE. Nein, Fraulein.

SLADE (*entering*). Well, I'll just wait. (SLADE KINNICOTT *is a good-looking, dark, high-spirited girl, a rather inspiriting and healthy example of the generation growing up on D. H. Lawrence. To her father and* NOLAN *as she crosses downstage between them*) Hello.

NOLAN. Slade!

KINNICOTT (*severely*). Daughter! What are you doing here?

SLADE. Came to have my picture painted. What are you?

KINNICOTT. Your coming here at this time is most inopportune, daughter. We are here on business.

SLADE (*mischievously*). I can imagine!

NOLAN. I'm very glad you came, Slade. I want you to meet the woman whom your father has just been accusing of the most reprehensible crimes!

SLADE. I'm pretty anxious to get a load of her myself. (*Looks about the room taking it in and then sits on the left end of the sofa below the piano*) Nice lay-out. Gee, I wish I were artistic. What a lucky gal she is! A paint-brush and an easel and she can set up shop anywhere in the world. That's independence for you! Gosh! (*She looks about, admiring and envious.*)

KINNICOTT. Why must you come here to get your picture painted? We have tolerable good artists in Knoxville.

SLADE. Well, if you *must* know I'm very keen to have a heart-to-heart talk with my fiancé's old girl. Natural, isn't it?

KINNICOTT. No, it isn't natural!

NOLAN (*crosses angrily to window and back toward* KINNICOTT *and sits down on stool right near sofa on which* SLADE *and her father are sitting*). This is what you get for telling her, Orrin.

SLADE. If you think I didn't suspect something was up ever since Froude arrived here, you don't know your little bride. Maybe I haven't been watching the clouds gather on that classic brow! Where is my rival? Don't tell me she's holding up two big shots like you two boys.

KINNICOTT. Slade, this is no time . . . please leave us before she comes.

SLADE. Not I! Just my luck; when a story is going to come out which has something in it *I* want to read, you two killjoys are going to suppress it!

NOLAN. This isn't exactly a joke, you know, Slade. . . .

SLADE. I mean it. . . .

KINNICOTT (*sadly*). I've spoiled you, Slade—I've been too easy with you. . . .

SLADE. At least I hope you'll buy the *manuscript*. My God, father, I'm curious. Can't you understand that? I want to find out what Leander was like before he became ambitious. I've a right to know! This story might hurt you with the voters in Tennessee, Leander, but it's given me a kick out of you I didn't know was there! How did she make you, Leander—that's what I'd like to know. You've been pretty unapproachable to me but I sort of took it for granted National Figures were like that. Also I'd gotten to the point when I was going to suggest that we break our engagement, but this little incident revives my interest.

NOLAN (*furious*). Indeed!

SLADE. Yes indeed. Where is this woman? What is that secret? How to Make National Figures . . . there's a title for you!

KINNICOTT. Slade, you're talking too much! Shut up!

NOLAN (*rises and moves stool toward them a bit*). No, she isn't at all. . . . (*To* SLADE) If your interest in me requires the artificial stimulus of an episode that happened twenty years ago . . .

SLADE (*leaning toward him*). It requires something. . . .

NOLAN (*leaning closer toward her. The three heads are now close together,* KINNICOTT's *in the center*). Does it?

SLADE. It does. We were getting so that conversation, when we were alone, was rather difficult. (NOLAN *starts to argue.*)

KINNICOTT (*pushes them apart*). Children! Children!

NOLAN. We're not children! (*To* SLADE) If our relationship is so—

SLADE. Tenuous . . . ?

NOLAN. . . . That it requires artificial . . .

SLADE. Respiration . . . ?

NOLAN. If it's as bad as that then I think perhaps we'd both better . . .

SLADE. Call it a day? . . . You'll need me in the Senate, Leander, to fill in the gaps when you get hung up in a speech. Consider carefully what you are discarding. . . .

NOLAN. If that is the case I tell you solemnly we'd better separate now.

SLADE (*mock tragedy*). Father, Leander is giving your daughter the air. Do something!

KINNICOTT. I don't blame him for being irritated. You should not be here. Please go home.

SLADE (*lights cigarette*). Don't worry, dad. I'll get him back.

KINNICOTT. This is a bad mess, Leander. And I must tell you frankly that I don't altogether approve of your attitude . . .

NOLAN. And I must tell you frankly that I don't approve of *yours*. . . .

KINNICOTT. Is that so!

NOLAN. I don't like your tone in speaking of a woman with whom at one time I had a relation of the tenderest emotion—for whom I still have a high regard. . . .

KINNICOTT. That's evident anyway!

NOLAN. When you apply to such a woman the terms you used before Slade came in, when you impute to her motives so base, you cast an equal reflection on my judgment and my character. . . .

SLADE. And that, pop, is lèse-majesté.

NOLAN. And it may be perfectly true, Slade, that knowing Miss Froude has spoiled me for the flippant modernisms with which you study. . . .

SLADE. I'm dying to ask her one thing: when you made love to her in the old days did it always sound like a prepared speech on tariff schedules?

KINNICOTT. This is getting us nowhere. . . .

SLADE. Well, dad, what do you expect? Leander and I have broken our engagement since I came into this room. That's progress, isn't it?

KINNICOTT. Your coming here at this time was most unfortunate.

SLADE. Leander doesn't think so. (*Ironically*) He's free now to pursue the lady for whom he still has a high regard. (*Rises*) Are we no longer engaged, Leander?

NOLAN. That's not for me to say.

SLADE (*rises and shakes hands with* NOLAN). Gentleman to the last! And at the very moment—

KINNICOTT (*in despair—speaks as* SLADE *starts to speak*). Slade, if you would only go home!

SLADE (*crosses left*). *Just* at the very moment when I was saying to myself: Well, if a brilliant and beautiful woman who has played footie with royalty in the capitals of the world loved him, maybe there's a secret charm in him that I've overlooked—just when I was saying that and preparing to probe and discover, (*Lightly*) he gives me the air. (*Sits on sofa left*) By God, Orrin, there's life for you. (*Bell rings*) Ah, that must be my rival! (NOLAN *gets up and fixes his tie, expecting* MARION. *But it is* KURT *who comes in. He faces them. He is in a white heat of anger.*)

KURT. Well, gentleman, I'm not surprised to find you here! (*Drops hat *on model stand and comes downstage left.)*

NOLAN (*about to introduce* KINNICOTT). How do you do, Mr. Kurt . . . this is. . . .

KURT. I can guess who it is. I can guess why you're here. Having failed to intimidate *me* you are here to intimidate Miss Froude. (SLADE *rises, excited by this tempest*) Well, I can advise you that you will fail with her too.

NOLAN. This is his usual style, Orrin. Don't mind him.

KURT. I have just come from my office where I have been informed by Mr. Neff— (SLADE *stands below* KURT *—just behind him—watching him*) whom *you* doubtless know, Mr. Kinnicott—that I could decide between publishing Miss Froude's story or giving up my job. I invited him to go to hell. That invitation I now cordially extend to you two gentlemen.

SLADE. Why doesn't somebody introduce me to this interesting young man? (*She comes toward him.* KURT *is embarrassed, but covers it in a gruff manner. He has actually not been aware of her in the room.*)

KURT. I'm sorry—I—I didn't know.

SLADE. Why are you sorry? I'm Slade Kinnicott. (*She gives him her hand. He takes it, limply.*)

KURT. Alright—alright. (*He is disarmed and feels, suddenly, rather foolish.*)

SLADE. Leander, why have you kept me apart from this young man?

KURT. I'm sorry—I . . .

SLADE. Nonsense. What's your name?

KURT. Richard Kurt.

SLADE. Go to it— (*Turns him toward others.*)

KINNICOTT (*impressively—interposing between them*). You're being very foolish, young man.

KURT (*crosses toward them—to right of model stand*). Possibly.

NOLAN. You can't argue with him. I've tried it. He's a fanatic.

KURT. But if you ask me I think *you're* being very foolish.

KINNICOTT (*who wants to find out what's in* KURT'S *mind*). Are we? How do you figure that, young man?

SLADE (*parroting—crosses and sits on model stand. She is having a wonderful time*). Yes, how!

KINNICOTT. Oh, hush your mouth.

KURT. Because I'm going to publish Miss Froude's book myself. And I promise you that it'll be the best-advertised first book that's come out in a long time.

SLADE. Thank God! Will you send me the advance sheets? I'll make it worth your while, Mr. Kurt.

KINNICOTT. I can see you are an extremely impulsive young man. Have you ever inquired, may I ask . . . ?

SLADE (*edges a bit closer to* KURT). This is going to be dangerous! Look out, Richard. . . . (NOLAN *sits on stool, disgusted with* SLADE.)

KINNICOTT (*smoothly*). Have you inquired into the penalties for libel, Mr. Kurt?

KURT. Libel! You're going to sue me for libel, are you?

KINNICOTT (*same voice*). Yes. You and Miss Froude both . . . yes. . . .

KURT. Well, you just go ahead and try it, that's all I can tell you. Go ahead and sue. (*Crosses to above* NOLAN) It'll put Mr. Nolan in a charming position before those *moral* constituents of his, won't it? (*Includes both* NOLAN *and* KINNICOTT) Go ahead and sue, both of you—sue year heads off . . . ! I promise the two of you I'll give you the fight of your lives!

SLADE (*delighted*). Good for you, Richard!
(MARION *comes in. She wears a long red velvet coat, and a little red cap stuck on the side of her golden head—she looks a little like Portia. She is at the top of her form.*)

MARION (*beaming with hospitality*). Well! How nice! Minnie!

KURT (*goes upstage to right of* MARION). This chivalrous gentleman has just been proposing to sue you for libel—he considers . . .

SLADE (*who rises and stands just below the model stand*). I'm Slade Kinnicott.

MARION (*crosses downstage to her and they shake hands over the model stand*). How very nice of you to come! (*Turns and faces* KINNICOTT) Is this Mr. Kinnicott? (*He bows*) I'm so glad to see you. (*They shake hands*) I'm so sorry to be late. (*Waves hello to* NOLAN) Hello, Bunny.

SLADE (*this is too much for her*). Oh, my God—BUNNY! (*She sits, overcome.*)

MARION (*to* NOLAN). I'm so sorry . . .

NOLAN (*glaring at* SLADE). It's all right, Marion!

MARION. Has Minnie given you tea? I'll just . . . Minnie! (MINNIE *enters*) Tea, Minnie, please. . . . (*To the men*) Or cocktails—highballs . . . ?

KINNICOTT. I never drink alcoholic mixtures.

NOLAN (*asserting his independence*). I'll have a highball!

KINNICOTT. I must tell you, Leander, that I do not approve—

NOLAN. I'll have *two* whiskies straight!

MARION. Good! Highball for you, Miss Kinnicott?

SLADE. Thanks.

MARION. I'll fix them myself, Minnie. Just bring us some tea, Minnie.

KINNICOTT. Nor do I wish any tea.

KURT (*crosses down left*). Nor do I.

MARION. Do you mind if I have a cup? Do sit down, Miss Kinnicott. A tiring day. . . . (SLADE *sits on model stand.* MARION *goes up to rear of piano)* Minnie, please bring me a cup of tea—

MINNIE. Ja, Fraulein. *(Remembering)* A telegram for you, Fraulein.

MARION. Oh, thank you, Minnie. Just put it there on the table. *(*MINNIE *leaves the telegram on the table rear of the sofa left and then exits left.* MARION *removes her coat and hat and crosses to rear of piano and starts to mix the highballs)* Now then! What is all this nice cheerful talk about a libel suit? That's what they're always having in England, isn't it, on the least provocation. It's when you've circulated a lie about someone—defamed someone—maliciously—isn't it? Bunny! *(She gives* NOLAN *his two drinks. He takes them and returns to his position.* MARION *picks up the other glass and crosses with it to* SLADE*)* Now then—whom have I defamed?

KURT. You've defamed the Honorable Mr. Nolan!

MARION *(hands drink to* SLADE*)*. Have I? Oh, I am tired. . . . *(She sits on sofa)* Sit by me, won't you, Miss Kinnicott?

SLADE *(sauntering over)*. Thanks. *(She sits by* MARION *on the sofa.)*

MARION. You're very pretty. . . .

SLADE *(more warmly)*. Thanks!

MARION. Bunny, I congratulate you. I've heard so much about you, Miss Kinnicott. And I think it's very gracious of you to come and see me. If Bunny lets me I'd like to paint you— *(*MINNIE *enters)* and give you the portrait for a wedding-present. *(She rises and crosses to above model stand to get cup of tea from* MINNIE. MINNIE *exits left.)* Thank you, Minnie.

SLADE. You're very lovely.

MARION. Thank you, my dear.

SLADE. I can't tell you how curious I've been about you—I—

KINNICOTT. This is all very well—but I'm a busy man . . .

MARION *(looks at* KINNICOTT *as she crosses and sits right of* SLADE. *A moment, then* MARION *speaks)*. It seems so strange to see you with all your clothes on. It seems a pity—as an artist I must say it seems a pity—to conceal that wonderful chest development that I've admired so often in The Body Beautiful.

KINNICOTT. That's neither here nor there.

MARION *(this is almost an aside to* SLADE*)*. It seems to me that it's decidedly *there.* *(*MARION *and* SLADE *laugh quietly together.)*

KINNICOTT. Slade, you've upset everything by coming here. . . .
*(*KURT *comes forward. He has been eaten up with irritation that the superb indignation he felt should have been so dissipated by this cascade of small talk. He can stand it no longer.)*

KURT *(crosses to right of model stand)*. If you understood better what these gentlemen mean to do. . . !

NOLAN *(protests)*. It wasn't my idea!

KURT. You wouldn't be quite so friendly, Marion. . . .

MARION. I couldn't possibly be unfriendly to anyone so frank—and—and gladiatorial—as Mr. Kinnicott.

KURT (*furious at her for not letting him launch into it*). A libel suit . . . !

MARION. Oh, yes! A libel suit! It sounds so cozy. Sit down, won't you? (KINNICOTT *sits on stool*) A libel suit. Now then—what shall it be about?

KURT. The Honorable Nolan is going to sue you for libel. . . .

NOLAN. I'll punch your head if you say that again. . . .

KURT. On the assumption that when you say in your story that you and he were lovers you are lying and defaming his character!

MARION. Dear Bunny, you must want to be a Senator very very badly!

NOLAN (*in despair*). I never said it, I tell you!

MARION. As a matter of fact, how could I prove it? Come to think of it, are there any letters? Did you ever write to me, Bunny?

NOLAN. I don't remember.

MARION. I don't think you ever did. You see—we were always—during that dim brief period of your youth—we were always so close—letters were hardly necessary, were they? Did I ever send you any letters, Bunny?

NOLAN. I don't remember, I tell you.

MARION. Neither do I. You might look around in old trunks and places and see if you can find some old letters of an affectionate nature—I'd love to read them—they'd probably make wonderful reading now. Why is it that the things one writes when one's young always sounds so foolish afterwards? Has that ever occurred to you, Mr. Kinnicott?

KINNICOTT. I don't admit the fact.

MARION. No.

KINNICOTT. No. I was looking over some old editorials of mine written in the depression of 1907 and they're just as apropos today. I haven't changed my ideas in twenty-five years.

MARION. Haven't you really? How very steadfast. Now if the world were equally changeless, how consistent that would make you. (*To* KURT) Well, there isn't any documentary evidence.

KURT. It doesn't matter. . . .

KINNICOTT. As I said before, this is getting us nowhere. Don't you think, Miss Froude, that the only way we can settle this is by ourselves? (*She smiles at him*) I can see you're a sensible woman.

MARION. I am very sensible.

KINNICOTT. And you and I can settle this matter in short order.

KURT. You don't have to talk to him at all if you don't want to.

MARION (*smiling at* KINNICOTT). But I'd love to. I've always wanted to meet Mr. Kinnicott. There are some questions I want very much to ask him. (*To the others*) You can all wait in my bedroom. It's fairly tidy, I think.

SLADE (*to* KURT— *Rises, crosses to him*). Why don't you take me for a walk, Richard?

MARION (*as* KURT *hesitates*). Do that, Dickie. A walk'll do you good.

NOLAN. What'll I do?

MARION (*as if it were another dilemma*). You wait in my bedroom. (*Aware suddenly of the proprieties*) No—in Minnie's bedroom. It's just next to the kitchen.

NOLAN (*defiantly*). I will! (*He exits into bedroom.*)

KURT (*sulky—he doesn't quite like the turn affairs have taken*). We'll be back in ten minutes.

SLADE (*as they go out*). You can't tell, Richard. (SLADE *and* KURT *exit.*)
(MARION *draws a deep breath. She assumes at once with* KINNICOTT *the air of two equals, mature people talking freely to each other after they've gotten rid of the children.*)

MARION (*they cross to sofa left*). Now we can talk! It's funny—I feel we've put the children to bed and can have a quiet talk after a lot of chatter.

KINNICOTT. Same here!

MARION. Please sit down. (*They do.*)

KINNICOTT. I feel sure you and I can come to an understanding.

MARION. I'm sure we can.

KINNICOTT. Now then, about this little matter of the story— You won't mind if I speak very frankly to you. . . . ?

MARION. Not at all.

KINNICOTT. You see, Miss Froude . . .

MARION. Oh, call me Marion. Everybody does.

KINNICOTT. Thanks. Call me Orrin.

MARION. Alright, I'll try. Not a very usual name. Orrin. Fits you. Strong. Rugged strength.

KINNICOTT. Thank you.

MARION. You're welcome. What were you going to say when I interrupted you? You were going to say something. . . .

KINNICOTT. I was going to say—you're not at all what I expected to meet.

MARION. No? What did you think I'd be like? Tell me—I'd love to know.

KINNICOTT. Well, you're kind of homey—you know—folksy . . .

MARION. Folksy. (*Smiles*) After all, there's no reason I shouldn't be, is there? I'm just a small-town girl from Tennessee. I sometimes wonder at myself—how I ever got so far away. . . .

KINNICOTT (*positively*). Metabolism!

MARION. I beg your pardon. . . .

KINNICOTT. I always say—take most of the bad men and most of the loose women and correct their metabolism and you'll correct them.

MARION. Really?

KINNICOTT (*seriously*). Absolutely. Trouble with our penology experts—so-called—is that they're psychologists—so-called—when they should be physiologists.

MARION. That is very interesting indeed. Have you ever written anything about that?

KINNICOTT. Off and on.

MARION. Any definitive work I mean?

KINNICOTT. I'm considering doing that right now.

MARION. Oh, I do wish you would! It's extraordinary how little one knows about one's own body, isn't it? I get so impatient of myself sometimes—of my physical limitations. My mind is seething with ideas but I haven't the physical energy to go on working. I tire so quickly—and often for no apparent reason. Why is that, Mr. Kinnicott?

KINNICOTT. Defective—
(*She says at same time with him.*)

MARION—KINNICOTT. Metabolism!

KINNICOTT. Tell me—

MARION. What?

KINNICOTT. Do you eat enough roughage?

MARION. I don't know, offhand.

KINNICOTT (*firmly*). Well, you should know!

MARION. As I say, Orrin—one is so ignorant of these fundamental things.

KINNICOTT (*definitely aware now of* MARION *as a personal possibility*). I can see this, Marion—if you'd met me—instead of Leander—when you were a young girl—you'd have been a different woman.

MARION. I'm sure I would. Imagine—with one's metabolism disciplined early in life—how far one could go.

KINNICOTT (*confidentially offering her hope*). It's not too late!

MARION. Isn't it?

KINNICOTT. Er. . . . (*He drops his voice still lower*) What are you doing tomorrow evenin'?

MARION. I—I'm free.

KINNICOTT (*same voice*). Will you have dinner with me?

MARION. I'd be delighted.

KINNICOTT. Fine! Then we can go over this little matter of the story and Leander quietly. Leander isn't strong on tact. . . .

MARION. You know, some men aren't.

KINNICOTT. You and I can make a friendly adjustment.

MARION. What fun! (*They chuckle.*)

KINNICOTT. What time shall we meet? Say seven-thirty?

MARION. Let's say eight . . . do you mind?

KINNICOTT. My apartment?

MARION. If you like.

KINNICOTT. Here's my card with the address. It's a roof apartment. I'm a widower.

MARION. Irresistible combination!

KINNICOTT. By the way—

MARION. What?

KINNICOTT. Don't mention our little date for tomorrow evenin' to Leander.

MARION (*rising*). No, I agree with you. I don't think that would be wise.

KINNICOTT (*nodding trustingly—rises*). Fine! At seven-thirty?

MARION. No—no. Eight.

KINNICOTT. Oh yes . . . eight. (*A moment's pause. He visibly preens before her, buttoning his beautifully-fitting frock coat across his heroic chest.*)

MARION (*approving*). Wonderful! Wonderful!

KINNICOTT (*going toward bedroom. To her*). Do you mind if I . . . Leander . . .

MARION. Not at all.

KINNICOTT. I'll take the load off his mind.
(*He goes out. She can't believe it. The whole situation is so fantastic. She flings off her little red cap and shaking with laughter collapses on the couch.* MINNIE *comes in to clear up the tea-things.*)

MARION (*as* MINNIE *enters*). It's too good to be true, Minnie. . . .

MINNIE. Vat is too good to be true?

MARION. I must write some of it down before I forget it . . . (*The bell again.* MARION *gets up to make notes on her script*) —A widower's penthouse— (*With an irritated sigh* MINNIE *goes out to answer bell.* MARION *sits at desk jotting notes very fast.* SLADE *and* KURT *come in.* KURT *is morose.* MARION *gets up to greet them*) Well, children?

SLADE. That walk was a total loss.

MARION (*laughing*). What did you expect?

SLADE. Well, a little encouragement —just a soupçon . . .

MARION. Dickie's very serious.

SLADE. How did you come out with dad?

MARION. Wonderful! I'm crazy about him!

SLADE. But he got you to renege on the story . . .

MARION. Well, he thinks so. However, we're going to discuss it tomorrow evenin'.

SLADE. Thought he'd date you up—could tell by the way he eyed you. . . .

MARION. He's going to teach me how to live in a state of virtuous metabolism.

SLADE. Oh! Don't you believe it! Dad's an awful old chaser.

MARION (*rather shocked*). Slade!

SLADE (*amused*). Are you shocked?

MARION. You make me feel a little old-fashioned. (KURT *is intensely irritated by this conversation.*)

KURT. Where are they?

MARION. They're in there sitting on Minnie's bed. Orrin is probably telling Bunny that everything'll be all right.

SLADE (*sits left of* MARION). Marion. . . .

MARION. Yes. . . .

SLADE. What is there about Bunny you can't help liking?
(*Utterly disgusted,* KURT *goes to sofa down left and sits staring moodily into a gloomily-tinted future.*)

MARION. He's a dear—there's something very touching about Bunny—sweet . . .

SLADE. Were you in love with him once?

MARION. Yes.

SLADE. Are you in love with him now?

MARION. No.

SLADE (*in a whisper*). Are you in love with—someone else?

MARION (*a moment's pause*). Yes.

SLADE. I thought you were. He's mad about you.— I envy you, Marion.

MARION. Do you? Why?

SLADE. You're independent. You're —yourself. You can do anything you like.

MARION. Yes, I know. But it's possible one can pay too much for independence. I'm adrift. Sometimes—you know what seems to me the most heavenly thing—the only thing—for a woman? Marriage, children—the dear boundaries of routine . . .

SLADE. If you had married Bunny he would've given 'em to you. He's still in love with you, but he doesn't quite know it. Shall I tell him?

MARION (*parrying*). What are you talking about?

SLADE. I wish we could change places, Marion. You can with me but I can't with you.
(KINNICOTT *and* NOLAN *come in from the bedroom.* KINNICOTT *is at his most oleaginous.*)

KINNICOTT (*to* KURT). Well, young man! Over your little temper?

KURT. No, I'm not over it! What makes you think I'm over it?

KINNICOTT. Well, well, well! As far as I'm concerned there are no hard feelings. I'm going to call up your employer myself when I get home and tell him, that as far as you are concerned, to let bygones be bygones. Can't do more than that, can I?

KURT. To what do I owe this generosity?

KINNICOTT. To the fact that in Miss Froude you have a most gracious friend and intercepter. (*He gives* MARION *a gallant, old-South bow*) Miss Froude—this has been a very great pleasure.

MARION (*rises—with an answering bow*). Thank you! (SLADE *also rises.*)

KINNICOTT (*giving her his hand*). Auf wiedersehen.

MARION. Auf wiedersehen. Ich kann es kaum **erwarten!**

KINNICOTT (*pretending to understand*). Yes, oh, yes, yes, of course! (*To* SLADE) Come, Slade. (*He goes to hall door.*)

SLADE. All right, dad. (*To* NOLAN) Coming—Bunny?

NOLAN. Well, yes—I'm coming.

SLADE (*to* NOLAN). You want to stay. Why don't you?

KINNICOTT (*quickly marshaling his little following with a military precision*). I think Leander had better come with us—

SLADE (*to* MARION). Good-bye, Marion.

MARION (*to* SLADE). Good-bye, Slade. (*They shake hands*) Come to see me.

SLADE. Thanks, I will.

KINNICOTT (*smiles at* MARION). Miss Froude! (*Bows to* MARION *who returns his bow*) Come, daughter. Come, Leander. (*To* KURT) Good-bye, young man. No hard feelings. (KURT *glares at him.* KINNICOTT *again bows to* MARION) Miss Froude! (MARION *is startled into still a third bow. He calls without looking back*) Come, Slade! Leander!!

SLADE (*as she exits*). Bunny!

NOLAN (*lingers an instant the crosses to* MARION). I'll be back.

MARION. When?

NOLAN. In a few minutes. All right

MARION. I'll be in. (*He goes ou quickly.* MARION *is in wonderfu spirits. She runs to* KURT *and throw her arms around him*) Oh, Dickie That Orrin! That Orrin!

KURT. What did you say to him tha put him in such good spirits?

MARION. Everything I said put hir in good spirits. I can't wait for tc morrow evenin'. I can't wait for tha dinner. It'll probably consist entirel of roughage—just imagine! He's th quaintest man I ever met in my life He's too good to be true. (*Sits righ of* KURT.)

KURT. Well, he may be quaint to yo but to me he's a putrescent old hypo crite and I don't see how you ca bear to have him come near you, sa less go to dinner with him!

MARION (*sobered by his intensity*) You're so merciless in your jud ments, Dickie. You quite frighte me sometimes—you do really.

KURT. And so do you me.

MARION. I do? That's absurd!

KURT. You do. It's like thinking person fastidious and exacting an finding her suddenly . . .

MARION. Gross—indiscriminating?

KURT (*bluntly*). Yes!

MARION. You know, Dickie, I adore you and I'm touched by you and I love you but I'd hate to live in a country where you were Dictator. It would be all right while you loved me but when you stopped. . . .

KURT. It wouldn't make any difference if I stopped—I shouldn't be that kind of a Dictator . . .

MARION (*glances at him. Almost sadly*). I see you've thought of it. . . .

KURT (*inexorably*). What did you say to Kinnicott?

MARION. Your manner is so—inquisitorial. I haven't been able to get used to it.

KURT (*angry and jealous*). I heard you tell Nolan to come back too . . . How do you think I feel?

MARION. Dickie!

KURT. When Nolan sat there and told me he had been your lover, I felt like socking him. Even when we're alone together, I can't forget that . . . yet you encourage him, and Kinnicott— My God, Marion, you seem to like these people!

MARION. I certainly like Slade.

KURT. Well I don't. She's conceited and overbearing. Thinks she can have anything she likes because she's Orrin Kinnicott's daughter.

MARION. That's where you're wrong. She's a nice girl—and she's unhappy.

KURT (*bitterly*). Maladjusted, I suppose!

MARION. Dickie, Dickie, Dickie! Studying you, I can see why so many movements against injustice become such absolute—tyrannies.

KURT. That beautiful detachment again. . . . (*He is white with fury. He hates her at this moment.*)

MARION (*with a little laugh*). You hate me, don't you . . . ?

KURT. Yes! Temporizing with these . . . ! Yes . . . ! I hate you. (*She says nothing, sits there looking at him*) These people flout you, they insult you in the most flagrant way. God knows I'm not a gentleman, but it horrifies me to think of the insufferable arrogance of their attitude toward you . . . as if the final insult to their pride and their honor could only come from the discovery that this stuffed shirt Nolan had once been your lover! The blot on the immaculate Tennessee scutcheon! Why, it's the God-damndest insolence I ever heard of. And yet you flirt and curry favor and bandy with them. And you're amused—always amused!

MARION. Yes. I am amused.

KURT. I can't understand such . . . !

MARION. Of course you can't. That's the difference—one of the differences—between 25 and 35!

KURT. If the time ever comes when I'm amused by what I should hate, I hope somebody shoots me. What did you tell Kinnicott?

MARION. Nothing. Simply nothing. I saw no point in having a scene with him so I inquired into his favorite subject. He gave me health hints. He thinks tomorrow night he will cajole me—through the exercise of his great personal charm—into giving up my plan to publish.

KURT. Well, why didn't you tell him right out that you wouldn't?

MARION. Because I wanted to avoid a scene.

KURT. You can't always avoid scenes. That's the trouble with you—you expect to go through life as if it were a beautifully-lit drawing room with modulated voices making polite chatter. Life isn't a drawing room . . . !

MARION. I have—once or twice—suspected it.

KURT (*rises*). What the devil are you afraid of, anyway? I had a scene today in the office and I was prepared for one here—until you let me down—

MARION (*lightly*). Prepared? I think you were eager. . . .

KURT. What if I was! It's in your behalf, isn't it?

MARION. Is it? But you forget, Dickie. You're a born martyr. I'm not. I think the most uncomfortable thing about martyrs is that they look down on people who aren't. (*Thinks—looks at him*) As a matter of fact, Dickie, I don't really understand. Why do you insist so on this story? Why is it so important—now wouldn't it be better to give it up?

KURT. Give it up!

MARION. Yes.

KURT. You'd give it up!

MARION. Why not?

KURT (*obeying a sudden manic impulse*). After all this—after all I've—! Oh, yes, of course! Then you could marry Nolan and live happily forever after. And be amused. Good-bye! (*He rushes up center, grabs his hat from the stand as he passes it, and continues on out the door.*)

MARION (*rises and runs after him*). Dickie!

KURT (*going out the door*). Good-bye!

MARION. Dickie! Dickie! (*The door slams.* MARION *walks back into the room. A pause. She stands still for a moment; she shakes her head. . . . She is very distressed and saddened and a deep unhappiness is gnawing in her heart, an awareness of the vast, uncrossable deserts between the souls of human beings. She makes a little helpless gesture with her hands, murmuring to herself*) Poor Dickie! Poor boy! (*In its Italian folder the manuscript of her book is lying on the piano before her. She picks it up—she gives the effect of weighing the script in her hand. Slowly, as if in a trance, she walks with the script to the Franklin stove downstage left and sits before it on a little stool. She opens the manuscript and then the isinglass door of the stove. The light from behind it glows on her face. She looks again down on her manuscript, at this morsel of her recorded past. She tears out a page or two and puts them into the fire. A moment and she has put the entire script into the stove and she sits there watching its cremation. The doorbell rings. As* MINNIE *comes in to answer it, she shuts the door of the stove quickly.*)

MARION. It's probably Mr. Nolan. (MINNIE *goes out.* MARION *makes a visible effort to shake herself out of her mood.* NOLAN *comes in followed by* MINNIE *who crosses stage and goes in the bedroom left.* NOLAN *is excited and distrait.*)

NOLAN. Hello, Marion. . . .

MARION. Hello, Bunny dear.

NOLAN (*sparring for time*). Excuse me for rushing in on you like this . . . I . . .

MARION. I've been expecting you.

NOLAN. That's right! I told you I was coming back, didn't I? . . .

MARION. You did—yes.

NOLAN. I must have known—I must have felt it—what would happen. . . . Marion . . .

MARION. Bunny dear, you're all worked up. Won't you have a highball?

NOLAN. No, thanks. Marion. . . .

MARION. Yes, Bunny . . .

NOLAN. I've done it!

MARION. You've done what?

NOLAN. I've broken with Slade. I've broken with Kinnicott. I've broken with all of them.

MARION. You haven't!

NOLAN. Yes! I have!

MARION. Oh—oh, Bunny!

NOLAN (*sits*). When Orrin told me what you'd done—that you were going to give up the story. . . .

MARION. But I—

NOLAN. He said he was sure he could get you to do it. It all came over me —your generosity—your wonderful generosity.

MARION (*beyond words*). Oh, Bunny! (*Sits. She is in a sort of laughing despair. He hardly notices her attitude. He rushes on.*)

NOLAN. I realized in that moment that in all this time—since I'd been seeing you—I'd been hoping you wouldn't give up the story, that you would go through with it, that my career would go to smash. . . .

MARION (*faintly*). Bunny. . . .

NOLAN. I saw then that all this—which I'd been telling myself I wanted—Slade, a career, Washington, public life—all of it—that I didn't want it, that I was sick at the prospect of it—that I wasn't up to it, that I was scared to death of it. I saw all that—and I told her—I told Slade. . . .

MARION. You did!

NOLAN. Yes.

MARION. What did she say?

NOLAN. She said she knew it. She's clever, that girl. She's cleverer than I am. She's cleverer than you are. I'm afraid of her cleverness. I'm uncomfortable with it. Marion, I know I seem stupid and ridiculous to you —just a Babbitt—clumsy—but I love you, Marion. I always have—never anyone else. Let me go with you wherever you go— (*Lest she think it a "proposition"*) I mean—I want to marry you.

MARION. I'm terribly touched by this, Bunny darling, but I can't marry you.

NOLAN. Why not?

MARION. If I married you it would be for the wrong reasons. And it wouldn't be in character really—neither for me—nor for you. Besides that, I think you're wrong about Slade. She's very nice, you know. I like her very much.

NOLAN. I don't understand her. I never will.

MARION. If you did you'd like her. You better have another try. Really, Bunny, I wish you would.

NOLAN. Letting me down easy, aren't you?

MARION. It's Slade's manner that shocks you—her modern—gestures. If you really understood me—as you think you do—I'd really shock you very much, Bunny.

NOLAN. I'll risk it. Marion, my dearest Marion, won't you give me some hope? . . .

MARION (*sees she must tell him*). Besides,—I'm in love.

NOLAN (*stunned*). Really! With whom?

MARION. Dickie . . . You see, Bunny . . . (*He can't get over this. There is a considerable pause*) You see, Bunny . . .

NOLAN (*slowly*). Do you mean that you and he—you don't mean that . . . ?

MARION. Yes, Bunny.

NOLAN (*dazed*). Are you going to marry him?

MARION. No.

NOLAN (*he passes his hand over his forehead*). This is a shock to me, Marion.

MARION (*gently*). I thought it only fair to tell you.

NOLAN (*in a sudden passion*). You —you. . . . (*He feels like striking her, controls himself with difficulty*) Anybody else but him. . . . !

MARION. You see, Bunny.

NOLAN (*after a moment—rises*). Sorry! Funny, isn't it? Joke, isn't it?

MARION. I'm terribly fond of you, Bunny. (*Takes his hand*) I always will be. That kind of tenderness outlasts many things.

NOLAN (*blindly*). I'll go on, I suppose.

MARION. Of course you will! (NOLAN *crosses to model stand and gets his hat.* KURT *comes in. There is a silence.* NOLAN *forces himself to look at him.* KURT *does not meet his glance.* KURT *is white and shaken—not in the least truculent*) Good-bye, Bunny dear. Bunny!

NOLAN. Yes, Marion.

MARION. Will you do me a favor?

NOLAN. Yes.

MARION. Will you please tell Mr. Kinnicott for me—that as I've been called out of town suddenly—I can't dine with him tomorrow night. You *will* see him, won't you, and you'll tell him?

NOLAN. Yes. (NOLAN *leaves. A silence again. . . . Suddenly* KURT *goes to her, embraces her with a kind of hopeless intensity.*)

KURT (*in a whisper, like a child*). Please forgive me. . . .

MARION. Yes.

KURT. These moods come over me—I can't control myself—afterwards I hate myself—it's because I love you so much—I can't bear to. . . .

MARION. I know, dear—I know. . . .

KURT. I'm torn up all the time—torn to bits.

MARION. I know, dear . . .

KURT. When this is all blown over—could we—do you think . . .

MARION. What, dear?

KURT. If we could only go away together, the two of us—somewhere away from people, by ourselves?

MARION. Why not, Dickie? We can go now, if you want to. . . .

KURT. Now? But you're crazy. How can we possibly leave now—with the book. . . .

MARION. Dickie—I must tell you . . .

KURT. You must tell me what?

MARION. You must be patient—you must hear me out for once—you must try to understand my point of view. (*She leads him to sofa left and sits beside him.*)

KURT. What do you mean?

MARION. You know, Dickie, I've been very troubled about you. I've been sad. I've been sad.

KURT. I was angry . . . I didn't mean . . . It was just that . . .

MARION. No, you don't understand—it wasn't your anger that troubled me. It was ourselves—the difference between us—not the years alone but the immutable difference in temperament. Your hates frighten me, Dickie. These people—poor Bunny, that ridiculous fellow Kinnicott—to you these rather ineffectual, blundering people symbolize the forces that have hurt you and you hate them. But I don't hate them. I can't hate them. Without feeling it, I can understand your hate but I can't bring myself to foster it. To you, this book has become a crusade. It couldn't be to me. Do you know, Dickie dear—and this has made me laugh so to myself—that there was nothing in the book about Bunny that would ever have been recognized by anybody. It was an idyllic chapter of first love—that's all—and there was nothing in it that could remotely have been connected with the Bunny that is now. . . .

KURT. So much the better—! Think of the spectacle they'll make of themselves—destroyed by laughter. . . .

MARION. I don't believe in destructive campaigns, Dickie . . . outside of the shocking vulgarity of it all—I couldn't do it—for the distress it would cause. . . .

KURT. You've decided not to publish then. . . .

MARION. I've destroyed the book, Dickie.

KURT. You've destroyed it!

MARION. Yes. I'm sorry.

KURT. You traitor!

MARION. It seemed the simple thing to do—the inevitable thing.

KURT. What about *me?* You might have consulted me—after what I've . . .

MARION. I'm terribly sorry—but I couldn't possibly have published that book.

KURT (*in a queer voice*). I see now why everything is this way. . . .

MARION. I couldn't . . . !

KURT. Why the injustice and the cruelty go on—year after year—century after century—without change—because—as they grow older—people become—*tolerant!* Things amuse them. I hate you and I hate your tolerance. I always did.

MARION. I know you do. You hate my essential quality—the thing that is me. That's what I was thinking just now and that's what made me sad.

KURT. Nothing to be said, is there? (*Rises*) Good-bye.

MARION (*rises*). All right! (KURT *starts to go. She calls after him, pitifully*) Won't you kiss me good-bye?

KURT. All right.

(MARION *goes up after him. They kiss each other passionately.*)

MARION (*whispering to him*). I would try to change you. I know I would. And if I changed you I should destroy what makes me love you. Good-bye, my darling. Good-bye, my dearest. Go quickly. (KURT *goes up stage and exits without a word. He is blinded by pain*) Dickie. . . . ! (MARION *is left alone. She is trembling a little. She feels cold. She goes to the stove and sits in front of it, her back to it, trying to get warm. She becomes aware that her eyes are full of tears. As* MINNIE *comes in, she brushes them away.*)

MINNIE. Are you worried from anything, Marion?

MARION. No, Minnie. I'm alright.

MINNIE. I tink maybe dot telegram bring you bad news.

MARION. Telegram? What telegram?

MINNIE. Dot telegram I bring you.

MARION. Of course—I haven't even—where is it?

MINNIE (*gets telegram from table rear of sofa left and hands it to* MARION). There it is!

MARION. Thank you, Minnie. (*Opens telegram and reads it*) This is from heaven! Minnie, I want you to pack right away. We're leaving! (*She springs up.*)

MINNIE. Leaving? Ven?

MARION. Right away. Tonight! This is from Feydie! Listen! (*Reads telegram aloud to* MINNIE) "Can get you commission to paint prize winners Motion Picture Academy—wire answer at once. Feydie." (*Hysterically grateful for the mercy of having something to do at once, of being busy, of not having time to think*) Something always turns up for me! Pack everything, Minnie. I want to get out right away. (*She rushes upstage right, picks up her hat and coat and then runs to the stairs left.*)

MINNIE. Don't you tink you better vait till tomorrow?

MARION. No, Minnie. Once the temptation to a journey comes into my head I can't bear it till I'm on my way! This time, Minnie, we'll have a real trip. From Hollywood we'll go to Honolulu and from Honolulu to China. How would you like that, Minnie? (*She starts up the stairs.*)

MINNIE (*for her, enthusiastic*). Fine, Marion! (*Calls after her as she runs upstairs*) Dot crazy Kurt he goes vit us?

MARION (*as she disappears into her bedroom*). No, Minnie—no one—we travel alone!

(*Quick curtain.*)

Ah, Wilderness!

BY EUGENE O'NEILL

TO

GEORGE JEAN NATHAN

who also, once upon a time, in peg-top trousers
went the pace that kills along the road to ruin

Ah, Wilderness! was first produced at the Guild Theatre, New York City, by the Theatre Guild, on October 2, 1933, and closed on June 7, 1934. Following is the original cast:

NAT MILLER, *owner of the* Evening Globe	George M. Cohan
ESSIE, *his wife*	Marjorie Marquis
ARTHUR, *their son*	William Post, Jr.
RICHARD, *their son*	Elisha Cook, Jr.
MILDRED, *their daughter*	Adelaide Bean
TOMMY, *their son*	Walter Vonnegut, Jr.
SID DAVIS, *Essie's brother, reporter on the* Waterbury Standard	Gene Lockhart
LILY MILLER, *Nat's sister*	Eda Heinemann
DAVID MCCOMBER, *dry-goods merchant*	Richard Sterling
MURIEL MCCOMBER, *his daughter*	Ruth Gilbert
WINT SELBY, *a classmate of Arthur's at Yale*	John Wynne
BELLE	Ruth Holden
NORA	Ruth Chorpenning
BARTENDER	Donald McClelland
SALESMAN	John Butler

Directed by Philip Moeller

Settings designed by Robert Edmond Jones

SCENES

ACT ONE

Sitting-room of the Miller home in a large small-town in Connecticut—early morning, July 4th, 1906

ACT TWO

Dining-room of the Miller home—evening of the same day

ACT THREE

SCENE I

Back room of a bar in a small hotel—10 o'clock the same night

SCENE II

Same as Act One—the sitting-room of the Miller home—a little after 11 o'clock the same night

ACT FOUR

SCENE I

The Miller sitting-room again—about 1 o'clock the following afternoon

SCENE II

A strip of beach along the harbor—about 9 o'clock that night

SCENE THREE

Same as Scene One—the sitting-room—about 10 o'clock the same night

AH, WILDERNESS!

ACT ONE

SCENE—*Sitting-room of the* MILLER *home in a large small-town in Connecticut—about 7:30 in the morning of July 4th, 1906.*

The room is fairly large, homely looking and cheerful in the morning sunlight, furnished with scrupulous medium-priced tastelessness of the period. Beneath the two windows at left, front, a sofa with silk and satin cushions stands against the wall. At rear of sofa, a bookcase with glass doors, filled with cheap sets, extends along the remaining length of wall. In the rear wall, left, is a double doorway with sliding doors and portières, leading into a dark, windowless, back parlor. At right of this doorway, another bookcase, this time a small, open one, crammed with boys' and girls' books and the best-selling novels of many past years—books the family really have read. To the right of this bookcase is the mate of the double doorway at its left, with sliding doors and portières, this one leading to a well-lighted front parlor. In the right wall, rear, a screen door opens on a porch. Farther forward in this wall are two windows, with a writing desk and a chair between them. At center is a big, round table with a green-shaded reading lamp, the cord of the lamp running up to one of five sockets in the chandelier above. Five chairs are grouped about the table—three rockers at left, right, and right rear of it, two armchairs at rear and left rear. A medium-priced, inoffensive rug covers most of the floor. The walls are papered white with a cheerful, ugly blue design

Voices are heard in a conversational tone from the dining-room beyond the back parlor, where the family are just finishing breakfast. Then MRS. MILLER'S *voice, raised commandingly, "Tommy! Come back here and finish your milk!" At the same moment* TOMMY *appears in the doorway from the back parlor—a chubby, sun-burnt boy of eleven with dark eyes, blond hair wetted and plastered down in a part, and a shiny, good-natured face, a rim of milk visible about his lips. Bursting with bottled-up energy and a longing to get started on the Fourth, he nevertheless has hesitated obediently at his mother's call.*

TOMMY (*calls back pleadingly*). Aw, I'm full, Ma. And I said excuse me and you said all right. (*His* FATHER'S *voice is heard speaking to his mother. Then she calls: "All right, Tommy,"* and TOMMY *asks eagerly*) Can I go out now?

MOTHER'S VOICE (*correctingly*). May I!

TOMMY (*fidgeting, but obediently*). May I, Ma?

MOTHER'S VOICE. Yes. (TOMMY *jumps for the screen door to the porch at right like a sprinter released by the starting shot.*)

FATHER'S VOICE (*shouts after him*). But you set off your crackers away from the house, remember! (*But* TOMMY *is already through the screen door, which he leaves open behind him.*)

(*A moment later the family appear from the back parlor, coming from the dining-room. First are* MILDRED *and* ARTHUR. MILDRED *is fifteen, tall and slender, with big, irregular features, resembling her father to the complete effacing of any pretense at prettiness. But her big, gray eyes are beautiful; she has vivacity and a fetching smile, and everyone thinks of her as an attractive girl. She is dressed in shirtwaist and skirt in the fashion of the period.*

(ARTHUR, *the eldest of the Miller children who are still living home, is nineteen. He is tall, heavy, barrel-chested and muscular, the type of football linesman of that period, with a square, stolid face, small blue eyes and thick sandy hair. His manner is solemnly collegiate. He is dressed in the latest college fashion of that day, which has receded a bit from the extreme of preceding years, but still runs to padded shoulders and pants half-pegged at the top, and so small at their wide-cuffed bottoms that they cannot be taken off with shoes on.*)

MILDRED (*as they appear—inquisitively*). Where are you going today, Art?

ARTHUR (*with superior dignity*). That's my business. (*He ostentatiously takes from his pocket a tobacco pouch with a big Y and class numerals stamped on it, and a heavy bulldog briar pipe with silver Y and numerals, and starts filling the pipe.*)

MILDRED (*teasingly*). Bet I know, just the same! Want me to tell you her initials? E. R.! (*She laughs.* ARTHUR, *pleased by this insinuation at his lady-killing activities, yet finds it beneath his dignity to reply. He goes to the table, lights his pipe and picks up the local morning paper, and slouches back into the armchair at left rear of table, beginning to whistle "Oh, Waltz Me Around Again, Willie" as he scans the headlines.* MILDRED *sits on the sofa at left, front.*)

(*Meanwhile, their mother and their* AUNT LILY, *their father's sister, have appeared, following them from the back parlor.* MRS. MILLER *is around fifty, a short, stout woman with fading light-brown hair sprinkled with gray, who must have been decidedly pretty as a girl in a round-faced, cute, small-featured, wide-eyed fashion. She has big brown eyes, soft and maternal—a bustling, mother-of-a-family manner. She is dressed in shirtwaist and skirt.*

(LILY MILLER, *her sister-in-law, is forty-two, tall, dark and thin. She conforms outwardly to the conventional type of old-maid school teacher, even to wearing glasses. But behind the glasses her gray eyes are gentle and tired, and her whole atmosphere is one of shy kindliness. Her voice presents the greatest contrast to her appearance—soft and full of sweetness. She, also, is dressed in a shirtwaist and skirt.*)

MRS. MILLER (*as they appear*). Getting milk down him is like— (*Suddenly she is aware of the screen door standing half open*) Goodness, look at that door he's left open! The house will be alive with flies! (*Rushing out to shut it*) I've told him again and again—and that's all the good it does! It's just a waste of breath! (*She slams the door shut.*)

LILY (*smiling*). Well, you can't expect a boy to remember to shut doors

—on the Fourth of July. (*She goes diffidently to the straight-backed chair before the desk at right, front, leaving the comfortable chairs to the others.*)

MRS. MILLER. That's you all over, Lily—always making excuses for him. You'll have him spoiled to death in spite of me. (*She sinks in rocker at right of table*) Phew, I'm hot, aren't you? This is going to be a scorcher. (*She picks up a magazine from the table and begins to rock, fanning herself.*)

(*Meanwhile, her husband and her brother have appeared from the back parlor, both smoking cigars.* NAT MILLER *is in his late fifties, a tall, dark, spare man, a little stoop-shouldered, more than a little bald, dressed with an awkward attempt at sober respectability imposed upon an innate heedlessness of clothes. His long face has large, irregular, undistinguished features, but he has fine, shrewd, humorous gray eyes.*

(SID DAVIS, *his brother-in-law is forty-five, short and fat, bald-headed, with the Puckish face of a Peck's Bad Boy who has never grown up. He is dressed in what had once been a very natty loud light suit but is now a shapeless and faded nondescript in cut and color.*)

SID (*as they appear*). Oh, I like the job first rate, Nat. Waterbury's a nifty old town with the lid off, when you get to know the ropes. I rang in a joke in one of my stories that tickled the folks there pink. Waterwagon—Waterbury—Waterloo!

MILLER (*grinning*). Darn good!

SID (*pleased*). I thought it was pretty fair myself. (*Goes on a bit ruefully, as if oppressed by a secret sorrow*) Yes, you can see life in Waterbury, all right—that is, if you're looking for life in Waterbury!

MRS. MILLER. What's that about Waterbury, Sid?

SID. I was saying it's all right in its way—but there's no place like home. (*As if to punctuate this remark, there begins a series of bangs from just beyond the porch outside, as* TOMMY *inaugurates his celebration by setting off a package of firecrackers. The assembled family jump in their chairs.*)

MRS. MILLER. That boy! (*She rushes to the screen door and out on the porch, calling*) Tommy! You mind what your Pa told you! You take your crackers out in the back yard, you hear me!

ARTHUR (*frowning scornfully*). Fresh kid! He did it on purpose to scare us.

MILLER (*grinning through his annoyance*). Darned youngster! He'll have the house afire before the day's out.

SID (*grins and sings*).

"Dunno what ter call 'im
But he's mighty like a Rose—velt."

(*They all laugh.*)

LILY. Sid, you Crazy! (SID *beams at her.* MRS. MILLER *comes back from the porch, still fuming.*)

MRS. MILLER. Well, I've made him go out back at last. Now we'll have a little peace. (*As if to contradict this, the bang of firecrackers and torpedoes begins from the rear of the house, left, and continues at intervals throughout the scene, not nearly so loud as the first explosion, but sufficiently emphatic to form a disturbing punctuation to the conversation.)*

MILLER. Well, what's on the tappee for all of you today? Sid, you're coming to the Sachem Club picnic with me, of course.

SID *(a bit embarrassedly)*. You bet. I mean I'd like to, Nat—that is, if—

MRS. MILLER *(regarding her brother with smiling suspicion)*. Hmm! I know what that Sachem Club picnic's always meant!

LILY *(breaks in in a forced joking tone that conceals a deep earnestness)*. No, not this time, Essie. Sid's a reformed character since he's been on the paper in Waterbury. At least, that's what he swore to me last night.

SID *(avoiding her eyes, humiliated—joking it off)*. Pure as the driven snow, that's me. They're running me for president of the W.C.T.U. *(They all laugh.)*

MRS. MILLER. Sid, you're a caution. You turn everything into a joke. But you be careful, you hear? We're going to have dinner in the evening tonight, you know—the best shore dinner you ever tasted and I don't want you coming home—well, not able to appreciate it.

LILY. Oh, I know he'll be careful today. Won't you, Sid?

SID *(more embarrassed than ever—joking it off melodramatically)*. Lily, I swear to you if any man offers me a drink, I'll kill him—that is, if he changes his mind! *(They all laugh except* LILY, *who bites her lip and stiffens.)*

MRS. MILLER. No use talking to him, Lily. You ought to know better by this time. We can only hope for the best.

MILLER. Now, you women stop picking on Sid. It's the Fourth of July and even a downtrodden newspaperman has a right to enjoy himself when he's on his holiday.

MRS. MILLER. I wasn't thinking only of Sid.

MILLER *(with a wink at the others)*. What, are you insinuating I ever—?

MRS. MILLER. Well, to do you justice, no, not what you'd really call—But I've known you to come back from this darned Sachem Club picnic— Well, I didn't need any little bird to whisper that you'd been some place besides to the well! *(She smiles good-naturedly.* MILLER *chuckles.)*

SID *(after a furtive glance at the stiff and silent* LILY*—changes the subject abruptly by turning to* ARTHUR*)*. How are you spending the festive Fourth, Boola-Boola? *(*ARTHUR *stiffens dignifiedly.)*

MILDRED *(teasingly)*. I can tell you, if he won't.

MRS. MILLER *(smiling)*. Off to the Rands', I suppose.

ARTHUR *(with dignity)*. I and Bert Turner are taking Elsie and Ethel Rand canoeing. We're going to have a picnic lunch on Strawberry Island. And this evening I'm staying at the Rands' for dinner.

MILLER. You're accounted for, then. How about you, Mid?

MILDRED. I'm going to the beach to Anne Culver's.

ARTHUR (*sarcastically*). Of course, there won't be any boys present! Johnny Dodd, for example?

MILDRED (*giggles—then with a coquettish toss of her head*). Pooh! what do I care for him? He's not the only pebble on the beach.

MILLER. Stop your everlasting teasing, you two. How about you and Lily, Essie?

MRS. MILLER. I don't know. I haven't made any plans. Have you, Lily?

LILY (*quietly*). No. Anything you want to do.

MRS. MILLER. Well, I thought we'd just sit around and rest and talk.

MILLER. You can gossip any day. This is the Fourth. Now, I've got a better suggestion than that. What do you say to an automobile ride? I'll get out the Buick and we'll drive around town and out to the lighthouse and back. Then Sid and I will let you off here, or anywhere you say, and we'll go on to the picnic.

MRS. MILLER. I'd love it. Wouldn't you, Lily?

LILY. It would be nice.

MILLER. Then, that's all settled.

SID (*embarrassedly*). Lily, want to come with me to the fireworks display at the beach tonight?

MRS. MILLER. That's right, Sid. You take her out. Poor Lily never has any fun, always sitting home with me.

LILY (*flustered and grateful*). I—I'd like to, Sid, thank you. (*Then an apprehensive look comes over her face*) Only not if you come home—you know.

SID (*again embarrassed and humiliated—again joking it off, solemnly*). Evil-minded, I'm afraid, Nat. I hate to say it of your sister. (*They all laugh. Even* LILY *cannot suppress a smile.*)

ARTHUR (*with heavy jocularity*). Listen, Uncle Sid. Don't let me catch you and Aunt Lily spooning on a bench tonight—or it'll be my duty to call a cop!

(SID *and* LILY *both look painfully embarrassed at this, and the joke falls flat, except for* MILDRED *who can't restrain a giggle at the thought of these two ancients spooning.*)

MRS. MILLER (*rebukingly*). Arthur!

MILLER (*dryly*). That'll do you. Your education in kicking a football around Yale seems to have blunted your sense of humor.

MRS. MILLER (*suddenly—startledly*). But where's Richard? We're forgetting all about him. Why, where is that boy? I thought he came in with us from breakfast.

MILDRED. I'll bet he's off somewhere writing a poem to Muriel McComber, the silly! Or pretending to write one. I think he just copies—

ARTHUR (*looking back toward the dining-room*). He's still in the dining-room, reading a book. (*Turning back—scornfully*) Gosh, he's always reading now. It's not my idea of having a good time in vacation.

MILLER (*caustically*). He read his school books, too, strange as that may seem to you. That's why he came out top of his class. I'm hoping before you leave New Haven they'll find time to teach you reading is a good habit.

MRS. MILLER (*sharply*). That reminds me, Nat. I've been meaning to speak to you about those awful books Richard is reading. You've got to give him a good talking to— (*She gets up from her chair*) I'll go up and get them right now. I found them where he'd hid them on the shelf in his wardrobe. You just wait till you see what— (*She bustles off, rear right, through the front parlor.*)

MILLER (*plainly not relishing whatever is coming—to* SID *grumblingly*). Seems to me she might wait until the Fourth is over before bringing up— (*Then with a grin*) I know there's nothing to it, anyway. When I think of the books I used to sneak off and read when I was a kid.

SID. Me, too. I suppose Dick is deep in Nick Carter or Old Cap Collier.

MILLER. No, he passed that period long ago. Poetry's his red meat nowadays, I think—love poetry—and socialism, too, I suspect, from some dire declarations he's made. (*Then briskly*) Well, might as well get him on the carpet. (*He calls*) Richard. (*No answer—louder*) Richard. (*No answer—then in a bellow*) Richard!

ARTHUR (*shouting*). Hey, Dick, wake up! Pa's calling you.

RICHARD'S VOICE (*from the dining-room*) All right. I'm coming.

MILLER. Darn him! When he gets his nose in a book, the house could fall down and he'd never—

(RICHARD *appears in the doorway from the back parlor, the book he has been reading in one hand, a finger marking his place. He looks a bit startled still, reluctantly called back to earth from another world. He is going on seventeen, just out of high school. In appearance he is a perfect blend of father and mother, so much so that each is convinced he is the image of the other. He has his mother's light-brown hair, his father's gray eyes; his features are neither large nor small; he is of medium height, neither fat nor thin. One would not call him a handsome boy; neither is he homely. But he is definitely different from both of his parents, too. There is something of extreme sensitiveness added—a restless, apprehensive, defiant, shy, dreamy, self-conscious intelligence about him. In manner he is alternately plain simple boy and a posey actor solemnly playing a role. He is dressed in prep school reflection of the college style of* ARTHUR.)

RICHARD. Did you want me, Pa?

MILLER. I'd hoped I'd made that plain. Come and sit down a while. (*He points to the rocking chair at the right of table near his.*)

RICHARD (*coming forward—seizing on the opportunity to play up his preoccupation—with apologetic superiority*). I didn't hear you, Pa. I was off in another world.

(MILDRED *slyly shoves her foot out so that he trips over it, almost falling. She laughs gleefully. So does* ARTHUR.)

ARTHUR. Good for you, Mid! That'll wake him up!

RICHARD (*grins sheepishly—all boy now*). Darn you, Mid! I'll show you! (*He pushes her back on the sofa and tickles her with his free hand, still holding the book in the other. She shrieks.*)

ARTHUR. Give it to her, Dick!

MILLER. That's enough, now. No more roughhouse. You sit down here, Richard. (RICHARD *obediently takes the chair at right of table, opposite his father*) What were you planning to do with yourself today? Going out to the beach with Mildred?

RICHARD (*scornfully superior*). That silly skirt party! I should say not!

MILDRED. He's not coming because Muriel isn't. I'll bet he's got a date with her somewheres.

RICHARD (*flushing bashfully*). You shut up! (*Then to his father*) I thought I'd just stay home, Pa—this morning, anyway.

MILLER. Help Tommy set off firecrackers, eh?

RICHARD (*drawing himself up—with dignity*). I should say not. (*Then frowning portentously*) I don't believe in this silly celebrating the Fourth of July—all this lying talk about liberty—when there is no liberty!

MILLER (*a twinkle in his eye*). Hmm.

RICHARD (*getting warmed up*). The land of the free and the home of the brave! Home of the slave is what they ought to call it—the wage slave ground under the heel of the capitalist class, starving, crying for bread for his children, and all he gets is a stone! The Fourth of July is a stupid farce!

MILLER (*putting a hand to his mouth to conceal a grin*). Hmm. Them are mighty strong words. You'd better not repeat such sentiments outside the bosom of the family or they'll have you in jail.

SID. And throw away the key.

RICHARD (*darkly*). Let them put me in jail. But how about the freedom of speech in the Constitution, then? That must be a farce, too. (*Then he adds grimly*) No, you can celebrate your Fourth of July. I'll celebrate the day the people bring out the guillotine again and I see Pierpont Morgan being driven by in a tumbril! (*His father and* SID *are greatly amused;* LILY *is shocked but, taking her cue from them, smiles.* MILDRED *stares at him in puzzled wonderment, never having heard this particular line before. Only* ARTHUR *betrays the outraged reaction of a patriot.*)

ARTHUR. Aw say, you fresh kid, tie that bull outside! You ought to get a punch in the nose for talking that way on the Fourth!

MILLER (*solemnly*). Son, if I didn't know it was you talking, I'd think we had Emma Goldman with us.

ARTHUR. Never mind, Pa. Wait till we get him down to Yale. We'll take that out of him!

RICHARD (*with high scorn*). Oh, Yale! You think there's nothing in the world besides Yale! After all, what is Yale?

ARTHUR. You'll find out what!

SID (*provocatively*). Don't let them scare you, Dick. Give 'em hell!

LILY (*shocked*). Sid! You shouldn't swear before—

RICHARD. What do you think I am, Aunt Lily—a baby? I've heard worse than anything Uncle Sid says.

MILDRED. And said worse himself, I bet!

MILLER (*with a comic air of resignation*). Well, Richard, I've always found I've had to listen to at least one stump speech every Fourth. I only hope getting your extra strong one right after breakfast will let me off for the rest of the day. (*They all laugh now, taking this as a cue.*)

RICHARD (*somberly*). That's right, laugh! After you, the deluge, you think! But look out! Supposing it comes before? Why shouldn't the workers of the world unite and rise? They have nothing to lose but their chains! (*He recites threateningly*) "The days grow hot, O Babylon! 'Tis cool beneath thy willow trees!"

MILLER. Hmm. That's good. But where's the connection, exactly? Something from that book you're reading?

RICHARD (*superior*). No. That's poetry. This is prose.

MILLER. I've heard there was a difference between 'em. What is the book?

RICHARD (*importantly*). Carlyle's "French Revolution."

MILLER. Hmm. So that's where you drove the tumbril from and piled poor old Pierpont in it. (*Then seriously*) Glad you're reading it, Richard. It's a darn fine book.

RICHARD (*with unflattering astonishment*). What, have you read it?

MILLER. Well, you see, even a newspaper owner can't get out of reading a book every now and again.

RICHARD (*abashed*). I—I didn't mean—I know you— (*Then enthusiastically*) Say, isn't it a great book, though—that part about Mirabeau—and about Marat and Robespierre—

MRS. MILLER (*appears from the front parlor in a great state of flushed annoyance*). Never you mind Robespierre, young man! You tell me this minute where you've hidden those books! They were on the shelf in your wardrobe and now you've gone and hid them somewheres else. You go right up and bring them to your father! (RICHARD, *for a second, looks suddenly guilty and crushed. Then he bristles defensively.*)

MILLER (*after a quick understanding glance at him*). Never mind his getting them now. We'll waste the whole morning over those darned books. And anyway, he has a right to keep his library to himself—that is, if they're not too— What books are they, Richard?

RICHARD (*self-consciously*). Well—there's—

MRS. MILLER. I'll tell you, if he won't—and you give him a good talking to. (*Then, after a glance at* RICHARD, *mollifiedly*) Not that I blame Richard. There must be some boy he knows who's trying to show off as advanced and wicked, and he told him about—

RICHARD. No! I read about them myself, in the papers and in other books.

MRS. MILLER. Well, no matter how, there they were on his shelf. Two by that awful Oscar Wilde they put in jail for heaven knows what wickedness.

ARTHUR (*suddenly — solemnly authoritative*). He committed bigamy. (*Then as* SID *smothers a burst of ribald laughter*) What are you laughing at? I guess I ought to know. A fellow at college told me. His father was in England when this Wilde was pinched—and he said he remembered once his mother asked his father about it and he told her he'd committed bigamy.

MILLER (*hiding a smile behind his hand*). Well then, that must be right, Arthur.

MRS. MILLER. I wouldn't put it past him, nor anything else. One book was called the Picture of something or other.

RICHARD. "The Picture of Dorian Gray." It's one of the greatest novels ever written!

MRS. MILLER. Looked to me like cheap trash. And the second book was poetry. The Ballad of I forget what.

RICHARD. "The Ballad of Reading Gaol," one of the greatest poems ever written. (*He pronounces it Reading Goal [as in goalpost].*)

MRS. MILLER. All about someone who murdered his wife and got hung, as he richly deserved, as far as I could make out. And then there were two books by that Bernard Shaw—

RICHARD. The greatest playwright alive today!

MRS. MILLER. To hear him tell it, maybe! You know, Nat, the one who wrote a play about—well, never mind—that was so vile they wouldn't even let it play in New York!

MILLER. Hmm. I remember.

MRS. MILLER. One was a book of his plays and the other had a long title I couldn't make head or tail of, only it wasn't a play.

RICHARD (*proudly*). "The Quintessence of Ibsenism."

MILDRED. Phew! Good gracious, what a name! What does it mean, Dick? I'll bet he doesn't know.

RICHARD (*outraged*). I do, too, know! It's about Ibsen, the greatest playwright since Shakespeare!

MRS. MILLER. Yes, there was a book of plays by that Ibsen there, too! And poems by Swin something—

RICHARD. "Poems and Ballads" by Swinburne, Ma. The greatest poet since Shelley! He tells the truth about real love!

MRS. MILLER. Love! Well, all I can say is, from reading here and there, that if he wasn't flung in jail along with Wilde, he should have been. Some of the things I simply couldn't read, they were so indecent— All about—well, I can't tell you before Lily and Mildred.

SID (*with a wink at* RICHARD—*jokingly*). Remember, I'm next on that one, Dick. I feel the need of a little poetical education.

LILY (*scandalized, but laughing*). Sid! Aren't you ashamed?

MRS. MILLER. This is no laughing matter. And then there was Kipling—but I suppose he's not so bad. And last there was a poem—a long one—the Rubay— What is it, Richard?

RICHARD. "The Rubaiyat of Omar Khayyam." That's the best of all!

MILLER. Oh, I've read that, Essie—got a copy down at the office.

SID (*enthusiastically*). So have I. It's a pippin!

LILY (*with shy excitement*). I—I've read it, too—at the library. I like—some parts of it.

MRS. MILLER (*scandalized*). Why, Lily!

MILLER. Everybody's reading that now, Essie—and it don't seem to do them any harm. There's fine things in it, seems to me—true things.

MRS. MILLER (*a bit bewildered and uncertain now*). Why, Nat, I don't see how you— It looked terrible blasphemous—parts I read.

SID. Remember this one: (*He quotes rhetorically*) "Oh Thou, who didst with pitfall and gin beset the path I was to wander in—" Now, I've always noticed how beset my path was with gin—in the past, you understand! (*He casts a joking side glance at* LILY. *The others laugh. But* LILY *is in a melancholy dream and hasn't heard him.*)

MRS. MILLER (*tartly, but evidently suppressing her usual smile where he is concerned*). You would pick out the ones with liquor in them!

LILY (*suddenly—with a sad pathos, quotes awkwardly and shyly*). I like—because it's true:

"The Moving Finger writes, and having writ,
Moves on: nor all your Piety nor Wit
Shall lure it back to cancel half a Line,
Nor all your Tears wash out a Word of it."

MRS. MILLER (*astonished, as are all the others*). Why, Lily, I never knew you to recite poetry before!

LILY (*immediately guilty and apologetic*). I—it just stuck in my memory somehow.

RICHARD (*looking at her as if he had never seen her before*). Good for you, Aunt Lily! (*Then enthusiastically*) But that isn't the best. The best is:

"A Book of Verses underneath the Bough,
A Jug of Wine, A Loaf of Bread—and Thou
Beside me singing in the Wilderness—"

ARTHUR (*who, bored to death by all this poetry quoting, has wandered over to the window at rear of desk, right*). Hey! Look who's coming up the walk— Old Man McComber!

MILLER (*irritably*). Dave? Now what in thunder does that damned old—Sid, I can see where we never are going to get to that picnic.

MRS. MILLER (*vexatiously*). He'll know we're in this early, too. No use lying. (*Then appalled by another thought*) That Norah—she's that thick, she never can answer the front door right unless I tell her each time. Nat, you've got to talk to Dave. I'll have her show him in here. Lily, you run up the back stairs and get your things on. I'll be up in a second. Nat, you get rid of him the first second you can! Whatever can the old fool want— (*She and* LILY *hurry out through the back parlor.*)

ARTHUR. I'm going to beat it—just time to catch the eight-twenty trolley.

MILDRED. I've got to catch that, too. Wait till I get my hat, Art! (*She rushes into the back parlor.*)

ARTHUR (*shouts after her*). I can't wait. You can catch up with me if you hurry. (*He turns at the back-parlor door—with a grin*) McComber may be coming to see if your intentions toward his daughter are dishonorable, Dick! You'd better beat it while your shoes are good! (*He disappears through the back-parlor door, laughing.*)

RICHARD (*a bit shaken, but putting on a brave front*). Think I'm scared of him?

MILLER (*gazing at him—frowning*). Can't imagine what— But it's to complain about something, I know that. I only wish I didn't have to be pleasant with the old buzzard—but he's about the most valuable advertiser I've got.

SID (*sympathetically*). I know. But tell him to go to hell, anyway. He needs that ad more than you.

(*The sound of the bell comes from the rear of the house, off left from back parlor.*)

MILLER. There he is. You clear out, Dick—but come right back as soon as he's gone, you hear? I'm not through with you, yet.

RICHARD. Yes, Pa.

MILLER. You better clear out, too, Sid. You know Dave doesn't approve jokes.

SID. And loves me like poison! Come on, Dick, we'll go out and help Tommy celebrate. (*He takes* RICHARD'S *arm and they also disappear through the back-parlor door.* MILLER *glances through the front parlor toward the front door, then calls in a tone of strained heartiness.*)

MILLER. Hello, Dave. Come right in here. What good wind blows you around on this glorious Fourth?

(*A flat, brittle voice answers him: "Good morning," and a moment later* DAVID MC COMBER *appears in the doorway from the front parlor. He is a thin, dried-up little man with a head too large for his body perched on a scrawny neck, and a long solemn horse face with deep-set little black eyes, a blunt formless nose and a tiny slit of a mouth. He is about the same age as* MILLER *but is entirely bald, and looks ten years older. He is dressed with a prim neatness in shiny old black clothes.*)

MILLER. Here, sit down and make yourself comfortable. (*Holding out the cigar box*) Have a cigar?

MC COMBER (*sitting down in the chair at the right of table—acidly*). You're forgetting. I never smoke.

MILLER (*forcing a laugh at himself*). That's so. So I was. Well, I'll smoke alone then. (*He bites off the end of the cigar viciously, as if he wished it were* MC COMBER'S *head, and sits down opposite him.*)

MC COMBER. You asked me what brings me here, so I'll come to the point at once. I regret to say it's something disagreeable – disgraceful would be nearer the truth—and it concerns your son, Richard!

MILLER (*beginning to bristle—but calmly*). Oh, come now, Dave, I'm sure Richard hasn't—

MC COMBER (*sharply*). And I'm positive he has. You're not accusing me of being a liar, I hope.

MILLER. No one said anything about liar. I only meant you're surely mistaken if you think—

MC COMBER. I'm not mistaken. I have proof of everything in his own handwriting!

MILLER (*sharply*). Let's get down to brass tacks. Just what is it you're charging him with?

MC COMBER. With being dissolute and blasphemous—with deliberately attempting to corrupt the morals of my young daughter, Muriel.

MILLER. Then I'm afraid I will have to call you a liar, Dave!

MC COMBER (*without taking offense—in the same flat, brittle voice*). I thought you'd get around to that, so I brought some of the proofs with me. I've a lot more of 'em at home. (*He takes a wallet from his inside coat pocket, selects five or six slips of paper, and holds them out to* MILLER) These are good samples of the rest. My wife discovered them in one of Muriel's bureau drawers hidden under the underwear. They're all in his handwriting, you can't deny it. Anyway, Muriel's confessed to me he wrote them. You read them and then say I'm a liar. (MILLER *has taken the slips and is reading them frowningly.* MC COMBER *talks on*) Evidently you've been too busy to take the right care about Richard's bringing up or what he's allowed to read—though I can't see why his mother failed in her duty. But that's your misfortune, and none of my business. But Muriel is my business and I can't and I won't have her innocence exposed to the contamination of a young man whose mind, judging from his choice of reading matter, is as foul—

MILLER (*making a tremendous effort to control his temper*). Why, you damned old fool! Can't you see Richard's only a fool kid who's just at the stage when he's out to rebel against all authority, and so he grabs at everything radical to read and wants to pass it on to his elders and his girl and boy friends to show off what a young hellion he is! Why, at heart you'd find Richard is just as innocent and as big a kid as Muriel is! (*He pushes the slips of paper across the table contemptuously*) This stuff doesn't mean anything to me—that is, nothing of what you think it means. If you believe this would corrupt Muriel, then you must believe she's easily corrupted! But I'll bet you'd find she knows a lot more about life than you give her credit for—and can guess a stork didn't bring her down your chimney!

MC COMBER. Now you're insulting my daughter. I won't forget that.

MILLER. I'm not insulting her. I think Muriel is a darn nice girl. That's why I'm giving her credit for ordinary good sense. I'd say the same about my own Mildred, who's the same age.

MC COMBER. I know nothing about your Mildred except that she's known all over as a flirt. (*Then more sharply*) Well, I knew you'd prove obstinate, but I certainly never dreamed you'd have the impudence, after reading those papers, to claim your son was innocent of all wrongdoing!

MILLER. And what did you dream I'd do?

MC COMBER. Do what it's your plain duty to do as a citizen to protect other people's children! Take and give him a hiding he'd remember to the last day of his life! You'd ought to do it for his sake, if you had any sense—unless you want him to end up in jail!

MILLER (*his fists clenched, leans across the table*). Dave, I've stood all I can stand from you! You get out! And get out quick, if you don't want a kick in the rear to help you!

MC COMBER (*again in his flat, brittle voice, slowly getting to his feet*). You needn't lose your temper. I'm only demanding you do your duty by your own as I've already done by mine. I'm punishing Muriel. She's not to be allowed out of the house for a month and she's to be in bed every night by eight sharp. And yet she's blameless, compared to that—

MILLER. I said I'd had enough out of you, Dave! (*He makes a threatening movement.*)

MC COMBER. You needn't lay hands on me. I'm going. But there's one thing more. (*He takes a letter from his wallet*) Here's a letter from Muriel for your son. (*Puts it on the table*) It makes clear, I think, how she's come to think about him, now that her eyes have been opened. I hope he heeds what's inside—for his own good and yours—because if I ever catch him hanging about my place again I'll have him arrested! And don't think I'm not going to make you regret the insults you've heaped on me. I'm taking the advertisement for my store out of your paper—and it won't go in again, I tell you, not unless you apologize in writing and promise to punish—

MILLER. I'll see you in hell first! As for your damned old ad, take it out and go to hell!

MC COMBER. That's plain bluff. You know how badly you need it. So do I. (*He starts stiffly for the door.*)

MILLER. Here! Listen a minute! I'm just going to call *your* bluff and tell you that, whether you want to reconsider your decision or not, I'm going to refuse to print your damned ad after tomorrow! Put that in your pipe and smoke it! Furthermore, I'll start a campaign to encourage outside capital to open a dry-goods store in opposition to you that won't be the public swindle I can prove yours is!

MC COMBER (*a bit shaken by this threat—but in the same flat tone*). I'll sue you for libel.

MILLER. When I get through, there won't be a person in town will buy a dishrag in your place!

MC COMBER (*more shaken, his eyes shifting about furtively*). That's all bluff. You wouldn't dare— (*Then finally he says uncertainly*) Well, good day. (*And turns and goes out.* NAT *stands looking after him. Slowly the anger drains from his face and leaves him looking a bit sick and disgusted.* SID *appears from the back parlor. He is nursing a burn on his right hand, but his face is one broad grin of satisfaction.*)

SID. I burned my hand with one of Tommy's damned firecrackers and came in to get some vaseline. I was listening to the last of your scrap. Good for you, Nat! You sure gave him hell!

MILLER (*dully*). Much good it'll do. He knows it was all talk.

SID. That's just what he don't know, Nat. The old skinflint has a guilty conscience.

MILLER. Well, anyone who knows me knows I wouldn't use my paper for a dirty, spiteful trick like that—no matter what he did to me.

SID. Yes, everyone knows you're an old sucker, Nat, too decent for your own good. But McComber never saw you like this before. I tell you you scared the pants off him. (*He chuckles.*)

MILLER (*still dejectedly*). I don't know what made me let go like that. The hell of skunks like McComber is that after being with them ten minutes you become as big skunks as they are.

SID (*notices the slips of paper on the table*). What's this? Something he brought? (*He picks them up and starts to read.*)

MILLER (*grimly*). Samples of the new freedom—from those books Essie found—that Richard's been passing on to Muriel to educate her. They're what started the rumpus. (*Then frowning*) I've got to do something about that young anarchist or he'll be getting me, and himself, in a peck of trouble. (*Then pathetically helpless*) But what can I do? Putting the curb bit on would make him worse. Then he'd have a harsh tyrant to defy. He'd love that, darn him!

SID (*has been reading the slips, a broad grin on his face—suddenly he whistles*). Phew! This is a warm lulu for fair! (*He recites with a joking intensity*)

"My life is bitter with thy love; thine eyes
Blind me, thy tresses burn me, thy sharp sighs
Divide my flesh and spirit with soft sound—"

MILLER (*with a grim smile*). Hmm. I missed that one. That must be Mr. Swinburne's copy. I've never read him, but I've heard something like that was the matter with him.

SID. Yes, it's labelled Swinburne—"Anactoria." Whatever that is. But wait, watch and listen! The worst is yet to come! (*He recites with added comic intensity*)

"That I could drink thy veins as wine, and eat
Thy breasts like honey, that from face to feet

Thy body were abolished and consumed,
And in my flesh thy very flesh entombed!"

MILLER (*an irrepressible boyish grin coming to his face*). Hell and hallelujah! Just picture old Dave digesting that for the first time! Gosh, I'd give a lot to have seen his face! (*Then a trace of shocked reproof showing in his voice*) But it's no joking matter. That stuff *is* warm—too damned warm, if you ask me! I don't like this a damned bit, Sid. That's no kind of thing to be sending a decent girl. (*More worriedly*) I thought he was really stuck on her—as one gets stuck on a decent girl at his age—all moonshine and holding hands and a kiss now and again. But this looks—I wonder if he is hanging around her to see what he can get? (*Angrily*) By God, if that's true, he deserves that licking McComber says it's my duty to give him! I've got to draw the line somewhere!

SID. Yes, it won't do to have him getting any decent girl in trouble.

MILLER. The only thing I can do is put it up to him straight. (*With pride*) Richard'll stand up to his guns, no matter what. I've never known him to lie to me.

SID (*at a noise from the back parlor, looks that way—in a whisper*). Then now's your chance. I'll beat it and leave you alone—see if the women folks are ready upstairs. We ought to get started soon—if we're ever going to make that picnic. (*He is halfway to the entrance to the front parlor as* RICHARD *enters from the back parlor, very evidently nervous about* MC COMBER'S *call.*)

RICHARD (*adopting a forced, innocent tone*). How's your hand, Uncle Sid?

SID. All right, Dick, thanks—only hurts a little. (*He disappears.* MILLER *watches his son frowningly.* RICHARD *gives him a quick side glance and grows more guiltily self-conscious.*)

RICHARD (*forcing a snicker*). Gee, Pa, Uncle Sid's a bigger kid than Tommy is. He was throwing firecrackers in the air and catching them on the back of his hand and throwing 'em off again just before they went off—and one came and he wasn't quick enough, and it went off almost on top of—

MILLER. Never mind that. I've got something else to talk to you about besides firecrackers.

RICHARD (*apprehensively*). What, Pa?

MILLER (*suddenly puts both hands on his shoulders—quietly*). Look here, Son. I'm going to ask you a question, and I want an honest answer. I warn you beforehand if the answer is "yes" I'm going to punish you and punish you hard because you'll have done something no boy of mine ought to do. But you've never lied to me before, I know, and I don't believe, even to save yourself punishment, you'd lie to me now, would you?

RICHARD (*impressed—with dignity*) I won't lie, Pa.

MILLER. Have you been trying to have something to do with Muriel—something you shouldn't—you know what I mean.

RICHARD (*stares at him for a moment, as if he couldn't comprehend—then, as he does, a look of shocked indignation comes over his face*). No! What do you think I am, Pa? I never would! She's not that kind! Why, I—I love her! I'm going to marry her—after I get out of college! She's said she would! We're engaged!

MILLER (*with great relief*). All right. That's all I wanted to know. We won't talk any more about it. (*He gives him an approving pat on the back.*)

RICHARD. I don't see how you could think— Did that old idiot McComber say that about me?

MILLER (*joking now*). Shouldn't call your future father-in-law names, should you? 'Tain't respectful. (*Then after a glance at* RICHARD'S *indignant face—points to the slips of paper on the table*) Well, you can't exactly blame old Dave, can you, when you read through that literature you wished on his innocent daughter?

RICHARD (*sees the slips for the first time and is overcome by embarrassment, which he immediately tries to cover up with a superior carelessness*). Oh, so that's why. He found those, did he? I told her to be careful— Well, it'll do him good to read the truth about life for once and get rid of his old-fogy ideas.

MILLER. I'm afraid I've got to agree with him, though, that they're hardly fit reading for a young girl. (*Then with subtle flattery*) They're all well enough, in their way, for you who're a man, but— Think it over, and see if you don't agree with me.

RICHARD (*embarrassedly*). Aw, I only did it because I liked them—and I wanted her to face life as it is. She's so darned afraid of life—afraid of her Old Man—afraid of people saying this or that about her—afraid of being in love—afraid of everything. She's even afraid to let me kiss her. I thought, maybe, reading those things—they're beautiful, aren't they, Pa?— I thought they would give her the spunk to lead her own life, and not be—always thinking of being afraid.

MILLER. I see. Well, I'm afraid she's still afraid. (*He takes the letter from the table*) Here's a letter from her he said to give you. (RICHARD *takes the letter from him uncertainly, his expression changing to one of apprehension.* MILLER *adds with a kindly smile*) You better be prepared for a bit of a blow. But never mind. There's lots of other fish in the sea. (RICHARD *is not listening to him, but staring at the letter with a sort of fascinated dread.* MILLER *looks into his son's face a second, then turns away, trouble and embarrassed*) Darn it! I better go upstairs and get rigged out or I never will get to that picnic. (*He moves awkwardly and self-consciously off through the front parlor.* RICHARD *continues to stare at the letter for a moment—then girds up his courage and tears it open and begins to read swiftly. As he reads his face grows more and more wounded and tragic, until at the end his mouth draws down at the corners, as if he were about to break into tears. With an effort he forces them back and his face grows flushed with humiliation and wronged anger.*)

RICHARD (*blurts out to himself*). The little coward! I hate her! She can't treat me like that! I'll show her! (*At the sound of voices from the front parlor, he quickly shoves the letter into the inside pocket of his coat and does his best to appear calm and indifferent, even attempting to whistle "Waiting at the Church." But the whistle peters out miserably as his mother,* LILY *and* SID *enter from the front parlor. They are dressed in all the elaborate paraphernalia of motoring at that period—linen dusters, veils, goggles,* SID *in a snappy cap.*)

MRS. MILLER. Well, we're about ready to start at last, thank goodness! Let's hope no more callers are on the way. What did that McComber want, Richard, do you know? Sid couldn't tell us.

RICHARD. You can search me. Ask Pa.

MRS. MILLER (*immediately sensing something "down" in his manner—going to him worriedly*). Why, whatever's the matter with you, Richard? You sound as if you'd lost your last friend! What is it?

RICHARD (*desperately*). I— I don't feel so well—my stomach's sick.

MRS. MILLER (*immediately all sympathy—smoothing his hair back from his forehead*). You poor boy! What a shame—on the Fourth, too, of all days! (*Turning to the others*) Maybe I better stay home with him, if he's sick.

LILY. Yes, I'll stay, too.

RICHARD (*more desperately*). No! You go, Ma! I'm not really sick. I'll be all right. You go. I want to be alone! (*Then, as a louder bang comes from in back as* TOMMY *sets off a cannon cracker, he jumps to his feet*) Darn Tommy and his darned firecrackers! You can't get any peace in this house with that darned kid around! Darn the Fourth of July, anyway! I wish we still belonged to England! (*He strides off in an indignant fury of misery through the front parlor.*)

MRS. MILLER (*stares after him worriedly—then sighs philosophically*). Well, I guess he can't be so very sick—after that. (*She shakes her head*) He's a queer boy. Sometimes I can't make head or tail of him.

MILLER (*calls from the front door beyond the back parlor*). Come along, folks. Let's get started.

SID. We're coming, Nat. (*He and the two women move off through the front parlor.*)

CURTAIN

ACT TWO

SCENE—*Dining-room of the* MILLER *home—a little after 6 o'clock in the evening of the same day.*

The room is much too small for the medium-priced, formidable dining-room set, especially now when all the leaves of the table are in. At left, toward rear, is a double doorway with sliding doors and portières leading into the back parlor. In the rear wall, left, is the door to the pantry. At the right of door is the china closet with its display of the family cut glass and fancy china. In the right wall are two windows looking out on a side lawn. In front of the windows is a heavy, ugly sideboard with three pieces of old silver on its top. In the left wall, extreme front, is a screen door opening on a side porch. A dark rug covers most of the floor. The table, with a chair at each end, left and right, three chairs on the far side, facing front, and two on the near side, their backs to front, takes up most of the available space. The walls are papered in a somber brown and dark-red design.

MRS. MILLER *is supervising and helping the Second Girl,* NORAH, *in the setting of the table.* NORAH *is a clumsy, heavy-handed, heavy-footed, long-jawed, beamingly good-natured young Irish girl—a "greenhorn."*

MRS. MILLER. I really think you better put on the lights, Norah. It's getting so cloudy out, and this pesky room is so dark, anyway.

NORAH. Yes, Mum. (*She stretches awkwardly over the table to reach the chandelier that is suspended from the middle of the ceiling and manages to turn one light on—scornfully*) Arrah, the contraption!

MRS. MILLER (*worriedly*). Careful!

NORAH. Careful as can be, Mum. (*But in moving around to reach the next bulb she jars heavily against the table.*)

MRS. MILLER. There! I knew it! I do wish you'd watch—!

NORAH (*a flustered appeal in her voice*). Arrah, what have I done wrong now?

MRS. MILLER (*draws a deep breath—then sighs helplessly*). Oh, nothing. Never mind the rest of the lights. You might as well go out in the kitchen and wait until I ring.

NORAH (*relieved and cheerful again*). Yes, Mum. (*She starts for the pantry.*)

MRS. MILLER. But there's one thing—(NORAH *turns apprehensively*) No, two things—things I've told you over and over, but you always forget. Don't pass the plates on the wrong side at dinner tonight, and do be careful not to let that pantry door slam behind you. Now you will try to remember, won't you?

NORAH. Yes, Mum. (*She goes into the pantry and shuts the door behind her with exaggerated care as* MRS. MILLER *watches her apprehensively.* MRS. MILLER *sighs and reaches up with difficulty and turns on another of the four lights in the chandelier. As she is doing so,* LILY *enters from the back parlor.*)

LILY. Here, let me do that, Essie. I'm taller. You'll only strain yourself. (*She quickly lights the other two bulbs.*)

MRS. MILLER (*gratefully*). Thank you, Lily. It's a stretch for me, I'm getting so fat.

LILY. But where's Norah? Why didn't she—?

MRS. MILLER (*exasperatedly*). Oh, that girl! Don't talk about her! She'll be the death of me! She's that thick, you honestly wouldn't believe it possible.

LILY (*smiling*). Why, what did she do now?

MRS. MILLER. Oh, nothing. She means all right.

LILY. Anything else I can do, Essie?

MRS. MILLER. Well, she's got the table all wrong. We'll have to reset it. But you're always helping me. It isn't fair to ask you—in your vacation. You need your rest after teaching a pack of wild Indians of kids all year.

LILY (*beginning to help with the table*). You know I love to help. It makes me feel I'm some use in this house instead of just sponging—

MRS. MILLER (*indignantly*). Sponging! You pay, don't you?

LILY. Almost nothing. And you and Nat only take that little to make me feel better about living with you. (*Forcing a smile*) I don't see how you stand me—having a cranky old maid around all the time.

MRS. MILLER. What nonsense you talk! As if Nat and I weren't only too tickled to death to have you! Lily Miller, I've no patience with you when you go on like that. We've been over this a thousand times before, and still you go on! Crazy, that's what it is! (*She changes the subject abruptly*) What time's it getting to be?

LILY (*looking at her watch*). Quarter past six.

MRS. MILLER. I do hope those men folks aren't going to be late for dinner. (*She sighs*) But I suppose with that darned Sachem Club picnic it's more likely than not. (LILY *looks worried, and sighs.* MRS. MILLER *gives her a quick side glance*) I see you've got your new dress on.

LILY (*embarrassedly*). Yes, I thought —if Sid's taking me to the fireworks— I ought to spruce up a little.

MRS. MILLER (*looking away*). Hmm. (*A pause—then she says with an effort to be casual*) You mustn't mind if Sid comes home feeling a bit—gay. I expect Nat to—and we'll have to listen to all those old stories of his about when he was a boy. You know what those picnics are, and Sid'd be running into all his old friends.

LILY (*agitatedly*). I don't think he will—this time—not after his promise.

MRS. MILLER (*avoiding looking at her*). I know. But men are weak. (*Then quickly*) That was a good notion of Nat's, getting Sid the job on the Waterbury *Standard*. All he ever needed was to get away from the rut he was in here. He's the kind that's the victim of his friends. He's easily led—but there's no real harm in him, you know that. (LILY *keeps silent, her eyes downcast.* MRS. MILLER *goes on meaningly*) He's making good money in Waterbury, too—thirty-five a week. He's in a better position to get married than he ever was.

LILY (*stiffly*). Well, I hope he finds a woman who's willing—though after he's through with his betting on horse races, and dice, and playing

Kelly pool, there won't be much left for a wife—even if there was nothing else he spent his money on.

MRS. MILLER. Oh, he'd give up all that—for the right woman. (*Suddenly she comes directly to the point*) Lily, why don't you change your mind and marry Sid and reform him? You love him and always have—

LILY (*stiffly*). I can't love a man who drinks.

MRS. MILLER. You can't fool me. I know darned well you love him. And he loves you and always has.

LILY. Never enough to stop drinking for. (*Cutting off* MRS. MILLER'S *reply*) No, it's no good in your talking, Essie. We've been over this a thousand times before and I'll always feel the same as long as Sid's the same. If he gave me proof he'd—but even then I don't believe I could. It's sixteen years since I broke off our engagement, but what made me break it off is as clear to me today as it was then. It was what he'd be liable to do now to anyone who married him—his taking up with bad women.

MRS. MILLER (*protests half-heartedly*). But he's always sworn he got raked into that party and never had anything to do with those harlots.

LILY. Well, I don't believe him—didn't then and don't now. I do believe he didn't deliberately plan to, but— Oh, it's no good talking, Essie. What's done is done. But you know how much I like Sid—in spite of everything. I know he was just born to be what he is—irresponsible, never meaning to harm but harming in spite of himself. But don't talk to me about marrying him—because I never could.

MRS. MILLER (*angrily*). He's a dumb fool—a stupid dumb fool, that's what he is!

LILY (*quietly*). No. He's just Sid.

MRS. MILLER. It's a shame for you—a measly shame—you that would have made such a wonderful wife for any man—that ought to have your own home and children!

LILY (*winces but puts her arm around her affectionately—gently*). Now don't you go feeling sorry for me. I won't have that. Here I am, thanks to your and Nat's kindness, with the best home in the world; and as for the children, I feel the same love for yours as if they were mine, and I didn't have the pain of bearing them. And then there are all the boys and girls I teach every year. I like to feel I'm a sort of second mother to them and helping them to grow up to be good men and women. So I don't feel such a useless old maid, after all.

MRS. MILLER (*kisses her impulsively—her voice husky*). You're a good woman, Lily—too good for the rest of us. (*She turns away, wiping a tear furtively—then abruptly changing the subject*) Good gracious, if I'm not forgetting one of the most important things! I've got to warn that Tommy against giving me away to Nat about the fish. He knows, because I had to send him to market for it, and he's liable to burst out laughing—

LILY. Laughing about what?

MRS. MILLER (*guiltily*). Well, I've never told you, because it seemed sort of a sneaking trick, but you know how Nat carries on about not being able to eat bluefish.

LILY. I know he says there's a certain oil in it that poisons him.

MRS. MILLER (*chuckling*). Poisons him, nothing! He's been eating bluefish for years—only I tell him each time it's weakfish. We're having it tonight—and I've got to warn that young imp to keep his face straight.

LILY (*laughing*). Aren't you ashamed, Essie?

MRS. MILLER. Not much, I'm not! I like bluefish! (*She laughs*) Where is Tommy? In the sitting-room?

LILY. No, Richard's there alone. I think Tommy's out on the piazza with Mildred. (MRS. MILLER *bustles out through the back parlor. As soon as she is gone, the smile fades from* LILY'S *lips. Her face grows sad and she again glances nervously at her watch.* RICHARD *appears from the back parlor, moving in an aimless way. His face wears a set expression of bitter gloom; he exudes tragedy. For* RICHARD, *after his first outburst of grief and humiliation, has begun to take a masochistic satisfaction in his great sorrow, especially in the concern which it arouses in the family circle. On seeing his aunt, he gives her a dark look and turns and is about to stalk back toward the sitting-room when she speaks to him pityingly*) Feel any better, Richard?

RICHARD (*somberly*). I'm all right, Aunt Lily. You mustn't worry about me.

LILY (*going to him*). But I do worry about you. I hate to see you so upset.

RICHARD. It doesn't matter. Nothing matters.

LILY (*puts her arm around him sympathetically*). You really mustn't let yourself take it so seriously. You know, something happens and things like that come up, and we think there's no hope—

RICHARD. Things like what come up?

LILY. What's happened between you and Muriel.

RICHARD (*with disdain*). Oh, her! I wasn't even thinking about her. I was thinking about life.

LILY. But then—if we really, *really* love—why, then something else is bound to happen soon that changes everything again, and it's all as it was before the misunderstanding, and everything works out all right in the end. That's the way it is with life.

RICHARD (*with a tragic sneer*). Life! Life is a joke! And everything comes out all wrong in the end!

LILY (*a little shocked*). You mustn't talk that way. But I know you don't mean it.

RICHARD. I do too mean it! You can have your silly optimism, if you like, Aunt Lily. But don't ask me to be so blind. I'm a pessimist! (*Then with an air of cruel cynicism*) As for Muriel, that's all dead and past. I was only kidding her, anyway, just to have a little fun, and she took it seriously, like a fool. (*He forces a cruel smile to his lips*) You know what they say about women and trolley cars, Aunt Lily: there's always another one along in a minute.

LILY (*really shocked this time*). I don't like you when you say such horrible, cynical things. It isn't nice.

RICHARD. Nice! That's all you women think of! I'm proud to be a cynic. It's the only thing you can be when you really face life. I suppose you think I ought to be heartbroken about Muriel—a little coward that's afraid to say her soul's her own, and keeps tied to her father's apron strings! Well, not for mine! There's plenty of other fish in the sea! (*As he is finishing, his mother comes back through the back parlor.*)

MRS. MILLER. Why, hello. You here, Richard? Getting hungry, I suppose?

RICHARD (*indignantly*). I'm not hungry a bit! That's all you think of, Ma—food!

MRS. MILLER. Well, I must say I've never noticed you to hang back at meal times. (*To* LILY) What's that he was saying about fish in the sea?

LILY (*smiling*). He says he's through with Muriel now.

MRS. MILLER (*tartly—giving her son a rebuking look*). She's through with him, he means! The idea of your sending a nice girl like her things out of those indecent books! (*Deeply offended,* RICHARD *disdains to reply but stalks woundedly to the screen door at left, front, and puts a hand on the knob*) Where are you going?

RICHARD (*quotes from "Candida" in a hollow voice*). "Out, then, into the night with me!" (*He stalks out, slamming the door behind him.*)

MRS. MILLER (*calls*). Well, don't you go far, 'cause dinner'll be ready in a minute, and I'm not coming running after you! (*She turns to* LILY *with a chuckle*) Goodness, that boy! He ought to be on the stage! (*She mimics*) "Out—into the night"—and it isn't even dark yet! He got that out of one of those books, I suppose. Do you know, I'm actually grateful to old Dave McComber for putting an end to his nonsense with Muriel. I never did approve of Richard getting so interested in girls. He's not old enough for such silliness. Why, seems to me it was only yesterday he was still a baby. (*She sighs—then matter-of-factly*) Well, nothing to do now till those men turn up. No use standing here like gawks. We might as well go in the sitting-room and be comfortable.

LILY (*the nervous, worried note in her voice again*). Yes, we might as well. (*They go out through the back parlor. They have no sooner disappeared than the screen door is opened cautiously and* RICHARD *comes back in the room.*)

RICHARD (*stands inside the door, looking after them—quotes bitterly*). "They do not know the secret in the poet's heart." (*He comes nearer the table and surveys it, especially the cut-glass dish containing olives, with contempt and mutters disdainfully*) Food! (*But the dish of olives seems to fascinate him and presently he has approached nearer, and stealthily lifts a couple and crams them into his mouth. He is just reaching out for more when the pantry door is opened slightly and* NORAH *peers in.*)

NORAH. Mister Dick, you thief, lave them olives alone, or the missus'll be swearing it was me at them!

RICHARD (*draws back his hand as if he had been stung—too flustered to be anything but guilty boy for a second*). I—I wasn't eating—

NORAH. Oho, no, of course not, divil fear you, you was only feeling their pulse! (*Then warningly*) Mind what I'm saying now, or I'll have to tell on you to protect me good name! (*She draws back into the pantry, closing the door.* RICHARD *stands, a prey to feelings of bitterest humiliation and seething revolt against everyone and everything. A low whistle comes from just outside the porch door. He starts. Then a masculine voice calls: "Hey, Dick." He goes over to the screen door grumpily—then as he recognizes the owner of the voice, his own as he answers becomes respectful and admiring.*)

RICHARD. Oh, hello, Wint. Come on in. (*He opens the door and* WINT SELBY *enters and stands just inside the door.* SELBY *is nineteen, a classmate of* ARTHUR'S *at Yale. He is a typical, good-looking college boy of the period, not the athletic but the hell-raising sport type. He is tall, blond, dressed in extreme collegiate cut.*)

WINT (*as he enters—warningly, in a low tone*). Keep it quiet, Kid. I don't want the folks to know I'm here. Tell Art I want to see him a second—on the Q.T.

RICHARD. Can't. He's up at the Rands'—won't be home before ten, anyway.

WINT (*irritably*). Damn, I thought he'd be here for dinner. (*More irritably*) Hell, that gums the works for fair!

RICHARD (*ingratiatingly*). What is it, Wint? Can't I help?

WINT (*gives him an appraising glance*). I might tell you, if you can keep your face shut.

RICHARD. I can.

WINT. Well, I ran into a couple of swift babies from New Haven this after, and I dated them up for tonight, thinking I could catch Art. But now it's too late to get anyone else and I'll have to pass it up. I'm nearly broke and I can't afford to blow them both to drinks.

RICHARD (*with shy eagerness*). I've got eleven dollars saved up. I could loan you some.

WINT (*surveys him appreciatively*) Say, you're a good sport. (*Then shaking his head*) Nix, Kid, I don't want to borrow your money. (*Then getting an idea*) But say, have you got anything on for tonight?

RICHARD. No.

WINT. Want to come along with me? (*Then quickly*) I'm not trying to lead you astray, understand. But it'll be a help if you would just sit around with Belle and feed her a few drinks while I'm off with Edith. (*He winks*) See what I mean? You don't have to do anything, not even take a glass of beer—unless you want to.

RICHARD (*boastfully*). Aw, what do you think I am—a rube?

WINT. You mean you're game for anything that's doing?

RICHARD. Sure I am!

WINT. Ever been out with any girls —I mean, real swift ones that there's something doing with, not these dead Janes around here?

RICHARD (*lies boldly*). Aw, what do you think? Sure I have!

WINT. Ever drink anything besides sodas?

RICHARD. Sure. Lots of times. Beer and sloe-gin fizz and—Manhattans.

WINT (*impressed*). Hell, you know more than I thought. (*Then considering*) Can you fix it so your folks won't get wise? I don't want your old man coming after me. You can get back by half-past ten or eleven, though, all right. Think you can cook up some lie to cover that? (*As Richard hesitates—encouraging him*) Ought to be easy—on the Fourth.

RICHARD. Sure. Don't worry about that.

WINT. But you've got to keep your face closed about this, you hear?—to Art and everybody else. I tell you straight, I wouldn't ask you to come if I wasn't in a hole—and if I didn't know you were coming down to Yale next year, and didn't think you're giving me the straight goods about having been around before. I don't want to lead you astray.

RICHARD (*scornfully*). Aw, I told you that was silly.

WINT. Well, you be at the Pleasant Beach House at half-past nine then. Come in the back room. And don't forget to grab some cloves to take the booze off your breath.

RICHARD. Aw, I know what to do.

WINT. See you later, then. (*He starts out and is just about to close the door when he thinks of something*) And say, I'll say you're a Harvard freshman, and you back me up. They don't know a damn thing about Harvard. I don't want them thinking I'm travelling around with any high-school kid.

RICHARD. Sure. That's easy.

WINT. So long, then. You better beat it right after your dinner while you've got a chance, and hang around until it's time. Watch your step, Kid.

RICHARD. So long. (*The door closes behind* WINT. RICHARD *stands for a moment, a look of bitter, defiant rebellion coming over his face, and mutters to himself*) I'll show her she can't treat me the way she's done! I'll show them all! (*Then the front door is heard slamming, and a moment later* TOMMY *rushes in from the back parlor.*)

TOMMY. Where's Ma?

RICHARD (*surlily*). In the sitting-room. Where did you think, Bonehead?

TOMMY. Pa and Uncle Sid are coming. Mid and I saw them from the front piazza. Gee, I'm glad. I'm awful hungry, ain't you? (*He rushes out through the back parlor, calling*) Ma! They're coming! Let's have dinner quick! (*A moment later* MRS. MILLER *appears from the back parlor accompanied by* TOMMY, *who keeps insisting urgently*) Gee, but I'm awful hungry, Ma!

MRS. MILLER. I know. You always are. You've got a tapeworm, that's what I think.

TOMMY. Have we got lobsters, Ma? Gee, I love lobsters.

MRS. MILLER. Yes, we've got lobsters. And fish. You remember what I told you about that fish. (*He snickers*) Now, do be quiet, Tommy! (*Then with a teasing smile at* RICHARD) Well, I'm glad to see you've got back out of the night, Richard. (*He scowls and turns his back on her.* LILY *appears through the back parlor, nervous and apprehensive. As she does so, from the front yard* SID'S *voice is heard singing "Poor John!"* MRS. MILLER *shakes her head forebodingly—but, so great is the comic spell for her even in her brother's voice, a humorous smile hovers at the corners of her lips*) Mmm! Mmm! Lily, I'm afraid—

LILY (*bitterly*). Yes, I might have known.

(MILDRED *runs in through the back parlor. She is laughing to herself a bit shamefacedly. She rushes to her mother.*)

MILDRED. Ma, Uncle Sid's— (*She whispers in her ear.*)

MRS. MILLER. Never mind! You shouldn't notice such things—at your age! And don't you encourage him by laughing at his foolishness, you hear!

TOMMY. You needn't whisper, Mid. Think I don't know? Uncle Sid's soused again.

MRS. MILLER (*shakes him by the arm indignantly*). You be quiet! Did I ever! You're getting too smart! (*Gives him a push*) Go to your place and sit right down and not another word out of you!

TOMMY (*aggrieved—rubbing his arm as he goes to his place*). Aw, Ma!

MRS. MILLER. And you sit down, Richard and Mildred. You better, too, Lily. We'll get him right in here and get some food in him. He'll be all right then. (RICHARD, *preserving the pose of the bitter, disillusioned pessimist, sits down in his place in the chair at right of the two whose backs face front.* MILDRED *takes the other chair facing back, at his left.* TOMMY *has already slid into the end chair at right of those at the rear of table facing front.* LILY *sits in the one of those at left, by the head of the table, leaving the middle one* [SID'S] *vacant. While they are doing this, the front screen door is heard slamming and* NAT'S *and* SID'S *laughing voices, raised as they come in and for a moment after, then suddenly cautiously lowered.* MRS. MILLER *goes to the entrance to the back parlor and calls peremptorily*) You come right in here! Don't stop to wash up or anything. Dinner's coming right on the table.

MILLER'S VOICE (*jovially*). All right, Essie. Here we are! Here we are!

MRS. MILLER (*goes to pantry door, opens it and calls*). All right, Norah. You can bring in the soup. (*She comes back to the back-parlor entrance just as* MILLER *enters. He isn't drunk by any means. He is just mellow and benignly ripened. His face is one large, smiling, happy beam of utter appreciation of life. All's right with the world, so satisfyingly right that he becomes sentimentally moved even to think of it.*)

MILLER. Here we are, Essie! Right on the dot! Here we are! (*He pulls her to him and gives her a smacking kiss on the ear as she jerks her head away.* MILDRED *and* TOMMY *giggle.*

RICHARD *holds rigidly aloof and disdainful, his brooding gaze fixed on his plate.* LILY *forces a smile.*)

MRS. MILLER (*pulling away—embarrassedly, almost blushing*). Don't, you Crazy! (*Then recovering herself—tartly*) So I see, you're here! And if I didn't, you've told me four times already!

MILLER (*beamingly*). Now, Essie, don't be critical. Don't be carpingly critical. Good news can stand repeating, can't it? 'Course it can! (*He slaps her jovially on her fat buttocks.* TOMMY *and* MILDRED *roar with glee. And* NORAH, *who has just entered from the pantry with a huge tureen of soup in her hands, almost drops it as she explodes in a merry guffaw.*)

MRS. MILLER (*scandalized*). Nat! Aren't you ashamed!

MILLER. Couldn't resist it! Just simply couldn't resist it!
(NORAH, *still standing with the soup tureen held out stiffly in front of her, again guffaws.*)

MRS. MILLER (*turns on her with outraged indignation*). Norah! Bring that soup here this minute! (*She stalks with stiff dignity toward her place at the foot of the table, right.*)

NORAH (*guiltily*). Yes, Mum. (*She brings the soup around the head of the table, passing* MILLER.)

MILLER (*jovially*). Why, hello, Norah!

MRS. MILLER. Nat! (*She sits down stiffly at the foot of the table.*)

NORAH (*rebuking him familiarly*). Arrah now, don't be making me laugh and getting me into trouble!

MRS. MILLER. Norah!

NORAH (*a bit resentfully*). Yes, Mum. Here I am. (*She sets the soup tureen down with a thud in front of* MRS. MILLER *and passes around the other side, squeezing with difficulty between the china closet and the backs of chairs at the rear of the table.*)

MRS. MILLER. Tommy! Stop spinning your napkin ring! How often have I got to tell you? Mildred! Sit up straight in your chair! Do you want to grow up a humpback? Richard! Take your elbows off the table!

MILLER (*coming to his place at the head of the table, rubbing his hands together genially*). Well, well, well. Well, well, well. It's good to be home again.
(NORAH *exits into the pantry and lets the door slam with a bang behind her.*)

MRS. MILLER (*jumps*). Oh! (*Then exasperatedly*) Nat, I do wish you wouldn't encourage that stupid girl by talking to her, when I'm doing my best to train—

MILLER (*beamingly*). All right, Essie. Your word is law! (*Then laughingly*) We did have the darndest fun today! And Sid was the life of that picnic! You ought to have heard him! Honestly, he had that crowd just rolling on the ground and splitting their sides! He ought to be on the stage.

MRS. MILLER (*as* NORAH *comes back with a dish of saltines—begins ladling soup into the stack of plates before her*). He ought to be at this table eating something to sober him up, that's what he ought to be! (*She *calls*) Sid! You come right in here! (*Then to* NORAH, *handing her a soup plate*) Here, Norah. (NORAH *begins passing soup*) Sit down, Nat, for goodness sakes. Start eating, everybody. Don't wait for me. You know I've given up soup.

MILLER (*sits down but bends forward to call to his wife in a confidential tone*). Essie—Sid's sort of embarrassed about coming—I mean I'm afraid he's a little bit—not too much, you understand—but he met such a lot of friends and—well, you know, don't be hard on him. Fourth of July is like Christmas—comes but once a year. Don't pretend to notice, eh? And don't you kids, you hear! And don't you, Lily. He's scared of you.

LILY (*with stiff meekness*). Very well, Nat.

MILLER (*beaming again—calls*). All right, Sid. The coast's clear. (*He begins to absorb his soup ravenously*) Good soup, Essie! Good soup!

(*A moment later* SID *makes his entrance from the back parlor. He is in a condition that can best be described as blurry. His movements have a hazy uncertainty about them. His shiny fat face is one broad, blurred, Puckish, naughty-boy grin; his eyes have a blurred, wondering vagueness. As he enters he makes a solemnly intense effort to appear casual and dead, cold sober. He waves his hand aimlessly and speaks with a silly gravity.*)

SID. Good evening. (*They all answer "Good evening," their eyes on their plates. He makes his way vaguely toward his place, continuing his grave effort at conversation*) Beautiful evening. I never remember seeing—more beautiful sunset. (*He bumps vaguely into* LILY'*s chair as he attempts to pass behind her—immediately he is all grave politeness*) Sorry—sorry, Lily—deeply sorry.

LILY (*her eyes on her plate—stiffly*). It's all right.

SID (*manages to get into his chair at last—mutters to himself*). Wha' was I sayin'? Oh, sunsets. But why butt in? Hasn't sun—perfect right to set? Mind y'r own business. (*He pauses thoughtfully, considering this—then looks around from face to face, fixing each with a vague, blurred, wondering look, as if some deep puzzle were confronting him. Then suddenly he grins mistily and nods with satisfaction*) And there you are! Am I right?

MILLER (*humoring him*). Right.

SID. Right! (*He is silent, studying his soup plate, as if it were some strange enigma. Finally he looks up and regards his sister and asks with wondering amazement*) Soup?

MRS. MILLER. Of course, it's soup. What did you think it was? And you hurry up and eat it.

SID (*again regards his soup with astonishment*). Well! (*Then suddenly*) Well, all right then! Soup be it! (*He picks up his spoon and begins to eat, but after two tries in which he finds it difficult to locate his mouth, he addresses the spoon plaintively*) Spoon, is this any way to treat a pal? (*Then suddenly comically angry, putting the spoon down with a bang*) Down with spoons! (*He raises his soup plate and declaims*) "We'll drink to the dead already, and hurrah for the next who dies." (*Bowing solemnly to right and left*) Your good health, ladies and gents. (*He starts drinking the soup.* MILLER *guffaws and* MILDRED *and* TOMMY *giggle. Even* RICHARD *forgets his melancholy and snickers, and* MRS. MILLER *conceals a smile. Only* LILY *remains stiff and silent.*)

MRS. MILLER (*with forced severity*). Sid!

SID (*peers at her muzzily, lowering the soup plate a little from his lips*). Eh?

MRS. MILLER. Oh, nothing. Never mind.

SID (*solemnly offended*). Are you—publicly rebuking me before assembled—? Isn't soup liquid? Aren't liquids drunk? (*Then considering this to himself*) What if they are drunk? It's a good man's failing. (*He again peers mistily about at the company*) Am I right or wrong?

MRS. MILLER. Hurry up and finish your soup, and stop talking nonsense!

SID (*turning to her—again offendedly*). Oh, no, Essie, if I ever so far forget myself as to drink a leg of lamb, then you might have some—excuse for— Just think of waste effort eating soup with spoons—fifty gruelling lifts per plate—billions of soup-eaters on globe—why, it's simply staggering! (*Then darkly to himself*) No more spoons for me! If I want to develop my biceps, I'll buy Sandow Exerciser! (*He drinks the rest of his soup in a gulp and beams around at the company, suddenly all happiness again*) Am I right, folks?

MILLER (*who has been choking with laughter*). Haw, haw! You're right, Sid.

SID (*peers at him blurredly and shakes his head sadly*). Poor old Nat! Always wrong—but heart of gold, heart of purest gold. And drunk again, I regret to note. Sister, my heart bleeds for you and your poor fatherless chicks!

MRS. MILLER (*restraining a giggle—severely*). Sid! Do shut up for a minute! Pass me your soup plates, everybody. If we wait for that girl to take them, we'll be here all night. (*They all pass their plates, which* MRS. MILLER *stacks up and then puts on the sideboard. As she is doing this,* NORAH *appears from the pantry with a platter of broiled fish. She is just about to place these before* MILLER *when* SID *catches her eye mistily and rises to his feet, making her a deep, uncertain bow.*)

SID (*raptly*). Ah, Sight for Sore Eyes, my beautiful Macushla, my star-eyed Mavourneen—

MRS. MILLER. Sid!

NORAH (*immensely pleased—gives him an arch, flirtatious glance*). Ah sure, Mister Sid, it's you that have kissed the Blarney Stone, when you've a drop taken!

MRS. MILLER (*outraged*). Norah! Put down that fish!

NORAH (*flusteredly*). Yes, Mum. (*She attempts to put the fish down hastily before* MILLER, *but her eyes are fixed nervously on* MRS. MILLER *and she gives* MILLER *a nasty swipe on the side of the head with the edge of the dish.*)

MILLER. Ouch! (*The children, even* RICHARD, *explode into laughter.*)

NORAH (*almost lets the dish fall*). Oh, glory be to God! Is it hurted you are?

MILLER (*rubbing his head—good-naturedly*). No, no harm done. Only careful, Norah, careful.

NORAH (*gratefully*). Yes, sorr. (*She thumps down the dish in front of him with a sigh of relief.*)

SID (*who is still standing—with drunken gravity*). Careful, Mavourneen, careful! You might have hit him some place besides the head. Always aim at his head, remember—so as not to worry us.
(*Again the children explode. Also* NORAH. *Even* LILY *suddenly lets out an hysterical giggle and is furious with herself for doing so.*)

LILY. I'm so sorry, Nat. I didn't mean to laugh. (*Turning on* SID *furiously*) Will you please sit down and stop making a fool of yourself!
(SID *gives her a hurt, mournful look and then sinks meekly down on his chair.*)

NORAH (*grinning cheerfully, gives* LILY *a reassuring pat on the back*). Ah, Miss Lily, don't mind him. He's only under the influence. Sure, there's no harm in him at all.

MRS. MILLER. Norah!
(NORAH *exits hastily into the pantry, letting the door slam with a crash behind her. There is silence for a moment as* MILLER *serves the fish and it is passed around.* NORAH *comes back with the vegetables and disappears again, and these are dished out.*)

MILLER (*is about to take his first bite—stops suddenly and asks his wife*). This isn't, by any chance, bluefish, is it, my dear?

MRS. MILLER (*with a warning glance at* TOMMY). Of course not. You know we never have bluefish, on account of you.

MILLER (*addressing the table now with the gravity of a man confessing his strange peculiarities*). Yes, I regret to say, there's a certain peculiar oil in bluefish that invariably poisons me. (*At this,* TOMMY *cannot stand it any more but explodes into laughter.* MRS. MILLER, *after a helpless glance at him, follows suit; then* LILY *goes off into uncontrollable, hysterical laughter, and* RICHARD *and* MILDRED *are caught in the contagion.* MILLER *looks around at them with a weak smile, his dignity now ruffled a bit*) Well, I must say I don't see what's so darned funny about my being poisoned.

SID (*peers around him—then with drunken cunning*). Aha! Nat, I suspect—plot! This fish looks blue to me—very blue—in fact despondent, desperate, and— (*He points his fork dramatically at* MRS. MILLER) See how guilty she looks—a ver—veritable Lucretia Georgia! Can it be this woman has been slowly poisoning you all these years? And how well—you've stood it! What iron constitution! Even now, when you are invariably at death's door, I can't believe—
(*Everyone goes off into uncontrollable laughter.*)

MILLER (*grumpily*). Oh, give us a rest, you darned fool! A joke's a joke, but— (*He addresses his wife in a wounded tone*) Is this true, Essie?

MRS. MILLER (*wiping the tears from her eyes—defiantly*). Yes, it is true.

if you must know, and you'd never have suspected it, if it weren't for that darned Tommy, and Sid poking his nose in. You've eaten bluefish for years and thrived on it and it's all nonsense about that peculiar oil.

MILLER (*deeply offended*). Kindly allow me to know my own constitution! Now I think of it, I've felt upset afterwards every damned time we've had fish! (*He pushes his plate away from him with proud renunciation*) I can't eat this.

MRS. MILLER (*insultingly matter-of-fact*). Well, don't then. There's lots of lobster coming and you can fill up on that.

(RICHARD *suddenly bursts out laughing again.*)

MILLER (*turns to him caustically*). You seem in a merry mood, Richard. I thought you were the original of the Heart Bowed Down today.

SID (*with mock condolence*). Never mind, Dick. Let them—scoff! What can they understand about girls whose hair sizzchels, whose lips are fireworks, whose eyes are red-hot sparks—

MILDRED (*laughing*). Is that what he wrote to Muriel? (*Turning to her brother*) You silly goat, you!

RICHARD (*surlily*). Aw, shut up, Mid. What do I care about her? I'll show all of you how much I care!

MRS. MILLER. Pass your plates as soon as you're through, everybody. I've rung for the lobster. And that's all. You don't get any dessert or tea after lobster, you know.

(NORAH *appears bearing a platter of cold boiled lobsters which she sets before* MILLER, *and disappears.*)

TOMMY. Gee, I love lobster!

(MILLER *puts one on each plate, and they are passed around and everyone starts in pulling the cracked shells apart.*)

MILLER (*feeling more cheerful after a couple of mouthfuls—determining to give the conversation another turn, says to his daughter*). Have a good time at the beach, Mildred?

MILDRED. Oh, fine, Pa, thanks. The water was wonderful and warm.

MILLER. Swim far?

MILDRED. Yes, for me. But that isn't so awful far.

MILLER. Well, you ought to be a good swimmer, if you take after me. I used to be a regular water rat when I was a boy. I'll have to go down to the beach with you one of these days—though I'd be rusty, not having been in in all these years. (*The reminiscent look comes into his eyes of one about to embark on an oft-told tale of childhood adventure*) You know, speaking of swimming, I never go down to that beach but what it calls to mind the day I and Red Sisk went in swimming there and I saved his life.

(*By this time the family are beginning to exchange amused, guilty glances. They all know what is coming.*)

SID (*with a sly, blurry wink around*). Ha! Now we—have it again!

MILLER (*turning on him*). Have what?

SID. Nothing—go on with your swimming—don't mind me.

MILLER (*glares at him—but immediately is overcome by the reminiscent *mood again*). Red Sisk—his father kept a blacksmith shop where the Union Market is now—we kids called him Red because he had the darnedest reddest crop of hair—

SID (*as if he were talking to his plate*). Remarkable!—the curious imagination—of little children.

MRS. MILLER (*as she sees* MILLER *about to explode—interposes tactfully*). Sid! Eat your lobster and shut up! Go on, Nat.

MILLER (*gives* SID *a withering look —then is off again*). Well, as I was saying, Red and I went swimming that day. Must have been—let me see—Red was fourteen, bigger and older than me, I was only twelve—forty-five years ago—wasn't a single house down there then—but there was a stake out where the whistling buoy is now, about a mile out. (TOMMY, *who has been having difficulty restraining himself, lets out a stifled giggle.* MILLER *bends a frowning gaze on him*) One more sound out of you, young man, and you'll leave this table!

MRS. MILLER (*quickly interposing, trying to stave off the story*). Do eat your lobster, Nat. You didn't have any fish, you know.

MILLER (*not liking the reminder—pettishly*). Well, if I'm going to be interrupted every second anyway—(*He turns to his lobster and chews in silence for a moment.*)

MRS. MILLER (*trying to switch the subject*). How's Anne's mother's rheumatism, Mildred?

MILDRED. Oh, she's much better, Ma. She was in wading today. She says salt water's the only thing that really helps her bunion.

MRS. MILLER. Mildred! Where are your manners? At the table's no place to speak of—

MILLER (*fallen into the reminiscent obsession again*). Well, as I was saying, there was I and Red, and he dared me to race him out to the stake and back. Well, I didn't let anyone dare me in those days. I was a spunky kid. So I said all right and we started out. We swam and swam and were pretty evenly matched; though, as I've said, he was bigger and older than me, but finally I drew ahead. I was going along easy, with lots in reserve, not a bit tired, when suddenly I heard a sort of gasp from behind me—like this—"help." (*He imitates. Everyone's eyes are firmly fixed on their plates, except* SID's) And I turned and there was Red, his face all pinched and white, and he says weakly: "Help, Nat! I got a cramp in my leg!" Well, I don't mind telling you I got mighty scared. I didn't know what to do. Then suddenly I thought of the pile. If I could pull him to that, I could hang on to him till someone'd notice us. But the pile was still—well, I calculate it must have been two hundred feet away.

SID. Two hundred and fifty!

MILLER (*in confusion*). What's that?

SID. Two hundred *and* fifty! I've taken down the distance every time you've saved Red's life for thirty years and the mean average to that pile is two hundred and fifty feet! (*There is a burst of laughter from around the table.* SID *continues complainingly*) Why didn't you let that

Red drown, anyway, Nat? I never knew him but I know I'd never have liked him.

MILLER (*really hurt, forces a feeble smile to his lips and pretends to be a good sport about it*). Well, guess you're right, Sid. Guess I have told that one too many times and bored everyone. But it's a good true story for kids because it illustrates the danger of being foolhardy in the water—

MRS. MILLER (*sensing the hurt in his tone, comes to his rescue*). Of course it's a good story—and you tell it whenever you've a mind to. And you, Sid, if you were in any responsible state, I'd give you a good piece of my mind for teasing Nat like that.

MILLER (*with a sad, self-pitying smile at his wife*). Getting old, I guess, Mother—getting to repeat myself. Someone ought to stop me.

MRS. MILLER. No such thing! You're as young as you ever were. (*She turns on* SID *again angrily*) You eat your lobster and maybe it'll keep your mouth shut!

SID (*after a few chews—irrepressibly*). Lobster! Did you know, Tommy, your Uncle Sid is the man invented lobster? Fact! One day—when I was building the Pyramids—took a day off and just dashed off lobster. He was bigger'n' older than me and he had the darnedest reddest crop of hair but I dashed him off just the same; Am I right, Nat? (*Then suddenly in the tones of a sideshow barker*) Ladies *and* Gents—

MRS. MILLER. Mercy sakes! Can't you shut up?

SID. In this cage you see the lobster. You will not believe me, ladies *and* gents, but it's a fact that this interesting bivalve only makes love to his mate once in every thousand years—but, dearie me, how he does enjoy it!

(*The children roar.* LILY *and* MRS. MILLER *laugh in spite of themselves—then look embarrassed.* MILLER *guffaws—then suddenly grows shocked.*)

MILLER. Careful, Sid, careful. Remember you're at home.

TOMMY (*suddenly in a hoarse whisper to his mother, with an awed glance of admiration at his uncle*). Ma! Look at him! He's eating that claw, shells and all!

MRS. MILLER (*horrified*). Sid, do you want to kill yourself? Take it away from him, Lily!

SID (*with great dignity*). But I prefer the shells. All famous epicures prefer the shells—to the less delicate, coarser meat. It's the same with clams. Unless I eat the shells there is a certain, peculiar oil that invariably poisons— Am I right, Nat?

MILLER (*good-naturedly*). You seem to be getting a lot of fun kidding me. Go ahead, then. I don't mind.

MRS. MILLER. He better go right up to bed for a while, that's what he better do.

SID (*considering this owlishly*). Bed? Yes, maybe you're right. (*He gets to his feet*) I am not at all well—in very delicate condition—we are praying for a boy. Am I right, Nat? Nat, I kept telling you all day I was in delicate condition and yet you kept forcing demon chowder on me, although you knew full well—even if you were full—that there is a certain peculiar oil in chowder that invariably— (*They are again all laughing*—LILY, *hysterically*.)

MRS. MILLER. *Will* you get to bed, you idiot!

SID (*mutters graciously*). Immediately—if not sooner. (*He turns to pass behind* LILY, *then stops, staring down at her*) But wait. There is still a duty I must perform. No day is complete without it. Lily, answer once and for all, will you marry me?

LILY (*with an hysterical giggle*). No, I won't—never!

SID (*nodding his head*). Right! And perhaps it's all for the best. For how could I forget the pre—precepts taught me at mother's dying knee. "Sidney," she said, "never marry a woman who drinks! Lips that touch liquor shall never touch yours!" (*Gazing at her mournfully*) Too bad! So fine a woman once—and now such a slave to rum! (*Turning to* NAT) What can we do to save her, Nat? (*In a hoarse, confidential whisper*) Better put her in institution where she'll be removed from temptation! The mere smell of it seems to drive her frantic!

MRS. MILLER (*struggling with her laughter*). You leave Lily alone, and go to bed!

SID. *Right!* (*He comes around behind* LILY'S *chair and moves toward the entrance to the back parlor—then suddenly turns and says with a bow*) Good night, ladies—*and* gents. We will meet—bye and bye! (*He gives an imitation of a Salvation Army drum*) Boom! Boom! Boom! Come and be saved, Brothers! (*He starts to sing the old Army hymn*)

"In the sweet
 Bye and bye
 We will meet on that beautiful
  shore."

(*He turns and marches solemnly out through the back parlor, singing*)

"Work and pray
 While you may.
 We will meet in the sky bye and
  bye."

(MILLER *and his wife and the children are all roaring with laughter.* LILY *giggles hysterically.*)

MILLER (*subsiding at last*). Haw, haw. He's a case, if ever there was one! Darned if you can help laughing at him—even when he's poking fun at you!

MRS. MILLER. Goodness, but he's a caution! Oh, my sides ache, I declare! I was trying so hard not to—but you can't help it, he's so silly! But I suppose we really shouldn't. It only encourages him. But, my lands—!

LILY (*suddenly gets up from her chair and stands rigidly, her face working—jerkily*). That's just it—you shouldn't—even I laughed—it does encourage—that's been his downfall—everyone always laughing, everyone always saying what a card he is, what a case, what a caution, so funny—and he's gone on—and we're all responsible—making it easy for him—we're all to blame—and all we do is laugh!

MILLER (*worriedly*). Now, Lily, now, you mustn't take on so. It isn't as serious as all that.

LILY (*bitterly*). Maybe—it is—to me. Or was—once. (*Then contritely*) I'm sorry, Nat. I'm sorry, Essie. I didn't mean to—I'm not feeling myself tonight. If you'll excuse me, I'll go in the front parlor and lie down on the sofa awhile.

MRS. MILLER. Of course, Lily. You do whatever you've a mind to.
(LILY *goes out.*)

MILLER (*frowning—a little shamefaced*). Hmm. I suppose she's right. Never knew Lily to come out with things that way before. Anything special happened, Essie?

MRS. MILLER. Nothing I know—except he'd promised to take her to the fireworks.

MILLER. That's so. Well, supposing I take her. I don't want her to feel disappointed.

MRS. MILLER (*shaking her head*). Wild horses couldn't drag her there now.

MILLER. Hmm. I thought she'd got completely over her foolishness about him long ago.

MRS. MILLER. She never will.

MILLER. She'd better. He's got fired out of that Waterbury job—told me at the picnic after he'd got enough Dutch courage in him.

MRS. MILLER. Oh, dear! Isn't he the fool!

MILLER. I knew something was wrong when he came home. Well, I'll find a place for him on my paper again, of course. He always was the best news-getter this town ever had. But I'll tell him he's got to stop his damn nonsense.

MRS. MILLER (*doubtfully*). Yes.

MILLER. Well, no use sitting here mourning over spilt milk. (*He gets up, and* RICHARD, MILDRED, TOMMY *and* MRS. MILLER *follow his example, the children quiet and a bit awed*) You kids go out in the yard and try to keep quiet for a while, so's your Uncle Sid'll get to sleep and your Aunt Lily can rest.

TOMMY (*mournfully*). Ain't we going to set off the skyrockets and Roman candles, Pa?

MILLER. Later, Son, later. It isn't dark enough for them yet anyway.

MILDRED. Come on, Tommy. I'll see he keeps quiet, Pa.

MILLER. That's a good girl. (MILDRED *and* TOMMY *go out through the screen door.* RICHARD *remains standing, sunk in bitter, gloomy thoughts.* MILLER *glances at him—then irritably*) Well, Melancholy Dane, what are you doing?

RICHARD (*darkly*). I'm going out—for a while. (*Then suddenly*) Do you know what I think? It's Aunt Lily's fault, Uncle Sid's going to ruin. It's all because he loves her, and she keeps him dangling after her, and eggs him on and ruins his life—like all women love to ruin men's lives! I don't blame him for drinking himself to death! What does he care if he dies, after the way she's treated him! I'd do the same thing myself if I were in his boots!

MRS. MILLER (*indignantly*). Richard! You stop that talk!

RICHARD (*quotes bitterly*).

"Drink! for you know not whence
you come nor why.

Drink! for you know not why you
go nor where!"

MILLER (*losing his temper—harshly*). Listen here, young man! I've had about all I can stand of your nonsense for one day! You're growing a lot too big for your size, seems to me! You keep that damn fool talk to yourself, you hear me—or you're going to regret it! Mind now! (*He strides angrily away through the back parlor.*)

MRS. MILLER (*still indignant*). Richard, I'm ashamed of you, that's what I am. (*She follows her husband.* RICHARD *stands for a second, bitter, humiliated, wronged, even his father turned enemy, his face growing more and more rebellious. Then he forces a scornful smile to his lips.*)

RICHARD. Aw, what the hell do I care? I'll show them! (*He turns and goes out the screen door.*)

CURTAIN

ACT THREE

SCENE I

SCENE—*The back room of a bar in a small hotel—a small, dingy room, dimly lighted by two fly-specked globes in a fly-specked gilt chandelier suspended from the middle of the ceiling. At left, front, is the swinging door leading to the bar. At rear of door, against the wall, is a nickel-in-the-slot player-piano. In the rear wall, right, is a door leading to the "Family Entrance" and the stairway to the upstairs rooms. In the middle of the right wall is a window with closed shutters. Three tables with stained tops, four chairs around each table, are placed at center, front, at right, toward rear, and at rear, center. A brass cuspidor is on the floor by each table. The floor is unswept, littered with cigarette and cigar butts. The hideous saffron-colored wallpaper is blotched and spotted.*

It is about 10 o'clock the same night. RICHARD *and* BELLE *are discovered sitting at the table at center,* BELLE *at left of it,* RICHARD *in the next chair at the middle of table, rear, facing front.*

BELLE *is twenty, a rather pretty peroxide blonde, a typical college "tart" of the period, and of the cheaper variety, dressed with tawdry flashiness. But she is a fairly recent recruit to the ranks, and is still a bit remorseful behind her make-up and defiantly careless manner.*

BELLE *has an empty gin-rickey glass before her,* RICHARD *a half-empty glass of beer. He looks horribly timid, embarrassed and guilty, but at the same time thrilled and proud of at last mingling with the pace that kills.*

The player-piano is grinding out "Bedelia." The BARTENDER, *a stocky young Irishman with a foxily cunning, stupid face and a cynically wise grin, stands just inside the bar entrance, watching them over the swinging door.*

BELLE (*with an impatient glance at her escort—rattling the ice in her empty glass*). Drink up your beer, why don't you? It's getting flat.

RICHARD (*embarrassedly*). I let it get that way on purpose. I like it better when it's flat. (*But he hastily gulps down the rest of his glass, as if it were some nasty-tasting medicine. The* BARTENDER *chuckles audibly.* BELLE *glances at him.*)

BELLE (*nodding at the player-piano scornfully*). Say, George, is "Bedelia" the latest to hit this hick burg? Well, it's only a couple of years old! You'll catch up in time! Why don't you get a new roll for that old box?

BARTENDER (*with a grin*). Complain to the boss, not me. We're not used to having Candy Kiddoes like you around—or maybe we'd get up to date.

BELLE (*with a professionally arch grin at him*). Don't kid me, please. I can't bear it. (*Then she sings to the music from the piano, her eyes now on* RICHARD) "Bedelia, I'd like to feel yer." (*The* BARTENDER *laughs. She smirks at* RICHARD) Ever hear those words to it, Kid?

RICHARD (*who has heard them but is shocked at hearing a girl say them—putting on a blasé air*). Sure, lots of times. That's old.

BELLE (*edging her chair closer and putting a hand over one of his*). Then why don't you act as if you knew what they were all about?

RICHARD (*terribly flustered*). Sure, I've heard that old parody lots of times. What do you think I am?

BELLE. I don't know, Kid. Honest to God, you've got me guessing.

BARTENDER (*with a mocking chuckle*). He's a hot sport, can't you tell it? I never seen such a spender. My head's dizzy bringing you in drinks!

BELLE (*laughs irritably—to* RICHARD) Don't let him kid you. You show him. Loosen up and buy another drink, what say?

RICHARD (*humiliated—manfully*). Sure. Excuse me. I was thinking of something else. Have anything you like. (*He turns to the* BARTENDER *who has entered from the bar*). See what the lady will have—and have one on me yourself.

BARTENDER (*coming to the table—with a wink at* BELLE). That's talking! Didn't I say you were a sport? I'll take a cigar on you. (*To* BELLE) What's yours, Kiddo—the same?

BELLE. Yes. And forget the house rules this time and remember a rickey is supposed to have gin in it.

BARTENDER (*grinning*). I'll try to—seeing it's you. (*Then to* RICHARD) What's yours—another beer?

RICHARD (*shyly*). A small one, please. I'm not thirsty.

BELLE (*calculatedly taunting*). Say, honest, are things that slow up at Harvard? If they had you down at New Haven, they'd put you in a kindergarten! Don't be such a dead one! Filling up on beer will only make you sleepy. Have a man's drink!

RICHARD (*shamefacedly*). All right. I was going to. Bring me a sloe-gin fizz.

BELLE (*to* BARTENDER). And make it a real one.

BARTENDER (*with a wink*). I get you. Something that'll warm him up, eh? (*He goes into the bar, chuckling.*)

BELLE (*looks around the room—irritably*). Christ, what a dump! (RICHARD *is startled and shocked by this curse and looks down at the table*) If this isn't the deadest burg I ever struck! Bet they take the sidewalks in after nine o'clock! (*Then turning on him*) Say, honestly, Kid, does your mother know you're out?

RICHARD (*defensively*). Aw, cut it out, why don't you—trying to kid me!

BELLE (*glances at him—then resolves on a new tack—patting his hand*). All right. I didn't mean to, Dearie. Please don't get sore at me.

RICHARD. I'm not sore.

BELLE (*seductively*). You see, it's this way with me. I think you're one of the sweetest kids I've ever met—and I could like you such a lot if you'd give me half a chance—instead of acting so cold and indifferent.

RICHARD. I'm not cold and indifferent. (*Then solemnly tragic*) It's only that I've got—a weight on my mind.

BELLE (*impatiently*). Well, get it off your mind and give something else a chance to work. (*The* BARTENDER *comes in, bringing the drinks.*)

BARTENDER (*setting them down—with a wink at* BELLE). This'll warm him for you. Forty cents, that is—with the cigar.

RICHARD (*pulls out his roll and hands a dollar bill over—with exaggerated carelessness*). Keep the change. (BELLE *emits a gasp and seems about to protest, then thinks better of it. The* BARTENDER *cannot believe his luck for a moment—then pockets the bill hastily, as if afraid* RICHARD *will change his mind.*)

BARTENDER (*respect in his voice*). Thank you, sir.

RICHARD (*grandly*). Don't mention it.

BARTENDER. I hope you like the drink. I took special pains with it. (*The voice of the* SALESMAN, *who has just come in the bar, calls "Hey! Anybody here?" and a coin is rapped on the bar.*) I'm coming. (*The* BARTENDER *goes out.*)

BELLE (*remonstrating gently, a new appreciation for her escort's possibilities in her voice*). You shouldn't be so generous, Dearie. Gets him in bad habits. A dime would have been plenty.

RICHARD. Ah, that's all right. I'm no tightwad.

BELLE. That's the talk I like to hear. (*With a quick look toward the bar, she stealthily pulls up her dress—to* RICHARD'S *shocked fascination—and takes a package of cheap cigarettes from her stocking*) Keep an eye out for that bartender, Kid, and tell me if you see him coming. Girls are only allowed to smoke upstairs in the rooms, he said.

RICHARD (*embarrassedly*). All right. I'll watch.

BELLE (*having lighted her cigarette and inhaled deeply, holds the package out to him*). Have a Sweet? You smoke, don't you?

RICHARD (*taking one*). Sure! I've been smoking for the last two years —on the sly. But next year I'll be allowed—that is, pipes and cigars. (*He lights his cigarette with elaborate nonchalance, puffs, but does not inhale—then, watching her, with shocked concern*) Say, you oughtn't to inhale like that! Smoking's awful bad for girls, anyway, even if they don't—

BELLE (*cynically amused*). Afraid it will stunt my growth? Gee, Kid, you are a scream! You'll grow up to be a minister yet! (RICHARD *looks shamefaced. She scans him impatiently—then holds up her drink*) Well, here's how! Bottoms up, now! Show me you really know how to drink. It'll take that load off your mind. (RICHARD *follows her example and they both drink the whole contents of their glasses before setting them down*) There! That's something like! Feel better?

RICHARD (*proud of himself—with a shy smile*). You bet.

BELLE. Well, you'll feel still better in a minute—and then maybe you won't be so distant and unfriendly, eh?

RICHARD. I'm not.

BELLE. Yes, you are. I think you just don't like me.

RICHARD (*more manfully*). I do too like you.

BELLE. How much? A lot?

RICHARD. Yes, a lot.

BELLE. Show me how much! (*Then as he fidgets embarrassedly*) Want me to come sit on your lap?

RICHARD. Yes—I— (*She comes and sits on his lap. He looks desperately uncomfortable, but the gin is rising to his head and he feels proud of himself and devilish, too.*)

BELLE. Why don't you put your arm around me? (*He does so awkwardly*) No, not that dead way. Hold me tight. You needn't be afraid of hurting me. I like to be held tight, don't you?

RICHARD. Sure I do.

BELLE. 'Specially when it's by a nice handsome kid like you. (*Ruffling his hair*) Gee, you've got pretty hair, do you know it? Honest, I'm awfully strong for you! Why can't you be about me? I'm not so awfully ugly, am I?

RICHARD. No, you're—you're pretty.

BELLE. You don't say it as if you meant it.

RICHARD. I do mean it—honest.

BELLE. Then why don't you kiss me? (*She bends down her lips toward his. He hesitates, then kisses her and at once shrinks back*) Call that kissing? Here. (*She holds his head and fastens her lips on his and holds them there. He starts and struggles. She laughs*) What's the matter, Honey Boy? Haven't you ever kissed like that before?

RICHARD. Sure. Lots of times.

BELLE. Then why did you jump as if I'd bitten you? (*Squirming around on his lap*) Gee, I'm getting just crazy about you! What shall we do about it, eh? Tell me.

RICHARD. I—don't know. (*Then boldly*) I—I'm crazy about you, too.

BELLE (*kissing him again*). Just think of the wonderful time Edith and your friend, Wint, are having upstairs—while we sit down here like two dead ones. A room only costs two dollars. And, seeing I like you so much, I'd only take five dollars—from you. I'd do it for nothing—for you—only I've got to live and I owe my room rent in New Haven—and you know how it is. I get ten dollars from everyone else. Honest! (*She kisses him again, then gets up from his lap—briskly*) Come on. Go out and tell the bartender you want a room. And hurry. Honest, I'm so strong for you I can hardly wait to get you upstairs!

RICHARD (*starts automatically for the door to the bar—then hesitates, a great struggle going on in his mind—timidity, disgust at the money element, shocked modesty, and the guilty thought of* MURIEL, *fighting it out with the growing tipsiness that makes him want to be a hell of a fellow and go in for all forbidden fruit, and makes this tart a romantic, evil vampire in his eyes. Finally, he stops and mutters in confusion*). I can't.

BELLE. What, are you too bashful to ask for a room? Let me do it, then. (*She starts for the door.*)

RICHARD (*desperately*). No—I don't want you to—I don't want to.

BELLE (*surveying him, anger coming into her eyes*). Well, if you aren't the lousiest cheap skate!

RICHARD. I'm not a cheap skate!

BELLE. Keep me around here all night fooling with you when I might be out with some real live ones—if there is such a thing in this burg!—and now you quit on me! Don't be such a piker! You've got five dollars! I seen it when you paid for the drinks, so don't hand me any lies!

RICHARD. I— Who said I hadn't? And I'm not a piker. If you need the five dollars so bad—for your room rent—you can have it without—I mean, I'll be glad to give— (*He has been fumbling in his pocket and pulls out his nine-dollar roll and holds out the five to her.*)

BELLE (*hardly able to believe her eyes, almost snatches it from his hand—then laughs and immediately becomes sentimentally grateful*). Thanks, Kid. Gee—oh, thanks—Gee, forgive me for losing my temper and bawling you out, will you? Gee, you're a regular peach! You're the nicest kid I've ever met! (*She kisses him and he grins proudly, a hero to himself now on many counts*) Gee, you're a peach! Thanks, again!

RICHARD (*grandly—and quite tipsily*). It's—nothing—only too glad. (*Then boldly*) Here—give me another kiss, and that'll pay me back.

BELLE (*kissing him*). I'll give you a thousand, if you want 'em. Come on, let's sit down, and we'll have another drink—and this time I'll blow you just to show my appreciation. (*She calls*) Hey, George! Bring us another round—the same!

RICHARD (*a remnant of caution coming to him*). I don't know as I ought to—

BELLE. Oh, another won't hurt you. And I want to blow you, see. (*They sit down in their former places.*)

RICHARD (*boldly draws his chair closer and puts an arm around her—tipsily*). I like you a lot—now I'm getting to know you. You're a darned nice girl.

BELLE. Nice is good! Tell me another! Well, if I'm so nice, why didn't you want to take me upstairs? That's what I don't get.

RICHARD (*lying boldly*). I did want to—only I— (*Then he adds solemnly*) I've sworn off. (*The* BARTENDER *enters with the drinks.*)

BARTENDER (*setting them on the table*). Here's your pleasure. (*Then regarding* RICHARD'S *arm about her waist*) Ho-ho, we're coming on, I see. (RICHARD *grins at him muzzily.*)

BELLE (*digs into her stocking and gives him a dollar*). Here. This is mine. (*He gives her change and she tips him a dime, and he goes out. She puts the five* RICHARD *had given her in her stocking and picks up her glass*) Here's how—and thanks again. (*She sips.*)

RICHARD (*boisterously*). Bottoms up! Bottoms up! (*He drinks all of his down and sighs with exaggerated satisfaction*) Gee, that's good stuff, all right. (*Hugging her*) Give me another kiss, Belle.

BELLE (*kisses him*). What did you mean a minute ago when you said you'd sworn off?

RICHARD (*solemnly*). I took an oath I'd be faithful.

BELLE (*cynically*). Till death do us part, eh? Who's the girl?

RICHARD (*shortly*). Never mind.

BELLE (*bristling*). I'm not good enough to talk about her, I suppose?

RICHARD. I didn't—mean that. You're all right. (*Then with tipsy gravity*) Only you oughtn't to lead this kind of life. It isn't right—for a nice girl like you. Why don't you reform?

BELLE (*sharply*). Nix on that line of talk! Can it, you hear! You can do a lot with me for five dollars—but you can't reform me, see. Mind your own business, Kid, and don't butt in where you're not wanted!

RICHARD. I—I didn't mean to hurt your feelings.

BELLE. I know you didn't mean. You're only like a lot of people who mean well, to hear them tell it. (*Changing the subject*) So you're faithful to your one love, eh? (*With an ugly sneer*) And how about her? Bet you she's out with a guy under some bush this minute, giving him all he wants. Don't be a sucker, Kid! Even the little flies do it!

RICHARD (*starting up in his chair—angrily*). Don't you say that! Don't you dare!

BELLE (*unimpressed—with a cynical shrug of her shoulders*). All right. Have it your own way and be a sucker! It cuts no ice with me.

RICHARD. You don't know her or—

BELLE. And don't want to. Shut up about her, can't you? (*She *stares before her bitterly.* RICHARD *subsides into scowling gloom. He is becoming perceptibly more intoxicated with each moment now. The* BARTENDER *and the* SALESMAN *appear just inside the swinging door. The* BARTENDER *nods toward* BELLE, *giving the* SALESMAN *a wink. The* SALESMAN *grins and comes into the room, carrying his highball in his hand. He is a stout, jowly-faced man in the late thirties, dressed with cheap nattiness, with the professional breeziness and jocular, kid-'em-along manner of his kind.* BELLE *looks up as he enters and he and she exchange a glance of complete recognition. She knows his type by heart and he knows hers.*)

SALESMAN (*passes by her to the table at right—grinning genially*). Good evening.

BELLE. Good evening.

SALESMAN (*sitting down*). Hope I'm not butting in on your party—but my dogs were giving out standing at that bar.

BELLE. All right with me. (*Giving* RICHARD *a rather contemptuous look*) I've got no party on.

SALESMAN. That sounds hopeful.

RICHARD (*suddenly recites sentimentally*).

"But I wouldn't do such, 'cause
  I loved her too much,
But I learned about women
  from her."

(*Turns to scowl at the* SALESMAN—*then to* BELLE) Let's have 'nother drink!

BELLE. You've had enough.

(RICHARD *subsides, muttering to himself.*)

SALESMAN. What is it—a child poet or a child actor?

BELLE. Don't know. Got me guessing.

SALESMAN. Well, if you could shake the cradle-robbing act, maybe we could do a little business.

BELLE. That's easy. I just pull my freight. (*She shakes* RICHARD *by the arm*) Listen, Kid. Here's an old friend of mine, Mr. Smith of New Haven, just come in. I'm going over and sit at his table for a while, see. And you better go home.

RICHARD (*blinking at her and scowling*). I'm never going home! I'll show them!

BELLE. Have it your own way—only let me up. (*She takes his arm from around her and goes to sit by the* SALESMAN. RICHARD *stares after her offendedly.*)

RICHARD. Go on. What do I care what you do? (*He recites scornfully.*) "For a woman's only a woman, but a good cigar's a smoke."

SALESMAN (*as* BELLE *sits beside him*). Well, what kind of beer will you have, Sister?

BELLE. Mine's a gin rickey.

SALESMAN. You've got extravagant tastes, I'm sorry to see.

RICHARD (*begins to recite sepulchrally*).

"Yet each man kills the thing
he loves,
By each let this be heard."

SALESMAN (*grinning*). Say, this is rich! (*He calls encouragement*) That's swell dope, young feller. Give us some more.

RICHARD (*ignoring him—goes on more rhetorically*).

"Some do it with a bitter look,
Some with a flattering word,
The coward does it with a kiss,
The brave man with a sword!"

(*He stares at* BELLE *gloomily and mutters tragically*) I did it with a kiss! I'm a coward.

SALESMAN. That's the old stuff, Kid. You've got something on the ball, all right, all right! Give us another—right over the old pan, now!

BELLE (*with a laugh*). Get the hook!

RICHARD (*glowering at her—tragically*).

" 'Oho,' they cried, 'the world is
wide,
But fettered limbs go lame!
And once, or twice, to throw the
dice
Is a gentlemanly game,
But he does not win who plays
with Sin
In the secret House of Shame!' "

BELLE (*angrily*). Aw, can it! Give us a rest from that bunk!

SALESMAN (*mockingly*). This gal of yours don't appreciate poetry. She's a lowbrow. But I'm the kid that eats it up. My middle name is Kelly and Sheets! Give us some more of the same! Do you know "The Lobster and the Wise Guy"? (*Turns to* BELLE *seriously*) No kidding, that's a peacherino. I heard a guy recite it at Poli's. Maybe this nut knows it. Do you, Kid? (*But* RICHARD *only glowers at him gloomily without answering.*)

BELLE (*surveying* RICHARD *contemptuously*). He's copped a fine skinful—and gee, he's hardly had anything.

RICHARD (*suddenly—with a dire emphasis*). "And then—at ten o'clock—Eilert Lovborg will come—with vine leaves in his hair!"

BELLE. And bats in his belfry, if he's you!

RICHARD (*regards her bitterly—then starts to his feet bellicosely—to the* SALESMAN). I don't believe you ever knew her in New Haven at all! You just picked her up now! You leave her alone, you hear! You won't do anything to her—not while I'm here to protect her!

BELLE (*laughing*). Oh, my God! Listen to it!

SALESMAN. Ssshh! This is a scream! Wait! (*He addresses* RICHARD *in tones of exaggerated melodrama*) Curse you, Jack Dalton, if I won't unhand her, what then?

RICHARD (*threateningly*). I'll give you a good punch in the snoot, that's what! (*He moves toward their table.*)

SALESMAN (*with mock terror—screams in falsetto*). Help! Help! (*The* BARTENDER *comes in irritably.*)

BARTENDER. Hey. Cut out the noise. What the hell's up with you?

RICHARD (*tipsily*). He's too—damn fresh!

SALESMAN (*with a wink*). He's going to murder me. (*Then gets a bright idea for eliminating* RICHARD *—seriously to the* BARTENDER) It's none of my business, Brother, but if I were in your boots I'd give this young souse the gate. He's under age; any fool can see that.

BARTENDER (*guiltily*). He told me he was over eighteen.

SALESMAN. Yes, and I tell you I'm the Pope—but you don't have to believe me. If you're not looking for trouble, I'd advise you to get him started for some other gin mill and let them do the lying, if anything comes up.

BARTENDER. Hmm. (*He turns to* RICHARD *angrily and gives him a push*) Come on, now. On your way! You'll start no trouble in here! Beat it now!

RICHARD. I will not beat it!

BARTENDER. Oho, won't you? (*He gives him another push that almost sends him sprawling.*)

BELLE (*callously*). Give him the bum's rush! I'm sick of his bull! (RICHARD *turns furiously and tries to punch the* BARTENDER.)

BARTENDER (*avoids the punch*). Oho, you would, would you? (*He grabs* RICHARD *by the back of the neck and the seat of the pants and marches him ignominiously toward the swinging door.*)

RICHARD. Leggo of me, you dirty coward!

BARTENDER. Quiet now—or I'll pin a Mary Ann on your jaw that'll quiet you! (*He rushes him through the screen door and a moment later the outer doors are heard swinging back and forth.*)

SALESMAN (*with a chuckle*). Hand it to me, Kid. How was that for a slick way of getting rid of him?

BELLE (*suddenly sentimental*). Poor kid. I hope he makes home all right. I liked him—before he got soused.

SALESMAN. Who is he?

BELLE. The boy who's upstairs with my friend told me, but I didn't pay much attention. Name's Miller. His old man runs a paper in this one-horse burg, I think he said.

SALESMAN (*with a whistle*). Phew! He must be Nat Miller's kid, then.

BARTENDER (*coming back from the bar*). Well, he's on his way—with a good boot in the tail to help him!

SALESMAN (*with a malicious chuckle*). Yes? well, maybe that boot will cost you a job, Brother. Know Nat Miller who runs the *Globe*? That's his kid.

BARTENDER (*his face falling*). The hell he is! Who said so?

SALESMAN. This baby doll. (*Getting up*) Say, I'll go keep cases on him—see he gets on the trolley all right, anyway. Nat Miller's a good scout. (*He hurries out.*)

BARTENDER (*viciously*). God damn the luck! If he ever finds out I served his kid, he'll run me out of town. (*He turns on* BELLE *furiously*) Why didn't you put me wise, you lousy tramp, you!

BELLE. Hey! I don't stand for that kind of talk—not from no hick beer-squirter like you, see!

BARTENDER (*furiously*). You don't, don't you! Who was it but you told me to hand him dynamite in that fizz? (*He gives her chair a push that almost throws her to the floor*) Beat it, you—and beat it quick—or I'll call Sullivan from the corner and have you run in for street-walking! (*He gives her a push that lands her against the family-entrance door*) Get the hell out of here—and no long waits!

BELLE (*opens the door and goes out—turns and calls back viciously*). I'll fix you for this, you thick Mick, if I have to go to jail for it. (*She goes out and slams the door.*)

BARTENDER (*looks after her worriedly for a second—then shrugs his shoulders*). That's only her bull. (*Then with a sigh as he returns to the bar*) Them lousy tramps is always getting this dump in Dutch!

CURTAIN

ACT THREE

SCENE II

SCENE—*Same as Act One—Sitting-room of the* MILLER *home—about* 11 *o'clock the same night.*

MILLER *is sitting in his favorite rocking-chair at left of table, front. He has discarded collar and tie, coat and shoes, and wears an old, worn, brown dressing-gown and disreputable-looking carpet slippers. He has his reading specs on and is running over items in a newspaper. But his mind is plainly preoccupied and worried, and he is not paying much attention to what he reads.*

MRS. MILLER *sits by the table at right, front. She also has on her specs. A sewing basket is on her lap and she is trying hard to keep her attention fixed on the doily she is doing. But, as in the case of her husband, but much more apparently, her mind is preoccupied, and she is obviously on tenterhooks of nervous uneasiness.*

LILY *is sitting in the armchair by the table at rear, facing right. She is pretending to read a novel, but her attention wanders, too, and her expression is sad, although now it has lost all its bitterness and become submissive and resigned again.*

MILDRED *sits at the desk at right, front, writing two words over and over again, stopping each time to survey the result critically, biting her tongue, intensely concentrated on her work.*

TOMMY *sits on the sofa at left, front. He has had a hard day and is ter ribly sleepy but will not acknowledge it. His eyes blink shut on him, his head begins to nod, but he isn't giving up, and every time he senses any of the family glancing in his direction, he goads himself into a bright-eyed wakefulness.*

MILDRED (*finally surveys the two words she has been writing and is satisfied with them*). There. (*She takes the paper over to her mother*) Look, Ma. I've been practising a new way of writing my name. Don't look at the others, only the last one. Don't you think it's the real goods?

MRS. MILLER (*pulled out of her preoccupation*). Don't talk that horrible slang. It's bad enough for boys, but for a young girl supposed to have manners—my goodness, when I was your age, if my mother'd ever heard me—

MILDRED. Well, don't you think it's nice, then?

MRS. MILLER (*sinks back into preoccupation—scanning the paper—vaguely*). Yes, very nice, Mildred—very nice, indeed. (*Hands the paper back mechanically.*)

MILDRED (*is a little piqued, but smiles*). Absent-minded! I don't believe you even saw it. (*She passes around the table to show her* AUNT LILY. MILLER *gives an uneasy glance at his wife and then, as if afraid of meeting her eye, looks quickly back at his paper again.*)

MRS. MILLER (*staring before her—sighs worriedly*). Oh, I do wish Richard would come home!

MILLER. There now, Essie. He'll be in any minute now. Don't you worry about him.

MRS. MILLER. But I do worry about him!

LILY (*surveying* MILDRED'S *handiwork—smiling*). This is fine, Mildred. Your penmanship is improving wonderfully. But don't you think that maybe you've got a little too many flourishes?

MILDRED (*disappointedly*). But, Aunt Lily, that's just what I was practising hardest on.

MRS. MILLER (*with another sigh*). What time is it now, Nat?

MILLER (*adopting a joking tone*). I'm going to buy a clock for in here. You have me reaching for my watch every couple of minutes. (*He has pulled his watch out of his vest pocket—with forced carelessness*) Only a little past ten.

MRS. MILLER. Why, you said it was that an hour ago! Nat Miller, you're telling me a fib, so's not to worry me. You let me see that watch!

MILLER (*guiltily*). Well, it's quarter to eleven—but that's not so late—when you remember it's Fourth of July.

MRS. MILLER. If you don't stop talking Fourth of July—! To hear you go on, you'd think that was an excuse for anything from murder to picking pockets!

MILDRED (*has brought her paper around to her father and now shoves it under his nose*). Look, Pa.

MILLER (*seizes on this interruption with relief*). Let's see. Hmm. Seems to me you've been inventing a new signature every week lately. What are you in training for—writing checks? You must be planning to catch a rich husband.

MILDRED (*with an arch toss of her head*). No wedding bells for me! But how do you like it, Pa?

MILLER. It's overpowering—no other word for it, overpowering! You could put it on the Declaratioin of Independence and not feel ashamed.

MRS. MILLER (*desolately, almost on the verge of tears*). It's all right for you to laugh and joke with Mildred! I'm the only one in this house seems to care— (*Her lips tremble.*)

MILDRED (*a bit disgustedly*). Ah, Ma, Dick only sneaked off to the fireworks at the beach, you wait and see.

MRS. MILLER. Those fireworks were over long ago. If he had, he'd be home.

LILY (*soothingly*). He probably couldn't get a seat, the trolleys are so jammed, and he had to walk home.

MILLER (*seizing on this with relief*). Yes, I never thought of that, but I'll bet that's it.

MILDRED. Ah, don't let him worry you, Ma. He just wants to show off he's heartbroken about that silly Muriel—and get everyone fussing over him and wondering if he hasn't drowned himself or something.

MRS. MILLER (*snappily*). You be quiet! The way you talk at times, I really believe you're that hard-hearted you haven't got a heart in you! (*With an accusing glance at her husband*) One thing I know, you don't get that from me! (*He meets her eye and avoids it guiltily. She sniffs and looks away from him around the room.* TOMMY, *who is nodding and blinking, is afraid her eye is on him. He straightens alertly and speaks in a voice that, in spite of his effort, is dripping with drowsiness.*)

TOMMY. Let me see what you wrote, Mid.

MILDRED (*cruelly mocking*). You? You're so sleepy you couldn't see it!

TOMMY (*valiantly*). I am not sleepy!

MRS. MILLER (*has fixed her eye on him*). My gracious, I was forgetting you were still up! You run up to bed this minute! It's hours past your bedtime!

TOMMY. But it's the Fourth of July. Ain't it, Pa?

MRS. MILLER (*gives her husband an accusing stare*). There! You see what you've done? You might know he'd copy your excuses! (*Then sharply to* TOMMY) You heard what I said, Young Man!

TOMMY. Aw, Ma, can't I stay up a *little* longer?

MRS. MILLER. I said, no! You obey me and no more arguing about it!

TOMMY (*drags himself to his feet*). Aw! I should think I could stay up till Dick—

MILLER (*kindly but firmly*). You heard your ma say no more arguing.

When she says git, you better git. (TOMMY *accepts his fate resignedly and starts around kissing them all good night.*)

TOMMY (*kissing her*). Good night, Aunt Lily.

LILY. Good night, dear. Sleep well.

TOMMY (*pecking at* MILDRED). Good night, you.

MILDRED. Good night, you.

TOMMY (*kissing him*). Good night, Pa.

MILLER. Good night, Son. Sleep tight.

TOMMY (*kissing her*). Good night, Ma.

MRS. MILLER. Good night. Here! You look feverish. Let me feel of your head. No, you're all right. Hurry up, now. And don't forget your prayers.
(TOMMY *goes slowly to the doorway —then turns suddenly, the discovery of another excuse lighting up his face.*)

TOMMY. Here's another thing, Ma. When I was up to the water closet last—

MRS. MILLER (*sharply*). When you were *where?*

TOMMY. The bathroom.

MRS. MILLER. That's better.

TOMMY. Uncle Sid was snoring like a fog horn—and he's right next to my room. How can I ever get to sleep while he's— (*He is overcome by a jaw-cracking yawn.*)

MRS. MILLER. I guess you'd get to sleep all right if you were inside a fog horn. You run along now. (TOMMY *gives up, grins sleepily, and moves off to bed. As soon as he is off her mind, all her former uneasiness comes back on* MRS. MILLER *tenfold. She sighs, moves restlessly, then finally asks*) What time is it now, Nat?

MILLER. Now, Essie, I just told you a minute ago.

MRS. MILLER (*resentfully*). I don't see how you can take it so calm! Here it's midnight, you might say, and our Richard still out, and we don't even know where he is.

MILDRED. I hear someone on the piazza. Bet that's him now, Ma.

MRS. MILLER (*her anxiety immediately turning to relieved anger*). You give him a good piece of your mind, Nat, you hear me? You're too easy with him, that's the whole trouble! The idea of him daring to stay out like this! (*The front door is heard being opened and shut, and someone whistling "Waltz Me Around Again, Willie."*)

MILDRED. No, that isn't Dick. It's Art.

MRS. MILLER (*her face falling*). Oh. (*A moment later* ARTHUR *enters through the front parlor, whistling softly, half under his breath, looking complacently pleased with himself.*)

MILLER (*surveys him over his glasses, not with enthusiasm—shortly*). So you're back, eh? We thought it was Richard.

ARTHUR. Is he still out? Where'd he go to?

MILLER. That's just what we'd like to know. You didn't run into him anywhere, did you?

ARTHUR. No. I've been at the Rands' ever since dinner. (*He sits down in the armchair at left of table, rear*) I suppose he sneaked off to the beach to watch the fireworks.

MILLER (*pretending an assurance he is far from feeling*). Of course. That's what we've been trying to tell your mother, but she insists on worrying her head off.

MRS. MILLER. But if he was going to the fireworks, why wouldn't he say so? He knew we'd let him.

ARTHUR (*with calm wisdom*). That's easy, Ma. (*He grins superiorly*). Didn't you hear him this morning showing off bawling out the Fourth like an anarchist? He wouldn't want to renege on that to you—but he'd want to see the old fireworks just the same. (*He adds complacently*) I know. He's at the foolish age.

MILLER (*stares at* ARTHUR *with ill-concealed astonishment, then grins*). Well, Arthur, by gosh, you make me feel as if I owed you an apology when you talk horse sense like that. (*He turns to his wife, greatly relieved*) Arthur's hit the nail right on the head, I think, Essie. That was what I couldn't figure out—why he—but now it's clear as day.

MRS. MILLER (*with a sigh*). Well, I hope you're right. But I wish he was home.

ARTHUR (*takes out his pipe and fills and lights it with solemn gravity*). He oughtn't to be allowed out this late at his age. I wasn't, Fourth or no Fourth—if I remember.

MILLER (*a twinkle in his eyes*). Don't tax your memory trying to recall those ancient days of your youth. (MILDRED *laughs and* ARTHUR *looks sheepish. But he soon regains his aplomb.*)

ARTHUR (*importantly*). We had a corking dinner at the Rands'. We had sweetbreads on toast.

MRS. MILLER (*arising momentarily from her depression*). Just like the Rands to put on airs before you! I never could see anything to sweetbreads. Always taste like soap to me. And no real nourishment to them. I wouldn't have the pesky things on my table!
(ARTHUR *again feels sat upon.*)

MILDRED (*teasingly*). Did you kiss Elsie good night?

ARTHUR. Stop trying to be so darn funny all the time! You give me a pain in the ear!

MILDRED. And that's where she gives me a pain, the stuck-up thing!—thinks she's the whole cheese!

MILLER (*irritably*). And it's where your everlasting wrangling gives me a pain, you two! Give us a rest! (*There is silence for a moment.*)

MRS. MILLER. (*sighs worriedly again*). I do wish that boy would get home!

MILLER (*glances at her uneasily, peeks surreptitiously at his watch—then has an inspiration and turns to* ARTHUR). Arthur, what's this I hear about your having such a good singing voice? Rand was telling me he liked nothing better than to hear you sing—said you did every night you were up there. Why don't you ever give us folks at home here a treat?

ARTHUR (*pleased, but still nursing wounded dignity*). I thought you'd only sit on me.

MRS. MILLER (*perking up—proudly*). Arthur has a real nice voice. He practises when you're not at home. I didn't know you cared for singing, Nat.

MILLER. Well, I do—nothing better—and when I was a boy I had a fine voice myself and folks used to say I'd ought— (*Then abruptly, mindful of his painful experience with reminiscence at dinner, looking about him guiltily*) Hmm. But don't hide your light under a bushel, Arthur. Why not give us a song or two now? You can play for him, can't you, Mildred?

MILDRED (*with a toss of her head*). I can play as well as Elsie Rand, at least!

ARTHUR (*ignoring her—clearing his throat importantly*). I've been singing a lot tonight. I don't know if my voice—

MILDRED (*forgetting her grudge, grabs her brother's hand and tugs at it*). Come on. Don't play modest. You know you're just dying to show off. (*This puts* ARTHUR *off it at once. He snatches his hand away from her angrily.*)

ARTHUR. Let go of me, you! (*Then with surly dignity*) I don't feel like singing tonight, Pa. I will some other time.

MILLER. You let him alone, Mildred! (*He winks at* ARTHUR, *indicating with his eyes and a nod of his head* MRS. MILLER, *who has again sunk into worried brooding. He makes it plain by this pantomime that he wants him to sing to distract his mother's mind.*)

ARTHUR (*puts aside his pipe and gets up promptly*). Oh—sure, I'll do the best I can. (*He follows* MILDRED *into the front parlor, where he switches on the lights.*)

MILLER (*to his wife*). It won't keep Tommy awake. Nothing could. And Sid, he'd sleep through an earthquake. (*Then suddenly, looking through the front parlor—grumpily*) Darn it, speak of the devil, here he comes. Well, he's had a good sleep and he'd ought to be sobered up. (LILY *gets up from her chair and looks around her huntedly, as if for a place to hide.* MILLER *says soothingly*) Lily, you just sit down and read your book and don't pay any attention to him. (*She sits down again and bends over her book tensely. From the front parlor comes the tinkling of a piano as* MILDRED *runs over the scales. In the midst of this,* SID *enters through the front parlor. All the effervescence of his jag has worn off and he is now suffering from a bad case of hangover—nervous, sick, a prey to gloomy remorse and bitter feelings of self-loathing and self-pity. His eyes are bloodshot and puffed, his face bloated, the fringe of hair around his baldness tousled and tufty. He sidles into the room guiltily, his eyes shifting about, avoiding looking at anyone.*)

SID (*forcing a sickly, twitching smile*). Hello.

MILLER (*considerately casual*). Hello, Sid. Had a good nap? (*Then, as* SID *swallows hard and is about to break into further speech,* MILDRED'S *voice comes from the front parlor, "I haven't played that in ever so long, but I'll try," and she starts an accompaniment.* MILLER *motions* SID *to be quiet*) Ssshh! Arthur's going to sing for us. (SID *flattens himself against the edge of the bookcase at center, rear, miserably self-conscious and ill-at-ease there but nervously afraid to move anywhere else.* ARTHUR *begins to sing. He has a fairly decent voice but his method is untrained sentimentality to a dripping degree. He sings that old sentimental favorite, "Then You'll Remember Me." The effect on his audience is instant.* MILLER *gazes before him with a ruminating melancholy, his face seeming to become gently sorrowful and old.* MRS. MILLER *stares before her, her expression becoming more and more doleful.* LILY *forgets to pretend to read her book but looks over it, her face growing tragically sad. As for* SID, *he is moved to his remorseful, guilt-stricken depths. His mouth pulls down at the corners and he seems about to cry. The song comes to an end.* MILLER *starts, then claps his hands enthusiastically and calls*). Well done, Arthur—well done! Why, you've got a splendid voice! Give us some more! You liked that, didn't you, Essie?

MRS. MILLER (*dolefully*). Yes—but it's sad—terrible sad.

SID (*after swallowing hard, suddenly blurts out*). Nat and Essie—and Lily —I—I want to apologize—for coming home—the way I did—there's no excuse—but I didn't mean—

MILLER (*sympathetically*). Of course, Sid. It's all forgotten.

MRS. MILLER (*rousing herself—affectionately pitying*). Don't be a goose, Sid. We know how it is with picnics. You forget it.

(*His face lights up a bit but his gaze shifts to* LILY *with a mute appeal, hoping for a word from her which is not forthcoming. Her eyes are fixed on her book, her body tense and rigid.*)

SID (*finally blurts out desperately*). Lily—I'm sorry—about the fireworks. Can you—forgive me? (*But* LILY *remains implacably silent. A stricken look comes over* SID'S *face. In the front parlor* MILDRED *is heard saying "But I only know the chorus"—and she starts another accompaniment.*)

MILLER (*comes to* SID'S *rescue*). Ssshh! we're going to have another song. Sit down, Sid. (SID, *hanging his head, flees to the farthest corner, left, front, and sits at the end of the sofa, facing front, hunched up, elbows on knees, face in hands, his round eyes childishly wounded and woebegone.* ARTHUR *sings the popular "Dearie," playing up its sentimental values for all he is worth. The effect on his audience is that of the previous song, intensified—especially upon* SID. *As he finishes,* MILLER *again starts and applauds*) Mighty fine, Arthur! You sang that darned well! Didn't he, Essie?

MRS. MILLER (*dolefully*). Yes—but I wish he wouldn't sing such sad songs. (*Then, her lips trembling*) Richard's always whistling that.

MILLER (*hastily—calls*). Give us something cheery, next one, Arthur. You know, just for variety's sake.

SID (*suddenly turns toward* LILY—*his voice choked with tears—in a pas-*

ion of self-denunciation). You're ight, Lily!—right not to forgive me! -I'm no good and never will be!— 'm a no-good drunken bum!—you houldn't even wipe your feet on me! -I'm a dirty, rotten drunk!—no good o myself or anybody else!—if I had ıny guts I'd kill myself, and good iddance!—but I haven't!—I'm yel-ow, too!—a yellow, drunken bum! *He hides his face in his hands and egins to sob like a sick little boy. This is too much for* LILY. *All her bit-ter hurt and steely resolve to ignore and punish him vanish in a flash, swamped by a pitying love for him. She runs and puts her arm around him—even kisses him tenderly and impulsively on his bald head, and soothes him as if he were a little boy.* MRS. MILLER, *almost equally moved, has half risen to go to her brother, too, but* MILLER *winks and shakes his head vigorously and motions her to sit down.*)

LILY. There! Don't cry, Sid! I can't bear it! Of course, I forgive you! Haven't I always forgiven you? I know you're not to blame— So don't, Sid!

SID (*lifts a tearful, humbly grateful, pathetic face to her—but a face that the dawn of a cleansed conscience is already beginning to restore to its natural Puckish expression*). Do you really forgive me— I know I don't deserve it—can you really—?

LILY (*gently*). I told you I did, Sid—and I do.

SID (*kisses her hand humbly, like a big puppy licking it*) Thanks, Lily. I can't tell you— (*In the front par-lor,* ARTHUR *begins to sing rollick-ingly "Waiting at the Church," and after the first line or two* MILDRED *joins in.* SID'S *face lights up with ap-preciation and, automatically, he be-gins to tap one foot in time, still holding fast to* LILY'S *hand. When they come to "sent around a note, this is what she wrote," he can no longer resist, but joins in a shaky bawl*) "Can't get away to marry you today, My wife won't let me!" (*As the song finishes, the two in the other room laugh.* MILLER *and* SID *laugh.* LILY *smiles at* SID'S *laughter. Only* MRS. MILLER *remains dolefully pre-occupied, as if she hadn't heard.*)

MILLER. That's fine, Arthur and Mil-dred. That's darned good.

SID (*turning to* LILY *enthusiastically*). You ought to hear Vesta Victoria sing that! Gosh, she's great! I heard her at Hammerstein's Victoria—you remember, that trip I made to New York.

LILY (*her face suddenly tired and sad again—for her memory of certain as-pects of that trip is the opposite from what he would like her to recall at this moment—gently disengaging her hand from his—with a hopeless sigh*). Yes, I remember, Sid. (*He is over-come momentarily by guilty confu-sion. She goes quietly and sits down in her chair again. In the front par-lor, from now on,* MILDRED *keeps starting to run over popular tunes but always gets stuck and turns to an-other.*)

MRS. MILLER (*suddenly*). What time is it now, Nat? (*Then without giving him a chance to answer*) Oh, I'm getting worried something dread-ful, Nat! You don't know what might have happened to Richard! You read in the papers every day about boys getting run over by automobiles.

LILY. Oh, don't say that, Essie!

MILLER (*sharply, to conceal his own reawakened apprehension*). Don't get to imagining things, now!

MRS. MILLER. Well, why couldn't it happen, with everyone that owns one out tonight, and lots of those driving, drunk? Or he might have gone down to the beach dock and fallen overboard! (*On the verge of hysteria*) Oh, I know something dreadful's happened! And you can sit there listening to songs and laughing as if— Why don't you do something? Why don't you go out and find him? (*She bursts into tears*).

LILY (*comes to her quickly and puts her arm around her*). Essie, you mustn't worry so! You'll make yourself sick! Richard's all right. I've got a feeling in my bones he's all right.

MILDRED (*comes hurrying in from the front parlor*). What's the trouble? (ARTHUR *appears in the doorway beside her. She goes to her mother and also puts an arm around her*) Ah, don't cry, Ma! Dick'll turn up in a minute or two, wait and see!

ARTHUR. Sure, he will!

MILLER (*has gotten to his feet, frowning—soberly*). I was going out to look—if he wasn't back by twelve sharp. That'd be the time it'd take him to walk from the beach if he left after the last car. But I'll go now, if it'll ease your mind. I'll take the auto and drive out the beach road—and likely pick him up on the way. (*He has taken his collar and tie from where they hang from one corner of the bookcase at rear, center, and is starting to put them on*) You better come with me, Arthur.

ARTHUR. Sure thing, Pa. (*Suddenly he listens and says*) Ssshh! There's someone on the piazza now—coming around to this door, too. That must be him. No one else would—

MRS. MILLER. Oh, thank God, thank God!

MILLER (*with a sheepish smile*). Darn him! I've a notion to give him hell for worrying us all like this. (*The screen door is pushed violently open and* RICHARD *lurches in and stands swaying a little, blinking his eyes in the light. His face is a pasty pallor, shining with perspiration, and his eyes are glassy. The knees of his trousers are dirty, one of them torn from the sprawl on the sidewalk he had taken, following the* BARTENDER'S *kick. They all gape at him, too paralyzed for a moment to say anything.*)

MRS. MILLER. Oh God, what's happened to him! He's gone crazy! Richard!

SID (*the first to regain presence of mind—with a grin*). Crazy, nothing. He's only soused!

ARTHUR. He's drunk, that's what! (*Then shocked and condemning*) You've got your nerve! You fresh kid! We'll take that out of you when we get you down to Yale!

RICHARD (*with a wild gesture of defiance—maudlinly dramatic*).

"Yesterday this Day's Madness did
prepare
Tomorrow's Silence, Triumph, or
Despair.
Drink! for—"

MILLER (*his face grown stern and angry, takes a threatening step toward him*). Richard! How dare—!

MRS. MILLER (*hysterically*). Don't you strike him, Nat! Don't you—!

SID (*grabbing his arm*). Steady, Nat! Keep your temper! No good bawling him out now! He don't know what he's doing!

MILLER (*controlling himself and looking a bit ashamed*). All right—you're right, Sid.

RICHARD (*drunkenly glorying in the sensation he is creating—recites with dramatic emphasis*). "And then—I will come—with vine leaves in my hair!" (*He laughs with a double-dyed sardonicism.*)

MRS. MILLER (*staring at him as if she couldn't believe her eyes*). Richard! You're intoxicated!—you bad, wicked boy, you!

RICHARD (*forces a wicked leer to his lips and quotes with ponderous mockery*). "Fancy that, Hedda!" (*Then suddenly his whole expression changes, his pallor takes on a greenish, seasick tinge, his eyes seem to be turned inward uneasily—and, all pose gone, he calls to his mother appealingly, like a sick little boy*) Ma! I feel—rotten! (MRS. MILLER *gives a cry and starts to go to him, but* SID *steps in her way.*)

SID. You let me take care of him, Essie. I know this game backwards.

MILLER (*putting his arm around his wife*). Yes, you leave him to Sid.

SID (*his arm around* RICHARD*—leading him off through the front parlor*). Come on, Old Sport! Upstairs we go! Your old Uncle Sid'll fix you up. He's the kid that wrote the book!

MRS. MILLER (*staring after them—still aghast*). Oh, it's too terrible! Imagine our Richard! And did you hear him talking about some Hedda? Oh, I know he's been with one of those bad women, I know he has—my Richard! (*She hides her face on* MILLER'S *shoulder and sobs heartbrokenly.*)

MILLER (*a tired, harassed, deeply worried look on his face—soothing her*). Now, now, you mustn't get to imagining such things! You mustn't, Essie! (LILY *and* MILDRED *and* ARTHUR *are standing about awkwardly with awed, shocked faces.*)

CURTAIN

ACT FOUR

SCENE I

SCENE—*The same—Sitting-room of the* MILLER *house—about 1 o'clock in the afternoon of the following day.*

As the curtain rises, the family, with the exception of RICHARD, *are discovered coming in through the back parlor from dinner in the dining-room.*

MILLER and his wife come first. His face is set in an expression of frowning severity. MRS. MILLER's face is drawn and worried. She has evidently had no rest yet from a sleepless, tearful night. SID is himself again, his expression as innocent as if nothing had occurred the previous day that remotely concerned him. And, outside of eyes that are bloodshot and nerves that are shaky, he shows no aftereffects except that he is terribly sleepy. LILY is gently sad and depressed. ARTHUR is self-consciously a virtuous young man against whom nothing can be said. MILDRED and TOMMY are subdued, covertly watching their father.

They file into the sitting-room in silence and then stand around uncertainly, as if each were afraid to be the first to sit down. The atmosphere is as stiltedly grave as if they were attending a funeral service. Their eyes keep fixed on the head of the house, who has gone to the window at right and is staring out frowningly, savagely chewing a toothpick.

MILLER (*finally—irritably*). Damn it, I'd ought to be back at the office putting in some good licks! I've a whole pile of things that have got to be done today!

MRS. MILLER (*accusingly*). You don't mean to tell me you're going back without seeing him? It's your duty—!

MILLER (*exasperatedly*). 'Course I'm not! I wish you'd stop jumping to conclusions! What else did I come home for, I'd like to know? Do I usually come way back here for dinner on a busy day? I was only wishing this hadn't come up—just at this particular time. (*He ends up very lamely and is irritably conscious of the fact.*)

TOMMY (*who has been fidgeting restlessly—unable to bear the suspense a moment longer*). What is it Dick's done? Why is everyone scared to tell me?

MILLER (*seizes this as an escape valve—turns and fixes his youngest son with a stern forbidding eye*). Young man, I've never spanked you yet, but that don't mean I never will! Seems to me that you've been just itching for it lately! You keep your mouth shut till you're spoken to—or I warn you something's going to happen!

MRS. MILLER. Yes, Tommy, you keep still and don't bother your pa. (*Then warningly to her husband*) Careful what you say, Nat. Little pitchers have big ears.

MILLER (*peremptorily*). You kids skedaddle—all of you. Why are you always hanging around the house? Go out and play in the yard, or take a walk, and get some fresh air. (*MILDRED takes TOMMY's hand and leads him out through the front parlor. ARTHUR hangs back, as if the designation "kids" couldn't possibly apply to him. His father notices this —impatiently*) You, too, Arthur. (*ARTHUR goes out with a stiff, wounded dignity.*)

LILY (*tactfully*). I think I'll go for a walk, too. (*She goes out through the front parlor. SID makes a movement as if to follow her.*)

MILLER. I'd like you to stay, Sid—for a while, anyway.

— Sure. (*He sits down in the rocking chair at right, rear, of table and immediately yawns*) Gosh, I'm dead. Don't know what's the matter with me today. Can't seem to keep awake.

MILLER (*with caustic sarcasm*). Maybe that demon chowder you drank at the picnic poisoned you! (SID *looks sheepish and forces a grin. Then* MILLER *turns to his wife with the air of one who determinedly faces the unpleasant*) Where is Richard?

MRS. MILLER (*flusteredly*). He's still in bed. I made him stay in bed to punish him—and I thought he ought to, anyway, after being so sick. But he says he feels all right.

SID (*with another yawn*). 'Course he does. When you're young you can stand anything without it feazing you. Why, I remember when I could come down on the morning after, fresh as a daisy, and eat a breakfast of pork chops and fried onions and—(*He stops guiltily.*)

MILLER (*bitingly*). I suppose that was before eating lobster shells had ruined your iron constitution!

MRS. MILLER (*regards her brother severely*). If I was in your shoes, I'd keep still! (*Then turning to her husband*) Richard must be feeling better. He ate all the dinner I sent up, Norah says.

MILLER. I thought you weren't going to give him any dinner—to punish him.

MRS. MILLER (*guiltily*). Well—in his weakened condition—I thought it best— (*Then defensively*) But you needn't think I haven't punished him. I've given him pieces of my mind he won't forget in a hurry. And I've kept reminding him his real punishment was still to come—that you were coming home to dinner on purpose—and then he'd learn that you could be terrible stern when he did such awful things.

MILLER (*stirs uncomfortably*). Hmm!

MRS. MILLER. And that's just what it's your duty to do—punish him good and hard! The idea of him daring—(*Then hastily*) But you be careful how you go about it, Nat. Remember he's like you inside—too sensitive for his own good. And he never would have done it, I know, if it hadn't been for that darned little dunce, Muriel, and her numbskull father—and then all of us teasing him and hurting his feelings all day—and then you lost your temper and were so sharp with him right after dinner before he went out.

MILLER (*resentfully*). I see this is going to work round to where it's all my fault!

MRS. MILLER. Now, I didn't say that, did I? Don't go losing your temper again. And here's another thing. You know as well as I, Richard would never have done such a thing alone. Why, he wouldn't know how! He must have been influenced and led by someone.

MILLER. Yes, I believe that. Did you worm out of him who it was? (*Then angrily*) By God, I'll make whoever it was regret it!

MRS. MILLER. No, he wouldn't admit there was anyone. (*Then triumphantly*) But there is one thing I did worm out of him—and I can tell you it relieved my mind more'n anything. You know, I was afraid he'd been with one of those bad women. Well, turns out there wasn't any Hedda. She was just out of those books he's been reading. He swears he's never known a Hedda in his life. And I believe him. Why, he seemed disgusted with me for having such a notion. (*Then lamely*) So somehow —I can't kind of feel it's all as bad as I thought it was. (*Then quickly and indignantly*) But it's bad enough, goodness knows—and you punish him good just the same. The idea of a boy of his age—! Shall I go up now and tell him to get dressed, you want to see him?

MILLER (*helplessly—and irritably*). Yes! I can't waste all day listening to you!

MRS. MILLER (*worriedly*). Now you keep your temper, Nat, remember! (*She goes out through the front parlor.*)

MILLER. Darn women, anyway! They always get you mixed up. Their minds simply don't know what logic is! (*Then he notices that* SID *is dozing—sharply*) Sid!

SID (*blinking—mechanically*). I'll take the same. (*Then hurriedly*) What'd you say, Nat?

MILLER (*caustically*). What I didn't say was what'll you have. (*Irritably*) Do you want to be of some help, or don't you? Then keep awake and try and use your brains! This is a damned sight more serious than Essie has any idea! She thinks there weren't any girls mixed up with Richard's spree last night—but I happen to know there were! (*He takes a letter from his pocket*) Here's a note a woman left with one of the boys downstairs at the office this morning —didn't ask to see me, just said give me this. He'd never seen her before —said she looked like a tart. (*He has opened the letter and reads*) "Your son got the booze he drank last night at the Pleasant Beach House. The bartender there knew he was under age but served him just the same. He thought it was a good joke to get him soused. If you have any guts you will run that bastard out of town." Well, what do you think of that? It's a woman's handwriting— not signed, of course.

SID. She's one of the babies, all righ —judging from her elegant language

MILLER. See if you recognize th handwriting.

SID (*with a reproachful look*). Nat I resent the implication that I correspond with all the tramps aroun this town. (*Looking at the letter* No, I don't know who this one coul be. (*Handing the letter back*) Bu I deduce that the lady had a run-i with the barkeep and wants revenge

MILLER (*grimly*). And I deduce tha before that she must have picked u Richard—or how would she kno who he was?—and took him to thi dive.

SID. Maybe. The Pleasant Beac House is nothing but a bed house- (*Quickly*) At least, so I've been told

MILLER. That's just the sort c damned fool thing he might do t spite Muriel, in the state of min he was in—pick up some tart. An she'd try to get him drunk so—

SID. Yes, it might have happened lik that—and it might not. How're w ever going to prove it? Everyone at the Pleasant Beach will lie their heads off.

MILLER (*simply and proudly*). Richard won't lie.

SID. Well, don't blame him if he don't remember everything that happened last night. (*Then sincerely concerned*) I hope you're wrong, Nat. That kind of baby is dangerous for a kid like Dick—in more ways than one. You know what I mean.

MILLER (*frowningly*). Yep—and that's just what's got me worried. Damn it, I've got to have a straight talk with him—about women and all those things. I ought to have long ago.

SID. Yes. You ought.

MILLER. I've tried to a couple of times. I did it all right with Wilbur and Lawrence and Arthur, when it came time—but, hell, with Richard I always get sort of ashamed of myself and can't get started right. You feel, in spite of all his bold talk out of books, that he's so darned innocent inside.

SID. I know. I wouldn't like the job. (*Then after a pause—curiously*) How were you figuring to punish him for his sins?

MILLER (*frowning*). To be honest with you, Sid, I'm damned if I know. All depends on what I feel about what he feels when I first size him up—and then it'll be like shooting in the dark.

SID. If I didn't know you so well, I'd say don't be too hard on him. (*He smiles a little bitterly*) If you remember, I was always getting punished—and see what a lot of good it did me!

MILLER (*kindly*). Oh, there's lots worse than you around, so don't take to boasting. (*Then, at a sound from the front parlor—with a sigh*) Well, here comes the Bad Man, I guess.

SID (*getting up*). I'll beat it. (*But it is* MRS. MILLER *who appears in the doorway, looking guilty and defensive.* SID *sits down again.*)

MRS. MILLER. I'm sorry, Nat—but he was sound asleep and I didn't have the heart to wake him. I waited for him to wake up but he didn't.

MILLER (*concealing a relief of which he is ashamed—exasperatedly*). Well, I'll be double damned! If you're not the—

MRS. MILLER (*defensively aggressive*). Now don't lose your temper at me, Nat Miller! You know as well as I do he needs all the sleep he can get today—after last night's ructions! Do you want him to be taken down sick? And what difference does it make to you, anyway? You can see him when you come home for supper, can't you? My goodness, I never saw you so savage-tempered! You'd think you couldn't bear waiting to punish him!

MILLER (*outraged*). Well, I'll be eternally— (*Then suddenly he laughs*) No use talking, you certainly take the cake! But you know darned well I told you I'm not coming home to supper tonight. I've got a date with Jack Lawson that may mean a lot of new advertising and it's important.

MRS. MILLER. Then you can see him when you do come home.

MILLER (*covering his evident relief at this respite with a fuming manner*). All right! All right! I give up! I'm going back to the office. (*He starts for the front parlor*) Bring a man all the way back here on a busy day and then you— No consideration— (*He disappears, and a moment later the front door is heard shutting behind him.*)

MRS. MILLER. Well! I never saw Nat so bad-tempered.

SID (*with a chuckle*). Bad temper, nothing. He's so tickled to get out of it for a while he can't see straight!

MRS. MILLER (*with a sniff*). I hope I know him better than you. (*Then fussing about the room, setting this and that in place, while* SID *yawns drowsily and blinks his eyes*) Sleeping like a baby—so innocent-looking. You'd think butter wouldn't melt in his mouth. It all goes to show you never can tell by appearances—not even when it's your own child. The idea!

SID (*drowsily*). Oh, Dick's all right, Essie. Stop worrying.

MRS. MILLER (*with a sniff*). Of course, you'd say that. I suppose you'll have him out with you painting the town red the next thing! (*As she is talking,* RICHARD *appears in the doorway from the sitting-room. He shows no ill effects from his experience the night before. In fact, he looks surprisingly healthy. He is dressed in old clothes that look as if they had been hurriedly flung on. His expression is one of hang-dog guilt mingled with a defensive defiance.*)

RICHARD (*with self-conscious unconcern, ignoring his mother*). Hello, Sid.

MRS. MILLER (*whirls on him*). What are you doing here, Young Man? I thought you were asleep! Seems to me you woke up pretty quick—just after your pa left the house!

RICHARD (*sulkily*). I wasn't asleep. I heard you in the room.

MRS. MILLER (*outraged*). Do you mean to say you were deliberately deceiving—

RICHARD. I wasn't deceiving. You didn't ask if I was asleep.

MRS. MILLER. It amounts to the same thing and you know it! It isn't enough your wickedness last night, but now you have to take to lying!

RICHARD. I wasn't lying, Ma. If you'd asked if I was asleep I'd have said no.

MRS. MILLER. I've a good mind to send you straight back to bed and make you stay there!

RICHARD. Ah, what for, Ma? It was only giving me a headache, lying there.

MRS. MILLER. If you've got a headache, I guess you know it doesn't come from that! And imagine me standing there, and feeling sorry for you, like a fool—even having a run-in with your pa because— But you wait till he comes back tonight! If you don't catch it!

RICHARD (*sulkily*). I don't care.

MRS. MILLER. You don't care? You talk as if you weren't sorry for what you did last night!

RICHARD (*defiantly*). I'm not sorry.

MRS. MILLER. Richard! You ought to be ashamed! I'm beginning to think you're hardened in wickedness, that's what!

RICHARD (*with bitter despondency*). I'm not sorry because I don't care a darn what I did, or what's done to me, or anything about anything! I won't do it again—

MRS. MILLER (*seizing on this to relent a bit*). Well, I'm glad to hear you say that, anyway!

RICHARD. But that's not because I think it was wicked or any such old-fogy moral notion, but because it wasn't any fun. It didn't make me happy and funny like it does Uncle Sid—

SID (*drowsily*). What's that? Who's funny?

RICHARD (*ignoring him*). It only made me sadder—and sick—so I don't see any sense in it.

MRS. MILLER. Now you're talking sense! That's a good boy.

RICHARD. But I'm not sorry I tried it once—curing the soul by means of the senses, as Oscar Wilde says. (*Then with despairing pessimism*) But what does it matter what I do or don't do? Life is all a stupid farce! I'm through with it! (*With a sinister smile*) It's lucky there aren't any of General Gabler's pistols around—or you'd see if I'd stand it much longer!

MRS. MILLER (*worriedly impressed by this threat—but pretending scorn*). I don't know anything about General Gabler—I suppose that's more of those darned books—but you're a silly gabbler yourself when you talk that way!

RICHARD (*darkly*). That's how little you know about me.

MRS. MILLER (*giving in to her worry*). I wish you wouldn't say those terrible things—about life and pistols! You don't want to worry me to death, do you?

RICHARD (*reassuringly stoical now*). You needn't worry, Ma. It was only my despair talking. But I'm not a coward. I'll face—my fate.

MRS. MILLER (*stands looking at him puzzledly—then gives it up with a sigh*). Well, all I can say is you're the queerest boy I ever did hear of! (*Then solicitously, putting her hand on his forehead*) How's your headache? Do you want me to get you some Bromo Seltzer?

RICHARD (*taken down—disgustedly*). No, I don't! Aw, Ma, you don't understand anything!

MRS. MILLER. Well, I understand this much: It's your liver, that's what! You'll take a good dose of salts tomorrow morning, and no nonsense about it! (*Then suddenly*) My goodness, I wonder what time it's getting to be. I've got to go upstreet. (*She goes to the front-parlor doorway—then turns*) You stay here, Richard, you hear? Remember you're not allowed out today—for a punishment. (*She hurries away.* RICHARD *sits in tragic gloom.* SID, *without opening his eyes, speaks to him drowsily.*)

SID. Well, how's my fellow Rum Pot, as good old Dowie calls us? Got a head?

RICHARD (*startled—sheepishly*). Aw, don't go dragging that up, Uncle

Sid. I'm never going to be such a fool again, I tell you.

SID (*with drowsy cynicism—not unmixed with bitterness at the end*). Seems to me I've heard someone say that before. Who could it have been, I wonder? Why, if it wasn't Sid Davis! Yes, sir, I've heard him say that very thing a thousand times, must be. But then he's always fooling; you can't take a word he says seriously; he's a card, that Sid is!

RICHARD (*darkly*). I was desperate, Uncle—even if she wasn't worth it. I was wounded to the heart.

SID. I like to the quick better myself—more stylish. (*Then sadly*) But you're right. Love is hell on a poor sucker. Don't I know it? (*RICHARD is disgusted and disdains to reply. SID's chin sinks on his chest and he begins to breathe noisily, fast asleep. RICHARD glances at him with aversion. There is a sound of someone on the porch and the screen door is opened and MILDRED enters. She smiles on seeing her uncle, then gives a start on seeing RICHARD.*)

MILDRED. Hello! Are you allowed up?

RICHARD. Of course, I'm allowed up.

MILDRED (*comes and sits in her father's chair at right, front, of table*). How did Pa punish you?

RICHARD. He didn't. He went back to the office without seeing me.

MILDRED. Well, you'll catch it later. (*Then rebukingly*) And you ought to. If you'd ever seen how awful you looked last night!

RICHARD. Ah, forget it, can't you?

MILDRED. Well, are you ever going to do it again, that's what I want to know.

RICHARD. What's that to you?

MILDRED (*with suppressed excitement*). Well, if you don't solemnly swear you won't—then I won't give you something I've got for you.

RICHARD. Don't try to kid me. You haven't got anything.

MILDRED. I have, too.

RICHARD. What?

MILDRED. Wouldn't you like to know! I'll give you three guesses.

RICHARD (*with disdainful dignity*). Don't bother me. I'm in no mood to play riddles with kids!

MILDRED. Oh, well, if you're going to get snippy! Anyway, you haven't promised yet.

RICHARD (*a prey to keen curiosity now*). I promise. What is it?

MILDRED. What would you like best in the world?

RICHARD. I don't know. What?

MILDRED. And you pretend to be in love! If I told Muriel that!

RICHARD (*breathlessly*). Is it—from her?

MILDRED (*laughing*). Well, I guess it's a shame to keep you guessing. Yes. It is from her. I was walking past her place just now when I saw her waving from their parlor window, and I went up and she said give this to Dick, and she didn't have a chance to say anything else because her mother called her and said she wasn't allowed to have company. So I took it—and here it is. (*She gives him a letter folded many times into a tiny square.* RICHARD *opens it with a trembling eagerness and reads.* MILDRED *watches him curiously—then sighs affectedly*) Gee, it must be nice to be in love like you are—all with one person.

RICHARD (*his eyes shining*). Gee, Mid, do you know what she says—that she didn't mean a word in that other letter. Her old man made her write it. And she loves me and only me and always will, no matter how they punish her!

MILDRED. My! I'd never think she had that much spunk.

RICHARD. Huh! You don't know her! Think I could fall in love with a girl that was afraid to say her soul's her own? I should say not! (*Then more gleefully still*) And she's going to try and sneak out and meet me tonight. She says she thinks she can do it. (*Then suddenly feeling this enthusiasm before* MILDRED *is entirely the wrong note for a cynical pessimist—with an affected bitter laugh*) Ha! I knew darned well she couldn't hold out—that she'd ask to see me again. (*He misquotes cynically*) "Women never know when the curtain has fallen. They always want another act."

MILDRED. Is that so, Smarty?

RICHARD (*as if he were weighing the matter*). I don't know whether I'll consent to keep this date or not.

MILDRED. Well, I know! You're not allowed out, you silly! So you can't!

RICHARD (*dropping all pretense—defiantly*). Can't I, though! You wait and see if I can't! I'll see her tonight if it's the last thing I ever do! I don't care how I'm punished after!

MILDRED (*admiringly*). Goodness! I never thought you had such nerve!

RICHARD. You promise to keep your face shut, Mid—until after I've left—then you can tell Pa and Ma where I've gone—I mean, if they're worrying I'm off like last night.

MILDRED. All right. Only you've got to do something for me when I ask.

RICHARD. 'Course I will. (*Then excitedly*) And say, Mid! Right now's the best chance for me to get away—while everyone's out! Ma'll be coming back soon and she'll keep watching me like a cat— (*He starts for the back parlor*) I'm going. I'll sneak out the back.

MILDRED (*excitedly*). But what'll you do till nighttime? It's ages to wait.

RICHARD. What do I care how long I wait! (*Intensely sincere now*) I'll think of her—and dream! I'd wait a million years and never mind it—for her! (*He gives his sister a superior scornful glance*) The trouble with you is, you don't understand what love means! (*He disappears through the back parlor.* MILDRED *looks after him admiringly.* SID *puffs and begins to snore peacefully.*)

CURTAIN

ACT FOUR

SCENE II

SCENE—*A strip of beach along the harbor. At left, a bank of dark earth, running half-diagonally back along the beach, marking the line where the sand of the beach ends and fertile land begins. The top of the bank is grassy and the trailing boughs of willow trees extend out over it and over a part of the beach. At left, front, is a path leading up the bank, between the willows. On the beach, at center, front, a white, flat-bottomed rowboat is drawn up, its bow about touching the bank, the painter trailing up the bank, evidently made fast to the trunk of a willow. Halfway down the sky, at rear, left, the crescent of the new moon casts a soft, mysterious, caressing light over everything. The sand of the beach shimmers palely. The forward half (left of center) of the rowboat is in the deep shadow cast by the willow, the stern section is in moonlight. In the distance, the orchestra of a summer hotel can be heard very faintly at intervals.*

RICHARD *is discovered sitting sideways on the gunwale of the rowboat near the stern. He is facing left, watching the path. He is in a great state of anxious expectancy, squirming about uncomfortably on the narrow gunwale, kicking at the sand restlessly, twirling his straw hat, with a bright-colored band in stripes, around on his finger.*

RICHARD (*thinking aloud*). Must be nearly nine. . . . I can hear the Town Hall clock strike, it's so still tonight . . . Gee, I'll bet Ma had a fit when she found out I'd sneaked out . . . I'll catch hell when I get back, but it'll be worth it . . . if only Muriel turns up . . . she didn't say for certain she could . . . gosh, I wish she'd come! . . . am I sure she wrote nine? . . . (*He puts the straw hat on the seat amidships and pulls the folded letter out of his pocket and peers at it in the moonlight*) Yes, it's nine, all right. (*He starts to put the note back in his pocket, then stops and kisses it —then shoves it away hastily, sheepish, looking around him shamefacedly, as if afraid he were being observed*) Aw, that's silly . . . no, it isn't either . . . not when you're really in love. . . . (*He jumps to his feet restlessly*) Darn it, I wish she'd show up! . . . think of something else . . . that'll make the time pass quicker . . . where was I this time last night? . . . waiting outside the Pleasant Beach House . . . Belle . . . ah, forget her! . . . now, when Muriel's coming . . . that's a fine time to think of—! . . . but you hugged and kissed her . . . not until I was drunk, I didn't . . . and then it was all showing off . . . darned fool! . . . and *I* didn't go upstairs with her . . . even if she was pretty . . . aw, she wasn't pretty . . . she was all painted up . . . she was just a whore . . . she was everything dirty . . . Muriel's a million times prettier anyway . . . Muriel and I will go upstairs . . . when we're married . . . but that will be beautiful . . . but I oughtn't even to think of that yet . . . it's not right . . . I'd never—now . . . and she'd never . . . she's a decent girl . . . I couldn't love her if she wasn't . . . but after we're married. . . . (*He gives a little shiver of passionate longing—then resolutely turns his mind away from these improper, almost desecrating thoughts*) That damned barkeep kicking me . . . I'll bet you if I hadn't been drunk I'd have given him one good punch in the nose, even if he could have licked me after! . . . (*Then with a shiver of shamefaced revulsion and self-disgust*) Aw, you deserved a kick in the pants . . . making such a darned slob of yourself . . . reciting the Ballad of Reading Gaol to those lowbrows! . . . you must have been a fine sight when you got home! . . . having to be put to bed and getting sick! . . . Phaw! . . . (*He squirms disgustedly*) Think of something else, can't you? . . . recite something . . . see if you remember . . .

"Nay, let us walk from fire unto fire
From passionate pain to deadlier delight—
I am too young to live without desire,
Too young art thou to waste this summernight—"

. . . gee, that's a peach! . . . I'll have to memorize the rest and recite it to Muriel the next time. . . . I wish I could write poetry . . . about her and me. . . . (*He sighs and stares around him at the night*) Gee, it's beautiful tonight . . . as if it was a special night . . . for me and Muriel. . . . Gee, I love tonight. . . . I love the sand, and the trees, and the grass, and the water and the sky, and the moon . . . it's all in me and I'm in it . . . God, it's so beautiful! (*He stands staring at the moon with a rapt face. From the distance the Town Hall clock begins to strike. This brings him back to earth with a start*) There's nine now. . . . (*He peers at the path apprehensively*) I don't see her . . . she must have got caught. . . . (*Almost tearfully*) Gee, I hate to go home and catch hell . . . without having seen her! . . . (*Then calling a manly cynicism to his aid*) Aw, who ever heard of a woman ever being on time. . . . I ought to know enough about life by this time not to expect . . . (*Then with sudden excitement*) There she comes now. . . . Gosh! (*He heaves a huge sigh of relief—then recites dramatically to himself, his eyes on the approaching figure*)

"And lo my love, mine own soul's heart, more dear
Than mine own soul, more beautiful than God,
Who hath my being between the hands of her—"

(*Then hastily*) Mustn't let her know I'm so tickled. . . . I ought to be mad about that first letter, anyway . . . if women are too sure of you, they treat you like slaves . . . let her suffer, for a change. . . . (*He starts to stroll around with exaggerated carelessness, turning his back on the path, hands in pockets, whistling with insouciance "Waiting at the Church."* MURIEL MC COMBER *enters from down the path, left front. She is fifteen, going on sixteen. She is a pretty girl with a plump, graceful little figure, fluffy, light-brown hair, big naïve wondering dark eyes, a round, dimpled face, a melting drawly voice. Just now she is in a great thrilled state of timid adventurousness. She hesitates in the shadow at the foot of the path, waiting for* RICHARD *to see her; but he resolutely goes on whistling with back turned, and she has to call him.)*

MURIEL. Oh, Dick.

RICHARD (*turns around with an elaborate simulation of being disturbed in the midst of profound meditation*). Oh, hello. Is it nine already? Gosh, time passes—when you're thinking.

MURIEL (*coming toward him as far as the edge of the shadow—disappointedly*). I thought you'd be waiting right here at the end of the path. I'll bet you'd forgotten I was even coming.

RICHARD (*strolling a little toward her but not too far—carelessly*). No, I hadn't forgotten, honest. But I got to thinking about life.

MURIEL. You might think of me for a change, after all the risk I've run to see you! (*Hesitating timidly on the edge of the shadow*) Dick! You come here to me. I'm afraid to go out in that bright moonlight where anyone might see me.

RICHARD (*coming toward her—scornfully*). Aw, there you go again—always scared of life!

MURIEL (*indignantly*). Dick Miller, I do think you've got an awful nerve to say that after all the risks I've run making this date and then sneaking out! You didn't take the trouble to sneak any letter to me, I notice!

RICHARD. No, because after your first letter, I thought everything was dead and past between us.

MURIEL. And I'll bet you didn't care one little bit! (*On the verge of humiliated tears*) Oh, I was a fool ever to come here! I've got a good notion to go right home and never speak to you again! (*She half turns back toward the path.*)

RICHARD (*frightened—immediately becomes terribly sincere—grabbing her hand*). Aw, don't go, Muriel! Please! I didn't mean anything like that, honest I didn't! Gee, if you knew how broken-hearted I was by that first letter, and how darned happy your second letter made me—!

MURIEL (*happily relieved—but appreciates she has the upper hand now and doesn't relent at once*). I don't believe you.

RICHARD. You ask Mid how happy I was. She can prove it.

MURIEL. She'd say anything you told her to. I don't care anything about what she'd say. It's you. You've got to swear to me—

RICHARD. I swear!

MURIEL (*demurely*). Well then, all right, I'll believe you.

RICHARD (*his eyes on her face lovingly—genuine adoration in his voice*). Gosh, you're pretty tonight, Muriel! It seems ages since we've been together! If you knew how I've suffered—!

MURIEL. I did, too.

RICHARD (*unable to resist falling into his tragic literary pose for a moment*).

The despair in my soul— (*He recites dramatically*) "Something was dead in each of us, And what was dead was Hope!" That was me! My hope of happiness was dead! (*Then with sincere boyish fervor*) Gosh, Muriel, it sure is wonderful to be with you again! (*He puts a timid arm around her awkwardly.*)

MURIEL (*shyly*). I'm glad—it makes you happy. I'm happy, too.

RICHARD. Can't I—won't you let me kiss you—now? Please! (*He bends his face toward hers.*)

MURIEL (*ducking her head away—timidly*). No. You mustn't. Don't—

RICHARD. Aw, why can't I?

MURIEL. Because—I'm afraid.

RICHARD (*discomfited—taking his arm from around her—a bit sulky and impatient with her*). Aw, that's what you always say! You're always so afraid! Aren't you ever going to let me?

MURIEL. I will—sometime.

RICHARD. When?

MURIEL. Soon, maybe.

RICHARD. Tonight, will you?

MURIEL (*coyly*). I'll see.

RICHARD. Promise?

MURIEL. I promise—maybe.

RICHARD. All right. You remember you've promised. (*Then coaxingly*) Aw, don't let's stand here. Come on out and we can sit down in the boat.

MURIEL (*hesitantly*). It's so bright out there.

RICHARD. No one'll see. You know there's never anyone around here at night.

MURIEL (*illogically*). I know there isn't. That's why I thought it would be the best place. But there might be someone.

RICHARD (*taking her hand and tugging at it gently*). There isn't a soul. (MURIEL *steps out a little and looks up and down fearfully.* RICHARD *goes on insistently*) Aw, what's the use of a moon if you can't see it!

MURIEL. But it's only a new moon. That's not much to look at.

RICHARD. But I want to see you. I can't here in the shadow. I want to—drink in—all your beauty.

MURIEL (*can't resist this*). Well, all right—only I can't stay only a few minutes. (*She lets him lead her toward the stern of the boat.*)

RICHARD (*pleadingly*). Aw, you can stay a little while, can't you? Please! (*He helps her in and she settles herself in the stern seat of the boat, facing diagonally left front.*)

MURIEL. A little while. (*He sits beside her*) But I've got to be home in bed again pretending to be asleep by ten o'clock. That's the time Pa and Ma come up to bed, as regular as clock work, and Ma always looks into my room.

RICHARD. But you'll have oodles of time to do that.

MURIEL (*excitedly*). Dick, you have no idea what I went through to get here tonight! My, but it was exciting! You know Pa's punishing me by sending me to bed at eight sharp, and I had to get all undressed and into bed 'cause at half-past he sends Ma up to make sure I've obeyed, and she came up, and I pretended to be asleep, and she went down again, and I got up and dressed in such a hurry—I must look a sight, don't I?

RICHARD. You do not! You look wonderful!

MURIEL. And then I sneaked down the back stairs. And the pesky old stairs squeaked, and my heart was in my mouth, I was so scared, and then I sneaked out through the back yard, keeping in the dark under the trees, and— My, but it was exciting! Dick, you don't realize how I've been punished for your sake. Pa's been so mean and nasty, I've almost hated him!

RICHARD. And you don't realize what I've been through for you—and what I'm in for—for sneaking out— (*Then darkly*) And for what I did last night—what your letter made me do!

MURIEL (*made terribly curious by his ominous tone*). What did my letter make you do?

RICHARD (*beginning to glory in this*). It's too long a story—and let the dead past bury its dead. (*Then with real feeling*) Only it isn't past, I can tell you! What I'll catch when Pa gets hold of me!

MURIEL. Tell me, Dick! Begin at the beginning and tell me!

RICHARD (*tragically*). Well, after your old—your father left our place I caught holy hell from Pa.

MURIEL. You mustn't swear!

RICHARD (*somberly*). Hell is the only word that can describe it. And on top of that, to torture me more, he gave me your letter. After I'd read that I didn't want to live any more. Life seemed like a tragic farce.

MURIEL. I'm so awful sorry, Dick—honest I am! But you might have known I'd never write that unless—

RICHARD. I thought your love for me was dead. I thought you'd never loved me, that you'd only been cruelly mocking me—to torture me!

MURIEL. Dick! I'd never! You know I'd never!

RICHARD. I wanted to die. I sat and brooded about death. Finally I made up my mind I'd kill myself.

MURIEL (*excitedly*). Dick! You didn't!

RICHARD. I did, too! If there'd been one of Hedda Gabler's pistols around, you'd have seen if I wouldn't have done it beautifully! I thought, when I'm dead, she'll be sorry she ruined my life!

MURIEL (*cuddling up a little to him*). If you ever had! I'd have died, too! Honest, I would!

RICHARD. But suicide is the act of a coward. That's what stopped me. (*Then with a bitter change of tone*) And anyway, I thought to myself, she isn't worth it.

MURIEL (*huffily*). That's a nice thing to say!

RICHARD. Well, if you meant what was in that letter, you wouldn't have been worth it, would you?

MURIEL. But I've told you Pa—

RICHARD. So I said to myself, I'm through with women; they're all alike!

MURIEL. I'm not.

RICHARD. And I thought, what difference does it make what I do now? I might as well forget her and lead the pace that kills, and drown my sorrows! You know I had eleven dollars saved up to buy you something for your birthday, but I thought, she's dead to me now and why shouldn't I throw it away? (*Then hastily*) I've still got almost five left, Muriel, and I can get you something nice with that.

MURIEL (*excitedly*). What do I care about your old presents? You tell me what you did!

RICHARD (*darkly again*). After it was dark, I sneaked out and went to a low dive I know about.

MURIEL. Dick Miller, I don't believe you ever!

RICHARD. You ask them at the Pleasant Beach House if I didn't! They won't forget me in a hurry!

MURIEL (*impressed and horrified*). You went there? Why, that's a terrible place! Pa says it ought to be closed by the police!

RICHARD (*darkly*). I said it was a dive, didn't I? It's a "secret house of shame." And they let me into a secret room behind the barroom. There wasn't anyone there but a Princeton Senior I know—he belongs to Tiger Inn and he's fullback on the football team—and he had two chorus girls from New York with him, and they were all drinking champagne.

MURIEL (*disturbed by the entrance of the chorus girls*). Dick Miller! I hope you didn't notice—

RICHARD (*carelessly*). I had a highball by myself and then I noticed one of the girls—the one that wasn't with the fullback—looking at me. She had strange-looking eyes. And then she asked me if I wouldn't drink champagne with them and come and sit with her.

MURIEL. She must have been a nice thing! (*Then a bit falteringly*) And did—you?

RICHARD (*with tragic bitterness*). Why shouldn't I, when you'd told me in that letter you'd never see me again?

MURIEL (*almost tearfully*). But you ought to have known Pa made me—

RICHARD. I didn't know that then. (*Then rubbing it in*) Her name was Belle. She had yellow hair—the kind that burns and stings you!

MURIEL. I'll bet it was dyed!

RICHARD. She kept smoking one cigarette after another—but that's nothing for a chorus girl.

MURIEL (*indignantly*). She was low and bad, that's what she was or she couldn't be a chorus girl, and her smoking cigarettes proves it! (*Then falteringly again*) And then what happened?

RICHARD (*carelessly*). Oh, we just kept drinking champagne—I bought a round—and then I had a fight with the barkeep and knocked him down because he'd insulted her. He was a great big thug but—

MURIEL (*huffily*). I don't see how he could—insult that kind! And why did you fight for her? Why didn't the Princeton fullback who'd brought them there? He must have been bigger than you.

RICHARD (*stopped for a moment—then quickly*). He was too drunk by that time.

MURIEL. And were you drunk?

RICHARD. Only a little then. I was worse later. (*Proudly*) You ought to have seen me when I got home! I was on the verge of delirium tremens!

MURIEL. I'm glad I didn't see you. You must have been awful. I hate people who get drunk. I'd have hated you!

RICHARD. Well, it was all your fault, wasn't it? If you hadn't written that letter—

MURIEL. But I've told you I didn't mean— (*Then faltering but fascinated*) But what happened with that Belle—after—before you went home?

RICHARD. Oh, we kept drinking champagne and she said she'd fallen in love with me at first sight and she came and sat on my lap and kissed me.

MURIEL (*stiffening*). Oh!

RICHARD (*quickly, afraid he has gone too far*). But it was only all in fun, and then we just kept on drinking champagne, and finally I said good night and came home.

MURIEL. And did you kiss her?

RICHARD. No, I didn't.

MURIEL (*distractedly*). You did, too! You're lying and you know it. You did, too! (*Then tearfully*) And there I was right at that time lying in bed not able to sleep, wondering how I was ever going to see you again and crying my eyes out, while you—! (*She suddenly jumps to her feet in a tearful fury*) I hate you! I wish you were dead! I'm going home this minute! I never want to lay eyes on you again! And this time I mean it! (*She tries to jump out of the boat but he holds her back. All the pose has dropped from him now and he is in a frightened state of contrition.*)

RICHARD (*imploringly*). Muriel! Wait! Listen!

MURIEL. I don't want to listen! Let me go! If you don't I'll bite your hand!

RICHARD. I won't let you go! You've got to let me explain! I never—! Ouch! (*For* MURIEL *has bitten his hand and it hurts, and, stung by the pain, he lets go instinctively, and she jumps quickly out of the boat and starts running toward the path.* RICHARD *calls after her with bitter despair and hurt*) All right! Go if you want to—if you haven't the decency to let me explain! I hate you, too! I'll go and see Belle!

MURIEL (*seeing he isn't following her, stops at the foot of the path—*

defiantly). Well, go and see her—if that's the kind of girl you like! What do I care? (*Then as he only stares before him broodingly, sitting dejectedly in the stern of the boat, a pathetic figure of injured grief*) You can't explain! What can you explain? You owned up you kissed her!

RICHARD. I did not. I said she kissed me.

MURIEL (*scornfully, but drifting back a step in his direction*). And I suppose you just sat and let yourself be kissed! Tell that to the Marines!

RICHARD (*injuredly*). All right! If you're going to call me a liar every word I say—

MURIEL (*drifting back another step*). I didn't call you a liar. I only meant—it sounds fishy. Don't you know it does?

RICHARD. I don't know anything. I only know I wish I was dead!

MURIEL (*gently reproving*). You oughtn't to say that. It's wicked. (*Then after a pause*) And I suppose you'll tell me you didn't fall in love with her?

RICHARD (*scornfully*). I should say not! Fall in love with that kind of girl! What do you take me for?

MURIEL (*practically*). How do you know what you did if you drank so much champagne?

RICHARD. I kept my head—with her. I'm not a sucker, no matter what you think!

MURIEL (*drifting nearer*). Then you didn't—love her?

RICHARD. I hated her! She wasn't even pretty! And I had a fight with her before I left, she got so fresh. I told her I loved you and never could love anyone else, and for her to leave me alone.

MURIEL. But you said just now you were going to see her—

RICHARD. That was only bluff. I wouldn't—unless you left me. Then I wouldn't care what I did—any more than I did last night. (*Then suddenly defiant*) And what if I did kiss her once or twice? I only did it to get back at you!

MURIEL. Dick!

RICHARD. You're a fine one to blame me—when it was all your fault! Why can't you be fair? Didn't I think you were out of my life forever? Hadn't you written me you were? Answer me that!

MURIEL. But I've told you a million times that Pa—

RICHARD. Why didn't you have more sense than to let him make you write it? Was it my fault you didn't?

MURIEL. It was your fault for being so stupid! You ought to have known he stood right over me and told me each word to write. If I'd refused, it would only have made everything worse. I had to pretend, so I'd get a chance to see you. Don't you see, Silly? And I had sand enough to sneak out to meet you tonight, didn't I? (*He doesn't answer. She moves nearer*) Still I can see how you felt the way you did—and maybe I am to blame for that. So I'll forgive and forget, Dick—if you'll swear to me you didn't even think of loving that—

RICHARD (*eagerly*). I didn't! I swear, Muriel. I couldn't. I love you!

MURIEL. Well, then—I still love you.

RICHARD. Then come back here, why don't you?

MURIEL (*coyly*). It's getting late.

RICHARD. It's not near half-past yet.

MURIEL (*comes back and sits down by him shyly*). All right—only I'll have to go soon, Dick. (*He puts his arm around her. She cuddles up close to him*). I'm sorry—I hurt your hand.

RICHARD. That was nothing. It felt wonderful—even to have you bite!

MURIEL (*impulsively takes his hand and kisses it*). There! That'll cure it. (*She is overcome by confusion at her boldness.*)

RICHARD. You shouldn't—waste that —on my hand. (*Then tremblingly*) You said—you'd let me—

MURIEL. I said, maybe.

RICHARD. Please, Muriel. You know —I want it so!

MURIEL. Will it wash off—her kisses —make you forget you ever—for always?

RICHARD. I should say so! I'd never remember—anything but it—never want anything but it—ever again.

MURIEL (*shyly lifting her lips*). Then—all right—Dick. (*He kisses her tremblingly and for a moment their lips remain together. Then she lets her head sink on his shoulder and sighs softly*) The moon *is* beautiful, isn't it?

RICHARD (*kissing her hair*). Not as beautiful as you! Nothing is! (*Then after a pause*) Won't it be wonderful when we're married?

MURIEL. Yes—but it's so long to wait.

RICHARD. Perhaps I needn't go to Yale. Perhaps Pa will give me a job. Then I'd soon be making enough to—

MURIEL. You better do what your pa thinks best—and I'd like you to be at Yale. (*Then patting his face*) Poor you! Do you think he'll punish you awful?

RICHARD (*intensely*). I don't know and I don't care! Nothing would have kept me from seeing you tonight—not if I'd had to crawl over red-hot coals! (*Then falling back on Swinburne—but with passionate sincerity*) You have my being between the hands of you! You are "my love, mine own soul's heart, more dear than mine own soul, more beautiful than God!"

MURIEL (*shocked and delighted*). Ssshh! It's wrong to say that.

RICHARD (*adoringly*). Gosh, but I love you! Gosh, I love you—Darling!

MURIEL. I love you, too—Sweetheart! (*They kiss. Then she lets her head sink on his shoulder again and they both sit in a rapt trance, staring at the moon. After a pause—dreamily*)

Where'll we go on our honeymoon, Dick? To Niagara Falls?

RICHARD (*scornfully*). That dump where all the silly fools go? I should say not! (*With passionate romanticism*) No, we'll go to some far-off wonderful place! (*He calls on Kipling to help him*) Somewhere out on the Long Trail—the trail that is always new—on the road to Mandalay! We'll watch the dawn come up like thunder out of China!

MURIEL (*hazily but happily*) That'll be wonderful, won't it?

CURTAIN

ACT FOUR

SCENE III

SCENE—*The sitting-room of the* MILLER *house again—about 10 o'clock the same night.* MILLER *is sitting in his rocker at left, front, of table, his wife in the rocker at right, front, of table. Moonlight shines through the screen door at right, rear. Only the green-shaded reading lamp is lit and by its light* MILLER, *his specs on, is reading a book while his wife, sewing basket in lap, is working industriously on a doily.* MRS. MILLER'S *face wears an expression of unworried content.* MILLER'S *face has also lost its look of harassed preoccupation, although he still is a prey to certain misgivings, when he allows himself to think of them. Several books are piled on the table by his elbow, the books that have been confiscated from* RICHARD.

MILLER (*chuckles at something he reads—then closes the book and puts it on the table.* MRS. MILLER *looks up from her sewing*). This Shaw's a comical cuss—even if his ideas are so crazy they oughtn't to allow them to be printed. And that Swinburne's got a fine swing to his poetry—if he'd only choose some other subjects besides loose women.

MRS. MILLER (*smiling teasingly*). I can see where you're becoming corrupted by those books, too—pretending to read them out of duty to Richard, when your nose has been glued to the page!

MILLER. No, no—but I've got to be honest. There's something to them. That Rubaiyat of Omar Khayyam, now. I read that over again and liked it even better than I had before—parts of it, that is, where it isn't all about boozing.

MRS. MILLER (*has been busy with her own thoughts during this last—with a deep sigh of relief*). My, but I'm glad Mildred told me where

Richard went off to. I'd have worried my heart out if she hadn't. But now, it's all right.

MILLER (*frowning a little*). I'd hardly go so far as to say that. Just because we know he's all right tonight doesn't mean last night is wiped out. He's still got to be punished for that.

MRS. MILLER (*defensively*). Well, if you ask me, I think after the way I punished him all day, and the way I know he's punished himself, he's had about all he deserves. I've told you how sorry he was, and how he said he'd never touch liquor again. It didn't make him feel happy like Sid, but only sad and sick, so he didn't see anything in it for him.

MILLER. Well, if he's really got that view of it driven into his skull, I don't know but I'm glad it all happened. That'll protect him more than a thousand lectures—just horse sense about himself. (*Then frowning again*) Still, I can't let him do such things and go scot-free. And then, besides, there's another side to it— (*He stops abruptly.*)

MRS. MILLER (*uneasily*). What do you mean, another side?

MILLER (*hastily*). I mean, discipline. There's got to be some discipline in a family. I don't want him to get the idea he's got a stuffed shirt at the head of the table. No, he's got to be punished, if only to make the lesson stick in his mind, and I'm going to tell him he can't go to Yale, seeing he's so undependable.

MRS. MILLER (*up in arms at once*). Not go to Yale! I guess he can go to Yale! Every man of your means in town is sending his boys to college! What would folks think of you? You let Wilbur go, and you'd have let Lawrence, only he didn't want to, and you're letting Arthur! If our other children can get the benefit of a college education, you're not going to pick on Richard—

MILLER. Hush up, for God's sake! If you'd let me finish what I started to say! I said I'd *tell* him that now—bluff—then later on I'll change my mind, if he behaves himself.

MRS. MILLER. Oh well, if that's all— (*Then defensively again*) But it's your duty to give him every benefit. He's got an exceptional brain, that boy has! He's proved it by the way he likes to read all those deep plays and books and poetry.

MILLER. But I thought you— (*He stops, grinning helplessly.*)

MRS. MILLER. You thought I what?

MILLER. Never mind.

MRS. MILLER (*sniffs, but thinks it better to let this pass*). You mark my words, that boy's going to turn out to be a great lawyer, or a great doctor, or a great writer, or—

MILLER (*grinning*). You agree he's going to be great, anyway.

MRS. MILLER. Yes, I most certainly have a lot of faith in Richard.

MILLER. Well, so have I, as far as that goes.

MRS. MILLER (*after a pause—judicially*). And as for his being in love with Muriel, I don't see but what it might work out real well. Richard could do worse.

MILLER. But I thought you had no use for her, thought she was stupid.

MRS. MILLER. Well, so I did, but if she's good for Richard and he wants her— (*Then inconsequentially*) Ma used to say you weren't overbright, but she changed her mind when she saw I didn't care if you were or not.

MILLER (*not exactly pleased by this*). Well, I've been bright enough to—

MRS. MILLER (*going on as if he had not spoken*). And Muriel's real cute-looking, I have to admit that. Takes after her mother. Alice Briggs was the prettiest girl before she married.

MILLER. Yes, and Muriel will get big as a house after she's married, the same as her mother did. That's the trouble. A man never can tell what he's letting himself in for— (*He stops, feeling his wife's eyes fixed on him with indignant suspicion.*)

MRS. MILLER (*sharply*). I'm not too fat and don't you say it!

MILLER. Who was talking about you?

MRS. MILLER. And I'd rather have some flesh on my bones than be built like a string bean and bore a hole in a chair every time I sat down —like some people!

MILLER (*ignoring the insult—flatteringly*). Why, no one'd ever call you fat, Essie. You're only plump, like a good figure ought to be.

MRS. MILLER (*childishly pleased—gratefully giving tit for tat*). Well, you're not skinny, either—only slender—and I think you've been putting on weight lately, too. (*Having thus squared matters she takes up her sewing again. A pause. Then* MILLER *asks incredulously.*)

MILLER. You don't mean to tell me you're actually taking this Muriel crush of Richard's seriously, do you? I know it's a good thing to encourage right now but—pshaw, why, Richard'll probably forget all about her before he's away six months, and she'll have forgotten him.

MRS. MILLER. Don't be so cynical (*Then, after a pause, thoughtfully*). Well, anyway, he'll always have it to remember—no matter what happens after—and that's something.

MILLER. You bet that's something. (*Then with a grin*) You surprise me at times with your deep wisdom.

MRS. MILLER. You don't give me credit for ever having common sense, that's why. (*She goes back to her sewing.*)

MILLER (*after a pause*). Where'd you say Sid and Lily had gone off to?

MRS. MILLER. To the beach to listen to the band. (*She sighs sympathetically*) Poor Lily! Sid'll never change, and she'll never marry him. But she seems to get some queer satisfaction out of fussing over him like a hen that's hatched a duck—though Lord knows I wouldn't in her shoes!

MILLER. Arthur's up with Elsie Rand, I suppose?

MRS. MILLER. Of course.

MILLER. Where's Mildred?

MRS. MILLER. Out walking with her latest. I've forgot who it is. I can't keep track of them. (*She smiles.*)

MILLER (*smiling*). Then, from all reports, we seem to be completely surrounded by love!

MRS. MILLER. Well, we've had our share, haven't we? We don't have to begrudge it to our children. (*Then has a sudden thought*) But I've done all this talking about Muriel and Richard and clean forgot how wild old McComber was against it. But he'll get over that, I suppose.

MILLER (*with a chuckle*). He has already. I ran into him upstreet this afternoon and he was meek as pie. He backed water and said he guessed I was right. Richard had just copied stuff out of books, and kids would be kids, and so on. So I came off my high horse a bit—but not too far—and I guess all that won't bother anyone any more. (*Then rubbing his hands together—with a boyish grin of pleasure*) And I told you about getting that business from Lawson, didn't I? It's been a good day, Essie—a darned good day!

(*From the hall beyond the front parlor the sound of the front door being opened and shut is heard.* MRS. MILLER *leans forward to look, pushing her specs up.*)

MRS. MILLER (*in a whisper*). It's Richard.

MILLER (*immediately assuming an expression of becoming gravity*). Hmm. (*He takes off his spectacles and puts them back in their case and straightens himself in his chair.* RICHARD *comes slowly in from the front parlor. He walks like one in a trance, his eyes shining with a dreamy happiness, his spirit still too exalted to be conscious of his surroundings, or to remember the threatened punishment. He carries his straw hat dangling in his hand, quite unaware of its existence.*)

RICHARD (*dreamily, like a ghost addressing fellow shades*). Hello.

MRS. MILLER (*staring at him worriedly*). Hello, Richard.

MILLER (*sizing him up shrewdly*). Hello, Son.

(RICHARD *moves past his mother and comes to the far corner, left front, where the light is dimmest, and sits down on the sofa, and stares before him, his hat dangling in his hand.*)

MRS. MILLER (*with frightened suspicion now*). Goodness, he acts queer! Nat, you don't suppose he's been—?

MILLER (*with a reassuring smile*). No. It's love, not liquor, this time.

MRS. MILLER (*only partly reassured—sharply*). Richard! What's the matter with you? (*He comes to himself with a start. She goes on scoldingly*) How many times have I told you to hang up your hat in the hall when you come in! (*He looks at his hat as if he were surprised at its existence. She gets up fussily and goes to him*) Here. Give it to me. I'll hang it up for you this once. And what are you sitting over here in the dark for? Don't forget your father's been waiting to talk to you! (*She comes back to the table and he follows her, still half in a dream, and stands by his father's chair.* MRS. MILLER *starts for the hall with his hat.*)

MILLER (*quietly but firmly now*). You better leave Richard and me alone for a while, Essie.

MRS. MILLER (*turns to stare at him apprehensively*). Well—all right. I'll go sit on the piazza. Call me if you want me. (*Then a bit pleadingly*) But you'll remember all I've said, Nat, won't you? (MILLER *nods reassuringly. She disappears through the front parlor.* RICHARD, *keenly conscious of himself as the about-to-be-sentenced criminal by this time, looks guilty and a bit defiant, searches his father's expressionless face with uneasy side glances, and steels himself for what is coming.*)

MILLER (*casually, indicating* MRS. MILLER'S *rocker*). Sit down, Richard. (RICHARD *slumps awkwardly into the chair and sits in a self-conscious, unnatural position.* MILLER *sizes him up keenly—then suddenly smiles and asks with quiet mockery*) Well, how are the vine leaves in your hair this evening?

RICHARD (*totally unprepared for this approach—shamefacedly mutters*). I don't know, Pa.

MILLER. Turned out to be poison ivy, didn't they? (*Then kindly*) But you needn't look so alarmed. I'm not going to read you any temperance lecture. That'd bore me more than it would you. And, in spite of your damn foolishness last night, I'm still giving you credit for having brains. So I'm pretty sure anything I could say to you you've already said to yourself.

RICHARD (*his head down—humbly*). I know I was a darned fool.

MILLER (*thinking it well to rub in this aspect—disgustedly*). You sure were—not only a fool but a downright, stupid, disgusting fool! (RICHARD *squirms, his head still lower*) It was bad enough for you to let me and Arthur see you, but to appear like that before your mother and Mildred—! And I wonder if Muriel would think you were so fine if she ever saw you as you looked and acted then. I think she'd give you your walking papers for keeps. And you couldn't blame her. No nice girl wants to give her love to a stupid drunk!

RICHARD (*writhing*). I know, Pa.

MILLER (*after a pause—quietly*). All right. Then that settles—the booze end of it. (*He sizes* RICHARD *up searchingly—then suddenly speaks sharply*) But there is another thing that's more serious. How about that tart you went to bed with at the Pleasant Beach House?

RICHARD (*flabbergasted—stammers*). You know—? But I didn't! If they've told you about her down there, they must have told you I didn't! She wanted me to—but I wouldn't. I gave her the five dollars just so she'd let me out of it. Honest, Pa, I didn't! She made everything seem rotten and dirty—and—I didn't want to do a thing like that to Muriel—no matter how bad I thought she'd treated me—even after I felt drunk, I didn't. Honest!

MILLER. How'd you happen to meet this lady, anyway?

RICHARD. I can't tell that, Pa. I'd have to snitch on someone—and you wouldn't want me to do that.

MILLER (*a bit taken aback*). No. I suppose I wouldn't. Hmm. Well, I believe you—and I guess that settles that. (*Then, after a quick, furtive glance at* RICHARD, *he nerves himself for the ordeal and begins with a shamefaced, self-conscious solemni ty*) But listen here, Richard, it's about time you and I had a serious talk about—hmm—certain matters pertaining to—and now that the subject's come up of its own accord, it's a good time—I mean, there's no use in procrastinating further—so, here goes. (*But it doesn't go smoothly and as he goes on he becomes more and more guiltily embarrassed and self-conscious and his expressions more stilted.* RICHARD *sedulously avoids even glancing at him, his own embarrassment made tenfold more painful by his father's*) Richard, you have now come to the age when— Well, you're a fully developed man, in a way, and it's only natural for you to have certain desires of the flesh, to put it that way— I mean, pertaining to the opposite sex—certain natural feelings and temptations—that'll want to be gratified—and you'll want to gratify them. Hmm—well, human society being organized as it is, there's only one outlet for—unless you're a scoundrel and go around ruining decent girls—which you're not, of course. Well, there are a certain class of women—always have been and always will be as long as human nature is what it is— It's wrong, maybe, but what can you do about it? I mean, girls like that one you—girls there's something doing with—and lots of 'em are pretty, and it's human nature if you— But that doesn't mean to ever get mixed up with them seriously! You just have what you want and pay 'em and forget it. I know that sounds hard and unfeeling, but we're talking facts and— But don't think I'm encouraging you to— If you can stay away from 'em, all the better—but if—why —hmm— Here's what I'm driving at, Richard. They're apt to be whited sepulchres—I mean, your whole life might be ruined if—so, darn it, you've got to know how to— I mean, there are ways and means— (*Suddenly he can go no farther and winds up helplessly*) But, hell, I suppose you boys talk all this over among yourselves and you know more about it than I do. I'll admit I'm no authority. I never had anything to do with such women, and it'll be a hell of a lot better for you if you never do!

RICHARD (*without looking at him*). I'm never going to, Pa. (*Then shocked indignation coming into his voice*) I don't see how you could think I could—now—when you know I love Muriel and am going to marry her. I'd die before I'd—!

MILLER (*immensely relieved—enthusiastically*). That's the talk! By God, I'm proud of you when you talk like that! (*Then hastily*) And now that's all of that. There's nothing more to say and we'll forget it, eh?

RICHARD (*after a pause*). How are you going to punish me, Pa?

MILLER. I *was* sort of forgetting that, wasn't I? Well, I'd thought of telling you you couldn't go to Yale—

RICHARD (*eagerly*). Don't I have to go? Gee, that's great! Muriel thought you'd want me to. I was telling her I'd rather you gave me a job on the paper because then she and I could get married sooner. (*Then with a boyish grin*) Gee, Pa, you picked a lemon. That isn't any punishment. You'll have to do something besides that.

MILLER (*grimly—but only half concealing an answering grin*). Then you'll go to Yale and you'll stay there till you graduate, that's the answer to that! Muriel's got good sense and you haven't! (RICHARD *accepts this philosophically*) And now we're finished, you better call your mother. (RICHARD *opens the screen door and calls "Ma," and a moment later she comes in. She glances quickly from son to husband and immediately knows that all is well and tactfully refrains from all questions.*)

MRS. MILLER. My, it's a beautiful night. The moon's way down low—almost setting. (*She sits in her chair and sighs contentedly.* RICHARD *remains standing by the door, staring out at the moon, his face pale in the moonlight.*)

MILLER (*with a nod at* RICHARD, *winking at his wife*). Yes, I don't believe I've hardly ever seen such a beautiful night—with such a wonderful moon. Have you, Richard?

RICHARD (*turning to them—enthusiastically*). No! It was wonderful—down at the beach— (*He stops abruptly, smiling shyly.*)

MILLER. (*watching his son—after a pause—quietly*). I can only remember a few nights that were as beautiful as this—and they were long ago, when your mother and I were young and planning to get married.

RICHARD (*stares at him wonderingly for a moment, then quickly from his father to his mother and back again, strangely, as if he'd never seen them before—then he looks almost disgusted and swallows as if an acrid taste had come into his mouth—but then suddenly his face is transfigured by a smile of shy understanding and sympathy. He speaks shyly*). Yes, I'll bet those must have been wonderful nights, too. You sort of forget the moon was the same way back then—and everything.

MILLER (*huskily*). You're all right, Richard. (*He gets up and blows his nose.*)

MRS. MILLER (*fondly*). You're a good boy, Richard. (RICHARD *looks dreadfully shy and embarrassed at this. His father comes to his rescue.*)

MILLER. Better get to bed early tonight, Son, hadn't you?

RICHARD. I couldn't sleep. Can't I go out on the piazza and sit for a while—until the moon sets?

MILLER. All right. Then you better say good night now. I don't know about your mother, but I'm going to bed right away. I'm dead tired.

MRS. MILLER. So am I.

RICHARD (*goes to her and kisses her*). Good night, Ma.

MRS. MILLER. Good night. Don't you stay up till all hours now.

RICHARD (*comes to his father and stands awkwardly before him*). Good night, Pa.

MILLER (*puts his arm around him and gives him a hug*). Good night, Richard. (RICHARD *turns impulsively and kisses him—then hurries out the screen door.* MILLER *stares after him—then says huskily*) First time he's done that in years. I don't believe in kissing between fathers and sons after a certain age—seems mushy and silly—but that meant something! And I don't think we'll ever have to worry about his being safe—from himself

—again. And I guess no matter what life will do to him, he can take care of it now. (*He sighs with satisfaction and, sitting down in his chair, begins to unlace his shoes*) My darned feet are giving me fits!

MRS. MILLER (*laughing*). Why do you bother unlacing your shoes now, you big goose—when we're going right up to bed?

MILLER (*as if he hadn't thought of that before, stops*). Guess you're right. (*Then getting to his feet—with a grin*) Mind if I don't say my prayers tonight, Essie? I'm certain God knows I'm too darned tired.

MRS. MILLER. Don't talk that way. It's real sinful. (*She gets up—then laughing fondly*) If that isn't you all over! Always looking for an excuse to— You're worse than Tommy! But all right. I suppose tonight you needn't. You've had a hard day. (*She puts her hand on the reading-lamp switch*) I'm going to turn out the light. All ready?

MILLER. Yep. Let her go, Gallagher. (*She turns out the lamp. In the ensuing darkness the faint moonlight shines full in through the screen door. Walking together toward the front parlor they stand full in it for a moment, looking out.* MILLER *puts his arm around her. He says in a low voice*) There he is—like a statue of Love's Young Dream. (*Then he sighs and speaks with a gentle nostalgic melancholy*) What's it that Rubaiyat says:

"Yet Ah, that Spring should
vanish with the Rose!
That Youth's sweet-scented
manuscript should close!"

(*Then throwing off his melancholy, with a loving smile at her*) Well, Spring isn't everything, is it, Essie? There's a lot to be said for Autumn. That's got beauty, too. And Winter —if you're together.

MRS. MILLER (*simply*). Yes, Nat. (*She kisses him and they move quietly out of the moonlight, back into the darkness of the front parlor.*)

CURTAIN

The Petrified Forest

BY ROBERT EMMET SHERWOOD

TO

MY MOTHER

The Petrified Forest was first produced at the Broadhurst Theatre, New York City, by Gilbert Miller and Leslie Howard, in association with Arthur Hopkins, on January 7, 1935, and closed on June 29, 1935. Following is the original cast:

Gramp Maple	Charles Dow Clark
Boze Hertzlinger	Frank Milan
A Telegraph Lineman	Milo Boulton
Another Lineman	James Doody
Jason Maple	Walter Vonnegut
Gabby Maple	Peggy Conklin
Paula	Esther Leeming
Alan Squier	Leslie Howard
Herb	Robert Porterfield
Mr. Chisholm	Robert Hudson
Mrs. Chisholm	Blanche Sweet
Joseph	John Alexander
Jackie	Ross Hertz
Duke Mantee	Humphrey Bogart
Ruby	Tom Fadden
Pyles	Slim Thompson
Legion Commander	Aloysius Cunningham
Another Legionnaire	Guy Conradi
Sheriff	Frank Tweddell
A Deputy	Eugene Keith
Another Deputy	Harry Sherwin

Staged by Arthur Hopkins

Setting by Raymond Sovey

SCENE

The scene is the Black Mesa Bar-B-Q, a gas station and lunch room at a lonely crossroads in the eastern Arizona desert

The action begins late in the afternoon of an autumn day in 1934, and continues into the evening of the same day

THE PETRIFIED FOREST

ACT ONE

The scene of the entire play is the lunch room of the Black Mesa Filling Station and Bar-B-Q on the desert in Eastern Arizona.

There is an atmosphere about the place of strenuous if not hearty welcome

At the upper right are double doors, with glass panels leading out to a covered porch. Off to the right, barely visible through these doors, are the red pumps of the filling station.

Downstage left is a door leading to the bedrooms of the MAPLE *family who own this establishment. Upstage left is a swinging door leading to the kitchen. Upstage is a lunch counter, with cash register, ketchup bottles, paper napkins, toothpicks, chewing-gum and Life-Saver rack, cigars, cigarettes, etc.*

In the right wall are wide windows, through which may be seen the porch and, beyond it, the desert purpling in the sunset. At the left is a stove, with a high-backed rocking chair beside it.

There are three small square tables—downstage left, downstage right and center. There are three chairs at each table. At the right, along the wall, is a wooden bench.

The walls are of phony adobe. The window and door trimmings are painted a dark, burnt red. Above the windows is a sign, with the words, "BLACK MESA BAR-B-Q," worked in rustic letters. This formerly hung outside, but was replaced by a Neon sign, the green gleam of which will be evident later on when darkness descends.

The walls are decorated with advertisements of Rye Whiskey, Gas and Oil, the NRA, the TVA, the Red Cross, the American Legion, the Santa Fé R. R., Apache Beer, etc. On the wall is a framed photograph of General Pershing and below it an old service flag with one star. Prominently displayed is a crudely lettered sign that shouts: "TIPPING IS UN-AMERICAN —KEEP YOUR CHANGE!"

At the table downstage right are two TELEGRAPH LINEMEN, *eating hamburger and drinking coffee. Both are young. The* FIRST *is thin and explosive in speech; the* SECOND *beefy and calm.*

Between them, and drawn back from the table, sits BOZE HERTZLINGER, *a stalwart, bronzed young man, who wears dirty white canvas pants and a filthy football jersey, on the back of which is a patch with the number 42. He is lighting a cigarette.*

At the left, in the rocking chair, sits GRAMP MAPLE*—an old, old man. His eyes are watery and his vision blurred. His skin is like leather that has been dried by a lifetime under the desert sun and worn thin by constant rough usage. He holds a tattered pink copy of the Denver Post, but he is paying more attention to the talk of the* LINEMEN *than to the screaming headlines.*

FIRST LINEMAN (*swallowing*). Certainly it's Revolution! And that's exactly what we got to come to, whether a lot of old fluffs back east like it or not . . .

SECOND LINEMAN. Yeah—and when it comes—how are *you* going to . . .

FIRST LINEMAN. When it comes, we're going to finally get some of that equality they talked about in the Declaration of Independence.

SECOND LINEMAN. Equality—hell! It's slavery. And how will you like that?

FIRST LINEMAN. What have we got *now,* I'd like to know? Do you call *this* freedom? (*He stows more food into his nimble mouth.*)

BOZE. Listen to me, kid. In school we had to read up a lot on that cockeyed system they got in Russia—and I'm here to tell you that if you were living over there you wouldn't be able to call your soul your own.

FIRST LINEMAN. And how do I know I've *got* a soul?

BOZE. You're alive, aren't you?

FIRST LINEMAN. Oh, sure—I'm alive. I got a heart—I can hear it beating. I got a stomach—I can hear it growling. I got blood—I can see it, when I stick myself with one of them God-damn splinters. But where's this soul that everybody hollers about?

BOZE. It's in your tongue, I guess. (*He winks broadly at the* SECOND LINEMAN. *A car is heard stopping off at the right.*)

FIRST LINEMAN. Yeah—and maybe they got it locked up in the safe at the Postal Telegraph Company, along with the rest of their doubtful assets.

(JASON MAPLE *has come in from the upper right. He is a dull, defeated man, of about forty, solemn, bespectacled, paunchy. He wears a gray alpaca cap, and a gray suit. In his lapel is an American Legion button.*)

JASON (*to* BOZE). Lady wants five gallons. Get going.

BOZE. O. K. boss. (*He pinches out the coal of his cigarette and places the butt behind his ear.*)

JASON. And you better keep on the alert out there so's customers don't have to wait. See?

BOZE. O. K. boss. (*He goes out. The* FIRST LINEMAN *laughs.*)

FIRST LINEMAN. And there's the guy who's here to tell me that in Russia you can't even call your soul your own.

JASON. You fellers want pie? (*His attitude toward the* FIRST LINEMAN *is not conspicuously amiable.*)

SECOND LINEMAN. Yeah.

FIRST LINEMAN. And another cuppa coffee. (JASON *picks up their cups and goes to the door at the left*) Rugged individualism! Every man for himself! That's the kind of liberty we've been getting.

JASON (*through the door at the left*). A couple of pies. (*He goes to the coffee boiler on the counter to refill the two cups.*)

SECOND LINEMAN. What are you complaining about? You're eating.

FIRST LINEMAN (*significantly*). "Man cannot live by bread alone."

SECOND LINEMAN. Who says he can't?

FIRST LINEMAN. God says so! That's who.

SECOND LINEMAN. Oh—is God a Russian?

FIRST LINEMAN. He certainly ain't with the Postal Telegraph.
(PAULA, *the Mexican cook, comes in, bearing the pie.* JASON *lights a cigar.*)

JASON. Take these. (JASON *gives the cups to* PAULA *as she passes.*)

FIRST LINEMAN. Why do you suppose it is that Russia's got the whole world scared? It's because they're pushing ahead. They're pioneering!

GRAMP. They're what?

FIRST LINEMAN. I said, they're pioneering. They're opening up new territory—and for the benefit of all, not so's a few land grabbers can step in and take the profits after somebody else has done the real work. Gracias. (*This is addressed to* PAULA, *who has delivered the pie and is now removing the remnants of the hamburger*) Those engineers in Russia are building something new! That's where they've got it on us. We ain't building—we're *repairing*. Just like you and me. What do we do—day after day? We climb up poles, and fix the wires, so that some broker in New York can telegraph in a split second to some guy in Los Angeles to tell him he's ruined.

GRAMP. Well, my friend—when you talk about pioneering—you're talking about something I can tell *you* a few things about. (*He has risen and is crossing to occupy the chair vacated by* BOZE.)

JASON. Shut up, Gramp.

GRAMP. I won't shut up.

JASON. I told you not to get into arguments with the guests.

GRAMP. Listen—I can tell these boys some things they'd be glad to hear. Wouldn't you, boys?

SECOND LINEMAN. Sure! Go ahead, Pop. Change the subject.
(*Both* LINEMEN *are devouring the pie.*)

GRAMP. Listen, my friend. I come down into this desert fifty-six years ago. I come down from Virginia City by way of Salt Lake and Mesa Verde. You had to be tough to cross this country in them days—Piyutes—Apaches—and plenty of white men with no love for their neighbors. Yes, *sir*! I was in your same line of business—wire stringing. I helped string the first line that run west out of Albuquerque, and we had one hell of a time doing it, too.
(BOZE *comes in.*)

BOZE. Lady wants a pack of Camels.

GRAMP. Do you want to know who was the Governor of this territory in them days? Well, I'll tell you. General Lew Wallace. He wrote "Ben Hur" right there in the palace in Santa Fé. He was a brave man and he had to be, because governing around here was dangerous work. It meant killing or being killed.

BOZE. Attaboy, Mr. Maple. Tell 'em about the time you took a shot at Billy the Kid.

(JASON *hands* BOZE *the Camels and the change.*)

GRAMP. I didn't take no shots at the Kid. I had too God-damn much sense. But he took a couple at me. I'm practically the only man he ever missed; but he was only doing it in fun, so it couldn't hardly count.

(GABBY MAPLE *comes in from the left on the cue "he ever missed." She is young and pretty, with a certain amount of style about her. Her principal distinguishing feature is an odd look of resentment in her large, dark eyes. She carries a thin book, her forefinger marking the place. She sits down at the table at the left and starts to read.*)

JASON. Get on out with those Camels.

BOZE. O. K. boss. (*He goes out, with a knowing look at* GABBY *which she ignores.*)

FIRST LINEMAN. Well, Pop, it's been very interesting, but I've got to be . . .

GRAMP. Wait a minute. I was just going to tell you about the first message we ever sent over that line. General Wallace dictated it and we sent it all the way through to Washington to President Hayes. And do you want to know what it said? It said, "God Save the Republic!" That's what General Wallace told us to say —and he was a great author.

FIRST LINEMAN (*who has risen*). You better send that same message through again, Pop—because the old republic's badly in need of assistance. How much do we owe? (*He has crossed to the lunch counter, the* SECOND LINEMAN *following.*)

JASON. That'll be fifty-five cents apiece.

GABBY. What did they have?

JASON. Hamburger special, pie, and two cups of coffee.

GABBY. All right. (*She puts down the book and picks up the pie plates and coffee mugs and goes out into the kitchen at the left. The* LINEMEN *are paying at the counter.*)

GRAMP. Hope you'll call in again, boys. I always enjoy talking to anybody in the telegraphing business.

SECOND LINEMAN. Maybe we will, Pop. Never can tell where we'll be sent next.

GRAMP. That's right—you can't.

JASON (*as he shoves change across the counter*). There's just one remark I'd like to pass to you, brother. Just watch out how you talk about the United States of America.

FIRST LINEMAN. What do you mean?

JASON. I mean simply this: belittling our system of government, preaching revolution and destruction, and red propaganda—well, it isn't a very healthy occupation. That's all.

GRAMP. I thought you said not to argue with the guests.

JASON. I'm only telling you, brother —for the sake of your own good.

FIRST LINEMAN. So it's unhealthy, eh! How do you think this government was started if it wasn't by revolution?

SECOND LINEMAN. Come on, Nick. We got to get going.

FIRST LINEMAN. Wait till he answers my question.

JASON. The American Revolution was fought to establish law and order. But the object of your dirty red propaganda is to destroy it . . .

FIRST LINEMAN. And how much law and order have *we* got? Did you read about that massacre yesterday in Oklahoma City? What kind of law and order is that?

SECOND LINEMAN. Listen, Nick. I got a dame waiting up for me in Gallup and I . . .

JASON. If some of you Bolsheviks would quit preaching disrespect for law, it wouldn't be possible for criminals to . . .

FIRST LINEMAN. Yeah? Do you want to know something? They don't have crime in Russia. And why? Because they've abolished the cause of crime. They've abolished greed! And I'll tell you something else . . .

SECOND LINEMAN. I'm going. (*He starts out.*)

JASON. You got your eats and there's your change. Now kindly get out.

FIRST LINEMAN (*pocketing his change*). O. K. Mr. Tin-horn Patriot. I only hope I'm around here when it happens. I want to see you when you've joined the mob and started waving the red flag. (*He turns and starts out.*)

GRAMP. 'Bye, boys.

FIRST LINEMAN. Good-bye, Pop. (*The* LINEMEN *go out.*)

GRAMP. You never should get into arguments with a boy like that, Jason. You only make a fool out of yourself.

JASON (*back of counter*). I'm sorry I didn't get his name, so's I could report him.

GRAMP. You tend to your own business, son, and stop fussing about other . . .

JASON (*with surprising vehemence*). My own business! That's a fine thing to say to me. What business have *I* got? Miserable little service station on the edge of nowheres.

GRAMP. It's a living, ain't it?

JASON. A living—yes—just barely. But it's one hell of a life for a man that ought to be getting some place in the world.

GRAMP. Maybe it's all you're good for.

JASON. I know—that's what *you* think. It's what you've always thought, since I was a boy. What chance have I ever had to prove what I can do?

GRAMP. You had a war, didn't you? Biggest war yet.

JASON. Yes—and you think I failed in that because I didn't come home with a lot of medals, and some German scalps hanging on my belt. Well, they didn't hand out medals to us soldiers that drove trucks—even if we did get right up into the danger zone time and time again.

GRAMP. All right, son—all right! You could have enlisted in the infantry if you'd had a mind to.

JASON (*hotly*). I enlisted in the branch of the service where my knowledge of mechanics could do the most good to my country. And I've still got that knowledge. And you know damned well it's your fault I don't get more scope for using it. (*He has come out from behind the counter.*)

GRAMP. My fault?

JASON. That's what I said. Hanging on to this place when you can sell it for good money.

GRAMP. I don't have to sell if I don't want to.

JASON. Dana Trimble's renewed his offer. Seven thousand dollars, and I know I can get him up to nine, maybe ten.

GRAMP. What makes him think this property's worth that much?

JASON. He knows perfectly well they're going to make this an interstate highway and run the bus route to El Paso through here.

GRAMP. All right—if it's good for him, it's good for us.

JASON. With seven thousand dollars I could buy a big piece of an Auto Camp on Redondo Boulevard in one of the best districts of Los Angeles. I'd put in a Bar-B-Q service and in a couple of years we'd *have* something . . .

GRAMP. Los Angeles! My God! You want to go to Los Angeles and Gabby wants to go to Europe. Ain't they nobody around here that's satisfied to stay put?

JASON. How about yourself? Were you ever satisfied to stay put, until you got so damned old you didn't have enough energy to move?

GRAMP. Listen to me, son. In my day, we had places to go—*new* places. But, my God—Los Angeles . . .
(GABBY *comes in from the kitchen.*)

GABBY. Paula's scared.

GRAMP. What's she scared of?

GABBY. The Mexicans are saying that Mantee is headed this way.

JASON. He was headed for the border and he's over it by now—if the Texas Rangers haven't got him.

GRAMP. They won't get him. Have you seen his picture? Straight black hair. Got Injun blood. He'll fool 'em.

JASON (*importantly*). You can't fool all the people all the time. (*He turns to go*) Watch the counter, will you, Gabby? I got to get dressed.

GRAMP. Dressed? For what?

JASON. Legion meeting.

GABBY. What time will you be home, Dad?

JASON. About ten, I guess—maybe later. There's a lot of important business coming up. (*He addresses* GRAMP, *with some defiance*) And I'm going to make some inquiries about those telegraph men. And if I can locate 'em, that Bolshevik will be out of a job and then he can go look for work pioneering in Russia.

GABBY. What'll you do—blow a bugle and turn the whole God-damn Legion loose on him?

JASON. Will you kindly control your language?

GABBY. I'll talk the only language I understand.

GRAMP. You'll never get Gabby to talk respectable. Never in all this world.

JASON. Well, I only hope some day my own daughter will learn to cultivate a little respect for the things I stand for. Maybe the time will come when you'll be thankful your father fought for his country. (*He goes out at the left.*)

GABBY (*going behind the counter*). What did that telegraph man say that got Dad in such a stew?

GRAMP. I don't know what he said—something about Russia and pioneering. But there's a lot in it, whatever it was. The trouble with this country is, it's got settled. It's camped down in the bed of a dried-up river, and whenever anybody says, "Let's get the hell out of here," all the rest start to holler, "If we move a step the Injuns'll get us." Well—say—if we'd been that way in my time, I'd like to know how this country'd ever have got rich enough to be able to support the American Legion. (*Two toots from an auto horn are heard*) Say! There's the mail.

(*With surprising alacrity,* GRAMP *jumps up and hurries out.* GABBY *has poured herself a cup of coffee and brought it down to the table at the left. She sits down, sips the coffee, opens her book, and reads. After a moment* BOZE *comes in, sees that she is alone, and closes the door behind him.* GABBY *looks up, sees who it is, indicates indifference, and resumes reading.* BOZE *comes up behind her, leans over and kisses the back of her neck. She brushes him off as though he were a fly.*)

GABBY (*without vehemence*). Cut it out.

(BOZE *grins, draws up a chair, and sits down close to her, his hefty forearms resting on the table.*)

BOZE. Not mad, are you, Gabby?

GABBY. Where's Gramp?

BOZE. He's out talking to the postman. Don't worry about him.

GABBY. I wasn't worrying.

BOZE. Don't you like me, honey sweet?

GABBY. No—not very much.

BOZE. O. K. I'll forgive you—seeing as I've been here only a little while and I haven't had much chance to go into my act. But when I do—you're going to change your attitude awful fast. (*She fails to comment on this threat. He is silent for a moment, his jaws confidently chewing on a small piece of gum*) What's that you're reading?

GABBY. You wouldn't like it.

BOZE. How do *you* know how I feel about things? Can I look?

GABBY. Sure. Go ahead and look. (*He takes the opened book and examines it.*)

BOZE. Hah—poems. (*He reads.*)

"The shapely slender shoulders small,
Long arms, hands wrought in glorious wise,

Round little breasts, the hips withal
High, full of flesh, not scant of size,
Fit for all amorous masteries . . ."

(*He whistles through his teeth*) Say! That's kind of pash! (*She snatches the book away from him*) So that's the kind of stuff you read. . . . Well, honey, I'm not a bit surprised. I've been suspecting all along that all you needed was a little encouragement. (*She looks at him, curiously, with a mixture of contempt and some slight interest*) And I don't wonder that in a God-forsaken place like this you'd have to get it out of poetry.

GABBY (*defensive*). It's great poetry!

BOZE. Certainly it's great. But I can think of something a whole lot better. . . . Look at me, honey. (*She looks at him*) I'm not so terrible looking, am I?

GABBY. Why do you wear that locket around your neck?

BOZE (*laughing*). Locket!

GABBY. It makes you look like a sissy.

BOZE. I've been waiting for you to notice that. That was my father's watch chain. My mother gave it to me when I graduated. I'd like you to know my mother. She lives in Grants Pass, Oregon, and she could tell you some pretty nice things about me. But wait till you see what's on the end. (*He draws the chain out and displays a gold football*) It's a gold football—solid gold! I got that for intercepting a pass and running sixty-eight yards for a touchdown.

GABBY. What was your school?

BOZE. Nevada Tech. If I'd been with Princeton or Minnesota or any of those big clubs, I'd have been All-American. Wait till I show you something. (*He produces a billfold from his hip pocket and extracts therefrom a frequently folded clipping*) That's from Sid Ziff's column in the *Los Angeles Herald*. He saw me play against Loyola. Listen to what he says: "Tip to the pigskin fraternity: When pondering your All-American selections for this current Anno Domini, just mull over the name of Boze Hertzlinger of Nevada Tech. Playing with an admittedly minor league club, and protected by interference of cellophane strength, Hertzlinger managed to remind some of us observers of the Illini Phantom himself." Do you know who the Illini Phantom was? Red Grange! (*He folds up the clipping and restores it to his pocket*) That's just a sample of the kind of notices I got. I could show you dozens more like it.

GABBY. You think a hell of a lot of yourself, don't you?

BOZE (*disarmingly*). Who wouldn't, in my position?

GABBY. Why do you have to work in a filling station?

BOZE. Well—that's a point that I don't know if I could explain so's you'd understand it. I could be making good money in a lot of ways right now—engineering, coaching, the insurance game—lots of ways. But—I just can't be tied down—not yet. I've got an itch inside here that keeps me on the move—chasing the rainbow.

GABBY. Do you ever expect to catch it?

BOZE. I'll catch it all right. I'll twist its tail, and make it do tricks. . . . Maybe I'm kind of close to it right now.

GABBY. You'd better look some place else. There aren't any rainbows around Black Mesa.

BOZE. I wouldn't bet on that. . . . You know, Gabby—you're a queer kid. Sometimes you seem too young to know anything. And then—sometimes—you seem like God's grandmother. And reading that pash poetry. That gives me an idea.

GABBY. An idea of what?

BOZE. Oh—it's easy to tell when a girl's ready for love.

GABBY. How do you tell that, Boze?

BOZE. Well—one pretty sure way is when she starts calling me by my own name for the first time. And another way is how I feel myself. It takes two to make a radio program, you know—the one that's sending, and the one that's receiving. And when I'm with a girl that's cute and appealing, with big, soft eyes—well—I can feel sort of electric waves running all through me—and I can be pretty sure she's doing some broadcasting, whether she knows it or not.

GABBY. Have you got a program coming in now?

BOZE. Listen— It's like the hottest torch song that ever was sung. Can't you kind of hear it, honey? (*She looks away from him, but says nothing. He reaches out and takes hold of her hand, entwining his fingers with hers*) You can call me a sap if you want to, Gabby—but I guess I'm falling in love with you. I'm getting so I want you more than is good for me.

GABBY (*looking at him, levelly*) Have you ever been in love before?

BOZE (*scornfully*). No!

GABBY. Have you ever *said* you were?

BOZE. Sure—plenty of times.

GABBY. Did they believe you?

BOZE (*amused*). Certainly they did. And I'll tell you why: it's because they were all dumb! But that's just where you're different. I couldn't fool you, Gabby.

GABBY. I'm smart, am I?

BOZE. Too smart—for most men. You'd catch on to 'em. But that's what I want. Because the more you see into me, the better you're going to like me. (*With his free hand, he takes hold of her chin.*)

GABBY. You'd better look out, if you want to hold on to your job. Dad might come in and he doesn't like to have the help making passes at me.

BOZE. That wouldn't bother me, honey sweet. There are plenty more jobs for anyone with the ambition I've got. But there aren't plenty more girls like you. (*He leans over and kisses her*) You're going to love me, Gabby. You're going to love me a lot.

GABBY. Look out! There's someone . . .

BOZE (*unconcerned*). We'll talk about it some more later.

(ALAN SQUIER *has appeared in the doorway, and, seeing that he has interrupted some amour, has paused to give them time to break. He is a thin, wan, vague man of about thirty-five. He wears a brown felt hat, brown tweed coat and gray flannel trousers —which came originally but much too long ago from the best Saville Row tailors. He is shabby and dusty but there is about him a sort of afterglow of elegance. There is something about him—and it is impossible in a stage direction to say just what it is —that brings to mind the ugly word "condemned." He carries a heavy walking stick and a rucksack is slung over his shoulders. He is diffident in manner, ultra-polite and soft spoken; his accent is that of an Anglicized American.*)

SQUIER. Good evening.

BOZE (*cordially*). Good evening! What can we do for you?

SQUIER. Can I order something to eat?

BOZE. Why, certainly. Miss Maple will take care of you. (*While* SQUIER *is taking off his rucksack and hat, and putting them on the bench at the right,* BOZE *turns to* GABBY *and speaks in a low tone*) Your father going into town?

GABBY. Yes. (*She is taking a menu card to the table at the center.*)

BOZE (*significantly*). O. K. (*He goes out.*)

GABBY. Will you sit down here, sir?

SQUIER. Thanks. (*He sits. She hands him the menu card.*)

GABBY. Driven far?

SQUIER. I've been walking.

GABBY. Do you live around here?

SQUIER. No. My last host of the road reached his own ranch, about ten miles back, and didn't ask me in. I had to continue on foot. It's wonderful what progress you can make just by doing this. (*He jerks his thumb and looks at the menu*) "Today's Special." . . . Just what is a Bar-B-Q?

GABBY. Well—here it's hamburger sandwich with vegetables on the side. It's always "Today's Special." But it's pretty good.

SQUIER. I want it. But first I'd like some of that cream of corn soup, and some beer, and—I'll order the dessert later.

GABBY. O. K. (*She takes the menu.*)

SQUIER. Another question. Where am I?

GABBY. This place is called Black Mesa, but there's nothing else here. Where were you planning to go?

SQUIER. My plans have been uncertain.

GABBY. You mean, you were just bumming along?

SQUIER. Call it gipsying. I had a vague idea that I'd like to see the Pacific Ocean, and perhaps drown in it. But that depends . . .

GABBY. Where did you come from?

SQUIER. Quite a long way, Miss Maple. Is that the name?

GABBY (*smiling*). Yes—that's it. Are you English?

SQUIER. No. You might call me an American once removed. . . . But—if you don't mind—

GABBY. The soup'll be right in. The washroom's through there, on your left, if you want it. (*She indicates the door at the left.*)

SQUIER Thank you.
(GABBY *goes out at the left.* SQUIER *rises. He sees the book of verse, picks it up and looks at it, wonderingly. The door at the left opens and* JASON *comes out, resplendent in the uniform of his Legion post. It is horizon blue, with white Sam Browne belt and pistol holster.* SQUIER *looks at* JASON *with amazement.*)

JASON. Good evening.

SQUIER. Good evening.

JASON. Anyone take your order?

SQUIER. Yes—a charming young lady. . . .

JASON. That's my daughter. (*He says this with a note of warning, as much as to add: "And don't try to get fresh."* JASON *crosses to the cash register, punches the "No Sale," and extracts five silver dollars from the till. He then reaches under the counter, takes out a revolver, breaks it to make sure it's loaded, and rubs it with a cloth.* SQUIER *has one more puzzled look at him, then goes out at the left.* GRAMP *comes in from the upper right, bearing a fresh copy of the Denver Post.*)

GRAMP (*at the end of the counter*). I was just talking to Roy Greeley and he says in town they're all certain that Mantee outfit is headed here. Look! They got the whole story here in The Post. Oklahoma City Massacre! Six killed—four wounded—two not expected to live. (JASON *glances at the paper*) The sheriff's got all his deputies out patrolling the roads. They think there's sure going to be some killing around here.

JASON. Well—if there is—we can't trust that sheriff to do a damn thing. We'll turn out the Legion.

GRAMP. You *would*?

JASON. Certainly! That's what we're there for. (*He thrusts the revolver in the holster of his Sam Browne belt, goes to the kitchen door, and calls through it: "Gabby!"*)

GABBY'S VOICE. Yes?

JASON. I'm leaving now. And I—I took five bucks. If anything delays me getting back, I'll phone.

GABBY'S VOICE. O. K.

JASON. Don't forget to light the Neon sign when it gets dark.

GABBY'S VOICE. I won't.
(*He shuts the kitchen door and crosses up front of the counter.*)

GRAMP. Well, by God, you'd better not try to do any shooting in that get-up. I never seed a better target.

JASON. You needn't be afraid about me.
(GABBY *comes in with the soup.*)

GRAMP. *I* ain't afraid. But I would be if I was you.

GABBY. How much did you say you took?

JASON. Five bucks.

GABBY. What do you need all that for?

JASON. Just in case of emergency. (*He decides to resent all this interference*) By God, between the two of you, you'd think I wasn't fit to be trusted with money or ideas or anything. But I'm here to tell you, both of you . . .

GABBY (*putting the soup on the table*). What, Dad?

JASON. Oh, never mind. (*He goes out.* GABBY *goes to the counter, opens a bottle of beer, and takes it to the centre table.*)

GRAMP (*while she is about this*). It's too bad they didn't wear a uniform like that when they fit the Germans. They wouldn't none of 'em have come home. . . . Who's that food for?

GABBY. Customer. He's in the washroom, I guess.

GRAMP. Is it that young feller that walked in with a little pack on his back? (*He goes to his rocking chair at the left.*)

GABBY. Yes—that's the one.

GRAMP. Looked to me like one of them things you see up around Taos. (*He sits down*) Hey, Gabby, how about letting your poor, weary old grandfather have a little drink now?

GABBY. No.

GRAMP. Aw—come on. I ain't got so long to live.

(SQUIER *comes in from the left.*)

GABBY. You can have one before you go to bed, and that's all. (*She goes out through the kitchen door.*)

GRAMP. Your soup's waiting for you, my friend.

SQUIER. Thank you.

GRAMP. Looks good, too.

SQUIER. Yes. It looks fine. (SQUIER *sits down and starts to eat, ravenously.* GRAMP *decides that the Denver Post will serve as a conversation opener. He crosses to* SQUIER'S *table.*)

GRAMP. Like to see a picture of that Duke Mantee? (*He holds out the newspaper.* SQUIER *looks at the clamorous headlines.*)

SQUIER. My God! Six killed. Did *he* do all that?

GRAMP. Him and his friends did, when they sprung him from the law. Fine lot of sheriffs they must have there in Oklahoma City—letting themselves get knocked over right out in front of the Court House.

SQUIER (*still eating*). He doesn't look very vicious, does he?

GRAMP (*sitting down*). Well—I'll tell you; you can't tell a killer from his picture, except by his chin. That's a funny thing about a killer—always holds his chin in. Ever notice that?

SQUIER (*buttering some bread*). I don't think I've ever seen a killer.

GRAMP. I have. Plenty of 'em. Ever hear of Billy the Kid?

SQUIER. Yes, indeed.

GRAMP. I knowed him well, down in the Pecos country. (*Proudly*) He took a couple of shots at me, once.

SQUIER. I congratulate you on still being with us.

GRAMP. Well—it was kind of dark, and he'd had a few—and, besides, I don't think he really meant to do me any real harm. Just wanted to scare the pants off of me.

SQUIER. Did he do it?

GRAMP. Naw—I seed he was just having some fun. So I said to him: "Kid—you're drunk!" And he said, "What makes you think that?" He was always soft-spoken. And I said: "Because you missed me!" Well, sir—he had to laugh. . . . You're kind of hongry, aren't you?

SQUIER. Yes. You can go just so long without food . . .

GRAMP. Been having some bad luck?

SQUIER. Yes.

GRAMPS Well—no disgrace in that these days. What line of work you in?

SQUIER. None, just now. I have been, at times, a writer.

GRAMP. A writer, eh? That's a funny thing. . . .

SQUIER (*laughing silently*). Yes—it is.

GRAMP. I knew the greatest writer that ever lived. Sam Clemens. Ever hear of him?

SQUIER (*trying hard to think*). Let me see . . .

GRAMP. Well, did you ever hear of Mark Twain?

SQUIER. Oh, *yes!*

GRAMP. Same feller!

SQUIER. Really?

(GABBY *comes in with "Today's Special," which she puts on the table.*)

GRAMP. Yes, sir. I knew him when I was a boy up in Virginia City. He was writing comical pieces for the paper there—The Enterprise—and he was the best God-damn liar I ever seed, and I've seed plenty. He used to say he did his writing on the principle that his readers wanted everything but the truth, so that's what he give 'em. (GABBY *is on the way out*) Are you a famous writer?

(*At the kitchen door,* GABBY *turns to look at* SQUIER, *then goes out.*)

SQUIER. No.

GRAMP. Maybe you're just modest. What's your name?

SQUIER. Alan Squier.

GRAMP. Well, maybe you are famous, for all I'd know. I don't get to do much reading, outside of the headlines. Eyes have gone back on me. But when I was your age, I could hit a running jack rabbit at fifty paces . . .

GABBY (*coming in*). Your supper's ready, Gramp.

GRAMP. And I'm ready for it. Got *me* hongry, watching him eat. (*He has risen*) Pleased to have met you, Mr. Squier.

SQUIER. Pleased to have met *you,* sir.

GRAMP. Yes, sir. Thank you, sir. (*He goes out.*)

GABBY. Like the soup?

SQUIER (*from the heart*). It was glorious!

GABBY. Want some coffee?

SQUIER. Will it mix with the beer?

GABBY. Oh, sure. Coffee will mix with anything. (*She goes to the counter to get his coffee.*)

SQUIER. That's a charming old gentleman. Your grandfather?

GABBY. Yes.

SQUIER. He told me he'd been missed by Billy the Kid.

GABBY. He tells everybody about that. Poor Gramp. You get terribly sick of him after a while. (*She has brought down the coffee*) Did I hear him say you're a writer?

SQUIER (*humbly*). Yes.

GABBY. I haven't met many writers —except Sidney Wenzell. Ever heard of him?

SQUIER. That's not Mark Twain, is it?

GABBY. No! Sidney Wenzell—he's with Warner Brothers. He stopped here once, when he was driving out to the Coast. He said I ought to go to Hollywood, and to be sure and look him up. But—what the hell! They never mean it.

SQUIER. No! They never mean a thing. (*She has picked up her book and started to go*) Please don't go. (*She pauses and turns.*)

GABBY. Something else you want? We got pie and layer cake.

SQUIER. No. I—I'd like to talk to you. Please sit down.

GABBY. All right. (*She sits down, across from him, at the center table.* SQUIER *eats rapidly, mechanically, during the subsequent dialogue, stowing the food away as he talks and listens.*)

SQUIER. I suppose you want to go into the movies?

GABBY (*scornfully*). God, *no!*

SQUIER. But—I thought every beautiful girl had her heart set on Hollywood.

GABBY. That's just it. It's too common. I want to go to Bourges. (*She fails to soften the "G."*)

SQUIER. Where?

GABBY. Bourges—in France. You'd never guess it, but that's where I came from.

SQUIER. You're not French?

GABBY. Partly. I was born in Bourges —but I left it almost before I was able to walk, so all I know about it is from the picture postcards my mother sends me. They got a cathedral there.

SQUIER. Your mother still lives there?

GABBY. Yes. Dad brought us back here after the war. Mother stuck it out in this desert for a couple of years, and then she packed up and went back to Bourges. We've never seen her since. Some people seem to think it was cruel of her to leave me. But what could she do? She didn't have any money to bring me up. She just couldn't *live* here—and you can't blame her for that. Do you think she was cruel?

SQUIER. Not if you don't, Miss Maple.

GABBY. Well—I *don't.* She's tried lots of times to get me over there to see her—but Dad won't allow it. She got a divorce and married a Frenchman that's got a bookstore. Mother was always a great reader, so I guess it's nice for her. She's got three more kids. Just think of that! I've got a half-brother and half-sisters that can't speak a word of English. I'd sure like to see them.

SQUIER. Can you speak French?

GABBY. Only what you learn in high school—like *table* for "table." (*She takes a photograph from the book*) Look—there's my mother's picture. That was just before she married Dad. She had her picture taken smelling a rose.

SQUIER. She's lovely! And I can see the resemblance.

GABBY. It's hard to imagine her being married to Dad, isn't it? But I guess he looked all right in his American uniform. Mother used to send me a book every year for my birthday, but they were all in French and I couldn't read them. So last year I wrote and asked if she'd mind sending me one in English, and she sent me this one. It's the Poems of François Villon. Ever read it?

SQUIER. Yes.

GABBY. It's wonderful poetry. She wrote in it: "*à ma chère petite Gabrielle.*" That means "To my dear little Gabrielle." She gave me that name. It's about the only French thing I've got.

SQUIER. Gabrielle. It's a beautiful name.

GABBY. Wouldn't you know it would get changed into "Gabby" by these ignorant bastards around here? I guess you think I use terrible language.

SQUIER. Oh, no! It—it's picturesque.

GABBY. Well—it suits this kind of country.

SQUIER. You share your mother's opinion of the desert? (*She nods*) But you can find solace in the Poems of François Villon.

GABBY. Yes. They get the stink of the gasoline and the hamburger out of my system.

SQUIER. Would you like to read me one of those poems, Gabrielle?

GABBY. You mean now?

SQUIER. Yes. While I'm finishing "Today's Special."

GABBY. O. K. I'll read you the one I like best. He wrote it about a friend of his who was getting married. (*She reads, with marked but inexpert emphasis*):

"At daybreak, when the falcon claps
his wings
No whit for grief, but noble heart
held high

With loud glad noise he stirs himself and springs,
And takes his meat and toward his lure draws nigh;
Such good I wish you! Yea, and heartily
I'm fired with hope of true love's meed to get;
Knowing Love writes it in his book; for why,
This is the end for which we twain are met."

Did you ever see a falcon?

SQUIER. Yes.

GABBY. What does it look like?

SQUIER. Not very pleasant. Like a hawk. Go on, Gabrielle.

GABBY (*resuming reading*).

"Mine own heart's lady with no gainsayings
You shall be always till I die;
And in my right against all bitter things
Sweet laurel with fresh rose its force shall try;
Seeing reason wills not that I cast love by
Nor here with reason shall I chide and fret

(*She closes the book and recites:*)

Nor cease to serve, but serve more constantly;
This is the end for which we twain are met."

(*She looks at him, and he at her. Then he resumes his attack on the hamburger*) You know—that's wonderful stuff. But that's the way the French people are: they can understand everything—like life, and love—and death—and they can enjoy it, or laugh at it, depending on how they feel.

SQUIER. And that's why you want to go to France—for understanding.

GABBY. I *will* go there! When Gramp dies, we can sell this place. Dad's going to take his share and move to Los Angeles, so that he can join a really big Legion post and get to be a political power. But I'm going to spend my part of the money on a trip to Bourges, where there's something beautiful to look at, and wine. and dancing in the streets.

SQUIER. If I were you—I'd stay here, Gabrielle, and avoid disappointment.

GABBY. What makes you think I'd be disappointed?

SQUIER. I've been to France.

GABBY. You were there in the war?

SQUIER. No, I missed that. But I lived there for eight years, through seventeen changes of government.

GABBY. What were you doing—writing books?

SQUIER. No—planning to write books. You know what a gigolo is?

GABBY. Were *you* one of those? (*He nods*) You danced with women for money?

SQUIER. Oh lord, no! I never was a good enough dancer for that. I—I married.

GABBY. Oh.

SQUIER. Please don't think too ill of me. I once actually wrote a book.

GABBY. What was it—fiction?

SQUIER. In a sense. It was a novel about the bleak, glacier-stripped hills of my native New England. I was twenty-two when I wrote it, and it was very, very stark. It sold slightly over six hundred copies. It cost the publisher quite a lot of money, and it also cost him his wife. You see, she divorced him and married me. She had faith in me, and she had the chance to display it, because her husband was very generous in the financial settlement. I suppose he had faith in me, too. She saw in me a major artist, profound, but inarticulate. She believed that all I needed was background, and she gave it to me—with southern exposure and a fine view of the Mediterranean. That was considered the thing to do in the period that followed Scott Fitzgerald. For eight years I reclined there, on the Riviera, on my background—and I waited for the major artist to step forth and say something of enduring importance. He preferred to remain inarticulate.

GABBY. And you've left your wife, now?

SQUIER. Yes.

GABBY. I'm glad you did.

SQUIER. I left her at her suggestion. She has taken up with a Brazilian painter—also a major artist. There was nothing for me to do but travel. I decided to go forth and discover America—and I've gone this far on my journey, thanks to the power of the thumb. (*He gestures with his thumb.*)

GABBY. What were you looking for?

SQUIER. Well—that's rather hard to say. I—I suppose I've been looking for something to believe in. I've been hoping to find something that's worth living for—and dying for.

GABBY. What have you found?

SQUIER. Nothing so interesting as an old man who was missed by Billy the Kid, and a fair young lady who reads Villon.

GABBY (*after a pause*). Well—I do other things that'd surprise you.

SQUIER. I'm sure you do.

GABBY. I wouldn't tell this to everybody—but you—well, you're kind of . . .

SQUIER. I'm kind of nobody. What is it, Gabrielle?

GABBY. I paint pictures.

SQUIER. Are they any good?

GABBY. Hell, *no!*

SQUIER. Could I see them?

GABBY. Oh—I never let people look at them. I'd only get kidded. They're kind of crazy pictures.

SQUIER. All the better. Please let me see them.

GABBY. You know anything about Art?

SQUIER. Oh—I've studied the whole cycle—right from El Greco through Burne Jones and back to El Greco again. Perhaps you're another genius. Perhaps it's my mission to introduce you to posterity.

GABBY. Are you kidding me?

SQUIER. No. Gabrielle. I've never kidded anybody outside of myself. (*The voice of* HERB, *a cowboy, is heard offstage.*)

GABBY. All right. But you've got to promise not to tell anybody.

SQUIER. My word of honor—for all it's worth.
(GABBY *goes out.*)

HERB'S VOICE. Sure, Boze. I know you've got all the inside dope. But I'll bet you four bits he flattens him inside of five rounds.

BOZE. Four bits to what?

HERB. No—I ain't giving you no odds.

BOZE. All *right*!

HERB. All *right*!
(HERB *has come in during this cheerful challenge. He wears a big black hat, gray shirt and blue overalls, and carries a gunnysack.*)

HERB (*genially, to* SQUIER). How de do.

SQUIER (*still eating*). Good evening.

HERB. Where's Gab?

SQUIER. She'll be back in a moment. (HERB *has crossed to the counter.*)

HERB. They sure give you a good meal here, don't they?

SQUIER. Superb!

HERB. Well—I'll tell you. Jason Maple's got a natural-born gift for hotel keeping, and by God I think Gabby's better at it than he is. The only trouble with 'em is, they ain't got a hotel. (*He has to laugh at that.*)

SQUIER. Yes—that does restrict the full play of their talents.
(GABBY *comes in with a sheaf of watercolor paintings of comparatively small size but of virulent color.*)

HERB. Hi, Gab.

GABBY. Hi, Herb.
(*Nervously she puts the pictures face down on the table by* SQUIER. *She cautions him with a look not to display them to* HERB. *But during the subsequent dialogue,* SQUIER *peeks at them with a certain amount of neck-stroking bewilderment.*)

HERB. Got any moon?

GABBY. Sure.

HERB. How much you asking for it?

GABBY. A dollar fifty a bottle.

HERB. *Holy* Cow! Well—give us a bottle, and half a dozen bottles of beer.

GABBY. You fellers going to get drunk to-night? (*She has gone to the counter to fill the order.*)

HERB (*leaning on the counter*). By God—that's the way it looks. Sheriff called up the old man and asked if we could be spared for patrolling the roads and the old man says sure and the sheriff says he'll come out and swear us in, but he ain't come yet, so we got a poker game started up the road a piece and thought we might as well have something to go along with it.

GABBY. There you are, Herb. That'll be two thirty.

HERB. All I got's two bucks. (*He tenders it*) Will you trust me for the thirty cents?

GABBY. I'll take back two bottles of beer. That'll make it even.

HERB (*as he dumps the bottles into the gunnysack*). Gosh—liquor sure is getting expensive these days. Well—I guess we got enough here seeing as there's only three of us.

GABBY. How you going to play poker if you haven't got any more money?

HERB. Oh, we got a book. So long, Gabby.

GABBY. So long, Herb. (*He goes out.* GABBY *rings up the $2.00 in the cash register and comes down. She is eager to know how* SQUIER *feels about her paintings, but she is trying desperately hard to be offhand about it*) They're terrible, aren't they?
(SQUIER *is now examining the pictures with rapt attention.*)

SQUIER. I—I don't know. Is—this a portrait of someone?

GABBY. That's Paula, our Mexican cook. She's the only one knows I ever try to do that junk. It isn't much of a likeness.

SQUIER. I'm sure it wasn't intended to be. (*He picks up another picture*) Certainly no critic could condemn you for being photographic.

GABBY. This is the one I like best. (SQUIER *looks at it*) I wanted to show how the storm clouds look when they roll down from the mountains.

SQUIER. What made you paint in this strange manner?

GABBY. It's—just the way I feel.

SQUIER. You're a product of the ultimate French school, all right.

GABBY (*pleased*). You think so?

SQUIER. These are somewhat in the Dufy manner—and yet—a lot less conventional.

GABBY. But are they any *good?*

SQUIER. I tell you, Gabrielle—I can't say. I'm tremendously impressed, and also, bewildered.

GABBY. I'll bet I could improve if I could get to France. You know, they've got some of the finest art schools in the world there. And they've got beautiful things to paint, too—flowers, and castles and rivers. But here in this desert—it's just the same thing over and over again.

SQUIER. Don't you realize—there are probably thousands of artists in France to-day who are saying, "I'd find a really big theme for my canvas if I could only get out to Arizona."

GABBY. I know. A lot of people come out here and go crazy about the desert. They say it's full of mystery, and it's haunted, and all that. Well—maybe it is. But there's something in me that makes me want something different.

SQUIER (*looking at her*). I know there's something in you. I wish I could figure out what it is.

GABBY. Listen—you've been in France. What are they like there?

SQUIER. Well—it's rather difficult to render a sweeping judgment.

GABBY. I've always imagined they must all be like Villon—gay, reckless, poetic.

SQUIER. No—I shouldn't call them any of those things. Especially, not reckless!

GABBY. But they're always having a good time, aren't they?

SQUIER. Not invariably.

GABBY. Maybe I know them better than you do, because it's in my blood. Sometimes I can feel as though I were sparkling all over, and I don't care what happens—I want to go out and do something that's absolutely crazy—and marvelous. But then the American part of me speaks up and spoils everything. It makes me go to work and figure out a lot of dull accounts; so many pounds of coffee, so many frankfurters, so many rolls. . . .

SQUIER. You keep the accounts correctly?

GABBY. If I didn't, this place would be bankrupt.

SQUIER. Then that's the French part of you. The sparkle must be 100% American. Would you like to marry a Frenchman?

GABBY. I don't want to marry anybody. I want to always be free!

SQUIER. How about that stalwart youth out there in the football jersey?

GABBY. What makes you think I'd take any notice of him?

SQUIER. Well—when I came in here . . .

GABBY. Oh, sure. He was kissing me. That's nothing.

SQUIER. Perhaps. But there's always the chance of development.

GABBY. He's trying to make me. That's all he wants.

SQUIER. Do you think he'll suceed?

GABBY. I haven't decided yet. It would be experience, and that's what I need. Do you think I ought to give in?

SQUIER. Don't ask me, Gabrielle. Let your French blood guide you. It's infallible, in matters like that.

GABBY. But you ought to know *something*. You've seen a lot, and you've written a book, and you've been married . . .

SQUIER. I don't know anything. You see—the trouble with me is, I belong to a vanishing race. I'm one of the intellectuals.

GABBY. That means you've got brains. I can see you have.

SQUIER. Yes—brains without purpose. Noise without sound. Shape without substance. Have you ever read The Hollow Men? (*She shakes her head*) Don't. It's discouraging, because it's true. It refers to the intellectuals, who thought they'd conquered Nature. They dammed it up, and used its waters to irrigate the wastelands. They built streamlined monstrosities to penetrate its resistance. They wrapped it up in cellophane and sold it to drugstores. They were so certain they had it subdued. And now—do you realize what it is that is causing world chaos?

GABBY. No.

SQUIER. Well, I'm probably the only living person who can tell you. . . . It's Nature hitting back. Not with the old weapons—floods, plagues, holocausts. We can neutralize them. She's fighting back with strange instruments called neuroses. She's deliberately afflicting mankind with the jitters. Nature is proving that she can't be beaten—not by the likes of us. She's taking the world away from the intellectuals and giving it back to the apes . . . Forgive me, Gabrielle . . . I can't tell you what a luxury it is to have some one to talk to. . . . But don't listen to me. I was born in 1901, the year Victoria died. I was just too late for the Great War—and too soon for the revolution. You're a war baby. You may be an entirely different species, for all I know. You can easily be one of Nature's own children, and therefore able to understand her, and laugh at her—or enjoy her—depending on how you feel. You're the only one who can say whether or not you should yield to the ardors of Number 42 out there. (*He finishes his glass of beer*) That beer is excellent.

GABBY. It's made in Phœnix. (*She is looking at him intently*) You know —you talk like a God-damn fool.

SQUIER. I know it. (*He is taking out the last of his cigarettes.*)

GABBY. No wonder your wife kicked you out. . . . And no wonder she fell for you in the first place.
(*He pauses in the act of lighting his cigarette.*)

SQUIRE. That sounds alarmingly like a compliment.

GABBY. It is a compliment. What did you say your name was?

SQUIER. Alan Squier. I've been calling you Gabrielle, so you'd better . . .

GABBY. Where are you going from here, Alan?

SQUIER. That depends on where this road leads.

GABBY. It leads to the petrified forest.

SQUIER. What's that?

GABBY. Oh—just a lot of dead old trees in the desert, that have turned to stone.

SQUIER. The petrified forest! A suitable haven for me. Perhaps that's what I'm destined for—to make an interesting fossil for future study. Homo Semi-Americanus—a specimen of the in-between age.

GABBY. I was just thinking—I'd like to go to France with you.
(*He looks at her, sharply—then looks sharply away.*)

SQUIER. Oh, no, Gabrielle! I could never retrace my footsteps.

GABBY. You mean you haven't enough money?

SQUIER. Even that is an understatement.

GABBY. I haven't enough, either—yet. But I can do this as well as you can. (*She gestures with her thumb.*)

SQUIER. We'd reach a point, on the Atlantic Coast, where even that gesture would be unavailing.

GABBY. You know, Alan—there's something about you that's very appealing.

SQUIER. Appealing! Yes—that's been my downfall. It was that very quality which led me into the gigolo trade.

GABBY. Why wouldn't you like to be a gigolo for me?

SQUIER. For one very good reason: you couldn't afford it.

GABBY. But I *will* be able to afford it.

SQUIER. On your share of this property? (*He shakes his head.*)

GABBY. Listen—I've got more than that coming to me. Do you know how much Gramp has got salted away in the bank in Santa Fé? Twenty-two thousand dollars! He had every cent of it in gold and silver in the safety vaults. Why—we didn't even know about it until the government passed a law against hoarding and they printed his name in the papers. It's in Liberty Bonds now, and it's all willed to me. I guess we could travel pretty far on that, couldn't we?

SQUIER. Too far.

GABBY. We could go to France, and you'd show me everything, all the cathedrals and the art—and explain everything. And you wouldn't have to marry me, Alan. We'd just live in sin and have one hell of a time.

SQUIER. That's a startling proposal, Gabrielle. I hadn't expected to receive anything like that in *this* desert.

GABBY. We'd have to wait—maybe years. But I could have Boze fired and give you the job tending the gas station.

SQUIER. You think you'd like to have me for a companion?

GABBY. I know I would. And I don't make mistakes. You're no ape-man, Alan—but you're lovable.

SQUIER. Lovable! The next grade below appealing.

GABBY. Wouldn't you like to be loved by me?

SQUIER (*looking at her intently*). Yes, Gabrielle . . . I should like to be loved by you.

GABBY. You think I'm attractive?

SQUIER. There are better words than that for what you are.

GABBY. Then why don't we at least make a start at it? You haven't got anything else to do.

SQUIER (*smiling*). No—that's just it. You couldn't live very long with a man who had nothing else to do but worship you. That's a dull kind of love, Gabrielle. It's the kind of love that makes people old, too soon. (*He rises*) But—I thank you for the suggestion. You've opened up a new channel of my imagination which will be pleasant to explore during my lonely wanderings. I'll think of the chimes of Bourges—and you—and sin.

GABBY. You're going now?

SQUIER. Yes. And I shall continue going until either I drop or that major artist emerges to announce his message to posterity.

GABBY (*rising*). Well—I can't stop you.

SQUIER. No, Gabrielle, you can't. But you can do me one great favor, before I go. . . . Would you mind very much if I kissed you good-bye? (GABBY *looks at him levelly.*)

GABBY. No. I wouldn't mind.

SQUIER. You'd understand that it would be nothing more . . .

GABBY. I'd understand. It'd be just a kiss—that's all.

SQUIER. That's absolutely all. (*He kisses her.* BOZE *is seen through the glass of the doorway. He bursts the door open.*)

BOZE. Ah-hah! So that's what's been going on in here! Necking, huh! (*He strides up to* SQUIER *and seizes him by the shoulder*) Who the hell are you?

GABBY. Lay off him, Boze. (*She has seized her paintings.*)

BOZE. Just because she's cute and sweet you thought you could get fresh, huh!

GABBY. He didn't get fresh! He only wanted to kiss me good-bye.

SQUIER. Yes—the impulse is rather hard to explain—but I . . .

BOZE. You needn't wait to explain it. Pay your check and get out.

SQUIER. Very well. How much do I owe, Miss Maple?

GABBY. Thirty cents.

BOZE. Is that all he ate? (*He looks down at the table at the remains of* SQUIER'S *meal.*)

GABBY. Yes! Shut up!

SQUIER. Thirty cents, eh. Very reasonable. Very reasonable indeed! But —that brings us to another embarrassment. I—I haven't got thirty cents. I haven't anything.

BOZE. Well—by God—I didn't expect to find such nerve in anybody that looked like you. What are you going to do about it?

SQUIER. I haven't the remotest . . .

BOZE. What have you got in your pack there?

SQUIER. Shirt, underwear, socks, toothbrush, passport, an insurance policy, and a copy of Modern Man in Search of a Soul, by Dr. Jung.

BOZE. You thought you could pay with a kiss, did you? (*He seizes* SQUIER *again. A car is heard stopping*) Thought if you brought a little romance into her poor, starved life the check'd be forgotten, did you?

GABBY. Take your hands off him, Boze. Go on, Alan, beat it!

SQUIER. I'll go.

BOZE. I'll just give you a little head start. (*He has* SQUIER *by the collar and is about to propel him out the door, when* MR. *and* MRS. CHISHOLM *come in.* MR. CHISHOLM *is about forty-five—thin, dry, sharp, persnickety, with pince-nez eyeglasses.* MRS. CHISHOLM *is about ten years younger—rather attractive, rather chic, very world-weary. The* CHISHOLMS *belong to the topmost layer of society in Dayton, Ohio.*)

MRS. CHISHOLM (*in an undertone to* GABBY). Where is the Ladies' Room, please?

GABBY. This way, madam. (*She directs* MRS. CHISHOLM *to the door at the left and points off*) That door there, on your left.

MRS. CHISHOLM. Thank you.
(JOSEPH, *the* CHISHOLMS' *Negro chauffeur, appears in the doorway. He is short, elegant, wears a neat uniform and yellow glasses.*)

JOSEPH. We want fifteen gallons and a quart of oil.

BOZE. Be right with you. (*In an undertone to* SQUIER) You ready to leave?

SQUIER. Just a moment—my rucksack.

GABBY. Get on the job, Boze. (*She goes up to the lunch counter and hides her paintings.* BOZE *mutters something unpleasant to* SQUIER *and goes out.* SQUIER *is putting on his rucksack.*)

CHISHOLM. What kind of cigars have you?

GABBY. Admiration, White Owl, and Texas Dandies.

CHISHOLM. How much are the Texas Dandies?

GABBY. Three for a dime.

CHISHOLM. Let me have an Admiration.

GABBY (*offering him the box*). Come far?

CHISHOLM (*selecting one*). Yes. We've driven from Dayton, Ohio. We're on our way out to Santa Barbara for the winter. (*As he pays for the cigar*) We lost a great deal of time today as I wanted Mrs. Chisholm to see the Gila cliff dwellings. She was rather disappointed. How far is it to the Phœnix Biltmore?

GABBY. It's a good two hundred miles from here. (*She hands him his change.*)

CHISHOLM (*consulting his watch*). I imagine we can make it by midnight.

GABBY. You'll have to step. What kind of car you driving?

CHISHOLM (*lighting the cigar*). Duesenberg.

SQUIER. Good-bye, Miss Maple.

GABBY. Just a minute, Alan. (*She turns again to* CHISHOLM) Excuse me, sir.

CHISHOLM. What?

GABBY. Would you have room in your car for another party?
(SQUIER *signals to her not to bother.*)

CHISHOLM (*suspicious*). Who is it?

GABBY. This friend of mine, Mr. Squier. He's on his way to the coast and he—he hasn't got a car just now. He's an author.

CHISHOLM (*to* SQUIER). Have you any luggage?

SQUIER. Just this, sir—on my back.
(CHISHOLM *looks him over, goes to the open door, and calls "Joseph."*)

CHISHOLM. Where'd you come from?

SQUIER. From Saint Tropez. That's on the Riviera.
(JOSEPH *comes in.*)

CHISHOLM. I know where it is. Do you think it's all right to give this man a lift to Phœnix?
(JOSEPH *subjects* SQUIER *to extremely critical inspection.*)

SQUIER. You've been there?

CHISHOLM. Yes . . .
(JOSEPH *taps* SQUIER *all over for concealed weapons.*)

SQUIER. It's a lovely spot, Saint Tropez.

CHISHOLM (*without enthusiasm*). Yes.

JOSEPH. I guess he's all right, Mr. Chisholm.

CHISHOLM. Very well. (JOSEPH *touches his cap and goes out*) Glad to have you with us.

SQUIER. Thank you very much, Mr. Chisholm. (GABBY *punches the "No Sale" key and takes out a silver dollar.* SQUIER *crosses to her*) And thank you, Miss Maple. I'll remember your kindness.

GABBY. I forgot to give you your change. (*She offers him the dollar.*)

SQUIER. Oh, no—I wanted you to keep that.

GABBY (*pointing to a sign*). Tipping is un-American and we don't allow it. Here—take it.

SQUIER. I—I can't very well pretend that I don't need . . .

GABBY. Perhaps Mr. Chisholm will take you all the way to the coast. When you get there, send me a post-card, with a view of the Pacific Ocean. I like pictures of the sea. (*She has forced the coin into his hand . . .* MRS. CHISHOLM *emerges.*)

CHISHOLM. This is Mr.—er—

GABBY. Mr. Squier.

CHISHOLM. Mr. Squier, darling. We're giving him a lift as far as the Phœnix Biltmore. (MRS. CHISHOLM *frowns*) It's all right; Joseph went over him.

SQUIER. How do you do, Mrs. Chisholm?

MRS. CHISHOLM. How do you do? Are we ready to start? (*She crosses toward the door.*)

CHISHOLM. Just been waiting for you. Come along, Mr. Squier.
(*The* CHISHOLMS *have gone out.*)

SQUIER. I suppose I'll never see you again.

GABBY. No. That's the way it is in a gas station. They come and they go.

SQUIER. But, somehow, or other, I'll repay that dollar. God knows when.

GABBY. Perhaps we'll run into each other some day in Bourges.
(*The horn of the Duesenberg is heard summoning, shrilly.*)

SQUIER. Good-bye, Gabrielle.

GABBY (*shaking hands*). Good-bye, Alan. (*He goes out. After a moment, she comes down and picks up the Poems of François Villon. The car is heard starting and charging off into the night.* GABBY *suddenly remembers the Neon sign, goes to a switch by the door and turns it on.* BOZE *comes in.*)

BOZE. Well—I took pity on that poor panhandler. I slipped him a dime.

GABBY. You *did?*

BOZE. I tried to—but he wouldn't take it. He said, "I don't deserve your kindness," and handed it back. It's a funny thing about a guy like that: he'll hold you up for a meal and think nothing of it. But when it comes to taking money, they suddenly discover they've got some pride.

GABBY. I appreciate that very much, Boze.

BOZE. Appreciate what, honey?

GABBY. Your wanting to help him. That was very kind.

BOZE. Why, say—you talk as if you were nuts about him.

GABBY. I'm not nuts about him. But now and then you see somebody that's just a natural object of charity.

BOZE (*pleased*). Well! If you appreciate it so much—how about being a little nice to me for a change? (*He goes to her and takes hold of her arms.*)

GABBY. I'd like to be nice to you . . . I'd like to be nice to everybody.

BOZE. You can be, Gabby. Listen—how about us taking a little walk around the Mesa? It's warm out and the moon's just coming up. How about it, sweetheart?

GABBY. But supposing a car came along wanting something?

BOZE. You know there's practically no traffic at this time of night.

GABBY. But suppose someone *did* come . . .

BOZE. Well—what if they did? In a pinch, the old man and that Mexican woman could take care of 'em. And you know how your grandfather is—he'd never notice anything peculiar about us being out for a while. . . . (*He goes after her*) Listen, honey sweet. You've got to grow up sometime. And before you can grow up, you've got to stop being afraid.

GABBY. I'm not afraid!

BOZE. Oh, yes, you are. You think I'm something terrible and you've got to keep away from me. But I'm not so bad, Gabby. I'm just a big guy with a good heart and plenty of hot blood. And I'm full of love, honey. (*He takes her in his arms*) And so are you. You don't know it yet—but you are. And when we get out there in the moonlight, you'll be glad I suggested it. Honestly you will, honey sweet. (*He kisses her lips passionately. After a moment, she struggles a little. He relaxes his hold on her. He is confident of progress*) All right—I'm not holding you against your will. I'm not trying to force you into anything that's wrong.

GABBY. I didn't say you were.

BOZE (*follows her*). It *isn't* wrong—except in the minds of old cranks that have forgotten how to love—if they ever knew. My God! It's the most natural thing in the world, for two people, like us, that are young, and clean, and . . . Why, it'd be wrong if we *didn't* take the chance when we've got it.

GABBY. Do you know what he said?

BOZE. What who said?

GABBY. He said we'd been trying to fight Nature, and we thought we'd licked it, because we've built a lot of dams, and cellophane and things like that. But that's where we're wrong, and that's what's the matter with the world. We've got to admit that Nature can't be beaten!

BOZE. Well—isn't that exactly what I've been trying to tell you all along?

GABBY. I guess it is, Boze. (*He takes her in his arms again.*)

BOZE. You're coming with me, aren't you, sweetheart? You're going to find out things about Nature more wonderful and exciting than anything you ever dreamed of. Aren't you, honey sweet?

GABBY. Oh, well—what the hell! I'll go out with you, Boze. (*He kisses her*) We'd better go now.

BOZE. Yes, Gabby. Oh, God—you're a beautiful kid! (*He kisses her again, passionately. A car is heard stopping. They break apart, quickly*) I'll get rid of 'em fast. (*He starts toward the door, but stops short when it opens and* JACKIE *appears. He is a short, chubby, cherubic gangster. He carries a sub-machine gun and wears a cheery smile.*)

JACKIE. Now—just behave yourselves, folks, and nobody'll get hurt. Who's the boss here?

BOZE. He's out.

JACKIE. Got any guns with you? (*He searches* BOZE *with practiced speed.*)

BOZE. No. (*He and* GABBY *have been retreating into the room as* JACKIE *has advanced. Following* JACKIE *has come* RUBY, *thin, sallow, adenoidal —and after him has come* DUKE MANTEE—*well-built but stoop-shouldered, with a vaguely thoughtful, saturnine face. He is about thirty-five and, if he hadn't elected to take up banditry, might have been a fine leftfielder. There is, about him, one quality of resemblance to* ALAN SQUIER: *he too is unmistakably condemned. He is hatless and unshaven and wears an ill-fitting suit with a gray prison shirt.* MANTEE *carries no visible arms, but* RUBY *has another machine-gun and a sawed-off shotgun.*)

JACKIE. This is Duke Mantee, folks. He's the world-famous killer and he's hungry.
(*The* DUKE *looks around.*)

DUKE. What's in there and in there? (*He speaks quietly, even gently, with an effortless ferocity.*)

GABBY. That's the kitchen, and in there's our bedrooms.

DUKE. You two married?

GABBY. No. He just works here.

JACKIE. Anybody else in?

BOZE. Only one old man and . . .

GABBY. My grandfather's in there and the cook. There's nobody in there.

DUKE. Bring 'em in, Jackie.

JACKIE. O. K., Duke. (*He goes out at the upper left.* DUKE *goes to the front door and calls out.*)

DUKE. Hey, Pyles. (PYLES' *voice is heard to reply: "Yeah, boss"*) Back that car into the shadow and stay with it.

PYLES' VOICE. Do I get to eat?

DUKE. You'll eat. (*The* DUKE *goes to the table, downstage right, and takes his coat off, revealing a harness over his waistcoat with two revolvers in holsters under either arm-pit. He folds his coat neatly and lays it on the bench, then turns to* RUBY) Hey, Ruby—pull that table over here.
(RUBY *moves the table to the right as directed.* BOZE *lowers his hands.*)

DUKE. Keep 'em up. (*The hands go up promptly.* RUBY *picks up his machine-gun*) Take a look around in there.

RUBY. How long do we stay here?

DUKE. Until they get here.

RUBY. You're going to wait for that blonde?

DUKE. Get out!

RUBY. O. K. (*He goes out at the lower left.*)

DUKE. You sit down there. (BOZE *sits down as directed at the center table*) What have you got to eat, sister? (GABBY *produces the menu card. The* DUKE *addresses* BOZE) Football player, eh?

BOZE. Yes. And you better not let me get close enough to take a sock at you.

DUKE (*unconcerned*). I used to be quite a fan. What's your school?

BOZE. Nevada Tech.

DUKE. Never heard of it.
(GRAMP *and* PAULA *the cook come in from the kitchen, followed by* JACKIE.)

PAULA. Don't shoot me, mister. Don't kill me, mister. In the name of the Holy Mother of God, don't kill me, mister.
(JACKIE *prods her with the machine-gun. She screams lustily.*)

JACKIE. Quiet, Pepita—quiet. We aren't going to do you any harm. (*In a ludicrously soothing voice*) All we're going to do is ask you to cook something. You wouldn't mind that, would you, Pepita?

PAULA. No, mister. I swear to God, I cook anything. You just tell me . . .

JACKIE. All right, Pepita. We got that settled.

GRAMP (*staring admiringly at* DUKE). So you're Mantee, are you? You're the killer!

DUKE. Would you mind sitting down over there, Pop? Take a look around that counter, Jackie.
(GRAMP *sits down at the left.* JACKIE *searches the counter.*)

JACKIE. Yes, Pop. That's the greatest killer alive today. Did you hear what happened in Oklahoma City? (*The* DUKE *inspects the menu.*)

GRAMP. Yes—I heard. You pulled off a massacre.

JACKIE. Who said it was a massacre? (*He comes down from the counter.*)

GRAMP. The Denver Post. (*He holds up the paper.*)

JACKIE (*snatching it*). Let me see it!

DUKE. Put that paper down! (JACKIE *drops the paper.*)

JACKIE. Did it say how many we killed?

GRAMP. Six killed and four wounded.

JACKIE. Did you hear that, Duke? We killed six and wounded four. (*He returns to the counter to empty the cash register.*)

DUKE (*to* GABBY). Got any steak?

GABBY. Only hamburger.

PAULA. And we got chicken, mister.

GRAMP. Two of the wounded's not expected to live.

DUKE. All right. Cook the chicken and four hamburgers. And plenty of onions.

JACKIE. Boy! That was some massacre!

GABBY. Anything else? (RUBY *comes in from the lower left.*)

RUBY. Nobody in there, boss. There's a good window at the end of the hall with a four-foot drop to the ground, right by where the car is.

DUKE. Take a look around outside. Tell Pyles not to hit that horn unless somebody comes up that really looks like trouble, and then to hit it plenty. (RUBY *goes out*) Bring us beer for the bunch, sister. (*He addresses* BOZE *and* GRAMP) You fellers like to join us?

BOZE. I never touch it.

GRAMP. I guess I'll have whiskey.

GABBY (*to* GRAMP). No, none for you, Gramp.

GRAMP (*disconsolate*). She says I can't have even a little one.

DUKE. Let him have it, sister.

JACKIE. Sure! He can only be young once.

PAULA. Can I begin cooking now, mister?

DUKE. Yeh. Go with her, Jackie. (RUBY *returns.*)

JACKIE. Come on, Pepita. And while the chicken's in the oven, you and me'll have a little fun, eh, kid? (*They go out into the kitchen.*)

DUKE. Hey, Ruby. Sit down there. (RUBY *sits down between the counter and the front door*) And keep that gun in your lap.

(RUBY *obeys, and from now on his eyes ceaselessly patrol the area from the front door to the kitchen door. The* DUKE *crosses with a convict's gait and goes out at the left.* GABBY *is behind the counter getting out the beer.* GRAMP *rises and starts to cross to his rocking chair.)*

RUBY. Sit down!

GRAMP (*sitting down hastily*). You needn't think I'm scared of you. I've known *real* killers in my time. And they knew how to make a six-shooter act like a machine-gun. Did you ever hear of fanning?

RUBY. No.

GRAMP. Well—you'd file down the trigger catch so that the hammer worked free, and then you'd fan it like this. (*He points his forefinger at* RUBY *and wiggles his thumb*) Wild Bill Hickock once knocked over five men that way. They was lined up at a bar and . . .
(SQUIER *comes in, hatless and breathless.* GABBY *is in the center of the stage, with the tray of bottles and glasses of beer.*)

GABBY. Alan! What did you come back for?

SQUIER (*panting*). There are some bandits around here.

BOZE. Yes. So we heard.

SQUIER. They cut in ahead of us about a mile down the road, and made us stop and get out, and then they got into Mr. Chisholm's car and drove off. They said we could take their car, but they'd left it locked. They were terrible-looking cut-throats, with a lot of guns and ammunition. (*He addresses* BOZE) Could you come with me back there and see if you can unlock that . . .
(*The* DUKE *comes in from the left.*)

GABBY. Look out, Alan!
(SQUIER *turns and sees the* DUKE. *Then he looks around and sees* RUBY *who has raised his machine-gun.*)

SQUIER (*lamely*). Oh—so we—meet again.

DUKE. Sit down, pal. Down there.

SQUIER. Why, thanks, I'd be delighted to.

DUKE. Wait a minute. (*He takes the rucksack from* SQUIER, *who then sits down opposite* BOZE *at the center table.*)

GRAMP (*proudly*). That's Duke Mantee. We were looking at his picture. Remember?

SQUIER. Yes—I remember.
(*The* DUKE *goes to the extreme right and sits down, his back to the wall.*)

DUKE. Join us in a glass of beer?

SQUIER. Why—thank you—but might I have some whiskey, instead?

DUKE. Certainly. Give him a drink, sister. And how about turning on the radio?
(GABBY *puts the bottle and a glass before* SQUIER. *He pours himself a stiff one.*)

GRAMP. What did I tell you? Look at that chin. He's a killer, all right!

BOZE. He's a gangster and a rat!

SQUIER. Sh!

GRAMP. *He* ain't a gangster! He's a real old-time desperado. Gangsters is foreigners. He's an American! And if the sheriffs find out he's here, we'll see some real killing—*won't* we?

(GABBY *turns on the radio. Soft, sticky music emerges.*)

DUKE. The cops ain't likely to catch up with us—not tonight. So we can all be quiet and peaceable, and have a few beers together, and listen to the music—and not make any wrong moves. Because—I may as well tell you, folks—old Ruby there, with the machine-gun—he's pretty nervous and jumpy and he's got the itch between his fingers. So let's everybody stay where they are.

SQUIER. Let there be killing! All evening long, I've had a feeling of Destiny closing in. (*To the* DUKE) Do you believe in astrology?

DUKE. I couldn't say, pal.

SQUIER. I don't—normally. But just now, as I was walking along that road, I began to feel the enchantment of this desert. I looked up at the sky and the stars seemed to be reproving me, mocking me. They were pointing the way to that gleaming sign, and saying, "There's the end of your tether! You thought you could escape it, and skip off to the Phœnix Biltmore. But we know better." That's what the stars told me, and perhaps they know that carnage is imminent, and that I'm due to be among the fallen. . . . It's a fascinating thought.

DUKE. Let's skip it. (*He lifts his glass*) Here's happy days.

GRAMP. Yes, *sir*—it sure is pleasant to have a killer around here again.

SQUIER. Yes. It's pleasant to be back again—among the living. (*He raises his glass*) Hooray! (*He drinks.*)

CURTAIN

ACT TWO

About half an hour has elapsed since the end of Act I.

DUKE *and* JACKIE *are finishing their meal at the right table.* RUBY *is sitting on a stool at the counter, drinking coffee, watching everything.* GRAMP *and* PAULA *are sitting at the table at the left.* BOZE *and* SQUIER *are at the center. The radio is murmuring faintly.*

GABBY *alone is permitted to move about—removing dishes, refilling coffee cups.*

GRAMP. That old Andy Anderson I was telling you about, he was a great character. He didn't kill for business reasons, like you fellers. He killed just for the fun of it. He was born somewheres up in Nova Scotia and come down to the State of Maine so's he could get into the Civil War and he fit all through it. And he never stopped talking about it as long as he lived. He always said that was a regular paradise for killing. He'd stick a Johnny Reb with his bayonet, throw him over his shoulder and then stick another. And he always said that the beauty of it was there was no sheriffs around to reprove him for it.

JACKIE. Say, Pop—I wish you wouldn't talk so much about blood while we're eating.

BOZE. Got it on your conscience, eh?

JACKIE. On my *what?*

BOZE. Yes—I thought so. A punk like you hasn't got any more conscience than a coyote.

JACKIE. Hmm! Listen to the halfback. How much did *you* get for playing on the team?

BOZE. I worked my way through college!

JACKIE. What were you doing? Peddling subscriptions to The American Boy?

BOZE. I worked for three whole years in the Student Laundry.

JACKIE. Oh—how *nice!* (*He lifts his coffee cup.*)

BOZE. Wait a minute—smart guy. I got something to show you. (*He reaches for his wallet.*)

RUBY. Keep your hand off your hip!

BOZE. I was only going to show him a newspaper clipping that said I ought to be All-America. . . . I scared you, did I? I know it. You're all yellow.

(*A none too pleasant expression appears in* JACKIE'*s eyes over the rim of his coffee cup.*)

SQUIER. I'd be a little tactful, Boze. Remember—they're your guests.
(GABBY *has sat down at the center table between* SQUIER *and* BOZE.)

BOZE. They're a bunch of yellow dogs. That's what made 'em turn crooked in the first place.

SQUIER. No—no. Cowardice isn't the cause of crime. It has something to do with glands.

BOZE. They just haven't got the guts to face the bigger problems of life. They've got to fight their way with guns instead of with *principles.*
(SQUIER *is by now slightly tight and is to become more so, by imperceptible degrees, as the Act proceeds.* JACKIE *sets down his coffee cup with ominous deliberateness and rises. picking up a sawed-off shotgun.*)

JACKIE. Step over to that side of the room, halfback.

GRAMP. You're going to kill him?

BOZE (*scared*). It's just what I said . . .

JACKIE. Come on. This shotgun scatters, and you wouldn't want me to hurt that cute dame, would you?
(*The dulcet chimes of the radio are heard.* BOZE *slowly rises.*)

SQUIER (*to* JACKIE). You know—you're taking this much too seriously.
(*The radio announcer's voice can be heard introducing the nightly news broadcast.*)

BOZE. I'm not afraid to die. (*But his voice is strained.*)

JACKIE. Come on! Move!

DUKE. Step up that radio—will you, sister? (*To* JACKIE) Sit down, Jackie Cooper.

JACKIE. Did you hear what he . . . ?

DUKE (*grinning*). Sit down! (*To* BOZE) You too.
(*They both sit down.* GABBY *has turned up the volume control dial.*)

RADIO VOICE (*very brisk*). . . . all anxious first off to hear latest bulletins concerning the greatest manhunt in human history. A monster dragnet has been cast over the entire southwest from St. Louis to the Pacific Coast. National Guardsmen are co-operating with state police and the famed Texas Rangers as well as countless local posses and Legion posts in a determined effort to apprehend the members of the notorious Mantee gang—to bring to justice this fierce, colorful band of murderers, kidnappers, bank-robbers, perpetrators of the shocking massacre in Oklahoma City. . . .

JACKIE. Take a bow, Duke.

RADIO VOICE. The gang made its escape in two cars, one of which contained Mantee and three other men, the other car containing three men and *one woman*. The Mantee car was seen early this morning at Tularosa and later at Hillsboro in New Mexico. The second car was positively identified at Estelline in the Texas Panhandle when it stopped at the local police station, held it up, and departed with a large supply of guns and ammunition.

JACKIE. Nice going, boys! I don't see how they did it with Doris along to . . .

DUKE. Shut up!

RADIO VOICE. Both cars are undoubtedly headed for the border, but it is considered certain they haven't reached it, due to the number and vigilance of the patrols. War-time conditions prevail on all the roads of Western Texas, New Mexico and Arizona and you know how the officers of the law are in this red-blooded frontier region: they shoot first and ask questions afterward.
(JACKIE *indicates his scorn, but* DUKE *withers him with a look.*)

RADIO VOICE. The Governor of Arizona has issued the following statement: "As long as Mantee and his followers are at large a blot of shame will mar the proud scutcheon of these United States. Any citizen who knowingly gives aid or comfort to these public enemies is a traitor to his country and will be answerable before the great bar of public opinion." . . . I'll now give you the scores of the leading football games of the day. Carnegie Tech—13, Miami—7; Washington State—19 . . .

DUKE. Turn it off, sister.

RADIO VOICE. U. S. C.—0; Navy—21, Virginia—6 . . .
(GABBY *switches off the radio.*)

JACKIE (*to* PAULA). Did you hear that, Pepita? You're a traitor for cooking for us. They'll string you up for that—if they can find a tree around here.

PAULA. The Holy Mother of God knows they put a gun in my stomach and said *you cook* . . .

JACKIE. Sure—*she* knows. But that don't count with the Governor. We're Public Enemies.

DUKE (*to* RUBY). Go on out to the car, Ruby, and tell Pyles to come in and get his supper. And tell him to bring in that sack of ammunition and the road map. And you stay there and keep awake.

RUBY. Yeah. O. K. (*He goes out.*)

GRAMP. Are you going to make a run for the Border, boys?

JACKIE. Oh, sure! We'll give you our whole route before we leave, so's you can tell the hick cops and have 'em give us a motorcycle escort.

SQUIER. I think I'm about ready for another whiskey, Gabrielle, if I may. (GABBY *goes behind the counter and brings forth a quart bottle and a bottle of drinking water, which she places on the table.*)

BOZE. Listen, Panhandler! Who told you you could call her by her first name?

SQUIER. Now, please, Boze—you and I must be friends, as long as they'll let us.

JACKIE. Why don't you take a sock at *him,* halfback? He hasn't got a gun.
(PYLES *comes in. He is a lean, lithe Negro, who carries a machine-gun and a bulging gunny sack.*)

PYLES. Hi, everybody! 'Bout time you got around to asking me in. Here's your map, boss. (*He puts the sack full of ammunition down on a bench at the back, and tosses the map down on the table before* DUKE) Lord, God! Look what you done to that chicken!

DUKE (*to* PAULA). Cook him some hamburger, sister.

PAULA. All right, mister. (*She rises*) But you people better tell that mister Governor I didn't . . .

DUKE. Go with her, Pyles.

PYLES. O. K., boss. I guess I don't get to eat with the white folks. (*He picks up the carcass of the chicken and starts to gnaw it as he crosses to the kitchen.*)

DUKE. Look around in there and see if you can find any rope.

PYLES. O. K., boss. (*He turns quickly to the* DUKE) When we going to lam out of here?

DUKE. When it's time.

JACKIE. Sure—as soon as the Duke connects with that heavy date. (*He winks broadly at* PYLES.)

PYLES (*as he goes*). Well—I don't like that dame stuff. I like to get out of range. (*He has gone out at the left after* PAULA.)
(*The* DUKE *has opened the Road Atlas to Arizona and New Mexico, and from now on he and* JACKIE *are studying it and murmuring to each other in inaudible tones.*)

GRAMP. How about passing that bottle over this way?

SQUIER. Why, certainly. Forgive me. . . . (*He is reaching for the bottle, but* GABBY *stops him.*)

GABBY. No! (*To* GRAMP) You've had all you're going to get.

SQUIER (*to* GRAMP). I'm very sorry.

GRAMP. Oh—that's all right. (*He reaches in his pocket for his pipe.*)

JACKIE. What are you doing?

GRAMP. Going to smoke my pipe.

DUKE. Go ahead, Pop.
(GRAMP *takes out the pipe, fills it with great care, lights it, and lapses into silence as he sits in his rocking chair.*)

BOZE. How long are you yeggs going to stick around here?

JACKIE. Keep quiet, halfback.

BOZE. The longer the better, to suit me. Because the U. S. Government is after you and pretty soon they'll be sending for your relatives to identify the bodies and it will probably be the first good look at you they've had in years.

GABBY. You'd better do what you're told and keep your trap shut.

SQUIER. That's good advice, Boze. Because those glandular phenomena I was talking about manifest themselves in sudden and violent ways.

BOZE (*savagely*). How are you going to pay for all that liquor you're drinking? (BOZE *is in an ugly mood, the result of humiliating frustration, and he is taking it out on the one completely defenseless person present.*)

SQUIER. I can pay, and will pay, Boze. For every drop! I have a dollar.

BOZE. Oh, you *have!* So you were holding out on us when you . . .

SQUIER. No— No. I've acquired it since then.

BOZE. Where did you get it?

GABBY. Probably those rich people gave it to him. Now lay off!
(*The kitchen door opens and* PYLES *appears.*)

PYLES. Here's some clothesline, boss.

DUKE. Throw it down.
(PYLES *tosses the coil on the floor and vanishes into the kitchen.*)

BOZE. So you turned down my dime and accepted their dollar. Your pride has its price, eh!

SQUIER. If you must know—I'll tell you the extent of my pride. Gabrielle gave me the dollar.

BOZE (*to* GABBY). You *did?*

GABBY. It's none of your God-damn business what I do.

BOZE. You were feeling kind of generous tonight, weren't you? (*He turns to* SQUIER) Would you like to know what she was just going to give me when those rats showed up? Would you like to know?

GABBY. Well—speaking of rats! Of all the low, slimy, stinking . . .

SQUIER. No, Gabby. You mustn't blame Boze for anything he says now. He's a man of muscle, and he's suffering from the pangs of frustration.

GABBY. I say, you're a dirty, low, stinking . . .

BOZE. I didn't mean it, Gabby.

GABBY. Then why the hell did you start . . . ?

BOZE. I'm terribly sorry, honey sweet. They've got me absolutely crazy mad, with those shotguns and machine-guns staring me in the face.

SQUIER. That's all it is.

BOZE. I didn't know what I was saying. Will you please forgive me, Gabby?

GABBY. No! Never!

BOZE (*humbly*). All right.

SQUIER. I sympathize with you utterly, Boze. Did you ever read "All Quiet on the Western Front"?

BOZE. No.

SQUIER. Well—all of us here tonight are under very much the same tension. You'd better have a drink, old man. (*He has one himself.*)

BOZE (*ignoring* SQUIER). I love you, Gabby. (*Startled by this sudden declaration* SQUIER *sets down his glass*) I love you, sweetheart—and if I thought I'd done or said anything to hurt you, I'd go over and I'd hang one on those yeggs and die for it, gladly. *Please* tell me you forgive me, honey sweet.

SQUIER. Excuse me. (*He stands up*) Would you rather I left?

JACKIE. Stay where you are!

SQUIER. But I'm intruding.

JACKIE. Sit down.
(SQUIER *sits.*)

GABBY. That's all right, Alan. We've got nothing to hide. Have we, Boze?

BOZE. No—worse luck.

GABBY (*to* SQUIER). I told you he'd been trying to make me.

BOZE. Now, listen . . .

GABBY. And tonight, just after you left, he went at it again. And I decided I was ready to give in to him, and find out what it's like.

BOZE. That's a dirty trick—telling that, before a total stranger.

SQUIER (*to* BOZE). Honestly, Boze—I'm not blaming you—not for an instant.

GABBY (*to* BOZE). I'll say this much for you: you're a pretty good lovemaker when you get going.

BOZE. I wasn't turning on any act. I told you I was full of love, and I was telling the truth, and I don't care who knows it.
(JACKIE *has arisen and started to cross toward the left with the map.*)

JACKIE. Full of love, are you, halfback?

DUKE. And don't let that Mexican hear you mention the names of any of those towns.

JACKIE. I'll be careful, Duke. I don't want to die. I got a dame, too. (*To* BOZE) Keep it up, halfback. I'm rooting for you. *Touch-down!* (*He goes into the kitchen.*)

BOZE (*to* GABBY). It doesn't make any difference to you what I'm trying to tell you—because you don't know

what it means to be really crazy about somebody.
(*She looks at him, through him, for a moment.*)

GABBY. For all you know, maybe I do.

BOZE. I don't believe it. Who have you ever . . . ?

DUKE. Get me a cigar, will you, sister?

GABBY (*rising*). We've got Admiration, White Owl, and Texas Dandies.

DUKE. Whatever costs the most.
(GABBY *has gone back of the counter to get a cigar box, which she takes down to the* DUKE.)

GRAMP. You fellers going to spend the night here?

DUKE. Can't say, Pop. Maybe we'll decide to get buried here. (GABBY *hands him the box of cigars and he takes a fistful*) Thanks.

SQUIER. You'd better come with me, Duke. I'm planning to be buried in the Petrified Forest. I've been evolving a theory about that that would interest you. It's the graveyard of the civilization that's been shot from under us. It's the world of outmoded ideas. Platonism—patriotism—Christianity—romance—the economics of Adam Smith—they're all so many dead stumps in the desert. That's where I belong—and so do you, Duke. For you're the last great apostle of rugged individualism. Aren't you?
(DUKE *has been calmly defoiling a cigar, biting the end off, and lighting it.*)

DUKE. Maybe you're right, pal.

SQUIER (*returning to his drink*). I'm eternally right. But what use do I make of it?

DUKE. I couldn't say.

BOZE (*to* GABBY, *who is resuming her seat*). Who were you ever crazy about?

GABBY. Is it any of your business?

BOZE. Everything about you is my business!

GABBY. Well—if you've got to know—it's him.

SQUIER (*startled*). What?

GABBY. I was just telling Boze that I'm crazy about you.

BOZE. That panhandler?

GABBY. You don't know the worst of him. He's more than a panhandler. He's a gigolo.

BOZE. Did you ever see him before?

GABBY. No. But that doesn't matter. I love him. I don't think I'll ever love anybody else.

SQUIER. Can I possibly be drunk?

GABBY. You will be if you keep hitting that rye.

BOZE. How did you happen to get that way, Gabby?

GABBY. I don't know. Just something.

SQUIER. I swear before God, Boze—I wasn't trying to be seductive.

BOZE (*scornfully*). No—I don't believe you could even try.

GABBY. After you left, Alan—I felt as if something had been taken out of me—or sort of as if I'd come out of a dream. I caught on to myself, and I knew I'm just another desert rat, and I'll never be anything else. I'd better get rid of all the girlish bunk that was in me, like thinking so much about going to France, and Art, and dancing in the streets. And I'd better make the most of what I can find right here—and it happened to be you, Boze. Do you know what I asked him? I asked him to let me go away with him, and live in sin. (*She turns again to* SQUIER) But you wouldn't have done it, even if we'd had the money—would you, Alan? (SQUIER *is looking straight into her eyes*) Would you?

SQUIER. No, Gabrielle.

GABBY (*to* BOZE). You see—he doesn't give a hoot in hell for me. I saw that, plainly enough. And it only made me love him all the more. And that's why I was willing to go out into the moonlight with you, when Duke Mantee came in.

DUKE. I'm sorry, sister. I don't like to interfere with anybody's fun.

BOZE (*with labored insincerity*). Oh —that's all right. It was probably all for the best.

DUKE. Yes. When I look at you, I guess it was. (*The* DUKE *turns and opens the window at his side about three inches.*)

SQUIER (*still looking at* GABBY). I'm sorry now that I came back.
(BOZE *has darted a look at the* DUKE, *and there is born in his mind an idea: by a sudden, tiger-like leap, he might get possession of the shotgun which is lying on the table.*)

BOZE. I'll take a drink of that stuff. (GABBY *passes him the bottle which has remained on the table.* BOZE *pours himself a stiff one, drinks it—and a moment later pours and consumes another. But he is constantly, furiously watching the* DUKE.)

SQUIER (*still looking at* GABBY). When I went out before—it was the poignant ending to a—an idyllic interlude. But now it's spoiled. I can't go forth quite so gracefully again.

GABBY. You're sorry you heard the real truth?

SQUIER. I told you that I'm the type of person to whom the truth is always distasteful.

GABBY. That wife of yours must have been terrible.

SQUIER. Why do you think so?

GABBY. Because she's talked all the heart out of you. I could put it back, Alan.

SQUIER (*with sudden irritability*). No! Don't delude yourself. If you have love, and don't know what to do with it, why don't you lavish it on Duke Mantee? There's your real mate—another child of Nature.

GABBY. You'd better not drink any more of that rye.

SQUIER. It's not the rye! It's the same disease that's afflicting Boze! Impotence! (*He stands up.*)

DUKE. Sit down, pal.

SQUIER. What do you care whether I sit or stand? What can *I* do to assail your superiority?

DUKE. I got to think about my health, pal.

SQUIER. If I had a machine-gun, I wouldn't know what to do with it. . . . I want to talk to him. (*Indicating* GRAMP.)

GRAMP. Me?

DUKE. You can talk sitting down. I heard you doing it.

SQUIER (*sitting down*). Very well . . .

GRAMP. What's on your mind?

SQUIER. Those Liberty Bonds of yours, buried in Santa Fé.

GRAMP (*sharply*). How do *you* know about them?

SQUIER. What are you going to do with them?

GRAMP. Going to leave 'em where they are!

SQUIER. Yes—leave them where they are! Your granddaughter is stifling and suffocating in this desert when a few of your thousands would give her the chance to claim her birthright.

GRAMP. Yes—and maybe give *you* the chance to steal it. I've heard what you've been saying.

SQUIER. That's a low way to justify your stinginess. Oh—I know you were a pioneer once. But what are you now? A mean old miser, hanging on to that money as though it meant something. Why in God's name don't you die and do the world some good?

GRAMP. Must be drunk.

DUKE (*rising menacingly*). Yes—drunk—or just about the lowest-grade son of a bitch I ever run across. What do you mean talking to an old man like that?
(RUBY *appears in the door.*)

RUBY. Say—there's three people coming down the road. Two men and a woman. Look to me like the owners of that Duesenberg.

DUKE. O. K. Keep quiet when they get here.

RUBY. It's all right out here. You can see plain in the moonlight. It's kind of nice to look at, too. (*He goes out.*)

SQUIER. I admit it, Duke. I was guilty of bad taste—and I apologize, Mr. Maple.

GRAMP. Sure.

DUKE. You'd better crawl, or I might have to put the lug on you. Talking to an old man like that . . .

SQUIER. Listen, Duke. If you had any of Robin Hood in you you'd go to Santa Fé, and rob that bank, and give it to her, before it's too late for her to use it as it should be used . . .

GRAMP. She'll get it when she needs it—when she has a family of her own to support—and probably a good-for-nothing unemployed husband . . . (DUKE *turns to look out the window.* BOZE *sees his chance. He effects the tiger-like leap, seizes the shotgun and wrests it from the* DUKE'*s frantic grasp.* BOZE *backs away quickly, covering the* DUKE.)

BOZE (*breathless with excitement*). Put' em up! Now I've got you. I've been waiting for this chance. I've been watching every move you . . .
(MR. *and* MRS. CHISHOLM *appear in the doorway, followed by* JOSEPH. *Seeing* BOZE *with the shotgun, and* DUKE *with hands up,* MRS. CHISHOLM *screams.* BOZE *whirls to cover them. As he does so,* DUKE *whips out one of his revolvers and fires.* BOZE *drops the shotgun and grabs his left hand with his right. The kitchen door flies open and* JACKIE *hurtles out.*)

DUKE. Get that gun.
(*As* JACKIE *dives for the shotgun, the* CHISHOLMS *turn to rush into the night.* PYLES *has followed* JACKIE *out of the kitchen, his machine-gun at the alert, his mouth full.*)

RUBY'S VOICE (*from off right*). Get back there or I'll shoot you dead!

GABBY. Are you hurt, Boze?

DUKE (*to* JACKIE). Give me that Tommy.
(JACKIE *gives his machine-gun to* DUKE. MR. *and* MRS. CHISHOLM *and* JOSEPH *return, followed by* RUBY.)

BOZE. He got me in the hand. (*His left hand is seen to be covered with blood.*)

JACKIE. So you tried to be brave, did you?

DUKE. Frisk 'em, Ruby.
(RUBY *hurriedly taps the* CHISHOLMS *all over.*)

MRS. CHISHOLM. Let us out of here! We didn't have anything to do with this.

JACKIE. Shut up.

MRS. CHISHOLM. I *won't* have that man pawing me.

DUKE. Get back to the car, Ruby.

RUBY. They're harmless, Duke. (*He goes.*)

DUKE. Sit down over there. Come on! Step! You down there. (*The* CHISHOLMS *sit at the center table, with* SQUIER. JOSEPH *sits upstage by the counter*) Take him in and bandage him, sister. He'll be all right. Go with 'em, Jackie—and you better take that line and tie him up and leave him in there.
(GABBY *and* BOZE *cross toward the left.*)

JACKIE (*picking up the clothes-line*). I'll tie him.

BOZE (*to the* CHISHOLMS). God damn you! Why did you have to pick that moment to come in here?

CHISHOLM. Why indeed!

GABBY. Come on, Boze.

BOZE. Oh, God! I had the chance and I muffed it. I could have got Mantee and got him good.

JACKIE. Tough luck, halfback. You made a nice try.
(GABBY *and* BOZE *go out at the left followed by* JACKIE.)

PYLES. Say, boss—we better lam out of here.

DUKE. We go when I say so.

PYLES (*contemplating the* CHISHOLMS). But if any more people come in here we'll have to be sending out for recruits. (*He turns to* JOSEPH) Hi-yah, colored brother!

JOSEPH (*with dignified asperity*). Good evening.

DUKE. Finish your supper, Pyles.

PYLES. Sure you don't need me? They almost got you that time.

DUKE. Almost ain't good enough. Go on.

PYLES. O. K., boss. (*He goes out into kitchen.*)

GRAMP. Say, Mantee—did you mean to hit him in the hand or was that a bad shot?

DUKE (*quietly*). It was a bad shot, Pop. But I had to get it off fast. Now, listen—I let that mugg make a mugg out of me. But—don't anybody try that again. Just keep in mind that I and the boys are candidates for hanging, and the minute anybody makes the wrong move, I'm going to kill the whole lot of you. So keep your seats. (*He returns his revolver to its holster, picks up the Tommy gun and sits down at the right. There is a dead pause.*)

CHISHOLM. Are *you* Mantee?

DUKE. Yes, pal.

MRS. CHISHOLM. I *knew* it was a mistake to take that hitchhiker into the car.

CHISHOLM. I don't see what *he* had to do with it.

MRS. CHISHOLM. He certainly didn't help matters much.
(SQUIER *was at first stunned by* BOZE's *spectacular action—then, as he thought it over, resentful—and then, as he thought still more, determined to do something spectacular himself. He has helped himself to another stiff slug of rye.*)

SQUIER (*gravely*). I'm afraid that's unanswerable, Mr. Chisholm. I have not helped matters at all—up to now. (*He finishes his drink and turns to* DUKE) Would you mind passing me that rucksack that's on the bench beside you?

DUKE. What do you want with it?

SQUIER. I want to get out my life-insurance policy. If you reach in there, you'll find it, in a bundle of papers.
(*The* DUKE *reaches with his left hand and extracts the papers.*)

GRAMP. What do you want with your insurance? Expecting to die?

SQUIER. You've guessed it, Mr. Maple. (*The* DUKE *tosses the bundle to* SQUIER) Thank you. Now can I take out my fountain pen? Here it is. (*He points to his breast pocket. The* DUKE *nods.* SQUIER *takes out his pen, and starts to write on the policy.*)

CHISHOLM (*to the* DUKE). What about my car?

DUKE. That's a nice bus you got there.

CHISHOLM. Are you going to restore it to me? And my luggage . . .

DUKE. You're likely to get the car back. Let's hope it won't be all full of bullet holes and blood.

MRS. CHISHOLM. There's one little travelling case with some—some things I need. Can I please have that?

DUKE. I took a look in that case.

MRS. CHISHOLM. You're going to steal it?

DUKE. Yes, ma'am. I got a friend that likes rubies.

MRS. CHISHOLM. You're a filthy *thief!*

DUKE. Yes, ma'am.

CHISHOLM. Look here, old man. How much will you take to let us out of here?

DUKE. How much have you got?

CHISHOLM. I could let you have—say —two hundred dollars in cash.

DUKE. Bring it here. (CHISHOLM *walks timorously over to the* DUKE, *produces his wallet and starts to take out some bills*) Just put down the whole wallet. (CHISHOLM *does so, with trembling hands*) Got any more?

CHISHOLM (*patting his pants pockets*). Only some small change.

DUKE. Keep it.

MRS. CHISHOLM (*rising*). Now can we go?

DUKE. No.

CHISHOLM. But I understood that you . . .

DUKE. Sit down where you were.

MRS. CHISHOLM. You are a cheap, contemptible, crooked thief . . .

CHISHOLM. Be quiet, Edith. (*He resumes his seat*) We're in his hands. There's nothing we can do—but hope that someday the United States Government will take some measures to protect the lives and property of its citizens.

(*The* DUKE *has been calmly taking all the money from the wallet.*)

DUKE. Here's your wallet, pal. (*He tosses it to* CHISHOLM, *who stoops to pick it up.*)

(SQUIER *has finished writing. He turns to the* DUKE *and from now on speaks rapidly and with a peculiar earnestness.*)

SQUIER. Duke—I have a great favor to ask of you.

DUKE. Yeah?

SQUIER. I don't think you'll refuse it. Because—you're a man of imagination. You're not afraid to do—rather outlandish things . . .

DUKE. What are you getting at?

SQUIER. This insurance policy—it's my only asset. It's for five thousand dollars—and it was made out in favor of my wife. She's a rich woman, and she doesn't need that money—and I know she doesn't *want* it, from me. I've written on the policy that I want the money paid to Miss Maple—that young lady in there. If Mr. and

Mrs. Chisholm will witness my signature, I'm sure it will be all right. My wife would never contest it. She's a good sort—really she is. Well—what I'm getting at is this, Duke: after they've signed, I wish—I'd be much obliged if you'd just—kill me. (*The* DUKE *looks at him levelly*) It couldn't make any difference to you, Duke. After all, if they catch you they can hang you only once—and you know better than anyone else they already have more than they need against you. And you can't be bothered by any humane considerations. You'd have a hard time finding a more suitable candidate for extermination. I'll be mourned by no one. In fact, my passing will evoke sighs of relief in certain quarters. You see, Duke—in killing me—you'd only be executing the sentence of the law—I mean, natural law—survival of the fittest . . .

GRAMP. My God—he *is* drunk!

DUKE. Sure—and having a fine time showing off.

SQUIER. Of course I'm showing off. I'm trying to outdo Boze in gallantry. But is there anything unnatural in that? Boze was ready to sacrifice his life to become an All-American star. And I'm ready to do likewise. (*He addresses the* CHISHOLMS) Can't you see I mean it?

CHISHOLM. I'm afraid I'm not greatly interested in your whimsicalities.

SQUIER. I don't blame you. But you must remember that this is a weird country we're in. These Mesas are enchanted—and you have to be prepared for the improbable. I'm only asking that you attest to my signature on this . . .

MRS. CHISHOLM. I believe you *do* mean it!

SQUIER. Good for you, Mrs. Chisholm! You're a kindred spirit! I'll bet that you, too, have been thrilled by "A Tale of Two Cities."

MRS. CHISHOLM. You're in love with her, aren't you?

SQUIER. Yes—yes, I suppose I am. And not unreasonably. She has heroic stuff in her. She may be one of the immortal women of France—another Joan of Arc, or Georges Sand, or Madame Curie. I want to show her that I believe in her—and how else can I do it? Living, I'm worth nothing to her. Dead—I can buy her the tallest cathedrals, and golden vineyards, and dancing in the streets. One well-directed bullet will accomplish that. And it will gain a measure of reflected glory for him who fired it and him who stopped it. (*He holds up the insurance policy*) This document will be my ticket to immortality. It will inspire people to say of me: "*There* was an artist, who died before his time!" Will you do it, Duke?

DUKE (*quietly*). I'll be glad to.

SQUIER. Then can I have this signed?

DUKE. Sure.

CHISHOLM (*to* GRAMP). Is he by any chance insane?

GRAMP. Don't ask *me*. He's no friend of mine.

MRS. CHISHOLM. Of *course* he's insane. But what of it?
(SQUIER *gives her the policy and the pen.*)

SQUIER. Thank you, Mrs. Chisholm. Please sign where I've written, "Witnessed this day." (*They start to sign*) I'm going to entrust this to you, Mr. Maple. And after I—after the Duke has obliged, put it in the hands of some good lawyer for collection. My passport is on that table for identification purposes. Thank you very much. (*As they hand him back the policy*) Here, Mr. Maple. (*He rises and hands the policy to* GRAMP.)

DUKE. Let me know when you want to be killed.

SQUIER. Pick your own moment, Duke. Say—just before you leave. (*He strides upstage nervously, aimlessly*) But I'd prefer to have her think that you did it in cold blood. Will you all please remember that? (PYLES *comes in.*)

DUKE. O. K., pal. But for the time being, you better sit down. You might get to feeling reckless.
(SQUIER *sits down.*)

SQUIER. I want to. Now—I think we'd all better have a drink.

MRS. CHISHOLM. Good!

SQUIER (*to* PYLES). Would you mind passing glasses to Mr. and Mrs. Chisholm?

PYLES. Sure. (*He goes behind the counter for glasses, while* SQUIER *pours himself another*) Say, boss—let's lam it out of here. I don't like all them big windows. (*He takes the glasses down to the* CHISHOLMS.)

DUKE. We got to give them more time.

PYLES. You oughtn't to trust a dame. They probably got lost down there in the Panhandle.

DUKE. They know this country like a book. Doris was the one who picked this place for meeting up.

PYLES. Well—I wish to God she'd show.

DUKE. Where's that cook?

PYLES. She's all right. I locked her up. (PYLES *has been passing glasses around.* GRAMP *has been reading the policy carefully. He turns his attention to* PYLES.)

GRAMP. Hey—I'll have a little of that, too.

PYLES (*pouring a drink*). Why—certainly.

DUKE. Don't give it to him, Pyles. The girl says he oughtn't to have it.

SQUIER. Better not, Mr. Maple, we'll all need clear heads for what is to come.

GRAMP. *My* head's never been muddled yet.

PYLES (*to* JOSEPH). Here, brother—you better take it.

JOSEPH. Is it all right, Mr. Chisholm?

PYLES (*ashamed for his race*). Listen to him! "Is it all right, Mr. Chisholm?" Ain't you heard about the big liberation? Come on—take your drink, weasel!

CHISHOLM. Go ahead, Joseph.

JOSEPH. Thank you, sir.

(PYLES *hands the drink to* JOSEPH, *then crosses to the right, and sits down on the bench by the* DUKE. GRAMP *has finished inspection of the policy and is putting it in his pocket.*)

SQUIER. Do you think it's legal?

GRAMP. Seems so to me. But I'd like to tell you just one thing, my friend.

SQUIER. And what is that, Mr. Maple?

GRAMP. There ain't a woman alive or ever did live that's *worth* five thousand dollars.

SQUIER. And let me tell *you* one thing—you're a forgetful old fool. Any woman is worth everything that any man has to give—anguish, ecstasy, faith, jealousy, love, hatred, life or death. Don't you see—that's the excuse for our existence? It's what makes the whole thing possible, and tolerable. When you've reached my age, you'll learn better sense.

MRS. CHISHOLM (*to her husband*). Did you hear that?

CHISHOLM (*wearily*). I heard.

SQUIER (*to* GRAMP). That lovely girl —that granddaughter of yours—do you know what she is? No—you don't. You haven't the remotest idea.

GRAMP. What is she?

SQUIER. She's the future. She's the renewal of vitality—and courage—and aspiration—all the strength that has gone out of you. Hell—I can't say what she is—but she's essential to me, and the whole damned country, and the whole miserable world. And please, Mrs. Chisholm—please don't look at me quizzically. I know how I sound.

MRS. CHISHOLM (*to* SQUIER). I'm wondering if you really believe all that—I mean, about women? (*She has already had one stiff drink and is about to have another.*)

SQUIER. Of course I do—and there's a man who agrees with me. (*Indicating the* DUKE) Don't you, Duke?

DUKE. I don't know, pal. I wasn't listening.

SQUIER. Then permit me to speak for you. (*He turns again to* MRS. CHISHOLM) He could have been over the border long ago, and safe—but he prefers to stay here and risk his life. And do you know why?

MRS. CHISHOLM. Why?

SQUIER. Because he has a rendezvous here with a girl. Isn't that true, Duke?

DUKE. Yes, pal—that's it.

MRS. CHISHOLM (*to the* DUKE). Do you mean to say you ever have *time* for romance?

DUKE. Not much, lady.

SQUIER. Certainly he has! Just like the Knights of the Round Table—between dragons.

DUKE. I guess we're *all* a lot of saps. But I wouldn't be surprised if he was the champion. (*He turns to* SQUIER) Did you think I was kidding when I said I'd be glad to knock you off?

SQUIER. I hope that neither of us was kidding. Did you think *I* was?

DUKE. I just wanted to make sure.

PYLES. Say! What you talking about?

DUKE. Shut up.

SQUIER. You gave me the idea, Duke, when you called me a low-grade son of a bitch. Forgive me, Mrs. Chisholm. I hope you don't object to that phrase.

MRS. CHISHOLM. Not in the least.

DUKE. I take it back. You're all right, pal. You've got good ideas. I'll try to fix it so's it won't hurt.

SQUIER (*raising his glass*). You're all right, too, Duke. I'd like to meet you again some day. (*He drinks.*)

DUKE. Maybe it'll be soon.

MRS. CHISHOLM. You know—this frightful place has suddenly become quite cosy. (*She finishes her second drink.*)

SQUIER. That's my doing, Mrs. Chisholm. You ought to thank me for having taken it out of the realms of reality.

MRS. CHISHOLM (*excitedly*). I'm going to *see* something at last—and after that dreadful dull day looking at cliff dwellings. (*She turns to her husband*) Do you realize that we're going to be witnesses at *murder*? He's actually going to shoot him . . .

SQUIER. Sh—please be careful, Mrs. Chisholm. (GABBY *comes in from the left, followed by* JACKIE) Hello. How's Boze?

GABBY. He'll be all right.

PYLES. Did you tie him up good?

JACKIE. Yeah—in the bathroom. Say, Duke, it's after ten o'clock.

PYLES. Yeah, boss.

DUKE. We'll give 'em a few more minutes.

SQUIER (*significantly*). A few minutes.

DUKE (*with a slight grin*). Not so much more time, pal.

(JACKIE *wanders out for a visit with* RUBY.)

GABBY. Listen, Gramp—I've got an idea we ought to sell out right away, tomorrow. It's the best chance we'll ever have, because this place is going to get advertised all over the country and people will be flocking here just to see where Duke Mantee stopped. I'll bet Dana Trimble will boost his offer sure. (*She is standing by the table at the left.*)

GRAMP (*significantly*). You're still aiming to take that trip to France?

GABBY. No—the hell with that! I'm asking you to do it for Dad's sake. Let him get located in Los Angeles—and maybe I'll find that writer with Warner Brothers, and maybe I'll get a job—and then we'll all be rich.

GRAMP. Don't sound likely to me.

GABBY. You can't tell, Gramp. There might be a great future for Dad in the Legion. That's what he wants, and you ought to give him a whack at it.

SQUIER. And would you be content with that?

GABBY (*savagely*). I'm not thinking about myself! I don't care what happens to me.

SQUIER. But you *must* think about yourself. You want to be a great painter, don't you? Then you'll have to get used to being a colossal egoist, selfish to the core.

GABBY. Are you going to give me more advice? You and your talk about Nature? I thought you told me never to listen to you.

SQUIRE. I did—but . . .

GABBY. Well, that's all the advice I'm going to take. (*She turns away from him.*)

MRS. CHISHOLM. Do you mind if I speak up, my dear? Perhaps I could tell you some things that . . .

GABBY. What do *you* know about me?

CHISHOLM. Nothing! If I were you, Edith, I'd keep out of . . .

MRS. CHISHOLM (*turning on him*). You haven't the remotest conception of what's inside me, and you never have had and never will have as long as you live out your stuffy, astigmatic life. (*She turns to* GABBY) I don't know about you, my dear. But I know what it means to repress yourself and starve yourself through what you conceive to be your duty to others. I've been through that. When I was just about your age, I went to Salzburg—because I'd had a nervous breakdown after I came out and I went to a psychoanalyst there and he told me I had every right to be a great actress. He gave me a letter to Max Reinhardt, and I might have played the Nun in "The Miracle." But my family of course started yapping about my obligations to *them*—who had given me everything, including life. At least, *they* called it "life." They whisked me back to Dayton, to take my place in the Junior League, and the Country Club, and the D. A. R.—and everything else that's foul and obscene. And before I knew it, I was married to *this* pillar of the mortgage, loan and trust. And what did *he* do? He took my soul and had it stencilled on a card, and filed. And where have I been ever since? In an art metal cabinet. That's why I think I have a *little* right to advise you.

CHISHOLM (*closing his tired eyes*). Dear God!

MRS. CHISHOLM. You needn't look so martyred! You know perfectly well that until this minute I've never complained. I've managed to play the part of a self-effacing . . .

CHISHOLM (*his eyes are now open*). Never complained, eh! Forgive me if I indulge in some quiet, mirthless laughter.

MRS. CHISHOLM. What you've wanted is a wife who's an ornamental cipher. And, God knows—I've tried and tried to be just that . . .

CHISHOLM. When?

MRS. CHISHOLM. I've given you what you wanted—at the cost of my individuality, my self-respect—and—and everything else . . .

CHISHOLM. At the cost of nothing! I suppose you've never come storming into the office and created a scene just when I was straining every faculty to find ways to pay for . . .

MRS. CHISHOLM (*to* GABBY). There —my dear!

CHISHOLM. Your insane extravagance . . .

MRS. CHISHOLM. Be quiet! (CHISHOLM *abandons the argument, as is his wont.* MRS. CHISHOLM *again to* GABBY) Perhaps you'll understand now what I mean. Profit by my example and realize that perhaps you have something important to give to the world. Don't let them stifle you with their talk about duty. Go to France—and *find* yourself!

GRAMP. Suppose she learns there's nothing there to find?

MRS. CHISHOLM. Even so—it would be better than endless doubt—which has been my portion. (*She pours herself another drink.* GABBY *sits down at the left.*)

SQUIER. You know—it's the damndest thing about this place. There's something here that stimulates the autobiographical impulse. (*To the* DUKE) What kind of life have *you* had, Duke?

DUKE. A hell of a life.

MRS. CHISHOLM. I don't believe it.

DUKE. Why not, lady?
(JACKIE *returns and sits on a stool at the counter.*)

MRS. CHISHOLM. Because you've had the one supreme satisfaction of knowing that at least you're a real man.

(MR. CHISHOLM *again shuts his eyes.*)

DUKE. Yeh—that's true. But what has it got me? I've spent most of my time since I grew up in jail, and it looks like I'll spend the rest of my life dead. So what good does it do me to be a real man when you don't get much chance to be crawling into the hay with some dame?

MRS. CHISHOLM (*after a slight, thoughtful pause*). I wonder if we could find any hay around *here?*

CHISHOLM (*past vehemence*). For the love of God, Edith . . .

JACKIE. *Say!* What's been going on here?

SQUIER. I'm not sure—but I *think* the Duke has had an offer.

MRS. CHISHOLM. He certainly has! And it was made with all sincerity, too.

PYLES. Now, listen, boss—don't you go getting into no hay with her. Because we got to lam it out of here.

DUKE. Thanks very much, lady. When I get settled down in Mexico, maybe I'll send you a postcard, with my address.

SQUIER. Excuse me, Duke—but how's the time getting along?

DUKE. It's just about up, pal.

SQUIER (*turning to* GABBY). I must talk to you, Gabrielle.

GABBY. You can wait until after they're gone.

SQUIER. I can't wait. I mean—when they go—I go. I have to tell you now that I love you.

GABBY. Now listen, Alan. I got sort of upset by all that blood, and I don't want to . . .

SQUIER. I tell you solemnly that I love you, with all the heart that is left in me.

JACKIE. Are we waiting just to listen to this?

MRS. CHISHOLM. He does love you, my dear. He told us so.

SQUIER. Please, Mrs. Chisholm. I'm capable of saying it. (*He turns to* GABBY) Even if I'm not capable of making you believe that I . . .

GABBY. Don't make a fool of yourself, Alan. They're all staring at you.

SQUIER. I know they are. But you've got to believe it, and you've got to remember it. Because—you see—it's my only chance of survival. I told you about that major artist, that's been hidden. I'm transferring him to you. You'll find a line in that verse of Villon's that fits that. Something about: "Thus in your field my seed of harvestry will thrive." I've provided barren soil for that seed—but you'll give it fertility and growth and fruition . . .

PYLES. Listen, boss—I got a wife and four children.

MRS. CHISHOLM. Be quiet—you black gorilla!

PYLES. What you call me? (*He rises, his machine-gun at the alert.*)

DUKE. She pegged you, all right, Pyles. Sit down!

(*Somewhat reluctantly,* PYLES *obeys.*)

SQUIER. You still think I was being comic?

GABBY. No, Alan. I just think that you—you're kind of crazy. And I guess so am I. And that's why I think we'd be terribly happy together.

(SQUIER *looks into her eyes.*)

SQUIER. Don't say that, Gabrielle.

GABBY. Why not—when I believe it, with all my heart.

SQUIER (*after a moment*). Well—maybe you're right . . .

GABBY. You're beginning to admit it . . .

SQUIER. Maybe we will be happy together in a funny kind of way.

GABBY. Alan! (*Impulsively, she goes forward and kneels beside him.*)

JACKIE. Hey!

DUKE. Leave 'em alone!

GABBY. Alan! If you're going away, I'm going with you—wherever it is.

SQUIER (*taking hold of her hand*). No, Gabrielle. I'm not going away, anywhere. I don't have to go any farther. Because I think I've found the thing I was looking for. I've found it—here, in the Valley of the Shadow.

GABBY. What, Alan? What have you found?

SQUIER. I can't say what it is, Gabrielle. Because I don't quite know, yet! (*He looks into her eyes for a moment, then turns suddenly to the* DUKE) All right, Duke. We needn't wait any longer.
(*Three sharp toots from the Duesenberg are heard.*)

DUKE. Watch it, boys!
(PYLES *and* JACKIE *hastily duck out of range of the windows.*)

CHISHOLM. What was that?

JOSEPH. It was our horn, Mr. Chisholm.
(JACKIE *is by the door,* DUKE *by the right window,* PYLES *is crouched, covering those in the room.*)

JASON'S VOICE. Who's that?

RUBY'S VOICE. Stick up your hands!
(THE DUKE *has levelled his machine-gun through the slightly open window.*)

DUKE. We got you covered by machine-guns. Open that door, Jackie. Come on, boys. Walk in the front door, and *keep 'em up!* Cover the door, Jackie.

JACKIE. I got it.

DUKE. Come on! Keep coming!
(JASON *comes in, followed by two fellow legionnaires—one, the* COMMANDER, *a peppery little man, and another who is burly and stupid. All are in the same gaudy uniforms and all look bewildered.*)

DUKE. Get those guns, Jackie.
(JACKIE *systematically disarms the legionnaires. He tosses the guns into the ammunition sack.* RUBY *comes to the door.*)

RUBY. All clear out here.

DUKE. Is their car in our way?

RUBY. No—it's a good mask.

DUKE. O. K. Get back to the car.
(RUBY *disappears into the night.*)

JASON. Is this a stick-up?

JACKIE. What a guesser!

GRAMP. Say—Jason. That there's Duke Mantee. Been here all evening. He and his gang picked this place out of the whole southwest.

DUKE. What's that uniform you're wearing?

JASON. It's the Ralph M. Kesterling Post of the American Legion.

COMMANDER. I'm the commander of this post, buddy, and I want to tell you that all of us men fought in the World War. You wouldn't shoot us down in cold blood?

JACKIE (*cheerfully*). Sure we would.

DUKE. Sit down, boys.

ANOTHER LEGIONNAIRE (*very basso*). Where?

JACKIE. On your cans, Legion.

DUKE. Down there on the floor—in a bunch—and stay there. (*With some little sacrifice of dignity, the* LEGIONNAIRES *sit down on the floor in a huddle in the centre*) Why did you come here?

JASON. This is where I live.

GABBY. That's my father.

DUKE. Why did you bring the whole regiment with you?

COMMANDER. We were trailing you. And by God we caught up with . . .

JASON. Shut up, Commander. The less we talk the better for all concerned.

JACKIE. Some legion! Out gunning for the bad men—and look at 'em now!

DUKE. What made you think I'd be around here?

COMMANDER. They caught your pals.

OTHER. Three men and a blonde.

PYLES. Don't you try to go get 'em out now, boss!

DUKE. Where was it? (*There is no reply.* DUKE *continues with unwonted ferocity*) Come on—tell me —or I'll tear holes a yard wide in them pansy uniforms!

JASON. They caught 'em at Buckhorn.

DUKE. Where's that?
(PYLES *pulls the map from his pocket.*)

OTHER. It's in New Mexico—'bout ninety—hundred miles southeast of here.

DUKE. When?

JASON. I don't know.

COMMANDER. We heard about it half an hour ago. Every man in this state that can bear arms has turned out to . . .

PYLES. Here it is, boss. Buckhorn—on Route 11.

JACKIE. How'd they get 'em?

COMMANDER. It was the regular army!

OTHER. Your friends run right into a troop of the U. S. Cavalry.

JASON. I warn you, Mantee—you'd better get out of here, for your own good.

DUKE. Is anybody else coming this way?

JASON. I don't know. I swear to God I don't. But there are posses all around here, and I don't want to get this place shot up.

COMMANDER. You got the whole mighty strength of this nation after you now, buddy.

JACKIE. Listen, Legion—when we're got it will be by *real* cops—not by any overgrown Boy Scouts in fancy dress.

JASON. All right—you can talk big, if you want to. But I'll tell you that the woman in that car has been doing some talking.

DUKE (*after a moment*). What?

JACKIE. It was Doris. She snitched. They always snitch!

DUKE. Shut up! (*To* JASON) What were you saying?

JASON. I'm telling you for your own good, Mantee—they know where you were heading—they've picked up your trail—and they'll get you . . .

JACKIE. She *has* snitched! Come on, Duke!

SQUIER. Don't listen to them, Duke! (SQUIER *is leaning forward, watching the* DUKE *with great intentness. He sees that the* DUKE, *for once, has been propelled into a state of turbulent, agonized indecision.*)

PYLES. Come on, boss—or we're all dead.

COMMANDER. The law's closing in on you!

JACKIE. What's the matter with you, Duke? Why the hell don't you . . .

DUKE (*with sudden savagery*). For Christ's sake, shut up! *Shut up!* Give me time to think.

SQUIER (*urgently*). No, Duke—don't waste any time thinking. That isn't your game. Don't listen to what they're telling you. You've got to keep going and going and going—

PYLES. Yeah—and go fast.

JACKIE. You've been double-crossed and bitched, and the next thing you'll be layed flat on a marble slab . . .

DUKE. Where'd they take her?

JASON. I don't know. Maybe to Albuquerque.

JACKIE. If we head for there, they'll take *us!*

SQUIER. You want revenge, don't you! You want to go out of your way again to get that blonde who snitched. Don't do it, Duke. Even if she did betray you, don't you commit a worse crime. Don't betray yourself. Go on, run for the border—and take your illusions with you!

JACKIE. He's right, Duke!

DUKE. I told you to shut up! (*He says that to* JACKIE, *but he is looking hard at* SQUIER, *who is talking with passionate earnestness.*)

SQUIER. You know they're going to get you, anyway. You're obsolete, Duke—like me. You've got to die. Then die for freedom. That's worth it. Don't give up your life for anything so cheap and unsatisfactory as revenge.

PYLES. I hear a car coming, boss. We better lam.
(*The* DUKE *looks at* SQUIER *curiously, for a moment.*)

DUKE. All right, pal. I'm going. Now, listen, folks; we've had a pleasant evening here and I'd hate to spoil it with any killing at the finish. So stay where you are until we're out of sight, because we'll be watching. Better cut that phone wire, Jackie. Pack up the ammunition, Pyles.
(PYLES *and* JACKIE *are galvanized into action.*)

SQUIER. Wait a minute! You're not forgetting me?
(JACKIE *is opening his knife,* PYLES *is picking up the ammunition sack, and* DUKE *is covering all, when the Duesenberg horn is heard again.* DUKE, PYLES *and* JACKIE *duck.*)

DUKE (*peering out the window*). Car's stopped out in the road. There's a guy with a rifle.

PYLES. Cops?

DUKE. Looks like it.

JACKIE. Hicks or G's?

DUKE. Hicks. Lay low!

COMMANDER. It's the Sheriff! He's got you, Mantee!

JASON. I warned you! You'd better surrender now before they start . . . (*A burst of machine-gun fire is heard from the left.*)

PYLES. That's Ruby shooting.

DUKE. The God-damn fool. Get out there to that window, Jackie, and tell him to hold his fire. We don't want 'em drilling that car. (JACKIE *starts to go*) Wait! Tell him to open up if they try to drift around that side.

JACKIE. O. K. (*Stooped over, he goes to the door at the lower left and out.*)

JASON. You have no right to endanger the lives of innocent people. You'd better surrender.

DUKE. Get behind that counter, Pyles. And keep this mob in here covered.

PYLES. O. K., boss. (*He crouches on the left end of the counter. The* DUKE *is marvellously alert, crouching by the window, the muzzle of his gun thrust out*) What they doing now, boss?
(*The* DUKE *delivers a short burst of machine-gun fire out the window.*)

DUKE. They're crawling into the sagebrush the other side of the road. Where are them pans?

PYLES. The sack's right there beside you. (*A shot from outside shatters one of the window panes*) Boy—I knowed this place wasn't safe!
(*Wails are heard from* PAULA, *off at the left.*)

DUKE. You folks better get down. Lie down all of you close together in the middle. Watch 'em, Pyles.

PYLES. I'm watching!
(*All hasten to obey, so that they are lying flat on their stomachs, close together.* JACKIE *returns.*)

JACKIE. O. K., Duke.

DUKE. Where's the light switch?

GRAMP. To the right of the door.

DUKE. Turn 'em out, Jackie.
(JACKIE *turns out the lights.*)

CHISHOLM (*to his wife*). Do you want any hay now?
(*The strip of faces and feet of the prone is illumined by the glow of light from the door at the right. Through the windows and the panes of the door come bright moonlight and the green Neon gleam to illumine, dimly, the* DUKE *and* JACKIE.)

DUKE. Get to the kitchen door, Jackie. Hold your fire, unless they try to rush it. They'll try to work around that direction to the shadow of that mesa. It's their only cover. When they get around there, we'll lam.

JACKIE. How many are there?

DUKE. Six or seven. Nothing to worry about. (*Another shot from outside*) When enough of 'em get across that road, give 'em a couple of bursts to scare 'em and then snap back here. And watch yourself, kid!

JACKIE. O. K., Duke. (*He crosses the line of bodies.*)

COMMANDER. Ouch!
(*Still another shot from outside breaks a window.* JACKIE *has gone out at the left.* BOZE'*s voice can be heard shouting: "Let me out of here! Let me out of here!"* PAULA *can be heard wailing prayers and imprecations in Spanish.*)

DUKE. Keeping 'em covered, Pyles?

PYLES. I got 'em, boss! I got 'em!
(*The subsequent dialogue is punctuated with shots from outside and bursts from* DUKE'*s Tommy-gun.*)

SQUIER. It's an inspiring moment—isn't it, Gabrielle? The United States of America versus Duke Mantee!
(*A volley from the* SHERIFF'*s posse and the Neon light goes out.*)

JASON. They've absolutely wrecked the Neon!

GRAMP. It's them deputies shooting. Probably all drunk.

SQUIER. It almost restores in me the will to live—and love—and conquer.

CHISHOLM. Listen, Edith—if I'm killed . . .

MRS. CHISHOLM. What did you say?

CHISHOLM. I said—if I'm killed—and you're not . . . notify Jack Lavery. He has full instructions.

MRS. CHISHOLM (*turning away*). All right.

COMMANDER. Hey—Mantee . . . you're not going to let 'em rush us, are you?
(*The* DUKE *replies with another burst.*)

PYLES. Getting any of 'em, boss?

DUKE. Can't get a good angle on 'em. But they're drifting over—and Jackie'll get 'em.

SQUIER. I feel as if I were sitting on top of a mountain . . . in the middle of Penguin Island. Watching . . . watching the odd little creatures. (MRS. CHISHOLM *starts to hum*) How do you feel about it, darling?

GABBY. I don't know, Alan. And I don't care.

JASON. I wish to God you'd stop that praying.

MRS. CHISHOLM. I'm not praying—I'm singing!
(*By now it is apparent that the attackers have been drifting over; the sound of shots comes more from the left.*)

PYLES. Why ain't Jackie shooting?

DUKE. The kid knows what he's doing.

COMMANDER. If you let 'em rush us . . . it'll be a massacre.

GABBY. Alan . . . Alan—when you get to France . . . what do you see first?

SQUIER. Customs Officers.

GABBY. But what's the first real sight you see?

SQUIER. The fields and forests of Normandy and then . . .

GABBY. What, Alan?

SQUIER. And then Paris.

PYLES. I better tell Jackie to open up.

DUKE. Stay where you are.

GABBY. Paris! That's the most marvellous place in the world for love—isn't it?

SQUIER. All places are marvellous.

GABBY. Even here.

SQUIER. Especially here, my darling.

JOSEPH (*swaying and chanting*). Oh, Lord! Oh, Lord! It is the judgment of thy wrath on these thy poor sinful children.
(*More wails from* PAULA *and shouts from* BOZE.)

JASON. The next thing you know those gas pumps will be up in flames.

SQUIER. As long as I live—I'll be grateful to the Duke . . .

GABBY. Alan . . . Alan . . . will you please kiss me? (*He kisses her.*)
(*The* DUKE *delivers a final prolonged burst, then turns from the window.*)

DUKE. O. K., Pyles. We're pulling out. Get Jackie.
(PYLES *ducks into the kitchen. The shooting from the left is now intense.*)

SQUIER. Oh, Lord— Now it's going to be all over.

GABBY (*clinging to him*). Not for us, Alan—never—

PYLES (*returning*). Jackie's got killed.

DUKE. How the hell did he do that?

PYLES. I don't know, boss.

DUKE. Well—we got to leave him. You and you and you and you are coming with us to hang on the running board. We got to have shields. (*He has designated the* CHISHOLMS, JOSEPH *and the two* LEGIONNAIRES.)

CHISHOLM. Me?

MRS. CHISHOLM. All right! All right! I don't care what happens to me now. I don't care a bit!

COMMANDER. For God's sake, Buddy, don't let us get shot down like . . .

JOSEPH. Oh, Lord God of Abraham. Oh, Holy Lord . . .

OTHER LEGIONNAIRE. This is the country I was ready to die for . . .
(*The foregoing is all jumbled together.*)

GRAMP. Me, too?

DUKE. No, not you, Pop. Come on, on your feet. Get moving out through that door. They won't shoot at you! You won't none of you get hurt if you keep your hands up and make plenty of noise. Come on—keep moving!

PYLES. And we're in one hell of a hurry. (*He is herding them out. Their hands are up and they are shouting lustily.*)

ALL. Don't shoot— Don't shoot. For God's sake, Buddies, don't shoot!
(*The* DUKE *is in the doorway, a crouched silhouette against the moonlit desert. His machine-gun is under his left arm, his revolver in his right hand.*)

DUKE (*to those remaining*). You'd better stay where you are for a while. Good night, folks.

SQUIER (*springing to his feet*). Duke!

GABBY. Alan! Keep down!

SQUIER. Duke!

DUKE. Do you still want it?

SQUIER (*desperately*). It's no matter whether I want it or not. You've got to . . .

DUKE. O. K., pal. (*He shoots.* SQUIER *spins against the lunch counter.* GABBY *screams*) I'll be seeing you soon. (*He goes.*)

GRAMP. God Almighty! He meant it!
(GABBY *rushes to* SQUIER. *There are more wails from* PAULA *and shouts from* BOZE, *but the shooting has stopped.*)

JASON. Keep *down!*
(*The motor of the car is heard starting. The door at the left bursts open and the* SHERIFF *comes in, holding a rifle. Behind him are* HERB *and two* DEPUTIES, *with rifles, pistols, shotguns.*)

SHERIFF. Where'd they go?

JASON (*rising*). Out there.

HERB (*full of enthusiasm and moon*). Let's get 'em, Sheriff! Come on, fellers—we'll shoot 'em dead!
(*The* SHERIFF *starts for the door, and bumps into* JASON.)

GABBY. Gramp! Go get Boze. He knows about first aid.
(GRAMP *goes out at the left.*)

SHERIFF. Get out of my way, you clumsy . . . (*The* SHERIFF *goes out the front door, followed by the* DEPUTIES *and* HERB. *They take cover, and raise their rifles.*)

JASON. Those are innocent people on the running board! (*He switches on the lights.*)

HERB. Never mind 'em. Let's shoot the hell out of 'em! (*He shoots.*)

SHERIFF. God damn! Come on. We'll go after 'em. (*He runs out of sight.*)

VOICE OF ANOTHER DEPUTY. Can't drive that car. The tires are all shot.

SHERIFF'S VOICE. Here's a car we can take.

JASON. Wait a minute. That's my car! You've done enough damage to my property.

HERB'S VOICE. Ah—shut up.
(SQUIER *lurches toward the center table.* GABBY *steadies him and helps him to slump down into a chair.*)

SQUIER. It doesn't hurt—or, at least, it doesn't seem. . . . It went into this lung, I think. (*He leans forward on the table.*)

GABBY. It's all right, Alan.

SQUIER. It isn't all right, Gabrielle. I'm practically dead.

GABBY. No! Alan! You said you wanted to live.

SQUIER. I know I did . . .

GABBY. And I'll live with you. I will!

SQUIER (*looking up at her and smiling, feebly*). I know I said it. I was blinded, then. But now I can see. . . .

GABBY (*shouting*). Boze! Gramp! Somebody! Come here quick!

SQUIER. They were right, Gabrielle . . . I mean the stars. I had to come all this way—to find a reason . . . Oh, —if people only had guts enough, they'd always find . . . (*He covers his eyes with his hand*) Death is funny-looking when . . . The Duke —understood what it was—I wanted . . . I hope you'll— (*His arms are stretched out on the table and his head has been sinking until it rests between them.*)

GABBY. What, Alan? What did you say? (*She takes hold of his shoulder and, frantically, shakes him*) *Alan . . .* (*He is finally silent. Her lip quivers, but she tightens her face*) No—don't worry, Alan. I'm not going to be a God-damned cry-baby about it . . . I know you died happy . . . Didn't you, Alan? *Didn't* you? (*After a moment,* BOZE *comes in, followed by* GRAMP. BOZE*'s right hand is in a blood-stained bandage.*)

BOZE. Are you all right, old kid?

GABBY. I guess he's dead.

GRAMP. Sure he is. Mantee couldn't have missed twice.

BOZE. Damned tough. He was a good guy, at that.
(*A wail from* PAULA *is again heard.*)

BOZE. What's that?

GABBY. It's Paula. Go in and let her out.
(BOZE *goes out at the left.* GRAMP *takes the insurance policy from his pocket.*)

GRAMP. Listen, Gabby—here's the funny thing. His life insurance for five thousand berries. He made it out to you, and it looks regular. Said he wanted you to spend it on a trip to France to see your mother. Of course, I don't know if it's collectible, but by God, I'm going to get it to Summerfield in the morning. (*He puts the policy back in his pocket*) He was the damnedest feller I ever did see. (*He turns and crosses to the left and sits down in his rocking chair*) Couldn't make him out.
(JASON *comes in quickly.*)

JASON. Mantee let 'em off the car 'bout a quarter of a mile up the road. You can see 'em walking back. (*He sees* SQUIER) Has he—

GRAMP. Yep—he's gone.

JASON (*removing his cap*). Poor feller. Well—he died a hero's death. We'll give him an honorable funeral.

GABBY. We'll bury him out there in the petrified forest.

JASON. *What?*

GABBY. That's what he wanted.

GRAMP. Yes—by God—he said so. (JASON *starts up to the telephone behind the counter.*)

JASON. Well, maybe his next of kin will have something to say about that.

I've got to 'phone the Sheriff's office. They'll never catch Mantee with my car—unless he wrecks that Duesenberg . . . Hello— Hello—get me the Sheriff's office in Morenci . . . Yeh. . . .

(GABBY *is still standing close to* SQUIER, *her hands on his shoulder.*)

GABBY (*almost to herself*).

"Thus in your field my seed of harvestry will thrive—
For the fruit is like me that I set—"

(BOZE *comes in, from the kitchen, laughing.*)

BOZE. Boy—it did me good to see that Jackie in a pool of blood. . . .

GABBY (*louder, almost defiantly*).

"God bids me tend it with good husbandry:
This is the end for which we twain are met."

JASON. Hello—who's this . . . Oh—hello, Ernie . . .

BOZE (*wildly*). Don't keep *staring* at him . . .

JASON. Jason Maple . . . Say—Mantee was here and escaped South in a yellow Duesenberg, Ohio license plate. Sheriff went after him, but you got to watch Route 71 and send out the alarm to watch Route 60. Yes—we had quite some shooting here. . . .

(*During this speech the curtain has fallen.*)

Waiting for Lefty

BY CLIFFORD ODETS

Waiting for Lefty was first produced at the Longacre Theatre, New York City, by the Group Theatre, on March 26, 1935, and closed on September 28, 1935. Following is the original cast:

FATT	Russell Collins
JOE	Lewis Leverett
EDNA	Ruth Nelson
MILLER	Gerrit Kraber
FAYETTE	Russell Collins
IRV	Walter Coy
FLORRIE	Paula Miller
SID	Herbert Ratner
CLAYTON	Bob Lewis
AGATE KELLER	Elia Kazan
HENCHMAN	Abner Biberman
SECRETARY	Dorothy Patten
ACTOR	William Challee
REILLY	Russell Collins
DR. BARNES	Roman Bohnen
DR. BENJAMIN	Clifford Odets
A MAN	George Heller
VOICES	Sam Roland, Lee J. Cobb, Wendell Keith Phillips, Harry Stone, Bernard Zanville

WAITING FOR LEFTY

As the curtain goes up we see a bare stage. On it are sitting six or seven men in a semicircle. Lolling against the proscenium down left is a young man chewing a toothpick: a gunman. A fat man of porcine appearance is talking directly to the audience. In other words he is the head of a union and the men ranged behind him are a committee of workers. They are now seated in interesting different attitudes and present a wide diversity of type, as we shall soon see. The fat man is hot and heavy under the collar, near the end of a long talk, but not too hot: he is well fed and confident. His name is HARRY FATT.

FATT. You're so wrong I ain't laughing. Any guy with eyes to read knows it. Look at the textile strike—out like lions and in like lambs. Take the San Francisco tie-up—starvation and broken heads. The steel boys wanted to walk out too, but they changed their minds. It's the trend of the times, that's what it is. All we workers got a good man behind us now. He's top man of the country—looking out for our interests—the man in the White House is the one I'm referrin' to. That's why the times ain't ripe for a strike. He's working day and night—

VOICE (*from the audience*). For who?
(*The* GUNMAN *stirs himself.*)

FATT. For you! The records prove it. If this was the Hoover régime, would I say don't go out, boys? Not on your tintype! But things is different now. You read the papers as well as me. You know it. And that's why I'm against the strike. Because we gotta stand behind the man who's standin' behind us! The whole country—

ANOTHER VOICE. Is on the blink!
(*The* GUNMAN *looks grave.*)

FATT. Stand up and show yourself, you damn red! Be a man, let's see what you look like! (*Waits in vain*) Yellow from the word go! Red and yellow makes a dirty color, boys. I got my eyes on four or five of them in the union here. What the hell'll they do for you? Pull you out and run away when trouble starts. Give those birds a chance and they'll have your sisters and wives in the whore houses, like they done in Russia. They'll tear Christ off his bleeding cross. They'll wreck your homes and throw your babies in the river. You think that's bunk? Read the papers! Now listen, we can't stay here all night. I gave you the facts in the case. You boys got hot suppers to go to and—

ANOTHER VOICE. Says you!

GUNMAN. Sit down, Punk!

ANOTHER VOICE. Where's Lefty? (*Now this question is taken up by the others in unison.* FATT *pounds with gavel.*)

FATT. That's what I wanna know. Where's your pal, Lefty? You elected him chairman—where the hell did he disappear?

VOICES. We want Lefty! Lefty! Lefty!

FATT (*pounding*). What the hell is this—a circus? You got the committee here. This bunch of cowboys you elected. (*Pointing to man on extreme right end.*)

MAN. Benjamin.

FATT. Yeah, Doc Benjamin. (*Pointing to other men in circle in seated order*) Benjamin, Miller, Stein, Mitchell, Phillips, Keller. It ain't my fault Lefty took a run-out powder. If you guys—

A GOOD VOICE. What's the committee say?

OTHERS. The committee! Let's hear from the committee! (FATT *tries to quiet the crowd, but one of the seated men suddenly comes to the front. The* GUNMAN *moves over to center stage, but* FATT *says*)

FATT. Sure, let him talk. Let's hear what the red boys gotta say!
(*Various shouts are coming from the audience.* FATT *insolently goes back to his seat in the middle of the circle. He sits on his raised platform and relights his cigar. The* GUNMAN *goes back to his post.* JOE, *the new speaker, raises his hand for quiet. Gets it quickly. He is sore.*)

JOE. You boys know me. I ain't a red boy one bit! Here I'm carryin' a shrapnel that big I picked up in the war. And maybe I don't know it when it rains! Don't tell me red! You know what we are? The black and blue boys! We been kicked around so long we're black and blue from head to toes. But I guess anyone who says straight out he don't like it, he's a red boy to the leaders of the union. What's this crap about goin' home to hot suppers? I'm asking to your faces how many's got hot suppers to go home to? Anyone who's sure of his next meal, raise your hand! A certain gent sitting behind me can raise them both. But not in front here! And that's why we're talking strike—to get a living wage!

VOICE. Where's Lefty?

JOE. I honest to God don't know, but he didn't take no run-out powder. That Wop's got more guts than a slaughterhouse. Maybe a traffic jam got him, but he'll be here. But don't let this red stuff scare you. Unless fighting for a living scares you. We gotta make up our minds. My wife made up my mind last week, if you want the truth. It's plain as the nose on Sol Feinberg's face we need a strike. There's us comin' home every night—eight, ten hours on the cab. "God," the wife says, "eighty cents ain't money—don't buy beans almost. You're workin' for the company," she says to me, "Joe! you ain't workin' for me or the family no more!" She says to me, "If you don't start. . . ."

I. JOE AND EDNA

The lights fade out and a white spot picks out the playing space within the space of seated men. The seated men are very dimly visible in the outer dark, but more prominent is FATT *smoking his cigar and often blowing the smoke in the lighted circle.*

A tired but attractive woman of thirty comes into the room, drying her hands on an apron. She stands there sullenly as JOE *comes in from the other side, home from work. For a moment they stand and look at each other in silence.*

JOE. Where's all the furniture, honey?

EDNA. They took it away. No installments paid.

JOE. When?

EDNA. Three o'clock.

JOE. They can't do that.

EDNA. Can't? They did it.

JOE. Why, the palookas, we paid three-quarters.

EDNA. The man said read the contract.

JOE. We must have signed a phony. . . .

EDNA. It's a regular contract and you signed it.

JOE. Don't be so sour, Edna. . . . (*Tries to embrace her.*)

EDNA. Do it in the movies, Joe—they pay Clark Gable big money for it.

JOE. This is a helluva house to come home to. Take my word!

EDNA. Take MY word! Whose fault is it?

JOE. Must you start that stuff again?

EDNA. Maybe you'd like to talk about books?

JOE. I'd like to slap you in the mouth!

EDNA. No you won't.

JOE (*sheepish*). Jeez, Edna, you get me sore some time. . . .

EDNA. But just look at me—I'm laughing all over!

JOE. Don't insult me. Can I help it if times are bad? What the hell do you want me to do, jump off a bridge or something?

EDNA. Don't yell. I just put the kids to bed so they won't know they missed a meal. If I don't have Emmy's shoes soled tomorrow, she can't go to school. In the meantime let her sleep.

JOE. Honey, I rode the wheels off the chariot today. I cruised around five hours without a call. It's conditions.

EDNA. Tell it to the A & P!

JOE. I booked two-twenty on the clock. A lady with a dog was lit . . . she gave me a quarter tip by mistake. If you'd only listen to me—we're rolling in wealth.

EDNA. Yeah? How much?

JOE. I had "coffee and—" in a beanery. (*Hands her silver coins*) A buck four.

EDNA. The second month's rent is due tomorrow.

JOE. Don't look at me that way, Edna.

EDNA. I'm looking through you, not at you. . . . Everything was gonna be so ducky! A cottage by the waterfall, roses in Picardy. You're a four-star bust! If you think I'm standing for it much longer, you're crazy as a bedbug.

JOE. I'd get another job if I could. There's no work—you know it.

EDNA. I only know we're at the bottom of the ocean.

JOE. What can I do?

EDNA. Who's the man in the family, you or me?

JOE. That's no answer. Get down to brass tacks. Christ, gimme a break, too! A coffee cake and java all day. I'm hungry, too, Babe. I'd work my fingers to the bone if—

EDNA. I'll open a can of salmon.

JOE. Not now. Tell me what to do!

EDNA. I'm not God!

JOE. Jeez. I wish I was a kid again and didn't have to think about the next minute.

EDNA. But you're not a kid and you do have to think about the next minute. You got two blondie kids sleeping in the next room. They need food and clothes. I'm not mentioning anything else—But we're stalled like a flivver in the snow. For five years I laid awake at night listening to my heart pound. For God's sake, do something, Joe, get wise. Maybe get your buddies together, maybe go on strike for better money. Poppa did it during the war and they won out. I'm turning into a sour old nag.

JOE (*defending himself*). Strikes don't work!

EDNA. Who told you?

JOE. Besides that means not a nickel a week while we're out. Then when it's over they don't take you back.

EDNA. Suppose they don't? What's to lose?

JOE. Well, we're averaging six-seven dollars a week now.

EDNA. That just pays for the rent.

JOE. That is something, Edna.

EDNA. It isn't. They'll push you down to three and four a week before you know it. Then you'll say, "That's somethin'," too!

JOE. There's too many cabs on the street, that's the whole damn trouble.

EDNA. Let the company worry about that, you big fool! If their cabs didn't make a profit, they'd take them off the streets. Or maybe you think they're in business just to pay Joe Mitchell's rent!

JOE. You don't know a-b-c, Edna.

EDNA. I know this—your boss is making suckers outa you boys every minute. Yes, and suckers out of all the wives and the poor innocent kids who'll grow up with crooked spines and sick bones. Sure, I see it in the papers, how good orange juice is for kids. But dammit our kids get colds one on top of the other. They look like little ghosts. Betty never saw a grapefruit. I took her to the store last week and she pointed to a stack of grapefruits. "What's that!" she said My God, Joe—the world is supposed to be for all of us.

JOE. You'll wake them up.

EDNA. I don't care, as long as I can maybe wake you up.

JOE. Don't insult me. One man can't make a strike.

EDNA. Who says one? You got hundreds in your rotten union!

JOE. The union ain't rotten.

EDNA. No? Then what are they doing? Collecting dues and patting your back?

JOE. They're making plans.

EDNA. What kind?

JOE. They don't tell us.

EDNA. It's too damn bad about you. They don't tell little Joey what's happening in his bitsie witsie union. What do you think it is—a ping pong game?

JOE. You know they're racketeers. The guys at the top would shoot you for a nickel.

EDNA. Why do you stand for that stuff?

JOE. Don't you wanna see me alive?

EDNA (*after a deep pause*). No . . . I don't think I do, Joe. Not if you can lift a finger to do something about it, and don't. No, I don't care.

JOE. Honey, you don't understand what—

EDNA. And any other hackie that won't fight . . . let them all be ground to hamburger!

JOE. It's one thing to—

EDNA. Take your hand away! Only they don't grind me to little pieces! I got different plans. (*Starts to take off her apron.*)

JOE. Where are you going?

EDNA. None of your business.

JOE. What's up your sleeve?

EDNA. My arm'd be up my sleeve darling, if I had a sleeve to wear. (*Puts neatly folded apron on back of chair.*)

JOE. Tell me!

EDNA. Tell you what?

JOE. Where are you going?

EDNA. Don't you remember my old boy friend?

JOE. Who?

EDNA. Bud Haas. He still has my picture in his watch. He earns a living.

JOE. What the hell are you talking about?

EDNA. I heard worse than I'm talking about.

JOE. Have you seen Bud since we got married?

EDNA. Maybe.

JOE. If I thought. . . . (*He stands looking at her.*)

EDNA. See much? Listen, boy friend, if you think I won't do this it just means you can't see straight.

JOE. Stop talking bull!

EDNA. This isn't five years ago, Joe.

JOE. You mean you'd leave me and the kids?

EDNA. I'd leave *you* like a shot!

JOE. No. . . .

EDNA. Yes!
(JOE *turns away, sitting in a chair with his back to her. Outside the lighted circle of the playing stage we hear the other seated members of the strike committee. "She will . . . she will . . . it happens that way," etc. This group should be used throughout for various comments, political, emotional and as general chorus. Whispering. . . . The fat boss now blows a heavy cloud of smoke into the scene.*)

JOE (*finally*). Well, I guess I ain't got a leg to stand on.

EDNA. No?

JOE (*suddenly mad*). No, you lousy tart, no! Get the hell out of here. Go pick up that bull-thrower on the corner and stop at some cushy hotel downtown. He's probably been coming here every morning and laying you while I hacked my guts out!

EDNA. You're crawling like a worm!

JOE. You'll be crawling in a minute.

EDNA. You don't scare me that much! (*Indicates a half inch on her finger.*)

JOE. This is what I slaved for!

EDNA. Tell it to your boss!

JOE. He don't give a damn for you or me!

EDNA. That's what I say.

JOE. Don't change the subject!

EDNA. This is the subject, the EXACT SUBJECT! Your boss makes this subject. I never saw him in my life, but he's putting ideas in my head a mile a minute. He's giving your kids that fancy disease called the rickets. He's making a jellyfish outa you and putting wrinkles in my face. This is the subject every inch of the way! He's throwing me into Bud Haas' lap. When in hell will you get wise—

JOE. I'm not so dumb as you think! But you are talking like a Red.

EDNA. I don't know what that means. But when a man knocks you down you get up and kiss his fist! You gutless piece of baloney.

JOE. One man can't—

EDNA (*with great joy*). I don't say one man! I say a hundred, a thousand, a whole million, I say. But start in your own union. Get those hack boys together! Sweep out those racketeers like a pile of dirt! Stand up like men and fight for the crying kids and wives. God damn it! I'm tired of slavery and sleepless nights.

JOE (*with her*). Sure, sure! . . .

EDNA. Yes. Get brass toes on your shoes and know where to kick!

JOE (*suddenly jumping up and kissing his wife full on the mouth*). Listen, Edna, I'm goin' down to 174th Street to look up Lefty Costello. Lefty was saying the other day . . . (*He suddenly stops*) How about this Haas guy?

EDNA. Get out of here!

JOE. I'll be back! (*Runs out.*) (*For a moment* EDNA *stands triumphant.*)

(*There is a blackout and when the regular lights come up,* JOE MITCHELL *is concluding what he has been saying.*)

JOE. You guys know this stuff better than me. We gotta walk out! (*Abruptly he turns and goes back to his seat and blackout.*)

II. LAB ASSISTANT EPISODE

Discovered: MILLER, *a lab assistant, looking around; and* FAYETTE, *an industrialist.*

FAY. Like it?

MILLER. Very much. I've never seen an office like this outside the movies.

FAY. Yes, I often wonder if interior decorators and bathroom fixture people don't get all their ideas from Hollywood. Our country's extraordinary that way. Soap, cosmetics, electric refrigerators—just let Mrs. Consumer know they're used by the Crawfords and Garbos—more volume of sale than one plant can handle!

MILL. I'm afraid it isn't that easy, Mr. Fayette.

FAY. No, you're right—gross exaggeration on my part. Competition is cutthroat today. Markets up flush against a stone wall. The astronomers had better hurry—open Mars to trade expansion.

MILL. Or it will be just too bad!

FAY. Cigar?

MILL. Thank you, don't smoke.

FAY. Drink?

MILL. Ditto, Mr. Fayette.

FAY. I like sobriety in my workers . . . the trained ones, I mean. The Pollacks and niggers, they're better drunk—keeps them out of mischief. Wondering why I had you come over?

MILL. If you don't mind my saying—very much.

FAY (*patting him on the knee*). I like your work.

MILL. Thanks.

FAY. No reason why a talented young man like yourself shouldn't string along with us—a growing concern.

Loyalty is well repaid in our organization. Did you see Siegfried this morning?

MILL. He hasn't been in the laboratory all day.

FAY. I told him yesterday to raise you twenty dollars a month. Starts this week.

MILL. You don't know how happy my wife'll be.

FAY. Oh, I can appreciate it. (*He laughs.*)

MILL. Was that all, Mr. Fayette?

FAY. Yes, except that we're switching you to laboratory A tomorrow. Siegfried knows about it. That's why I had you in. The new work is very important. Siegfried recommended you very highly as a man to trust. You'll work directly under Dr. Brenner. Make you happy?

MILL. Very. He's an important chemist!

FAY (*leaning over seriously*). We think so, Miller. We think so to the extent of asking you to stay within the building throughout the time you work with him.

MILL. You mean sleep and eat in?

FAY. Yes. . . .

MILL. It can be arranged.

FAY. Fine. You'll go far, Miller.

MILL. May I ask the nature of the new work?

FAY (*looking around first*). Poison gas. . . .

MILL. Poison!

FAY. Orders from above. I don't have to tell you from where. New type poison gas for modern warfare.

MILL. I see.

FAY. You didn't know a new war was that close, did you?

MILL. I guess I didn't.

FAY. I don't have to stress the importance of absolute secrecy.

MILL. I understand!

FAY. The world is an armed camp today. One match sets the whole world blazing in forty-eight hours. Uncle Sam won't be caught napping!

MILL (*addressing his pencil*). They say 12 million men were killed in that last one and 20 million more wounded or missing.

FAY. That's not our worry. If big business went sentimental over human life there wouldn't be big business of any sort!

MILL. My brother and two cousins went in the last one.

FAY. They died in a good cause.

MILL. My mother says "no!"

FAY. She won't worry about you this time. You're too valuable behind the front.

MILL. That's right.

FAY. All right, Miller. See Siegfried for further orders.

MILL. You should have seen my brother—he could ride a bike without hands. . . .

FAY. You'd better move some clothes and shaving tools in tomorrow. Remember what I said—you're with a growing organization.

MILL. He could run the hundred yards in 9:8 flat.

FAY. Who?

MILL. My brother. He's in the Meuse-Argonne Cemetery. Momma went there in 1926. . . .

FAY. Yes, those things stick. How's your handwriting, Miller, fairly legible?

MILL. Fairly so.

FAY. Once a week I'd like a little report from you.

MILL. What sort of report?

FAY. Just a few hundred words once a week on Dr. Brenner's progress.

MILL. Don't you think it might be better coming from the Doctor?

FAY. I didn't ask you that.

MILL. Sorry.

FAY. I want to know what progress he's making, the reports to be purely confidential—between you and me.

MILL. You mean I'm to watch him?

FAY. Yes!

MILL. I guess I can't do that. . . .

FAY. Thirty a month raise . . .

MILL. You said twenty. . . .

FAY. Thirty!

MILL. Guess I'm not built that way.

FAY. Forty. . . .

MILL. Spying's not in my line, Mr. Fayette!

FAY. You use ugly words, Mr. Miller!

MILL. For ugly activity? Yes!

FAY. Think about it, Miller. Your chances are excellent. . . .

MILL. No.

FAY. You're doing something for your country. Assuring the United States that when those God-damn Japs start a ruckus we'll have offensive weapons to back us up! Don't you read your newspapers, Miller?

MILL. Nothing but Andy Gump.

FAY. If you were on the inside you'd know I'm talking cold sober truth! Now, I'm not asking you to make up your mind on the spot. Think about it over your lunch period.

MILL. No. . . .

FAY. Made up your mind already?

MILL. Afraid so.

FAY. You understand the consequences?

MILL. I lose my raise—

(*Simultaneously*) { MILL. And my job! FAY. And your job! MILL. You misunderstand—

MILL. Rather dig ditches first!

FAY. That's a job for foreigners.

MILL. But sneaking—and making poison gas—that's for Americans?

FAY. It's up to you.

MILL. My mind's made up.

FAY. No hard feelings?

MILL. Sure hard feelings! I'm not the civilized type, Mr. Fayette. Nothing suave or sophisticated about me. Plenty of hard feelings! Enough to want to bust you and all your kind square in the mouth!
(*Does exactly that.*)

BLACKOUT

III. THE YOUNG HACK AND HIS GIRL

Opens with girl and brother. FLORENCE *waiting for* SID *to take her to a dance.*

FLOR. I gotta right to have something out of life. I don't smoke, I don't drink. So if Sid wants to take me to a dance, I'll go. Maybe if you was in love you wouldn't talk so hard.

IRV. I'm saying it for your good.

FLOR. Don't be so good to me.

IRV. Mom's sick in bed and you'll be worryin' her to the grave. She don't want that boy hanging around the house and she don't want you meeting him in Crotona Park.

FLOR. I'll meet him anytime I like!

IRV. If you do, yours truly'll take care of it in his own way. With just one hand, too!

FLOR. Why are you all so set against him?

IRV. Mom told you ten times—it ain't him. It's that he ain't got nothing. Sure, we know he's serious, that he's stuck on you. But that don't cut no ice.

FLOR. Taxi drivers used to make good money.

IRV. Today they're makin' five and six dollars a week. Maybe you wanta raise a family on that. Then you'll be back here living with us again and I'll be supporting two families in one. Well . . . over my dead body.

FLOR. Irv, I don't care—I love him!

IRV. You're a little kid with half-baked ideas!

FLOR. I stand there behind the counter the whole day. I think about him—

IRV. If you thought more about Mom it would be better.

FLOR. Don't I take care of her every night when I come home? Don't I cook supper and iron your shirts and . . . you give me a pain in the neck, too. Don't try to shut me up! I bring a few dollars in the house, too. Don't you see I want something else out of life. Sure, I want romance, love, babies. I want everything in life I can get.

IRV. You take care of Mom and watch your step!

FLOR. And if I don't?

IRV. Yours truly'll watch it for you!

FLOR. You can talk that way to a girl. . . .

IRV. I'll talk that way to your boy friend, too, and it won't be with words! Florrie, if you had a pair of eyes you'd see it's for your own good we're talking. This ain't no time to get married. Maybe later—

FLOR. "Maybe later" never comes for me, though. Why don't we send Mom to a hospital? She can die in peace there instead of looking at the clock on the mantelpiece all day.

IRV. That needs money. Which we don't have!

FLOR. Money, Money, Money!

IRV. Don't change the subject.

FLOR. This is the subject!

IRV. You gonna stop seeing him? (*She turns away*) Jesus, kiddie, I remember when you were a baby with curls down your back. Now I gotta stand here yellin' at you like this.

FLOR. I'll talk to him, Irv.

IRV. When?

FLOR. I asked him to come here tonight. We'll talk it over.

IRV. Don't get soft with him. Nowadays is no time to be soft. You gotta be hard as a rock or go under.

FLOR. I found that out. There's the bell. Take the egg off the stove I boiled for Mom. Leave us alone, Irv. (SID *comes in—the two men look at each other for a second.* IRV *exits.*)

SID (*enters*). Hello, Florrie.

FLOR. Hello, Honey. You're looking tired.

SID. Naw, I just need a shave.

FLOR. Well, draw your chair up to the fire and I'll ring for brandy and soda . . . like in the movies.

SID. If this was the movies I'd bring a big bunch of roses.

FLOR. How big?

SID. Fifty or sixty dozen—the kind with long, long stems—big as that. . . .

FLOR. You dope. . . .

SID. Your Paris gown is beautiful.

FLOR (*acting grandly*). Yes, Percy, velvet panels are coming back again. Madame La Farge told me today that Queen Marie herself designed it.

SID. Gee . . . !

FLOR. Every princess in the Balkans is wearing one like this. (*Poses grandly.*)

SID. Hold it. (*Does a nose camera—thumbing nose and imitating grinding of camera with other hand. Suddenly she falls out of the posture and swiftly goes to him, to embrace him, to kiss with love. Finally*)

SID. You look tired, Florrie.

FLOR. Naw, I just need a shave. (*She laughs tremorously.*)

SID. You worried about your mother?

FLOR. No.

SID. What's on your mind?

FLOR. The French and Indian War.

SID. What's on your mind?

FLOR. I got us on my mind, Sid. Night and day, Sid!

SID. I smacked a beer truck today. Did I get hell! I was driving along thinking of US, too. You don't have to say it—I know what's on your mind. I'm rat poison around here.

FLOR. Not to me. . . .

SID. I know to who . . . and I know why. I don't blame them. We're engaged now for three years. . . .

FLOR. That's a long time. . . .

SID. My brother Sam joined the navy this morning—get a break that way. They'll send him down to Cuba with the hootchy-kootchy girls. He don't know from nothing, that dumb basketball player!

FLOR. Don't you do that.

SID. Don't you worry, I'm not the kind who runs away. But I'm so tired of being a dog, Baby, I could choke. I don't even have to ask what's going on in your mind. I know from the word go, 'cause I'm thinking the same things, too.

FLOR. It's yes or no—nothing in between.

SID. The answer is no—a big electric sign looking down on Broadway!

FLOR. We wanted to have kids. . . .

SID. But that sort of life ain't for the dogs which is us. Christ, Baby! I get like thunder in my chest when we're together. If we went off together I could maybe look the world straight in the face, spit in its eye like a man should do. God damn it, it's trying to be a man on the earth. Two in life together.

FLOR. But something wants us to be lonely like that—crawling alone in the dark. Or they want us trapped.

SID. Sure, the big-shot money men want us like that.

FLOR. Highly insulting us—

SID. Keeping us in the dark about what is wrong with us in the money sense. They got the power and mean to be damn sure they keep it. They know if they give in just an inch, all the dogs like us will be down on them together—an ocean knocking them to hell and back and each singing cuckoo with stars coming from their nose and ears. I'm not raving, Florrie—

FLOR. I know you're not, I know.

SID. I don't have the words to tell you what I feel. I never finished school. . . .

FLOR. I know. . . .

SID. But it's relative, like the professors say. We worked like hell to send him to college—my kid brother Sam, I mean—and look what he done—joined the navy! The damn fool don't see the cards is stacked for all of us. The money man dealing himself a hot royal flush. Then giving you and me a phony hand like a pair of tens or something. Then keep on losing the pots 'cause the cards is stacked against you. Then he says, what's the matter you can't win—no stuff on the ball, he says to you. And kids like my brother believe it 'cause they don't know better. For all their education, they don't know from nothing. But wait a minute! Don't he come around and say to you—this millionaire with a jazz band—listen Sam or Sid or what's-your-name, you're no good, but here's a chance. The whole world'll know who you are. Yes sir, he says, get up on that ship and fight those bastards who's making the world a lousy place to live in. The Japs, the Turks, the Greeks. Take this gun—kill the slobs like a real hero, he says, a real American. Be a hero! And the guy you're poking at? A real louse, just like you, 'cause they don't let him catch more than a pair of tens, too. On that foreign soil he's a guy like me and Sam, a guy who wants his baby like you and hot sun on his face! They'll teach Sam to point the guns the wrong way, that dumb basketball player!

FLOR. I got a lump in my throat, Honey.

SID. You and me—we never even had a room to sit in somewhere.

FLOR. The park was nice . . .

SID. In Winter? The hallways . . . I'm glad we never got together. This way we don't know what we missed.

FLOR (*in a burst*). Sid, I'll go with you—we'll get a room somewhere.

SID. Naw . . . they're right. If we can't climb higher than this together—we better stay apart.

FLOR. I swear to God I wouldn't care.

SID. You would, you would—in a year, two years, you'd curse the day. I seen it happen.

FLOR. Oh, Sid. . . .

SID. Sure, I know. We got the blues, Babe—the 1935 blues. I'm talkin' this way 'cause I love you. If I didn't, I wouldn't care. . . .

FLOR. We'll work together, we'll—

SID. How about the backwash? Your family needs your nine bucks. My family—

FLOR. I don't care for them!

SID. You're making it up, Florrie. Little Florrie Canary in a cage.

FLOR. Don't make fun of me.

SID. I'm not, Baby.

FLOR. Yes, you're laughing at me.

SID. I'm not.
(They stand looking at each other, unable to speak. Finally, he turns to a small portable phonograph and plays a cheap, sad, dance tune. He makes a motion with his hand; she comes to him. They begin to dance slowly. They hold each other tightly, almost as though they would merge into each other. The music stops, but the scratching record continues to the end of the scene. They stop dancing. He finally unlooses her clutch and seats her on the couch, where she sits, tense and expectant.)

SID. Hello, Babe.

FLOR. *Hello. (For a brief time they stand as though in a dream.)*

SID *(finally)*. Good-by, Babe. *(He waits for an answer, but she is silent. They look at each other.)*

SID. Did you ever see my Pat Rooney imitation? *(He whistles Rosy O'Grady and soft shoes to it. Stops. He asks)*

SID. Don't you like it?

FLOR *(finally)*. No. *(Buries her face in her hands.)*
(Suddenly he falls on his knees and buries his face in her lap.)

BLACKOUT

IV. LABOR SPY EPISODE

FATT. You don't know how we work for you. Shooting off your mouth won't help. Hell, don't you guys ever look at the records like me? Look in your own industry. See what happened when the hacks walked out in Philly three months ago! Where's Philly? A thousand miles away? An hour's ride on the train.

VOICE. Two hours!

FATT. Two hours . . . what the hell's the difference. Let's hear from someone who's got the practical experience to back him up. Fellers, there's a man here who's seen the whole parade in Philly, walked out with his pals, got knocked down like the rest—and blacklisted after they went back. That's why he's here. He's got a mighty interestin' word to say. *(Announces)* TOM CLAYTON! *(As* CLAYTON *starts up from the audience,* FATT *gives him a hand which is sparsely followed in the audience.* CLAYTON *comes forward)* Fellers, this is a man with practical strike experience—Tom Clayton from little ole Philly.

CLAYTON *(a thin, modest individual)*. Fellers, I don't mind your booing. If I thought it would help us hacks get better living conditions, I'd let you walk all over me, cut me up to little pieces. I'm one of you myself. But what I wanna say is that Harry Fatt's right. I only been working here in the big town five weeks, but I know conditions just like the rest of you. You know how it is—don't take long to feel the sore spots, no matter where you park.

CLEAR VOICE (*from audience*). Sit down!

CLAYTON. But Fatt's right. Our officers is right. The time ain't ripe. Like a fruit don't fall off the tree until it's ripe.

CLEAR VOICE. Sit down, you fruit!

FATT (*on his feet*). Take care of him, boys.

VOICE (*in audience, struggling*). No one takes care of me.
(*Struggle in house and finally the owner of the voice runs up on stage, says to speaker.*)

SAME VOICE. Where the hell did you pick up that name? Clayton! This rat's name is Clancy, from the old Clancys, way back! Fruit! I almost wet myself listening to that one!

FATT (*gunmen with him*). This ain't a barn! What the hell do you think you're doing here!

SAME VOICE. Exposing a rat!

FATT. You can't get away with this. Throw him the hell outa here.

VOICE (*preparing to stand his ground*). Try it yourself. . . . When this bozo throws that slop around. You know who he is? That's a company spy.

FATT. Who the hell are you to make—

VOICE. I paid dues in this union for four years, that's who's me! I gotta right and this pussy-footed rat ain't coming in here with ideals like that. You know his record. Lemme say it out—

FATT. You'll prove all this or I'll bust you in every hack outfit in town!

VOICE. I gotta right. I gotta right. Looka *him*, he don't say boo!

CLAYTON. You're a liar and I never seen you before in my life!

VOICE. Boys, he spent two years in the coal fields breaking up any organization he touched. Fifty guys he put in jail. He's ranged up and down the east coast—shipping, textiles, steel—he's been in everything you can name. Right now—

CLAYTON. That's a lie!

VOICE. Right now he's working for that Bergman outfit on Columbus Circle who furnishes rats for any outfit in the country before, during, and after strikes.
(*The man who is the hero of the next episode goes down to his side with other committee men.*)

CLAYTON. He's trying to break up the meeting, fellers!

VOICE. We won't search you for credentials. . . .

CLAYTON. I got nothing to hide. Your own secretary knows I'm straight.

VOICE. Sure. Boys, you know who this sonovabitch is?

CLAYTON. I never seen you before in my life! !

VOICE. Boys, I slept with him in the same bed sixteen years. HE'S MY OWN LOUSY BROTHER! !

FATT (*after pause*). Is this true? (*No answer from* CLAYTON.)

VOICE (*to* CLAYTON). Scram, before I break your neck!
(CLAYTON *scrams down center aisle.*)

VOICE (*watching him*). Remember his map—he can't change that—Clancy! (*Standing in his place*) Too bad you didn't know about this, Fatt! (*After a pause*) The Clancy family tree is bearing nuts!
(*Standing isolated clear on the stage is the hero of the next episode.*)

BLACKOUT

V. THE YOUNG ACTOR

A New York theatrical producer's office. Present are a stenographer and a young actor. She is busy typing; he, waiting with card in hand.

STEN. He's taking a hot bath . . . says you should wait.

PHILIPS (*the actor*). A bath did you say? Where?

STEN. See that door? Right through there—leads to his apartment.

PHIL. Through there?

STEN. Mister, he's laying there in a hot perfumed bath. Don't say I said it.

PHIL. You don't say!

STEN. An oriental den he's got. Can you just see this big Irishman burning Chinese punk in the bedroom? And a big old rose canopy over his casting couch. . . .

PHIL. What's that—casting couch?

STEN. What's that? You from the sticks?

PHIL. I beg your pardon?

STEN (*rolls up her sleeves, makes elaborate and dumb signs*). No from side walkies of New Yorkie . . . savvy?

PHIL. Oh, you're right. Two years of dramatic stock out of town. One in Chicago.

STEN. Don't tell him, Baby Face. He wouldn't know a good actor if he fell over him in the dark. Say you had two years with the Group, two with the Guild.

PHIL. I'd like to get with the Guild. They say—

STEN. He won't know the difference Don't say I said it!

PHIL. I really did play with Watson Findlay in "Early Birds."

STEN (*withering him*). Don't tell him!

PHIL. He's a big producer, Mr. Grady. I wish I had his money. Don't you?

STEN. Say, I got a clean heart, Mister. I love my fellow man! (*About to exit with typed letters*) Stick around —Mr. Philips. You might be the type. If you were a woman—

PHIL. Please. Just a minute . . . please . . . I need the job.

STEN. Look at him!

PHIL. I mean . . . I don't know what buttons to push, and you do. What my father used to say—we had a gas station in Cleveland before the crash—"Know what buttons to push," Dad used to say, "and you'll go far."

STEN. You can't push me, Mister! I don't ring right these last few years!

PHIL. We don't know where the next meal's coming from. We—

STEN. Maybe . . . I'll lend you a dollar?

PHIL. Thanks very much: it won't help.

STEN. One of the old families of Virginia? Proud?

PHIL. Oh, not that. You see, I have a wife. We'll have our first baby next month . . . so . . . a dollar isn't much help.

STEN. Roped in?

PHIL. I love my wife!

STEN. Okay, you love her! Excuse me! You married her. Can't support her. No . . . not blaming you. But you're fools, all you actors. Old and young! Watch you parade in and out all day. You still got apples in your cheeks and pins for buttons. But in six months you'll be like them—putting on an act: phony strutting "pishers"—that's French for dead codfish! It's not their fault. Here you get like that or go under. What kind of job is this for an adult man?

PHIL. When you have to make a living—

STEN. I know, but—

PHIL. Nothing else to do. If I could get something else—

STEN. You'd take it!

PHIL. Anything!

STEN. Telling me! With two brothers in my hair! (*Mr. Grady now enters; played by* FATT) Mr. Brown sent this young man over.

GRADY. Call the hospital: see how Boris is.
(*She assents and exits.*)

PHIL. Good morning, Mr. Grady. . . .

GRADY. The morning is lousy!

PHIL. Mr. Brown sent me. (*Hands over card.*)

GRADY. I heard that once already.

PHIL. Excuse me. . . .

BRADY. What experience?

PHIL. Oh, yes. . . .

GRADY. Where?

PHIL. Two years in stock, sir. A year with the Goodman Theatre in Chicago. . . .

GRADY. That all?

PHIL (*abashed*). Why no . . . with the Theatre Guild . . . I was there. . . .

GRADY. Never saw you in a Guild show!

PHIL. On the road, I mean . . . understudying Mr. Lunt . . .

GRADY. What part? (*Philips can not answer*) You're a lousy liar, son.

PHIL. I did. . . .

GRADY. You don't look like what I want. Can't understand that Brown. Need a big man to play a soldier. Not a lousy soldier left on Broadway! All in pictures, and we get the nances! (*Turns to work on desk.*)

PHIL (*immediately playing the soldier*). I was in the ROTC in college . . . Reserve Officers' Training Corps. We trained twice a week. . . .

GRADY. Won't help.

PHIL. With real rifles. (*Waits*) Mr. Grady, I weigh a hundred and fifty-five!

GRADY. How many years back? Been eating regular since you left college?

PHIL (*very earnestly*). Mr. Grady, I could act this soldier part. I could build it up and act it. Make it up—

GRADY. Think I run a lousy acting school around here?

PHIL. Honest to God I could! I need the job—that's why I could do it! I'm strong. I know my business! YOU'll get an A-1 performance. Because I need this job! My wife's having a baby in a few weeks. We need the money. Give me a chance!

GRADY. What do I care if you can act it? I'm sorry about your baby. Use your head, son. Tank town stock is different. Here we got investments to be protected. When I sink fifteen thousand in a show I don't take chances on some youngster. We cast to type!

PHIL. I'm an artist! I can—

GRADY. That's your headache. Nobody interested in artists here. Get a big bunch for a nickel on any corner. Two flops in a row on this lousy street nobody loves you—only God, and He don't count. We protect investments: we cast to type. Your face and height we want, not your soul, son. And Jesus Christ himself couldn't play a soldier in this show . . . with all his talent. (*Crosses himself in quick repentance for this remark.*)

PHIL. Anything . . . a bit, a walk-on?

GRADY. Sorry: small cast. (*Looking at papers on his desk*) You try Russia, son. I hear it's hot stuff over there.

PHIL. Stage manager? Assistant?

GRADY. All filled, sonny. (*Stands up; crumples several papers from the desk*) Better luck next time.

PHIL. Thanks. . . .

GRADY. Drop in from time to time. (*Crosses and about to exit*) You never know when something— (*The* STENOGRAPHER *enters with papers to put on desk*) What did the hospital say?

STEN. He's much better, Mr. Grady.

GRADY. Resting easy?

STEN. Dr. Martel said Boris is doing even better than he expected.

GRADY. A damn lousy operation!

STEN. Yes. . . .

GRADY (*belching*). Tell the nigger boy to send up a bromo seltzer.

STEN. Yes, Mr. Grady. (*He exits*) Boris wanted lady friends.

PHIL. What?

STEN. So they operated . . . poor dog!

PHIL. A dog?

STEN. His Russian Wolfhound! They do the same to you, but you don't know it! (*Suddenly*) Want advice? In the next office, don't let them see you down in the mouth. They don't like it—makes them shiver.

PHIL. You treat me like a human being. Thanks. . . .

STEN. You're human!

PHIL. I used to think so.

STEN. He wants a bromo for his hangover. (*Goes to door*) Want that dollar?

PHIL. It won't help much.

STEN. One dollar buys ten loaves of bread, Mister. Or one dollar buys nine loaves of bread and one copy of The Communist Manifesto. Learn while you eat. Read while you run. . . .

PHIL. Manifesto? What's that? (*Takes dollar*) What is that, what you said. . . . Manifesto?

STEN. Stop off on your way out—I'll give you a copy. From Genesis to Revelation, Comrade Philips! "And I saw a new earth and a new heaven; for the first earth and the first heaven were passed away; and there was no more sea."

PHIL. I don't understand that. . . .

STEN. I'm saying the meek shall not inherit the earth!

PHIL. No?

STEN. The MILITANT! Come out in the light, Comrade.

BLACKOUT

VI. INTERNE EPISODE

DR. BARNES, *an elderly distinguished man, is speaking on the telephone. He wears a white coat.*

DR. BARNES. No, I gave you my opinion twice. You outvoted me. You did this to Dr. Benjamin yourself. That is why you can tell him yourself. (*Hangs up phone, angrily. As he is about to pour himself a drink from a bottle on the table, a knock is heard.*)

BARNES. Who is it?

BENJAMIN (*without*). Can I see you a minute, please?

BARNES (*hiding the bottle*). Come in, Dr. Benjamin, come in.

BENJ. It's important—excuse me—they've got Leeds up there in my place—He's operating on Mrs. Lewis—the hysterectomy—it's my job. I washed up, prepared . . . they told me at the last minute. I don't mind being replaced, Doctor, but Leeds is a damn fool! He shouldn't be permitted—

BARNES (*dryly*). Leeds is the nephew of Senator Leeds.

BENJ. He's incompetent as hell.

BARNES (*obviously changing subject, picks up lab. jar*). They're doing splendid work in brain surgery these days. This is a very fine specimen. . . .

BENJ. I'm sorry, I thought you might be interested.

BARNES (*still examining jar*). Well, I am, young man, I am! Only remember it's a charity case!

BENJ. Of course. They wouldn't allow it for a second, otherwise.

BARNES. Her life is in danger?

BENJ. Of course! You know how serious the case is!

BARNES. Turn your gimlet eye elsewhere, Doctor. Jiggling around like a cricket on a hot grill won't help. Doctors don't run these hospitals. He's the Senator's nephew and there he stays.

BENJ. It's too bad.

BARNES. I'm not calling you down either. (*Plopping down jar suddenly*) God damn it, do you think it's my fault?

BENJ. (*about to leave*). I know . . . I'm sorry.

BARNES. Just a minute. Sit down.

BENJ. Sorry, I can't sit.

BARNES. Stand then!

BENJ. (*sits*). Understand, Dr. Barnes, I don't mind being replaced at the last minute this way, but . . . well, this flagrant bit of class distinction—because she's poor—

BARNES. Be careful of words like that —"class distinction." Don't belong here. Lots of energy, you brilliant young men, but idiots. Discretion! Ever hear that word?

BENJ. Too radical?

BARNES. Precisely. And some day like in Germany, it might cost you your head.

BENJ. Not to mention my job.

BARNES. So they told you?

BENJ. Told me what?

BARNES. They're closing Ward C next month. I don't have to tell you the hospital isn't self-supporting. Until last year that board of trustees met deficits. . . . You can guess the rest. At a board meeting Tuesday, our fine feathered friends discovered they couldn't meet the last quarter's deficit—a neat little sum well over $100,000. If the hospital is to continue at all, its damn—

BENJ. Necessary to close another charity ward!

BARNES. So they say. . . . (*A wait.*)

BENJ. But that's not all?

BARNES (*ashamed*). Have to cut down on staff too. . . .

BENJ. That's too bad. Does it touch me?

BARNES. Afraid it does.

BENJ. But after all I'm top man here. I don't mean I'm better than others, but I've worked harder.

BARNES. And shown more promise. . . .

BENJ. I always supposed they'd cut from the bottom first.

BARNES. Usually.

BENJ. But in this case?

BARNES. Complications.

BENJ. For instance?

BARNES (*hesitant*). I like you, Benjamin. It's one ripping shame.

BENJ. I'm no sensitive plant—what's the answer?

BARNES. An old disease, malignant, tumescent. We need an antitoxin for it.

BENJ. I see.

BARNES. What?

BENJ. I met that disease before—at Harvard first.

BARNES. You have seniority here, Benjamin.

BENJ. But I'm a Jew! (BARNES *nods his head in agreement.* BENJ. *stands there a moment and blows his nose.*)

BARNES (*blows his nose*). Microbes!

BENJ. Pressure from above?

BARNES. Don't think Kennedy and I didn't fight for you!

BENJ. Such discrimination, with all those wealthy brother Jews on the board?

BARNES. I've remarked before—doesn't seem to be much difference between wealthy Jews and rich Gentiles. Cut from the same piece!

BENJ. For myself I don't feel sorry. My parents gave up an awful lot to get me this far. They ran a little drygoods shop in the Bronx until their pitiful savings went in the crash last year. Poppa's peddling neckties. . . . Saul Ezra Benjamin—a man who's read Spinoza all his life.

BARNES. Doctors don't run medicine in this country. The men who know their jobs don't run anything here, except the motormen on trolley cars. I've seen medicine change—plenty—anesthesia, sterilization—but not because of rich men—in *spite* of them! In a rich man's country your true self's buried deep. Microbes! Less. . . . Vermin! See this ankle, this delicate sensitive hand? Four hundred years to breed that. Out of a revolutionary background! Spirit of '76! Ancestors froze at Valley Forge! What's it all mean? Slops! The honest workers were sold out then, in '76. The Constitution's for rich men then and now. Slops! (*The phone rings.*)

BARNES (*angrily*). Dr. Barnes. (*Listens a moment, looks at* BENJAMIN) I see. (*Hangs up, turns slowly to the younger Doctor*) They lost your patient.

(BENJ. *stands solid with the shock of this news but finally hurls his operation gloves to the floor.*)

BARNES. That's right . . . that's right. Young, hot, go and do it! I'm very ancient, fossil, but life's ahead of you, Dr. Benjamin, and when you fire the first shot say, "This one's for old Doc Barnes!" Too much dignity—bullets. Don't shoot vermin! Step on them! If I didn't have an invalid daughter— (*Goes back to his seat, blows his nose in silence*) I have said my piece, Benjamin.

BENJ. Lots of things I wasn't certain of. Many things these radicals say . . . you don't believe theories until they happen to you.

BARNES. You lost a lot today, but you won a great point.

BENJ. Yes, to know I'm right? To really begin believing in something? Not to say, "What a world!" but to say, "Change the world!" I wanted to go to Russia. Last week I was thinking about it—the wonderful opportunity to do good work in their socialized medicine—

BARNES. Beautiful, beautiful!

BENJ. To be able to work—

BARNES. Why don't you go? I might be able—

BENJ. Nothing's nearer what I'd like to do!

BARNES. Do it!

BENJ. No! Our work's here—America! I'm scared. . . . What future's ahead, I don't know. Get some job to keep alive—maybe drive a cab—and study and work and learn my place—

BARNES. And step down hard!

BENJ. Fight! Maybe get killed, but God damn! We'll go ahead! (BENJAMIN *stands with clenched fist raised high.*)

BLACKOUT

AGATE. LADIES AND GENTLEMEN, and don't let anyone tell you we ain't got some ladies in this sea of upturned faces! Only they're wearin' pants. Well, maybe I don't know a thing; maybe I fell outa the cradle when I was a kid and ain't been right since—you can't tell!

VOICE. Sit down, cockeye!

AGATE. Who's paying you for those remarks, Buddy?—Moscow Gold? Maybe I got a *glass eye*, but it come from working in a factory at the age of eleven. They hooked it out because they didn't have a shield on the works. But I wear it like a medal 'cause it tells the world where I belong—deep down in the working class! We had delegates in the union there—all kinds of secretaries and treasurers . . . walkin' delegates, but not with blisters on their feet! Oh, no! On their fat little ass from sitting on cushions and raking in mazuma. (SECRETARY *and* GUNMAN *remonstrate in words and actions here*) Sit down, boys. I'm just sayin' that about unions in general. I know it ain't true here! Why no, our officers is all aces. Why, I seen our own secretary Fatt walk outa his way not to step on a cockroach. No, boys, don't think—

FATT (*breaking in*). You're out of order!

AGATE (*to audience*). Am I outa order?

ALL. No, no. Speak. Go on, etc.

AGATE. Yes, our officers is all aces. But I'm a member here—and no experience in Philly either! Today I couldn't wear my union button. The damnedest thing happened. When I take the old coat off the wall, I see she's smoking. I'm a sonovagun if the old union button isn't on fire! Yep, the old celluloid was makin' the most god-awful stink: the landlady come up and give me hell! You know what happened?—that old union button just blushed itself to death! Ashamed! Can you beat it?

FATT. Sit down, Keller! Nobody's interested!

AGATE. Yes they are!

GUNMAN. Sit down like he tells you!

AGATE (*continuing to audience*). And when I finish—
(*His speech is broken by* FATT *and* GUNMAN *who physically handle him. He breaks away and gets to other side of stage. The two are about to make for him when some of the committeemen come forward and get in between the struggling parties.* AGATE'*s shirt has been torn.*)

AGATE (*to audience*). What's the answer, boys? The answer is, if we're reds because we wanna strike, then we take over their salute too! Know how they do it? (*Makes Communist salute*) What is it? An uppercut! The good old uppercut to the chin! Hell, some of us boys ain't even got a shirt to our back. What's the boss class tryin' to do—make a nudist colony outa us?
(*The audience laughs and suddenly* AGATE *comes to the middle of the stage so that the other cabmen back him up in a strong clump.*)

AGATE. Don't laugh! Nothing's funny! This is your life and mine! It's skull and bones every incha the road! Christ, we're dyin' by inches! For what? For the debutant-ees to have their sweet comin' out parties in the Ritz! Poppa's got a daughter she's gotta get her picture in the papers. Christ, they make 'em with our blood. Joe said it. Slow death or fight. It's war! (*Throughout this whole speech* AGATE *is backed up by the other six workers, so that from their activity it is plain that the whole group of them are saying these things. Several of them may take alternate lines out of this long last speech*) You Edna, God love your mouth! Sid and Florrie, the other boys, old Doc Barnes—fight with us for right! It's war! Working class, unite and fight! Tear down the slaughterhouse of our old lives! Let freedom really ring. These slick slobs stand here telling us about bogeymen. That's a new one for the kids—the reds is bogeymen! But the man who got me food in 1932, he called me Comrade! The one who picked me up where I bled —he called me Comrade too! What are we waiting for. . . . Don't wait for Lefty! He might never come. Every minute— (*This is broken into by a man who has dashed up the center aisle from the back of the house. He runs up on stage, says*)

MAN. Boys, they just found Lefty!

OTHERS. What? What? What?

SOME. Shhh. . . . Shhh. . . .

MAN. They found Lefty. . . .

AGATE. Where?

MAN. Behind the car barns with a bullet in his head!

AGATE (*crying*). Hear it, boys, hear it? Hell, listen to me! Coast to coast! HELLO AMERICA! HELLO. WE'RE STORMBIRDS OF THE WORKING CLASS. WORKERS OF THE WORLD. . . . OUR BONES AND BLOOD! And when we die they'll know what we did to make a new world! Christ, cut us up to little pieces. We'll die for what is right! put fruit trees where our ashes are! (*To audience*) Well, what's the answer?

ALL. STRIKE!

AGATE. LOUDER!

ALL. STRIKE!

AGATE *and* OTHERS (*on stage*). AGAIN!

ALL. STRIKE, STRIKE, STRIKE!!!

CURTAIN

NOTES FOR PRODUCTION

The background of the episodes, a strike meeting, is not an excuse. Each of the committeemen shows in his episode the crucial moment of his life which brought him to this very platform. The dramatic structure on which the play has been built is simple but highly effective. The form used is the old blackface minstrel form of chorus, end men, specialty men and interlocutor.

In FATT's *scenes before the "Spy Exposé," mention should again be made of* LEFTY's *tardiness. Sitting next to* FATT *in the center of the circle is a little henchman who sits with his back to the audience. On the other side of* FATT *is* LEFTY's *empty chair. This is so indicated by* FATT *when he himself asks: "Yeah, where's your chairman?"*

FATT, *of course, represents the capitalist system throughout the play. The audience should constantly be kept aware of him, the ugly menace which hangs over the lives of all the people who act out their own dramas. Perhaps he puffs smoke into the spotted playing space; perhaps during the action of a playlet he might insolently walk in and around the unseeing players. It is possible that some highly gratifying results can be achieved by the imaginative use of this character.*

The strike committee on the platform during the acting out of the playlets should be used as chorus. Emotional, political, musical, they have in them possibilities of various comments on the scenes. This has been indicated once in the script in the place where JOE's *wife is about to leave him. In the climaxes of each scene, slogans might very effectively be used—a voice coming out of the dark. Such a voice might announce at the appropriate moments in the "Young Interne's" scene that the USSR is the only country in the world where anti-Semitism is a crime against the State.*

Do not hesitate to use music wherever possible. It is very valuable in emotionally stirring an audience.

Dead End

BY SIDNEY KINGSLEY

"The contrast of affluence and wretchedness is like dead and living bodies chained together."

THOMAS PAINE

Dead End was first produced at the Belasco Theatre, New York City, by Norman Bel Geddes on October 28, 1935, and closed on June 12, 1937. Following is the original cast:

GIMPTY	Theodore Newton
T.B.	Gabriel Dell
TOMMY	Billy Hallop
DIPPY	Huntz Hall
ANGEL	Bobby Jordon
SPIT	Charles R. Duncan
DOORMAN	George Cotton
OLD LADY	Marie R. Burke
OLD GENTLEMAN	George N. Price
1ST CHAUFFEUR	Charles Benjamin
"BABY-FACE" MARTIN	Joseph Downing
HUNK	Martin Gabel
PHILIP GRISWALD	Charles Bellin
GOVERNESS	Sidonie Espero
MILTY	Bernard Punsly
DRINA	Elspeth Eric
MR. GRISWALD	Carroll Ashburn
MR. JONES	Louis Woods
KAY	Margaret Mullen
JACK HILTON	Cyril Gordon Weld
LADY WITH DOG	Margaret Linden
THREE SMALL BOYS	Billy Winston, Joseph Taibi Sidney Lumet
2ND CHAUFFEUR	Richard Clark
SECOND AVENUE BOYS	David Gorcey, Leo Gorcey
MRS. MARTIN	Marjorie Main
PATROLMAN MULLIGAN	Robert J. Mulligan
FRANCEY	Sheila Trent

G MEN	Francis de Sales, Dan Duryea Edward P. Goodnow
POLICEMEN	Francis G. Cleveland William Toubin
PLAINCLOTHESMAN	George Steele
INTERNE	Philip Bourneuf
MEDICAL EXAMINER	Lewis L. Russel
SAILOR	Bernard Zanville

Directed by Sidney Kingsley

DEAD END

ACT ONE

Dead end of a New York street, ending in a wharf over the East River. To the left are a high terrace and a white iron gate leading to the back of the exclusive East River Terrace Apartments. Hugging the terrace and filing up the street are a series of squalid tenement houses.

Beyond the wharf is the East River, covered by a swirling scum an inch thick. A brown river, mucky with floating refuse and offal. A hundred sewers vomit their guts into it. Up-town of the wharf as we float down Hell Gate, the River voices its defiant protest in fierce whirlpools and stumbling rapids, groaning. Farther down, we pass under the arch of the Queensboro Bridge, spired, delicate, weblike in superstructure, powerful and brutal in the stone and steel which it plants like uncouth giant feet on the earth. In its hop, skip, and jump over the River it has planted one such foot on the Island called Welfare, once the home of hospital, insane asylum, and prison, now being dismantled, an eyesore to the fastidious who have recently become its neighbors. And here on the shore, along the Fifties, is a strange sight. Set plumb down in the midst of slums, antique warehouses, discarded breweries, slaughterhouses, electrical works, gas tanks, loading cranes, coal-chutes, the very wealthy have begun to establish their city residence in huge, new, palatial apartments.

The East River Terrace is one of these. Looking up this street from the vantage of the River, we see only a small portion of the back terrace and a gate; but they are enough to suggest the towering magnificence of the whole structure. The wall is of rich, heavy masonry, guarded at the top by a row of pikes. Beyond the pikes, shutting off the view of the squalid street below, is a thick edging of lush green shrubbery. And beyond that, a glimpse of the tops of gaily colored sun umbrellas. Occasionally the clink of glasses and laughter filter through the shrubs. The exposed sidewall of the tenement is whitewashed and ornamented with an elaborate, ivy-covered trellis to hide its ugliness. The gate posts are crowned with brass ship lanterns, one red, one green. Through the gateway is a catwalk which leads to a floating dock, where the inhabitants of this apartment moor their boats and yachts.

Contrasting sharply with all this richness is the diseased street below, filthy, strewn with torn newspapers and garbage from the tenements. The tenement houses are close, dark and crumbling. They crowd each other. Where there are curtains in the windows, they are streaked and faded; where there are none, we see through to hideous, water-stained, peeling wallpaper, and old broken-down furniture. The fire escapes are cluttered with gutted mattresses and quilts, old clothes, bread boxes, milk bottles, a canary cage, an occasional potted plant struggling for life.

To the right is a huge, red sand hopper standing on stilts of heavy timber several stories tall. Up the street, blocking the view, is a caterpillar steam shovel. Beyond it, way over to the west, are the sky-scraping parallelepipeds of Radio City. An alley-way between two tenements, tied together by drooping lines of wash, gives us a distant glimpse of the mighty Empire State Building rearing its useless mooring tower a quarter of a mile into the clouds.

At the juncture of tenement house and terrace is a police call-box; at the juncture of the street and wharf is a police stanchion bearing the warning, "Dead End."

The boards of the wharf are weatherbeaten and deeply grained; the piles are stained green with algae to where the water licks, and brown above. A ladder nailed to the beams dips down into the river. The sunlight tossed from the waves dances across the piles to the musical lap of the water. Other river sounds counterpoint the orchestration: the bells and the whistles, the clink and the chug of passing boats.

A gang of boys are swimming in the sewerage at the foot of the wharf, splashing about and enjoying it immensely. Some of them wear torn bathing trunks, others are nude. Their speech is a rhythmic, shocking jargon that would put a truck-driver to blush.

There are a few onlookers. A fat, greasy WOMAN *leans out of a tenement window. She is peeling an orange and throwing the peels into the street. A sensitive-faced young* MAN, *in a patched, frayed shirt, open at the neck, is sitting on one of the piles. In his lap is a drawing board. Occasionally he will work feverishly, using pencil and triangular ruler, then he will let the pencil droop, and stare out over the river with deep-set eyes, dream-laden, moody.*

A tubercular-looking BOY *about sixteen is up near the hopper, pitching pennies to the sidewalk. There is a splash of water, a loud derisive laugh, and up the ladder climbs a* BOY, *lean, lithe, long-limbed, snub-nosed, his cheeks puffed with water. Reaching the top of the ladder, he leans over and squirts out the water. A yelp below. He laughs again and cries: "Gotcha dat time!"*

TWO BOYS *come running down the street toward the wharf. One, a tiny Italian with a great shock of blue-black hair, is dangling a shoe box almost as big as himself; the other, a gawky Polack, head shaven, cretinous, adenoidal, is slapping his thigh with a rolled newspaper as he runs. They shout: "Hi ya, Tommy?"*

TOMMY. H'lo, Angel! H'lo, Dippy! (ANGEL *unslings his box, and starts tearing off his clothes. A squat boy with a brutish face, snot bubbling from his nostrils, climbs up after* TOMMY. *As he reaches the top and sees the others, he shouts in a mocking sing-song, "Dopey Dippy, dopey Dippy, dopey Dippy!"*)

DIPPY. Shat ap, will ya, Spit!

SPIT (*spitting through his teeth at* DIPPY, *who is stripping his jersey over his head*). Right inna belly-button! (*Laughs and climbs onto the wharf to sprawl next to* TOMMY. DIPPY *mumbles and wipes out his navel with his finger.*)

TOMMY. Lay off 'im, why doncha?

SPIT. I'll knock 'im innis eye!

TOMMY. Wassamattuh? Yuh a wise guy er a boy scout? C'mon in, Dippy!

ANGEL. Howza wawda, Tommy?

TOMMY. Boy! Duh nuts!

SPIT. Geeze, great!

ANGEL. Cold?

TOMMY. Nah. Swell. Jus' right. (*Wiping off some of the river filth that has clung to him*) Boy, deah's a lot a junk inna wawda tuhday!

DIPPY (*pointing to some dirt on* SPIT'*s back*). Wat's at? (*He touches* SPIT, *smells his finger and makes a wry face*) Pee-ew, whadda stink! (SPIT *plucks off a huge gob of filth and throws it at* DIPPY. DIPPY *whines*) What yuh wanna do dat fuh?

SPIT. Aw, I'll mobilize yuh!

TOMMY. Leave 'im alone! (*To* DIPPY) Whyn't yuh keep yuh trap shut, huh?

DIPPY. He trew dat crap on me! I wuz . . .

TOMMY. O.K. O.K. O.K. (*Pointing at some imaginary object near the sand hopper*) Hey, felluhs, look! (*All look off.* TOMMY *sticks his forefinger next to* SPIT'*s averted nose*) Hey, Spit! (SPIT *turns his head and bumps his nose on* TOMMY'*s finger. The boys laugh*) Nex' time leave 'im alone, see?

(*The cadaverous-looking lad picks up his pennies, and comes down to the others, boasting, "Boy, I git a crack all a time!"*)

TOMMY (*rising*). Yeah? Aw right, T.B., I'll pitch yuh.

T.B. O.K. C'mon.

TOMMY. Lemme a couple.

T.B. Yuh ain' got 'ny?

TOMMY. Come on! I'll pay yuh back. (TOMMY *and* T.B. *go up to the hopper and pitch pennies to the side walk.*)

SPIT (*turning to* DIPPY, *makes a swipe at him.* DIPPY *backs away*). Two fuh flinchin' . . . two fuh flinchin'!

DIPPY. I di' not.

SPIT. Yuh did so.

DIPPY. I di' not.

ANGEL. Whyn't cha choose? Choose 'im. Choose fer it!

SPIT (*scrambling to his feet*). O.K. Odds!

ANGEL. Go on!

DIPPY. Evens! (SPIT *and* DIPPY *match fingers*) Once fuh me. See? Cheatin' shows!

SPIT. Come on! Once fuh me. Twice fuh me. An' tree fuh me. Cheatin' shows? Yeah. Boy, ahl knock yuh fer a loop!

ANGEL. Go on, Dippy, yuh lost. Yuh git yer lumps.

DIPPY (*whining*). Hey, Tommy. . . .

SPIT (*grabbing* DIPPY'*s rolled newspaper*). Come on! (*He bangs* DIPPY *twice on the head.*)

DIPPY. Ow! . . . Ow! . . . Ow! Ah, yuh louse. Yuh didn't have tuh hit me so hahd. Wid all his might he hit me. Wid all his might, duh son uva bitch!

TOMMY (*still absorbed in pitching pennies with* T.B.). Whyn't yuh pick on a kid who kin fight back?

SPIT. Aw-ww!

TOMMY. Ah!
(*The* DOORMAN, *a giant in powder-blue uniform with gilt buttons and braid, opens the gate of the apartment house, crosses to the end of the sidewalk and blows a whistle, then signals to someone up the street to come down. He turns to speak to an aristocratic* OLD GENTLEMAN *and* OLD LADY *who appear in the gateway of the East River Terraces.*)

DOORMAN. I'm so sorry, ma'am, but it'll only be for a day or two.

OLD LADY. That's quite all right.

OLD GENTLEMAN (*arthritic, grumpy, walking slowly and with effort*). It isn't at all. There's no reason why we should have to walk half a block to the car.
(*A* COLORED MAN *in chauffeur's uniform comes down the sidewalk.*)

DOORMAN. I'm so sorry, sir.

OLD LADY. That's quite all right. (*She pauses a moment, surveying the boys*) Look at this!

OLD GENTLEMAN. Humph! I've seen it from the balcony.

ANGEL. Hey, look, guys! Dey usin' a back daw.

TOMMY. I wonduh why.

DIPPY (*familiarly, to the young man who is sketching*). Duh yuh know, Gimpty? Hey, Gimpty?

GIMPTY. What?

DIPPY. Duh yuh know why?

GIMPTY. Why what?

DIPPY. Why dey usin' a back daw.

GIMPTY. Are they?

DIPPY. Yeah.

GIMPTY. No . . . no, I don't.
(*The* COLORED CHAUFFEUR *salutes the* OLD MAN *and offers him an arm to lean on.*)

CHAUFFEUR. Good afternoon, sir. I'm sorry I couldn't drive the car around the . . .

OLD LADY. That's all right, Jordan. Look at these youngsters! Aren't they sweet?

OLD GENTLEMAN. Sweet? Yes . . . from a distance!
(*They walk up the street, out of sight. A passing tug blasts the air with its foghorn.* TOMMY, *having won at penny-pitching, puts the pennies in the pocket of his trousers, which are hanging on the hopper.* T.B. *disconsolate, goes to* ANGEL.)

T.B. Dat cleans me. I dunno. I kin always git a crack when I'm playin' by myself. (*He watches* ANGEL, *who is fussing with a scrap of newspaper and some strange, brown substance*) Watcha got deah?

ANGEL. It's a dried up hawse-ball.

T.B. Watcha doin'?

ANGEL. I'm gonna make some cigarettes. Some guy tole me—yuh kin make cigarettes outta dem.

T.B. Yeah?

ANGEL. Yeah. I'm gonna try it.

T.B. I never hoid a dat.

ANGEL. It's good. Some guy tole me.

TOMMY. Aw, yuh crazy.

ANGEL. Naw . . . it's good.

T.B. Deah wuz a guy at rifawm school once used tuh smoke marywanna. Yuh know what dat is? Dope. It's like dope. It's dope. It gives yuh dreams.

ANGEL. Didja try it?

T.B. Nah. I can't smoke on accoun' a my T.B. It gits me. I cough like anyt'ing.

ANGEL (*rises and crosses to* GIMPTY). Hey, Gimpty, got a match?

T.B. (*murmurs*). My pratt and your face. Dat's a good match! (*Laughs to himself.*)

GIMPTY. What for?

DIPPY. He's makin' cigarettes outta hawse-balls.

GIMPTY. Out of what?

ANGEL. Hawse-balls.

GIMPTY. Throw it away, you crazy fool. You want to get sick?

ANGEL. I kin smoke. Whadda yuh tink I yam?

GIMPTY. Listen. I read about a guy once who smoked that stuff. You know what happened to him.

ANGEL. What?

GIMPTY. Great, big things grew right out of his head.

ANGEL (*turning away from* GIMPTY, *with disgust*). Aw—w—w, go wan.

GIMPTY. Listen . . . if I give you a good one, will you throw that away?

ANGEL (*turning back eagerly*). Sure!

GIMPTY (*appropriates* ANGEL'S *horrible cigarette and throws it into the water; then takes a sack of tobacco from his pocket, adeptly rolls a cigarette and holds it out to* ANGEL). Here! Stick out your tongue. (ANGEL *licks the paper.* GIMPTY *completes rolling the cigarette and gives it to him*) There you are! Now don't try that again. You'll get sick as a dog. Remember . . . I'm tellin' you.

ANGEL (*proudly exhibiting his cigarette*). Boy! Hey, felluhs, look! Gimpty gimme a butt. (*To* T.B.) Gimme a light, T.B. (T.B. *fishes some matches from his pocket and lights* ANGEL'S *cigarette.*)

DIPPY (*dashing over to* GIMPTY). Me too, Gimpty! Gimme! Yew know me! Yew know me! (DIPPY, TOMMY *and* SPIT *descend on* GIMPTY, *swarming over him like a horde of locusts. They hold out their hands and beg plaintively. "Give us one! Yew know us, Gimpty."*)

GIMPTY. No! No! No more! Beat it! That's all! (*They only plead the louder*) I said that's all. Don't you understand English? You want a boot in the behind?

(TWO MEN *come down the street. One, tall, young, rather good looking in a vicious way: the other, older, shorter, squat, a sledge-hammer build. The first has thin nervous lips, narrow agate eyes, bloodshot. A peculiarly glossy face, as if the skin had been stretched taut over the cheekbones which are several sizes too large for the lean jaw underneath. Here is a man given to sudden volcanic violences that come and are gone in a breath. His movements are sharp, jerky; his reflexes exaggerated, those of a high-strung man whose nerves are beginning to snap under some constant strain. He covers it, though, with a cocky swagger. He walks leaning forward, hips thrown back, almost as if out of joint. He wears a gray, turned-down fedora, an expensive suit, sharpy style, the coat a bit too tight at the waist, pleated trousers, and gray suede shoes. His squat companion is dressed almost identically, but was not designed to wear such clothes. His trousers hang on his hips, revealing a bulge of shirtwaist between vest and trouser-top, his barrel of a chest is too thick for his jacket, his arms too long for the sleeves. His huge fingers you notice at once! Thick stubs sticking out of the shapeless bags of his hands like the teats of a cow. The* TWO MEN *come down almost to the edge of the wharf. The tall one lights a cigarette, looks about, smiles, shakes his head, and talks* sotto voce *to his companion.)*

TOMMY (*to* GIMPTY). Aw, ta hell wid yuh! Cheap skate!
(*The boys walk away, disgusted.* GIMPTY *rolls another cigarette, lights it, and returns to his drawing-board.*)

SPIT. Yeah, ta hell wid 'im!

DIPPY. Yeah, ta hell wid 'im!

SPIT (*crosses to his clothes, which are hanging from a nail on the hopper*). I dun need hisn. I gotta stack a butts I picked up I'm savin'.

TOMMY. Give us one.

DIPPY. Yeah! Give us one!

SPIT. Nah. I'm savin' 'em.

TOMMY. Don' be a miser. (SPIT *takes out a tobacco tin, opens it, exposing a rare collection of cigarette ends gleaned from the streets. Grudgingly he hands* TOMMY *and* DIPPY *a butt each, then selects a choice one for himself*) Gimme a light, T.B. (*They all light up and puff away with huge satisfaction.*)

ANGEL (*suddenly aware of the two strangers*). Shine, mistah? (*The tall fellow shakes his head and turns away*) A good shine. Come on! (*To the other*) Yew? (*The squat man glares at him and growls, "Yuh cockeyed? Can't yuh see we got one?"*)

ANGEL (*turns away, muttering*). Aw . . . call 'at a shine?
(*The* DOORMAN *comes to the gate and holds it open. A* GOVERNESS, *accompanied by a well-dressed, delicate-featured, little boy, comes out of the Terrace Apartments. The* GOVERNESS *talks with a marked French accent. She nods to the* DOORMAN.)

GOVERNESS. Good afternoon.

DOORMAN. Good afternoon, ma'am.

GOVERNESS. But . . . where is our chauffeur?

DOORMAN. I think he's on the corner with the cab-drivers. Shall I get him?

GOVERNESS. Never mind. (*To the little boy*) Wait here. *Attends moi ici, mon cheri.*
(*The* DOORMAN *goes in, closing the gate behind him. The little boy, surveying the curious scene, answers, a bit distracted, "All right, I'll . . ." When he opens his mouth, he shows a shiny, gold orthodontic brace.*)

GOVERNESS. *Mais, Philippe! En français!*

PHILIP (*obediently*). *Oui, mademoiselle, j'attendrai.*

GOVERNESS. *Très bien. J'y reviendrai de suite . . . dans deux minutes.*

PHILIP. *Oui, oui, mademoiselle.*
(*She hurries up the sidewalk and out of sight.*)

TOMMY. Wee-wee! He's godda go wee-wee!
(*All the boys shout with laughter.*)

DIPPY. Do a swan-dive, Tommy. At's wad I like.

TOMMY. O.K. Hole my butt. (*He hands his cigarette to* DIPPY) Hey, kid! Hey, yew! Hey, wee-wee! (PHILIP *looks at him*) Yuh wanna see sumpm? A swan-dive. Watch! (TOMMY *dashes off, under the hopper. We hear his "Whe-e-e" and a splash. The boys cluck approval.*)

PHILIP. What's so wonderful about that?

ANGEL. Aw, yuh fat tub a buttuh, it's more'n yew kin do.

PHILIP. That shows how much you know.

T.B. I bet a dollar he can't even swim.

PHILIP. I can too.

T.B. Ah, balonee!

PHILIP. Balonee yourself! We've a pool in there and I swim every day . . . with instruction.

SPIT. Aw, bushwah!
(TOMMY *appears on the ladder.* DIPPY *hands him his cigarette.*)

DIPPY. He sez dey godda pool in ere.

TOMMY. How wuzat swan-dive?

DIPPY. He sez it wuz lousy.

TOMMY (*climbing over the parapet and crossing to* PHILIP, *belligerently*). Oh yeah? What wuza mattuh wid it? Kin yew do betta?

PHILIP. A trillion times.

TOMMY. Awright. Lessee yuh.

PHILIP. Where?

TOMMY. Heah!

PHILIP. Here?

TOMMY. Yeah, heah. Yew hoid me. Yew ain' deef. (*Turns to the others*) His eahs ovuhlap, dat's it! (*They roar with laughter.*)

PHILIP. I wouldn't swim here.

T.B. He's yelluh, dat's what! Dat's what! He's godda yelluh streak up 'is back a mile wide.

PHILIP. It's dirty here.

DIPPY (*shocked*). Doity!

T.B. (*very indignant*). Doity! He sez doity. He sez it's doity! I'll sock 'im!

ANGEL. Lil fairy!

SPIT. Wassamattuh? Yuh sca'd yuh git a lil doit on yuh?

PHILIP. Besides, I haven't got my suit.

TOMMY. Well, go in bareass.

T.B. Yeah, wassamattuh wid bareass?

PHILIP. And besides, I'm not allowed to.

DIPPY (*sing-song*). Sissy, sissy, sucks his mamma's titty!

PHILIP. Sticks and stones may break my bones, but names will never hurt me.
(*The boys crowd him back against the gate.*)

TOMMY. Ah, ahl spit in yuh eye an' drown yuh. Hey, what's 'at junk yuh got in yuh mout . . . like a hawse?

PHILIP. It's a brace, to make my teeth straight.

TOMMY. Wha-a-at? I could do dat wit one wallop!
(*The gang roar with laughter.*)

PHILIP. You try and you'll be arrested.

SPIT. Yeah?

TOMMY (*contemptuously*). Look who's gonna arrest us!

PHILIP. My uncle's a judge.

TOMMY. Balonee!

PHILIP. Did you ever hear of Judge Griswald?

ANGEL. So what? So I know a guy whose brudduh's a detective. He'll git us out.

T.B. Yeah? Did yuh evuh hear a Judge Poikins! Well, he's a frien' a mine, see? He sent me to rifawm school once.

DOORMAN (*appears, bellowing*). What's the matter? Get away from here, you! (*They scatter, razzing him. He turns to* PHILIP) Were they bothering you?

PHILIP. No, I don't pay any attention to them.
(*The* DOORMAN *opens the gate and both he and* PHILIP *go in. The boys laugh and mock them.* DIPPY, *preoccupied with the phenomena of his body, suddenly discovers a lone hair on his chest.*)

DIPPY. Boy! Gee! Hey, I godda hair! (*He caresses it, proudly.* T.B. *comes over, inspects the hair, admires it, then suddenly plucks it out, and runs away laughing and holding up the trophy.* DIPPY *yips, first with pain, then with rage.* TOMMY *finds an old discarded broom in the litter under the hopper. He balances it skillfully on the palm of his hand.*)

SPIT. Gese, I'm hungry!

TOMMY. Me too!

ANGEL. Boy, I'm so hungry I could eat a live dog.

DIPPY (*looks up from his wounded chest*). Boy, I could eat a hot dog.

ANGEL. Wid sauerkraut!

DIPPY. Yeah.

ANGEL (*licking his lips and patting his belly*). Yum.

SPIT. Hey, should we go tuh Schultzie's 'n' see if we kin snitch sumpn?

TOMMY (*balancing the broom*). Nah, Schultzie's wise tuh us.

ANGEL. We could try some udduh staws.

TOMMY (*still balancing the broom*). Nah, dey're all wise tuh us. Duh minute we walk in 'ey asks us wadda we want. If we had some dough, while one uv us wuz buyin' sumpm de udduh guys could swipe some stuff, see? I got faw cents, but 'at ain' enough. (*He drops the broom, and becomes the man of action*) Anybody got any dough heah? Hey, yew, Angel, yuh got some?

ANGEL. No, I ain'.

TOMMY. Come on! Don' hole out!

ANGEL. Honest! I didn' git no customuh dis mawnin'.

TOMMY. Wheah's 'is pants? Look in 'is pants!

(T.B. *and* SPIT *rush to the hopper, grab* ANGEL'*s pants, and start rifling the pockets.* ANGEL *follows them, yelling.*)

ANGEL. Hey! Git outta deah! Git outta deah!

T.B. Nuttn but a couple a stamps 'n' a boy-scout knife.

SPIT (*taking the knife himself*). Oh baby, kin I have dis?

ANGEL (*follows* SPIT). No, I need it.

SPIT. No, yuh don't.

ANGEL. Aw, Spit, gimme my knife!

SPIT (*mocking his accent*). Watsa ma'? Piza Taliana? (*He spits at him*) Right inee ear! Ha!

ANGEL (*backs a step and wipes out his ear with a finger*). Ah, yuh louse! Ast me fuh sumpm sometime 'n' see watcha git.

TOMMY. Give 'im 'is knife!

SPIT. Da hell I will!

ANGEL. Aw, Spit, gimme my knife! Tommy, make 'im, will yuh?

TOMMY. Gimme dat knife!

SPIT. What fuh?

TOMMY (*makes a fist and waves it in front of* SPIT'*s nose*). Fuh dis . . . right in yuh bugle! (*He grabs the knife and examines it*) Gese, dat's a knife! Five blades! Boy, I'd like one like 'at.

(*Enter from the lower tenement door, a young* BOY *of about twelve, a bit timid, neatly dressed, obviously Semitic features.*)

ANGEL. Aw, Tommy, I need it. I godda use it. Honest!

TOMMY (*gives him his knife*). Here! Stop squawkin'! Don' say I nevuh gave yuh nuttin'!

ANGEL. Tanks, Tommy. Dat's white.

TOMMY (*good-naturedly*). Ah, shar ap! (*To* DIPPY, *who sits reflectively picking his nose*) Hey, Dippy! Pick me a big juicy one! (DIPPY *grins, rolls the resinous matter into a little ball, and flicks it at* TOMMY. TOMMY *laughs, and trots up the street to join the others who are seated on a tenement stoop. The* TALL MAN *turns from his conversation with his companion, and calls to* DIPPY, *"Hey, you!")*

DIPPY. What?

THE TALL ONE. Wanna run a errand fuh me?

THE SQUAT ONE *(offers)*. I'll go, chief. What is it?

DIPPY. Sure. Wheah?

THE TALL ONE *(points to a tenement house up the block)*. 418 . . . fourth floor . . . Mrs. Martin. Tell her a friend a hers wants a see her here.

DIPPY. O.K. 418? O.K. *(He trots off.)*

GIMPTY *(who has looked up at the sound of* THE TALL MAN'S *voice)*. Don't I know you from somewhere? *(The stranger's lips compress—"no")* I could've sworn I . . .

SQUAT MAN *(comes over and mutters in a thick voice full of threat)*. He said no, didn' he? *(The other restrains him with a touch on the arm.)*

GIMPTY. Sorry. *(He looks down at his drawing. The two walk away, and stand leaning against the wall, talking in low tones. The boys on the stoop suddenly notice the little Jewish boy who is peering over the wharf.)*

T.B. Hey, look! Deah's 'at new kid 'at moved aroun' a block.

SPIT. 'At's 'at Jew kid! *(They rise and come down toward him.)*

TOMMY. Hey, kid!

ANGEL. Hey, kid!

THE JEWISH BOY *(looks up)*. Wadda yuh want?

SPIT. Come heah, Ikey! Come on! Don' be so slow.
(He comes over, eager to join them, yet scared.)

TOMMY. Yew da noo kid onna block, aintcha?

THE JEWISH BOY. Yeah.

TOMMY. Watsya name?

THE JEWISH BOY. Milton. Milton Schwartz.

TOMMY. Yuh wanna belong tuh are gang?

MILTY *(eagerly)*. Yeah. Shuah.

TOMMY. Got 'ny dough? Yuh godda be ineetiated.

MILTY. I god tree sants.

TOMMY. Gimme it!

SPIT *(prodding him in the ribs)*. Give it tuh 'im!

T.B. *(prodding him harder and pulling him around)*. Go on!

TOMMY *(pulling him back)*. Come on! Don' hole out! *(*MILTY *fishes out three cents and hands them to* TOMMY*)* 'At's all yuh got?

MILTY. Yeah.

SPIT. Sure?

MILTY. Hones'.

TOMMY. Soich 'im!
(They start to go through his pockets.)

MILTY *(turns his pockets inside out)*. Don'! Yuh don' haf tuh. Look!

SPIT. Ah, you punk!

TOMMY. Listen, yew! If yuh wanna belong to dis gang, yuh godda git a quatuh.

MILTY. A quatuh? Wheah ahm gonna git a quatuh fum?

SPIT. Fum yuh ole lady.

MILTY. She woodn gimme no quatuh.

SPIT. Yuh know wheah she keeps huh money, doncha?

MILTY. Dat's a sin tuh steal.

SPIT *(mocking his accent)*. Wassamattuh, Ikey?

MILTY. Don' make fun on me, I can' help it.

SPIT *(contemptuously)*. Yuh scared tuh snitch a quatuh? Gese, she won' fin' out.

MILTY. Yes, she would.

SPIT *(still mocking him)*. Oh, she counts huh money all a time, huh, Jakey Ikey?

MILTY. Stop dat! Gimme back my tree sants. I don' wanna hang out wid youse.

TOMMY *(to* SPIT*)*. Yuh godda watchpocket, aintcha?

SPIT. Yeah.

TOMMY. Guard dis dough! *(He hands the money to* SPIT*, who puts it in his pocket. They walk away, completely ignoring* MILTY.*)*

MILTY *(follows them, murmuring tremulously)*. Gimme back my tree sants!

SPIT *(whispers to the others)*. Let's cockalize him!

ANGEL. Wadda yuh say, Tommy?

TOMMY. O.K.

T.B. Come on!
*(*ANGEL *crosses nonchalantly behind* MILTY*, then crouches on his hands and knees unnoticed. The others turn and slowly approach him. Suddenly* TOMMY *pushes* MILTY*, who stumbles backward and trips over* ANGEL*, feet flying up. They all pounce on the prostrate boy, pin his arms and legs to the ground, unbutton his pants, pull up his shirt.)*

TOMMY. Gimme some a dat doit!

SPIT *(scoops up a handful of dirt)*. Heah!
(They rub it into MILTY*'s groin. He kicks and screams, hysterically laughing at the sensation. When he's through rubbing in the filth,* TOMMY *coughs up a huge wad of saliva and spits on* MILTY*'s organ. Each of them spit, once round the circle. The* TALL ONE *and the* SQUAT ONE *laugh. A tattoo of heels running down the street! A whirlwind hits the group, and the boys are dispersed right and left. The whirlwind is a girl not much bigger than* TOMMY*, with a face resembling his—pushed-up nose and freckles. She slaps and pulls and*

pushes the boys, who scatter away, laughing and shouting. She stands there, eyes blazing.)

TOMMY. Aw, scram, will yuh, Drina! Scram!

DRINA. Shut up! (*She helps the sobbing* MILTY *to his feet, brushes him off, and wipes his face, comforting him. On second glance she is not the child she seemed. Her simple dress, her hair combed back of the ears and held in place with a cheap celluloid clasp, her lithe, boyish figure combine to create the illusion of a very young girl. When she comforts* MILTY, *however, it is apparent in the mature quality of her solicitude that she is much older—in her earlier twenties. The* TALL ONE *grins at her. She throws him a contemptuous side glance and rebukes him sharply.*)

DRINA. You ought to be ashamed of yourself, standing there and letting them pile up on this kid.

TOMMY. Aw, Drina, will yuh butt outta this?

DRINA (*to the sniveling boy*). Are you hurt? (*To the* TALL ONE) Why didn't you stop 'em?

THE TALL ONE. What fer? It'll do 'im good.

DRINA (*furiously*). Oh, yeah? I suppose it'll do you good if I crack your face, huh?

THE TALL ONE. Oh, lady, yuh scare me!

DRINA. Fresh guy, huh?

THE SQUAT ONE (*walks over to her, his face screwed up in disgust*). Shut yuh big mouth or I'll . . .

THE TALL ONE (*sharply*). Hunk! Cut it! (HUNK *obeys instantly. They walk away to the bulwark.*)

TOMMY. Aw, Drina, why dontcha butt outta my business?

DRINA. Wait till I get you home, I'll show you butt out of . . . (TOMMY *scratches his head. She places her hands on her hips and frowns*) What are you scratchin' your head for? Are you buggy again? (*Her authoritative, maternal concern gives her the air of a little girl playing house.*)

TOMMY. Aw, git out a heah or I'll bust yuh one!

DRINA. That's fine talk, Tommy . . . bust you one! (*He scratches again*) There you go again! Scratchin'! (*She crosses to him*) Come on home! I'm gonna wash your head.

TOMMY. Aw, lemme alone. All a time yuh bodderin' me. . . . (*Runs away from* DRINA *and climbs up the hopper like a monkey, out of her reach.*)

DRINA (*to* GIMPTY). Pete, why didn't you stop 'em?

GIMPTY. I'm sorry, Drina. I didn't notice what was happenin'. I was thinkin' about somethin'.

DRINA. Yeah? (*She turns to* TOMMY, *dangling high on his perch*) Tommy, did you go to school today?

TOMMY. Sure.

DRINA. If you're lying, Tommy, I'll kill you.

TOMMY (*wiggling his toes at her*). Aw, nuts!

DRINA (*to* MILTY, *who is still sobbing*). What's the matter? Did they hurt you?

MILTY. Dey took my money.

DRINA. They did? How much?

MILTY. Tree sants.

DRINA. Tommy!

TOMMY. What?

DRINA. Did you take this boy's three cents?

TOMMY. Nope.

DRINA. You did so!

TOMMY. I di' not!

DRINA. You did so!

TOMMY. Well, I ain't got it.

DRINA. Who has? Who's got it? (*To* ANGEL) You?

ANGEL. Not me.
(DRINA *looks accusingly at* T.B.)

T.B. (*walks away, indignantly*). Don't look at me!

TOMMY. Go on, Spit, give 'im back 'is tree cents.

DRINA (*turns on* SPIT). Oh, so you're the one! Come on!

SPIT (*thumbs his nose*). Like hell I will.

DRINA. Come on!

SPIT. Frig you!

DRINA (*flaring*). I'll crack you . . . you talk like that!

SPIT. Ah, I'll sock yuh inna tit. (*She smacks him. He clenches his fist and draws it back ready to swing.*)

TOMMY (*jumps from the hopper and rushes at* SPIT, *fists clenched, arms raised in fighting position*). Cut dat out, yuh louse!

SPIT. Well . . . she smacked me foist. She smacked me foist. No dame kin smack me foist an' get away wid it.

TOMMY. Give 'er dat dough.

SPIT. What fuh?

TOMMY. Give her da dough. Dat's what fuh.

SPIT. Yeah?

TOMMY. Yeah.

SPIT. Ah, yuh mudduh's chooch!

TOMMY. Ah, yuh fadduh's doop!

DRINA. Keep quiet, Tommy! (*To* SPIT) Come on! *Come on!*

TOMMY. Hurry up! Give 'er dat dough! (*Pause.* SPIT *grudgingly gives her the money.* TOMMY *drops his hands and returns to the hopper, whistling.* DRINA *hands the money back to* MILTY.)

DRINA. Here.

MILTY. Tanks!

DRINA. That's all right. You look like a nice boy. Stay away from them. They're no good. They're bums.

SPIT (*sullen, but seeking an ally*). Come on, Angel. Y'ain' bin in yet. Wanna go in?

ANGEL. O.K.

SPIT. Last one in's a stinkin' rotten egg!
(*They rush off and jump into the water with great splashes.* T.B. *remains near the hopper, watching. Off right voices are heard. A tall, lean, soft-spoken gentleman, middle-aged, wearing shell-rimmed glasses and carrying a pipe, appears at the gate. He is followed by a plumpish man of about the same age.* PHILIP *opens the gate for them, smiling.*)

PHILIP. Hello, daddy!

PHILIP'S FATHER. Hello, son. Shoulders back! (PHILIP *straightens*) Attaboy. Where's Jeanne?

PHILIP. She went to find Charles.

PHILIP'S FATHER. Oh? And where's he?

PHILIP. I don't know.

PHILIP'S FATHER (*goes up the street, looks into the tenement hallway. He shakes his head in disapproval and turns to his companion*). Say, Jones! Look at this at our back door!
(JONES *nods.*)

DRINA (*to* GIMPTY). You let them take his money without even interfering. Shame on you!

GIMPTY. I told you I didn't notice what was happening. My mind was on somethin' else.

DRINA. Ah, you're always sticking up for them. (*To* TOMMY) Tommy! I'm gonna get some kerosene and clean your head right away.

TOMMY. Aw—w—w.

DRINA. Don't aw—w—w me! (*She walks up the street.* TOMMY *jumps down from the hopper and dives into the water.*)

PHILIP'S FATHER. Hm! Whose property is this?

JONES. I think J. and J. I'm not sure, Griswald.

GRISWALD. Why don't they keep it in repair?

JONES. What for! It's valuable stuff as it is. No upkeep.

GRISWALD (*gasps at the stench that comes out of the building*). Phew! What do they do? Use this hallway as a latrine?

JONES. Probably.

GRISWALD. Hm! Terrible!

JONES. Well, these people have to live some place.

GRISWALD (*groping in his coat pockets*). Hm. Forgot my tobacco pouch. Will you run up and get it for me, son?

PHILIP. Sure, daddy! Where is it?

GRISWALD. Now, let me see. I think it's . . . I'd better go myself. (*Turns to* JONES.)

JONES. I'll go up with you.

GRISWALD. We'll be down in a minute. Ask Charles to wait for us.

PHILIP. Certainly, daddy.

GRISWALD. Thanks, son. (*They go off into the apartment house.* DIPPY *comes running down the sidewalk.*)

DIPPY. I fuhgot. Wot wuzat name? Moitle?

THE TALL ONE. Martin!
(HUNK, *the squat man, cautions him with a tug.* GIMPTY'S *head jerks up. He stares at the* TALL ONE.)

HUNK. Maybe I better go.

THE TALL ONE. O.K. 418, fourth floor. (*To* DIPPY) Nevuh mind, kid. (*To* HUNK) And while yuh at it, look in at tailor's I tole yuh.

HUNK (*nods*). Check! (*Exit* HUNK *up the sidewalk.*)

DIPPY. I'll go. I'll go git her.

THE TALL ONE. Beat it!

DIPPY. Don' I git nuttin'? I went part a da way.

THE TALL ONE. Nuttin' fer nuttin'. Beat it!

DIPPY. Ah, dat's a lousy trick tuh play on a kid.

THE TALL ONE (*raises his foot to kick* DIPPY). Come on! . . .
(DIPPY *runs to the ladder, grumbling, climbs over, yells.*)

DIPPY. Hey! Yew! (*The* TALL ONE *turns to look*) Go tuh hell! (*And he quickly jumps into the water. The* TALL ONE *laughs, comes down to the edge of the wharf, and watches* DIPPY *splash away.*)

GIMPTY (*snaps his fingers. Sudden recollection*). Martin! Baby-face Martin!

THE TALL ONE (*wheels to face* GIMPTY, *one hand reaching under his coat for a shoulder holster*). I ain't Martin, you bastard!

GIMPTY. Don't you remember me?

MARTIN. O.K. Yew asked fer it an' yuh git it!

GIMPTY. I'm Gimpty. . . . Remember?

MARTIN. Gimpty?

GIMPTY. Sure, Baby-face. I . . .

MARTIN. Sh! Shat ap! My name's Johnson. Git it? Johnson.

GIMPTY. We were kids here. Don't you remember? I was one of the gang.

MARTIN (*squints at him carefully for a long time*). Yeah.

GIMPTY. You don't have to worry about me.

MARTIN. I ain't worryin' about you. I'm worryin' about me. (*His hand emerges slowly from under his coat*) You wuz dat funny kid who used to mind my clothes when I went swimmin'.

GIMPTY. Yeah.

MARTIN. Yeah. 'At's right. Kin yuh still keep yer lips buttoned up?

GIMPTY. I guess so.

MARTIN. Yuh guess so! Yuh better find out. And God-damn quick!

GIMPTY. You know me, Marty, I . . . (*A man comes out of the East River Terrace.*)

MARTIN. Sh! (MARTIN *waits till the man is out of hearing, then relaxes*) O.K. Ony, I'm tellin' yuh, if it wuz anybody else, so help me God, I'd . . . (*Gestures with thumb and forefinger, as if reaching for his gun.*)

GIMPTY. Thanks. . . . What did you do to your face?

MARTIN. Operation. Plastic, dey call it.

GIMPTY. Oh! And you dyed your hair, too.

MARTIN. Yeah. I guess yuh read about me.

GIMPTY. Sure. You're the headliner these days.

MARTIN. God-damn right! (*Pauses. Looks around reminiscently and nods toward the East River Terrace Apartments*) Hey, dat's somethin' new, ain't it?

GIMPTY. No. It's been up a couple of years.

MARTIN. Yeah? What is it?

GIMPTY. One of the swellest apartment houses in town.

MARTIN. Yuh don' tell me! Well, what do yuh know!

GIMPTY. Yeah. You have to have blue blood, a million bucks, and a yacht to live in there, or else you have to . . . (*Breaks off, moodily.*)

MARTIN. What?

GIMPTY. Oh, nothin'.

MARTIN. Come on! I don' like 'at. If you're gonna say it, say it.

GIMPTY. It's nothin'. You see over there? They got a floatin' dock.

MARTIN. Yeah. . . . What's it doin' there? Right by de ole wharf. We used to pee over deah . . . remember?

GIMPTY. Yeah.

MARTIN. Uh-huh. (*Regards* GIMPTY *quizzically*) What's your racket?

GIMPTY. I'm an architect.

MARTIN. What's dat?

GIMPTY. I design houses.

MARTIN. Yuh don' say! What do yuh know! Little Gimpty, an' look at 'im! An architect! Well, I always knew yuh'd come trew. Yuh had somethin' here, kid! (*Taps his head*) Yep. Well, I'm glad tuh see yuh doin' O.K., Gimpty. Not like dese udder slobs. Yuh must be in a big dough, huh?

GIMPTY (*laughs*). Nine out of ten architects are out of work.

MARTIN. Yeah?

GIMPTY. Yeah.

MARTIN. So what da hell's a good?

GIMPY. That's the question. Don't ask me. I don't know. . . . Strictly speakin', I'm not even an architect. You see, before you're an architect, you got to build a house, an' before anybody'll let you build 'em a house, you got to be an architect.

MARTIN. Sounds screwy.

GIMPTY. Yeah, I guess it is. Besides, nobody's building any more, anyway.

MARTIN. An' fer dat yuh had tuh go tuh high school?

GIMPTY. College, too.

MARTIN. College? Yuh went tuh college?

GIMPTY. Six years.

MARTIN. Six years? Why, yuh son uv a bitch, yuh're marvelous!

GIMPTY. Well, I won a scholarship, and Mom worked like hell . . . and here I am. I was doin' a little work for the government, but . . .

MARTIN. Oh, yeah?

GIMPTY. No . . . don't get excited. . . . On a slum clearance project. But that folded up. I'm on home relief now.

MARTIN. Oh!
(*A* MAN *comes down the street and enters the tenement. He bangs the door.* MARTIN *starts and looks back jerkily.*)

GIMPTY. Say, is it so smart for you to come here? With that big reward.

MARTIN. I ain' here. I'm out West. Read da papers.

GIMPTY. Have you seen your mother yet?

MARTIN. No. Dat's one reason why I come back. I ain't see de old lady 'n seven years. I kind a got a yen. Yuh know?

GIMPTY. Sure. . . . I saw her here day before yesterday.

MARTIN. Yeah? I taught she might be aroun'. How's she look?

GIMPTY. All right.

MARTIN. Gese. Seven years! Since a day I come out a reform school. Say, yew came down 'ere wid her tuh meet me, didn' cha?

GIMPTY. Yeah.

MARTIN. Sure. 'At's right.

GIMPTY. Well, you've gone a long way since then.

MARTIN. Yeah.

GIMPTY. You know, Marty, I never could quite believe it was you.

MARTIN. Why not?

GIMPTY. To kill eight men?

MARTIN. Say, what ta hell a yuh tryin' tuh do? Tell me off, yuh bastard. Why, I'll . . .

GIMPTY. No, Marty. . . .

MARTIN. Say, maybe yuh changed, huh? Maybe yuh become a rat. Maybe yuh'd like tuh git dat faw grand 'at's up fuh me. . . .

GIMPTY. You know better.

MARTIN. I'm not so sure. Fawty-two hundred bucks is pretty big dough fer a joik like yew.

GIMPTY. You can trust me.

MARTIN. Den don' gimme any a dat crap! What ta hell did yuh tink I wuz gonna do, hang aroun' 'is dump waitin' fer Santa Claus tuh take care a me, fer Chris' sake? Looka yew! What a yew got? Six years yuh went tuh college an what da hell a yuh got? A lousy handout a thoity bucks a month! Not fer me! I yain't like yew punks . . . starvin' an' freezin' . . . fuh what? Peanuts? Coffee an'? Yeah, I got mine, but I took it. Look! (*Pulls at his shirt*) Silk. Twenty bucks. Look a dis! (*Pulls at his jacket*) Custom tailored—a hunderd an' fifty bucks. Da fat a da land I live off of. An' I got a flock a dames at'd make yew guys water at da mout'. At'd make yew slobs run off in a dark corner when yuh see dere pichure an play pocket-pool.

GIMPTY. Ain't you ever scared?

MARTIN. Me? What of? What ta hell, yuh can't live faever. Ah, I don' know. Sure! Sometimes I git da jitters. An' sometimes I git a terrific yen tuh stay put, an' . . . Ah, ta hell wid it! Say, do yew remember dat kid Francey?

GIMPTY. Francey?

MARTIN. She wuz my goil when we were kids.

GIMPTY. Oh, yeah. She was a fine girl. I remember.

MARTIN. Yew bet. Ey don' make no more like her. I know. I had 'em all. Yuh ain't seen her around, have yuh?

GIMPTY. No.

MARTIN. Hoid anyt'hin' about her?

GIMPTY. No.

MARTIN. Gee, I got a terrific yen tuh see dat kid again. At's why I come back here. I wonder what she's doin'. Maybe she got married. Nah, she couldn't! Maybe she died. Nah, not Francey! She had too much on a ball, too much stuff . . . guts. Yeah, she wuz like me. Nuttin' kin kill Babyface Martin an' nuttin' kin kill her. Not Francey. Gese, I wonder what's become a her?

GIMPTY. She's the girl whose uncle owns a tailor shop around the corner, isn't she?

(MILTY *strolls over to the parapet and stands looking into the water.*)

MARTIN. Yeah. Yuh remember her now.

GIMPTY. Sure I remember her, all right.

MARTIN. I tole Hunk, he's one a my boys, tuh look in 'ere an' see if he could git her address. Gese, I gotta see dat kid again!

(SPIT *climbs out of the water, goes to* MILTY *and, in one sweep of his arm, tears* MILTY'*s fly open.*)

SPIT. Tree bagger!

MILTY. Stop dat!

SPIT (*threatening him*). What?

TOMMY (*follows* SPIT *over the parapet*). Aw, cut it out, Spit. We gave 'im enough fuh one time.

SPIT. I'll knock 'im intuh da middle a next week!

TOMMY (*tearing open* SPIT'*s fly*). Home run!

(*The rest of the* KIDS *climb out of the water.* MILTY *joins them in laughing at* SPIT'S *discomfiture.*)

SPIT (*turning on* MILTY). What a yuh laughin' at?

DIPPY. Yeah, what?

SPIT. Sock 'im, Dippy.

DIPPY. Aw, I could lick 'im wid one han' tied behin' my back. (*Taps* MILTY'S *shoulder with his clenched fist in rhythm to*) Tree, six, nine, da fight is mine, I kin lick yew any ole time. Tree, six, nine, da . . .

MILTY. Git outa heah. Lemme alone. (*He swings at* DIPPY, *who retreats frightened.*)

SPIT (*grabbing* MILTY *roughly by his shirt*). Oh . . . a tough guy, huh?

TOMMY. I said leave 'im alone. We give 'im enough fuh one time.

SPIT (*releases* MILTY *and goes to* TOMMY, *threateningly*). Wheah da hell a yuh come off, all a time tellin' me what tuh do?

TOMMY. I'll put yew out like a light.

SPIT (*spitting at* TOMMY). Right inna nose!

TOMMY (*ducks, and the wad of saliva flies over his head*). Miss! Now yuh git yer lumps!

SPIT. Try it! Wanna make somethin' out uv it? Come on! Come on! (*He starts dancing in front of* TOMMY, *waves his fists and mutters dire threats.* TOMMY *suddenly gives him one terrific blow and* SPIT *collapses, his nose bleeding.*)

GIMPTY. Hey!

TOMMY. Hay fuh hosses! It wuz comin' tuh him. (*To* MILTY, *patting his back*) O.K., kid! Yew kin stick aroun'.
(HUNK *enters down the sidewalk.*)

T.B. Hey, Tommy, len' me a couple a my pennies. I wanna practice pitchin'.

TOMMY. O.K.
(*They pitch pennies from the hopper to the sidewalk.*)

MARTIN (*to* GIMPTY). Da kids aroun' here don' change! (*Turns, meets* HUNK'S *suspicious stare at* GIMPTY; *to* HUNK) He ain' nuttin' tuh worry about.

HUNK. It's your funeral as well as mine.

MARTIN. Did yuh git huh address?

HUNK. Yuh mudder's out. Deah wuz no answer.

MARTIN. Francey. What about huh?

HUNK. Dee old joker said ee didn' know, but ee gimme da address of her aunt in Brooklyn. She might know.

MARTIN. Well, hop a cab an' git it.

HUNK (*making a wry face*). Brooklyn?

MARTIN. Yeah.

HUNK. Oh, hell!

MARTIN. Come on! Stop crappin' aroun'.

HUNK. Awright.
(*Exit up the sidewalk.*)

SPIT (*to* PHILIP, *who has appeared on the terrace to watch the fight*). Whadda yuh lookin' at, huh. Yuh nosey li'l . . .

PHILIP. Nosey nothing. It's a free country, isn't it?

TOMMY. Hey, wee-wee, what ah yuh, a boy 'r a goil?

T.B. He's a goil, cantcha see?

PHILIP. I'm a man!
(T.B. *razzes him loudly. Philip razzes loudly back.*)

T.B. Wassamattuh? Yew a wise guy?

PHILIP. Yes, I am.

T.B. Oh, yeah?

PHILIP. I can name all the Presidents of the United States. Can you?

T.B. What? Tommy kin . . .

PHILIP. Ah-h-h!

TOMMY. I used tuh be able tuh.

T.B. Ah, I bet yuh. I bet yuh a dollar ee kin. I bet yuh . . .

PHILIP. All right.

T.B. Aw right what?

PHILIP. I'll bet you a dollar.

T.B. What?

PHILIP (*takes a dollar bill from his pocket and proudly waves it aloft*). Put up your dollar!

DIPPY. Gese, a buck!

T.B. (*slaps his cheek in amazement*). A whole real live dollar . . . my gawd! (ANGEL *and* SPIT, *impressed, exclaim and whistle.*)

PHILIP. Aw, you haven't even got a dollar.

T.B. Yeah, well . . . show 'im, Tommy, anyway. Show 'im! Jus' show 'im up, will yuh?

PHILIP. Washington, Adams, Jefferson. Go on! Name the next three!

TOMMY. Madison . . . Harrison . . . no . . .

PHILIP. Wrong!

TOMMY. Well, I used tuh know 'em. I fergit.

PHILIP. Aw-w.

TOMMY. Well, who cares, anyway? Yuh li'l sissy! Let's cockalize 'im! Whadda yuh say? Come on! (*Chorus of approval. They start climbing up the wall, but the* DOORMAN *appears just in time.*)

DOORMAN. Get out of here! (*He gives them a dirty look, then exits, closing the gate.*)

TOMMY. Wait till I git yew . . . I'll fix your wagon! Come heah, guys. We gotta git dat kid away from deah. We gotta git him. . . .
(*The gang all huddle about* TOMMY, *whispering. Three smaller* BOYS *straggle down the street and sit on the curb. They try to insinuate their way into the conclave.*)

TOMMY (*to the three smaller* BOYS). Hey, whata yew want? (*The three smaller* BOYS *don't answer, but are ready for a fight*) Angel, tell yuh kid brudder tuh git da hell outta heah!

ANGEL. Beat it!

TOMMY. Go home and tell yuh mudder she wants yuh!

ANGEL (*rises, rushes the kids. The smallest stops to fight him, but* ANGEL *routs them and they flee up the sidewalk*). Dat crazy brudduh a mine! (DRINA *enters down the street, carrying a can of kerosene.*)

MARTIN. Well, keep yer nose clean, Gimpty, an' yer lips buttoned up tight, see?

GIMPTY. Forget it!
(MARTIN *exits up the sidewalk, eyeing* DRINA *as she passes him.*)

DRINA. Come on, Tommy.

TOMMY. Not now, I'm busy.

DRINA. Tommy, don't be like that, will you? You can't go around with a head full of livestock.

TOMMY. I ain't got no bugs.

DRINA (*grabbing him, as he pulls away*). Let me see . . . come here! (*She examines his head*) Whew! You ain't! You got an army with a brass band. Come on home.

TOMMY. Wassamattuh wid tuhnight?

DRINA. Tonight I got a strike meetin'. I don't know what time I'll be home.

TOMMY. Aw, yew an' yuh lousy meetin's.

DRINA. It ain't no fun for me, Tommy. Come on an' let's get you cleaned up.

TOMMY. Aw, Drina!

DRINA. I don't like it any more than you do.

TOMMY. Gese, look it! (*He points up the street, and* DRINA *relaxes her hold on him.* TOMMY *rushes off under the hopper and dives into the water with a "Whee-ee." The other* KIDS *laugh and then straggle up the street to sit in a huddle on the doorstep of a tenement house.*)

DRINA. Tommy!

GIMPTY (*laughs.* DRINA *looks at him. He smiles understandingly*). You've got a tough job on your hands, Drina.

DRINA (*peering over the wharf, following* TOMMY *with her eyes*). He's really a good kid.

GIMPTY (*also watches* TOMMY, *whom we can hear thrashing the water with a clock-work, six-beat crawl*). Sure.

DRINA. Just a little wild.

GIMPTY. Hey . . . Tommy's got a good crawl-kick!

DRINA (*calling*). Tommy! Come on! (TOMMY *shouts under the water, making a noise like a seal.* DRINA *laughs against her will*) What are you gonna do with a kid like that?

GIMPTY (*laughs*). I don't know.

DRINA (*seating herself on the parapet, next to* GIMPTY). It's not that he's dumb, either. I went to see his teacher yesterday. She said he's one of the smartest pupils she's got. But he won't work. Two weeks he played hookey.

GIMPTY. I don't blame him.

DRINA. I can't seem to do anything with him. It was different when Mom was alive. She could handle him . . . and between us we made enough money to live in a better neighborhood than this. If we win this strike, I'm gonna move, get him outta here the first thing.

GIMPTY. Yeah. That's the idea.

DRINA (*noticing his drawings*). What've you got there? More drawings?

GIMPTY. Couple a new ideas in community housing. Here! See? (*He passes the drawing pad to her.*)

DRINA (*studies them and nods admiration*). Yeah. They're beautiful houses, Pete. But what's the good? Is anybody going to build them?

GIMPTY. No.

DRINA (*handing back the drawings*). So what?

GIMPTY. All my life I've wanted to build houses like these. Well . . . I'm gonna build 'em, see? Even if it's only on paper.

DRINA. A lot of good they'll do on paper. Your mother told me you've even given up looking for a job lately.

GIMPTY (*suddenly bitter and weary*). Sure. What's the use? How long have you been on strike now?

DRINA. A month.

GIMPTY. Picketin' an' fightin' an' broken heads. For what?

DRINA. For what? For two dollars and fifty cents a week extra. Eleven dollars a month, Pete. All toward rent. So's Tommy an' I can live in a decent neighborhood.

GIMPTY. Yeah. You're right there. I've seen this neighborhood make some pretty rough guys. You've heard about Baby-face Martin? He used to live around here.

DRINA. Yeah. I read about it.

GIMPTY. I used to know him.

DRINA. You did? What was he like? (TOMMY *climbs up out of the water, breathless. He lies on the parapet, listening.*)

GIMPTY. As a kid, all right . . . more than all right. Yeah, Drina, the place you live in is awfully important. It can give you a chance to grow, or it can twist you— (*He twists an imaginary object with grim venom*) —like that. When I was in school, they used to teach us that evolution made men out of animals. They forgot to tell us it can also make animals out of men.

TOMMY. Hey, Gimpty.

GIMPTY. Yeah?

TOMMY. What's evilushin? (*He clambers along the parapet and lies on his stomach in front of* DRINA.)

GIMPTY (*looks at* TOMMY *a moment, smiles, and comes out of his dark mood*). What's evolution, Tommy? Well, I'll tell you. A thousand million years ago we were all worms in the mud, and that evolution made us men.

DRINA. And women!

GIMPTY. And women.

TOMMY. An' boys and goils?

GIMPTY. And boys and girls.

TOMMY. Ah, I wuzn't even born a tousan' million years ago.

GIMPTY. No, but your great, great, great, great grandfather and mother were; and before them their great, great, great, great, great grandfather and mother were worms.

TOMMY. Blah-h-h!

DRINA (*impressed*). It's like God!

GIMPTY. It is God! Once it made dinosaurs—animals as big as that house.

TOMMY. As big as 'at?

DRINA. Sure.

TOMMY. Wow!

GIMPTY. Then it didn't like its work and it killed them. Every one of them! Wiped 'em out!

TOMMY. Boy! I'd like tuh see one a dem babies.

GIMPTY. I'll show you a picture some time.

TOMMY. Will yuh?

GIMPTY. Sure.

TOMMY. 'At'll be swell, Gimpty. (SPIT *appears on the ladder and stops to listen, hanging from the top rung.*)

GIMPTY. Once evolution gave snakes feet to walk on.

TOMMY. Snakes? No kiddin'!

SPIT (*sings in mockery*). Te-da-da-da-da-bushwah, te-da-da bushwah!

TOMMY. Shat ap! Right innee eye! (*He spits.* SPIT *jumps back into the water.*)

DRINA. Tommy, cut that out! See? You're like an animal.

TOMMY. Well . . . he does it tuh all ee udduh kids. . . . Anyhow, what happened tuh duh snakes' feet?

GIMPTY. Evolution took 'em away. The same as ostriches could once fly. I bet you didn't know that.

TOMMY. No.

GIMPTY. Well, it's true. And then it took away their power to fly. The same as it gave oysters heads.

TOMMY. Oysters had heads?

GIMPTY. Once, yeah.

TOMMY. Aw-w!

DRINA. Sh, listen!

GIMPTY. Then it took them away. "Now men," says Evolution, "now men"— (*Nods to* DRINA, *acknowledging her contribution*) —"and women

. . . I made you walk straight, I gave you feeling, I gave you reason, I gave you dignity, I gave you a sense of beauty, I planted a God in your heart. Now let's see what you're going to do with them. An' if you can't do anything with them, then I'll take 'em away. Yeah, I'll take away your reason as sure as I took away the head of the oyster, and your sense of beauty as I took away the flight of the ostrich, and men will crawl on their bellies on the ground like snakes . . . or die off altogether like the dinosaur."
(*A very attractive, smartly-groomed* YOUNG LADY *in a white linen suit comes out of the gate. She brings a clean coolness into this sweltering street. She has a distinctive, lovely face; high forehead, patrician nose, relieved by a warm, wide, generous mouth and eyes that shut and crinkle at the corners when she smiles—which she is doing now.*

TOMMY. Gee!

GIMPTY. That scare you?

TOMMY. Wow!

ANGEL (*who has been sitting on the tenement steps up the street watching* T.B. *and* DIPPY *climb the steam shovel, notices the woman come out of the gate*). Hey, Gimpty, heah's yuh goil friend!

GIMPTY. Oh, hello, Kay!

KAY. Hello, Pete. (*Her manner is simple, direct, poised and easy. She is a realist; no chichi, no pretense. And she is obviously very fond of* GIMPTY.)

DIPPY (*to* T.B.). Hey, Gimpty's goil fren come outta deah.

T.B. (*rising*). No kid! No kid!

ANGEL. Gee whiz! (*The* THREE BOYS *saunter down to* KAY.)

DIPPY. Do yew live in deah?

GIMPY (*embarrassed*). Hey!

KAY (*laughs*). Yes.

ANGEL. Have dey really got a swimmin' pool in 'at joint?

KAY. Yes. A big one.

DIPPY. Ah you a billionairess?

KAY. No.

DIPPY. Millionairess?

KAY. No.

GIMPTY. Hey-y-y!

ANGEL. Den what a yuh doin' comin' out a deah?

DRINA. Angelo! (*To* KAY) Don't mind him!

KAY (*smiling*). Oh, he's all right.

DIPPY. I got it. She's a soivant goil.

T.B. Nah, she's too swell-dressed all a time.
(KAY *laughs*).

GIMPTY (*squirming with embarrassment*). Look! Will you kids beat it? Scram! Get outta here! Go on!

DRINA. Come on, Tommy! I'm gonna wash your head.

TOMMY (*crawling over to the ladder*). Nah! Hey, Gimpty . . . 'at evilushin guy . . .

GIMPTY. What about him?

TOMMY. Did he make everything?

GIMPTY. Yeah.

TOMMY. Bugs too?

GIMPTY. Yeah.

TOMMY (*to* DRINA). Deah yuh ah! God makes bugs an' yew wanna kill 'em. (*Gently chiding her as if she were a naughty child*) Is 'at nice? (*He dives off the ladder into the water*) Whee-e-e!

KAY. He's very logical.

DRINA. Yeah. That part's all right, but he's very lousy too, an' that part ain't. (*She calls*) Tommy! Come on! (*More splashing of the water from* TOMMY.)

DIPPY. Whee! Look! He's a flyin' fish! Do dat again, Tommy! Wait, I'm comin', Tommy! (*He mounts the parapet*) Look a me! I'm divin' . . . a backjack! (*He stands poised for a backjack, then looks back and downward, fearfully. It's awfully high*) Wait a minute! Wait . . . wait! (*He climbs two rungs down the ladder. Looks down. Nods. This is better*) I'm divin' a backjack! Watch out, Tommy! (*He jumps sprawling out of sight. A tremendous splash.* KAY *looks over the parapet laughing.* DIPPY *calls up*) How wuz 'at?

KAY. Beautiful!

T.B. Stinks! (*He walks off toward the hopper arm in arm with* ANGEL. TWO *girls come out of the Terrace, and walk up the street, chattering.* T.B. *and* ANGEL *follow them, mimicking their mincing walk, and making indecent remarks. One of the* GIRLS *stops and turns to slap* ANGEL. *The* BOYS *laugh and run off behind the hopper. The* TWO GIRLS *go up the street, one indignant, the other giggling.* KAY *has picked up* GIMPTY'S *drawings and is admiring them.* DRINA *stares enviously at* KAY, *at her modish coiffeur, at her smart suit, at her shoes.* KAY *becomes conscious of the scrutiny and turns.* DRINA, *embarrassed, drops her eyes, then calls to* TOMMY.

DRINA. Tommy! Coming?

TOMMY (*from the water*). No-o-o!

DRINA. Well, I'm goin' home. I can't wait here all day. (*She goes.*)

GIMPTY. They're using the back entrance to-day. . . .

KAY (*handing him the drawing pad*). Yes. There's some trouble in front. They've ripped up the whole street. (*She looks out across the river, and breathes deep*) It's a grand day, isn't it?

GIMPTY. Yeah.

KAY. Oh! . . . I was talking to some of Jack's friends last night. I thought they could find something for you. (*Produces a business card from her pocket*) Here's a man who said you might come up and speak to him. Here's his card.

GIMPTY (*takes the card from her, and reads it*). Del Block. Oh, yeah . . . he's a good man. Thanks! Gee! Thanks!

KAY. I don't know if it'll help much.

GIMPTY. This is swell of you! (*He looks at her a moment, lost in admiration. Then shyly, with a good deal *of hesitation and groping for the right words*) I was telling Mom about you last night. I been kind of going around the house like a chicken with its head chopped off . . . and Mom asked me why. So I told her.

KAY. What?

GIMPTY. Oh, just a little about you. How we'd got to talking here, and meeting every day, and what great friends we've become. How you've been trying to help me. And . . . that I worship you!

KAY. You didn't!

GIMPTY. Well, I do. Do you mind?

KAY (*deeply touched*). Mind? You fool! What'd she say?

GIMPTY. She said you sounded like a very real, good person.

KAY. Good? Did you tell her all about me? About Jack?

GIMPTY. Yeah.

KAY. Your mother must be a sweet woman. I'd like to meet her some time.

GIMPTY (*enthusiastically*). She'd be tickled. Will you?

KAY. Right now, if you like.

GIMPTY. Well, she's out for the afternoon.

KAY. Oh!

GIMPTY. Maybe I can get her down here day after tomorrow, huh?

KAY (*pauses, then, a bit depressed*). I may not be here then. I may leave tomorrow.

GIMPTY. Tomorrow?

KAY. Night. Jack's going on a fishing trip. He wants me with him.

GIMPTY. Isn't that sudden?

KAY. He's been planning it for some time.

GIMPTY. How long will you be gone?

KAY. About three months.

GIMPTY. That's a long time.

KAY. Yes.
(*Down the street strides a well-dressed, rather handsome man in his early forties, hard lines around the eyes. At the moment he is hot and uncomfortable. He eyes the tenements curiously as he passes them. The* DOORMAN *appears as he starts to enter the gate. He asks the* DOORMAN *in a cultured, quiet voice, "What happened in front?"*)

DOORMAN. I'll tell you, Mr. Hilton. You see, the gas mains . . .

KAY (*rises*). Hello, Jack!

HILTON (*turns around, sees* KAY. *Surprised*). Hello! What're you doing here? *He crosses to her.*)

KAY. Oh, I just came out.

HILTON (*takes off his panama, wipes the sweat band and mops his brow with a handkerchief*). Phew! It's been a hell of a day, arranging things at the office. Well, I've made the plans for the trip. Everything's set.

The boat's in shape. I've talked to Captain Swanson.
(DIPPY *climbs up over the parapet, talking to himself.*)

DIPPY. Hooray fuh me! I did a back-jack! (*To* GIMPTY) Wuz 'at good, Gimpty?

GIMPTY. All right!

DIPPY (*to* KAY). Hey, Gimpty's goil friend, wuz 'at good?

KAY. Beautiful.
(DIPPY, *patting his chest and gloating "Attaboy, Dippy!" goes back into the water.* HILTON *is puzzled and annoyed. He looks at* KAY.)

HILTON. What's all this about?

KAY Nothing.

HILTON. What's all this about?

KAY. Nothing.

HILTON (*his voice begins to rasp*). Come on. Let's go in.

KAY. It's nice out. I'd like to take a walk first.

HILTON. You'll do that later. Come on.

KAY. I have a little headache. I want to stay out a few minutes more.

HILTON. Take an aspirin and you'll be all right. Come on!

KAY. Please!

HILTON. We've a million things to do.

KAY. You go ahead. I'll be right in.

HILTON (*casts a glance at* GIMPTY). What's the big attraction out here?

KAY. Nothing.

HILTON. Then stop acting like a prima donna and come on in.

KAY. Please don't make a fuss.

HILTON (*suddenly loses his temper and snaps*). It's not me . . . it's you! Damn it, I've been tearing around all day like a madman, and I come home and find you behaving like a cheap . . .

KAY. Jack!

HILTON (*bites his lip, controls himself, and mutters curtly*). All right! Stay there! (*He goes in.* KAY *follows him to the gate, pauses there, uncertain. Then indulges in a momentary flash of temper, herself.*)

KAY. Oh . . . let him! (*She returns slowly.*)

GIMPTY. Is that the guy?

KAY. Yes. (*Then, not to be unfair*) Don't judge him by this. He's really not so bad. He's going to be sorry in a few minutes. He's so darn jealous. His wife gave him a pretty raw deal. You can't blame him for . . .

GIMPTY (*suddenly inflamed*). All right! If it were anybody else, all right! But you? He can't treat *you* like that!

KAY (*sits there a while in silence, thinking. Finally, she speaks, slowly, almost in explanation to herself*). I've been living with Jack a little over a year now. He isn't usually like this You see, he really loves me.

GIMPTY. He has a funny way of showing it.

KAY. He wants me to marry him.

GIMPTY. Are you going to?

KAY. I don't know.

GIMPTY. Do you love him?

KAY. I like him.

GIMPTY. Is that enough?

KAY. I've known what it means to scrimp and worry and never be sure from one minute to the next. I've had enough of that . . . for one lifetime.

GIMPTY (*intensely*). But Kay, not to look forward to love . . . God, that's not living at all!

KAY (*not quite convincing*). I can do without it.

GIMPTY. That's not true. It isn't, is it?

KAY (*smiles wryly*). Of course not.
(*A very stout* LADY *with much bosom comes out of the gate, fondling a tiny, black dog.*)

TOMMY (*clambering over the parapet, sees the dog and chuckles*). Look a dat cockaroach, will yuh? Hey, lady, wheah didja git dat cockaroach?

FAT LADY. Well, of all the little . . . ! (TOMMY *starts to bark. The dog yaps back, and struggles to escape. The other boys climb up and bark in various keys. The three* SMALLER BOYS *appear and join in the medley. The stout* LADY *is distraught. She shouts at them, but to no avail*) Get away from here, you little beasts!

SPIT. In yuh hat, fat slob! (*And he continues barking.*)

FAT LADY. Wha-a-at? Doorman! (*To the frantic dog*) Quiet. Buddy darling! Quiet! Doorman!
(*The* DOORMAN *comes out on the run and chases the boys away. They run en masse to the hopper.* TOMMY *climbs up on it. The* SMALLER BOYS *retire to the steps of an upper tenement doorway.* MR. GRISWALD, PHILIP, *and* MR. JONES *come out of the East River Terrace Apartments.*)

GRISWALD. What's the matter?

DOORMAN. Those kids! They're terrible, sir.

PHILIP. They wanted to hit me, too, daddy!

GRISWALD. Oh, yes? Why? What did you do to them? (*Smiles at* JONES.)

PHILIP. Nothing.

GRISWALD. Sure?

PHILIP. Honest, daddy, I didn't say anything to them.

DOORMAN. It's all their fault, sir.

FAT LADY. They're really horrible brats. And their language! . . .

TOMMY (*hanging from the hopper*). Ah, shat ap, yuh fat bag a hump!

GRISWALD. You touch him again and I'll break your necks.

TOMMY. Balls to yew, faw eyes!

GRISWALD (*to* PHILIP, *as he takes his arm and walks him up the street*). The next time you hit them back.

PHILIP. But they all pile up on you, daddy.

GRISWALD. Oh, is that so? Well, I think I'm going to buy you a set of gloves and teach you how to box. (*They continue up the sidewalk, followed by* JONES.)

PHILIP. Will you, daddy?
(THE GOVERNESS *and a young* CHAUFFEUR *in maroon livery meet them.*)

GOVERNESS. *Bonjour, monsieur.*

CHAUFFEUR (*saluting*). I'm sorry to keep you waiting, sir, but . . .

GRISWALD (*waves them ahead*). That's all right. Never mind. (*To* PHILIP) The next time someone attacks you, you'll be able to defend yourself.

MR. JONES. That's the idea!

TOMMY (*shouts up the street after them*). Yeah! Wid ee army an' navy behin' 'im! (*Gang laughs and shouts.* TOMMY *jumps down from the hopper. The* FAT LADY *waddles across to* KAY.)

TOMMY. Come 'ere, guys, I got a scheme how we kin git dat kid an' cockalize 'im. (*They gather in a huddle.*)

ANGEL. How?

TOMMY (*subsiding to a whisper*). Foist we git 'im inna hallway, an' . . .

FAT LADY. The little Indians! They oughtn't to be allowed in the street with decent people.
(*Exit the* DOORMAN, *closing the gate.*)

GIMPTY. No? What would you do with them?

FAT LADY. Send them all away.

GIMPTY. Where?

FAT LADY. I'm sure I don't know.

GIMPTY. Huh!
(*Great outburst of laughter from the huddle.*)

T.B. Dat'll woik! You'll see! Dat'll git 'im!

TOMMY. Wait! Shat ap! I got maw . . .
(*The conclave becomes a whispered one again.*)

FAT LADY. The little savages! They're all wicked. It's born in them. They inherit it.

GIMPTY (*suddenly bursts out, a bitter personal note in his passion*). Inheritance? Yeah. You inherit a castle thirty stories over the river, or a stinkin' hole in the ground! Wooden heads are inherited, but not wooden legs . . . nor legs twisted by rickets! (*The* FAT LADY *is completely taken aback by this unexpected antipathy. She looks at* KAY, *gasps, and walks away, head high, patting her animal.* KAY *smiles at* GIMPTY *sadly, sympathetically.*)

GIMPTY. I'm sorry.

KAY (*touches his hand*). Oh, Pete!
(*Another outburst. The three smaller* BOYS *have crept down and joined the fringe of the huddle.*)

TOMMY. Dey're back again! Angel, will yuh tell yuhr kid brudduh tuh git tuh hell outta heah?

(ANGEL *swings at the tiniest of the* BOYS, *who kicks him in the shin, spits at him, and runs away, thumbing his nose.* ANGEL *chases the* BOYS *part of the way up the street, then returns rubbing his shin and shaking his head.*)

ANGEL. 'At crazy kid brudduh a mine, I'm gonna kill 'im when I git 'im home!
(*The huddle reorganizes.*)

GIMPTY. Gosh, I wish we could be alone for a minute!

KAY. Pete, I've thought of that so many times. I've wanted to invite you inside, but . . .

GIMPTY. You couldn't, of course.

KAY. Cockeyed, isn't it? Couldn't we go to your place?

GIMPTY. Gee, I . . . ! No, you wouldn't like it.

KAY. Why not?

GIMPTY. It's an awful dump. It would depress you.

KAY. Oh!

GIMPTY. I'd love to have you, Kay, but I'm ashamed to let you see it. Honestly.

KAY (*rises and offers him her hand*). Oh, Pete, that's silly. I wasn't born in a penthouse. Come on! (*With the aid of a cane he rises. They walk up the street. For the first time we notice that one of his legs is withered and twisted—by rickets.*)
(MILTY *rises and crosses to within a few steps of the huddle.*)

MILTY (*timidly*). Hey.

TOMMY. What?

MILTY. Look, I . . . (*He approaches* TOMMY *slowly*). If yuh want, I t'ink I kin snitch 'at quatuh fuh yuh.
(*The chug of an approaching tugboat is faintly heard.*)

TOMMY (*thinks it over*). O.K., Milt! O.K. Den yuhr inna gang, see? (*Turns to the others.*) Anybody gits snotty wid Milt, gits snotty wid me, see? (*To* MILTY) Now git dat quatuh. Come on, git duh lead outta yuh pants!
(*The chug-chug grows louder.*)

MILTY (*jubilant*). O.K., Tommy! (*Runs off into the tenement house. The chug-chug grows louder.*)

TOMMY. See? He's a good kid. He loins fast. Remember da time I moved aroun' heah? I wuz wearin' white socks an' I wouldn't coise, so yuh all taught I wuz a sissy.
(*The chug-chug grows louder.*)

DIPPY. 'Cept me, Tommy.

TOMMY. Yeah, 'cept yew. Everybody else. I hadda beat da pants off a yuh foist. (*Down to business again*) Now here's how we git Wee-wee. Yew, T.B. . . . (*His voice is drowned out by the chug-chug-chug-chug—*)

CURTAIN

ACT TWO

SCENE—*The same, the following day, lit by a brilliant afternoon sun. The boys are playing poker with an ancient deck of cards, greasy and puffed, inches thick. Match sticks are their chips. Their faces are grave and intense. They handle their cards familiarly, caressing them like old gamblers.*

MARTIN *lounges against the terrace wall and watches them with grim nostalgia.*

ANGEL (*throwing two match sticks into the pot*). I'll open fuh two. Hey, Spit, it's rainin'. Come on, decorate da mahogany!

T.B. (*adds his two*). O.K. I'm in.

SPIT (*follows suit*). Heah's my two, Dippy.

DIPPY (*tosses in his match sticks, deliberately, one at a time*). I'm in.

ANGEL (*slapping down two cards*). Gimme . . . two.

SPIT (*deals*). Aw, he's got tree uva kin'.

T.B. (*throws away one*). Gimme one. Make it good. (SPIT *deals him one.*)

ANGEL. Ah, yuh ain' got nuttin'.

SPIT. He's got a monkey. I ain' takin' any. How many fuh yew, Dippy?

DIPPY (*studies his hand with grave deliberation*). I'll take five.

SPIT. Yuh can' take five.

DIPPY (*the mental effort contorts his face*). Faw.

SPIT. Yuh kin only take t'ree.

DIPPY (*after considerable hesitation*). Gimme one!

ANGEL (*inclining his head toward* T.B.) Say, T.B., feel 'at bump I got. Feel it!

T.B. (*explores* ANGEL'S *head with a finger*). Wow! Feel 'at bump Angel's got!

DIPPY (*leans over and feels the bump*). Boy! 'At's like 'n egg!

SPIT. Wheah juh git it?

ANGEL. Me ole man give it tuh me.

DIPPY. Fuh what?

ANGEL. Fuh nuttin. Just like 'at, fuh nuttin. Last night me ole man cumzin drunk.

SPIT (*impatiently*). Cum on, cum on . . . whadda yuh do?

ANGEL (*raps his knuckles on the sidewalk*). I blow.

T.B. (*raps*). I blow.

SPIT (*raps*). I blow, too. Dippy?

DIPPY (*raps*). I blow.

T.B. Watcha got?

ANGEL (*reveals a pair of Jacks*). A pair of Johnnies. You?

T.B. (*exhibits two pair, twos and threes*). Two pair. Deuces and trays. (*He reaches for the pot.*)

ANGEL. Aw hell!

SPIT. Wait a minute! (*Lays down three tens*). Read 'em an' weep! Judge Schmuck . . . thoity days!

DIPPY. I guess I ain't got nuttin'. (SPIT *gleefully rakes in the match sticks. Enter* TOMMY, *kicking a tin can before him. The* BOYS *greet him.*)

TOMMY. Hi yuh, guys. Howza wawda?

SPIT. Cold.

TOMMY. Whatcha playin' fuh?

SPIT. Owins. Wanna play?

TOMMY (*starts undressing*). Deal me inna next han'. Who's winnin'?

T.B. I yam.

TOMMY. How much?

T.B. Twenty-eight matches.

TOMMY. Twenty-eight cents . . . boy, 'at's putty good! Hey, didja heah about it?

SPIT. What?

ANGEL. About what?

DIPPY. What, Tommy?

Together

TOMMY. Dincha heah? Boy, deah wuz a big fight at da Chink laundry las' night.

ANGEL. No kiddin'!

TOMMY. Yeah.

DIPPY. How did it staht, Tommy?

TOMMY. Oh . . . a couple handkuhchifs got snotty. (*They all roar with laughter*). Did Wee-wee show up yet?

DIPPY. No, Tommy.

ANGEL. Don' worry. I bin on a lookout furrim.

DIPPY. Yeah, we bin on a lookout furrim.

ANGEL. So, like I wuz tellin' yuh, las' night me old man come in stinkin' drunk. So he stahts beatin' hell outta me ole lady. Boy, he socks 'er all ovah da place! (SPIT *laughs.*)

TOMMY. What da hell a yuh laughin at? Dat ain' so funny.

ANGEL. No, dat ain' so funny. Cause den ee picks up a chair and wants a wallop me wid it.

DIPPY. Whatcha do den?

ANGEL. So I grabs a kitchen knife . . . dat big . . . an' I sez, "Touch me, yuh louse, an' I give yuh dis."

T.B. Yeah?

ANGEL. Yeah, yeah, I did. So he laughs, so he falls on a flaw, an' he goes tuh sleep . . . so he snores—(*imitates a rasping snore*)— like at. Boy, wuz ee drunk! Boy, he wuz stinkin'!
(*Enter* MILTY *down the sidewalk.*)

TOMMY. Hi, yuh, Milty! How's evyting?

MILTY. Swell.

TOMMY. Attaboy.
(MILTY *goes to* MARTIN.)

MARTIN. Well?

MILTY. She wuz deah. I tole huh. She said not tuh come up. She said tuh meet huh down heah.

MARTIN. O.K. Heah, kid, buy yerself a Rolls Royce. (*He gives* MILTY *a half-dollar.*)

MILTY. Gee!

SPIT. Whatcha git?

MILTY. Oh, momma! Haffa buck!

SPIT (*shouting quickly*). Akey! Akey! Haffies!

MILTY (*also shouting quickly, topping* SPIT *and holding up crossed fingers*). Fens! No akey! No akey!

SPIT (*throws down his cards and rises threateningly*). I said akey. Come on, haffies.

MILTY. Yuh didn' have yuh finguhs crossed.

SPIT. Don' han' me dat balonee! Gimme two bits.

MILTY. Yuh didn't cross yuh finguhs.

SPIT (*thrusting his face into* MILTY'S). Gimme two bits 'r I kick yuh inna slats.

MILTY. Yeah?

SPIT. Yeah.

MILTY. Ah, yuh mudduh's chooch!

SPIT. Ah, yuh fadduh's doop!

MILTY. Hey, Tommy, do I gotta givim?

TOMMY. Naw. He didn' have 'is finguhs crossed.

SPIT. I'll choose yuh fer it.

MILTY. Whadduh yuh tink I yam, a dope?

SPIT. Ah, yuh damn jip ahdist!

MILTY. Look who's talkin'!

SPIT. Ah, yew stink on ice!

TOMMY. Stan' up tuh him Milty! Stan' up tuh him.

MILTY (*suddenly thrusts his jaw forward*). Watsamatteh? Yew wanna fight?

SPIT. Yeah.

MILTY. Join ee ahmy! . . . Ha!
(*The boys roar at* SPIT.)

SPIT (*raising a fist and twisting his face fiercely*). Ah!

MILTY (*raising his fist and returning the grimace*). Ah!

SPIT (*fiercer in grimace and growl*). Mah!

MILTY (*tops him*).Wah!
(*They stand there a moment, glaring at each other in silence, fists raised, faces almost touching, then* SPIT *turns in disgust and sits down again to his cards.*)

TOMMY (*grins at* MILTY'S *triumph*). Kimmeah, Milty! Yuh wanna play?

MILTY. I dunna how.

TOMMY. Kimmeah, watch me. I'll loin yuh.
(*Two strange, tough-looking* BOYS *come down the street. They pause, watch a moment, confer, then wander over to the group.*)

FIRST BOY. Hey, which one a youse guys is a captain a dis gang?

TOMMY (*doesn't even deign to look up*). Who wantsa know?

SECOND BOY. Weah fum up da blocks.

TOMMY. Second Avenya gang?

FIRST BOY. Yeah.

TOMMY (*assorting his cards*). Yeah? Well, go take a flyin' jump at ta moon!

SECOND BOY. Whooza leaduh?

TOMMY. Me. What about it? I pass. (*Throws down his cards, rises, turns to the enemy*) Wanna make sumpm out uv it?

SECOND BOY (*a bit frightened*). Yew tell 'im.

FIRST BOY. Yuh wanna fight are gang?

TOMMY. *Sure.* (*Turns to his gang*) O.K. felluhs? Yuh wanna fight da Second Avenyoo gang? (*They approve raucously*) TOMMY (*Turns back to the emissaries*) Sure!

FIRST BOY. O.K. On are block?

TOMMY. Yeah. O.K.

SECOND BOY. Satiday?

TOMMY (*asks the gang*). O.K., Satiday, felluhs? (*They shout approval*) Faw o'clock? (*A little bickering about time, but they agree*) O.K. We'll be up deah Satiday faw o'clock an' boy, we'll kick the stuffin's outa youse!

SECOND BOY. Yeah?

TOMMY. Yeah! No bottles 'r rocks, jus' sticks 'n' bare knucks. Flat sticks. No bats.

SECOND BOY. Sure.

TOMMY. O.K.?

SECOND BOY. O.K.!

TOMMY. O.K. Now git da hell out a heah befaw I bust yuh one! Scram! (*The two* BOYS *run off. From a safe distance they yell.*)

FIRST BOY. Nuts tuh yew! Son uva bitch! son uva bitch!

SECOND BOY. *Satiday!* We be waitin' faw yuh. We kick da pants offa yuh!
(TOMMY *picks up a rock, hurls it after them.* DIPPY *rises, does the same.* MARTIN *laughs.*)

ANGEL (*first noticing* MARTIN). Shine, mistuh?

MARTIN. O.K., kid.

ANGEL (*moves his box down to* MARTIN *and begins to shine his shoes*).

SPIT (*sneers at* DIPPY). Look at 'im trow, will yuh? Like a goil. Yuh godda glass ahm? Cantcha trow a rock even?

DIPPY. Yeah. Kin yew trow bettuh?

SPIT (*picks up a rock, rises, looks for a target. He spots a flower pot on a fire escape*). Watch! See at flowuh pot? (*He throws the rock and breaks the pot.*)

TOMMY. Pot shot! Pot shot!

MARTIN. Say, at waz good pitchin'. Yew kids like tuh git some dope on gang fightin'?

ANGEL. Sure! Hey, felluhs, come heah! (*They crowd about* MARTIN.)

MARTIN. Foist ting is tuh git down ere oiliuh' an yuh. . . . (GIMPTY *enters down the sidewalk, whistling cheerfully*) Hello, Gimpty!

GIMPTY. Hello.

MARTIN (*continues the lesson.* GIMPTY *stops and listens*). Oiliuh an yuh said, see? Dey won't be ready fuh yuh. En I tell yuh kids what yuh wanna do. Git a lot of old electric bulbs, see? Yuh trow 'em, and den yuh trow a couple a milk bottles . . . an' some a dee udder kids git hoit, an' den yuh charge 'em.

TOMMY. Yeah, but we made up no milk bottles, ony bare knucks an' sticks.

MARTIN. Yuh made up! Lissen, kid . . . When yuh fight, dee idee is tuh win. It don' cut no ice how. An' in gang fightin' remember, take out da tough guys foist. Tree aw faw a yuh gang up on 'im. Den one a yuh kin git behin' 'im an' slug 'im. A stockin' fulla sand an' rocks is good fuh dat. An' if ey're lickin' yuh, pull a knife. Give 'em a little stab in ee arm. Ey'll yell like hell an' run.

TOMMY. Yeah, but we made up no knives. Gese, 'at ain' fair. . . .

GIMPTY. What's a matter with you? What are you trying to teach these kids?

MARTIN. Yew shut yer trap. (*To* TOMMY) Lissen. If yuh wanna win, yuh gotta make up yer own rules, see?

TOMMY. But we made up dat . . .

MARTIN. Yuh made up . . .

TOMMY. We kin lick 'em wid bare knucks . . . fair and square.

MARTIN. Lissen, kid . . . Ere ain' no fair an' ere ain' no square. It's winnah take all. An' it's easier tuh lick a guy by sluggin' 'im fum behin' 'en it is by sockin' it out wid 'im toe tuh toe. Cause if yuhr lickin' 'im, en he pulls a knife on yuh, see? En wheah are yuh?

TOMMY. Den I pull a knife back on him.

MARTIN. Yeah, but what's a good unless uh got one an' know how tuh use it?

TOMMY. I know how tuh.

GIMPTY. Don't pay any attention to him, guys!

MARTIN. Yew lookin' fer a sock in a puss?

GIMPTY. If you kids listen to that stuff, you'll get yourselves in Dutch.

TOMMY. Aw, shat ap.
(*The boys razz* GIMPTY.)

MARTIN. Git out a heah, yuh monkey! (GIMPTY, *angry but impotent, walks away.* MARTIN *turns to the boys again*) See what I mean?

TOMMY. Yeah, well, if I had a knife . .

MILTY. Angel's godda knife.

ANGEL. Aw, I need it.

MARTIN (*hands* ANGEL *a dime for the shine*).

TOMMY. Yuh kin jus' loan it tuh me. I'll give it back tuh yuh.

ANGEL. No, yuh won't. Honest, I need it.

SPIT. Give it tuh him! Go on, or I'll crack yuh one!

ANGEL. No!

TOMMY. Nevuh mind . . . tuh hell wid 'im!

T.B. (*to* ANGEL). Ah, you stink on ice!

ANGEL. Aw, shat ap!

T.B. Shat ap yuhself!

MILTY. Look, Angel, I tell yuh what. Ahl give yuh a quarteh fuh it. Whadda yuh say?

ANGEL. Sure!

MILTY (*to* MARTIN). Change, Misteh?

MARTIN. Yeah. . . . (*He gives* MILTY *two quarters in exchange for the half, then rises. A newspaper in the gutter catches his attention. He frowns, picks it up, reads it, wandering off to the tenement stoop, where he sits on a step, absorbed in the newspaper item.* ANGEL *runs to the hopper, finds his trousers, fumbles in the pocket, produces the knife and returns with it. He completes the transaction with* MILTY, *who hands the knife to* TOMMY.)

MILTY. Heah, Tommy.

TOMMY (*rises*). Wha' faw?

MILTY. Fuh a present.

TOMMY. Yuh mean yuh givin' it tuh me?

MILTY. Yeah. Yuh kin keep it.

TOMMY. Gee, t'anks, Milty! Gese, 'at's swell . . . t'anks!

MILTY. Aw, dat's nuttin.

TOMMY. Aw, dat's a whole lot. T'anks! Gee!

CHARLES (*the chauffeur, enters from the gate of the East River Terrace followed by* PHILIP.)

T.B. Hey, Tommy . . . ! (*He points to* PHILIP. *The gang gathers under the hopper, in huddled consultation.*)

PHILIP. I think I'll wait here, Charles.

CHARLES. Wouldn't you rather come with me to the garage?

PHILIP. No.

CHARLES. But your mother said . . .

PHILIP. I'll wait here for them.

CHARLES. Yes, sir.
(*Exit* CHARLES *up the street.* PHILIP *examines his wrist watch ostentatiously.* KAY *appears on the terrace, finds a space in the shrubbery, leans over the balustrade, and signals to* GIMPTY.)

KAY. Pete!

GIMPTY (*rising and crossing toward her, beaming*). Hello, Kay! How are you feeling?

KAY. All right. And you?

GIMPTY. Like a million dollars!

KAY. I'll be down in a second. (*She disappears behind the shrubs. The conclave finished, all the boys saunter off in different directions, pretending disregard of* PHILIP. TOMMY, *whistling a funeral dirge, signals* T.B. *with a wink and a nod of the head.* T.B. *approaches* PHILIP *casually.*)

T.B. Hello, what time is it?

PHILIP. Half past four.

T.B. T'anks. Gee, dat's a nice watch yuh got deah. What kine is it?

PHILIP. A Gruen.

T.B. Boy, at's as nice as 'n Ingersoll. (*Coughs, then proudly tapping his chest, boasts*) T.B. I got T.B.

TOMMY (*on the tenement stoop*). Hey, felluhs, come on inna hall heah. I got sumpm great tuh show yuhs. Come on, T.B. (*They all whip up loud, faked enthusiasm.*)

T.B. O.K. (*To* PHILIP) Yuh wanna come see?

TOMMY. Nah, he can't come. Dis is ony fuh da gang.
(*The others agree volubly that* PHILIP *can't join them in the mystery.*)

T.B. Aw, why not? He's a good kid.

TOMMY (*supported by a chorus of "Nahs"*). Nah, he can't see dis. Dis is ony fuh da gang.

PHILIP. What is it?

T.B. Gee, I can't tell yuh . . . but it's . . . Gese, it's sumpm great!

TOMMY (*to* T.B.) Come on! Git da lead out a yuh pants!

T.B. Too bad dey won' letcha see it. Boy, yuh nevuh saw anyting like dat.

PHILIP. Well, I don't care. I can't anyway. I'm waiting for my father and mother. We're going to the country.

T.B. It'll ony take a minute. . . . Hey, felluhs, let 'im come 'n' see it, will yuh? He's O.K.

TOMMY (*consenting with a great show of reluctance*). Well . . . awright. Let 'im come.

TOMMY (*enters the tenement, followed by the others.*)

T.B. Come on.

PHILIP. I don't know. I expect my . . .

T.B. Awright, it's yuhr loss!

T.B. (*starts up the sidewalk.*)

PHILIP. Wait! Wait! I'm coming! (*Runs to catch up with* T.B. *As they reach the steps and enter,* T.B. *pushes him in the doorway, spits on his hands and follows him in.* KAY *enters.*)

GIMPTY (*beams. He is very happy*). Hello!

KAY. Hello, darling. (*There is a slight strain in her voice and attitude, which manifests itself in over-kindness and too much gentleness, as if she were trying to mitigate some hurt she is about to give him. They sit on the coping.*)

GIMPTY. Well . . . I got up early this morning and went down to a stack of offices looking for a job.

KAY. That's swell. Did you find one?

GIMPTY. Not yet. But I will. Wait and see.

KAY. Of course you will.

GIMPTY. Thanks to you.

SPIT (*runs from the hallway, stops a second on the sidewalk, looking about, then grabs a large barrel stave, whacks his hand with it, whistles, and runs back into the tenement hallway.*)

KAY. Did you see Del Block?

GIMPTY. Yep.

KAY. Didn't he have anything for you?

GIMPTY. Oh, we had a nice talk. He's a very interesting guy. He showed me some of his work. He's done some pretty good stuff. (*Grins*) He asked me if I knew where *he* could find a job. (*They both have to laugh at this*) He thinks you're pretty swell, too.

KAY. Pete . . . you've got to get something.

GIMPTY. I will.

KAY. I didn't know how important it was until yesterday.

GIMPTY. Hey, there!

KAY. I used to think we were poor at home because I had to wear a made-over dress to a prom. Yesterday I saw the real thing. If I hadn't seen it, I couldn't have believed it. I dreamt of it all night . . . the filth, the smells, the dankness! I touched a wall and it was wet. . . . (*She touches her finger-tips, recalling the unpleasant tactile sensation. She shivers.*)

GIMPTY. That house was rotten before I was born. The plumbing is so old and broken . . . it's been dripping through the building for ages.

KAY. What tears my heart out is the thought that you have to live there. It's not fair! It's not right!

GIMPTY. It's not right that anybody should live like that, but a couple a million of us do.

KAY. Million?

GIMPTY. Yeah, right here in New York . . . New York with its famous skyline . . . its Empire State, the biggest God-damned building in the world. The biggest tombstone in the world! They wanted to build a monument to the times. Well, there it is, bigger than the pyramids and just as many tenants. (*He forces her to smile with him. Then he sighs, and adds, hopelessly*) I wonder when they'll let us build houses for men to live in? (*Suddenly annoyed with himself*) Ah, I should never have let you see that place!

KAY. I'm glad you did. I know so much more about you now. And I can't tell you how much more I respect you for coming out of that fine, and sweet . . . and sound.

GIMPTY (*his eyes drop to his withered limb*). Let's not get started on that.
(PHILIP *can be heard sobbing in the tenement hallway. He flings open the door and rushes out, down the street into the apartment, crying convulsively, his clothes all awry. The gang follows him from the hallway, yelling and laughing.*)

TOMMY (*holding* PHILIP'S *watch*). Come on, let's git dressed an' beat it!

SPIT. Let's grab a quick swim foist.

TOMMY. Nah!

SPIT. Come on!

MILTY. Betteh not. . . .

SPIT (*rushes off under the hopper and dives into the water*). Las' one in's a stinkin' rotten egg!

TOMMY (*throws the watch to* T.B.) Guard 'at watch and lay chickee! (*All the boys except* T.B. *dive into the water.*)

GIMPTY. When I see what it's doing to those kids I get so mad I want to tear down these lice nests with my fingers!

KAY. You can't stay here. You've got to get out. Oh, I wish I could help you!

GIMPTY. But you have. Don't you see?

KAY. No. I'm not that important.

GIMPTY. Yes, you are!

KAY. I mustn't be. Nobody must. For your own good, you've got to get out of here.

GIMPTY. I will, damn it! And if I do . . . maybe I'm crazy . . . but will you marry me?

KAY. Listen!

GIMPTY. Don't get me wrong. I'm not askin' you to come and live there with me. But you see, if. . . .

KAY. Listen! First I want you to know that I love you . . . as much as I'll allow myself to love anybody. Maybe I shouldn't have gone with you yesterday. Maybe it was a mistake. I didn't realize quite how much I loved you. I think I ought to leave tonight.

GIMPTY. Why?

KAY. Yes, I'd better.
(*The chug of a small boat is heard.*)

GIMPTY. Why?

KAY. I'd better get away while we can still do something about this.

GIMPTY. How will that help?

KAY. If I stay, I don't know what will happen, except that . . . we'll go on and in the end make ourselves thoroughly miserable. We'd be so wise to call it quits now.

GIMPTY. Gee, I don't see it.

KAY. I do, and I think I'm right. (*Pause. She looks out over the river*) There's the boat.

GIMPTY (*pauses. Turns to look*). Is that it?

KAY. Yes.

GIMPTY (*irrelevantly, to conceal his emotion. In a dull monotone*). It's a knockout. I'm crazy about good boats. They're beautiful, because they're designed to work. That's the way houses should be built . . . like boats.

KAY. Pete, will you be here . . . tonight . . . before I leave?
(MARTIN *looks up from his newspaper to eye* KAY.)

GIMPTY. Don't go, Kay. I'll do anything. Isn't there some way . . . something?

KAY (*hopelessly*). What? (*Rises*) I guess I'll go in now, and get my things ready . . . I'll see you later? (*She presses his shoulder and exits.* MARTIN *rises, throws down his newspaper and approaches* GIMPTY.)

MARTIN (*sucks his lips, making a nasty, suggestive sound*). Say . . . dat's a pretty fancy lookin' broad. High class, huh? How is she? Good lay? (GIMPTY *glares at him.* MARTIN *laughs*) Well, fer Chris' sake, what's a matter? Can't yuh talk?

GIMPTY. Cut it out, Martin. Just cut it out!

MARTIN. Lissen, kid, why don' yuh git wise tuh yerself? Dose dames are pushovers, fish fuh duh monkeys!

GIMPTY (*half rising, furious*). I said cut it out!

MARTIN (*roughly pushes him back*). Sit down, yew! (*A chuckle of contempt*) Look what wantsa fight wid me! Little Gimpty wansa fight wid me! Wassamattuh, Gimpty? Wanna git knocked off?
(HUNK *slouches down the street, followed in a painfully weary shuffle by a gaunt, raw-boned, unkempt woman, sloppy and disheveled. Her one garment an ancient house dress retrieved from some garbage heap, black with grease stains. Her legs are stockingless, knotted and bulging with blue, twisted, cord-like veins. Her feet show through the cracks in her house slippers. In contrast to the picture of general decay is a face that looks as if it were carved out of granite; as if infinite suffering had been met with dogged unyielding strength.*)

HUNK. Hey!
(*She comes to a dead stop as she sees* MARTIN. *There is no other sign of recognition, no friendliness on her lips. She stares at him out of dull, hostile eyes.*)

MARTIN (*his face lights, he grins. He steps rapidly toward her*). Hello, Mom! How are yuh? (*Pause*) It's me. (*No recognition*) I had my face fixed. (*There is a moment of silence. She finally speaks in an almost inaudible monotone.*)

MRS. MARTIN. Yuh no-good tramp!

MARTIN. Mom!

MRS. MARTIN. What're yuh doin' here?

MARTIN. Aintcha glad tuh see me? (*She suddenly smacks him a sharp crack across the cheek.*)

MRS. MARTIN. That's how glad I am.

MARTIN (*rubs his cheek, stunned by this unexpected reception. He stammers*). 'At's a great hello.

MRS. MARTIN. Yuh dog! Yuh stinkin' yellow dog yuh!

MARTIN. Mom! What kin' a talk is 'at? Gese, Mom . . .

MRS. MARTIN. Don't call me Mom! Yuh ain't no son a mine. What do yuh want from me now?

MARTIN. Nuttin'. I just . . .

MRS. MARTIN (*her voice rises, shrill hysterical*). Then git out a here! Before I crack yuh God-damn face again. Git out a here!

MARTIN (*flaring*). Why, yuh ole tramp, I killed a guy fer lookin' at me da way yew are!

MRS. MARTIN (*her voice rises, shrill, slowly. Then, quietly*). Yeah . . . You're a killer all right . . . You're a murderer . . . you're a butcher, sure! Why don't yuh leave me ferget yuh? Ain' I got troubles enough with the cops and newspapers botherin' me? An' Johnny and Martha . . .

MARTIN. What's a mattuh wid 'em?

MRS. MARTIN. None a yer business! Just leave us alone! Yuh never brought nothin' but trouble. Don't come back like a bad penny! . . . Just stay away and leave us alone . . . an' die . . . but leave us alone! (*She turns her back on him, and starts to go.*)

MARTIN. Hey, wait.

MRS. MARTIN (*pauses*). What?

MARTIN. Need any dough?

MRS. MARTIN. Keep yer blood money

MARTIN. Yuh gonna rat on me . . gonna tell a cops?

MRS. MARTIN. No. They'll get yuh soon enough.

MARTIN. Not me! Not Martin! Huh, not Baby-face Martin!

MRS. MARTIN (*mutters*). Baby-face! Baby-face! I remember . . . (*She begins to sob, clutching her stomach*) In here . . . in here! Kickin'! That's where yuh come from. God! I ought to be cut open here fer givin' yuh life . . . murderer!!! (*She shuffles away, up the street, weeping quietly.* MARTIN *stands there looking after her for a long time. His hand goes to his cheek.* HUNK *comes down to him, clucking sympathetically. A boat whistle is heard.*)

HUNK. How da yuh like 'at! Yuh come all away across a country jus' tuh see yer ole lady, an' what da yuh git? Crack inna face! I dunno, my mudder ain' like dat. My mudder's always glad tuh see me. . . .

MARTIN (*low, without turning*). Shut up! Gese, I must a been soft inna head, so help me!

HUNK. Yuh should a slugged 'er one.

MARTIN. Shut up! I must a bin crazy inna head. I musta bin nuts.

HUNK. Nah! It's jus' she ain't gotta heart. Dat ain' . . .

MARTIN (*turns on* HUNK, *viciously, barking*). Screw, willyuh? Screw! (*Exit* HUNK *up the sidewalk.* MARTIN *turns, looking after his mother. Turns slowly onto the sidewalk, then notices* GIMPTY) Kin yuh picture dat?

GIMPTY. What did you expect . . . flags and a brass band?

MARTIN (*suddenly wheels and slaps* GIMPTY). Why—yew—punk!

GIMPTY. What's the idea?

MARTIN. Dat's ee idea . . . fer shootin' off yer mout'. I don' like guys 'at talk outa toin. Not tuh me!

GIMPTY. Who the hell do you think you are?

MARTIN (*claws his fingers and pushes* GIMPTY'S *face against the wall*). Why, yuh lousy cripple, I'll . . .

GIMPTY (*jerks his head free of* MARTIN'S *clutch*). Gee, when I was a kid I used to think you were something, but you're rotten . . . see? You ought to be wiped out!

MARTIN (*his face twitching, the veins on his forehead standing out, kicks* GIMPTY'S *crippled foot and shouts*). Shut up!

GIMPTY (*gasps in pain, glaring at* MARTIN. *After a long pause, quietly, deliberately*). All right. O.K., Martin! Just wait!

MARTIN. What? (*Reaches for his shoulder holster*) What's 'at?

GIMPTY. Go on! Shoot me! That'll bring 'em right to you! Go on!

MARTIN (*hesitates. He is interrupted by the excited voices of* GRISWALD *and* PHILIP. *Cautiously he restrains himself and whispers*). I'll talk to yuh later. I'll be waitin' right up thuh street, see? Watch yuh step.
(GRISWALD *appears behind the gate with* PHILIP, *who is sobbing. The* GOVERNESS *tries to quiet* PHILIP *while she dabs his face with her handkerchief.* MARTIN *goes up the street.*)

GRISWALD. It's all right, son! Now stop crying! What happened? Stop crying! Tell me just what happened?

GOVERNESS. *Attends, mon pauvre petit* . . . 'ere, let me wipe your face . . . *attends, attends!*

PHILIP. They hit me with a stick!

GRISWALD. A stick!

PHILIP (*spread-eagling his arms*). That big!

GRISWALD (*furious*). I'll have them locked up . . . I swear I'll send them to jail. Would you know them if you saw them?

PHILIP. Yes, daddy.

GRISWALD (*to the* GOVERNESS). You should have been with him. After yesterday . . .

GOVERNESS. I told him to stay in the garden. Madame said it was all right and she asked me to help Clara with the curtains in his room.
(SPIT *starts up the ladder, followed by the other boys.* DIPPY *is frozen. He is blue and shaking with cold. His teeth are chattering.*)

DIPPY. Look, I'm shiverin'. My teet' 'r' knockin'.

TOMMY. Yeah. Yuh lips 'r' blue! Yuh bettuh git dressed quick, aw yuh'll ketch cold. (*Looks down at* MILTY *who is climbing the ladder, behind him.*) How do yuh like it, Milty?

MILTY (*grins from ear to ear*). Swell! (*As the boys appear over the parapet,* T.B. *rises from under the hopper, points to* GRISWALD, *and calls the danger-cry.*)

T.B. Chickee! Putzo! Hey, felluhs! Chickee! Tommy!
(PHILIP *sees the boys and points them out to* GRISWALD.)

PHILIP. There they are! They're the ones. (*Points out* TOMMY) He's the leader!

GRISWALD. That one?

PHILIP. Yes.
(SPIT, DIPPY, MILTY *and* ANGEL *dash to the hopper, all yelling "Chickee!" They gather up their clothes and run madly up the street, followed by* T.B. TOMMY, *stooping to pick up his clothes, trips, falls and is grabbed by* GRISWALD, *who shakes him violently.*)

GRISWALD. What right did you have to beat this boy? What makes you think you can get away with that?

TOMMY (*struggling to escape*). Lemme go! Lemme go, will yuh? I didn' do nuttin' . . . lemme go!

PHILIP (*jumping up and down with excitement*). He's the one! He's the got the watch, daddy!

TOMMY (*tries to break away and get at* PHILIP). I have not, yuh fat li'l bastid!

GOVERNESS (*frightened, screams*).
GRISWALD (*jerks* TOMMY *back*). Oh, no! Not this time! I'll break your neck!

PHILIP. He's the one!

GRISWALD. Give me that watch!

TOMMY. I yain't got it!

PHILIP. He has! He's got it!

GRISWALD (*turns to the* GOVERNESS, *peremptorily*). Jeanne! Call an officer! (*To* TOMMY *again*) Give me that watch!

TOMMY (*frightened by the police threat*). I yain't got it. Honest, I yain't! (*Suddenly shouts up the street for help*) Hey, felluhs!
(*The* GOVERNESS *stands there, paralyzed.*)

GRISWALD. Jeanne, *will* you call an officer! Come on! Hurry!

GOVERNESS. *Oui, oui, monsieur! (She runs up the sidewalk in a stiff-legged trot.)*

TOMMY (*stops struggling for a moment*). Aw, Mister, don't toin me ovuh tuh da cops, will yuh? I won' touch 'im again. We do it to allee udduh kids, an 'ey do it tuh us. Dat ain' nuttin'.

GRISWALD. No? I ought to break your neck.

TOMMY. Oh, yeah? (*He suddenly pulls away, almost escaping.* GRISWALD *puts more pressure on the arm.* TOMMY *calls to the gang*) Hey, felluhs! (GRISWALD *twists his arm double.* TOMMY *begins to cry with pain, striking at* GRISWALD) Yuh joik! Ow, yuh breakin' my ahm! Hey, Gimpty!

GIMPTY. Have a heart! You're hurting that kid. You don't have to . . .

GRISWALD. Hurt him! I'll kill him! (MILTY *runs down the street, holding out the watch.*)

MILTY. Heah yuh ah! Heah's duh watch! Leave 'em go misteh! He didn' do nuttin'! Leave 'im go! (*He starts pounding* GRISWALD. TOMMY *frees his hand.* GRISWALD *hooks his arm around* TOMMY *in a stranglehold, and with the free arm pushes* MILTY *away.*)

GRISWALD (*to* MILTY). Get out of here, you . . .

TOMMY. Hey, yer chokin' me! Yer chokin' me! (*Both hands free, he gropes in the trousers he has clung to. Suddenly he produces an open jackknife and waves it.*) Look out! I gotta knife. I'll stab yuh! (GRISWALD *only holds him tighter, trying to capture the knife. A flash of steel!* GRISWALD *groans and clutches his wrist, releasing* TOMMY. TOMMY *and* MILTY *fly up the street.* GRISWALD *stands there stunned, staring at his bleeding wrist.*)

PHILIP. Daddy! Daddy! Daddy! (*He begins to sob at the sight of blood.*) (*The* DOORMAN *comes out of the gateway and is immediately excited.*)

DOORMAN. What's the matter?

GRISWALD (*jerking his head toward the fleeing boys*). Catch those boys! (*The* DOORMAN *lumbers up the street in pursuit.* GRISWALD *takes a handkerchief from his breast pocket and presses it to his wrist. Blood seeps through.* GRISWALD, *self-controlled now, tries to quiet the sobbing* PHILIP.) It's all right, son, it's all right! No, no, no! Now stop crying. Let me have your handkerchief!

GIMPTY. Are you hurt?

GRISWALD. What do you think?

GIMPTY. Can I help?

GRISWALD. It's a little late for that now.

PHILIP (*fishes out a crumpled handkerchief and hands it to his father*). *Here.*

GRISWALD. Haven't you a clean one?

PHILIP. No.

GIMPTY. You can have mine.

GRISWALD. Never mind. (*To* PHILIP, *who puts his own handkerchief back*) You should always carry two clean handkerchiefs. Put your hand in my pocket. You'll find one there. No, the other pocket.
(PHILIP *finds the handkerchief. The* GOVERNESS *comes down the sidewalk with a* POLICEMAN.)

POLICEMAN. What's the matter?

GRISWALD. Plenty.

GOVERNESS (*sees the blood and shrieks*). Oh! He's bleeding! (*To* PHILIP) *Qu'est ce qui passe, mon petit?*

PHILIP. That boy stuck him with a knife!

GOVERNESS (*to* GRISWALD) *Mon Dieu!* Are you hurt, monsieur?
(GRISWALD *ignores her and tightens the bandage.*)

POLICEMAN. Is it deep?

GRISWALD. Deep enough.

POLICEMAN. Better let me make a tourniquet.

GRISWALD. Never mind.

POLICEMAN. Who did it?

GRISWALD. One of these hoodlums around here. I want that boy arrested.

POLICEMAN. Sure. Do you know who he was?

GRISWALD. No.

GOVERNESS. Can I help you, monsieur?

GRISWALD. Yes. Go up and call Dr. Merriam at once. I'm afraid of infection. (*The* DOORMAN *returns, empty-handed, puffing, and mopping his brow.* GRISWALD *frowns*) Where is he?

DOORMAN (*panting*). Phew . . . I couldn't catch them.

GRISWALD (*angry*). You let them go?

DOORMAN. I tried, sir. They were like flies . . . in and out. . . . Just when I though I had one of them . . . he ran down the cellar . . . I went after him, but he got away.

GRISWALD. Officer, I want you to find that boy and arrest him. Understand?

POLICEMAN (*takes out a notebook and pencil*). Well, that ain't gonna be so easy, you know.

GRISWALD. Never mind. That's your job! It's pretty serious that a thing like this can happen on your beat in broad daylight.

POLICEMAN. Well, I can't be everywhere at once.

GRISWALD. Before he stabbed me, he and some others beat up my boy and stole his watch. You should have been around some of that time.

POLICEMAN (*annoyed at his officiousness. Brusquely*). Well . . . what's your name?

GRISWALD. My name's Griswald . . . I live here. (*Nods toward the East River Terrace.*)

POLICEMAN. What did the boy look like?

GRISWALD. He was about so high . . . black hair . . . oh, I don't know. I didn't notice. Did you, son?

PHILIP. One of them coughs.

POLICEMAN. Didn't you notice anything else?

PHILIP. No.

GRISWALD. Jeanne?

GOVERNESS. Let me see . . .

POLICEMAN. How was he dressed?

GOVERNESS. They'd been in swimming here. They were practically naked . . . and filthy. And their language was 'orrible.

GRISWALD (*irritated*). He knows that, he knows that! What were they like, though? Didn't you see?

GOVERNESS. It all happened so quickly, I didn't have a chance to, monsieur.

PHILIP. He hit me with a stick.

POLICEMAN. Hm!

GRISWALD (*suddenly a bit faint*). These men can tell you better. They saw it. Jeanne, will you please call Dr. Merriam right away? I'm feeling a little sick.

GOVERNESS. *Oui, monsieur!* Come, Philippe! (*She goes in, accompanied by* PHILIP.)

GRISWALD. I don't want to make any trouble, officer, but I want that boy caught and arrested. Understand?

POLICEMAN. I'll do the best I can. (*Exit* GRISWALD. *The* POLICEMAN *mutters*) I wonder who the hell that guy thinks he is. . . .

DOORMAN (*impressively, rolling the sound on his tongue*). Mr. Griswald. (CHARLES, *the chauffeur, saunters down the sidewalk.*)

POLICEMAN. What of it?

DOORMAN. Don't you know? He's Judge Griswald's brother.

POLICEMAN (*his attitude changes*). Oh!

DOORMAN (*to the* CHAUFFEUR, *who has reached the gate*). Oh, I don't think Mr. Griswald'll be using the car now. He was just hurt.

CHARLES. Wha-a-at? What happened?

DOORMAN. He was stabbed. It's a long story. I'll tell you later.

CHARLES (*concerned*). Well, will you call him and see if he wants me?

DOORMAN (*starting off*). Yeah.

POLICEMAN. Hey, wait!

DOORMAN. I'll be right out, officer. Mr. Griswald may need him.

POLICEMAN. Oh, all right.
(DOORMAN *and* CHARLES *go in through the gate.*)

CHARLES. What happened?

DOORMAN. These kids around here have been raising an awful rumpus all day, and just now one of them . . . (*Their voices die off.*)

POLICEMAN (*to* GIMPTY) Did you see the kids who did this?

GIMPTY. I didn't notice them.

POLICEMAN. You come around here often?

GIMPTY. Yes.

POLICEMAN. Didn't you recognize any of 'em?

GIMPTY. No.

POLICEMAN. Can you describe 'em?

GIMPTY. Not very clearly.

POLICEMAN (*annoyed*). Well, what were they like?

GIMPTY. About so high . . . dirty an' naked. . . .

POLICEMAN (*impatiently*). And they socked that young jalopee in the eye. Yeah. I got that much myself. But that might be any kid in this neighborhood. Anything else?

GIMPTY. No.

POLICEMAN (*slaps his book shut*) Why the hell didn't I learn a trade? (*He starts toward the gate.* DRINA *comes down the street and approaches* GIMPTY. *She looks tired and bedraggled. She has an ugly bruise on her forehead.*)

GIMPTY (*to* DRINA). Hey, what's the matter with your head ?

DRINA (*looking at the* POLICEMAN *and raising her voice*) We were picketing the store, an' some lousy cop hit me.

POLICEMAN (*wheels around, insulted*). What's that?

DRINA (*deliberately*). One a you lousy cops hit me.

POLICEMAN. You better watch your language or you'll get another clout!

DRINA. Go on and try it!

GIMPTY (*urging discretion*). Sh!

POLICEMAN. Listen! I'm in no mood to be tampered with. I'm in no mood! . . . Not by a lousy Red.

DRINA (*quietly*). I ain't no Red

POLICEMAN (*thick-skulled*). Well you talk like one.

DRINA. Aw nuts!

POLICEMAN. You were strikin', weren't you?

DRINA. Sure. Because I want a few bucks more a week so's I can live decent. God knows I earn it!

POLICEMAN (*who has had enough*). Aw, go on home! (*He turns and goes in the gate, addressing someone*] Hey, Bill, I wanna see you. . . . (*Pause.*)

DRINA (*to* GIMPTY). We were only picketing. We got a right to picket. They charged us. They hit us right and left. Three of the girls were hurt bad.

GIMPTY. I'll give you some advice about your brother.

DRINA. I was just lookin' for him. Did you see him?

GIMPTY. Tell him to keep away from here . . . or he's in for a lot of trouble.

DRINA (*sits down, exhausted, and sighs*). What's he done now?

GIMPTY. Plenty.

DRINA. What?

GIMPTY. Just tell him to keep away.

DRINA. Gosh, I don't know what to do with that boy! (*A passing boat hoots twice.* DRINA *ponders her problem a moment*) There's a feller I know . . . is always askin' me to marry him. . . . Maybe I ought to do that, hm? . . . For Tommy . . . he's rich. . . . What should I do?

GIMPTY (*disinterested, too absorbed in his own problem*) That's up to you.

DRINA. Most of the girls at the store are always talkin' about marryin' a rich guy. I used to laugh at 'em. (*She laughs now at herself.*)

GIMPTY. Maybe they're right.

DRINA (*looks at him*). That doesn't sound like you.

GIMPTY. No? How do you know what goes on inside of me?

DRINA (*shakes her head and smiles sadly*). I know.

GIMPTY (*curtly*). Smart girl!

DRINA (*very tender and soft. She knows he's suffering*). What's the matter?

GIMPTY. Nothing.

DRINA. I understand.

GIMPTY. You can't.

DRINA. Why can't I? (*Suddenly exasperated*) Sometimes for a boy as bright as you, with your education, you talk like a fool. Don't you think I got a heart too? Don't you think there are nights when I cry myself to sleep? Don't you think I know what it means to be lonely and scared and to want somebody? God, ain't I human? Am I so homely that I ain't got a right to . . .

GIMPTY. No, Drina! I think you're a swell girl. You are.

DRINA (*turns away, annoyed at his patronage*). Oh, don't give me any of that taffy! You don't even know I'm alive!

GIMPTY. Why do you say that?

DRINA. What's the difference? It don't matter. . . . Only I hate to see you butting your head against a stone wall. You're only going to hurt yourself.

GIMPTY. What're you talking about?

DRINA. You know. . . . Oh, I think that lady's beautiful . . . and I think she's nice. . . .

GIMPTY (*angry*). Look! Will you be a good girl and mind your own business?

DRINA. She's not for you!

GIMPTY. Why not?

(*The* POLICEMAN *comes out of the East River Terrace, notebook and pencil in hand. He goes to* GIMPTY.)

POLICEMAN. Well, I got something to work on, anyway. . . . Do you know a kid named Tommy something around here?

(DRINA *starts, but checks herself.*)

GIMPTY. No.

POLICEMAN. They heard the others call him Tommy. (*Jerks his head toward the gate*) You know what he's liable to do? With his pull? Have me broke, maybe. The first thing I know, I'll be pounding a lousier post than this! Harlem, maybe. Get a knife in my back. . . . (*Looks up from his notebook to* DRINA) Hey, you!

DRINA. What?

POLICEMAN. You live around here?

DRINA (*very docile, frightened*). Yes.

POLICEMAN. Know a kid named Tommy something?

DRINA. No . . . no, I don't.

POLICEMAN (*studying his notes*). I'll catch him. I'll skin him alive!

DRINA (*finally ventures*). What'd he do?

POLICEMAN. Pulled a knife on some high muck-a-muck in there.

DRINA. No!

POLICEMAN. Yeah. Ah, it don't pay to be nice to these kids. It just don't pay.

DRINA. Was the man hurt?

POLICEMAN. Yeah. It looks like a pretty deep cut. Lord, he's fit to be tied! I never seen a guy so boined up! (DRINA *turns and goes up the street, restraining her impulse to run. The* POLICEMAN *jabbers on, complainingly*) This is a rough enough precinct . . . but Harlem?—There's a lousy precinct! A pal of mine got killed there last year. Left a wife and a couple a kids.

GIMPTY. Is that so?

POLICEMAN. Yeah.

GIMPTY. Too bad! (*As the idea begins to take form*) Well . . . maybe you can catch Baby-face Martin or one of those fellows, and grab off that forty-two-hundred-dollar reward.

POLICEMAN. Yeah.

GIMPTY. Then you could retire.

POLICEMAN. Yeah, you could do a lot on that.

GIMPTY. Yeah, I guess you could. . . . Say . . . tell me something . . .

POLICEMAN. What?

GIMPTY. Supposin' . . . supposin' a fellow knew where that . . . er . . . Baby-face Martin is located. How would he go about reporting him . . . and making sure of not getting gypped out of the reward?

POLICEMAN. Just phone police headquarters . . . or the Department of Justice direct. They'd be down here in two minutes. (*He looks at* GIMPTY *and asks ironically*) Why? You don't know where he is, do you?

GIMPTY (*smiles wanly back at him*). Colorado, the newspapers say. . . . No, I was just wonderin'.

POLICEMAN. Well, whoever turns that guy in is taking an awful chance He's a killer.

GIMPTY. Well . . . you can't live forever.
(*A passing tug shrieks its warning signal. And shrieks again.* MARTIN *walks, cat-footed, down the street.*)

POLICEMAN. That's right.
(GIMPTY *turns, sees* MARTIN, *and rises.*)

GIMPTY (*to the* POLICEMAN). Excuse me.

POLICEMAN. Sure.
(GIMPTY *crosses to the other side of the street, and walks away, pretending not to notice* MARTIN.)

MARTIN. Hello, Gimpty! (GIMPTY *accelerates his pace and hobbles off.* MARTIN *sucks his teeth for a second, thinking. Then he adopts an amiable smile and approaches the* POLICEMAN) Kinda quiet today, ain' it, officer?

POLICEMAN. Not with these kids around.

MARTIN (*jerks his head in* GIMPTY'S *direction*). Dat's a nice feller. Friend a mine.
(HUNK *has entered from up the street just after* GIMPTY'S *exit. He is lighting a cigar, when he sees* MARTIN *in friendly conversation with the arch enemy. He stands there, transfixed, match to cigar.*)

POLICEMAN. I had quite a talk with him.

MARTIN (*fishing*). What about?

POLICEMAN. Oh . . . about these kids here.

MARTIN. Zat all?

POLICEMAN. Say, that's plenty! (*He puts his notebook in his pocket*) You don't happen to know a kid around here named Tommy something, do you?

MARTIN (*shakes his head*). Uh-uh!

POLICEMAN. Well, I'll catch him all right! (*He strides up the sidewalk.* MARTIN *watches him, then laughs. The match burns* HUNK'S *fingers. He drops it.*)

HUNK. Jesus!

MARTIN (*laughing*). A pal a mine.

HUNK. Dat's crazy.

MARTIN. Dey don' know me . . . wid dis mug.

HUNK (*sighs. This is too much for him. Then he remembers his errand*). Say, dat dame is heah.

MARTIN. Who?

HUNK. Er . . . Francey, or whatevah yuh call huh.

MARTIN. She is?

HUNK. Yeah. I got 'er waitin' on a corner. (*Puzzled*) I dunno what yuh wanna bodder wid a cheap hustlah like dat fuh.

MARTIN (*sharply*). Wha da yuh mean? Francey ain' no hustluh!

HUNK (*skeptical*). No?

MARTIN. No.

HUNK (*smiles weakly*). O.K. My mistake. We all make mistakes, boss.

Dat's what dey got rubbuhs on ee end a pencils faw. (*Laughs feebly.*)

MARTIN. Pretty cute, ain't cha? Maybe yuhr a mistake. Maybe yuhr liable tuh git rubbed out yuhself.

HUNK (*frightened*). I'll git huh now. (*He starts off. A young girl comes down the street, an obvious whore of the lowest class, wearing her timeless profession defiantly. A pert, pretty little face still showing traces of quality and something once sweet and fine. Skin an unhealthy pallor, lips a smear of rouge. Her mop of dyed red hair is lustreless, strawy, dead from too much alternate bleach and henna. She carries herself loosely. Droop-shouldered. Voluptuous S-shaped posture. There are no clothes under her cheap, faded green silk dress, cut so tight that it reveals the nipples of her full breasts, her navel, the "V" of her crotch, the muscles of her buttocks. She has obviously dressed hastily, carelessly; one stocking streaked with runs dribbles down at the ankle. She accosts* HUNK, *impatiently.*)

FRANCEY. Hey, what ta hell's ee idear, keepin' me standin' on a corner all day? I'm busy. I gotta git back tuh da house. Yuh want Ida tuh break my face?
(MARTIN *looks at her.*)

MARTIN. Francey! Jesus, what's come over yuh?

FRANCEY (*turning sharply to* MARTIN). How do yew know my name? Who are yew? (*Impatiently*) Well, who th' hell . . . (*Then she recognizes him, and gasps*) Fuh th' love a God! Marty!

MARTIN (*never taking his eyes off the girl*). Yeah. Hunk . . . scram!

(HUNK *goes up the street, stops at the tenement stoop and lounges there, within ear shot.*)

FRANCEY (*eagerly*). How are yuh, Marty?

MARTIN. Read duh papers!

FRANCEY. Yuh did somethin' to yuh face.

MARTIN. Yeah. Plastic, dey call it.

FRANCEY. They said yuh wuz out aroun' Coloradah—th' noospapuhs! Gee, I'm glad to see yuh!
(MARTIN *slips his arm around her waist and draws her tight to his body. As his lips grope for hers,* FRANCEY *turns her face away.* MARTIN *tries to pull her face around. She cries furiously*) No . . . don' kiss me on a lips!

MARTIN (*releasing her, puzzled*). What? What's a matter? (*He can't believe this. He frowns*) I ain't good enough for yuh?

FRANCEY (*quickly*). No. It ain't dat. It ain't yew. It's me. I got a sore on my mouth. Fuh yuhr own good, I don't want yuh to kiss me, dat's why.

MARTIN. I ain't nevuh fuhgot da way yew kiss.

FRANCEY (*wistfully*). I ain't niethuh. (*She laughs*) Go on! You wit all yer fancy dames. Where do I come off?

MARTIN. Dey don't mean nuttin'.

FRANCEY. Dat chorus goil . . . what's 'er name?

MARTIN. Nuttin'. She ain't got nuttin' . . . no guts, no fire. . . . But yew been boinin' in my blood . . . evuh since . . .

FRANCEY. An' yew been in mine . . . if yuh wanna know.

MARTIN. Remembuh dat foist night . . . on a roof?

FRANCEY. Yeah, I remembuh . . . da sky was full a stars, an' I was full a dreamy ideas. Dat was me foist time. I was fourteen, goin' on fifteen.

MARTIN. Yeah. It wuz mine too. It wuz terrific. Hit me right wheah I live . . . like my back wuz meltin'. An I wuz so sca'd when yuh started laffin' an' cryin', crazy like. . . . (*They both laugh, enjoying the memory, a little embarrassed by it.*)

FRANCEY. Yeah.

MARTIN. Gee, I nevuh wuz so sca'd like 'at time.

FRANCEY. Me too.

MARTIN (*draws her to him again, more gently*). Come eah! Close to me!

FRANCEY (*acquiescing*). Ony don' kiss me on a lips!

MARTIN. Closuh! (*They stand there a moment, bodies close, passionate.* MARTIN *buries his face in her hair.*)

FRANCEY (*eyes closed, whispers*). Marty!

MARTIN. Dose times unduh da stairs. . . .

FRANCEY. A couple a crazy kids we were! We wuz gonna git married. I bought a ring at da five an' dime staw.

MARTIN. Yeah. Ony we didn' have money enough fuh de license. Gee, it seems like yestiddy. We wuz talkin' about it right heah.

FRANCEY. Yestiddy! It seems like a million yeahs!

MARTIN (*as voices are heard coming from the East River Terrace*). Wait! (*They separate. He draws his hat over his eyes and turns away as a young couple come out of the gate and walk up the street.*)

GIRL. So many people standing around. What's all the excitement? What's happened?

MAN. The elevator man said someone was stabbed.

GIRL. Really? Who was it, do you know?

MAN. Mr. Griswald, I think he said. Twelfth floor.

GIRL. Oh! Yes? Did he say who did it?

MAN. He said one of the kids around here somewhere. . . . (*When they are well out of sight,* FRANCEY *clutches* MARTIN'S *arm.*)

FRANCEY. Marty, listen! Yuh got ta take care a yuhself. Yuh gotta go way an' hide. I don' want 'em to git yuh! I don' wan' 'em to git yuh!

MARTIN. Whatsa diffrince wheah I go? Ey got thuh finger on me every-wheah. Ah, frig 'em.

FRANCEY. Dey won't reco'nize yuh. Dey won't! Even I didn't.

MARTIN. Yeah, but yuh can' change ese, Francey. Look! (*He holds up his fingers. The tips are yellow and scarred*) Tree times I boined 'em wid acid an' t'ings. No good. Dere are some t'ings yuh can't change. But I'll tell yuh what . . . I'll scram out a heah. I'll scram . . . if yew come wit me.

FRANCEY. Ah, what do yuh want me fer? A broken-down hoor.

MARTIN. Shut up!

FRANCEY. I wouldn' be good fuh yuh.

MARTIN. I know what I want.

FRANCEY (*laughs, crazily*). Yeah. Dis is a swell pipe-dream I'm havin'! I'm Minnie de Moocher kickin' a gong aroun'!

MARTIN. Listen! I got de dough now, kid. We kin do it now.

FRANCEY. But I'm sick, Marty! Don't yuh see? I'm sick!

MARTIN. What's a matter wid yuh?

FRANCEY (*almost inaudibly*). What do yuh think?
(MARTIN *looks at her for a long time. He sees her. The nostalgic dream is finished. His lips begin to curl in disgust.*)

MARTIN. Why didncha git a job?

FRANCEY. Dey don' grow on trees!

MARTIN. Why didncha starve foist?

FRANCEY. Why didnchou?
(MARTIN *makes no effort to conceal his growing disgust. Turns away.*)

FRANCEY (*suddenly shouts, fiercely, at the top of her lungs*). Well, what ta hell did yuh expect?

MARTIN. I don' know.
(*A passing tug shrieks hoarsely. The echo floats back.*)

FRANCEY (*quietly, clutching at a hope*). Maybe . . . if yuh got da dough . . . yuh git a doctuh an' he fixes me up . . .

MARTIN. Nah. Once at stuff gits in yuh . . . nah! (*Again the tug shrieks and is answered by its echo. He reaches into his inner breast pocket, extracts a fat roll of bills, peels off several and hands them to her*) Heah. Buy yerself somethin'.

FRANCEY (*her eyes suddenly glued to the money*). Baby! Dat's some roll yuh got. Yuh cud choke a hoss wid dat.

MARTIN (*thrusting it at her*). Heah!

FRANCEY (*takes the money*). Is it hot?

MARTIN. Yeah. Bettah be careful where yuh spend it.

FRANCEY. Sure.

MARTIN. An' keep yuh lips buttoned up!

FRANCEY. I wouldn' tell on yuh, Marty. Not if dey tied me ta wild hosses, I wouldn't.

MARTIN. Bettuh not.

FRANCEY (*folds her money, still fascinated by the huge roll of bills in his hand. Her voice takes on a peculiar whining, wheedling quality*). Honey!

MARTIN. Yeah?

FRANCEY. Cud yuh spare another twenty bucks? I godda . . .

MARTIN. No!

FRANCEY. Aw, come on, dearie!

MARTIN. No!

FRANCEY. Don' be a tightwad!

MARTIN (*reaching the limit of his disgust*). What ta hell do yuh tink I am? Some guy yuh got up in yuh room? I'll . . . (*He raises his hand, ready to slap her. Again the shriek of a tug, and the echo.*)

FRANCEY (*quickly, frightened*). Nah, ferget it, Marty! I wuz just . . .

MARTIN. Awright! Awright! Now beat it!

FRANCEY. O.K., Marty. (*She starts to go, pauses, turns back*) Fer old times' sakes, will yuh do me a favor? Please?

MARTIN (*shoves the money back into his pocket*). No!

FRANCEY. Not dat.

MARTIN. What?

FRANCEY. Will yuh kiss me? Heah? Ona cheek? Jus' fuh old times' sakes? Come on. (*He hesitates. She comes close, presses her cheek against his lips. He pecks her cheek, and turns away, scowling. She laughs, a low bitter laugh, at his obvious disrelish*) Thanks! (*She goes up the street slowly, her purse swinging carelessly, her body swaying invitation, the tired march of her profession. The shriek of the tug is drawn out and distant now. The echo lingers.* MARTIN *spits and wipes the kiss off his lips with a groan of distaste.*)

HUNK (*comes down the sidewalk, slowly*). Well?

MARTIN. Huh?

HUNK. See?

MARTIN. Yeah. Yeah!

HUNK. Twice in one day. Deah yuh ah! I toldja we shouldn' a come back. But yuh wouldn' lissen a me. Yuh nevah lissen a me.

MARTIN. Yeah.

HUNK (*trying to console him*). I know how yuh feel, Marty. Les go back to St. Louis, huh? Now dat dame yuh had deah—Deedy Cook—Now dat wuz a broad. Regaler. Bet she's waitin fuh yuh . . . wid welcome ona doormat.

MARTIN. Awright! Don' talk about dames, Hunk, will yuh? Fuhget 'em. All cats look alike inna dahk. Fuhget 'em.
(*A little girl comes out of the gate bouncing a rubber ball.* MARTIN *looks at her, thinks a moment, turns to watch her go up the street. He sucks his teeth a moment, thinking.*)

HUNK. Listen, Marty . . . Let's git outta heah. Too many people know yuh heah. Whaddaya say?

MARTIN. Sh! I'm thinkin'.
(*Pause.*)

HUNK. Well, guess I'll go shoot a game a pillpool. (*Starts to go up the street.*)

MARTIN (*motions him back, turns to stare at the Terrace Apartments*).

Wait a minute . . . (HUNK *returns*) Yuh know, Hunk. (*He shakes a thumb at the Apartment*) Der's a pile a tin in ere.

HUNK. Yeah.

MARTIN. Didja see what dese kids did heah today?

HUNK. No.

MARTIN. Ey got one a dese rich little squoits in a hallway, slapped him around an' robbed his watch.

HUNK. So what?
(*A man appears on the terrace, watches them for a second, and then slips away. Two men come down the street talking casually, one of them goes into the tenement, the other, waiting for him, wanders over back of the hopper and is hidden from view.*)

MARTIN (*glances at them, lowers his voice*). Maybe we kin pull a snatch . . . kidnap one a dese babies.

HUNK. We're too hot. Foolin' round wid kids ain' our racket.

MARTIN. Scared?

HUNK. No . . . ony . . . I. . . .

MARTIN. Stop yuh yammerin'! Git a hold a Whitey. See wot he knows about duh mugs in heah! (HUNK *hesitates*) Come on, Hunk, git goin'!

HUNK. O.K. Yuh duh boss! (*He goes reluctantly.*)
(*The tap of* GIMPTY'*s cane on the sidewalk is heard approaching, its rhythmic click ominous.* GIMPTY *appears, tight-lipped, pale, grim.* MARTIN *smiles out of one corner of his lips, and throws him a conciliatory greeting.*)

MARTIN. Hello, Gimpty!
(GIMPTY *turns away without answering.* MARTIN, *amused, laughs. He is suddenly in a good mood. The man who spied on him from the terrace appears in the gateway and catches* GIMPTY'*s eye.* GIMPTY *points his cane at* MARTIN. *The good mood passes.* MARTIN'*s eyebrows pull together in one puzzled line.*)

MARTIN. What's eatin' yuh, wise guy?
(*The man behind the gate draws a revolver, comes quickly up behind* MARTIN *and digs the gun in his back.*

G MAN. Get 'em up, Martin! The Department of Justice wants you!

MARTIN. What ta hell . . . ! (*Tries to turn, but the revolver prods him back.*)

G MAN. Come on, get' em up!

MARTIN (*hands up*). I ain't Martin. My name's Johnson. Wanna see my license? (*He slides his hand into his breast pocket.*)

G MAN. If you're smart, you'll behave yourself!

MARTIN (*wheels around, draws his gun, and fires in one motion*). No, yuh don't . . . (*The* G MAN *drops his gun, crumples onto the sidewalk holding his belly and kicking.* MARTIN *turns to face* GIMPTY, *who has backed away to the hopper.* MARTIN, *his face black and contorted, aims at* GIMPTY) So yuh ratted, yuh. . . . (*From behind the hopper and the tenement doorway guns explode*

Two other G MEN *appear and descend on* MARTIN, *firing as they come.* MARTIN *groans, wheels, and falls, his face in the gutter, his fingers clawing the sidewalk. One of the* G MEN *goes to aid his wounded comrade. The other* G MAN *stands over* MARTIN's *body, pumping bullet after bullet into him, literally nailing him to the ground. The* G MAN *kicks him to make sure he's dead. No twitch!* MARTIN *lies there flat. The* G MAN *takes out a handkerchief, picks up* MARTIN's *gun gingerly, wraps it in the handkerchief, puts it in his pocket.)*

SECOND G MAN. Where 'd he get you, Bob? Come on, sit up here! (*Helps him to sit against the coping.* FIRST G MAN *presses his hand in agony to his wound. From the street there is a rising babble of voices. Tenement windows are thrown up, heads thrust out; the curious crowd to the edge of the terrace, come to the gate, run down the street, collect in small groups, discussing the macabre scene in excited, hushed murmur. A* LADY *comes out of the gate, sees the dead man, screams hysterically, and is helped off by the* DOORMAN. *The* POLICEMAN *comes tearing down the street, revolver drawn. He forces his way through the crowd.)*

POLICEMAN. Out a my way! Look out! (*To the* THIRD G MAN) What's this?

THIRD G MAN (*taking out a badge in a leather case from inside his coat pocket and holding it up*). It's all right, officer. Department of Justice! (*Replaces the badge.)*

POLICEMAN. What happened? Who's this guy?

THIRD G MAN. Baby-face Martin.

POLICEMAN. Is that him?

THIRD G MAN. Yep.

POLICEMAN. Gese, I was talkin' to him a couple a minutes ago.

SECOND G MAN. Get an ambulance, quick! Will you?

POLICEMAN (*crosses to the police box, opens it*). Box 10 . . . Mulligan. Send ambulance! Make all notifications! Baby-face Martin was just shot by Federal men. He winged one of 'em . . . I don't know . . . yeah . . . here. Gese, I was talking to him myself a few minutes ago . . . Hell, Sarge, I couldn't recognize him. His face is all made over. (*He hangs up. The shrill siren of a radio car mounts to a crescendo, mingles with the screech of brakes, and is suddenly silent. Two more policemen dash on, forcing their path through the crowd. They are followed by* SPIT, *wearing a single roller skate. He edges his way to the front of the crowd.)*

SECOND POLICEMAN. Hi, Mulligan. What have yuh got here?

MULLIGAN. Baby-face Martin!

THIRD POLICEMAN. Did you git him?

MULLIGAN. No such luck. The Federal men got him. He winged one of them. (*Gestures toward the wounded* G MAN.)

SECOND POLICEMAN. Did you notify the house?

MULLIGAN. Yeah. I gave 'em everything . . . Lend us a hand, will yuh. Git rid of this crowd. (MULLIGAN *stands by* MARTIN's *body, writing in a notebook. The other* POLICEMEN *push back the crowd.* SPIT *slips through, and looks at the dead man with scared curiosity.)*

SECOND POLICEMAN (*pushing the crowd*). Break it up! This is no circus. Come on, break it up!

GIRL IN THE CROWD. Don't push me!

SECOND POLICEMAN. Well, go on home! Go on, break it up!

SECOND G MAN (*to the wounded agent*). How you feelin', Bob?

FIRST G MAN. Lousy.

SECOND G MAN. You'll be O.K.

FIRST G MAN. I don't know . . . I don't know! I should've plugged him right away . . . in the back. You don't give a snake like that a break. . . . Anyway, we got him! That's something!

SECOND G MAN. Sure you did, Bob. You'll get cited for this.

FIRST G MAN. That's dandy! That's just dandy! Give the medal to my old lady for the kids to play with . . . an' remember they once had an old man who was a . . . hero!

THIRD G MAN. Aw, cut it, Bob. You'll be O.K. Don't talk like that!

DOORMAN (*pushing through the crowd*). Officer! Officer!

MULLIGAN. Get outa here! You with the rest of them. Come on, get back!

DOORMAN. Officer, this is important! That's one of the boys . . . there, that one! He's one of the gang!

MULLIGAN. What boy? What the hell are you talkin' about?

DOORMAN. The one who stabbed Mr. Griswald.

MULLIGAN. What? Oh, where?

DOORMAN (*pointing*). That one there! He's one of the gang.

MULLIGAN. Are you sure?

DOORMAN. Yes . . . yes . . . I'll swear to it!

MULLIGAN. Come here! Hey you! (*Runs over to* SPIT, *grabs his arm. The murmur of the crowd rises.)*

SPIT. Lemme go! I didn' do nuttin'. Lemme go!

SECOND POLICEMAN. What is this kid got to do with it?

MULLIGAN. That's somethin' else. (*The clang of an approaching ambulance comes to a sudden halt. Enter, pushing their way down the street, an* INTERNE *carrying a doctor's bag, followed by an* AMBULANCE MAN *carrying a folded stretcher, which encloses a pillow and a rolled blanket. The murmur of the crowd hushes.)*

INTERNE. Hello, Mulligan.

MULLIGAN. Hello, doc. (*To* SECOND POLICEMAN) Hold this kid a minute.
(SECOND POLICEMAN *grabs* SPIT'S *arm and drags him back to the crowd on the sidewalk.)*

INTERNE. What's up? (*He comes down to the body.)*

MULLIGAN. Just got Baby-face Martin!
(The murmur rises again as the news is spread.)

INTERNE. You did? *(He glances at the body)* He won't need me!

SECOND G MAN. Hey, doc, look at this man! *(The* INTERNE *kneels to the wounded man, examines his wound, sponges it, places a pad over it)* It's not bad, is it, doc?

INTERNE *(cheerfully)*. Not very bad, but we'd better rush him off to the hospital. Here, somebody help get him on the stretcher.
(The AMBULANCE MAN *opens the stretcher, places the pillow at the head.* SECOND G MAN *and* MULLIGAN *lift the wounded* G MAN *carefully and lay him on the stretcher with words of encouragement. The* AMBULANCE MAN *unrolls the blanket over him.* SECOND G MAN *and the* AMBULANCE DRIVER *carry the wounded man up the sidewalk calling "Gangway." The* THIRD G MAN *accompanies them, holding the wounded man's hand and talking to him. The crowd open a path, and stare, their murmur silenced for a moment.)*

MULLIGAN *(pointing to* BABY-FACE*)*. Want to look at this guy, doc?

INTERNE *(kneels by the body, rips open the coat and vest, cursorily inspects the wounds, rolls back the eyelid, applies a stethoscope to the heart)*. Phew! They certainly did a job on him! Nothing left to look at but chopped meat. God, they didn't leave enough of him for a good p.m.! *(Rises, takes pad and pencil from his pocket, glances at* MULLIGAN'S *shield, writes)* Mulligan . . . 10417 . . . 19th Precinct. Have you got his pedigree?

MULLIGAN *(reading from his own notebook)*. Joe Martin. 28. White . . . U.S. 5 ft., 9 in. 170 lbs. Unmarried. Occupation . . . *(Shrugs his shoulders.)*

INTERNE. All right. Dr. Flint. Mark him D.O.A.!

MULLIGAN *(writing)*. Dead . . . on . . . arrival. . . .
(Enter, pushing their way through the crowd, the MEDICAL EXAMINER, *followed by the* POLICE PHOTOGRAPHER. *The* PHOTOGRAPHER *opens his camera, adjusts it, and photographs the body from several angles.)*

INTERNE *(as the* EXAMINER *approaches)*. Hello, doc!

EXAMINER. Hello, Doctor. So they finally got him, did they?

INTERNE. Yes, they sure did.

EXAMINER. It's about time. What have you got on him?

INTERNE. Twelve gunshot wounds. Five belly, four chest, three head. *(Picks up his bag and goes. The* EXAMINER *inspects the body.)*

MULLIGAN *(to the* DOORMAN*)*. Hey, find something to cover this up with. *(The* DOORMAN *nods and disappears through the gateway.* MULLIGAN *turns to the* THIRD POLICEMAN, *who is still holding back the crowd)* Hey, Tom! Stand by while I go through this bum! *(He kneels, and goes through* MARTIN'S *pockets, handing his findings to the* THIRD POLICEMAN *who jots them down in his notebook.* MULLIGAN *takes a ring off* MARTIN'S *finger)* Diamond ring. Look at that rock! *(He hands it to the* THIRD POLICEMAN *who pockets it, and* *makes a note.* MULLIGAN *extracts* MARTIN'*s wad of bills*) And this roll of bills! What a pile! You count it!

EXAMINER. Through with him, boys?

MULLIGAN (*rising*). Yeah.

PHOTOGRAPHER. One second! (*Takes a last photograph.*)

EXAMINER. Well, as soon as the wagon comes, send him down to the morgue. I'll look him over in the morning. Mulligan, you report to me there first thing in the morning, too.

MULLIGAN. Yes, sir.
(*The* EXAMINER *goes. The* PHOTOGRAPHER *folds his camera and follows.*)

WOMAN IN THE CROWD (*to the* SECOND POLICEMAN, *who is holding* SPIT). Officer! What did this boy have to do with it? Why are you holding him?

SECOND POLICEMAN. Never mind. Stand back!

SPIT. Lemme go! I didn't do nuttin'! Whadda yuh want?

MULLIGAN (*goes to* SPIT). You're one of the gang who beat up a boy here today and stabbed his father, ain't you?

SPIT. No, I yain't. I didn' 'ave nuttn tuh do wid it. It wuz a kid named Tommy McGrath.

(*The murmur of the crowd fades as they all listen.*)

MULLIGAN. Tommy McGrath! Where does he live?

SPIT. On Foist Avenoo between Fifty-toid and Fifty-fawt.

MULLIGAN. Sure?

SPIT. Yeah.

MULLIGAN (*to the* SECOND POLICEMAN). Take this kid around there, will yuh? Get ahold a Tommy McGrath. He's wanted for stabbin some guy. I got to wait for the morgue wagon.

SECOND POLICEMAN. O.K. (*Drags* SPIT *through the crowd*) Come on! You show us where he lives and we'll let you go. (*As they go off, the murmur of the crowd rises again. The* THIRD G MAN *crosses to* GIMPTY, *who is leaning against the hopper, white and shaking. The* DOORMAN *comes out with an old discarded coat, the gold braid raveled and rusty, the cloth dirty and oil-stained.* MULLIGAN *takes it from him.*)

THIRD G MAN (*to* GIMPTY). Good work, Mac: Come over to the office and pick up your check. (*He makes his way up the street.* MULLIGAN *throws the coat over* MARTIN'*s body. The murmur of the crowd rises high. A boat horn in the river bellows hoarsely and dies away.*)

CURTAIN

ACT THREE

SCENE—*The same. That night. A very dark night. From the dock the sounds of a gay party, music, babble, laughter.* GIMPTY, *a bent silhouette, sits on the coping leaning against the terrace wall. There's a lamp shining up the street. The lights from the tenement windows are faint and yellow and glum. The lanterns on the gateposts, one red, one green, are lit and look very decorative. There's a blaze of fire crackling out of an old iron ash-can in the center of the street. The* BOYS *hover over it, roasting potatoes skewered on long sticks. Their impish faces gleam red one minute and are wiped by shadows the next as they lean over the flames.*

ANGEL (*gesturing wildly*). All uv a sudden da shots come . . . bing . . . bing . . . bam . . . biff . . .

T.B. (*superior*). I hoid da shots foist. I wuz jus walkin' up . . .

ANGEL (*angrily*). Yuh di'not.

T.B. I did so.

ANGEL. Yuh tought it wuz a rivitin' machine, yuh said.

T.B. I di'not.

ANGEL (*tops him*). Yuh did so.

T.B. (*tops him*). I di'not.

ANGEL (*tops him*). Yuh did so.

T.B. (*tops him*). Ah, yuh mudduh's chooch!

ANGEL (*tops him*). Yeah, yuh fadduh's doop!

T.B. (*crescendo*). Fongoola!
(DIPPY *runs down the street waving two potatoes.*)

DIPPY. Hey, guys, I swiped two maw mickeys. Look!

ANGEL. Boy, 'at's good!

SPIT. O.K. Put 'em in.

DIPPY. Wheah's Tommy?

SPIT. Put 'em in!

DIPPY. Dis big one's mine, remembuh!

SPIT. Put 'em in, I said!

DIPPY. Don' fugit, dis big one's mine!

SPIT. Shat ap!

DIPPY. Yeah . . . yew . . . yew shat ap!

SPIT. Wha-a-at?

DIPPY (*cowed, moves away from* SPIT). Wheah's Tommy?

ANGEL. I dunno. He didn' show up yet.

T.B. (*reflectively, referring to* MARTIN). Da papuhs said dey found twenty gran' in 'is pockets.

ANGEL. Twenty G's. Boy, 'at's a lot a dough!

SPIT. Boy, he must a bin a putty smaht guy.

T.B. Baby-face? Sure! He wuz a tops. Public enemy numbuh one. Boy, he had guts. He wasn' a scared a nobody. Boy, he could knock 'em all off like dat . . . like anyt'ing! Boy, like nuttn!
(DIPPY *takes a stick from the can and holds it against his shoulder, pointed at* ANGEL, *maneuvering it as if it were a machine gun.*)

DIPPY (*makes a rapid, staccato bleating sound*). Ah-ah-ah-ah-ah! Look, I godda machine gun! Ah-ah-ah-ah!

ANGEL (*pointing his kazoo at* DIPPY). Bang Bang!

DIPPY (*sore*). Nah, yuh can't do dat. Yuh'r dead. I shot yuh foist.

ANGEL (*ignores that salient point, raises the kazoo again, takes dead aim at* DIPPY). Bang!

DIPPY (*lets loose with his improvised machine gun*). Ah-ah-ah-ah! Deah. Now I gotcha! Now yuh dead!

ANGEL. Bang!

DIPPY (*disgusted*). Aw-w-w! (*He throws the stick into the fire and turns away.*)

T.B. Gese . . . what I could do wid twenty G's!

ANGEL. What?

SPIT. Snot!

T.B. Yeah, I bet I could buy a boat like dat, huh? (*He points off toward the dock.*)

ANGEL. Look! Dey got lights an' flags an' music!

SPIT. Dey got some hot party on, hey guys?

DIPPY. Look! Look! Dey're dancin'! (*Cavorts about with an imaginary partner, making ribald gestures and singing*) Yuh're da top, yuh're da coliseum. Hey! I'm dancin'! Look, felluhs! Look on me! I'm dancin'! Look on me! (*He whirls around and looks at them for approval.*)

T.B. (*sour-faced*). Sit down! Yew stink!
(DIPPY *stops grinning and dancing simultaneously. He sits down, squelched.*)

ANGEL. Twenty grand! . .

SPIT. Yeah . . . so what's it got 'im?

ANGEL. Yeah. Yuh see duh pitchuh uv 'is broad inna papuhs? Deedy Cook aw sump'm . . .

T.B. Boy, some nice nooky, huh?

SPIT. Boy, she's got some contrac's now! I heah she's gonna do a bubble dance in a boilesque, I t'ink.

ANGEL. Yeah. My fadduh took one look at huh pitchuh. So 'ee said 'ee'd let 'em shoot 'im too, fuh half an hour wid a fancy floozy like dat. So my mudduh gits mad. So she sez dey wouldn' haf tuh shoot cha. Haf an hour wid at cockamamee yuh'd be dead! (*They all laugh*) So she spills some boilin' watuh on 'im. So 'ee yells like a bastid an' runs outta da house mad.

(MILTY *comes down the sidewalk, breathless with excitement.*)

MILTY. Hey, felluhs, yuh know what?

ANGEL. What?

SPIT. Snot!

MILTY. Balls tuh yew!

SPIT. Ah, I'll mobilize yuh!

MILTY. Yuh know what, guys? Duh cops ah wise tuh Tommy.

ANGEL. Gese!

T.B. No kid! No kid!

SPIT. Aw, bushwah!

MILTY. No bushwah! Deah' lookin' fuh 'im. He tole me hisself. (*To* SPIT) Fot smelleh! Dey went up tuh his house. Some guy snitched.

T.B. No kid!

SPIT. Did dey git 'im?

MILTY. Nah. Tommy's too wise fuh dem. Dey come in tru de daw. He goes out tru de fire-escape, down a yahrd, oveh de fence, tru de celleh, up de stayuhs, out dee udduh street.

SPIT. Wheah's he now?

MILTY. He's hidin' out.

SPIT. Wheah?

MILTY. Wheah duh yuh tink, wheah? Wheah dey don' ketch 'im, dat's wheah.

SPIT. Ah, dey'll ketch 'im.

MILTY. Dey don' ketch Tommy so quick.

SPIT (*nervously, looking into the fire*). How're de mickeys comin'?

T.B. Gese, I bet a dollah dey sen' 'im tuh rifawm school.

SPIT. Sure. Dat's what dey do.

DIPPY. Yeah, dat's what. Ain' it, T.B.?

T.B. Yeah. Dey sent me tuh rifawm school fuh jus' swipin' a bunch a bananas. An' 'ey wuz all rotten too, most a dem.

MILTY. I pity duh guy who snitched. Tommy's layin' fuh him, awright.

DIPPY. Does 'ee know who?

SPIT (*trying to change the subject*). Hey, guys, duh mickeys ah awmost done!

ANGEL (*fishing out his potato and poking it with his kazoo*). Nah, not yet. Look, dis one's hard inside.

DIPPY *reaches to feel* ANGEL'S *mickey*). Yeah. Like a rock . . . Ouch! Dat's hot! (*Licks his fingers.*)

ANGEL (*dipping the mickey back into the embers*). Gese, poor Tommy! If dey ketch 'im, he don' git no maw mickeys like dis fer a long time.

DIPPY. Dey git mickeys in rifawm school, don' dey?

T.B. Slop dey git, slop . . . unless dey git some dough tuh smeah da jailies wid.

SPIT. Aw, shat ap! All a time yuh shoot yuh mout' off about rifawm school . . . like yew wuz 'ee ony one who evuh went.

DIPPY. Yeah. Yew wuz ony deah six mont's.

ANGEL. Tom'll git two yeahs.

DIPPY. T'ree, maybe, I bet.

MILTY. Gese, dat's lousy.

SPIT. Ah, shat ap, will yuh?

T.B. Yeah, nevuh mind. Yuh loin a barrel a good tings in rifawm school.
(*The* DOORMAN *comes out of the gate, exasperated.*)

DOORMAN. Now I'm not going to tell you again!
(SPIT, T.B. *and* ANGEL *speak simultaneously.*)

SPIT. Ah, go frig!
T.B. Deah're awmost done.
ANGEL. Jus' a li'l while.

DOORMAN. No! Get away from here . . . all of you . . . right now!

GIMPTY (*approaches the* DOORMAN *and addresses him in a voice tight and hoarse, hardly recognizable*). Did you give her my note?

DOORMAN. Yes. She said she'd be out in a moment.

GIMPTY. Thanks. (*He retires to sit again in the shadows.*)

DOORMAN. If you kids don't beat it, I'm going to call a cop! (*Turns to the gate.*)

SPIT. Aw, hold yuh hawses!

DOORMAN (*wheels about, threateningly*). Wha-a-at?

SPIT (*scared*). Nuttn.
(*A* LADY *in evening gown and a* MAN *in tuxedo come down the street, talking quietly. The* WOMAN *laughs. As they reach the gate, the* DOORMAN *touches his hat.*)

DOORMAN. Good evening.

MAN AND WOMAN. Good evening.
(*The* DOORMAN *follows them through the gateway.*)

SPIT (*when the* DOORMAN *is well out of earshot*), Ah, yuh louse, I'll mobilize yuh!
(*The boys all roar.*)

ANGEL. Hey, de fire's dyin' down.

T.B. Yeah, we need maw wood.

SPIT. Let's scout aroun' an' soich out some maw wood. I'll stay heah an' guard de mickeys.

T.B. Me too.

SPIT. Yew, too, balls!

T.B. What's a mattuh wit me?

SPIT. What's a mattuh wit yew? Yew stink on ice, 'at's what's a mattuh wit' yew!

T.B. Yeah, well, yew ain' no lily a da valley.

SPIT. Go on now, or yuh git dis mickey . . . red hot . . . up yuh bunny!

T.B. Yeah? (*He begins to cough.*)

SPIT. Yeah! Wanna make sumpm otuv it?

T.B. If it wasn't fuh my T.B. . . .

SPIT. Ah, dat's a gag. Any time yuh put it straight up tuh 'im, he goes . . . (*Imitates the cough*) My T.B. . . . Balls!

T.B. Oh, yeah? . . . Look, smart guy! (*He has been holding his hand to his lips. He coughs again, spits, opens his hand, holds it out and displays a bloody clot in the palm. Proudly*) Blood! (*The boys gasp.*)

ANGEL. Wow!

T.B. Smart guy!

SPIT. Ah, I could do dat. Yuh suck yuh mout'!

DIPPY (*sucks his mouth audibly, spits into his hand*). I can't . . . I can't. How do yuh do it?
(DRINA *comes down the street, sees the boys and hurries to them.*)

MILTY. Hello, Drina.

DRINA. Did you see Tommy? (*There is a tired, desperate quality in her tone.*)

MILTY. No.

DRINA (*to* DIPPY). Did you?

DIPPY. Nope.

DRINA. Did anybody see him? He hasn't been home at all.

MILTY. No. Nobody saw 'im, Drina.

DRINA (*tired, very tired*). Thanks. Thanks, Milty. (*She notices* GIMPTY *and approaches him.*)

ANGEL (*in a whisper*). Whyn't yuh tell huh?

MILTY (*also whispering*). No. Tommy said no.

SPIT (*aloud*). Ah, balonee!

MILTY (*whispers*). Sh! Shat ap!

SPIT (*deliberately loud*). Who fuh! I'll give yuh yuh lumps in a minute.

DRINA (*to* GIMPTY). Pete, did you see Tommy?

GIMPTY. What?

DRINA. My brother? Have you seen him at all?

GIMPTY. Oh! No.

DRINA. Gee, he hasn't showed up yet. The cops are looking for him. I'm scared to death.

GIMPTY. I'm sorry.

SPIT. Hey, Drina! Milty knows, but he won't tell!

DRINA (*turns quickly*). Does he?

MILTY. No.

SPIT. He does.

MILTY (*quietly to* SPIT). Ah, yuh louse! (*Aloud to* DRINA) I do not!

SPIT (*to* MILTY). I'll mobilize yuh! (*To* DRINA) He does so.
(DRINA *takes* MILTY *by both shoulders and shakes him.*)

DRINA. Milty, please tell me if you know . . . please! I'm half crazy.

MILTY. Tommy said not tuh tell.

DRINA (*pleading*). But I wouldn't hurt him. You know that. It's for his good. I've got to talk to him. I've got to find out what we're gonna do. (*Pause*) Milty, you've gotta tell me . . . please!

MILTY (*reluctantly*). Aw right! Come on. . . .

DRINA (*as they go up the street*). How is he? Is he all right? Is he hurt or anything?

MILTY. Nah!

DRINA. Why didn't he come home?

MILTY. Don' worry, Drina. Dey won' catch 'im.
(*They're out of sight and the voices fade off.*)

SPIT. Hey, Angel. You stay heah wid me. Youse guys git some wood. Go on!

DIPPY. O.K. Watch my mickey.

T.B. Mine too.
(DIPPY *and* T.B. *exit up the sidewalk.*)

DIPPY. Me, I'm goin' ovuh on Toid Avenoo.

T.B. I'm goin' ovuh tuh Schultzie's.

DIPPY. Naw, whyn't cha go ovuh on Second Avenoo?
(*Their voices fade away.*)

SPIT. Hey, Angel, yew stay heah an' guard dose mickeys.

ANGEL. Wheah yuh goin'?

SPIT. I'm gonna trail Milty an' fin' out wheah Tommy is.

ANGEL. What faw!

SPIT. None a yuh beeswax! (*He lopes up the street.* ANGEL *watches him for a while, puzzled, then fishes his kazoo from a pocket, relaxes by the fireside, and hums into the instrument. A shadow detaches itself from the hopper and creeps stealthily toward* ANGEL. *It whispers "Psst! Hey! Angel!"* ANGEL *wheels around, startled.*)

ANGEL. Tommy! Gese!

TOMMY (*his face glowing red as he leans over the fire toward* ANGEL). Sh! Shat ap! (*In a hoarse whisper*) Wheah ah da guys?
(*They both talk in whispers.*)

ANGEL. Dey went tuh look fuh wood.

TOMMY. What?

ANGEL. Fuh wood. Maw wood. Milty jus' took yuh sistuh . . .

TOMMY. Is Spit wit de guys?

ANGEL. Yeah.

TOMMY. O.K.

ANGEL. Milty jus' took yuh sistuh tuh yer hideout.

TOMMY. He did? De louse!

ANGEL. Whatcha gonna do, Tommy?

TOMMY. Run away . . . so de bulls don' git me.

ANGEL (*impressed*). Gese!

TOMMY (*quietly*). But foist I'm gonna ketch de guy who snitched. Do yuh know who it wuz?

ANGEL. Me? No.

TOMMY (*flaring*). Don' lie tuh me . . . I'll kill yuh!

ANGEL. Yew know me, Tommy.

TOMMY. O.K. I tink I'm wise tuh who done it.

ANGEL. Who?

TOMMY. Spit.

ANGEL. Yuh tink so?

TOMMY. Yeah.

ANGEL. Gese!

TOMMY. Now I'm gonna hide, see? Right back a deah. (*Points up behind the hopper*) If yuh let on I'm heah . . . (*Ominously*) I'll put yuh teet' down yuh troat!

ANGEL. Aw, Tommy, yuh know me . . . yuh know me!

TOMMY. O.K. Den do like I tell yuh. When Spit comes back, yew tell 'im like dis . . . Duh guy I stabbed wuz down heah lookin' fuh Spit tuh givvim five bucks fuh snitchin' on who done it. Yuh got dat straight?

ANGEL. Duh guy what he got stabbed . . . wuz down heah lookin' fuh Spit . . . tuh givvim five bucks fuh snitchin' on who done it.

TOMMY. Right.

ANGEL. O.K.

TOMMY. An' rememba . . . yew let on I'm heah, I'll . . .

ANGEL. Aw, Tommy, yew know me.

TOMMY. Aw right. Jus' do like I tole yuh.

ANGEL. Whadda yuh gonna do tuh Spit if 'ee done it? (TOMMY *takes a knife from his pocket, and nips open the blade. The firelight runs along the blade. It looks bright and sharp and hard.* TOMMY *grimly draws it diagonally across his cheek.* ANGEL *grunts*) Mark a de squealuh?

TOMMY (*snaps the blade home and pockets the knife*). Right.

ANGEL. Gese!

TOMMY. Now, go on playin' yuh kazoo like nuttn happened . . . like I wuzn't heah.

(*Footsteps and voices from the gate.* TOMMY *ducks and melts into the shadows of the hopper.* ANGEL *plays his kazoo a bit ostentatiously. The* DOORMAN *opens the gate.* KAY *appears in a shimmering evening gown, lovely and scented.*)

GIMPTY (*his voice dull and tired*). Hello, Kay!

KAY. Hello, Pete! (GIMPTY *looks past* KAY *at the* DOORMAN) Yes?

DOORMAN. Ma'am?

KAY. Anything you want?

DOORMAN. Oh no . . . no, ma'am. Excuse me. (*Exit.*)

GIMPTY. I sent you a note this afternoon. Did you get it?

KAY. Yes. I was out. I didn't get back till late. I'm so sorry, Pete. Forgive me.

GIMPTY. Forget it!

(*Two couples in evening clothes come down the street. They are all hectic, gay, and a trifle drunk. They greet* KAY *merrily. She laughs and jests with them, tells them she'll join them shortly, and in the gate they go. Not, however, without one or two backward glances at* GIMPTY. *Their chatter, off, ends in a burst of laughter that fades away.* KAY *turns to* GIMPTY.)

KAY. What a brawl that's turning into!

GIMPTY. Yeah. It seems like quite a party.

KAY. Yes, it is.

GIMPTY (*after a pause, in a voice so low, it can scarcely be heard*). Kay . . . did you hear what happened here this afternoon?

KAY. What do you . . . ?

GIMPTY. The shooting.

KAY (*making talk. Evading*). Oh, yes. And we just missed it. It must have been exciting. I'm . . .

GIMPTY. I didn't miss it.

KAY. No? . . . Oh, tell me . . . was it very . . . ?

GIMPTY (*begins to give way to the terror and remorse pent up in him*). It was pretty horrible.

KAY. Oh . . . of course.

GIMPTY. Horrible!

KAY (*realizing by his tone that something dreadful lies in all this, she becomes very tender and soothing*). Pete, give me your hand. Come here. (*She leads him to the edge of the wharf*) Sit down. . . . Now, what happened?

GIMPTY. I'd rather not talk about it for a minute.

KAY. If it upsets you, let's not talk about it at all.

GIMPTY. Yes, I've got to . . . but not for a minute. . . .

KAY. All right.

(*Underneath them, the river splashes against the bulwark. Off, on the yacht, the band is playing a soft, sentimental melody. The chatter and the laughter from the party float faintly over the water. They sit there for a long time just staring across the river, at its lights, at the factories and signs on the opposite shore, at the bridge with its glittering loops, at the string of ghostly barges silently moving across the river. For a long time. Then she speaks, quietly.*)

KAY. I love the river at night. . . . It's beautiful . . . and a bit frightening.

GIMPTY (*stares down at the black water swirling under him. He begins to talk, faster and faster, trying to push back into his unconscious the terror that haunts him, to forget that afternoon if only for a few seconds*). It reminds me of something. . . . What is it? . . . Oh, yeah . . . when I was a kid. In the spring the sudden sun showers used to flood the gutters. The other kids used to race boats down the street. Little boats: straws, matches, lollipop-sticks. I couldn't run after them, so I guarded the sewer and caught the boats to keep them from tumbling in. Near the sewer . . . sometimes, I remember . . . a whirlpool would form. . . . Dirt and oil from the street would break into rainbow colors . . . iridescent

. . . (*For a moment he does escape*) Beautiful, I think . . . a marvel of color out of dirty water. I can't take my eyes off it. And suddenly a boat in danger. (*The terror in him rises again*) I try to stop it. . . . Too late! It shoots into the black hole of the sewer. I used to dream about falling into it myself. The river reminds me of that. . . . Death must be like this . . . like the river at night. (*There is no comfort in her big enough for his needs. They sit in brooding silence, which is finally interrupted by the* DOORMAN'S *voice, off.*)

DOORMAN. Miss Mitchell came out here only a moment ago. Yes, there she is now.
(*The* DOORMAN *and a* SAILOR *come out of the gate.*)

SAILOR. Miss Mitchell?

KAY. Yes?

SAILOR. Mr. Hilton says we're ready to cast off. We're waiting for you, ma'am.

KAY. Tell him I'll be there in a minute.

SAILOR. Yes'm.
(*Exit* SAILOR.)

DOORMAN (*turns to* ANGEL, *who is still hovering over the fire*). Why don't you kids beat it?

ANGEL. Aw-w!

DOORMAN. All right! I'll fix you! (*He strides off up the street.*)

GIMPTY (*desperately*). Kay, there's still time. You don't have to go.

KAY (*finality in her quiet voice*). I'm afraid I do.

GIMPTY. Listen . . . I knew wher Martin was. And I told the police.

KAY. You? How did you recogniz him?

GIMPTY. I used to know him when was a kid.

KAY. Oh!

GIMPTY. I know it was a stinkin thing to do.

KAY. No. It had to be done.

GIMPTY. There was a reward.

KAY. Yes, I know. I read about it That's a break for you, Pete. You ca help your mother now. And you ca live decently.

GIMPTY. How about you?

KAY. This isn't the miracle we wer looking for.

GIMPTY (*after a long pause*). No. guess you're right.

KAY. How long would it last us? Per haps a year, then what? I've bee through all that. I couldn't g through it again.

GIMPTY. I guess it's asking too much

KAY (*softly, trying to make him se the picture realistically, reasonably*) It's not all selfishness, Pete. I'n thinking of you too. I could do this I could go and live with you and b happy— (*And she means it*) —an then when poverty comes . . . and w begin to torture each other, wha would happen? I'd leave you and g back to Jack. He needs me too, yo see. I'm pretty certain of him. Bu what would become of you then? That sounds pretty bitchy, I suppose.

GIMPTY. No . . . no, it's quite right. I didn't see things as clearly as you did. It's just that I've been . . . such a dope.

KAY. No! It's just that we can't have everything . . . ever. (*She rises.*)

GIMPTY. Of course.

KAY. Good-bye, darling.

GIMPTY (*rises*). Good-bye, Kay. Have a pleasant trip.

KAY (*one sob escaping her*). Oh, Pete, forgive me if I've hurt you. Please forgive me!

GIMPTY. Don't be foolish. You haven't hurt me. It's funny, but you know, I never honestly expected anything. I didn't. It was really just a . . . whimsy I played on myself.

KAY. Pete.

GIMPTY. Yes?

KAY. Will you stay here and wave good-bye to me when the boat goes?

GIMPTY. Naturally. I expected to.

KAY. Thanks. (*She kisses him*) Take care of yourself! (*She goes quickly.* GIMPTY *follows her to the gate, standing there, peering through the bars, catching a last glimpse of her.* SPIT *trots down the street.*)

SPIT. He wuzn't deah.

ANGEL. No?

SPIT. Nah. Milty's a lot of bushwah. I tole yuh. (*He looks at the fire. Spits into it.* ANGEL *glances backward at the shadows under the hopper.*)

ANGEL. Hey, Spit!

SPIT. What?

ANGEL. Dey wuz a guy heah . . . (T.B. *appears, dragging an egg crate.*)

T.B. Look what I got! Whew! Boy, dat'll go up like wildfire!

SPIT. Babee! Dat's good!

ANGEL. Yeah! Dat's swell!
(*They smash up the crate by jumping on it. Then they tear off the slats and break them across the curb. The noise of the crashing and splintering exhilarates them. They laugh and chatter.* DIPPY *enters, puffing and grunting, dragging an old discarded automobile seat by a rope.*)

DIPPY (*proud of his contribution*). Hey, yuh t'ink dis'll boin? I t'ink it'll boin, don' chew? Boy, like a house afire I bet.

ANGEL. Nah, dat'll stink up da place.

DIPPY (*disappointed*). Aw, Gese, I dragged it a mile. I dragged it fuh five blocks. It wuz way ovuh by Toid Avenoo.
(*The* BOYS *throw some of the wood into the fire. It flares up with a great crackling. Tongues of flame shoot up out of the can. The band on the boat plays, "Anchors Aweigh!" There is much laughter and shouting of "Bon Voyage!" "Have a pleasant trip," etc. from the party who have disembarked. The bells and the whistles of the boat blow, the engines throb, and the propellers churn the water.*

GIMPTY *stands strained and tense, looking off, through the gate.)*

T.B. Hey, look! Look! Duh boat! She's goin' like sixty. Babee! *(They rush over to the gate.)*

ANGEL. Boy, dat's some boat! Dat's a crackerjack.

DIPPY. Yeah. *(He imitates the sound of the bells, the foghorn, the engine)* Clang, clang! Oooh! Ch, ch, ch! Poo! Poo! I'm a boat! Look, felluhs, I'm a boat. Ch! Ch! Ch! *(He shuffles around, hands fore and aft.)*

ANGEL *(points at the departing boat)*. Lookit duh dame wavin' at us.

DIPPY *(waves vigorously)*. Yoo, hoo! Yoo hoo!

T.B. She ain't wavin' at us, yuh dope.

SPIT. At Gimpty.

T.B. How'd you like tuh be on 'at boat?

DIPPY. Boy! I bet yew cud cross 'ee ocean in 'at boat. Yuh cud cross 'ee ocean in 'at boat, couldn't yuh, Gimpty?

GIMPTY. What?

DIPPY. Yuh cud cross 'ee ocean in 'at boat, couldn't yuh?
(ANGEL returns to the fire and pokes around in it.)

GIMPTY. Oh, yeah, I guess you could.

T.B. A cawse yuh could, yuh dope, anybody knows 'at.

SPIT *(sees ANGEL fishing out a mickey)*. Hey, watcha doin'?

ANGEL *(testing his mickey)*. My mickey's done. Dey're done now, felluhs!
(The sounds of the yacht die off in the distance.)

SPIT. Look out! Look out! Wait a minute!
(They all rush to haul out their mickeys. SPIT pushes them aside, and spears the biggest potato with a stick.)

DIPPY. Hey, Spit, dat big one's mine. Remembuh . . . I swiped it!

SPIT. Shat ap, yuh dope! *(He punches DIPPY, who begins to snivel.)*

DIPPY. If Tommy wuz heah, yuh wouldn't do dat.

SPIT. Nuts tuh yew! Who's got da salt?

ANGEL *(takes a small packet of newspaper from his shoe-shine box)*. Heah, I got it! *(The salt is passed around. They eat their mickeys with much smacking of lips.)*

DIPPY *(who has gotten the smallest mickey)*. Ahl git even witcha!

SPIT. Nuts!

DIPPY. Yew wait till yuh ast me tuh do sumpm fuh yew some day. Jus' wait. See watcha git!

SPIT *(spits at DIPPY)*. Right inne eye!

DIPPY *(wiping his eye)*. Ah, yuh louse!

ANGEL *(remembering the conspiracy. Slowly and deliberately, between munches)*. Hey, Spit.

SPIT. What?

ANGEL. Dey wuz a guy heah . . . yuh know da guy what Tommy stabbed? . . . Well, he wuz heah.

SPIT. What fuh?

ANGEL. He wuz lookin' fuh yew.

SPIT. Fuh me?

ANGEL. Yeah.

SPIT. What faw?

ANGEL. He said he wuz gonna give yuh five bucks fuh snitchin' on who done it.

SPIT. Wheah izee? Wheah'd ee go?

DIPPY. Did yew snitch on Tommy?

SPIT. Sure. Sure I did. (*A chorus of disapproval follows this confession.* SPIT *rises and doubles up his fists. To* DIPPY) What's it to yuh?

DIPPY. Nuttin'! (SPIT *looks at* ANGEL.)

ANGEL. Nuttin'!

T.B. Yew snitched on Tommy! Gese!

SPIT. Aw, shat ap, 'r I'll give yuh yuhr lumps! (*He turns, looking for the benefactor*) Wheah'd he go? Which way? I want dat five bucks. (TOMMY *runs from behind the hopper, leaps onto* SPIT's *back, bearing him to the ground.*)

TOMMY (*sits astride* SPIT, *his knees pinning* SPIT's *arms down*). Yuh'll git it, yuh stool pigeon! In a pig's kapooch yuh will!

DIPPY. Tommy!
ANGEL. Gese!
T.B. Wow! } (*Simultaneously.*)

TOMMY. Ahl give yuh sumpm yuh won' fuhgit so easy. Say yuh prayuhs, yuh louse!

SPIT. Lemme go! Lemme go!

TOMMY. Oh, no, yuh don't!

SPIT. Aw, Tommy, I didn't mean tuh. Dey had me! De cops had me! What could I do?

TOMMY. Yuh know watcha gonna git fuh it? (*He takes out his knife.* SPIT *squeals with terror.* TOMMY *jams his hand over* SPIT's *mouth*) Shat ap!

DIPPY. What's ee gonna do?

ANGEL. Gash his cheek fum heah tuh heah!

T.B. No kid!

ANGEL. Yeah.

DIPPY. Gee whiz! Wow!

SPIT (*crying and pleading*). Tommy, don't, will yuh? I'll give yuh dose bike wheels I swiped. I'll give yuh me stamps. I'll give yuh me immies. I'll give yuh dat five bucks. Ony lemme go, will yuh?

TOMMY. Dis time yuh don' git away wid it so easy, see?

SPIT. Hey, felluhs! Hey, Gimpty! He's got a knife!

GIMPTY (*notices for the first time what's happening*). Stop that, you crazy kid!

TOMMY. No!

GIMPTY (*starts toward* TOMMY). Let him go, Tommy!

TOMMY. Come near me, Gimpty, an' I'll give it tuh yew. Stay back, or I'll give it tuh 'im right now! (*He places the knife point at* SPIT'S *throat.* GIMPTY *stops short.*)

GIMPTY. Getting easy, isn't it?

TOMMY. Yeah, it's a cinch.

GIMPTY. Let him up, Tommy!

TOMMY. No!

GIMPTY. Tommy, give me that knife.

TOMMY. No!

GIMPTY. Sell it to me! I'll buy it from you!

TOMMY. No!

GIMPTY. What's a matter? You a yellow-belly, Tommy?

TOMMY. Who's a yeller-belly?

GIMPTY. Only a yellow-belly uses a knife, Tommy. You'll be sorry for this!

TOMMY. Well, he squealed on me! (MILTY *and* DRINA *come down the street.*)

MILTY. I dunno. He wuz heah be-faw . . . honest! (*Seeing the fight, he rushes to* TOMMY *and* SPIT) Wassa-mattuh, Tommy?

DRINA (*rushing to* TOMMY *and* SPIT). Tommy! Tommy! Where've you been?

SPIT. Drina! Drina, he's godda knife! He wants a stab me!

TOMMY (*slaps* SPIT). Shat ap!

DRINA. Tommy! . . . Give me that knife! . . . What's the matter with you? Aren't you in enough hot water now? Don't you understand what you're doing? (*Screams*) Give me that knife!

GIMPTY. Go on, Tommy! (*Pause.*)

TOMMY (*reluctantly hands the knife to* DRINA). Heah! (*He rises, releasing* SPIT. *As* SPIT *scrambles to his feet,* TOMMY *kicks him in the rump, yelling*). Beat it, yuh son uv a . . . (SPIT *runs up the sidewalk.*)

DRINA (*sharply*). Sh, Tommy!

SPIT (*from a safe distance, turns*). Tuh hell witcha, yuh bastid! (*Then he redoubles his speed, disappearing around the corner.*)

TOMMY. I'll kill yuh! (*He starts after* SPIT, *but* DRINA *grabs his arm, and pulls him back.*)

DRINA. Tommy, behave yourself!

TOMMY. But 'ee squealed on me, Drina!

DRINA. That's no excuse for this. Now it's knives! (*She snaps the blade shut*) What'll it be next? What's happening to you, Tommy?

TOMMY. I wuz ony gonna scare 'im.

DRINA (*grasps him by the shoulders and shakes him to emphasize what she's saying*). Listen to me! The cops came up to the house ten minutes ago. They were lookin' for you. You stabbed some man! Why! *Why!* (TOMMY *turns away*) Don't you see what you're doing? They'll send you to jail, Tommy!

TOMMY (*all the fight gone*). No, dey won't. Dey gotta ketch me foist.

DRINA. What do you mean?

TOMMY. I'm gonna run away.

DRINA. Run away? Where to?

TOMMY. I dunno.

DRINA. Where?

TOMMY. Dere a plenty a places I kin hitch tuh. Lots a guys do.

DRINA. And what are you gonna eat? Where you gonna sleep?

TOMMY. I'll git along.

DRINA. How?

TOMMY. I dunno. Some way. I'll hitch stuff. I dunno. (*Belabored and uncertain*) Aw, lemme alone!

DRINA. I can see what's gonna happen to you. (*Fiercely*) You'll become a bum!

TOMMY. Aw right! I'll become a bum, den!

DRINA (*hurls the knife onto the sidewalk, and screams*). That's fine! That's what Mamma worked her life away for! That's what I've worked since I was a kid for! So you could become a bum. That's great.

TOMMY (*shouting back*). Aw right! It's great. Well, Gese, whadda yuh want me tuh do? Let da cops git me an' sen' me up the rivuh, Drina? I don' wanna be locked up till I'm twenty-one. Izzat what yuh want me tuh do?

DRINA (*suddenly very soft and tender, maternally*). No, darling, no. I won't let that happen. I won't let them touch you, Tommy. Don't worry.

TOMMY. Well, what else kin we do?

DRINA. I'll run away with you, Tommy. We'll go away, together, some place.

TOMMY. No, Drina, yuh couldn't do dat. Yer a goil. (*Pause*) Yuh know what? Maybe, if I give myself up, an' tell em I didn' mean tuh do it, an if I swear on a Bible I'll nevuh do it again, maybe dey'll let me go.

DRINA. No, Tommy, I'm not gonna let you give yourself up. No!

TOMMY. Yeah, Drina.
(*Enter* DOORMAN *with a* POLICEMAN.)

DOORMAN (*pointing to the boys*). There!

POLICEMAN (*roars*). Get ta hell out a here! Go wan home!

T.B. Chickee da cop! (*The* BOYS *scatter.* DIPPY *and* T.B. *duck into the tenement doorway.* ANGEL *and* MILTY *scramble under the hopper.*)

POLICEMAN (*to the* DOORMAN). Get some water! Put this out. (MULLIGAN, *the policeman, turns to the cringing figures under the hopper*) Yuh wanna set fire to these houses? Lemme ketch you doin' this again and I'll beat the b'jesus out a you! (*He slaps the blazing can with his night stick to punctuate the warning. Sparks fly up.*)

TOMMY (*slowly*). Yuh know, Drina, I tink 'at's what I ought tuh do.

DRINA (*holding him tight, terrified. In a hoarse whisper*). No. I won't let you do that.

TOMMY. Yeah. (*He detaches her arm, and goes to* MULLIGAN) Hey, mister!

MULLIGAN. What do you want? Come on, beat it!

TOMMY. Wait a minute! I'm Tommy McGrath.

MULLIGAN. What of it? (*The other* BOYS *creep back.*)

TOMMY. I'm da kid dat stabbed dat man today.

MULLIGAN. What!!! (*He grabs* TOMMY'S *arm. The* DOORMAN *comes running over to verify this.*)

TOMMY (*his voice shrill and trembly*). Yeah. He wuz chokin' me an breakin' my ahm . . . so I did it.

MULLIGAN. So, you're the kid. I bin lookin' fuh you.

DOORMAN (*who has been staring at* TOMMY, *suddenly elated*). That's him all right. That's him! Wait, I'll call Mr. Griswald. He'll tell you! (*He rushes off through the gateway.*)

MULLIGAN. All right. I'll keep him here. Don't you worry.

DRINA (*goes to* MULLIGAN, *pleading*). Tommy! No, no, they can't take him. Let him go, officer! Please!

MULLIGAN. I can't do that, miss.

DRINA. He didn't know what he wa[s] doing. He's only a baby.

MULLIGAN. You tell it to the judge[.] Tell it to the judge.

DRINA (*trying to wrench* TOMMY *free*). No! Let him go! Let him go[!]

MULLIGAN (*pushes her away roughly*). Get away. Don't try that[.] (*To* GIMPTY. You better take he[r] away or she'll get hurt.

GIMPTY. Drina, come here.

DRINA. No.

MULLIGAN. In a minute I'll take he[r] to the station-house, too.

TOMMY. Aw, Drina, cut it out, wil[l] yuh? Dat ain' gonna help.

GIMPTY. He's right, you know.

T.B. (*sidles over to* TOMMY, *whispering*). Hey, Tommy, if yuh go tu[h] rifawmatory, look up a guy named . .[.]

MULLIGAN (*shoving* T.B. *away*). Gi[t] outta here! (T.B. *flies across th[e] street.*)

DRINA. Yes, of course he's right. I'[m] so . . . I just don't know what I'm . .[.]

DOORMAN (*enters with* MR. GRISWALD). Yes, Mr. Griswald, I'm sur[e] it's the boy. (GRISWALD *pushes him aside, and walks briskly to* MULLIGAN.)

GRISWALD. So you've caught him.

MULLIGAN. Yes, sir.

DRINA. He gave himself up!

GRISWALD. Let me look at him. (*He looks searchingly at* TOMMY'S *face and nods*) Yes, this is the boy, all right.

MULLIGAN. Good.

DRINA. He gave himself up.

GRISWALD (*turns to her*). What's that?

DRINA (*trying desperately to be calm*). I'm his sister!

GRISWALD. Oh. Well . . . a fine brother you've got.

MULLIGAN (*to* ANGEL *and* MILTY, *who have crept to the foreground*). Come on, get out a here! Beat it! (*They scramble back again under the hopper.*)

DRINA. Listen, mister! Give him another chance. . . . (*She clutches his arm. He winces and draws his breath in pain*) Please, will you?

GRISWALD. Careful of that arm!

DRINA. Oh! I'm sorry. . . . Give him another chance! Let him go!

GRISWALD. Another chance to what? To kill somebody?

TOMMY. I won' evuh do it again. Yew wuz chokin' me an' I wuz seein' black already, an' I . . .

DRINA. Have a heart, mister! He's only a kid. He didn't know what he was doing.

GRISWALD. No?

DRINA. No.

GRISWALD. Then you should have taught him better.

DRINA (*her impulse is to fight back, but she restrains herself*). Listen! He's a good boy. And he's got brains. Ask his teacher . . . Miss Judell, P.S. 59. He used to get A,A,A . . . all the time. He's smart.

GRISWALD. Then I can't see any excuse at all for him.

DRINA (*flaring*). All right! He made a mistake! He's sorry! What's so terrible about that?

GIMPTY. Sh! Drina!

GRISWALD. I have a gash half an inch deep in my wrist. The doctor is afraid of infection. What do you say to that?

DRINA (*with such an effort at self-control that she trembles*). I'm sorry! I'm awfully sorry!

GRISWALD. Sorry! That won't help, will it?

DRINA. Will it help to send him to reform school?

GRISWALD. I don't know. It'll at least keep him from doing it to someone else.

DRINA. But you heard him. He swore he wouldn't ever do it again.

GRISWALD. I'm afraid I can't believe that. He'll be better off where they'll send him. They'll take him out of the gutters and teach him a trade.

DRINA (*explodes again*). What do you know about it?

GRISWALD. I'm sorry. I've no more time. I can't stand here arguing with you. (*To* MULLIGAN). All right, officer! I'll be down to make the complaint. (*Starts to exit.*)

GIMPTY (*stepping in front of* GRISWALD *and blocking his path*). Wait a minute, mister!

GRISWALD. Yes?

GIMPTY. May I talk to you a moment?

GRISWALD. There's no use, really.

GIMPTY. Just a moment, please?

GRISWALD. Well, what is it?

GIMPTY. You know what happened here today? A man was shot . . . killed.

GRISWALD. You mean that gangster?

GIMPTY. Yes.

GRISWALD. What about it?

GIMPTY. I killed him.

GRISWALD. You what?

MULLIGAN. He's crazy. (*To* GIMPTY) What are you trying to do?

GIMPTY. It was I who told them where to find him.

GRISWALD. Well, that may be so. Then you were doing your duty. It's simple enough. And I'm doing mine.

DRINA (*hysterically*). No! It ain't the same! Martin was a butcher, he was like a mad dog. He deserved to die. But Tommy's a baby . . .

GIMPTY. Please! That's not the point

DRINA. It is!

MULLIGAN (*to* ANGEL *and* MILTY *who are back again*). How many times have I gotta tell you! . . . (*They retreat.*)

GIMPTY. Yes, maybe it is. Anyway I turned him over for my own selfish reasons. And yet the thing I did, Griswald, was nothing compared to what you're doing. . . . Yeah . . . Martin was a killer, he was bad, he deserved to die, true! But I knew him when we were kids. He had a lot of fine stuff. He was strong. He had courage. He was a born leader. He even had a sense of fair play. But living in the streets kept making him bad. . . Then he was sent to reform school. Well, they reformed him all right. They taught him the ropes. He came out tough and hard and mean, with all the tricks of the trade.

GRISWALD. But I don't see what you're driving at.

GIMPTY. I'm telling you! That's what you're sending this kid to.

GRISWALD. I'm afraid there's no alternative.

DRINA. Are you so perfect? Didn't you ever do anything you were sorry for later? (*Screams*). God! Didn't anybody ever forgive you for anything?

GRISWALD (*looks at her in silence for a moment. Then gently, and sympathetically*). Of course. I'm sorry. I'm very sorry. Believe me, I'm not being vindictive. I'm not punishing him for hurting me. As far as this goes— (*Touches his bandaged wrist*.)

—I would forgive him gladly. But you must remember that I'm a father . . . that today he, unprovoked, beat my boy with a stick and stole his watch. There are other boys like mine. They've got to be protected, too. I feel awfully sorry for you, but your brother belongs in a reformatory. (*To* MULLIGAN) All right, officer! (*He shakes his head and disappears in the gateway.*)

DRINA (*with a cry of despair*). What?

MULLIGAN. All right! Let's go! (*To* TOMMY) Come along.

T.B. (*edges over to* TOMMY). Hey, Tommy, wait! Look up a guy named Smokey! . . .

MULLIGAN. Get away from here. I'll bounce one off your head!

TOMMY (*looking back to* DRINA). Don' worry, Drina. I ain' scared.

DRINA (*trying to smile for* TOMMY). Of course not, darling. I'm coming with you. (*Starts up.*)

MULLIGAN. Yeah, I think you better. Come on! (*He calls over his shoulder to the* DOORMAN) Put out that fire!

DOORMAN. Oh, yes . . . yes, officer! (*Hurries off, through the gate.* MULLIGAN *and* TOMMY *go up the street.* DRINA *starts to follow.* T.B. *catches her arm.*)

T.B. Drina! Drina! Wait!

DRINA. No, I can't, I gotta . . .

T.B. It's important. It's about Tommy!

DRINA (*turns*). What?

T.B. (*very knowing and very helpful. He's been through this before*). Look, Drina, dere's a guy at rifawm school named Smokey . . . like dat, Smokey, dey call him Smokey. Yew tell Tommy tuh be nice tuh him and give im t'ings like cigarettes an dat. Cause dis guy Smokey, he knows a lot of swell rackets fuh Tommy when ee gits out . . . cause Tommy's a wise kid an . . .

DRINA (*scared, helpless, begins to sob*). Oh, Mom, why did you leave us? I don't know what to do, Mom. I don't know where to turn. I wish I was dead and buried with you.

T.B. (*puzzled by this unexpected reaction to his good advice*). What's a mattuh? What'd I say? I didn' say nuttin'. What'd I say?

GIMPTY. Sh. Shut up! (*He goes to* DRINA, *who is sobbing her heart out, and puts a protective arm around her*). You poor kid! You poor kid. Stop crying. Stop crying now.

DRINA. I'm all right. I'll be all right in a minute.

GIMPTY. Now you stop crying and listen to me. Tomorrow morning you meet me right here at half past nine. We're going downtown. We're going to get the best lawyer in this city, and we'll get Tommy free.

DRINA. But that'll cost so much!

GIMPTY. Don't worry about that. We'll get him out.

DRINA. Do you really think so?

GIMPTY. I know so.

DRINA. Oh, God bless you . . . you're so . . . (*She breaks into sobs again.*)

GIMPTY. Now, now. You go along now and stick by Tommy.

DRINA (*controlling herself*). You've been so awfully good to us, I . . . I hate to ask for anything else, but . . .

GIMPTY. Sure, what is it?

DRINA. I wish you'd come along with us now. I know if you're there . . . they wouldn't dare touch . . . (*Her voice catches*) Tommy!

GIMPTY. Me? I'm nobody. I can't . . .

DRINA. I wish you would. Please?

GIMPTY (*softly*). All right. (*They go up the street, his arm still around her, his cane clicking on the sidewalk even after they've disappeared from sight. Awed by the scene, the kids gather about the fire again.*)

ANGEL. Gese, wadda yuh tink'll happen tuh Tommy?

MILTY. Dey'll git 'im off. Dey'll git 'im off. Yuh'll see.

T.B. Even if dey don't, yuh loin a barrel of good tings at rifawm school. Smokey once loined me how tuh open a lock wid a hair pin. Boy! It's easy! It's a cinch! I loined one-two-three, but now I fuhgit . . .
(*The* DOORMAN *appears uncoiling a garden hose. He pushes* ANGEL *aside, points the nozzle into the can, and releases the stream. The fire hisses, spits, and dies. A thick pillar of smoke ascends skyward out of the can.*)

ANGEL (*looks upward, entranced*). Holy smokes!

DIPPY. Whee!

ANGEL. Look a dat!

T.B. Boy! Right up tuh duh sky!

ANGEL. Right up tuh duh stahs!

DIPPY. How high ah dey? How high ah duh stahs?

DOORMAN (*turning back at the gate*). And you rats better not start any more trouble, if you know what's good for you! (*He goes in. The boys wait till he is out of ear-shot, then they hurl a chorus of abuse.*)

MILTY. Gay cock of'm yam!
ANGEL. Fongoola!
DIPPY. Nuts ta yew!
T.B. In yuhr hat!
(*Simultaneously*)

ANGEL (*plays a mocking tune on his kazoo.* T.B. *sings the lyrics*). Te da da da da bushwah. Te da da bushwah.

ANGEL. Ahl goul him!

DIPPY (*laughs*). Yeah.
(*After this outburst, there is a long pause. They watch the smoke coiling upward.*)

MILTY (*softly*). Gee! Looka dat smoke!

T.B. Dat reminds me—all a time at rifawm school Smokey usta sing a song about Angel—"If I had de wings of a Angel."
(*They laugh.*)

MILTY. Angel ain't got no wings.

DIPPY. Real ones got wings. I saw it in a pitcha once.

(ANGEL *starts playing "If I had the wings of an angel" on his kazoo.*)

T.B. Dat's right. Dat's it! (*In a quavery voice he accompanies* ANGEL) If I had de wings of a angel. Ovuh dese prison walls I wud fly . . . (*The others join in, swelling the song*). Straight tuh dee yahms a my muddah. Ta da da, da da . . . (*A passing tramp steamer hoots mournfully. The smoke continues to roll out of the can, as their cacophony draws out to a funereal end*) Da . . . Da . . . da . . . dum.

CURTAIN

Boy Meets Girl

BY BELLA AND SAMUEL SPEWACK

TO

JO DAVIDSON

WHOSE HOSPITALITY AND

ENCOURAGEMENT DELAYED THE COMPLETION OF

THIS PLAY THREE MONTHS.

Boy Meets Girl was first produced at the Cort Theatre, New York City, by George Abbott, on November 27, 1935, and closed on June 19, 1937. Following is the original cast:

ROBERT LAW	Allyn Joslyn
LARRY TOMS	Charles McClelland
J. CARLYLE BENSON	Jerome Cowan
ROSETTI	Everett H. Sloane
MR. FRIDAY (C.F.)	Royal Beal
PEGGY	Peggy Hart
MISS CREWS	Lea Penman
RODNEY BEVAN	James MacColl
GREEN	Garson Kanin
SLADE	Maurice Sommers
SUSIE	Joyce Arling
A NURSE	Helen Gardner
DOCTOR	Perry Ivins
CHAUFFEUR	Edison Rice
YOUNG MAN	Philip Faversham
STUDIO OFFICER	George W. Smith
CUTTER	Robert Foulk
ANOTHER NURSE	Marjorie Lytell
MAJOR THOMPSON	John Clarke

Directed by George Abbott

Settings by Arne Lundborg

SCENES

ACT ONE

Mr. Friday's Office, the Royal Studios in Hollywood

ACT TWO

SCENE I

A Neighborhood Theatre. Seven months later

SCENE II

Mr. Friday's office

SCENE III

The same. Several hours later

ACT THREE

SCENE I

A hospital corridor. Three weeks later

SCENE II

In your home

SCENE III

Mr. Friday's office

BOY MEETS GIRL

ACT ONE

The room we see is one of a suite of three, comprising the sanctum of MR. C. ELLIOT FRIDAY, *a supervisor, sometimes called a producer, who is engaged in manufacturing motion pictures in Hollywood, California.*

In its present state the room is a happy combination of the Regency and Russell Wright periods—given over to pale green, mauve and canary yellow, with Rodier-cloth-covered easy chairs and couch. A magnificent, be-French-phoned desk is at one end of the room. On it rests the inter-office dictograph, over which in the course of the play we hear the voice of the great B.K., chief executive of the studio. Beside it, appropriately, stands an amiable photograph of Mrs. C. Elliot Friday, a cultured if fatuous lady; a copy of "Swann's Way" (leaves uncut), a bronze nude astride an ash tray, a bottle of Pyramidon and a copy of "Variety." In the trash basket is a copy of "Hollywood Reporter." (It was very unkind to MR. FRIDAY.) *On the wall back of the desk are bookshelves with pots of hanging ivy on the top shelf, the rest given over, curiously enough, to books—and occasional bric-a-brac. There are a few end tables with ash trays and boxes of cigarettes, for it is the unwritten law in Hollywood that supervisors must provide cigarettes for writers during conferences and other times of stress. The two windows, although of the old-fashioned, non-casement kind, are framed by tasteful, expensive drapes and are partially concealed by half-drawn Venetian blinds. (A supervisor would lose caste without Venetian blinds.) The door left leads to an anteroom where sits* MISS CREWS, *secretary to* MR. FRIDAY. *The door at right rear leads to a smaller office where* MR. FRIDAY *sometimes thinks in solitude. This room contains* MR. FRIDAY'S *Commencement Day photograph (Harvard '19), snapshots of B.K.'s wedding, at which* MR. FRIDAY *served as an usher, and a huge picture of Pola Negri inscribed "Sincerely yours." There are other photographs with more florid inscriptions upon faces once famous and since vanished in film dust. The room is also memorable for the fact that* MR. FRIDAY—*a bit of a diplomat in his way—sometimes keeps earnest writers here while he submits their scripts to other writers in his inner office. At times as many as fifteen bright minds are thus let loose upon a C. Elliot Friday production, with sometimes startling results.*

All this, however, is very much by the by. It is really more important to note that through those Venetian blinds you can feel the sweet sterility of the desert that is so essentially Southern California. The sun is bright of course, and it pours endlessly through the windows. The time is two o'clock, and the boys have been at it since noon.

One of the boys is BENSON—J. CARLYLE BENSON, *whom we discover prone on a couch. He is in his thirties and in his flannels. Years ago, as he will tell you, he worked as a scene painter and a property boy. He became a writer because he learned how bricks were made and laid. He knows every cliché, every formula, and in his heart of hearts he really believes the fairy tale is a credo of life. And he's a damned nice guy; handicapped somewhat by the fact that he married a beautiful but extravagant young woman who obviously doesn't love him. They live in a gorgeous home, have four dogs, two cars and, as* MR. FRIDAY *would put it, "a menage."*

The other member of the writing team is ROBERT LAW *whom you will find listed in O'Brien's "Best Short Stories" of five years ago. He came to Hollywood to make a little money and run right back to Vermont where he could really write. He is rather handsome, a little round-shouldered; smokes incessantly. He's a damned nice guy, too.*

There is a deep and abiding affection between the two men, even though LAW'S *nostalgia for realism and sincerity and substance finds no echoing response in* MR. BENSON. *They have one great thing in common—their mutual love of a great gag, a practical joke to enliven the monotony of the writing factory.*

For we are dealing here with a factory that manufactures entertainment in approved sizes; that puts the seven arts right on the belt. And it is this very quality that makes MR. FRIDAY'S *office as fascinating as a power house and a good deal more entertaining.*

The other inmates of the room are LARRY TOMS—*you know* LARRY TOMS—*a Western star, and one* ROSETTI, *an agent. It is* MR. ROSETTI'S *business to see to it that* MR. TOMS *is profitably employed, for* MR. ROSETTI *collects ten per cent of* MR. TOM'S *weekly salary which, despite the star's fading popularity, is still a respectable sum.* MR. TOMS *is handsome, of course. He is also parsimonious. He leads a completely righteous life, and if you don't like him it isn't our fault; in all respects he is an extremely admirable character.*

As the curtain goes up we see that LAW *is on his feet and obviously he has been telling a story to* MR. TOMS—*a story that* MR. TOMS *is expected to re-enact before the camera.*

LAW. And this bozo comes up to you and you look him straight in the eye and you say, "Why, damn your soul, I loved her before you ever married her." And then in walks the bitch, and she cries, "Larry, I heard everything you said." And you just look at her, and there's a long pause —a *long* pause. And then finally you say, "Did you?" That's all. Just a plain, quiet, simple "Did you?" Boy, what a moment! (*He lies down on the couch beside* BENSON.)

LARRY. But what's the story about?

BENSON (*rolling over*). Love!

LAW (*singing*). "Love is the sweetest thing—"

LARRY. Now, come on, boys—get off the couch. This ain't fair. I got a lot at stake in this picture. It's the last one in my contract. If I get a poor story I'm out in the cold.

LAW. Shivering with a million dollar annuity.

ROSETTI. Now, gentlemen, don't let's get personal.

LARRY (*rises and crosses to couch*). When they told me I was getting the star team of writers on the lot, I was all for it. But you've done nothing but clown around, and the shooting date's only two weeks off. I've got to play this picture.

LAW. Why?

LARRY (*swallowing*). Tell me your story in a few simple words.

LAW. Mr. Benson, what's our story?

BENSON. How the hell do I know?

LAW (*sits up*). Didn't you listen?

BENSON. No. We ought to have a stenographer.

LAW. But they won't wear tights. And I can't dictate to a stenographer who won't wear tights.

LARRY. Now listen, boys—

LAW. Don't speak to me. You don't like our story.

LARRY. I didn't say I didn't like it. I couldn't follow it. (*He slumps in disgust.*)

BENSON (*indignantly*). You couldn't follow it? Listen, I've been writing stories for eleven years. Boy meets girl. Boy loses girl. Boy gets girl.

LAW. Or—girl meets boy. Girl loses boy. Girl gets boy. Love will find a way. Love never loses. Put your money on love. You can't lose. (*Rises and saunters to window*) I'm getting hungry.

BENSON. It's a sorry state of affairs when an actor insists on following a story. Do you think this is a golf tournament?

ROSETTI (*earnestly*). If I may make a point, I don't think you're showing the proper respect to one of the biggest stars in this studio. A man who's not only captivated millions of people but is going to captivate millions more—

BENSON (*wearily*). With his little lasso—

LARRY. Just because I don't get Gable's fan mail don't mean I ain't got his following. A lot of those that want to write me ain't never learned how.

LAW. Benson, injustice has been done. We've been lacking in respect for the idol of illiteracy.

BENSON. Do we apologize?

LAW. No!

ROSETTI. Well, let me tell you something. Before I became an agent I taught diction for years, and Larry Toms is potentially the greatest actor I've ever met. And I can prove it with X-rays. I was just taking them up to show B.K. He's got the Barrymore larynx. I'll put his larynx against John Barrymore's and I defy you to tell me which is which. (*Takes X-rays from brief case. Gives one to* BENSON, *one to* LAW.)

LARRY. I couldn't tell it myself and it's my own larynx.

BENSON (*drawling*). Say—are you sure this is his *larynx*?

ROSETTI (*the diplomat; retrieving X-rays*). Gentlemen, I wouldn't be surprised with the proper training if Larry couldn't sing. That opens up the whole field of musicals. (*Puts brief case on chair.*)

BENSON (*to* LAW). What are we waiting for?

LAW. Lunch.

LARRY (*angrily rising*). I'm getting fed up with this. I got writers who are just plain crazy—a producer who can't concentrate—and ain't even here—and— (*Throws hat on floor and starts for* BENSON *and* LAW. LAW *moves to back of couch and* BENSON *goes up to door.*)

ROSETTI (*crossing down on* LARRY'S *left*). Now . . . now . . . Larry . . . don't lose your temper.

LARRY (*righteously*). The idea of writers getting fifteen hundred a week for acting like hoodlums.

LAW. I agree with you.

LARRY. Huh?

LAW. We're not writers. We're hacks. If we weren't, would I be sitting here listening to your inarticulate grunts?

LARRY. Huh?

LAW. That's exactly what I mean. For two cents, Benson, I'd take the next train back to Vermont.

LARRY. That's all right with me.

BENSON. Will you forget Vermont?

LAW. At least I wouldn't have to sit around with *that* in Vermont. I'd write—really write. My God, I wrote once. I wrote a book. A darn good book. I was a promising young novelist. O'Brien reprinted three of my stories. 1928-1929-1930. And in 1935 I'm writing dialogue for a horse!

LARRY (*enraged*). Now, listen—

ROSETTI (*pleading*). Larry—Larry, take a deep breath. The boys mean no harm. . . . Exhale!

LAW (*sniffing*). I smell carbon monoxide.

LARRY. One more crack, that's all—just one more crack! (*Phone rings.*)

ROSETTI (*at phone*). Hello . . . oh, yes . . . just a minute. For you, Benson.

BENSON (*taking up phone*). Yes, speaking. Who? Of course, Mrs. Benson's check is good. How much is it for? Thirty-five hundred? Oh! I hope it was real ermine. . . . Certainly it's all right. You put the check through tomorrow. (*Hangs up; dials phone.*)

ROSETTI (*with a feline purr*). Ermine is a nice fur.
(MISS CREWS *enters regally; puts letters on desk.*)

LARRY (*grumbling*). Miss Crews, what's keeping C.F.?

MISS CREWS. He's still up with B.K. (*She exits regally.*)

BENSON (*into phone*). Jim? Benson. Listen, sell three of my Municipal Fives this afternoon, will you? And put it in my joint account in the Security. I've got a check to meet. Never mind about that. I'll talk to her. Right. (*Hangs up.*)

LAW. Pearl is certainly spreading prosperity.

BENSON. What the hell? She's only a kid. She's having a good time. What's money for? (C.F. *enters.* C.F. *is, of course,* C. ELLIOTT FRIDAY.)

C.F. (*briskly*). Good morning.

ROSETTI (*rises*). Good morning, C.F.

LARRY (*rises and sits*). Hello, C.F. (BENSON *lies on sofa.* LAW *rises and salaams Hindu fashion, as popularized by Mr. De Mille.*)

C.F. Boys, no antics, please. We've got a heavy day ahead of us. (*Sits at desk; picks up phone. Into phone*) I don't want to be disturbed by anybody—understand? And order some lunch. A plate of raw carrots, and a bottle of certified raw milk. See that it's *raw*. Bring enough for everybody. (*About to hang up.*)

LAW (*rises*). Just a moment. (*Takes phone*) Mr. Benson and Mr. Law want two cups of chicken broth—some ham hocks—cabbage—lemon meringue pie—and some bicarbonate of soda. (*Hangs up; returns to couch.*)

C.F. You're slaughtering yourselves, boys. You won't be able to think with that poison in your stomachs, and we've got to think. I've just seen the front office. Boys, we're facing a crisis.

ROSETTI (*eagerly*). Any truth in the report, C.F., that Gaumont British wants to buy the studio?

C.F. You know as much about it as I do, Rosetti.

LAW. Why sell? I thought we were sitting pretty. We're in receivership.

ROSETTI. Well, I'm going up to see B.K. I hope you boys get a good story foı Larry.

C.F. (*ignoring him;* C.F. *can ignore beautifully*). As a matter of fact, you may as well know it. There may be a reorganization.

BENSON. Again?

C.F. And you know my position. I'm the only college-bred man in the studio. They resent me.

LAW. The big snobs.

C.F. Just because I've always tried to do something fine, something dignified, something worth while, I'm being hammered on all sides. Boys, if my next picture fails, I'm out. And you're out, Larry. And it won't do you boys any good either. Of course you can always write plays.

LAW. I don't see why not. We never wrote any.

C.F. I have an idea for a play I want to discuss with you sometime. You'll be wild about it. Just one set, too—simple to produce, and practically anybody can play it. Katharine Cornell would be marvelous for the girl. She dies in the first act.

LARRY. Listen here, C.F., I ain't in the theatre. What about my picture?

C.F. Boys, we need a big picture. Not just a good story. I want to do something fine—with sweep, with scope—stark, honest, gripping, adult, but with plenty of laughs and a little hokum.

LARRY (*bitterly*). And no "Did you?" scenes.

C.F. Something we'll be proud of. Not just another picture, but the picture of the year. A sort of Bengal Lancer, but as Kipling would have done it. Maybe we could wire Kipling and get him to write a few scenes. It would be darned good publicity. (PEGGY *enters;* PEGGY *is the manicurist on the lot*) Oh, come in . . . come in, Peggy. (PEGGY *puts tray of manicurist's paraphernalia on desk; moves small chair at* C.E.'s *side; takes bowl and exits for water.*)

BENSON (*in astonishment*). He doesn't think we're as good as Kipling.

C.F. (*quickly*). Mind you, not that I think Kipling is a great writer. A storyteller, yes. But greatness? Give me Proust anytime. Now, boys, how about a story?

LAW. Nestling on your desk for two weeks there's a script we wrote for Larry Toms.

BENSON. A beautiful script. That one with my fingerprints on the cover.

C.F. (*picking up script, holding it in his hands as if weighing it*). This? This won't do.

LAW. That's where you're wrong. I had it weighed at the A. & P. and the manager went wild over it. (C.F. *puts script on top of dictograph.* MISS CREWS *enters.*)

MISS CREWS. Excuse me, Mr. Friday, but Casting wants to know how many midgets you'll need.

C.F. (*irritably*). Midgets? I don't need any midgets.

MISS CREWS. Casting says you ordered midgets and they've got them.

C.F. They're crazy. I'm not doing a horror story. (*Phone rings; at phone*) Hello. . . . It's for you, Benson.

BENSON. For me?

C.F. I think it's Mrs. Benson. Listen, Miss Crews, we're in conference. Please don't disturb us again.

MISS CREWS. Yes, Mr. Friday. (*She exits.*)

BENSON (*into telephone*). Oh, hello, darling. . . . Yes, I know you've been shopping. . . . Why don't you try Woolworth's? . . . No, I'm not mad. . . . Oh, you're taking the dogs for a walk? That's good. . . . Oh, no, I can't take you to lunch. I'm in a story conference. . . . But look, darling, I'm in a story conference. . . . Hello . . . (*He mops his brow and tries to shake off his gloom.*)

C.F. How is Mrs. Benson?

BENSON. Swell.

C.F. I must get Mrs. Friday to invite her over to her French class. All the wives are taking it up very seriously. Gives them something to do, and as I said to Mrs. Friday: I'm a linguist—why shouldn't you be? That's the great thing in marriage—mutual interests. (BENSON *crosses to couch*) Of course, Mrs. Benson isn't the studious type, is she? Beautiful girl, though. . . . Where were we? What was I saying?

BENSON (*crosses back to desk; sighs; indicates script*). You were saying that this is one of the greatest picture scripts ever written.

C.F. (*with a superior smile*). Now, just a minute—

LAW (*quickly*). And do you know why? Because it's the same story Larry Toms has been doing for years.

BENSON. We *know* it's good.

LAW. Griffith used it. Lubitsch used it. And Eisenstein's coming around to it.

BENSON. Boy meets girl. Boy loses girl. Boy gets girl.

LAW. The great American fairy tale. Sends the audience back to the relief rolls in a happy frame of mind.

BENSON. And why not?

LAW. The greatest escape formula ever worked out in the history of civilization . . .

C.F. Of course, if you put it that way . . . but, boys, it's hackneyed.

LAW. You mean classic.

C.F. (*triumphantly*). *Hamlet* is a classic—but it isn't hackneyed!

LAW. *Hamlet* isn't hackneyed? Why, I'd be ashamed to use that poison gag. He lifted that right out of the Italians. (PEGGY *enters and crosses to her chair and sits*) Ask Peggy. (PEGGY *puts the bowl now half filled with water down on the desk.*)

BENSON. Yes, let's ask Peggy . . . if she wants to see Larry Toms in a different story. She's your audience.

PEGGY. Don't ask me anything, Mr. Benson. I've got the damnedest toothache. (*She takes* C.F.'s *hand and looks up at him suddenly*) Relax! (*She begins filing.*)

BENSON (*wheedling*). But, Peggy. you go to pictures, don't you?

PEGGY. No.

BENSON. But you've seen Larry's pictures and enjoyed them?

PEGGY. No.

BENSON. . . . As millions of others have . . .

LAW. Why, one man sent him a rope all the way from Manila—with instructions.

C.F. Boys, this isn't getting us anywhere.

BENSON (*assuming the manner of a district attorney; barking at* PEGGY). Peggy, do you mean to sit there and tell me you haven't seen *one* Larry Toms picture?

PEGGY. I saw one.

BENSON. Ah!

PEGGY. *Night in Death Valley.*

BENSON. This isn't getting us anywhere, eh? How would you like to see *Night in Death Valley* again—with a new title?

PEGGY. I wouldn't.

BENSON. That's all. Step down. (*Crosses to couch; slaps* LAW *on shoulder*) May I point out to this court that the body was found only two feet away, in an open field, with every door and window shut? (*To* LAW) Your witness. (*He exits.*)

LAW (*rises*). I've got to see a man about a woman. (*He exits. Our writers have vanished. They love to vanish from story conferences.*)

C.F. (*rises*). Come back here! (*Picks up phone.*)

LARRY. That's what I mean—clowning.

C.F. (*at phone*). Miss Crews, leave word at the gate Benson and Law are not to be allowed off the lot. They're to come right back to my office. (*Hangs up.*)

LARRY. Why do you stand for it?

C.F. Larry, those boys are crazy, but they've got something.

LARRY. They've been fired off every other lot.

C.F. I'll fire them off this one, after they've produced a story. I've made up my mind to that. Meanwhile, patience.

LARRY. That's easy to say.

C.F. You can't quibble with the artistic temperament when it produces.

LARRY (*grumbling*). They've been producing nothing but trouble around here.
(YOUNG ACTOR *enters in the resplendent uniform of the Coldstream Guards. His name is* RODNEY. *Both uniform and actor explain themselves as the play proceeds.*)

MISS CREWS. Right in here.

RODNEY. How do you do?

C.F. What do *you* want?

RODNEY. Why, Wardrobe sent me. Do you approve the uniform?

C.F. Uniform for what?

RODNEY. *Young England.*

C.F. You see, Larry—three pictures in production—all going on at the same time—I'm standing on my head—and then they wonder what's wrong with the industry. (*Rises; barks at* RODNEY) Stand over there. (MISS CREWS *exits.* C.F. *surveys the actor judicially*) I can't say I like the hat. (*He is referring, of course, to the awe-inspiring busby.*)

RODNEY (*mildly*). The hat is authentic, sir.

C.F. I still don't like it. You can't photograph it. (*Phone rings*) Yes?—What midgets? I didn't send out any call for midgets. Get rid of them. (*Hangs up. He jiggles the phone*) Get me Wardrobe. (*Hubbub is heard outside window*) Who's making all that noise? (PEGGY *goes to the window*) This is C.F.—I don't like the hat.—I don't care if it's authentic or not— Who's making all that noise?

PEGGY (*at window*). Midgets.

C.F. (*into phone*). Change the hat. . . . You can't photograph it. . . . We want to see faces, not hats. (*Hangs up. Stone crashes through the window left*) Good God! Somebody's thrown a rock through my window. (*To* RODNEY) Here, you—pull down those blinds.

RODNEY (*always the little gentleman*). Yes, sir.

C.F. (*in phone*). Get me Casting. . . . This is C.F. . . . Somebody's thrown a rock through my window. One of the midgets. Of course they're indignant! Sour grapes! I'm telling you to get rid of them. (*Hangs up.*)

RODNEY. What shall I tell Wardrobe, sir?

C.F. Tell them I don't like the hat.

RODNEY (*smiles diffidently*). Well, it's very peculiar that you should take umbrage at the hat as it happens to be the only correct item in the entire outfit.

C.F. What's that?

RODNEY. This coat doesn't hang properly—these buttons are far too large. These shoulder straps are absurd, of course. And the boots . . . if I may say so . . . are too utterly fantastic. Any Guardsman would swoon away at the sight of them.

C.F. So!

RODNEY. The hat, however, *is* authentic.

C.F. It is, eh? What's your salary.

RODNEY. As I understand it, I'm to receive seven dollars a day Monday and Tuesday, when I speak no lines, and fifteen dollars a day Thursday, Friday and Saturday, when I propose a toast.

C.F. And you're telling a fifty-thousand-dollar-a-year man how to run his picture. Look here—I spent two weeks in London, my man, at the Savoy, and I watched them change the Guards, personally.

RODNEY. At the Savoy?

C.F. Young man, we have a technical adviser on this picture. And it doesn't happen to be you.

RODNEY. Quite. He's a splendid fellow, but he's a third-generation Canadian. He's never even been to London.

C.F. So you don't like the uniform and you don't like the technical expert. (*Smoothly*) What's your name?

RODNEY. Rodney Bevan. Of course, it's a sort of *nom de plume,* or *nom de guerre*—

C.F. Rodney Bevan. (*Picks up phone*) Give me Casting. . . . This is C.F. Extra here by the name of Rodney Bevan doesn't like his uniform. Fire him.

RODNEY (*aghast*). Fire? Have you given me the sack?

C.F. I've enough trouble without extras telling me how to make pictures. That's the trouble with this business. A man spends his life at it, and anybody can walk in and tell him how to run it.

RODNEY. But I merely suggested—(MISS CREWS *enters.*)

MISS CREWS. Mr. Green and Mr. Slade are outside, Mr. Friday. They want you to hear the song.

RODNEY. I've waited a long time for this opening—

C.F. Get out! (*To* MISS CREWS) I'm in no mood for *music.* (GREEN *and* SLADE *enter.*)

GREEN. We've got it, and you're going to listen. If you don't like it,

Schulberg's nuts about it. (SLADE *crosses to piano and starts playing the song*) We wrote it for *Young England,* but it's flexible— Flexible as hell.

(MISS CREWS *exits.* RODNEY *turns forlornly and fades out through the door. What else can he do?*)

C.F. Boys, I'm in no mood for—

GREEN. It's a touching little thing, but, boy, what power! There's a "Pain in My Heart, and My Heart's on My Sleeve." Like the title? (SLADE *is one of those who glues himself to a piano. He's all pasted together now, and his fingers fly.* GREEN *sings with all the fervid sincerity of Georgie Jessel with a cold.*)

You promised love undying,
And begged me to believe;
Then you left, and left me crying
With a pain in my heart, and my
  heart on my sleeve.

It isn't right to show it,
To flaunt the way I grieve;
But the world will quickly know it,
For the pain's in my heart and my
  heart on my sleeve.

I confess that I'm a mess—
The way I lived my life,
But what does it matter?
Yes, I guess that happiness
Is only for a wife;
Sorrow isn't served on a silver platter.

I really shouldn't blame you
Because you chose to leave;
But one thing forever will shame
  you—
It's the pain in my heart, and my
  heart on my sleeve.

(*During the song* MISS CREWS *enters with glass of orange juice. She crosses around desk, puts glass in front of* C.F., *gets book from lower drawer.*)

C.F. (*as* GREEN *finishes song*). Miss Crews, get hold of Benson and Law! (MISS CREWS *exits.*)

LARRY (*as the din grows*). I've worked for Biograph. . . . I've worked for Monogram. . . . I've worked for Columbia. . . . I've worked for Warners. . . . I've worked for Metro . . . but a screwier outfit I never did see! (BENSON *and* LAW *enter in costume of beefeaters. They, too, wear busbies.*)

C.F. (*whose nails are being buffed*). What do you want? (*At the musicians*) Quiet! (*At the busbies, for* C.F. *doesn't deign to look at actors' faces*) I told Wardrobe I don't like the hats.

BENSON. He doesn't like the hats.

LAW. Call Jock Whitney. We want to be in color.

C.F. (*exasperated*). For God's sake! This is a fine time to be masquerading.

BENSON (*leaping into character; picking up stone*). Wait! What a pretty stone! I wonder where that came from.

LAW (*in his own big scene*). I wonder.

BENSON (*transporting himself to the desert*). I think we've found gold, partner.

LAW (*grabbing for it*). Gold!

BENSON. Stand back—you desert rat!

LAW. Gold—after all these years! I'm going mad . . . mad . . . mad. . . .

C.F. Oh, stop it, boys.

LARRY (*suddenly inspired. To* C.F.). I wouldn't be surprised if they threw that there rock through the window.

BENSON. What an innuendo!

C.F. You didn't do that, did you, boys? Smash my Vita-glass?

LAW. To think—after all these years of loyal, faithful service— Larry Toms, you ought to be ashamed!

BENSON. The man with the poison-pen mind. We're going to tell Louella Parsons on you.

C.F. (*impatiently*). *Very* well . . . *very* well. . . . But I still have my suspicions. (*Snaps*) Now what about our story?

BENSON. Right here. (*Indicating script on desk.*)

LAW (*takes a statuette from top of desk*). Mr. Benson, for the most brilliant script of the year, the Academy takes great pleasure in presenting to you this little gargoyle—

BENSON. Wrap it up, please.
(LAW *drops it in* LARRY'S *hat and stands back of couch. Music plays.*)

LARRY (*rising in a dither*). Now, listen—
(C.F. *crosses below desk, retrieves statue, places it back on desk.*)

GREEN (*to* SLADE *at piano*). What do you say to this, Otto, for the second chorus:

Yes, I've been kissed,
But like Oliver Twist,
I'm still crying for more.

(*Without waiting for an answer, to* C.F.) How did you like the song, C.F.?

LAW. Darn good. Can you play *Over the Waves?*

C.F. Boys, can't you be sensible for a moment? You're trying my patience. What about our story?

LAW. What about it? It's a rich, protean part for Larry.

LARRY. It just don't make sense.

LAW. I resent that as a gentleman and a grammarian.

C.F. Now really, boys, I'm tolerant, but I've got to see results. I'm not one to put the creative urge in a strait jacket. But you've been fired off every other lot in this industry for your pranks. Perhaps you've forgotten, Benson, but when I hired you for this job you promised me to behave in no uncertain terms. And you promised me Law would toe the line. Now, I'm warning you, boys. Let's get to work. Let's concentrate. (*Crosses above desk to chair back of desk*) Do you realize you boys are making more than the President of the United States?

LAW. But look at the fun he's having!

LARRY (*angrily*). Now looka here—

GREEN. How do you like the song, C. F.?

C.F. It lacks body.

LAW. No breasts.

C.F. That's exactly it— Pallid.

GREEN. Come on, Otto.

SLADE (*starts for door*). This isn't my idea of a fair audition.

GREEN. Wait'll they hear it at the Cocoanut Grove. They'll be sorry. (GREEN *and* SLADE *exit.* PEGGY *enters and* LAW, *humming "Merry Widow," intercepts her, dances a few measures with her.*)

C.F. Listen, boys—we've had enough of this.
(SUSIE *enters carrying a tray.* SUSIE *is a waitress. We worship* SUSIE. *Why describe her? We'll tell you what she wears—the full-blown costume of a Hollywood waitress. Of her blonde fragility, her intricate but blameless sex life, and the ineffable charm of her touching naïveté we won't say a word.*)

LAW. *Lunch!*

BENSON. Grub! Susie, I love you. (PEGGY *exits. She never comes back. Why should she?*)

C.F. Wait a minute—wait a minute— (LAW *gets end table and places it in front of couch.* BENSON *takes tray from* SUSIE.)

SUSIE (*weakly*). Please, Mr. Benson, be careful.

LAW. Put that tray right down here.

SUSIE (*quavering*). Thanks. . . . It's not very heavy . . . (*She then collapses neatly on the floor.*)

C.F. Good Lord!

LAW (*bending over her*). Susie— Susie—

BENSON (*grabbing phone*). Get the doctor over here—right away—

LAW. Somebody give me water. (BENSON *takes glass from tray on table.*)

C.F. (*disapprovingly*). This is a nice thing to happen in my office. . . . Who is this girl, anyway?

LAW (*putting water to her as he kneels beside her*). Come on, Susie. (*Lifting her head up to glass.*)

LARRY (*whose father wrote letters to the papers*). That commissary shouldn't employ people with epilepsy.

C.F. (*bitter, still*). I had an actor who did that to me once. Held up my shooting schedule fourteen days.

LAW. She's all right. Here.

SUSIE. Did you all get napkins? (*Opens her eyes for the first time.*)

BENSON. Now, Susie—get into this chair.

SUSIE. Thanks. (*She sits.*)

C.F. (*sharply*). What's wrong with you, young woman?

SUSIE (*still quavering*). Nothing. . . . I'm much better now. . . . Thanks.

C.F. Where's that doctor?

SUSIE. Did you call for a doctor? You didn't have to.

C.F. Do you get these epileptic fits often?

SUSIE. I didn't have an epileptic fit.

C.F. Then what's wrong with you?

SUSIE. There's nothing wrong . . . it's only natural.

C.F. Only natural for you to come into my office and collapse on the floor.

SUSIE. Oh, no, sir . . . it's only natural for you to feel sick when you're going to have a baby.

LAW. A baby!

BENSON. Susie, you're not going to have a baby!

SUSIE. That's what they told me. . . .

BENSON. Susie's going to have a baby!

LAW. Let's get drunk!

C.F. (*into phone*). Tell that doctor not to come. You heard me. I don't want him. (*He hangs up*) I won't have my office converted into a maternity ward! (*He turns on* SUSIE) I don't think much of your husband—letting you work at a time like this!

SUSIE. Oh, but I haven't got a husband.

C.F. Huh?

SUSIE (*rises*). You'd better eat your lunch before it gets cold. Have you all got napkins?

LAW (*humbly*). The new generation! Faces the facts of nature without squeamishness, without subterfuge. "I haven't got a husband," she says. "It's only natural," she says. "I'm going to have a baby." . . . Susie, you're magnificent.

SUSIE. I'm quitting at the end of the week so I thought I'd tell everybody why. I wouldn't want them to think I was discontented.

LAW. Our little mother!

SUSIE. Oh, don't make fun of me.

LAW (*rises*). Fun? I've never been so touched in my life. Susie, I feel purified.

BENSON. Susie—can we be godfather?

SUSIE. Do you mean it?

BENSON. Do we mean it? We haven't got a baby. And we've been collaborating for years.

SUSIE. Oh, I think that would be wonderful for Happy to have writers for a godfather.

BENSON. Happy?

SUSIE. I'm going to call him Happy—even if he's a girl. Because I want him to be happy—even if he's a girl.

BENSON. Beautiful! A beautiful thought! Where are you going to have this baby, Susie?

SUSIE. In the County Hospital. It's all fixed. I was very lucky because I've only lived in the county three months and I'm not eligible.

C.F. Now, listen, boys—enough of this.

LAW (*into phone*). Give me the Cedars of Lebanon Hospital—and make it snappy.

BENSON (*jubiliant*). We've got a baby!

C.F. Just a minute. Hang up that phone. (BENSON *good-naturedly brushes his arm down.*)

LAW. Dr. Marx, please. . . . Willy, this is Law of Benson and Law. Reserve the best suite in the house for us. I'm serious. Dead serious. A little friend of ours is going to have a baby and we want the goddamnedest confinement you've got in stock . . . .

BENSON. Day and night nurse.

LAW (*To* BENSON) And not the one with the buck teeth either. She's dynamite. (*Into phone*) We want everything that Gloria Swanson had —only double. What's that? Bill? Bill the studio, of course. (*He hangs up.*)

C.F. You'll do no such thing! What kind of a gag is this?
(MISS CREWS *enters.*)

MISS CREWS. Do you want to hear the trumpet call? The men are here. Music Department wants your O.K.

C.F. Trumpets?

MISS CREWS. For *Young England.*

C.F. Look here—I haven't time to listen to them now. Come back here at two o'clock. And give it tc me from out there. I don't want them blasting in my ear.
(*Meanwhile* BENSON *and* LAW *have been in whispered conference.*)

MISS CREWS. Yes, Mr. Friday. (*Exits.*)

C.F. Now, boys—let's get together on this. (*Turns on* SUSIE *from below desk*) And you—what are you sitting here for? Get out! (SUSIE *tries to rise.*)

LAW. Sit right where you are. (*Crosses to front of desk*) Don't you bark at our inspiration! We've got it!

C.F. What?

LAW (*with mounting excitement*). A baby!

C.F. Boys, I'm a patient man, but you're trying me.

BENSON (*awed*). *Larry Toms and a baby!*

LAW (*to* C.F.) Do you see it?

LARRY (*bellowing*). Wait a minute —wait a minute!

LAW (*quickly*). He finds a baby—in the Rockies—

BENSON (*inspired; quickly to* C.F.). Girl with a no-good gambler—out of Las Vegas—has a baby . . . gambler is killed. Girl leaves baby on the ranger's door step. Larry is the ranger.

LAW (*dramatizing it all*). My God, he says—a baby!

BENSON (*awed*). A baby!

LAW. The most precious thing in life. The cutest, God-damn little bastard you ever saw.

BENSON. Tugging at every mother's heart. And every potential mother.

LAW. And who isn't?

BENSON. A love story between Larry and the baby—

LAW. The two outcasts! Get it?

BENSON. And then he meets the mother!

LAW. She wants her baby back.

BENSON. She's been through the fires of hell.

LAW. The man she loved . . . let her down. . . .

BENSON. She hates men . . . all men. . . .

LAW. She won't look at Larry.

BENSON (*to* LARRY). No. There she sits . . . bitter, brooding, cynical, but underneath—a mother's heart.

LAW. Out on the Rockies—

BENSON. The hell with the Rockies —back to the Foreign Legion!

LAW. Right! Larry's joined to forget. He's out on the march. We can use all that stock stuff—and he finds a baby!

BENSON. He's gone off to fight the Riffs.

LAW. The hell with the Riffs! Ethiopians!

BENSON. Stick to the Riffs. We don't want any race problem.

LAW. Right! She doesn't know if he's coming back.

BENSON. She's waiting—waiting!

LAW. We cut to the Riffs—

BENSON. Cut back—

LAW (*to* BENSON). Right into the battle.

BENSON (*really inspired now*). His father's the Colonel!

LAW. Talk about Kipling—

BENSON. Talk about scope—sweep—what a set-up!

LAW. A love story!

BENSON. A great love story!

LAW. Mary Magdalen of the Foreign Legion and the West Point man who wanted to forget!

BENSON (*rises*). The baby brings them together, splits them apart, brings them together—

LAW. Boy meets girl—

BENSON. Boy loses girl—

LAW. Boy gets girl!

C.F. (*rising in excitement*). Boys, I think you've got something! Let's go up and try it on B.K. while it's hot.

LAW. Let's go! (*They move forward.*)

LARRY (*crosses to behind couch*). Wait a minute—you can't act with a baby. They steal every scene— Look what happened to Chevalier.

LAW. Are you selling motherhood short? (LAW, BENSON *and* C.F. *exit through next speech.*)

LARRY. They'll be looking at the baby when they should be looking at me. I tell you—I won't play it. (*Follows off.* SUSIE *tries to rise, now she is left alone. She sits down again.* RODNEY, *in the Coldstream Guards uniform, enters.* SUSIE *turns.*)

RODNEY. Oh, I'm sorry. I hope I didn't startle you.

SUSIE. Oh, no. (*Then, as he looks at* C.F.'s *desk*). They all stepped out and they didn't even touch their lunch.

RODNEY (*licking his lips involuntarily*). Lunch?— You don't happen to know when Mr. Friday is coming back?

SUSIE. No, I don't.

RODNEY. I did want to see him. It's rather urgent. Do you mind if I wait here?

SUSIE. No, of course not. (*He seats himself on couch, near a tray. There is an awkward silence.* SUSIE *stares straight ahead.* RODNEY *plays with a cracker. Finally* SUSIE *breaks the silence*) What are you supposed to be?

RODNEY. Eh? Oh! That's just it. . . . I'm supposed to be a Buckingham Palace Guard, sergeant major— (*He pops the cracker into his mouth and swallows it.* SUSIE *looks at him rather intently*) Good Lord! What am I doing?

SUSIE. You're eating Mr. Friday's cracker.

RODNEY. I'm awfully sorry. I don't understand how I—

SUSIE. You must be very hungry.

RODNEY. Not a bit. Not at all.

SUSIE. You *look* hungry.

RODNEY. Do I?

SUSIE. Why don't you have something? They'll never eat it. They're always sending things back they order—never even touched.

RODNEY. Really?

SUSIE. You'll only be doing me a favor.

RODNEY. Oh?

SUSIE. I won't have so much to carry back to the commissary. Sometimes I think I carry back more than I bring.

RODNEY. You're pulling my leg, of course.

SUSIE. What did you say?

RODNEY. You're not really a waitress.

SUSIE. Sure I am.

RODNEY (*triumphantly*). Waitresses don't usually sit in producers' offices.

SUSIE. They do when they don't feel well.

RODNEY. You don't feel well? Oh, I'm sorry. Is there anything I can do?

SUSIE. No, thanks.

RODNEY. But what's wrong?

SUSIE. Oh, there's no use telling you. I told Mr. Friday and he made such a fuss about it I guess I better keep it to myself.

RODNEY. I'm afraid I don't quite understand.

SUSIE. Try the chicken soup. It's very good.

RODNEY. Are you seriously suggesting that I filch some of this broth?

SUSIE. We make it special for B.K. with nine chickens.

RODNEY. Well, dash it, I will eat it. Just to make the joke good! (*He laughs weakly and picks up the bowl and puts it to his lips, and sips it.*)

SUSIE (*warningly*). It's hot!

RODNEY (*now quite gay*). So I've learned.

SUSIE. When did you eat last?

RODNEY (*lying, of course*). I had my lunch an hour ago.

SUSIE. Have some crackers with it.

RODNEY. Thanks.

SUSIE. You're English, aren't you?

RODNEY. Yes, of course.

SUSIE. So is Ronald Colman.

RODNEY (*bolting his food*). So he is.

SUSIE. I like the way the English talk.

RODNEY. Do you?

SUSIE. It's very soothing.

RODNEY. What an idea!

SUSIE. Of course, that's only *my* idea. I'm very ignorant.

RODNEY. Oh, please don't say that. I think you're very intelligent.

SUSIE. Oh, I'm intelligent. But I don't know anything.

RODNEY. You're an extraordinary girl.

SUSIE. I've never been to high school.

RODNEY (*gallantly*). May I say that's the high school's loss?

SUSIE. But some day I'll go to high school. That's my secret ambition. Try the ham hocks. The cook eats them himself. He comes from Czechoslovakia.

RODNEY. Does he really? Look here—I feel an awful swine guzzling by myself. Won't you join me?

SUSIE. Well, I'm not very hungry, but I can eat.

RODNEY. Good! (*He rises and adjusts a chair for her.*)

SUSIE. It's funny how I keep on eating.

RODNEY. Some ham hocks?

SUSIE. No. Happy doesn't like ham. He likes milk.

RODNEY (*mystified*). I beg your pardon? (*But he doesn't press the point*) Did you say milk?

SUSIE. Yes. Milk.

RODNEY (*as he pours*). There you are.

SUSIE. Thanks.

RODNEY. Cozy, this—what?

SUSIE. It's good milk. Have some.

RODNEY. Do you know, I think you're the most extraordinary girl I ever met.

SUSIE. Why?

RODNEY. You're so kind. You're so direct, so sincere. Most girls one meets play about with words so. They're so infernally smart. They make one feel like a worm.

SUSIE. Of course, I'm different on account of my condition. Most girls aren't in my condition.

RODNEY. Your condition?

SUSIE. The minute I found out about Happy I said to myself: I'm going to be very good and very sincere, because then Happy will be very good and very sincere.

RODNEY. I'm afraid I don't quite follow.

SUSIE (*sighing*). Nobody does.

RODNEY. Eh? Oh, yes. . . . As I was saying— What was I saying?

SUSIE (*looking into his eyes and feeling strangely stirred*). Have some mustard.

RODNEY. Do you know, I must confess. I was hungry. As a matter of fact, I was close to wiring home for funds today. But I didn't. (*Looks very determined, righteous.*)

SUSIE. You mean you need money, and you can get it—and you won't wire for it?

RODNEY. I can't—and keep my pride. I told *them* I was on my own. You see, my family didn't want me to act. Not that they've any prejudices against the stage—or the films. Not at all. In fact, one of my aunts was a Gaiety girl. Quite all right. But they don't think I *can* act. That's what hurts.

SUSIE. Can you act?

RODNEY. No.

SUSIE. Not at all?

RODNEY. Not at all. I'm awful!

SUSIE. Oh, that's too bad.

RODNEY. But I only realized it in the stock company . . . out in Pasadena. I was the worst member of the company. At first I thought it was because they were always giving me character parts—American gangsters—and that sort of thing. And then one week I played a Cambridge undergraduate. And, mind you, I've been a Cambridge undergraduate. And do you know that I was utterly unconvincing?

SUSIE. Then why don't you give it up?

RODNEY. Pride.

SUSIE. I can understand that— Pride.

RODNEY. Can you really?

SUSIE. Sure I can.

RODNEY. That's why I simply must see Mr. Friday. (*Suddenly*) Look here— (*He takes a book from couch and opens it*) Look at this color plate. Does this uniform remotely resemble the one I'm wearing? (*He crosses down right.*)

SUSIE (*looks at book; then at* RODNEY). Yes, I think so.

RODNEY (*crosses to her left*). But, my dear girl, look at the coat and the buttons—and the boots—note the heels—and look at mine. (*Steps back.*)

SUSIE. Well, come to think of it, I guess it is different.

RODNEY. Of course. And I've taken this book right out of their own research department. When I show this to Mr. Friday he's bound to be sporting enough to admit an error.

SUSIE. Oh, sure.

RODNEY (*leaning over her*). You see, all I want is to appear in *one* picture —and then I can tell the family: "I've done it. But it's not good enough. I'm chucking it." But I'll have my pride.

SUSIE (*gazing at him*). I see.

RODNEY. Oh . . . I say . . . I'm not boring you?

SUSIE. Oh, no. Finish your ham.

RODNEY. Eh! Oh! Don't mind if I do. A bit of pie for you? (*He extends plate with fork.*)

SUSIE (*brightly. Almost flirting*). Well, I'll try. (*She smiles at him and he at her, fork poised in mid-air.*)

RODNEY. Do you know, I've never enjoyed a lunch quite as much as this one—thanks to you. (*Suddenly*) Would it bore you if I tried out my lines—in *Young England*, you know?

SUSIE. Oh, no.

RODNEY. Very well. (*He rises, holding glass of milk*) Gentlemen, the Queen— (*He waits.*)

SUSIE. Is that all?

RODNEY. That's all. But of course I could say: "Gentlemen, I give you the Queen." Fatten up the part a bit, what? . . . Gentlemen, I give you the Queen! . . . Sounds rather better, doesn't it? (*Then with profound bass*) Gentlemen, I give you the Queen!

(LARRY *enters followed by* C.F. C.F. *stares.*)

LARRY. I don't cotton to the whole idea, and if B.K.'s got any sense, he won't listen to those maniacs.

C.F. What's going on here?

RODNEY. How'd you do. . . . I . . . I . . . (*Puts glass of milk back on tray.*)

C.F. What is this? A tête-à-tête in my office! Good Gad! You've been drinking my milk!

SUSIE. It's all right, Mr. Friday. I told him he could have it.

C.F. *You* told him?

RODNEY. I'm awfully sorry. I owe you an apology, and money, of course. Will you accept my I.O.U.? And I have the book—from Research. I can show you the really authentic uniform. I'm sure if you study this— (SUSIE *finds the page and hands book to* RODNEY.)

C.F. I've a good mind to call the studio police.

SUSIE (*rises*). Oh, please don't do that, Mr. Friday.

LARRY. That's what you get for having foreign actors around. Take the food right out of your mouth!

RODNEY. I'm terribly sorry, of course.

C.F. Get out!

RODNEY. I realize there's nothing I can say— (*He turns to* SUSIE) except —my eternal gratitude. (*He grabs her by the hand and shakes it. Exits.*)

SUSIE. Oh, you shouldn't have done that. He's been having a terrible time.

C.F. (*glaring at* SUSIE). Get these dishes out of here.

SUSIE (*meekly*). Yes, sir. (*She begins piling up dishes on tray.*)

LARRY. The idea of a baby! The more I think of it, the less I like it.

C.F. (*crosses to chair at desk*). Larry, you're driving me into a nervous breakdown. I had to take you out of B.K.'s office so you'd stop arguing before he could make a decision.

LARRY. There's nothing to decision. I won't play it.

C.F. If B.K. likes the idea, you'll play it.

LARRY. Maybe—and maybe not. I'm willing to bet ten to one right now B.K. kicks the whole story in the ash can. He's no fool. (BENSON *and* LAW *enter in shirt sleeves. They've obviously had a hot session with* B.K.)

BENSON. Sold! Lock, stock and baby! B.K. says it's the best mother-love story he's heard in years.

LARRY. What? What's that?

LAW (*magnificently*). Susie, put that tray down!

SUSIE. Please, Mr. Law, I've got to get back to the commissary.

LARRY. You sold him that story, huh?

BENSON. Lie down, actor!

LARRY. I'll see about this. (*He exits.*)

BENSON. Now listen, Susie—and listen carefully.

LAW. Let me tell her, will you? (*He faces her*) Susie, nature meant you for a sucker. You were designed to get the short end of the stick. The girl who gets slapped.

BENSON (*quickly*). But we're changing all that.

LAW. Susie, in real life, you'd have your baby in the County Hospital . . . get yourself a job, if lucky, with a philanthropic Iowa family of fourteen adults and twelve minors for twenty bucks a month. And when your grateful son grew up he'd squirt tobacco juice in your eye and join the Navy.

BENSON. There you go with your God-damn realism. (*Turns to* SUSIE *with paper and pencil*) Sign, please—

SUSIE. Here? (*She signs; and then turns, brightly*) What is it?

BENSON. Just a power of attorney authorizing us to deal for you in all matters with this studio.

C.F. What power of attorney? What are you boys up to?

LAW. We said to ourselves upstairs—why shouldn't Susie have the good things of life?

BENSON. After all, we're godfathers.

SUSIE. I—I don't feel very good.

LAW. Get this, Susie. We've just sold a story about a baby.

BENSON. Sweetest story ever told!

LAW. A new-born baby.

BENSON. Brand new.

LAW. We're going to watch that baby—the first hair—the first tooth—the first smile—

BENSON. The same baby. No switching—first time in the history of pictures. That baby's going to grow up before your eyes.

LAW. Open up like a flower. . . . Just like the Dionne quintuplets.

BENSON. Minute he's born we set the cameras on him. We stay with him—

LAW. That baby's going to gurgle and google and drool his way to stardom!

SUSIE. But—

LAW. And that baby, Susie, is Happy. Upstairs in B.K.'s office we put your unborn child into pictures!

SUSIE (*transported*). Happy—in pictures! Oh—that's wonderful—(*Then, with a sudden gasp*) Oh!

LAW (*quickly*) Susie! What's the matter?

SUSIE. I don't know . . . I . . . I . . . I don't feel so good . . . I think . . . I . . . (*In these broken words,* SUSIE *tells all.* BENSON *helps* SUSIE *to lie on couch.* LAW *looks over* SUSIE*'s shoulder; whistles; runs to phone.*)

LAW (*into phone*). *Emergency! Get the ambulance over to Mr. Friday's office right away—get the doctor—get the nurse. . . .*

C.F. (*staring*). What is it? In *my* office. Good Gad! Miss Crews! (*Door opens.*)

MISS CREWS (*at door*). The trumpets are here!
(*Trumpets sound their triumphant clarion call.*)

LAW (*through the Wagnerian brass, to* BENSON, *awed*). Happy's on his way!

CURTAIN

ACT TWO

SCENE I

We are in your neighborhood theatre, seven months later.

As the curtain rises we face a motion-picture screen, and to the sound-track accompaniment of "Home on the Range," these glaring titles pop out at us:

IF YOU LIKED HAPPY
IN
"WANDERING HEARTS"
YOU'LL ADORE HIM
IN
"GOLDEN NUGGET"

This is what is known as a trailer, in technical terms. It is shown at neighborhood theatres prior to the release of the picture so that the customers will be teased into returning the following week.

There are, of course, beautifully composed shots of horses, men and open spaces, and finally we come upon a series of close-ups of HAPPY, *over which these titles dance:*

HAPPY!
HAPPY!
HAPPY!

The sound track blares forth "Ride of the Valkyries."

CROWN PRINCE OF COMEDY!
KING OF TRAGEDY!
EMPEROR OF EMOTION!

Just prior to these titles we have seen a Chinese, who has emerged from God knows where, but what is a ranch without a Chinese? The general idea is that the Chinese finds HAPPY *on the doorstep and communicates his discovery to* LARRY TOMS. *There follows a title which explains all:*

THE DESERT WAIF WHO MADE
A SOFTIE OF A BAD MAN

The picture is further described as:

THE BIG GOLD STRIKE
OF MOTHER LOVE

We see horses galloping, men falling, revolvers barking, and nice, big, wavy

THRILLS

CHILLS

The credit card is as follows:

FROM A STORY BY H. G. WELLS
ADAPTED BY J. CARLYLE BENSON AND ROBERT LAW
DIRECTED BY SERGE BORODOKOV

and, appropriately enough, in solitary grandeur:

PRODUCED BY C. ELLIOT FRIDAY

SCENE II

The screen lifts, and once more we are in MR. FRIDAY'S *office.*

C.F. *is at his desk,* MISS CREWS *is seated upstage and at desk;* BENSON *is on the couch beside* LARRY. ROSETTI *is seated on the piano bench.*

BENSON. Read those figures, Miss Crews.

MISS CREWS. Eighty-two thousand at the Music Hall. Forty-eight thousand five hundred and thirty-eight in Des Moines.

BENSON. Without a stage show.

LARRY. I always went big in Des Moines.

MISS CREWS. Twenty-eight thousand in Newark.

LARRY. That's one of my big towns.

MISS CREWS. Forty-two thousand three hundred and eighty-four in San Francisco.

LARRY. I'm big there, too.

MISS CREWS. Twenty-six thousand eight hundred and seventy-five in Detroit.

BENSON (*to* C.F.). And you sit there and tell me Happy isn't worth thirty-five hundred a week?

C.F. But, Benson, be reasonable. I can't go to B.K. with any such fantastic figure.

BENSON (*sighing*). Read that list again, Miss Crews.

C.F. Never mind, Miss Crews.

LARRY. What about me? *Wandering Hearts* was my picture, wasn't it? Folks came to see me. They didn't come to see Happy.

BENSON (*taking "Variety" from his pocket*). Let me read "Variety" to the assembled multitude. *Wandering Hearts* socko in Minneapolis despite Larry Toms . . .

LARRY. Huh?

BENSON. Mexico nuts about Happy but no like Larry Toms—

LARRY. Where? Where does it say that? (*He takes paper.* ROSETTI *rises and looks over* LARRY's *shoulder.*)

BENSON. This is an accidental business in an accidental world. Happy is going to get it while it's hot.

C.F. Benson, you owe me something.

BENSON. What?

C.F. Gratitude. . . . After all, the idea of a baby was mine—more or less.

BENSON. More or less.

C.F. I made that baby act.

BENSON. All right, Svengali.

C.F. Shall we say three hundred a week for Happy?

BENSON. Shall we say thirty-five hundred a week for Happy?

C.F. I've a good mind to have you thrown out of this studio.

BENSON. All right. Happy goes with us. We've still got that power of attorney.

C.F. Of course, I didn't mean that literally.

BENSON. I did. (*Telephone rings.*)

C.F. Hello. . . . Yes, Miss Goodwin. . . . What? You can't write about Brussels because you've never been there? My dear girl, why do you think we have a research department? After all, Bernard Shaw wrote *Don Juan* and he never went to Bulgaria. Imagination, my dear girl—imagination. (*Hangs up*) Look here. Benson, I knew I couldn't deal with Law. I thought I could with you. After all, you're in no position to antagonize this studio. Some day you may need my friendship.

BENSON. I'm supposed to be working with our Mr. Law on a story. To wit: *Tiger Tamer*. Do you mind if I join my partner in a little English composition?

C.F. Some day you may be very sorry for this, Benson.

BENSON. What do you think, Miss Crews.

MISS CREWS. I think Happy ought to get it while it's hot.

C.F. Get back to your desk.

MISS CREWS. Yes, Mr. Friday. (*She exits.*)

LARRY (*waving "Variety"*). I said that baby'd ruin me! Well, he ain't going to steal no more pictures! I won't play that new scene.

C.F. (*irritably*). What new scene?

LARRY. I'm supposed to wash Happy.

C.F. That's a cute scene. I read it.

LARRY. Am I the type that washes babies?

C.F. Why not?

LARRY. 'Tain't manly!

BENSON. No. You want the baby to wash you!

LARRY. Listen!

BENSON. Any further business before the house? (*Turns to* LARRY) By the way, I saw you with Susie at the Trocadero last night. We don't approve of you as an escort. Remind me to speak to her about that.

C.F. Benson, I'm asking you once more. Be fair—be reasonable.

BENSON. I am. We're asking thirty-five hundred a week. We'll consider three thousand and settle for twenty-five hundred. But not a penny less. Incidentally, Fox'll pay twenty-five hundred for Happy. We promised to let them know by Saturday. No hurry, of course. (*Exits.*)

C.F. Have you ever seen anything more damnably unfair? Imagine *writers* holding up this studio at the point of a gun. It's nothing but blackmail.

ROSETTI (*rises*). I've got a hunch, C.F. When did you sign Happy? Do you remember?

C.F. Of course I remember . . . July fourteenth . . . Fall of the Bastille. I remember my wife pointing out the coincidence at the time. Why?

ROSETTI (*crosses to desk*). I've got a hunch that power of attorney expires pretty soon. I want to be prepared.

C.F. Rosetti, I'm not interested in the future. I'm interested in signing Happy right now—before we lose him to Fox. (*Phone rings.*)

ROSETTI. You've got to have vision in this business, C.F. (*He reaches for other phone, changes his mind, and then exits.*)

C.F. (*into phone*). Hello. . . . Yes, listen, Gregg. . . . I ran the sound track on *Young England* last night. I don't like the trumpets. They're sour. They spoil the whole mood. . . . What? . . . What's that? You can't walk out on a picture like that. What kind of a director are you if you can't take constructive criticism . . . hello . . . hello . . . (*Hangs up*) Gregg is walking out on *Young England,* I can't sign Happy—

LARRY. What about me?

C.F. Ten thousand feet of film sick —and he walks out. I'll have to run the picture all the afternoon and sit up all night cutting it.
(MISS CREWS *enters.*)

MISS CREWS. Happy's through for the day.

NURSE (*wheeling in a streamlined baby carriage*). Through for the day.

DOCTOR (*as he enters*). Through for the day. Is his mother here?

MISS CREWS. No, Doctor, but she should be here very soon.

NURSE (*backing carriage in front of desk*). Say da-da to Mr. Friday.

C.F. (*waving obediently*). Da-da, Happy.

DOCTOR. Nurse, take the little trouper out into the garden and keep him in the sunshine.

LARRY. He's through for the day and I'm working until eight. He's sure got it soft.
(NURSE *exits with* HAPPY. ROSETTI *enters.*)

DOCTOR. They've been overworking you, have they?

LARRY. I ain't feeling so hearty, doc. I wish you'd look me over.

C.F. (*rises and goes below desk*). Just your imagination. I wish I had your constitution. I've got to see B.K. (*He exits.*)

DOCTOR. All you picture people are hypochondriacs. However, come up to my office and I'll look you over. (*He exits.*)

LARRY. I'm a star. I've been a star for ten years. I've worked hard to get where I'm at— (*He rises. Phone rings.*)

ROSETTI (*at phone*). Hello. . . . Yes . . . speaking—

LARRY. I don't drink. I don't smoke. I don't swear. I don't get into no scandal. And the girls I passed up!

ROSETTI (*into phone*). Oh, you've got that, Mr. Williams? Fine. When does it expire? . . . It *did* expire? Last week? . . . No, don't do that. I'll tell the boys. . . . You see, I may be handling Happy's new contract. Right. (*He hangs up.*)

LARRY. They ain't making pictures here no more. They're shooting nothing but close-ups of babies. Happy laughing! Happy crying! Happy! . . . Happy! . . .

ROSETTI. Larry, I've just checked with the Legal Department. The boys' power of attorney expired last week. And they don't even know it.

LARRY. What's that got to do with me?

ROSETTI. Larry, there's been something developing in the back of my mind for some weeks. Why do you think I asked you to take Susie to the Trocadero?

LARRY. She talked me deaf, dumb, and blind about going to high school. Set me back fourteen bucks. Lucky she don't drink.

ROSETTI (*the dreamer*). I wanted you to get friendly with her because I visualized a way for you and me to get Happy—for life.

LARRY. Huh?

ROSETTI (*with Napoleonic intensity*). Larry, here's the tactical move. You marry Susie.

LARRY. Marry her?

ROSETTI. That's what I said.

LARRY. I won't do it.

ROSETTI (*who knows his client*). All right, suit yourself.

LARRY. We got community property in California. If there's a bust-up the woman gets half.

ROSETTI. Larry, I don't want to hurt your feelings, but I can't get you a new contract the way things are now. B.K. is dickering to borrow Clark Gable or Gary Cooper for Happy's next picture.

LARRY (*touched to the quick*). What?

ROSETTI. I'd marry her myself if I was free. Show me a girl with a better heart—with more culture—

LARRY. You don't expect me to believe what the studio hands out—her husband was a prominent portrait painter who went down on the *Morro Castle*?

ROSETTI (*indignantly*). Who are you to cast the first stone?

LARRY. I don't want to marry nobody. Anyways, there's no sense to it.

ROSETTI (*patiently*). If you marry her, you're Happy's legal guardian and we control the situation. A father and son team off the screen as well as on! Is that practical or am I just an idealist? Look at Guy Lathrop! He argued with me when I told him to marry Betty Bird. But he finally had the sense to play along with me and we've been drawing top money ever since.

LARRY. I don't want to marry nobody.

ROSETTI. Larry, you're at the crossroads right now. One road leads to stardom and big pictures, with Happy and me. The other leads to Poverty Row and cheap Westerns. Will you put your hand in mine and let me guide you?
(MISS CREWS *enters.*)

MISS CREWS. Mr. Toms, you're wanted on the set.

LARRY (*growling*). All right.

MISS CREWS. Oh, hello, Mrs. Seabrook . . . how nice you look. (*For* SUSIE *enters. She wears a white middy blouse and a navy blue, pleated skirt.*)

SUSIE. We had gym today. . . . Hello, Larry. . . . Hello, Mr. Rosetti. I hope I didn't interrupt anything important.

ROSETTI. Not at all. . . . (*Significantly*) I'll be in the Legal Department, Larry. (*He exits.*)

SUSIE. Where's Happy?

MISS CREWS. Happy's in the garden with his nurse. He's all through for the day.

SUSIE. Oh, that's wonderful. I don't get to see him very much. He's working and I'm going to high school. (CHAUFFEUR *enters.*)

CHAUFFEUR. Excuse me, Miss.

SUSIE. What is it, Simpson?

CHAUFFEUR. You forgot your algebra book, Miss.

SUSIE. Oh, thank you, Simpson. That was very thoughtful.
(CHAUFFEUR *exits.*)

MISS CREWS. And I have a new batch of fan mail for you and Happy (*Exits.*)

SUSIE. It's wonderful to get mail. Nobody used to write me before. Now I even get letters from Japan. (MISS CREWS *enters with letters*) All those letters? Thank you, Miss Crews.

LARRY (*sighs*). Miss Crews, call the set and tell 'em I may be a little late.

MISS CREWS. Very well. (*She exits.*)

SUSIE (*sitting on desk, poring over her hand-written, moronic literature*). Here's one from North Carolina. Oh, the poor thing! There's so much sadness in this world. (LARRY *sighs; she looks up at him*) You look sad, too, Larry. What's the matter?

LARRY. Well—(*He rises and crosses to* SUSIE)—uh—I been waiting a long time to talk to you, Susie. I couldn't go to the high school. All those girls would mob me for autographs, especially when I tell them who I am.

SUSIE. All the girls are crazy about Clark Gable.

LARRY (*clears his throat*). Susie—I can get two tickets for the opening at the Chinese—the de Mille picture.

SUSIE. Can you?

LARRY. I knew that'd knock you over.

SUSIE. Oh, it'll be wonderful.

LARRY. I'm always thinkin' of little things to make life wonderful—for you.

SUSIE (*nods*). Everybody is.

LARRY (*bridling*). What do you mean—everybody?

SUSIE. Only the other day Mr. Benson said something very true. He said: "Susie, you're Cinderella." And that's just what I feel like. And you know what else he said? He said: "All you need now is a Prince Charming."

LARRY. He did, huh? Who did he have in mind?

SUSIE. Oh, nobody.

LARRY. He didn't mention me, did he?

SUSIE. Oh, no. (LARRY *grunts*) Of course, I've never met a Prince Charming. I wouldn't know what he looks like. Although, one day an awful nice boy came in here.

LARRY. Who?

SUSIE. I don't even know his name. He was in uniform and I was in my condition—I've never seen him since.

LARRY. You shouldn't be thinking of him. You should be thinking of Happy.

SUSIE. But I do . . . only sometimes it gets lonesome for me, especially at night. And of course, Mr. Benson and Mr. Law are busy all the time. Happy used to say good night to them on the telephone. Not really good night—just goo-n'—just like that. But they're so busy they won't come to the telephone any more.

LARRY. Happy needs a father.

SUSIE. Do you think so?

LARRY. Well, you want him to be able to look the whole world in the face, don't you?

SUSIE (*twinkling*). He does!

LARRY. I mean when he grows up. He's gonna be ashamed when he finds out he never had a father.

SUSIE. Of course he had a father.

LARRY. I mean—a married father.

SUSIE. He was married—but I didn't know it.

(LARRY *winces.*)

LARRY. Uh — listen, Susie — I'm mighty fond of you and Happy. (*He tries playing the bashful Western hero*) Mighty fond.

SUSIE. Are you really, Larry?

LARRY. Mighty fond.

SUSIE. Who would have thought six months ago that I'd be sitting in the same room with Larry Toms and he'd be saying to me he was—

LARRY. Mighty fond.

SUSIE. Do you know something very odd? When I first came to California, it was raining very hard—oh, it rained for three weeks—it was very unusual—and I was looking for a job, and I couldn't find one—and I had fifteen cents—and I just had to get out of the rain—and I went into a theatre and there you were—on the screen—

LARRY. Mighty fond—

SUSIE (*awed*). That's just what you were saying to Mary Brian—and now you're saying it to me.

LARRY. What was the picture?

SUSIE. *Thunder over Arizona.* It was a beautiful picture. I don't remember what it was about, but I saw it four times. Until I got dry.

LARRY. Susie, soon's this picture's over, how'd you like to come up to my ranch? You and Happy—

SUSIE (*rises*). Ranch? Oh, that would be lovely! Maybe Mr. Benson and Mr. Law could come, too?

LARRY. Maybe they could, but they won't.

SUSIE. But I couldn't go alone—without a chaperon.

LARRY. Susie—you and Happy'll love that ranch. I got a mighty nice house, big and rambling. I got plenty of barns and a corral and plenty of livestock. But no baby.

SUSIE. I know Happy'll just love it.

LARRY. Susie—I know you don't expect this, and I don't want you to get too excited—but, Susie, I been thinkin' about you and Happy—thinkin' a lot. Ever since the day you come into this office and fell on that there floor, I said to myself: Larry, there's your leadin' lady—for life.

SUSIE. Me?

LARRY. Nobody else.

SUSIE. But I don't—you won't get mad?—but I'm not in love with you.

LARRY. You shouldn't be thinking of yourself—I'm not thinking of myself—you should be thinking of Happy.

SUSIE. I guess you're right. I don't know what to say. (*Pauses*) I'll ask Mr. Benson and Mr. Law—

LARRY. Huh?

SUSIE. They've been so good to me.

LARRY. I'm not proposing to them!

SUSIE. I know, but—

LARRY. You don't mean nothing to them. Before you came along they had a Spanish snake charmer until they got tired of her. And before that they had a broken-down pug who wiggled his ears. They was groomin' him for my place. There ain't nothin' holy to them!

SUSIE. But they've done everything for me.

LARRY (*crosses to* SUSIE). I'm offering you my ranch—my name—and a father Happy'll be proud of!

SUSIE. I know, but—

LARRY. Don't give me your answer now. Think it over. (*Pats her arm*) Only don't think too long. I'll be waiting for your answer in the Legal Department. You know where that is?

SUSIE. Oh, yes.
(MISS CREWS *opens the door.*)

LARRY. I'll be there. (*He exits.* SUSIE *looks a little dazed.*)

MISS CREWS. Oh, Mrs. Seabrook—I've located that young man you were looking for. He's outside.

SUSIE. Oh, you have? Really?

MISS CREWS (*at door*). Come in.
(SUSIE *tenses herself. A strange* YOUNG MAN *enters and stops.*)

SUSIE (*staring at him*). Oh! Oh, no, that's not him—I mean—he.

YOUNG MAN (*earnestly*). Won't I do? I've just finished a short for Hal Roach—I'm making a test for Metro tomorrow, and—

MISS CREWS (*firmly escorting him out*). Thank you for coming! (YOUNG MAN *shrugs and exits, and* MISS CREWS *closes the door.*)

SUSIE. He's not English.

MISS CREWS. English? We didn't have any English actors in *Young England.*

SUSIE. This boy was an extra.

MISS CREWS. Does he owe you a lot of money?

SUSIE. Oh, no. It was nothing like that.

MISS CREWS (*as it dawns on her*). Oh, I see! A personal matter! Well, I'll try again. (*Brightly.*)

SUSIE. I guess it's no use, Miss Crews. (*Sighs*) He probably swallowed his pride and went back to England.
(BENSON *and* LAW *enter.* BENSON *carries paper and pencil.* BENSON *sits upstage end of desk.* LAW *crosses to front of couch.*)

LAW. Hi, Susie! How's the little mother? Clear out. We're trying to work and a hundred chorus boys are practicing fencing underneath our windows. (*Turns to* MISS CREWS) Miss Crews, leave a note for C.F. He's got to change our office. We can't work with fencing fairies! (*Sits on couch.*)

MISS CREWS. Yes, Mr. Law. (*She exits.*)

SUSIE. Are you very busy?

BENSON. We still need an opening.

LAW. Fade-in. . . . A zoo!

SUSIE (*crossing to* BENSON). I just wanted to thank you, Mr. Benson, for the beautiful white teddy bear.

BENSON. What teddy bear?

SUSIE. Mrs. Benson brought it herself.

BENSON (*looking up from typewriter*). Oh, she did?

SUSIE. She played with Happy, too. And even after he went for his nap, she stayed and looked at him.

BENSON (*to* LAW—*covering*). Where were we?

SUSIE. When she left, she was crying. I think she ought to have a baby of her own.

BENSON (*angered*). Come on, Law—come on—fade-in on the zoo.

LAW. I've got it! Larry's carrying a hunk of meat for his pet tiger. He's crossing the road. Bang! The dame comes tearing down ninety miles an hour.

BENSON. Give her a little character.

LAW. She's a high-handed rich bitch. Bang! She almost runs the bastard down. . . . Where the hell do you think you're going? . . . She burns. . . . Society girl. . . . She's never been talked to like that before. . . . Why, you lousy bum, she snarls. . . . Listen, here's a cute piece of business. She bawls the hell out of him and he throws the hunk of meat right in her puss!

BENSON (*enthusiastically*). That's charming!

LAW. Listen, Susie, what are you standing there for? Go home and write in your diary.

SUSIE. Boys, I wanted to ask you something . . .

BENSON. Fade-out!

LAW. Fade-in!

SUSIE. . . .and then I'll go.

LAW (*wearily*). What is it?

SUSIE. Do you think I should marry Larry Toms?

LAW. Who?

SUSIE. Larry Toms.

LAW (*rises, crosses below couch*). No. . . . Fade-in. . . .

BENSON. Better get a different background. We've been staying in the zoo too long.

LAW. Right! Girl's home—a Pan shot—fifteen hundred butlers with white socks. . . . (*Turns to* SUSIE) Did he ask you to marry him?

SUSIE. Yes.

LAW. Did you spit in his face?

SUSIE. He's taking me to the opening tonight. He says he's mighty fond of Happy and me.

LAW (*crosses to back of couch*). Why shouldn't he be? His contract depends on it. Even Wilkes Barre doesn't want him and they're still calling for Theda Bara—

SUSIE. Don't you think he'd be good for Happy? He's an outdoor man.

LAW. So is the fellow who collects my garbage.

BENSON. Listen, let's get on with this. Introducing the fiancé. A pale anemic louse. A business man!

LAW. Right! The minute the audience sees him they yell: Don't marry that heel.

SUSIE. I know you're very busy. . . .

LAW. Go away, Susie.

SUSIE. You boys were so sweet to me. I felt I had somebody. But lately I've been awfully alone. . . .

LAW. Sure! Everybody's alone. What do you think life is? Why do you have crowds? Because everybody's alone. (*Stops; crosses above couch to front*) That's a thought. That's what I should be writing instead of this titivating drivel. Life as it is. People as they are.

SUSIE. But that would be terrible. You don't know, Mr. Law; you don't know how awful life can be.

BENSON. When you philosophers are through I'd like to get on with this story.

SUSIE (*eagerly, to* BENSON). You wouldn't like to come out and say hello to Happy? He's in the garden. (LAW *waves her away; crosses and sits on couch.* SUSIE *is quite defeated now.*)

BENSON (*ignoring her*). I've got it. (*To* SUSIE) Don't bother me! (SUSIE *crosses to desk, gets mail, and fades from the scene*) I've got it! Introducing Happy! Back to the zoo—Larry gets up in the morning and there, curled up with his pet tiger cub, is a baby! Happy!

LAW. Not bad!

BENSON. Larry looks at him. "How'd you get here?" (*He mimics* LARRY'S *voice.*)

LAW. The baby can't answer. The tiger begins to growl. Happy cries. Larry takes the baby to his hut.

BENSON. We meet Larry's drunken pal, the comic. (*Rises and crosses to* LAW) That's where we have swell business. Two clumsy men pinning up his diapers—

LAW (*his enthusiasm gone*). Formula 284 . . . Diapers gag.

BENSON (*exulting*). Ah, yes, but the tiger runs away with the diapers! Fade-out! Now we need excitement. The tigers are loose—

LAW. How did they get loose?

BENSON (*crosses to* LAW). The comic's drunk. He opens the cages by accident. Christ! I see it! The city in uproar—the police—National Guard—the girl's come down to the zoo—she's trapped with Larry—and the baby. Fifty tigers snapping at Happy's throat.

LAW. And where does my priceless dialogue come in? (*Rises and crosses to chair back of desk*) That's the worst of hack writing. It's hard work.

BENSON. Suppose—Larry—thinks—it's—the girl's baby?

LAW. Society girls go around leaving foundlings in the zoo? (*Drinking*) Prostitution of a God-given talent!

(*Sits*) Pasteboard pictures of pasteboard people.

BENSON. Will you shut up? I've got to get this line-up today. Pearl expects me to take her to the opening.

LAW (*fiddling with the dictograph*). Eenie . . . Meenie . . . Mina . . . Mo . . . (*Dictograph buzzes*) Music Department?

GREEN'S VOICE. Yes, this is the Music Department. This is Mr. Green.

LAW (*mimics* C.F.'s *voice*). Not Mr. Green! This is C.F. . . . can you write me a roundelay with a symphonic undertone in about fifteen minutes? . . . Do it! (*Dictograph buzzes*) Yes?

GREEN'S VOICE. Look, Mr. Friday, did you say a lullaby?

LAW. No, I didn't say a lullaby. I said a roundelay. The sort of thing Beethoven dashes off. (*He clicks the dictograph off.* ROSETTI *enters.*)

ROSETTI (*genially*). Hello, boys . . . have a cigar.

LAW. Hello, buzzard. What's the occasion?

BENSON. Fade-out, stooge, we're busy.

ROSETTI. Same old boys! Anything for a gag! Well, I'm feeling pretty good myself. I've just set Larry to a long-term contract. And he didn't have to take a cut, either. I got him a nice little set-up. A joint contract with Happy!

BENSON. With Happy?

LAW (*rises*). Huh? You're crazy!

ROSETTI. Well, the mother came to me just now and said you two were tired of her. And I happened to look up your power of attorney, and it seems you didn't even care to get a new one when it expired.

BENSON. Is this on the level?

LAW. Where's that power of attorney?

BENSON. I thought you had it.

LAW (*aghast*). What'd you get for Happy?

ROSETTI. Three hundred!

LAW. Why, we turned down fifteen hundred from Fox!

ROSETTI. You should have taken it. But three hundred's a lot of money. Anyway, what's the difference? It's all in the family—now.

LAW. Where's Susie?

ROSETTI. She went out with Larry. They're going to the opening tonight. They're celebrating.

LAW. Who thought this up—you?

ROSETTI. Sure.

LAW. Why, you scavenging son of a—

ROSETTI. You better be careful how you talk to me. And you'd better be careful how you talk to Larry from now on. He's fed up with your gags and insults. You got away with a lot of stuff around here because you had Happy. Well, Larry's got him now, and he's going to have plenty to say around here. I'm warning you. He'd like to see you boys off this lot. And he's in a position to do it—now. So be careful. If you want to keep your jobs. (*Turns away to door*) And if I had a wife who was throwing my money away before I even made it, I'd be plenty careful.

BENSON. Why, you— (ROSETTI *exits quickly.* BENSON *crosses to door, then turns to* LAW) Why the hell didn't you keep track of that power of attorney?

LAW. Why didn't *I*?

BENSON. Why the hell didn't you talk to Susie? She was in here.

LAW. Yeah.

BENSON. I see it—I see it now. Larry—Rosetti—and we let her walk right into it. Do you realize what this means? We're on our way out. (*Crosses to piano.*)

LAW. That's fine.

BENSON. Fine?

LAW. Now I'll have to go back to Vermont. Now I'll have to write.

BENSON. Pearl doesn't like Vermont.

LAW. The whims of your wife don't interest me. I've got a book—all planned.

BENSON. Listen—I want to stay in pictures. I love pictures. I'm knee-deep in debts. We've got to bust this Larry thing wide open. We've got to get Happy back.

LAW. But it's closed.

BENSON. Well, what of it? We'll open it. We've got to get Happy back.

LAW. How?

BENSON. Suppose we get Larry Toms to break that joint contract.

LAW. All right—but how?

BENSON. He's scared green of scandal. Suppose we show up at the opening tonight with a drunken dame. *Larry's deserted wife!*

LAW. Has he got one?

BENSON. We'll get one of your tarts.

LAW. That's too damned obvious.

BENSON. Can you top it?

LAW. Let me think.

BENSON. How about a poor deserted mother? I'll bet he's got one.

LAW (*rises, carried away*). I know! *Happy's father!*

BENSON. Huh?

LAW. We're going to produce Happy's father on the air—tonight. (*Crosses to phone.*)

BENSON. Happy's father! That's swell! That's marvellous. . . . (*Pause*) But where'll we get a father?

LAW (*into phone*). *Central Casting, please.* . . . Hello. I want a handsome young extra, a gentleman, a little down at the heel, not too well

fed, neat business suit—shiny but well pressed; quiet manner . . .
(*Door opens and* RODNEY *enters.*)

BENSON. What do you want?

RODNEY. I received a message from Miss Crews but apparently she's stepped out. Is Mr. Friday here? I assume I've been called for a part.

LAW (*into phone, as his eyes refuse to leave* RODNEY). Never mind—cancel it. (*Hangs up.*)

BENSON. Will you shut the door, please? (RODNEY *complies*) So you're an actor, my boy? (*Paternally.*)

RODNEY. Of course, I haven't had much experience. As a matter of fact, I never appeared in a picture. I almost did. Since then I've been out of the profession, so to speak. Odd jobs—barbecue stand, and when that closed I offered to show tourists homes of the movie stars. Unfortunately I haven't a motor car and they won't walk. . . . I don't mind saying this call was an extremely pleasant surprise.

LAW. He's perfect!

RODNEY. Do you really think I'll do?

LAW (*inspired*). Benson, take these lines. . . .
(BENSON *goes to chair.*)

RODNEY. Oh, are there lines? Then the fee will be fifteen dollars, I assume?

LAW. Fifteen? One hundred for you.

RODNEY. I'm afraid I'm not worth that.

LAW. This is a trailer we're making tonight. We pay more for trailers.

RODNEY. Oh, I say!

BENSON (*at desk, with paper and pencil*). We're going to shoot this at Grauman's Chinese in the lobby. There'll be a girl at the microphone. Her name is Susie. You come running up . . . you say . . .

LAW (*at downstage end of desk*). "Susie, why did you leave me?" . . . Say it.

RODNEY. Susie, why did you leave me?

BENSON. With feeling.

RODNEY (*with feeling*). Susie, why did you leave me?

LAW. I'm Happy's father.

RODNEY. I'm Happy's father.

BENSON. Louder.

RODNEY. *I'm Happy's father.*

LAW. I did not go down on the *Morro Castle*. . . . Susie, I've searched for you in the four corners of the earth. . . . *Susie, why did you leave me?*

RODNEY (*who has been repeating the ends of the phrases in* LAW'S *speech*). *Susie, why did you leave me?*

BENSON (*jubilant*). Right!

BLACKOUT AND CURTAIN

SCENE III

A radio voice is heard in the theatre before the rise of the curtain. We're right in Grauman's Chinese Theatre in Hollywood

RADIO ANNOUNCER. Folks, this is the première of Cecil B. de Mille's super-spectacle of Egyptian life—*King Saul*—at Grauman's Chinese. Your favorite stars, folks, in person—and the *crowds*. They're pushing and shoving and yelling for autographs, but it's all in good-natured fun. Only two hurt and they've refused medical treatment. There's Constance Bennett, folks, with her husband, the Marquis de la Falaise. No, I'm wrong. Sorry. It's not the Marquis . . . it's not Constance Bennett. It's Mary Pickford. By the way, I've been reading our Mary's book, folks. She's selling God, folks, and that's something we all ought to be in the market for. Give a thought to God and He'll give a thought to you. That's the big lesson in *King Saul,* folks. Oh, there's Leotta Marvin. . . .

As the curtain rises, the booming voice softens to the normal tone of a radio.

Again we are in MR. FRIDAY'S *office, later in the evening. At the rise of the curtain,* C.F. *is seated with* A CUTTER, *and* BENSON *sits a little apart from him, in chair back of couch, near the radio, which is on.*

RADIO ANNOUNCER. . . . And if you've seen her on the screen, I don't have to tell you she's blonde, beautiful and gorgeous. Folks, I want to tell you that this is the most thrilling première it's been my privilege to cover. *King Saul,* de Mille's super-spectacle of Egyptian life at Grauman's Chinese—

C.F. Benson, turn down that radio. We've got to get three thousand feet out of *Young England.* It's a sick picture, Benson. Where's Law? I left word at his hotel.

BENSON. He'll be here. I'm inside man tonight. He's outside.

C.F (*to* CUTTER). Cut the coronation scene—it drags. And give me an underlying something that means something. I want a stirring Britannic quality.
(BENSON *turns up the radio.*)

RADIO ANNOUNCER. . . . And that, folks, was Mr. Stanley Oswald, veteran of old silent films. . . . This is the première of *King Saul,* Cecil B. de Mille's super-spectacle at Grauman's Chinese . . .

C.F. Benson, turn to page 94 and read that scene. I want to lap-dissolve through Queen Victoria. Simmons, you're supposed to be a cutter. Give me some ideas.

RADIO ANNOUNCER. . . . And now, folks, I'm told that none other than Larry Toms is with us tonight. And he's not altogether by his lonesome for hanging on his manly arm is none other than Mrs. Susan Seabrook, mother of America's Crown Prince—Happy!

BENSON. Hooray!

CUTTER. I got a way of cutting all that Boer War stuff so you won't even miss it.

RADIO ANNOUNCER. . . . And now I have the honor to present Mrs. Seabrook, the mother of Happy . . .

C.F. Will you turn that infernal thing off? (*To* CUTTER) I can't cut the Boer War. It's historically valuable.

RADIO ANNOUNCER. . . . And now I have the honor to present Mrs. Seabrook, the mother of Happy—

SUSIE'S VOICE. But I don't know what to say!

BENSON. Susie's on the air.

RADIO ANNOUNCER. Is it true, Mrs. Seabrook, that you and Larry have been window shopping?

SUSIE'S VOICE (*and it's very nervous indeed*). Well—

RADIO ANNOUNCER. The microphone is yours.

SUSIE'S VOICE. I would like to thank all of you for the thousands of letters and gifts that you've sent my baby Happy. I read all your letters and some of them make me cry—they're so pathetic. I would like to send all of you money only I haven't got that much and the studio won't let me. I'd like to say a few words about the letters asking about Happy's diet. You read a lot of advertisements of what he eats but if Happy ate everything they said he ate I guess he'd be a giant, and he's really got a very little stomach.

BENSON. Good for Susie! Truth in advertising!

C.F. (*struck by appalling thought*). Benson, was Queen Victoria alive during the Boer War?

BENSON. If she's alive in the picture, she was.

RADIO ANNOUNCER (*through this*) Folks, this is the première of Cecil B. de Mille's super-spectacle of Egyptian life, *King Saul,* at Grauman's Chinese—

SUSIE'S VOICE. Can I say hello to all my girl friends at the Julia Marshall High School? . . . *Hello!*

C.F. Benson—

BENSON. Ssssh . . . Susie's talking.

SUSIE'S VOICE. A lot of you wonder in your letters how a grown woman can go to high school. Well, it's not easy. I'm a mother, and the other girls aren't . . .

BENSON. Let's hope not.

SUSIE'S VOICE (*brightly*). . . . although some of the girls are very developed.

RADIO ANNOUNCER (*quickly*). Folks, this is the première of *King Saul,* Cecil B. de Mille's super-spectacle of Egyptian life. . . .

C.F. Shut that infernal thing off.
(BENSON *lifts hand like traffic signal "Stop."*)

SUSIE'S VOICE. I didn't finish. I wanted to explain that I'm going to high school so I can keep up with Happy when he goes to college. Because I'm the only one Happy can go to. He hasn't got a father, and—

RADIO ANNOUNCER (*very, very firmly*). That was Happy's mother, folks. . . . She was wearing a white evening gown. And folks, meet Larry Toms, the lucky man.

C.F. Benson, can we lap-dissolve through, do you think, on page 94?

LARRY'S VOICE. I know this is going to be a wonderful picture.

RADIO ANNOUNCER. A little bird has whispered to me that you and Mrs. Seabrook are contemplating marriage, Larry.

BENSON. Well, what do you know about that?

C.F. Will you come here, Benson, with that script?

LARRY'S VOICE. Well, to tell you the truth—

BENSON. He's blushing.

LARRY'S VOICE. I kinda missed the little fella after the day's work was done. So I guess pretty soon I'll be Happy's father off the screen as well as on—

BENSON. Who wrote his speech? You or Rosetti?

RODNEY'S VOICE. Stop! I'm Happy's father!

C.F. (*rises*). What's that?

RODNEY'S VOICE. I did not go down on the *Morro Castle.* I've searched for you in the four corners of the earth. Susie, why did you leave me?

C.F. (*excitedly*). Did you hear that?

BENSON (*softly*). Yes. I wonder what that was . . .
(*Cries are heard of "Here, Officer"—inarticulate shouts—a siren.*)

RADIO ANNOUNCER. Folks, there was a slight interruption. That voice you heard was a young man . . . he . . . well, he threw his arms about Mrs. Seabrook and kissed her. There's some confusion—a police officer is making his way through—they've got the young man . . . no, they haven't got him . . . Folks, this is the opening of Cecil B. de Mille's super-spectacle of Egyptian life, *King Saul,* at Grauman's Chinese . . .
(BENSON *turns it off.*)

C.F. (*stunned*). Good Gad! (*Phone rings. He moves to it.*)

BENSON (*shakes his head*). Strangest thing I ever heard.

C.F. Oh, hello, B.K. . . . Yes, I've just heard it over the radio . . . (*Miserable*) I'm sitting here trying to cut *Young England* . . . what? . . . But, B.K., . . . yes, of course, it's a serious situation . . . I agree with you . . . yes, . . . yes . . . of course . . . I'll get hold of the mother immediately. (*He rises; hangs up, still dazed. To* BENSON) B.K.'s coming down to the studio! (*Phone rings*) Yes . . . Look here, I've nothing to say to the press. It's a canard. (*He hangs up. Phone rings again*) I won't answer it.
(MISS CREWS *enters.*)

MISS CREWS. Doctor Tompkins is calling you, Mr. Friday. He says it's important.

C.F. What's he want? I'm not in. Call Mrs. Seabrook's house and have her ring me the minute she comes in.

MISS CREWS. Yes, Mr. Friday. (*She exits.*)

C.F. Benson, do you think that young man was genuine?

BENSON (*rises, crosses around downstage end of couch*). Search me.

C.F. Well, we'll soon find out. B.K.'s set the police after him.

BENSON (*a little disturbed*). Why do that? Best thing the studio can do is ignore it.

C.F. We can't ignore it. This has brought up the whole paternity issue.

BENSON. What of it?

C.F. Suppose Happy has a skeleton in his closet?

BENSON (*lies on couch*). I don't even know if he's got a closet.

C.F. Save your gags for your pictures. They need them. I've never heard B.K. so excited. (*Crosses to window*) What do you think the reaction will be in the sticks—in the provinces? An illegitimate baby!

BENSON. This is 1935.

C.F. To me, yes. But how many intellectuals have we in America?

BENSON. One.

C.F. You don't seem to realize—

BENSON. Why, this is going to send Happy's stock up one hundred per cent. From now on he's not only cute, he's romantic.

C.F. He's illegitimate! I know America!

CUTTER (*studying the script*). What about Prince Albert? I can cut him out of the picture and you won't even miss him.

C.F. (*crossing below desk*). Yes, yes, Simmons. You go to the cutting room and do the best you know how. (SIMMONS *rises and puts chair up against wall*) I've something more urgent right now. (*Crosses to* SIMMONS) And, for God's sake, Simmons, get me some trumpets that sound like trumpets.

CUTTER (*not gruffly, but politely*). You sure you don't mean a trombone, C.F.?

C.F. No. I mean trumpets. I'm not a musician but I know what I mean. Trumpets—that slide. (*He pantomimes a trombone, of course.*)

BENSON (*to* CUTTER). He wants a slide trumpet.
(CUTTER *exits. Simultaneously through other door* GREEN *and* SLADE *appear.*)

GREEN. Well, we've got that roundelay.

C.F. What do you want? What roundelay?
(*Phone rings.*)

GREEN. Park it, Otto. (*Both go to piano.*)

C.F. (*at phone*). Yes—yes—no, Mr. Friday is not here. He has nothing to say to the press. (*He hangs up.*)

GREEN. You're going to be enthusiastic about this. We've been up all night working on it. (SLADE *starts playing Beethoven's Turkish March. As* C.F. *starts toward the piano, the phone rings*) Smooth, ain't it?

C.F. (*at phone*). Miss Crews? Where's Mrs. Seabrook? Why haven't you got her? (*To* GREEN) I will not listen to any more music.

GREEN. Get a load of this. It's the real McCoy.

C.F. (*at phone*). Yes—I'm holding the line—all right, never mind. Call me. (*Hangs up. To* SLADE *and* GREEN) I'll call the studio guards if you don't stop that infernal din I'll report you to B.K. for insubordination. I'll have your contracts torn up!

GREEN. Are you kidding, or is this on the level?

C.F. Get out!

GREEN. O.K. Don't get tough! Come on, Otto. (*Crosses back of couch to door*) But it's a fine how-do-you-do when you call up a couple of artists late at night and put 'em to work going through Beethoven's symphonies for a little inspiration and then give them the bum's rush just because you ain't in the mood. (GREEN *and* SLADE *exit.*)
(LARRY *and* ROSETTI *enter, both in tails and toppers.*)

ROSETTI. Now calm down, Larry, calm down—

LARRY. I'm not saying a word.

C.F. Where's Mrs. Seabrook? What did you do with her?

LARRY. I don't know, and I don't care.

BENSON (*mockingly*). "I kinda missed the little fella after the day's work was done—"

C.F. (*quickly*). Look here, Larry, I want to know what Susie said. Did she know the young man? What did she say?

LARRY. You listen to what *I* gotta say. I ain't goin' to go through with no contract to play with no unbaptized baby!

ROSETTI (*placatingly*). Just a moment, Larry—

LARRY. I'm through! (*Overwhelmed with the memory*) On the air—with all my fans listening in! I'm serving you notice now. I ain't marrying her. I ain't doing no more pictures with Happy.

ROSETTI. Larry, will you listen to reason?

LARRY. There's only one thing you can do for me, Rosetti. Get me a doctor. I'm going up to my dressing room. I need a sedative.
(LAW *enters quietly.*)

BENSON. Don't stand there. Get him a doctor—

LAW. Take me. I'm a qualified veterinary.
(ROSETTI *exits with* LARRY.)

C.F. Law—
(BENSON *sits up.*)

LAW. Hello, C.F. I just got your message at the hotel. *Young England* in trouble? Well, the old salvaging crew will pitch in. (*Takes off his coat.*)

C.F. Were you there?

LAW. Where? At the opening? Yes. Extraordinary, wasn't it?

BENSON (*significantly*). *We* heard it over the radio.

LAW (*casually*). How'd it come over?

BENSON (*admiringly*). Clear as a bell!

LAW. It certainly broke Larry up. You should have seen our chivalrous hero running from the rescue. Why, the wind whistled right past me!

C.F. Law, do you think that fellow was a crank, or do you think he was really—

LAW (*judicially*). Hard to say. He had a sinister underlip.

C.F. (*into phone*). Miss Crews, did you get Mrs. Seabrook's house? No one answers? Someone *must* answer—she has a ménage! (*Hangs up. Dictograph buzzes*) Hello?

B.K.'S VOICE. Look here, Friday . . .

C.F. Yes, B.K.

B.K.'S VOICE. Did you get any dope on that young man?

C.F. No. I can't get any information. No one seems to know.

B.K.'S VOICE. Why not? I ask you to do the simplest little thing and, as usual, you fall down on me.

C.F. (*piteously*). Why blame me? I was sitting here cutting *Young England.*

B.K.'S VOICE. Don't bother me with *Young England.* You come up here—I want to talk with you.

C.F. Yes, B.K. I'll be right up. (*He moves to the door; sighs*) Sometimes I wonder if this industry is worth the sacrifice. (*He exits.*)

BENSON (*smiles*). What'd you do with him?

LAW. Put him in an office across the hall.

BENSON (*aghast*). What? Why here?

LAW. They won't look for him here.

BENSON. Why didn't you dump him somewhere else?

LAW. And leave him free to roam—and blab? Listen, Benson, B.K.'s called the Chief personally and the whole damn police department is scouring the town for Rodney. (*Crosses to liquor cabinet; pours a drink*) And you don't know what I've been up against with Rodney. (*He drinks*) In his own peculiar English fashion, he's not entirely nitwitted. I had to shove him at the mike, and he's been demanding explanations ever since.

BENSON. One question: What'll we do with him?

LAW (*crossing back to couch; sits*). Frankly, I planned everything but Rodney's disposal. I don't know. But given a little time we'll work this problem out.

BENSON (*really aghast now*). Time?

LAW. Rodney's all right. He doesn't know it, but I've locked him in.

BENSON. Listen: I've got a wife to support! I've got a job to keep! I haven't got Vermont on my mind! I *like* writing pictures! I'm no goddamn realist!

LAW (*soothingly*). Easy, there, easy—

BENSON. If B.K. even dreamed we had anything to do with this we'd be blacklisted in the industry.

LAW (*rising*). Give me a chance to think, will you? Why the panic? I'll admit I've overlooked a few details.

BENSON. Get that guy out of the studio. Put him on a plane to Mexico. Strangle him! I don't care what you do.

LAW. No—no. Murder leads to theft and theft leads to deceit. Haven't you read De Quincey?

BENSON. C.F. may breeze in here any minute. Will you get going?

LAW. Very well, my sweet—I go. (*He starts for door, remembers that he had a coat, looks around room and finally locates it on couch. Gets it and exits. Phone rings.*)

BENSON (*into phone*). Hello . . . Yes, right here. Oh, hello, darling. How are you feeling? (*Tenderly*) Of course I recognized your voice . . . Pearl, I'll be home in half an hour. . . . Less . . . Well, what are you crying about? . . . But I told you I couldn't take you to the opening. Well, if Louise was going why didn't you go with them? They'd be tickled to have you . . . Listen, darling . . . I know . . . I know . . . Yes, I'm listening. . . . (LAW *re-enters—a changed* LAW. *He goes right to the second telephone.*)

LAW (*picking up the second telephone*). Give me the front gate!

BENSON (*into phone*). Yes, darling . . . yes . . . (*Sincerely*) Darling, please—please don't say that.

LAW. Smitty, this is Mr. Law. Any stranger go through the gate in the last ten minutes? . . . No?

BENSON (*sighs*). Yes, darling. . . .

LAW. Well, listen. The fellow that was on the air tonight—Happy's father—yes! He's loose in the studio . . . Yeah. . . .

BENSON (*turns to* LAW, *still holding the phone*). What?

LAW. Grab him and hold him. Don't let anyone come near him. Report to me personally . . . yeah . . .

BENSON. Darling, I'll call you back. (*Slams down the phone.*)

LAW (*hangs up*). The damn cleaning woman let him out!

BENSON (*apoplectic*). I told you, didn't I? I told you you shouldn't have brought him here! (SUSIE *enters. She has been magnificently decked out for the opening, but despite her splendor she seems extremely unhappy.*)

SUSIE. Oh, Mr. Benson . . . I tried to get you at your house but Mrs. Benson said you were here. I tried to get you, too, Mr. Law, at the hotel.

LAW. Now, now, Susie—I know—I know.

SUSIE. Oh, I should never have gone to that opening. I didn't want to go. When I was dressing I put my slip on the wrong side. I knew something terrible was going to happen. And then in the nursery when I went to say good night to Happy, he wouldn't eat his formula. And he wouldn't say good night to me. He was so cross. I told Larry I didn't want to leave Happy—but he insisted—and then the way Larry ran out on me—

LAW (*consolingly*). Now, now—

SUSIE. Why should he do that? Oh, I was so ashamed . . . I didn't even see the picture. And then when I got home—I knew I shouldn't have gone—I should never have left Happy. When I went to the hospital. . . .

LAW. Hospital?

BENSON. Hospital?

SUSIE. They won't let me in . . . not for two weeks.

BENSON (*crosses to* SUSIE). Happy's in the hospital?

SUSIE (*puzzled*). Happy's got the measles.

LAW. What?

SUSIE. And they won't let me come near him.

BENSON. Measles!

LAW. He certainly picked the right time for it!

SUSIE. That's why he wouldn't eat his formula.

C.F.'S VOICE (*offstage; grimly*). Well, we'll see— (*As he opens the door*) I brought you some visitors, boys. Come in. (RODNEY *enters with* STUDIO OFFICER. *To* RODNEY). Are these the men?

RODNEY. They most certainly are.

SUSIE (*crosses to* RODNEY). You know you're not Happy's father.

RODNEY. Of course not, but—

SUSIE. You couldn't be!

RODNEY. Of course not! My dear, I'm very sorry. Look here, we always seem to meet under extraordinary circumstances . . . I never dreamt . . . I'd no idea . . . It was all so spectacular . . . And to do this to you—You were so kind to me . . . They said it was a trailer . . . I didn't realize until I was in the midst of it . . . And then I found myself in a car . . . with him . . . (*Indicates* LAW) I asked him to bring me to you at once. Instead, he locked me in a dusty office.

C.F. So you boys put him up to it!

LAW. Before you say anything you'll be sorry for, C.F. . . . (*Turns to* OFFICER) Smitty, who called you tonight to tell you this unfortunate young man was loose in the studio?

OFFICER. *You* did, Mr. Law.

LAW (*grandly*). That's all.

BENSON. Take him away.

LAW. It's an obvious psychiatric case, C.F.

BENSON (*to* C.F.). I wouldn't be surprised if he's the boy that's been springing out of bushes.

LAW. Certainly. Look at the way he kissed Susie!

RODNEY (*appalled*). But you coached me for hours. Both of you. Wait—here are my lines. (*He fumbles in his pocket*) I know I have them—unless I've lost them.

LAW. So you're an author, too! And I thought it was extemporaneous.

RODNEY. Here—here they are! My dear, will you please read these lines? (*He hands the paper to* SUSIE) They're the very words I spoke over the radio.

SUSIE (*reads and backs away from* RODNEY). You never said *these* lines. You *must* be a crank. Maybe you do spring out of bushes.

RODNEY (*stares*). Oh, I beg your pardon. My lines are on the other side.

LAW (*grabs for paper*). I'll take that! Susie—

C.F. (*taking paper out of* SUSIE'S *hand, brushes* LAW *aside*). Just a minute. (*Reads*) "She's a high-handed rich bitch."—*Tiger Tamer!* —There it is in the corner. *Tiger Tamer* by J. Carlyle Benson and Robert Law!

LAW (*hurt to the quick*). It's a forgery. Benson, we've been framed!

C.F. (*grimly*). This is the last prank you'll ever play. (*Clicks the dictograph.*)

MISS CREWS (*enters*). The new trumpets are here. (*For once,* C.F. *is not interested. The trumpets blare out.*)

C.F. (*into dictograph*). B.K.? I just found out—Benson and Law put that young man on the radio.

B.K.'S VOICE. Are you sure of that?

C.F. I have the proof. The young man is in my office.

B.K.'S VOICE. All right, fire them. I don't want them on this lot. If they think they can get away with that—

C.F. Fire them? Of course I'll fire them.

(LARRY'S *voice is heard as he enters.*)

LARRY. Don't tell me nothing—let go of me. (DOCTOR *and* ROSETTI *enter, following* LARRY *and struggling with him.*)

C.F. Quiet there—

LARRY. Let go of me!

C.F. Larry, I have neither the time nor the patience to pander to actors!

LARRY (*bellowing with the hurt roar of a wounded bull*). No? Babies, huh . . . (*Turns on* SUSIE) You—you—

SUSIE (*frightened; runs to* BENSON). What do you want?

LARRY. What do I want? That goddamn baby of yours has given me the measles!

CURTAIN

ACT THREE

A hospital corridor. Several weeks later. Facing us are several doors, punctuated by the little white cards identifying the patients within.

As the curtain rises, a white-clad NURSE *is walking down the corridor bearing a covered tray. Before she disappears,* BENSON *enters. He knocks on the door of the room where* HAPPY *is ensconced.* SUSIE *opens the door.*

SUSIE. Oh, hello, Mr. Benson. I'd ask you to come in but Happy's still sleeping. The doctor says he can be discharged tomorrow or the day after, he's getting along so fine. Where's Mr. Law?

BENSON. I don't know. We haven't been patronizing the same barrooms.

SUSIE. You look as if you didn't get much sleep.

BENSON (*slumping into a wheel chair*). I didn't.

SUSIE (*pityingly*). Why don't you go home?

BENSON. Home?

SUSIE. Is there anything wrong?

BENSON. Not a thing! Everything's fine.

SUSIE. How's Mrs. Benson?

BENSON. She's fine.

SUSIE. That's good. I called your house to thank her for the radio for Happy but they said you moved.

BENSON. We *were* moved.

SUSIE. You mean you were thrown out?

BENSON. If you want to be technical about it, yes.

SUSIE. Oh, I'm sorry.

BENSON (*broodingly*). What hurts is Aggrafino Jesus.

SUSIE. Who?

BENSON. My favorite Filipino butler. He slapped a lien on my brand-new Packard.

SUSIE. Oh!

BENSON. That's what the missionaries taught *him!*

SUSIE. You boys shouldn't have played that joke on me. You only hurt yourselves. Please don't drink any more, Mr. Benson.

BENSON. So it's come to that! You're going to reform me.

SUSIE. Well, I feel just like a sister to you boys. That's why I couldn't stay mad at you. Please, Mr. Benson, if you need money—I can give you some. I mean—when the studio sends

Happy's checks. They haven't sent them yet.

BENSON (*looking up*). They haven't? How many do they owe you?

SUSIE. Two. I called Mr. Friday but he wouldn't talk to me. Do you think they're docking Happy?

BENSON. They can't do that. Measles are an act of God.
(NURSE *enters with a box of flowers.*)

NURSE. Some flowers for you, Mrs. Seabrook.

SUSIE (*extending her hand for it*). Oh, thank you.

NURSE. And he'd like to know if he can come up to see you. He's downstairs.

SUSIE (*embarrassed*). Oh . . .

BENSON. Who's downstairs? Who's sending you flowers?

SUSIE (*reluctantly*). It's Mr. Bevan. You know—

BENSON. You haven't been seeing our Nemesis?

SUSIE. Oh, no. But he's been writing me every day and sending me flowers. I didn't tell you. I didn't want to get you excited.

BENSON (*to* NURSE; *sweetly*). Tell him to come up, Nurse. And stand by.

SUSIE (*quickly*). Oh, no, Nurse. He's not to come up. I don't want to see him. Ever. And give him back his flowers. (*She hands box back to* NURSE.)

NURSE (*taking it*). Very well. (*She exits.*)

BENSON. Why deprive me of the pleasure of kicking an actor?

SUSIE. It wasn't his fault. After all, you put him up to it.

BENSON (*outraged*). Are you defending him?

SUSIE. Oh, no, I'm just as disappointed in him as you are. But I'm trying to be fair. (*She pauses*) He writes very nice letters. (*A far-away look comes into her eyes.*)

BENSON (*suspiciously*). What kind of letters do you write him?

SUSIE (*hastily*). Oh, I don't write *any* letters.

BENSON. Good!

SUSIE. I'm afraid of my spelling. (LAW *enters. There's an air of on-my-way about him.*)

LAW. Hello, Susie. . . . And goodbye, Susie.

SUSIE. Hello, Mr. Law. Are you going away?

LAW. I am.

SUSIE. Where?

LAW. Where I belong. Vermont. Where you can touch life and feel life, and write it! (*Glares at* BENSON.)

BENSON. When does the great exodus begin?

LAW. In exactly thirty-five minutes. I'm flying back to my native hills, like a homing pigeon. No stopping in New York for me! I've chartered a plane—right to Vermont.

BENSON. Chartered a plane! Where'd you get the money?

LAW (*grudgingly*). Well, there are twelve Rotarians coming along.

BENSON. You'll be back in a week.

SUSIE (*eagerly*). Will you, Mr. Law?

LAW (*scornfully*). Back to what? Sunshine and psyllium seed? Listen, I've got me a little shack overlooking the valley . . . I'm going to cook my own food, chop my own wood, and *write*—

BENSON (*sardonically*). At twenty below?

LAW (*rapturously*). Snow! . . . God, how I love snow! (*He raises his eyes to Heaven.*)

> And since to look at things in
> bloom
> Fifty springs are little room,
> About the woodlands I will go
> To see the cherry—hung with
> snow!

SUSIE. That's poetry.

LAW. A. E. Housman! *Shropshire Lad.* (*He pats the book in his pocket.*)

BENSON. There's plenty of snow in Arrowhead.

LAW. Yeah; they deliver it in trucks. And even when it's real you think it's cornflakes.

SUSIE. You won't drink too much in Vermont, will you, Mr. Law?

LAW. Only the heady wine air that has no dregs!

SUSIE. Because you're crazy enough without drinking.

LAW (*defensively*). I drank for escape . . . escape from myself . . . but now I'm free! I've found peace!

SUSIE. You'll say good-bye to Happy before you go? I want him to remember you.

LAW. Right now!

SUSIE. Wait! I'll see if he's awake. (*She enters* HAPPY'S *room.*)

BENSON. Will you send me a copy of the book—autographed?

LAW. You get copy number one—first edition.

BENSON. What's the book about?

LAW. I'm going to bare my soul . . . I'm going to write life in the raw. I've got the opening all planned—two rats in a sewer!

BENSON. Sounds delightful.

LAW (*scornfully*). You wouldn't appreciate real writing. You've been poisoned. On second thought, I won't send you a book.

BENSON. Tell me more about the rats. What's your story?

LAW (*slightly patronizing*). This isn't a picture that you paste together, Mr. Benson. I'm going to write Life. Life isn't a story . . . it's a discordant overture to death!

BENSON. Well, if you want people to read it, the boy had better meet the girl.

LAW. There is no girl. There is no boy. These are people—real, live people—listen! I'm not even going to use a typewriter! I'm going to weigh every word—with a pencil!

BENSON. Well, maybe you're on the right track. You've got something to say—and the talent to say it with.

LAW. It's finally penetrated!

BENSON. You're probably doing the right thing.

LAW. The only thing. It's different with you—you've got a wife.

BENSON. I had.

LAW. Huh?

BENSON. Oh—uh—Pearl left last night.

LAW. No! I'm sorry.

BENSON (*shrugs*). You can't blame her. She wasn't wild about marrying me in the first place. I coaxed her into it. I painted some pretty pictures for her. It just didn't pan out.

LAW. You still want her?

BENSON (*almost to himself*). I guess I do.

LAW. Personally, I'd say the hell with her.

BENSON (*smiles bitterly*). The trouble is I don't mean it when I say it. (ROSETTI *enters.*)

ROSETTI. Hello, boys.

LAW (*cheerily*). Hello, louse. Get Benson a job, will you? He wants to stay in this God-forsaken hole.

ROSETTI. Listen! I'm not handling second-hand writers. Chicken feed! Right now I'm immersed in a three million dollar deal.

LAW (*interested*). Yeah?

ROSETTI. Yeah. With Gaumont British, and I'm underestimating when I say three million because B.K.'s turned down three million. Why should I bother with writers on the blacklist? So don't go calling me a louse! (SUSIE *enters.*)

SUSIE (*gaily*). Happy has his eyes open. You want to come in now, Mr. Law?

LAW. Coming, Susie. (*He follows* SUSIE *into* HAPPY'S *room.*)

BENSON. Rosetti— (*Going to him, whispering*) Law wants to leave. He's flying in half an hour. Can you call up the studios? Can you get us a one-picture contract? We'll make you our agent for life. *He's leaving!*

ROSETTI. Sure, he's leaving. Nobody wants him.

BENSON. How do you know? You haven't tried.

ROSETTI. I've tried. I don't let my personal feelings interfere with commissions.

BENSON. Listen, I've been a scene painter, prop boy, camera man, director, producer . . . I even sold film in Australia . . . They can't throw me out of this business!

ROSETTI (*crosses to a door and throws it back*). They won't touch you with a ten-foot pole. You, Law, or Happy.

BENSON. Or Happy?

ROSETTI. I gave B.K. a swell angle. Listen in on KNX this afternoon.

BENSON. Huh?

ROSETTI. The world is full of babies. You can get them two for a nickel. (*He opens inner door and meets* LARRY *coming out*) Hello, Larry. I was just coming in to see you. (NURSE *pushes* LARRY *in wheel chair into corridor.*)

LAW'S VOICE. Good-bye, Happy. (*He enters with* SUSIE) Good-bye, Susie.

SUSIE. Good-bye, Mr. Law.

LAW. Hello, Larry. How's every little spot?

LARRY. What's the idea?

LAW. What idea?

LARRY. What's the idea of sending me a box of dead spiders?

LAW. Didn't you like the box?

LARRY. You wait until I'm through convalescing!

NURSE. Now, don't excite yourself. You heard what the doctor said. You're going for your sun bath now. (*She wheels him out.*)

ROSETTI. I'll go along with you, Larry. I've got some great news for you. B.K.'s lending you out to Mascot! (*He exits.*)

LARRY (*as he goes out*). What?

LAW. Well, Susie, take good care of Happy.

SUSIE. Oh, I will.

LAW. Continue your education.

SUSIE. I'm doing that.

LAW (*quickly*). What's the capital of Nebraska?

SUSIE. Lincoln.

LAW. Who hit Sir Isaac Newton on the bean with an apple?

SUSIE. The law of gravity.

LAW. Who said, "Don't give up the ship?"

SUSIE. Captain James Lawrence in the battle of Lake Erie, 1813.

LAW. Don't give up the ship, Susie. I'll write you. (*He kisses her on the forehead.*)

SUSIE. Good-bye, Mr. Law. I've got to go back to Happy. (*Her voice breaks*) I feel awful funny—your going away. (*Exits.*)

BENSON (*finally*). Well, you bastard—get out of here.

LAW. I'm going, stinker. (*Crosses to* BENSON. *They look at each other. A pause. Then* LAW *extends hand. They shake.* LAW *moves to go.*)

BENSON (*without turning*). Say—(LAW *stops*) I don't suppose you'll be interested—Rosetti finally admitted Paramount wants us. Two thousand bucks a week to save Dietrich. We can close the deal in three or four days.

LAW (*turns slowly*). My plane leaves in twenty-five minutes. And you're a liar!

BENSON. I'm not trying to hold you back. But I figured this time you might *save* your money and—

LAW. I can live on twelve dollars a week in Vermont—in luxury!

BENSON. It would kind of help *me* out— If I could lay my hands on some ready dough Pearl might listen to reason.

LAW (*casually*). Well, we loaned out a lot of money in our time. Collect it. And send me my share.

BENSON. I thought of that. The trouble is I don't remember just who it was—and how much. The only one I remember is Jascha Simkovitch.

LAW. Who?

BENSON. Jascha Simkovitch. The fellow that came over with Eisenstein. Don't you remember? You made a wonderful crack about him. He said "There's a price on my head in Russia." And you said, "Yeah—two roubles." (*Laughs. He is flattering* LAW *smoothly.*)

LAW (*laughs with him*). Sure, I remember him. Why, we gave that bed-bug three thousand bucks! Get hold of him and collect it.

BENSON. He's in Paris. What's-his-name came over and said Jascha was living at the Ritz bar.

LAW. Then you can't collect it. Well, I'm off. (*He moves to exit once more.*)

BENSON (*as if struck with sudden thought*). Wait a minute! I've got a great gag for you! Let's call Jascha up in Paris—on Larry's phone! (*Chuckles, throws arms around* LAW. *Both laugh*) Can you imagine Larry's face when he gets the bill? A farewell rib!

LAW (*hesitates*). Have I got time?

BENSON (*reassuringly; looks at his watch*). You've got plenty of time.

LAW. I'll work fast. Stand guard, Benson. (*He enters* LARRY'S *room.* BENSON *follows and partly closes door.*)

LAW'S VOICE. I'm talking for Mr. Toms. I want to put a call through to Paris, France. . . . I want Jascha Simkovitch . . . Hotel Ritz, Paris. . . . Listen, don't worry about the charges . . . That's right—Jascha, as in Heifetz . . . S-i-m-k-o-v-i-t-c-h. (BENSON *closes door on* LAW. NURSE *enters with registered letter, knocks on* SUSIE'S *door.* BENSON *looks at his watch.* SUSIE *appears.*)

NURSE. Registered letter for you, Mrs. Seabrook.

SUSIE. For me?

NURSE. You'll have to sign for it. There's a return receipt on it. (SUSIE *signs.*)

SUSIE. Now what do I do?

NURSE. Now you give me the receipt back and I'll give it to the postman. He's waiting for it. Here's your letter. (NURSE *exits.* SUSIE *opens letter.*)

SUSIE (*cheerily*). Why—it's from Mr. Friday. (LAW *emerges, as she opens the letter.*)

LAW. The service had better be good or there'll be no farewell rib. I haven't got much time.

SUSIE. Oh, didn't you go yet, Mr. Law?

LAW. I'm on my way!

SUSIE (*reading letter*). What does Mr. Friday mean when he says they're taking advantage of Clause 5A?

LAW. What? Let me see that. (*He reads the letter.* BENSON *looks over his shoulder*) Well, this is the goddamnedest . . .

SUSIE. You mustn't swear so much. I don't mind—I'm used to it—but Happy might hear you. What does it mean?

LAW (*reading*). Clause 5A—when an artist through illness—for a period of more than fourteen days—

BENSON. They're just using that for an excuse. It's the paternity issue!

SUSIE. What paternity issue?

BENSON. They're crazy! That kid's going to be as good as he ever was—better.

SUSIE. What does it mean?

LAW. It means, Susie—Happy is out.

SUSIE. Out?

BENSON. Yeah. Finished—done. At the age of eight months— In his prime!

SUSIE. Out of pictures?

BENSON (*turning on* LAW). And there's the man who did it. It was your brilliant idea!

SUSIE (*such a nice girl!*). Oh, no. After all, it was just like a dream. I had to wake up some time.

LAW (*as phone rings*). I guess that's Paris.

SUSIE. What's Paris? (*Phone still rings.*)

BENSON. Go ahead and have your farewell rib, and get out, author! (*Phone still rings.* LAW *enters room.*)

SUSIE. What's Paris?

BENSON (*going to door of* LARRY'S *room*). A city in France.

LAW (*in room*). Hello—right here.—Yes—yes—I'm ready. Hello! . . . Hello—Jascha? Jascha Simkovitch? This is Bobby Law. Is it raining in Paris? . . . well, it's not raining here!

BENSON. Wonderful age we're living in!

LAW (*in room*). Listen, Jascha, are you sober? . . . How come? . . . Oh, you just got there! . . . You're going to London? . . . Today? . . . Hold the wire. (LAW *enters*) I've got an idea! *Let's buy the studio!*

BENSON. What?

LAW. You heard Rosetti. Gaumont British is offering three million. Let's get Jascha to send a cable—sign it Gaumont British—offering four!

BENSON. Why be petty? Offer five!

LAW (*judicially*). Right! (*Exits into room.*)

SUSIE. You boys are very peculiar.

LAW (*in room*). Jascha—got a pencil and paper? Fine. Listen, Jascha, we want you to send a cable from London as follows: Quote. . . .
(LARRY *enters in his wheel chair.* BENSON *closes the door hurriedly.*)

LARRY. Hey, that's my room!

BENSON (*firmly shutting the door*). A private conversation should be private.

LARRY. What's the idea of using my phone?

BENSON. Do you object?

LARRY. Certainly I object. I ain't gonna pay for your calls.

BENSON. All right, if that's the way you feel about it—here's your nickel!

BLACKOUT AND CURTAIN

SCENE II

In Your Own Home. That is, if you have one, and if you listen to the raido.

RADIO ANNOUNCER. Ladies and Gentlemen, this is Station KNX—the Voice of Hollywood. At this time we take great pleasure in announcing the winner of the Royal Studios' Baby Star Contest to find the successor to Happy, who retired from the screen after his illness. Ladies and Gentlemen, the lucky baby is Baby Sylvester Burnett, infant son of Mr. and Mrs. Oliver Burnett of Glendale, California. Congratulations, Mr. and Mrs. Burnett. Contracts for your baby are waiting in Mr. C. Elliot Friday's office at the Royal Studios. Incidentally, Mr. Friday asks that you bring your baby's birth certificate and your marriage license. This is KNX, the Voice of Hollywood. (*Chimes are heard.*)

SCENE III

MR. FRIDAY'S *office, the following day.* MR. FRIDAY *is sitting at his desk, dictating to* MISS CREWS.

C.F. My dear Mr. Pirandello. . . . On second thought, you'd better make that Signor Pirandello. . . . I am writing to ascertain if possibly you have something in your trunk—every author has—which would be uitable as a vehicle for our new baby star, Baby Sylvester Burnett. It can be either a short story or sketch or a few lines which you can jot down at your leisure and which we can whip up into suitable material. I am writing of my own volition as both Mrs. Friday and I are great admirers of you. Very truly yours. . . . Now take a letter to Stark Young. (*Dictograph buzzes*) Yes?

B.K.'S VOICE. Listen, Friday—

C.F. What, B.K.?

B.K.'S VOICE. Come right up here. I want to see you. We've got a new cable from Gaumont British.

C.F. Gaumont British? Yes, sir, I'll be right up. (*He rises*) Miss Crews, have you the contracts for the Burnett baby?

MISS CREWS. Right on your desk, Mr. Friday. And the parents are in the commissary.

C.F. Good. I've got to go up and see B.K. (*Exits.*)

GREEN (*who enters almost simultaneously, followed by* SLADE). Where is he? Where's C.F.?

MISS CREWS. You can't shoot him today.

GREEN. It's a wonder we don't. We're walking up and down in front of the projection room developing an idea when we hear a number—our number— We go in, and it's in *Young England!* Our song! They don't even tell us about it—they murdered it! They run dialogue over it. You got to spot a song—we ask for Guy Lombardo and they give us a six-piece symphony orchestra!

MISS CREWS. If you buy me a handkerchief I promise to cry. Lace, if you don't mind.

GREEN. Lissen—play her the number the way it should be.

MISS CREWS. Must you?

SLADE. Oh, what's the use?

GREEN. Give her the chorus.

SLADE. I'm losing my pep.

GREEN. You might as well hear it. Nobody else will. (SLADE *plays*) Will you listen to that? Ain't it a shame?

You promised love undying,
And begged me to believe;
Then you left, and left me crying
With pain in my heart, and my heart on my sleeve.

I really shouldn't blame you
Because you chose to leave;
But one thing forever will shame you—
It's the pain in my heart, and my heart on my sleeve.

(C.F. *has entered.*)

C.F. Miss Crews!

MISS CREWS. Yes, Mr. Friday?

C.F. Miss Crews, get hold of Benson and Law right away!

MISS CREWS. Who?

C.F. Have Benson and Law come here—immediately.

MISS CREWS. Yes, Mr. Friday.

GREEN (*as* SLADE *pounds away*). That's the chorus! That's the chorus that you murdered!

C.F. Wait a minute, Miss Crews! Get me the hospital. I want to talk to Happy's mother.

MISS CREWS. Yes, Mr. Friday. (*She exits.*)

C.F. Miss Crews! Call my florist and tell him to send Happy a bouquet of roses. And some orchids for his mother, right away. (*He turns to* GREEN) Will you stop that noise! (*He picks up telephone.*)

GREEN. Noise? The song that you murdered? We just wanna see if you got a conscience.

C.F. (*into phone*). Miss Crews, call up Magnin's and tell them to send a radio to the hospital for Happy. One of those slick, modernistic sets in white. And don't forget to have my card put in with the flowers. Did you get Benson and Law? . . . Well, did you get Happy's mother? . . . Well, get them! (*Hangs up.*)

GREEN. Is that a song that you run dialogue over, C.F.?

C.F. What are you babbling about, Green? I haven't used any of your songs in *Young England!*

GREEN (*outraged*). How about *Westminster Abbey in the Moonlight?* They wasn't our lyrics, but it was our tune!

C.F. I used an old Jerome Kern number we've had for years, out of the library.

GREEN (*crestfallen*). You did? (T SLADE) I thought you said it came t you in the middle of the nigh Where? In the library?

C.F. Will you get out of my office

GREEN (*with sudden enthusiasm* We got a new number you'll be craz about.

C.F. I've got too much on my min to listen to your tinny effusions. told the studio to hire Richard Straus and no one else. One great compose is worth twenty of your ilk! (ROSETTI *enters with* LARRY.)

LARRY. Looka here, C.F., I just g out of a sick bed to see you.

C.F. What do you want, Larr (SLADE *plays on*) What do you wan I'm very busy. (*Turns to* GREEN Will you please go? I will not liste

GREEN (*as the worm turns*). . . O.K., music lover! (GREEN *an* SLADE *exit.*)

LARRY. I shouldn't be here. I shou be on my ranch convalescing. I' weak.

C.F. Come to the point, Larry. Com to the point.

LARRY (*bitterly*). What's the idea lending me out to Mascot? I'm a sta I ain't goin' to degrade myself b playing in no undignified thirty-tho sand-dollar feature.

C.F. Larry, face the facts—you' through.

LARRY. That's a nice thing to tell a sick man.

ROSETTI. Now, Larry, I told you. Your attitude is all wrong.

LARRY. Never mind about my attitude.

C.F. (*at the phone*). Miss Crews, have you got Benson and Law? . . . Who's gone to Vermont? . . . What about Susie? . . . What? They left the hospital? (*He hangs up.*)

ROSETTI (*eagerly*). What's up, C.F.?

C.F. (*finally*) This is confidential, Rosetti. (*Lowers his voice*) Gaumont British wants to buy the company intact.

LARRY. Gaumont British?

C.F. They want all our stars, including Happy. Naturally they want him. He's the sensation of London.

ROSETTI. But B.K. turned down three million. I've been handling that deal myself.

C.F. They've raised it. They've just cabled an offer of five million.

ROSETTI. They did? Say, that's marvellous. I'm in on that!

LARRY. Well, you better get me back from Mascot quick. Gaumont British wants *me*. Why, they made me an offer a year ago, only I was tied up.

C.F. They made no mention of you.

LARRY. What?

C.F. Rosetti, we've got to sign Happy immediately. Get hold of Susie and let's close.

ROSETTI. You can sign the three of 'em for a hundred a week. They're broke. And they're low. I'm going right after it. (*He starts for door.*)

LARRY. Come back here. You're supposed to be *my* agent! What are you going to do about *me?*

ROSETTI. You're all right where you are—with Mascot. I'll call you later C.F. (*Exits.*)

LARRY (*to* C.F.) My agent! I been distrustin' that guy for years. (*Exits.*)

C.F. (*Who can balance a budget, picks up phone*). Miss Crews, you didn't send those flowers off, did you? . . . What? . . . But they've left the hospital. What about the radio? . . . Well, call them up right away and cancel it. . . . Who? . . . She's here? Send her right in! (*He crosses to greet* SUSIE. *He is now cordial; hearty, a thing of beauty and a joy forever*). Well, Susie, I'm delighted to see you. You're looking well. I must say we've missed you. I hear the boys are in Vermont.

SUSIE (*stands in door*). Mr. Law was going but he missed the plane.

C.F. (*taken aback*). Well, where are they?

SUSIE. They're in B.K.'s office, getting the contracts.

C.F. Without consulting me?

SUSIE. They said they don't trust you, Mr. Friday.

C.F. Gad! After all I've done for them!

SUSIE (*seating herself on the couch*). Do you mind if I sit here and do my homework? I'm way behind and I don't want to be left back. I'm supposed to wait here until they get B.K.'s signature, and then I'm going to sign.

C.F. I'm going right up to see B.K. (MISS CREWS *enters.*)

MISS CREWS. Mr. and Mrs. Burnett have had their coffee and now they want their contracts.

C.F. What contracts?

MISS CREWS. The parents of the other infant.

C.F. What other infant? What other infant is there except Happy?

MISS CREWS. But what'll I do with them?

C.F. Send them away. (*Now he sees* RODNEY *looking in through door.* RODNEY *has a large box of flowers*) What do you want?

RODNEY. Here's the check for the milk—and other odd items.

C.F. Check.

RODNEY. I think you'll find it correct. I verified it at the commissary. And of course I included a service charge —and interest at six per cent. The total is two dollars and eighty-four cents. Thank you. (*Dictograph buzzes.*)

C.F. (*into dictograph*). Hello—

B.K.'S VOICE. Listen, Friday, you might as well be here. I'm settling the Happy contract with Benson and Law.

C.F. Yes, B.K. I'm coming right up. (*Phone rings; into phone*) What? . . . I never asked for trumpets in the first place. I don't want any trumpets. I want a period of utter silence. See that I get it. (*Hangs up. To* RODNEY) *You* get out!

RODNEY (*firmly*). I've something to say to Mrs. Seabrook. (SUSIE *turns away. Softly*) I brought you some flowers.

C.F. Give her her flowers, and get out And don't let me find you here when I come back. Miss Crews, I'll be up in B.K.'s office. (*He exits.*)

RODNEY. I know you don't want to see me. (*Extends flowers*) Won't you take them? (MISS CREWS *exits*) I wrote, you know. I explained everything.

SUSIE (*still not facing him*). Happy's not allowed to have flowers.

RODNEY. Oh, but they're for Happy's mother—from Happy's father.

SUSIE (*turning; aghast*). Are you joking about what you did?

RODNEY. I'm not joking. Lord, no. I mean it. Look here—will you marry me? (SUSIF *stares at him*) I've thought it all out. I owe it to you. Shall we consider it settled?

SUSIE. Did Mr. Law and Mr. Benson put you up to this, too?

RODNEY. Good Lord, no. I haven't seen them and, what's more, I don't intend to.

SUSIE. Then why do you want to marry me?

RODNEY. I owe it to you.

SUSIE (*angrily*). That's no reason.

RODNEY. My visa's expired—I've two days' grace. I must get a train this afternoon. Are you coming with me?

SUSIE. I don't think you'd make a very sensible father for Happy. I don't think so at all.

RODNEY. I'm not at all sensible. I'm frightfully stupid—impulsive—emotional—but I'm not really at my best these days. Most people aren't when they're infatuated.

SUSIE. You couldn't be infatuated with me!

RODNEY. But I am. Look here, it's no good debating. My mind's made up. I don't frequently make it up, but when I do, I stick to the end.

SUSIE. But you don't know about my past.

RODNEY. I've been through all that, in my mind. It doesn't matter.

SUSIE. But it does. I'm ashamed to tell you.

RODNEY. Please don't, then.

SUSIE. Happy's father was a bigamist.

RODNEY. Eh?

SUSIE. He married twice.

RODNEY. Is that it?

SUSIE. What did you think?

RODNEY. It doesn't really matter.

SUSIE. I didn't know he was married before.

RODNEY. But, good Lord, nobody can blame *you*.

SUSIE. His wife did.

RODNEY. Naturally.

SUSIE. How was I to know? And it wasn't his fault, either. He got a Mexican divorce and he didn't know it wasn't good.

RODNEY. Oh!

SUSIE (*drawing herself up à la Fairfax*). So I said to him, "Your duty is to your first wife." And I ran away. I didn't know I was going to have Happy, then.

RODNEY. Have you—heard from him?

SUSIE. Oh, no. Of course, he should have told me in the first place. But he was infatuated, too, and I didn't know any better.

RODNEY. Well, have you divorced him?

SUSIE. No.

RODNEY. You'll have to clear that matter up, I think—immediately.

SUSIE. I can't clear it up. He's dead.

RODNEY. Oh!

SUSIE. She shot him.

RODNEY. His wife?

SUSIE. Yes.

RODNEY. Good Lord!

SUSIE. I hear from her sometimes. She's awfully sorry.

RODNEY (*brightly*). Well then, you're free to marry, aren't you?

SUSIE. Oh, I'm free, but the point is —do I want to? After all, I don't know you very well, and every time we meet something terrible happens. I didn't know Jack very well, either, and look what happened to him. I've go to be careful.

RODNEY. But I'm not a bigamist.

SUSIE. Maybe not. You may be something else.

RODNEY. But the British Consul'll vouch for me. He knows my family. I haven't had much of a life, but it's an open book.

SUSIE. Oh, I believe you. But I can't listen to my heart. I've got to listen to my head.

RODNEY. Of course, I haven't much to offer you. I've just come into a little money, and on my thirtieth birthday I come into a great deal more. We can have a flat in London and one of my aunts is going to leave me a place in the country.

SUSIE. That's in Europe, isn't it?

RODNEY. Yes, of course.

SUSIE. Oh, I couldn't go to Europe.

RODNEY. But why not?

SUSIE. The boys want to put Happy back in pictures.

RODNEY. I wouldn't hear of it. That's no life for a baby. Thoroughly abnormal. And, furthermore, I don't like the California climate. Now in England we have the four seasons.

SUSIE. You have?

RODNEY (*ardently*). Summer, winter, spring and fall.

SUSIE (*finally*). I want to ask you something.

RODNEY. Certainly.

SUSIE. When I come into a room—does something happen to you?

RODNEY. Eh? Of course—very much so.

SUSIE (*rises and turns away*). Well, I'll think it over.

RODNEY (*rises and takes* SUSIE'S *arm*). Look here, I couldn't possibly take no for an answer.

SUSIE. Of course, when you come into a room, something happens to me, too.

RODNEY. Does it really? (SUSIE *nods. He takes her in his arms. They kiss. Door opens and* LAW *enters with* BENSON.)

LAW. Susie, did my eyes deceive me? Were you kissing an actor?

BENSON. What's that?

LAW (*to* BENSON). An English actor!

BENSON. What? Didn't I tell you—?

SUSIE. Boys, I've been thinking it over—

BENSON (*wearily drops down to piano;* LAW *down to end of couch*) With what?

SUSIE. I'm going to marry Rodney and I'm going to Europe. They've got the four seasons over there, and Happy'll be normal.

RODNEY. Well put, my dear.
(C.F. *enters.*)

SUSIE. So I don't think I'd better sign the contract.

RODNEY. Most certainly not!

C.F. You're not going to sign Happy?

LAW. Susie, I've just given up Vermont for a whole year—for you. A whole year out of my life—because B.K. begged me to stay and handle Happy. I've sacrificed a great book—for what? A paltry fifteen hundred dollars a week? I didn't want it!

C.F. If she doesn't sign, we'll break that contract with you, Law.

LAW. Try and do it.

SUSIE. I'm going to Europe with Rodney.

LAW. Do you want to tell Happy he's out of pictures? Do you want to break his little heart?

SUSIE. He'll understand.

BENSON (*suddenly*). Do you know who Rodney is? English Jack! Confidence man.

LAW (*quickly*). Yes! Ship's gambler, petty racketeer and heartbreaker.
(RODNEY *tries to speak.*)

BENSON. Served two terms for bigamy!

SUSIE. Bigamy?

RODNEY. But that's absurd.

BENSON (*bitterly*). I've seen hundreds of your kind in Limehouse.

C.F. So have I!

BENSON (*quietly*). Listen, C.F., stay off our side!

RODNEY (*to* SUSIE). You don't believe this, of course. They can't possibly believe it themselves.

LAW. Brazening it out, eh? As sure as God made little green apples—and He did—you're not coming near Susie. We'll have you in the can and out of the country by morning.

BENSON. No sooner said— (*Into phone*) Get me the Department of Justice.

SUSIE (*to* RODNEY). You see? Something terrible always happens when you come.

LAW (*to* SUSIE). And you—sign that contract immediately.

RODNEY. She'll do nothing of the sort. You're not to intimidate her. Do you hear?
(*Door opens and* LARRY *enters, accompanied by middle-aged English gentleman.*)

LARRY. Come on in here, Major.

C.F. What do you want, Larry? I'm busy.

BENSON (*into telephone*). Department of Justice? I want two of your best operatives to come down to the Royal Studios immediately. Report to Mr. Friday's office.

SUSIE. Oh, but you can't do that—

LARRY (*angrily*). Just a minute. Major Thompson is the representative here of Gaumont British.

C.F. Oh! I'm sorry. We've been rather upset. How do you do, Major? I'm Mr. Friday.

MAJOR. How do you do, sir? I won't be a moment. Mr. Toms suggested I come down here. He told me you'd received a cable from my home office.

C.F. Yes—yes—

MAJOR. He was rather upset because his name wasn't mentioned.

C.F. Yes, yes—

MAJOR. I called my home office, and they assure me they never sent such a cable.

C.F. What?

LARRY. That's what! It was a phony!

RODNEY (*who has been trying to attract attention for some time*). Major!

MAJOR. Well! Aren't you— Why, how do you do? I thought I recognized you. Met up with your brother. By the way, I saw him a few weeks ago just before I sailed. Particularly asked me to look you up.

RODNEY. Is my name English Jack? Am I a ship's gambler? Have I served sentences for bigamy?

MAJOR. Good Gad, no!

RODNEY. Will you vouch for me?

MAJOR (*a bore of bores*). Vouch for Puffy Bevan? Delighted! His brother —splendid chap— I met him first in India—he's a captain in the Coldstream Guards. His father is Lord Severingham. His sister is Lady Beasley—lectures, I believe. Now, let me see—

LAW (*interrupting*). Did you say—Lord Severingham?

MAJOR. Yes.

BENSON. I beg your pardon, sir—*his* father? (*He indicates* RODNEY.)

MAJOR. Yes.
(BENSON *shakes his head in wonder.*)

SUSIE. Is your father a lord?

RODNEY. It doesn't matter, does it?

SUSIE. If you don't care, I don't care.

MAJOR. If I can be of any further service—

RODNEY. No. I think we'll sail along beautifully now. Thanks.

MAJOR. Good afternoon. (*Shakes hands with* RODNEY.)

C.F. Who sent that cable? That's all I want to know! Who sent that cable! (MAJOR *and* LARRY *exit*) Who perpetrated this hoax? Who's responsible for this outrage? By Gad, I'll find out! (*Exits.*)

RODNEY (*turns to* SUSIE). Shall we go?

SUSIE. Good-bye, boys. Take care of yourselves.

LAW (*bows; bitterly*). Thank you, milady.

SUSIE. Don't drink too much.

LAW. Thank you, milady.

SUSIE. You were awful good to me. Yes, they were, Rodney. They were awful good to me sometimes.

RODNEY. In that case, I don't mind shaking hands with you. (*Starts toward* LAW.)

LAW (*quickly*). Don't shake hands. Just go. Dissolve—*slow fade-out!*

BENSON (*pantomiming*). Shimmer away!

RODNEY. Eh? (*Shrugs*) Well—come, Susie.

SUSIE (*waving a delicate little hand*). Good-bye, boys. (*Pause. They exit in silence.*)

LAW (*tense*). I wonder what C.F.'s up to?

BENSON (*struck all of a heap*).The hell with that. Look at it—it checks! Cinderella—Prince Charming—Boy meets girl. . . . Boy loses girl. . . . Boy gets girl! Where's your damned realism now?

(C.F. *enters. He looks grimly at the boys.*)

C.F. (*finally*) Well—it's a good thing you boys are not mixed up in this! (*He goes to desk.*)

BENSON (*slowly*). What?

LAW (*slowly*). What happened, C.F.?

C.F. I don't understand it at all. The cable was sent from London all right. But B.K. should have known it was a fake. It was sent collect. (*He picks up phone.*)

LAW. Jascha always sends collect.

C.F. Huh? (*Into phone*) Miss Crews, get hold of the Burnett baby immediately. . . . Who? . . . the *what* is here? (*Puzzled. The answer comes in the clarion call of the trumpets, blaring their gay, lilting notes through the windows. Ta-ra-ta-ta-ta-ta-tata-tata-tata! So much pleasanter than a factory whistle, don't you think?*)

CURTAIN

The Women

BY CLARE BOOTHE

TO BUFF COBB

WITH LOVE

The Women was first produced at the Ethel Barrymore Theatre, New York City, by Max Gordon, on December 26, 1936, and closed on July 9, 1938. Following is the original cast:

JANE	Anne Teeman
SYLVIA (Mrs. Howard Fowler)	Ilka Chase
NANCY BLAKE	Jane Seymour
PEGGY (Mrs. John Day)	Adrienne Marden
EDITH (Mrs. Phelps Potter)	Phyllis Povah
MARY (Mrs. Stephen Haines)	Margalo Gillmore
MRS. WAGSTAFF	Ethel Jackson
OLGA	Ruth Hammond
FIRST HAIRDRESSER	Mary Stuart
SECOND HAIRDRESSER	Jane Moore
PEDICURIST	Ann Watson
EUPHIE	Eloise Bennett
MISS FORDYCE	Eileen Burns
LITTLE MARY	Charita Bauer
MRS. MOREHEAD	Jessie Busley
FIRST SALESWOMAN	Doris Day
SECOND SALESWOMAN	Jean Rodney
HEAD SALESWOMAN	Lucille Fenton
FIRST MODEL	Beryl Wallace
THIRD SALESWOMAN	Martina Thomas
CRYSTAL ALLEN	Betty Lawford
A FITTER	Joy Hathaway
SECOND MODEL	Beatrice Cole
PRINCESS TAMARA	Arlene Francis
EXERCISE INSTRUCTRESS	Anne Hunter
MAGGIE	Mary Cecil
MISS WATTS	Virgilia Chew
MISS TRIMMERBACK	Mary Murray
A NURSE	Lucille Fenton
LUCY	Marjorie Main
COUNTESS DE LAGE	Margaret Douglass
MIRIAM AARONS	Audrey Christie

Helene	Arlene Francis
Sadie	Marjorie Wood
Cigarette Girl	Lillian Norton

Directed by Robert B. Sinclair
Settings designed by Jo Mielziner
Costumes supervised by John Hambleton

SCENES

ACT ONE

SCENE I

Mary Haines' living room. A winter afternoon

SCENE II

A hairdresser's. An afternoon, a few days later

SCENE III

Mary's boudoir, an hour later

SCENE IV

A fitting room. An afternoon, two months later

ACT TWO

SCENE I

An exercise room, two weeks later

SCENE II

Mary's kitchen, midnight, a few days later

SCENE III

Mary's living room, a month later

SCENE IV

A hospital room, a month later

SCENE V

A Reno hotel room, a few weeks later

ACT THREE

SCENE I

Crystal's bathroom, early evening, two years later

SCENE II

Mary's bathroom, eleven-thirty, the same night

SCENE III

The Powder Room at the Casino Roof, near midnight, the same night

THE WOMEN

ACT ONE

SCENE I

MARY HAINES' *living room. Today, Park Avenue living rooms are decorated with a significant indifference to the fact that ours is still a bisexual society. Period peacock alleys, crystal-hung prima-donna roosts, they reflect the good taste of their mistresses in everything but a consideration of the master's pardonable right to fit into his own home decor.* MARY HAINES' *living room is not like that. It would be thought a comfortable room by a man. This, without sacrificing its own subtle, feminine charm. Above the fireplace, there is a charming portrait of Mary's children— a girl of 11, a boy of 5 or 6. Right, a door to the living quarters. Left, another to the hall. Center, a sofa, armchair, tea-table group; and in the good light from the window, a bridge-table group.*

As the curtain rises JANE, *a pretty and quite correct little Irish-American maid, is arranging the tea table.* FOUR WOMEN *are playing bridge in a smoking-car cloud of smoke. They are:*

NANCY, *who is sharp, but not acid; sleek but not smart; a worldly and yet virginal 35. And her partner—*

PEGGY, *who is pretty, sweet, 25.* PEGGY'S *character has not, will never quite, "jell." And—*

SYLVIA, *who is glassy, elegant, feline, 34. And her partner—*

EDITH, *who is a sloppy, expensively dressed (currently, by Lane Bryant) matron of 33 or 34. Indifferent to everything but self,* EDITH *is incapable of either deliberate maliciousness or spontaneous generosity.*

SYLVIA. So I said to Howard, "What do you expect me to do? Stay home and darn your socks? What do we all have money for? Why do we keep servants?"

NANCY. You don't keep them long, God knows—(*Placing the pack of cards*) Yours, Peggy.

PEGGY. Isn't it Mrs. Potter's? I opened with four spades. (SYLVIA *firmly places the pack before* PEGGY. PEGGY *wrong again, deals.*)

SYLVIA. Second hand, you did. And went down a thousand. (*Patronizingly*) Peggy, my pet, you can't afford it.

PEGGY. I can too, Sylvia. I'm not a pauper.

SYLVIA. If your bridge doesn't improve, you soon will be.

NANCY. Oh, shut up, Sylvia. She's only playing till Mary comes down.

SYLVIA (*querulously*). Jane, what's Mrs. Haines doing up there?

JANE (*reproachfully*). It's that lingerie woman *you* sent her, Mrs. Fowler.

SYLVIA. I didn't expect Mrs. Haines to buy anything. I was just trying to get rid of the creature. (JANE *exits*) Peggy, bid.

PEGGY. Oh, mine? By.

SYLVIA (*looking at* PEGGY). She won't concentrate.

NANCY. She's in love, bless her. After the child's been married as long as you girls, she may be able to concentrate on vital matters like bridge.

SYLVIA (*bored*). Another lecture on the Modern Woman?

NANCY. At the drop of a hat. By.

SYLVIA. I consider myself a perfectly good wife. I've sacrificed a lot for Howard Fowler—two spades. I devote as much time to my children as any of my friends.

NANCY. Except Mary.

SYLVIA. Oh, Mary, of course. Mary is an exception to all of us.

NANCY. Quite right. (*They are waiting for* PEGGY *again*) Peggy?

PEGGY (*uncertainly*). Two no trumps?
(EDITH *rises suddenly. Plainly, she feels squeamish.*)

SYLVIA (*wearily*). Edith, not *again*?

EDITH. I shouldn't have eaten that alligator pear. Morning sickness! I heave the whole darn day. This is positively the last time I go through this lousy business for any man! Four spades. If men had to bear babies, there'd never be—

NANCY. —more than one child in a family. And he'd be a boy. By.
(EDITH *sinks on the edge of her chair, lays down her cards.*)

PEGGY. I wish *I* were having a baby. We can't afford one now.

SYLVIA. And you'll never be able to, until you know Culbertson. (*Arranging* EDITH'S *cards*) Honestly, Edith! Why didn't you show a slam?

EDITH (*rising hurriedly*). Oh, I *have* got to unswallow. Wait till you've had three, Peggy. You'd wish you'd never gotten past the bees and flowers. (*Exits precipitously.*)

NANCY (*disgusted*). Poor, frightened, bewildered madonna!

SYLVIA. I'm devoted to Edith Potter. But she does get me down. You'd think she had a hard time. Dr. Briggs says she's like shelling peas. She ought to go through what *I* went through. Nobody *knows!*

NANCY. No clubs, partner?

SYLVIA. So when Cynthia came, I had a Cæsarian. You should see my stomach— It's a slam!

NANCY. Are you sure?

SYLVIA. Got the king, Peggy? (PEGGY *obligingly plays the king*) Thanks, dear, it's a slam. And the rubber. (*Rises, lights a fresh cigarette, goes to armchair and perches*) But I've kept my figure. I must say, I don't blame Phelps Potter for playing around.

PEGGY. Oh, does her husband . . . ?

SYLVIA. Oh, Phelps has made passes at all us girls. I do think it's bad taste for a man to try to make his wife's friends, *especially* when he's bald and fat. I told him once, "Phelps Potter," I said, "the next time you grab at me, I'm going straight to Edith."

NANCY. And did you?

SYLVIA. Certainly not. I wouldn't say anything to hurt Edith for the world. Well, you can't blame the men. But I'll say one thing for Edith. She's not as dumb as *some* of my friends. She's on to her husband.

PEGGY (*bravely*). Do you think *he* is on to her?

SYLVIA. What do you mean?

PEGGY. If he could only hear her talk about him!

SYLVIA. Listen, Peggy, do we know how men talk about us when we're not around?

NANCY. I've heard rumors.

SYLVIA. Exactly. Peggy, you haven't been married long enough to form a private opinion of your husband.

PEGGY. Well, if I had one, I'd keep it to myself. Do you think I'd tell anybody in the world about the quarrels John and I have over money? I'd be too proud!
(*Enter* EDITH. *Goes to tea table, and gathers a handful of sandwiches.*)

SYLVIA. All over, dear?

EDITH. Oh, that was a false alarm. What happened?

SYLVIA. Only a slam, dear. You do underbid.

EDITH. I'll bet you had me on the pan.

SYLVIA. I never say behind my friends' backs what I won't say to their faces. I said you ought to diet.

EDITH. There's no use dieting in my condition. I've got to wait until I can begin from scratch. Besides, I've got the most wonderful cook. She was with Mary. She said Mary let her go because she was too extravagant. I think this cook Mary has is too, too homey. (*Examines sandwich*) Water cress. I'd just as soon eat my way across a front lawn.

SYLVIA. I think Mary's gone off terribly this winter. Have you noticed those deep lines, here? (*Draws her finger around her mouth.*)

NANCY. Smiling lines. Tragic, aren't they?

SYLVIA. Perhaps they *are*. Maybe a woman's headed for trouble when she begins to get too—smug.

NANCY. Smug? Don't you mean, happy?

PEGGY. Mr. Haines adores her so!

SYLVIA (*snickering and flashing* EDITH *a significant glance*). Yes, doesn't he?

NANCY (*coldly*). You just can't bear it, Sylvia, can you?

SYLVIA. Bear what?

NANCY. Mary's happiness. It gets you down.

SYLVIA. Nancy Blake, if there's one thing I can say for myself, I've never been jealous of another woman. Why should I be jealous of Mary?

NANCY. Because she's contented. Contented to be what she is.

SYLVIA. Which is what?

NANCY. A woman.

EDITH. And what, in the name of my revolting condition, are we?

NANCY. Females.

SYLVIA. Really. And what are you, pet?

NANCY. What nature abhors. I'm—a virgin—a frozen asset.

EDITH. I wish I were a virgin again. The only fun I ever had was holding out on Phelps. Nancy, you ought to thank God every night you don't have to make sacrifices for some man.

PEGGY. I wish I could make a little money writing, the way you do, Miss Blake.

NANCY. If you wrote the way I do, that's just what you'd make.

SYLVIA. You're not exactly a popular author, are you, dear?

NANCY. Not with you. Well, good news, Sylvia. My book is finished and once again I'm about to leave your midst.

PEGGY. Oh, I wish we could afford to travel. Where do you go this time, Miss Blake?

NANCY. Africa, shooting.

SYLVIA. Well, darling, I don't blame you. I'd rather face a tiger any day than the sort of things the critics said about your last book.
(*Enter* MARY. *She is a lovely woman in her middle thirties. She is what most of us think our happily married daughters are like. She is carrying several white boxes.*)

MARY. Sorry, girls. (*Teasing*) Sylvia, must you always send me woebegone creatures like that lingerie woman? It's been a very expensive half hour for me.

PEGGY (*looking at* SYLVIA). For me too, Mrs. Haines.

MARY (*laughing*). Nonsense, Peggy, you were playing for me. Here. (*Hands* PEGGY *a box*) Don't open it now. It's a bed-jacket. Or a tea cozy. Or something padded. I wouldn't know. I was crying so hard.

SYLVIA. You didn't believe that woman's sob story?

MARY. Of course I did. (*She really didn't*) Anyway, she's a lot worse off than you and I. (*Putting down another box*) Edith, wee garments—

EDITH. Darling, how sweet! (*It comes over her again*) Oh, my God! I'm sick as a cat. (*Sits.*)

SYLVIA. It's a girl. Girls always make you sicker.

NANCY. Even before they're born?

EDITH. I don't care what it is. I've lost everything including my curiosity. Why did God make it take nine months?

NANCY (*helpfully*). It takes an elephant seven years.

EDITH. I wish I were an elephant. I'll look like one anyway before I'm finished. And it would be heaven not to worry for seven years.

MARY (*laughing*). Oh, Edith, it is rather trying. But when it's all over, isn't it the grandest thing in the world to have them?

EDITH. Well, I'd love mine just as much if they came out of cabbages.

NANCY. And I dare say your husband would hardly notice the difference.

JANE (*entering with teakettle*). Ma'am, Mr. Haines would like to speak to you on the phone.

MARY. Oh, I can feel what it is in my bones, Jane. (*To the others*) Stephen's going to be kept at the office again tonight. (*Exits.*)

SYLVIA. Give him my love, pet.

MARY (*offstage*). I will.

SYLVIA (*she never lets anything pass*). Nancy, you couldn't be more wrong about me and Mary.

NANCY. Still rankling?

SYLVIA. Jealous? As a matter of fact, I'm sorry for her.

NANCY. Oh-ho? Why?

SYLVIA (*mysteriously*). Well, for all *we* know she may be living in a fool's paradise with Stephen.

NANCY. Let's check that one for a moment, Sylvia. Jane, are the children in?

JANE. Yes, Miss. Just back from the Park.

(EDITH *rises*—SYLVIA, *in pantomime, signals her not to leave room. This is not lost on* NANCY. *For a moment she hesitates at the door.*)

PEGGY. Oh, I'd love to see Mrs. Haines' little girl, Miss Blake—

NANCY (*following* PEGGY). Come along, child. Anyway, it's our turn to go on the pan. But we don't have to worry. You've got a poor man. I've got no man at all. (*They exit.*)

EDITH (*goes to tea table—pours two cups.* JANE *empties ash trays*). This is positively the last time I play bridge with Nancy. She never misses a chance to get in a dig. What has a creature like her got but her friends? (JANE *exits, closing door, left.* SYLVIA *stealthily closes door, right*) The way she kept at you about Mary made me so nervous, I thought I'd scream. And in my condition—

SYLVIA. Edith, I've got to tell you! I'll burst if I wait!

EDITH. I *knew* you had something! (*She brings her well-laden plate and teacup and settles herself happily beside* SYLVIA *on the sofa.*)

SYLVIA. You'll die!

EDITH. Mary?

SYLVIA. No, Stephen. Guess!

EDITH. You couldn't mean . . . ?

SYLVIA (*nodding*). Stephen Haines is cheating on Mary!

EDITH. I don't believe you; is it true?

SYLVIA. Wait till you hear. (*Now she is into it*) You know I go to Michael's for my hair. You ought to go, pet. I despise whoever does yours. Well, there's the most wonderful new manicurist there. (*Shows her scarlet nails*) Isn't that divine? Jungle Red—

EDITH. Simply divine. Go on.

SYLVIA. It all came out in the most extraordinary way, this morning. I tried to get you on the phone—

EDITH. I was in the tub. Go on.

SYLVIA. This manicurist, she's marvelous, was doing my nails. I was looking through *Vogue*, the one with Mary in the Beaux Arts Ball costume—

EDITH. —in that white wig that flattered her so much?

SYLVIA (*nodding*). Well, this manicurist: "Oh, Mrs. Fowler," she said, "is that that Mrs. Haines who's so awfully rich?"

EDITH. Funny how people like that think people like us are awfully rich.

SYLVIA. I forget what she said next. You know how those creatures are, babble, babble, babble, babble, and never let up for a minute! When suddenly she said: "I know the girl who's being *kept* by Mr. Haines!"

EDITH. No!

SYLVIA. I swear!

EDITH (*thrilled*). Someone *we* know?

SYLVIA. No! That's what's so awful about it. She's a friend of this manicurist. Oh, it wouldn't be so bad if Stephen had picked someone in his own class. But a blonde floosie!

EDITH. But how did Stephen ever meet a girl like that?

SYLVIA. How do men ever meet girls like that? That's what they live for, the rats!

EDITH. But—

SYLVIA. I can't go into all the details, now. They're utterly fantastic—

EDITH. You suppose Mary knows?

SYLVIA. Mary's the kind who couldn't help showing it.

EDITH (*nodding, her mouth full of her third cake*). No self-control. Well, she's bound to find out. If a woman's got any instincts, she feels when her husband's off the reservation. I know *I* would.

SYLVIA. Of course you do, darling. Not Mary— (*Rises, and walks about the room, wrestling with* MARY'S *sad problem*) If only there were some way to *warn* her!

EDITH (*horrified, following her*). Sylvia! You're not going to tell her?

SYLVIA. Certainly not. I'd *die* before I'd be the one to hurt her like that!

EDITH. Couldn't someone shut that manicurist up?

SYLVIA. A good story like that? A lot those girls care whose life they ruin.

EDITH. *Isn't* it a dirty trick?

SYLVIA. Isn't it *foul?* It's not as though only Mary's friends knew. We could keep our mouths shut.

EDITH. I know plenty that I never *breathe* about my friends' husbands!

SYLVIA. So do I! (*They exchange a sudden glance of sharp suspicion*) Anyway, the whole thing's disgustingly unfair to Mary. I feel like a disloyal skunk, just knowing about it—

EDITH. I adore her—

SYLVIA. I *worship* her. She's my dearest friend in all the world— (*Voices, offstage. They sit down at the card table and begin to play solitaire hastily. Enter* NANCY *and* PEGGY.)

NANCY. Well, Sylvia, feeling better?

SYLVIA (*innocently*). Meaning what?

NANCY. Must've been choice. You both look so *relaxed.*

SYLVIA. Nancy, were you listening at that door?

PEGGY. Oh, Mrs. Fowler, we were in the nursery.
(MARY *enters.*)

SYLVIA (*quickly*). Well, darling, how is Stephen, the old dear? And did you give him my love?

MARY. I did. Stephen's not so well. Sylvia.

SYLVIA. Oh? What's the trouble?

MARY. Nervous indigestion. That's why I have such a plain cook now.

EDITH. Phelps has had indigestion for years. You should hear that man rumble in the night. Like a truck on cobblestones.

SYLVIA. There's nothing—worrying Stephen?

MARY. Oh. no, he's just been working late. He's not coming home tonight. Oh, I wish— (*Abruptly, with an indulgent laugh*) Well, man's love is of man's life a thing apart, 'tis woman's whole—et cetera.

SYLVIA. Are you sure it's *work,* darling, and not a beautiful blonde?

MARY. Stephen? (*Laughing, and perhaps a little smugly, too*) Oh, Sylvia.

EDITH (*afraid that* SYLVIA *will go too far*). Sylvia, let's play!

SYLVIA. Stephen's a very attractive man.

MARY. Isn't he? I can't imagine why he hasn't deserted me for some glamorous creature long ago.

NANCY (*alarmed*). Mary, you *do* sound smug.

MARY. Oh, let me be, Nancy. How can you be too sure of what you believe in most?

SYLVIA. I wouldn't be sure of the Apostle Paul. I always tell Howard, "If you ever manage to make a fool of me, I'll deserve what I get."

NANCY. You certainly will. (*Faces* SYLVIA *squarely*) Now, Sylvia, let's have it.

SYLVIA. Have what?

NANCY. Just what did you mean when you said Mary was living in a fool's paradise?

MARY. What?

SYLVIA (*angrily*). Nancy, don't be absurd. (*A pause. Then, wriggling out of it*) Oh, Mary, I was just trying to make a typical Nancy Blake wisecrack about marriage. I said, "A woman's paradise is always a fool's paradise!"

MARY. That's not bad, is it, Nancy? Well, Sylvia, whatever I'm living in, I like it. Nancy, cut.

SYLVIA (*examines her nails minutely, suddenly shows them to* MARY). Mary, how do you like that?

NANCY (*not looking*). Too, too adorable.

SYLVIA. You can't imagine how it stays on. I get it at Michael's—you ought to go, Mary!

EDITH (*protestingly*). Oh, Sylvia!—

SYLVIA. A wonderful new manicurist. Olga's her name. She's marvelous.

EDITH. Will you cut, Sylvia?

SYLVIA. Look, Jungle Red.

NANCY. Looks as if you'd been tearing at somebody's throat.

SYLVIA. I'll be damned, Nancy, if I'll let you ride me any more!

MARY. Now, Sylvia, Nancy's just being clever too.

SYLVIA. She takes a crack at everything about me. Even my nails!

MARY (*laughing*). Well, I like it. I really do! It's new and smart. (*Pats her hand*) Michael's, Olga, Jungle Red? I'll remember that. (*Cuts cards*) You and I, Sylvia. I feel lucky today.

SYLVIA (*with a sweet, pitying smile*). *Do* you, darling? Well, you know what they say, "Lucky in cards"—

CURTAIN

SCENE II

An afternoon, a few days later. A hairdressing booth in Michael's. An elegantly functional cubbyhole. Right, a recessed mirror in the wall. Left, from the high partition pole, a curtain to the floor. The rear wall is a plain partition. Center, a swivel hairdressing chair. Above it from an aluminum tree, the hanging thicket of a permanent-wave machine. In the wall, gadgets for curling irons, electric outlets which connect with wires to the drying machine, the hand drier, the manicurists' table-light; stools for the pedicurist, the manicurist, OLGA.

As the curtain rises, the booth is, to put it mildly, full.

MRS. WAGSTAFF, *a fat, elderly woman, is in the chair, undergoing the punishment of a permanent. Wires and clamps, Medusa-like, rise from her head to the cap of the machine.*

OLGA, *at her right, is doing her nails. Her fat bare feet rest in the lap of the* PEDICURIST. *The* FIRST HAIRDRESSER *cools her steaming locks with a hand-drier. The* SECOND HAIRDRESSER, *watch in hand, fiddles with the wires, times the operation. When the machine is working, a small, red light glows among the wires.*

MRS. WAGSTAFF, *apparently inured to public execution, smokes, reads a magazine on her lap, occasionally nibbles a sandwich which the* MANICURIST *passes her from a tray near her instruments. The drier, whenever it is on, makes a loud noise, drowning out voices, which must be harshly raised above it. Now the drier is on, the voices loud.*

MRS. WAGSTAFF. It's burning my neck!

SECOND HAIRDRESSER. Be brave! One minute more!

MRS. WAGSTAFF (*in pain*). O-o-oo!

FIRST HAIRDRESSER. It's going to be so worth it, Mrs. Wagstaff.

MRS. WAGSTAFF. My ears!

SECOND HAIRDRESSER. Be brave!

MRS. WAGSTAFF. O-o-o-o! My nerves – Oo–my God! (*To* PEDICURIST) My sandwich– (OLGA *hands her sandwich.*)

SECOND HAIRDRESSER. Ten seconds. We must suffer to be beautiful. (*The curtain parts;* A FIGURE *in flowing white half-enters. It is, judging by the voice, a woman, but its face is completely obliterated by a mud-mask.*)

MUD-MASK. Oh, pardon–I thought I was in here. Why, hello, Mrs. Wagstaff. (*Coyly*) Guess who I am? (*A second* FACE *appears over this intruder's shoulder. At first, it looks like another mud-mask. It's not. It's the colored maid,* EUPHIE. *She clutches the shoulder of the mud mask.*)

EUPHIE. Mustn't talk, ma'am. You'll crack yo'self. (*Exit* MUD-MASK *followed by* EUPHIE.)

MRS. WAGSTAFF. Who was it?

FIRST HAIRDRESSER. Mrs. Phipps– (*Switches off the drier. Now they all lower their voices to a normal pitch*) There, dear, the agony's over. (*They take the permanent clamps off* MRS. WAGSTAFF's *hair. A drier is on in the next booth. A voice is heard offstage, screaming above it.*)

VOICE. –so I feel awful. I ate a lobster at the opening of the Ritz– (*The drier goes off.*)

OLGA (*to* MRS. WAGSTAFF). Mrs. Mordie Barnes. She's been in the hospital. It wasn't ptomaine at all. It was a mis–

SECOND HAIRDRESSER. Olga! She'll hear you–

MRS. WAGSTAFF (*thoughtfully*). I think I'll have a mud-mask.

SECOND HAIRDRESSER (*calling outside*). Euphie! Tell the desk Mrs. Wagstaff's working in a mud!

MRS. WAGSTAFF (*enviously*). Mrs. Phipps has such a lovely skin.

FIRST HAIRDRESSER. Not lovelier than yours, Mrs. Wagstaff.

CHORUS (SECOND HAIRDRESSER, OLGA, PEDICURIST). Oh, yours is lovely! Why, not nearly as lovely! Lovelier than yours?

MRS. WAGSTAFF (*coyly*). I do think it's rather good for a woman my age.

FIRST HAIRDRESSER. You talk as if you were an old woman, dear.

MRS. WAGSTAFF (*lying*). I'm 42.

SECOND HAIRDRESSER. Mustn't tell anyone. You don't look a day over 35!

CHORUS (SECOND HAIRDRESSER, PEDICURIST, OLGA). Why, no one would believe it! Why, not a day! Oh, you don't look it!

SECOND HAIRDRESSER. —now you've gotten so much slimmer!

MRS. WAGSTAFF. I have slimmed down, haven't I?

CHORUS (PEDICURIST, OLGA, FIRST HAIRDRESSER). Oh, thin as a shadow! Why, terribly thin! Oh, just right, now!

MRS. WAGSTAFF (*admiring her nail polish*). That's lovely.

OLGA. Jungle Red. Everybody loves it. Do you know Mrs. Howard Fowler?

PEDICURIST (*rising, gathering up her things*). Don't put your stockings on yet, Mrs. Wagstaff, you'll smear your beautiful big toe— (*Exits.*)

OLGA. They say Mr. Fowler made a fortune in some stock. But one of the ladies Mrs. Fowler sent in was telling me Mr. Fowler does like to drink! Only the other day—

FIRST HAIRDRESSER (*sharply*). We're ready now, Mrs. Wagstaff. (*Gets* MRS. WAGSTAFF *up*) We'll unwind you in the shampoo. (*Calling*) Euphie!

SECOND HAIRDRESSER (*taking* MRS. WAGSTAFF *to door*). This way, dear. How does your permanent feel? And it's going to look lovely, too— (SECOND HAIRDRESSER *herds* MRS. WAGSTAFF *out of the booth,* MRS. WAGSTAFF *walking on her heels, her toes still wadded with cotton. Enter* EUPHIE, *who, during the ensuing dialogue, cleans up the debris on the floor of the booth.*)

OLGA. That old gasoline truck! Fifty-two if she's a day!

FIRST HAIRDRESSER. One more permanent and she won't have a hair left on her head.

OLGA. There's plenty on her upper lip.

EUPHIE. She sho' does shed, don't she?

OLGA. Any woman who's fool enough to marry a man ten years younger! Know what a client told me? Her husband's a pansy! (HAIRDRESSER *exits followed by* OLGA.)

SECOND HAIRDRESSER (*entering*). Ready?

EUPHIE. Yes, ma'am.
(*The* SECOND HAIRDRESSER *holds back the curtain.*)

MARY (*offstage*). So I woke up this morning and decided for no reason at all to change the way— (*She enters, followed by* NANCY) I do my hair. (*Exit* EUPHIE.)

SECOND HAIRDRESSER. Mr. Michael will be ten minutes, ma'am. Anyone in particular for your manicure?

MARY. Who does Mrs. Fowler's nails?

HAIRDRESSER. Olga. I'll see. (*Exits.*)

NANCY. God, I'd love to do Mrs. Fowler's nails, right down to the wrist, with a nice big buzz saw.

MARY. Sylvia's all right. She's a good friend underneath.

NANCY. Underneath what?

MARY. Nancy, you don't humor your friends enough.

NANCY. So that's the big idea coming here? You're humoring Sylvia?

MARY. Oh, you did hurt her. I had it all over again at lunch. (*She catches a glimpse of herself in the mirror*) Nancy, am I getting old?

NANCY. Who put that in your head? Sylvia?

MARY. Tell me the truth.

NANCY. Beauty is in the eye of the beholder, and twaddle to that effect.

MARY. But it's such a scary feeling when you see those little wrinkles creeping in.

NANCY. Time's little mice.

MARY. And that first gleam of white in your hair. It's the way you'd feel about autumn if you knew there'd never be another spring—

NANCY (*abruptly*). There's only one tragedy for a woman.

MARY. Growing old?

NANCY. Losing her man.

MARY. That's why we're all so afraid of growing old.

NANCY. Are you afraid?

MARY. Well, I was very pretty when I was young. I never thought about it twice then. Now I know it's why Stephen loved me.

NANCY. Smart girl.

MARY. Now I think about it all the time.

NANCY. Love is not love which alters when it alteration finds. Shakespeare.

MARY. Well, he told me, on my birthday, I'd always look the same to him.

NANCY. Nice present. No jewels?

MARY. It rained that day. He brought me a bottle of perfume called "Summer Rain."

NANCY. How many ounces?

MARY. Nancy, you've never been in love.

NANCY. Says who?

MARY (*surprised*). Have you?

NANCY. Yes.

MARY. You never told me.

NANCY. You never asked— (*Wistfully*) Neither did *he.* (OLGA *enters with fresh bowl of water*) Here, innocent. (*Gives a book to* MARY) The book my readers everywhere have been waiting for with such marked apathy.

MARY. "All the Dead Ladies"?

NANCY. Originally called, "From the Silence of the Womb." My publisher thought that would make too much noise.

MARY. What's it about? (OLGA *begins to file* MARY'S *nails.*)

NANCY. Women I dislike: "Ladies"—

MARY. Oh, Nancy!

OLGA. Don't soak it yet. (*Taking* MARY'S *hand out of the water.*)

NANCY. No good? Too bad. It's a parting shot. I'm off.

MARY. Off?

NANCY. Africa.

MARY. But not today?

NANCY. I knew if I told you you'd scurry around and do things. A party. Steamer baskets of sour fruit. Not nearly as sour as the witty cables your girl friends would send me— So don't move. No tears. For my sake —just soak it? Good-bye, Mary—

MARY. Good-bye, Nancy. I'll miss you.

NANCY. I doubt it. Practically nobody ever misses a clever woman. (*Exits.*)

OLGA. Funny, isn't she?

MARY. She's a darling.

OLGA (*filing* MARY'S *nails*). She's a writer? How do those writers think up those plots? I guess the plot part's not so hard to think up as the end. I guess anybody's life'd make a interesting plot if it had a interesting end —Mrs. Fowler sent you in? (MARY, *absorbed in her book, nods*) She's sent me three clients this week. Know Mrs. Herbert Parrish that was Mrs. Malcolm Leeds? Well, Mrs. Parrish was telling me herself about her divorce. Seems Mr. Parrish came home one night with lipstick on his undershirt. Said he always explained everything before. But *that* was something he just wasn't going to try to explain. Know Mrs. Potter? She's awful pregnant—

MARY (*she wants to read*). I know.

OLGA. Soak it, please. (*Puts* MARY'S *hand in water. Begins on other hand*) Know Mrs. Stephen Haines?

MARY. What? Why, yes, *I*—

OLGA. I guess Mrs. Fowler's told you about that! Mrs. Fowler feels awfully sorry for her.

MARY (*laughing*). Oh, she does! Well, I don't. I—

OLGA. You would if you knew this girl.

MARY. What girl?

OLGA. This Crystal Allen.

MARY. Crystal Allen?

OLGA. Yes, you know. The girl who's living with Mr. Haines. (MARY *starts violently*) Don't you like the file? Mrs. Potter says it sets her unborn child's teeth on edge.

MARY (*indignant*). Whoever told you such a thing?

OLGA. Oh, I thought you knew. Didn't Mrs. Fowler—?

MARY. No—

OLGA. Then you will be interested. You see, Crystal Allen is a friend of mine. She's really a terrible man-trap. Soak it, please. (MARY, *dazed, puts her hand in the dish*) She's behind the perfume counter at Saks'. So was I before I got fi—left. That's how she met him.

MARY. Stephen Haines?

OLGA. Yeah. It was a couple a months ago. Us girls wasn't busy. It was an awful rainy day, I remember. So this gentleman walks up to the counter. He was the serious type, nice-looking, but kind of thin on top. Well, Crystal nabs him. "I want some perfume," he says. "May I awsk what type of woman for?" Crystal says, very Ritzy. That didn't mean a thing. She was going to sell him Summer Rain, our feature anyway. "Is she young?" Crystal says. "No," he says, sort of embarrassed. "Is she the glamorous type?" Crystal says. "No, thank God," he says. "Thank God?" Crystal says and bats her eyes. She's got those eyes which run up and down a man like a searchlight. Well, she puts perfume on her palm and in the crook of her arm for him to smell. So he got to smelling around and I guess he liked it. Because we heard him tell her his name, which one of the girls recognized from Cholly Knickerbocker's column—Gee, you're nervous—Well, it was after that I left. I wouldn't of thought no more about it. But a couple of weeks ago I stopped by where Crystal lives to say hello. And the landlady says she'd moved to the kind of house where she could entertain her gentleman friend—"What gentleman friend?" I says. "Why, that Mr. Haines that she's had up in her room all hours of the night," the landlady says—Did I hurt? (MARY *draws her hand away*) One coat, or two? (*Picks up a red bottle.*)

MARY. None. (*Rises and goes to the chair, where she has left her purse.*)

OLGA. But I thought that's what you came for? All Mrs. Fowler's friends—

MARY. I think I've gotten what all Mrs. Fowler's friends came for. (*Puts coin on the table.*)

OLGA (*picks up coin*). Oh, thanks—Well, good-bye. I'll tell her you were in, Mrs. —?

MARY. Mrs. Stephen Haines.

OLGA. Mrs. —? Oh, gee, gee! Gee, Mrs. Haines—I'm sorry! Oh, isn't there something I can do?

MARY. Stop telling that story!

OLGA. Oh, sure, sure, I will!

MARY. And please, don't tell anyone— (*Her voice breaks*) that you told it to *me*—

OLGA. Oh, I won't, gee, I promise! Gee, that would be kind of humiliating for you! (*Defensively*) But in a way, Mrs. Haines, I'm kinda *glad* you know. Crystal's a terrible girl—I mean, she's terribly clever. And she's terribly pretty, Mrs. Haines—I mean, if I was you I wouldn't waste no time getting Mr. Haines away from her—(MARY *turns abruptly away*) I mean, now you *know*, Mrs. Haines!

(OLGA *eyes the coin in her hand distastefully, suddenly puts it down on the table and exits.* MARY, *alone, stares blankly in the mirror, then suddenly focusing on her image, leans forward, searching her face between her trembling hands. A drier goes on in the next booth. A shrill voice rises above its drone.*)

VOICE. —Not too hot! My sinus! So *she* said: "I wouldn't want anybody in the world to know," and *I* said: "My dear, you know you can trust *me!*"

CURTAIN

SCENE III

An hour later. MARY'S *boudoir. Charming, of course. A door to bedroom, right. A door to the hall, left. A chaise-longue; next to it, a table with books, flowers, a telephone. A dressing table.*

As the curtain rises, MARY *is discovered on the chaise-longue, trying to read.* JANE *enters from the hall. She is upset about something. She keeps daubing at her eyes.*

MARY. Tea, Jane?

JANE. It's coming, ma'am.

MARY. My mother will be here in a few minutes. A cup for her.

JANE. Yes, ma'am. (*Sniffling*) Ma'am—

MARY. And tell cook please, dinner on time. We're going to the theatre. Mr. Haines likes to be there for the curtain. I'll wear my old black, Jane.

JANE (*looking nervously at the door behind her*). Yes, ma'am.

MARY. No, I'll wear my new blue, Jane.

JANE. Ma'am, it's cook. She wants to see you. (*Defensively*) It's about *me*. She says I—

MARY. Later, Jane.

JANE. Don't you believe a word she says, ma'am. It's all his fault.

MARY (*aware of* JANE'S *distress for the first time*). Whose fault?

JANE. Her husband's. Ford's.

MARY (*surprised*). What's the matter with Ford? He's a very good butler.

JANE. Oh, he does his work, ma'am. But you don't know how he is in the pantry. Always kidding around with us girls. He don't mean any harm, but cook—

(*Enter* COOK *abruptly with* MARY'S *tea tray. She is a fat, kind woman, with a strong Scandinavian accent. At the moment she is very mad.*)

COOK. Afternoon, ma'am. (*Glaring at* JANE) I'd like to talk to you alone, ma'am.

JANE. I told you, it isn't my fault.

COOK. You led him on!

JANE. I didn't. (*Bursting into tears*) I've been with Mrs. Haines seven years. She knows I never make trouble downstairs. (*Exits to hall.*)

MARY. Yes, Ingrid?

COOK. Ma'am, you're the nicest I ever had. But I go. I got to get Ford away from that bad girl.

MARY (*very firmly*). Jane is not a bad girl.

COOK (*bursts into tears*). Oh, course she ain't. He was always like that! Sometimes I could die, for the shame!

MARY (*kindly*). I'll send him away. You can stay.

COOK (*more soberly*). No, I don't do that, ma'am.

MARY. I'll give you a hundred dollars. That's more than half of what you make together.

COOK. Thank you, ma'am. We both go.

MARY. Is that sensible?

COOK. No. It's plain dumb.

MARY. Then why?

COOK (*she pauses, rocking from foot to foot*). I guess nobody understand. Sure it was no good to marry him. My mother told me he's a lady-killer. Don't marry them, she said. His wife is the lady he kills. Oh, he's terrible. But except for women he's a good man. He always says, "Ingrid, you take the money. You manage good." Oh, he don't want nobody but me for his wife! That's an awful big thing, ma'am.

MARY. Is that the thing that really matters?

COOK. With women like us, yes ma'am— You give us references? (MARY *nods*) And don't say nothing about his ways?

MARY. I won't.

COOK (*moving to the door*). Black bean soup, a fricassee, fried sweets and apple pie for dinner, ma'am— (*She opens the door.* JANE *has been eavesdropping.*)

COOK (*in a low, fierce voice*). Slut! (*Exit* COOK.)

JANE (*entering with extra cup on tray*). Did you hear what she called me, Mrs. Haines?

MARY. Please, Jane.

JANE (*cheerfully*). I'd rather be that any day than have some man make a fool of me!

(*Enter* MISS FORDYCE. *She is a raw-*

boned, capable English spinster of 32.)

MISS FORDYCE. May I see you, Mrs. Haines?

MARY. Of course, Miss Fordyce.

MISS FORDYCE. It's about little Mary—Really, Mrs. Haines, you'll have to talk to your child. She's just smacked her little brother, hard. Pure temper.

MARY. What did little Stevie do to her, Miss Fordyce?

MISS FORDYCE. Well, you see, it happened while I was down getting my tea. When I came up, she'd had such a tantrum, she'd made herself ill. She positively refuses to discuss the incident with me. But I'm quite sure the dear boy hadn't done a thing.

MARY. You're very apt to take the boy's side, Miss Fordyce.

MISS FORDYCE. Not at all. But in England, Mrs. Haines, our girls are not so wretchedly spoiled. After all, this *is* a man's world. The sooner our girls are taught to accept the fact *graciously—*

MARY (*gently*). Send her in to me, Miss Fordyce. (*Exit* MISS FORDYCE) Oh, Jane, I don't understand it. Miss Fordyce really prefers Mary, but she insists we all make a little god of Stevie. (*Exits to bedroom, leaving the door open.*)

JANE. Them English ones always hold out for the boys. But they say since the War, ma'am, there's six women over there to every man. Competition is something fierce! Over here, you can treat the men the way they deserve—Men aren't so scarce.

(*Enter* LITTLE MARY. *She is a broad-browed, thoughtful, healthy little girl, physically well developed for her age.)*

LITTLE MARY. Where's Mother?

JANE. You're going to catch it. Smacking your little brother. (*Mimicking* MISS FORDYCE) Such a dear, sweet little lad—shame. (LITTLE MARY *does not answer*) I'll bet you wish you were Mother's girl, instead of Daddy's girl today, don't you? (LITTLE MARY *doesn't answer*) What's the matter, the cat got your tongue? (*Enter* MARY, *wearing a negligée.)*

MARY. Hello, darling—Aren't you going to kiss me? (LITTLE MARY *doesn't move*) What red eyes!

LITTLE MARY. I was mad. I threw up. When you throw up, doesn't it make you cry?

MARY (*smiling*). Stevie tease you? (LITTLE MARY, *embarrassed, looks at* JANE. JANE *snickers, takes the hint and goes out*) Well, darling?

LITTLE MARY. Mother, I don't know how to begin.

MARY (*sitting on the chaise-longue, and putting out her hand*). Come here. (LITTLE MARY *doesn't budge*) Would you rather wait until tonight and tell Dad?

LITTLE MARY (*horrified*). Oh, Mother, I couldn't tell him! (*Fiercely*) And I'd be killed to death before I'd tell skinny old Miss Fordyce—

MARY. That's not the way for my dear little girl to talk.

LITTLE MARY (*setting her jaw*). I don't want to be a dear little girl. (*She suddenly rushes to her mother's outstretched arms in tears*) Oh, Mother dear, Mother dear!

MARY. Baby, what?

LITTLE MARY. What brother said!

MARY. What did he say, the wretched boy?

LITTLE MARY (*disentangling herself*). He said I had bumps!

MARY. Bumps? You don't mean mumps?

LITTLE MARY. No, bumps. He said I was covered with disgusting bumps!

MARY (*alarmed*). Mary, *where?*

LITTLE MARY (*touching her hips and breasts with delicate, ashamed finger tips*). *Here* and *here!*

MARY. Oh— (*Controlling her relieved laughter, and drawing her daughter to her side*) Of course you have bumps, darling. Very pretty little bumps. And you have them because—you're a little girl.

LITTLE MARY (*wailing*). But, Mother dear, I don't want to be a little girl. I hate girls! They're so silly, and they tattle, tattle—

MARY. Not really, Mary.

LITTLE MARY. Yes, Mother, I know. Oh, Mother, what *fun* is there to be a lady? What can a lady do?

MARY (*cheerfully*). These days, darling, ladies do all the things men do. They fly aeroplanes across the ocean, they go into politics and business—

LITTLE MARY. *You* don't, Mother.

MARY. Perhaps I'm happier doing just what I do.

LITTLE MARY. What do you do, Mother?

MARY. Take care of you and Stevie and Dad.

LITTLE MARY. You don't, Mother. Miss Fordyce and the servants do.

MARY (*teasing*). I see. I'm not needed around here.

LITTLE MARY (*hugging her*). Oh, Mother, I don't mean that. It wouldn't be any fun at all without *you*. But, Mother, even when the ladies *do* do things, they stop it when they get the lovie-dovies.

MARY. The what?

LITTLE MARY. Like in the movies, Mother. Ladies always end up so *silly*. (*Disgusted*) Lovey-dovey, lovey-dovey all the time!

MARY. Darling, you're too young to understand—

LITTLE MARY. But, Mother—

MARY. "But Mother, but Mother!" There's one thing a woman can do, no man can do.

LITTLE MARY (*eagerly*). What?

MARY. Have a child. (*Tenderly*) Like you.

LITTLE MARY. Oh, that! Everybody knows that. But is that any fun, Mother dear?

MARY. Fun? No. But it is—joy. (*Hugging her*) Of a very special kind.

LITTLE MARY (*squirming away*). Well, it's never sounded specially exciting to me—I love you, Mother. But I bet you anything you like, Daddy has more *fun* than you! (*She slips away from* MARY. *Then sees her mother's dispirited face, turns and kisses her warmly*) Oh, I'm sorry, Mother. But you just *don't understand!* (*A pause*) Am I to be punished, Mother?

MARY (*she is thinking about something else*). What do you think?

LITTLE MARY. I smacked him awful hard—Shall I punish myself?

MARY. It will have to be pretty bad.

LITTLE MARY (*solemnly*). Then I won't go down to breakfast with Daddy tomorrow, or the next day—O. K., Mother?

MARY. O. K.
(LITTLE MARY *walks, crestfallen, to the door as* JANE *enters.* LITTLE MARY *sticks out her tongue.*)

LITTLE MARY. There's my tongue! So what? (*Exits skipping.*)

JANE (*laughing*). She never lets anybody get the best of her, does she, Mrs. Haines?

MARY. My poor baby. She doesn't want to be a woman, Jane.

JANE. Who does?

MARY. Somehow, I've never minded it, Jane. (*Enter* MRS. MOREHEAD. *She is a bourgeois aristocrat of 55.* MARY *rises, kisses her.*)

MRS. MOREHEAD. Hello, child. Afternoon, Jane.

JANE. Afternoon, Mrs. Morehead. (*Exits to bedroom.*)

MARY. Mother, dear! (*She walks slowly to the dressing table.*)

MRS. MOREHEAD (*cheerfully*). Well, what's wrong? (*Sits.*)

MARY (*turning*). How did you know something's wrong?

MRS. MOREHEAD. Your voice on the phone. Is it Stephen?

MARY. How did you know?

MRS. MOREHEAD. You sent for *Mother*. So it must be he. (*A pause.*)

MARY. I don't know how to begin, Mother.

MRS. MOREHEAD (*delighted to find that her instincts were correct*). It's a woman! Who is she?

MARY. Her name is Crystal Allen. She—she's a salesgirl at Saks'. (*Her mother's cheerful and practical manner discourages tears, so she begins to cream and tonic her face instead.*)

MRS. MOREHEAD. She's young and pretty, I suppose.

MARY. Well, yes. (*Defensively*) But common.

MRS. MOREHEAD (*soothingly*). Of course—Stephen told you?

MARY. No. I—I found out—this afternoon.

MRS. MOREHEAD. How far has it gone?

MARY. He's known her about three months.

MRS. MOREHEAD. Does Stephen know you know?

MARY (*shaking her head*). I—I wanted to speak to you first. (*The tears come anyway*) Oh, Mother dear, what am I going to say to him?

MRS. MOREHEAD. *Nothing.*

MARY. Nothing?
(*Enter* JANE *with the new dress.*)

JANE. I'll give it a touch with the iron.

MARY. Look, Schiaparelli— (JANE *holds dress up*) It's rather trying, though, one of those tight skirts with a flared tunic—

MRS. MOREHEAD. Personally, I always thought you looked best in things not too extreme.
(*Exit* JANE.)

MARY. But, Mother, you don't really mean I should say nothing?

MRS. MOREHEAD. I do.

MARY. Oh, but Mother—

MRS. MOREHEAD. My dear, I felt the same way twenty years ago.

MARY. Not Father?

MRS. MOREHEAD. Mary, in many ways your father was an exceptional man. (*Philosophically*) That, unfortunately, was not one of them.

MARY. Did you say nothing?

MRS. MOREHEAD. Nothing. I had a wise mother, too. Listen, dear, this is not a new story. It comes to most wives.

MARY. But Stephen—

MRS. MOREHEAD. Stephen is a man. He's been married twelve years—

MARY. You mean, he's tired of me!

MRS. MOREHEAD. Stop crying. You'll make your nose red.

MARY. I'm not crying. (*Patting tonic on her face*) This stuff stings.

MRS. MOREHEAD (*going to her*). Stephen's tired of himself. Tired of feeling the same things in himself year after year. Time comes when every man's got to feel something new—when he's got to feel young again, just because he's growing old. Women are just the same. But when *we* get that way we change our hair dress. Or get a new cook. Or redecorate the house from stem to stern. But a man can't do over his office, or fire his secretary. Not even change the style of his hair. And the urge usually hits him hardest just when he's beginning to lose his hair. No, dear, a man has only one escape from his old self: to see a different self—in the mirror of some woman's eyes.

MARY. But, Mother—

MRS. MOREHEAD. This girl probably means no more to him than that new dress means to you.

MARY. But, Mother—

MRS. MOREHEAD. "But Mother, but Mother!" He's not giving anything to her that belongs to you, or you would have felt that yourself long ago.

MARY (*bewildered*). Oh, I always thought I would. I love him so much.

MRS. MOREHEAD. And he loves you, baby. (*Drawing* MARY *beside her on the chaise-longue*) Now listen to me: Go away somewhere for a month or two. There's nothing like a good dose of another woman to make a man appreciate his wife. Mother knows!

MARY. But, there's never been a lie between us before.

MRS. MOREHEAD. You mean, there's never been a *silence* between you before. Well, it's about time. Keeping still, when you *ache* to talk, is about the only sacrifice spoiled women like us ever have to make.

MARY. But, I'd forgive him—

MRS. MOREHEAD. Forgive him? (*Impatiently*) For what? For being a man? Accuse him, and you'll never get a chance to forgive him. He'd have to justify himself—

MARY. How can he?

MRS. MOREHEAD (*sighing*). He can't and he *can*. Don't make him try. Either way you'd lose him. And remember, dear, it's being together at the *end* that really matters. (*Rising*) One more piece of motherly advice: Don't confide in your girl friends!

MARY. I think they all know.

MRS. MOREHEAD. They think you don't? (MARY *nods*) Leave it that way. If you let them advise you, they'll see to it, in the name of friendship, that you lose your husband and your home. I'm an old woman, dear, and I know my sex. (*Moving to the door*) I'm going right down this minute and get our tickets.

MARY. Our—tickets?

MRS. MOREHEAD. You're taking me to Bermuda, dear. My throat's been awfully bad. I haven't wanted to worry you, but my doctor says—

MARY. Oh, Mother darling! Thank you!

MRS. MOREHEAD. Don't thank me, dear. It's rather—*nice* to have you need Mother again. (*Exits. The telephone rings.* MARY *answers it.*)

MARY. Yes?—Oh, Stephen—Yes, dear?— (*Distressed*) Oh, Stephen! Oh, no—I'm not angry. It's—it's just that I wanted to see the play. Yes, I can get Mother. Stephen, will you be very—late? (*It's a bit of a struggle, but she manages a cheerful voice*) Oh, it's—all right. Have a good time. Of course, I know it's just business—No, dear—I won't wait up—Stephen, I love— (*A click. The other end has hung up.* JANE *enters.* MARY *turns her back. Her face would belie the calmness of her voice*) Jane—The children and I will have dinner alone—

CURTAIN

SCENE IV

Two months later. A dressmaker's shop. We see two fitting booths, the same in appointment: triplex pier glasses, dress racks, smoking stands, two small chairs. They are divided by a mirrored partition. At the rear of each booth, a curtain and a door, off a corridor, which leads to "the floor."

As the curtain rises the booth on the left is empty. The other booth is cluttered with dresses. Two SALESGIRLS *are loading them over their arms.*

FIRST GIRL (*with vivid resentment against a customer who has just departed*). Well, now we can put them all back again. Makes you drag out everything in the damn store, and doesn't even buy a brassiere!

SECOND GIRL. And that's the kind who always needs one.

FIRST GIRL. This isn't her type. That isn't her type. I'd like to tell her what her type is.

SECOND GIRL. I'd like to know.

FIRST GIRL. It's the type that nobody gives a damn about! Gee, I'd like to work in a men's shop once. What can a man try on?

SECOND GIRL. Ever see a man try on hats? What they go through, you'd think a head was something peculiar. (*Both* GIRLS *exit.* FIRST SALESWOMAN *enters the booth on the left, hereafter called "Mary's Booth."*)

FIRST SALESWOMAN. Miss Myrtle, step in here a moment.
(*A handsome wench, in a slinky negligée, enters.*)

MODEL. Yes, Miss Shapiro.

FIRST SALESWOMAN. If I've told you once, I've told you a thousand times, when you're modelling that dress, your stomach must lead. If you walk like this (*Pantomimes*) you take away all the seduction. *This* is seduction! (*Shows* MISS MYRTLE *her rather unconvincing conception of a seductive walk.*)

MODEL. I'll try, Miss Shapiro. (*Tearfully*) But if you had my appendix!

FIRST SALESWOMAN. Well, Miss Myrtle, you can take your choice: You will either lose your job or lose your appendix!
(*Exit* MODEL. *In right booth, hereafter called "Crystal's Booth," enter* SECOND SALESWOMAN.)

SECOND SALESWOMAN (*to the* FIRST *and* SECOND GIRLS *who have returned for another load of dresses*). Quickly, please. I have a client waiting. (SECOND GIRL *exits with last of clothes as enter* CRYSTAL, *followed by* SALESWOMAN. THIRD SALESWOMAN *is seen crossing corridor from right to left.*)

(*Mary's Booth*)
FIRST SALESWOMAN (*giving little white slip to the* SALESWOMAN *who*

passes). Bring down Mrs. Haines' fittings. (*Exits, leaving booth empty.*)

(*Crystal's Booth*)

SECOND SALESWOMAN. Will you open a charge?

CRYSTAL (*taking off her gloves and hat*). Please.

SECOND SALESWOMAN. May I have the name?

CRYSTAL (*she is quite self-assured*). Allen. Miss Crystal Allen. The Hotel Waverly.

SECOND SALESWOMAN. May I have your other charges? Saks, Bergdorf, Cartier—?

CRYSTAL (*putting it on*). Oh, I'll be opening those, in the next few days—

SECOND SALESWOMAN. Then may I have your bank?

CRYSTAL. I've no checking account either, at the moment.

(*Enter* MARY *in her booth, with* FITTER *and* FIRST SALESWOMAN, *who carries her try-on gown. During the following scene* MARY *undresses, gets into gay evening gown, fits.*)

FIRST SALESWOMAN (*to* MARY, *as they enter*). Shall we show the things that came in while you were away?

MARY. Please. But I'd like to see some younger things than I usually wear.

(*Crystal's Booth*)

SECOND SALESWOMAN. I'm sorry, Miss Allen. But we *must* ask for one business reference—

CRYSTAL (*lightly; she was prepared for this*). Oh, of course. Mr. Stephen Haines, 40 Wall. He's an old friend of my family.

SECOND SALESWOMAN (*writing*). That will do. Mrs. Haines is a very good client of ours.

CRYSTAL (*unprepared for that*). Oh?

SECOND SALESWOMAN. Will you try on now, or finish seeing the collection?

CRYSTAL. By the way, I've never met Mrs. Haines.

SECOND SALESWOMAN. She's lovely.

CRYSTAL. So—I'd rather you didn't mention to her, that I gave her husband as reference. (*Beguiling*) Do you mind?

SECOND SALESWOMAN (*with a faint smile*). Oh, of course not, Miss Allen. (*Indulgently*) We understand.

CRYSTAL (*angrily*). Do you! What do you understand?

SECOND SALESWOMAN (*flustered*). I mean—

CRYSTAL (*very injured*). Never mind.

SECOND SALESWOMAN. Please, I hope you don't think I meant—

CRYSTAL (*laughing and very charming again*). Of course not. Oh, it's dreadful, living in a strange city alone. You have to be so careful not to do anything people can misconstrue. You see, I don't know Mrs. Haines yet. So I'd hate to get off on the wrong foot, before I've met her *socially*.

SECOND SALESWOMAN (*she sounds convinced*). Naturally. Women are funny about little things like that.

(*Mary's Booth—Enter* SYLVIA.)
SYLVIA. Yoo-hoo! May I come in?

MARY (*not at all pleased to see her*). Hello, Sylvia.

(*In Crystal's Booth.*)
SECOND SALESWOMAN. What are you most interested in, Miss Allen, evening gowns?

CRYSTAL. Until I—I organize my social life—I won't have much use for evening gowns.

SECOND SALESWOMAN. I'll show you some smart daytime things. (*Deliberately toneless*) And we have very *exciting* negligées— (*They exit.*)

(*Mary's Booth.*)
(SYLVIA *circles around* MARY, *appraising her fitting with a critical eye.*)

MARY. Oh, sit down, Sylvia.

SYLVIA (*to the fitter*). I don't like that underslung line. (*Demonstrating on* MARY) It cuts her across the fanny. Makes her look positively duck-bottomed.

MARY (*pulling away*). It's so tight, Mrs. Fowler can't sit down.

FIRST SALESWOMAN. Mrs. Fowler, shall I see if your fittings are ready?

SYLVIA. They'll call me.

MARY (*pointing to dress* FIRST SALESWOMAN *has over her arm*). Have you seen that?

FIRST SALESWOMAN (*holding up dress*). It's a lovely shape on. It doesn't look like a thing in the hand. (*Hands dress to someone outside and calls*) Show this model, girls.

SYLVIA (*settling in a chair and smoking a cigarette*). So you had a marvelous time in Bermuda.

MARY. I had a good rest.

SYLVIA (*with unconscious humor*). Howard wants *me* to take a world cruise. By the way, dear, how is Stephen?

MARY. Splendid. (*Smiling, and very glad to be able to tell* SYLVIA *this*) He's not nearly so busy. He hasn't spent an evening—in the office, since I've come home. (*Enter* FIRST MODEL *in an elaborate negligée.* MARY *shakes her head, very practical*) Pretty, but I never need a thing like that—

SYLVIA. Of course *you* don't. A hot little number, for intimate afternoons. (*Exit* FIRST MODEL) Howard says nobody's seen Stephen in the Club, in the afternoon, for months—

MARY (*The thought flashes across her mind that* STEPHEN *could, of course, have revised his extra-marital schedule, from an evening to an afternoon one, but she quickly dismisses it;* STEPHEN *has never let anything interfere with his hours downtown*). Don't worry so much about Stephen, Sylvia. He's my concern.
(*Enter* SECOND MODEL *in a corset. She is prettily fashioned from head to toe. She does a great deal for the wisp of lace she wears. It does nothing that nature didn't do better for her.*)

SECOND MODEL. This is our new one-piece lace foundation garment. (*Pirouettes*) Zips up the back, and no bones. (*She exits.*)

SYLVIA. Just that uplift, Mary, you need. I always said you'd regret nursing. Look at me. I don't think there's another girl our age who has bazooms like mine. I've taken care of them. Ice water every morning, camphor at night.

MARY. Doesn't it smell like an old fur coat? (PRINCESS TAMARA *passes in the corridor.*)

SYLVIA. Who cares?

MARY. Howard?

SYLVIA (*laughing harshly*). Howard!

FIRST SALESWOMAN (*calling out door*). Princess Tamara, show here. (*Enter* PRINCESS TAMARA *in a very extreme evening gown. She is Russian, regal, soignée.*)

MARY. Oh, Tamara, how lovely!

TAMARA. You must have it. Stephen would be amazed.

MARY. He certainly would. It's too extreme for me.

SYLVIA (*rises*) And you really haven't the figure. (*Yanks at gown*) Tamara, you wear it wrong. I saw it in *Vogue*. (*Jerks*) Off here, and down there.

TAMARA (*slapping* SYLVIA'S *hand down*). Stop mauling me!

FIRST SALESWOMAN. Princess!

TAMARA. What do you know how to wear clothes?

SYLVIA. *I* am not a model, Tamara, but no one disputes how *I* wear clothes!

TAMARA. No one has mistaken you for Mrs. Harrison Williams yet!

FIRST SALESWOMAN. Princess Tamara, you'd better apologize.

MARY (*to* SALESWOMAN). It's just professional jealousy. They're really good friends!

SYLVIA (*maliciously*). You mean Tamara and *Howard* are friends.

TAMARA (*disgusted at the thought*). Do you accuse me of flirting with *your* husband?

SYLVIA (*pleasantly*). Go as far as you can, Tamara! If I know Howard, you're wasting valuable time.

TAMARA (*very angry*). Perhaps I am. But perhaps somebody else is not! (*The* SALESWOMAN *gives her an angry shove*) You are riding for a fall-off, Sylvia dear! (*Exit* TAMARA *angrily, followed by* SALESWOMAN.)

SYLVIA. Did you get that innuendo? I'd like to see Howard Fowler put anything over on me. Oh, I've always hated that girl, exploiting her title the way she does! (CRYSTAL *and* SECOND SALESWOMAN *enter Crystal's Booth.*)

SECOND SALESWOMAN (*calling down the corridor*). Princess Tamara, show in here, to Miss Allen. (MARY'S SALESWOMAN *enters Mary's Booth, picking up the call.*)

FIRST SALESWOMAN. Girls show in Number 3 to Miss Allen.

SYLVIA (*alert*). Did you say Miss Allen?

FIRST SALESWOMAN. Yes.

SYLVIA. Not—Crystal Allen?

FIRST SALESWOMAN. Why, yes—I just saw her on the floor. She's so attractive I asked her name.

SYLVIA (*watching* MARY *closely*). Oh, so Crystal Allen gets her things here? (MARY *sits down suddenly.*)

FIRST SALESWOMAN. She's a new client— Why, Mrs. Haines, are you ill? (MARY *has caught* SYLVIA'S *eye in the mirror.* SYLVIA *knows now that* MARY *knows.*)

MARY. No, no. I'm just tired. (TAMARA *enters Crystal's Booth.*)

FITTER. We've kept you standing too long—

FIRST SALESWOMAN. I'll get you a glass of sherry. (*Exit* MARY'S FITTER *and* SALESWOMAN. SYLVIA *closes door.*)

(*Crystal's Booth.*)

CRYSTAL (*admiring* TAMARA'S *extreme evening gown*). I'm going to have that, if I have to wear it for breakfast.

SECOND SALESWOMAN. Send it in here, Princess. (TAMARA *exits.*)

(*Mary's Booth.*)

SYLVIA. Mary, you do know! (*Deeply sympathetic*) Why didn't you confide in me?

MARY. Sylvia, go away.

SYLVIA (*fiercely*). Stephen is a louse. Spending your money on a girl like that.

MARY. Sylvia, please mind your own affairs.

SYLVIA. She's already made a fool of you before all your friends. And don't you think the salesgirls know who gets the bills?

MARY (*distraught*). I don't care, I tell you. I don't care!

SYLVIA. Oh, yes, you do. (*Pointing to* MARY'S *stricken face in the mirror*) Don't be an ostrich, Mary. (*A pause*) Go in there.

MARY. Go in there? I'm going home. (*She rises and begins to dress.*)

FIRST SALESWOMAN (*half enters*). Mrs. Haines' sherry—

SYLVIA (*taking it from her, and closing the door in her face*). All right.

SYLVIA. You've caught her cold. It's *your* chance to humiliate her. Just say a few *quiet* words. Tell her you'll make Stephen's life *hell* until he gives her up.

MARY. Stephen will give her up when he's tired of her.

SYLVIA. When he's tired of her? Look where she was six months ago. Look where she is now.

MARY. Stephen's not in love with that girl.

SYLVIA. Maybe not. But you don't know women like that when they get hold of a man.

MARY. Sylvia, please let me decide what is best for me, and my home. (CRYSTAL, *in her booth, has been undressing, admiring herself as she does so in the mirror. Now she slips into a "really exciting" negligée.*)

SYLVIA. Well, she may be a perfectly marvelous influence for Stephen, but she's not going to do your children any good.

MARY (*turning to her*). What do you mean?

SYLVIA (*mysteriously*). Never mind.

MARY (*going to her*). Tell me!

SYLVIA. Far be it from *me* to tell you things you don't care to hear. I've known this all along. (*Nobly*) Have I *uttered?*

MARY (*violently*). What have my children to do with this?

SYLVIA (*after all*, MARY'S *asking for it*). It was while you were away. Edith saw them. Stephen, and that tramp, and your children—together, lunching in the Park.

MARY. It's not true!

SYLVIA. Why would Edith lie? She said they were having a hilarious time. Little Stevie was eating his lunch sitting on that woman's lap. She was kissing him between every bite. When I heard that, I was positively *heart-sick*, dear! (*Sees she has scored. Celebrates by tossing down* MARY'S *sherry.*)

(*Crystal's Booth.*)

CRYSTAL. Oh, go get that evening gown. This thing bores me.

SECOND SALESWOMAN. Right away, Miss Allen. (*Exits.*)

(*Mary's Booth.*)

SYLVIA. But, as you say, dear, it's your affair, not mine. (*Goes to the door, looking very hurt that* MARY *has refused her good advice*) No doubt that girl will make a perfectly good *step-mamma* for your children! (*Exits.* MARY, *now dressed, is alone. She stares at the partition which separates her from that still unmeasured enemy to her well-ordered domesticity, "the other woman." Her common sense dictates she should go home, but now she violently experiences the ache to talk. She struggles against it, then goes, bitterly determined, to the door. Exits. A second later, there is a knock on* CRYSTAL'S *door.* CRYSTAL *is alone.*)

CRYSTAL. Come in! (*Enter* MARY. *She closes door*) I beg your pardon?

MARY. I am—Mrs. Stephen Haines.

CRYSTAL (*her poise is admirable*). Sorry—I don't think I know you!

MARY. Please don't pretend.

CRYSTAL. So Stephen finally told you?

MARY. No. I found out.
(SECOND SALESWOMAN *half enters.*)

CRYSTAL. Stay out of here! (*Exit* SALESWOMAN.)

MARY. I've known about you from the beginning.

CRYSTAL. Well, that's news.

MARY. I kept still.

CRYSTAL. Very smart of you.

(SECOND SALESWOMAN *pantomimes down the corridor, to another girl to join her. Enters* MARY'S *booth. One by one, during the rest of this scene, the* FITTERS, SALESWOMEN *and* MODELS *tiptoe into* MARY'S *booth and plaster their ears against the partition.*)

MARY. No, not smart. I wanted to spare Stephen. But you've gone a little too far— You've been seeing my children. I won't have you touching my children!

CRYSTAL. For God's sake, don't get hysterical. What do I care about your children? I'm sick of hearing about them.

MARY. You won't have to hear about them any more. When Stephen realizes how humiliating all this has been to me, he'll give you up instantly.

CRYSTAL. Says who? The dog in the manger?

MARY. That's all I have to say.

CRYSTAL. That's plenty.

MARY (*more calmly*). Stephen would have grown tired of you anyway.

CRYSTAL (*nastily*). Speaking from your *own* experience? Well, he's not tired of me yet, Mrs. Haines.

MARY (*contemptuous*). Stephen is just amusing himself with you.

CRYSTAL. And he's amusing himself plenty.

MARY. You're very hard.

CRYSTAL. I can be soft—on the *right* occasions. What do you expect me to do? Burst into tears and beg you to forgive me?

MARY. I found exactly what I expected!

CRYSTAL. That goes double!

MARY (*turning to the door*). You'll have to make other plans, Miss Allen.

CRYSTAL (*going to her*). Listen, I'm taking my marching orders from Stephen.

MARY. Stephen doesn't love you.

CRYSTAL. He's doing the best he can in the circumstances.

MARY. He couldn't love a girl like you.

CRYSTAL. What do you think we've been doing for the past six months? Crossword puzzles? What have you got to kick about? You've got everything that matters. The name, the position, the money—

MARY (*losing control of herself again*). Nothing matters to me but Stephen—!

CRYSTAL. Oh, can the sob-stuff, Mrs. Haines. You don't think this is the first time Stephen's ever cheated? Listen, I'd break up your smug little roost if I could. I have just as much right as you have to sit in a tub of butter. But I don't stand a chance!

MARY. I'm glad you know it.

CRYSTAL. Well, don't think it's just because he's *fond* of you—

MARY. *Fond?*

CRYSTAL. You're not what's stopping him— You're just an old *habit* with him. It's just those brats he's afraid of losing. If he weren't such a sentimental fool about those kids, he'd have walked out on *you* years ago.

MARY (*fiercely*). That's not true!

CRYSTAL. Oh, yes, it is. I'm telling you a few plain truths you won't get from Stephen.

MARY. Stephen's always told me the truth—!

CRYSTAL (*maliciously*). Well, look at the record. (*A pause*) Listen, Stephen's satisfied with this arrangement. So don't force any issues, unless you want plenty of trouble.

MARY. You've made it impossible for me to do anything else—!

CRYSTAL (*rather pleased*). Have I?

MARY. You haven't played fair—!

CRYSTAL. Where would any of us get if we played fair?

MARY. Where do you hope to get?

CRYSTAL. Right where *you* are, Mrs. Haines!

MARY. You're very confident.

CRYSTAL. The longer you stay in here, the more confident I get. Saint or no saint, Mrs. Haines, you are a hell of a *dull woman!*

MARY (*stares at* CRYSTAL *wide-eyed at the horrid thought that this may be the truth. She refuses to meet the challenge. She equivocates*). By your standards, I probably am. I— (*Suddenly ashamed that she has allowed herself to be put so pathetically on the defensive*) Oh, why am I standing here talking to you? This is something for Stephen and me to settle! (*Exits.*)

CRYSTAL (*slamming the door after her*). Oh, what the hell!

(*Mary's Booth.*)

SECOND SALESWOMAN. So that's what she calls meeting Mrs. Haines *socially*.

FIRST SALESGIRL. Gee, I feel sorry for Mrs. Haines. She's so nice.

NEGLIGÉE MODEL. She should have kept her mouth shut. Now she's in the soup.

FIRST SALESWOMAN. It's a terrible mistake to lay down ultimatums to a man.

FIRST MODEL. Allen's smart. She's fixed it so anything Mr. Haines says is going to sound wrong.

FIRST SALESGIRL. She'll get him sure.

FIRST FITTER. Look at that body. She's got him now.

SECOND SALESGIRL. You can't trust any man. *That's* all they want.

CORSET MODEL (*plaintively, her hands on her lovely hips*). What else have we got to give?

CURTAIN

ACT TWO

SCENE I

Two weeks later. A small exercise room in Elizabeth Arden's beauty salon. Right, a mirrored wall. Rear, a door. Left, a cabinet victrola beneath an open window. On the floor, a wadded pink satin mat. As the curtain rises, SYLVIA, *in a pair of shorts, is prone on the mat, describing lackadaisical arcs with her legs, to the sensuous rhythm of a tango record. The* INSTRUCTRESS, *a bright, pretty girl, in a pink silk bathing suit, stands above her, drilling her in a carefully cultured voice. Until the cue "stretch," the* INSTRUCTRESS' *lines are spoken through* SYLVIA'S *prattle, which she is determined, for the honor of the salon, to ignore, and, if possible, to discourage. From the word "up," this is a hopeless task.*

INSTRUCTRESS. Up — over — up — down. Up—stretch--up—together. Up—stretch—up—

SYLVIA. Of course, my sympathies are for Mrs. Haines. They always are for a woman against a man—

INSTRUCTRESS (*louder*). Up—over —up—down. Up—stretch—up—together. Up—

SYLVIA. But she did behave like an awful idiot—

INSTRUCTRESS. Stretch — up — together. Please don't try to talk, Mrs. Fowler.

SYLVIA. But you know how some women are when they lose their heads—

INSTRUCTRESS (*grimly*). Stretch—up—together—up—

SYLVIA. They do things they regret all their lives—

INSTRUCTRESS (*grabs* SYLVIA'S *languid limb and gives it a corrective yank*). Ster-retch!

SYLVIA. Ouch, my scars!

INSTRUCTRESS (*callously*). This is very good for adhesions. Up—

SYLVIA (*resolutely inert*). It's got me down.

INSTRUCTRESS. Rest. (SYLVIA *groans her relief*) And relax your diaphragm muscles, Mrs. Fowler, (*Bitterly*) if you can. (*Goes to the victrola, changes the record for a fox trot.*)

SYLVIA. Of course, I do wish Mrs. Haines would make up her mind if she's going to get a divorce. It's terrible on all her friends, not knowing. Naturally, you can't ask them anywhere—

INSTRUCTRESS. Of course not. Now, on your side. (SYLVIA *rolls to her side, reclining on her elbow*) Ready? Up—down—up—down— (*Snaps her fingers.* SYLVIA *flaps a limp leg up, down*—) Don't bend the knee—

SYLVIA (*thoughtfully*). Of course, for the children's sake, I think Mrs. Haines ought to stay. (*Piously*) I know I would. (*Her knees look bent, not to say broken.*)

INSTRUCTRESS (*imploring*). Don't crook it, please.

SYLVIA. And she ought not to have faced Mr. Haines with the issue. When a man's got himself in that deep he has to have time to taper it off—

INSTRUCTRESS (*straightening out* SYLVIA'S *offending member with considerable force*). Thigh in, not out.

SYLVIA (*pained, but undaunted*). But Mrs. Haines never listens to any of her friends. She is a very peculiar woman.

INSTRUCTRESS. She must be. Now, please—up—down—up—down—

SYLVIA (*redoubling her efforts, and her errors*). Oh, I tell everybody whatever she wants to do is the right thing. I've got to be loyal to Mrs. Haines, you know . . . Oh, I'm simply exhausted. (*Flops over, flat on her stomach, panting.*)

INSTRUCTRESS. Then suppose you try something simple—like crawling up the wall? (SYLVIA *lifts a martyred face. The* INSTRUCTRESS *changes the record for a waltz.*)

SYLVIA (*scrambling to her feet*). What I go through to keep my figure! Lord, it infuriates me at dinner parties when some fat lazy man asks, "What do you do with yourself all day, Mrs. Fowler?" (*Sits alongside the rear wall.*)

INSTRUCTRESS. You rotate on your buttocks. (SYLVIA *rotates, then lies back, her knees drawn up to her chin, the soles of her feet against the wall*) Arms flat. Now you crawl slowly up the wall.

SYLVIA (*crawling*). I wish you wouldn't say that. It makes me feel like vermin—

INSTRUCTRESS (*kneeling beside her*). Don't talk.

SYLVIA. There's a couple of people I'd like to exterminate, too—

INSTRUCTRESS. Let's reverse the action. (SYLVIA *crawls down, as* PEGGY *enters in an exercise suit. The* INSTRUCTRESS *brightens.*)

INSTRUCTRESS. How do you do, Mrs. Day? (*To* SYLVIA) Down slowly—

PEGGY (*gaily*). How do you do? Hello, Sylvia.

SYLVIA. You're late again, Peggy.

PEGGY (*crestfallen*). I'm sorry.

SYLVIA (*sitting up*). After all, dear, I am paying for this course.

PEGGY. You know I'm grateful, Sylvia—

SYLVIA. Well, don't cry about it. It's only fifty dollars.

PEGGY. That's a lot to me—

SYLVIA (*sweetly*). To you, or just to your husband, dear?

INSTRUCTRESS. Please, ladies. Let us begin with posture. (SYLVIA *rises*) A lady always enters a room erect.

SYLVIA. Lots of my friends exit horizontally. (PEGGY *and* SYLVIA *go to the mirrored wall, stand with their backs to it.*)

INSTRUCTRESS. Now—knees apart. Sit on the wall. (*They sit on imaginary seats*) Relax. (*They bend forward from the waist, finger-tips brushing the floor*) Now, roll slowly up the wall . . . pressing each little vertebra against the wall as hard as you can . . . shoulders back, and where they belong. Heads back. Mrs. Fowler, lift yourself behind the ears. Pretend you're just a silly little puppet dangling on a string. Chin up. (*She places her hand at the level of* PEGGY'S *straining chin*) No, Mrs. Day, your chin is resting comfortably on a little table. Elbows bent—up on your toes—arms out—shove with the small of your back—you're off! (SYLVIA *and* PEGGY, *side by side, mince across the room.*)

PEGGY (*whispering*). Oh, Sylvia, why do you always insinuate that John is practically a—miser?

INSTRUCTRESS (*she refers to* PEGGY'S *swaying hips*). Tuck under!

SYLVIA. You have your own little income, Peggy. And what do you do with it? You give it to John—

INSTRUCTRESS. Now, back, please! (*They mince backwards across the room.*)

PEGGY (*staunchly*). John makes so little—

INSTRUCTRESS (*she refers to* SYLVIA'S *relaxed tummy*). Steady center control!

SYLVIA. Peggy, you're robbing John of his manly sense of responsibility. You're turning him into a gigolo. A little money of her own she lets no man touch is the only protection a woman has. (*They are against the mirror again.*)

INSTRUCTRESS. Now, are you both the way you were when you left the wall?

SYLVIA (*brightly*). Well, I am.

INSTRUCTRESS. No, Mrs. Fowler, you're not. (*She imitates* SYLVIA'S *posture, showing how* SYLVIA'S *posterior protrudes, against the dictates of fashion, if not of nature*) Not this, Mrs. Fowler—("*Bumps*") *That!* (*She leads* SYLVIA *forward*). Try it, please. (*Facing one another, they do an elegant pair of "bumps"*) Now, relax on the mat.

(*This piece of business defies description, but to do the best one can: the* GIRLS *stand side by side, arms straight above their heads. At the* INSTRUCTRESS' *count of "one," each drops a hand, limp, from the wrist. At "two," the other hand drops, then their heads fall upon their breasts, their arms flap to their sides, their waists cave in, their knees buckle under, and they swoon, or crumble like boneless things, to the mat.*)

INSTRUCTRESS (*she has changed the record*) Now, ready? Bend—stretch, you know. Begin— (*They do another leg exercise on the mat*) Bend—

stretch—bend—down—plenty of pull on the hamstrings, please! Bend—stretch—bend—down—

(*Enter* EDITH. *She is draped in a white sheet. Her head is bound in a white towel. Her face is undergoing a "tie-up," that is, she wears broad white straps under her chin and across her forehead. She appears very distressed.*)

EDITH. Oh, Sylvia! Hello, Peggy—

SYLVIA (*sitting up*). Why, Edith, what are you doing up here?

EDITH. Having a facial, downstairs. Oh, Sylvia. I'm so glad you're here. I've done the most *awful* thing, I—

INSTRUCTRESS. We're right in the middle of of our exercises, Mrs. Potter—

SYLVIA (*to* INSTRUCTRESS). Will you tell them outside—I want my paraffine bath now? There's a dear.

INSTRUCTRESS. But, Mrs. Fowler—

SYLVIA (*cajoling*). I'm simply exhausted.

INSTRUCTRESS. You've hardly moved a muscle.

SYLVIA (*with elaborate patience*). Look, whose carcass is this? Yours or mine?

INSTRUCTRESS. It's yours, Mrs. Fowler, but I'm paid to exercise it.

SYLVIA. You talk like a horse-trainer.

INSTRUCTRESS. Well, Mrs. Fowler, you're getting warm. (*Exits.*)

EDITH. I've done the most *ghastly* thing. Move over. (PEGGY *and* SYLVIA *move over;* EDITH *plumps between them on the mat*) But it wasn't until I got here, in the middle of my facial, that I realized it—I could bite my tongue off when I think of it—

SYLVIA. Well, what is it, Edith?

EDITH. I was lunching with Frances Jones, and—

SYLVIA. Edith Potter, I know exactly what you're going to say!

EDITH. I forgot she—

SYLVIA. You forgot she's Dolly de Peyster.

EDITH. But I never read her awful column—

SYLVIA (*fiercely*). You told her something about me? What did you tell her?

EDITH. Oh, darling, you know I never give *you* away. (*Remorsefully*) I—I—told her all about Stephen and Mary—

SYLVIA (*relieved*). Oh! That!

EDITH. It wasn't until the middle of my facial—

PEGGY. Oh, Edith! It will be in all those dreadful tabloids!

EDITH. I know—I've been racking my brains to recall what I said—I think I told her that when Mary walked into the fitting room, she yanked the ermine coat off the Allen girl—

SYLVIA. You didn't!

EDITH. Well, I don't know whether I said ermine or *sable*—but I know I told her that Mary *smacked* the Allen girl!

PEGGY. Edith!

EDITH. Well, that's what Sylvia told me!

SYLVIA. I didn't!

EDITH. You did, too!

SYLVIA (*hurt*). Anyway, I didn't expect you to tell it to a cheap reporter—

EDITH. Well, it doesn't really make much difference. The divorce is practically settled—

SYLVIA (*eagerly*). Who says so?

EDITH. You did!

SYLVIA (*patiently*). I said, Mary couldn't broadcast her domestic difficulties, and not expect them to wind up in a scandal.

PEGGY. Mary didn't broadcast them!

SYLVIA. Who did?

PEGGY. *You* did. You—you're all making it impossible for her to do anything now but get a divorce!

SYLVIA. You flatter us. We didn't realize how much influence we had on our friends' lives!

PEGGY. Everybody calling her up, telling her how badly she's been treated—

SYLVIA. As a matter of fact, I told her she'd make a great mistake. What has any woman got to gain by a divorce? No matter how much he gives her, she won't have what they have together. And you know as well as I do, he'd marry that girl. What he's spent on her, he'd have to, to protect his investment. (*Sorrowfully*) But, I have as much influence on Mary as I have on *you*, Peggy. (*The* INSTRUCTRESS *re-enters.*)

INSTRUCTRESS. The paraffine bath is ready, Mrs. Fowler.

SYLVIA (*rises*). Well, don't worry, Edith, I'll give de Peyster a ring. I can fix it.

EDITH. How?

SYLVIA (*graciously*). Oh, I'll tell her you were lying.

EDITH. You'll do no such thing!

SYLVIA (*shrugging*). Then let the story ride. It will be forgotten tomorrow. You know the awful things they printed about—what's her name?—before she jumped out the window? Why, I can't even remember her name, so who cares, Edith? (*Exits.*)

INSTRUCTRESS. Mrs. Potter, you come right back where you belong.

EDITH. Why, you'd think this was a boarding school!

INSTRUCTRESS. But, Mrs. Potter, it's such a foolish waste of money—

EDITH. Listen, relaxing is part of my facial.

INSTRUCTRESS (*coolly*). Then you should relax completely, Mrs. Potter, from the chin up. (*Exits.*)

EDITH. Honestly, the class feeling you run into these days! (*Struggles to her feet*) I'm so tired of paying creatures like that to insult me—

PEGGY (*going to her*). Edith! Let's call Mary up and warn her!

EDITH. About what?

PEGGY. The newspapers!

EDITH. My dear, how could we do that, without involving Sylvia—

PEGGY. But it's *her* fault— Oh, she's such a dreadful woman!

EDITH. Oh, she can't help it, Peggy. It's just her tough luck she wasn't born deaf and dumb. But what can we do about it? She's always gotten away with murder. Why, she's been having an affair for a year with that young customers' man in Howard's office.

PEGGY (*shocked*). Edith!

EDITH. Right under Howard's nose! But Howard doesn't care! So what business is it of yours or mine? (*Earnestly*) Peggy, take a tip from me—keep out of other women's troubles. I've never had a fight with a girl friend in all my life. Why? I hear no evil, I see no evil, I speak no evil!

CURTAIN

SCENE II

A few days later.

MARY'S *pantry, midnight. Left, a swinging door, to the kitchen. Rear, a sink under a curtained window. A small, built-in refrigerator. Center, a table, two chairs.*

As the curtain rises, JANE, *the maid, and* MAGGIE, *the new cook, are having a midnight snack.* MAGGIE, *a buxom, middle-aged woman, wears a wrapper and felt bedroom slippers.*

JANE (*folding a tabloid newspaper which she has been reading to* MAGGIE). So *he* says, "All you can do with a story like that, is live it down, Mary."

MAGGIE. I told you they'd begin all over. Once a thing like that is out between a married couple, they've got to fight it out. Depends which they get sick of first, each other, or the argument.

JANE. It's enough to make you lose your faith in marriage.

MAGGIE. Whose faith in marriage?

JANE. You don't believe in marriage?

MAGGIE. Sure I do. For women. (*Sighs*) But it's the sons of Adam they got to marry. Go on.

JANE. Well, finally he said to the madam, "I gave her up, didn't I? And

I was a swine, about the way I did it." How do you suppose he did it, Maggie?

MAGGIE. Maybe he just said, "Scram, the wife is onto us."

JANE. Well, the madam didn't believe him. She says, "Stephen, you really ain't seen her?"

MAGGIE. He lied in his teeth—

JANE. Oh, the way he said it, I kind of believed him. But the madam says, "Oh, but can I ever trust you again?"

MAGGIE You can't trust none of 'em no further than I can kick this lemon pie.

JANE. Oh, it was terrible sad. He said, "Mary, dear Mary, Mary, dear Mary, Mary—"

MAGGIE. Dear Mary. But it ain't exactly convincing.

JANE. Then, I guess he tried to kiss her. Because she says, "Please don't. I'll never be able to kiss you again, without thinking of her in your arms."

MAGGIE (*appreciatively*). Just like in the movies— Imagine him taking up with a girl like that.

JANE. He was telling the madam: She's a virgin.

MAGGIE. She *is*? Then what's all the rumpus about?

JANE. Oh, she ain't a virgin now. She was.

MAGGIE. So was Mae West—once.

JANE. He told the madam he'd beer faithful for twelve years.

MAGGIE. Well, that's something these days, that beats flying the Atlantic. Did the madam believe him?

JANE. She said, "How do I know you've been faithful?"

MAGGIE. She don't.

JANE. But the way he said it—

MAGGIE. Listen, if they lay off six months, they feel themselves busting out all over with haloes.

JANE. Anyway, he says this girl was really a nice girl. So sweet and interested in him and all. And how it happened one night, unexpected, in her room—

MAGGIE. Did he think it was going to happen in Roxy's?

JANE. He said she wouldn't take nothing from him for months—

MAGGIE. Only her education. Oh, that one knew her onions. She certainly played him for a sucker.

JANE. That's what the madam said. She said, "Stephen, can't you see that girl's only interested in you for your money?"

MAGGIE. Tch, tch, tch. I'll bet that made him sore. A man don't like to be told no woman but his wife is fool enough to love him. It drives 'em nutty.

JANE. Did it! "Mary, I told you what kind of girl she is," he says. You know—I just told you—

MAGGIE. I had her number. You didn't convey no information.

JANE. Well, then they both get sore.

MAGGIE (*rises, goes out for coffee*). I knew it.

JANE. So, he began to tell her all over, what a good husband he'd been. And how hard he'd worked for her and the kids. And she kept interrupting with what a good wife she'd been and how proud she was of him. Then they began to exaggerate themselves—

MAGGIE (*enters with coffee pot*). Listen, anybody that's ever been married knows that line backwards and forwards. What happened?

JANE. Well, somewhere in there the madam says, "Stephen, you do want a divorce. Only you ain't got the courage to ask it." And he says, "Oh, my God, no I don't, Mary. Haven't I told you?" And she says, "But you don't love me!" And he says, "But oh, my God, Mary, I'm awful *fond* of you." And she says, very icy, "Fond, fond? Is that all?" And he says, "No, Mary, there's the children." Maggie, that's the thing I don't understand. Why does she get so mad every time he says they've got to consider the children? If children ain't the point of being married, what is?

MAGGIE. A woman don't want to be told she's being kept on just to run a kindergarten. (*Goes to the icebox for a bottle of cream.*)

JANE. Well, the madam says, "Stephen, I want to keep the children out of this. I haven't used the children. I ain't asked you to sacrifice yourself for the children." Maggie, that's where he got so terrible mad. He says, "But why, in God's name, Mary? You knew about us all along. Why did you wait until now to make a fool of me?"

MAGGIE. As if he needed her help.

JANE. So then, suddenly she says, in a awful low voice, "Stephen, oh, Stephen, we can't go on like this. It ain't worthy of what we been to each other!" And he says, "Oh, no, it's not, Mary!"

MAGGIE. Quite a actress, ain't you?

JANE. My boy friend says I got eyes like Claudette Colbert's.

MAGGIE. Did he ever say anything about your legs? Have a cup of coffee. (*Pours coffee.*)

JANE. That's when the madam says what you could have knocked me down with a feather! The madam says, "Stephen, I want a divorce. Yes, Stephen, *I* want a divorce!"

MAGGIE. Tch. Tch. Abdicating!

JANE. Well, Maggie, you could have knocked him down with a feather!

MAGGIE (*waving coffee pot*). I'd like to knock him down with this.

JANE. "My God! Mary," he says, "you don't mean it!" So she says, in a funny voice, "Yes, I do. You've killed my love for you, Stephen."

MAGGIE. He's just simple-minded enough to believe that.

JANE. So he says, "I don't blame you. My God, how can I blame you?"

MAGGIE. My God, he can't!

JANE. So then she said it was all over, because it was only the children he minded losing. She said that made their marriage a mockery.

MAGGIE. A mockery?

JANE. Something funny.

MAGGIE. I ain't going to die laughing.

JANE. He said she was talking nonsense. He said she was just upset on account of this story in the papers. He said what else could she expect if she was going to spill her troubles to a lot of gabby women? He said she should go to bed until she could think things over. He was going out for a breath of fresh air.

MAGGIE. The old hat trick.

JANE. So the madam says, "You're going to see that girl." And he says, "Oh, for God's sake, Mary, one minute you never want to see me again, the next I can't even go out for a airing!"

MAGGIE. You oughtn't to let none of 'em out except on a leash.

JANE. And she says, "Are you going to see her, or ain't you?" And he says, "Well, what difference does it make, if you're going to divorce me?" And she says, "It don't make no difference to *you,* I guess. Please go, Stephen. And don't come back *ever.*" (*Begins to cry.*)

MAGGIE (*impatiently*). Yes?

JANE. I didn't hear his last words. Because naturally, when he said he was going, I scooted down the hall. But I heard her call, "Stephen?" And he stops on the landing and says, "Yes, Mary?" and she says, "Nothing. Just don't slam the front door— The servants will hear you!" So I came down here. Oh, Maggie, what's going to happen?

MAGGIE. She's going to get a divorce.

JANE. Oh, dear. I'm so sad for her.

MAGGIE. I ain't.

JANE. What?

MAGGIE. She's indulging a pride she ain't entitled to. Marriage is a business of taking care of a man and rearing his children. It ain't meant to be no perpetual honeymoon. How long would any husband last if he was supposed to go on acting forever like a red-hot Clark Gable? What's the difference if he don't love her?

JANE. How can you say that, Maggie!

MAGGIE. That don't let her off her obligation to keep him from making a fool of himself, does it?

JANE. Do you think he'll marry that girl?

MAGGIE. When a man's got the habit of supporting some woman, he just don't feel natural unless he's doing it.

JANE. But he told the madam marrying her was the furthest thing from his mind.

MAGGIE. It don't matter what he's got in his mind. It's what those two women got in theirs will settle the matter.

JANE. But the madam says it's up to *him*. She said, "You love her, or you love me, Stephen."

MAGGIE. So what did he say to that?

JANE. Nothing for a long time. Just walked up and down—up and down—up and—

MAGGIE. He was thinking. Tch—tch. The first man who can think up a good explanation how he can be in love with his wife *and* another woman, is going to win that prize they're always giving out in Sweden!

CURTAIN

SCENE III

A month later.

MARY'S *living room. The room is now denuded of pictures, books, vases, etc. The rug is rolled up. The curtains and chairs are covered with slips.*

As the curtain rises, MARY, *dressed for traveling, is pacing up and down.* MRS. MOREHEAD, *dressed for the street, watches her from the sofa.*

MRS. MOREHEAD. What time does your train go?

MARY (*looking at her wrist watch*). An hour. His secretary ought to be here. I never knew there could be so many papers to sign.

MRS. MOREHEAD. You showed everything to your lawyers—

MARY. They always say the same thing! I'm getting a "raw deal"—

MRS. MOREHEAD (*alarmed*). But, Mary—

MARY. Oh, I know it's not true. Stephen's been very generous.

MRS. MOREHEAD. Oh, I wouldn't say that. If Stephen is a rich man now, he owes it largely to you.

MARY. Stephen would have gotten where he is, with or without me.

MRS. MOREHEAD. He didn't have a penny when you married him.

MARY. Mother, are you trying to make me bitter, too?

MRS. MOREHEAD (*helplessly*). I'm sure I don't know what to say. If I sympathize with Stephen, you accuse me of taking his side. And when I sympathize with you, I'm making you bitter. The thing for me to do is keep still. (*There is a pause. Then, emphatically*) You're both making a terrible mistake!

MARY. Mother, please!

MRS. MOREHEAD. But the children, Mary. The children—

MARY. What good will it do them to be brought up in a home full of quarreling and suspicion? They'll be better off just with me.

MRS. MOREHEAD. No, they won't. A child needs both its parents in one home.

MARY. A home without love?

MRS. MOREHEAD. He's terribly fond of you—

MARY. Mother, don't use that word! Oh, Mother, please. Every argument goes round in circles. And, it's too late now—

MRS. MOREHEAD. It's never too late when you love. Mary, why don't you call this thing off? I'm sure that's what Stephen's waiting for.

MARY (*bitterly*). Is it? He hasn't made any sign of it to me. Isn't he the one to come to me?

MRS. MOREHEAD. You're the one, Mary, who insisted on the divorce.

MARY. But don't you see; if he hadn't wanted it, he'd have fought me—

MRS. MOREHEAD. Stephen's not the fighting kind.

MARY. Neither am I.

MRS. MOREHEAD. Damn these modern laws!

MARY. Mother!

MRS. MOREHEAD. Damn them, I say! Fifty years ago, when women couldn't get divorces, they made the best of situations like this. And sometimes, out of situations like this they made very good things indeed! (*Enter* JANE, *right.*)

JANE. Mr. Haines' secretary, ma'am.

MRS. MOREHEAD. Tell her to come in. (*Exit* JANE) Now, go bathe your eyes. Don't let that adding machine see you like this. And don't be long. Remember, you have one more unpleasant task.

MARY. Mary?

MRS. MOREHEAD. The child must be told.

MARY (*miserably, and a little guiltily*). I have been putting it off. Because—

MRS. MOREHEAD. Because you hope at the last minute a miracle will keep you from making a mess of your life. Have you thought: Stephen might marry that girl?

MARY (*very confident*). He won't do that.

MRS. MOREHEAD. What makes you so sure?

MARY. Because, deep down, Stephen does love me— But he won't find it out, until I've—really gone away— (*At the door*) You'll take good care of the children, Mother? And make them write to me to Reno, once a week? And please, Mother, don't spoil them so. (*Exits left.*)

MRS. MOREHEAD. Gracious! You'd think I'd never raised children of my own! (*Enter* MISS WATTS *and* MISS TRIMMERBACK, *right. They are very tailored, plain girls.* MISS WATTS, *the older and the plainer of the two carries a brief case*) How do you do, Miss Watts?

MISS WATTS. How do you do, Mrs. Morehead? This is Miss Trimmerback from our office.

MISS TRIMMERBACK. How do you do?

MISS WATTS. She's a notary. We have some papers for Mrs. Haines to sign.

MRS. MOREHEAD. Anything I can do?

MISS WATTS. The children will be with you? (MRS. MOREHEAD *nods*) Any incidental bills, Mrs. Morehead, send to the office. But you understand, bills arriving after the divorce will be assumed by Mrs. Haines under the terms of the settlement.

MRS. MOREHEAD. Mrs. Haines will be with you in a minute. Please don't bother her with unnecessary details. She's—she's pressed for time. (*Exits right.*)

MISS TRIMMERBACK. Gee, don't you feel sorry for Mrs. Haines?

MISS WATTS (*bitterly*). I don't feel sorry for any woman who thinks the world owes her breakfast in bed.

MISS TRIMMERBACK. You don't like her.

MISS WATTS. Oh, she never interfered at the office.

MISS TRIMMERBACK. Maybe that's why he's been a success.

MISS WATTS. He'd have gotten further without her. Everything big that came up, he was too cautious, because of her and the kids. (*Opens the brief case, takes out papers and pen, arranges the papers, for signing, on the table*) Well, thank heavens it's almost over. He and I can go back to work. (*Sits.*)

MISS TRIMMERBACK. What about Allen?

MISS WATTS (*guardedly*). What about her?

MISS TRIMMERBACK. Is he going to marry her?

MISS WATTS. I don't butt into his private affairs. Oh, I hold no brief for Allen. But I must say knowing *her* gave him a new interest in his work. Before her, he was certainly going stale. That had me worried.

MISS TRIMMERBACK (*sinking on the sofa*). Well, she's lucky, I'll say.

MISS WATTS. Oh?

MISS TRIMMERBACK. I wish I could get a man to foot my bills. I'm sick and tired, cooking my own breakfast, sloshing through the rain at 8 A. M., working like a dog. For what? Independence? A lot of independence you have on a woman's wages. I'd chuck it like that for a decent, or an indecent, home.

MISS WATTS. I'm sure you would.

MISS TRIMMERBACK. Wouldn't you?

MISS WATTS. I have a home.

MISS TRIMMERBACK. You mean Plattsburgh, where you were born?

MISS WATTS. The office. That's my home.

MISS TRIMMERBACK. Some home! I see. The office-wife?

MISS WATTS (*defiantly*). He could get along better without Mrs. Haines or Allen than he could without me.

MISS TRIMMERBACK. Oh, you're very efficient, dear. But what makes you think you're indispensable?

MISS WATTS. I relieve him of a thousand foolish details. I remind him of things he forgets, including, very often these days, his good opinion of himself. I never cry and I don't nag. I guess I *am* the office-wife. And a lot better off than Mrs. Haines. He'll never divorce me!

MISS TRIMMERBACK (*astonished*). Why, you're in love with him! (*They both rise, face each other angrily.*)

MISS WATTS. What if I am? I'd rather work for him than marry the kind of a dumb cluck I could get— (*Almost tearful*) just because he's a *man*— (*Enter* MARY, *left.*)

MARY. Yes, Miss Watts.

MISS WATTS (*collecting herself quickly*). Here are the inventories of the furniture, Mrs. Haines. I had the golf cups, the books, etchings, and the ash stands sent to Mr. Haines' club. (*Pauses*) Mr. Haines asked if he could also have the portrait of the two children.

MARY (*looking at the blank space over the mantel*). Oh, but—

MISS WATTS. He said it wouldn't matter, if you really didn't *care* for him to have it.

MARY. It's in storage.

MISS WATTS (*laying a paper on the table*). This will get it out. Sign there. The cook's letter of reference. Sign here. (MARY *sits, signs*) The insurance papers. You sign here. (MISS TRIMMERBACK *signs each paper after* MARY) The transfer papers on the car. What do you want done with it?

MARY. Well, I—

MISS WATTS. I'll find a garage. Sign here. What do you want done if someone meets your price on this apartment?

MARY. Well, I thought—

MISS WATTS. This gives us power of attorney until you get back. Sign here.

MARY. But—I—

MISS WATTS. Oh, it's quite in order, Mrs. Haines. Now, Mr. Haines took the liberty of drawing you a new will. (*Places a blue, legal-looking document before* MARY.)

MARY (*indignantly*). But—really—

MISS WATTS. If anything were to happen to you in Reno, half your property would revert to him. A detail your lawyers overlooked. Mr. Haines drew up a codicil cutting himself out—

MARY. But, I don't understand legal language, Miss Watts. I -I must have my lawyer—

MISS WATTS. As you please. (*Stiffly*) Mr. Haines suggested this for *your* sake, not his. I'm sure you realize, he has nothing but your interests at heart. (*A pause*) Sign here. (MARY *signs,* MISS WATTS *signs*) We need three witnesses. (*Enter* JANE, right, *with a box of flowers*) Your maid will do.

MARY. Jane, please witness this. It's my will.

JANE (*in tears*). Oh, Mrs. Haines! (*Signs.*)

MISS WATTS (*gathering all the papers*). You can always make changes, in the event of your remarriage. (MARY *rises*) And don't hesitate to let me know at the office, if there is anything *I* can ever do for you.

MARY (*coldly*). There will be nothing, Miss Watts.

MISS WATTS (*cheerfully*). Oh, there are always tag ends to a divorce, Mrs. Haines. And you know how Mr. Haines hates to be bothered with inconsequential details. Good day, Mrs. Haines, and pleasant journey to you! (*Exit* MISS WATTS *right, followed by* MISS TRIMMERBACK.)

JANE (*sniveling as she places the box on the table*). Mr. Haines said I was to give you these to wear on the train. (*Exits abruptly.* MARY *slowly opens the box, takes out a corsage of orchids and a card. Reads aloud: "What can I say? Stephen." Then throws them violently in the corner. Enter* MRS. MOREHEAD, LITTLE MARY, *dressed for street.*)

MRS. MOREHEAD. All set, dear?

MARY (*grimly*). All set— Mary, Mother wants to talk to you before she goes away.

MRS. MOREHEAD. Brother and I will wait for you downstairs. (*Exit* MRS. MOREHEAD.)

MARY. Mary, sit down, dear. (LITTLE MARY *skips to the sofa, sits down. A pause.* MARY *discovers that it's going to be even more painful and difficult than she imagined*) Mary—

LITTLE MARY. Yes, Mother?

MARY. Mary—

LITTLE MARY (*perplexed by her mother's tone, which she feels bodes no good to her*). Have I done something wrong, Mother?

MARY. Oh, no, darling, no. (*She sits beside her daughter, and takes her two hands*) Mary, you know Daddy's been gone for some time.

LITTLE MARY (*sadly*). A whole month.

MARY. Shall I tell you why?

LITTLE MARY (*eagerly*). Why?

MARY (*plunging in*). You know, darling, when a man and woman fall in love what they do, don't you?

LITTLE MARY. They kiss a lot—

MARY. They get married—

LITTLE MARY. Oh, yes. And then they have those children.

MARY. Well, sometimes, married people don't stay in love.

LITTLE MARY. What, Mother?

MARY. The husband and the wife—fall out of love.

LITTLE MARY. Why do they do that?

MARY. Well, they do, that's all. And when they do, they get unmarried. You see?

LITTLE MARY. No.

MARY. Well, they do. They—they get what is called a divorce.

LITTLE MARY (*very matter-of-fact*). Oh, do they?

MARY. You don't know what a divorce is, but—

LITTLE MARY. Yes, I do. I go to the movies, don't I? And lots of my friends have mummies and daddies who are divorced.

MARY (*relieved, kisses her*). You know I love you very much, don't you, Mary?

LITTLE MARY (*a pause*). Of course, Mother.

MARY. Your father and I are going to get a divorce. That's why I'm going away. That's why— Oh, darling, I can't explain to you quite. But I promise you, when you are older you will understand. And you'll forgive me. You really will! Look at me, baby, please!

LITTLE MARY (*her lips begin to tremble*). I'm looking at you, Mother— Doesn't Daddy love you any more?

MARY. No, he doesn't.

LITTLE MARY. Don't you love him?

MARY. I—I—no, Mary.

LITTLE MARY. Oh, Mother, why?

MARY. I—I don't know—But it isn't either Daddy's or Mother's fault.

LITTLE MARY. But, Mother, when you love somebody I thought you loved them until the day you die!

MARY. With children, yes. But grown-ups are different. They can fall out of love.

LITTLE MARY. I won't fall out of love with you and Daddy when I grow up. Will you fall out of love with me?

MARY. Oh, no, darling, that's different, too.

LITTLE MARY (*miserable*). I don't see *how*.

MARY. You'll have to take my word for it, baby, it is. This divorce has nothing to do with our love for you.

LITTLE MARY. But if you and Daddy—

MARY (*rising and drawing her daughter up to her*). Darling, I'll explain it better to you in the taxi. We'll go alone in the taxi, shall we?

LITTLE MARY. But, Mother, if you and Daddy are getting a divorce, which one won't I see again? Daddy or you?

MARY. You and Brother will live with me. That's what happens when—when people get divorced. Children must go with their mothers. But you'll see Daddy—sometimes. Now, darling, come along.

LITTLE MARY. Please, Mother, wait for me downstairs.

MARY. Why?

LITTLE MARY. I have to go to the bathroom.

MARY. Then hurry along, dear— (*Sees the orchids on the floor, and as she moves to the door stoops, picks them up, goes out.* LITTLE MARY *stands looking after her, stricken. Suddenly she goes to the back of the chair, hugs it, as if for comfort. Then she begins to cry and beat the back of the chair with her fists.*)

LITTLE MARY. Oh, please, please, Mother dear— Oh! Daddy, Daddy darling! Oh, why don't you do something—*do something*—Mother dear!

CURTAIN

SCENE IV

A month later.

A room in a lying-in hospital. Left, a door to the corridor. Right, a window banked to the sill with expensive flowers. Center, a hospital bed, in which EDITH, *propped up in a sea of lace pillows, lies with a small bundle at her breast. A white-uniformed nurse sits by the window. The droop of her shoulders is eloquent:* EDITH *is a trying patient. As the curtain rises,* EDITH *reaches across the bundle to the bedside table for a cigarette. She can't make it.*

EDITH (*whining*). Nurse!

NURSE (*rising wearily*). Yes, Mrs. Potter.

EDITH. Throw me a cigarette.

NURSE. Can't you wait, at least until you're through nursing?

EDITH. How many children have you nursed? I've nursed four. (NURSE *lights her cigarette;* EDITH *shifts the bundle slightly*) Ouch! Damn it! It's got jaws like a dinosaur.
(*Enter* PEGGY *with a box of flowers.*)

PEGGY. Hello, Edith.

EDITH (*in a faint voice*). Hello, Peggy.

PEGGY (*putting flowers on bed*). Here—

EDITH. How thoughtful! Nurse, will you ask this damn hospital if they're equipped with a decent vase?
(NURSE *takes the box, opens flowers and arranges them, with others, in the window.*)

PEGGY (*leans over baby*). Oh, let me see. Oh, Edith, isn't he divine!

EDITH. I hate that milky smell.

PEGGY (*alarmed*). What's that on his nose?

EDITH. What nose? Oh, that's an ash. (*Blows away the ash. Hands* PEGGY *a letter from beside table.*)

PEGGY. Mary?

EDITH (*nodding*). All about how healthy Reno is. Not a word about how she feels. I thought she cared more about Stephen than that. She sends her love to you and John. (PEGGY *reads. The wail of a new-born is heard outside.*)

EDITH. Nurse, close that door. (*The* NURSE *closes the door*) I can't tell you what that new-born yodel does to my nerves. (*To* PEGGY) What're you so down in the mouth about? I feel as badly about it as you do, but it was the thing Mary wanted to do, or she wouldn't have done it. Judging by that, she's reconciled to the whole idea.

PEGGY. She's just being brave!

EDITH. Brave? Why should she bother to be brave with her friends? Here, Nurse, he's through. (*The* NURSE *takes the bundle from her*) I told Phelps to be sure to tell Stephen that Mary's perfectly happy. It will cheer Stephen up. He's been going around like a whipped dog.

PEGGY. Oh, Edith, please let me hold him! (*The* NURSE *gives* PEGGY *the baby.*)

NURSE (*smiling*). Careful of his back, Mrs. Day.

PEGGY (*goes to the window, hugging the bundle*). Oh, I *like* the feeling so!

EDITH. You wouldn't like it so much if you'd just had it. (*Whimpering*) I had a terrible time, didn't I, Nurse?

NURSE. Oh, no, Mrs. Potter. You had a very easy time. (*She is suddenly angry*) Why, women like you don't know what a terrible time is. Try bearing a baby and scrubbing floors. Try having one in a cold filthy kitchen, without ether, without a change of linen, without decent food, without a cent to bring it up—and try getting up the next day with your insides falling out, to cook your husband's—! (*Controls herself*) No. Mrs. Potter, you didn't have a terrible time at all—I'll take the baby, please. (*Sees the reluctant expression on* PEGGY'S *face*) I hope some day you'll have one of your own, Mrs. Day. (*The* NURSE *exits with the baby.* PEGGY *breaks into tears.*)

EDITH. Well, for God's sake, Peggy, that old battle-axe didn't hurt my feelings a bit! They're all the same. If you don't get peritonitis or have quintuplets, they think you've had a picnic— (PEGGY *sits beside the bed, crying*) What's the matter?

PEGGY. Oh, Edith—John and I are getting a divorce!

EDITH (*patting her hand*). Well, darling, that's what I heard!

PEGGY (*surprised*). But—but we didn't decide to until last night.

EDITH (*cheerfully*). Oh, darling, everybody could see it was in the cards. Money, I suppose?

PEGGY (*nodding*). Oh, dear! I wish Mary were here—

EDITH. Well, she'll be there, (*Laughs*) Oh, forgive me, dear. I do feel sorry for you. But it is funny.

PEGGY. What's funny?

EDITH. It's going to be quite a gathering of the clan. (*Sitting up in bed, full of energy to break the news*) Howard Fowler's bounced Sylvia out right on her ear! He's threatened to divorce her right here in New York if she doesn't go to Reno. And name her young customers' man—

PEGGY. But—Howard's always known—

EDITH. Certainly. He hired him, so he'd have plenty of time for his own affairs. Howard's got some girl he wants to marry. But nobody, not even Winchell, knows who she is! Howard's a coony cuss. (*Laughing*) I do think it's screaming. When you remember how Sylvia always thought she was putting something over on us girls! (*She laughs so hard, she gives herself a stitch. She falls back among her pillows, limp and martyred.*)

PEGGY (*bitterly*). Life's awfully unattractive, isn't it?

EDITH (*yawning*). Oh, I wouldn't complain if that damned stork would take the Indian sign off me.

CURTAIN

SCENE V

A few weeks later. MARY'S *living room in a Reno hotel. In the rear wall, a bay window showing a view of Reno's squat rooftops and distant Nevada ranges. Left, doors to the kitchenette, the bedroom. Right, a door to the corridor. A plush armchair, a sofa. In the corner,* MARY'S *half-packed trunks and bags. It is all very drab and ugly. As the curtain rises,* LUCY, *a slatternly, middle-aged, husky woman in a house-dress, is packing the clothes that are strewn on the armchair and the table. She is singing in a nasal falsetto.*

LUCY.

Down on ole Smokey, all covered
 with snow,
I lost my true lov-ver, from courtin'
 too slow.
Courtin' is pul-leasure, partin' is grief,
Anna false-hearted lov-ver is worse
 thanna thief —

(PEGGY *enters, right. She wears a polo coat and a wool tam. She is on the verge of tears.*)

PEGGY. Lucy, where's Mrs. Haines?

LUCY. Down waiting for the mail. You'll miss her a lot when she goes tomorrow? (PEGGY *nods, sinks, dejected, on the sofa*) Mrs. Haines is about the nicest ever came here.

PEGGY. I hate Reno.

LUCY. You didn't come for fun. (*Goes on with her packing and singing.*)

The grave'll de-cay you, an' change you tuh dust,
Ain't one boy outta twenty, a poor gal kin trust—

PEGGY. You've seen lots of divorcees, haven't you, Lucy?

LUCY. Been cookin' for 'em for ten years.

PEGGY. You feel sorry for us?

LUCY. Well, ma'am, I don't. You feel plenty sorry enough for yourselves. (*Kindly*) Lord, you ain't got much else to do.

PEGGY (*resentfully*). You've never been married, Lucy.

LUCY (*indignant*). I've had three—

PEGGY. Husbands?

LUCY. Kids!

PEGGY. Oh, then you're probably very happy—

LUCY. Lord, ma'am, I stopped thinking about being happy years ago.

PEGGY. You don't think about being happy?

LUCY. Ain't had the time. With the kids and all. And the old man such a lemon when he's drinking— Them big, strong, red-headed men. They're fierce.

PEGGY. Oh, Lucy, he beats you? How terrible!

LUCY. Ain't it? When you think what a lot of women in this hotel need a beating worse than me.

PEGGY. But you live in Reno. You could get a divorce overnight.

LUCY. Lord, a woman can't get herself worked up to a thing like that overnight. I had a mind to do it once. I had the money, too. But I had to call it off.

PEGGY. Why?

LUCY. I found out I was in a family way. (*There is a rap on the door.*)

PEGGY (*going to her*). Lucy, tell Mrs. Haines I must talk to her—alone— before supper—

(*Enter* COUNTESS DE LAGE, *left. She is a silly, amiable, middle-aged woman, with carefully waved, bleached hair. She wears a gaudily-checked riding habit, carries an enormous new sombrero and a jug of corn liquor.*)

COUNTESS. Ah, Peggy, how are you, dear child?

PEGGY. All right, Countess de Lage.

COUNTESS. I've been galloping madly over the desert all day. Lucy, here's a wee juggie. We must celebrate Mrs. Haines' divorce.

PEGGY. Oh, Countess de Lage, I don't think a divorce is anything to celebrate.

COUNTESS. Wait till you've lost as many husbands as I have, Peggy. (*Wistfully*) Married, divorced, married, divorced! But where Love leads I always follow. So here I am, in Reno.

PEGGY. Oh, I wish I were anywhere else on earth.

COUNTESS. My dear, you've got the Reno jumpy-wumpies. Did you go to the doctor? What did he say?

PEGGY. He said it was—the altitude.

COUNTESS. Well, la, la, you'll get used to that. My third husband was a Swiss. If one lives in Switzerland, Peggy, one has simply got to accept the Alps. As I used to say to myself, Flora, there those damn Alps are, and there's very little even you can do about it.

PEGGY. Yes, Countess de Lage. (*Exits, hurriedly, left.*)

COUNTESS. Oh, I wish she hadn't brought up the Alps, Lucy. It always reminds me of that nasty moment I had the day Gustav made me climb to the top of one of them. (*Sits in armchair*) Lucy, pull off my boots. (LUCY *kneels, tugs at her boots*) Anyhow, there we were. And suddenly it struck me that Gustav had pushed me. (*Tragically*) I slid halfway down the mountain before I realized that Gustav didn't love me any more. (*Gaily*) But Love takes care of its own, Lucy. I slid right into the arms of my fourth husband, the Count.

LUCY (*rises, with boots*). Ain't that the one you're divorcing now?

COUNTESS. But, of course, Lucy. (*Plaintively*) What could I do when I found out he was putting arsenic in my headache powders. Ah! L'amour! L'amour! Lucy, were you ever in love?

LUCY. Yes, ma'am.

COUNTESS. Tell me about it, Lucy.

LUCY. Well, ma'am, ain't much to tell. I was kinda enjoyin' the courtin' time. It was as purty a sight as you ever saw, to see him come lopin across them hills. The sky so big and blue and that hair of his, blazing like the be-jesuss in the sun. Then we'd sit on my back fence and spark. But ma'am, you know how them big strong, red-headed men are. They just got to get to the point. So we got married, ma'am. And natcheraly, I ain't had no chanct to think about love since—

COUNTESS (*she has not been listening*). The trouble with me, Lucy, is I've been marrying too many foreigners. I think I'll go back to marrying Americans.

(*Enter* MIRIAM, *right. She is a breezy, flashy redhead, about 28 years old. She is wearing a theatrical pair of lounging pajamas.*)

MIRIAM. Hya, Lucy?

LUCY. Evening, Mrs. Aarons. (*Exits right.*)

MIRIAM. Hya, Countess, how's rhythm on the range? (*Sees the jug on the table, pours the* COUNTESS *and herself drinks.*)

COUNTESS. Gallop, gallop, gallop madly over the sagebrush! But now Miriam, I'm having an emotional relapse. In two weeks I'll be free, free as a bird from that little French bastard. But whither, oh, whither shall I fly?

MIRIAM. To the arms of that cowboy up at the dude ranch?

COUNTESS (*modestly*). Miriam Aarons!

MIRIAM. Why, he's nuts for you, Countess. He likes you better than his horse, and it's such a damn big horse.

COUNTESS (*rises, and pads in her stocking feet to the sofa*). Well, Buck Winston is nice. So young. So strong. Have you noticed the play of his muscles? (*Reclining*) Musical. Musical.

MIRIAM. He could crack a coconut with those knees. If he could get them together. Say, Countess, that guy hasn't been arousing your honorable intentions, has he?

COUNTESS. Yes, Miriam, but I'm different from the rest of you. I've always put my faith in love. Still, I've had four divorces. Dare I risk a fifth?

MIRIAM. What are you risking, Countess, or maybe I shouldn't ask?

COUNTESS. I mean, Miriam, I could never make a success of Buck at Newport.

MIRIAM. Even Mrs. Astor would have to admit Buck's handsome. If I had your dough, I'd take him to Hollywood first, then Newport.

COUNTESS. Hollywood? Why *not?* I might turn him into a picture star. After all, my second husband was a gondolier, and a month after I married him, a Duchess eloped with him. Ah! L'amour!

(*Enter* SYLVIA, *right. She is wearing a smart dinner dress. Her trip to Reno has embittered her, but it has not subdued her.*)

MIRIAM. Hya, Sylvia? Going to a ball?

SYLVIA (*pours a drink*). Doing the town with a boy friend.

MIRIAM. Where'd you pick him up?

SYLVIA. The Silver State Bar. I'm not going to sit around, moping, like Mary.

COUNTESS. Poor Mary. If her husband gave her the flimsiest excuse, she'd take him back.

SYLVIA. She has no pride. I'd roast in hell before I'd take Howard Fowler back. Kicking me out like that! After all I sacrificed!

MIRIAM. Such as what?

SYLVIA. I gave him my *youth!*

COUNTESS (*dreamily*). Hélas, what else can a woman do with her youth, but give it to a man?

MIRIAM. Hélas, she can't preserve it in alcohol.

COUNTESS (*practical*). But, Sylvia, how could your husband kick you out, if you were a femme fidèle?

SYLVIA. Of course, I was a faithful wife. (MIRIAM *snorts*) What are you laughing at?

MIRIAM. Two kinds of women, Sylvia, owls and ostriches. (*Raises her glass*) To the feathered sisterhood! To the girls who *get* paid and paid. (*Parenthetically*) And you got paid *plenty!*

SYLVIA. You bet I got plenty! The skunk!

COUNTESS. I never got a sou from any of my husbands, except my first husband, Mr. Straus. He said the most touching thing in his will. I remember every word of it. "To my beloved wife, Flora, I leave all my estate in trust to be administered by executors, because she is an A No. 1 schlemeil." (*Touched anew*) Wasn't that sweet?

(*Enter* MARY, *right. She is subdued. She is carrying some letters.*)

MIRIAM. Hya, queen?

MARY. Fine.

MIRIAM. Ya lie.

COUNTESS. Mary, I'm starved.

(LUCY *enters, left, takes* MARY'S *hat.*)

MARY. Supper's nearly ready. As my last official act in Reno, I cooked the whole thing with my hands, didn't I, Lucy?

LUCY. All but the steak and tomatoes and dessert, Mrs. Haines. (*Exits, left.*)

MARY (*gives a letter to* SYLVIA, *glancing, as she does so, at the inscription*). For you, Sylvia. From Edith?

SYLVIA. You couldn't miss that infantile handwriting. (*Pointedly*) You didn't hear from anyone?

MARY. No.

SYLVIA. Well, darling, Stephen's hardly worth a broken heart.

MARY. The less you have to say about me and Stephen the better I like it!

SYLVIA. I'm only trying to cheer you up. That's more than you do for me.

MARY. I'm doing enough, just being pleasant to you.

SYLVIA. My, you have got the jitters, dear.

MIRIAM. Hey, Sylvia, we're all out here in the same boat. Mary's laid off you. Why don't you lay off her?

SYLVIA. Oh, I'm just trying to make her see life isn't over just because Stephen let her down. (*Opens her letter. A batch of press clippings falls out. The* COUNTESS *picks them up, reads them idly, as* SYLVIA *goes on with the letter.*)

COUNTESS. You see, Miriam? What else is there for a woman but l'amour?

MIRIAM. There's a little corn whiskey left. (*She pours another drink.*)

COUNTESS. Cynic, you don't believe in Cupid.

MIRIAM. That double-crossing little squirt! Give me Donald Duck. (*To* MARY) Have a drink? (MARY *shakes her head*) Listen, Babe, why not—give out? You'd feel better—

MARY (*laughing*). Miriam, you're not very chatty about your own affairs.

COUNTESS (*suddenly engrossed by the clippings from* SYLVIA'S *letter*). Miriam, you sly puss, you never told us you even knew Sylvia's husband.

SYLVIA (*looking up from her letter*). What?

COUNTESS (*rises*). Sylvia, listen to this: "Miriam Vanities Aarons is being Renovated. Three guesses, Mrs. Fowler, for whose Ostermoor?"

(SYLVIA *snatches the clippings from her.*)

IRIAM. Why can't those lousy rags ave a successful divorce alone?

OUNTESS (*reading another clipping*). "Prominent stockbroker and x-chorine to marry."

YLVIA (*to* MIRIAM). Why, you little hypocrite! (*During this,* PEGGY *as entered and goes back of the sofa. he listens but does not join the roup.*)

ARY (*going to her*). Now, Sylvia—

YLVIA. Did you know this?

ARY. Oh, Sylvia, why do you care? ou don't love Howard—

YLVIA (*brushing her aside*). That as nothing to do with it. (*To* IRIAM, *fiercely*) How much did he ettle on you?

IRIAM. I made Howard pay for hat he wants; you made him pay or what he doesn't want.

YLVIA. You want him for his money.

IRIAM. So what do you want him or? I'll stay bought. That's more than ou did, Sylvia.

YLVIA. Why, you dirty little trollop!

IRIAM. Don't start calling names, ou Park Avenue push-over! (SYLVIA *ives* MIRIAM *a terrific smack. In the winkling of an eye, they are pulling air.* MARY *seizes* SYLVIA'S *arm;* SYL-IA *breaks loose. The* COUNTESS *tugs t* MIRIAM'S *belt, as* LUCY *comes in, ooks at the fight with a rather proessional eye, and exits for the smelling salts.*)

COUNTESS. Tiens! Miriam. Don't be vulgar. (*Her interference enables* SYLVIA *to slap* MIRIAM *unimpeded.*)

MIRIAM (*shoving the* COUNTESS *on the sofa*). Out of the way, you fat old—! (SYLVIA *grabs* MIRIAM'S *hair*) Ouch, let go! (SYLVIA *is about to use her nails.* MARY *takes a hand.*)

MARY. I won't have this, you hear! (MARY'S *interference allows* MIRIAM *to give* SYLVIA *a terrific kick in the shins.*)

SYLVIA (*routed, in sobs*). Oh, you hurt me, you bitch, you! (*As she turns away,* MIRIAM *gives her another well-placed kick, which straightens* SYLVIA *up.*)

MIRIAM. Take that! (SYLVIA, *shrieking with rage and humiliation, grabs* MIRIAM *again, sinks her white teeth into* MIRIAM'S *arm. At this mayhem,* MARY *seizes her, shakes her violently, pushes her sobbing into the armchair.*)

MARY (*to* MIRIAM). That's enough.

MIRIAM. Where's the iodine? (MARY *points to bedroom*) Gotta be careful of hydrophobia, you know. (*Exits, right.*)

SYLVIA (*blubbering, nursing her wounds*). Oh, Mary, how could you let her do that to me!

MARY (*coldly*). I'm terribly sorry, Sylvia.

SYLVIA. The humiliation! You're on her side. After all I've done for you!

MARY. What have you done for me?

SYLVIA. I warned *you!*

MARY (*bitterly*). I'm not exactly grateful for that.

SYLVIA (*hysterical*). Oh, aren't you? Listen to me, you ball of conceit. You're not the object of pity you suppose. Plenty of the girls are tickled to death you got what was coming to you. You deserved to lose Stephen, the stupid way you act. But I always stood up for you, like a loyal friend. What thanks do I get? You knew about that woman, and you stood by, gloating, while she—

MARY. Get out of here! (LUCY *enters from the bedroom, with a bottle of spirits of ammonia, as* SYLVIA *gives way completely to hysteria, and, screaming with rage, picks up ash trays, glasses, and cigarette boxes, and hurls them violently against the wall.*)

SYLVIA (*at the top of her lungs*). I hate you! I hate you! I hate *everybody*—

LUCY (*takes* SYLVIA *firmly by the shoulders, forces the bottle under her nose*). Listen, Mrs. Fowler! You got the hy-strikes! (*Rushes her gasping, sobbing, to the door.*)

SYLVIA. You wait. Some day you'll need a woman friend. Then you'll think of me— (*Exit* LUCY *and* SYLVIA, *struggling helplessly, right.*)

COUNTESS (*rising from the sofa*). Poor creatures. They've lost their equilibrium because they've lost their faith in love. (*Philosophically*) L'amour. Remember the song Buck made up, just for me? (*Pours herself a drink, sings*) "Oh, a man can ride a horse to the range above, But a woman's got to ride on the wings of love, Coma a ti-yi-yippi." (*Throws the jug over her shoulder, and exit right, still singing, as* MIRIAM *enters, the ravages of her fight repaired.*)

MIRIAM. The coast clear?

PEGGY. Oh, that was the most disgusting thing I ever saw.

MIRIAM. Right, kid, we're a pair of alley cats—

MARY. You should not be here, Peggy, to see it at all. (*She picks up the ash trays, etc.*)

MIRIAM. What the hell are you doing here?

MARY. Peggy wanted to buy a car.

PEGGY. With my own money!

MARY. John said they couldn't afford a car.

PEGGY. He couldn't. I could.

MARY. What was his—is yours. What is yours—is your own. Very fair.

PEGGY. A woman's best protection is a little money of her own.

MARY. A woman's best protection is —the right man. (*With gentle sarcasm*) Obviously, John isn't the right man and Peggy will forget all about him in another month.

PEGGY. No, I won't. I can't. Because —because— (*Bursts into tears*) Oh, Mary, I'm going to have a baby. Oh, Mary, what shall I do?

MARY. Peggy, what's his telephone number?

PEGGY (*quickly*). Eldorado 5-2075. (MIRIAM *goes at once to the phone*

;ets the operator, gives the number*) 3ut, oh, Mary, I can't tell him!

IRIAM. Why? Isn't it his?

EGGY. Oh, of course!

IIRIAM. And make it snappy, oper-tor.

EGGY. I always wanted it. But what an I do with it now?

IIRIAM. Land it with the Marines—

IARY. Peggy, you've shared your ove with him. Your baby will share our blood, your eyes, your hair, your irtues—and your faults— But your ttle pin-money, that, of course, you ould not share.

EGGY. Oh, Mary, I know I'm wrong. 3ut, it's no use—you don't know the hings he said to me. I have my pride.

IARY (*bitterly*). Reno's full of wom-n who all have their pride.

EGGY. You think I'm like them.

IIRIAM. You've got the makings, ear.

IARY. Love has pride in nothing—ut its own humility.

IIRIAM (*at telephone*). Mr. Day, lease. Reno calling—Mr. Day? My ;od, he must live by the phone. Just old the—
PEGGY *leaps to the phone.*)

EGGY. Hello, John. (*Clears her hroat of a sob*) No, I'm not sick! 'hat is, I am sick! That is, I'm sick o my stomach. Oh, John! I'm going o have a baby— Oh, darling, are ou?— Oh, darling, do you?— Oh, darling, so am I! So do I! Course, I forgive you.— Yes, precious. Yes, lamb. On the very next train! John? (*A kiss into the phone. It is returned*) Oh, Johnny, when I get back, things are going to be so different—! John, do you mind if I reverse the charges? (*Hangs up*) I can't stay for supper. I've got to pack.

MARY. When you get back—don't see too much of the girls.

PEGGY. Oh, I won't, Mary. It's all their fault we're here.

MARY. Not—entirely.

PEGGY. Good-bye! Oh, I'm so happy, I could cry. (*Exits, right.*)

MIRIAM. Getting wise, aren't you?

MARY. Know all the answers.

MIRIAM. Then, why're you here?

MARY. I had plenty of advice, Miriam.
(*The telephone rings.* MIRIAM *goes to it.*)

MIRIAM. Hello. No, we completed that call, operator. (*Hangs up.*)

MARY. Cigarette?

MIRIAM (*suddenly*). Listen.

MARY. There's nothing you can say I haven't heard.

MIRIAM. Sure? I come from a world where a woman's got to come out on top—or it's just too damned bad. Maybe I got a new slant.

MARY (*wearily*). All right, Miriam. Talk to me about my—lawful husband. Talk to me about security—What does it all come to? Compromise.

MIRIAM. What the hell? A woman's compromised the day she's born.

MARY. You can't compromise with utter defeat. He doesn't want me.

MIRIAM. How do you know?

MARY. How do I know—why else am I here?

MIRIAM (*a pause. Then, mock-tragically*). Because you've got no guts, Mary Haines. It happened to me—I lost my man, too.

MARY (*smiling*). You?

MIRIAM. Oh, it only happened once. Got wise to myself after that. Look, how did I lose him? We didn't have enough dough to get married. I wouldn't sleep with him until we did. I had ideals—God knows where I got 'em. I held out on him— (*Sighs*) Can you beat it? I liked him a lot better than I've ever liked anybody since. I never held out again—What'd my Romeo do? Got himself another girl. I made a terrible stink. Why shouldn't I? I should. But what I ought not to have done was say—good-bye. I was like you.

MARY. I don't understand.

MIRIAM. Then get a load of this. I should of licked that girl where she licked me—in the hay.

MARY. Miriam!

MIRIAM. That's where you win in the first round. And if I know men, that's still Custer's Last Stand. (MARY *walks away from her*) Shocked yo You're too modest. You're ashame O.K., sister. But my idea of love that love isn't ashamed of nothing.

MARY (*turning to her*). A good argu ment, Miriam. So modern. So sim ple. Sex the cause, sex the cure. It too simple, Miriam. Your love battle are for — lovers — or professional (*Gently*) Not for a man and woma who've been married twelve qui years! Oh, I don't mean I wouldn love Stephen's arms around m again. But I wouldn't recapture, if could, our—young passion. That wa the wonderful young thing we ha That was part of our youth, like th —babies. But not the thing that mad him my husband, that made me hi wife—Stephen needed me! He *need ed* me for twelve years. Stephe doesn't need me any more.

MIRIAM. I get it. (*Phone rings* That's why I'm marrying this gu Fowler. He needs me like hell. If don't marry him he'll drink himse to death in a month, the poor dop

MARY (*at the telephone*). Yes? No operator, we completed—you say New York is calling Mrs. Haines I'll take that call— (*To* MIRIAM Stephen!

MIRIAM. Listen, make him tha speech you just made me!

MARY (*radiant*). I knew he'd call. knew when the last moment came he'd realize he needed me.

MIRIAM. For God's sake, tell hin that *you* need him!

MARY. Hello—hello? Stephen? Mary Yes. I'm very cheerful. It's so goo to hear your voice, Stephen. I—why yes, it's scheduled for tomorrow at 12—but, Stephen, I can— (*Frightened*) but, Stephen! No—of course—I haven't seen the papers. How could I, out here? (*There is a long pause*) Yes, I'd rather *you* told me. Of course I understand the position you're both in. No, I'm not bitter, not bitter at all—I—I hope you'll both be very happy. No, I have no plans, no plans at all—Stephen, do you mind if I hang up? Good-bye, Stephen— Good-bye—

MIRIAM. He's marrying her?

MARY. Oh, God, why did I let this happen? We were married. We were one person. We had a good life. Oh, God, I've been a *fool!*

MIRIAM. Sure you have. Haven't we all, sister?

MARY. But she doesn't love him. I *do*. That's the way it is. (*She goes to the window, and looks out. There is a pause. Then, violently*) But it's not ended if your heart doesn't say so. It's not ended!

CURTAIN

ACT THREE

SCENE I

Early evening, two years later. CRYSTAL'*s bathroom. Left, a black marbleized tub with frilled shower curtains. In a niche, back of the tub, a gilded French telephone. Right, a satin-skirted dressing table, covered with glittering toilet bottles and cosmetic jars. Towel racks piled with embroidered bathtowels. Center, a door to* CRYSTAL'*s bedroom. As the curtain rises,* CRYSTAL *is lolling in the bath, reading a magazine, smoking, as* HELENE, *a chic French maid, enters.*

HELENE. Madame has been soaking an hour.

CRYSTAL (*rudely*). So what?

HELENE. But, monsieur—

CRYSTAL. Monsieur is going out with me and my friends, whether he likes it or not. Has that kid gone home yet?

HELENE. Mademoiselle Mary has just finished the supper with her daddy. Madame, monsieur is so anxious that you say good night to her.

CRYSTAL. Listen, that kid doesn't want to bid me beddy-bye any more than I do. He's tried for two years to cram us down each other's throat. Let her go home to her mommer. (*Passes* HELENE *a brush*) Here—scrub— Some day I'm going to slap that kid down. She's too— (*As* HELENE *scrubs too hard*) Ow! You're taking my skin off— Oh, I'm so bored

I could— (*Hurls the soap across the room*) Helene, never marry a man who's deserted a "good woman." He's as cheerful as a man who's murdered his poor old mother. (*Telephone rings*) Get out! And, Helene, when Mrs. Fowler comes, keep her downstairs, if you have to *sit* on her. (*Exit* HELENE. CRYSTAL *picks up the telephone. Her voice melts*) Hello, darling, I'm in the tub. I'm shrivelled to a peanut waiting for this call. No, I'm not afraid of a shock. You ought to know— Oh, Buck, I'm going to miss you like nobody's business. I can't tell you what it did to me, locking the door on our little apartment— I'll say we had fun! Coma ti-yi-yippy, what? Oh, no, say anything you like. This is the one place where I have some privacy— (CRYSTAL's *back is to the door. She does not hear a brief rap*) Listen, baby, must you really go to the coast? Oh, the hell with Mr. Goldwyn. (*Enter* LITTLE MARY. *She stands hesitantly against the door*) Listen, you don't have to tell me what you sacrificed to have a movie career. I've seen that cartoon you married. If Flora was ever a Countess, I'm the Duchess of Windsor. Well, Buck, maybe she's not such a half-wit, but— (*Sees* LITTLE MARY) Oh— call me back in two minutes. I've had a small interruption. (*Hangs up*) Who told you to come in here?

LITTLE MARY (*politely*). Daddy. Good night. (*Turns to go.*)

CRYSTAL (*sweetly*). Oh, don't go, darling. Hand me that brush.

LITTLE MARY (*gently*). Please?

CRYSTAL. Please. (LITTLE MARY *gives her the brush.*)

LITTLE MARY. Good night. (*Goes to the door.*)

CRYSTAL. My, you're in a hurry to tell Daddy about it.

LITTLE MARY. About what?

CRYSTAL. My talk on the telephone.

LITTLE MARY. I don't understand grown-ups on the telephone. They all sound silly. Good night.

CRYSTAL. Good night, who? (*A pause*) You've been told to call me Aunty Crystal. (*A pause*) Why don't you do it?

LITTLE MARY (*still edging to the door*). Yes.

CRYSTAL. Yes, what?

LITTLE MARY (*lamely*). Yes, good night.

CRYSTAL (*angry*). You sit down!

LITTLE MARY. Oh, it's awfully hot in here. I've got my coat on.

CRYSTAL. You heard me! (LITTLE MARY *sits on the stool before the dressing table, squirms*) We're going to have this out. I've done my damn —my level best to be friends with you, but you refuse to co-operate.

LITTLE MARY. What?

CRYSTAL. Co-operate.

LITTLE MARY (*nodding mechanically*). Co-operate.

CRYSTAL (*exasperated*). Answer my question. You don't like me. Why?

LITTLE MARY (*rising*). Well, good night, Crystal—

CRYSTAL. I said, why?

LITTLE MARY (*very patiently*). Listen, Crystal, my mother told me I wasn't to be rude to you.

CRYSTAL. For the last time, young lady, you give me one good reason why you don't like me.

LITTLE MARY. I never said I didn't like you, Crystal.

CRYSTAL. But you don't like me, do you?

LITTLE MARY. No, but I never *said* so. I've been very polite, Crystal, considering you're something awful!

CRYSTAL. Wait till your father hears this!

LITTLE MARY (*suddenly defiant*). Listen— Daddy doesn't think you're so wonderful any more!

CRYSTAL. Did he tell you that?

LITTLE MARY. No. Daddy always pretends you're all right, but he's just ashamed to have Mother know what a mean, silly wife he's got. And I don't tell Mother what *we* think, because you've made her cry enough, Crystal. So I'm not going to co-operate, *ever!*

CRYSTAL. Get out!

LITTLE MARY (*goes to the door, then turns, rather superior*). And *another* thing, I think this bathroom is perfectly ridiculous! Good night, Crystal! (*Exits. The telephone rings.* CRYSTAL *grabs it, irritable.*)

CRYSTAL. Yes, darling— That Haines brat. God, she gets under my skin!— No, she didn't hear anything. What good would it do her, anyhow? You're off in the morning, and Lord knows we've been discreet— What? You are? (*Giggling*) Dining with the first Mrs. Haines— Well, darling, lay off the gin. It makes you talk too much— Well, just be careful, darling.

(*Enter* SYLVIA, *without knocking. She wears an elaborate evening gown, and carries a cocktail. These two years have had no appreciable effect on* SYLVIA. *She is her old Act One self again.*)

SYLVIA. Yoohoo! May I come in?

CRYSTAL (*in the telephone*). No, this is not the Aquarium. It's Grand Central Station. (*Hangs up.*)

SYLVIA. Who was that?

CRYSTAL. A wrong number.

SYLVIA. You were talking to a man.

CRYSTAL. Pass me that sponge.— Please.

SYLVIA (*waiting on* CRYSTAL). Oh, Crystal, you know you can trust me.

CRYSTAL. And that eye cup.

SYLVIA. There must be someone. After all, I've known Stephen for years. He's really not your type. I often wonder how you two got together. I was telling my psychoanalyst about it. You know, I've got to tell him everything.

CRYSTAL. That must be an awful effort.

SYLVIA. I don't mind discussing myself. But talking about my friends does make me feel disloyal. He says Stephen has a Guilt Complex.

CRYSTAL. What?

SYLVIA (*cheerfully*). He says men of Stephen's generation were brought up to believe that infidelity is a sin. That's why he allowed Mary to divorce him, and that's why he married you, Crystal. He had to marry you just to convince himself he was not a sexual monster.

CRYSTAL. Yes? Well, if Stephen is a sexual monster, psychoanalysis is through.

SYLVIA. And he says you've got a Cinderella Complex. He says most American women have. They're all brought up to believe that marriage to a rich man should be their aim in life. He says we neither please the men nor function as child-bearing animals—

CRYSTAL (*bored and angry*). Will you function yourself into the bedroom?

SYLVIA (*hurt*). I don't think that's the way to talk to me, after all I've done for you. When you married Stephen you didn't know a soul. It wasn't easy to put *you* over. Everybody was on Mary's side.

CRYSTAL. They still are. They never miss a chance to remind me what a noble, useful woman Mary has become since she left Stephen.

SYLVIA (*comforting*). My dear, she's miserable! Why, she never sees a soul.

CRYSTAL. She's having a dinner party tonight.

SYLVIA. Edith told me. She's going. And Flora.

CRYSTAL. Flora?

SYLVIA. The Countess de Lage. Mrs. Buck Winston? My God, I have to laugh when I think of Flora actually turning that cowboy into a movie star. Of course he's not my type, but he's positively the Chambermaid's Delight—

CRYSTAL (*fiercely*). Will you shut up?

SYLVIA. But, Crystal—

CRYSTAL. I said shut up— (*Calling*) Helene!

SYLVIA. Well, I think you're very ungrateful!

CRYSTAL. Well, take it up with your psychoanalyst. (HELENE *enters*) Helene, draw the curtains. I want to take a shower. (SYLVIA *goes to the door as* HELENE *draws the curtains*) That's right, Sylvia—wait in the bedroom.

SYLVIA (*sees the scales, decides to weigh herself*). Oh, dear, I've lost another pound. I must remember to tell my analyst. You know, everything means something. (*The shower goes on.* HELENE *exits.* SYLVIA *gets off the scales. During the following monologue, she goes to* CRYSTAL'*s dressing table, where she examines all the bottles and jars*) But even my analyst says no woman should try to do as much as I do. He says I attach too much value to my feminine friendships. He says I have a Damon and Pythias Complex. I guess I have given too much of myself to other women. He says women are natural enemies— (*Picks up bottle*) Why, Crystal, I thought you didn't touch up your hair— (*Sniffing perfume*)

My dear, I wouldn't use this. You smell it on every tart in New York. That reminds me— (*Going to the shower curtains*) if you do have an affair, Crystal, for heaven's sake, be discreet. Remember what Howard did to me, the skunk. (*Peeking in*) My, you're putting on weight. (*Going back to dressing table, she sits down, and begins to pry in all the drawers*) But men are so mercenary. They think they own you body and soul, just because they pay the bills— I tried this cream. It brought out pimples— Of course, Crystal, if you were smart, you'd have a baby. It's the only real hold a woman has—
(HELENE *enters.*)

HELENE. Monsieur says will madame be long?

SYLVIA. Can't you see she's rushing?— (HELENE *exits. The shower goes off*) Men are so selfish! When you're only making yourself beautiful for them. (*Opens another drawer*) I wish I could find a man who would understand my need for a companion— (*Finds a key, examines it*) Why, Crystal, what are *you* doing with a key to the Gothic Apartments? (CRYSTAL'S *head pops from behind the curtain.*)

CRYSTAL. What?— Oh— (*Nervously*) Oh, that! (*Playing for time*) Throw me a towel, Sylvia!

SYLVIA (*bringing her towel*). That's where Howard had me followed. The doorman there is a professional blackmailer! (CRYSTAL *has wrapped herself in a big towel, now steps from behind the shower curtains and sits on the rim of the tub to dry her legs*) I asked my psychoanalyst about him, and he said blackmailers are really perverts who can't think of a good perversion. So they blackmail people instead.

CRYSTAL (*going to the dressing-table*). Really? Well, he can't blackmail me now. (*As she passes* SYLVIA, *she lightly snatches the key from her*) The Gothic Apartments are where Stephen and I had to go before the divorce. I keep it for sentimental reasons. (*Smiling, she drops the key back in the drawer, locks it.*)

SYLVIA. Poor Stephen! My dear, I thought tonight how tired he looked, and old. Crystal, I've told you everything. Tell me: how long do you think you can be faithful to Stephen?

CRYSTAL (*making up her face*). Well, life plays funny tricks. The urge might hit me tomorrow.

SYLVIA. I doubt it, pet. You're a typical blonde.

CRYSTAL. So what?

SYLVIA (*loftily*). Most *blondes* are frigid.

CRYSTAL. Really? Well, maybe that's just a dirty piece of *brunette* propaganda!

CURTAIN

SCENE II

Eleven o'clock the same night. MARY'S *bedroom. A charming, simple room. Left, a door to the dressing-room. Right, a door to the hall. As the curtain rises,* JANE *is arranging a number of evening wraps on the bed.* MIRIAM, MARY *and* NANCY *are entering.*

MIRIAM. Thanks, baby, a lot! I never was at a wetter dinner.

MARY. It was a success. I left Reno two years ago today. This was a memorial dinner for you old Renoites, and your new husbands.

MIRIAM. I get it. Listen, there's no soap eating out your heart, sister!

NANCY. Mary, if I had a heroine in one of my books who behaved the way you do, my two readers would never believe it. No one man is worth it.

MIRIAM. Say, the whole Racquet Club's not worth it— Speaking of my dear husband Howard—the skunk—can I have a whiskey and soda?

NANCY. Make it two.
(JANE *exits, right.*)

MIRIAM. I lay off when Howard's around. I'm weaning him from the bottle by easy stages. He's in the secondary stage now.

NANCY. What stage is that?

MIRIAM. He puts ice in.

MARY. How's matrimony, Miriam? Making a go of it?

MIRIAM. I'm doing a reconstruction job that makes Boulder Dam look like an egg-cup.
(*Enter* PEGGY, *right.*)

PEGGY. Oh, Mary, can't we get off to the party? I have to get home early. Little John always wakes up. Little John said the cutest thing the other day. (*A dramatic pause*) He said da-da—!

NANCY. When does he enter Columbia?
(*Enter* JANE *with tray and highballs.*)

MARY. Jane, tell Mrs. Winston the ladies are ready to go.

JANE. Mrs. Winston, ma'am, is drinking with the gentlemen.

MARY. Well, tell her to come up.
(*Exit* JANE.)

MIRIAM. What's the hurry? Two more snootfuls, and Flora will float up on her own breath.
(*Enter* EDITH, *right.*)

EDITH (*petulantly*). Mary, I wish you had an elevator in this house. It's so difficult to walk upstairs in my condition.

MARY. Edith, are you Catholic or just careless?

EDITH. Mary, isn't this your old furniture?

MARY. Yes.

EDITH. I think you should get rid of it. There's nothing that keeps a woman so in the dumps as sleeping in a bed with old associations. Mary, you're carrying this nunnery business too far. How do you expect to find anyone else, if you don't make an effort?

MARY. I don't want anyone, Edith. (*Mock cynical*) I hate men! Men are awful—

EDITH. Oh, they're not all like Stephen, dear.

MARY. I saw plenty of men when I came back from Reno. They're all alike. They never leave you at your own front door without a wrestling-match.

EDITH. You know I asked Phelps about that once. I said, "Why does a man always act like a Don Juan in a taxi?" And he said it was a hang-over from their bachelor days when a man's sex life was conditioned by the click of the meter.

MIRIAM. It beats me how in a taxi, the nicest guy turns into Harpo Marx.

EDITH. Mary, want to hear something about Sylvia? (MARY, MIRIAM, NANCY *and* PEGGY: *chorus, "No!"*) Well, Sylvia's going to a psychoanalyst. She says you destroyed all her faith in friendship.

MARY. As if any woman needed to go to a psychoanalyst to find out she can't trust women.

EDITH. Mary, you've grown awfully hard since you deserted your old friends.

MARY. Isn't "wise" the word? I'm beginning to understand women.

NANCY. Too bad! It's the beginning of woman's inhumanity to woman.

EDITH (*moving to door, left*). Oh, they're going to talk philosophy, Peggy. Come on in here while I powder my nose.

PEGGY. Edith, did I tell you how little John said da-da?

EDITH. Listen, I wouldn't care if *this* one stood up and sang the Star Spangled Banner! (*They exit, as enter* MRS. MOREHEAD, *in street clothes, right.*)

MRS. MOREHEAD. Oh, hello, girls Hello, dear. Party over?

MARY. Enjoy the movies, Mother?

MRS. MOREHEAD. I wish I could make up my mind whether or not I like Shirley Temple.
(*Enter the* COUNTESS DE LAGE, *right She is a tangle of tulle and jewels. She has a slight "edge" on.*)

COUNTESS. Such a lovely dinner! It's so wonderful to see all our lives temporarily settled!

MARY. My mother, Mrs. Morehead, Mrs. Winston. Mrs. Buck Winston.

MRS. MOREHEAD (*trying to place the name*). Buck Winston?

MARY. The movie star.

MRS. MOREHEAD. Ah, yes! (*Pleasantly*) My granddaughter adores your son on the screen.

COUNTESS (*good-naturedly*). I daresay the public does see Buck as just a boy. And it is a trifle absurd *me* being married to a movie star. But, Mrs. Morehead, you wouldn't believe how many of my Newport friends who ridiculed Buck when I married him positively claw for invitations to Hollywood. Mais là, East is East and West is West, but I always say Le Cinema is the Great Leveller!

MRS. MOREHEAD. You don't say! (*Edges to the hall door.*)

COUNTESS. Mrs. Morehead, do whip into something, and come along with Mary to my party. The Casino Roof. Everyone's clamored to come. I have no idea who's going to be there.

MRS. MOREHEAD. Well, you're sure to know somebody. (*To* MARY) Later, dear? (MARY *nods*, MRS. MOREHEAD *escapes, right.*)

COUNTESS (*gathering her wrap*). Mary, you're not coming?

MARY. I'm very tired, Flora.

COUNTESS. Oh, you're cross because Buck's had a wee droppie.

MIRIAM. Don't be modest, Flora. Your ducky is stinko.

COUNTESS. I do wish he wouldn't drink straight gin. You know, he's not allowed to. Mr. Goldwyn put that in the new contract.

MIRIAM. I wish I'd had my marriag license drawn up by Mr. Goldwyr

COUNTESS. Mary, do come. This i *really* our farewell party. I'm neve coming back to New York.

MARY. What's wrong with Nev York, Flora?

COUNTESS. Well, when Buck isn working we're not going to live any where. (*Whispering*) Mary, can trust you?

MARY. Of course, Flora!

COUNTESS (*to the others*). You wi keep this just between the four of us

MIRIAM. Shoot, Flora, it's a nation wide hookup!

COUNTESS (*settling herself besid* MARY *on the foot of the bed*). Well you know how Buck was? (*Wistful* So--so impassioné?

MIRIAM. The boy had something.

COUNTESS (*tartly*). Well, he hasn got it any more, Miriam! First, thought it was just gin, interferin with his libido— (*Tearfully*) Bu now I think Buck is deceiving me–

NANCY. How incredible!

COUNTESS. Well, I have no proof Except he comes home every after noon smelling of a strange perfume

MARY. Where does he say he's been.

COUNTESS. Visiting his horse. Bu Trixie was shipped to Hollywood las week. You remember, I was photo graphed with her in the baggage-car. Now he says he's been going to the

Grand Central Gymnasium. But I telephoned today. Some great oaf answered. I said: "Is Buck Winston there?" he said: "Who? No." So I said: "My dear good man, he comes every day." So he said: "My mistake, lady, he's inside now boxing with Rudolph Valentino."

MARY. Poor Flora!

COUNTESS (*practical*). That's why I think it's safer just to keep floating around.

MARY. I understand—l'amour.

COUNTESS. L'amour, yes, but jamais, (*She has her lucid moments*) jamais *lopsided* amour!

MARY (*laughing*). Lopsided amour is better than no amour at all. Flora, let him make a fool of you. Let him do anything he wants, as long as he stays. He's taking the trouble to deceive you. (*Half to herself*) And if he took the trouble, he really must have cared—

NANCY. The Voice of Experience.

MIRIAM (*to* COUNTESS). Come on, chin up.

NANCY. That's right. Both of them! (*Enter* PEGGY *and* EDITH.)

COUNTESS (*rising*). Oh, cheries, you missed it! I was just saying—now will you keep this just among the six of us?—I suspect Buck of being unfaithful. Of course, it's my own fault. I should have had him watched. The way I did all the others. I wish I'd found out where he's had that apartment!

PEGGY. An apartment—?

COUNTESS. Where would you expect him to go? Central Park? Why, it's winter.

PEGGY. Oh, I've always heard people went to hotels.

COUNTESS. But, cherie, *Buck* couldn't go to a hotel. You know what would happen. At the most inopportune moment someone would say: "Mr. Winston, may I have your autograph?" It happened to us on our wedding night. I would have sent for the manager, but it was the manager asking for the autograph. Ah, well, off to Hollywood in the morning! That's safe! (*Moving to door*) Dear Mr. Hays will protect me from Dietrich and Harlow. (*Exits, right.*)

EDITH (*getting her wrap*). Darling, you really won't come to Flora's party?

MARY. No, Edith!

EDITH. Then I can tell you. Of course, I know how you feel about your Ex—and his New Deal—though I think you'd be glad he's so happy.

MARY. I am.

EDITH. Sylvia telephoned tonight. She and Crystal and Stephen are going on to the Roof with a theatre party. Well, darling, I don't feel much like going myself. I loathe this dress. My husband says I look as though I were going to sing in it. (*Exits, right.*)

NANCY. Think I'll go, too, Mary! It's a good chance to study Park Avenue's flora and fauna. And I'm writing a new book. It's called "Gone with the Ice-man," or "Sex Has No Place in the Home." (*Exits with* PEGGY.)

MIRIAM (*to* MARY). Listen, Queen, change your mind! Let's go on to the party!

MARY. No, Miriam.

MIRIAM. Well, I'm going. Wish you could see the cooing-fest Howard and I put on for Sylvia— Shall I spit in Crystal's eye for you? (MARY *shakes her head*) You're passing up a swell chance, sister! Where I spit no grass grows ever! (*Exits.* JANE *enters, right.* MARY *begins to unfasten her dress, takes off her jewels, lays them on the dresser.*)

MARY. Jane, turn down my bed.

JANE. Yes, ma'am.
(MARY *goes into the boudoir, left.*)

MARY (*offstage*). Did Mary have a nice time with her father?

JANE (*turning down the bed*). Well, ma'am, you know how she is when she comes home.

MARY (*offstage*). I'm afraid she's never going to get used to it.

JANE. She takes after you, ma'am, if you'll pardon me. Always brooding. Sometimes, ma'am, I think it would be better if she didn't see her father. Or maybe, ma'am—though it's none of my business—if you could find some nice man—
(*Enter* MRS. MOREHEAD, *right, in a wrapper and slippers.*)

MRS. MOREHEAD. Going to bed, darling?

MARY (*offstage*). Yes, Mother.

MRS. MOREHEAD. Shall we chat for a moment? Jane, I'll have a cigarette.

JANE (*surprised*). Mrs. Morehead!

MRS. MOREHEAD. Those dreadful women made me nervous. Why Mrs. Haines tolerates them even once a year is beyond me!

MARY (*entering, in a nightgown*). An object lesson. Smoking, Mother?

MRS. MOREHEAD. Oh, you, too?

MARY. Me too?

MRS. MOREHEAD. I just felt that spooky pinch. You'd think after ten years your father's ghost might have grown more tolerant.

JANE. Good night, ma'am. (*Switches off side-lights.*)

MARY AND MRS. MOREHEAD. Good night, Jane. (*Exit* JANE. MARY *gets into bed, opens a book, flips through it.*)

MRS. MOREHEAD (*sitting on the bed*). Good book?

MARY. Don't know. Nancy just gave it to me. It's about—love. Poetry. All about love. (*Reads*) "When love beckons to you, follow him, though his ways are hard and steep. And when his wings enfold you, yield to him— Though his voice may shatter your dreams as the North Wind lays waste the garden."

MRS. MOREHEAD. Well, all I can say is, that's very tactless of Nancy. (*Suddenly*) Oh, Mary, I wish you could find—

MARY (*slams book shut*). Some nice man. We've been all over that before, Mother. I had the only one I ever wanted, I lost him—

MRS. MOREHEAD. It wasn't entirely your fault.

MARY. If I hadn't listened to everyone, everything but my own heart!

MRS. MOREHEAD. He loved her.

MARY. He still does. Though you know, Mother, I'm just beginning to doubt it.

MRS. MOREHEAD. Why?

MARY. Because so many people, like Edith, make a point of telling me how much he loves her. Oh, Mother, I'm terribly tired.

MRS. MOREHEAD. Well, do cheer up, darling. Living alone has its compensations. You can go where you please, wear what you please and eat what you please. I had to wait twenty years to order the kind of meal I liked! Your father called it bird-food— And, heaven knows, it's marvelous to be able to sprawl out in bed, like a swastika. Good night, darling.

MARY. Good night, Mother.

MRS. MOREHEAD. Don't read by that light. You'll hurt your eyes. (*Exits.* MARY *props herself against the pillows, begins to read.*)

MARY. "But if in your fear you would seek only love's peace and love's pleasure, then it is better for you to pass out of love's threshing-floor, into the seasonless world; where you shall laugh, but not all of your laughter, and weep, but not all of your tears." (*Enter* LITTLE MARY, *in a nightgown, barefooted, and very sleepy.*)

LITTLE MARY. Mother?

MARY. Darling, what's the matter?

LITTLE MARY (*goes to the bed*). I had a bad dream!

MARY. Darling, what was it?

LITTLE MARY. I forget. Let me crawl in with you, Mother.

MARY (*helping her in*). I'm so restless.

LITTLE MARY. I don't mind if you kick me. You know, that's the only good thing about divorce; you get to sleep with your mother. (*She kisses her. A pause*) I taste lipstick.

MARY. I haven't washed yet. Good night, darling.

LITTLE MARY. You know, you're a very sympathetic mother.

MARY. Am I?

LITTLE MARY. Oh, yes. So would you just tickle my back?

MARY. All right. But go to sleep— (*A pause.*)

LITTLE MARY. She's so silly!

MARY. Who?

LITTLE MARY. Crystal.

MARY. Ssh—

LITTLE MARY. I told Daddy so tonight.

MARY. Oh, you mustn't hurt Daddy's feelings.

LITTLE MARY. Mother?

MARY. Sssh!

LITTLE MARY. I think Daddy doesn't love her as much as you any more.

MARY. What makes you think so, Mary?

LITTLE MARY. He told me so after I saw Crystal.

MARY. What?

LITTLE MARY. But he said I mustn't tell you because, naturally, why do you care how he feels. (*A pause*) Oh, don't stop tickling, Mother. (*A pause*) Mother?

MARY. Yes?

LITTLE MARY. What's anyone want with a telephone in the bathroom?

MARY. I don't know. Sssh!

LITTLE MARY. Crystal has one. She was awful mad when I walked in on her while she was talking.

MARY. Sleep, Mary!

LITTLE MARY. Mother, who's the Duchess of Windsor?

MARY. What a question!

LITTLE MARY. Well, Crystal said on the telephone if somebody else was a Countess, she was the Duchess of Windsor!

MARY. Really!

LITTLE MARY. Good night, Mother.

MARY. Good night, baby. (*A pause.*)

LITTLE MARY. I wonder if it was the same man you had for dinner.

MARY. Maybe, ssh!

LITTLE MARY. I thought so.

MARY (*curiously*). If who was the same man?

LITTLE MARY. Crystal was talking to, so lovey-dovey.

MARY (*protestingly*). Oh, Mary!

LITTLE MARY. Well, the front part was the same, Mother.

MARY (*a pause*). The front part of what?

LITTLE MARY. His name, Mother!

MARY (*taking her by the shoulders*). What are you talking about?

LITTLE MARY. That man Crystal was talking to in the bathtub.

MARY (*half shaking her*). Mary, what do you mean?

LITTLE MARY. I mean his front name was *Buck*, Mother! (MARY *gets quickly out of bed, rings bell on table*) Oh, Mother, what are you doing?

MARY. Go to sleep, darling. (*Begins to pull on her stockings.*)

LITTLE MARY. Grown-ups are so sudden. Are you dressing?

MARY. Yes, Mary.

LITTLE MARY. You forgot you were invited to a party?

MARY. Almost, Mary.

LITTLE MARY. What are you going to do when you get there, Mother?

MARY. I don't know yet. But I've got to do something.

LITTLE MARY. Well, have a good time! (*Rolls over. Then suddenly sits up*) Mother!

MARY. Yes?

LITTLE MARY. I remember now I had something to tell you!

MARY (*eagerly*). Yes?

LITTLE MARY (*dolefully*). I was awfully rude to Crystal.

MARY. I'll forgive you this time. (*Enter* JANE.)

JANE. You rang, ma'am?

MARY. Yes. My evening dress, Jane, and a taxi—and don't stand there gaping! Hurry! Hurry!

CURTAIN

SCENE III

Later, the same night. The Powder Room at the Casino Roof. The decoration is rich, tawdry and modernistic. Right, a swinging door from the lobby. Left, another to the washrooms. The rest of the wall space, left and right, is taken up by counter-like dressing tables and mirrors. The rear wall is a great window overlooking the glitter of midnight Manhattan. An overstuffed sofa and an armchair upholstered in modernistic fabric. Near the door, right, a screen hides the coat-rack. By this, a chair for SADIE, *a little old woman in a black maid's uniform and apron. As the curtain rises,* SADIE *is reading a tabloid, which she puts down when two flashily-dressed* GIRLS *enter from the lobby. They check their wraps.*

FIRST GIRL. It's jammed.

SECOND GIRL. Oh, my boy friend'll get a table. (*Enter two* SOCIETY WOMEN. *They move directly across the stage to the washroom.*)

FIRST WOMAN. My dear, won't he let you?

SECOND WOMAN. No, he won't.

FIRST WOMAN. How incredibly foul!

SECOND WOMAN. I'm heartbroken. But I have to be philosophical; after all, missing one winter in Palm Beach really won't kill me. (*Enter* "CIGARETTES," *a pretty girl in a white satin blouse and short black skirt. She carries a tray of cigarettes.*)

FIRST GIRL (*moving left*). Thought you and the boy friend had a row?

SECOND GIRL. We did.

FIRST GIRL. What about?

SECOND GIRL. His wife.

FIRST GIRL. His wife? What right has she got to butt in?

SECOND GIRL. He's got some cock-eyed idea that after twenty years he can't kick her out. (*They exit, left.*)

CIGARETTES. Jeepers, why don't they get sick of this joint night after night! Same music, same act, same faces.

SADIE. They like familiarity. It gives them confidence.

CIGARETTES. I'll say they like familiarity. Most of them shoving around that floor would be more comfortable with each other in bed.

SADIE. In bed? If they was to get that over, what would they use for conversation? (*Enter a* DOWAGER *and a* DEBUTANTE, *right. They move directly across stage.*)

DOWAGER. —Dancing like that! What can those boys think of you?

DEBUTANTE (*wearily*). Oh, Mother.

DOWAGER. Guzzling champagne like that! After all I spent on your education!

DEBUTANTE. Oh, Mother.

DOWAGER. It's one thing to come out. It's quite another to go under the table! (*They exit, left.*)

SADIE. Getting married, dearie?

CIGARETTES (*sinking, very tired, on the arm of a chair*). As soon as Mike gets a job. It ain't fair! Why, we could get married and have a family on that coat— Sadie, wh'd'ya say if I was to tell you I'm a Commyanist?

SADIE. I'd say ya was bats. I was a Townsendite. Where'd it get me? (*Enter the* COUNTESS, *piloted by* NANCY *and* MIRIAM. *She is tight and tearful.* MIRIAM *and* NANCY *get her, with some difficulty, to the sofa.*)

COUNTESS (*tacking*). How could Buck do such a thing to me! Oh, the Dr. Jekyll! The Mr. Hyde! Which was which?

MIRIAM. Pipe down or you'll put an awful dent in his career, Flora.

COUNTESS. What of my career? I've had five husbands. Buck's the first one who ever told me what he really thought of me—in public.

NANCY. It takes all kinds of husbands to round out a career like yours, Flora.

COUNTESS. He told me he'd been deceiving me for months. Right in the middle of the Organ-Grinder. (*Kicks off shoes*) Oh, I feel so—superfluous!

MIRIAM (*to* SADIE). A bromo-seltzer.

COUNTESS. Bromo-seltzer? Qu'-est-que c'est que ca?

NANCY. It will settle your—superfluity. Flora, did he tell you the lady's name?

COUNTESS (*indignant*). Certainly not, Nancy. He's not that drunk.

MIRIAM (*as* SADIE *exits, right*). And another drink for Mrs. Winston!

COUNTESS. No, Miriam. He wouldn't tell me her name, because she's a married woman. Buck is very proletarian, but he's not a bounder. He just said *she* was a natural blonde.

NANCY. That ought to narrow down the field considerably.

COUNTESS. He said she was pretty as a painted wagon.

MIRIAM. Oh, you're not such a bad calliope. Snap out of it, Flora. You know, you're going to forgive him.

COUNTESS (*firmly*). I'd forgive unfaithfulness, but not base ingratitude. I rescued him from those prairies. I married him. What thanks do I get? (*Wailing*) He says he'll be a cockeyed coyote if he'll herd an old beef like me back to the coast!

NANCY. Let this be your lesson. Don't let your next husband become financially independent of you.

COUNTESS. Now, don't lecture me, Nancy. Every time I marry I learn something. This has taught me once and for all—you can't expect *noblesse oblige* from a cowboy— (*Sitting up*) Ohhh, my eyes! They're full of mascara.

NANCY (*helping her off the couch. To* MIRIAM). We've got to get her home. Get Buck, and meet us in the lobby.

MIRIAM (*exits, right*). We're headin' for the last round-up!

COUNTESS. If there's a telephone in here I'm going to call up Mr. Goldwyn. (*Exits, left, with* NANCY, *as* SADIE, *with a bromo-seltzer, enters, right, followed by* CIGARETTES.)

CIGARETTES. What's it all about?

SADIE (*picks up* COUNTESS' *shoes, as she crosses, left*). Some man.

CIGARETTES. Bet he isn't worth it.

SADIE. You can always collect on that one. (*Exits, left, as re-enter, left, the* DOWAGER *and the* DEBUTANTE.)

DOWAGER. —Laughing and joking with those boys like that!

DEBUTANTE. Yes, Mother.

DOWAGER. What can they think of you?

DEBUTANTE. Yes, Mother.

DOWAGER. And don't think I didn't overhear that Princeton boy call me an old drizzle-puss, either! (*Exits, right.*)

SADIE (*enters, left; to* CIGARETTES) She wants gin in her bromo-seltzer. (*Enter* MARY *and* MIRIAM, *right.*)

MIRIAM (*protesting*). Crystal's not in here. I don't think she's in the joint.

MARY. She's coming. I know it.

MIRIAM. So what are you going to do when you find her? (SADIE *takes* MARY'*s wrap.*)

MARY. I don't know. But I've got to find her tonight. Buck's going to Hollywood in the morning.

MIRIAM. Say, why don't you settle this matter with Stephen?

MARY. I have no proof, I tell you! But if Buck is as drunk as you say, he'll give away something.

MIRIAM. Listen, he's been trying all night to give Flora away to the doorman. Got a twenty-dollar bill?

MARY. Yes.

MIRIAM. That'll lock him in the men's room till we need him. (*Exits, right, with* MARY, *as enter, left, the two* SOCIETY WOMEN. *They cross the stage.*)

FIRST WOMAN. Not three pounds?

SECOND WOMAN. Three pounds!

FIRST WOMAN. How divine! Aren't you ecstatic?

SECOND WOMAN. Yes, but it's the moral satisfaction. Just bananas and milk for one whole week! That called for enormous character! (*They exit, right.*)

CIGARETTES (*to* SADIE). Enormous character! Well, she'll need it, all right. Comes the Revolution, she'll diet plenty. (*Enter* PEGGY *and* EDITH, *right. They powder, at the mirror, right.*)

PEGGY. I wish I hadn't come.

EDITH. Well, your husband didn't want you to.

PEGGY (*goes for her wrap*). Flora was disgusting!

EDITH. But it was funny. Even the kettledrummer was laughing.

PEGGY. You never miss anything. (SADIE *gives* EDITH *and* PEGGY *their wraps.*)

EDITH. My dear, who could stand the life we lead without a sense of humor? But Flora is a fool. Always remember, Peggy, it's matrimonial suicide to be jealous when you have a really good reason.

PEGGY. Edith, don't you ever get tired of giving advice?

EDITH. Listen, Peggy, I'm the only happy woman you know. Why? I don't ask Phelps or any man to understand me. How could he? I'm a woman. (*Pulls down her corset*) And I don't try to understand them. They're just animals. Who am I to quarrel with the way God made them? I've got security. So I put my faith in the law. And I say: "What the hell?" And let nature take its course—it's going to, anyway. (*They exit, right, as enter the two* GIRLS, *left.*)

SECOND GIRL (*powdering at the mirror, left*). —So there we were on Sattiday night and it's Atlantic City. And he says: "I gotta go home tomorrow, baby!" And I says: (*Pulls up her stockings*) "Why dja got to?" And he says: "My wife always expects me home on Easter Sunday." So I says: "What's she expect ya to do? Lay an egg?"

FIRST GIRL. They got no sentiment. (*Enter, right, a* GIRL, *in distress. The shoulder strap of her very low décolletage has broken.*)

GIRL IN DISTRESS (*to* SADIE). Have you got a safety pin? I was never so embarrassed! (SADIE *gets pin.*)

SECOND GIRL (*crossing, right*). So I told him, "I had a great career until you made me give up the stage, you lunkhead. For what? A couple of cheesy diamond bracelets? A lousy car, which every time it breaks down you got to have the parts shipped over from Italy. (*The* GIRLS *exit.*)

GIRL IN DISTRESS. So he says, "Don't look now, you've just dropped something!" (*Enter* CRYSTAL *and* SYLVIA, *right. They move to check their wraps with* SADIE.)

SADIE. Just a minute, please.

SYLVIA (*they go to mirror, left*). Stephen is in a mood.

CRYSTAL. He can take it and like it.

GIRL IN DISTRESS (*to* SADIE). Does it show now?

SADIE. Not what it did before, miss.

GIRL IN DISTRESS. Thank you. (*She exits, right.* SADIE *takes* CRYSTAL'S *and* SYLVIA'S *wraps.*)

CRYSTAL. Is my mouth on straight?

SYLVIA. Crystal, you didn't come here to see somebody, did you?

CRYSTAL. Oh, Sylvia, can't you lay off that for a minute? (*Enter* MARY *and* MIRIAM, *left.*)

MARY (*moving forward resolutely*). Mrs. Haines, this is a great pleasure!

CRYSTAL (*turning*). I beg your pardon?

MARY. Such a lovely party! I was afraid you weren't coming. (*Introducing* CRYSTAL *and* MIRIAM, MIRIAM *and* SYLVIA) Mrs. Fowler, Mrs. Haines, Mrs. Fowler, Mrs. Fowler.

MIRIAM (*graciously*). Chawmed.

SYLVIA (*bridling*). This is humiliating.

MARY. Modern life is complicated. When you came in I was just telling Miriam—

CRYSTAL. Oh, come along, Sylvia The lady is tight.

SYLVIA. Mary, when did you begin drinking?

MARY (*to* CRYSTAL). Early in the evening, with Mr. Winston. You *know* Mr. Winston, don't you?

CRYSTAL (*at the door*). I'm afraid I don't.

SYLVIA. Of course you do, Crystal. I introduced you to him. Don't you remember?

CRYSTAL. Oh, yes, a cocktail party.

MARY. Well, he's in the lobby now, waiting for someone, Mrs. Haines, and drunker than you can possibly imagine. You'd find him very difficult to handle, in front of Stephen. (CRYSTAL *suddenly changes her mind about going into the lobby, moves toward the washroom.*)

SYLVIA. Crystal, where are you going?

CRYSTAL. I won't stand here and listen to drivel!

MARY. I wouldn't go in there, either, Mrs. Haines. His wife's in there now, having hysterics. She's found out that Buck has been deceiving her.

CRYSTAL. Really! What has that to do with me?

MARY. A good deal, I'm afraid. You seem to be the woman.

SYLVIA (*delighted*). Why, Crystal! —*Are* you?

CRYSTAL. If he used my name, it's a lie! He's just the cheap sort— I'll tell my husband.

MARY. You'll have to. Tomorrow it will be common gossip. I don't think Stephen will like it.

SYLVIA. Oh, Crystal, he's going to loathe it! But my psychoanalyst is going to adore it.

CRYSTAL (*going to her*). What are you trying to do? Pin something on me, in front of witnesses?

SYLVIA. Whatever she's driving at, Crystal— (*Pointing to* MIRIAM) that little tramp put her up to it!

CRYSTAL (*to* SYLVIA). Keep out of this!

MIRIAM. Yeah, check it, Sylvia, we're minor league this evening.

CRYSTAL. All right, Mrs. Haines, you've been listening to the ravings of a conceited fool. What did he tell you?

MARY (*playing for time, or inspiration*). Really, Mrs. Haines, this is very embarrassing.

CRYSTAL (*brazening it out*). Yes, Mrs. Haines, isn't it? Exactly what do you think you know about me?

MARY. Everything! (*A pause,* CRYSTAL *laughs.*)

CRYSTAL. Then why are you standing here talking to me. You ought to be outside spilling it to Stephen. You're bluffing. Come along, Sylvia!

MARY (*also moving to door.* CRYSTAL *stops*). That's very good advice. I will tell Stephen.

CRYSTAL. Oh, he wouldn't believe you.

SYLVIA. Oh, you can't tell, Crystal! He's terribly fond of Mary.

CRYSTAL. Now get this straight, Mrs. Haines. I like what I got, and I'm going to keep it. You handed me your husband on a silver platter. (*Enter* NANCY, *left*) But I'm not returning the compliment. I can't be stampeded by gossip. What you believe and what Stephen believes will cut no ice in a divorce court. You need proof and you haven't got it. When Mr. Winston comes to his senses, he'll apologize. And Stephen will have no choice, but to accept—my explanations. Now that's that! Good night!

MARY (*desperately*). I hope Mrs. Winston will accept your explanations.

CRYSTAL. What have I got to explain to her?

MARY (*with a conviction she does not feel*). What about the apartment?

CRYSTAL. What apartment?

MARY. You know as well as I do.

CRYSTAL. Oh, stop trying to put two and two together—

MARY. Oh, Mrs. Winston did that. She had you watched—she's seen you both.

CRYSTAL (*defiantly*). Where?

MARY. Going in, and coming out!

CRYSTAL. Going in and coming out *where?* (*A pause*) You're lying!

SYLVIA (*warningly*). I wouldn't be so sure, Crystal!

MIRIAM. Sounds like the McCoy to me, Crystal.

CRYSTAL. Shut up!

SYLVIA. Oh, Crystal, why didn't you confide in me? (CRYSTAL *turns to the door again, triumphant.*)

MARY (*dismayed*). Sylvia, didn't she?

SYLVIA. Certainly *not!* (CRYSTAL *smiles very pleased with herself*) She's the cat that walks alone. (*Goes to* CRYSTAL) Why, Crystal, I could have told you some place *much safer* than the Gothic Apartments!

CRYSTAL (*exploding*). Why, you big, loud-mouthed idiot!

SYLVIA. How dare you!

CRYSTAL. I'd like to slap your stupid face.

SYLVIA (*backing up*). Oh, Mary, how dare she?

MIRIAM. Oh, I've got a job to do on Flora. (*She pats* SYLVIA *affectionately*) Kiss you when I get back, Sylvia. (*Exits, left.*)

NANCY. And I'll explain the facts of life to Stephen. (NANCY *exits, right.*)

CRYSTAL (*to* MARY, *fiercely*). You're trying to break up my marriage!

SYLVIA. The way you did hers, you floosie!

CRYSTAL (*nasty*). Well, maybe you're welcome to my—left-overs.

MARY (*calmly*). I'll take them, thank you.

SYLVIA. Why, Mary, haven't you any *pride?*

MARY. That's right. No, no pride; that's a luxury a woman in love can't afford.
(*Enter* COUNTESS *and* MIRIAM, *left.* MIRIAM *goes to* SADIE, *gets the* COUNTESS' *and her own wraps.*)

COUNTESS (*rushing for* CRYSTAL). Oh, mon Dieu, mon Dieu!

MARY (*stopping her*). Flora, it's really too bad—

COUNTESS (*to* CRYSTAL) You—you painted wagon!

CRYSTAL. So you're determined to have a scandal, Mrs. Haines.

COUNTESS. I'm the one who's going to have the scandal. Why, Mary, she's no more a blonde naturelle than I am. What's the creature's name? Miriam forgot to tell me.

MARY. Mrs. Stephen Haines, currently.

COUNTESS. Is that the thing Stephen left you for? Well, cherie, all I can say is, you're an idiot! I hope I never live to see the day when an obvious piece like that conquers *me* on the champs d'amour! (*She exits, right, followed by* MIRIAM.)

CRYSTAL (*to* MARY). That damn fool didn't know. (SADIE *gives* MARY *her wrap.*)

MARY. I'm afraid she didn't. (*Enter* NANCY, *right.*)

NANCY. There's a gentleman called Mr. Haines. He says he's been waiting a long time for his wife— (CRYSTAL *moves to get her wrap.*)

MARY (*stepping between her and* SADIE). Tell him, *I* am coming. (*Exit* NANCY *quickly.*)

SYLVIA. Mary, what a dirty female trick!

CRYSTAL. Yes! From the great, noble little woman! You're just a cat, like all the rest of us!

MARY. Well, I've had two years to sharpen my claws. (*Waves her hand gaily to* SYLVIA) Jungle-red, Sylvia! Good night, ladies! (*Exits.*)

CURTAIN

"Having Wonderful Time"

BY ARTHUR KOBER

TO MARC

WITH MANY THANKS

Note: The characters and situations in this play are wholly fictional and imaginative, do not portray, and are not intended to portray, any actual person or parties.

"Having Wonderful Time" was first produced at the Lyceum Theatre, New York City, by Marc Connelly, on February 20, 1937, and closed on January 8, 1938. Following is the original cast:

Lois	Connie Lent
Sophie	Kay Loring
Rosalind	Ann Thomas
Teddy Stern	Katherine Locke
Fay Fromkin	Janet Fox
Mac Finkle	B. D. Kranz
Henrietta Brill	Lois Reichard
Miriam Robbins	Muriel Campbell
Chick Kessler	Jules Garfield
Hi	Mitchell Grayson
Eli	Shimen Ruskin
Schmutz	Solen Burry
Barney	Edward Mann
Abe Tobias	Wolfe Barzell
Charlie	Herbert Ratner
Joe	William Swetland
Mr. G.	Hudy Block
Mrs. G.	Ann Brody
Birdie	Helen Golden
Reba	Irene Winston
Tiny	Irving Israel
The Honeymooners	Herbert Vigran Sandra Gould
Itchy Flexner	Philip Van Zandt
Sammy	Tony Kraber
Maxine	Henriette Kaye
Gussie	Mona Conrad
Pinkie Aaronson	Sheldon Leonard

KITTY	Lily Winton
DOC	Cornel Wilde
A CERTAIN PARTY	Frank Gould
CAMP GUESTS, WAITERS, ETC.	Helen Edwards, Estelle Raymond, Laura Windsor, Connie Ernst, Peggy Craven, Richard Allen, MacFarlane Roberts, Bob Strauss, Juanita Beatty, Tony Heath and others.

Associate Producer Bèla Blau

Settings by Stewart Chaney

SCENES

The action of the play takes place at CAMP KARE-FREE, in the Berkshires, during August

ACT ONE

SCENE I

Teddy's Bungalow. About noon

SCENE II

The Dining Room. Ten minutes later

SCENE III

Back Porch of the Social Hall. That night

ACT TWO

SCENE I

Eagle Rock. Six days later

SCENE II

Teddy's Bungalow. Eleven P.M. that night

SCENE III

Pinkie's Bungalow. A short time later

ACT THREE

SCENE I

Teddy's Bungalow. The following morning

SCENE II

The Dining Room. A short time later

"HAVING WONDERFUL TIME"

ACT ONE

SCENE I

"A brilliant grammarian," reads the Camp Kare-Free brochure with which owner ABE TOBIAS *woos potential guests, "will try through picturesque verbiage to glowingly paint a beautiful picture of camp life."* MR. TOBIAS *then quickly sounds a note of warning. "One must remember, however, that there is an ancient adage which goes, 'Seeing is believing.' Because we are disciples of this motto, we have prepared this little booklet, profusely illustrated with photographs, in the hopes that these pictures will tell you more than we can utter, no matter how flowery our language. Perhaps, as you scan the pages, you will be inspired to visit Camp Kare-Free, where friendships are formed which endure a lifetime, where dull care and trouble quickly vanish 'neath Nature's magic spell."*

The photographs show the Kare-Free lake front with its many canoes and rowboats prominently banked in the foreground; it calls attention to the social hall facing the lake, and assures you that it has a staff of well-known artists and musicians captained by "that jovial personality, an expert technician in the art of Thespis," "ITCHY" FLEXNER; *it emphasizes the Kare-Free sunset, "a glorious, colorful souvenir you will talk about for years."*

Turn the pages and your eye will be met with camera studies of the championship tennis courts, the eighteen-hole tournament golf course, the dining hall showing a group of happy vacationists seated on the steps "after a wholesome meal prepared by a staff of expert cooks well versed in the culinary art." There are many more examples of happy campers as captured by the camera: on horseback (looking even more frightened than the horses), in hiking costume as they file along a mountain trail, on the diving platform participating in aquatic sports, on romantic Eagle Rock dreamily ushering in that lifetime friendship, on the porch of the writing lodge in the throes of composition, and, finally, in front of one of the bungalows.

"Beautiful landscaped roads lead to our semi-private bungalows," MR. TOBIAS'S *minnesinger ecstatically chants. "Spaciousness and comfort are the keynotes of Kare-Free's comfy cabins. You will note that all our bunks are shaded by tall, towering pines, thus assuring cool comfort by day and likewise by night. Each bungalow is modern in every respect. It has its own private porch and is equipped with complete toilet facilities, including hot and cold running water and shower."*

For some inexplicable reason there is no photograph of the interior of any of the bungalows.

The first scene of the first act takes place in TEDDY'S *bungalow.*

It is a crude structure, slapped together with a lot of storm-beaten planks. It is one of several dozen cabins spattered over the camp grounds, and differs only slightly from the shacks on the men's side: this has a closet, lower right, concealed by a curtain. There are four bed-cots squeezed into the room—two on either side. Over the cots are towel racks and over them are several hooks on which are hung shirts, shorts, a deflated automobile tube, etc. There are two cheap dressers with large mirrors attached, several wicker chairs and one or two lamps. A pair of shoes, just whitened, rests on the ledge of one of the two screen windows in the background. A yellow satin evening gown is suspended from one of the hooks. (It is Saturday and the girls are expected to be "strictly formal" that night.) A door, left, leads into the bathroom. The door opening into the bungalow is in the dead center of the room and leads to the porch which runs along the side of the shack. Bags are visible under beds, several rackets and golf bags are placed in corners, books and magazines are strewn over dressers, chairs, etc.

TEDDY STERN, *still wearing her city clothes, stands framed in the doorway, her back toward the audience. It is a somewhat upset* TEDDY *we shall soon meet. Won by the captivating phrases of* MR. TOBIAS'S *booklet, lured by the blandishments contained in the letters of her girl friend,* FAY FROMKIN, TEDDY *has come to camp, a lost soul with nobody on hand to meet her. Three of the campers,* ROSALIND, LOIS *and* SOPHIE *have taken her in hand and have escorted her to her bunk.* TEDDY'S *open suitcase rests on a cot in the foreground. The three girls—*ROSALIND *in overalls, a bandanna over her head,* SOPHIE *in linen culottes, her hair in curlers, and* LOIS *in a bright red bathing suit, are rummaging through* TEDDY'S *effects.* LOIS *picks up a bottle of perfume, shakes it and applies the glass stopper to the back of her ear.*

LOIS. Oh, don't worry. Fay'll be here in a minute.

SOPHIE (*finding a new camera and clicking jigger*). She must've gone down to meet you at the awfice.

ROSALIND (*marveling at* TEDDY'S *set*). This toilet set must've cost a pretty coupla dollars. (*Sights name on bag handle*) Your name's Teddy Stern. (*Calling to* TEDDY) How come your first name's Teddy? Teddy, that's a fella's name.

TEDDY (*shyly, as she turns and comes into room*). It's only my nickname, Teddy. It stands for Tessie.

ROSALIND (*a trigger mind*). Oh, I get it.

LOIS (*in alarm, to* SOPHIE). Put that down. You'll break it. (*To* TEDDY) Was it very hot in the city when you left?

TEDDY. Not so warm as it was sticky.

SOPHIE. Oh, lots of humidity, ha? (ROSALIND *has walked toward* TEDDY *and now stands at her right.*)

ROSALIND. Oh, there must be a load of humidity in the city. (*Suddenly fascinated by* TEDDY'S *printed dress, she fingers the material*) That's very nice material.

TEDDY. Thank you. (SOPHIE *has unearthed a stenographic notebook and holds it up.*)

SOPHIE. Look! A note-book!

LOIS (*outraged, and prepared, if necessary, to picket*). You're not going to do any work while you're on your vacation, are you?

TEDDY. Oh, no. (*Self-consciously*) I thought I'd make some notes for myself—you know, my impressions of camp life. Then some day I'll have something to look back on.

ROSALIND. Like a diary, huh? Say, that's a very good idear.

SOPHIE. I wonder why we din think of it.

LOIS (*eyeing her admiringly*). Your friend, Fay, is right. You must have a very good head on your shoulders. (*She looks at wrist watch and starts for door*) Come on, if we're going to be there.

SOPHIE (*following her out*). See you in the dining room. (*After a quick survey of the room*) Say, this bunk's even bigger than ours.

TEDDY (*aware of the amenities*). Thanks for showing me the way.

ROSALIND. Don't worry about Fay, Teddy. She's prolly looking all over camp for you. (*Hurries after the others on porch. Their voices can be heard as they trail off*) Dijja see that evening gown? It was beaudyful.

LOIS. That must cost a good ninedy semny-five wholesale.

(TEDDY *crosses to bed, notices her effects which the girls have thrown into violent disorder, and starts to arrange them. The cloppety-clop of running feet is heard, the door is flung open and the breathless* FAY FROMKIN *comes rushing in to hurl herself at* TEDDY. FAY *is the complete apotheosis of that snug and self-sufficient borough of New York, the Bronx. Her features, manners, gestures, the sing-song intonation of her voice are unmistakably identified with that struggling horde of workers who, during rush hour, squeeze themselves into the subway trains bearing the red and green lights.*)

FAY. Teddy, dolling!

TEDDY. Hello, Fay.

FAY. I din know till just this minute—(MAC FINKLE *appears in the doorway, in tennis costume. He is a pleasant, ineffectual young man who exudes considerable dental charm. He watches the girls in close embrace.*)

TEDDY (*after they part*). Well, I'm glad to see I'm in the right place after all.

FAY. I din even know the bus was in yet. (*Aware of* MAC's *presence*) Come on in, Mac. I want you should meet my girl friend, Miss Teddy Stern, I told you so much about. (*She places her hand on* MAC's *neck with a proprietary air*) Teddy, this is Mac Finkle.

TEDDY. Hoddeya do?

MAC. Pleased to make your acquaintanceship.

FAY. You got lipstick where I kissed you. (*Erasing it with her handkerchief*) Here, hold still.

MAC. You remaining here fa long, Teddy?

FAY (*picks up* TEDDY's *coat and walks to closet*). Now we'll put your coat in here.

TEDDY. I'm supposed to stay for two weeks, but now— (*Dubiously as she looks around room*) Oh, I don't know.

FAY (*shocked*). Teddy!

TEDDY (*casting an apathetic eye on the cots*). This isn't at all what I expected, Fay. Semi-private bungalows, they said in the little booklet. And look, four in a room! (*To* MAC) Why, it's like living at home with my mother and father and my brother, Charlie, and his wife. I purposely came here to get away from them.

FAY. You're gonna love it here. Won't she, Mac?

MAC. You just gotta get used to it. Now you take when I first came—

FAY (*sitting on cot*). Say, what about the argument you had?

MAC. Yes, we heard about it. Chick told us.

TEDDY. Who's Chick?

MAC. The fella you had the argument with. What happened?

TEDDY (*with a dismissive wave of the hand*). Oh, that. Well, I'm not feeling so good lately. All I want is some peace and quiet.

FAY (*anxious to elaborate*). Teddy's had a little trouble with a certain young—

TEDDY (*quickly, before all is disclosed*). That's neither here nor there. Well, I was sitting in the bus, thinking over some personal matters, when this young man, this—

FAY. Chick. Go on.

TEDDY. He speaks to me, a complete stranger—out of a clear sky! And on and on he goes, about the view and the mountains. Finally I had to say to him: "Look, I'm not interested in mountains. Do you mind, please?" Well, you should've heard his answer!

MAC. He saw you was alone and was oney trying to be sociable.

TEDDY (*appealing to the widely-traveled* FAY). But at the seashore porters don't act that way. Do they, Fay?

FAY. Chick's not a porter; he's a waiter.

MAC. And they're like us. They pay for their jobs.

FAY. They're not like hired help at all.

TEDDY (*spurred by a pang of conscience*). Oh, then maybe I shouldn't've been so annoyed. (*As* MAC *moves away to inspect the room*) But waiter or no waiter, he said some very fresh things to me. Do you know what he—? (HENRIETTA BRILL, *a stout girl, comes out of bathroom dressed in a slip, skirt, stockings and high-heeled shoes. She has on severe-looking glasses which make her seem more formidable than ever.* HENRIETTA *is a sectarian radical who has recently discovered The Cause. She is full of political rubber-stamps and platitudes and, like a new convert, makes up for her ignorance by taking a dogmatic stand on all matters. She sights* MAC, *gasps, and takes refuge in the bathroom.*)

HENRIETTA. Oh!

MAC. I better get outta here.

FAY. I din know Henrietta was in there.

MAC (*waving to* TEDDY). Pleased to've made your acquaintanceship. (*Significantly to* FAY) See you later.

FAY. Surely. (*He exits. She crosses toward center*) It's aw right now, Henrietta. He's gone.
(HENRIETTA *appears and spears* FAY *with a withering glance. Her voice is coated with outraged indignation.*)

HENRIETTA. For heaven's sakes, Fay Fromkin, why don't you inform a person when you have mixed company in the bungalow?

FAY. I din even know you were in there. Oh, I want you should meet—

HENRIETTA (*without changing her tone*). I had the pleasure already. (*Walking toward closet*) Honestly, it's very embarrassing to have people intrude on your privacy, especially when you have nothing on. (*She disappears into closet.* TEDDY *sidles up to* FAY *and speaks in a whisper.*)

TEDDY. Who is she?

FAY. A floor-lady in Newark. She's a radical. Evveything is with her a speech.

TEDDY (*shrugging her shoulders*). Beyond me.

FAY. Well, waddeya think of Mac?

TEDDY. Who?

FAY. Mac. The boy who was just here. (*Parenthetically, as* TEDDY *holds up slacks and blouse*) You put them in there. I wrote you about him.

TEDDY (*on way to bathroom*). Oh, so he's the one. (*She pauses, suddenly remembering the rhapsodic passages in* FAY'*s letters to her*) But he doesn't look like Robert Taylor.

FAY (*lamely*). Oh, I think so—a little bit.

TEDDY. Oh, Fay! Is he a college man?

FAY. No, he's in business fa himself. (*Feigning indifference*) Anyway it's nothing serious. He's going back tomorra. He's just a nice contact to know in the city doong the winter, that's all.

TEDDY (*she has made a quick flight in and out of bathroom*). Now you know you like him, and why shouldn't you if he's a nice boy? (*Pats her gently on the back.* HENRIETTA *comes from closet in time to hear part of the conversation.*)

HENRIETTA. Parm me for interrupting, but when it comes to the male sex this camp is very inferior. You're going to be disillusioned, Betty.

TEDDY. Teddy.

HENRIETTA. Teddy. They're very common, I regret to say. Their conversation is mostly physical, not intellectual.

TEDDY (*her eyes traveling from* HENRIETTA *to* FAY) Really?

HENRIETTA. Oh, emphatically! The ad in the Nation says, "A summer camp for adults," but it should be for adultery judging how forward they are. And such audacity you've never seen!

FAY (*moved to salvage the camp's honor*). Far be it fomm me to conterdict you, but I—

HENRIETTA (*diving into her speech*). Parm me for interrupting, but I've been coming here for four years steadily. (*With complete finality*) I know whereof I speak. (*As* TEDDY *crosses to bathroom with towel*) Oh, the hot water there doesn't function.

TEDDY (*vaguely*). Doesn't it? (*Enters bathroom.*)

HENRIETTA (*picks up a brush and pastes her hair*). Even in camp they exploit us. You'd think for the price you pay the faucets would at least function.

(*Just then a voice is heard coming over the Public Address System. The announcer cherishes the fond hope that some day a radio scout will hear and discover him. For this reason the local broadcasts are delivered in the sweet, oozy, Crisco-like tones employed by professional announcers.*)

P. A. VOICE. Attention, please. All boats in.

FAY (*as* TEDDY *comes flying out of bathroom*). That's the announcer.

P. A. VOICE. All boats in. Thaaank you.

FAY. Gee, it's nearly lunch time.

HENRIETTA (*now fully dressed*). If we presented a united front and demanded better service, we'd get it all right. (*Pauses at the door*) But go activize a bunch of petty bourgeois! (*She exits.*)

TEDDY. Who in the world let her loose?

FAY. Dijja ever!

TEDDY. What's the matter with her, anyway?

FAY. Sour grapes. She believes in free love, but none of the fellas will give her a tumble.

TEDDY. Aw, the poor girl.

FAY. It's no wonder. Just lookit her form—chunky—a regella Kate Smith.

TEDDY (*examining her stained hands*). Look at my hands! (*Returns to bathroom.*)

FAY (*removes* TEDDY'S *evening gown from bed and holds it up*). Lookit this! A new evening gown she's got. Oh, it's simply stunning—a genuwine knockout! (*There is a knock at the door*) Come! (CHICK KESSLER *enters carrying a new and handsome bag with foreign travel labels pasted conspicuously on it. He is young, intelligent, sensitive—but not in the shirt-open-at-the-collar sort of way. He wears a gray sweat-shirt with the camp's letters on it—C. K. F., white duck trousers and black shoes.*)

CHICK (*smiles engagingly*). Here's your friend's suitcase. (*Places it at foot of* TEDDY'S *cot*) Look. Give her some advice for me. Tell her to relax. (*Starts for door.*)

FAY. Chick, I gotta bone to pick with you.

CHICK. Yes? What's the bone?

FAY. D'you think Mr. Tobias would like to know you offended one of the guests here?

CHICK. Waddeya mean—offended?

FAY. You think it's the right spirit to pass a remark to my girl friend, 'specially when she's new to this camp?

CHICK (*tolerantly*). You think it's the right spirit for her to insult me?

FAY. Perhaps she was justified.

CHICK. Perhaps she wasn't justified. I'm not a bellboy, and I'm not fresh, and she shouldn't have provoked me by her attitude.

FAY. What attitude?

CHICK (*pointing to labels on bag*). Maybe your friend is very rich. Maybe she travels a lot with servants who are constantly at her beck and call. That doesn't necessarily mean that every person she meets should be treated like a menial.

FAY. Wait a minute. She *borrowed* that bag! Why, Teddy's never been away from home before. (*Puzzled*) Say, wadde you talking about?

CHICK (*impatiently*). I made some innocent comment to her about the scenery. I didn't give a damn about the scenery. She seemed all alone, and I just wanted to be pleasant. (*His voice rising as he recalls the scene*) Well, the way she snapped at me you wouldn't even snap at a dog! Where does she get off, this Miss High-and-Mighty—?

(*The bathroom door is flung open and the enraged* TEDDY *flounces out, adjusting slacks into which she has changed.*)

TEDDY. I'll show you where Miss High-and-Mighty gets off when I have you reported. Of all the impudent, fresh individuals I ever—

FAY. Teddy, dolling, you're oney aggravating yesself.

TEDDY. I didn't come to this camp to be insulted.

CHICK (*coldly*). Perhaps if you talked a little more civilly and with less temper you—

TEDDY. Don't you tell me how to talk. For the money I pay I can talk exactly as I please!

CHICK (*with heavy sarcasm*). Oh, I beg your pardon. You're a customer here, so naturally you're right. You have the privilege of stepping on the help, and the help must meekly submit. Why not? You're a paying guest. So I beg your pardon. Excuse me for living!

FAY (*stepping toward* CHICK). Is that necessary, that sarcasm?

TEDDY. I guess that's what you get around here.

FAY. Honestly, Chick, I'm surprised at you. A boy with your brain matter. My girl friend is just here.

CHICK. Wadde you want me to do?

FAY. The lease you can do is to apologize to her.

TEDDY (*almost crying*). Please, Fay. I don't want any favors.

FAY (*sweetly as she sidles up to him*). Go on, Chick. Do like I say.

CHICK (*reluctantly to* TEDDY). Look. Maybe I—I said something I shouldn'a said—

TEDDY. Huh! I like this maybe!

CHICK. All right, I said something I shouldn'a said. Satisfied? So if I hurt you—

TEDDY (*tearfully*). Don't worry. You didn't have the satisfaction!

CHICK. Aw, what's the use! (*He exits, slamming door.*)

TEDDY (*sinks on cot, her back to audience*). A fine camp you recommended! They certainly have some very polite people here, I must say!

FAY. I'm so supprised at him. He's a very polite fella ordinarily.

TEDDY. Dope!

FAY (*rushing to* CHICK'S *defense: what's right is right*). Oh, Chick's a college grad.

TEDDY. He must've studied how to be rude. I didn't mean to hurt his feelings.

FAY (*walking toward her*). Come on. It'll soon be time for lunch.

TEDDY (*dully*). You know something? (*Rising*) I've got halfa mind to pack up and leave. Let them keep the deposit!

FAY. Teddy, what're you talking!

TEDDY. Honestly, I mean it. (*Her voice breaking*) With all the troubles of the past few months—

FAY (*putting arm around her*). Teddy!

TEDDY. Fay, I'm so sick and disgusted you have no idea.

FAY. That's foolish, that kinda talk.

TEDDY. Everything in the world seems to be happening to me.

FAY (*fixes her with a look of reproval*). Now who's the girl who wasn't gonna say one word about her engagement? Listen to her! (*Sits on end of cot.*)

TEDDY. Oh, I'm not even thinking about it, and besides I don't wanna be reminded. That's all my family's been talking about for weeks. Oh, God, it'll be a relief not to have mama nagging at me. "Tessie, you're gonna be an old maid! Tessie, it's gonna serve you right!" Tessie this, and Tessie that, till I could almost bust.

FAY. Gee, you'd think Sam Rappaport was the oney man left in the world!

TEDDY (*wearily*). I don't even wanna talk about it any more.

FAY. How you could allow a man to make a nervous wretch outta you is beyond me.

TEDDY. Sam's a dead issue in my life. He could drop dead this minute, God forbid, and I wouldn't care. I—I'd only feel sorry, that's all.

FAY. I wouldn't waste a single drop of sympathy on him. (*A note of censure, now that the subject is up*) If I was in your shoes I wouldn't've returned the ring either. Why, you never even had it appraised!

TEDDY. Let's not talk about it. He's past and forgotten.

FAY (*her voice flaked with indignation*). I can't get over the lousy crust of a man! You're formally engaged, with the furniture all picked out—a beaudyful bedroom suit—

TEDDY (*testily*). Please, Fay, I told you I don't wish to revive Sam.

FAY. Listen, if a person thinks more of setting up their brother in business insteada taking that money and making a nice home fa their intended, I say the hell with him!

TEDDY (*getting to her feet*). O.K. O.K., already! (*Bitterly after a slight pause*) Another whole year he wanted me to wait till he got his investment back. Three years' waiting wasn't enough!

FAY. You never really liked him. Old Man of the Mountains!

TEDDY. He's only forty-two.

FAY. Forty-two! Then let him find somebody his own age. A young girl like you! It's like—like marrying your own father. (*Guilty of a social lapse*) Excuse the expression.

TEDDY (*musingly*). My brother, Charlie, is married. My sisters are all married. Mama was so afraid I'd be the only single one. "A man in his forties is just right," she'd say. "He doesn't run around. He's settled already." Sam certainly was settled all right. He wouldn't budge at night. He didn't like concerts; he didn't like dances; he didn't like this; he didn't like that. Only one thing he liked—the radio. God, how Sam adored the radio! (*Picks up her bag, places it on cot and starts to snap it open*) I tell you it'll feel wonderful to have dinner again without those two extra guests— (*Glances toward* FAY) Amos an' Andy.

FAY (*swinging around to face* TEDDY). Well, I wanted to tell you in the beginning it was a mistake, but I was afraid I'd hurtcha feelings.

TEDDY. Oh, I guess I was sick and tired of my job and my family. I thought it'd be fun to have my own home. So every summer I took my vacation money and bought dishes and flatware and blankets. What a fool I was! (*Softly as she touches the Paris label on her bag*) I—I thought surely by this time I'd be honeymooning in some place like Paris. My cousin, Sid, told me so much about Paris. "Paree," he calls it. (*Takes comb and brush from bag and crosses*) Well, anyway, here I am—at Camp Kare-Free. My first vacation in three years.

FAY. Never mind, Teddy. (*Rising*) A girl with your brains and your personality will have no trouble. He'll be a hundred times better than Sam Rappaport. Wait and see.

TEDDY. Oh, Sam's a dead issue with me. (*Fingering a dress hanging on hook*) I don't even wanna discuss it.

FAY (*pointing to dress*). She copied it from Joan Crawford's last pickcha.

TEDDY. Who did?

FAY. Miriam. She occupies this bed. Mmmm, is she raging mad! Her boy-friend, Pinkie, stood her up on a horseback date.

TEDDY. Is she here with her boy-friend?

FAY. Nah! She met him here at camp, and you should see the way she chases him around. It's a disgrace! (*Suddenly*) Say, there's somebody you'd like—Pinkie Aaronson. He's got two millinery stores and he's young—

MIRIAM'S VOICE (*from offstage, left*). Go on, Reba. I'll meetcha in the dining room.

FAY. Speak of the devil, she's sure to appear.

(*The door opens and* MIRIAM ROBBINS *enters. She is pretty, feminine and a complete bird-brain. Her vacation is dedicated to the task of bagging the elusive* PINKIE AARONSON. *She is in her riding habit: black jodhpurs, green blouse, yellow scarf. Her hair is piled high, giving the curious impression of a nest balanced on her head. During the scene she changes her blouse and scarf.*)

FAY. Oh, Miriam, I want you should meet my girl friend, Teddy. Teddy, this is Miriam.

TEDDY. Pleased to meet you.

MIRIAM. Likewise.

FAY. We were just complimenting your evening dress.

MIRIAM. It's a Jo-an Craw-ford copy I designed fomm her last pitcha. (*Alive with news*) Oh, guess why Pinkie din keep the date— Mrs. Sklar!

FAY. Mrs. Sklar!

MIRIAM. That married woman. You know, the heavy drinker with the antique jewlerry.

FAY. She's in the canteen all the time? (*Confidentially, to* TEDDY) Whenever you look at her she's got a glass of Scotch highball in her hand.

MIRIAM. She's a married woman.

FAY. With the cutest baby—Donald. A little boy.

MIRIAM. She occupies a cottage in the married section. She's here fa the whole season.

TEDDY. Her husband here with her?

FAY. Nah! He oney comes down week-ends.

MIRIAM. But this week-end he hadda be detained by business.

FAY (*knowingly*). That's what he said!

MIRIAM. So what has she got to do but go after the single boys?

FAY. Some of the married women here are so common, you got no idear.

MIRIAM. And the boys like the married women. One or two of them are positively wild!

TEDDY (*the smart conversationalist*). If their husbands only knew! (*She goes off to bathroom.*)

MIRIAM (*with a sigh of resignation*). Well, that's what we got to content with here at camp. Trouble enough finding a nice serious type boy without some flighty married woman snatching him away. (*Primping her-*

self at dresser) Of course, if Pinkie wishes to make a spectacle of hisself with Mrs. Sklar, far be it fomm me to stand in the way.

P. A. VOICE. Attention, please. Luncheon is now being served. Luncheon is now being served. Thaank you.

TEDDY *(coming from bathroom and smoothing her slacks and blouse)*. Maybe we'd better hurry.

MIRIAM. Take it easy. There's plenty of time yet.

TEDDY. I hope the food is good. I'm famished.

FAY *(after a careful scrutiny of* TEDDY*)*. What you need is earrings!

TEDDY. Not with slacks, Fay.

FAY *(goes to dresser and rummages through box)*. Here. I got an extra pair that'd go good with your blouse.

TEDDY. But I don't want them, Fay.

FAY *(sadly, shaking her head)*. You haven't really changed the lease bit. Have you, Teddy?

TEDDY. Why should I wear earrings when I hate them?

FAY. You oughta look your best. After all, even in a barrel of rotten apples there's bound to be a good one. Who knows, there may be a fella here exactly your type?

TEDDY. Look, Fay. I came here not because I wanted to, but I didn't know where else to go. I thought maybe it would be nice to breathe some fresh air and get a sunburn. The way I feel people don't interest me one little bit. *(Kindly, as she looks up from a couple of Modern Library books she has taken from her bag)* I mean with the exception of yourself.

FAY. Aw right, Miss Crazy. It's your life, not mine. Hurry up. *(Exits to porch.)*

TEDDY *(busily engaged in relaying her effects from bag to dresser)*. All I wanna do is get away from two things: my family and my awfice. I'm not even going to write any letters so I won't see any envelopes—printed and plain, clasp and open, button and string, cellophane and glassine. It'll be wonderful— *(Looks around and notices that she is alone)* Oh, she's gone. *(She closes her bag.* MIRIAM *comes out of bathroom brushing her hair. She turns, and her attention is immediately captured by the labels on* TEDDY'S *suitcase.)*

MIRIAM. Are those foreign labels?

TEDDY. Yes.

MIRIAM. Oh, *parly voo Fransay?*

TEDDY. No. That's my cousin's bag. *(Buries it under cot.)*

MIRIAM *(admiringly)*. Some bag! *(The impatient* FAY *shouts to* TEDDY *through screen window.)*

FAY. Well, Teddy? Howz about it?

TEDDY. I'm coming. *(Then to* MIRIAM*)* Well, good-bye for a little while—Miriam. *(*MIRIAM *starts for bathroom carrying a towel)* Oh— *(Points off)* the hot water doesn't function.

CURTAIN

ACT ONE

SCENE II

The Dining Room. The stage represents a corner of a vast dining room. Several tables, set for two, are in the center right of stage. Two large tables, arranged for four, are placed prominently, left. A screened window along the back wall affords a view of the tall pines in the distance. Backed against the rear wall is a long service table which holds bottles of ketchup, condiments, mustard, etc. There is a bandstand, lower right, against which rests another service table. Tacked on the wall above the stand is an ornate banner in purple and gold. It bears the legend, "Camp Kare-Free, 1921" and a design representing a rising sun flanked by two pine trees. Nor is this the only decoration on the walls: there are several homemade murals nailed on the ell going off, left, into the wings. They represent the camp's romantic settings: Eagle Rock, Crystal Lake, Honeymoon Hollow. Two doors, upper right, lead into and out of kitchen. Another door, upper left, takes one on to porch and the grounds.

"A staff of well-trained waiters," the Kare-Free folder brags, "of whom we are forced to boast they are college grads, assist in bringing to our guests the fullest possible enjoyment from each and every dish in the hearty meals we serve." As a matter of fact, two of the waiters we meet have actually gone to college: CHICK, *who has his law degree, and* BARNEY, *the camp Lothario, who is taking a post-graduate course in dentistry. Of the others, several years of intensive training at an evening high school haven't completely erased* ELI'S *accent, nor can* SCHMUTZ *conceal the fact that his East Side intonation represents an individual triumph over an institution of learning no higher than public school.*

At the rise of the curtain CHICK *is seated at a table folding napkins.* HI, *another waiter, is finishing the setting of one of the smaller tables.* SCHMUTZ, *followed by another waiter, enters from kitchen carrying a large tray containing platters of chopped liver.* ELI *comes in from door, upper left. All the waiters are dressed in white shirts, black snap bow-ties, white duck trousers and black shoes.* ELI *walks to* CHICK *and gives him an envelope.*

ELI. Janet told me to say good-bye and to give you this.

HI. It must be your tip.

SCHMUTZ. Open it. (CHICK *does so, extracting a single bill which he holds up.*)

ELI (*in disgust*). A one-dollar bill!

HI. Why din she put it in an eye-dropper instead of an envelope?

ELI. That's the thanks you get fa waiting on her like a slave, and trotting your feet off at night.

CHICK (*handing bill to* SCHMUTZ). Here, give it to Tobias.

SCHMUTZ. Don't worry about it, Chick. These disappointed dames always take it out on us.

CHICK. At this rate my share of the tips won't even cover the sixty dollars I paid Tobias for the job.

ELI. I heard he might give us our money back at the end of the season.

SCHMUTZ. A dreamer!
(BARNEY *enters and hangs a poster on the wall. It reads: Basket-Ball, This Friday Night at the Social Hall. Camp Kare-Free vs. Mount Topmore.*)

HI. Aha, the Magnificent Obsession!

ELI. Guess he's been examining the new arrivals.

HI. Well, Casanova, dijja see what landed?

BARNEY. Yeah. Not bad.

HI. Not bad!

SCHMUTZ. Dincha see their faces? At lease with a pretty dame—

BARNEY. The pretty dames *you* can keep. With them you've got to argue—to debate. But with these dogs, you do 'em a favor when you show some attention. And they're grateful. They come across with tips.

ELI (*snorts contemptuously*). Peeew! One buck!

BARNEY. I saw one that came in—not so bad. (*Turns to* CHICK) You took her valise.

CHICK. I'll *shenk* her to you.

BARNEY. What's the matter?

CHICK. Very refined! A little too rich for my blood. I told her off already!

BARNEY. You're gonna wind up behind the eight ball with the tips, Chick.

HI. And he needs 'em.

BARNEY. And how he needs 'em! Schmutz, at least, can go back to his old man's shop. I have my P. G. course to take up. But with you—well.

CHICK. With me there's nothing! Go on, say it!

SCHMUTZ. It pays to have a college degree! You hadda go and study law yet!
(ABE TOBIAS'S *voice, heard from kitchen, spurs them into activity.* HI *and* SCHMUTZ *exit left.* BARNEY, CHICK *and* ELI *busy themselves at the large table center.*)

TOBIAS'S VOICE. A check fa this, a check fa that! What'm I made of, fourteen-karat gold, fa heaven's sakes?
(TOBIAS *enters, followed by* CHARLIE, *the headwaiter. The former is a harassed little man obsessed with the idea he is constantly being taken advantage of.* CHARLIE *no longer takes his employer's complaints very seriously. A moment or two later* JOE, *the camp handyman, shuffles out of kitchen and stands meekly by waiting for attention. He is a tired-looking cadaver, and wears dirty shirt, trousers and hat.*)

TOBIAS (*examining a handful of bills*). Try to cut down! Reduce a little the bills! No! Abe Tobias is paying, so why worry?

CHARLIE. But, Abe, the expenses are bound to be heavier—

TOBIAS. Why? Answer me, why!

CHARLIE. Because we've got twenty-four more guests than last week. Because—

TOBIAS. For evveything he's awways got an answer. But awways! (*He notices two patties of butter on plate which he holds up. He glares at* CHARLIE) Such big pieces! Who's the Sandy Clause around here?

CHARLIE. Regulation size.

TOBIAS (*to* JOE *who has been tugging at his sleeve*). What is it, Joe? What's the matter?

JOE. I gotta get some supplies fomm the village.

TOBIAS (*reading paper* JOE *gives him*). What is this—new washers, new plungers?

JOE. A coupla terlets ain't woikin' on the goils' side.

TOBIAS. Let 'em wait a few days.

JOE. But they're raisin' holy hell wit' me. They want the hot water fixed and I—

TOBIAS (*waving him away*). What're you bothering me with hot water for?

JOE. But Mr. Tobias—

TOBIAS. O.K., Joe.

CHARLIE (*to waiters who have been whispering at table*). For God's sakes, fellas, what is this—a coffee klotch? Come on, break it up!

TOBIAS. A gold mine you gotta have the way money pours out around here. (*Excitedly, to waiters*) Listen, boys, the next time— (*His features break into a smile; several guests have come in*) Hoddeya do? (*He greets* MR. *and* MRS. G., *who are followed in by* HENRIETTA. MR. G., *a retired merchant, is at camp for his wife's health. He has long ago taken possession of her ailments as a subject for discussion, and in any argument concerning medicine, he is the final authority.* MRS. G. *is a small, roly-poly, motherly woman who accepts each of her husband's statements as a personal challenge.*)

MR. G. Hoddeya do, Abe? Hoddeya do?

(TOBIAS *exits, left.* CHARLIE *enters kitchen.*)

HENRIETTA (*loading her plate with celery and olives*). I certainly could relish a nice piece of fried chicken despite my diet.

MR. G. (*counting set-ups at next table*). Four places today. So who is the new persin? Must be a girl.

MRS. G. And why is with you a "must be"?

MR. G. (*spreading his napkin before him*). Because is all the time more girls in camp than boyess. That's why must be. (HENRIETTA *has dug into the food before her, after carefully wiping the cutlery and dishes with her napkin. She now lowers fork with a bang and turns to address* CHICK *who has come on.*)

HENRIETTA. Chick, would you kindly come here? (*As* CHICK *approaches*) I simply must protest.

CHICK. What's the matter?

HENRIETTA (*holding up her plate*). You call this chopped liver? (*He eyes it apathetically*) Just taste this if you wanna taste something disagreeable. Go on.

CHICK. No, thanks. What would you like instead?

HENRIETTA. Anything but that. That isn't liver—it's sabotage! (CHICK *hurries into kitchen.* ROSALIND *comes on with* BIRDIE, *another camper, and they take their chairs at the* G.S' *table.* REBA *and* TINY *enter and go to table at right, center. The former's back and arms are burned a lobster-red. Throughout scene waiters rush in and out of kitchen. A cloud of sound soon hangs over the room, a blend of voices, cutlery, dishes and conversation.*)

ROSALIND. Hearty appetite.

MR. G. Denk you.

ROSALIND (*stretching to reach for the bread*). Believe me I'm always glad when it's Sattiday. Excuse my boarding-house reach. (*She spills salt*) Look what I did. That means a fight. (*Throws some salt over her shoulder.* TEDDY *and* FAY *come in.*)

FAY. . . . and that's our table there. (*Pausing near* MR. G.) Folks, I want you should meet my girl friend, Teddy. Teddy, the folks.

TEDDY. How do you do?

MR. G. Please to meetchoo.

TEDDY (*noticing plate before* MR. G.) That looks very good. (*She goes to table, center, and sits.* FAY *has already taken her place there.*)

HENRIETTA (*through a mouthful of celery*). Parm my full mouth, but the food gets more atrocious every meal. I just hadda change my liver

MR. G. (*holding a forkful of liver*). Meat, meat! Is all the time meat! Too much meat makes high the blood pressure. (CHICK *has come in from kitchen with a fruit cup which he places before* HENRIETTA. ROSALIND *notices this.*)

ROSALIND. That looks tasty. Canya change my *forshspice*, Chick?

CHICK (*to* FAY). Shall I change yours, Fay?

FAY. Surely.

CHICK (*to* TEDDY). What about you?

HENRIETTA. Better change. The liver is unbearable.

TEDDY (*pointing to* MRS. G. *who is dumping oysterettes into her glass of tomato juice*). I'll have some of that tomahto juice, please.

CHICK. Tomato juice isn't on the menu, but—

TEDDY (*bristling*). If it's not, then why has she—?

CHICK (*as he leaves for kitchen*). But I dare say we can get some for a new guest. (*Exits.*)

FAY. Please don't do her any favors! (*But he is gone. She turns to* TEDDY) Ignore him. That's the best way.

MR. G. (*seeing in* TEDDY *a new customer for his story*). Mrs. G. gets special the temeteh juice.

MRS. G. (*proudly as she rises*). I'm suffering from diabetis.

MR. G. From a long time awready.

MRS. G. Comes September will be two years.

MR. G. We din even know about it. Alluva sudden I see she's losing ten, maybe fiftin pounds.

MRS. G. And a heavy water drinkeh. Ten glesses is by me a notting.

MR. G. Alluva sudden! So I say to myself, "Mr. G., must be something the metteh with Mrs. G.—"

MRS. G. Was like a blood condition. And the docteh says—

MR. G. (*with exasperation*). Let a persin tukk! (*Continuing to others*) So we go to a specialist and he gives Mrs. G. a blood test, and this kine test, and that kine test—

ROSALIND (*looking off*). The honeymooners! (*All turn as* AARON *and* BESSIE BERLINER *enter. They are shy and self-conscious.*)

AARON. Hello, evveybody.

MR. G. Hoddeya do, Mr. and Mrs. Berliner? How eye you? (*He rises and crosses to* TEDDY.)

BESSIE (*as* AARON *assists her into chair at table down right*). Hearty appetite. Enjoy your lunch.

MR. G. Denk you. Denk you.

AARON. Ah, chopt liver! Just what I like.

BESSIE. Oh, I can make that. You just take liver and chop it up.

MR. G. (*to* TEDDY *in loud whisper*) Lest year he was in the bend a fiddler. So she comes to camp and one-two-three they falling in love. Now look —honeymooners!

FAY. Isn't that romantic, Teddy?

MR. G. Now they here fa a vacation, and it don't cust them a penny even.

TEDDY. Don't they pay anything?

HENRIETTA. Couples whose romance emerge from this camp get their honeymoon free, gratis and for nothing.
(MR. G. *spears her with a glance and returns to his table.*)

ROSALIND. It's like an inducement. (*Sighs*) But you gotta have luck. (BESSIE *sneezes.* AARON, *lost in his food, isn't aware of any contretemps.*)

BESSIE (*glaring at him*). Poopsy!

AARON (*uxoriously, through a mouthful*). Hello, you little weasel, you!

BESSIE (*a wounded pigeon*). I just now sneezed.

AARON. Oh, *gesundheit.*

BESSIE. Thank you. (*The martyr*) Gee, a person could sneeze a thousand times before getting a *gesundheit* outta you!

AARON. But, baby, I just now said *gesundheit.*

BESSIE. Sure, after I hadda beg you for it. (*He reaches across table for her hand but she withdraws it petulantly*) No, I'm mad. (*She refutes this by bestowing a smile on him. Both return to their food.*)

AARON. You little weasel, you!

(*During later part of scene* CHICK *has come in from kitchen, and* MIRIAM *from door, left. Latter takes her place at* TEDDY'S *table.*)

CHICK. Good afternoon, or rather, good evening.

MIRIAM. So I'm late fa the appetizer. Don't be so sarcastical. (*Turning to* ROSALIND) Rosalind, please pass the celry.

ROSALIND (*passing plate which has only one piece of celery on it*). To take the last piece means you're gonna be an old maid.

MIRIAM (*tearing off stalk so that one piece is still left*). See, I'm leaving some over. (*Suddenly* MIRIAM'S *attention is arrested by some one she sees offstage. She pushes chair back, rises and hurries off*) There's Pinkie!

ROSALIND (*staring after her*). My goodness, lookit her rush!

HENRIETTA. No wonder there's no sex equality in camp—with the girls constantly running after the fellas.

ROSALIND (*excitedly, pointing toward other end of dining room*). Look. Here comes Itchy, our social director!

FAY (*chuckles, and turns to* TEDDY). Some wonderful sense a yewma he's got—a little risky, but comical.

ROSALIND. I consider him much better than Milton Berle.

(ITCHY FLEXNER *enters followed by his assistant,* SAMMY. *That* ITCHY *is a comedian is known at once by his costume: a bright blazer, bell-bottom sailor trousers and a sailor's hat.* SAMMY, *hiding behind an accordion he carries, wears a pith helmet. Both mount the bandstand.*)

TEDDY. That's a very funny get-up.

OFFSTAGE VOICES (*in a cheer as* ITCHY *mounts stand*) Forty-seven, forty-eight, forty-nine, raaaazberries!

ITCHY. Hoddeya like that? The Master of Cemeteries gets the razzberry! (*Whips out false beard which he puts on*) Comes the revolution I'll get razzberries with crimm! (*There is laughter from the diners.*)

FAY. What'd I tell you? Some sense a yewma!

ITCHY (*removing beard*). Seriously, folks, I wanna extend in the name of Mr. Tobias a welcome to the newcomers who are new to this camp. To the old-timers I wanna say that Camp Kare-Free's still got the old carefree spirit and—well, we wanna get your co-operation to keep the camp spirit as such.

FAY. He talks a very nice grammar.

ROSALIND He's got a sister who's a liberrian.

ITCHY. I wanna tell the newcomers that we are informal at this camp. You can dress how you like.

SAMMY. So long as you wear clothes.

ITCHY. Fa my part you can even be a nudist. Remember, where there's life, buoy, there's soap. Ong, ong, ong! (*Again there is laughter from the listeners. The loudest laugh, however, can be traced to* ITCHY: *he slays himself*) But seriously, folks, tonight is dress-up night. We want the girls to spruce yesselves up and show the fellas what you really look like. I mean with your clothes on.

FAY. What'd I tell you? He's very risky.

HENRIETTA. He's coarse—but not offensive.

ITCHY (*looking around room*). And now folks, being as there's lotsa newcomers here today— (FAY'S *hand shoots up and she points to* TEDDY) Ah, there's one— (*Consults his list*) Fay Fromkin's girl friend, Miss Teddy Stern! (*Applause from diners*) Stand up, Teddy, and take a bow.

FAY. Go on, Teddy. Stand up.

TEDDY (*lowering her head in embarrassment*). No, no! Lemme alone!

ITCHY. Ah, she's a little bashful. Looks like Teddy can't bear it. Ouch! Well, suppose we give her and the other newcomers here the good old Camp Kare-Free song. Now, all together—evveybody sing! Hit it, Sammy!
(*A steady procession of waiters come from kitchen carrying trays laden with soup, and exit left above the tables. During the song* TEDDY *can be seen in whispered remonstration with* FAY.)

ITCHY AND DINERS (*to the tune of "Mother"*)

C is for this camp with pleasures many;
A means active, always on the go;
M is for the meals, and they are plenty;
P is for our plays—a wond'rous show;
K is class, and that's the very highest;
F is fun. That means you're never blue.
Put them all together that spells Kare-Free.
(*A cheer*)
Kare-Free, rah, rah, rah! Kare-Free, sis, boom bah!
(*Again the song*)
And sweetest memories for you.

(*As* ITCHY *comes to the concluding line of song he pauses to slap* REBA *across her sunburned back.*)

REBA. Geez!
(ITCHY *and* SAMMY *leave, left, as the diners applaud them.* CHICK *and* ELI *are on stage serving* MR. G. *and others.*)

FAY. Gee whiz, what's the harm in taking a little bow? If it was me—

TEDDY. But it's not you, and I'm not going to make an exhibition of myself.

HENRIETTA. I know precisely how you feel. I remember one time—
(MIRIAM *returns to her table, unaware of the curious glances fixed on her.*)

MIRIAM. Listen, I gotta sit with Pinkie and hold his hand. He's like a baby.

HENRIETTA. And what's the matter with him?

MIRIAM. He's sick. That's why he wasn't in a horseback mood.

FAY. He wasn't too sick to keep a date in the canteen last night.

MIRIAM. You think I won't tell him about it? He's gonna get a mighty good piece of my mind in the canoe this afternoon. (*She walks off up-stage as* MAC *comes on from down, left.*)

MAC. Hearty appetite, folks.

MR. G. Denk you. Denk you.

MAC (*to* FAY). I just came to remind you we got a date fa a canoe-ride later.

FAY (*hesitates and directs a glance toward* TEDDY). I don't think I can—

TEDDY. Oh, don't worry about me. There's lotsa things I wanna do.

HENRIETTA. If you wish canoe-company, I'm not occupied.

TEDDY. No, thanks. I haven't finished unpacking. (*To* FAY) But you two go ahead.

FAY. No, Mac. Some other time.

MAC. But there's no other time. I'm leaving tomorrow.

TEDDY. Go ahead, Fay—please. It's silly to change your plans on my account. Fay—please!

FAY. O.K., Mac. See you later. (MAC *withdraws. For a moment or two there is silence broken only by the diners lost in their soup.*)

TEDDY (*idly digging at her food*). Everybody suddenly seems to be going canoe-riding.

MR. G. (*brightening*). Look. She don't know why! Iggle Rock, uv cuss!

TEDDY. What?

MR. G. Iggle Rock. Sure! The boyess and the girls, they go there in boats. In the night-time is the moon shining and they holding hands—

MRS. G. (*beaming*). And right away—(*Smacks her lips*) monkey business!

MR. G. Wait! You'll make monkey business, too.

TEDDY. I beg your pardon.
(CHICK *comes on with several plates of food which he serves at* MR. G.'s *table.*)

MR. G. What'sa metteh, a nice girl like you won't find a boy? Don't worry. So if not a camper, he's a waiter.

TEDDY (*embarrassed, she turns to* ROSALIND). Could we have the bread, please?

ROSALIND. Russian rye or plain white?

TEDDY. Any kind.

MR. G. (*refusing to drop the subject*) Listen, the waiters, they the best. Collitch boyess. The finest from the finel (*Takes* CHICK's *arm*) Lookit Chick. A lawyer. Smott like anything!

CHICK. O.K., Mr. G., O.K.!

MR. G. Look, look, how beshful he is.

TEDDY. I wish this man would stop it.

MR. G. Listen! Maybe I can fix it op so you should be honeymooners next year. Ha?

FAY. Can'tcha see you're embarrassing my girl friend?

MR. G. But he's such a nice boy, this Chick. Aw right, he don't make a good living now, but—

CHICK (*furiously*). You'd do me a great favor, Mr. G., if you'd keep that big mouth of yours shut.

MRS. G. Say, hold the tongue, you fresh thing, you!
(CHARLIE *walks on from kitchen.*)

MR. G. Who you tukking to like this? Respect show!

CHICK. Please keep your two cents outta my affairs!

CHARLIE. What's this? What's going on here?

MRS. G. A refined boy should insult Mr. G. Such fresh woids he used—like a regelleh tremp.

TEDDY (*rising*). I beg your pardon, but with all due respect to this gentleman here— (*Nods toward* MR. G.) it really wasn't the waiter's fault.

CHICK. Don't bother about me—please.

TEDDY. I was only trying to— (*Glares at him and then rushes off.*)

FAY. Teddy! (*Rises and dashes after* TEDDY.)

MR. G. (*waving finger at* CHICK). Tips I'll give you? You should live so long!

CHICK. You can take your tips and—

CHARLIE. Shut up, Chick! Just for that you'll be fined fifty cents. Hear that?

CHICK. Why fifty? Why not make it a dollar?

CHARLIE (*pushing* CHICK *toward kitchen*). Maybe I will if you don't shut up.
(MR. G. *is tearing a roll into shreds and throwing the pieces into his bowl of soup.*)

CHICK. Go on, make it five dollars—ten dollars! Who cares?

CHARLIE (*as they exit into kitchen*). Keep it up and I'll report you to Mr. Tobias. I'm much too lenient around here, and that's no kidding.

MRS. G. (*to her husband who is eating madly*). Some noive from a collitch boy!

MR. G. (*lowering spoon with a bang and pushing plate aside*). Ehhh, who can eat now?

CURTAIN

ACT ONE

SCENE III

The Rear Porch of the Social Hall. The left of porch is in complete darkness; the right is outlined by the moon's rays which cast a shadow of leaves against the top of the porch. The door leading to this balcony is in the dead center of the stage and is decorated with streamers and lanterns.

Although informality is the note stressed at camp, Saturday night finds the female guests arrayed in all their sartorial splendor. This is the night they seem more exotic than Garbo, more fashionable than Kay Francis. They are all glamour girls, all clothes-horses exhibiting the most fashionable in gowns. The boys, with the exception of a few rebels, wear flannels and sports coats.

At the rise of the curtain the concluding strains of a fox-trot are heard, there is offstage chatter and applause, and a number of couples come from the Social Hall to join their friends hidden in the shadows of the porch. There is ad lib conversation from the groups as they come on: "We're gonna get some of those green things with ice in them. Know what I mean?" "Oh, cromm de mint. I had that tonight awready." "Your Gary Cooper is nothing but a string bean. Go love a string bean!" "I suppose your Nelson Eddy is better?" "At least my Nelson Eddy can sing." "Has anyone here seen Gertrude?" "She's on the front porch." "Thaaank you."

BARNEY *and* SOPHIE *come out of Social Hall and walk toward rail which runs along front of porch.*

BARNEY. You better go to your bunk and get a blanket.

SOPHIE. A blanket?

BARNEY. Certainey. We're going to Eagle Rock.

SOPHIE. But why do we need a blanket?

BARNEY. You wanna catch cold?

SOPHIE (*affectionately as she takes his arm*). Oh, you want me to put it over my back?

BARNEY. Sure, dopey—over your back! Don't you know the grass gets kinda wet this time of night? (*They go off, left, as* CHICK *and* SCHMUTZ *come on right.*)

SCHMUTZ. Once a head-waiter, awways a louse! I knew that Charlie would blab to Tobias.

CHICK (*wearily*). So what?

SCHMUTZ. So you hadda wash windows all afternoon, that's what!

CHICK. It was almost worth it. Maybe Mr. G. will learn to keep his nose out of other people's business.

SCHMUTZ. Not Mr. G.'s nose.

CHICK. I don't mind getting up at five in the morning, or waiting all day on these well-fed nature lovers, or trotting my feet off at night dancing with them. That's my job. All right. But it's not my job to be insulted by them and—

SCHMUTZ. They're the ones who give the tips. And after all, that's why we're here.

CHICK. One of the reasons I'm here was to play tennis every day, and swim in the lake every morning. That's what Tobias promised us. God, I haven't been near that lake in weeks. And with four hours' sleep a night I'm just all in. (*As music starts*) Well, here we go again—picking flowers off the wall.

SCHMUTZ (*stopping him*). You're about ready to fold up like an accordion. Give yesself a break, why don'tcha? Stay out here and give your dogs a rest.

CHICK. How can I? If Tobias sees me it's good-bye job.

SCHMUTZ. Don't let him see you. And if I run into him, I'll cover you up.

CHICK (*with a sigh*). I am pretty pooped. (*Dreamily studying the sky*) And it certainly is one swell night.

SCHMUTZ. I'm getting sick of this double life I'm leading—waiter by day, gigolo by night! (*He goes into Social Hall.* CHICK *crosses to left center, leans over the rail and scans the sky. The* BERLINERS *have come from right.*)

BESSIE. Jerry says it's O.K. with him, provided we can dig up a fourth.

AARON. Ah, that's the problem. Whom can we get for a fourth? (*A sudden inspiration*) Sylvia Retnick!

BESSIE. Bridge is with her a passion. Wait here a minute while I see if she's in there. (*She hurries into hall.*)

AARON. Hurry, sweets. (*Looks off and observes* CHICK *leaning against a pillar*) Hello, Chick.

CHICK. Hello, Aaron.

(*A girl comes on from right, sights* CHICK *and hurries toward him.* GUSSIE, *one of the "wallflowers," is short, undulating and unprepossessing.*)

GUSSIE. I thought that was you. What'sa matter you're not dancing?

CHICK (*affecting limp*). It's my toe. It's all swollen.

AARON. What happened, Chick?

CHICK. I must've sprained it or something.

AARON. You oughta take care of it.

CHICK. That's exactly what I'm going to do. I hope Doc is still up. (*He limps off.*)

GUSSIE (*eyes* AARON *for a moment and then speaks*). A good frienda mine suffered something terrible fomm her finger. She let a rusty pin get near it and it became infected and, my goodness, she thought she was gonna lose it. (*Holding up digit*) It was the pinkie.

AARON. With those things it's best to take care of them right away.

GUSSIE (*drawing closer*). I never take a chance. Let something happen, a scratch even, I simply must put on iodeen. Or mercurichrome— (*Takes another step toward him*) That's like iodeen—oney it's red. (*Pauses to listen to music*) That's very nice music, isn't it? (*Looks at him hopefully.*)

AARON (*patronizingly*). It's aw right.

GUSSIE. Kinda makes you wanna dance. Doesn't it?

AARON (*shedding the ash of his cigar*). Ah, this band don't compare to last year. I was in that one.

GUSSIE. Is that so?

AARON. I did a little fiddle-scratching.

GUSSIE. Isn't that funny? I noticed you before but I thought you were a newcomer.

AARON. Nah! I was here fa a whole summer last year.

GUSSIE (*now at his side*). Oh, fa goodness sake!
(BESSIE *comes out of Social Hall and walks directly to* AARON.)

BESSIE. In fifteen minutes— (*Suddenly freezes as she sees another girl at her husband's side, she says*) Suppose we go in and have a dance.

GUSSIE (*snatching* AARON'S *arm*). Wait a minute. I saw him first.

BESSIE (*with icy hauteur*). I beg your pardon, but you did not see him first. Aaron Berliner happens to be my husband.

GUSSIE. Oh, I—I din know. Excuse me. (*She hurries off.*)

AARON. What nerve! She comes over to me and—

BESSIE (*returning to the Social Hall*). You must've given her some encouragement—

AARON. Poopsy! May I drop dead this minute if I so much as looked at her!

BESSIE (*entering hall, followed by* AARON). Never mind—without fire there's never any smoke!

AARON. But Poopsy, I'm standing right here—
(HENRIETTA *and* TEDDY *have both come on during this. The former wears a flaming-red gown. Her billowy bosom is a shelf of cheap jewelry.* TEDDY, *attractively dressed in white, takes a position against the rail.*)

HENRIETTA. Your Miss Fay is a fine girl friend.

TEDDY. She's probably out with Mac somewheres.

HENRIETTA. That's what I mean. A real friend wouldn't desert you when you just arrived.

TEDDY. If I couldn't take care of myself she'd be with me. I've known Fay all my life. We were in the same class in business school together. She even got me my first job—L. Gallagher and Company. And I met several nice girls there, and lots since. But none of them compare with Fay. That's why I'm glad if she's with Mac. Besides, it's his last night.

HENRIETTA. His last night! My God, you'd think he was going to be liquidated tomorrow! (*Crosses up and stares longingly into hall!*) The atmosphere appears fairly lively. Perhaps we should participate.

TEDDY. No, thanks. I'd rather be out here. (*Takes a deep breath*) My, this night air feels marvelous. And look at that moon.

HENRIETTA (*still staring into Social Hall*). We could obtain a dance from the staff.

TEDDY. They must have a special moon here in the country. It's so—so bright and so big.

HENRIETTA. They're supposed to oblige us, you know.

TEDDY. What?

HENRIETTA. The staff.

TEDDY. Oh, I couldn't go up to a stranger and ask him for a dance. I just couldn't. It would be different if somebody came to me. But this way—(*Shakes her head and smiles*) Anyways, I haven't been on a dance floor in so long I wouldn't know how to follow. My feet would— (SCHMUTZ, *seeking escape, appears in doorway. He sees the girls and quickly retreats but not before* HENRIETTA *has drawn a bead on him.*)

HENRIETTA (*the Northwest Mounted out to get her man*). Parm me, but I'm going in and partake of this dance! (*She goes after* SCHMUTZ. TEDDY *sighs, reaches into her bag for mirror and lipstick and primps herself. From the darkened corner muffled voices are heard.*)

MAXINE. Ouch!

HI. What'sa matter?

MAXINE. When did you shave last?

HI. Before lunch. Why?

MAXINE. You're scratching me up with your whiskers.

HI. Aw, baby, I din mean—

MAXINE (*petulantly*). Go 'way. My face feels like it's been resting on a pincushion!

(MIRIAM *and* PINKIE AARONSON *come on from right. Latter is a suave, dapper young man in his early thirties. There is an unctuous, man-of-the-world quality about his manner. It is apparent at once that self-doubt has never tortured him.*)

MIRIAM. Come on, Pinkie. The music will be nearly over.

PINKIE. Let's go to the canteen. I gotta have a drink.

MIRIAM. After this dance. Please, Pinkie.

TEDDY (*approaching* MIRIAM). Pardon me, but have you seen Fay by any chance?

MIRIAM. No, I haven't.

PINKIE (*surveying the newcomer*). Well, bless mah *mezzuzah* and look who's here!

MIRIAM (*reluctantly*). This is Pinkie Aaronson. Pinkie, meet Teddy.

PINKIE (*extending hand*). Welcome, young lady. And where've you been hiding?

MIRIAM. She's my new bunk-mate. Well—

PINKIE. Not the one with the French label? (*Patting her hand*) Say, we've gotta have a long talk about la belle France.

TEDDY. Oh, have you been there?

PINKIE. Have I been there? (*Laughs and turns to* MIRIAM) Listen to that, will ya?

MIRIAM (*impatiently*). Pinkie, I'm afraid it'll be over before you know it.

PINKIE (*as* TEDDY *withdraws her hand*). You and I are having the next dance, and I'll tell you about what happened to me on the Champs-Elysee—

MIRIAM. There is no next dance. This is the last one, Pinkie, and it'll be nearly over. Come on, awready.

PINKIE. Don't go 'way. I'll be right back after I give *schmiggeggie* here a work-out. (*Enters Social Hall.*)

MIRIAM. Pay no attention to him. (*In furious whisper to* PINKIE *as she follows him in*) I can't unnastand what pleasure you get fomm making me feel unnecessary—

(*A group of* GIRLS, *laughing uproariously, come out of darkness, walk across porch and exit.* MAXINE, *one of the* GIRLS, *is giggling.*)

MAXINE. I din even see them in the dark. Oh, are my cheeks red!

ROSALIND. Lookit Maxine! She's hysterical!

(TEDDY *has strolled to right of porch.* CHICK *comes on from left followed by* HI *who is accompanied by a* GIRL.)

HI. Tobias is coming! Better grab yourself a horse. (*Pointing to* TEDDY *who is leaning against a pillar*) There's one. (HI *and* GIRL *disappear into room.*)

CHICK. Good evening. (*Awkwardly, as she stiffens*) I—I just wanted to tell you I'm sorry I lost my temper this afternoon. I mean that squabble with Mr. G. At the table, I mean, when you started in to explain to Charlie. I'm sorry about it— (ELI *hurries in, notices* CHICK, *points frantically off-stage and speaks in tense whisper.*)

ELI. Tobias! (*Exits into hall.*)

CHICK (*quickly*). And I just wanted to ask if you have this dance taken.

TEDDY. Yes, I have.

CHICK (*sunk*). Oh!

TEDDY. Besides, I'm not in the habit of dancing with people who are rude in their remarks.

CHICK. Well, I—I thought if this dance wasn't taken— (*Glances nervously off and starts to withdraw*) Well, thank you just the same.

TEDDY (*after a brief struggle with herself*). It—it looks as if this person I'm waiting for is late. (*Looks off, left and right*) He seems to be detained somewheres.

CHICK. You mean, perhaps you wouldn't mind dancing?

TEDDY. Well—all right. (TEDDY *enters hall and* CHICK *is about to follow when* TOBIAS *comes on, accompanied by* CHARLIE.)

TOBIAS. Just a minute, Kessler. I wanna have a serious talk with you.

CHICK. Can't it wait, Mr. Tobias? (TEDDY *appears in doorway*) I have this dance with one of the guests.

TOBIAS (*forcing a broad grin to his face*). Oh. Oh, certainey. I din know. (TEDDY *and* CHICK *withdraw*) What're you bothering me with Kessler? He's dancing.

CHARLIE. Sure. Now he's showing co-operation. But where was he the resta the night? No place! (*They cross porch and almost collide with* ITCHY *who has* REBA *in tow.*)

ITCHY. Hey, stupid, watch— (*Apologetically*) Oh, Mr. Tobias. I din know it was you. Excuse me.

TOBIAS. I've been looking fa you, Itchy. A new show you're supposed to put on each week. That show tonight was simply terrible.

ITCHY. Terrible?

TOBIAS. Two repeats you served up tonight. The whole camp was complaining they seen them before.

ITCHY. I had two new numbers set but you wouldn't get me the costooms. You said—

TOBIAS. Hear that, Charlie? Evveything is my fault—but evveything! (*Turning to* ITCHY) And that number tonight with the radio—was that a piece of cheese! Feh!

ITCHY (*to* REBA, *stung to the quick*). Phil Baker's whole routine! I copied it word fa word.

TOBIAS. Excuse the expression, Itchy, but it— (*Catching himself*) it's no good. "Hello, Beetle" and "Hello, Bottle." You can't copy something better?

ITCHY. Yeah, what?

TOBIAS. Me he's asking! I'm the social director here?

ITCHY. What about giving that Japanese fiesta?

TOBIAS. Again that fiesta!

ITCHY. Why not try it? Look. We fix up the canoes with Japanese lantins. Then evveybody gets into Japanese costooms—the girls with fans and the fellas with—well, in Japanese costooms. It won't cost much, and it's a big novelty.

TOBIAS (*again appealing to* CHARLIE). You hear? He spends my money and that's with him a novelty. Listen, Itchy, forget this foreign stuff, this Japanese canoeing, and think of something good. *That* would be a novelty. (*Laughs and exits followed by* CHARLIE. ITCHY, *his arm around* REBA'S *waist, looks off at* TOBIAS'S *retreating figure.*)

ITCHY (*his hand traveling along* REBA'S *side*). He's such a darling! I rack my brain copying down material and he says it—

REBA (*yanking his hand away*). Itchy! Take away the hand!

ITCHY. I just wanted to see if you carry a gun, that's all.

REBA. Well, I don't, so there! (*The orchestra swings from a fox-trot to "Good Night, Ladies"*) It's the last dance. Come on. (*There is a flurry of activity as couples disentangle themselves and follow* ITCHY *and* REBA *in. From right, clusters of* GIRLS *come scurrying to dance with each other.* MAC *and* FAY *come out of darkened corner.*)

FAY. Let's dance out here. It's more romantic. (MAC *puts her coat on rail and takes her in his arms. They dance slowly and gracefully.*)

MAC. Gee, tomorra back to the same old grind.

FAY. Then you'll forget all about me. Outta sight, outta mind.

MAC. This winter you'll be throwing me outta your house at lease twice a week. (*Pressing her closer*) You're such a dolling. (*He stops to kiss her. They part and he reaches for her coat.*)

FAY. No, Mac. No.

MAC (*surprised*). Why not?

FAY. My girl friend, Teddy, is here.

MAC. Say, she's probably on Eagle Rock this very minute.

FAY. Oh, no—not Teddy.

MAC. Dijja tell her about us?

FAY. Mac!

MAC. I dunno. I thought maybe girls, you know—they talk.

FAY. Surely they talk. But I could never tell things to Teddy. About myself, I mean. She's from another world altogether.

MAC. My farewell to camp! (*As she hesitates*) Say, what is she, anyway? Your mother or something?

FAY. But suppose she asts me where I been the whole evening?

MAC. Say you've been with me. Tell her you hadda say good-bye because —well, after all, it is my last night!

FAY (*taking his arm and exiting left*). Gee, Mac, you're awways so ultra-practical!

(*The music stops, there is laughter and applause, and the* CAMPERS *file out of the hall. The porch becomes a scene of much activity and animation. Farewells are exchanged,* GIRLS *are propelled in the direction of Eagle Rock and there are ad lib fragments of chatter exchanged:*

ROSALIND. *So I says to Itchy, "With your sense a yewma you oughta be on the stage." He's much better than Al Jolson.*

BIRDIE. *Well, who ain't?*

LOIS. *So why should I go mountain climbing? My God, don't I climb enough stairs?*

KITTY. *Of all the places fa me to have a sunburn. Mama will kill me when she finds out.*

HENRIETTA. *How about a little drink, Eli?*

ELI. *Aw right, I'll let you buy me a double Scotch.*

TEDDY *and* CHICK *are the last to appear. They smile shyly at each other.* CHICK *becomes aware he is holding her purse and returns it.*)

CHICK. Would you like some refreshment?

TEDDY. No, thanks ever so much. I'll just enjoy the view for a minute and then I think I'll retire—to bed. (*At the railing, looking off*) Very pretty, the mountains.

CHICK. Yes, they are. Cigarette?

TEDDY. Thank you. (*As he lights it for her*) Again thank you. Don't you indulge?

CHICK (*whipping pipe from pocket*). Pipe! You're a very graceful dancer.

TEDDY. Considering it's a camp, it's a very nice orchestra.
(GUSSIE *crosses porch, sees* CHICK *and approaches.*)

GUSSIE. Funny how remockable you recovered fomm your sore foot! (*Having delivered this thrust she stalks off.*)

TEDDY. What in the world provoked that?

CHICK. I didn't wish to dance with her so I invented an excuse. I believe she's annoyed.

TEDDY. I'm beginning to understand what your job is like. You must get pretty aggravated with people like us.

CHICK. Surely you're not placing yourself in the same category with her.

TEDDY. You must think so judging from my outburst this morning.

CHICK. Suppose we forget about today. It was just a misunderstanding.

TEDDY (*looks over rail as voices are heard in the distance*). What's that?

CHICK (*embarrassed*). That—that's Eagle Rock. (*The porch light is extinguished*) They turn it out at midnight.

TEDDY (*overwhelmed by Nature*). One feels so little in all this vastness. But I suppose you're used to it.

CHICK. Oh, sure. But then all enjoyment is relative.

TEDDY. And pray, what do you mean by relative?

CHICK (*the pipe-puffing philosopher*). Well, take anything. Take a one-dollar bill. To some one poor a dollar represents a fortune. To a rich person—poof—a mere nothing.

TEDDY. I'm afraid I don't quite comprehend the connection.

CHICK (*indicating the moon*). Well, pardon me for pointing, but take the moon for instance.

TEDDY. Yes?

CHICK. To us that moon is beautiful. Right?

TEDDY. It's exquisite.

CHICK. So bright, so luminous. Observe how it lights up that tree over there.

TEDDY. Oh, yes. (*About to point but checks the impulse*) Is—is that a chestnut tree?

CHICK. No, those are all pines. And that's the tallest in the Berkshires.

TEDDY. "Poems are made by fools like me, but only God can make a tree." (*Turns to* CHICK) Are you familiar with—? (PINKIE *comes on from right and goes to* TEDDY.)

PINKIE. I bet you thought I'd forgotten— (*Observes* CHICK) Excuse me. I mighta known you'd be snapped up. Well, back I go to little Miss Screwball. (*Exits.*)

TEDDY. Good night (*Giving her attention to* CHICK) Excuse the interruption.

CHICK. That's quite all right. (*The mood isn't broken: the rail is still the rail of the "Normandie"*) Now look across the lake. It's so still and tranquil.

TEDDY. Indeed it is.

CHICK. Now the moon there shows us how beautiful nature is. And that's where my point comes in. Somewhere in a wretched hovel some poor, penniless man is tossing in bed because this very same moon is shining in his eyes. He cannot sleep. Let us say he has no window blinds. So he looks around, and what does he see? His hovel, squalid and bare. "Ah," he thinks, "why do I have to be reminded at night of what I cannot help seeing all day?" In other words, this moon which reveals to us how beautiful *our* world is, reveals to this poor individual how wretched *his* world is.

TEDDY (*her face aglow with understanding*). At last I comprehend what you mean! Now take me, for instance. It so happens that all my life I've desired to go to Paris. I've wanted to see the Eiffel Tower and the Arc de—you know, where the unknown soldier is buried, and the Champ Elysee—I guess that's how you call it. And yet you take a Frenchman. He is *so* sick of the Eiffel Tower, he's probably dying to come to this country and see the skyline and the Empire State Building. Correct?

CHICK (*amazed at her perception*). That's exactly what I mean! Everything is relative— (*Diffidently*) I'm sorry, but I didn't get your name.

TEDDY. Teddy. Teddy Stern.

CHICK (*extending his hand*). My name is Chick Kessler. I'm very pleased to meet you.

TEDDY (*with conviction*). The feeling is mutual, I'm sure! (*They shake hands.*)

CURTAIN

ACT TWO

SCENE I

Eagle Rock, six days later. A huge bowlder jutting from the right, an elevated sweep of greensward carpeted with pine needles, a birch tree gleaming in the sun, hint of the beauty and charm of romantic Eagle Rock.

TEDDY *and* CHICK *have known each other now for almost a week. In sharp contrast to the cold and hostile attitude which marked their first meeting, they are now on warm and friendly terms. They have found many things in common, particularly a feeling of intellectual superiority over many of the other campers.*

TEDDY is seated on a canoe cushion and is making a queue by sewing two pieces of black cloth to the top of a silk stocking. She is attractively costumed in blue overalls, a satin cut-out top, blue bandanna and sandals. The freshly-shaven CHICK wears a black crew-neck sweater, flannel trousers and sports shoes. He is lying on the ground and is gazing off in rapt admiration of the scenery.

CHICK. Gosh, it—it's beautiful! Every day Eagle Rock becomes more and more enchanting.

TEDDY. "This is the forest primeval, the murmuring pines and the hemlocks." (*Looking up*) Poetry.

CHICK. I know that. "Evangeline."

TEDDY. Oh, that Henry Wadsworth Longfellow. I'll never forget the long white beard he had on.

CHICK. Where did you see him?

TEDDY. Just his picture. It used to hang over the blackboard in our class. "Exhale," I called it.

CHICK (*laughs*). You called the picture, "Exhale"?

TEDDY. No, the whiskers. Whenever we had deep-breathing exercises I hadda breathe in— (*Illustrates by inhaling and bringing her head back*) and every time my eyes came to the whiskers, it was time to exhale. That's why I called the whiskers "Exhale."

CHICK. Crazy kid.

TEDDY. Oh, I was just a child in those days. (*She puts silk top over his head. He squirms*) Hoddeya expect me to fix this when you twist and turn so much?

CHICK (*looking at queue*). Hey, this is going to be a Japanese fiesta, isn't it? Y'know, strictly speaking the Japanese don't wear queues.

TEDDY. Since when?

CHICK. Since never!

TEDDY. Listen, tonight they'll wear queues! (*Takes mirror from handbag and holds it up*) Here, Chickie, look. Your own mother wouldn't recognize you.

CHICK. I hope not. What're you wearing?

TEDDY. All the girls will be wearing kimonos so I thought I'd have on pajamas. (*Suddenly*) They wear pajamas, don't they? (*CHICK sits up, looks at her, smiles and leans over to peck her on cheek.*)

TEDDY (*without any emotion*). And pray, what brought on this sudden outburst of osculation?

CHICK (*affectionately*). You're so cute, I couldn't resist. What's the matter? You disapprove?

TEDDY. And perhaps I do.

CHICK. Very well, so I return the kiss. (*Does so.*)

TEDDY (*placing queue in bag and removing bottle of lotion*). A nut. What can I do with him?

CHICK. Y'know, Teddy, the more I see of you the more goofy I get. Right now I'm overwhelmed with goofiness.

TEDDY. You make me feel like some disease. Six days with me and you're overwhelmed with goofiness.

CHICK. Oh, I know you only six days, do I? Well, apparently you're unaware that time in the country is different from time in the city.

TEDDY (*spreading lotion on legs*). Ah, ha! We have Professor Einstein with us today.

CHICK. I mean it. I figgered it out after I left you last night.

TEDDY. This morning, you mean.

CHICK (*rising*). Supposing a fella was seeing you in the city. Regularly, I mean. Let's say two or three times a week.

TEDDY. Go on.

CHICK. Of those two-three times a week he spends, let's say, four hours a night. But— (*Holding up finger, significantly*) but he doesn't spend those four hours solidly with you. I mean, you take in a lecture here, a movie there—you know. So of the four hours, he spends two solid hours with you. Now two hours times two nights a week, that's four solid hours you're in each other's company. Follow me?

TEDDY. Proceed.

CHICK. Let's multiply four hours a week by four weeks a month and we have sixteen hours a month he sees you. Suppose, merely for the sake of argument, it's a close relationship Say six months. Right?

TEDDY (*modestly lowering her eyes*). Continue.

CHICK. Sixteen times six months— six, three to carry— Ninety-six hours you've known each other to warrant a steady relationship.

TEDDY. So what's the point?

CHICK. Simply this. Up to and including today I've been seeing you for breakfast, lunch and supper. I've been with you till two-three o'clock in the morning. Correct?

TEDDY. Granted.

CHICK. That's fifteen hours a day we've been seeing each other really solidly. Multiply that by six and that's—that's ninety hours!

TEDDY. Proving?

CHICK. Proving a very significant fact. Namely, that we've known each other the approximate equivalent of six months in the city. Six months! (*Sitting beside her*) Think of it, Teddy!

TEDDY. You missed your vocation. You should've been an accountant, not a lawyer.

CHICK. My God, Teddy, I know you thoroughly!

TEDDY. Yes? And what conclusions have you formed?

CHICK. Tons of conclusions, believe me. Tons of 'em!

TEDDY (*consumed with curiosity*). That's no answer. Enumerate, why don't you?

CHICK. Well, for one thing, you're different from the average girl around here.

TEDDY. That's a wonderful compliment—comparing me with hill-billies from the Bronx!

CHICK. I mean, well, I'll be very frank with you, Teddy. When we had that little squabble the first day I thought you were like the others. That's why I was so frigid to you.

TEDDY. Frigid! An icebox couldn't've been more frigid than the way you were!

CHICK. I just didn't know you—how sweet you are and what fun it is to be with you. It's seldom you find a girl who is charming and bright at the same time.

TEDDY. Oh, I'm not bright, Chick. Really, I'm not.

CHICK. Yes? Well, I consider you very intelligent.

TEDDY. My mind is—is passable, that's all. (*In a sudden burst of confidence*) Chick, I'll tell you something I wouldn't tell any one else. I even hate to admit it to myself. I'm a bluff, and what's more, I know it. (*As he starts to speak*) Now, wait. I like to use big words so people will think I'm a college grad. I try to give the impression I'm brainy, but when it comes down to it I'm just like the other girls around here. (*Quickly*) Maybe on a little higher mental plane or something, but that's about all.

CHICK. Listen to Miss Inferiority Complex! You think I'd waste my time on you if I thought you were a dope?

TEDDY. Now wait a minute. I didn't say my mind was bad. But I ought to develop it, you know—with lectures and courses at night. But all day long I'm busy typing Mr. Faber's dictation, all day long. Comes night-time I'm a total wreck, too tired to go any place, except a movie occasionally.

CHICK. We're going places this winter—museums and concerts and exhibitions. I've been waiting to find the right person to take.

TEDDY (*reminiscently*). My brother, Charlie, used to take me to the Stadium concerts, before he was married. The music was over my head, but it was nice to sit there, out in the open, with all those intelligent people. You go to concerts all the time, don't you?

CHICK. Pretty often. (*Smiles*) To tell you the truth, Teddy, some of the music's over my head, too.

TEDDY. I wish I didn't have to work. There's so much I could do if I had the time—books I wanna read, places I'd like to go to.

CHICK. Poor, sweet Teddy. You got such a raw deal from life!

TEDDY. I certainly did! (*Suddenly puzzled*) Hoddeya mean that, Chick?

CHICK. I'm thinking of what you told me about your erstwhile engagement to this fella—this Sam what's-his-name.

TEDDY. Sam Rappaport.

CHICK. For three whole years you've been waiting to throw up your job. You've been laying out your life like you lay out a table for supper—everything neat and orderly. Then alluva sudden—bang! The table is pushed over. The engagement broken. Goodbye to marriage!

TEDDY (*quietly*). I believe in things being all for the best.

CHICK. The nicest years of your life, torn up like a piece of paper. I know what that means, Teddy. The same happened to me.

TEDDY. You were formally engaged?

CHICK. I'm talking about the years I tore up studying law, clerking for buttons before I could take my bar exams. And for what? So I could be a stinking, lousy failure!

TEDDY. I'm surprised to hear you talk that way.

CHICK (*bitterly*). Why not? What's ahead for me, Teddy? Maybe you know the answer.

TEDDY. But you're not the only one in that position—

CHICK. Isn't that peachy? My hand is chopped off and I'm bleeding, so you tell me about somebody whose foot is chopped off. That's gonna relieve my bleeding, huh?

TEDDY. No, but you must realize—

CHICK. I realize plenty—plenty, believe me! (*Desperately*) God, if it's gonna to be the same as last year, I—Oh, I dunno.

TEDDY. I've never seen you in such a morbid mood.

CHICK (*reminiscently*). Gee, I remember when I was a kid I had the world by the tail. I used to see rich men in their automobiles and I'd say to myself, "Don't worry, Chick. Some day you'll have a boat like that—only better. With your full name on the side, not just your initials." Or else I'd read about some famous man and I'd say, "O.K. O.K., Chick. There's no hurry. Shh! Just take it easy. You'll get there and you'll be even more famous." (*Smiles ruefully*) Funny, when you're a kid nothing seems impossible.

TEDDY. I wanted to grow up to be a letter-carrier's wife. (*Laughs*) Of all things!

CHICK. Y'know, even after I was admitted to the bar I still thought I was a big shot. I was a professional man, see? I had a sheepskin with my name on it in fancy letters—Charles Kessler, LL.B. The world was waiting for me! (*Snorts*) Sure it was!

TEDDY. Seems to me I'm detecting a little sarcasm.

CHICK. Sarcasm is right! It was waiting—with a club in each hand.

TEDDY (*as lotion runs down her arm*). Hand me that towel, please.

CHICK. So now I have an education and a degree, and what the hell good is it? I can't even get a job as relief investigator at twenty-five smackers a week. There're too many other lawyers ahead of me. (TEDDY *sits up, hands bottle to* CHICK *and turns so that her back is toward him.*)

TEDDY. Rub some of this on my back Chickie.

CHICK (*applying it ever so gently*). It's all a lotta baloney, Teddy. Study hard, they tell you. Get a lotta knowledge—knowledge is power. A lotta bunk is what I say!

TEDDY. That's enough, thank you.

CHICK. There's something rotten about the whole set-up. We're licked. We're up against a brick wall, all of us.

TEDDY. Well, I still have my job, thank goodness—

CHICK. And you hate it worse than poison! For three years you've been dreaming of giving it up, of having a home—your own home that you and Sam what's-his-name were gonna share. Where is it?

TEDDY (*turning her head away*). It's none of your business.

CHICK. You haven't got it. His brother was licked, so in the neck you got it.

TEDDY. Please! I don't wanna hear—

CHICK. I know you thoroughly, Teddy. You want a decent home, a husband and some kids. But husbands don't grow on trees these days. What're you gonna do while you're waiting?

TEDDY. I'll—I'll wait, that's all.

CHICK (*getting to his feet*). God, if things only weren't so bitched up. (*Quickly*) Excuse me.

TEDDY. Wadde you mean by that remark?

CHICK. Once in a blue moon I meet a girl who hits me so hard she leaves me winded. I start doing some serious thinking about how I'd like to settle down. But how can I—without a job and no prospects? And look at you.

TEDDY. What about me?

CHICK. You've got a job, and how you despise it! You can't quit and settle down till somebody comes along who's ready to make things comfortable for you. Correct?

TEDDY (*sadly*). Correct.

CHICK. It looks as if we're just a couple of *shnooks*.

TEDDY (*pushing canoe cushions back and rising*). Yes, it certainly looks that way. (*There is a thoughtful silence.* CHICK *directs his gaze toward* TEDDY *who seems deeply troubled. She looks up and notices his fixed stare. Suddenly his features break into a smile.*)

CHICK (*walking toward her*). Come here, funny face. (*He draws her close to him and they embrace. After a long kiss they part and she studies his face.*)

TEDDY. I like you, Mr. Kessler.

CHICK. Mr. Kessler is my father. Just call me Chick.

TEDDY. I like you, Chick.

CHICK. Yeah?

TEDDY. Yeah.

CHICK. Why?

TEDDY (*coquettishly*). "Y" is a crooked letter.

CHICK. Go on. Tell me why you like me.

TEDDY (*flippantly*). Oh, 'cause you're such a clean-cut boy, I guess, with a very cute face, and you're so—well, you're a clean-cut college man.

CHICK. That's not much of a reason.

TEDDY. I'll tell you, Chick. All my life I've been wanting to meet some one with nice, refined instincts, some one whose mind I could respect—a person aware of other things in life besides business and the radio. That's all Sam Rappaport could ever talk about. (*Shaking her head*) The difference between you two fellas!

CHICK (*after a pause*). Teddy?

TEDDY. What?

CHICK. We're both in a spot. It's not my fault I can't get a job, and it's not your fault that you can't have your own home.

TEDDY. I suppose you're right.

CHICK. While we're both marking time these next few years, maybe we can help each other.

TEDDY. How?

CHICK. By admitting that we're two normal, human beings and grabbing some fun out of life. Then we can say to the world, "We fooled you! We're not licked! Look—we're laughing!"

TEDDY. You still didn't say how.

CHICK. You like me—you just said so. And you know how I feel about you.

TEDDY. I know, Chick.

CHICK. Well, since we can't get married, why don't we— (*They exchange glances. There is a moment or two of silence before she grasps the import.*)

TEDDY (*shocked*). Chick!

CHICK. Why should we let life deny us everything? It isn't right! We're entitled to some happiness. My God, we're still young!

TEDDY. No, Chick.

CHICK. Why not?

TEDDY. It's obvious why not.

CHICK. I must be blind. I don't see it.

TEDDY. Don't spoil everything. Please, Chick.

CHICK. You're evading the issue. I'm still asking why not?

TEDDY. 'Cause I simply can't. You don't know what my family would—

CHICK. What has your family to do with—?

TEDDY. I can't. I just can't. Even though this might be the real thing, I—

CHICK. Might be? Teddy, do you think I'd talk to any one else the way I talk to you?

TEDDY. I know that, Chick.

CHICK. I don't. I assure you I don't. Somehow you struck me right between the eyes with a terrific bang. Boy, I see a million stars, every one with your face on it. And all I can say is if things were only different—

TEDDY. If! If! But they're not!

CHICK. I know they're not. I know I can't earn a living and I've no right to ask you to starve with me. But this other hunger—that's something where you can help me. Where I can help you. That's something the two of us can share.

TEDDY. No, Chick! No!

CHICK (*shouting*). Why not, for God's sake?

TEDDY (*tearfully*). I'll thank you not to shout at me!

CHICK. I—I'm sorry. Excuse me. (*Calmly*) Why not, Teddy?

TEDDY. Honestly, Chick, I can't understand a sweet and clean-cut boy like you asking me to behave like some cheap, ordinary thing—

CHICK. Cheap, ordinary thing. You call—? (*Eyes her coldly*) Come on. Let's get out of here.

TEDDY. Look, Chick. A girl isn't at all like a fella. She's got her family to think of— (*Righteously*) This would be a fine world if every girl—

CHICK. Shut up! Shut up, you damn fool! (*He rushes off.* TEDDY *watches him, stunned. She picks up her sewing bag and walks slowly down the hill.*)

CURTAIN

ACT TWO

SCENE II

TEDDY'*s bungalow, 11:30 that night.*

At rise of the curtain the door opens and FAY *enters carrying several Japanese lanterns which she hangs up on the hooks. She is dressed in pajamas, and has a bright red sash around her waist. Her hair is parted, and flowers placed over each ear represent the final Oriental fillip.* SCHMUTZ, *also attired in what he hopes is a Japanese costume, follows her in carrying a basket of supplies. He quickly disappears and returns with several boxes which he arranges. He then throws a tablecloth over this improvised bar.* ELI, *appropriately attired, enters carrying a bench which he places down right.*

ELI. Make it snappy, kiddies. I gotta heavy date.

FAY. Who was that girl, Eli?

ELI. I just met her. I made a big hit with my Japanese costume. She wants me to handle her laundry. (*There is a great deal of bustle and activity on the part of the trio as they arrange the room, pushing chairs and cots aside to make a clearing in the center.*)

FAY. It certainey was some fiesta. We all looked like regella Chinks, huh? I coulda closed my eyes and imagined I was right back in Japan.

SCHMUTZ. During the rainy season.

FAY. Too bad the weather came along and drizzled up evveything.

ELI. What became of Teddy tonight? She wasn't at our table fa supper.

FAY. She prolly sat somewhere else fa a change. I guess she was in Chick's canoe doong the fiesta.

SCHMUTZ. I was in Chick's canoe. And we had a stowaway—Gussie.

FAY. Teddy wasn't with Chick?

SCHMUTZ. Not unless she came dressed as Gussie.
(*The boys have finished arranging the bar and now head for the door.*)

ELI. Anything else?

FAY. No, thanks very much.
(*They exit to porch, left, as* TEDDY *comes on from right.*)

SCHMUTZ. Here she is.

FAY. And about time.
(TEDDY *comes in dressed in the same costume she wore on Eagle Rock. She looks off at the boys and laughs.*)

TEDDY. Those are very funny costumes. (*To* FAY) How was the fiesta?

FAY. Fine.

TEDDY (*surveying the rearranged room*). Say, what's been going on here?

FAY. We're gonna have a party.

TEDDY. Who is?

FAY. The whole gang. Itchy heard it was my last night, so he's giving me a blow-out. (*Sternly*) Teddy, I wanna have a serious talk with you.

TEDDY. Huh?

FAY. Where were you fa suppa?

TEDDY. Why, I—I had it at our table.

FAY. When?

TEDDY (*without conviction*). After you left. Then I went back to the writing lodge and finished reading a novel I started this morning. That's why I was late for supper.

FAY. There's something wrong, Teddy. Go on—tell me.
(TEDDY *is about to confide in her but hesitates, feeling that the subject is much too personal for discussion. She decides to dodge the issue.*)

TEDDY. I'm worried about Mama. I wonder whether I oughtn't to leave with you tomorrow.

FAY (*seeing through her*). You do!

TEDDY. She hasn't been feeling any too well lately—

FAY. Listen, Teddy. I'm no dope. I still can add two and two.

TEDDY. Of course you can.

FAY (*hurt*). Aw right, you don't hafta tell me. (*Suddenly*) Did—did Chick try to get a little personal?

TEDDY. What makes you say that?

FAY. So that's it! (*Laughs*) My God, I thought it was something serious! (MAXINE *opens door, deposits a large bag of food on the floor, speaks excitedly and vanishes.*)

MAXINE. Corn-beef, American cheese, cream cheese, franks! I gotta get pickles. Good-bye!

FAY (*mechanically*). Good-bye. (TEDDY *goes to bag, takes out sandwich, looks at it, and, aware that* FAY *is watching her, puts it back.*)

FAY. Why don'tcha go ahead? You know you've had no suppa.

TEDDY. Oh, I ate very heartily.

FAY. And you've had no fight with Chick. Listen, Teddy, you might as well know he's coming to the party with Gussie.

TEDDY (*with forced gayety*). The more the merrier! (*She crosses to get her pajamas hanging from hook.*)

FAY. I see. So you're gonna act like Pagliacci.

TEDDY (*heading for bathroom with pajamas*). Fay, that mind of yours imagines more things! After three years I'm here for a good time. And that's what I'm certainly having! (*Enters bathroom.*)

MIRIAM'S VOICE. Quick, somebody—open up the door! (FAY *rushes to door and opens it to admit* MIRIAM *who is laden with a portable victrola and a batch of records. She wears a topcoat over her pajamas.*)

FAY. Look who's here—Mrs. Sandy Clause!

MIRIAM. Take those records off before I bust.

(FAY *removes records and clears a place on cot for the victrola.*)

TEDDY'S VOICE. Hello, Miriam.

MIRIAM. Hello. (*Turning to* FAY) I got a lend of the machine fomm Pinkie. What I din hafta go through to get it!

FAY. Is—is Pinkie coming?

MIRIAM. Nachelly he's coming—if he can stop guzzling at the canteen. I wish Mr. Tobias would padlock that saloon.

TEDDY'S VOICE. Is it still wet outside?

MIRIAM. Yeah, it's drizzling the weather. (*To* FAY) Oh, I ran into Henrietta, and guess what?

FAY. What?

MIRIAM. She's not coming. She's got a date.

TEDDY'S VOICE. *Our* Henrietta? You know, I'm kinda glad.

MIRIAM. Can you imagine!

FAY. I bet she's out galvinating with some radical. The two of them must be talking of blowing up places with bombs. You know how it is when them communists get together.

MIRIAM (*prophetically*). Some day those people are gonna get arrested. (*She has doffed her coat and now comes forward pirouetting in the manner of a mannikin*) Hoddeya like these? They're genuwine Japanese pajamas. Very chop-suey, ha?

FAY. They new?

MIRIAM. Eh, heh.

FAY. Wear them in good health.

MIRIAM. Thank you. The exact same thing retails at Hearn's fa four ninety-eight, not counting that goddamn tax. (*Anxiously as she holds out pajama pants and turns her back*) Can you see the foundation garment I got on?

FAY. Nah. You can't see a thing.

MIRIAM. You feel so untidy when you can see through. (*Crossing over to bar*) Well, we'd better get ready. (TEDDY *comes out of bathroom dressed in pajamas. She wears a garland of flowers in her hair, and a sash around her waist. She minces across stage, her hands raised in Japanese fashion.*)

FAY. Don't you look like Miss Anna May Wong!

TEDDY. Now what I need is earrings.

FAY. Sure, help yesself.
(MIRIAM *has started to open a jar of olives with a carving knife, and has quite a time of it.*)

MIRIAM. Gee, I'm worried about that Pinkie. You got no idear how the girls keep pestering him and pestering him. They all hadda hear about his stores. (*Walks toward* TEDDY) He's got two big hat stores, and is that a business! Evvy winter he goes to Europe. To Paris, France.

TEDDY. Does he really go abroad?

MIRIAM. Of course—fa the new styles. (*Sighs*) Believe me, I'd like to go to Europe. Of course, I don't know the langwich—

TEDDY. I thought he was joking the first night, talking about Paris.

MIRIAM. Oh, no! Evvy winter—regella like clock-work, off he goes to Paris, France. His suitcases are covered with labels galore— (*She prods jar with knife and comes dangerously near decapitating herself*) like the one you got.

FAY (*taking knife from her*). Gimme that knife. Wanna kill yesself?

ITCHY'S VOICE. Open up in the name a the law!

FAY. It's Itchy! (*She dashes forward and opens door.* ITCHY *and* REBA *enter and deposit gin bottles and mixings at the bar.* ITCHY *wears a pigtail, drooping mustache, and his eyes are made up in Oriental fashion. A brightly-colored robe covers his costume. His headgear consists of an electric plate, the cable serving as a pigtail. He shuffles to* TEDDY *and genuflects.*)

ITCHY. Hoy chung a fong foo moy yung. Honable ladies, me belly happy meeting you. Me name? (*Coughing violently*) One Lung Gone! Get it?

FAY. *Meshugeh!*

MIRIAM. Look at Charlie Chan at Camp Kare-Free!

ITCHY (*placing gin bottle on his head*). Me putee firewater on toupee. Know why? To keepee wig-warm. Ong, ong, ong. (*This is met with an appreciative roar.* ITCHY *takes his place behind the bar and starts to prepare cocktails.*)

MIRIAM. I thought you were bringing Pinkie with you.

ITCHY. The nurse is giving him his bottle—in the canteen.

MIRIAM (*picking up a drink at the bar*). Him and that liquor! Y'know what? (*Grimly*) I'm gonna get plastered tonight. I'm gonna get so plastered, I'll be drunk!

ITCHY. Past out, you mean. Two drinks and you're under. Poor Butterfly, she no can take it. (*To* TEDDY) Say, Teddy, is Chick pulling a gag or something? He ast me if it's O.K. to bring Gussie.

TEDDY (*with forced enthusiasm*). I hope you said it was all right.

ITCHY. Sure. "Bring her along," I says. "She'll be the death of the party!"
(*All the* GIRLS *laugh,* TEDDY *a bit too heartily.*)

TEDDY. Oh, you mustn't talk that way about Gussie. She's a very nice girl.

FAY (*laughing as she walks to* TEDDY). "The death of the party!" Isn't he a scream, Teddy? (*Sotto voce*) Y'know, you're not fooling me!

ITCHY (*crossing to them with drinks*). Here we are, my chickadees. A little something fa the throat.

FAY (*plucking olive from her glass*). I don't like olives in my drink. To me an olive belongs on a plate next to a piece celry.
(*Suddenly offstage voices are heard in song, faintly at first and louder as* SINGERS *approach.*)

VOICES.

There's a long, long trail awindin
Along Camp Kare-Free's mountai
road,
Where good times and pleasure
wait you,
And life's an easy load—

ITCHY (*through this*). Here come Captain Henry's Showboat. Got everything ready?

FAY. Gee, the cigarettes I forgot t put out. (*Hurries to do this.*)

MIRIAM (*extending glass*). Here gimme another drink. I might's we catch up with Pinkie.

VOICES (*now directly at door*).

There's a long, long time of froli
And of dreams all come true—

(*The door opens and about a doze* CAMPERS, *led by* SAMMY *playing th guitar, stand framed in doorway Their assorted costumes make them look more like Jewish night-rider than celestials.* GUSSIE, *an exotic siren, has a firm grip on* CHICK's *arm.*)

ALL.

So when summer time is over
You'll feel fresh and clean and
new.

(*There are ad lib cries and greeting as they pour into room and dives themselves of their coats, robes and blankets.* TEDDY *is an energetic and smiling hostess, greeting each gues just a bit too enthusiastically.*)

TEDDY (*to* BARNEY). Oh, don't you look wonderful? Please let me have your blanket.

BARNEY. Shoy tung foo yung how ming moy low ung. Rang chop chop soy.

SOPHIE. That really means something?

BARNEY. Sure. It means hello in Japan.

ITCHY. So carbolic acid, carbolic acid. That's good-bye in any langwich!

GUSSIE (*coming forward with* CHICK). That walk we had along the lake knocked me out. I gotta have a drink, Chick.

CHICK (*eyeing* TEDDY). O.K.

GUSSIE (*following his gaze*). I'll get one glass so we'll make it a loving cup! (*She joins the others at the bar where* ITCHY *is shaking cocktails.* CHICK *crosses to* TEDDY *who has picked up a tray of sandwiches from bench.*)

CHICK. Look. I don't want you to get me wrong—

TEDDY (*regally*). Are you addressing me by any chance?

CHICK. No, I just like to hear myself talk.

TEDDY. I beg your pardon, but I happen to be extremely choosy about who talks to me. (*She starts away but he grabs her wrist.*)

CHICK. Listen, Miss Stern. It is not that I wish to talk to you—

TEDDY (*the Dorothy Parker!*). So I notice!
(CHICK *releases his grip, and looks self-consciously about him.*)

CHICK. I—I just wanna say one thing and then, as far as you're concerned, I'll forever hold my peace.

TEDDY. Can I count on that?

CHICK (*heatedly*). You certainly can! (*Collecting himself*) All I wanna say is that you weren't at the table for supper, so I set aside some food for you. It's on the shelf of that little stand outside the kitchen door, under a napkin. And believe me, I do not care whether you eat it or not!

GUSSIE (*coming between them, holding a glass of beer*). Here, Chickie.

CHICK. Ah, here we are!

TEDDY. Excuse me, Gussie. I would like to give a final word to your escort. Tell him I'm grateful for the details, but he's mistaken. I ate very substantially, thank him.

GUSSIE. You want me to tell him? He's not deef. (*To* CHICK) Are you?

CHICK. We're just kidding around, Gussie. Ask her where?

GUSSIE (*sitting on bench*). He wants to know where.

TEDDY. At another table— (*Quickly*) Tell him. (*Picking up the tray of sandwiches*) Excuse me.

GUSSIE. Oh, sandwiches! I'll have some of them, please.

CHICK. Gussie, how on earth can you be so hungry after what we had at the canteen?

GUSSIE. I dunno. Guess I developed an appetite.

TEDDY (*impatiently*). Please make your selection. Some people may be hungry, you know.

CHICK (*significantly*). Yes. I know one.

(TEDDY *starts for door with the sandwiches and is about to exit when* BARNEY *shouts to her.*)

BARNEY. Hey, don't run away with the food! (*She allows him to take the tray from her. The victrola music is now on and several couples are dancing.* TEDDY *smiles at* SCHMUTZ.)

TEDDY. Wanna dance, Schmutz?

GUSSIE (*ready to share everything with* CHICK). Wanna go halfies, Chick?

CHICK. You wanted them so much. Go on—eat them.

GUSSIE (*as* ITCHY *raps for attention*). I'll eat 'em later.

ITCHY. Folks, I wanna welcome you to this farewell Japanese party given tonight in honor of Miss Fay Fromkin's going away. But I don't wanna welcome you unless you join in the spirit of the thing. That means you gotta take off that robe, Barney.

BARNEY. Why don'tcha speak fa yesself, Jake? What about the one you got on?

SOPHIE. Yeah, why not take off your own robe?

ITCHY. O.K. If that's the way you feel about it, I will. (*He removes his robe revealing a costume made of a false dickey on which a grotesque design has been painted, and a pair of bright red pajama trousers. This sight is met with hearty laughter, the heartiest roar coming from* ITCHY.)

BARNEY. The biggest mustard plaster in the world!

GUSSIE. He looks like a Japanese cannibal. (CHICK *goes to bar accompanied by* GUSSIE *who glances over her shoulder at* TEDDY.)

ITCHY. I've been waiting to flash these all night but the damn weather spoiled evveything.

CHICK. Suppose we have another drink, Gussie?

GUSSIE. Sure. Why not?

(PINKIE *enters, removes coat and throws it on cot.* MIRIAM *weaves unsteadily toward him.*)

MIRIAM. Pinkie! I've been waiting fa you. Where you been?

PINKIE. I've been to New York and back. Where do you think—?

MIRIAM (*smiles fatuously and taps him*). Hello.

PINKIE. You look pale. What's the matter? (*She sways unsteadily. He grabs her around waist and pulls her toward her cot.*)

FAY. Fresh drinks. Who'll have a nice— (*Sees* MIRIAM *being put to bed and rushes forward to assist* PINKIE) What happened?

PINKIE. A couple drinks and out she goes like a *Chanukeh* light. (*To* MIRIAM) Come on, *Schmiggeggie*—flop!

MIRIAM. Oh, my goodness! The room is going round and round just like a bicycle. Round and round it goes.

FAY. Poor girl, the drinks made her topsy.

PINKIE (*taking blanket from* HENRIETTA'S *cot*). Here, put this over you—(*He finds an enormous brassiere in the folds of the blanket, and holds it up*) My God, a straitjacket! (*He looks at* FAY.)

FAY. Don't look at me. It's Henrietta's.

PINKIE. What does she carry around—cannon balls?

FAY (*placing blanket over* MIRIAM). Cover up, Miriam. You'll be aw right. (TEDDY *looks over and notices the outstretched* MIRIAM.)

MIRIAM. Round and round it goes.

TEDDY (*approaching*). What happened?

HI (*dancing by with one of the* GIRLS). Victim number one! The party's a success!

PINKIE (*as* TEDDY *comes closer*). Well, look who's here! Yum, yum, don't you look nice?

TEDDY. Aw, poor Miriam.

PINKIE. Serves the little screwball right. She shouldn't drink—with her stomach. Lookit her—dead to the world.

TEDDY. The poor kid.
(PINKIE *glances around room and observes* GUSSIE *staring lovingly into* CHICK'S *eyes*.)

PINKIE. Say, how come you're in circulation alluva sudden?

TEDDY (*looks up, sees* CHICK *and turns quickly away*). Sorry, but I don't understand.

PINKIE. You understand. With a nice dish like you here, why is the boy friend trotting that horse around?

TEDDY. He's not my boy friend, and furthermore I'd rather we dropped the subject.

PINKIE. Ah, ha, a lovers' quarrel! What a lucky break fa me. (*Taking her arm*) You owe me a dance, young lady.

TEDDY. Oh, do I?

PINKIE. Yes, ma'am. (*They start dancing*) You dance a very nice fox-trot. I've watched you.

TEDDY. But I have to serve— (*They inadvertently collide with* CHICK *and* GUSSIE.)

CHICK (*starting for bar*). Let's have another drink, Gussie. The floor seems very crowded.

GUSSIE. Aw, Chick, we were dancing so nice. (*The door opens and* TOBIAS *comes into the room. Conversation quickly dies as all eyes turn to him.*)

TOBIAS (*unctuously*). Excuse me fa butting in on the party. (*He takes a confidential tone. The tension is relieved*) There's a coupla soreheads on the girls' side and evveything is with them a complaint—the food, the bunks, the boats—but evveything. So go ahead—enjoy yesselves—oney quiet, see, these soreheads shouldn't complain.

AD LIB. Sure, sure. Don't worry, we'll keep very still. We'll pipe down.

CHICK. We'll be as quiet as mice.

TOBIAS (*walking toward him*). Oh, so you're here, too, Chick. You having a good time?

CHICK (*smiling*). Yes, Mr. Tobias. I'm having a swell time.

TOBIAS (*with forced heartiness*). That's fine, 'cause I run this camp just fa you alone. I run up heavy expenses just so you should be happy, Mr. Sport.

CHICK. I don't know what you mean.

TOBIAS. Look. My name is Tobias, not Rockefeller. *I* spend good money on canoe-cushions, not *you*. (*To others*) So he takes out a boat fa a good time and now—good-bye the cushions.

CHICK. Gee, I—I must've forgotten them.

TOBIAS. What's the matter with you these days, Kessler? Maybe if I make you pay fa the cushions you lost—

TEDDY. They're not lost, Mr. Tobias. They were left on Eagle Rock.

ITCHY (*giving his hands a dry-wash*). Aha, they were on Eagle Rock!

SCHMUTZ. Boy, if them cushions could oney talk—oh, Mama!

TOBIAS (*turning to* CHICK). You get the cushions first thing in the morning. Keep up this foolishness and you'll be canoe-riding back to New York. You understand me? (CHICK *lowers his head in embarrassment.* TOBIAS *turns to the others and puts on his faucet smile*) Well, go on evveybody—have a good time—enjoy yesselves. (*There are ad lib good-nights as* TOBIAS *exits.* ITCHY *looks from* CHICK *to* TEDDY.)

ITCHY. What were you two doing on Eagle Rock all afternoon? Go on, deny it!

SCHMUTZ. What does anybody do on Eagle Rock? (*Sharpening his fingers*) Naughty, naughty.

CHICK. All right, have your fun at my expense—

TEDDY (*stung by the taunts*). There are some people who might like to enjoy the scenery and the mountain-side. There are some people whose minds aren't so coarse they must constantly think of only one subject alone!

GUSSIE. Yeah, and there are some people who forget to take canoe cushions back with them.

BARNEY. What's the matter? Wasn't the ground soft enough?

TEDDY (*furiously*). Shut up!

CHICK. Another crack like that, Barney, and you won't be able to talk for a week. I mean it!

BARNEY. Aw, keep your shirt on. I was oney kidding.

GUSSIE. Say, is this a party or a funeral? Let's have some music.

ITCHY. You're the music, Gussie. Don'tcha know when you're playing second fiddle?

GUSSIE (*crossing to* CHICK). Yeah? Well, come around to Eagle Rock tomorra and you'll see me leading the whole orchester. Am I right, Chick?

ITCHY (*as victrola is turned on*). Come on, soaks—on with the dance. Let joy be unrefined!

PINKIE (*sympathetically, to* TEDDY *who is sitting on bench*). You're not having such a good time, are you? (*As she starts to speak*) Now don't lie.

TEDDY. I—I've got a headache.

PINKIE. This noise don't help much. Why don't we get some fresh air?

TEDDY. It's kinda wet outside, isn't it?

PINKIE (*reaching for his coat*). We can walk to my bunk where it's nice and quiet and we can have a heart to heart talk. Waddeya say? (*Holds the coat up invitingly for her.* GUSSIE'*s shrill laugh pierces the room.*)

GUSSIE. Now Chickie!

TEDDY (*quickly rising*). Will you tell me about your trips to Paris?

PINKIE. Well, I'll do my best. I din expect to give a lecture or else I woulda brought along my lantin-slides— (FAY *comes into scene and notices* TEDDY *in coat.*)

FAY. Say, where do you think—?

PINKIE. She's perfectly O.K.

FAY. Oh, I—I din know. (*She smiles approval and watches them exit.*)

ITCHY (*in imitation of Mae West*). I dunno. Evvey time I have a drink I wanna do something desperate.

GUSSIE. That ain't like her at all. Look. This is the way Mae West goes. (*Indicating victrola*) Shut that thing off. (*The music is stopped. She heaves her hips and looks seductively at* CHICK) Hello, tall, dark and handsome. Why don'tcha come up and see me some time? (CHICK, *embarrassed, looks nervously around.*)

CHICK. Cut it out, Gussie. Cut it out.

GUSSIE. Oh, so you're the bashful type. What you need is a little coaxing.

CHICK (*pushing her hands away*) Don't do that!

GUSSIE. Look. He can't take it. (CHICK *forces a smile to his face and idly glances around room.* FAY, *watching him closely, approaches.*)

FAY. If you're looking fa Teddy, it may innerest you to know she's gone.

CHICK. That's very kind of you to furnish me with information that doesn't concern me in the slightest.

GUSSIE. We're getting along very fine and dandy. Thank you fa asking.

CHICK. Sure!

FAY (*casually*). She went out a coupla minutes ago—with Pinkie.

CHICK (*sharply*). She went out—with him?

FAY. I thought you said you wasn't innerested. (CHICK *hurries toward the door.*)

GUSSIE. Just a minute, Mr. Chick. You can't rush off and leave me flat. (*But he goes. She turns around and stares at the others in amazement*) He did!

CURTAIN

ACT TWO

SCENE III

PINKIE'S *bungalow. The room is smaller than* TEDDY'S *and contains only two cots: one, lower right, is made up, the other, upper left, has an uncovered pillow and a rolled blanket on its bare mattress. Above* PINKIE'S *bed is the bathroom, and left of it the dresser on which rest several magazines, some hairbrushes and a bottle of Scotch. Entrance into room is made through door down left. Two wicker side chairs and a small table are in center, a wicker armchair up left. The room is sloppy and disorderly with shirts, shorts and other articles of apparel hung carelessly on hooks.* PINKIE'S *wardrobe trunk plastered with foreign travel labels stands in a corner.*

The curtain rises and PINKIE *hurries to window near his cot to lower the canvas flaps.* TEDDY *drapes the coat over a chair and wrings the cuffs of her pajamas. The sound of rain is heard as it beats against the roof.*

TEDDY. Leaving the party wasn't such a good idea.

PINKIE. It's lucky fa me we left that party or else I'd be swimming in that cot tonight.

TEDDY (*raises rear flap and stares out*) Just listen to it come down. I —I hope it lets up soon.

PINKIE. Thirty-seven fifty they soak me fa a bunk on the lake-front. And what do I get? The lake-front in my bunk! If we could've found that damn path we could've got here in ten minutes.

TEDDY. You better be careful you don't catch cold.

PINKIE. Thanks for reminding me. I've got a very good cure fa a cold. (*Taking whisky bottle from dresser*) You like Scotch?

TEDDY (*the woman of the world*). Oh, I don't mind indulging once in a while.

PINKIE. We might as well make ourselves comftible as long as it's raining. (*Produces several glasses and pours a stiff drink.*)

TEDDY. Not so much! You'll have me drunk in no time.

PINKIE. Please, young lady, whatever you do, don't pull a Miriam on me. One dead pigeon is plenty!

TEDDY (*taking proffered drink*). Thank you. Do you—do you happen to have any ginger ale?

PINKIE. What kinda saloon do you think I run here? Ginger ale I should have yet! If you wanna travel and see the world you might as well learn how to drink. Take it plain. That's the best way. (*Raising his glass*) Here's hoping you get your wish and that your next vacation will be in Paris.

TEDDY. Thank you. (*Takes a sip and slowly sinks into chair*). Oooh, this burns! It's just like fire. Have you any water?

PINKIE. Don't take a chaser—that spoils a drink. Drink like we do in Paris: bottoms up with the rest.

TEDDY. I—I can't. I'm afraid I'm not that used to it.

PINKIE (*filling the glasses*). It's simple. Look. (*He takes a generous swig*) Come on now. Lemme see you do it. (*Thus challenged* TEDDY *rises, sips, winces, smiles nervously and glances toward door.*)

TEDDY. And now I think I better be getting back. It's late and it's such a long walk—

PINKIE. Aw, that's too bad—just when we're getting to know each other. Why don'tcha wait till it stops raining? Then you can—
(*The door opens and* CHICK, *a figure of wrath—a very wet and breathless figure of wrath—storms in. He addresses* TEDDY *in a voice heavy with icy sarcasm.* PINKIE, *amused, seats himself at table and follows the quarrel with considerable interest.*)

CHICK. So this is the highly respectable young lady who bawled me out something fierce today! And now look at her!

PINKIE (*dryly*) Hello, Chick.

CHICK. I'm not talking to you!

PINKIE. Not even a tiny little hello? Aw!

TEDDY. You certainly have one great big nerve following me here.

CHICK. As I was leaving the party your charming friend, Fay, was only too anxious to tell me you went off with this person here, and I knew exactly the result. But exactly!

TEDDY. I hope you're not disappointed.

CHICK. Far from it, I assure you. What I visualized in my mind is precisely what happened—right to the dot!

TEDDY. Maybe you can visualize yourself right out of here. I'm not used to having people intrude on me and then bawling me out in the bargain.

CHICK. I'm exceedingly sorry I'm hurting your feelings, Miss Teddy Stern. It won't happen again, let me assure you from the bottom of my heart. (*Starts to go and then turns*) And furthermore, may I remind you that you were the righteous one who was so shocked by what I said today?

TEDDY. And may I remind you that I'm not deaf, God forbid? (*Laughs and looks at* PINKIE *for approval of this mot.*)

CHICK. It gives me a big laugh to behold the marvelous spectacle of you, all alone, in your pajamas—

TEDDY. It so happens there's an Oriental party going on in my bunk—

CHICK. But this isn't your bunk, and you're here, in your pajamas— (*Point-*

ing to whisky bottle) boozing around with a certain person—

PINKIE (*waving hand*). Hi, Chick!

TEDDY. If you think that what you're saying disturbs me in the slightest, you're greatly mistaken. In the meantime, you'll oblige me greatly by getting out of here. Or can't you take a hint?

CHICK (*quietly, concealing his rage*). I'm sure I have no wish to continue this disgusting matter one bit further. Good-bye!

TEDDY. Good-bye! (CHICK *exits, slamming door.*)

PINKIE. You know, I think he's sore.

TEDDY (*miserably*). He's sore? And how do you suppose I feel?

PINKIE. I dunno.

TEDDY. The nerve! Spying on me and breaking in here and bawling me out! Who does he think he is, my owner or somebody?

PINKIE. I'll tell you one thing, tootsie. That tray-carrier's cuckoo over you.

TEDDY. He certainly has a remarkable way of showing it. (*In sudden anger*) Why I didn't slap him one—!

PINKIE (*rising to pour another drink*). Calm down and drink this. You'll feel better.

TEDDY. No, thanks.

PINKIE. Don't tell me it struck home?

TEDDY. What did?

PINKIE. What he said about boozing around here?

TEDDY. Oh, that. (*Quickly picking up drink*) Here's to your health (*She gulps it and almost chokes in a fit of coughing*) Get me some water—quick! (*He hurries into bathroom as she falls into chair*) That's not Scotch—that's a red-hot rivet. My insides are on fire. Oh, I feel terrible That damn Chick! (PINKIE *appears with the glass of water*) Thank you

MR. G.'S VOICE (*accompanying a knock on the door*). Somebody is in bunk fife?

PINKIE (*in whisper to the frightened* TEDDY). That sounds like Mr. G.

TEDDY. My God, what'll he think—me in my pajamas! (*There is another knock on the door.*)

PINKIE. Don't worry, I'll take care of him. (*Propelling her toward bathroom*) Get into the bathroom. (*She goes in, closing door behind her.*)

MR. G.'S VOICE. Hello, in bunk fife.

PINKIE (*to himself as he crosses*). What the hell is this—a public liberry? (*Opens door and admits* MR. G. *who is wearing raincoat, hat, overshoes*) Oh, Mr. G., it's—it's you.

MR. G. (*coming into room*). I was pessing and I seen boining the 'lectric light. So I say to myself, "Mr. G., maybe Pinkie's sick inside." So I figger— (*Seats himself at table.*)

PINKIE. I was just going to bed.

MR. G. (*pointing to bottle of Scotch*). Look, a regellch saloon is here. A bummer you wanna be, a nice boy like you?

PINKIE. I caught a cold, and now with this rain—

MR. G. (*leaping to his feet*). A cold? Listen! I got by me in bunk a special meditzin, in two minutes guzz quick away the cold. You want I should bring it?

PINKIE. Not now, Mr. G. I'm gonna hit the hay.

MR. G. (*walking toward door*). So how long it takes to bring it? A secont!

PINKIE. Cant'cha see I'm dead tired and I wanna get some sleep?

MR. G. (*taken aback by his tone*). O.K., so in the munning I'll bring it. (*Sits on edge of cot and prepares to go into detail*) I got it a special 'scription fomm mine docteh. You take a spoon in the munning, and comes night time—

PINKIE (*helping him up*). Yeah, yeah, but if I don't get some sleep, I'll need a doctor. Good night!

MR. G. (*good-naturedly*). Good night. Good night. (*Pauses at door and turns*) So in the munning I'll come. (*He exits.* PINKIE *closes the door and heaves a sigh of relief.*)

PINKIE. He's gone. (*As* TEDDY *appears from bathroom*) It was Mr. G.

TEDDY. And now I really must go home.

PINKIE. What for?

TEDDY (*weakly*). I—I haven't had a bite of food since morning.

PINKIE. No kidding?

TEDDY. All I had at the party was some of that cocktail stuff Itchy made—

PINKIE. And on top of that some Scotch. Say, what keeps you on your feet? (*She shrugs her shoulders to convey that this drinking bout is quite common with her. She then extends her hands and smiles.*)

TEDDY. Well, good night. I certainly had a very nice time.

PINKIE. But you can't walk to your bunk in this weather. You'd never find your way alone, and you'd be soaked to the skin. It'll let up soon. (*He picks up bottle and fills his glass.*)

TEDDY. I don't know what to do. It must be awfully late. (*Turns and sees* PINKIE *pouring drink*) No more for me. (*As he raises glass*) Don't you think you've had enough?

PINKIE. Don't worry, I can stand it. It don't burn me. (TEDDY *goes to rear window, lifts the flap and stares anxiously out.*)

PINKIE. You poor kid. You're worried, aren't you? (*She nods*) And it ain't the weather.

TEDDY (*wheeling around*). Why, what on earth—?

PINKIE. It's this guy, Chick. He's got you tied in knots, hasn't he? Take my advice and forget it. He's strictly small-time stuff. These college boys, they know fomm nothing.

TEDDY. Please don't worry about me. As far as Chick's concerned, I don't even know he exists.

PINKIE (*going toward her*). Sit down, young lady.

TEDDY. Sure. (*She is about to take the armchair and then stops*) It's wet!

PINKIE. O.K., so we'll dry it. (*He picks up a striped silk shirt from top of dresser and hands it to her.*)

TEDDY. Not with your shirt! (*Fingering material*) Is that silk?

PINKIE (*modestly*). Yes, ma'am. Solid silk. Feel it. My pajamas, socks—the same way. That's the oney thing I wear. (*As* TEDDY *dries chair*) Too bad you're nuts about that Chick.

TEDDY. I'm not nuts about Chick, and I don't know what you mean by too bad.

PINKIE. I had my eye on you fomm the very first time I saw you.

TEDDY. Haven't you got me mixed up with a girl named Miriam?

PINKIE. That *schmiggeggie!* She's strictly hit-and-run stuff! You're more my type, Teddy. (*Surveying her slowly*) Yes, sir, with a little breaking in and the rough edges taken off, you'd be a very tasty dish, honey.

TEDDY (*uncomfortably*). Honey! Another drink and there's no telling what you'll be calling me.

PINKIE. You've got me wrong. I'm not drunk, young lady. I'm leveling with you.

TEDDY. You're what with me?

PINKIE. Sit down. (*She sits on edge of armchair*) I'm stricly right-fomm-the-shoulder. No beating around the bush. I don't hand out a line of *shmoos*—not even in business. Me, I talk plain turkey.

TEDDY. I must be stupid or something, but I just don't get your drift.

PINKIE. Here we are, the two of us, alone in the bunk together. Outside it's pouring with rain. Listen. (*He pauses. The patter of rain punctuates the silence*) What a perfect set-up! You're in your pajamas, and it'd take me two minutes to get into mine. (TEDDY *jumps to her feet and throws the wet shirt she has been holding at him.*)

TEDDY. You filthy, no-good tramp! What do you think I am anyway?

PINKIE. Sha, sha! Don't get so excited. Want the whole camp to hear you? (*Now takes bantering tone*) I thought with Chick moving out, I could sorta take his place.

TEDDY (*furiously*). I wish he were here this minute so that he could smash you right in that rotten mouth of yours!

PINKIE. Yep, I bet he would. Just like he did a little while ago when he was here.

TEDDY. So this is how a young business man behaves! This is what all your traveling on boats and going to Paris teaches you!

PINKIE. You said it, kid! (*Turns to her*) Now get me straight. I'm not gonna keep on begging you. With three dames to evvey fella a guy is nuts to argue— (*As* TEDDY *picks up his coat*) Oh, no, you don't! That's my coat and I'm particular who wears it. You wanna leave, leave in your pajamas.

TEDDY. I'm getting out of here.

PINKIE. Good-bye, please. (TEDDY *leaves.* PINKIE *removes his shirt, takes off his shoes and reaches for his pajama top—a gaudy affair with his monogram prominently scrolled on it. There is a knock; he rises and speaks, exasperatedly*) Come in, Mr. G. (TEDDY, *more frightened than ever, enters.*)

TEDDY. It—it's worse than ever outside. I'm scared.

PINKIE. Wait a minute. Maybe I changed my mind. I got pride, too.

TEDDY. It's pitch-black outside. Will you lend me your flashlight? (*As he hesitates*) I promise to return it.

PINKIE. Now I gotta go hunting flashlights!

TEDDY (*moving unsteadily toward chair*). If it's too much trouble—

PINKIE (*rummaging through drawer*). I'll see if I can find it.

TEDDY. Don't bother.

PINKIE. It's in this drawer some place—unless some tootsie's taken it. (*With a sigh*) Ah, I might as well get dressed and take you home.

TEDDY (*sitting on arm of chair*). No, thanks. I'd rather go home with the flashlight.

PINKIE. I never argue with a lady. (*Digs deeper into drawer and unearths the flashlight*) Ah, here it is. (*Gives it to her, gets his pajama trousers and exits into bathroom*) And now, ladies and gentlemen—(*In imitation of Ben Bernie*) the time has come to lend thine ears and say, "Au revoir" until the same time tomorrow night. Your broadcaster is Pincus J. Aaronson who's had a little tough luck tonight trying to do a little broadcasting of his own. Nighty-night and pleasant dree-ums. (*The flashlight falls from* TEDDY'S *hand.* PINKIE, *in his pajamas, comes from bathroom and observes* TEDDY *slumped in chair*) Hey, I just said, "Nighty-night." Bong, bong, bong! (TEDDY'S *head sinks to her chest and her hand falls to her side. He rushes to her*) Aw, fa God's sakes! (*He lifts her gently and places her full length on cot. He pauses, shakes his head, picks up the blanket and covers her. He crosses to turn out light, stops and looks back at the slumbering* TEDDY *with amused resignation*) I shoot more dead pigeons!

CURTAIN

ACT THREE

SCENE I

TEDDY's *bungalow, the following morning. The room is a shambles. The bar, piled high with débris, and several tattered lanterns suspended from the hooks are forceful reminders of the party.*

FAY, *in beach pajamas, walks slowly from the bathroom wiping her hands on a towel. She walks to* TEDDY's *empty cot, stares pensively at it, gets her watch, consults it and shakes her head, deeply troubled. The door-knob rattles and she wheels around to meet* HENRIETTA *who enters briskly with several letters she has received.*

HENRIETTA. Good morning, lazy-bones.

FAY. Good morning.

HENRIETTA (*slumping into chair and examining her mail*). What's happened to everybody? The dining-room appears like a regular morgue. Completely deserted!

FAY (*attempting to be casual*). Well, Teddy's having breakfist, isn't she?

HENRIETTA. No. And she was already out when I got up. I guess she's already concluded her breakfast.

FAY. Was it very late when you got in last night?

HENRIETTA. To tell you the honest truth, I didn't even notice the time.

FAY. I mean, was—was evvebody asleep when you got in?

HENRIETTA. I guess so. All I know is that I was so exhausted, I barely had the strength to take off my clothes and— (MIRIAM *comes in from bathroom and shuffles toward her cot. She is wearing rompers*) Lo and behold, the sleeping beauty is up!

MIRIAM (*balefully*). Is it late?

FAY. They awready announced breakfist.

MIRIAM (*grimaces and gingerly feels her head*). God, it feels like an elephant is having a baby in my head!

FAY. You got a hangover, that's all.

MIRIAM (*flopping on bed*). That's enough! (*There is a knock on the door.*)

FAY. Come! (ELI *enters and looks around.*)

ELI. Teddy isn't here?

FAY. What is it?

ELI. I gotta message fa her.

FAY. So what's the message? I'll give it to her.

ELI. No. This is strictly private. This certain party told me to give it oney to Teddy.

FAY. What party?

ELI (*hunching his shoulders*). I'm not saying. This certain party don't want their name known. She isn't here, huh?

FAY. She may be in the dining room having breakfist.

ELI (*starting for the door*). I'm going over there now, and I'll look.

HENRIETTA (*rising and going toward* MIRIAM). Wait a minute, Eli. Miriam, what your system requires is a little nourishment. Why don't you order some breakfast?

MIRIAM (*groaning*). I'm sick. I don't wanna thing.

HENRIETTA. But you've gotta have something. After all, the human body is like a machine—

ELI (*crosses to her and yanks her sleeve*). Anyway, it's against the rules to serve breakfist in the bunks unless Mr. Tobias says—

HENRIETTA. You'll kindly inform Mr. Tobias that we've got a sick person here, and even an invalid has to eat. (*Solicitously, to* MIRIAM) What do you wish, Miriam?

MIRIAM. Nothing.

FAY. You better have a large glass of temata juice.

HENRIETTA. That's precisely what a dietician would recommend.

MIRIAM. Oh, O.K.

ELI. Temata juice—that's all?

HENRIETTA. In a very large glass. (*As* ELI *starts to withdraw*) Wait, Eli. (*Turning to* MIRIAM) You might as well order some eggs while you're about it. They don't charge you extra. Go on, Miriam.

MIRIAM (*weakly as she gets into sitting position*). Well, maybe I'll have a coupla medium-boiled eggs, and some crisp bacon— (*This is too much for* ELI: *he whips his pad and pencil from pocket and writes*) and some cawfee and a few pieces Melba toast. The Melba toast should be very thin. (*She sinks back, exhausted.*)

HENRIETTA. Got that?

ELI. I got it, but I don't know if you'll get it. (*He leaves.* FAY *continues packing her bag which she has placed on* TEDDY'S *cot.*)

P. A. VOICE. Attention, please. Attention, please. Last call for breakfast. Last call for breakfast. Thaaank you.

MIRIAM. Oh, my God!

FAY. What'sa matter?

MIRIAM (*leaping out of bed*). Pinkie! He must've been up hours ago.

FAY (*feeling her heart*). Did you gimme a *shreck* just now!

MIRIAM. Listen, after working awmost two weeks on Pinkie I'd certainey hate to lose him now. (*Flees into bathroom.*)

HENRIETTA (*sweeping crumbs from bed*). So that's why I could hardly sleep last night—pretzels in my bed! Such aggravation my class enemies should have! (*Noticing* FAY'S *open bag*) What time are you departing?

FAY. I'd planned to take the afternoon bus. I've still got lunch coming to me.

MIRIAM (*rushing out of bathroom*). Gosh, I hope nobody's got him dated up awready. (*She gets into her sandals, turning her back on* FAY *to do so.*)

FAY (*going to closet to get a linen suit*). I think I'll give my suit a little air.

MIRIAM (*suddenly aware of the amenities*). Parm my back.

FAY. It's gonna seem funny getting into city clothes. I bet I gained—(*To* MIRIAM) Did you say something just now?

MIRIAM. I just said, "Parm my back."

FAY. Oh, surely. (*Turning to* HENRIETTA) Listen, I wanna go over the tip situation with you.

MIRIAM. I must look like a wreck. (*With a wave of the hand*) Oh, the hell with it! See you later. (*She exits.*)

HENRIETTA. What's there to go over? You give Clara, the cleaning woman, two dollars. Eli gets a dollar, and you give Chick five dollars.

FAY. Five dollars! You must think I'm Mrs. J. P. Morgan.

HENRIETTA. That isn't so much. I figgered a ten-cent tip for each meal would come to four dollars and change at the end of two weeks. Very well, so you make it an extra dollar.

FAY. I dunno about that. I've been mauling it over in my mind, and Chick's attitude lately, specially to my girl friend, Teddy—

HENRIETTA (*primping herself at mirror*). I'm merely telling you what I'm leaving. After all, tipping is a matter of individual preference entirely optional with the patron. (*Fixes her hat and looks at her watch*) Say, you're gonna miss your breakfast.

FAY. I think I'll leave Teddy a note. (HENRIETTA *exits.* FAY *finds pencil and paper and starts writing a note.*)

P. A. VOICE. Attention please. Aaron Berliner, go to your bunk, your wife is waiting. Aaron Berliner, go to your bunk, your wife is waiting. Thaaank you. (FAY *sits on bed writing. She is interrupted by a knock on the door.*)

FAY. Come!
(PINKIE *enters. He wears a bright silk shirt, flannel trousers and gray suède shoes. He carries* TEDDY'S *pajamas in a rolled bundle.*)

FAY. Oh, hello, Pinkie. Funny you din run into her.

PINKIE. Run into who?

FAY. Miriam. Why, she left just two seconds—

PINKIE. I've come here about Teddy.

FAY (*nervously, as she rises*). Oh, Teddy. She'll be back in a minute. She—she went out fa a walk and she—

PINKIE. Look. Don't kid me, see? This is serious.

FAY (*noticing the pajamas*). Why, they're—they're Teddy's pajamas! Wadde you doing with her pajamas? (*Angrily*) See here, Pinkie Aaronson, if this is some dirty trick you're playing on my girl friend, lemme tell you I think it's a rotten shame—!

PINKIE. Will you kindly button that lip and lemme talk?

FAY. What'd you do to her? Where is she? Please, Pinkie. It's aw right to tell me. I'm her friend.

PINKIE. I'll be glad to tell you if you'll oney pipe down. (*He tosses pajamas on cot.*)

FAY. O.K. I'm piped down. So what happened?

PINKIE. She comes to my bunk last night and chews my ear off asting me all about Paris. So it starts in to rain. Pretty soon Chick comes over and bawls her out fa being in my bunk.

FAY. I wish some people would learn to mind their own business.

PINKIE. Well, he leaves and I see it's oney a lover's quarrel. So I says, "Nighty-night. I'm hitting the hay so you better go back to your bunk." Then Teddy says to me, "It's pouring." Would I mind if she stays till the rain lets up. "Go ahead," I says, "but I'm a dead herring. I'm hitting the hay." Well, sir, I hit the hay, and I wake up, and there it is—the next day awready, and who do you suppose is on the other cot, fast asleep—?

FAY. Teddy!

PINKIE. So I wake her up and she gets scared stiff. Here she is, on the men's side, with nothing on but her pajamas. Right away she starts yelping about her reputation. (*Placing hand on hip and tossing his head*) "Suppose somebody finds me in your bunk so early," she says. "They'll put two and two together." "O.K.," I says, "so stay here till the fellas go in fa breakfist, then you can sneak out," I says, "and beat it over to the girls' side."

FAY. A very good idear!

PINKIE. "Oh, no!" says your friend, Miss Teddy. "Chick saw me here last night and if I don't get back to the table fa breakfist he'll know I slept here."

FAY. Again that Chick!

PINKIE. Well, so she climbs into some of my things, and as soon as the coast is clear she jumps right off my porch and into the lake. Steve Brody, the second!

FAY (*in alarm*). Must be at lease halfa mile fomm your bunk to the float. My God, that takes years to swim!

PINKIE. I tried to stop her. I says to her, "Teddy, that's foolish—"

FAY (*hysterically*). Suppose she catches a terrible cramp in her foot or something! Suppose—suppose she drowns, God fabbid!

PINKIE. Suppose you pipe down! Teddy's aw right. The damn fool is sitting out there on the float. (*As* FAY *starts for door*) Where're you going?

FAY. To the lake. If there's no sign of her I'll get Hal and some life-guards to go out in a boat—

PINKIE. Wait a minute. I'll go with you, but get this straight. You don't get me into any trouble, see. I'm not to blame for this. I kept asting her— (*The rattle of dishes is heard and* CHICK *appears in doorway with a tray of breakfast dishes.*)

FAY (*brushing him aside*). Excuse me.

CHICK (*shouting after her*). Where's Miriam?

PINKIE. She'll be back in a minute. I'm waiting for her. (CHICK *comes into room and places tray on bar. He stares at* PINKIE *and shifts awkwardly from side to side.*)

CHICK. I—I'm sorry about last night, Pinkie. I guess you think I acted pretty strangely.

PINKIE. You were doing aw right.

CHICK. I realize now I had no business breaking into your place like a wild man. I don't know why you didn't haul off and take a sock at me.

PINKIE (*smiling*). What for? I was having too good a time listening to you.

CHICK. I was listening, too. I could hear myself shouting at her, saying mean and nasty things. And all the time I was hating myself for saying them. Yet I—I just couldn't help it. (*Lowering head in shame*) I behaved like some neurotic.

PINKIE. I had the sneaking feeling you were kinda sore.

CHICK. You see, Pinkie, I can't be like you when it comes to girls. You can take them in your stride, and you'd 've been tactful. But that is unusual with me, and I get out of my element.

PINKIE (*the Don Juan*). You ought never to let them know where they stand.

CHICK. Sure. You've had lots and lots of experience with them.

PINKIE. You never can have too much is what I awways say.

CHICK. You see, I happen to be very fond of Miss Teddy Stern. And when I heard she went to your bunk I was so—so furious, my first impulse was to do something desperate. (*Reflectively*) I suppose you call it jealousy. Then I started blaming you. "That Pinkie rat!" I said to myself.

PINKIE. Lucky you din say it to me.

CHICK. All right, but you know you've got a pretty bad reputation with girls. And when I ran out of here last night I kept thinking all kinds of terrible things. My mind was like one of those old-fashioned movies. I had visions of Teddy struggling with you —and you struggling with Teddy. I ran through the rain hoping I'd get to your bunk in time to—

PINKIE (*sharply*). To what?

CHICK (*lamely*). Well, to—to break things up.

PINKIE. Too bad we disappointed you.

CHICK. I saw enough there to make me boil. There she was, wearing pajamas, in another fella's bungalow, after midnight, and she's drinking Scotch and feeling very much at home! When I saw that I almost wished there had been something to break up!

PINKIE (*paternally*). Lemme take a load off your mind, Chick. I'm not innerested in your Teddy, and the oney reason she was in my bunk was to burn you up. Sure enough, she did. So when she saw how you took it she starts in to cry. So I let her cry and then I walked her back here. (*Starts walking away from him and stops*) I guess you din come back here, dijja?

CHICK. No.

PINKIE (*quickly resuming*). So I says— (*He picks up* TEDDY's *pajamas and addresses them*) "Here you are. Now sit tight," I says, "and if Chick really likes you he'll come to you and say so." (*Turning to him, benevolently*) Now, young fella, insteada chewing my ear off about what a sap you was last night, suppose you go tell it to Teddy. I gotta go and get me some more experience with girls.

CHICK (*smiling*). Thanks, Pinkie. And look, I wanna take back everything I thought about you. (FAY, *wild-eyed, comes tearing in.*)

FAY. There's not a sign of anybody on the lake. Pinkie, we've got to do something. We've got to see Mr. Tobias and tell him Teddy's drowned—

CHICK. Teddy's what? What're you talking about?

FAY (*furiously*). You're the real cause of this! If Teddy's drowned it's because she hadda swim all the way back fomm Pinkie's bunk so that you wouldn't know where she spent the night!

PINKIE. Shut up, you dumb cluck!

FAY (*tearfully as she sits on* TEDDY'S *cot*). Oh, my poor Teddy! God oney knows what's happened to you!

PINKIE. Will you pull yesself together and stop acting like a hysterical *yenteh!*

CHICK. You must've gotten a lotta satisfaction outta me making a fool of myself. Of all the cheap, tin-horn tricks— (*He lunges at* PINKIE *who grabs his arm.*)

PINKIE. Hey, before I split you in two, you oughta know this. Your girl friend's just as pure— (*The door opens and the bedraggled* TEDDY *comes stumbling in, her hair stringy and dripping. Her shorts are much too large for her, and the improvised halter just manages to serve its purpose.*)

TEDDY. Thank God, I'm here—

FAY. Teddy, dolling, where've you been? You had me scared to death. (*Embracing her*) Honestly, I thought —Say, you're wet!

TEDDY. Get me a towel.

CHICK (*icily, as he tries to leave*). Would you be so kind as to step aside? I feel superfluous being in this room.

(TEDDY *stares at him in amazement as he exits.*)

FAY. How'd you get here? I looked at the lake and you weren't there. You ast Pinkie what I din go through the last few minutes.

TEDDY (*staring off at porch*). What's the matter with Chick?

PINKIE. This bright hunk girl here just told your boy friend where you slept last night.

TEDDY. Fay, you didn't!

FAY (*apologetically*). Well, Teddy, I din hear fomm you a whole morning and I thought surely you were drowned or something and nachelly I started in blaming Chick. So it slipped out and—

TEDDY (*crossing to get into her slippers*). There are times when you can be an awful fool, Fay!

FAY. That's the thanks I get fa going crazy with worry over you! Gee whiz!

PINKIE. I—I brought you your pajamas. Listen, young lady, if you ever visit me again, God fabbid, will you please bring a rowboat with you? It'll save wear and tear on the nerves.

TEDDY (*mopping herself with towel*). After I go to all that trouble so that Chick won't know—

PINKIE. Yeah, and what about me? I turn into a boy scout and tell him fairy stories about how you left my place last night crying tears over him. And he believed it! But *schmiggeggie* here hadda take her thumb out of her mouth and talk!

FAY. You leave me alone!

TEDDY (*heading for bathroom*). I've got to get to Chick right away. I've got to tell him he's mistaken and I'm not what he thinks. (*In response to knock*) Come! (ELI *enters*. TEDDY *gives him a dismissive look and is about to hurry on.*)

FAY. Oh, he's got a message fa you, Teddy.

ELI. He says he's tired of waiting and you should meet him fa breakfist.

TEDDY. Who?

ELI. This certain party who's been waiting fa you.

TEDDY. Well, who is it?

ELI. The first time it was a surprise, but now he says to tell you Sam Rappaport is here.

TEDDY (*stunned*). Sam Rappaport!

ELI. Uh, huh! He's unpacked his stuff and he's ready fa breakfist.

TEDDY (*sinking slowly to cot*). Oh, my God!

PINKIE (*to* FAY). Who is this guy?

FAY. The fella she's been engaged to. (*Falling into chair*) Well, waddeya know? Sam is here!
(PINKIE *looks from the stricken* TEDDY *to the dumbfounded* FAY. *His features break into a broad grin. He, too, sits down and stretches his legs.*)

ELI. So what'll I tell him?

FAY. She'll be there soon.

TEDDY. Wait a minute, Eli. Tell Sam Rappaport to read the little booklet while he's waiting. "Here at Camp Kare-Free, dull care and trouble quickly vanish— (*Her voice breaking*) 'neath Nature's magic spell."

CURTAIN

ACT THREE

SCENE II

The Dining Room. There are only slight changes in the setting of the dining room: one of the smaller tables has been removed, and a poster announcing aquatic sports with prizes as the bait replaces the basketball announcement.

MR. *and* MRS. G. *are at their table. The latter is digging industriously into her grapefruit, gutting the yellow shell which she soon picks up to drain the juice into her spoon. The garrulous* MR. G. *is chatting with* SCHMUTZ, *who is serving them. There is a steady stream of waiters moving in and out of kitchen.*

MR. G. And when Mr. G. makes a promise, let me tell you is a promise! So I'm bringing to Pinkie the special meditzin should go away his cold, and I'm wukking to his bungalow, and what I see on his puttch I'm not believing mine eyes! Is coming out a girl —quick, in a hurry-like. (*Using the water glass to illustrate*) Look. This is Pinkie's puttch, and I'm stending like here— (*He places his coffee cup near him. During the latter part of his recital* CHARLIE *comes on escorting* SAM RAPPAPORT, *a prosaic-looking man with accordion-pleated features. A dull sports suit hangs wearily from his thin body. He wears pencils and pens clipped to his pocket, proudly, like medals. Several newspapers and a magazine serve to anchor his coat.* MRS. G. *and* SCHMUTZ *turn to stare.* MR. G., *deserted by his audience, is forced to examine the newcomer.*)

CHARLIE. Right this way. (*To* HI, *who comes out of kitchen*) Oney cawffee—

HI. —and rolls for the late-comers. (CHARLIE *glares at the disappearing* HI *and then directs his attention to* SAM.)

CHARLIE. Take a seat anywhere. This is Mr. and Mrs. Gottlieb.

MR. G. Plain Mr. G. call me.

CHARLIE. And this is— (*Severely, to* SCHMUTZ *who is bringing coffee to* MRS. G.) What're you doing at these tables?

SCHMUTZ. Relieving Chick. Miriam is sick, and he's bringing her breakfist.

CHARLIE. Who gave him permission?

MR. G. (*anxious to resume*). So like I'm saying—

CHARLIE. I wanna have a serious talk with that young fella. (*To* SAM, *before he exits*) Oh, your waiter is Schmutz.

SCHMUTZ. I—I din catch your name.

SAM. Rappaport. Sam Rappaport.

SCHMUTZ. Hi ya, Sam. What'cha having fa breakfist?

SAM. I ain't so hungry. Just bring me some cawffee with a roll.

MR. G. *Nu,* so I'm stending like here—

MRS. G. (*to* SAM). You came here lest night?

SAM. No. This morning I came. I drove up.

MRS G. In a machine?

SAM. In my own car.

MRS. G. Say, that's some long ride.

SAM. I wouldn't 've minded so much, but my radio hadda go dead on me. (SCHMUTZ *places coffee and a basket of rolls in front of* SAM. MR. G., *his audience before him, quickly resumes.*)

MR. G. So listen. I'm stending here— (*Turning to* SAM *who is breaking roll in half and dunking it into coffee*) I'm just now telling a story is something funny heppening this munning. So like I say, I'm looking on Pinkie's puttch— (*Parenthetically, to* SAM) Pinkie is here in camp a fella. And I see this girl, and she's coming fomm the bungalow, and right away quick she's jumping in lake. (*Plunges his finger into water glass to illustrate.*)

SCHMUTZ. Dijja see her face?

MR. G. A question! Uf cuss I see the face!

SCHMUTZ. Who is she?

MR. G. Never mind. You know who she is awready. (*Apologetically, to* SAM) Excuse me, please. I'm not saying the name 'cause maybe you'll see her and it wouldn't look so nice. *Nu,* so I say to myself, "Mr. G., why is jumping this girl fomm puttch in the first place, and in the second place, what business she got in Pinkie's bungalow so early? Aha!" I say to myself. "Remember lest night, Mr. G., you was tukking to Pinkie? Was there on table a bottle *shnopps?* *Nu,* so was there by him in bungalow a guest—this girl, and she was staying there, the two of them together!"

MRS. G. (*rushing to the defense of her sex*). You know she was there a whole night! You was maybe under the bed. (*Scornfully, turning to* SCHMUTZ) He knows positively was there the two together!

MR. G. (*witheringly*). Excuse me. I know notting. Evveything oney you know! Mrs. Smott-like-anything!

MRS. G. I know you shouldn't tukk fomm such things. Maybe it was Pinkie's fault—not the goil's!

MR. G. I'm saying something fomm the girl? I'm telling her name? I'm just saying was a young lady coming from Pinkie's place, and she was there a whole night. That's all. (*He rises.* MRS. G. *also pushes chair back and gets to her feet.*)

SCHMUTZ. Why dincha say something to her?

MR. G. I said something to her. I gave out a scrimm, "Teddy!" (*There is a

violent reaction from MRS. G.) But she din hear.
(SAM *slowly lowers his saturated roll.*)

MRS. G. Mr. Dope! You're not saying the name, hah?

MR. G. It—it slipt out by me.

MRS. G. Why you don't advettice it in noocepapers? (*Exits slowly left followed out by* MR. G.) Why you don't make a spitch bime radio should the whole woild know Teddy Stern was in Pinkie's bungalow a whole night? (SAM *freezes, unable to dig into his roll.* SCHMUTZ, *marveling at the news, turns to him.*)

SCHMUTZ. Gee, does that Pinkie knock 'em over! You don't know this dame, but to look at her you'd think she was sweet Miss Innocence herself. Still, you never can tell! (*He picks up tray and enters kitchen.* FAY *comes on from porch, sights* SAM, *turns in door to grab* TEDDY'S *wrist, and escorts her in.*)

FAY. Sam Rappaport, where in the world did you spring fomm?

TEDDY (*nervously*). Hello, Sam. I—I didn't expect to see you here.

SAM (*his voice in his shoes*). Hello, Tessie.

SCHMUTZ (*coming in from kitchen*). Oney cawffee and rolls fa the latecomers.

TEDDY. That's all right. I don't want anything else. (*She moves up to* FAY *and speaks in a whisper*) Why is SCHMUTZ waiting on the table? Where's Chick?

FAY. Hodda I know?

TEDDY. Uh, huh!

SAM. Well, Tessie, your mama told me to come up here as a supprise. And lemme tell you something. I'm the party getting the supprise. What I din just hear about you! (*Stares at her and shakes his head*) Tchk, tchk, tchk!

TEDDY. What'd you hear?

FAY (*raising her hand*). Whatever it is, it's not true, and I'm a witness.

SAM. An elderly-looking man—he reminded me of Schlepperman on the radio—he had on a gold tooth and sat over there—

FAY (*trading glances with the unhappy* TEDDY). That Mr. G.!

SAM (*querulously, as he rises*). Who is this Pinkie-Schminkie fella who's turned you into—into something wild?

TEDDY. I don't know what you're talking about, Sam.

FAY. It's Greek to me, too.

SAM. You think it's nice to sit at the table eating a piece roll and cawffee, and alluva sudden there's people talking about *you?* (*Slumping into chair*) I can still feel a piece roll choking me, like a lump lead.

P. A. VOICE. Attention, Fay Fromkin. Attention, Fay Fromkin.

FAY (*leaping to her feet*). My God—that's me!

P. A. VOICE. Report to the awfice. It's about some letters.

FAY. I bet I forgot to put on stamps like a dope.

P. A. VOICE. It's about some letters. Thaaank you.

FAY (*a parting admonition to* TEDDY). Don't let him put anything over on you till I get back. (*She rushes off.* HI *and* CHICK'S *voice can be heard coming from kitchen. The door opens and* HI *comes out carrying bread basket. He almost collides with* CHARLIE *who comes on from left.*)

HI. Say, Charlie, what's the matter with Chick?

CHARLIE. Huh?

HI (*pointing to kitchen*). Go look. (CHARLIE *brushes him aside and hurries into kitchen.* TEDDY, *who has heard this, rises and takes a step toward kitchen.* HI *exits.*)

SAM (*brooding, his head on hand*). I felt you acted kinda hasty about that engagement proposition, Tessie, so I went and had a long talk with your mama. I promised her I'd drive up here and stay a week. Maybe you and me, we still could get together on our deal— (CHARLIE *and* CHICK *can be heard in an argument.* TEDDY *stands at kitchen door listening*) our engagement. But I dunno. (*The determined* SAM *now* rises) I'm a business man, Tessie. With me my merchandise must be in A-1 condition or else no sale.

TEDDY. That's fine.

SAM. The same is true with this marriage business. So what happens? I come here, and this elderly party tells me my goods ain't like in the invoice!

TEDDY (*about to enter kitchen*). Excuse me, Sam.

SAM. He'll bring you your breakfist! (*Taking her arm and bringing her forward*) Let's get out of here.

TEDDY. Sam, I've got to see someone.

SAM. Frankly, Tessie, I don't like this camp. It's no place fa a young girl. (*Generously*) I'll forget what I heard— (*He is interrupted by the entrance of* CHARLIE *and* CHICK *from kitchen. Latter is in city clothes and carries a suitcase which he brings to table near stand. He opens it and starts packing law books, baseball glove, etc., which he takes from the shelves of serving stand near kitchen door.*)

CHARLIE. You can't do this on a Saturday with the week-end so heavy. If you wanna quit, wait till Monday at least.

CHICK. I don't wanna wait. I'm leaving now.

CHARLIE. What's the great rush, fa God's sakes, that you can't remain a coupla extra days?
(TEDDY *has crossed toward the two.* SAM *watches her reactions with growing interest.*)

CHICK. It's imperative that I'm on that morning bus and outta here as quickly as possible.

CHARLIE. You know what this means, don'tcha? Abe Tobias will keep every nickel you made in tips.

TEDDY. Wait a minute. He earned those tips. He's got to have them! (*To* CHICK) You were counting on that money. What don't—?

CHICK. Will you please keep outta my affairs?

SAM (*making a great discovery*). So this is that so-called Pinkie!

SCHMUTZ (*entering from left and heading for kitchen*). No, that's Chick!
(*This is too much for* SAM, *who shakes his head, bewildered.*)

CHICK (*to* TEDDY, *pausing in his packing*). I'm free, white and twenty-one, and able to make my own decisions.

SAM. The waiter's right, Tessie.

CHARLIE. We'll see what Abe Tobias has to say about this! (*Enters kitchen.*)

SAM (*through this*). Tessie, we're leaving! You finish your breakfist, and I'll be back as soon as I pack my things. (*Ominously*) But we're gonna have a very long talk on the way home! (*Exits.*)

TEDDY (*as* CHICK *snaps his suitcase shut*). Look. If you'll be calm for only two seconds I'd like to explain something to you.

CHICK. You owe me no explanation whatsoever!

TEDDY. I know why you're leaving, Chick, and I give you my word you're jumping at the wrong conclusions.

CHICK. Oh, am I? Well, let me inform you that I was ready to apologize to you this morning for what I said and the way I acted. In fact, I made a humiliating spectacle of myself by telling your dear and charming friend—

TEDDY. He's no friend of mine!

CHICK. Pardon me. Friend doesn't quite express what he is to you, does it? Well, to me he's nothing but a rotten, low-down, contemptible chaser!

TEDDY (*quietly, as she studies her shoes*). He's worse than a chaser.

CHICK. A flashy, blow-mouth sport, that's what he is! A rat of the lowest order!

TEDDY. Even worse than that. (*Looking up*) You should've heard the things he said about you last night.

CHICK. And I suppose you agreed with him!

TEDDY. I did nothing of the kind! I give you my word, Chick—may I never leave this room again if—

CHICK. Please! You're under no obligations to me. What you do is your own responsibility. (*Bridling*) But what gets me is how you, a girl who likes fine things, could fall for a cheap, petty chaser who'd go after anything in skirts—but anything!

TEDDY. I didn't fall for him!
(*A group of campers gather outside window attracted by the raised voices. Several others come from dining room, napkin in hand, and stand listening.*)

CHICK (*the lawyer cross-questioning the defendant*). Is a certain statement concerning your whereabouts true?

TEDDY. That type is the last one in the world I'd—

CHICK. Don't evade the issue! Is a certain statement true?

TEDDY. This is what happened, Chick. I went—

CHICK (*unrelentingly*). Answer my question. Yes or no?

TEDDY. Yes! Yes! But—

CHICK. Yes, she says!

SCHMUTZ (*coming on from kitchen and crossing stage*). You've oney got five minutes to make that bus.

CHICK (*picking up bag*). I'll make it.

TEDDY. But Chick, you've got to listen to me. I—I don't even know your address in New York. I—

CHICK (*scornfully*). I admit I haven't got your Mr. Pinkie's material means. But, as I pointed out, we've known each other virtually six months! And yet you let a relationship like ours go to hell for a hat salesman with a pocketful of pennies!

TEDDY (*seething*). You finished, Mr. Kessler?

SCHMUTZ (*crossing room*). Haven't much time, Chick.

CHICK. All right. (*Surveys* TEDDY *and sadly shakes his head*) I once had respect for you. But now, now all I've got left is contempt. (*He starts to go. She grabs his arm and wheels him around.*)

TEDDY. I've stood just about enough of your insults. Now I'm going to tell you something. Nothing happened between me and that Pinkie—not one single, solitary thing. I couldn't leave his bunk because it was pouring, and he wouldn't even give me his coat to put over my pajamas. But I'll tell you this how much money means to me! I was in that bunk, thinking and thinking, and I kept wishing I could get away and see you, and talk to you, and tell you how sorry I was because I behaved so silly on Eagle Rock. I was going to ask you to marry me, money or no money, 'cause I had a job, and I'd be willing to go on working just to support you. But I wasn't willing to wait a whole year for Sam—and he earns a very nice living. And the reason I wouldn't wait, in spite of my mother's begging me and begging me, was that way down deep in my heart I didn't love Sam. (*Her voice breaking*) But for you, I'd work my fingers to the bone. So that's how much money means to me, Chick Kessler! (*Tearfully*) And now, please do me a favor, and go to hell! (TEDDY *goes to chair and weeps into her arms. There are ad lib comments from the spectators.* CHICK *turns and sees them for the first time.*)

CHICK. I hope you're having a good time!

(SCHMUTZ *comes from the kitchen and shoos them off with his towel.*)

SCHMUTZ. Come on, give 'em a break, why don'tcha?

BARNEY (*coming from dining room, to group at entrance*). What is this, a public meeting place or something? Break it up! Come on—out we go. (*The campers slowly dissolve.* CHICK *stares helplessly at the weeping* TEDDY.)

CHICK. Aw, Teddy—Teddy, baby. I can't stand it when you cry. (*She checks her tears*) I didn't mean it, darling. I swear I didn't mean it. I was so jealous, I didn't know what I was saying.

SCHMUTZ (*again crossing stage*). Well, there goes the bus!

TEDDY. Honestly, Chick, nothing happened. I just didn't wanna catch pneumonia, that's all.

CHICK. I know, baby. I could tear my tongue out for saying such mean things.

TEDDY. I didn't mean them either—all except our getting married. Oh, I meant that all right. (*Glancing shyly at him*) Provided you still love me.

CHICK. I do. I do. But—

TEDDY. But what?

CHICK. I can't have you support me, Teddy. You know that's impossible.

TEDDY. But why? There're so many girls doing it these days—girls who make far less than I do.

CHICK. But it's not right. I've no job. Who knows how long it'll last?

TEDDY. Look, Chick. (*Turns in chair toward him*) I know you'll say its awfully dopey, but I figger this way. If there was a war, the men would go to the front and the women would stay behind and take care of their homes and children while the husbands were out there fighting. (*Rising*) Well, it's almost like a war now, isn't it? With so many people fighting for jobs!

CHICK. Oh, you darling! (*Takes her in his arms*) You'd hang onto a job you hate, for God knows how long, just to marry me? (*She nods*) You'd really do it, wouldn't you?

TEDDY (*again nodding*). Yes— (*As she turns away*) and I'm not thinking of the two weeks' free honeymoon next year either!

CHICK (*after kissing her*). I'll tell you what. As soon as I clean up here we'll go to Eagle Rock and talk it over.

TEDDY. All right. (CHICK *starts clearing dishes from table.* TEDDY *picks up law book he has left there and eyes it in admiration. She riffles several pages and says, "A law book!"* TOBIAS'S *voice is heard coming from dining room.*)

TOBIAS. Let him carry his own grips to the train, nobody should give him a lift to the station. Hear me, Charlie? We'll see how far that Chick— (*Enters, followed, as usual, by* CHARLIE. *He sights* CHICK, *and scowls*) So, Kessler, alluva sudden you're going away, huh! No excuse, no notice—nothing! Just plain, "I quit!" and "Good-bye!"

CHICK. It's a mistake, Mr. Tobias. (*Grinning*) I'm not leaving.

TEDDY (*rushing into* CHICK'S *outstretched arms*). He's my intended! (TOBIAS *watches them in embrace and then turns to* CHARLIE.)

TOBIAS (*irritably*). Listen, Charlie, why do you pick so much on Chick—? (ELI *comes ont of kitchen carrying pail and mop. He starts piling the chairs on table preparatory to cleaning the dining room when he sees* TEDDY *in* CHICK'S *arms. He suppresses a yawn and turns away. Such sights are not uncommon at camp.* MR. TOBIAS, *on the other hand, beams with delight at the embraced lovers. He is already planning an announce-*

ment for the bulletin board: "Just as advertised in the little booklet, ABE TOBIAS, *proprietor of Camp Kare-Free, takes pleasure in giving* MISS TEDDY STERN *and* MR. CHICK KESSLER *two weeks' free vacation next season being as they met each other at camp and are now hereby engaged. Two weeks' free vacation with positively no charge!"* MR. TOBIAS'S *grin broadens. "Say," he muses, "they're the first couple this season so it won't kill me if I throw in free transportation—both ways!")*

(But this has nothing to do with the fact that the final curtain has already fallen.)

Our Town

BY THORNTON WILDER

TO

ALEXANDER WOOLLCOTT

OF CASTLETON TOWNSHIP, RUTLAND COUNTY, VERMONT

Our Town was first produced at the Henry Miller Theatre, New York City, by Jed Harris, on February 4, 1938, and closed on November 19, 1938. Following is the original cast:

STAGE MANAGER	Frank Craven
DR. GIBBS	Jay Fassett
JOE CROWELL	Raymond Roe
HOWIE NEWSOME	Tom Fadden
MRS. GIBBS	Evelyn Varden
MRS. WEBB	Helen Carew
GEORGE GIBBS	John Craven
REBECCA GIBBS	Marilyn Erskine
WALLY WEBB	Charles Wiley, Jr.
EMILY WEBB	Martha Scott
PROFESSOR WILLARD	Arthur Allen
MR. WEBB	Thomas W. Ross
WOMAN IN THE BALCONY	Carrie Weller
MAN IN THE AUDITORIUM	Walter O. Hill
LADY IN THE BOX	Aline McDermott
SIMON STIMSON	Philip Coolidge
MRS. SOAMES	Doro Merande
CONSTABLE WARREN	E. Irving Locke
SI CROWELL	Billy Redfield
BASEBALL PLAYERS	Alfred Ryder, William Roehrick, Thomas Coley
SAM CRAIG	Francis G. Cleveland
JOE STODDARD	William Wadsworth
ASSISTANT STAGE MANAGERS	Thomas Morgan, Alfred Ryder, William Roehrick, Thomas Coley.

Technical direction by Raymond Sovey

Costumes designed by Helene Pons

The entire play takes place in Grover's Corners, N. H., 1901 to 1913.

OUR TOWN

ACT ONE

No curtain.

No scenery.

The audience, arriving, sees an empty stage in half-light.

Presently the STAGE MANAGER, *hat on and pipe in mouth, enters and begins placing a table and several chairs downstage left, and a table and chairs downstage right.*

"Left" and "right" are from the point of view of the actor facing the audience. "Up" is toward the back wall.

As the house lights go down he has finished setting the stage and leaning against the right proscenium pillar watches the late arrivals in the audience.

When the auditorium is in complete darkness he speaks:

STAGE MANAGER. This play is called "Our Town." It was written by Thornton Wilder; produced and directed by A . . . . [or: produced by A . . . .; directed by B . . . .]. In it you will see Miss C . . . . ; Miss D . . . . ; Miss E . . . . ; and Mr. F . . . . ; Mr. G . . . . ; Mr. H . . . . ; and many others. The name of the town is Grover's Corners, New Hampshire,—just across the Massachusetts line: longitude 42 degrees 40 minutes; latitude 70 degrees 37 minutes. The First Act shows a day in our town. The day is May 7, 1901. The time is just before dawn. (*A rooster crows.*) The sky is beginning to show some streaks of light over in the East there, behind our mount'in. The morning star always gets wonderful bright the minute before it has to go. (*He stares at it for a moment, then goes upstage.*) Well, I'd better show you how our town lies. Up here— (*That is: parallel with the back wall*) is Main Street. Way back there is the railway station; tracks go that way. Polish Town's across the tracks and some Canuck families. (*Toward the left*) Over there is the Congregational Church; across the street's the Presbyterian. Methodist and Unitarian are over there. Baptist is down in the holla' by the river. Catholic Church is over beyond the tracks. Here's the Town Hall and Post Office combined; jail's in the basement. Bryan once made a speech from these steps here. Along here's a row of stores. Hitching-posts and horse blocks in front of them. First automobile's going to come along in about five years,—belonged to Banker Cartwright, our richest citizen . . . lives in the big white house up on the hill. Here's the grocery store and here's Mr. Morgan's drugstore. Most everybody in town manages to look into those two stores once a day. Public School's over yonder. High School's still farther over. Quarter of nine mornings, noontimes, and three o'clock afternoons, the hull town can hear the yelling and screaming from those schoolyards. (*He approaches the table and chairs downstage right*) This is our doctor's house,—Doc Gibbs. This is the back door. (*Two arched trellises are pushed out, one by each proscenium pillar.*) There's some scenery for those who think they have to have scenery. There's a garden here. Corn . . . peas . . . beans . . . hollyhocks . . . heliotrope . . . and a lot of burdock. (*Crosses the stage*) In those days our newspaper come out twice a week,—The Grover's Corners *Sentinel*,—and this is Editor Webb's house. And this is Mrs. Webb's garden. Just like Mrs. Gibbs's, only it's got a lot of sunflowers, too. Right here,—big butternut tree. (*He returns to his place by the right proscenium pillar and looks at the audience for a minute.*) Nice town, y'know what I mean? Nobody very remarkable ever come out of it, —s'far as we know. The earliest tombstones in the cemetery up there on the mountain say 1670-1680—they're Grovers and Cartwrights and Gibbses and Herseys—same names as are around here now. Well, as I said: it's about dawn. The only lights on in town are in a cottage over by the tracks where a Polish mother's just had twins. And in the Joe Crowell house, where Joe Junior's getting up so as to deliver the paper. And in the depot, where Shorty Hawkins is gettin' ready to flag the 5:45 for Boston. (*A train whistle is heard. The* STAGE MANAGER *takes out his watch and nods*) Naturally, out in the country—all around—they've been lights on for some time, what with milkin's and so on. But town people sleep late. So—another day's begun. There's Doc Gibbs comin' down Main Street now, comin' back from that baby case. And here's his wife comin' downstairs to get breakfast. Doc Gibbs died in 1930. The new hospital's named after him. Mrs. Gibbs died first—long time ago in fact. She went out to visit her daughter, Rebecca, who married an insurance man in Canton, Ohio, and died there—pneumonia—but her body was brought back here. She's up in the cemetery there now—in with a whole mess of Gibbses and Herseys—she was Julia Hersey 'fore she married Doc Gibbs in the Congregational Church over there. In our town we like to know the facts about everybody.—That's Doc Gibbs. And there comes Joe Crowell, Jr., delivering Mr. Webb's *Sentinel*.

(DR. GIBBS *has been coming along Main Street from the left. At the point where he would turn to approach his house, he stops, sets down his—imaginary—black bag, takes off his hat, and rubs his face with fatigue, using an enormous handkerchief.* MRS. GIBBS *has entered her kitchen, gone through the motions of putting wood into a stove, lighting it, and preparing breakfast. Suddenly,* JOE CROWELL, JR., *starts down Main Street from the right, hurling imaginary newspapers into doorways.*)

JOE CROWELL, JR. Morning, Doc Gibbs.

DR. GIBBS. Morning, Joe.

JOE CROWELL, JR. Somebody been sick, Doc?

DR. GIBBS. No. Just some twins born over in Polish Town.

JOE CROWELL, JR. Do you want your paper now?

DR. GIBBS. Yes, I'll take it.—Anything serious goin' on in the world since Wednesday?

JOE CROWELL, JR. Yessir. My schoolteacher, Miss Foster, 's getting married to a fella over in Concord.

DR. GIBBS. I declare.—How do you boys feel about that?

JOE CROWELL, JR. Well, of course, it's none of my business,—but I think if a person starts out to be a teacher, she ought to stay one.

DR. GIBBS. How's your knee, Joe?

JOE CROWELL, JR. Fine, Doc, I never think about it at all. Only like you said, it always tells me when it's going to rain.

DR. GIBBS. What's it telling you today? Goin' to rain?

JOE CROWELL, JR. No, sir.

DR. GIBBS. Sure?

JOE CROWELL, JR. Yessir.

DR. GIBBS. Knee ever make a mistake?

JOE CROWELL, JR. No, sir.
(JOE *goes off.* DR. GIBBS *stands reading his paper.*)

STAGE MANAGER. Here comes Howie Newsome delivering the milk.
(HOWIE NEWSOME *comes along Main Street, passes* DOCTOR GIBBS, *comes down the center of the stage, leaves some bottles at* MRS. WEBB'S *back door, and crosses the stage to* MRS. GIBBS'S.)

HOWIE NEWSOME. Git-ap, Bessie. What's the matter with you?—Morning, Doc.

DR. GIBBS. Morning, Howie.

HOWIE NEWSOME. Somebody sick?

DR. GIBBS. Pair of twins over to Mrs. Goruslawski's.

HOWIE NEWSOME. Twins, eh? This town's gettin' bigger every year.

DR. GIBBS. Going to rain, Howie?

HOWIE NEWSOME. No, no. Fine day—that'll burn through. Come on, Bessie.

DR. GIBBS. Hello, Bessie. (*He strokes her*) How old is she, Howie?

HOWIE NEWSOME. Going on seventeen. Bessie's all mixed up about the route ever since the Lockharts stopped takin' their quart of milk every day. She wants to leave 'em a quart just the same—keeps scolding me the hull trip. (*He reaches* MRS. GIBBS'S *back door. She is waiting for him.*)

MRS. GIBBS. Good morning, Howie.

HOWIE NEWSOME. Morning, Mrs. Gibbs. Doc's just comin' down the street.

MRS. GIBBS. Is he? Seems like you're late today?

HOWIE NEWSOME. Yes. Somep'n went wrong with the separator. Don't know what 'twas. (*He goes back to Main Street, clucks for Bessie and goes off right.* DR. GIBBS *reaches his home and goes in.*)

MRS. GIBBS. Everything all right?

DR. GIBBS. Yes. I declare—easy as kittens.

MRS. GIBBS. Bacon'll be ready in a minute. Set down and drink your coffee. Child-*run!* Child-*run!* Time to get up.—George! Rebecca!—you can catch a couple hours' sleep this morning, can't you?

DR. GIBBS. Hm! . . . Mrs. Wentworth's coming at eleven. Guess I know what it's about, too. Her stummick ain't what it ought to be.

MRS. GIBBS. All told, you won't get more'n three hours' sleep. Frank Gibbs, I don't know what's goin' to become of you. I do wish I could get you to go away some place and take a rest. I think it would do you good.

MRS. WEBB. Emileeee! Time to get up! Wally! Seven o'clock!

MRS. GIBBS. I declare, you got to speak to George. Seems like something's come over him lately. He's no help to me at all. I can't even get him to cut me some wood.

DR. GIBBS. Is he sassy to you?

MRS. GIBBS. No. He just whines! All he thinks about is that baseball—George! Rebecca! You'll be late for school.

DR. GIBBS. M-m-m. . . .

MRS. GIBBS. George!

DR. GIBBS. George, look sharp!

GEORGE'S VOICE. Yes, Pa!

DR. GIBBS (*as he goes off the stage*). Don't you hear your mother calling you?

MRS. WEBB. Walleee! Emileee! You'll be late for school! Walleee! You wash yourself good or I'll come up and do it myself.

REBECCA GIBBS'S VOICE. Ma! What dress shall I wear?

MRS. GIBBS. Don't make a noise. Your father's been out all night and needs his sleep. I washed and ironed the blue gingham for you special.

REBECCA. Ma, I hate that dress.

MRS. GIBBS. Oh, hush-up-with-you.

REBECCA. Every day I go to school dressed like a sick turkey.

MRS. GIBBS. Now, Rebecca, don't be impossible. You always look *very* nice.

REBECCA. Mama, George's throwing soap at me.

MRS. GIBBS. I'll come up and slap the both of you,—that's what I'll do.
(*A factory whistle sounds. The children enter and take their places at the breakfast tables:* EMILY *and* WALLY WEBB; GEORGE *and* REBECCA GIBBS.)

STAGE MANAGER. We've got a factory in our town too,—hear it? Makes blankets. Cartwrights own it and it brung 'em a fortune.

MRS. WEBB. Children! Now I won't have it. Breakfast is just as good as any other meal and I won't have you gobbling like wolves. It'll stunt your growth,—that's a fact. Put away your book, Wally.

WALLY. Aw, Ma!

MRS. WEBB. You know the rule's well as I do—no books at table. As for me, I'd rather have my children healthy than bright.

EMILY. I'm both, Mama: you know I am. I'm the brightest girl in school for my age. I have a wonderful memory.

MRS. WEBB. Eat your breakfast.

WALLY. I'm bright, too, when I'm looking at my stamp collection.

MRS. GIBBS. I'll speak to your father about it when he's rested. Seems to me twenty-five cents a week's enough for a boy your age. I declare I don't know how you spend it all.

GEORGE. Aw, Ma,—I gotta lotta things to buy.

MRS. GIBBS. Strawberry phosphates—that's what you spend it on.

GEORGE. I don't see how Rebecca comes to have so much money. She has more'n a dollar.

REBECCA (*spoon in mouth, dreamily*). I've been saving it up gradual.

MRS. GIBBS. Well, dear, I think it's a good thing every now and then to spend some.

REBECCA. Mama, do you know what I love most in the world—do you? —Money.

MRS. GIBBS. Eat your breakfast.
(*The school bell is heard.*)

THE CHILDREN. Mama, there's first bell.—I gotta hurry.—I don't want any more.

MRS. WEBB. Walk fast, but you don't have to run. Wally, pull up your pants at the knee. Stand up straight, Emily.

MRS. GIBBS. Tell Miss Foster I send her my best congratulations—can you remember that?

REBECCA. Yes, Ma.

MRS. GIBBS. You look real nice, Rebecca. Pick up your feet.

ALL. Good-by.
(*The children from the two houses join at the center of the stage and go up to Main Street, then off left.* MRS. GIBBS *fills her apron with food for the chickens and comes down to the footlights.*)

MRS. GIBBS. Here, chick, chick, chick. No, go away, you. Go away. Here, chick, chick, chick. What's the matter with *you?* Fight, fight, fight,—that's all you do. Hm . . . *you* don't belong to me. Where'd you come from? (*She shakes her apron*) Oh, don't be so scared. Nobody's going to hurt you.
(MRS. WEBB *is sitting by her trellis, stringing beans.*)

MRS. GIBBS. Good morning, Myrtle. How's your cold?

MRS. WEBB. Well, it's better; but I told Charles I didn't know as I'd go to choir practice tonight. Wouldn't be any use.

MRS. GIBBS. Just the same, you come to choir practice, Myrtle, and try it.

MRS. WEBB. Well, if I don't feel any worse than I do now I probably will. While I'm resting myself I thought I'd string some of these beans.

MRS. GIBBS (*rolling up her sleeves as she crosses the stage for a chat*). Let me help you. Beans have been good this year.

MRS. WEBB. I've decided to put up forty quarts if it kills me. The children say they hate 'em but I notice they're able to get 'em down all winter.

(*Pause.*)

MRS. GIBBS. Now, Myrtle. I've got to tell you something, because if I don't tell somebody I'll burst.

MRS. WEBB. Why, Julia Gibbs!

MRS. GIBBS. Here, give me some more of those beans. Myrtle, did one of those second-hand furniture men from Boston come to see you last Friday?

MRS. WEBB. No—o.

MRS. GIBBS. Well, he called on me. First I thought he was a patient wantin' to see Dr. Gibbs. 'N he wormed his way into my parlor, and, Myrtle Webb, he offered me three hundred and fifty dollars for Grandmother Wentworth's highboy, as I'm sitting here!

MRS. WEBB. Why, Julia Gibbs!

MRS. GIBBS. He did! That old thing! Why, it was so big I didn't know where to put it and I almost give it to Cousin Hester Wilcox!

MRS. WEBB. Well, you're going to take it, aren't you?

MRS. GIBBS. I don't know.

MRS. WEBB. You don't know—three hundred and fifty dollars. What's come over you?

MRS. GIBBS. Well, if I could get the Doctor to take the money and go away some place on a real trip I'd sell it like that.—Myrtle, ever since I was *that* high I've had the thought that I'd like to see Paris, France. I suppose I'm crazy.

MRS. WEBB. Oh, I know what you mean.—How does the Doctor feel about it?

MRS. GIBBS. Well, I did beat about the bush a little and said that if I got a legacy—that's the way I put it—I'd make him take me somewhere.

MRS. WEBB. M-m-m. . . . What did he say?

MRS. GIBBS. You know how he is. I haven't heard a serious word out of him, ever since I've known him. No, he said, it might make him discontented with Grover's Corners to go traipsin' about Europe; better let well enough alone, he says. Every two years he makes a trip to the battlefields of the Civil War and that's enough treat for anybody, he says.

MRS. WEBB. Well, Mr. Webb just *admires* the way Dr. Gibbs knows everything about the Civil War. Mr. Webb's a good mind to give up Napoleon and move over to the Civil War, only Dr. Gibbs being one of the greatest experts in the country just makes him despair.

MRS. GIBBS. It's a fact! Doctor Gibbs is never so happy as when he's at Antietam or Gettysburg. The times I've walked over those hills, Myrtle, stopping at every bush and pacing it all out, like we was going to buy it.

MRS. WEBB. Well, if that second-hand man's really serious about buyin' it, Julia, you sell it. And then you'll get to see Paris, all right.

MRS. GIBBS. Oh, I'm sorry I mentioned it. Only it seems to me that once in your life before you die you ought to see a country where they don't talk and think in English and don't even want to.
(*The* STAGE MANAGER *returns to the center of the stage.*)

STAGE MANAGER. That'll do. That'll do. Thank you very much, ladies. (MRS. GIBBS *and* MRS. WEBB *gather up their things, return into their homes and disappear*) Now we're going to skip a few hours in the day at Grover's Corners. But before we go on I want you to know some more things about the town,—all kinds of things. So I've asked Prof. Willard of our State University to come down here and sketch in a few details of our past history,—kind of scientific account, you might say. Is Prof. Willard here? (PROF. WILLARD, *a rural savant, pince-nez on a wide satin ribbon, enters from the right with some notes in his hand*) May I introduce Prof. Willard of our University. A few brief notes, thank you, Professor,—unfortunately our time is limited.

PROF. WILLARD. Grover's Corners . . . let me see . . . Grover's Corners lies on the old Archaeozoic granite of the Appalachian range. I may say it's some of the oldest land in the world. We're very proud of that. A shelf of Devonian basalt crosses it with vestiges of Mesozoic shale, and some sandstone outcroppings; but that's all more recent: two hundred, three hundred million years old. Some highly interesting fossils have been found. . . . I may say: unique fossils . . . two miles out of town, in Silas Peckham's cow pasture. They can be seen at the museum in our University at any time. Did you wish the meteorological conditions?

STAGE MANAGER. Thank you. We would.

PROF. WILLARD. The mean precipitation is 40 inches. The mean annual temperature is 43 degrees, ranging between 102 degrees in the shade, and 38 degrees below zero in winter. The . . . the . . . uh . . .

STAGE MANAGER. Thank you, Professor. And have you Prof. Gruber's notes on the history of human life here?

PROF. WILLARD. Hm . . . yes . . . anthropological data: Early Amerindian stock. Cotahatchee tribes . . . no evidence before the Tenth Century of this era . . . hm . . . now entirely disappeared . . . possible traces in three families. Migration toward the end of the Seventeenth Century of English brachycephalic blue-eyed stock . . . for the most part. Since then some influx of Slav and Mediterranean types. . . .

STAGE MANAGER. And the population, Prof. Willard?

PROF. WILLARD. Within the town limits: 2,640. The postal district brings in 507 more. Mortality and birth-rates are constant; by MacPherson's gauge: 6.032.

STAGE MANAGER. Thank you very much, Professor. We're all very much obliged to you, I'm sure.

PROF. WILLARD. Not at all, sir; not at all.

STAGE MANAGER. This way, Professor, and thank you again. (*Exit* PROF.

WILLARD) Now the political and social report: Editor Webb.—Oh, Mr. Webb?

(MRS. WEBB *appears at her back door.*)

MRS. WEBB. He'll be here in a minute. . . . He just cut his hand while he was eatin' an apple.

STAGE MANAGER. Thank you, Mrs. Webb.

MRS. WEBB. Charles! Everybody's waitin'. (*Exit* MRS. WEBB.)

STAGE MANAGER. Mr. Webb is Publisher and Editor of The Grover's Corners *Sentinel*. That's our local paper, y'know.

(MR. WEBB *enters from his house, pulling on his coat. His finger is bound in a handkerchief.*)

MR. WEBB. Hm. . . . I don't have to tell you that we're run here by a Board of Selectmen.—All males vote at the age of 21. Women vote indirect. We're lower middle-class, sprinkling of professional men . . . 10% illiterate laborers. Politically, we're 86% Republicans; 6% Democrats; 4% Socialists; rest, indifferent. Religiously, we're 85% Protestants; 12% Catholics; rest, indifferent. Do you want the poverty and insanity statistics?

STAGE MANAGER. Thank you, no. Have you any comments, Mr. Webb?

MR. WEBB. Very ordinary town, if you ask me. Little better behaved than most. Probably a lot duller. But our young people here seem to like it well enough: 90% of 'em graduating from High School settle down right here to live—even when they've been away to college.

STAGE MANAGER. Thank you, Mr. Webb. Now, is there anyone in the audience who would like to ask Editor Webb anything about the town?

WOMAN IN THE BALCONY. Is there much drinking in Grover's Corners?

MR. WEBB. Well, ma'am, I wouldn't know what you'd call *much*. Satiddy nights the farmhands meet down in Ellery Greenough's stable and holler some. Fourth of July I've been known to taste a drop myself—and Decoration Day, of course. We've got one or two town drunks, but they're always having remorses every time an evangelist comes to town. No, ma'am, I'd say likker ain't a regular thing in the home here, except in the medicine chest. Right good for snake bite, y'know—always was.

TALL MAN AT BACK OF AUDITORIUM. Is there no one in town aware of—

STAGE MANAGER. Come forward, will you, where we can all hear you—What were you saying?

TALL MAN. Is there no one in town aware of social injustice and industrial inequality?

MR. WEBB. Oh, yes, everybody is,—somethin' terrible. Seems like they spend most of their time talking about who's rich and who's poor.

TALL MAN. Then why don't they do something about it?

MR. WEBB. Well, we're ready to listen to everybody's suggestion as to how you can see that the diligent and sensible 'll rise to the top and the lazy and quarrelsome sink to the bottom. We'll listen to anybody. Meantime until that's settled, we try to take care of those that can't help themselves, and those that can we leave alone.—Are there any more questions?

LADY IN A BOX. Oh, Mr. Webb? Mr. Webb, is there any culture or love of beauty in Grover's Corners?

MR. WEBB. Well, ma'am, there ain't much—not in the sense you mean. Come to think of it, there's some girls that play the piano at High School Commencement; but they ain't happy about it. Yes, and I see where my daughter's been made to read "The Merchant of Venice" over to the school. Seems all pretty remote to 'em, y'know what I mean. No, ma'am, there isn't much culture; but maybe this is the place to tell you that we've got a lot of pleasures of a kind here: we like the sun comin' up over the mountain in the morning, and we all notice a good deal about the birds. We pay a lot of attention to them, and trees and plants. And we watch the change of the seasons: yes, everybody knows about them. But those other things—you're right, ma'am—there ain't much—"Robinson Crusoe" and the Bible; and Handel's "Largo," we all know that; and Whistler's "Mother"—those are just about as far as we go.

LADY IN A BOX. So I thought. Thank you, Mr. Webb.

STAGE MANAGER. All right! All right! Thank you, everybody. (MR. WEBB *retires*) We'll go back to the town now. It's middle of the afternoon. All 2,640 have had their dinners and all the dishes have been washed. There's an early afternoon calm in our town: a buzzin' and a hummin' from the school buildings; only a few buggies on Main Street—the horses dozing at the hitching-posts; you all remember what it's like. Doc Gibbs is in his office, tapping people and making them say "ah." Mr. Webb's cuttin' his lawn over there; one man in ten thinks it's a privilege to push his own lawn mower. No, sir. It's later than I thought. There are the children coming home from school already.

(EMILY WEBB *comes sedately down Main Street carrying some school books. There are some signs that she is imagining herself to be a lady of striking elegance. Her father's movements to and fro with the lawn mower bring him into her vicinity.*)

EMILY. I *can't,* Lois. I've got to go home and help my mother. I *promised.*

MR. WEBB. Emily, walk simply. Who do you think you are today?

EMILY. Papa, you're terrible. One minute you tell me to stand up straight and the next minute you call me names. I just don't listen to you (*She gives him an abrupt kiss.*)

MR. WEBB. Golly, I never got a kiss from such a great lady before. (*He goes out of sight.* EMILY *leans over and picks some flowers by the gate of her house.* GEORGE GIBBS *comes careening down Main Street. He is throwing a ball up to dizzying heights, and waiting to catch it again. This sometimes requires his taking six steps backward.*)

GEORGE. Excuse me, Mrs. Forrest.

STAGE MANAGER (*as* MRS. FORREST). Go out and play in the fields, young man. You got no business playing baseball on Main Street.

GEORGE. Awfully sorry, Mrs. Forrest. —Hello, Emily.

EMILY. H'lo.

GEORGE. You made a fine speech in class.

EMILY. Well . . . I was really ready to make a speech about the Monroe Doctrine, but at the last minute Miss Corcoran made me talk about the Louisiana Purchase instead. I worked an awful long time on both of them.

GEORGE. Gee, it's funny, Emily. From my window up there I can just see your head nights when you're doing your homework over in your room.

EMILY. Why, can you?

GEORGE. You certainly do stick to it, Emily. I don't see how you can sit still that long. I guess you like school.

EMILY. Well, I always feel it's something you have to go through.

GEORGE. Yeah.

EMILY. I don't mind it really. It passes the time.

GEORGE. Yeah.—Emily, what do you think? We might work out a kinda telegraph from there to there; and once in a while you could give me a kinda hint or two about one of those algebra problems. I don't mean the answers, Emily, of course not . . . just some little hint. . . .

EMILY. Oh, I think *hints* are allowed. —So-ah—if you get stuck, George, you whistle to me; and I'll give you some hints.

GEORGE. Emily, you're just naturally bright, I guess.

EMILY. I figure that it's just the way a person's born.

GEORGE. Yeah. But, you see, I want to be a farmer, and my Uncle Luke says whenever I'm ready I can come over and work on his farm and if I'm any good I can just gradually have it.

EMILY. You mean the house and everything?

(*Enter* MRS. WEBB.)

GEORGE. Yeah. Well, thanks . . . I better be getting out to the baseball field. Thanks for the talk, Emily.—Good afternoon, Mrs. Webb.

MRS. WEBB. Good afternoon, George.

GEORGE. So-long, Emily.

EMILY. So-long, George.

MRS. WEBB. Emily, come and help me string these beans for the winter. George Gibbs let himself have a real conversation, didn't he? Why, he's growing up. How old would George be?

EMILY. I don't know.

MRS. WEBB. Let's see. He must be almost sixteen.

EMILY. Mama, I made a speech in class today and I was very good.

MRS. WEBB. You must recite it to your father at supper. What was it about?

EMILY. The Louisiana Purchase. It was like silk off a spool. I'm going to make speeches all my life.—Mama, are these big enough?

MRS. WEBB. Try and get them a little bigger if you can.

EMILY. Mama, will you answer me a question, serious?

MRS. WEBB. Seriously, dear—not serious.

EMILY. Seriously,—will you?

MRS. WEBB. Of course, I will.

EMILY. Mama, am I good-looking?

MRS. WEBB. Yes, of course you are. All my children have got good features; I'd be ashamed if they hadn't.

EMILY. Oh, Mama, that's not what I mean. What I mean is: am I *pretty?*

MRS. WEBB. I've already told you, yes. Now that's enough of that. You have a nice young pretty face. I never heard of such foolishness.

EMILY. Oh, Mama, you never tell us the truth about anything.

MRS. WEBB. I *am* telling you the truth.

EMILY. Mama, were *you* pretty?

MRS. WEBB. Yes, I was, if I do say it. I was the prettiest girl in town next to Mamie Cartwright.

EMILY. But, Mama, you've got to say *some*thing about me. Am I pretty enough . . . to get anybody . . . to get people interested in me?

MRS. WEBB. Emily, you make me tired. Now stop it. You're pretty enough for all normal purposes. Come along now and bring that bowl with you.

EMILY. Oh, Mama, you're no help at all.

STAGE MANAGER. Thank you. Thank you! That'll do. We'll have to interrupt again here. Thank you, Mrs. Webb; thank you, Emily. (MRS. WEBB *and* EMILY *withdraw*) There are some more things we've got to explore about this town. This time we're going to go about it in another way: we're going to look back on it from the future. I'm not going to tell you what became of these two families we're seeing most of, because the rest of the play will tell you about them. But take some of these others: Take Joe Crowell, Jr.: Joe was a very bright fellow. He graduated with honors and got a scholarship to Boston Tech.,—M.I.T., that is. But the War broke out and Joe died in France. All that education for nothing. Howie Newsome's still delivering milk at Grover's Corners. He's an old man now, has a lot of help, but he still delivers it himself. Says he gets the feel of the town that way. Carries all the accounts in his head; never has to write down a word. Mr. Morgan's drug store ain't the same,—it's all citified. Mr. Morgan retired and went out to live in San Diego, California, where his daughter married a real estate man, name of Kerby. Mr. Morgan died there in 1935 and was buried in a lot of palm trees. Kinda lost his religion at the end and took up New Thought or something. They read some new-fangled poetry over him and cremated him. The New Hampshire in him sort of broke down in him in that climate, seems like. The Cartwrights got richer and richer. The house is closed most of the year. They're off eating big dinners in hotels now,—in Virginia Hot Springs and Miami Beach. They say the winters are cold here. I see where they've become 'Piscopalians. The Cartwright interests have just begun building a new bank in Grover's Corners—had to go to Vermont for the marble, sorry to say. And they've asked a friend of mine what they should put in the cornerstone for people to dig up a thousand years from now. Of course, they've put in a copy of the New York *Times* and a copy of Mr. Webb's *Sentinel.* We're kind of interested in this because some scientific fellas have found a way of painting all that reading matter with a kind of glue—silicate glue—that'll make it keep a thousand—two thousand years. We're putting in a Bible . . . and the Constitution of the United States and a copy of William Shakespeare's plays. What do you say, folks? What do you think? Y'know—Babylon once had two million people in it, and all we know about 'em is the names of the kings and some copies of wheat contracts and . . . the sales of slaves. Yet, every night all those families sat down to supper, and the father came home from his work, and the smoke went up the chimney,—same as here. And even in Greece and Rome, all we know about the real life of the people is what we can piece together out of the joking poems and the comedies they wrote for the theater back then. So I'm going to have a copy of this play put in the cornerstone and the people a thousand years from now'll know a few simple facts about us—more than the Treaty of Versailles and the Lindbergh flight. See what I mean? Well,—you people a thousand years from now,—in the provinces north of New York at the beginning of the Twentieth Century, people et three times a day: soon after sunrise; at noon; and at sunset. Every seventh day, by law and by religion, was a day of rest and all work come to a stop. The religion at that time was Christianity. I guess you have some other records about Christianity. The domestic set-up was marriage: a binding relation between a male and one female that lasted for life. Christianity strictly forbade killing, but you were allowed to kill animals, and you were allowed to kill human beings in war and government punishings. I guess we don't have to tell you about the government and business forms, because that's the kind of thing people seem to hand down first of all. Let me see now if there's anything else. Oh, yes,—at death people were buried in the ground just as they are. So, friends, this is the way we were in our growing up and in our marrying and in our doctoring and in our living and in our dying. Now we'll return to our day in Grover's Corners. A lot of time has gone by. It's evening. You can hear choir practice going on in the Congregational Church. All the children are at home doing their school work. The day is running down like a tired clock.

(*A choir partially concealed in the orchestra pit has begun singing "Blessed be the tie that binds."* SIMON STIMSON *stands directing them. Two ladders have been pushed on to the stage; they serve as indication of the second story in the Gibbs and Webb houses.* GEORGE *and* EMILY *mount them, and apply themselves to their school work.* DR. GIBBS *has entered and is seated in his kitchen reading.*)

SIMON STIMSON. Now look here, everybody. Music come into the world to give pleasure.—Softer! Softer! Get it out of your heads that music's only good when it's loud. You leave loudness to the Methodists. You couldn't beat 'em, even if you wanted to. Now again. Tenors!

GEORGE. Hssst! Emily!

EMILY. Hello.

GEORGE. Hello!

EMILY. I can't work at all. The moonlight's so *terrible*.

GEORGE. Emily, did you get the third problem?

EMILY. Which?

GEORGE. The *third?*

EMILY. Why, yes, George—that's the easiest of them all.

GEORGE. I don't see it. Emily, can you give me a hint?

EMILY. I'll tell you one thing: the answer's in yards.

GEORGE. !!! In yards? How do you mean?

EMILY. In *square* yards.

GEORGE. Oh . . . in square yards.

EMILY. Yes, George, don't you see?

GEORGE. Yeah.

EMILY. In square yards of *wallpaper*.

GEORGE. Wallpaper,—oh, I see. Thanks a lot, Emily.

EMILY. You're welcome. My, isn't the moonlight *terrible?* And choir practice going on.—I think if you hold your breath you can hear the train all the way to Contookuck. Hear it?

GEORGE. M-m-m—What do you know!

EMILY. Well, I guess I better go back and try to work.

GEORGE. Good night, Emily. And thanks.

EMILY. Good night, George.

SIMON STIMSON. Before I forget it: how many of you will be able to come in Tuesday afternoon and sing at Fred Hersey's wedding?—show your hands. That'll be fine; that'll be right nice. We'll do the same music we did for Jane Trowbridge's last month.—Now we'll do: "Art thou weary; art thou languid?" It's a question, ladies and gentlemen, make it talk. Ready.

DR. GIBBS. Oh, George, can you come down a minute?

GEORGE. Yes, Pa. (*He descends the ladder.*)

DR. GIBBS. Make yourself comfortable, George; I'll only keep you a minute. George, how old are you?

GEORGE. I? I'm sixteen, almost seventeen.

DR. GIBBS. What do you want to do after school's over?

GEORGE. Why, you know, Pa, I want to be a farmer on Uncle Luke's farm.

DR. GIBBS. You'll be willing, will you, to get up early and milk and feed the stock . . . and you'll be able to hoe and hay all day?

GEORGE. Sure, I will. What are you . . . what do you mean, Pa?

DR. GIBBS. Well, George, while I was in my office today I heard a funny sound . . . and what do you think it was? It was your mother chopping wood. There you see your mother—getting up early; cooking meals all day long; washing and ironing;—and still she has to go out in the back yard and chop wood. I suppose she just got tired of asking you. She just gave up and decided it was easier to do it herself. And you eat her meals, and put on the clothes she keeps nice for you, and you run off and play baseball,—like she's some hired girl we keep around the house but that we don't like very much. Well, I knew all I had to do was call your attention to it. Here's a handkerchief, son. George, I've decided to raise your spending money twenty-five cents a week. Not, of course, for chopping wood for your mother, because that's a present you give her, but because you're getting older—and I imagine there are lots of things you must find to do with it.

GEORGE. Thanks, Pa.

DR. GIBBS. Let's see—tomorrow's pay day. You can count on it—Hmm. Probably Rebecca'll feel she ought to have some more too. Wonder what could have happened to your mother. Choir practice never was as late as this before.

GEORGE. It's only half-past eight, Pa.

DR. GIBBS. I don't know why she's in that old choir. She hasn't any more voice than an old crow. . . . Traipsin' around the streets at this hour of the night. . . . Just about time you retired, don't you think?

GEORGE. Yes, Pa. (GEORGE *mounts to his place on the ladder. Laughter and good nights can be heard on stage left and presently* MRS. GIBBS, MRS. SOAMES *and* MRS. WEBB *come down Main Street. When they arrive at the center of the stage they stop.*)

MRS. SOAMES. Good night, Martha. Good night, Mr. Foster.

MRS. WEBB. I'll tell Mr. Webb; I *know* he'll want to put it in the paper.

MRS. GIBBS. My, it's late!

MRS. SOAMES. Good night, Irma.

MRS. GIBBS. Real nice choir practice, wa'n't it? Myrtle Webb! Look at that moon, will you! Tsk-tsk-tsk. Potato weather, for sure.

MRS. SOAMES. Naturally I didn't want to say a word about it in front of those others, but now we're alone—really, it's the worst scandal that ever was in this town!

MRS. GIBBS. What?

MRS. SOAMES. Simon Stimson!

MRS. GIBBS. Now, Louella!

MRS. SOAMES. But, Julia! To have the organist of a church drink and drink year after year. You know he was drunk tonight.

MRS. GIBBS. Now, Louella! We all know about Mr. Stimson, and we all know about the troubles he's been through, and Dr. Ferguson knows too, and if Dr. Ferguson keeps him on there in his job the only thing the rest of us can do is just not to notice it.

MRS. SOAMES. Not to notice it! But it's getting worse.

MRS. WEBB. No, it isn't, Louella. It's getting better. I've been in that choir twice as long as you have. It doesn't happen anywhere near so often. . . . My, I hate to go to bed on a night like this.—I better hurry. Those children'll be sitting up till all hours. Good night, Louella. (*She hurries downstage, enters her house and disappears.*)

MRS. GIBBS. Can you get home safe, Louella?

MRS. SOAMES. It's as bright as day. I can see Mr. Soames scowling at the window now. You'd think we'd been to a dance the way the menfolk carry on.
(*Repeated good nights.* MRS. GIBBS *arrives at her home.*)

MRS. GIBBS. Well, we had a real good time.

DR. GIBBS. You're late enough.

MRS. GIBBS. Why, Frank, it ain't any later 'n usual.

DR. GIBBS. And you stopping at the corner to gossip with a lot of hens.

MRS. GIBBS. Now, Frank, don't be grouchy. Come out and smell my heliotrope in the moonlight. (*They stroll out arm in arm along the footlights*) Isn't that wonderful? What did you do all the time I was away?

DR. GIBBS. Oh, I read—as usual. What were the girls gossiping about tonight?

MRS. GIBBS. Well, believe me, Frank —there is something to gossip about.

DR. GIBBS. Hmm! Simon Stimson far gone, was he?

MRS. GIBBS. Worst I've ever seen him. How'll that end, Frank? Dr. Ferguson can't forgive him forever.

DR. GIBBS. I guess I know more about Simon Stimson's affairs than anybody in this town. Some people ain't made for small town life. I don't know how that'll end; but there's nothing we can do but just leave it alone. Come, get in.

MRS. GIBBS. No, not yet. . . . Oh, Frank, I'm worried about you.

DR. GIBBS. What are you worried about?

MRS. GIBBS. I think it's my duty to make plans for you to get a real rest and change. And if I get that legacy, well, I'm going to insist on it.

DR. GIBBS. Now, Julia, there's no sense in going over that again.

MRS. GIBBS. Frank, you're just *unreasonable!*

DR. GIBBS. Come on, Julia, it's getting late. First thing you know you'll catch cold. I gave George a piece of my mind tonight. I reckon you'll have your wood chopped for a while anyway. No, no, start getting upstairs.

MRS. GIBBS. Oh, dear. There's always so many things to pick up, seems like. You know, Frank, Mrs. Fairchild always locks her front door every night. All those people up that part of town do.

DR. GIBBS. They're all getting citified, that's the trouble with them. They haven't got nothing fit to burgle and everybody knows it. (*They dis-*

appear. REBECCA *climbs up the ladder beside* GEORGE.)

GEORGE. Get out, Rebecca. There's only room for one at this window. You're always spoiling everything.

REBECCA. Well, let me look just a minute.

GEORGE. Use your own window.

REBECCA. I did; but there's no moon there. . . . George, do you know what I think, do you? I think maybe the moon's getting nearer and nearer and there'll be a big 'splosion.

GEORGE. Rebecca, you don't know anything. If the moon were getting nearer, the guys that sit up all night with telescopes would see it first and they'd tell about it, and it'd be in all the newspapers.

REBECCA. George, is the moon shining on South America, Canada and half the whole world?

GEORGE. Well—prob'ly is.
(*The* STAGE MANAGER *strolls on.*)

STAGE MANAGER. Nine-thirty. Most of the lights are out. No, there's Constable Warren trying a few doors on Main Street. And here comes Editor Webb, after putting his newspaper to bed.

MR. WEBB. Good evening, Bill.

CONSTABLE WARREN. Evenin', Mr. Webb.

MR. WEBB. Quite a moon!

CONSTABLE WARREN. Yepp.

MR. WEBB. All quiet tonight?

CONSTABLE WARREN. Simon Stimson is rollin' around a little. Just saw his wife movin' out to hunt for him so I looked the other way—there he is now.
(SIMON STIMSON *comes down Main Street from the left, only a trace of unsteadiness in his walk.*)

MR. WEBB. Good evening, Simon. . . . Town seems to have settled down for the night pretty well. . . . (SIMON STIMSON *comes up to him and pauses a moment*) Good evening. . . . Yes, most of the town's settled down for the night, Simon. . . . I guess we better do the same. Can I walk along a ways with you? (SIMON STIMSON *continues on his way without a word and disappears at the right*) Good night.

CONSTABLE WARREN. I don't know how that's goin' to end, Mr. Webb.

MR. WEBB. Well, he's seen a peck of trouble, one thing after another. . . . Oh, Bill . . . if you see my boy smoking cigarettes, just give him a word, will you? He thinks a lot of you, Bill.

CONSTABLE WARREN. I don't think he smokes no cigarettes, Mr. Webb. Leastways, not more'n two or three a year. He don't belong to that crowd that hangs out down by the gully.

MR. WEBB. Hm. . . . I hope not.—Well, good night, Bill.

CONSTABLE WARREN. Good night, Mr. Webb. (*Exit.*)

MR. WEBB. Who's that up there? Is that you, Myrtle?

EMILY. No, it's me, Papa.

MR. WEBB. Why aren't you in bed?

EMILY. I don't know. I just can't sleep yet, Papa. The moonlight's so *won*-derful. And the smell of Mrs. Gibbs's heliotrope. Can you smell it?

MR. WEBB. Hm. . . . Yes. Haven't any troubles on your mind, have you, Emily?

EMILY. *Troubles,* Papa. *No.*

MR. WEBB. Well, enjoy yourself, but don't let your mother catch you. Good night, Emily.

EMILY. Good night, Papa.

(MR. WEBB *crosses into the house, whistling "Blessed Be the Tie that Binds" and disappears.*)

REBECCA. I never told you about that letter Jane Crofut got from her minister when she was sick. The minister of her church in the town she was in before she came here. He wrote Jane a letter and on the envelope the address was like this: It said: Jane Crofut; The Crofut Farm; Grover's Corners; Sutton County; New Hampshire; United States of America.

GEORGE. What's funny about that?

REBECCA. But listen, it's not finished: the United States of America; Continent of North America; Western Hemisphere; the Earth; the Solar System; the Universe; the Mind of God,—that's what it said on the envelope.

GEORGE. What do you know!

REBECCA. And the postman brought it just the same.

GEORGE. What do you know!

STAGE MANAGER. That's the end of the First Act, friends. You can go and smoke now, those that smoke.

ACT TWO

The tables and chairs of the two kitchens are still on the stage.

The ladders have been withdrawn.

The STAGE MANAGER *has been at his accustomed place watching the audience return to its seats.*

STAGE MANAGER. Three years have gone by. Yes, the sun's come up over a thousand times. Summers and winters have cracked the mountains a little bit more and the rains have brought down some of the dirt. Some babies that weren't even born before have begun talking regular sentences already; and a number of people who thought they were right young and spry have noticed that they can't bound up a flight of stairs like they used to, without their heart fluttering a little. Some older sons are sitting at the head of the table, and some people I know are having their meat cut up for them.—All that can happen in a thousand days. Nature's been pushing and contriving in other ways, too: a number of young people fell in love and got married. Yes, the mountain got bit away a few fractions of an inch; millions of gallons of water went by the mill; and here and there a new home was set up under a roof. Almost everybody in the world gets married,—you know what I mean? In our town there aren't hardly any exceptions. Most everybody in the world climbs into their graves married. The First Act was called the Daily Life. This Act is called Love and Marriage. There's another Act coming after this: I reckon you can guess what that's about. So: It's three years later. It's 1904. It's July 7th, just after High School Commencement. That's the time most of our young people jump up and get married. Soon as they've passed their last examinations in solid geometry and Cicero's Orations, looks like they suddenly feel themselves fit to be married. It's early morning. Only this time it's been raining. It's been pouring and thundering. Mrs. Gibbs's garden, and Mrs. Webb's here: drenched. All those bean poles and pea vines: drenched. All yesterday over there on Main Street, the rain looked like curtains being blown along. Hm . . . it may begin again any minute. There! You can hear the 5:45 for Boston. And here comes Howie Newsome delivering the milk. And there's Si Crowell delivering the papers like his brother before him.—You remember about his brother?—all that education he's going to get and that'll be wasted. And there's Mrs. Gibbs and Mrs. Webb come down to make breakfast, just as though it were an ordinary day. I don't have to point out to the women in my audience that those ladies they see before them, both those ladies cooked three meals a day,—one of 'em for twenty years, the other for forty,—and no summer vacation. They brought up two children apiece; washed; cleaned the house,—and never a nervous breakdown. Never thought themselves hard-used, either. It's like what one of those Middle West poets said: You've got to love life to have life, and you've got to have life to love life. . . . It's what they call a vicious circle.

(SI CROWELL *has entered hurling imaginary newspapers into doorways;* HOWIE NEWSOME *has come along Main Street with* BESSIE.)

HOWIE NEWSOME. Git-ap, Bessie.

SI CROWELL. Morning, Howie.

HOWIE NEWSOME. Morning, Si.—Anything in the papers I ought to know?

SI CROWELL. Nothing much, except we're losing about the best baseball pitcher Grover's Corners ever had.

HOWIE NEWSOME. Reckon he was. He's been standing off the whole of South New Hampshire singlehanded, looks like.

SI CROWELL. He could hit and run bases, too.

HOWIE NEWSOME. Yep. Mighty fine ball player.—Bessie! I guess I can stop and talk if I've a mind to!

SI CROWELL. I don't see how he could give up a thing like that just to get married. Would you, Howie?

HOWIE NEWSOME. Can't tell, Si. Never had no talent that way. (CONSTABLE WARREN *enters. They exchange mornings.*) You're up early, Bill.

CONSTABLE WARREN. Seein' if there's anything I can do to prevent a flood. River's been risin' all night.

HOWIE NEWSOME. Si Crowell's all worked up here about George Gibbs retiring from baseball.

CONSTABLE WARREN. Yes, sir; that's the way it goes. Back in '84 we had a player, Si,—even George Gibbs couldn't touch him. Name of Hank Todd. Went down to Maine and become a parson. Wonderful ball player.—Howie, how did the weather look to you?

HOWIE NEWSOME. No, 'tain't bad. Think maybe it'll clear up for good. (CONSTABLE WARREN *and* SI CROWELL *continue on their way.* HOWIE NEWSOME *brings the milk first to* MRS. GIBBS'S *house. She meets him by the trellis.*)

MRS. GIBBS. Good morning, Howie. Do you think it's going to rain again?

HOWIE NEWSOME. Morning, Mrs. Gibbs. It rained so heavy, I think maybe it'll clear up.

MRS. GIBBS. Certainly hope it will.

HOWIE NEWSOME. How much did you want today?

MRS. GIBBS. I guess I'll need three-a-milk and two-a-cream, Howie. I'm going to have a house full of relations.

HOWIE NEWSOME. My wife says to tell you we both hope they'll be very happy, Mrs. Gibbs. Know they *will.*

MRS. GIBBS. Thanks a lot, Howie. Tell your wife I hope she gits there to the wedding.

HOWIE NEWSOME. Yes, she'll be there; she'll be there if she kin. (HOWIE NEWSOME *crosses to* MRS. WEBB'S *house.*) Morning, Mrs. Webb.

MRS. WEBB. Oh, good morning, Mr. Newsome. I told you four quarts of milk, but I hope you can spare me another.

HOWIE NEWSOME. Yes'm . . . and the two of cream.

MRS. WEBB. Will it rain all day, Mr. Newsome?

HOWIE NEWSOME. No'm. Just sayin' to Mrs. Gibbs as how it may lighten up. Mrs. Newsome told me to tell you as how we hope they'll both be very happy, Mrs. Webb. Know they *will.*

MRS. WEBB. Thank you, and thank Mrs. Newsome and we hope to see you all at the wedding.

HOWIE NEWSOME. Yes, Mrs. Webb We hope to git there. Couldn't miss that. Chck! Bessie!

(*Exit* HOWIE NEWSOME. DR. GIBBS *descends in shirt sleeves, and sits down at his breakfast table.*)

DR. GIBBS. Well, Ma, the day has come. You're losin' one of your chicks.

MRS. GIBBS. Frank Gibbs, don't you say another word. I feel like crying every minute. Sit down and drink your coffee.

DR. GIBBS. The groom's up shaving himself. Whistling and singing, like he's glad to leave us.—Every now and then he says "I do" to the mirror, but it don't sound convincing to me.

MRS. GIBBS. I declare I don't know how he'll get along. I've arranged his clothes and seen to it he's put warm things on,—Frank! they're too young. Emily won't think of such things. He'll catch his death of cold within a week.—Here's something I made for you.

DR. GIBBS. Why, Julia Hersey! French toast!

MRS. GIBBS. 'Tain't hard to make, and I had to do something.

DR. GIBBS. I remember my wedding morning, Julia.

MRS. GIBBS. Now don't start that, Frank Gibbs. I tell you I can't stand it.

DR. GIBBS. I was the scaredest young fella in the State of New Hampshire. I thought I'd made a mistake for sure. And when I saw you comin' down that aisle I thought you were the prettiest girl I'd ever seen, but the only trouble was that I'd never seen you before. There I was in the Congregational Church marryin' a total stranger.

MRS. GIBBS. And how do you think I felt!—Did you hear Rebecca stirring about upstairs?

DR. GIBBS. Only morning in the year she hasn't been managing everybody's business. She's shut up in her room. I got the impression that maybe she's crying.

MRS. GIBBS. Good Lord! This has got to stop.—Rebecca! Rebecca! Everything's getting cold down here.
(GEORGE *comes rattling down the stairs very brisk.*)

GEORGE. Good morning, everybody. Only five more hours to live.
(*Makes the gesture of cutting his throat.*)

MRS. GIBBS. Where are you going?

GEORGE. Just stepping across the grass to see my girl.

MRS. GIBBS. Now, George! You take an umbrella or I won't let you out of this house.

GEORGE. Aw, Ma. It's just a *step!*

MRS. GIBBS. From tomorrow on you can kill yourself in all weathers, but while you're in my house you live wisely, thank you. There are your overshoes right there in the hall. And here's an umbrella.

GEORGE. Aw, Ma!

DR. GIBBS. George, do as your mother tells you.

MRS. GIBBS. Maybe Mrs. Webb isn't used to callers at seven in the morning. Take a cup-a coffee first.

GEORGE. Be back in a minute. (*He crosses the stage, leaping over the puddles*) Good morning, Mother Webb.

MRS. WEBB. Goodness! You frightened me!—Now, George, you can come in a minute out of the wet, but you know I can't ask you in.

GEORGE. Why not—?

MRS. WEBB. George, you know's well as I do: the groom can't see his bride on his wedding day, not until he sees her in church.

GEORGE. Aw!—that's just a superstition.
(*Enter* MR. WEBB.)

MR. WEBB. Good morning, George.

GEORGE. Mr. Webb, you don't believe in that superstition, do you?

MR. WEBB. There's a lot of common sense in some superstitions, George.

MRS. WEBB. Millions have folla'd it, George, and you don't want to be the first to fly in the face of custom.

GEORGE. How is Emily?

MRS. WEBB. She hasn't waked up yet. I haven't heard a sound out of her.

GEORGE. Emily's *asleep!!!*

MRS. WEBB. No wonder! We were up till all hours,—sewing and packing. I'll tell you what I'll do; you set down here a minute with Mr. Webb and drink this cup of coffee; and I'll go upstairs and see she doesn't come down and surprise you. There's some bacon, too; but don't be long about it.
(*Exit* MRS. WEBB. *Embarrassed silence.*)

MR. WEBB. Well, George, how are you?

GEORGE. Oh, fine. I'm fine. (*Pause*) Mr. Webb, what sense could there be in a superstition like that?

MR. WEBB. Well, you see,—on her wedding morning a girl's head's apt to be full of . . . clothes and things like that. Don't you think that's probably it?

GEORGE. Ye-e-s. I never thought of that.

MR. WEBB. A girl's apt to be a mite nervous on her wedding day.
(*Pause.*)

GEORGE. I wish a fellow could get married without all that marching up and down.

MR. WEBB. Well, every man that's ever lived has felt that way about it, George; but it hasn't done much good. It's the women that have built up weddings, my boy. From now on they have it pretty much as they like. . . . All those good women standing shoulder to shoulder making sure that the knot's tied in a mighty public way.

GEORGE. But . . . you *believe* in it, don't you, Mr. Webb?

MR. WEBB. Oh, yes; oh, yes. Don't you misunderstand me, my boy. Marriage is a wonderful thing,—wonderful thing. And don't you forget that, George.

GEORGE. No, sir—Mr. Webb, how old were you when you got married?

MR. WEBB. Well, you see: I'd been to college and I'd taken a little time to get settled. But Mrs. Webb,—she wasn't much older than what Emily is. Oh, age hasn't much to do with it, George,—not compared to other things.

GEORGE. What were you going to say, Mr. Webb?

MR. WEBB. Oh, I don't know,—was I going to say something? (*Pause*) George, I was thinking the other night of some advice my father gave me when I got married. Charles, he said, Charles, start out early showing who's boss, he said. Best thing to do is to give an order, even if it don't make sense; just so she'll learn to obey. And he said: if anything about your wife irritates you,—her conversation, or anything,—just get up and leave the house. That'll make it clear to her, he said. And, oh, yes! he said never, *never* let your wife know how much money you have, never.

GEORGE. Well, Mr. Webb . . . I don't think I could . . .

MR. WEBB. So I took the opposite of my father's advice and I've been happy ever since. And let that be a lesson to you, George, never to ask advice on personal matters,— George, are you going to raise chickens on your farm?

GEORGE. What?

MR. WEBB. Are you going to raise chickens on your farm?

GEORGE. Uncle Luke's never been much interested, but I thought—

MR. WEBB. A book came into my office the other day, George, on the Philo System of raising chickens. I want you to read it. I'm thinking of beginning in a small way in the back yard, and I'm going to put an incubator in the cellar—

(*Enter* MRS. WEBB.)

MRS. WEBB. Charles, are you talking about that old incubator again? I thought you two'd be talking about things worth while.

MR. WEBB. Well, Myrtle, if you want to give the boy some good advice, I'll go upstairs and leave you alone with him.

MRS. WEBB. Now, George, I'm sorry, but I've got to send you away so that Emily can come down and get some breakfast. She told me to tell you that she sends you her love but that she doesn't want to lay eyes on you. So good-by, George.

(GEORGE *crosses the stage to his own home and disappears.*)

MR. WEBB. Myrtle, I guess you don't know about that older superstition.

MRS. WEBB. What do you mean, Charles?

MR. WEBB. Since the cave-men: the groom shouldn't be left alone with his father-in-law on the day of the wedding, or near it. Now don't forget that!

STAGE MANAGER. Thank you. Thank you, everybody. Now I have to interrupt again here. You see, we want to know how all this began,—this wedding, this plan to spend a lifetime together. I'm awfully interested in how big things like that begin. You know how it is: you're twenty-one or twenty-two and you make some decisions; then whisssh! you're seventy: you've been a lawyer for fifty years, and that white-haired lady at your side has eaten over fifty thousand meals with you. How do such things begin? George and Emily are going to show you now the conversation they had when they first knew that . . . that . . . as the saying goes . . . they were meant for one another. But before they do it I want you to try and remember what it was like when you were young, when you were fifteen or sixteen. For some reason it is very hard to do: those days when even the little things in life could be almost too exciting to bear. And particularly the days when you were first in love; when you were like a person sleep-walking, and you didn't quite see the street you were in, and didn't quite hear everything that was said to you. You're just a little bit crazy. Will you remember that, please? Now they'll be coming out of High School at three o'clock. George has just been elected President of the Junior Class, and as it's June, that means he'll be President of the Senior Class all next year. And Emily's just been elected Secretary and Treasurer. I don't have to tell you how important that is. (*He places a board across the backs of two chairs, parallel to the foot-lights, and places two high stools behind it. This is the counter of* MR. MORGAN'S *drugstore.*) All ready!

(EMILY, *carrying an armful of—imaginary—school books, comes along Main Street from the left.*)

EMILY. I can't, Louise. I've got to go home. Good-by. Oh, Ernestine! Ernestine! Can you come over tonight and do algebra? I did the first and third in Study Hall. No, they're not hard. But, Ernestine, that Caesar's awful hard. I don't see why we have to do a thing like that. Come over about seven. Tell your mother you *have* to. G'by. G'by, Helen. G'by, Fred.

(GEORGE, *also carrying books, catches up with her.*)

GEORGE. Can I carry your books home for you, Emily?

EMILY (*coldly*). Thank you. (*She gives them to him.*)

GEORGE. Excuse me a minute, Emily. —Say, Bob, get everything ready. I'll be there in a quarter of an hour. If I'm a little late start practice anyway. And give Herb some long high ones. His eye needs a lot of practice. Seeya later.

EMILY. Good-by, Lizzy.

GEORGE. Good-by, Lizzy.—I'm awfully glad you were elected, too, Emily.

EMILY. Thank you.

(*They have been standing on Main Street, almost against the back wall.* GEORGE *is about to take the first steps towards the audience when he stops again and says:*)

GEORGE. Emily, why are you mad at me?

EMILY. I'm not mad at you.

GEORGE. You . . . you treat me so funny.

EMILY. Well, I might as well say it right out, George. I don't like the whole change that's come over you in the last year. I'm sorry if that hurts your feelings, but I've just got to tell the truth and shame the devil.

GEORGE. I'm awfully sorry, Emily. Wha-a-what do you mean?

EMILY. Well, up to a year ago I used to like you a lot. And I used to watch you as you did everything . . . because we'd been friends so long . . . and then you began spending all your time at baseball . . . and you never even spoke to anybody any more; not even to your own family you didn't . . . and, George, it's a fact, you've got awful conceited and stuck-up, and all the girls say so. They may not say so to your face, but that's what they say about you behind your back, and it hurts me to hear them say it, but I've got to agree with them a little. I'm sorry if it hurts your feelings . . . but I can't be sorry I said it.

GEORGE. I . . . I'm glad you said it, Emily. I never thought that such a thing was happening to me. I guess it's hard for a fella not to have faults creep into his character.
(*They take a step or two in silence, then stand still in misery.*)

EMILY. I always expect a man to be perfect and I think he should be.

GEORGE. Oh . . . I don't think it's possible to be perfect, Emily.

EMILY. Well, my father is, and as far as I can see your father is. There's no reason on earth why you shouldn't be, too.

GEORGE. Well, Emily . . . I feel it's the other way round. That men aren't naturally good; but girls are. Like you and your mother and my mother.

EMILY. Well, you might as well know right now that I'm not perfect. It's not as easy for a girl to be perfect as a man, because we girls are more nervous.—Now I'm sorry I said all that about you. I don't know what made me say it.

GEORGE. No, no,—I guess if it's the truth you ought to say it. You stick to it, Emily.

EMILY. I don't know if it's the truth or not. And I suddenly feel that it isn't important at all.

GEORGE. Emily, would you like an ice-cream soda, or something, before you go home?

EMILY. Well, thank you. . . . I would. (*They come into the drugstore and seat themselves on the stools.*)

STAGE MANAGER (*as* MR. MORGAN). Hello, George. Hello, Emily. What'll you have? Why, Emily Webb, what've you been crying about?

GEORGE (*he gropes for an explanation*). She . . . she just got an awful scare, Mr. Morgan. She almost got run over by that hardware store wagon. Everybody always says that Tom Huckins drives like a crazy man.

STAGE MANAGER. Here, take a drink of water, Emily. You look all shook up. There!—Now, what'll you have?

EMILY. I'll have a strawberry phosphate, thank you, Mr. Morgan.

GEORGE. No, no. You go and have an ice-cream soda with me, Emily.—Two strawberry ice-cream sodas, Mr. Morgan.

STAGE MANAGER (*working the faucets*). Yes, sir. I tell you, you've got to look both ways before you cross Main Street these days. Gets worse every year. There are a hundred and twenty-five horses in Grover's Corners this minute I'm talking to you. State Inspector was in here yesterday. And now they're bringing in these auto-mo-biles, the best thing to do is to just stay home. Why, I can remember the time when a dog could lie down all day in the middle of Main Street and nothing would come to disturb him.—Yes, Miss Ellis; be with you in a minute. Here are your sodas. Enjoy 'em. (*He goes off.*)

EMILY. They're so expensive.

GEORGE. No, no,—don't you think of that. We're celebrating. First, we're celebrating our election. And then do you know what else I'm celebrating?

EMILY. No.

GEORGE. I'm celebrating because I've got a friend who tells me all the things that ought to be told me.

EMILY. George, *please* don't think of that. I don't know why I said it. It's not true. You're—

GEORGE. No, you stick to it, Emily. I'm glad you spoke to me like you did. But you'll see: I'm going to change so quick—you bet I'm going to change. And, Emily, I want to ask you a favor.

EMILY. What?

GEORGE. Emily, if I go away to State Agriculture College next year, will you write me a letter once in a while?

EMILY. I certainly will. I certainly will, George. . . . (*Pause*) It certainly seems like being away three years you'd get out of touch with things.

GEORGE. No, no. I mustn't do that. You see I'm not only going to be just a farmer. After a while maybe I'll run for something to get elected. So your letters'll be very important to me; you know, telling me what's going on here and everything. . . .

EMILY. Just the same, three years is a long time. Maybe letters from Grover's Corners wouldn't be so interesting after a while. Grover's Corners isn't a very important place when you think of all New Hampshire; but I think it's a very nice town.

GEORGE. The day wouldn't come when I wouldn't want to know everything that's happening here. I know *that's* true, Emily.

EMILY. Well, I'll try to make my letters interesting. (*Pause.*)

GEORGE. Y'know, Emily, whenever I meet a farmer I ask him if he thinks it's important to go to Agriculture School to be a good farmer.

EMILY. Why, George—

GEORGE. Yeah, and some of them say that it's even a waste of time. You can get all those things, anyway, out of the pamphlets the government sends out. And Uncle Luke's getting old,—he's about ready for me to start in taking over his farm tomorrow, if I could.

EMILY. My!

GEORGE. And, like you say, being gone all that time . . . in other places and meeting other people . . . If anything like that can happen I don't want to go away. I guess new people aren't any better than old ones. I'll bet they almost never are. Emily . . . I feel that you're as good a friend as I've got. I don't need to go and meet the people in other towns.

EMILY. But, George, maybe it's very important for you to go and learn all that about cattle-judging and soils and those things. And if you're going into politics, maybe you ought to meet people from other parts of the State . . . of course, I don't know.

GEORGE (*after a pause*). Emily, I'm going to make up my mind right now. I won't go. I'll tell Pa about it tonight.

EMILY. Why, George, I don't see why you have to decide right now. It's a whole year away.

GEORGE. Emily, I'm glad you spoke to me about that . . . that fault in my character. And what you said was right; but there was *one* thing wrong in it, and that was when you said that for a year I wasn't noticing people, and . . . you, for instance. Listen, Emily . . . you say you were watching me when I did everything. . . . Why, I was doing the same about you all the time. Why, sure,—I always thought about you as one of the chief people I thought about. I always made sure where you were sitting on the bleachers, and who you were with. And we've always had lots of talks . . . and joking, in the halls; and they always meant a lot to me. Of course, they weren't as good as the talk we're having now. Lately I'd been noticing that you'd been acting kind of funny to me, and for three days I've been trying to walk home with you, but something's always got in the way. Yesterday I was standing over against the wall waiting for you, and you walked home with Miss Corcoran.

EMILY. George! . . . Life's awful funny! How could I have known that? Why, I thought—

GEORGE. Listen, Emily, I'm going to to tell you why I'm not going to Agriculture School. I think that once you've found a person that you're very fond of . . . I mean a person who's fond of you, too,—at least enough to be interested in your character . . . Well, I think that's just as important as college is, and even more so. That's what I think.

EMILY. I think it's awfully important, too.

GEORGE. Emily.

EMILY. Yes, George.

GEORGE. Emily, if I improve and make a big change . . . would you be . . . I mean: *could* you be . . .

EMILY. I . . . I am now; I always have been.

GEORGE (*pause*). So I guess this is an important talk we've been having.

EMILY. Yes.

GEORGE (*takes a deep breath and straightens his back*). Wait just a minute and I'll take you home. (*He rises and goes to the* STAGE MANAGER *who appears and comes toward him.*) Mr. Morgan, I'll have to go home and get the money to pay you for this. It'll only take me a minute.

STAGE MANAGER. What's that? George Gibbs, do you mean to tell me—!

GEORGE. Yes, but I had reasons, Mr. Morgan.—Look, here's my gold watch to keep until I come back with the money.

STAGE MANAGER. That's all right. Keep your watch. I'll trust you.

GEORGE. I'll be back in five minutes.

STAGE MANAGER. I'll trust you ten years, George,—not a day more.—Got all over your shock, Emily?

EMILY. Yes, thank you, Mr. Morgan. It was nothing.

GEORGE (*taking up the books from the counter*). I'm ready.
(*They walk in grave silence down the stage, turn, and pass through the trellis at the Webbs' back door and disappear.*)

STAGE MANAGER. Thank you, Emily. Thank you, George. Now before we go on to the wedding, there are still some more things we ought to know about this—about this marriage. I want to know some more about how the parents took it; but what I want to know most of all is: oh, you know what I mean,—what Grover's Corners thought about marriage anyway. You know's well as I do: people are never able to say right out what they think of money, or death, or fame, or marriage. You've got to catch it between the lines; you've got to *over*-hear it. Oh, Doctor! Mrs. Gibbs!
(*They appear at their side of the stage and exchange a glance of understanding with him. The* STAGE MANAGER *lays the same plank across two chairs that served as a drugstore counter and it has now become* MRS. GIBBS'S *ironing board.* DR. GIBBS *sits down in a rocker and smokes.* MRS. GIBBS *irons a moment in silence; then goes to the foot of the stairs and calls:*)

MRS. GIBBS. Rebecca! It's time you turned out your light and went to sleep. George, you'd better get some sleep, too.

REBECCA'S VOICE. Ma, I haven't finished my English.

MRS. GIBBS. What? Well, I bet you haven't been working, Rebecca. You've been reading that Sears, Roebuck catalogue, that's what you've been doing.—All right, I'll give you ten more minutes. If you haven't finished by then you'll just have to fail the course and be a disgrace to your father and me.—George, what are you doing?

GEORGE'S VOICE (*hurt*). I'm doing history.

MRS. GIBBS. Well, you'd better go to bed. You're probably sleeping at the desk as it is. (*She casts an amused eye at her husband and returns to her ironing.*)

DR. GIBBS. I had a long talk with the boy today.

MRS. GIBBS. Did you?

DR. GIBBS. I tell you, Mrs. G., there's nothing so terrifying in the world as a son. The relation of a father to a son is the damnedest, awkwardest—I always come away feeling like a soggy sponge of hypocrisy.

MRS. GIBBS. Well, a mother and a daughter's no picnic, let me tell you.

DR. GIBBS. George is set on it: he wants to marry Emily 'soon as school's out and take her right on to the farm. (*Pause*) He says he can sit up nights and learn agriculture from government pamphlets, without going to college for it.

MRS. GIBBS. He always was crazy about farming. Gets that from my people.

DR. GIBBS. At a pinch, I guess he could start in farming;—but I swear I think he's too young to get married. Julia, he's just a green half-grown kid. He isn't ready to be a family man.

MRS. GIBBS. No, he ain't. You're right.—But he's a good boy and I wouldn't like to think of him being alone out there . . . coming into town Satiddy nights, like any old farm hand, tuckered out from work and looking for excitement. He might get into bad ways. It wouldn't be enough fun for him to come and sit by our stove,—and holding hands with Emily for a year mightn't be enough either. He might lose interest in her.

DR. GIBBS. Hm.

MRS. GIBBS. Frank, I' been watching her. George is a lucky boy when you think of all the silly girls in the world.

DR. GIBBS. But, Julia,—George *married*. That great gangling selfish nincompoop.

MRS. GIBBS. Yes, I know. (*She takes up a collar and examines it*) Frank, what do you do to your collars? Do you gnaw 'em? I never saw such a man for collars.

DR. GIBBS. Julia, when I married you, do you know what one of my terrors was in getting married?

MRS. GIBBS. Pshaw! Go on with you!

DR. GIBBS. I was afraid we weren't going to have material for conversation more'n 'ld last us a few weeks. I was afraid we'd run out and eat our meals in silence, that's a fact. You and I've been conversing for twenty years now without any noticeable barren spells.

MRS. GIBBS. Well, good weather, bad weather, 'tain't very choice, but I always manage to find something to say.
(*Pause.*)

DR. GIBBS. What do you think? What do you think, Julia? Shall we tell the boy he can go ahead and get married?

MRS. GIBBS. Seems like it's up to us to decide. Myrtle and Charles Webb are willing. They think it's a good idea to throw the young people into the sea and let'm sink or swim, as soon as they're ready.

DR. GIBBS. What does that mean? Must we decide right now? This minute?

MRS. GIBBS. There you go putting the responsibility on me!

DR. GIBBS. Here it is, almost April. —I'll go up and say a word to him right now before he goes to bed. (*He rises*) You're sure, Julia? You've nothing more to add?

MRS. GIBBS (*stops ironing a moment*) I don't know what to say. Seems like it's too much to ask, for a big outdoor boy like that to go and get shut up in classrooms for three years. And once he's on the farm, he might just as well have a companion, seeing he's found a fine girl like Emily. . . . People are meant to live two-by-two in this world. . . . Yes, Frank, go up and tell him it's all right.

DR. GIBBS (*crosses and is about to call when—*)

MRS. GIBBS (*her hands on her cheeks staring into the audience, in sharp alarm*). Wait a minute! Wait a minute!—(*Then resuming her ironing*) No,—go and tell him.

DR. GIBBS. Why did you stop then, Julia?

MRS. GIBBS. Oh, you know: I thought of all those times we went through in the first years when George and Rebecca were babies,—you walking up and down with them at three in the morning; the whooping-cough; the time George fell off the porch. You and I were twenty-five years old, and more. It's wonderful how one forgets one's troubles, like that.—Yes, Frank, go upstairs and tell him. . . . It's worth it.

DR. GIBBS. Yes, they'll have a lot of troubles, but that's none of our business. Let'm. Everybody has a right to his own troubles.—You ought to be present, Julia,—important occasion like that. I'll call him.—George! Oh, George!

GEORGE'S VOICE. Yes, Pa.

DR. GIBBS. Can you come down a minute? Your mother and I want to speak to you.

GEORGE. Yeah, sure.

MRS. GIBBS (*putting her arm through her husband's*). Lord, what a fool I am: I'm trembling all over. There's nothing to tremble about.

STAGE MANAGER. Thank you! Thank you! Now we're ready to go on with the wedding. (*While he talks, the actors remove the chair and tables and trellises from the Gibbs and Webb homes. They arrange the pews for the church in the back of the stage. The congregation will sit facing the back wall. The aisle of the church is in the middle of the scene. A small platform is placed against the back wall on which the* STAGE MANAGER *as Minister can stand.*) There are a lot of things to be said about a wedding; there are a lot of thoughts that go on during a wedding. We can't get them all into one wedding, naturally, and especially not into a wedding at Grover's Corners where they're awfully plain and short. In this wedding I play the minister. That gives me the right to say a few more things about it. For a while now, the play gets pretty serious. Y'see, some churches say that marriage is a sacrament. I don't quite know what that means, but I can guess. Like Mrs. Gibbs said a few minutes ago: People were made to live two-by-two. This is a good wedding, but people are so put together that even at a good wedding there's a lot of confusion way down deep in people's minds and we thought that that ought to be in our play, too. The real hero of this scene isn't on the stage at all, and you know who that is. It's like what one of those European fellas said: every child born into the world is Nature's attempt to make a perfect human being. Well, we've seen Nature pushing and contriving for some time now. We all know that nature's interested in quantity; but I think she's interested in quality, too,—that's why I'm in the ministry.—Maybe she's trying to make another good governor for New Hampshire. And don't forget the other witnesses at this wedding,—the ancestors. Millions of them. Most of them set out to live two-by-two, also. Millions of them. Well, that's all my sermon. 'Twan't very long, anyway. (*The organ starts playing Handel's "Largo." The congregation streams into the church and sits in silence.* MRS. WEBB, *on the way to her place, turns back and speaks to the audience.)*

MRS. WEBB. I don't know why on earth I should be crying. I suppose there's nothing to cry about. It came over me at breakfast this morning; there was Emily eating her breakfast as she's done for seventeen years and now she's going off to eat it in someone else's house. I suppose that's it. And Emily! She suddenly said: I can't eat another mouthful, and she put her head down on the table and she cried. (*She starts toward her seat in the church, but turns back and adds*) Oh, I've got to say it: you know, there's something downright cruel about sending our girls out into marriage this way. I hope some of her girl friends have told her a thing or two. It's cruel, I know, but I couldn't bring myself to say anything. I went into it blind as a bat myself. The whole world's wrong, that's what's the matter. There they come.

(*She hurries to her place in the pew.* GEORGE *starts to come down the right aisle of the theatre, through the audience. Suddenly three members of his baseball team appear by the right proscenium pillar and start whistling and catcalling to him. They are dressed for the ball field.*)

THE BASEBALL PLAYERS. Eh, George, George! Hsst—yaow! If things don't go right, call us in. We know what to do. Eh, fellas? Yaow! George, don't look so innocent, you old geezer. We know what you're thinking. Don't disgrace the team, big boy. Whoo-oo-oo.

STAGE MANAGER. All right! All right! That'll do. That's enough of that. (*Smiling, he pushes them off the stage. They lean back to shout a few more catcalls.*) There used to be an awful lot of that kind of thing at weddings in the old days,—Rome, and later. We're more civilized now,—so they say.

(*The choir starts singing "Love divine, all love excelling—."* GEORGE *has reached the stage. He stares at the congregation a moment, then takes a few steps of withdrawal, toward the right proscenium pillar.*)

GEORGE (*darkly, to himself*). I wish I were back at school. . . . I don't want to get married.

(*His mother has left her seat and comes toward him. She stops, looking at him anxiously.*)

MRS. GIBBS. George, what's the matter?

GEORGE. Ma, I don't want to grow *old*. Why's everybody pushing me so?

MRS. GIBBS. Why, George . . . you wanted it.

GEORGE. Why do I have to get married at all? Listen, Ma, for the last time I ask you—

MRS. GIBBS. No, no, George . . . you're a man now.

GEORGE. Listen, Ma, you never listen to me. All I want to do is to be a fella . . . why do—

MRS. GIBBS. George! If anyone should hear you! Now stop. Why, I'm ashamed of you!

GEORGE (*passing his hand over his forehead*). What's the matter? I've been dreaming. Where's Emily?

MRS. GIBBS. Gracious! You gave me such a turn.

GEORGE. Cheer up, Ma. What are you looking so funny for? Cheer up; I'm getting married.

MRS. GIBBS. Let me catch my breath a minute.

GEORGE. Now, Ma, you save Thursday nights. Emily and I are coming over to dinner every Thursday night . . . you'll see. Ma, what are you crying for? Come on; we've got to get ready for this.

(*In the meantime,* EMILY, *in white and wearing her wedding veil, has come through the audience and mounted on to the stage. She too draws back when she sees the congregation in the church. The choir begins: "Blessed be the tie that binds."*)

EMILY. I never felt so alone in my whole life. And George over there, looking so . . . ! I *hate* him. I wish I were dead. Papa! Papa!

MR. WEBB (*leaves his seat in the pews and comes toward her anxiously*). Emily! Emily! Now don't get upset. . . .

EMILY. But, Papa,—I don't want to get married. . . .

MR. WEBB. Sh-sh—Emily. Everything's all right.

EMILY. Why can't I stay for a while just as I am? Let's go away.

MR. WEBB. No, no, Emily. Now stop and think.

EMILY. Don't you remember that you used to say,—all the time you used to say that I was *your* girl. There must be lots of places we can go to. Let's go away. I'll work for you. I could keep house.

MR. WEBB. Sh. . . . You mustn't think of such things. You're just nervous, Emily. Now, now,—you're marrying the best young fellow in the world. George is a fine fellow.

EMILY. But, Papa,—

MR. WEBB. George! George! (MRS. GIBBS *returns to her seat.* GEORGE *hears* MR. WEBB *and looks up.* MR. WEBB *beckons to him. They move to the center of the stage*) I'm giving away my daughter, George. Do you think you can take care of her?

GEORGE. Mr. Webb, I want to . . . I want to try. Emily, I'm going to do my best. I love you, Emily. I need you.

EMILY. Well, if you love me, help me. All I want is someone to love me.

GEORGE. I will, Emily.

EMILY. If ever I'm sick or in trouble, that's what I mean.

GEORGE. Emily, I'll try. I'll try.

EMILY. And I mean for *ever.* Do you hear? For ever and ever.

(*They fall into each other's arms. The March from "Lohengrin" is heard.*)

MR. WEBB. Come, they're waiting for us. Now you know it'll be all right. Come, quick.

(GEORGE *slips away and takes his place beside the* STAGE MANAGER-CLERGYMAN. EMILY *proceeds up the aisle on her father's arm.*)

STAGE MANAGER. Do you, George, take this woman, Emily, to be your wedded wife, to have . . .

(MRS. SOAMES *has been sitting in the last row of the congregation. She now turns to her neighbors and in a shrill voice says:*)

MRS. SOAMES. Perfectly lovely wedding! Loveliest wedding I ever saw. Oh, I do love a good wedding, don't you? Doesn't she make a lovely bride?

GEORGE. I do.

STAGE MANAGER. Do you, Emily, take this man, George, to be your wedded husband,—

MRS. SOAMES. Don't know *when* I've seen such a lovely wedding. But I always cry. Don't know why it is, but I always cry. I just like to see young people happy, don't you? Oh, I think it's lovely.

(The ring. The kiss. The stage is suddenly arrested into silent tableau. The STAGE MANAGER, *his eyes on the distance, says to the audience:)*
I've married two hundred couples in my day. Do I believe in it? I don't know. M . . . . marries N . . . . millions of them. The cottage, the gocart, the Sunday afternoon drives in the Ford, the first rheumatism, th grandchildren, the second rheuma tism, the deathbed, the reading o the will.—Once in a thousand time it's interesting. Well, let's have Men delssohn's "Wedding March"!
(The organ picks up the March. Th bride and groom come down the aisle radiant, but trying to be very digni fied.)

MRS. SOAMES. Aren't they a lovel couple? Oh, I've never been to suc a nice wedding. I'm sure they'll b happy. I always say: *happiness,* that' the great thing! The important thin is to be happy.
(The bride and groom reach th steps leading into the audience. bright light is thrown upon them They descend into the auditoriu and run up the aisle joyously.)

STAGE MANAGER. That's all th Second Act. Ten minutes' intermi sion, folks.

ACT THREE

During the intermission the audience has seen the actors arranging the stage On the right-hand side, a little right of the center, ten or twelve ordinar chairs have been placed in three openly spaced rows facing the audience.

These are graves in the cemetery.

Towards the end of the intermission the actors enter and take their place. The front row contains: toward the center of the stage, an empty chair; the MRS. GIBBS; SIMON STIMSON. *The second row contains, among others,* MR SOAMES. *The third row has* WALLY WEBB.

The dead sit in a quiet without stiffness, and in a patience without lis lessness.

The STAGE MANAGER *takes his accustomed place and waits for the hous lights to go down.*

STAGE MANAGER. This time nine years have gone by, friends—summer, 1913. Gradual changes in Grover's Corners. Horses are getting rare Farmers coming into town in Ford Chief difference is in the young pe ple, far as I can see. They want to go to the moving pictures all the time. They want to wear clothes like they see there . . . want to be citified. Everybody locks their house doors now at night. Ain't been any burglars in town yet, but everybody's heard about 'em. But you'd be surprised though—on the whole, things don't change much at Grover's Corners. Guess you want to know what all these chairs are here fur. Smarter ones have guessed it already. I don't know how you feel about such things; but this certainly is a beautiful place. It's on a hilltop—a windy hilltop—lots of sky, lots of clouds,—often lots of sun and moon and stars. You come up here on a fine afternoon and you can see range on range of hills—awful blue they are—up there by Lake Sunapee and Lake Winnipesaukee . . . and way up, if you've got a glass, you can see the White Mountains and Mt. Washington—where North Conway and Conway is. And, of course, our favorite mountain, Mt. Monadnock, 's right here—and all around it lie these towns—Jaffrey, 'n East Jaffrey, 'n Peterborough, 'n Dublin and (*Then pointing down in the audience*) there, quite a ways down, is Grover's Corners. Yes, beautiful spot up here. Mountain laurel and li-lacks. I often wonder why people like to be buried in Woodlawn and Brooklyn when they might pass the same time up here in New Hampshire. Over in that corner—(*Pointing to stage left*) are the old stones,—1670, 1680. Strong-minded people that come a long way to be independent. Summer people walk around there laughing at the funny words on the tombstones . . . it don't do any harm. And genealogists come up from Boston—get paid by city people for looking up their ancestors. They want to make sure they're Daughters of the American Revolution and of the *Mayflower*. . . . Well, I guess that don't do any harm, either. Wherever you come near the human race, there's layers and layers of nonsense. . . . Over there are some Civil War veterans too. Iron flags on their graves. . . . New Hampshire boys . . . had a notion that the Union ought to be kept together, though they'd never seen more than fifty miles of it themselves. All they knew was the name, friends —the United States of America. The United States of America. And they went and died about it. This here is the new part of the cemetery. Here's your friend, Mrs. Gibbs. 'N let me see— Here's Mr. Stimson, organist at the Congregational Church. And over there's Mrs. Soames who enjoyed the wedding so—you remember? Oh, and a lot of others. And Editor Webb's boy, Wallace, whose appendix burst while he was on a Boy Scout trip to Crawford Notch. Yes, an awful lot of sorrow has sort of quieted down up here. People just wild with grief have brought their relatives up to this hill. We all know how it is . . . and then time . . . and sunny days . . . and rainy days . . . 'n snow . . . tz-tz-tz. We're all glad they're in a beautiful place and we're coming up here ourselves when our fit's over. This certainly is an important part of Grover's Corners. A lot of thoughts come up here, night and day, but there's no post office. Now I'm going to tell you some things you know already. You know'm as well as I do; but you don't take'm out and look at'm very often. I don't care what they say with their mouths—everybody knows that *something* is eternal. And it ain't houses and it ain't names, and it ain't earth, and it ain't even the stars . . . everybody knows in their bones that *some-*

thing is eternal, and that something has to do with human beings. All the greatest people ever lived have been telling us that for five thousand years and yet you'd be surprised how people are always losing hold of it. There's something way down deep that's eternal about every human being. (*Pause*) You know as well as I do that the dead don't stay interested in us living people for very long. Gradually, gradually, they let hold of the earth . . . and the ambitions they had . . . and the pleasures they had . . . and the things they suffered . . . and the people they loved. They get weaned away from earth—that's the way I put it,—weaned away. Yes, they stay here while the earth part of 'em burns away, burns out, and all that time they slowly get indifferent to what's goin' on in Grover's Corners. They're waitin'. They're waitin' for something that they feel is comin'. Something important and great. Aren't they waitin' for the eternal part in them to come out clear? Some of the things they're going to say maybe'll hurt your feelings—but that's the way it is: mother 'n daughter . . . husband 'n wife . . . enemy 'n enemy . . . money 'n miser . . . all those terribly important things kind of grow pale around here. And what's left? What's left when memory's gone, and your identity, Mrs. Smith? (*He looks at the audience a minute, then turns to the stage*) Well! There are some *living* people. There's Joe Stoddard, our undertaker, supervising a new-made grave. And here comes a Grover's Corners boy, that left town to go out West.

(JOE STODDARD *has hovered about in the background.* SAM CRAIG *enters left, wiping his forehead from the exertion. He carries an umbrella and strolls front.*)

SAM CRAIG. Good afternoon, Joe Stoddard.

JOE STODDARD. Good afternoon, good afternoon. Let me see now: do I know you?

SAM CRAIG. I'm Sam Craig.

JOE STODDARD. Gracious sakes alive! Of all people! I should'a knowed you'd be back for the funeral. You've been away a long time, Sam.

SAM CRAIG. Yes, I've been away over twelve years. I'm in business out in Buffalo now, Joe. But I was in the East when I got news of my cousin's death, so I thought I'd combine things a little and come and see the old home. You look well.

JOE STODDARD. Yes, yes, can't complain. Very sad, our journey today, Samuel.

SAM CRAIG. Yes.

JOE STODDARD. Yes, yes. I always say, I hate to supervise when a young person is taken. I see you brought your umbrella. It's going to rain and make it sadder still, seems like. They'll be here in a few minutes now. I had to come here early today—my son's supervisin' at the home.

SAM CRAIG (*reading stones*). Old Farmer McCarty, I used to do chores for him—after school. He had the lumbago.

JOE STODDARD. Yes, we brought Farmer McCarty here a number of years ago now.

SAM CRAIG (*staring at* MRS. GIBBS' *knees*). Why, this is my Aunt Julia

. . . I'd forgotten that she'd . . . of course, of course.

JOE STODDARD. Yes, Doc Gibbs lost his wife two-three years ago . . . about this time. And today's another pretty bad blow for him, too.

MRS. GIBBS (*to* SIMON STIMSON: *in an even voice*). That's my sister Carey's boy, Sam. . . . Sam Craig.

SIMON STIMSON. I'm always uncomfortable when *they're* around.

MRS. GIBBS. Simon.

SIMON STIMSON. They and their nonsense and their damned glee at being alive. . . .

MRS. GIBBS. Simon, be patient. . . .

SAM CRAIG. Do they choose their own verses much, Joe?

JOE STODDARD. No . . . not usual. Mostly the bereaved pick a verse.

SAM CRAIG. Doesn't sound like Aunt Julia. There aren't many of those Hersey sisters left now. Let me see: where are . . . I wanted to look at my father's and mother's . . .

JOE STODDARD. Over there with the Craigs. . . . Avenue F.

SAM CRAIG (*reading* SIMON STIMSON'S *epitaph*). He was organist at church, wasn't he?—Hm, drank a lot, we used to say.

JOE STODDARD. Nobody was supposed to know about it. He'd seen a peck of trouble. Those musical fellas ain't like the rest of us, I reckon. (*Behind his hand*) Took his own life, y' know?

SAM CRAIG. Oh, did he?

JOE STODDARD. Hung himself in the attic. They tried to hush it up, but of course it got around. His wife's just married Senator Barstow. Many a time I've seen her, eleven o'clock at night, goin' around the streets huntin' for her husband. Think o' that! Now she's married to Senator Barstow over at Manchester. He chose his own epytaph. You can see it there. It ain't a verse exactly.

SAM CRAIG. Why, it's just some notes of music—what is it?

JOE STODDARD. Oh, I wouldn't know. It was wrote up in the Boston papers at the time.

SAM CRAIG. Joe, what did she die off?

JOE STODDARD. Who?

SAM CRAIG. My cousin.

JOE STODDARD. Oh, didn't you know? Had some trouble bringing a baby into the world. Let's see, today's Friday—'twas almost a week ago now.

SAM CRAIG (*putting up his umbrella*). Did the baby live?

JOE STODDARD (*raising his coat collar*). No. 'Twas her second, though. There's a little boy 'bout four years old.

SAM CRAIG. The grave's going to be over there?

JOE STODDARD. Yes, there ain't much more room over here among the Gibbses, so they're opening up a whole new Gibbs section over by Avenue B. You'll excuse me now. I see they're comin'.

THE DEAD (*not lugubrious; and strongly New England in accent*). Rain'll do a lot of good.—Yes, reckon things were gettin' downright parched. Don't look like it's goin' to last long, though.—Lemuel, you remember the floods of '79? Carried away all the bridges but one.

(*From left to right, at the back of the stage, comes a procession. Four men carry a casket, invisible to us. All the rest are under umbrellas. One can vaguely see* DR. GIBBS, GEORGE, *the* WEBBS, *etc. They gather about a grave in the back center of the stage, a little to the left of center.*)

MRS. SOAMES. Who is it, Julia?

MRS. GIBBS (*without raising her eyes*). My daughter-in-law, Emily Webb.

MRS. SOAMES (*a little surprised, but no emotion*). Well, I declare! The road up here must have been awful muddy. What did she die of, Julia?

MRS. GIBBS. In childbirth.

MRS. SOAMES. Childbirth. (*Almost with a laugh*) I'd forgotten all about that! My, wasn't life awful— (*With a sigh*) and wonderful?

SIMON STIMSON (*with a sideways glance*). Wonderful, was it?

MRS. GIBBS. Simon! Now, remember!

MRS. SOAMES. I remember Emily's wedding. Wasn't it a lovely wedding? And I remember her reading the class poem at Graduation Exercises. Emily was one of the brightest girls ever graduated from High School. I've heard Principal Wilkins say so time after time. I called on them at their new farm, just before I died. Perfectly beautiful farm.

A WOMAN FROM AMONG THE DEAD. It's on the same road we lived on.

A MAN AMONG THE DEAD. Yes, just near the Elks' picnic grounds. Remember, Joe? By the lake where we always used to go Fourth of July? Right smart farm.

(*They subside. The group by the grave starts singing "Blessed be the tie that binds."*)

A WOMAN AMONG THE DEAD. I always liked that hymn. I was hopin' they'd sing a hymn.

A MAN AMONG THE DEAD. My wife—my second wife—knows all the verses of about every hymn there is. It just beats the Dutch . . . she can go through them all by heart.

(*Pause. Suddenly* EMILY *appears from among the umbrellas. She is wearing a white dress. Her hair is down her back and tied by a white ribbon like a little girl. She comes slowly, gazing wonderingly at the dead, a little dazed. She stops halfway and smiles faintly.*)

EMILY. Hello.

VOICES AMONG THE DEAD. Hello, Emily. H'lo, M's. Gibbs.

EMILY. Hello, Mother Gibbs.

MRS. GIBBS. Emily.

EMILY. Hello. (*The hymn continues.* EMILY *looks back at the funeral. She says dreamily*) It's raining.

MRS. GIBBS. Yes. . . . They'll be gone soon, dear. Just rest yourself.

(EMILY *sits down in the empty chair by* MRS. GIBBS.)

EMILY. It seems thousands and thousands of years since I. . . . How stupid they all look. They don't have to look like that!

MRS. GIBBS. Don't look at them now, dear. They'll be gone soon.

EMILY. Oh, I wish I'd been here a long time. I don't like being new here. —How do you do, Mr. Stimson?

SIMON STIMSON. How do you do, Emily?
(EMILY *continues to look about her with a wan and wondering smile; but for a moment her eyes do not return to the funeral group. As though to shut out from her mind the thought of that group she starts speaking to* MRS. GIBBS *with a touch of nervousness.*)

EMILY. Mother Gibbs, George and I have made that farm into just the best place you ever saw. We thought of you all the time. We wanted to show you the new barn and a great long ce-ment drinking fountain for the stock. We bought that out of the money you left us.

MRS. GIBBS. I did?

EMILY. Don't you remember, Mother Gibbs—the legacy you left us? Why, it was over three hundred and fifty dollars.

MRS. GIBBS. Yes, yes, Emily.

EMILY. Well, there's a patent device on this drinking fountain so that it never overflows, Mother Gibbs, and it never sinks below a certain mark they have there. It's fine. (*Her voice trails off and her eyes return to the funeral group*) It won't be the same to George without me, but it's a lovely farm. (*Suddenly she looks directly at* MRS. GIBBS) Live people don't understand, do they?

MRS. GIBBS. No, dear—not very much.

EMILY. They're sort of shut up in little boxes, aren't they? I feel as though I knew them last a thousand years ago. . . . My boy is spending the day at Mrs. Carter's. (*She sees* MR. CARTER *among the dead*) Oh, Mr. Carter, my little boy is spending the day at your house.

MR. CARTER. Is he?

EMILY. Yes, he loves it there.—Mother Gibbs, we have a Ford, too. Never gives any trouble. I don't drive, though. Mother Gibbs, when does this feeling go away?—Of being . . . one of *them?* How long does it . . . ?

MRS. GIBBS. Sh! dear. Just wait and be patient.

EMILY (*with a sigh*). I know.—Look, they're finished. They're going.

MRS. GIBBS. Sh—. (*The umbrellas leave the stage.* DR. GIBBS *comes over to his wife's grave and stands before it a moment.* EMILY *looks up at his face.* MRS. GIBBS *does not raise her eyes.*)

EMILY. Look! Father Gibbs is bringing some of my flowers to you. He looks just like George, doesn't he? Oh, Mother Gibbs, I never realized before how troubled and how . . . how in the dark live persons are. From morning till night, that's all they are—troubled.
(DR. GIBBS *goes off.*)

THE DEAD. Little cooler than it was. —Yes, that rain's cooled it off a little. Those northeast winds always do the same thing, don't they? If it isn't a rain, it's a three-day blow.—Reckon it may clear up before night; often does.

(*A patient calm falls on the stage. The* STAGE MANAGER *appears at his proscenium pillar, smoking.* EMILY *sits up abruptly with an idea.*)

EMILY. But, Mother Gibbs, one can go back; one can go back there again . . . into living. I feel it. I know it. Why, just then for a moment I was thinking about . . . about the farm . . . and for a minute I *was* there, and my baby was on my lap as plain as day.

MRS. GIBBS. Yes, of course you can.

EMILY. I can go back there and live all those days over again . . . why not?

MRS. GIBBS. All I can say is, Emily, don't.

EMILY (*takes a few steps toward the* STAGE MANAGER). But it's true, isn't it? I can go and live . . . back there . . . again.

STAGE MANAGER. Yes, some have tried—but they soon come back here.

MRS. GIBBS. Don't do it, Emily.

MRS. SOAMES. Emily, don't. It's not what you think it'd be.

EMILY. But I won't live over a sad day. I'll choose a happy one— I'll choose the day I first knew that I loved George. Why should that be painful?

(*They are silent. Her question turns to the* STAGE MANAGER.)

STAGE MANAGER. You not only live it; but you watch yourself living it.

EMILY. Yes.

STAGE MANAGER. And as you watch it, you see the thing that they—down there—never know. You see the future. You know what's going to happen afterwards.

EMILY. But is that—painful? Why?

MRS. GIBBS. That's not the only reason why you shouldn't do it, Emily. When you've been here longer you'll see that our life here is our hope that soon we'll forget all that, and think only of what's ahead, and be ready for what's ahead. When you've been here longer you'll understand.

EMILY (*softly*). But, Mother Gibbs, how can I ever forget that life? It's all I know. It's all I had. (MRS. GIBBS *does not answer*) Mr. Stimson, did you go back?

SIMON STIMSON (*sharply*). No.

EMILY. Did you, Mrs. Soames?

MRS. SOAMES. Oh, Emily. It isn't wise. Really, it isn't. All we can do is just warn you. It won't be what you expect.

EMILY (*slowly*). But it's a thing I must know for myself. I'll choose a happy day, anyway.

MRS. GIBBS. No. At least, choose an unimportant day. Choose the least important day in your life. It will be important enough.

:MILY (*to the* STAGE MANAGER). Then it can't be since I was married; r since the baby was born. I can hoose a birthday at least, can't I?— choose my twelfth birthday.

TAGE MANAGER. All right. February 1th, 1899. A Tuesday.—Do you vant any special time of day?

:MILY. Oh, I want the whole day.

TAGE MANAGER. We'll begin at lawn. You remember it had been nowing for several days; but it had topped the night before, and they nad begun clearing the roads. The un's coming up.

MILY (*with a cry*). There's Main Street . . . why, that's Mr. Morgan's Irugstore before he changed it! . . . And there's the livery stable. *She walks toward the back of the tage.*)

TAGE MANAGER. Yes, it's 1899. This s fourteen years ago.

MILY. Oh, that's the town I knew as little girl. And, look, there's the ld white fence that used to be round our house. Oh, I'd forgotten hat! Oh, I love it so! Are *they* inide?

TAGE MANAGER. Yes, your mother'll e coming downstairs in a minute to nake breakfast.

MILY (*softly*). Will she?

TAGE MANAGER. And you remember: your father had been away for everal days; he came back on the arly morning train.

MILY. No . . . ?

STAGE MANAGER. He'd been back to his college to make a speech—in Western New York, at Clinton.

EMILY. Look! There's Howie Newsome. There's our policeman. But he's *dead;* he *died.*
(*The* STAGE MANAGER *retires to his corner. The voices of* HOWIE NEWSOME, CONSTABLE WARREN *and* JOE CROWELL, JR., *are heard at the left of the stage.*)

HOWIE NEWSOME. Whoa, Bessie!-Bessie! Morning, Bill.

BILL. Morning, Howie.

HOWIE NEWSOME. You're up early.

BILL. Been rescuin' a party; darn near froze to death, down by Polish Town thar. Got drunk and lay out in the snowdrifts. Thought he was in bed when I shook'm.

EMILY. Why, there's Joe Crowell. . . .

JOE CROWELL. Good morning, Mr. Warren. Morning, Howie.
(MRS. WEBB *has appeared in her kitchen, but* EMILY *does not see her until she calls.*)

MRS. WEBB. Chil-*dren!* Wally! Emily! . . . Time to get up.

EMILY. Mama, here I am! Oh! how young Mama looks! I didn't know Mama was ever that young. Oh!

MRS. WEBB. You can come and dress by the kitchen fire, if you like; but hurry. (HOWIE NEWSOME *has entered along Main Street and brings the milk to* MRS. WEBB'S *door*) Good morning, Mr. Newsome. Whhhh—it's cold.

HOWIE NEWSOME. Ten below by my barn, Mrs. Webb.

MRS. WEBB. Think of it! Keep yourself wrapped up. (*She takes her bottles in, shuddering.*)

EMILY (*with an effort*). Mama, I can't find my blue hair ribbon anywhere.

MRS. WEBB. Just open your eyes, dear, that's all. I laid it out for you special—on the dresser, there. If it were a snake it would bite you.

EMILY. Yes, yes. . . .
(*She puts her hand on her heart.* MR. WEBB *comes along Main Street, where he meets* CONSTABLE WARREN.)

MR. WEBB. Good morning, Bill.

BILL. Good morning, Mr. Webb. You're up early.

MR. WEBB. Yes, just been back to my old college in New York State. Been any trouble here?

BILL. Well, I was called up this mornin' to rescue a Polish fella—darn near froze to death he was.

MR. WEBB. We must get it in the paper.

BILL. 'Twan't much.

EMILY (*whispers*). Papa.
(MR. WEBB *shakes the snow off his feet and enters his house.*)

MR. WEBB. Good morning, Mother.

MRS. WEBB. How did it go, Charles?

MR. WEBB. Oh, fine, I guess. I told'm a few things.

MRS. WEBB. Did you sit up on the train all night?

MR. WEBB. Yes. Never could sleep on a Pullman anyway.

MRS. WEBB. Charles, seems to me—we're rich enough so that you could sleep in a train once in a while.

MR. WEBB. Everything all right here?

MRS. WEBB. Yes—can't think of anything that's happened, special. Been right cold. Howie Newsome says it's ten below over to his barn.

MR. WEBB. Yes, well, it's colder than that at Hamilton College. Students' ears are falling off. It ain't Christian. —Paper have any mistakes in it?

MRS. WEBB. None that I noticed. Coffee's ready when you want it. (*He starts upstairs*) Charles! Don't forget it's Emily's birthday. Did you remember to get her something?

MR. WEBB (*patting his pocket*). Yes I've got something here.

MRS. WEBB. Goodness sakes! I hope she likes what I got for her. I hunted hard enough for it. Child*ren!* Hurry up! Hurry up!

MR. WEBB. Where's my girl? Where's my birthday girl? (*He goes off left.*

MRS. WEBB. Don't interrupt her now Charles. You can see her at breakfast. She's slow enough as it is. Hurry up, children! It's seven o'clock. Now I don't want to call you again.

EMILY (*softly, more in wonder than in grief*). I can't bear it. They're so young and beautiful. Why did they ever have to get old? Mama, I'm here I'm grown up. I love you all, every thing.—I can't look at everything hard enough. There's the butternut tree. (*She wanders up Main Street*) There's Mr. Morgan's drugstore. And there's the High School, forever and ever, and ever. And there's the Congregational Church where I got married. Oh, dear. Oh, dear. Oh, dear! (*The* STAGE MANAGER *beckons partially to her. He points to the house. She says a breathless "yes" and goes to the house*) Good morning, Mama.

MRS. WEBB (*at the foot of the stairs, kissing her in a matter-of-fact way*). Well, now, dear, a very happy birthday to my girl and many happy returns. There are some surprises waiting for you on the kitchen table.

EMILY. Oh, Mama, you *shouldn't* have. (*She throws an anguished glance at the* STAGE MANAGER) I can't—I can't.

MRS. WEBB (*facing the audience, over her stove*). But birthday or no birthday, I want you to eat your breakfast good and slow. I want you to grow up and be a good strong girl. (*She goes to the stairs and calls*) Wally! Wally, wash yourself good. Everything's getting cold down here. (*She returns to the stove with her back to* EMILY. EMILY *opens her parcels*) That in the blue paper is from your Aunt Carrie and I reckon you can guess who brought the post card album. I found it on the doorstep when I brought in the milk—George Gibbs . . . must have come over in the cold pretty early . . . right nice of him.

EMILY (*to herself*). Oh, George! I'd forgotten that. . . .

MRS. WEBB. Chew that bacon slow. It'll help keep you warm on a cold day.

EMILY (*beginning softly but urgently*). Oh, Mama, just look at me one minute as though you really saw me. Mama, fourteen years have gone by. I'm dead. You're a grandmother, Mama. I married George Gibbs, Mama. Wally's dead, too. Mama, his appendix burst on a camping trip to North Conway. We felt just terrible about it—don't you remember? But, just for a moment now we're all together. Mama, just for a moment we're happy. Let's look at one another.

MRS. WEBB. That in the yellow paper is something I found in the attic among your grandmother's things. You're old enough to wear it now, and I thought you'd like it.

EMILY. And this is from you. Why, Mama, it's just lovely and it's just what I wanted. It's beautiful! (*She flings her arms around her mother's neck. Her mother goes on with her cooking, but is pleased.*)

MRS. WEBB. Well, I hoped you'd like it. Hunted all over. Your Aunt Norah couldn't find one in Concord, so I had to send all the way to Boston. (*Laughing*) Wally has something for you, too. He made it at Manual Training class and he's very proud of it. Be sure you make a big fuss about it.—Your father has a surprise for you, too; don't know what it is myself. Sh—here he comes.

MR. WEBB (*off stage*). Where's my girl? Where's my birthday girl?

EMILY (*in a loud voice to the* STAGE MANAGER). I can't. I can't go on. Oh! Oh. It goes so fast. We don't have time to look at one another. (*She breaks down sobbing. At a gesture from the* STAGE MANAGER, MRS WEBB *disappears*) I didn't realize. So all that was going on and we never noticed. Take me back—up the hill—to my grave. But first: Wait! One more look. Good-by, good-by, world. Good-by, Grover's Corners . . . Mama and Papa. Good-by to clocks ticking . . . and Mama's sunflowers. And food and coffee. And new-ironed dresses and hot baths . . . and sleeping and waking up. Oh, earth, you're too wonderful for anybody to realize you. (*She looks toward the* STAGE MANAGER *and asks abruptly, through her tears*) Do any human beings ever realize life while they live it?—every, every minute?

STAGE MANAGER. No. (*Pause*) The saints and poets, maybe—they do some.

EMILY. I'm ready to go back. (*She returns to her chair beside* MRS. GIBBS) Mother Gibbs, I should have listened to you. Now I want to be quiet for a while.—Oh, Mother Gibbs, I saw it all. I saw your garden.

MRS. GIBBS. Did you, dear?

EMILY. That's all human beings are! —Just blind people.

MRS. GIBBS. Look, it's clearing up. The stars are coming out.

EMILY. Oh, Mr. Stimson, I should have listened to them.

SIMON STIMSON (*with mounting violence; bitingly*). Yes, now you know. Now you know! That's what it was to be alive. To move about in a cloud of ignorance; to go up and down trampling on the feelings of those . . . of those about you. To spend and waste time as though you had a million years. To be always at the mercy of one self-centered passion, or another. Now you know—that's the happy existence you wanted to go back and see. Did you shout to 'em? Did you call to 'em?

EMILY. Yes, I did.

SIMON STIMSON. Now you know them as they are: in ignorance and blindness.

MRS. GIBBS (*spiritedly*). Simon Stimson, that ain't the whole truth and you know it.
(*The dead have begun to stir.*)

THE DEAD. Lemuel, wind's coming up, seems like.—Oh, dear,—I keep remembering things tonight.—It's right cold for June, ain't it?

MRS. GIBBS. Look what you've done, you and your rebellious spirit stirring us up here.—Emily, look at that star. I forget its name.

THE DEAD. I'm getting to know them all, but I don't know their names.—My boy Joel was a sailor,—knew 'em all. He'd set on the porch evenings and tell 'em all by name. Yes, sir, it was wonderful.—A star's mighty good company.—Yes, yes.—Yes, 'tis.

SIMON STIMSON. Here's one of *them* coming.

THE DEAD. That's funny. 'Tain't no time for one of them to be here.—Goodness sakes.

EMILY. Mother Gibbs, it's George.

MRS. GIBBS. Sh, dear. You just rest yourself.

EMILY. It's George.
(GEORGE *enters from the left, and slowly comes toward them.*)

A MAN FROM AMONG THE DEAD. And my boy, Joel, who knew the stars-he used to say it took millions of years for that speck o' light to git to the earth. Don't seem like a body could believe it, but that's what he used to say—millions of years.

ANOTHER. That's what they say.
(GEORGE *flings himself on* EMILY'S *grave.*)

THE DEAD. Goodness! That ain't no way to behave!—He ought to be home.

EMILY. Mother Gibbs?

MRS. GIBBS. Yes, Emily?

EMILY. They don't understand much, do they?

MRS. GIBBS. No, dear, not very much.
(*The* STAGE MANAGER *appears at the right, one hand on a dark curtain which he slowly draws across the scene. In the distance a clock is heard striking the hour very faintly.*)

STAGE MANAGER. Most everybody's asleep in Grover's Corners. There are a few lights on: Shorty Hawkins, down at the depot, has just watched the Albany train go by. And at the livery stable somebody's setting up late and talking.—Yes, it's clearing up. There are the stars—doing their old, old criss-cross journeys in the sky. Scholars haven't settled the matter yet, but they seem to think there are no living beings up there. They're just chalk . . . or fire. Only this one is straining away, straining away all the time to make something of itself. The strain's so bad that every sixteen hours everybody lies down and gets a rest. (*He winds his watch*) Hm. . . . Eleven o'clock in Grover's Corners. —You get a good rest, too. Good-night.

The Little Foxes

BY LILLIAN HELLMAN

"Take us the foxes, the little foxes,
that spoil the vines; for our vines
have tender grapes."

FOR ARTHUR KOBER AND LOUIS KRONENBERGER
WHO HAVE BEEN MY GOOD FRIENDS

The Little Foxes was first produced at the National Theatre, New York City, by Herman Shumlin, on February 15, 1939, and closed on January 20, 1940. Following is the original cast:

ADDIE	Abbie Mitchell
CAL	John Marriott
BIRDIE HUBBARD	Patricia Collinge
OSCAR HUBBARD	Carl Benton Reid
LEO HUBBARD	Dan Duryea
REGINA GIDDENS	Tallulah Bankhead
WILLIAM MARSHALL	Lee Baker
BENJAMIN HUBBARD	Charles Dingle
ALEXANDRA GIDDENS	Florence Williams
HORACE GIDDENS	Frank Conroy

Produced and staged by Herman Shumlin

Settings designed by Howard Bay

Costumes designed by Aline Bernstein

SCENES

The scene of the play is the living room of the Giddens house, in a small town in the South

ACT ONE

The spring of 1900, evening

ACT TWO

A week later, early morning

ACT THREE

Two weeks later, late afternoon

There has been no attempt to write Southern dialect. It is to be understood that the accents are Southern.

THE LITTLE FOXES

ACT ONE

SCENE—*The living room of the Giddens house, in a small town in the deep South, the spring of 1900. Upstage is a staircase leading to the second story. Upstage, right, are double doors to the dining room. When these doors are open we see a section of the dining room and the furniture. Upstage, left, is an entrance hall with a coat rack and umbrella stand. There are large lace-curtained windows on the left wall. The room is lit by a center gas chandelier and painted china oil lamps on the tables. Against the wall is a large piano. Downstage, right, are a high couch, a large table, several chairs. Against the left back wall are a table and several chairs. Near the window there are a smaller couch and tables. The room is good-looking, the furniture expensive; but it reflects no particular taste. Everything is of the best and that is all.*

AT RISE—ADDIE, *a tall, nice-looking Negro woman of about fifty-five, is closing the windows. From behind the closed dining-room doors there is the sound of voices. After a second,* CAL, *a middle-aged Negro, comes in from the entrance hall carrying a tray with glasses and a bottle of port.* ADDIE *crosses, takes the tray from him, puts it on table, begins to arrange it.*

ADDIE (*pointing to the bottle*). You gone stark out of your head?

CAL. No, smart lady, I ain't. Miss Regina told me to get out that bottle. (*Points to bottle*) That very bottle for the mighty honored guest. When Miss Regina changes orders like that you can bet your dime she got her reason.

ADDIE (*points to dining room*). Go on. You'll be needed.

CAL. Miss Zan she had two helpings frozen fruit cream and she tell that honored guest, she tell him that you make the best frozen fruit cream in all the South.

ADDIE (*smiles, pleased*). Did she? Well, see that Belle saves a little for her. She like it right before she go to bed. Save a few little cakes, too, she like—

(*The dining-room doors are opened and quickly closed again by* BIRDIE HUBBARD. BIRDIE *is a woman of about forty, with a pretty, well-bred, faded face. Her movements are usually nervous and timid, but now, as she comes running into the room, she is gay and excited.* CAL *turns to* BIRDIE.)

BIRDIE. Oh, Cal. (*Closes door*) I want you to get one of the kitchen boys to run home for me. He's to look in my desk drawer and— (*To* ADDIE) My, Addie. What a good supper! Just as good as good can be.

ADDIE. You look pretty this evening, Miss Birdie, and young.

BIRDIE (*laughing*). Me, young? (*Turns back to* CAL) Maybe you better find Simon and tell him to do it himself. He's to look in my desk, the left drawer, and bring my music album right away. Mr. Marshall is very anxious to see it because of his father and the opera in Chicago. (*To* ADDIE) Mr. Marshall is such a polite man with his manners and very educated and cultured and I've told him all about how my mamma and papa used to go to Europe for the music— (*Laughs. To* ADDIE) Imagine going all the way to Europe just to listen to music. Wouldn't that be nice, Addie? Just to sit there and listen and— (*Turns and steps to* CAL) Left drawer, Cal. Tell him that twice because he forgets. And tell him not to let any of the things drop out of the album and to bring it right in here when he comes back.

(*The dining-room doors are opened and quickly closed by* OSCAR HUBBARD. *He is a man in his late forties.*)

CAL. Yes'm. But Simon he won't get it right. But I'll tell him.

BIRDIE. Left drawer, Cal, and tell him to bring the blue book and—

OSCAR (*sharply*). Birdie.

BIRDIE (*turning nervously*). Oh, Oscar. I was just sending Simon for my music album.

OSCAR (*to* CAL). Never mind about the album. Miss Birdie has changed her mind.

BIRDIE. But, really, Oscar. Really I promised Mr. Marshall. I— (CAL *looks at them, exits.*)

OSCAR. Why do you leave the dinner table and go running about like a child?

BIRDIE (*trying to be gay*). But, Oscar, Mr. Marshall said most specially he *wanted* to see my album. I told him about the time Mama met Wagner, and Mrs. Wagner gave her the signed program and the big picture. Mr. Marshall wants to see that. Very, very much. We had such a nice talk and—

OSCAR (*taking a step to her*). You have been chattering to him like a magpie. You haven't let him be for a second. I can't think he came South to be bored with you.

BIRDIE (*quickly, hurt*). He wasn't bored. I don't believe he was bored. He's a very educated, cultured gentleman. (*Her voice rises*) I just don't believe it. You always talk like that when I'm having a nice time.

OSCAR (*turning to her, sharply*). You have had too much wine. Get yourself in hand now.

BIRDIE (*drawing back, about to cry, shrilly*). What am I doing? I am not doing anything. What am I doing?

OSCAR (*taking a step to her, tensely*). I said get yourself in hand. Stop acting like a fool.

BIRDIE (*turns to him, quietly*). I don't believe he was bored. I just don't believe it. Some people like music and like to talk about it. That's all I was doing.

(LEO HUBBARD *comes hurrying through the dining-room door. He is a young man of twenty, with a weak kind of good looks.*)

LEO. Mama! Papa! They are coming in now.

OSCAR (*softly*). Sit down, Birdie. Sit down now. (BIRDIE *sits down, bows* her head as if to hide her face.)

(The dining-room doors are opened by CAL. *We see people beginning to rise from the table.* REGINA GIDDENS *comes in with* WILLIAM MARSHALL. REGINA *is a handsome woman of forty.* MARSHALL *is forty-five, pleasant-looking, self-possessed. Behind them comes* ALEXANDRA GIDDENS, *a very pretty, rather delicate-looking girl of seventeen. She is followed by* BENJAMIN HUBBARD, *fifty-five, with a large jovial face and the light graceful movements that one often finds in large men.)*

REGINA. Mr. Marshall, I think you're trying to console me. Chicago may be the noisiest, dirtiest city in the world but I should still prefer it to the sound of our horses and the smell of our azaleas. I should like crowds of people, and theatres, and lovely women— *Very* lovely women, Mr. Marshall?

MARSHALL *(crossing to sofa)*. In Chicago? Oh, I suppose so. But I can tell you this: I've never dined there with three *such* lovely ladies.

*(*ADDIE *begins to pass the port.)*

BEN. Our Southern women are well favored.

LEO *(laughs)*. But one must go to Mobile for the ladies, sir. Very elegant worldly ladies, too.

BEN *(looks at him very deliberately)*. Worldly, eh? *Worldly*, did you say?

OSCAR *(hastily, to* LEO*)*. Your uncle Ben means that worldliness is not a mark of beauty in any woman.

LEO *(quickly)*. Of course, Uncle Ben. I didn't mean—

MARSHALL. Your port is excellent, Mrs. Giddens.

REGINA. Thank you, Mr. Marshall. We had been saving that bottle, hoping we could open it just for you.

ALEXANDRA *(as* ADDIE *comes to her with the tray)*. Oh. May I *really*, Addie?

ADDIE. Better ask Mama.

ALEXANDRA. May I, Mama?

REGINA *(nods, smiles)*. In Mr. Marshall's honor.

ALEXANDRA *(smiles)*. Mr. Marshall, this will be the first taste of port I've ever had.

*(*ADDIE *serves* LEO.*)*

MARSHALL. No one ever had their first taste of a better port. *(He lifts his glass in a toast; she lifts hers; they both drink)* Well, I suppose it is all true, Mrs. Giddens.

REGINA. What is true?

MARSHALL. That you Southerners occupy a unique position in America. You live better than the rest of us, you eat better, you drink better. I wonder you find time, or want to find time, to do business.

BEN. A great many Southerners don't.

MARSHALL. Do all of you live here together?

REGINA. Here with me? *(Laughs)* Oh, no. My brother Ben lives next door. My brother Oscar and his family live in the next square.

BEN. But we are a very close family. We've always *wanted* it that way.

MARSHALL. That is very pleasant. Keeping your family together to share each other's lives. My family moves around too much. My children seem never to come home. Away at school in the winter; in the summer, Europe with their mother—

REGINA (*eagerly*). Oh, yes. Even down here we read about Mrs. Marshall in the society pages.

MARSHALL. I dare say. She moves about a great deal. And all of you are part of the same business? Hubbard Sons?

BEN (*motions to* OSCAR). Oscar and me. (*Motions to* REGINA) My sister's good husband is a banker.

MARSHALL (*looks at* REGINA, *surprised*). Oh.

REGINA. I am so sorry that my husband isn't here to meet you. He's been very ill. He is at Johns Hopkins. But he will be home soon. We think he is getting better now.

LEO. I work for Uncle Horace. (REGINA *looks at him*) I mean I work for Uncle Horace at his bank. I keep an eye on things while he's away.

REGINA (*smiles*). Really, Leo?

BEN (*looks at* LEO, *then to* MARSHALL). Modesty in the young is as excellent as it is rare. (*Looks at* LEO *again.*)

OSCAR (*to* LEO). Your uncle means that a young man should speak more modestly.

LEO (*hastily, taking a step to* BEN). Oh, I didn't mean, sir—

MARSHALL. Oh, Mrs. Hubbard. Where's that Wagner autograph you promised to let me see? My train will be leaving soon and—

BIRDIE. The autograph? Oh. Well. Really, Mr. Marshall, I didn't mean to chatter so about it. Really I— (*Nervously, looking at* OSCAR) You must excuse me. I didn't get it because, well, because I had—I—I had a little headache and—

OSCAR. My wife is a miserable victim of headaches.

REGINA (*quickly*). Mr. Marshall said at supper that he would like you to play for him, Alexandra.

ALEXANDRA (*who has been looking at* BIRDIE). It's not I who play well, sir. It's my aunt. She plays just wonderfully. She's my teacher. (*Rises. Eagerly*) May we play a duet? May we, Mama?

BIRDIE (*taking* ALEXANDRA'S *hand*). Thank you, dear. But I have my headache now. I—

OSCAR (*sharply*). Don't be stubborn, Birdie. Mr. Marshall wants you to play.

MARSHALL. Indeed I do. If your headache isn't—

BIRDIE (*hesitates, then gets up, pleased*). But I'd like to, sir. Very much. (*She and* ALEXANDRA *go to the piano.*)

MARSHALL. It's very remarkable how you Southern aristocrats have kept together. Kept together and kept what belonged to you.

BEN. You misunderstand, sir. Southern aristocrats have *not* kept together and have *not* kept what belonged to them.

MARSHALL (*laughs, indicates room*). You don't call this keeping what belongs to you?

BEN. But we are not aristocrats. (*Points to* BIRDIE *at the piano*) Our brother's wife is the only one of us who belongs to the Southern aristocracy.
(BIRDIE *looks towards* BEN.)

MARSHALL (*smiles*). My information is that you people have been here, and solidly here, for a long time.

OSCAR. And so we have. Since our great-grandfather.

BEN (*smiles*). Who was *not* an aristocrat, like Birdie's.

MARSHALL (*a little sharply*). You make great distinctions.

BEN. Oh, they have been made for us. And maybe they are important distinctions. (*Leans forward, intimately*) Now you take Birdie's family. When my great-grandfather came here they were the highest-tone plantation owners in this state.

LEO (*steps to* MARSHALL. *Proudly*). My mother's grandfather was *governor* of the state before the war.

OSCAR. They owned the plantation, Lionnet. You may have heard of it, sir?

MARSHALL (*laughs*). No, I've never heard of anything but brick houses on a lake, and cotton mills.

BEN. Lionnet in its day was the best cotton land in the South. It still brings us in a fair crop. (*Sits back*) Ah, they were great days for those people—even when I can remember. They had the best of everything. (BIRDIE *turns to them*) Cloth from Paris, trips to Europe, horses you can't raise any more, niggers to lift their fingers—

BIRDIE (*suddenly*). We were good to our people. Everybody knew that. We were better to them than—
(MARSHALL *looks up at* BIRDIE.)

REGINA. Why, Birdie. You aren't playing.

BEN. But when the war comes these fine gentlemen ride off and leave the cotton, *and* the women, to rot.

BIRDIE. My father was killed in the war. He was a fine soldier, Mr. Marshall. A fine man.

REGINA. Oh, certainly, Birdie. A famous soldier.

BEN (*to* BIRDIE). But that isn't the tale I am telling Mr. Marshall. (*To* MARSHALL) Well, sir, the war ends. (BIRDIE *goes back to piano*) Lionnet is almost ruined, and the sons finish ruining it. And there were thousands like them. Why? (*Leans forward*) Because the Southern aristocrat can adapt himself to nothing. Too high-tone to try.

MARSHALL. Sometimes it is difficult to learn new ways. (BIRDIE *and* ALEXANDRA *begin to play*. MARSHALL *leans forward, listening*.)

BEN. Perhaps, perhaps. (*He sees that* MARSHALL *is listening to the music. Irritated, he turns to* BIRDIE *and* ALEXANDRA *at the piano, then back to* MARSHALL) You're right, Mr.

Marshall. It is difficult to learn new ways. But maybe that's why it's profitable. *Our* grandfather and *our* father learned the new ways and learned how to make them pay. They work. (*Smiles nastily*) *They* are in trade. Hubbard Sons, Merchandise. Others, Birdie's family, for example, look down on them. (*Settles back in chair*) To make a long story short, Lionnet now belongs to *us*. (BIRDIE *stops playing*) Twenty years ago we took over their land, their cotton, and their daughter. (BIRDIE *rises and stands stiffly by the piano.* MARSHALL, *who has been watching her, rises.*)

MARSHALL. May I bring you a glass of port, Mrs. Hubbard?

BIRDIE (*softly*). No, thank you, sir. You are most polite.

REGINA (*sharply, to* BEN). You are boring Mr. Marshall with these ancient family tales.

BEN. I hope not. I hope not. I am trying to make an important point—(*Bows to* MARSHALL) for our future business partner.

OSCAR (*to* MARSHALL). My brother always says that it's folks like us who have struggled and fought to bring to our land some of the prosperity of your land.

BEN. Some people call that patriotism.

REGINA (*laughs gaily*). I hope you don't find my brothers too obvious, Mr. Marshall. I'm afraid they mean that this is the time for the ladies to leave the gentlemen to talk business.

MARSHALL (*hastily*). Not at all. We settled everything this afternoon. (MARSHALL *looks at his watch*) I have only a few minutes before I must leave for the train. (*Smiles at her*) And I insist they be spent with you.

REGINA. *And* with another glass of port.

MARSHALL. Thank you.

BEN (*to* REGINA). My sister is right. (*To* MARSHALL) I am a plain man and I am trying to say a plain thing. A man ain't only in business for what he can get out of it. It's got to give him something here. (*Puts hand to his breast*) That's every bit as true for the nigger picking cotton for a silver quarter, as it is for you and me. (REGINA *gives* MARSHALL *a glass of port*) If it don't give him something here, then he don't pick the cotton right. Money isn't all. Not by three shots.

MARSHALL. Really? Well, I always thought it was a great deal.

REGINA. And so did I, Mr. Marshall.

MARSHALL (*leans forward. Pleasantly, but with meaning*). Now you don't have to convince me that you are the right people for the deal. I wouldn't be here if you hadn't convinced me six months ago. You want the mill here, and I want it here. It isn't my business to find out *why* you want it.

BEN. To bring the machine to the cotton, and not the cotton to the machine.

MARSHALL (*amused*). You have a turn for neat phrases, Hubbard.

Well, however grand your reasons are, mine are simple: I want to make money and I believe I'll make it on you. (*As* BEN *starts to speak, he smiles*) Mind you, I have no objections to more high-minded reasons. They are mighty valuable in business. It's fine to have partners who so closely follow the teachings of Christ. (*Gets up*) And now I must leave for my train.

REGINA. I'm sorry you won't stay over with us, Mr. Marshall, but you'll come again. Any time you like.

BEN (*motions to* LEO, *indicating the bottle*). Fill them up, boy, fill them up. (LEO *moves around filling the glasses as* BEN *speaks*) Down here, sir, we have a strange custom. We drink the *last* drink for a toast. That's to prove that the Southerner is always still on his feet for the last drink. (*Picks up his glass*) It was Henry Frick, your Mr. Henry Frick, who said, "Railroads are the Rembrandts of investments." Well, *I* say, "Southern cotton mills *will be* the Rembrandts of investment." So I give you the firm of Hubbard Sons and Marshall, Cotton Mills, and to it a long and prosperous life.

(*They all pick up their glasses.* MARSHALL *looks at them, amused. Then he, too, lifts his glass, smiles.*)

OSCAR. The children will drive you to the depot. Leo! Alexandra! You will drive Mr. Marshall down.

LEO (*eagerly, looks at* BEN *who nods*). Yes, sir. (*To* MARSHALL) Not often Uncle Ben lets *me* drive the horses. And a beautiful pair they are. (*Starts for hall*) Come on, Zan.

ALEXANDRA. May I drive tonight, Uncle Ben, please? I'd like to and—

BEN (*shakes his head, laughs*). In your evening clothes? Oh, no, my dear.

ALEXANDRA. But Leo always—(*Stops, exits quickly.*)

REGINA. I don't like to say good-bye to you, Mr. Marshall.

MARSHALL. Then we won't say goodbye. You have promised that you would come and let me show you Chicago. Do I have to make you promise again?

REGINA (*looks at him as he presses her hand*). I promise again.

MARSHALL (*touches her hand again, then moves to* BIRDIE). Good-bye, Mrs. Hubbard.

BIRDIE (*shyly, with sweetness and dignity*). Good-bye, sir.

MARSHALL (*as he passes* REGINA). Remember.

REGINA. I will.

OSCAR. We'll see you to the carriage. (MARSHALL *exits, followed by* BEN *and* OSCAR. *For a second* REGINA *and* BIRDIE *stand looking after them. Then* REGINA *throws up her arms, laughs happily.*)

REGINA. And there, Birdie, goes the man who has opened the door to our future.

BIRDIE (*surprised at the unaccustomed friendliness*). What?

REGINA (*turning to her*). *Our future.* Yours and mine, Ben's and Oscar's, the children— (*Looks at* BIRDIE's *puzzled face, laughs*) Our future! (*Gaily*) You were charming at supper, Birdie. Mr. Marshall certainly thought so.

BIRDIE (*pleased*). Why, Regina! Do you think he did?

REGINA. Can't you tell when you're being admired?

BIRDIE. Oscar said I bored Mr. Marshall. (*Then quietly*) But he admired *you*. He told me so.

REGINA. What did he say?

BIRDIE. He said to me, "I hope your sister-in-law will come to Chicago. Chicago will be at her feet." He said the ladies would bow to your manners and the gentlemen to your looks.

REGINA. Did he? He seems a lonely man. Imagine being lonely with all that money. I don't think he likes his wife.

BIRDIE. Not like his wife? What a thing to say.

REGINA. She's away a great deal. He said that several times. And once he made fun of her being so social and high-tone. But that fits in all right. (*Sits back, arms on back of sofa, stretches*) Her being social, I mean. She can introduce me. It won't take long with an introduction from her.

BIRDIE (*bewildered*). Introduce you? In Chicago? You mean you really might go? Oh, Regina, you can't leave here. What about Horace?

REGINA. Don't look so scared about everything, Birdie. I'm going to live in Chicago. I've always wanted to. And now there'll be plenty of money to go with.

BIRDIE. But Horace won't be able to move around. You know what the doctor wrote.

REGINA. There'll be millions, Birdie, millions. You know what I've always said when people told me we were rich? I said I think you should either be a nigger or a millionaire. In between, like us, what for? (*Laughs. Looks at* BIRDIE) But I'm not going away tomorrow, Birdie. There's plenty of time to worry about Horace when he comes home. If he ever decides to come home.

BIRDIE. Will we be going to Chicago? I mean, Oscar and Leo and me?

REGINA. You? I shouldn't think so (*Laughs*) Well, we must remember tonight. It's a very important night and we mustn't forget it. We shall plan all the things we'd like to have and then we'll really have them. Make a wish, Birdie, any wish. It's bound to come true now.
(BEN *and* OSCAR *enter.*)

BIRDIE (*laughs*). Well. Well, I don't know. Maybe. (REGINA *turns to look at* BEN) Well, I guess I'd know right off what I wanted.
(OSCAR *stands by the upper window, waves to the departing carriage.*)

REGINA (*looks up at* BEN, *smiles. He smiles back at her*). Well, you did it.

BEN. Looks like it might be we did.

REGINA (*springs up, laughs*). Looks like it! Don't pretend. You're like a cat who's been licking the cream. (*Crosses to wine bottle*) Now we must all have a drink to celebrate.

OSCAR. The children, Alexandra and Leo, make a very handsome couple,

Regina. Marshall remarked himself what fine young folks they were. How well they looked together!

REGINA (*sharply*). Yes. You said that before, Oscar.

BEN. Yes, sir. It's beginning to look as if the deal's all set. I may not be a subtle man—but— (*Turns to them. After a second*) Now somebody ask me how I know the deal is set.

OSCAR. What do you mean, Ben?

BEN. You remember I told him that down here we drink the *last* drink for a toast?

OSCAR (*thoughtfully*). Yes. I never heard that before.

BEN. Nobody's ever heard it before. God forgives those who invent what they need. I already had his signature. But we've all done business with men whose word over a glass is better than a bond. Anyway it don't hurt to have both.

OSCAR (*turns to* REGINA). You understand what Ben means?

REGINA (*smiles*). Yes, Oscar. I understand. I understood immediately.

BEN (*looks at her admiringly*). Did you, Regina? Well, when he lifted his glass to drink, I closed my eyes and saw the bricks going into place.

REGINA. And *I* saw a lot more than that.

BEN. Slowly, slowly. As yet we have only our hopes.

REGINA. Birdie and I have just been planning what we want. I know what I want. What will you want, Ben?

BEN. Caution. Don't count the chickens. (*Leans back, laughs*) Well, God would allow us a little daydreaming. Good for the soul when you've worked hard enough to deserve it. (*Pauses*) I think I'll have a stable. For a long time I've had my good eye on Carter's in Savannah. A rich man's pleasure, the sport of kings, why not the sport of Hubbards? Why not?

REGINA (*smiles*). Why not? What will you have, Oscar?

OSCAR. I don't know. (*Thoughtfully*) The pleasure of seeing the bricks grow will be enough for me.

BEN. Oh, of course. Our *greatest* pleasure will be to see the bricks grow. But we are all entitled to a little side indulgence.

OSCAR. Yes, I suppose so. Well, then, I think we might take a few trips here and there, eh, Birdie?

BIRDIE (*surprised at being consulted*). Yes, Oscar. I'd like that.

OSCAR. We might even make a regular trip to Jekyll Island. I've heard the Cornelly place is for sale. We might think about buying it. Make a nice change. Do you good, Birdie, a change of climate. Fine shooting on Jekyll, the best.

BIRDIE. I'd like—

OSCAR (*indulgently*). What would you like?

BIRDIE. *Two* things. Two things I'd like most.

REGINA. Two! I should like a thousand. You are modest, Birdie.

BIRDIE (*warmly, delighted with the unexpected interest*). I should like to have Lionnet back. I know you own it now, but I'd like to see it fixed up again, the way Mama and Papa had it. Every year it used to get a nice coat of paint—Papa was very particular about the paint—and the lawn was so smooth all the way down to the river, with the trims of zinnias and red-feather plush. And the figs and blue little plums and the scuppernongs— (*Smiles. Turns to* REGINA) The organ is still there and it wouldn't cost much to fix. We could have parties for Zan, the way Mama used to have for me.

BEN. That's a pretty picture, Birdie. Might be a most pleasant way to live. (*Dismissing* BIRDIE) What do you want, Regina?

BIRDIE (*very happily, not noticing that they are no longer listening to her*). I could have a cutting garden. Just where Mama's used to be. Oh, I do think we could be happier there. Papa used to say that *nobody* had ever lost their temper at Lionnet, and *nobody* ever would. Papa would never let anybody be nasty-spoken or mean. No, sir. He just didn't like it.

BEN. What do you want, Regina?

REGINA. I'm going to Chicago. And when I'm settled there and know the right people and the right things to buy—because I certainly don't now—I shall go to Paris and buy them. (*Laughs*) I'm going to leave you and Oscar to count the bricks.

BIRDIE. Oscar. Please let me have Lionnet back.

OSCAR (*to* REGINA). You are serious about moving to Chicago?

BEN. She is going to see the great world and leave us in the little one. Well, we'll come and visit you and meet all the great and be proud to think you are our sister.

REGINA (*gaily*). Certainly. And you won't even have to learn to be subtle, Ben. Stay as you are. You will be rich and the rich don't have to be subtle.

OSCAR. But what about Alexandra? She's seventeen. Old enough to be thinking about marrying.

BIRDIE. And, Oscar, I have one more wish. Just one more wish.

OSCAR (*turns*). What is it, Birdie? What are you saying?

BIRDIE. I want you to stop shooting. I mean, so much. I don't like to see animals and birds killed just for the killing. You only throw them away—

BEN (*to* REGINA). It'll take a great deal of money to live as you're planning, Regina.

REGINA. Certainly. But there'll be plenty of money. You have estimated the profits very high.

BEN. I have—

BIRDIE (OSCAR *is looking at her furiously*). And you never let anybody else shoot, and the niggers need it so much to keep from starving. It's wicked to shoot food just because you like to shoot, when poor people need it so—

BEN (*laughs*). I have estimated the profits very high—for myself.

REGINA. What did you say?

BIRDIE. I've always wanted to speak about it, Oscar.

OSCAR (*slowly, carefully*). What are you chattering about?

BIRDIE (*nervously*). I was talking about Lionnet and—and about your shooting—

OSCAR. You are exciting yourself.

REGINA (*to* BEN). I didn't hear you. There was so much talking.

OSCAR (*to* BIRDIE). You have been acting very childish, very excited, all evening.

BIRDIE. Regina asked me what I'd like.

REGINA. What did you say, Ben?

BIRDIE. Now that we'll be so rich everybody was saying what they would like, so *I* said what *I* would like, too.

BEN. I said— (*He is interrupted by* OSCAR.)

OSCAR (*to* BIRDIE). Very well. We've all heard you. That's enough now.

BEN. I am waiting. (*They stop*) I am waiting for you to finish. You and Birdie. Four conversations are three too many. (BIRDIE *slowly sits down.* BEN *smiles, to* REGINA) I said that I had, and I do, estimate the profits very high—for myself, and Oscar, of course.

REGINA (*slowly*). And what does that mean?
(BEN *shrugs, looks towards* OSCAR.)

OSCAR (*looks at* BEN, *clears throat*). Well, Regina, it's like this. For forty-nine per cent Marshall will put up four hundred thousand dollars. For fifty-one per cent— (*Smiles archly*) a controlling interest, mind you, we will put up two hundred and twenty-five thousand dollars besides offering him certain benefits that our (*Looks at* BEN) local position allows us to manage. Ben means that two hundred and twenty-five thousand dollars is a lot of money.

REGINA. I know the terms and I know it's a lot of money.

BEN (*nodding*). It is.

OSCAR. Ben means that we are ready with our two-thirds of the money. Your third, Horace's I mean, doesn't seem to be ready. (*Raises his hand as* REGINA *starts to speak*) Ben has written to Horace, I have written, and you have written. He answers. But he never mentions this business. Yet we have explained it to him in great detail, and told him the urgency. Still he never mentions it. Ben has been very patient, Regina. Naturally, you are our sister and we want you to benefit from anything we do.

REGINA. And in addition to your concern for me, you do not want control to go out of the family. (*To* BEN) That right, Ben?

BEN. That's cynical. (*Smiles*) Cynicism is an unpleasant way of saying the truth.

OSCAR. No need to be cynical. We'd have no trouble raising the third share, the share that you want to take.

REGINA. I am sure you could get the third share, the share you were sav ing for me. But that would give you a strange partner. And strange partners sometimes want a great deal. (*Smiles unpleasantly*) But perhaps it would be wise for you to find him.

OSCAR. Now, now. Nobody says we *want* to do that. We would like to have you in and you would like to come in.

REGINA. Yes. I certainly would.

BEN (*laughs, puts up his hand*). But we haven't heard from Horace.

REGINA. I've given my word that Horace will put up the money. That should be enough.

BEN. Oh, it was enough. I took your word. But I've got to have more than your word now. The contracts will be signed this week, and Marshall will want to see our money soon after. Regina, Horace has been in Baltimore for five months. I know that you've written him to come home, and that he hasn't come.

OSCAR. It's beginning to look as if he doesn't want to come home.

REGINA. Of course he wants to come home. You can't move around with heart trouble at any moment you choose. You know what doctors are like once they get their hands on a case like this—

OSCAR. They can't very well keep him from answering letters, can they? (REGINA *turns to* BEN) They couldn't keep him from arranging for the money if he wanted to—

REGINA. Has it occurred to you that Horace is also a good business man?

BEN. Certainly. He is a shrewd trader. Always has been. The bank is proof of that.

REGINA. Then, possibly, he may be keeping silent because he doesn't think he is getting enough for his money. (*Looks at* OSCAR) Seventy-five thousand he has to put up. That's a lot of money, too.

OSCAR. Nonsense. He knows a good thing when he hears it. He knows that we can make *twice* the profit on cotton goods manufactured *here* than can be made in the North.

BEN. That isn't what Regina means. (*Smiles*) May I interpret you, Regina? (*To* OSCAR) Regina is saying that Horace wants *more* than a third of our share.

OSCAR. But he's only putting up a third of the money. You put up a third and you get a third. What else *could* he expect?

REGINA. Well, *I* don't know. I don't know about these things. It would seem that if you put up a third you should only get a third. But then again, there's no law about it, is there? I should think that if you knew your money was very badly needed, well, you just might say, I want more, I want a bigger share. You boys have done that. I've heard you say so.

BEN (*after a pause, laughs*). So you believe he has deliberately held out? For a larger share? (*Leaning forward*) Well, I *don't* believe it. But I *do* believe that's what *you* want. Am I right, Regina?

REGINA. Oh, I shouldn't like to be too definite. But I *could* say that I wouldn't like to persuade Horace unless he did get a larger share. I must look after his interests. It seems only natural—

OSCAR. And where would the larger share come from?

REGINA. I don't know. That's not my business. (*Giggles*) But perhaps it could come off your share, Oscar. (REGINA *and* BEN *laugh.*)

OSCAR (*rises and wheels furiously on both of them as they laugh*). What kind of talk is this?

BEN. I haven't said a thing.

OSCAR (*to* REGINA). *You* are talking very big tonight.

REGINA (*stops laughing*). Am I? Well, you should know me well enough to know that I wouldn't be asking for things I didn't think I could get.

OSCAR. Listen. I don't believe you can even get Horace to come home, much less get money from him or talk quite so big about what you want.

REGINA. Oh, I can get him home.

OSCAR. Then why haven't you?

REGINA. I thought I should fight his battles for him, before he came home. Horace is a very sick man. And even if *you* don't care how sick he is, I do.

BEN. Stop this foolish squabbling. How can you get him home?

REGINA. I will send Alexandra to Baltimore. She will ask him to come home. She will say that she *wants* him to come home, and that *I* want him to come home.

BIRDIE (*suddenly*). Well, of course she wants him here, but he's sick and maybe he's happy where he is.

REGINA (*ignores* BIRDIE, *to* BEN). You agree that he will come home if she asks him to, if she says that I miss him and want him—

BEN (*looks at her, smiles*). I admire you, Regina. And I agree. That's settled now and— (*Starts to rise.*)

REGINA (*quickly*). But before she brings him home, I want to know what he's going to get.

BEN. What do you want?

REGINA. Twice what you offered.

BEN. Well, you won't get it.

OSCAR (*to* REGINA). I think you've gone crazy.

REGINA. I don't want to fight, Ben—

BEN. I don't either. You won't get it. There isn't any chance of that. (*Roguishly*) You're holding us up, and that's not pretty, Regina, not pretty. (*Holds up his hand as he sees she is about to speak*) But we need you, and I don't want to fight. Here's what I'll do: I'll give Horace forty per cent, instead of the thirty-three and a third he really should get. I'll do that, provided he is home and his money is up within two weeks. How's that?

REGINA. All right.

OSCAR. I've asked before: where is this extra share coming from?

BEN (*pleasantly*). From you. From your share.

OSCAR (*furiously*). From me, is it? That's just fine and dandy. That's my reward. For thirty-five years I've worked my hands to the bone for you. For thirty-five years I've done all the things you didn't want to do. And this is what I—

BEN (*turns slowly to look at* OSCAR. OSCAR *breaks off*). My, my. I am being attacked tonight on all sides. First by my sister, then by my brother. And I ain't a man who likes being attacked. I can't believe that God wants the strong to parade their strength, but I don't mind doing it if it's got to be done. (*Leans back in his chair*) You ought to take these things better, Oscar. I've made you money in the past. I'm going to make you more money now. You'll be a very rich man. What's the difference to any of us if a little more goes here, a little less goes there—it's all in the family. And it will stay in the family. I'll never marry. (ADDIE *enters, begins to gather the glasses from the table.* OSCAR *turns to* BEN) So my money will go to Alexandra and Leo. They may even marry some day and— (ADDIE *looks at* BEN.)

BIRDIE (*rising*). Marry—Zan and Leo—

OSCAR (*carefully*). That would make a great difference in my feelings. If they married.

BEN. Yes, that's what I mean. Of course it would make a difference.

OSCAR (*carefully*). Is that what *you* mean, Regina?

REGINA. Oh, it's too far away. We'll talk about it in a few years.

OSCAR. I want to talk about it now.

BEN (*nods*). Naturally.

REGINA. There's a lot of things to consider. They are first cousins, and—

OSCAR. That isn't unusual. Our grandmother and grandfather were first cousins.

REGINA (*giggles*). And look at us. (BEN *giggles.*)

OSCAR (*angrily*). You're both being very gay with my money.

BEN (*sighs*). These quarrels. I dislike them so. (*Leans forward to* REGINA) A marriage might be a very wise arrangement, for several reasons. And then, Oscar has given up something for you. You should try to manage something for him.

REGINA. I haven't said I was opposed to it. But Leo is a wild boy. There were those times when he took a little money from the bank and—

OSCAR. That's all past history—

REGINA. Oh, I know. And I know all young men are wild. I'm only mentioning it to show you that there are considerations—

BEN (*irritated because she does not understand that he is trying to keep* OSCAR *quiet*). All right, so there are. But please assure Oscar that you will think about it very seriously.

REGINA (*smiles, nods*). Very well. I assure Oscar that I will think about it seriously.

OSCAR (*sharply*). That is not an answer.

REGINA (*rises*). My, you're in a bad humor and you shall put me in one. I have said all that I am willing to say now. After all, Horace has to give his consent, too.

OSCAR. Horace will do what you tell him to.

REGINA. Yes, I think he will.

OSCAR. And I have your word that you will try to—

REGINA (*patiently*). Yes, Oscar. You have my word that I will think about it. Now do leave me alone.
(*There is the sound of the front door being closed.*)

BIRDIE. I—Alexandra is only seventeen. She—

REGINA (*calling*). Alexandra? Are you back?

ALEXANDRA. Yes, Mama.

LEO (*comes into the room*). Mr. Marshall got off safe and sound. Weren't those fine clothes he had? You can always spot clothes made in a good place. Looks like maybe they were done in England. Lots of men in the North send all the way to England for their stuff.

BEN (*to* LEO). Were you careful driving the horses?

LEO. Oh, yes, sir. I was.
(ALEXANDRA *has come in on* BEN'S *question, hears the answer, looks angrily at* LEO.)

ALEXANDRA. It's a lovely night. You should have come, Aunt Birdie.

REGINA. Were you gracious to Mr. Marshall?

ALEXANDRA. I think so, Mama. I liked him.

REGINA. Good. And now I have great news for you. You are going to Baltimore in the morning to bring your father home.

ALEXANDRA (*gasps, then delighted*). Me? Papa said I should come? That must mean— (*Turns to* ADDIE) Addie, he must be well. Think of it, he'll be back home again. We'll bring him home.

REGINA. You are going alone, Alexandra.

ADDIE (ALEXANDRA *has turned in surprise*). Going alone? Going by herself? A child that age! Mr. Horace ain't going to like Zan traipsing up there by herself.

REGINA (*sharply*). Go upstairs and lay out Alexandra's things.

ADDIE. He'd expect me to be along—

REGINA. I'll be up in a few minutes to tell you what to pack. (ADDIE *slowly begins to climb the steps. To* ALEXANDRA) I should think you'd like going alone. At your age it certainly would have delighted me. You're a strange girl, Alexandra. Addie has babied you so much.

ALEXANDRA. I only thought it would be more fun if Addie and I went together.

BIRDIE (*timidly*). Maybe I could go with her, Regina. I'd really like to.

REGINA. She is going alone. She is getting old enough to take some responsibilities.

OSCAR. She'd better learn now. She's almost old enough to get married. (*Jovially, to* LEO, *slapping him on shoulder*) Eh, son?

LEO. Huh?

OSCAR (*annoyed with* LEO *for not understanding*). Old enough to get married, you're thinking, eh?

LEO. Oh, yes, sir. (*Feebly*) Lots of girls get married at Zan's age. Look at Mary Prester and Johanna and—

REGINA. Well, she's not getting married tomorrow. But she is going to Baltimore tomorrow, so let's talk about that. (*To* ALEXANDRA) You'll be glad to have Papa home again.

ALEXANDRA. I wanted to go before, Mama. You remember that. But you said *you* couldn't go, and that *I* couldn't go alone.

REGINA. I've changed my mind. (*Too casually*) You're to tell Papa how much you missed him, and that he must come home now—for your sake. Tell him that you *need* him home.

ALEXANDRA. Need him home? I don't understand.

REGINA. There is nothing for you to understand. You are simply to say what I have told you.

BIRDIE (*rises*). He may be too sick. She couldn't do that—

ALEXANDRA. Yes. He may be too sick to travel. I couldn't make him think he had to come home for me, if he is too sick to—

REGINA (*looks at her, sharply, challengingly*). You *couldn't* do what I tell you to do, Alexandra?

ALEXANDRA (*quietly*). No. I couldn't. If I thought it would hurt him.

REGINA (*after a second's silence, smiles pleasantly*). But you are doing this for Papa's own good. (*Takes* ALEXANDRA'S *hand*) You must let me be the judge of his condition. It's the best possible cure for him to come home and be taken care of here. He mustn't stay there any longer and listen to those alarmist doctors. You are doing this entirely for his sake. Tell your papa that I want him to come home, that I miss him very much.

ALEXANDRA (*slowly*). Yes, Mama.

REGINA (*to the others. Rises*). I must go and start getting Alexandra ready now. Why don't you all go home?

BEN (*rises*). I'll attend to the railroad ticket. One of the boys will bring it over. Good night, everybody. Have a nice trip, Alexandra. The food on the train is very good. The celery is so crisp. Have a good time and act like a little lady. (*Exits.*)

REGINA. Good night, Ben. Good night, Oscar— (*Playfully*) Don't be so glum, Oscar. It makes you look as if you had chronic indigestion.

BIRDIE. Good night, Regina.

REGINA. Good night, Birdie. (*Exits upstairs.*)

OSCAR (*starts for hall*). Come along.

LEO (*to* ALEXANDRA). Imagine your not wanting to go! What a little fool you are. Wish it were me. What I could do in a place like Baltimore!

ALEXANDRA (*angrily, looking away from him*). Mind your business. I can guess the kind of things *you* could do.

LEO (*laughs*). Oh, no, you couldn't. (*He exits.*)

REGINA (*calling from the top of the stairs*). Come on, Alexandra.

BIRDIE (*quickly, softly*). Zan.

ALEXANDRA. I don't understand about my going, Aunt Birdie. (*Shrugs*) But anyway, Papa will be home again. (*Pats* BIRDIE'S *arm*) Don't worry about me. I can take care of myself. Really I can.

BIRDIE (*shakes her head, softly*). That's not what I'm worried about. Zan—

ALEXANDRA (*comes close to her*). What's the matter?

BIRDIE. It's about Leo—

ALEXANDRA (*whispering*). He beat the horses. That's why we were late getting back. We had to wait until they cooled off. He always beats the horses as if—

BIRDIE (*whispering frantically, holding* ALEXANDRA'S *hands*). He's my son. My own son. But you are more to me—more to me than my own child. I love you more than anybody else—

ALEXANDRA. Don't worry about the horses. I'm sorry I told you.

BIRDIE (*her voice rising*). *I am not worrying about the horses.* I am worrying about *you*. You are *not* going to marry Leo. I am not going to let them do that to you—

ALEXANDRA. Marry? To Leo? (*Laughs*) I wouldn't marry, Aunt Birdie. I've never even thought about it—

BIRDIE. But they have thought about it. (*Wildly*) Zan, I couldn't stand to think about such a thing. You and—

(OSCAR *has come into the doorway on* ALEXANDRA'S *speech. He is standing quietly, listening.*)

ALEXANDRA (*laughs*). But I'm not going to marry. And I'm certainly not going to marry Leo.

BIRDIE. Don't you understand? They'll make you. They'll make you—

ALEXANDRA (*takes* BIRDIE'S *hands, quietly, firmly*). That's foolish, Aunt Birdie. I'm grown now. Nobody can make me do anything.

BIRDIE. I just couldn't stand—

OSCAR (*sharply*). Birdie. (BIRDIE *looks up, draws quickly away from* ALEXANDRA. *She stands rigid, frightened. Quietly*) Birdie, get your hat and coat.

ADDIE (*calls from upstairs*). Come on, baby. Your mama's waiting for you, and she ain't nobody to keep waiting.

ALEXANDRA. All right. (*Then softly, embracing* BIRDIE) Good night, Aunt Birdie. (*As she passes* OSCAR) Good night, Uncle Oscar. (BIRDIE *begins to move slowly towards the door as* ALEXANDRA *climbs the stairs.* ALEXANDRA *is almost out of view when* BIRDIE *reaches* OSCAR *in the doorway. As* BIRDIE *quickly attempts to pass him, he slaps her hard, across the face.* BIRDIE *cries out, puts her hand to her face. On the cry,* ALEXANDRA *turns, begins to run down the stairs*) Aunt Birdie! What happened? What happened? I—

BIRDIE (*softly, without turning*) Nothing, darling. Nothing happened. (*Quickly, as if anxious to keep* ALEXANDRA *from coming close*) Now go to bed. (OSCAR *exits*) Nothing happened. (*Turns to* ALEXANDRA *who is holding her hand*) I only—I only twisted my ankle. (*She goes out.* ALEXANDRA *stands on the stairs looking after her as if she were puzzled and frightened.*)

CURTAIN

ACT TWO

SCENE—*Same as Act One. A week later, morning.*

AT RISE—*The light comes from the open shutter of the right window; the other shutters are tightly closed.* ADDIE *is standing at the window, looking out. Near the dining-room doors are brooms, mops, rags, etc. After a second,* OSCAR *comes into the entrance hall, looks in the room, shivers, decides not to take his hat and coat off, comes into the room. At the sound of the door,* ADDIE *turns to see who has come in.*

ADDIE (*without interest*). Oh, it's you, Mr. Oscar.

OSCAR. What is this? It's not night. What's the matter here? (*Shivers*) Fine thing at this time of the morning. Blinds all closed. (ADDIE *begins to open shutters*) Where's Miss Regina? It's cold in here.

ADDIE. Miss Regina ain't down yet.

OSCAR. She had any word?

ADDIE (*wearily*). No, sir.

OSCAR. Wouldn't you think a girl that age could get on a train at one place and have sense enough to get off at another?

ADDIE. Something must have happened. If Zan say she was coming last night, she's coming last night. Unless something happened. Sure fire disgrace to let a baby like that go all that way alone to bring home a sick man without—

OSCAR. You do a lot of judging around here, Addie, eh? Judging of your white folks, I mean.

ADDIE (*looks at him, sighs*). I'm tired. I been up all night watching for them.

REGINA (*speaking from the upstairs hall*). Who's downstairs, Addie? (*She appears in a dressing gown, peers down from the landing.* ADDIE *picks up broom, dustpan and brush and exits*) Oh, it's you, Oscar. What are you doing here so early? I haven't been down yet. I'm not finished dressing.

OSCAR (*speaking up to her*). You had any word from them?

REGINA. No.

OSCAR. Then something certainly has happened. People don't just say they are arriving on Thursday night, and they haven't come by Friday morning.

REGINA. Oh, nothing has happened. Alexandra just hasn't got sense enough to send a message.

OSCAR. If nothing's happened, then why aren't they here?

REGINA. You asked me that ten times last night. My, you do fret so, Oscar. Anything might have happened. They may have missed connections in Atlanta, the train may have been delayed—oh, a hundred things could have kept them.

OSCAR. Where's Ben?

REGINA (*as she disappears upstairs*). Where should he be? At home, probably. Really, Oscar, I don't tuck him in his bed and I don't take him out of it. Have some coffee and don't worry so much.

OSCAR. Have some coffee? There isn't any coffee. (*Looks at his watch, shakes his head. After a second* CAL *enters with a large silver tray, coffee urn, small cups, newspaper*). Oh, there you are. Is everything in this fancy house always late?

CAL (*looks at him surprised*). You ain't out shooting this morning, Mr. Oscar?

OSCAR. First day I missed since I had my head cold. First day I missed in eight years.

CAL. Yes, sir. I bet you. Simon he say you had a mighty good day yesterday morning. That's what Simon say. (*Brings* OSCAR *coffee and newspaper.*)

OSCAR. Pretty good, pretty good.

CAL (*laughs, slyly*). Bet you got enough bobwhite and squirrel to give every nigger in town a Jesus-party. Most of 'em ain't had no meat since the cotton picking was over. Bet they'd give anything for a little piece of that meat—

OSCAR (*turns his head to look at* CAL). Cal, if I catch a nigger in this town going shooting, you know what's going to happen.
(LEO *enters.*)

CAL (*hastily*). Yes, sir, Mr. Oscar. I didn't say nothing about nothing. It was Simon who told me and— Morning, Mr. Leo. You gentlemen having your breakfast with us here?

LEO. The boys in the bank don't know a thing. They haven't had any message.
(CAL *waits for an answer, gets none, shrugs, moves to door, exits.*)

OSCAR (*peers at* LEO). What you doing here, son?

LEO. You told me to find out if the boys at the bank had any message from Uncle Horace or Zan—

OSCAR. I told *you* if they had a message to bring it here. I told you that if they didn't have a message to stay at the bank and do your work.

LEO. Oh, I guess I misunderstood.

OSCAR. You didn't misunderstand. You just were looking for any excuse to take an hour off. (LEO *pours a cup of coffee*) You got to stop that kind of thing. You got to start settling down. You going to be a married man one of these days.

LEO. Yes, sir.

OSCAR. You also got to stop with that woman in Mobile. (*As* LEO *is about to speak*) You're young and I haven't got no objections to outside women. That is, I haven't got no objections so long as they don't interfere with serious things. Outside women are all right in their place, but *now* isn't their place. You got to realize that.

LEO (*nods*). Yes, sir. I'll tell her. She'll act all right about it.

OSCAR. Also, you got to start working harder at the bank. You got to convince your Uncle Horace you going to make a fit husband for Alexandra.

LEO. What do you think has happened to them? Supposed to be here last night— (*Laughs*) Bet you Uncle Ben's mighty worried. Seventy-five thousand dollars worried.

OSCAR (*smiles happily*). Ought to be worried. Damn well ought to be. First he don't answer the letters, then he don't come home—(*Giggles.*)

LEO. What will happen if Uncle Horace don't come home or don't—

OSCAR. Or don't put up the money? Oh, we'll get it from outside. Easy enough.

LEO (*surprised*). But *you* don't want outsiders.

OSCAR. What do I care who gets my share? I been shaved already. Serve Ben right if he had to give away some of his.

LEO. Damn shame what they did to you.

OSCAR (*looking up the stairs*). Don't talk so loud. Don't you worry. When I die, you'll have as much as the rest. You might have yours *and* Alexandra's. I'm not so easily licked.

LEO. I wasn't thinking of myself, Papa—

OSCAR. Well, you should be, you should be. It's every man's duty to think of himself.

LEO. You think Uncle Horace don't want to go in on this?

OSCAR (*giggles*). That's my hunch. He hasn't showed any signs of loving it yet.

LEO (*laughs*). But he hasn't listened to Aunt Regina yet, either. Oh, he'll go along. It's too good a thing. Why wouldn't he want to? He's got plenty and plenty to invest with. He don't even have to sell anything. Eighty-eight thousand worth of Union Pacific bonds sitting right in his safe deposit box. All he's got to do is open the box.

OSCAR (*after a pause. Looks at his watch*). Mighty late breakfast in this fancy house. Yes, he's had those bonds for fifteen years. Bought them when they were low and just locked them up.

LEO. Yeah. Just has to open the box an take them out. That's all. Easy as easy can be. (*Laughs*) The things in that box! There's all those bonds, looking mighty fine. (OSCAR *slowly puts down his newspaper and turns to* LEO) Then right next to them is a baby shoe of Zan's and a cheap old cameo on a string, and, *and*—nobody'd believe this—a piece of an old violin. Not even a whole violin. Just a piece of an old thing, a piece of a violin.

OSCAR (*very softly, as if he were trying to control his voice*). A piece of a violin! What do you think of that!

LEO. Yes, sirree. A lot of other crazy things, too. A poem, I guess it is, signed with his mother's name, and two old schoolbooks with notes and — (LEO *catches* OSCAR'S *look. His voice trails off. He turns his head away.*)

OSCAR (*very softly*). How do you know what's in the box, son?

LEO (*stops, draws back, frightened, realizing what he has said*). Oh, well. Well, er. Well, one of the boys, sir. It was one of the boys at the bank. He took old Manders' keys. It was Joe Horns. He just up and took Manders' keys and, and—well, took the box out. (*Quickly*) Then they all asked me if I wanted to see, too. So I looked a little, I guess, but then I made them close up the box quick and I told them never—

OSCAR (*looks at him*). Joe Horns, you say? He opened it?

LEO. Yes, sir, yes, he did. My word of honor. (*Very nervously, looking away*) I suppose that don't excuse *me* for looking— (*Looking at* OSCAR) but I did make him close it up and put the keys back in Manders' drawer—

OSCAR (*leans forward, very softly*). Tell me the truth, Leo. I am not going to be angry with you. Did you open the box yourself?

LEO. *No, sir, I didn't.* I told you I didn't. No, I—

OSCAR (*irritated, patient*). I am *not* going to be angry with you. (*Watching* LEO *carefully*) Sometimes a young fellow deserves credit for looking round him to see what's going on. Sometimes that's a good sign in a fellow your age. (OSCAR *rises*) Many great men have made their fortune with their eyes. Did you open the box?

LEO (*very puzzled*). No. I—

OSCAR (*moves to* LEO). Did you open the box? It may have been—well, it may have been a good thing if you had.

LEO (*after a long pause*). I opened it.

OSCAR (*quickly*). Is that the truth? (LEO *nods*) Does anybody else know that you opened it? Come, Leo, don't be afraid of speaking the truth to me.

LEO. No. Nobody knew. Nobody was in the bank when I did it. But—

OSCAR. Did your Uncle Horace ever know you opened it?

LEO (*shakes his head*). He only looks in it once every six months when he cuts the coupons, and sometimes Manders even does that for him. Uncle Horace don't even have the keys. Manders keeps them for him. Imagine not looking at all that. You can bet if I had the bonds, I'd watch 'em like—

OSCAR. If you had them. (LEO *watches him*) If you had them. Then you could have a share in the mill, you and me. A fine, big share, too. (*Pauses, shrugs*) Well, a man can't be shot for wanting to see his son get on in the world, can he, boy?

LEO (*looks up, begins to understand*). No, he can't. Natural enough. (*Laughs*) But I haven't got the bonds and Uncle Horace has. And now he can just sit back and wait to be a millionaire.

OSCAR (*innocently*). You think your Uncle Horace likes you well enough to lend you the bonds if he decides not to use them himself?

LEO. Papa, it must be that you haven't had your breakfast! (*Laughs loudly*) Lend me the bonds! My God—

OSCAR (*disappointed*). No, I suppose not. Just a fancy of mine. A loan for three months, maybe four, easy enough for us to pay it back then. Anyway, this is only April— (*Slowly counting the months on his fingers*) and if he doesn't look at them until Fall, he wouldn't even miss them out of the box.

LEO. That's it. He wouldn't even miss them. Ah, well—

OSCAR. No, sir. Wouldn't even miss them. How could he miss them if he never looks at them? (*Sighs as* LEO *stares at him*) Well, here we are sitting around waiting for him to come home and invest his money in something he hasn't lifted his hand to get. But I can't help thinking he's acting strange. You laugh when I say he could lend you the bonds if he's not going to use them himself. But would it hurt him?

LEO (*slowly looking at* OSCAR). No. No, it wouldn't.

OSCAR. People ought to help other people. But that's not always the way it happens. (BEN *enters, hangs his coat and hat in hall. Very carefully*) And so sometimes you got to think of yourself. (*As* LEO *stares at him,* BEN *appears in the doorway*) Morning, Ben.

BEN (*coming in, carrying his newspaper*). Fine sunny morning. Any news from the runaways?

REGINA (*on the staircase*). There's no news or you would have heard it. Quite a convention so early in the morning, aren't you all? (*Goes to coffee urn.*)

OSCAR. You rising mighty late these days. Is that the way they do things in Chicago society?

BEN (*looking at his paper*). Old Carter died up in Senateville. Eighty-one is a good time for us all, eh? What do you think has really happened to Horace, Regina?

REGINA. Nothing.

BEN (*too casually*). You don't think maybe he never started from Baltimore and never intends to start?

REGINA (*irritated*). Of course they've started. Didn't I have a letter from Alexandra? What is so strange about people arriving late? He has that cousin in Savannah he's so fond of. He may have stopped to see him. They'll be along today some time, very flattered that you and Oscar are so worried about them.

BEN. I'm a natural worrier. Especially when I am getting ready to close a business deal and one of my partners remains silent *and* invisible.

REGINA (*laughs*). Oh, is that it? I thought you were worried about Horace's health.

OSCAR. Oh, that too. Who could help but worry? I'm worried. This is the first day I haven't shot since my head cold.

REGINA (*starts towards dining room*). Then you haven't had your breakfast. Come along. (OSCAR *and* LEO *follow her.*)

BEN. Regina. (*She turns at dining-room door*) That cousin of Horace's has been dead for years and, in any case, the train does not go through Savannah.

REGINA (*laughs, continues into dining room, seats herself*). Did he die? You're always remembering about people dying. (BEN *rises*) Now I intend to eat my breakfast in peace, and read my newspaper.

BEN (*goes towards dining room as he talks*). This is second breakfast for me. My first was bad. Celia ain't the cook she used to be. Too old to have taste any more. If she hadn't belonged to Mama, I'd send her off to the country.

(OSCAR *and* LEO *start to eat.* BEN *seats himself.*)

LEO. Uncle Horace will have some tales to tell, I bet. Baltimore is a lively town.

REGINA (*to* CAL). The grits isn't hot enough. Take it back.

CAL. Oh, yes'm. (*Calling into kitchen as he exits*) Grits didn't hold the heat. Grits didn't hold the heat.

LEO. When I was at school three of the boys and myself took a train once and went over to Baltimore. It was so big we thought we were in Europe. I was just a kid then—

REGINA. I find it very pleasant (ADDIE *enters*) to have breakfast alone. I hate chattering before I've had something hot. (CAL *closes the dining-room doors*) Do be still, Leo.

(ADDIE *comes into the room, begins gathering up the cups, carries them to the large tray. Outside there are the sounds of voices. Quickly* ADDIE *runs into the hall. A few seconds later she appears again in the doorway, her arm around the shoulders of* HORACE GIDDENS, *supporting him.* HORACE *is a tall man of about forty-five. He has been good looking, but now his face is tired and ill. He walks stiffly, as if it were an enormous effort, and carefully, as if he were unsure of his balance.* ADDIE *takes off his overcoat and hangs it on the hall tree. She then helps him to a chair.*)

HORACE. How are you, Addie? How have you been?

ADDIE. I'm all right, Mr. Horace. I've just been worried about you.

(ALEXANDRA *enters. She is flushed and excited, her hat awry, her face dirty. Her arms are full of packages, but she comes quickly to* ADDIE.)

ALEXANDRA. Now don't tell me how worried you were. We couldn't help it and there was no way to send a message.

ADDIE (*begins to take packages from* ALEXANDRA). Yes, sir, I was mighty worried.

ALEXANDRA. We had to stop in Mobile overnight. Papa— (*Looks at him*) Papa didn't feel well. The trip was too much for him, and I made him stop and rest— (*As* ADDIE *takes the last package*) No, don't take that. That's father's medicine. I'll hold it. It mustn't break. Now, about the stuff outside. Papa must have his wheel chair. I'll get that and the valises—

ADDIE (*very happy, holding* ALEXANDRA's *arms*). Since when you got to carry your own valises? Since when I ain't old enough to hold a bottle of medicine? (HORACE *coughs*) You feel all right, Mr. Horace?

HORACE (*nods*). Glad to be sitting down.

ALEXANDRA (*opening package of medicine*). He doesn't feel all right. (ADDIE *looks at her, then at* HORACE) He just says that. The trip was very hard on him, and now he must go right to bed.

ADDIE (*looking at him carefully*). Them fancy doctors, they give you help?

HORACE. They did their best.

ALEXANDRA (*has become conscious of the voices in the dining room*). I bet Mama was worried. I better tell her we're here now. (*She starts for door.*)

HORACE. Zan. (*She stops*) Not for a minute, dear.

ALEXANDRA. Oh, Papa, you feel bad again. I knew you did. Do you want your medicine?

HORACE. No, I don't feel that way. I'm just tired, darling. Let me rest a little.

ALEXANDRA. Yes, but Mama will be mad if I don't tell her we're here.

ADDIE. They're all in there eating breakfast.

ALEXANDRA. Oh, are they all here? Why do they *always* have to be here? I was hoping Papa wouldn't have to see anybody, that it would be nice for him and quiet.

ADDIE. Then let your papa rest for a minute.

HORACE. Addie, I bet your coffee's as good as ever. They don't have such good coffee up North. (*Looks at the urn*) Is it as good, Addie? (ADDIE *starts for coffee urn.*)

ALEXANDRA. No. Dr. Reeves said not much coffee. Just now and then. I'm the nurse now, Addie.

ADDIE. You'd be a better one if you didn't look so dirty. Now go and take a bath, Miss Grown-up. Change your linens, get out a fresh dress and give your hair a good brushing—go on—

ALEXANDRA. Will you be all right, Papa?

ADDIE. Go on.

ALEXANDRA (*on stairs, talks as she goes up*). The pills Papa must take once every four hours. And the bottle only when—only if he feels very bad. Now don't move until I come back and don't talk much and remember about his medicine, Addie—

ADDIE. Ring for Belle and have her help you and then I'll make you a fresh breakfast.

ALEXANDRA (*as she disappears*). How's Aunt Birdie? Is she here?

ADDIE. It ain't right for you to have coffee? It will hurt you?

HORACE (*slowly*). Nothing can make much difference now. Get me a cup, Addie. (*She looks at him, crosses to urn, pours a cup*) Funny. They can't make coffee up North. (ADDIE *brings him a cup*) They don't like red pepper, either. (*He takes the cup and gulps it greedily*) God, that's good. You remember how I used to drink it? Ten, twelve cups a day. So strong it had to stain the cup. (*Then slowly*) Addie, before I see anybody else, I want to know why Zan came to fetch me home. She's tried to tell me, but she doesn't seem to know herself.

ADDIE (*turns away*). I don't know. All I know is big things are going on. Everybody going to be high-tone rich. Big rich. You too. All because smoke's going to start out of a building that ain't even up yet.

HORACE. I've heard about it.

ADDIE. And, er— (*Hesitates—steps to him*) And—well, Zan, she going to marry Mr. Leo in a little while.

HORACE (*looks at her, then very slowly*). What are you talking about?

ADDIE. That's right. That's the talk, God help us.

HORACE (*angrily*). *What's* the talk?

ADDIE. I'm telling you. There's going to be a wedding— (*Angrily turns away*) Over my dead body there is

HORACE (*after a second, quietly*). Go and tell them I'm home.

ADDIE (*hesitates*). Now you ain't to get excited. You're to be in your bed—

HORACE. Go on, Addie. Go and say I'm back. (ADDIE *opens dining-room doors. He rises with difficulty, stands stiff, as if he were in pain, facing the dining room.*)

ADDIE. Miss Regina. They're home They got here—

REGINA. Horace! (REGINA *quickly rises, runs into the room. Warmly*). Horace! You've finally arrived. (*As she kisses him, the others come forward, all talking together.*)

BEN (*in doorway, carrying a napkin*) Well, sir, you had us all mighty worried. (*He steps forward. They shake hands.* ADDIE *exits.*)

OSCAR. You're a sight for sore eyes

HORACE. Hello, Ben.
(LEO *enters, eating a biscuit.*)

OSCAR. And how you feel? Tip-top, I bet, because that's the way you're looking.

HORACE (*coldly, irritated with* OSCAR's *lie*). Hello, Oscar. Hello, Leo, how are you?

LEO (*shaking hands*). I'm fine, sir. But a lot better now that you're back.

REGINA. Now sit down. What did happen to you and where's Alexandra? I am so excited about seeing you that I almost forgot about her.

HORACE. I didn't feel good, a little weak, I guess, and we stopped overnight to rest. Zan's upstairs washing off the train dirt.

REGINA. Oh, I am so sorry the trip was hard on you. I didn't think that—

HORACE. Well, it's just as if I had never been away. All of you here—

BEN. Waiting to welcome you home. (BIRDIE *bursts in. She is wearing a flannel kimono and her face is flushed and excited.*)

BIRDIE (*runs to him, kisses him*). Horace!

HORACE (*warmly pressing her arm*). I was just wondering where you were, Birdie.

BIRDIE (*excited*). Oh, I would have been here. I didn't know you were back until Simon said he saw the buggy. (*She draws back to look at him. Her face sobers*). Oh, you don't look well, Horace. No, you don't.

REGINA (*laughs*). Birdie, what a thing to say—

HORACE (*looking at* OSCAR). Oscar thinks I look very well.

OSCAR (*annoyed. Turns on* LEO). Don't stand there holding that biscuit in your hand.

LEO. Oh, well. I'll just finish my breakfast, Uncle Horace, and then I'll give you all the news about the bank— (*He exits into the dining room.*)

OSCAR. And what is that costume you have on?

BIRDIE (*looking at* HORACE). Now that you're home, you'll feel better. Plenty of good rest and we'll take such fine care of you. (*Stops*) But where is Zan? I missed her so much.

OSCAR. I asked you what is that strange costume you're parading around in?

BIRDIE (*nervously, backing towards stairs*). Me? Oh! It's my wrapper. I was so excited about Horace I just rushed out of the house—

OSCAR. Did you come across the square dressed that way? My dear Birdie, I—

HORACE (*to* REGINA, *wearily*). Yes, it's just like old times.

REGINA (*quickly to* OSCAR). Now, no fights. This is a holiday.

BIRDIE (*runs quickly up the stairs*). Zan! Zannie!

OSCAR. Birdie! (*She stops.*)

BIRDIE. Oh. Tell Zan I'll be back in a little while. (*Whispers*) Sorry, Oscar. (*Exits.*)

REGINA (*to* OSCAR *and* BEN). Why don't you go finish your breakfast and let Horace rest for a minute?

BEN (*crossing to dining room with* OSCAR). Never leave a meal unfinished. There are too many poor people who need the food. Mighty glad to see you home, Horace. Fine to have you back. Fine to have you back.

OSCAR (*to* LEO *as* BEN *closes dining-room doors*). Your mother has gone crazy. Running around the streets like a woman—

(*The moment* REGINA *and* HORACE *are alone, they become awkward and self-conscious.*)

REGINA (*laughs awkwardly*). Well. Here we are. It's been a long time. (HORACE *smiles*) Five months. You know, Horace, I wanted to come and be with you in the hospital, but I didn't know where my duty was. Here, or with you. But you know how much I *wanted* to come.

HORACE. That's kind of you, Regina. There was no need to come.

REGINA. Oh, but there was. Five months lying there all by yourself, no kinfolks, no friends. Don't try to tell me you didn't have a bad time of it.

HORACE. I didn't have a bad time. (*As she shakes her head, he becomes insistent*) No, I didn't, Regina. Oh, at first when I—when I heard the news about myself—but after I got used to that, I liked it there.

REGINA. You *liked* it? (*Coldly*) Isn't that strange. You liked it so well you didn't want to come home?

HORACE. That's not the way to put it. (*Then, kindly, as he sees her turn her head away*) But there I was and I got kind of used to it, kind of to like lying there and thinking. (*Smiles*) I never had much time to think before. And time's become valuable to me.

REGINA. It sounds almost like a holiday.

HORACE (*laughs*). It was, sort of. The first holiday I've had since I was a little kid.

REGINA. And here I was thinking you were in pain and—

HORACE (*quietly*). I was in pain.

REGINA. And instead you were having a holiday! A holiday of thinking. Couldn't you have done that here?

HORACE. I wanted to do it before I came here. I was thinking about us.

REGINA. About us? About you and me? Thinking about you and me after all these years. (*Unpleasantly*) You shall tell me everything you thought—some day.

HORACE (*there is silence for a minute*). Regina. (*She turns to him*) Why did you send Zan to Baltimore?

REGINA. Why? Because I wanted you home. You can't make anything suspicious out of that, can you?

HORACE. I didn't mean to make anything suspicious about it. (*Hesitantly, taking her hand*) Zan said you wanted me to come home. I was so pleased at that and touched, it made me feel good.

REGINA (*taking away her hand, turns*). Touched that I should want you home?

HORACE (*sighs*). I'm saying all the wrong things as usual. Let's try to get along better. There isn't so much more time. Regina, what's all this crazy talk I've been hearing about Zan and Leo? Zan and Leo marrying?

REGINA (*turning to him, sharply*). Who gossips so much around here?

HORACE (*shocked*). Regina!

REGINA (*annoyed, anxious to quiet him*). It's some foolishness that Oscar thought up. I'll explain later. I have no intention of allowing any such arrangement. It was simply a way of keeping Oscar quiet in all this business I've been writing you about—

HORACE (*carefully*). What has Zan to do with any business of Oscar's? Whatever it is, you had better put it out of Oscar's head immediately. You know what I think of Leo.

REGINA. But there's no need to talk about it now.

HORACE. There is no need to talk about it ever. Not as long as I live. (HORACE *stops, slowly turns to look at her*) As long as I live. I've been in a hospital for five months. Yet since I've been here you have not once asked me about—about my health. (*Then gently*) Well, I suppose they've written you. I can't live very long.

REGINA (*coldly*). I've never understood why people have to talk about this kind of thing.

HORACE (*there is a silence. Then he looks up at her, his face cold*). You misunderstand. I don't intend to gossip about my sickness. I thought it was only fair to tell you. I was not asking for your sympathy.

REGINA (*sharply, turns to him*). What do the doctors think caused your bad heart?

HORACE. What do you mean?

REGINA. They didn't think it possible, did they, that your fancy women may have—

HORACE (*smiles unpleasantly*). Caused my heart to be bad? I don't think that's the best scientific theory. You don't catch heart trouble in bed.

REGINA (*angrily*). I didn't think you did. I only thought you might catch a bad conscience—in bed, as you say.

HORACE. I didn't tell them about my bad conscience. Or about my fancy women. Nor did I tell them that my wife has not wanted me in bed with her for— (*Sharply*) How long is it, Regina? (REGINA *turns to him*) Ten years? Did you bring me home for this, to make me feel guilty again? That means you want something. But you'll not make me feel guilty any more. My "thinking" has made a difference.

REGINA. I see that it has. (*She looks towards dining-room door. Then comes to him, her manner warm and friendly*) It's foolish for us to fight this way. I didn't mean to be unpleasant. I was stupid.

HORACE (*wearily*). God knows I didn't either. I came home wanting so much not to fight, and then all of a sudden there we were. I got hurt and—

REGINA (*hastily*). It's all my fault. I didn't ask about—about your illness because I didn't want to remind you of it. Anyway I never believe doctors when they talk about—(*Brightly*) when they talk like that.

HORACE (*not looking at her*). Well, we'll try our best with each other. (*He rises.*)

REGINA (*quickly*). I'll try. Honestly, I will. Horace, Horace, I know you're tired but, but—couldn't you stay down here a few minutes longer? I want Ben to tell you something.

HORACE. Tomorrow.

REGINA. I'd like to now. It's very important to me. It's very important to all of us. (*Gaily, as she moves toward dining room*) Important to your beloved daughter. She'll be a very great heiress—

HORACE. Will she? That's nice.

REGINA (*opens doors*). Ben, are you finished breakfast?

HORACE. Is this the mill business I've had so many letters about?

REGINA (*to* BEN). Horace would like to talk to you now.

HORACE. Horace would not like to talk to you now. I am very tired, Regina—

REGINA (*comes to him*). Please. You've said we'll try our best with each other. I'll try. Really, I will. Please do this for me now. You will see what I've done while you've been away. How I watched your interests. (*Laughs gaily*) And I've done very well too. But things can't be delayed any longer. Everything must be settled this week— (HORACE *sits down.* BEN *enters.* OSCAR *has stayed in the dining room, his head turned to watch them.* LEO *is pretending to read the newspaper*) Now you must tell Horace all about it. Only be quick because he is very tired and must go to bed. (HORACE *is looking up at her. His face hardens as she speaks*) But I think your news will be better for him than all the medicine in the world.

BEN (*looking at* HORACE). It could wait. Horace may not feel like talking today.

REGINA. What an old faker you are! You know it can't wait. You know it must be finished this week. You've been just as anxious for Horace to get here as I've been.

BEN (*very jovial*). I suppose I have been. And why not? Horace has done Hubbard Sons many a good turn. Why shouldn't I be anxious to help him now?

REGINA (*laughs*). Help him! Help him when you need him, that's what you mean.

BEN. What a woman you married, Horace! (*Laughs awkwardly when* HORACE *does not answer*) Well, then I'll make it quick. You know what I've been telling you for years. How I've always said that every one of us little Southern business men had great things— (*Extends his arm*) right beyond our finger tips. It's been my dream: my dream to make those fingers grows longer. I'm a lucky man, Horace, a lucky man. To dream and to live to get what you've dreamed of. That's *my* idea of a lucky man. (*Looks at his fingers as his arm drops slowly*) For thirty years I've cried bring the cotton mills to the cotton. (HORACE *opens medicine bottle*) Well, finally I got up nerve to go to Marshall Company in Chicago.

HORACE. I know all this. (*He takes the medicine.* REGINA *rises, steps to him.*)

BEN. Can I get you something?

HORACE. Some water, please.

REGINA (*turns quickly*). Oh, I'm sorry. Let me. (*Brings him a glass of water. He drinks as they wait in silence*) You feel all right now?

HORACE. Yes. You wrote me. I know all that.
(OSCAR *enters from dining room.*)

REGINA (*triumphantly*). But you don't know that in the last few days Ben has agreed to give us—you, I mean—a much larger share.

HORACE. Really? That's very generous of him.

BEN (*laughs*). It wasn't so generous of me. It was smart of Regina.

REGINA (*as if she were signaling* HORACE). I explained to Ben that perhaps you hadn't answered his letters because you didn't think he was offering you enough, and that the time was getting short and you could guess how much he needed you—

HORACE (*smiles at her, nods*). And I could guess that he wants to keep control in the family?

REGINA (*to* BEN, *triumphantly*). Exactly. (*To* HORACE) So I did a little bargaining for you and convinced my brothers they weren't the only Hubbards who had a business sense.

HORACE. Did you have to convince them of that? How little people know about each other! (*Laughs*) But you'll know better about Regina next time, eh, Ben? (BEN, REGINA, HORACE *laugh together* OSCAR'*s face is angry*) Now let's see. We're getting a bigger share. (*Looking at* OSCAR) Who's getting less?

BEN. Oscar.

HORACE. Well, Oscar, you've grown very unselfish. What's happened to you?
(LEO *enters from dining room.*)

BEN (*quickly, before* OSCAR *can answer*). Oscar doesn't mind. Not worth fighting about now, eh, Oscar?

OSCAR (*angrily*). I'll get mine in the end. You can be sure of that. I've got my son's future to think about.

HORACE (*sharply*). Leo? Oh, I see. (*Puts his head back, laughs.* REGINA *looks at him nervously*) I am beginning to see. Everybody will get theirs.

BEN. I knew you'd see it. Seventy-five thousand, and that seventy-five thousand will make you a million.

REGINA (*steps to table, leaning forward*). It will, Horace, it will.

HORACE. I believe you. (*After a second*) Now I can understand Oscar's self-sacrifice, but what did you have to promise Marshall Company besides the money you're putting up?

BEN. They wouldn't take promises. They wanted guarantees.

HORACE. Of what?

BEN (*nods*). Water power. Free and plenty of it.

HORACE. You got them that, of course.

BEN. Cheap. You'd think the Governor of a great state would make his price a little higher. From pride, you know. (HORACE *smiles.* BEN *smiles*) Cheap wages. "What do you mean by cheap wages?" I say to Marshall. "Less than Massachusetts," he says to me, "and that averages eight a week." "Eight a week! By God," I tell him, "*I'd* work for eight a week myself." Why, there ain't a mountain white or a town nigger but wouldn't give his right arm for three silver dollars every week, eh, Horace?

HORACE. Sure. And they'll take less than that when you get around to playing them off against each other. You can save a little money that way, Ben. (*Angrily*) And make them hate each other just a little more than they do now.

REGINA. What's all this about?

BEN (*laughs*). There'll be no trouble from anybody, white or black. Marshall said that to me. "What about strikes? That's all we've had in Massachusetts for the last three years." I say to him, "What's a strike? I never heard of one. Come South, Marshall. We got good folks and we don't stand for any fancy fooling."

HORACE. You're right. (*Slowly*) Well, it looks like you made a good deal for yourselves, and for Marshall, too. (*To* BEN) Your father used to say he made the thousands and you boys would make the millions. I think he was right. (*Rises.*)

REGINA (*They are all looking at* HORACE. *She laughs nervously*). Millions for *us*, too.

HORACE. Us? You and me? I don't think so. We've got enough money, Regina. We'll just sit by and watch the boys grow rich. (*They watch* HORACE *tensely as he begins to move towards the staircase. He passes* LEO, *looks at him for a second*) How's everything at the bank, Leo?

LEO. Fine, sir. Everything is fine.

HORACE. How are all the ladies in Mobile? (HORACE *turns to* REGINA, *sharply*) Whatever made you think I'd let Zan marry—

REGINA. Do you mean that you are turning this down? Is it possible that's what you mean?

BEN. No, that's not what he means. Turning down a fortune. Horace is tired. He'd rather talk about it tomorrow—

REGINA. We can't keep putting it off this way. Oscar must be in Chicago by the end of the week with the money and contracts.

OSCAR (*giggles, pleased*). Yes, sir. Got to be there end of the week. No sense going without the money.

REGINA (*tensely*). I've waited long enough for your answer. I'm not going to wait any longer.

HORACE (*very deliberately*). I'm very tired now, Regina.

BEN (*hastily*). Now, Horace probably has his reasons. Things he'd like explained. Tomorrow will do. I can—

REGINA (*turns to* BEN, *sharply*). I want to know his reasons now! (*Turns back to* HORACE).

HORACE (*as he climbs the steps*). I don't know them all myself. Let's leave it at that.

REGINA. We shall not leave it at that! We have waited for you here like children. Waited for you to come home.

HORACE. So that you could invest my money. So this is why you wanted me home? Well, I had hoped—(*Quietly*) If you are disappointed, Regina, I'm sorry. But I must do what I think best. We'll talk about it another day.

REGINA. We'll talk about it now. Just you and me.

HORACE (*looks down at her. His voice is tense*). Please, Regina. It's been a hard trip. I don't feel well. Please leave me alone now.

REGINA (*quietly*). I want to talk to you, Horace. I'm coming up. (*He looks at her for a minute, then moves on again out of sight. She begins to climb the stairs.*)

BEN (*softly.* REGINA *turns to him as he speaks*). Sometimes it is better to wait for the sun to rise again. (*She does not answer*) And sometimes, as our mother used to tell you, (REGINA *starts up stairs*) it's unwise for a good-looking woman to frown. (BEN *rises, moves towards stairs*) Softness and a smile do more to the heart of men—(*She disappears.* BEN *stands looking up the stairs. There is a long silence. Then, suddenly,* OSCAR *giggles.*)

OSCAR. Let us hope she'll change his mind. Let us hope. (*After a second* BEN *crosses to table, picks up his newspaper.* OSCAR *looks at* BEN. *The silence makes* LEO *uncomfortable.*)

LEO. The paper says twenty-seven cases of yellow fever in New Orleans. Guess the flood waters caused it. (*Nobody pays attention*) Thought they were building the levees high enough. Like the niggers always say: a man born of woman can't build nothing high enough for the Mississippi. (*Gets no answer. Gives an embarrassed laugh.*)

(*Upstairs there is the sound of voices. The voices are not loud, but* BEN, OSCAR, LEO *become conscious of them.* LEO *crosses to landing, looks up, listens.*)

OSCAR (*pointing up*). Now just suppose she don't change his mind? Just suppose he keeps on refusing?

BEN (*without conviction*). He's tired. It was a mistake to talk to him today. He's a sick man, but he isn't a crazy one.

OSCAR. (*giggles*). But just suppose he is crazy. What then?

BEN (*puts down his paper, peers at* OSCAR). Then we'll go outside for the money. There's plenty who would give it.

OSCAR. And plenty who will want a lot for what they give. The ones who are rich enough to give will be smart enough to want. That means we'd be working for them, don't it, Ben?

BEN. You don't have to tell me the things I told you six months ago.

OSCAR. Oh, you're right not to worry. She'll change his mind. She always has. (*There is a silence. Suddenly* REGINA'S *voice becomes louder and sharper. All of them begin to listen now. Slowly* BEN *rises, goes to listen by the staircase.* OSCAR, *watching him, smiles. As they listen* REGINA'S *voice becomes very loud.* HORACE'S *voice is no longer heard*) Maybe. But I don't believe it. I never did believe he was going in with us.

BEN (*turning on him*). What the hell do you expect me to do?

OSCAR (*mildly*). Nothing. You done your almighty best. Nobody could blame you if the whole thing just dripped away right through our fingers. You can't do a thing. But there may be something I could do for us. (OSCAR *rises*) Or, I might better say, Leo could do for us. (BEN *stops, turns, looks at* OSCAR. LEO *is staring at* OSCAR) Ain't that true, son? Ain't it true you might be able to help your own kinfolks?

LEO (*nervously taking a step to him*). Papa, I—

BEN (*slowly*). How would he help us, Oscar?

OSCAR. Leo's got a friend. Leo's friend owns eighty-eight thousand dollars in Union Pacific bonds. (BEN *turns to look at* LEO) Leo's friend don't look at the bonds much—not for five or six months at a time.

BEN (*after a pause*). Union Pacific. Uh, huh. Let me understand. Leo's friend would—would lend him these bonds and he—

OSCAR (*nods*). Would be kind enough to lend them to us.

BEN. Leo.

LEO (*excited, comes to him*). Yes, sir?

BEN. When would your friend be wanting the bonds back?

LEO (*very nervous*). I don't know. I—well, I—

OSCAR (*sharply. Steps to him*). You told me he won't look at them until Fall—

LEO. Oh, that's right. But I—not till Fall. Uncle Horace never—

BEN (*sharply*). Be still.

OSCAR (*smiles at* LEO). Your uncle doesn't wish to know your friend's name.

LEO (*starts to laugh*). That's a good one. Not know his name—

OSCAR. Shut up, Leo! (LEO *turns away slowly, moves to table.* BEN *turns to* OSCAR) He won't look at them again until September. That gives us five months. Leo will return the bonds in three months. And we'll have no trouble raising the money once the mills are going up. Will Marshall accept bonds?

(BEN *stops to listen to sudden sharp voices from above. The voices are now very angry and very loud.*)

BEN (*smiling*). Why not? Why not? (*Laughs*) Good. We are lucky. We'll take the loan from Leo's friend—I think he will make a safer partner than our sister. (*Nods towards stairs. Turns to* LEO) How soon can you get them?

LEO. Today. Right now. They're in the safe-deposit box and—

BEN (*sharply*). I don't want to know where they are.

OSCAR (*laughs*). We will keep it secret from you. (*Pats* BEN'*s arm.*)

BEN (*smiles*). Good. Draw a check for our part. You can take the night train for Chicago. Well, Oscar, (*Holds out his hand*) good luck to us.

OSCAR. Leo will be taken care of?

LEO. I'm entitled to Uncle Horace's share. I'd enjoy being a partner—

BEN (*turns to stare at him*). You would? You can go to hell, you little— (*Starts towards* LEO.)

OSCAR (*nervously*). Now, now. He didn't mean that. I only want to be sure he'll get something out of all this.

BEN. Of course. We'll take care of him. We won't have any trouble about that. I'll see you at the store.

OSCAR (*nods*). That's settled then. Come on, son. (*Starts for door.*)

LEO (*puts out his hand*). I didn't mean just that. I was only going to say what a great day this was for me and— (BEN *ignores his hand.*)

BEN. Go on.
(LEO *looks at him, turns, follows* OSCAR *out.* BEN *stands where he is, thinking. Again the voices upstairs can be heard.* REGINA'*s voice is high and furious.* BEN *looks up, smiles, winces at the noise.*)

ALEXANDRA (*upstairs*). Mama—Mama—don't . . . (*The noise of running footsteps is heard and* ALEXANDRA *comes running down the steps, speaking as she comes*) Uncle Ben! Uncle Ben! Please go up. Please make Mama stop. Uncle Ben, he's sick, he's so sick. How can Mama talk to him like that—please, make her stop. She'll—

BEN. Alexandra, you have a tender heart.

ALEXANDRA (*crying*). Go on up, Uncle Ben, please—
(*Suddenly the voices stop. A second later there is the sound of a door being slammed.*)

BEN. Now you see. Everything is over. Don't worry. (*He starts for the door*) Alexandra, I want you to tell your mother how sorry I am that I had to leave. And don't worry so, my dear. Married folk frequently raise their voices, unfortunately. (*He starts to put on his hat and coat as* REGINA *appears on the stairs.*)

ALEXANDRA (*furiously*). How can you treat Papa like this? He's sick. He's very sick. Don't you know that? I won't let you.

REGINA. Mind your business, Alexandra. (*To* BEN. *Her voice is cold and calm*) How much longer can you wait for the money?

BEN (*putting on his coat*). He has refused? My, that's too bad.

REGINA. He will change his mind. I'll find a way to make him. What's the longest you can wait now?

BEN. I could wait until next week. But I can't wait until next week. (*He giggles, pleased at the joke*) I could but I can't. Could and can't. Well, I must go now. I'm very late—

REGINA (*coming downstairs towards him*). You're not going. I want to talk to you.

BEN. I was about to give Alexandra a message for you. I wanted to tell you that Oscar is going to Chicago to-night, so we can't be here for our usual Friday supper.

REGINA (*tensely*). Oscar is going to Chi— (*Softly*) What do you mean?

BEN. Just that. Everything is settled. He's going on to deliver to Marshall—

REGINA (*taking a step to him*). I demand to know what— You are lying. You are trying to scare me. *You haven't got the money*. How could you have it? You can't have— (BEN *laughs*) You will wait until I— (HORACE *comes into view on the landing.*)

BEN. You are getting out of hand. Since when do I take orders from you?

REGINA. Wait, you— (BEN *stops*) How *can* he go to Chicago? Did a ghost arrive with the money? (BEN *starts for the hall*) I don't believe you. Come back here. (REGINA *starts after him*) Come back here, you— (*The door slams. She stops in the doorway, staring, her fists clenched. After a pause she turns slowly.*)

HORACE (*very quietly*) It's a great day when you and Ben cross swords. I've been waiting for it for years.

ALEXANDRA. Papa, Papa, please go back! You will—

HORACE. And so they don't need you, and so you will not have your millions, after all.

REGINA (*turns slowly*). You hate to see anybody live now, don't you? You hate to think that I'm going to be alive and have what I want.

HORACE. I should have known you'd think that was the reason.

REGINA. Because you're going to die and you know you're going to die.

ALEXANDRA (*shrilly*). Mama! Don't— Don't listen, Papa. Just don't listen. Go away —

HORACE. Not to keep you from getting what you want. Not even partly that. (*Holding to the rail*) I'm sick of you, sick of this house, sick of my life here. I'm sick of your brothers and their dirty tricks to make a dime. There must be better ways of getting rich than cheating niggers on a pound of bacon. Why should I give you the money? (*Very angrily*) To pound the bones of this town to make dividends for you to spend? You wreck the town, you and your brothers, *you* wreck the town and live on it. Not me. Maybe it's easy for the dying to be honest. But it's not my fault I'm dying. (ADDIE *enters, stands at door quietly*) I'll do no more harm now. I've done enough. I'll die my own way. And I'll do it without making the world any worse. I leave that to you.

REGINA (*looks up at him slowly, calmly*). I hope you die. I hope you die soon. (*Smiles*) I'll be waiting for you to die.

ALEXANDRA (*shrieking*). Papa! Don't— Don't listen— Don't—

ADDIE. Come here, Zan. Come out of this room.

(ALEXANDRA *runs quickly to* ADDIE, *who holds her.* HORACE *turns slowly and starts upstairs.*)

CURTAIN

ACT THREE

SCENE—*Same as Act One. Two weeks later. It is late afternoon and it is raining.*

AT RISE—HORACE *is sitting near the window in a wheel chair. On the table next to him is a safe deposit box, and a small bottle of medicine.* BIRDIE *and* ALEXANDRA *are playing the piano. On a chair is a large sewing basket.*

BIRDIE (*counting for* ALEXANDRA). One and two and three and four. One and two and three and four. (*Nods—turns to* HORACE) We once played together, Horace. Remember?

HORACE (*has been looking out of the window*). What, Birdie?

BIRDIE. We played together. You and me.

ALEXANDER. *Papa* used to play?

BIRDIE. Indeed he did. (ADDIE *appears at the door in a large kitchen apron. She is wiping her hands on a towel*) He played the fiddle and very well, too.

ALEXANDRA (*turns to smile at* HORACE). I never knew—

ADDIE. Where's your mama?

ALEXANDRA. Gone to Miss Safronia's to fit her dresses.
(ADDIE *nods, starts to exit.*)

HORACE. Addie.

ADDIE. Yes, Mr. Horace.

HORACE (*speaks as if he had made a sudden decision*). Tell Cal to get on his things. I want him to go an errand.
(ADDIE *nods, exits.* HORACE *moves nervously in his chair, looks out of the window.*)

ALEXANDRA (*who has been watching him*). It's too bad it's been raining all day, Papa. But you can go out in the yard tomorrow. Don't be restless.

HORACE. I'm not restless, darling.

BIRDIE. I remember so well the time we played together, your papa and me. It was the first time Oscar brought me here to supper. I had never seen all the Hubbards together before, and you know what a ninny I am and how shy. (*Turns to look at* HORACE) You said you could play the fiddle and you'd be much obliged if I'd play with you. *I* was obliged to *you*, all right, all right. (*Laughs when he does not answer her*) Horace, you haven't heard a word I've said.

HORACE. Birdie, when did Oscar get back from Chicago?

BIRDIE. Yesterday. Hasn't he been here yet?

ALEXANDRA (*stops playing*). No. Neither has Uncle Ben since—since that day.

BIRDIE. Oh, I didn't know it was *that* bad. Oscar never tells me anything—

HORACE (*smiles, nods*). The Hubbards have had their great quarrel. I knew it would come some day. (*Laughs*) It came.

ALEXANDRA. It came. It certainly came all right.

BIRDIE (*amazed*). But Oscar was in such a good humor when he got home, I didn't—

HORACE. Yes, I can understand that. (ADDIE *enters carrying a large tray with glasses, a carafe of elderberry wine and a plate of cookies, which she puts on the table.*)

ALEXANDRA. Addie! A party! What for?

ADDIE. Nothing for. I had the fresh butter, so I made the cakes, and a little elderberry does the stomach good in the rain.

BIRDIE. Isn't this nice! A party just for us. Let's play party music, Zan. (ALEXANDRA *begins to play a gay piece.*)

ADDIE (*to* HORACE, *wheeling his chair to center*). Come over here, Mr. Horace, and don't be thinking so much. A glass of elderberry will do more good.
(ALEXANDRA *reaches for a cake.* BIRDIE *pours herself a glass of wine.*)

ALEXANDRA. Good cakes, Addie. It's nice here. Just us. Be nice if it could always be this way.

BIRDIE (*nods happily*). Quiet and restful.

ADDIE. Well, it won't be that way long. Little while now, even sitting here, you'll hear the red bricks going into place. The next day the smoke'll be pushing out the chimneys and by church time that Sunday every human born of woman will be living on chicken. That's how Mr. Ben's been telling the story.

HORACE (*looks at her*). They believe it that way?

ADDIE. Believe it? They use to believing what Mr. Ben orders. There ain't been so much talk around here since Sherman's army didn't come near.

HORACE (*softly*). They are fools.

ADDIE (*nods, sits down with the sewing basket*). You ain't born in the South unless you're a fool.

BIRDIE (*has drunk another glass of wine*). But we didn't play together after that night. Oscar said he didn't like me to play on the piano. (*Turns to* ALEXANDRA) You know what he said that night?

ALEXANDRA. Who?

BIRDIE. Oscar. He said that music made him nervous. He said he just sat and waited for the next note. (ALEXANDRA *laughs*) He wasn't poking fun. He meant it. Ah, well—(*She finishes her glass, shakes her head.* HORACE *looks at her, smiles*) Your papa don't like to admit it, but he's been mighty kind to me all these years. (*Running the back of her hand along his sleeve*) Often he'd step in when somebody said something and once— (*She stops, turns away, her face still*) Once he stopped Oscar from— (*She stops, turns. Quickly*) I'm sorry I said that. Why, here I am so happy and yet I think about bad things. (*Laughs nervously*) That's not right, now, is it? (*She pours a drink.* CAL *appears in the door. He has on an old coat and is carrying a torn umbrella.*)

ALEXANDRA. Have a cake, Cal.

CAL (*comes in, takes a cake*). Yes'm. You want me, Mr. Horace?

HORACE. What time is it, Cal?

CAL. 'Bout ten minutes before it's five.

HORACE. All right. Now you walk yourself down to the bank.

CAL. It'll be closed. Nobody'll be there but Mr. Manders, Mr. Joe Horns, Mr. Leo—

HORACE. Go in the back way. They'll be at the table, going over the day's business. (*Points to the deposit box*) See that box?

CAL (*nods*). Yes, sir.

HORACE. You tell Mr. Manders that Mr. Horace says he's much obliged to him for bringing the box, it arrived all right.

CAL (*bewildered*). He know you got the box. He bring it himself Wednesday. I opened the door to him and he say, "Hello, Cal, coming on to summer weather."

HORACE. You say just what I tell you. Understand?

(BIRDIE *pours another drink, stands at table.*)

CAL. No, sir. I ain't going to say I understand. I'm going down and tell a man he give you something he already know he give you, and you say "understand."

HORACE. Now, Cal.

CAL. Yes, sir. I just going to say you obliged for the box coming all right. I ain't going to understand it, but I'm going to say it.

HORACE. And tell him I want him to come over here after supper, and to bring Mr. Sol Fowler with him.

CAL. (*nods*). He's to come after supper and bring Mr. Sol Fowler, your attorney-*at*-law, with him.

HORACE (*smiles*). That's right. Just walk right in the back room and say your piece. (*Slowly*) In front of everybody.

CAL. Yes, sir. (*Mumbles to himself as he exits.*)

ALEXANDRA (*who has been watching* HORACE). Is anything the matter, Papa?

HORACE. Oh, no. Nothing.

ADDIE. Miss Birdie, that elderberry going to give you a headache spell.

BIRDIE (*beginning to be drunk. Gaily*). Oh, I don't think so. I don't think it will.

ALEXANDRA (*as* HORACE *puts his hand to his throat*). Do you want your medicine, Papa?

HORACE. No, no. I'm all right, darling.

BIRDIE. Mama used to give me elderberry wine when I was a little girl. For hiccoughs. (*Laughs*) You know, I don't think people get hiccoughs any more. Isn't that funny? (BIRDIE *laughs.* HORACE *and* ALEXANDRA *laugh*) I used to get hiccoughs just when I shouldn't have.

ADDIE (*nods*). And nobody gets growing pains no more. That is funny. Just as if there was some style in what you get. One year an ailment's stylish and the next year it ain't.

BIRDIE (*turns*). I remember. It was my first big party, at Lionnet I mean, and I was so excited, and there I was with hiccoughs and Mama laughing. (*Softly. Looking at carafe*) Mama always laughed. (*Picks up carafe*) A big party, a lovely dress from Mr. Worth in Paris, France, and hiccoughs. (*Pours drink*) My brother pounding me on the back and Mama with the elderberry bottle, laughing at me. Everybody was on their way to come, and I was such a ninny, hiccoughing away. (*Drinks*) You know, that was the first day I ever saw Oscar Hubbard. The Ballongs were selling their horses and he was going there to buy. He passed and lifted his hat—we could see him from the window—and my brother, to tease Mama, said maybe we should have invited the Hubbards to the party. He said Mama didn't like them because they kept a store, and he said that was old-fashioned of her. (*Her face lights up*) And then, and *then*, I saw Mama angry for the first time in my life. She said that wasn't the reason. She said she was old-fashioned, but not that way. She said she was old-fashioned enough not to like people who killed animals they couldn't use, and who made their money charging awful interest to poor, ignorant niggers and cheating them on what they bought. She was very angry, Mama was. I had never seen her face like that. And then suddenly she laughed and said, "Look, I've frightened Birdie out of the hiccoughs." (*Her head drops. Then softly*) And so she had. They were all gone. (*Moves to sofa, sits.*)

ADDIE. Yeah, they got mighty well off cheating niggers. Well, there are people who eat the earth and eat all the people on it like in the Bible with the locusts. Then there are people who stand around and watch them eat it. (*Softly*) Sometimes I think it ain't right to stand and watch them do it.

BIRDIE (*thoughtfully*). Like I say, if we could only go back to Lionnet. Everybody'd be better there. They'd be good and kind. I like people to be kind. (*Pours drink*) Don't you, Horace; don't you like people to be kind?

HORACE. Yes, Birdie.

BIRDIE (*very drunk now*). Yes, that was the first day I ever saw Oscar. Who would have thought— (*Quickly*) You all want to know something? Well, I don't like Leo. My very own son, and I don't like him. (*Laughs, gaily*) My, I guess I even like Oscar more.

ALEXANDRA. Why did you marry Uncle Oscar?

ADDIE (*sharply*). That's no question for you to be asking.

HORACE (*sharply*). Why not? She's heard enough around here to ask anything.

ALEXANDRA. Aunt Birdie, why did you marry Uncle Oscar?

BIRDIE. I don't know. I thought I liked him. He was kind to me and I thought it was because he liked me too. But that wasn't the reason—(*Wheels on* ALEXANDRA) Ask why *he* married *me*. I can tell you that: He's told it to me often enough.

ADDIE (*leaning forward*). Miss Birdie, don't—

BIRDIE (*speaking very rapidly, tensely*). My family was good and the cotton on Lionnet's fields was better. Ben Hubbard wanted the cotton and (*Rises*) Oscar Hubbard married it for him. He was kind to me, then. He used to smile at me. He hasn't smiled at me since. Everybody knew that's what he married me for. (ADDIE *rises*) Everybody but me. Stupid, stupid me.

ALEXANDRA (*to* HORACE, *holding his hand, softly*). I see. (*Hesitates*) Papa, I mean—when you feel better couldn't we go away? I mean, by ourselves. Couldn't we find a way to go—

HORACE. Yes, I know what you mean. We'll try to find a way. I promise you, darling.

ADDIE (*moves to* BIRDIE) Rest a bit, Miss Birdie. You get talking like this you'll get a headache and—

BIRDIE (*sharply, turning to her*). I've never had a headache in my life. (*Begins to cry hysterically*) You know it as well as I do. (*Turns to* ALEXANDRA) I never had a headache, Zan. That's a lie they tell for me. I drink. All by myself, in my own room, by myself, I drink. Then, when they want to hide it, they say, "Birdie's got a headache again"—

ALEXANDRA (*comes to her quickly*). Aunt Birdie.

BIRDIE (*turning away*). Even you won't like me now. You won't like me any more.

ALEXANDRA. I love you. I'll always love you.

BIRDIE (*furiously*). Well, don't. Don't love me. Because in twenty years you'll just be like me. They'll do all the same things to you. (*Begins to laugh hysterically*) You know what? In twenty-two years I haven't had a whole day of happiness. Oh, a little, like today with you all. But never a single, whole day. I say to myself, if only I had one more *whole* day, then— (*The laugh stops*) And that's the way you'll be. And you'll trail after them, just like me, hoping they won't be so mean that day or say something to make you feel so bad—only you'll be worse off because you haven't got my Mama to remember— (*Turns away, her head drops. She stands quietly, swaying a little, holding onto the sofa.* ALEXANDRA *leans down, puts her cheek on* BIRDIE'*s arm.*)

ALEXANDRA (*to* BIRDIE). I guess we were all trying to make a happy day. You know, we sit around and try to pretend nothing's happened. We try to pretend we are not here. We make believe we are just by ourselves, some place else, and it doesn't seem to work. (*Kisses* BIRDIE'*s hand*) Come now, Aunt Birdie, I'll walk you home. You and me. (*She takes* BIRDIE'*s arm. They move slowly out.*)

BIRDIE (*softly as they exit*). You and me.

ADDIE (*after a minute*). Well. First time I ever heard Miss Birdie say a word. (HORACE *looks at her*) Maybe it's good for her. I'm just sorry Zan had to hear it. (HORACE *moves his head as if he were uncomfortable*) You feel bad, don't you? (*He shrugs.*)

HORACE. So you didn't want Zan to hear? It would be nice to let her stay innocent, like Birdie at her age. Let her listen now. Let her see everything. How else is she going to know that she's got to get away? I'm trying to show her that. I'm trying, but I've only got a little time left. She can even hate me when I'm dead, if she'll only learn to hate and fear this.

ADDIE. Mr. Horace—

HORACE. Pretty soon there'll be nobody to help her but you.

ADDIE (*crossing to him*). What can I do?

HORACE. Take her away.

ADDIE. How can I do that? Do you think they'd let me just go away with her?

HORACE. I'll fix it so they can't stop you when you're ready to go. You'll go, Addie?

ADDIE (*after a second, softly*). Yes, sir. I promise. (*He touches her arm, nods.*)

HORACE (*quietly*). I'm going to have Sol Fowler make me a new will. They'll make trouble, but you make Zan stand firm and Fowler'll do the rest. Addie, I'd like to leave you something for yourself. I always wanted to.

ADDIE (*laughs*). Don't you do that, Mr. Horace. A nigger woman in a white man's will! I'd never get it nohow.

HORACE. I know. But upstairs in the armoire drawer there's seventeen hundred dollar bills. It's money left from my trip. It's in an envelope with your name. It's for you.

ADDIE. Seventeen hundred dollar bills! My God, Mr. Horace, I won't know how to count up that high. (*Shyly*) It's mighty kind and good of you. I don't know what to say for thanks—

CAL (*appears in doorway*). I'm back. (*No answer*) I'm back.

ADDIE. So we see.

HORACE. Well?

CAL. Nothing. I just went down and spoke my piece. Just like you told me. I say, "Mr. Horace he thank you mightily for the safe box arriving in good shape and he say you come right after supper to his house and bring Mr. Attorney-at-law Sol Fowler with you." Then I wipe my hands on my coat. Every time I ever told a lie in my whole life, I wipe my hands right after. Can't help doing it. Well, while I'm wiping my hands, Mr. Leo jump up and say to me, "What box? What you talking about?"

HORACE (*smiles*). Did he?

CAL. And Mr. Leo say he got to leave a little early cause he got something to do. And then Mr. Manders say Mr. Leo should sit right down and finish up his work and stop acting like somebody made him Mr. President. So he sit down. Now, just like I told you, Mr. Manders was mighty surprised with the message because he knows right well he brought the box— (*Points to box, sighs*) But he took it all right. Some men take everything easy and some do not.

HORACE (*puts his head back, laughs*). Mr. Leo was telling the truth; he *has* got something to do. I hope Manders don't keep him too long. (*Outside there is the sound of voices.* CAL *exits.* ADDIE *crosses quickly to* HORACE, *puts basket on table, begins to wheel his chair towards the stairs. Sharply*) No. Leave me where I am.

ADDIE. But that's Miss Regina coming back.

HORACE (*nods, looking at door*). Go away, Addie.

ADDIE (*hesitates*). Mr. Horace. Don't talk no more today. You don't feel well and it won't do no good—

HORACE (*as he hears footsteps in the hall*). Go on. (*She looks at him for a second, then picks up her sewing from table and exits as* REGINA *comes in from hall.* HORACE'*s chair is now so placed that he is in front of the table with the medicine.* REGINA *stands in the hall, shakes umbrella, stands it in the corner, takes off her cloak and throws it over the banister. She stares at* HORACE.)

REGINA (*as she takes off her gloves*). We had agreed that you were to stay in your part of this house and I in mine. This room is *my* part of the house. Please don't come down here again.

HORACE. I won't.

REGINA (*crosses towards bell-cord*). I'll get Cal to take you upstairs.

HORACE (*smiles*). Before you do I want to tell you that after all, we have invested our money in Hubbard Sons and Marshall, Cotton Manufacturers.

REGINA (*stops, turns, stares at him*). What are you talking about? You haven't seen Ben— When did you change your mind?

HORACE. I didn't change my mind. *I* didn't invest the money. (*Smiles*) It was invested for me.

REGINA (*angrily*). What—?

HORACE. I had eighty-eight thousand dollars' worth of Union Pacific bonds in that safe-deposit box. They are not there now. Go and look. (*As she stares at him, he points to the box*) Go and look, Regina. (*She crosses quickly to the box, opens it*) Those bonds are as negotiable as money.

REGINA (*turns back to him*). What kind of joke are you playing now? Is this for my benefit?

HORACE. I don't look in that box very often, but three days ago, on Wednesday it was, because I had made a decision—

REGINA. I want to know what you are talking about.

HORACE (*sharply*). Don't interrupt me again. Because I had made a decision, I sent for the box. The bonds were gone. Eighty-eight thousand dollars gone. (*He smiles at her.*)

REGINA (*after a moment's silence, quietly*). Do you think I'm crazy enough to believe what you're saying?

HORACE (*shrugs*). Believe anything you like.

REGINA (*stares at him, slowly*). Where did they go to?

HORACE. They are in Chicago. With Mr. Marshall, I should guess.

REGINA. What did they do? Walk to Chicago? Have you really gone crazy?

HORACE. Leo took the bonds.

REGINA (*turns sharply, then speaks softly, without conviction*). I don't believe it.

HORACE (*leans forward*). I wasn't there but I can guess what happened. This fine gentleman, to whom you were willing to marry your daughter, took the keys and opened the box. You remember that the day of the fight Oscar went to Chicago? Well, he went with my bonds that his son Leo had stolen for him. (*Pleasantly*) And for Ben, of course, too.

REGINA (*slowly, nods*). When did you find out the bonds were gone?

HORACE. Wednesday night.

REGINA. I thought that's what you said. Why have you waited three days to do anything? (*Suddenly laughs*) This *will* make a fine story.

HORACE (*nods*). Couldn't it?

REGINA (*still laughing*). A fine story to hold over their heads. How could they be such fools? (*Turns to him.*)

HORACE. But I'm not going to hold it over their heads.

REGINA (*the laugh stops*). What?

HORACE (*turns his chair to face her*). I'm going to let them keep the bonds—as a loan from you. An eighty-eight-thousand-dollar loan; they should be grateful to you. They will be, I think.

REGINA (*slowly, smiles*). I see. You are punishing me. But I won't let you punish me. If you won't do anything, I will. Now. (*She starts for door.*)

HORACE. You won't do anything. Because you can't. (REGINA *stops*) It won't do you any good to make trouble because I shall simply say that I lent them the bonds.

REGINA (*slowly*). You would do that?

HORACE. Yes. For once in your life I am tying your hands. There is nothing for you to do. (*There is silence. Then she sits down.*)

REGINA. I see. You are going to lend them the bonds and let them keep all the profit they make on them, and there is nothing I can do about it. Is that right?

HORACE. Yes.

REGINA (*softly*). Why did you say that I was making this gift?

HORACE. I was coming to that. I am going to make a new will, Regina, leaving you eighty-eight thousand dollars in Union Pacific bonds. The rest will go to Zan. It's true that your brothers have borrowed your share for a little while. After my death I advise you to talk to Ben and Oscar. They won't admit anything and Ben, I think, will be smart enough to see that he's safe. Because I knew about the theft and said nothing. Nor will I say anything as long as I live. Is that clear to you?

REGINA (*nods, softly, without looking at him*). You will not say anything as long as you live.

HORACE. That's right. And by that time they will probably have replaced your bonds, and then they'll belong to you and nobody but us will ever know what happened. (*Stops, smiles*) They'll be around any minute to see what I am going to do. I took good care to see that word reached Leo. They'll be mighty relieved to know I'm going to do nothing and Ben will think it all a capital joke on you. And that will be the end of that. There's nothing you can do to them, nothing you can do to me.

REGINA. You hate me very much.

HORACE. No.

REGINA. Oh, I think you do. (*Puts her head back, sighs*) Well, we haven't been very good together. Anyway, I don't hate you either. I have only contempt for you. I've always had.

HORACE. From the very first?

REGINA. I think so.

HORACE. I was in love with *you*. But why did *you* marry *me*?

REGINA. I was lonely when I was young.

HORACE. *You* were lonely?

REGINA. Not the way people usually mean. Lonely for all the things I wasn't going to get. Everybody in this house was so busy and there was so little place for what I wanted. I wanted the world. Then, and then—(*Smiles*) Papa died and left the money to Ben and Oscar.

HORACE. And you married me?

REGINA. Yes, I thought— But I was wrong. You were a small-town clerk then. You haven't changed.

HORACE (*nods, smiles*). And that wasn't what you wanted.

REGINA. No. No, it wasn't what I wanted. (*Pauses, leans back, pleasantly*) It took me a little while to find out I had made a mistake. As for you—I don't know. It was almost as if I couldn't stand the kind of man you were— (*Smiles, softly*) I used to lie there at night, praying you wouldn't come near—

HORACE. Really? It was as bad as that?

REGINA (*nods*). Remember when I went to Doctor Sloan and I told you he said there was something the matter with me and that you shouldn't touch me any more?

HORACE. I remember.

REGINA. But you believed it. I couldn't understand that. I couldn't understand that anybody could be such a soft fool. That was when I began to despise you.

HORACE (*puts his hand to his throat, looks at the bottle of medicine on table*). Why didn't you leave me?

REGINA. I told you I married you for something. It turned out it was only for this. (*Carefully*) This wasn't what I wanted, but it was something. I never thought about it much but if I had (HORACE *puts his hand to his throat*) I'd have known that you would die before I would. But I couldn't have known that you would get heart trouble so early and so bad. I'm lucky, Horace. I've always been lucky. (HORACE *turns slowly to the medicine*) I'll be lucky again. (HORACE *looks at her. Then he puts his hand to his throat. Because he cannot reach the bottle he moves the chair closer. He reaches for the medicine, takes out the cork, picks up the spoon. The bottle slips and smashes on the table. He draws in his breath, gasps.*)

HORACE. Please. Tell Addie— The other bottle is upstairs. (REGINA *has not moved. She does not move now. He stares at her. Then, suddenly as if he understood, he raises his voice. It is a panic-stricken whisper, too small to be heard outside the room*) Addie! Addie! Come— (*Stops as he hears the softness of his voice. He makes a sudden, furious spring from the chair to the stairs, taking the first few steps as if he were a desperate runner. On the fourth step he slips, gasps, grasps the rail, makes a great effort to reach the landing. When he reaches the landing, he is on his knees. His knees give way, he falls on the landing, out of view.* REGINA *has not turned during his climb up the stairs. Now she waits a second. Then she goes below the landing, speaks up.*)

REGINA. Horace. Horace. (*When there is no answer, she turns, calls*) Addie! Cal! Come in here. (*She starts up the steps.* ADDIE *and* CAL *appear. Both run towards the stairs*) He's had an attack. Come up here. (*They run up the steps quickly.*)

CAL. My God. Mr. Horace— (*They cannot be seen now.*)

REGINA (*her voice comes from the head of the stairs*). Be still, Cal. Bring him in here.

(*Before the footsteps and the voices have completely died away,* ALEXANDRA *appears in the hall door, in her raincloak and hood. She comes into the room, begins to unfasten the cloak, suddenly looks around, sees the empty wheel chair, stares, begins to move swiftly as if to look in the dining room. At the same moment* ADDIE *runs down the stairs.* ALEXANDRA *turns and stares up at* ADDIE.)

ALEXANDRA. Addie! What?

ADDIE (*takes* ALEXANDRA *by the shoulders*). I'm going for the doctor. Go upstairs. (ALEXANDRA *looks at her, then quickly breaks away and runs up the steps.* ADDIE *exits. The stage is empty for a minute. Then the front-door bell begins to ring. When there is no answer, it rings again. A second later* LEO *appears in the hall, talking as he comes in.*)

LEO (*very nervous*). Hello. (*Irritably*) Never saw any use ringing a bell when a door was open. If you are going to ring a bell, then somebody should answer it. (*Gets in the room, looks around, puzzled, listens, hears no sound*) Aunt Regina. (*He moves around restlessly*) Addie. (*Waits*) Where the hell— (*Crosses to the bell cord, rings it impatiently, waits, gets no answer, calls*) Cal! Cal! (CAL *appears on the stair landing.*)

CAL (*his voice is soft, shaken*). Mr. Leo. Miss Regina says you stop that screaming noise.

LEO (*angrily*). Where is everybody?

CAL. Mr. Horace he got an attack. He's bad. Miss Regina says you stop that noise.

LEO. Uncle Horace— What— What happened? (CAL *starts down the stairs, shakes his head, begins to move swiftly off.* LEO *looks around wildly*) But when— You seen Mr. Oscar or Mr. Ben? (CAL *shakes his head. Moves on.* LEO *grabs him by the arm*) Answer me, will you?

CAL. No, I ain't seen 'em. I ain't got time to answer you. I got to get things. (CAL *runs off.*)

LEO. But what's the matter with him? When did this happen— (*Calling after* CAL) You'd think Papa'd be some place where you could find him. I been chasing him all afternoon. (OSCAR *and* BEN *come into the room, talking excitedly.*)

OSCAR. I hope it's not a bad attack.

BEN. It's the first one he's had since he came home.

LEO. Papa, I've been looking all over town for you and Uncle Ben—

BEN. Where is he?

OSCAR. Addie said it was sudden.

BEN (*to* LEO). Where is he? When did it happen?

LEO. Upstairs. Will you listen to me, please? I been looking for you for—

OSCAR (*to* BEN). You think we should go up? (BEN, *looking up the steps, shakes his head.*)

BEN. I don't know. I don't know.

OSCAR (*shakes his head*). But he was all right—

LEO (*yelling*). *Will you listen to me?*

OSCAR (*sharply*). What is the matter with you?

LEO. I been trying to tell you. I been trying to find you for an hour—

OSCAR. Tell me what?

LEO. Uncle Horace knows about the bonds. He knows about them. He's had the box since Wednesday—

BEN (*sharply*). Stop shouting! What the hell are you talking about?

LEO (*furiously*). I'm telling you he knows about the bonds. Ain't that clear enough—

OSCAR (*grabbing* LEO's *arm*). You God-damn fool! Stop screaming!

BEN. Now what happened? Talk quietly.

LEO. You heard me. Uncle Horace knows about the bonds. He's known since Wednesday.

BEN (*after a second*). How do you know that?

LEO. Because Cal comes down to Manders and says the box came O.K. and—

OSCAR (*trembling*). That might not mean a thing—

LEO (*angrily*). No? It might not huh? Then he says Manders should come here tonight and bring So

Fowler with him. I guess that don't mean a thing either.

OSCAR (*to* BEN). Ben— What— Do you think he's seen the—

BEN (*motions to the box*). There's the box. (*Both* OSCAR *and* LEO *turn sharply.* LEO *makes a leap to the box*) You ass. Put it down. What are you going to do with it, eat it?

LEO. I'm going to— (*Starts.*)

BEN (*furiously*). Put it down. Don't touch it again. Now sit down and shut up for a minute.

OSCAR. Since Wednesday. (*To* LEO) You said he had it since Wednesday. Why didn't he say something— (*To* BEN) I don't understand—

LEO (*taking a step*). I can put it back. I can put it back before anybody knows.

BEN (*who is standing at the table, softly*). He's had it since Wednesday. Yet he hasn't said a word to us.

OSCAR. *Why? Why?*

LEO. What's the difference why? He was getting ready to say plenty. He was going to say it to Fowler tonight—

OSCAR (*angrily*). Be still. (*Turns to* BEN, *looks at him, waits.*)

BEN (*after a minute*). I don't believe that.

LEO (*wildly*). *You* don't believe it? What do I care what *you* believe? I do the dirty work and then—

BEN (*turning his head sharply to* LEO). I'm remembering that. I'm remembering that, Leo.

OSCAR. What do you mean?

LEO. You—

BEN (*to* OSCAR). If you don't shut that little fool up, I'll show you what I mean. For some reason he knows, but he don't say a word.

OSCAR. Maybe he didn't know that *we*—

BEN (*quickly*). That *Leo*— He's no fool. Does Manders know the bonds are missing?

LEO. How could I tell? I was half crazy. I don't think so. Because Manders seemed kind of puzzled and—

OSCAR. But we got to find out— (*He breaks off as* CAL *comes into the room carrying a kettle of hot water.*)

BEN. How is he, Cal?

CAL. I don't know, Mr. Ben. He was bad. (*Going towards stairs.*)

OSCAR. But when did it happen?

CAL (*shrugs*). He wasn't feeling bad early. (ADDIE *comes in quickly from the hall*) Then there he is next thing on the landing, fallen over, his eyes tight—

ADDIE (*to* CAL). Dr. Sloan's over at the Ballongs. Hitch the buggy and go get him. (*She takes the kettle and cloths from him, pushes him, runs up the stairs*) Go on. (*She disappears.* CAL *exits.*)

BEN. Never seen Sloan anywhere when you need him.

OSCAR (*softly*). Sounds bad.

LEO. He would have told *her* about it. Aunt Regina. He would have told his own wife—

BEN (*turning to* LEO). Yes, he might have told her. But they weren't on such pretty terms and maybe he didn't. Maybe he didn't. (*Goes quickly to* LEO) Now, listen to me. If she doesn't know, it may work out all right. If she does know, you're to say he lent you the bonds.

LEO. Lent them to me! Who's going to believe that?

BEN. Nobody.

OSCAR (*to* LEO). Don't you understand? It can't do no harm to say it—

LEO. Why should I say he lent them to me? Why not to you? (*Carefully*) Why not to Uncle Ben?

BEN (*smiles*). Just because he didn't lend them to me. Remember that.

LEO. But all he has to do is say he didn't lend them to me—

BEN (*furiously*). But for some reason, he doesn't seem to be talking, does he?
(*There are footsteps above. They all stand looking at the stairs.* REGINA *begins to come slowly down.*)

BEN. What happened?

REGINA. He's had a bad attack.

OSCAR. Too bad. I'm so sorry we weren't here when—when Horace needed us.

BEN. When *you* needed us.

REGINA (*looks at him*). Yes.

BEN. How is he? Can we—can we g up?

REGINA (*shakes her head*). He's no conscious.

OSCAR (*pacing around*). It's that—it's that bad? Wouldn't you thinl Sloan could be found quickly, jus once, just once?

REGINA. I don't think there is mucl for him to do.

BEN. Oh, don't talk like that. He' come through attacks before. He wil now.
(REGINA *sits down. After a secon she speaks softly.*)

REGINA. Well. We haven't seen eacl other since the day of our fight.

BEN (*tenderly*). That was nothing Why, you and Oscar and I used t fight when we were kids.

OSCAR (*hurriedly*). Don't you thin we should go up? Is there anythin we can do for Horace—

BEN. You don't feel well. Ah—

REGINA (*without looking at them* No, I don't. (*Slight pause*) Horac told me about the bonds this afte noon. (*There is an immedia shocked silence.*)

LEO. The bonds. What do you mean What bonds? What—

BEN (*looks at him furiously. The to* REGINA). The Union Pacifi bonds? *Horace's* Union Pacif bonds?

REGINA. Yes.

OSCAR (*steps to her, very nervously*). Well. Well what—what about them? What—what could he say?

REGINA. He said that Leo had stolen the bonds and given them to you.

OSCAR (*aghast, very loudly*). That's ridiculous, Regina, absolutely—

LEO. I don't know what you're talking about. What would I— Why—

REGINA (*wearily to* BEN). Isn't it enough that he stole them from me? Do I have to listen to this in the bargain?

OSCAR. You are talking—

LEO. I didn't steal anything. I don't know why—

REGINA (*to* BEN). Would you ask them to stop that, please?

(*There is silence for a minute.* BEN *glowers at* OSCAR *and* LEO.)

BEN. Aren't we starting at the wrong end, Regina? What did Horace tell you?

REGINA (*smiles at him*). He told me that Leo had stolen the bonds.

LEO. I didn't steal—

REGINA. Please. Let me finish. Then he told me that he was going to pretend that he had lent them to you (LEO *turns sharply to* REGINA, *then looks at* OSCAR, *then looks back at* REGINA) as a present from me—to my brothers. He said there was nothing I could do about it. He said the rest of his money would go to Alexandra. That is all.

(*There is a silence.* OSCAR *coughs,* LEO *smiles slyly.*)

LEO (*taking a step to her*). I told you he had lent them— I could have told you—

REGINA (*ignores him, smiles sadly at* BEN). So I'm very badly off, you see. (*Carefully*) But Horace said there was nothing I could do about it as long as he was alive to say he had lent you the bonds.

BEN. You shouldn't feel that way. It can all be explained, all be adjusted. It isn't as bad—

REGINA. So you, at least, are willing to admit that the bonds were stolen?

BEN (OSCAR *laughs nervously*). I admit no such thing. It's possible that Horace made up that part of the story to tease you— (*Looks at her*) Or perhaps to punish you. Punish you.

REGINA (*sadly*). It's not a pleasant story. I feel bad, Ben, naturally. I hadn't thought—

BEN. Now you shall have the bonds safely back. That was the understanding, wasn't it, Oscar?

OSCAR. Yes.

REGINA. I'm glad to know that. (*Smiles*) Ah, I had greater hopes—

BEN. Don't talk that way. That's foolish. (*Looks at his watch*) I think we ought to drive out for Sloan ourselves. If we can't find him we'll go over to Senateville for Doctor Morris. And don't think I'm dismissing this other business. I'm not. We'll have it all out on a more appropriate day.

REGINA (*looks up, quietly*). I don't think you had better go yet. I think you had better stay and sit down.

BEN. We'll be back with Sloan.

REGINA. Cal has gone for him. I don't want you to go.

BEN. Now don't worry and—

REGINA. You will come back in this room and sit down. I have something more to say.

BEN (*turns, comes towards her*). Since when do I take orders from you?

REGINA (*smiles*). You don't—yet. (*Sharply*) Come back, Oscar. You too, Leo.

OSCAR (*sure of himself, laughs*). My dear Regina—

BEN (*softly, pats her hand*). Horace has already clipped your wings and very wittily. Do I have to clip them, too? (*Smiles at her*) You'd get farther with a smile, Regina. I'm a soft man for a woman's smile.

REGINA. I'm smiling, Ben. I'm smiling because you are quite safe while Horace lives. But I don't think Horace will live. And if he doesn't live I shall want seventy-five per cent in exchange for the bonds.

BEN (*steps back, whistles, laughs*). Greedy! What a greedy girl you are! You want so much of everything.

REGINA. Yes. And if I don't get what I want I am going to put all three of you in jail.

OSCAR (*furiously*). You're mighty crazy. Having just admitted—

BEN. And on what evidence woul you put Oscar and Leo in jail?

REGINA (*laughs, gaily*). Oscar, liste to him. He's getting ready to swea that it was you and Leo! What d you say to that? (OSCAR *turns fur ously towards* BEN) Oh, don't be ar gry, Oscar. I'm going to see that h goes in with you.

BEN. Try anything you like, Regin (*Sharply*) And now we can stop a this and say good-bye to you. (ALE ANDRA *comes slowly down the steps* It's his money and he's obviously wil ing to let us borrow it. (*More plea antly*) Learn to make threats whe you can carry them through. For ho many years have I told you a goo looking woman gets more by bein soft and appealing? Mama used t tell you that. (*Looks at his watch* Where the hell is Sloan? (*To* OSCAR Take the buggy and— (*As* BEN *turn to* OSCAR, *he sees* ALEXANDRA. *Sh walks stiffly. She goes slowly to th lower window, her head bent. The all turn to look at her.*)

OSCAR (*after a second, moving t ward her*). What? Alexandra— (*Sh does not answer. After a second,* A DIE *comes slowly down the stair moving as if she were very tired. A foot of steps, she looks at* ALEXAN DRA, *then turns and slowly crosses door and exits.* REGINA *rises.* BE *looks nervously at* ALEXANDRA, REGINA.)

OSCAR (*as* ADDIE *passes him, irritab to* ALEXANDRA). Well, what is (*Turns into room—sees* ADDIE *at fo of steps*) What's— (BEN *puts up hand, shakes his head*) My God, didn't know—who *could* have know —I didn't know he was that sic Well, well—I—

(REGINA *stands quietly, her back to them.*)

BEN (*softly, sincerely*). Seems like yesterday when he first came here.

OSCAR (*sincerely, nervously*). Yes, that's true. (*Turns to* BEN) The whole town loved him and respected him.

ALEXANDRA (*turns*). Did you love him, Uncle Oscar?

OSCAR. Certainly, I— What a strange thing to ask! I—

ALEXANDRA. Did you love him, Uncle Ben?

BEN (*simply*). He had—

ALEXANDRA (*suddenly starts to laugh very loudly*). And you, Mama, did you love him, too?

REGINA. I know what you feel, Alexandra, but please try to control yourself.

ALEXANDRA (*still laughing*). I'm trying, Mama. I'm trying very hard.

BEN. Grief makes some people laugh and some people cry. It's better to cry, Alexandra.

ALEXANDRA (*the laugh has stopped. Tensely moves toward* REGINA). What was Papa doing on the staircase?
(BEN *turns to look at* ALEXANDRA.)

REGINA. Please go and lie down, my dear. We all need time to get over shocks like this. (ALEXANDRA *does not move.* REGINA'S *voice becomes softer, more insistent*) Please go, Alexandra.

ALEXANDRA. No, Mama. I'll wait. I've got to talk to you.

REGINA. Later. Go and rest now.

ALEXANDRA (*quietly*). I'll wait, Mama. I've plenty of time.

REGINA (*hesitates, stares, makes a half shrug, turns back to* BEN). As I was saying. Tomorrow morning I am going up to Judge Simmes. I shall tell him about Leo.

BEN (*motioning toward* ALEXANDRA). Not in front of the child, Regina. I—

REGINA (*turns to him. Sharply*). I didn't ask her to stay. Tomorrow morning I go to Judge Simmes—

OSCAR. And what proof? What proof of all this—

REGINA (*turns sharply*). None. I won't need any. The bonds are missing and they are with Marshall. That will be enough. If it isn't, I'll add what's necessary.

BEN. I'm sure of that.

REGINA (*turns to* BEN). You can be quite sure.

OSCAR. We'll deny—

REGINA. Deny your heads off. You couldn't find a jury that wouldn't weep for a woman whose brothers steal from her. And you couldn't find twelve men in this state you haven't cheated and hate you for it.

OSCAR. What kind of talk is this? You couldn't do anything like that! We're your own brothers. (*Points upstairs*) How can you talk that way when upstairs not five minutes ago—

REGINA (*slowly*). There are people who can never go back, who must finish what they start. I am one of those people, Oscar. (*After a slight pause*) Where was I? (*Smiles at* BEN) Well, they'll convict you. But I won't care much if they don't. (*Leans forward, pleasantly*) Because by that time you'll be ruined. I shall also tell my story to Mr. Marshall, who likes me, I think, and who will not want to be involved in your scandal. A respectable firm like Marshall and Company. The deal would be off in an hour. (*Turns to them angrily*) And you know it. Now I don't want to hear any more from any of you. *You'll do no more bargaining in this house.* I'll take my seventy-five per cent and we'll forget the story forever. That's one way of doing it, and the way I prefer. You know me well enough to know that I don't mind taking the other way.

BEN (*after a second, slowly*). None of us have ever known you well enough, Regina.

REGINA. You're getting old, Ben. Your tricks aren't as smart as they used to be. (*There is no answer. She waits, then smiles*) All right. I take it that's settled and I get what I asked for.

OSCAR (*furiously to* BEN). Are you going to let her do this—

BEN (*turns to look at him, slowly*). You have a suggestion?

REGINA (*puts her arms above her head, stretches, laughs*). No, he hasn't. All right. Now, Leo, I have forgotten that you ever saw the bonds. (*Archly, to* BEN *and* OSCAR) And as long as you boys both behave yourselves, I've forgotten that we ever talked about them. You can draw up the necessary papers tomorrow. (BEN *laughs.* LEO *stares at him, starts for door. Exits.* OSCAR *moves towards door angrily.* REGINA *looks at* BEN, *nods, laughs with him. For a second,* OSCAR *stands in the door, looking back at them. Then he* exits.)

REGINA. You're a good loser, Ben. I like that.

BEN (*he picks up his coat, then turns to her*). Well, I say to myself, what's the good? You and I aren't like Oscar. We're not sour people. I think that comes from a good digestion. Then, too, one loses today and wins tomorrow. I say to myself, years of planning and I get what I want. Then I don't get it. But I'm not discouraged. The century's turning, the world is open. Open for people like you and me. Ready for us, waiting for us. After all this is just the beginning. There are hundreds of Hubbards sitting in rooms like this throughout the country. All their names aren't Hubbard, but they are all Hubbards and they will own this country some day. We'll get along.

REGINA (*smiles*). I think so.

BEN. Then, too, I say to myself things may change. (*Looks at* ALEXANDRA) I agree with Alexandra. What is a man in a wheel chair doing on a staircase? I ask myself that.

REGINA (*looks up at him*). And what do you answer?

BEN. I have no answer. But maybe some day I will. Maybe never, but maybe some day. (*Smiles. Pats her arm*) When I do, I'll let you know. (*Goes towards hall.*)

REGINA. When you do, write me. I will be in Chicago. (*Gaily*) Ah, Ben, if Papa had only left me his money!

BEN. I'll see you tomorrow.

REGINA. Oh, yes. Certainly. You'll be sort of working for me now.

BEN (*as he passes* ALEXANDRA, *smiles*) Alexandra, you're turning out to be a right interesting girl. (*Looks at* REGINA) Well, good night all. (*He exits.*)

REGINA (*sits quietly for a second, stretches, turns to look at* ALEXANDRA). What do you want to talk to me about, Alexandra?

ALEXANDRA (*slowly*). I've changed my mind. I don't want to talk. There's nothing to talk about now.

REGINA. You're acting very strange. Not like yourself. You've had a bad shock today. I know that. And you loved Papa, but you must have expected this to come some day. You knew how sick he was.

ALEXANDRA. I knew. We all knew.

REGINA. It will be good for you to get away from here. Good for me, too. Time heals most wounds, Alexandra. You're young, you shall have all the things I wanted. I'll make the world for you the way I wanted it to be for me. (*Uncomfortably*) Don't sit there staring. You've been around Birdie so much you're getting just like her.

ALEXANDRA (*nods*). Funny. That's what Aunt Birdie said today.

REGINA (*nods*). Be good for you to get away from all this.
(ADDIE *enters.*)

ADDIE. Cal is back, Miss Regina. He says Dr. Sloan will be coming in a few minutes.

REGINA. We'll go in a few weeks. A few weeks! That means two or three Saturdays, two or three Sundays. (*Sighs*) Well, I'm very tired. I shall go to bed. I don't want any supper. Put the lights out and lock up. (ADDIE *moves to the piano lamp, turns it out*) You go to your room, Alexandra. Addie will bring you something hot You look very tired. (*Rises. To* ADDIE) Call me when Dr. Sloan gets here. I don't want to see anybody else. I don't want any condolence calls tonight. The whole town will be over.

ALEXANDRA. Mama, I'm not coming with you. I'm not going to Chicago.

REGINA (*turns to her*). You're very upset, Alexandra.

ALEXANDRA (*quietly*). I mean what I say. With all my heart.

REGINA. We'll talk about it tomorrow. The morning will make a difference.

ALEXANDRA. It won't make any difference. And there isn't anything to talk about. I am going away from you. Because I want to. Because I know Papa would want me to.

REGINA (*puzzled, careful, polite*). You *know* your papa wanted you to go away from me?

ALEXANDRA. Yes.

REGINA (*softly*). And if I say no?

ALEXANDRA (*looks at her*). Say it, Mama, say it. And see what happens.

REGINA (*softly, after a pause*). And if I make you stay?

ALEXANDRA. That would be foolish. It wouldn't work in the end.

REGINA. You're very serious about it, aren't you? (*Crosses to stairs*) Well, you'll change your mind in a few days.

ALEXANDRA. You only change your mind when you want to. And I won't want to.

REGINA (*going up the steps*) Alexandra, I've come to the end of my rope. Somewhere there has to be what I want, too. Life goes too fast. Do what you want; think what you want; go where you want. I'd like to keep you with me, but I won't make you stay. Too many people used to make me do too many things. No, I won't make you stay.

ALEXANDRA. You couldn't, Mama, because I want to leave here. As I've never wanted anything in my life before. Because now I understand what Papa was trying to tell me. (*Pause*) All in one day: Addie said there were people who ate the earth and other people who stood around and watched them do it. And just now Uncle Ben said the same thing. Really, he said the same thing. (*Tensely*) Well, tell him for me, Mama, I'm not going to stand around and watch you do it. Tell him I'll be fighting as hard as he'll be fighting (*Rises*) some place where people don't just stand around and watch.

REGINA. Well, you have spirit, after all. I used to think you were all sugar water. We don't have to be bad friends. I don't want us to be bad friends, Alexandra. (*Starts, stops, turns to* ALEXANDRA) Would you like to come and talk to me, Alexandra? Would you—would you like to sleep in my room tonight?

ALEXANDRA (*takes a step towards her*). Are you afraid, Mama? (REGINA *does not answer. She moves slowly out of sight.* ADDIE *comes to* ALEXANDRA, *presses her arm.*)

CURTAIN

The Man Who Came to Dinner

BY MOSS HART AND GEORGE S. KAUFMAN

TO

ALEXANDER WOOLLCOTT

FOR REASONS

THAT ARE NOBODY'S BUSINESS

The Authors

The Man Who Came to Dinner was first produced at the Music Box Theatre, New York City, by Sam H. Harris, on October 16, 1939. Following is the original cast:

Mrs. Ernest W. Stanley	Virginia Hammond
Miss Preen	Mary Wickes
Richard Stanley	Gordon Merrick
June Stanley	Barbara Wooddell
John	George Probert
Sarah	Mrs. Priestley Morrison
Mrs. Dexter	Barbara Adams
Mrs. McCutcheon	Edmonia Nolley
Mr. Stanley	George Lessey
Maggie Cutler	Edith Atwater
Dr. Bradley	Dudley Clements
Sheridan Whiteside	Monty Woolley
Harriet Stanley	Ruth Vivian
Bert Jefferson	Theodore Newton
Professor Metz	LeRoi Operti
The Luncheon Guests	Phil Sheridan Charles Washington William Postance
Mr. Baker	Carl Johnson
Expressman	Harold Woolf
Lorraine Sheldon	Carol Goodner
Sandy	Michael Harvey
Beverly Carlton	John Hoysradt
Westcott	Edward Fisher
Radio Technicians	Rodney Stewart Carl Johnson
Six Young Boys	Daniel Leone Jack Whitman Daniel Landon Donald Landon DeWitt Purdue Robert Rea
Banjo	David Burns
Two Deputies	Curtis Karpe Phil Sheridan
A Plainclothes Man	William Postance

Stage Manager—Bernard Hart

Setting by Donald Oenslager

With thanks to Cole Porter for the music and lyrics.

SCENES

The scene is the home of Mr. and Mrs. Stanley, in a small town in Ohi

ACT ONE

SCENE I

A December morning

SCENE II

About a week later

ACT TWO

Another week has passed

Christmas Eve

ACT THREE

Christmas morning

THE MAN WHO CAME TO DINNER

ACT ONE

SCENE I

The curtain rises on the attractive living room in the home of MR. *and* MRS. ERNEST W. STANLEY, *in a small town in Ohio. The* STANLEYS *are obviously people of means. The room is large, comfortable, tastefully furnished. Double doors lead into a library; there is a glimpse of a dining room at the rear, and we see the first half dozen steps of a handsome curved staircase. At the other side, bay windows, the entrance hall, the outer door.*

MRS. STANLEY *is hovering nervously near the library doors, which are tightly closed. She advances a step or two, retreats, advances again and this time musters up enough courage to listen at the door. Suddenly the doors are opened and she has to leap back.*

A NURSE *in full uniform emerges—scurries, rather, out of the room.*

An angry voice from within speeds her on her way: "Great dribbling cow!"

MRS. STANLEY (*eagerly*). How is he? Is he coming out?

(*But the* NURSE *has already disappeared into the dining room. Simultaneously the doorbell rings—at the same time a young lad of twenty-one,* RICHARD STANLEY, *is descending the stairs.*)

RICHARD. I'll go, Mother.

(JOHN, *a white-coated servant, comes hurrying in from the dining room and starts up the stairs, two at a time.*)

MRS. STANLEY. What's the matter? What is it?

JOHN. They want pillows. (*And he is out of sight.*)

(*Meanwhile the* NURSE *is returning to the sickroom. The voice is heard again as she opens the doors. "Don't call yourself a doctor in my presence! You're a quack if I ever saw one!"* RICHARD *returns from the hall, carrying two huge packages and a sheaf of cablegrams.*)

RICHARD. Four more cablegrams and more packages. . . . Dad is going crazy upstairs, with that bell ringing all the time.

(*Meanwhile* JUNE, *the daughter of the house, has come down the stairs. An attractive girl of twenty. At the same time the telephone is ringing.*)

MRS. STANLEY. Oh, dear! . . . June, will you go? . . . What did you say, Richard?

RICHARD (*examining the packages*). One's from New York and one from San Francisco.

MRS. STANLEY. There was something from Alaska early this morning.

JUNE (*at the telephone*). Yes? . . . Yes, that's right.

MRS. STANLEY. Who is it?
(*Before* JUNE *can answer, the double doors are opened again and the* NURSE *appears. The voice calls after her: "Doesn't that bird-brain of yours ever function?"*)

THE NURSE. I—I'll get them right away. . . . He wants some Players Club cigarettes.

MRS. STANLEY. Players Club?

RICHARD. They have 'em at Kitchener's. I'll run down and get' em. (*He is off.*)

JUNE (*still at the phone*). Hello. . . . Yes, I'm waiting.

MRS. STANLEY. Tell me, Miss Preen, is he—are they bringing him out soon?

MISS PREEN (*wearily*). We're getting him out of bed now. He'll be out very soon . . . Oh, thank you.
(*This last is to* JOHN, *who has descended the stairs with three or four pillows.*)

MRS. STANLEY. Oh, I'm so glad. He must be very happy.
(*And again we hear the invalid's voice as* MISS PREEN *passes into the room. "Trapped like a rat in this hell-hole! Take your fishhooks off me!"*)

JUNE (*at the phone*). Hello. . . . Yes, he's here, but he can't come to the phone right now . . . London? (*She covers the transmitter with her hand*) It's London calling Mr. Whiteside.

MRS. STANLEY. London? My, my!

JUNE. Two o'clock? Yes, I think he could talk then. All right. (*She hangs up*) Well, who do you think that was? Mr. H. G. Wells.

MRS. STANLEY (*wild-eyed*). H. G. Wells? On our telephone?
(*The doorbell again.*)

JUNE. I'll go. This is certainly a busy house.
(*In the meantime* SARAH, *the cook, has come from the dining room with a pitcher of orange juice.*)

MRS. STANLEY (*as* SARAH *knocks on the double doors*). Oh, that's fine, Sarah. Is it fresh?

SARAH. Yes, ma'am.
(*The doors are opened;* SARAH *hands the orange juice to the nurse. The voice roars once more: "You have the touch of a sex-starved cobra!"*)

SARAH (*beaming*). His voice is just the same as on the radio.
(*She disappears into the dining room as* JUNE *returns from the entrance hall, ushering in two friends of her mother's,* MRS. DEXTER *and* MRS. MC CUTCHEON. *One is carrying a flowering plant, partially wrapped; the other is holding, with some care, what turns out to be a jar of calf's-foot jelly.*)

THE LADIES. Good morning!

MRS. STANLEY. Girls, what do you think? He's getting up and coming out today!

MRS. MC CUTCHEON. You don't mean it!

MRS. DEXTER. Can we stay and see him?

MRS. STANLEY. Why, of course—he'd love it. Girls, do you know what just happened?

JUNE (*departing*). I'll be upstairs, Mother, if you want me.

MRS. STANLEY. What? . . . Oh, yes. June, tell your father he'd better come down, will you? Mr. Whiteside is coming out.

MRS. DEXTER. Is he really coming out today? I brought him a plant— Do you think it's all right if I give it to him?

MRS. STANLEY. Why, I think that would be lovely.

MRS. MC CUTCHEON. And some calf's-foot jelly.

MRS. STANLEY. Why, how nice! Who do you think was on the phone just now? H. G. Wells, from London. And look at those cablegrams. He's had calls and messages from all over this country and Europe. The New York *Times,* and Radio City Music Hall—I don't know why *they* called—and Felix Frankfurter, and Dr. Dafoe, the Mount Wilson Observatory—I just can't tell you what's been going on.

MRS. DEXTER. There's a big piece about it in this week's *Time*. Did you see it? (*Drawing it out of her bag.*)

MRS. STANLEY. No—really?

MRS. MC CUTCHEON. Your name's in it too, Daisy. It tells all about the whole thing. Listen: "Portly Sheridan Whiteside, critic, lecturer, wit, radio orator, intimate friend of the great and near great, last week found his celebrated wit no weapon with which to combat a fractured hip. The Falstaffian Mr. Whiteside, trekking across the country on one of his annual lecture tours, met his Waterloo in the shape of a small piece of ice on the doorstep of Mr. and Mrs. Ernest W. Stanley, of Mesalia, Ohio. Result: Cancelled lectures and disappointment to thousands of adoring clubwomen in Omaha, Denver, and points west. Further result: The idol of the air waves rests until further notice in home of surprised Mr. and Mrs. Stanley. Possibility: Christmas may be postponed this year." What's *that* mean?

MRS. STANLEY. Why, what do you think of that? (*She takes the magazine; reads*) "A small piece of ice on the doorstep of Mr. and Mrs. Ernest"—think of it!

MRS. MC CUTCHEON. Of course if it were *my* house, Daisy, I'd have a bronze plate put on the step, right where he fell.

MRS. STANLEY. Well, of course I felt terrible about it. He just never goes to dinner anywhere, and he finally agreed to come here, and then *this* had to happen. Poor Mr. Whiteside! But it's going to be so wonderful having him with us, even for a little while. Just think of it! We'll sit around in the evening and discuss books and plays, all the great people he's known. And he'll talk in that wonderful way of his. He may even read "Good-bye, Mr. Chips" to us.

(MR. STANLEY, *solid, substantial—the American business man—is descending the stairs.*)

STANLEY. Daisy, I can't wait any longer. If—ah, good morning, ladies.

MRS. STANLEY. Ernest, he's coming out any minute, and H. G. Wells telephoned from London, and we're in *Time*. Look!

STANLEY (*taking the magazine*). I don't like this kind of publicity at all, Daisy. When do you suppose he's going to leave?

MRS. STANLEY. Well, he's only getting up this morning—after all, he's had quite a shock, and he's been in bed for two full weeks. He'll certainly have to rest a few days, Ernest.

STANLEY. Well, I'm sure it's a great honor, his being in the house, but it *is* a little upsetting—phone going all the time, bells ringing, messenger boys running in and out—
(*Out of the sickroom comes a business-like-looking young woman about thirty. Her name is* MARGARET CUTLER—MAGGIE *to her friends.*)

MAGGIE. Pardon me, Mrs. Stanley—have the cigarettes come yet?

MRS. STANLEY. They're on the way, Miss Cutler. My son went for them.

MAGGIE. Thank you.

MRS. STANLEY. Ah—this is Miss Cutler, Mr. Whiteside's secretary.
(*An exchange of "How do you do's?"*)

MAGGIE. May I move this chair?

MRS. STANLEY (*all eagerness*). You mean he's—coming out now?

MAGGIE (*quietly*). He is indeed.

MRS. STANLEY. Ernest, call June. June! June! Mr. Whiteside is coming out!

(JOHN, *visible in the dining room, summons* SARAH *to attend the excitement. "Sarah! Sarah!"* SARAH *and* JOHN *appear in the dining-room entrance,* JUNE *on the stairs.* MRS. STANLEY *and the two other ladies are keenly expectant; even* MR. STANLEY *is on the qui vive. The double doors are opened once more, and* DR. BRADLEY *appears, bag in hand. He has taken a good deal of punishment, and speaks with a rather false heartiness.*)

DR. BRADLEY. Well, here we are, merry and bright. Good morning, good morning. Bring our little patient out, Miss Preen.
(*A moment's pause, and then a wheelchair is rolled through the door. It is full of pillows, blankets, and* SHERIDAN WHITESIDE. SHERIDAN WHITESIDE *is indeed portly and Falstaffian. He is wearing an elaborate velvet smoking jacket and a very loud tie, and he looks like every caricature ever drawn of him. There is a hush as the wheelchair rolls into the room. Welcoming smiles break over every face. The chair comes to a halt;* MR. WHITESIDE *looks slowly around, into each and every beaming face. His fingers drum for a moment on the arm of the chair. He looks slowly around once more. And then he speaks.*)

WHITESIDE (*quietly, to* MAGGIE). I may vomit.

MRS. STANLEY (*with a nervous little laugh*). Good morning, Mr. Whiteside. I'm Mrs. Ernest Stanley—remember? And this is Mr. Stanley.

STANLEY. How do you do, Mr. Whiteside? I hope that you are better.

WHITESIDE. Thank you. I am suing you for a hundred and fifty thousand dollars.

STANLEY. How's that? What?

WHITESIDE. I said I am suing you for a hundred and fifty thousand dollars.

MRS. STANLEY. You mean—because you fell on our steps, Mr. Whiteside?

WHITESIDE. Samuel J. Liebowitz will explain it to you in court. . . . Who are those two harpies standing there like the kiss of death?
(MRS. MC CUTCHEON, *with a little gasp, drops the calf's-foot jelly. It smashes on the floor.*)

MRS. MC CUTCHEON. Oh, dear! My calf's-foot jelly.

WHITESIDE. Made from your own foot, I have no doubt. And now, Mrs. Stanley, I have a few small matters to take up with you. Since this corner druggist at my elbow tells me that I shall be confined in this mouldy mortuary for at least another ten days, due entirely to your stupidity and negligence, I shall have to carry on my activities as best I can. I shall require the exclusive use of this room, as well as that drafty sewer which you call the library. I want no one to come in or out while I am in this room.

STANLEY. What do you mean, sir?

MRS. STANLEY (*stunned*). But we have to go up the stairs to get to our rooms, Mr. Whiteside.

WHITESIDE. Isn't there a back entrance?

MRS. STANLEY. Why—yes.

WHITESIDE. Then use that. I shall also require a room for my secretary, Miss Cutler. I shall have a great many incoming and outgoing calls, so please use the telephone as little as possible. I sleep until noon and require quiet through the house until that hour. There will be five for lunch today. Where is the cook?

STANLEY. Mr. Whiteside, if I may interrupt for a moment—

WHITESIDE. You may not, sir. . . . Will you take your clammy hand off my chair? (*This last to the nurse*) . . . And now will you all leave quietly, or must I ask Miss Cutler to pass among you with a baseball bat?
(MRS. DEXTER *and* MRS MC CUTCHEON *are beating a hasty retreat, their gifts still in hand.*)

MRS. MC CUTCHEON. Well—goodbye, Daisy. We'll call you— Oh, no, we mustn't use the phone. Well—we'll see you. (*And they are gone.*)

STANLEY (*boldly*). Now look here, Mr. Whiteside—

WHITESIDE. There is nothing to discuss, sir. Considering the damage I have suffered at your hands, I am asking very little. Good day.

STANLEY (*controlling himself*). I'll call you from the office later, Daisy.

WHITESIDE. Not on this phone, please.
(STANLEY *gives him a look, but goes.*)

WHITESIDE. Here is the menu for lunch. (*He extends a slip of paper to* MRS. STANLEY.)

MRS. STANLEY. But—I've already ordered lunch.

WHITESIDE. It will be sent up to you on a tray. I am using the dining room for my guests. . . . Where are those cigarettes?

MRS. STANLEY. Why—my son went for them. I don't know why he —here, Sarah. (*She hands* SARAH *the luncheon slip*) I'll—have mine upstairs on a tray. (SARAH *and* JOHN *depart.*)

WHITESIDE (*to* JUNE, *who has been posed on the landing during all this*). Young lady, will you either go up those stairs or come down them? I cannot stand indecision.
(JUNE *is about to speak, decides against it, and ascends the stairs with a good deal of spirit.* MRS. STANLEY *is hovering uncertainly on the steps as* RICHARD *returns with the cigarettes.*)

RICHARD. Oh, good morning. I'm sorry I was so long—I had to go to three different stores.

WHITESIDE. How did you travel? By ox-cart?
(RICHARD *is considerably taken aback. His eyes go to his mother, who motions to him to come up the stairs. They disappear together, their eyes unsteadily on* WHITESIDE.)

WHITESIDE. Is there a man in the world who suffers as I do from the gross inadequacies of the human race? (*To the* NURSE, *who is fussing around the chair again*) Take those canal boats away from me! (*She obeys, hastily*) Go in and read the life of Florence Nightingale and learn how unfitted you are for your chosen profession. (MISS PREEN *glares at him, but goes.*)

DR. BRADLEY (*heartily*). Well, I think I can safely leave you in Miss Cutler's capable hands. Shall I loo[k] in again this afternoon?

WHITESIDE. If you do, I shall spi[t] right in your eye.

DR. BRADLEY. What a sense of humo[r] you writers have! By the way, it isn'[t] really worth mentioning, but—I'v[e] been doing a little writing myself[.] About my medical experiences.

WHITESIDE (*quietly*). Am I to b[e] spared nothing?

DR. BRADLEY. Would it be too muc[h] to ask you to—glance over it whil[e] you're here?

WHITESIDE (*eyes half closed, a[s] though the pain were too exquisite t[o] bear*). Trapped.

DR. BRADLEY (*delving into his bag*) I just happen to have a copy wit[h] me. (*He brings out a tremendou[s] manuscript*) "Forty Years an Ohi[o] Doctor. The Story of a Humbl[e] Practitioner."

WHITESIDE. I shall drop everything[.]

DR. BRADLEY. Much obliged, and [I] hope you like it. Well, see you o[n] the morrow. Keep that hip quiet an[d] don't forget those little pills. (*H[e] goes.*)

WHITESIDE (*handing the manu[-] script to* MAGGIE). Maggie, will yo[u] take *Forty Years Below the Nave[l]* or whatever it's called?

MAGGIE (*surveying him*). I must sa[y] you have certainly behaved with al[l] of your accustomed grace and charm[.]

WHITESIDE. Look here, Puss—I am i[n] no mood to discuss my behavio[r] good or bad.

MAGGIE. These people have done everything in their power to make you comfortable. And they happen, God knows why, to look upon you with a certain wonder and admiration.

WHITESIDE. If they had looked a little more carefully at their doorstep I would not be troubling them now. I did not wish to cross their cheerless threshold. I was hounded and badgered into it. I now find myself, after two weeks of racking pain, accused of behaving without charm. What would you have me do? Kiss them?

MAGGIE (*giving up*). Very well, Sherry. After ten years I should have known better than to try to do anything about your manners. But when I finally give up this job I may write a book about it all. *Cavalcade of Insult*, or *Through the Years with Prince Charming*.

WHITESIDE. Listen, Repulsive, you are tied to me with an umbilical cord made of piano wire. And now if we may dismiss the subject of my charm, for which, incidentally, I receive fifteen hundred dollars per appearance, possibly we can go to work . . . Oh, no, we can't. Yes?
(*This last is addressed to a wraith-like lady of uncertain years, who has more or less floated into the room. She is carrying a large spray of holly, and her whole manner suggests something not quite of this world.*)

THE LADY (*her voice seems to float, too*). My name is Harriet Stanley. I know you are Sheridan Whiteside. I saw this holly, framed green against the pine trees. I remembered what you had written, about *Tess* and *Jude the Obscure*. It was the nicest present I could bring you. (*She places the holly in his lap, and drifts out of the room again.*)

WHITESIDE (*his eyes following her*). For God's sake, what was that?

MAGGIE. That was Mr. Stanley's sister, Harriet. I've talked to her a few times—she's quite strange.

WHITESIDE. Strange? She's right out of *The Hound of the Baskervilles*. . . . You know, I've seen that face before somewhere.

MAGGIE. Nonsense. You couldn't have.

WHITESIDE (*dismissing it*). Oh, well! Let's get down to work. (*He hands her the armful of holly*) Here! Press this in the doctor's book. (*He picks up the first of a pile of papers*) If young men keep asking me how to become dramatic critics— (*He tears up the letter and drops the pieces on the floor.*)

MAGGIE (*who has picked up the little sheaf of messages from the table*). Here are some telegrams.

WHITESIDE (*a letter in his hand*). What date is this?

MAGGIE. December tenth.

WHITESIDE. Send a wire to Columbia Broadcasting. "You can schedule my Christmas Eve broadcast from the New York studio, as I shall return East instead of proceeding to Hollywood. Stop. For special New Year's Eve broadcast will have as my guests Jascha Heifetz, Katharine Cornell, Schiaparelli, the Lunts, and Dr. Alexis Carrel, with Anthony Eden on short wave from England. Whiteside."

MAGGIE. Are you sure you'll be all right by Christmas, Sherry?

WHITESIDE. Of course I will. Send a cable to Sacha Guitry: "Will be in Paris June ninth. Dinner seven-thirty. Whiteside." . . . Wire to *Harper's Magazine*: "Do not worry, Stinky. Copy will arrive. Whiteside." . . . Send a cable to the Maharajah of Jehraput, Bombay: "Dear Boo-Boo: Schedule changed. Can you meet me Calcutta July twelfth? Dinner eight-thirty. Whiteside." . . . Arturo Toscanini. Where *is* he?

MAGGIE. I'll find him.

WHITESIDE. "Counting on you January 4th Metropolitan Opera House my annual benefit Home for Paroled Convicts. As you know this is a very worthy cause and close to my heart. Tibbett, Rethberg, Martinelli and Flagstad have promised me personally to appear. Will you have quiet supper with me and Ethel Barrymore afterwards? Whiteside." (*The telephone rings*) If that's for Mrs. Stanley tell them she's too drunk to talk.

MAGGIE. Hello . . . Hollywood?

WHITESIDE. If it's Goldwyn, hang up.

MAGGIE. Hello . . . Banjo! (*Her face lights up.*)

WHITESIDE. Banjo! Give me that phone!

MAGGIE. Banjo, you old so-and-so! How are you, darling?

WHITESIDE. Come on—give me that!

MAGGIE. Shut up, Sherry! . . . Are you coming East, Banjo? I miss you . . . No, we're not going to Hollywood . . . Oh, he's going to live.

WHITESIDE. Stop driveling and give me the phone.

MAGGIE. In fact, he's screaming at me now. Here he is.

WHITESIDE (*taking the phone*). How are you, you fawn's behind? And what are you giving me for Christmas? (*He roars with laughter at* BANJO'S *answer*) What news, Banjo, my boy? How's the picture coming? . . . How are Wacko and Sloppo? . . . No, no, I'm all right. . . . Yes, I'm in very good hands. Dr. Crippen is taking care of me. . . . What about you? Having any fun? . . . Playing any cribbage? . . . What? (*Again he laughs loudly*) . . . Well, don't take all his money—leave a little bit for me . . . You're what? . . . Having your portrait painted? By whom? Milt Gross? . . . No, I'm going back to New York from here. I'll be there for twelve days, and then I go to Dartmouth for the Drama Festival. You wouldn't understand . . . Well, I can't waste my time talking to Hollywood riffraff. Kiss Louella Parsons for me. Good-bye. (*He hangs up and turns to* MAGGIE) He took fourteen hundred dollars from Sam Goldwyn at cribbage last night, and Sam said, "Banjo, I will never play garbage with you again."

MAGGIE. What's all this about his having his portrait painted?

WHITESIDE. Mm. Salvador Dali. That's all that face of his needs—a surrealist to paint it. . . . Now what do *you* want, Miss Bed Pan? (*This is addressed to the* NURSE, *who has returned somewhat apprehensively to the room.*)

MISS PREEN. It's—it's your pills. One every—forty-five minutes. (*She drops them into his lap and hurries out of the room.*)

WHITESIDE. Now where were we?

MAGGIE (*the messages in her hand*). Here's a cable from that dear friend of yours, Lorraine Sheldon.

WHITESIDE. Let me see it.

MAGGIE (*reading the message in a tone that gives* MISS SHELDON *none the better of it*). "Sherry, my poor sweet lamb, have been in Scotland on a shooting party with Lord and Lady Cunard and only just heard of your poor hip." (MAGGIE *gives a faint raspberry, then reads on*) "Am down here in Surrey with Lord Bottomley. Sailing Wednesday on the *Normandie* and cannot wait to see my poor sweet Sherry. Your blossom girl, Lorraine." . . . In the words of the master, I may vomit.

WHITESIDE. Don't be bitter, Puss, just because Lorraine is more beautiful than you are.

MAGGIE. Lorraine Sheldon is a very fair example of that small but vicious circle you move in.

WHITESIDE. Pure sex jealousy if ever I saw it . . . Give me the rest of those.

MAGGIE (*mumbling to herself*). Lorraine Sheldon . . . Lord Bottomley . . . My Aunt Fanny.

WHITESIDE (*who has opened the next message*). Ah! It's from Destiny's Tot.

MAGGIE (*peering over his shoulder*). England's little Rover Boy?

WHITESIDE. Um-hm. (*He reads*) "Treacle Face, what is this I hear about a hip fractured in some bordello brawl? Does this mean our Hollywood Christmas party is off? Finished the new play in Pago-Pago and it's superb. Myself and a ukulele leave Honolulu tomorrow, in that order. By the way, the Sultan of Zanzibar wants to meet Ginger Rogers. Let's face it. Oscar Wilde."

MAGGIE. He does travel, doesn't he? You know, it'd be nice if the world went around Beverly Carlton for a change.

WHITESIDE. Hollywood next week—why couldn't he stop over on his way to New York? Send him a cable: "Beverly Carlton, Royal Hawaiian Hotel, Honolulu—" (*The door bell rings.* MR. WHITESIDE *is properly annoyed*) If these people intend to have their friends using the front door—

MAGGIE. What do you want them to use—a rope ladder?

WHITESIDE. I will not have a lot of mildewed pus-bags rushing in and out of this house— (*He stops as the voice of* JOHN *is heard at the front door. "Oh, good morning, Mr. Jefferson." The answering voice of* MR. JEFFERSON *is not quite audible.*)

WHITESIDE (*roaring*). There's nobody home! The Stanleys have been arrested for counterfeiting! Go away! (*But the visitor, meanwhile, has already appeared in the archway.* MR. JEFFERSON *is an interesting-looking young man in his early thirties.*)

JEFFERSON. Good morning, Mr. Whiteside. I'm Jefferson, of the Mesalia *Journal.*

WHITESIDE (*sotto voce, to* MAGGIE). Get rid of him.

MAGGIE (*brusquely*). I'm sorry—Mr. Whiteside is seeing no one.

JEFFERSON. Really?

MAGGIE. So will you please excuse us? Good day.

JEFFERSON (*not giving up*). Mr. Whiteside seems to be sitting up and taking notice.

MAGGIE. I'm afraid he isn't taking notice of the Mesalia *Journal.* Do you mind?

JEFFERSON. You know, if I'm going to be insulted I'd like it to be by Mr. Whiteside himself. I never did like road companies.

WHITESIDE (*looking around, interested*). Mm. Touché if I ever heard one. And in Mesalia too, Maggie dear.

MAGGIE (*still on the job*). Will you please leave?

JEFFERSON (*ignoring her*). How about an interview, Mr. Whiteside?

WHITESIDE. I never give them. Go away.

JEFFERSON. Mr. Whiteside, if I don't get this interview, I lose my job.

WHITESIDE. That would be quite all right with me.

JEFFERSON. Now you don't mean that, Mr. Whiteside. You used to be a newspaperman yourself. You know what editors are like. Well, mine's the toughest one that ever lived.

WHITESIDE. You won't get around me that way. If you don't like him, get off the paper.

JEFFERSON. Yes, but I happen to think it's a good paper. William Allen White could have got out of Emporia, but he didn't.

WHITESIDE. You have the effrontery, in my presence, to compare yourself with William Allen White?

JEFFERSON. Only in the sense that William Allen White stayed in Emporia, and I want to stay here and say what I want to say.

WHITESIDE. Such as what?

JEFFERSON. Well, I can't put it into words, Mr. Whiteside—it'd sound like an awful lot of hooey. But the *Journal* was my father's paper. It's kind of a sentimental point with me, the paper. I'd like to carry on where he left off.

WHITESIDE. Ah—just a minute. Then this terrifying editor, this dread journalistic Apocalypse is—you?

JEFFERSON. Ah—yes, in a word. (WHITESIDE *chuckles with appreciation.*)

MAGGIE (*annoyed*). In the future, Sherry, I wish you would let me know when you don't want to talk to people. I'll usher them right in. (*She goes into the library.*)

WHITESIDE. Young man, that kind of journalistic trick went out with Richard Harding Davis . . . Come over here. I suppose you've written that novel?

JEFFERSON. No, I've written that play.

WHITESIDE. Well, I don't want to read it. But you can send me your paper—I'll take a year's subscription. Do you write the editorials, too?

JEFFERSON. Every one of them.

WHITESIDE. I know just what they're like. Ah, me! I'm afraid you're that noble young newspaperman—crusading, idealistic, dull. (*He looks him up and down*) Very good casting, too.

JEFFERSON. You're not bad casting yourself, Mr. Whiteside.

WHITESIDE. We won't discuss it. . . . Do these old eyes see a box of goodies over there? Hand them to me on your way out.

JEFFERSON (*as he passes over the candy*). The trouble is, Mr. Whiteside, that your being in this town comes under the heading of news. Practically the biggest news since the Armistice.

WHITESIDE (*examining the candy*). Mm. Pecan butternut fudge.

(MISS PREEN, *on her way to the kitchen from the library, stops short as she sees* MR. WHITESIDE *with a piece of candy in his hand.*)

MISS PREEN. Oh, my! You mustn't eat candy, Mr. Whiteside. It's very bad for you.

WHITESIDE (*turning*). My great-aunt Jennifer ate a whole box of candy every day of her life. She lived to be a hundred and two, and when she had been dead three days she looked better than you do now. (*He swings blandly back to his visitor*) What were you saying, old fellow?

JEFFERSON (*as* MISS PREEN *makes a hasty exit*). I can at least report to my readers that chivalry is not yet dead.

WHITESIDE. We won't discuss it. . . . Well, now that you have won me with your pretty ways, what do you want?

JEFFERSON. Well, how about a brief talk on famous murders? You're an authority on murder as a fine art.

WHITESIDE. My dear boy, when I talk about murder I get paid for it. I have made more money out of the Snyder-Gray case than the lawyers did. So don't expect to get it for nothing.

JEFFERSON. Well, then, what do you think of Mesalia, how long are you going to be here, where are you going, things like that?

WHITESIDE. Very well. (a) Mesalia is a town of irresistible charm, (b) I cannot wait to get out of it, and (c) I am going from here to Crockfield, for my semi-annual visit to the Crockfield Home for Paroled Convicts, for which I have raised over half a million dollars in the last five years. From there I go to New York. . . . Have you ever been to Crockfield, Jefferson?

JEFFERSON. No, I haven't. I always meant to.

WHITESIDE. As a newspaperman you ought to go, instead of wasting your time with me. It's only about seventy five miles from here. Did you ever hear how Crockfield started?

JEFFERSON. No, I didn't.

WHITESIDE. Ah! Sit down, Jefferson. It is one of the most endearing and touching stories of our generation. One misty St. Valentine's Eve—the year was 1901—a little lady who had given her name to an era, Victoria, lay dying in Windsor Castle. Maude Adams had not yet caused every young heart to swell as she tripped across the stage as Peter Pan; Irving Berlin had not yet written the first note of a ragtime rigadoon that was to set the nation's feet a-tapping, and Elias P. Crockfield was just emerging from the State penitentiary. Destitute, embittered, cruel of heart, he wandered, on this St. Valentine's Eve, into a little church. But there was no godliness in his heart that night, no prayer upon his lips. In the faltering twilight, Elias P. Crockfield made his way toward the poor box. With callous fingers he ripped open this poignant testimony of a simple people's faith. Greedily he clutched at the few pitiful coins within. And then a child's wavering treble broke the twilight stillness. "Please, Mr. Man," said a little girl's voice, "won't you be my Valentine?" Elias P. Crockfield turned. There stood before him a bewitching little creature of five, her yellow curls cascading over her shoulders like a golden Niagara, in her tiny outstretched hand a humble valentine. In that one crystal moment a sealed door opened in the heart of Elias P. Crockfield, and in his mind was born an idea. Twenty-five years later three thousand ruddy-cheeked convicts were gamboling on the broad lawns of Crockfield Home, frolicking in the cool depths of its swimming pool, broadcasting with their own symphony orchestra from their own radio station. Elias P. Crockfield has long since gone to his Maker, but the little girl of the golden curls, now grown to lovely womanhood, is known as the Angel of Crockfield, for she is the wife of the warden, and in the main hall of Crockfield, between a Rembrandt and an El Greco, there hangs, in a simple little frame, a humble valentine.

MAGGIE (*who has emerged from the library in time to hear the finish of this*). And in the men's washroom, every Christmas Eve, the ghost of Elias P. Crockfield appears in one of the booths . . . Will you sign these, please?
(*The doorbell is heard.*)

WHITESIDE. This aging ingénue, Mr. Jefferson, I retain in my employ only because she is the sole support of her two-headed brother.

JEFFERSON. I understand. . . . Well, thank you very much, Mr. Whiteside—you've been very kind. By the way, I'm a cribbage player, if you need one while you're here.

WHITESIDE. Fine. How much can you afford to lose?

JEFFERSON. I usually win.

WHITESIDE. We won't discuss that. Come back at eight-thirty. We'll play three-handed with Elsie Dinsmore . . . Metz!
(JOHN, *who has answered the door bell, has ushered in a strange-looking little man in his fifties. His hair runs all over his head and his clothes are too big for him.*)

WHITESIDE. Metz, you incredible beetle-hound! What are you doing here?

METZ (*with a mild Teutonic accent*). I explain, Sherry. First I kiss my little Maggie.

MAGGIE (*embracing him*). Metz darling, what a wonderful surprise!

WHITESIDE. The enchanted Metz! Why aren't you at the university? . . . Jefferson, you are standing in the presence of one of the great men of our time. When you write that inevitable autobiography, be sure to record the day that you met Professor Adolph Metz, the world's greatest authority on insect life. Metz, stop looking at me adoringly and tell me why you're here.

METZ. You are sick, Sherry, so I come to cheer you.

MAGGIE. Metz, you tore yourself away from your little insects and came here? Sherry, you don't deserve it.

WHITESIDE. How are all your little darlings, Metz? Jefferson, would you believe that eight volumes could be written on the mating instinct of the female white ant? He did it.

METZ. Seven on the female, Sherry. One on the male.

WHITESIDE. Lived for two years in a cave with nothing but plant lice. He rates three pages in the *Encyclopaedia Britannica*. Don't you, my little hookworm?

METZ. Please, Sherry you embarrass me. Look—I have brought you a present to while away the hours.
(*He motions to* JOHN, *who comes forward bearing a great box, wrapped in brown paper. He unwraps it as he speaks.*)

METZ. I said to my students: "Boys and girls, I want to give a present to my sick friend, Sheridan Whiteside." So you know what we did? We made for you a community of *Periplaneta Americana*, commonly known as the American cockroach. Behold, Sherry! (*He strips off the paper*) Roach City! Inside here are ten thousand cockroaches.

JOHN. Ten thousand— (*Heading for the kitchen in great excitement*) Sarah! Sarah!

METZ. Here in Roach City they play, they make love, they mate, they die. See—here is the graveyard. They even bury their own dead.

MAGGIE. I'm glad of that, or I'd have to do it.

WHITESIDE (*glaring at her*). Ssh!

METZ. You can watch them, Sherry, while they live out their whole lives. It is fascinating. Look! Here is where they store their grain, here is the commissary of the aristocracy, here is the maternity hospital.

WHITESIDE. Magnificent! This is my next piece for the London *Mercury*.

METZ. With these earphones, Sherry, you listen to the mating calls. There are microphones down inside. Listen! (*He puts the earphones over* WHITESIDE's *head.*)

WHITESIDE (*listening, rapt*). Mm. How long has this been going on?
(MRS. STANLEY *starts timorously to descend the stairs. She tiptoes as far as the landing, then pauses as she sees the group below. Meanwhile* PROF. METZ, *his mind ever on his work, has moved in the direction of the dining room.*)

METZ (*suddenly his face lights up*). Aha! *Periplaneta Americana!* There are cockroaches in this house!

MRS. STANLEY (*shocked into speech*). I beg your pardon! (*The doorbell rings*) Mr. Whiteside, I don't know who this man is, but I will not stand here and—

WHITESIDE. Then go upstairs. These are probably my luncheon guests. Metz, you're staying for the day, of course? Jefferson, stay for lunch? Maggie, tell 'em there'll be two more. Ah, come right in, Baker. Good morning, gentlemen. (*The gentlemen addressed are three in number—two white, one black. They are convicts, and they look the part. Prison gray, handcuffed together.* BAKER, *in uniform, is a prison guard. He carries a rifle*) Jefferson, here are the fruits of that humble valentine. These men, now serving the final months of their prison terms, have chosen to enter the ivy-covered walls of Crockfield. They have come here today to learn from me a little of its tradition . . . Gentlemen, I envy you your great adventure.

JOHN (*in the dining-room doorway*). Lunch is ready, Mr. Whiteside.

WHITESIDE. Good! Let's go right in. (*To one of the convicts, as they pass*) You're Michaelson, aren't you? Butcher-shop murders?

MICHAELSON. Yes, sir.

WHITESIDE. Thought I recognized you. . . . After you, Baker. . . . The other fellow, Jefferson— (*He lowers his tone*) is Henderson, the hatchet fiend. Always did it in a bathtub—remember? (*His voice rises as he wheels himself into the dining room*) We're having chicken livers Tetrazzini, and Cherries Jubilee for dessert. I hope every little tummy is a-flutter with gastric juices. Serve the white wine with the fish, John, and close the doors. I don't want a lot of people prying on their betters.

(*The doors close. Only* MRS. STANLEY *is left outside. She collapses quietly into a chair.*)

CURTAIN

ACT ONE

SCENE II

Late afternoon, a week later. Only a single lamp is lit.

The room, in the week that has passed, has taken on something of the character of its occupant. Books and papers everywhere. Stacks of books on the tables, some of them just half out of their cardboard boxes. Half a dozen or so volumes, which apparently have not appealed to the Master, have been thrown onto the floor. A litter of crumpled papers around the WHITESIDE *wheelchair; an empty candy box has slid off his lap. An old pair of pants has been tossed over one chair, a seedy bathrobe over another. A handsome Chinese vase has been moved out of its accustomed spot and is doing duty as an ash receiver.*

MR. WHITESIDE *is in his wheelchair, asleep. Roach City is on a stand beside him, the earphones over his head. He has apparently dozed off while listening to the mating calls of* Periplaneta Americana.

For a moment only his rhythmic breathing is heard. Then MISS PREEN *enters from the library. She brings some medicine—a glass filled with a murky mixture. She pauses when she sees that he is asleep, then, after a good deal of hesitation, gently touches him on the shoulder. He stirs a little; she musters up her courage and touches him again.*

WHITESIDE (*slowly opening his eyes*). I was dreaming of Lillian Russell, and I awake to find *you.*

MISS PREEN. Your—your medicine, Mr. Whiteside.

WHITESIDE (*taking the glass*). What time is it?

MISS PREEN. About half-past six.

WHITESIDE. Where is Miss Cutler?

MISS PREEN. She went out.

WHITESIDE. Out?

MISS PREEN. With Mr. Jefferson. (*She goes into the library.* JOHN, *meanwhile, has entered from the dining room.*)

JOHN. All right if I turn the lights up, Mr. Whiteside?

WHITESIDE. Yes. Go right ahead, John.

JOHN. And Sarah has something for you, Mr. Whiteside. Made it special.

WHITESIDE. She has? Where is she? My Soufflé Queen!

SARAH (*proudly entering with a tray on which reposes her latest delicacy*). Here I am, Mr. Whiteside.

WHITESIDE. She walks in beauty like the night, and in those deft hands there is the art of Michelangelo. Let me taste the new creation. (*With one hand he pours the medicine into the Chinese vase, then swallows at a gulp one of* SARAH'S *not so little cakes. An ecstatic expression comes over his face*) Poetry! Sheer poetry!

SARAH (*beaming*). I put a touch of absinthe in the dough. Do you like it?

WHITESIDE (*rapturously*). Ambrosia!

SARAH. And I got you your terrapin Maryland for dinner.

WHITESIDE. I have known but three great cooks in my time. The Khedive of Egypt had one, my great-aunt Jennifer another, and the third, Sarah, is you.

SARAH. Oh, Mr. Whiteside!

WHITESIDE (*lowering his voice*). How would you like to come to New York and work for me? You and John.

SARAH. Why, Mr. Whiteside!

JOHN. Sarah! . . . It would be wonderful, Mr. Whiteside, but what would we say to Mr. and Mrs. Stanley?

WHITESIDE. Just "good-bye."

SARAH. But—but they'd be awfully mad, wouldn't they? They've been very kind to us.

WHITESIDE (*lightly*). Well, if they ever come to New York we can have them for dinner, if I'm not in town. Now run along and think it over. This is our little secret—just between us. And put plenty of sherry in that terrapin . . . Miss Preen! (SARAH *and* JOHN *withdraw in considerable excitement.* WHITESIDE *raises his voice to a roar*) Miss Preen!

MISS PREEN (*appearing, breathless*). Yes? Yes?

WHITESIDE. What have you got in there, anyway? A sailor?

MISS PREEN. I was—just washing my hands.

WHITESIDE. What time did Miss Cutler go out?

MISS PREEN. A couple of hours ago.

WHITESIDE. Mr. Jefferson called for her?

MISS PREEN. Yes, sir.

WHITESIDE (*impatiently*). All right, all right. Go back to your sex life.

(MISS PREEN *goes.* WHITESIDE *tries to settle down to his book, but his mind is plainly troubled. He shifts a little, looks anxiously toward the outer door.* HARRIET STANLEY *comes softl down the steps. She seems delighte to find* MR. WHITESIDE *alone.*)

HARRIET (*opening an album that sh has brought with her*). Dear Mr Whiteside, may I show you a few mementos of the past? I somehow fee that you would love them as I do.

WHITESIDE. I'd be delighted. (*Observing her*) Miss Stanley, haven' we met somewhere before?

HARRIET. Oh, no. I would have re membered. It would have been on of my cherished memories—like these (*She spreads the portfolio befor him*) Look! Here I am with my firs sweetheart, under our lovely beech wood tree. I was eight and he wa ten. I have never forgotten him. Wha happy times we had! What— (*Sh stops short as she hears footsteps o the stairway*) There's someone com ing! I'll come back! . . . (*She gath ers up her album and vanishes int the dining room.*)

(WHITESIDE *looks after her, puzzle It is* MR. STANLEY *who comes dow the stairs. He is carrying a slip o paper in his hand, and he is obviousl at the boiling point. A few steps b hind comes* MRS. STANLEY, *appreher sive and nervous.*)

MRS. STANLEY. Now, Ernest, please-

STANLEY. Be quiet, Daisy. . . . M Whiteside, I want to talk to you. don't care whether you're busy or no I have stood all that I'm going stand.

WHITESIDE. Indeed?

STANLEY. This is the last straw. have just received a bill from the tel phone company for seven hundre and eighty-four dollars. (*He reads from the slip in his hand*) Oklahoma City, Calcutta, Hollywood, Paris, Brussels, Rome, New York, New York, New York, New York, New York, New York— (*His voice trails off in an endless succession of New Yorks*) Now I realize, Mr. Whiteside, that you are a distinguished man of letters—

MRS. STANLEY. Yes, of course. We both do.

STANLEY. Please . . . But in the past week we have not been able to call our souls our own. We have not had a meal in the dining room *once.* I have to tiptoe out of the house in the mornings.

MRS. STANLEY. Now, Ernest—

STANLEY (*waving her away*). I come home to find convicts sitting at my dinner table—butcher-shop murderers. A man putting cockroaches in the kitchen.

MRS. STANLEY. They just escaped, Ernest.

STANLEY. That's not the point. I don't like coming home to find twenty-two Chinese students using my bathroom. I tell you I won't stand for it, no matter *who* you are.

WHITESIDE. Have you quite finished?

STANLEY. No, I have not. I go down into the cellar this morning and trip over that octopus that William Beebe sent you. I tell you I won't stand it. Mr. Whiteside, I want you to leave this house as soon as you can and go to a hotel. . . . Stop pawing me, Daisy. . . . That's all I've got to say, Mr. Whiteside.

WHITESIDE. And quite enough, I should say. May I remind you again, Mr. Stanley, that I am not a willing guest in this house? I am informed by my doctor that I must remain quiet for another ten days, at which time I shall get out of here so fast that the wind will knock you over, I hope. If, however, you insist on my leaving before that, thereby causing me to suffer a relapse, I shall sue you for every additional day that I am held inactive, which will amount, I assure you, to a tidy sum.

STANLEY (*to his wife*). This is outrageous. Do we have to—

WHITESIDE. As for the details of your petty complaints, those twenty-two Chinese students came straight from the White House, where I assure you they used the bathroom too.

MRS. STANLEY. Mr. Whiteside, my husband didn't mean—

STANLEY. Yes, I did. I meant every word of it.

WHITESIDE. There is only one point that you make in which I see some slight justice. I do not expect you to pay for my telephone calls, and I shall see to it that restitution is made. Can you provide me with the exact amount?

STANLEY. I certainly can, and I certainly will.

WHITESIDE. Good. I shall instruct my lawyers to deduct it from the hundred and fifty thousand dollars that I am suing you for.

(MR. STANLEY *starts to speak, but simply chokes with rage. Furious, he storms up the steps again,* MRS. STANLEY *following.*)

WHITESIDE (*calling after him*). And I'll thank you not to trip over that octopus, which is very sensitive. (*Left alone,* MR. WHITESIDE *enjoys his triumph for a moment, then his mind jumps to more important matters. He looks at his watch, considers a second, then wheels himself over to the telephone.*)

WHITESIDE. Give me the Mesalia *Journal,* please. (*He peers at Roach City while waiting*) Hello, *Journal?* . . . Is Mr. Jefferson there? . . . When do you expect him? . . . No. No message. (*He hangs up, drums impatiently on the arm of his chair. Then he turns sharply at the sound of the outer door opening. But it is the younger Stanleys,* RICHARD *and* JUNE, *who enter. They are in winter togs, with ice skates under their arms. In addition,* RICHARD *has a camera slung over his shoulder. Their attitudes change as they see that* WHITESIDE *is in the room. They slide toward the stairs, obviously trying to be as unobtrusive as possible.*)

WHITESIDE. Come here, you two. . . . Come on, come on. I'm not going to bite you. . . . Now look here. I am by nature a gracious and charming person. If I err at all it is on the side of kindness and amiability. I have been observing you two for this past week, and you seem to me to be extremely likeable young people. I am afraid that when we first met I was definitely unpleasant to you. For that I am sorry, and I wish that in the future you would not treat me like something out of Edgar Allan Poe. How do you like my new tie?

JUNE. Thank you, Mr. Whiteside. This makes things much pleasanter. And I think the tie is very pretty.

RICHARD. Well, now that we're on speaking terms, Mr. Whiteside, I don't mind telling you that I have been admiring all your ties.

WHITESIDE. Do you like this one?

RICHARD. I certainly do.

WHITESIDE. It's yours. (*He takes it off and tosses it to him*) Really, this curious legend that I am a difficult person is pure fabrication. . . . Ice-skating, eh? Ah, me! I used to cut figure eights myself, arm in arm with Betsy Ross, waving the flag behind us.

JUNE It was wonderful on the ice today. Miss Cutler and Mr. Jefferson were there.

WHITESIDE. Maggie? Skating?

RICHARD. Yes, and she's good, too. I got a marvelous picture of her.

WHITESIDE. Were they still there when you left?

RICHARD. I think so. Say, Mr. Whiteside, mind if I take a picture of you? I'd love to have one.

WHITESIDE. Very well. Do you want my profile? (*He indicates his stomach.*)

JUNE (*starting up the stairs*) I'm afraid you're done for, Mr. Whiteside. My brother is a camera fiend.

RICHARD (*clicking his camera*). Thank you, Mr. Whiteside. I got a great one.
(*He and* JUNE *go up the stairs as* MAGGIE *enters from the hallway. They call a "Hello, Miss Cutler!" as they disappear.*)

MAGGIE. Hello, there. . . . Good evening, Sherry. Really Sherry, you've got this room looking like an old parrot-cage. . . . Did you nap while I was out? (WHITESIDE *merely glowers at her*) What's the matter, dear? Cat run away with your tongue? (*She is on her knees, gathering up debris.*)

WHITESIDE (*furious*). Don't look up at me with those great cow-eyes, you sex-ridden hag. Where have you been all afternoon? Alley-catting around with Bert Jefferson?

MAGGIE (*her face aglow*). Sherry—Bert read his play to me this afternoon. It's superb. It isn't just that play written by a newspaperman. It's superb. I want you to read it *tonight.* (*She puts it in his lap*) It just cries out for Cornell. If you like it, will you send it to her, Sherry? And will you read it tonight?

WHITESIDE. No, I will not read it tonight or any other time. And while we're on the subject of Mr. Jefferson, you might ask him if he wouldn't like to pay your salary, since he takes up all your time.

MAGGIE. Oh, come now, Sherry. It isn't as bad as that.

WHITESIDE. I have not even been able to reach you, not knowing what haylofts you frequent.

MAGGIE. Oh, stop behaving like a spoiled child, Sherry.

WHITESIDE. Don't take that patronizing tone with me, you flea-bitten Cleopatra. I am sick and tired of your sneaking out like some lovesick high-school girl every time my back is turned.

MAGGIE. Well, Sherry— (*She pulls together the library doors and faces*

WHITESIDE. I'm afraid you've hit the nail on the head. (*With a little flourish, she removes her hat.*)

WHITESIDE. Stop acting like Zasu Pitts and explain yourself.

MAGGIE. I'll make it quick, Sherry. I'm in love.

WHITESIDE. Nonsense. This is merely delayed puberty.

MAGGIE. No, Sherry, I'm afraid this is it. You're going to lose a very excellent secretary.

WHITESIDE. You are out of your mind.

MAGGIE. Yes, I think I am, a little. But I'm a girl who's waited a long time for this to happen, and now it has. Mr. Jefferson doesn't know it yet, but I'm going to try my darnedest to marry him.

WHITESIDE (*as she pauses*). Is that all?

MAGGIE. Yes, except that—well—I suppose this is what might be called my resignation—as soon as you've got someone else.

WHITESIDE (*there is a slight pause*). Now listen to me, Maggie. We have been together for a long time. You are indispensable to me, but I think I am unselfish enough not to let that stand in the way where your happiness is concerned. Because, whether you know it or not, I have a deep affection for you.

MAGGIE. I know that, Sherry.

WHITESIDE. That being the case, I will not stand by and allow you to make a fool of yourself.

MAGGIE. I'm not, Sherry.

WHITESIDE. You are, my dear. You are behaving like a Booth Tarkington heroine. It's—it's incredible. I cannot believe that a girl who for the past ten years has had the great of the world served up on a platter before her—I cannot believe that it is anything but a kind of temporary insanity when you are swept off your feet in seven days by a second-rate, small-town newspaperman.

MAGGIE. Sherry, I can't explain what's happened. I can only tell you that it's so. It's hard for me to believe too, Sherry. Here I am, a hard-bitten old cynic, behaving like *True Story Magazine,* and liking it. Discovering the moon, and ice-skating—I keep laughing to myself all the time, but there it is. What can I do about it, Sherry? I'm in love.

WHITESIDE (*with sudden decision*). We're leaving here tomorrow. Hip or no hip, we're leaving here tomorrow. I don't care if I fracture the other one. Get me a train schedule and start packing. *I'll* pull you out of this, Miss Stardust. *I'll* get the ants out of those moonlit pants.

MAGGIE. It's no good, Sherry. I'd be back on the next streamlined train.

WHITESIDE. It's completely unbelievable. Can you see yourself, the wife of the editor of the Mesalia *Journal,* having an evening at home for Mr. and Mrs. Stanley, Mr. and Mrs. Poop-Face, and the members of the Book-of-the-Month Club?

MAGGIE. Sherry, I've had ten years of the great figures of our time, and don't think I'm not grateful to you for it. I've loved every minute of it. They've been wonderful years, Sherry. Gay and stimulating—why, I don't think anyone has ever had the fun we've had. But a girl can't laugh all the time, Sherry. There comes a time when she wants—Bert Jefferson. You don't know Bert, Sherry. He's gentle, and he's unassuming, and—well, I love him, that's all.

WHITESIDE. I see. Well, I remain completely unconvinced. You are drugging yourself into this Joan Crawford fantasy, and before you become completely anesthetized I shall do everything in my power to bring you to your senses.

MAGGIE (*wheeling on him*). Now listen to me, Whiteside. I know you. Lay off. I know what a devil you can be. I've seen you do it to other people, but don't you dare to do it to me. Don't drug *yourself* into the idea that all you're thinking of is my happiness. You're thinking of yourself a little bit, too, and all those months of breaking in somebody new. I've seen you in a passion before when your life has been disrupted, and you couldn't dine in Calcutta on July twelfth with Boo-Boo. Well, that's too bad, but there it is. I'm going to marry Bert if he'll have me, and don't you dare try any of your tricks. I'm on to every one of them. So lay off. That's my message to *you,* Big Lord Fauntleroy. (*And she is up the stairs. Left stewing in his own juice,* MR. WHITESIDE *is in a perfect fury. He bangs the arm of his chair, then slaps at the manuscript in his lap. As he does so, the dawn of an idea comes into his mind. He sits perfectly still for a moment, thinking it over. Then, with a slow smile, he takes the manuscript out of its envelope. He looks at the title page, ruffles through the script, then stops and thinks again. His face breaks out into one great smile. Then he quickly wheels himself over to the table and hunts hurriedly through a pile of old cablegrams and letters, until he finds the one he wants. With this in his hand, he takes up the telephone receiver.)*

WHITESIDE (*in a lowered voice*). Long distance, please. I want to put in a trans-Atlantic call. (*He looks at the cablegram again for confirmation*) Hello. Trans-Atlantic operator? . . . This is Mesalia one four two. I want to talk to Miss Lorraine Sheldon—S-h-e-l-d-o-n. She's on the *Normandie*. It sailed from Southampton day before yesterday. . . . Will it take long? . . . All right. My name is Whiteside. . . . Thank you. (*He hangs up as the door bell rings. He goes back to the manuscript again and looks through it.* JOHN *then ushers in* DR. BRADLEY.)

DR. BRADLEY (*hearty, as usual*). Well, well! Good evening, Mr. Whiteside!

WHITESIDE. Come back tomorrow—I'm busy.

DR. BRADLEY (*turning cute*). Now what would be the best news that I could possibly bring you?

WHITESIDE. You have hydrophobia.

DR. BRADLEY (*laughing it off*). No, no. . . . Mr. Whiteside, you are a well man. You can get up and walk *now*. You can leave here tomorrow.

WHITESIDE. What do you mean?

DR. BRADLEY. Well, sir! I looked at those X-rays again this morning, and do you know what? I had been looking at the wrong X-rays. I had been looking at old Mrs. Moffat's X-rays. You are perfectly, absolutely well!

WHITESIDE. Lower your voice, will you?

DR. BRADLEY. What's the matter? Aren't you pleased?

WHITESIDE. Delighted. . . . Naturally. . . . Ah—this is a very unexpected bit of news, however. It comes at a very curious moment. (*He is thinking fast; suddenly he gets an idea. He clears his throat and looks around apprehensively*) Dr. Bradley, I—ah—I have some good news for you, too. I have been reading your book—ah—*Forty Years*—what is it?

DR. BRADLEY (*eagerly*). *An Ohio Doctor*—yes?

WHITESIDE. I consider it extremely close to being one of the great literary contributions of our time.

DR. BRADLEY. Mr. Whiteside!

WHITESIDE. So strongly do I feel about it, Dr. Bradley, that I have a proposition to make to you. Just here and there the book is a little uneven, a little rough. What I would like to do is to stay here in Mesalia and work with you on it.

DR. BRADLEY (*all choked up*). Mr. Whiteside, I would be so terribly honored—

WHITESIDE. Yes. But there is just one difficulty. You see, if my lecture bureau and my radio sponsors were to learn that I am well, they would insist on my fulfilling my contracts, and I would be forced to leave Mesalia. Therefore, we must not tell anyone —not anyone at all—that I am well.

DR. BRADLEY. I see. I see.

WHITESIDE. Not even Miss Cutler, you understand.

DR. BRADLEY. No, I won't. Not a soul. Not even my wife.

WHITESIDE. That's fine.

DR. BRADLEY. When do we start work—tonight? I've got just one patient that's dying and then I'll be perfectly free.
(*The phone rings.*)

WHITESIDE (*waving him away*). Ah —tomorrow morning. This is a private call—would you forgive me? . . . Hello. . . . Yes, I'm on. (*He turns again to the* DOCTOR) Tomorrow morning.

DR. BRADLEY. Tomorrow morning it is. Good night. You've made me very proud, Mr. Whiteside. (*He goes.*)

WHITESIDE (*again on the phone*). Yes, yes, this is Mr. Whiteside on the phone. Put them through. . . . Hello. Is this my Blossom Girl? How are you, my lovely? . . . No, no, I'm all right. . . . Yes, still out here. . . . Lorraine dear, when do you land in New York? . . . Tuesday? That's fine. . . . Now listen closely, my pet. I've great news for you. I've discovered a wonderful play with an enchanting part it in for you. Cornell would give her eye teeth to play it, but I think I can get it for you. . . . Now wait, wait. Let me tell you. The author is a young newspaper man in this town. Of course he wants Cornell, but if you jump on a train and get right out here, I think you could swing it, if you play your cards right. . . . No, he's young, and very attractive, and just your dish, my dear. It just takes a little doing, and you're the girl that can do it. Isn't that exciting, my pet? . . . Yes. . . . Yes, that's right. . . . And look. Don't send me any messages. Just get on a train and arrive. . . . Oh, no, don't thank me, my darling. It's perfectly all right. Have a nice trip and hurry out here. Goodbye, my blossom. (*He hangs up and looks guiltily around. Then he straightens up and gleefully rubs his hands together.* MISS PREEN *enters, medicine in hand, and frightened, as usual.*)

WHITESIDE (*jovial as hell*). Hello, Miss Preen. My, you're looking radiant this evening.

MISS PREEN (*staggered*). What?

WHITESIDE. Nothing. Nothing at all. Just said you are ravishing.
(*He takes the medicine from her and swallows it at one gulp.* MISS PREEN, *still staggered, retreats into the library, just as* MAGGIE *comes down the stairs. She is dressed for the street.*)

MAGGIE (*pausing on the landing*). Sherry, I'm sorry for what I said before. I'm afraid I was a little unjust.

WHITESIDE (*all nobility*). That's all right, Maggie dear. We all lose our tempers now and then.

MAGGIE. I promised to have dinner

with Bert and go to a movie, but we'll come back and play cribbage with you instead.

WHITESIDE. Fine.

MAGGIE. See you soon, Sherry dear. (*She kisses him lightly on the forehead and goes on her way.* WHITESIDE *looks after her until he hears the doors close. Then his face lights up again and he bursts happily into song as he wheels himself into the library.*)

WHITESIDE.

"I'se des a 'ittle wabbit in the sunshine,
I'se des a 'ittle wabbit in the wain—"

CURTAIN

ACT TWO

A week later, late afternoon.

The room is now dominated by a large Christmas tree, set in the curve of the staircase, and hung with the customary Christmas ornaments.

SARAH *and* JOHN *are passing in and out of the library, bringing forth huge packages which they are placing under the tree.* MAGGIE *sits at a little table at one side, going through a pile of correspondence.*

JOHN. Well, I guess that's all there are, Miss Cutler. They're all under the tree.

MAGGIE. Thank you, John.

SARAH. My, I never saw anyone get so many Christmas presents. I can hardly wait to see what's in 'em.

JOHN. When'll Mr. Whiteside open them, Miss Cutler?

MAGGIE. Well, John, you see Christmas is Mr. Whiteside's personal property. He invented it and it belongs to him. First thing tomorrow morning, Mr. Whiteside will open each and every present, and there will be the damnedest fuss you ever saw.

SARAH (*bending over the packages*). My, look who he's got presents from! Shirley Temple, William Lyon Phelps, Billy Rose, Ethel Waters, Somerset Maugham—I can hardly wait for tonight.
(*The doorbell rings.* JOHN *departs for the door.*)

SARAH. My, it certainly is wonderful. And Mr. Whiteside's tree is so beautiful, too. Mr. and Mrs. Stanley had to put theirs in their bedroom, you know. They can hardly undress at night.
(*It is* BERT JEFFERSON *who enters.*)

BERT. Hello, Maggie. Merry Christmas, Sarah.

SARAH. Merry Christmas, Mr. Jefferson.

(*She and* JOHN *disappear into the dining room.*)

BERT (*observing the pile of packages under the tree*). Say, business is good, isn't it? My, what a little quiet blackmail and a weekly radio hour can get you. What did his sponsors give him?

MAGGIE. They gave him a full year's supply of their product, Cream of Mush.

BERT. Well, he'll give it right back to them over the air.

MAGGIE. Wait until you hear tonight's broadcast, old fellow. It's so sticky I haven't been able to get it off my fingers since I copied it.

BERT. I'll bet . . . Look, I'll come clean. Under the influence of God knows what I have just bought you a Christmas present.

MAGGIE (*surprised*). Why, Mr. Jefferson, sir.

BERT. Only I'd like you to see it before I throw away my hard-earned money. Can you run downtown with me and take a look at it?

MAGGIE. Bert, this is very sweet of you. I'm quite touched. What is it? I can't wait.

BERT. A two years' subscription to *Screen Romances*. . . . Listen, do you think I'm going to tell you? Come down and see.

MAGGIE (*she calls into the library*). Sherry! Sherry, I'm going out for a few minutes. With Horace Greeley I won't be long. (*She goes into the hallway for her coat and hat.*)

BERT (*raising his voice*). Noel, Noel, Mr. W.! How about some cribbage after your broadcast tonight?

(*The* WHITESIDE *wheelchair is rolling into the room.*)

WHITESIDE. No, I will not play cribbage with you, Klondike Harry. You have been swindling the be-jesus out of me for two weeks. . . . Where are you off to now, Madame Butterfly?

MAGGIE. I'm being given a Christmas present. Anything you want done downtown?

WHITESIDE. 'Es. B'ing baby a lollipop. . . . What are *you* giving me for Christmas, Jefferson? I have enriched your feeble life beyond your capacity to repay me.

BERT. Yes, that's what I figured, so I'm not giving you anything.

WHITESIDE. I see. Well, I was giving you my old truss, but now I shan't. . . . Maggie, what time are those radio men coming?

MAGGIE. About six-thirty—I'll be here. You've got to cut, Sherry. You're four minutes over. Oh, by the way, there was a wire from Beverly. It's there somewhere. He doesn't know what train he can get out of Chicago, but he'll be here some time this evening.

WHITESIDE. Good! Is he staying overnight?

MAGGIE. No, he has to get right out again. He's sailing Friday on the *Queen Mary*.

BERT. Think I could peek in at the window and get a look at him? Beverly Carlton used to be one of my heroes.

WHITESIDE. Used to be, you inkstained hack? Beverly Carlton is the greatest single talent in the English theatre today. Take this illiterate numbskull out of my sight, Maggie, and don't bring him back.

BERT. Yes, Mr. Whiteside, sir. I won't come back until Beverly Carlton gets here.

MAGGIE (*as they go on their way*). Where are we going, Bert? I want to know what you've bought me—I'm like a ten-year-old kid.

BERT (*laughing a little*). You know, you look like a ten-year-old kid right now, Maggie, at that.
(*They are out of earshot by this time.* WHITESIDE *looks after them intently, listens until the door closes. He considers for a second, then wheels himself over to the telephone.*)

WHITESIDE (*on the phone*). Will you give me the Mansion House, please? . . . No, I don't know the number. . . . Hello? Mansion House? . . . Tell me, has a Miss Lorraine Sheldon arrived yet? . . . Yes, that's right—Miss Lorraine Sheldon. From New York. . . . She hasn't, eh? Thank you. (*He hangs up, drums with his fingers on the armchair, looks at his watch. He slaps his knees impatiently, stretches. Then, vexed at his self-imposed imprisonment, he looks cautiously around the room, peers up the stairs. Then, slowly, he gets out of his chair; standing beside it, he indulges in a few mild calisthenics, looking cautiously around all the while. Then the sound of the library doors being opened sends him scurrying back to his chair. It is* MISS PREEN *who emerges.*)

WHITESIDE (*annoyed*). What do you want, coming in like that? Why don't you knock before you come into a room?

MISS PREEN. But—I wasn't coming in. I was coming out.

WHITESIDE. Miss Preen, you are obviously *in* this room. That is true, isn't it?

MISS PREEN. Yes, it is, but—

WHITESIDE. Therefore you came in. Hereafter, please knock.
(*Before* MISS PREEN *can reply, however,* JOHN *enters from the dining room.*)

JOHN (*en route to the front door*). There're some expressmen here with a crate, Mr. Whiteside. I told them to come around the front.

WHITESIDE. Thank you, John. . . . Don't stand there, Miss Preen. You look like a frozen custard. Go away.

MISS PREEN (*controlling herself as best as she can*). Yes, sir. (*She goes.*)
(*At the same time two* EXPRESSMEN, *carrying a crate, enter from the front door.*)

JOHN. Bring it right in here. Careful there—don't scrape the wall. Why, it's some kind of animals.

EXPRESSMAN. I'll say it's animals. We had to feed 'em at seven o'clock this morning.

WHITESIDE. Bring it over here, John. Who's it from?

JOHN (*reading from the top of the crate as they set it down*) Admiral Richard E. Byrd. Say!

WHITESIDE (*peering through the slats*). Why, they're penguins. Two —three—four penguins. Hello, my pretties.

EXPRESSMAN. Directions for feeding are right on top. These two slats are open.

JOHN (*reading*). "To be fed only whale blubber, eels and cracked lobster."

EXPRESSMAN. They got Coca-Cola this morning. And liked it. (*They go.*)

WHITESIDE (*peering through the slats again*). Hello, hello, hello. You know, they make the most entrancing companions, John. Admiral Byrd has one that goes on all his lecture tours. I want these put right in the library with me. Take 'em right in.

JOHN (*picking up the crate*). Yes, sir.

WHITESIDE. Better tell Sarah to order a couple of dozen lobsters. I don't suppose there's any whale blubber in Mesalia.
(*At which point* DR. BRADLEY *obligingly enters from the hall*. MR. WHITESIDE *is equal to the occasion.*)

WHITESIDE (*with just the merest glance at the* DOCTOR). Oh, yes, there is.

DR. BRADLEY. The door was open, so I— Good afternoon, Mr. Whiteside. And Merry Christmas.

WHITESIDE. Merry Christmas, Merry Christmas. Do you happen to know if eels are in season, Doctor?

DR. BRADLEY. How's that?

WHITESIDE. Never mind. I was a fool to ask you.
(JOHN *returns from the library, carefully closing the doors.*)

JOHN. I opened those two slats a little, Mr. Whiteside—they seemed so crowded in there.

WHITESIDE. Thank you, John. (JOHN *goes on his way*) On your way downtown, Doctor, will you send these air mail? Miss Cutler forgot them. (*He hands him a few letters*) Goodbye. Sorry you dropped in just now. I have to do my Yogi exercises. (*He folds his arms, leans back and closes his eyes.*)

DR. BRADLEY. But, Mr. Whiteside, it's been a week now. My book, you know—when are we going to start work on the book? (WHITESIDE, *his eyes still closed, places his fingers to his lips, for absolute silence*) I was hoping that today you'd be— (*He stops short as* MISS PREEN *returns from the dining room*) Good afternoon, Miss Preen.

MISS PREEN. Good afternoon, Dr. Bradley. (*She opens the doors to enter the library, then freezes in her tracks. She closes the doors again and turns to the* DOCTOR, *glassy-eyed. She raises a trembling hand to her forehead*) Doctor, perhaps I'm—not well, but—when I opened the doors just now I thought I saw a penguin with a thermometer in its mouth.

WHITESIDE. What's this? Have those penguins got out of their crate?

MISS PREEN. Oh, thank God. I thought perhaps the strain had been too much.

DR. BRADLEY (*incredulous*). Penguins?

WHITESIDE. Yes. Doctor, will you go in and capture them, please, and put them back in the crate? There're four of them.

DR. BRADLEY (*somewhat staggered*). Very well. Do you suppose that later on, Mr. Whiteside, we might—

WHITESIDE. We'll see, we'll see. First catch the penguins. And, Miss Preen, will you amuse them, please, until I come in?

MISS PREEN (*swallowing hard*). Yes, sir.
(*Meanwhile* JOHN *has descended the stairs.*)

JOHN. The Christmas tree just fell on Mr. Stanley. He's got a big bump on his forehead.

WHITESIDE (*brightly*). Why, isn't that too bad? . . . Go ahead, Doctor. Go on, Miss Preen.
(RICHARD *pops in from the hallway.*)

RICHARD. Hello, Mr. Whiteside.

WHITESIDE. Hello, Dickie, my boy.

DR. BRADLEY (*still lingering*). Mr. Whiteside, will you have some time later?

WHITESIDE (*impatient*). I don't know, Doctor. I'm busy now.

DR. BRADLEY. Well, suppose I wait a little while? I'll—I'll wait a little while. (*He goes into the library.*)

WHITESIDE. Dr. Bradley is the greatest living argument for mercy killings. . . . Well, Dickie, would you like a candid camera shot of my left nostril this evening?

RICHARD. I'm sort of stocked up on those. Have you got a minute to look at some new ones I've taken?

WHITESIDE. I certainly have. . . . Why, these are splendid, Richard. There's real artistry in them—they're as good as anything by Margaret Bourke-White. I like all the things you've shown me. This is the essence of photographic journalism.

RICHARD. Say, I didn't know they were as good as that. I just like to take pictures, that's all.

WHITESIDE. Richard, I've been meaning to talk to you about this. You're not just a kid fooling with a camera any more. These are good. This is what you ought to do. You ought to get out of here and do some of the things you were telling me about. Just get on a boat and get off wherever it stops. Galveston, Mexico, Singapore—work your way through and just take pictures—everything

RICHARD. Say, wouldn't I like to, though! It's what I've been dreaming of for years. If I could do that I'd be the happiest guy in the world.

WHITESIDE. Well, why can't you do it? If I were your age, I'd do it like a shot.

RICHARD. Well, you know why. Dad.

WHITESIDE. Richard, do you really want to do this more than anything else in the world?

RICHARD. I certainly do.

WHITESIDE. Then do it.
(JUNE *comes quietly in from the dining room. Obviously there is something on her mind.*)

JUNE. Hello, Dick. Good afternoon, Mr. Whiteside.

WHITESIDE. Hello, my lovely. . . . So I'm afraid it's up to *you*, Richard.

RICHARD. I guess it is. Well, thank you, Mr. Whiteside. You've been swell and I'll never forget it.

WHITESIDE. Righto, Richard.

RICHARD. June, are you coming upstairs?

JUNE. Ah—in a few minutes, Richard.

RICHARD. Well— knock on my door, will you? I want to talk to you.

JUNE. Yes, I will.
(RICHARD *disappears up the stairs.*)

WHITESIDE (*brightly, opening his book*). June, my lamb, you were too young to know about the Elwell murder, weren't you? Completely fascinating. I have about five favorite murders, and the Elwell case is one of them. Would you like to hear about it?

JUNE. Well, Mr. Whiteside, I wanted to talk to you. Would you mind, for a few minutes? It's important.

WHITESIDE. Why, certainly, my dear. I take it this is all about your young Lothario at the factory?

JUNE. Yes. I just can't seem to make Father understand. It's like talking to a blank wall. He won't meet him—he won't even talk about it. What are we going to do, Mr. Whiteside? Sandy and I love each other. I don't know where to turn.

WHITESIDE. My dear, I'd like to meet this young man. I'd like to see him for myself.

JUNE. Would you, Mr. Whiteside? Would you meet him? He's—he's outside now. He's in the kitchen.

WHITESIDE. Good! Bring him in.

JUNE (*hesitating*). Mr. Whiteside, he's—he's a very sensitive boy. You will be nice to him, won't you?

WHITESIDE. God damn it, June, when will you learn that I am *always* kind and courteous! Bring this idiot in!

JUNE (*calling through the dining room in a low voice*). Sandy. . . . Sandy. . . . (*She stands aside as a young man enters. Twenty-three or -four, keen-looking, neatly but simply dressed*) Here he is, Mr. Whiteside. This is Sandy.

SANDY. How do you do, sir?

WHITESIDE. How do you do? Young man, I've been hearing a good deal about you from June this past week. It seems, if I have been correctly informed, that you two babes in the woods have quietly gone out of your minds.

JUNE. There's another name for it. It's called love.

WHITESIDE. Well, you've come to the right place. Dr. Sheridan Whiteside, Broken Hearts Mended, Brakes Relined, Hamburgers. Go right ahead.

SANDY. Well, if June has told you anything at all, Mr. Whiteside, you know the jam we're in. You see, I work for the union, Mr. Whiteside. I'm an organizer. I've been organizing the men in Mr. Stanley's factory, and Mr. Stanley's pretty sore about it.

WHITESIDE. I'll bet.

SANDY. Did June tell you that?

WHITESIDE. Yes, she did.

SANDY. Well, that being the case, Mr. Whiteside, I don't think I have the right to try to influence June. If she marries me it means a definite break with her family, and I don't like to bring that about. But Mr. Stanley's so stubborn about it, so arbitrary. You know, this is not something I've done just to spite him. We fell in love with each other. But Mr. Stanley behaves as though it were all a big plot—John L. Lewis sent me here just to marry his daughter.

JUNE. He's tried to fire Sandy twice, out at the factory, but he couldn't on account of the Wagner Act, thank God!

SANDY. Yes, he thinks I wrote that, too.

JUNE. If he'd only let me talk to him. If he'd let Sandy talk to him.

SANDY. Well, we've gone over all that, June. Anyway, this morning I got word I'm needed in Chicago. I may have to go on to Frisco from there. So you see the jam we're in.

JUNE. Sandy's leaving tonight, Mr. Whiteside. He'll probably be gone a year. We've simply got to decide. *Now.*

WHITESIDE. My dear, this is absurdly simple. It's no problem at all. Now to my jaundiced eye— (*The telephone rings*) Oh-h! Hello. . . . Yes. . . . This is Whiteside. . . . Excuse me—it's a trans-Atlantic call. . . . Yes? . . . Yes, I'm on. Who's calling me? (*His tone suddenly becomes one of keen delight*) All right—put her through. (*He turns to the young pair*) It's Gertrude Stein, in Paris. . . . Hello. . . . Hello, Gertie! How's my little nightingale? . . . Yes, I hoped you would. How'd you know I was here? . . . I see. Well, it's wonderful of you to call. . . . Yes. Yes, I'm listening. Ten seconds more? (*A quick aside to the others*) It'll be Christmas in Paris in ten seconds, and every year—yes? . . . Yes, Gertie, I hear them. It's wonderful. As though they were right outside. . . . June! (*He holds the receiver out to* JUNE *for a second*) Thank you, my dear, and a very Merry Christmas to *you.* Don't forget we're dining on June tenth. . . . Pourquoi ne pas se réunir chez vous après? Tachez d'avoir Picasso, Matisse, Cocteau. Je serai seulement là pour quelques jours et je veux voir tout le monde. N'est-ce pas? Ah! Bon! Au revoir—au revoir. (*He hangs up*) You know what that was you listened to? The bells of Notre Dame.

JUNE. Not really!

WHITESIDE. Miss Stein calls me every Christmas, no matter where I am, so that I can hear them. Two years ago I was walking on the bottom of the ocean in a diving suit with William Beebe, but she got me. . . . Now, where were we? Oh, yes. . . . June, I like your young man. I have an unerring instinct about people—I've never been wrong. That's why I wanted to meet him. My feeling is that you two will be very happy together. Whatever his beliefs are, he's entitled to them, and you shouldn't let anything stand in your way. As I see it, it's no problem at all. Stripped of its externals, what does it come down to? Your father. The possibility of making him unhappy. Is that right?

JUNE. Very unhappy.

WHITESIDE. That isn't the point. Suppose your parents *are* unhappy—it's good for them. Develops their characters. Look at me. I left home at the age of four and haven't been back since. They hear me on the radio and that's enough for them.

SANDY. Then—your advice is to go ahead, Mr. Whiteside?

WHITESIDE. It is. Marry him tonight, June.

JUNE (*almost afraid to make the leap*). You—you mean that, Mr. Whiteside?

WHITESIDE (*bellowing*). No, I mean you should marry Senator Borah. If I didn't mean it I wouldn't say it. What do you want me to do—say it all over again? My own opinion is— (*The voice of* MR. STANLEY *is heard at the head of the stairs. "Come on, Daisy—stop dawdling."* JUNE *quickly pushes her young man out of the room, as* MR. *and* MRS. STANLEY *descend the stairs.*)

STANLEY (*with deep sarcasm*). Forgive us for trespassing, Mr. Whiteside.

WHITESIDE. Not at all, old fellow—not at all. It's Christmas, you know. Merry Christmas, Merry Christmas.

MRS. STANLEY (*nervously*). Ah—yes. Merry Christmas. . . . Would you like to come along with us, June? We're taking some presents over to the Dexters.

JUNE. No—no, thank you, Mother. I—I have to write some letters. (*She hurries up the stairs.*)

STANLEY (*who has been donning his coat*). Come along, Daisy. (*Turning, he reveals a great patch of court plaster on his head*).

WHITESIDE (*entirely too sweetly*). Why, Mr. Stanley, what happened to your forehead? Did you have an accident?

STANLEY (*just as sweetly*). No, Mr. Whiteside. I'm taking boxing lessons. . . . Come, Daisy. (*They go.*) (HARRIET, *who has been hovering at the head of the stairs, hurries down as the* STANLEYS *depart. She is carrying a little Christmas package.*)

HARRIET. Dear Mr. Whiteside, I've been trying all day to see you. To give you—*this.*

WHITESIDE. Why, Miss Stanley. A Christmas gift for me?

HARRIET. It's only a trifle, but I wanted you to have it. It's a picture of me as I used to be. It was taken on another Christmas Eve, many years ago. Don't open it till the stroke of midnight, will you? (*The doorbell rings.* HARRIET *looks apprehensively over her shoulder*) Merry Christmas, dear Mr. Whiteside. Merry Christmas.

WHITESIDE. Merry Christmas to you, Miss Stanley, and thank you.

(*She glides out of the room. In the hallway, as* JOHN *opens the door, we hear a woman's voice, liquid and melting. "This* IS *the Stanley residence, isn't it?" "Yes, it is." "I've come to see Mr. Whiteside. Will you tell him Miss Sheldon is here?"*)

WHITESIDE. Lorraine! My Blossom Girl!

LORRAINE (*coming into view*). Sherry, my sweet! (*And quite a view it is.* LORRAINE SHELDON *is known as the most chic actress on the New York or London stage, and justly so. She glitters as she walks. She is beautiful, and even, God save the word, glamorous. . . . Her rank as one of the Ten Best-Dressed Women of the World is richly deserved. She is, in short, a siren of no mean talents, and knows it.*)

LORRAINE (*wasting no time*). Oh, darling, look at that poor sweet tortured face! Let me kiss it! You poor darling, your eyes have a kind of gallant compassion. How drawn you are! Sherry, my sweet, I want to cry.

WHITESIDE. All right, all right. You've made a very nice entrance. Now relax, dear.

LORRAINE. But, Sherry, darling, I've been so worried. And now seeing you in that chair . . .

WHITESIDE. This chair fits my fanny as nothing else ever has. I feel better than I have in years, and my only concern is news of the outside world. So take that skunk off and tell me everything. How are you, my dear?

LORRAINE (*removing a cascade of silver fox from her shoulders*). Darling, I'm so relieved. You look perfectly wonderful—I never saw you look better. My dear, do I look a wreck? I just dashed through New York. Didn't do a thing about Christmas. Hattie Carnegie and had my hair done, and got right on the train. And the *Normandie* coming back was simply hectic. Fun, you know, but simply exhausting. Jock Whitney, and Cary Grant, and Dorothy di Frasso—it was *too* exhausting. And of course London before that was so magnificent, my dear—well, I simply never got to bed at all. Darling, I've so much to tell you I don't know where to start.

WHITESIDE. Well, start with the dirt first, dear—that's what I want to hear.

LORRAINE. Let me see. . . . Well, Sybil Cartwright got thrown right out of Ciro's—it was the night before I sailed. She was wearing one of those new cellophane dresses, and you could absolutely see Trafalgar Square. And, oh, yes—Sir Harry Montrose—the painter, *you* know—is suing his mother for disorderly conduct. It's just shocked *every*one. Oh, and before I forget—Anthony Eden told me he's going to be on your New Year's broadcast, and he gave me a message for you. He said for God's sake not to introduce him again as the English Grover Whalen.

WHITESIDE. Nonsense. . . . Now come, dear, what about *you?* What about your love life? I don't believe for one moment that you never got to bed at all, if you'll pardon the expression.

LORRAINE. Sherry dear, you're dreadful.

WHITESIDE. What about that splendid bit of English mutton, Lord Bottomley? Haven't you hooked him yet?

LORRAINE. Sherry, please. Cedric is a very dear friend of mine.

WHITESIDE. Now, Blossom Girl, this is Sherry. Don't try to pull the bed clothes over *my* eyes. Don't tell *me* you wouldn't like to be Lady Bottomley, with a hundred thousand pounds a year and twelve castles. By the way, has he had his teeth fixed yet? Every time I order Roquefort cheese I think of those teeth.

LORRAINE. Sherry, really! . . . Cedric may not be brilliant, but he's rather sweet, poor lamb, and he's very fond of me, and he does represent a kind of English way of living that I like. Surrey, and London for the season—shooting box in Scotland—that lovely old castle in Wales. You were there, Sherry—you know what I mean.

WHITESIDE. Mm. I do indeed.

LORRAINE. Well, really, Sherry, why not? If I can marry Cedric I don't know why I shouldn't. Shall I tell you something, Sherry? I think, from something he said just before I sailed, that he's finally coming around to it. It wasn't definite, mind you, but—don't be surprised if I *am* Lady Bottomley before very long.

WHITESIDE. Lady Bottomley! Won't Kansas City be surprised! However, I shall be a flower girl and give the groom an iron toothpick as a wedding present. Come ahead, my blossom—let's hear some more of your skullduggery.
(*The library doors are quietly opened at this point and the* DOCTOR'S *head appears.*)

DR. BRADLEY (*in a heavy whisper*). Mr. Whiteside.

WHITESIDE. What? No, no—not now. I'm busy.
(*The* DOCTOR *disappears.*)

LORRAINE. Who's that?

WHITESIDE. He's fixing the plumbing. . . . Now come on, come on—I want more news.

LORRAINE. But, Sherry, what about this play? After all, I've come all the way from New York—even on Christmas Eve—I've been so excited ever since your phone call. Where is it? When can I read it?

WHITESIDE. Well, here's the situation. This young author—his name is Bert Jefferson—brought me the play with the understanding that I send it to Kit Cornell. It's a magnificent part, and God knows I feel disloyal to Kit, but there you are. Now *I've* done *this* much—the rest is up to you. He's young and attractive—now, just how you'll go about persuading him, I'm sure you know more about that than I do.

LORRAINE. Darling, how can I ever thank you? Does he know I'm coming—Mr. Jefferson, I mean?

WHITESIDE. No, no. You're just out here visiting me. You'll meet him, and that's that. Get him to take you to dinner, and work around to the play. Good God, I don't have to tell you how to do these things. How did you get all those other parts?

LORRAINE. Sherry! . . . Well, I'll go back to the hotel and get into something more attractive. I just dumped my bags and rushed right over here. Darling, you're wonderful. (*Lightly kissing him.*)

WHITESIDE. All right—run along and get into your working clothes. Then come right back here and spend Christmas Eve with Sherry and I'll have Mr. Jefferson on tap. By the way, I've got a little surprise for you. Who do you think's paying me a flying visit tonight? None other than your old friend and fellow actor, Beverly Carlton.

LORRAINE (*not too delighted*). Really? Beverly? I thought he was being glamorous again on a tramp steamer.

WHITESIDE. Come, come, dear—mustn't be bitter because he got better notices than you did.

LORRAINE. Don't be silly, Sherry. I never read notices. I simply wouldn't care to act with him again, that's all. He's not staying here, is he? I *hope* not!

WHITESIDE. Temper, temper, temper. No, he's not. . . . Where'd you get that diamond clip, dear? That's a new bit of loot, isn't it?

LORRAINE. Haven't you seen this before? Cedric gave it to me for his mother's birthday. . . . Look, darling, I've got a taxi outside. If I'm going to get back here—
(*At this point the voice of* MAGGIE *is heard in the hallway.*)

MAGGIE. Sherry, what do you think? I've just been given the most beautiful . . . (*She stops short and comes to a dead halt as she sees* LORRAINE.)

LORRAINE. Oh, hello, Maggie. I knew you must be around somewhere. How are you, my dear?

WHITESIDE. Santa's been at work, my pet. Blossom Girl just dropped in out of the blue and surprised us.

MAGGIE (*quietly*). Hello, Lorraine.

WHITESIDE (*as* JEFFERSON *appears*). Who's that—Bert? This is Mr. Bert Jefferson, Lorraine. Young newspaperman. Miss Lorraine Sheldon.

BERT. How do you do, Miss Sheldon?

LORRAINE. How do you do? I didn't quite catch the name—Jefferson?

WHITESIDE (*sweetly*). That's right, Pet.

LORRAINE (*full steam ahead*). Why, Mr. Jefferson, you don't look like a newspaperman. You don't look like a newspaperman at all.

BERT. Really? I thought it was written all over me in neon lights.

LORRAINE. Oh, no, not at all. I should have said you were—oh, I don't know—an aviator or an explorer or something. They have that same kind of dash about them. I'm simply enchanted with your town, Mr. Jefferson. It gives one such a warm, gracious feeling. Tell me—have you lived here all your life?

BERT. Practically.

WHITESIDE. If you wish to hear the story of his life, Lorraine, kindly do so on your own time. Maggie and I have work to do. Get out of here, Jefferson. On your way, Blossom.

LORRAINE. He's the world's rudest man, isn't he? Can I drop you, Mr. Jefferson? I'm going down to the—Mansion House, I think it's called.

BERT. Thank you, but I've got my car. Suppose I drop you?

LORRAINE. Oh, would you? That'd be lovely—we'll send the taxi off. See you in a little while. Sherry. 'Bye, Maggie.

BERT. Good-bye, Miss C. (*He turns to* WHITESIDE). I'm invited back for dinner, am I not?

WHITESIDE. Yes—yes, you are. At Christmas I always feed the needy. Now please stop oozing out—*get* out.

LORRAINE. Come on, Mr. Jefferson. I want to hear more about this charming little town. And I want to know a good deal about you, too.
(*And they are gone. There is a slight but pregnant pause after they go.* MAGGIE *simply stands looking at* WHITESIDE, *waiting for what may come forth.*)

WHITESIDE. (*as though nothing had happened*). Now let's see, have you got a copy of that broadcast? How much did you say they wanted out —four minutes?

MAGGIE. That's right—four minutes. . . . She's looking very well, isn't she?

WHITESIDE (*busy with his manuscript*). What's that? Who?

MAGGIE. The Countess di Pushover. . . . Quite a surprise, wasn't it—her dropping in?

WHITESIDE. Yes—yes, it was. Now come on, Maggie, come on. Get to work.

MAGGIE. Why, she must have gone through New York like a dose of salts. How long's she going to stay?

WHITESIDE. (*completely absorbed*). What? Oh, I don't know—a few days . . . (*He reads from his manuscript*) "At this joyous season of the year, when in the hearts of men—" I can't cut that.

MAGGIE. Isn't it curious? There was Lorraine, snug as a bug in somebody's bed on the *Normandie*—

WHITESIDE (*so busy*). "Ere the Yuletide season pass—"

MAGGIE (*quietly taking the manuscript out of his hands*). Now, Sherry dear, we will talk a bit.

WHITESIDE. Now look here, Maggie. Just because a friend of mine happens to come out to spend Christmas with me— (*The doorbell rings*) I have a hunch that's Beverly. Maggie, see if it is. Go ahead—run! Run!
(MAGGIE *looks at him—right through him, in fact. Then she goes slowly toward the door. We hear her voice at the door: "Beverly!" Then, in clipped English tones: "Magpie! A large, moist, incestuous kiss for my magpie!"*)

WHITESIDE (*roaring*). Come in here, you Piccadilly pen-pusher, and gaze upon a soul in agony.
(BEVERLY CARLTON *enters, arm in arm with* MAGGIE. *Very confident, very British, very Beverly Carlton.*)

BEVERLY. Don't tell me how you are, Sherry dear. I want none of the tiresome details. I have only a little time, so conversation will be entirely about *me,* and I shall love it. Shall I tell you how I glittered through the South Seas like a silver scimitar, or would you rather hear how I frolicked through Zambesia, raping the Major General's daughter and finishing a three-act play at the same time? . . . Magpie dear, you are the moonflower of my middle age, and I love you very much. Say something beautiful to me. Sherry dear, without going into mountainous waves of self-pity, how are you?

WHITESIDE. I'm fine, you presumptuous cockney. . . . Now, how was the trip, wonderful?

BEVERLY. Fabulous. I did a fantastic amount of work. By the way, did I glimpse that little boudoir butterfly, La Sheldon, in a motor-car as I came up the driveway?

MAGGIE. You did indeed. She's paying us a Christmas visit.

BEVERLY. Dear girl! They do say she set fire to her mother, but I don't believe it. . . . Sherry, my evil one, not only have I written the finest comedy since Molière, but also the best revue since my last one and an operetta that frightens me—it's so good. I shall play it for eight weeks in London and six in New York—that's all. No matinees. Then I am off to the Grecian Islands. . . . Magpie, why don't you come along? Why don't you desert this cannonball of fluff and come with me?

MAGGIE. Beverly dear, be careful. You're catching me at a good moment.

WHITESIDE (*changing the subject*). Tell me, did you have a good time in Hollywood? How long were you there?

BEVERLY. Three unbelievable days. I saw everyone from Adrian to Zanuck. They came, poor dears, as to a shrine I was insufferably charming and ruthlessly firm in refusing seven million dollars for two minutes' work.

WHITESIDE. What about Banjo? Did you see my wonderful Banjo in Hollywood?

BEVERLY. I did. He gave a dinner for me. I arrived, in white tie and tails, to be met at the door by two bewigged flunkies, who quietly proceeded to take my trousers off. I was then ushered, in my lemon silk drawers, into a room full of Norma Shearer, Claudette Colbert, and Aldous Huxley, among others. Dear, sweet, incomparable Banjo.

WHITESIDE. I'll never forget that summer at Antibes, when Banjo put a microphone in Lorraine's mattress, and then played the record the next day at lunch.

BEVERLY. I remember it indeed. Lorraine left Antibes by the next boat.

MAGGIE (*half to herself*). I wish Banjo were here now.

BEVERLY. What's the matter, Magpie? Is Lorraine being her own sweet sick-making self?

MAGGIE. You wouldn't take her to the Grecian Islands with you, would you, Beverly? Just for me?

WHITESIDE. Now, now. Lorraine is a charming person who has gallantly given up her own Christmas to spend it with me.

BEVERLY. Oh, I knew I had a bit of dirt for us all to nibble on. (*He draws a letter out of his pocket. Again the library doors are opened and the* DOCTOR'*s head comes through.*)

DR. BRADLEY. Mr. Whiteside.

WHITESIDE. No, no, not now. Go away.
(*The* DOCTOR *withdraws.*)

BEVERLY. Have you kidnapped someone, Sherry?

WHITESIDE. Yes, that was Charley Ross . . . Go ahead. Is this something juicy?

BEVERLY. Juicy as a pomegranate. It is the latest report from London on the winter maneuvers of Miss Lorraine Sheldon against the left flank—in fact, all flanks—of Lord Cedric Bottomley. Listen: "Lorraine has just left us in a cloud of Chanel Number Five. Since September, in her relentless pursuit of His Lordship, she has paused only to change girdles and check her oil. She has chased him, panting, from castle to castle, till he finally took refuge, for several week-ends, in the gentlemen's lavatory of the House of Lords. Practically no one is betting on the Derby this year; we are all making book on Lorraine. She is sailing tomorrow on the *Normandie*, but would return on the *Yankee Clipper* if Bottomley so much as belches in her direction." Have you ever met Lord Bottomley, Magpie dear? (*He goes immediately into an impersonation of His Lordship. Very British, very full of teeth, stuttering*) "No v-v-very good shooting today, blast it. Only s-s-six partridges, f-f-four grouse, and the D-D-Duke of Sutherland."

WHITESIDE (*chuckling*). My God, that's Bottomley to the very bottom.

BEVERLY (*still in character*). "R-r-ripping debate in the House today. Old Basil spoke for th-th-three hours. D-d-dropped dead at the end of it. Ripping."

MAGGIE. You're making it up, Beverly. No one sounds like that.

WHITESIDE. It's so good it's uncanny. . . . Damn it, Beverly, why must you race right out of here? I never see enough of you, you ungrateful moppet.

BEVERLY. Sherry darling, I can only tell you that my love for you is so great that I changed trains at Chicago to spend ten minutes with you and wish you a Merry Christmas. Merry Christmas, my lad. My little Magpie. (*A look at his watch*) And now I have just time for one magnificent number, to give you a taste of how brilliant the whole thing is. It's the second number in the revue. (*He strikes a chord on the piano, but before he can go further the telephone rings.*)

WHITESIDE. Oh, damn! Get rid of them, Maggie.

MAGGIE. Hello . . . Oh, hello, Bert . . . . Oh! Well, just a minute. . . . Beverly, would you talk to a newspaperman for just two minutes? I kind of promised him.

BEVERLY. Won't have time, Magpie, unless he's under the piano.

MAGGIE. Oh! (*Into the phone*) Wait a minute. (*To* BEVERLY *again*) Would you see him at the station, just for a minute before the train goes? (BEVERLY *nods*) Bert, go to the station and wait for him. He'll be there in a few minutes. . . . 'Bye.

WHITESIDE. The stalls are impatient, Beverly. Let's have this second-rate masterpiece.

BEVERLY (*his fingers rippling over the keys*). It's called: "What Am I to Do?"

"Oft in the nightfall
I think I might fall
Down from my perilous height;
Deep in the heart of me,
Always a part of me,
Quivering, shivering light.
Run, little lady,
Ere the shady
Shafts of time
Barb you with their winged desire,
Singe you with their sultry fire.
Softly a fluid
Druid
Meets me,
Olden
and golden
the dawn that greets me;
Cherishing,
Perishing,
Up to the stars
I climb.
What am I to do
Toward ending this madness,
This sadness,
That's rending me through?
The flowers of yesteryear
Are haunting me,
Taunting me,
Darling, for wanting you.
What am I to say
To warnings of sorrow
When morning's tomorrow
Greets the dew?
Will I see the cosmic Ritz
Shattered and scattered to bits?
What *not* am I to do?"

(*As he swings into the chorus for a second time the doorbell rings, and* JOHN *is glimpsed as he goes to the door. It is a trio of* RADIO MEN *who appear in the doorway, their arms filled with equipment for* MR. WHITESIDE'*s broadcast.*)

WHITESIDE. Oh, come in, Westcott. . . . Beverly, it's superb. The best thing you've ever written. It'll be played by every ragtag orchestra from Salem to Singapore.

BEVERLY. Please! Let *me* say that . . . Ah, the air waves, eh? Well, I shan't have to hear you, thank God. I shall be on the train.

MAGGIE. Come on, Whiteside, say good-bye. Mr. Westcott, he's still four minutes over—you'll have to chisel it out.

WHITESIDE (*as* MAGGIE *starts to wheel him into the library*). Stop this nonsense. Beverly, my lamb—

MAGGIE. You can kiss Beverly in London on July twelfth. (*Then to the technicians*) The microphone set-up is right there, gentlemen, and you can connect up outside. John, show them where it is.

WHITESIDE. Maggie, what the hell are you—

BEVERLY (*calling after the fast-disappearing* WHITESIDE). Au revoir, Sherry. Merry Christmas. Magpie, come get a kiss.

MAGGIE (*emerging from the library and closing the doors behind her*). Beverly, I want one minute. I must have it. You'll make the train. The station's a minute and a half from here.

BEVERLY. Why, what's the matter, Magpie?
(*At which the library doors are*

opened and the DOCTOR *emerges, rather apologetically. He is sped on his way by* MR. WHITESIDE'S *roaring voice—"Oh, get out of here!")*

DR. BRADLEY. I'm—I'm just waiting in the kitchen until Mr. Whiteside is— Excuse me. (*He darts out through the dining room.*)

BEVERLY. Who *is* that man?

MAGGIE. Never mind . . . Beverly, I'm in great trouble.

BEVERLY. Why, Magpie dear, what's the matter?

MAGGIE. I've fallen in love. For the first time in my life. Beverly, I'm in love. I can't tell you about it—there isn't time. But Sherry is trying to break it up. In his own fiendish way he's doing everything he can to break it up.

BEVERLY. Why, the old devil! What's he doing?

MAGGIE. Lorraine. He's brought Lorraine here to smash it.

BEVERLY. Oh, it's somebody *here?* In this town?

MAGGIE (*nodding*). He's a newspaperman—the one you're going to see at the station—and he's written a play, and I know Sherry must be using that as bait. You know Lorraine—she'll eat him up alive. You've got to help me, Beverly.

BEVERLY. Of course I will, Magpie. What do you want me to do?

MAGGIE. I've got to get Lorraine out of here—the farther away the better—and you can do it for me.

BEVERLY. But how? How can I? I'm leaving.

(*The library doors are opened and* WESTCOTT, *the radio man, emerges.*)

WESTCOTT. Have you a carbon copy of the broadcast, Miss Cutler?

MAGGIE. It's on that table.

WESTCOTT. Thank you. One of those penguins ate the original.

(*The voice of* WHITESIDE *is now heard calling from his room.*)

WHITESIDE. Beverly, are you still there?

MAGGIE. No, he's gone, Sherry. (*She lowers her voice*) Come out here. (*Maneuvering him into the hall, we see her whisper to him; his head bobs up and down quickly in assent. Then he lets out a shriek of laughter.*)

BEVERLY. I'd love it. I'd absolutely love it. (MAGGIE *puts a quick finger to his lips, peers toward the* WHITESIDE *room. But* MR. WESTCOTT *has gone in; the doors are closed*) It's simply enchanting, and bitches Sherry and Lorraine at the same time. It's pure heaven! I adore it, and I shall do it up brown. (*He embraces her.*)

MAGGIE. Darling, the first baby will be named Beverly. You're wonderful.

BEVERLY. Of course I am. Come to Chislewick for your honeymoon and I'll put you up. Good-bye, my lovely. I adore you. (*And he is gone.* MAGGIE *comes back into the room, highly pleased with herself. She even sings a fragment of* BEVERLY'S *song. "What am I to do? Tra-la-la-la-la-la."* JOHN, *entering from the dining room, breaks the song.*)

JOHN. Shall I straighten up the room for the broadcast, Miss Cutler?

MAGGIE. No, John, it isn't television, thank God. They only hear that liquid voice.

JOHN. He's really wonderful, isn't he? The things he finds time to do.

MAGGIE. Yes, he certainly sticks his nose into everything, John. (*She goes into the library.* JOHN *is putting the room in order when suddenly* JUNE *comes quietly down the stairs. She is dressed for the street and is carrying a suitcase.*)

JOHN. Why, Miss June, are you going away?

JUNE. Why—no, John. No. I'm just—Mr. Whiteside is inside, I suppose?

JOHN. Yes, he's getting ready to go on the radio.

JUNE. Oh! Well, look, John— (*And then* RICHARD *darts down the stairs. A light bag, two cameras slung over his shoulder.*)

RICHARD (*to* JUNE, *in a heavy whisper*). Where's Mr. Whiteside? In there?

JUNE. Yes, he is.

RICHARD. Oh! Well, maybe we ought to— (*The doorbell rings.* RICHARD *and* JUNE *exchange looks, then scurry out quickly through the dining room.* JOHN *looks after them for a second, puzzled, then goes to the door. It is* LORRAINE *who comes in, resplendent now in evening dress and wrap, straight from Paris. At the same time* MAGGIE *emerges from the library and* JOHN *goes on his way.*)

LORRAINE. Hello, dear. Where's Sherry?

MAGGIE. Inside, working—he's broadcasting very soon.

LORRAINE. Oh, of course—Christmas Eve. What a wonderful man Sheridan Whiteside is! You know, my dear, it must be such an utter joy to be secretary to somebody like Sherry.

MAGGIE. Yes, you meet such interesting people. . . . That's quite a gown, Lorraine. Going anywhere?

LORRAINE. This? Oh, I just threw on anything at all. Aren't you dressing for dinner?

MAGGIE. No, just what meets the eye. (*She has occasion to carry a few papers across the room at this point.* LORRAINE'*s eye watches her narrowly.*)

LORRAINE. Who does your hair, Maggie?

MAGGIE. A little French woman named Maggie Cutler comes in every morning.

LORRAINE. You know, every time I see you I keep thinking your hair could be so lovely. I always want to get my hands on it.

MAGGIE (*quietly*). I've always wanted to get mine on yours, Lorraine.

LORRAINE (*absently*). What, dear? (*One of the radio men drifts into the room, plugs into the control board, drifts out again.* LORRAINE'*s eyes follow him idly. Then she turns to* MAGGIE *again*) By the way, what time does Beverly get here? I'm not over anxious to meet him.

MAGGIE. He's been and gone, Lorraine.

LORRAINE. Really? Well, I'm very glad. . . . Of course you're great friends, aren't you—you and Beverly?

MAGGIE. Yes, we are. I think he's a wonderful person.

LORRAINE. Oh, I suppose so. But when I finished acting with him I was a perfect wreck. All during that tender love scene that the critics thought was so magnificent he kept dropping peanut shells down my dress. I wouldn't act with him again if I were starving.

MAGGIE (*casually*). Tell me, Lorraine, have you found a new play yet?

LORRAINE (*at once on guard*). No. No, I haven't. There was a pile of manuscripts waiting in New York for me, but I hurried right out here to Sherry.

MAGGIE. Yes, it was wonderful of you, Lorraine—to drop everything that way and rush to Sherry's wheelchair.

LORRAINE. Well, after all, Maggie dear, what else has one in this world but friends? . . . How long will Sherry be in there, I wonder?

MAGGIE. Not long. . . . Did you know that Mr. Jefferson has written quite a good play? The young man that drove you to the hotel.

LORRAINE. Really? No, I didn't. Isn't that interesting?

MAGGIE. Yes, isn't it? (*There is a considerable pause. The ladies smile at each other.*)

LORRAINE (*evading* MAGGIE'S *eyes*). They've put a polish on my nails I simply loathe. I don't suppose Elizabeth Arden has a branch in this town.

MAGGIE (*busy with her papers*). Not if she has any sense.

LORRAINE. Oh, well, I'll just bear it, but it does depress me. (*She rises, wanders aimlessly for a moment, picks up a book from the table*) Have you read this, Maggie? Everybody was reading it on the boat. I hear you simply can't put it down.

MAGGIE. *I* put it down—right there. (LORRAINE *casually strikes a note or two on the piano. The telephone rings.*)

MAGGIE (*taking up the receiver a little too casually*). Hello . . . Yes . . . Yes . . . Miss Lorraine Sheldon? Yes, she's here . . . There's a trans-Atlantic call coming through for you, Lorraine.

LORRAINE. Trans-Atlantic—for me? Here? Why, what in the world—

MAGGIE (*as she hands over the receiver*). It's London.

LORRAINE. London? . . . Hello. (*Then in a louder tone*) Hello . . . Cedric! Cedric, is this you? . . . Why, Cedric, you darling! Why, what a surprise! How'd you know I was here? . . . Darling, don't talk so fast and you won't stutter so . . . That's better . . . Yes, now I can hear you . . . Yes, very clearly. It's as though you were just around the corner. . . .

I see . . . What? . . . Darling! Cedric, dearest, would you wait just one moment? (*She turns to* MAGGIE) Maggie, would you mind? It's Lord Bottomley—a *very* personal call. Would you mind?

MAGGIE. Oh, not at all. (*She goes into the dining room; almost does a little waltz step as she goes.*)

LORRAINE. Yes, my dearest—now tell me . . . Cedric, please don't stutter so. Don't be nervous. (*She listens for a moment again*) Oh, my darling. Oh, my sweet. You don't know how I've prayed for this, every night on the boat . . . Darling, yes! YES, a thousand times Yes! . . . I'll take a plane right out of here and catch the next boat. Oh, my sweet, we're going to be the happiest people in the world. I wish I were there now in your arms, Cedric . . . What? . . . Cedric, don't stutter so . . . Yes, and I love *you,* my darling—oh, so much! . . . Oh, my dear sweet. My darling, my darling. . . . Yes, yes! I will, I will, darling! I'll be thinking of you every moment . . . You've made me the happiest girl in the world . . . Good-bye, good-bye, darling. Good-bye. (*Bursting with her news, she throws open the library doors*) Sherry, Sherry! Do you know what's happened? Cedric just called from London— He's asked me to marry him. Sherry, think of it! At last! I've got to get right out of here and catch the next boat. How far are we from Chicago? I can get a plane from there.

MAGGIE (*emerging, mouse-like, from the dining room*). May I come in?

LORRAINE. Maggie dear, can I get a plane out of here right away? Or I'll even take a train to Chicago and fly from there. I've simply got to get the next boat for England. When is it—do you know? Is there a newspaper here?

MAGGIE. The *Queen Mary* sails Friday. Why, what's all the excitement Lorraine? What's happened?

LORRAINE. Maggie, the most wonderful thing in the world has happened. Lord Bottomley has asked me to marry him . . . Oh, Maggie! (*And in her exuberance she throws her arms around her.*)

MAGGIE. Really? Well, what do you know?

LORRAINE. Isn't it wonderful? I'm so excited I can hardly think. Maggie dear, you must help me get out of here.

MAGGIE. I'd be delighted to, Lorraine.

LORRAINE. Oh, thank you, thank you. Will you look things up right away?

MAGGIE. Yes, I've a time-table right here. And don't worry, because if there's no train I'll drive you to Toledo and you can catch the plane from there.

LORRAINE. Maggie darling, you're wonderful. . . . Sherry, what's the matter with you? You haven't said a word. You haven't even congratulated me.

WHITESIDE (*who has been sitting through this like a thundercloud*). Let me understand this, Lorraine. Am I to gather from your girlish squeals that you are about to toss your career into the ashcan?

LORRAINE. Oh, not at all. Of course I may not be able to play this season, but there'll be other seasons, Sherry.

WHITESIDE. I see. And everything goes into the ashcan with it— Is that right?

LORRAINE. But, Sherry, you couldn't expect me to—

WHITESIDE (*icily*). Don't explain, Lorraine. I understand only too well. And I also understand why Cornell remains the First Actress of our theatre.

MAGGIE (*busy with her time-tables*). Oh, this is wonderful! We're in luck, Lorraine. You can get a plane out of Toledo at ten-three. It takes about an hour to get there. Why, it all works out wonderfully, doesn't it, Sherry?

WHITESIDE (*through his teeth*). Peachy!

LORRAINE (*heading for the phone*). Maggie, what's the number of that hotel I'm at? I've got to get my maid started packing.

MAGGIE. Mesalia three two.

LORRAINE (*into the phone*). Mesalia three two, please . . . Let's see—I sail Friday, five-day boat, that means I ought to be in London Wednesday night. . . . Hello. This is Miss Sheldon. . . . That's right. Connect me with my maid.

MAGGIE (*at the window*). Oh, look, Sherry, it's starting to snow. Isn't that wonderful, Sherry? Oh, I never felt more like Christmas in my life. Don't you, Sherry dear?

WHITESIDE. Shut your nasty little face!

LORRAINE (*on the phone*). Cosette? . . . Now listen carefully, Cosette. Have you got a pencil? . . . We're leaving here tonight by plane and sailing Friday on the *Queen Mary*. Start packing immediately and I'll call for you in about an hour . . . Yes, that's right . . . Now I want you to send these cables for me . . . Ready? . . . The first one goes to Lord and Lady Cunard—you'll find all these addresses in my little book. It's in my dressing case. "Lord and Lady Cunard. My darlings. Returning Friday *Queen Mary*. Cedric and I being married immediately on arrival. Wanted you to be the first to know. Love.—Lorraine." . . . Now send the same message—what? . . . Oh, thank you, Cosette. Thank you very much . . . Send the same message to Lady Astor, Lord Beaverbrook, and the Duchess of Sutherland . . . Got that? . . . And send a cable to Molyneaux, in Paris. "Please meet me Claridge's Thursday of next week with sketches of bridal gown and trousseau.—Lorraine Sheldon." And then send one to Monsieur Pierre Cartier, Cartier's, Paris: "Can you bring over to London the triple string of pearls I picked out in October? Cable me *Queen Mary*.—Lorraine Sheldon." . . . Have you got all that straight, Cosette? . . . That's fine. Now you'll have to rush, my dear—I'll be at the hotel in about an hour, so be ready. . . Good-bye. (*She hangs up*) Thank goodness for Cosette— I'd die without her. She's the most wonderful maid in the world. . . . Well! Life is really just full of surprises, isn't it? Who'd have thought an hour ago that I'd be on my way to London?

MAGGIE. An *hour* ago? No, I certainly wouldn't have thought it an hour ago.

WHITESIDE (*beside himself with temper*). Will you both stop this female drooling? I have a violent headache.

MAGGIE (*all solicitude*). Oh, Sherry! Can I get you something?

LORRAINE. Look here, Sherry, I'm sorry if I've offended you, but after all my life is my own and I'm not going to— (*She stops as* BERT JEFFERSON *comes in from the outside.*)

BERT. Hello, everybody. Say, do you know it's snowing out? Going to have a real old-fashioned Christmas.

WHITESIDE. Why don't you telephone your scoop to the New York Times?

MAGGIE. Bert, Miss Sheldon has to catch a plane tonight, from Toledo. Can we drive her over, you and I?

BERT. Why, certainly. Sorry you have to go, Miss Sheldon. No bad news, I hope?

LORRAINE. Oh, on the contrary—very good news. Wonderful news.

MAGGIE. Yes, indeed—calls for a drink, I think. You're not being a very good host, Sherry. How about a bottle of champagne?

BERT. Oh, I can do better than that—let me mix you something. It's a Jefferson Special. Okay, Mr. Whiteside?

WHITESIDE. Yes, yes, yes, yes, yes. Mix anything. Only stop driveling.

BERT (*on his way to the dining room*). Anybody admired my Christmas present yet, Maggie?

MAGGIE. Oh, dear, I forgot. (*She raises her arm, revealing a bracelet*) Look, everybody! From Mr. Jefferson to me.

LORRAINE. Oh, it's charming. Let me see it. Oh! Why, it's inscribed, too. "To Maggie. Long may she wave. Bert." Maggie, it's a lovely Christmas present. Isn't it sweet, Sherry?

WHITESIDE (*glowering*). Ducky!

MAGGIE. I told you it was beautiful, Bert. See?

BERT. Well, shows what you get if you save your coupons.

LORRAINE (*looking from* BERT *to* MAGGIE). Well, what's going on between you two, anyhow? Maggie, are you hiding something from us?

WHITESIDE (*a hand to his head*). Great God, will this drivel never stop? My head is bursting.

BERT. A Jefferson Special will cure anything. . . . By the way, I got a two-minute interview with Beverly Carlton at the station. You were right, Mr. Whiteside— He's quite something.

MAGGIE (*uneasily*). Go ahead, Bert—mix the drinks.

BERT. I was lucky to get even two minutes. He was in a telephone booth most of the time. Couldn't hear what he was saying, but from the faces he was making it looked like a scene from one of his plays.

MAGGIE (*hiding her frenzy*). Bert, mix those drinks, will you?

WHITESIDE (*suddenly galvanized*). Just a minute, if you please, Jefferson. Mr. Carlton was in a telephone booth at the station?

BERT. Certainly was—I thought he'd never come out. Kept talking and making the damnedest faces for about five minutes.

MAGGIE (*tensely*). Bert, for goodness sake, will you—

WHITESIDE (*ever so sweetly*). Bert, my boy, I have an idea I shall love the Jefferson Special. Make me a double one, will you? My headache has gone with the wind.

BERT. Okay. (*He goes.* WHITESIDE, *his eyes gleaming, immediately whirls his wheelchair across the room to the telephone.*)

WHITESIDE (*a finger to his lips*). Sssh! Philo Vance is now at work.

LORRAINE. What?

WHITESIDE. Sssh! (*He picks up the telephone. His voice is absolutely musical*) Operator! Has there been a call from England over this telephone within the past half hour? . . . Yes, I'll wait.

LORRAINE. Sherry, what *is* all this?

WHITESIDE. What's that? There have been no calls from England for the past three days? Thank you . . . Now, will you repeat that, please? . . . Blossom Girl. (*He beckons to* LORRAINE, *then puts the receiver to her ear*) Hear it, dear? (*Then again to the operator*) Thank you, and a Merry Christmas. (*He hangs up*) Yes, indeed, it seems we're going to have a real old-fashioned Christmas.

LORRAINE (*stunned*). Sherry, what is all this? What's going on? What does this mean?

WHITESIDE. My dear, you have just played the greatest love scene of your career with your old friend, Beverly Carlton.

LORRAINE. Why—why, that's not true. I was talking to Cedric. What do you mean?

WHITESIDE. I mean, my blossom, that that was Beverly you poured out your girlish heart to, not Lord Bottomley. Ah, me, who'd have thought five minutes ago that you would not be going to London!

LORRAINE. Sherry, stop it! What is this? I want this explained.

WHITESIDE. Explained? You heard the operator, my dear. All I can tell you is that Beverly was indulging in one of his famous bits of mimicry, that's all. You've heard him do Lord Bottomley before, haven't you?

LORRAINE (*as it dawns on her*). Yes . . . Yes, of course . . . But—but why would he want to do such a thing? This is one of the most dreadful—oh, my God! Those cables! (*In one bound she is at the telephone*) Give me the hotel—whatever it's called—I want the hotel—I'll pay him off for this if it's the last thing that I— Why, the cad! The absolute unutterable cad! The dirty rotten— Mansion House? Connect me with my maid . . . What? . . . Who the hell do you *think* it is? Miss Sheldon, of course . . . Oh, God! Those cables! If only

Cosette hasn't—Cosette! Cosette! Did you send those cables? . . . Oh, God! Oh, God. . . . Now listen, Cosette! I want you to send another cable to every one of those people, and tell them somebody has been using my name, and to disregard anything and everything they hear from me—except this, of course . . . Don't ask questions—do as you're told . . . Don't argue with me, you French bitch—God damn it, do as you're told . . . And unpack—we're not going! (*She hangs up.*)

WHITESIDE. Now steady, my blossom. Take it easy.

LORRAINE (*in a white rage*). What do you mean take it easy? Do you realize I'll be the laughingstock of England? Why, I won't dare show my face! I always knew Beverly Carlton was low, but not this low. Why? WHY? It isn't even funny. Why would he do it, that's what I'd like to know. Why would he do it? Why would anyone in the world want to play a silly trick like this? I can't understand it. Do you, Sherry? Do you, Maggie? You both saw him this afternoon. Why would he walk out of here, go right to a phone booth, and try to ship me over to England on a fool's errand? There must have been some reason—there must have. It doesn't make sense otherwise. Why would Beverly Carlton, or anybody else for that matter, want me to— (*She stops as a dim light begins to dawn*) Oh! Oh! (*Her eye, which has been on* MAGGIE, *goes momentarily to the dining room, where* BERT *has disappeared. Then her gaze returns to* MAGGIE *again*) I—I think I begin to—of course! Of course! That's it. Of course that's it. Yes, and that's a very charming bracelet that Mr. Jefferson gave you—isn't it, Maggie dear? Of course. It makes complete sense now. And to think that I nearly—well! Wild horses couldn't get me out of here *now*, Maggie. And if I were you I'd hang onto that bracelet, dear. It'll be something to remember him by!

(*Out of the library comes* MR. WESTCOTT, *his hands full of papers. At the same time the two technicians emerge from the dining room and go to the control board.*)

WESTCOTT (*his eyes on his watch*). All right, Mr. Whiteside. Almost time. Here's your new copy. Hook her up, boys. Start testing.

WHITESIDE. How much time?

WESTCOTT (*bringing him a microphone*). Couple of minutes.

(*One of the radio technicians is talking into a microphone, testing: "One, two, three, four, one, two, three, four. How are we coming in, New York? . . . A, B, C, A, B, C. Mary had a little lamb, Mary had a little lamb."* MR. *and* MRS. STANLEY, *having delivered their Christmas presents, enter from the hallway and start up the stairs.* MRS. STANLEY *looks hungrily at the radio goings-on, but* MR. STANLEY *delivers a stern "Come, Daisy," and she follows him up the stairs. The voices of the technicians drone on: "One, two, three, four, one, two, three, four. O.K., New York. Waiting."* MR. WESTCOTT *stands with watch in hand. From the dining room comes* BERT JEFFERSON, *a tray of drinks in hand.*)

BERT. Here comes the Jefferson Special . . . Oh! Have we time?

LORRAINE. Oh, I'm sure we have. Mr. Jefferson, I'm not leaving after all. My plans are changed.

BERT. Really? Oh, that's good.

LORRAINE. And I hear you've written a simply marvelous play, Mr. Jefferson. I want you to read it to me—tonight. Will you? We'll go back to the Mansion House right after dinner, and you'll read me your play.

BERT. Why—why, I should say so. I'd be delighted. . . . Maggie, did you hear that? Say! I'll bet *you* did this. You arranged the whole thing. Well, it's the finest Christmas present you could have given me.
(MAGGIE *looks at him for one anguished moment. Then, without a word, she dashes into the hall, grabs her coat and flings herself out of the house.* BERT, *bewildered, stands looking after her.* MR. *and* MRS. STANLEY *come pellmell down the stairs. Each clutches a letter, and they are wild-eyed.*)

STANLEY. *Mr.* Whiteside! My son has run off on a freighter and my daughter is marrying an anarchist! They say *you* told them to do it!

MRS. STANLEY. My poor June! My poor Richard! This is the most awful—

WESTCOTT. Quiet! Quiet, please! We're going on the air.

STANLEY. How dare you! This is the most outrageous—

WESTCOTT (*raising his voice*). Please! *Please!* Quiet! We're going on the air.
(STANLEY *chokes and looks with fury.* MRS. STANLEY *is softly crying. In this moment of stillness,* DR. BRADLEY *emerges from the dining room.*)

DR. BRADLEY. Oh! I see you're still busy.

STANLEY (*bursting forth*). Mr. Whiteside, you are the—

WESTCOTT (*yelling*). *Quiet!* For God's sake, quiet! QUIET! . . . All right, boys!
(*From the hallway come six* CHOIR BOYS, *dressed in their robes. They take their places by the microphone as the voice of the technician completes the hook-up.*)

TECHNICIAN. O.K., New York. (*He raises his arm, waiting to give the signal.* WESTCOTT *is watching him. There is a dead pause of about five seconds.* JOHN *and* SARAH *are on tiptoe in the dining room. Then the arm drops.*)

WESTCOTT (*into the microphone*). Good evening, everybody. Cream of Mush brings you Sheridan Whiteside. (*The* LEADER *gestures to the* CHOIR BOYS, *and they raise their lovely voices in "Heilige Nacht." Another gesture from* WESTCOTT, *and* WHITESIDE *begins to speak, with the boys singing as a background.*)

WHITESIDE. This is Whiteside speaking. On this eve of eves, when my own heart is overflowing with peace and kindness, I think it is most fitting to tell once again the story of that still and lustrous night, nigh onto two thousand years ago, when first the star of Bethlehem was glimpsed in a wondrous sky . . . (*The famous* WHITESIDE *voice goes out over the air to the listening millions as the curtain falls.*)

ACT THREE

Christmas morning.

The bright December sunlight streams in through the window.

But the Christmas calm is quickly broken. From the library comes the roaring voice of MR. WHITESIDE. *"Miss Preen! Miss Preen!"*

MISS PREEN, *who is just coming through the dining room, rushes to open the library doors.*

MISS PREEN (*nervously*). Yes, sir. Yes, sir.
(MR. WHITESIDE, *in a mood, rolls himself into the room.*)

WHITESIDE. Where *do* you disappear to all the time, My Lady Nausea?

MISS PREEN (*firmly*). Mr. Whiteside, I can only be in one place at a time.

WHITESIDE. That's very fortunate for this community. . . . Go away, Miss Preen. You remind me of last week's laundry.
(MISS PREEN *goes indignantly into the library and slams the doors after her.* JOHN *emerges from the dining room.*)

JOHN. Good morning, Mr. Whiteside. Merry Christmas.

WHITESIDE (*testily*). Merry Christmas, John. Merry Christmas.

JOHN. And Sarah and I want to thank you for the wonderful present.

WHITESIDE. That's quite all right, John.

JOHN. Are you ready for your breakfast, Mr. Whiteside?

WHITESIDE. No, I don't think I want any breakfast. . . . Has Miss Cutler come down yet?

JOHN. No, sir, not yet.

WHITESIDE. Is she in her room, do you know?

JOHN. Yes, sir, I think she is. Shall I call her?

WHITESIDE. No, no. That's all, John.

JOHN. Yes, sir.
(MAGGIE *comes down the stairs. She wears a traveling suit, and carries a bag.* WHITESIDE *waits for her to speak.*)

MAGGIE. I'm taking the one o'clock train, Sherry. I'm leaving.

WHITESIDE. You're doing nothing of the kind!

MAGGIE. Here are your keys—your driving license. The key to the safe-deposit vault is in the apartment in New York. I'll go in here now and clear things up. (*She opens the library doors.*)

WHITESIDE. Just a moment, Mrs. Siddons! Where *were* you until three o'clock this morning? I sat up half the night in this station wagon, worrying about you. You heard me calling to you when you came in. Why didn't you answer me?

MAGGIE. Look, Sherry, it's over, and you've won. I don't want to talk about it.

WHITESIDE. Oh, come, come, come, come, come. What are you trying to do—make me feel like a naughty, naughty boy? Honestly, Maggie, sometimes you can be very annoying.

MAGGIE (*looking at him in wonder*). You know, you're quite wonderful, Sherry, in a way. *You*'re annoyed. I wish there was a laugh left in me. Shall I tell you something, Sherry? I think you are a selfish, petty egomaniac who would see his mother burned at the stake if that was the only way he could light his cigarette. I think you'd sacrifice your best friend without a moment's hesitation if he disturbed the sacred routine of your self-centered, paltry little life. I think you are incapable of any human emotion that goes higher up than your stomach, and I was the fool of the world for ever thinking I could trust you.

WHITESIDE (*pretty indignant at this*). Well, as long as I live, I shall never do anyone a good turn again. I won't ask you to apologize, Maggie, but six months from now you will be thanking me instead of berating me.

MAGGIE. In six months, Sherry, I expect to be so far away from you— (*She is halted by a loud voice from the hallway, as the door bangs. "Hello—hello—hello!" It is* BERT JEFFERSON *who enters, full of Christmas cheer.*)

BERT. Merry Christmas, everybody! Merry Christmas! I'm a little high, but I can explain everything. Hi, Maggie! Hi, Mr. Whiteside! Shake hands with a successful playwright. Maggie, why'd you run away last night? Where were you? Miss Sheldon thinks the play is wonderful. I read her the play and she thinks it's wonderful. Isn't that wonderful?

MAGGIE. Yes, that's fine, Bert.

BERT. Isn't that wonderful, Mr. Whiteside?

WHITESIDE. Jefferson, I think you ought to go home, don't you?

BERT. What? No—biggest day of my life. I know I'm a little drunk, but this is a big day. We've been sitting over in Billy's Tavern all night. Never realized it was daylight until it was daylight. . . . Listen, Maggie—Miss Sheldon says the play needs just a little bit of fixing—do it in three weeks. She's going to take me to a little place she's got in Lake Placid—just for three weeks. Going to work on the play together. Isn't it wonderful? Why don't you say something, Maggie?

WHITESIDE. Look, Bert, I suggest you tell us all about this later. Now, why don't you— (*He stops as* DR. BRADLEY *enters from the hallway.*)

DR. BRADLEY. Oh, excuse me! Merry Christmas, everybody. Merry Christmas.

BERT. God bless us all, and Tiny Tim.

DR. BRADLEY. Yes. . . . Mr. Whiteside, I thought perhaps if I came very early—

BERT. You know what, Doc? I'm going to Lake Placid for three weeks—isn't that wonderful? Ever hear of Lorraine Sheldon, the famous actress? Well, we're going to Lake Placid for three weeks.

WHITESIDE. Dr. Bradley, would you do me a favor? I think Mr. Jefferson would like some black coffee and a little breakfast. Would you take care of him, please?

DR. BRADLEY (*none too pleased*). Yes, yes, of course.

BERT. Dr. Bradley, I'm going to buy breakfast for *you*—biggest breakfast you ever had.

DR. BRADLEY. Yes, yes. Come along, Jefferson.

BERT. You know what, Doctor? Let's climb down a couple of chimneys. I got a friend doesn't believe in Santa Claus—let's climb down his chimney and frighten the hell out of him. (*He goes out with the* DOCTOR.)

WHITESIDE (*in a burst of magnanimity*). Now listen to me, Maggie. I am willing to forgive your tawdry outburst and talk about this calmly.

MAGGIE (*now crying openly*). I love him so terribly. Oh, Sherry, Sherry, why did you do it? Why did you do it? (*She goes stumblingly into the library.* WHITESIDE, *left alone, looks at his watch; heaves a long sigh. Then* HARRIET *comes down the steps, dressed for the street.*)

HARRIET. Merry Christmas, Mr. Whiteside.

WHITESIDE. Oh! . . . Merry Christmas, Miss Stanley.

HARRIET (*nervously*). I'm afraid I shouldn't be seen talking to you, Mr. Whiteside—my brother is terribly angry. I just couldn't resist asking—did you like my Christmas present?

WHITESIDE. I'm very sorry, Miss Stanley — I haven't opened it. I haven't opened any of my presents yet.

HARRIET. Oh, dear. I was so anxious to—it's right here, Mr. Whiteside. (*She goes to the tree*) Won't you open it now?

WHITESIDE (*as he undoes the string*). I appreciate your thinking of me, Miss Stanley. This is very thoughtful of you. (*He takes out the gift*) Why, it's lovely. I'm very fond of these old photographs. Thank you very much.

HARRIET. I was twenty-two when that was taken. That was my favorite dress. . . . Do you really like it?

WHITESIDE. I do indeed. When I get back to town I shall send *you* a little gift.

HARRIET. Will you? Oh, thank you, Mr. Whiteside. I shall treasure it. . . . Well, I shall be late for church. Good-bye. Good-bye.

WHITESIDE. Good-bye, Miss Stanley. (*As she goes out the front door,* WHITESIDE'S *eyes return to the gift.*

He puzzles over it for a second, shakes his head. Mumbles to himself—"What is there about that woman?" Shakes his head again in perplexity. JOHN *comes from the dining room, en route to the second floor with* MRS. STANLEY'S *tray.*)

JOHN. Sarah's got a little surprise for you, Mr. Whiteside. She's just taking it out of the oven.

WHITESIDE. Thank you, John.
(JOHN *disappears up the stairs. Then suddenly there is a great ringing of the doorbell. It stops for a second, then picks up violently again—rhythmically, this time. It continues until the door is opened.*)

WHITESIDE. Miss Preen! Miss Preen!
(MISS PREEN *comes hurrying from the library.*)

MISS PREEN. Yes, sir. Yes, sir.

WHITESIDE. Answer the door, will you? John is upstairs.
(MISS PREEN, *obviously annoyed, hurries to the door. We hear her voice from the hallway: "Who is it?" An answering male voice: "Polly Adler's?" Then a little shriek from* MISS PREEN, *and in a moment we see the reason why. She is carried into the room in the arms of a pixie-like gentleman, who is kissing her over and over.*)

THE GENTLEMAN CARRYING MISS PREEN. I love you madly—madly! Did you hear what I said—madly! Kiss me! Again! Don't be afraid of my passion. Kiss me! I can feel the hot blood pounding through your varicose veins.

MISS PREEN (*through all this*). Put me down! Put me down, do you hear? Don't you dare kiss me! Who are you? Put me down or I'll scream. Mr. Whiteside! Mr. Whiteside!

WHITESIDE. Banjo! Banjo, for God's sake!

BANJO (*quite calmly*). Hello, Whiteside. Will you sign for this package, please?

WHITESIDE. Banjo, put that woman down. That is my nurse, you mental delinquent.

BANJO (*putting* MISS PREEN *on her feet*). Come to my room in half an hour and bring some rye bread. (*And for good measure he slaps* MISS PREEN *right on the fanny.*)

MISS PREEN (*outraged*). Really, Mr. Whiteside! (*She adjusts her clothes with a quick jerk or two and marches into the library.*)

BANJO. Whiteside, I'm here to spend Christmas with you. Give me a kiss! (*He starts to embrace him.*)

WHITESIDE. Get away from me, you reform-school fugitive. How did you get here anyway?

BANJO. Darryl Zanuck loaned me his reindeer. . . . Whiteside, we finished shooting the picture yesterday and I'm on my way to Nova Scotia. Flew here in twelve hours—borrowed an airplane from Howard Hughes. Whiteside, I brought you a wonderful Christmas present. (*He produces a little tissue-wrapped package.*) This brassière was once worn by Hedy Lamarr.

WHITESIDE. Listen, you idiot, how long can you stay?

BANJO. Just long enough to take a bath. I'm on my way to Nova Scotia. Where's Maggie?

WHITESIDE. Nova Scotia? What are you going to Nova Scotia for?

BANJO. I'm sick of Hollywood and there's a dame in New York I don't want to see. So I figured I'd go to Nova Scotia and get some good salmon. . . . Where the hell's Maggie? I want to see her. . . . What's the matter with you? Where is she?

WHITESIDE. Banjo, I'm glad you're here. I'm very annoyed at Maggie. Very!

BANJO. What's the matter? . . . (*To his considerable surprise, at this point, he sees* WHITESIDE *get up out of his chair and start to pace up and down the room*) Say, what *is* this? I thought you couldn't walk.

WHITESIDE. Oh, I've been all right for weeks. That isn't the point. I'm furious at Maggie. She's turned on me like a viper. You know how fond I am of her. Well, after all these years she's repaying my affection by behaving like a fish-wife.

BANJO. What are you talking about?

WHITESIDE. But I never believed for a moment she was really in love with him.

BANJO. In love with *who*? I just got here—remember.

WHITESIDE. Great God, I'm telling you, you Hollywood nitwit. A young newspaperman here in town.

BANJO (*surprised and pleased*). Maggie finally fell—well, what do you know? What kind of a guy is he?

WHITESIDE. Oh, shut up and listen, will you?

BANJO. Well, go on. What happened?

WHITESIDE. Well, Lorraine Sheldon happened to come out here and visit me.

BANJO. Old Hot-pants—here?

WHITESIDE. Now listen! He'd written a play—this young fellow. You can guess the rest. He's going away with Lorraine this afternoon. To "re-write." So there you are. Maggie's in there now, crying her eyes out.

BANJO. Gee! . . . (*Thinking it over*) Say, wait a minute. What do you mean Lorraine Sheldon *happened* to come out here? I smell a rat, Sherry —a rat with a beard. (*And it might be well to add, at this point, that* MR. SHERIDAN WHITESIDE *wears a beard.*)

WHITESIDE. Well, all right, all right. But I did it for Maggie—because I thought it was the right thing for her.

BANJO. Oh, sure. You haven't thought of yourself in years. . . . Gee, poor kid. Can I go in and talk to her?

WHITESIDE. No—no. Leave her alone

BANJO. Any way I could help, Sherry? Where's this guy live—this guy she likes? Can we get hold of him?

WHITESIDE. Now, wait a minute, Banjo. We don't want any phony warrants, or you pretending to be J. Edgar Hoover. I've been through all that with you before. (*He paces again*) I got Lorraine out here and I've got to get her away.

BANJO. It's got to be good, Sherry. Lorraine's no dope. . . . Now, there must be *some*thing that would get her out of here like a bat out of hell. . . . Say! I think I've got it! That fellow she's so crazy about over in England—Lord Fanny or whatever it is. Bottomley—that's it!

WHITESIDE (*with pained expression*). No, Banjo. No.

BANJO. Wait a minute—you don't catch on. We send Lorraine a cablegram from Lord Bottomley—

WHITESIDE. I catch on, Banjo. Lorraine caught on, too. It's been tried.

BANJO. Oh! . . . I told you she was no dope. . . . (*Seeing* WHITESIDE'S *chair, he sits in it and leans back with a good deal of pleasure*) Well, you've got a tough proposition on your hands.

WHITESIDE. The trouble is there's so damned little time. . . . Get out of my chair! (WHITESIDE *gets back into it*) Lorraine's taking him away with her this afternoon. Oh, damn, damn, damn. There must be some way out. The trouble is I've done this job too well. Hell and damnation.

BANJO (*pacing*). Stuck, huh?

WHITESIDE. In the words of one of our greatest lyric poets, you said it.

BANJO. Yeh. . . . Gee, I'm hungry. We'll think of something, Sherry—you watch. We'll get Lorraine out of here if I have to do it one piece at a time.
(SARAH *enters from the dining room bearing a tray on which reposes the culinary surprise that* JOHN *has mentioned. She holds it behind her back.*)

SARAH. Merry Christmas, Mr. Whiteside. . . . Excuse me. (*This last is to* BANJO) I've got something for you. . . .
(BANJO *blandly lifts the latest delicacy and proceeds to eat it as* SARAH *presents the empty plate to* WHITESIDE.)

SARAH (*almost in tears*). But, Mr. Whiteside, it was for you.

WHITESIDE. Never mind, Sarah. He's quite mad.

BANJO. Come, Petrouchka, we will dance in the snow until all St. Petersburg is aflame with jealousy. (*He clutches* SARAH *and waltzes her toward the kitchen, loudly humming the Merry Widow waltz.*)

SARAH (*as she is borne away*). Mr. Whiteside! Mr. Whiteside!

WHITESIDE. Just give him some breakfast, Sarah. He's harmless.
(MR. WHITESIDE *barely has a moment in which to collect his thoughts before the library doors are opened and* MISS PREEN *emerges. It is* MISS PREEN *in street clothes this time, and with a suitcase in her hand. She plants herself squarely in front of* WHITESIDE, *puts down her bag and starts drawing on a pair of gloves.*)

WHITESIDE. And just what does this mean?

MISS PREEN. It means, Mr. Whiteside, that I am leaving. My address is on the desk inside; you can send me a check.

WHITESIDE. You realize, Miss Preen, that this is completely unprofessional.

MISS PREEN. I do indeed. I am not only walking out on this case, Mr.

Whiteside—I am leaving the nursing profession. I became a nurse because all my life, ever since I was a little girl, I was filled with the idea of serving a suffering humanity. After one month with you, Mr. Whiteside, I am going to work in a munitions factory. From now on anything that I can do to help exterminate the human race will fill me with the greatest of pleasure. If Florence Nightingale had ever nursed *you*, Mr. Whiteside, she would have married Jack the Ripper instead of founding the Red Cross. Good day. (*And she sails out.*)

(*Before* WHITESIDE *has time to digest this little bouquet,* MRS. STANLEY, *in a state of great fluttery excitement, rushes down the stairs.*)

MRS. STANLEY. Mr. Stanley is here with June. He's brought June back. Thank goodness, thank goodness. (*We hear her at the door*) June, June, thank God you're back. You're not married, are you?

JUNE (*from the hallway*). No, Mother, I'm not. And please don't be hysterical.

(MRS. STANLEY *comes into view, her arms around a rebellious* JUNE. *Behind them looms* MR. STANLEY, *every inch the stern father.*)

MRS. STANLEY. Oh, June, if it had been anyone but that awful boy. You know how your father and I felt. . . . Ernest, thank goodness you stopped it. How did you do it?

STANLEY. Never mind that, Daisy. Just take June upstairs. I have something to say to Mr. Whiteside.

MRS. STANLEY. What about Richard? Is there any news?

STANLEY. It's all right, Daisy—all under control. Just take June upstairs.

JUNE. Father, haven't we had enough melodrama? I don't have to be taken upstairs—I'll go upstairs. . . . Merry Christmas, Mr. Whiteside. It looks bad for John L. Lewis. Come on, Mother—lock me in my room.

MRS. STANLEY. Now, June, you'll feel much better after you've had a hot bath, I know. Have you had anything to eat? (*She follows her daughter up the stairs.* STANLEY *turns to* MR. WHITESIDE.)

STANLEY. I am pleased to inform you, sir, that your plans for my daughter seem to have gone a trifle awry. She is not, nor will she ever be, married to that labor agitator that you so kindly picked out for her. As for my son, he has been apprehended in Toledo, and will be brought back home within the hour. Not having your gift for invective, I cannot tell you what I think of your obnoxious interference in my affairs, but I have now arranged that you will interfere no longer. (*He turns toward the hallway*) Come in, gentlemen. (*Two burly* MEN *come into view and stand in the archway*) Mr. Whiteside, these gentlemen are deputy sheriffs. They have a warrant by which I am enabled to put you out of this house, and I need hardly add that it will be the greatest moment of my life. Mr. Whiteside—(*He looks at his watch*) I am giving you fifteen minutes in which to pack up and get out. If you are not gone in fifteen minutes, Mr. Whiteside, these gentlemen will forcibly eject you. (*He turns to the deputies*) Thank you, gentlemen. Will you wait outside, please? (*The* TWO MEN *file out*) Fifteen minutes, Mr.

Whiteside—and that means bag, baggage, wheelchair, penguins, octopus and cockroaches. I am now going upstairs to smash our radio, so that not even accidentally will I ever hear your voice again.

WHITESIDE. Sure you don't want my autograph, old fellow?

STANLEY. Fifteen minutes, Mr. Whiteside. (*And he goes.* BANJO, *still eating, returns from the kitchen.*)

BANJO. Well, Whiteside, I didn't get an idea. Any news from the front?

WHITESIDE. Yes. The enemy is at my rear, and nibbling.

BANJO. Where'd you say Maggie was? In there?

WHITESIDE. It's no use, Banjo. She's taking the one o'clock train out.

BANJO. No kidding? You didn't tell me that. You mean she's quitting you, after all these years? She's really leaving?

WHITESIDE. She is!

BANJO. That means you've only got till one o'clock to do something?

WHITESIDE. No, dear. I have exactly fifteen minutes— (*He looks at his watch*) ah — fourteen minutes — in which to pull out of my hat the Goddamnedest rabbit you have ever seen.

BANJO. What do you mean fifteen minutes?

WHITESIDE. In exactly fifteen minutes Baby's rosy little body is being tossed into the snow. My host has sworn out a warrant. I am being kicked out.

BANJO. What? I never heard of su a thing. What would he do a thi like that for?

WHITESIDE. Never mind, never mir The point is, I have only fifteen mi utes. Banjo dear, the master is gro ing a little desperate.

BANJO (*paces a moment*). Wh about laying your cards on the tal with Lorraine?

WHITESIDE. Now, Banjo. You kno Dream Girl as well as I do. What *you* think?

BANJO. You're right. . . . Say! If knew where she was I could get car and run her over. It wouldn't hu her much.

WHITESIDE (*wearily*). Banjo, f God's sake. Go in and talk to Magg for a minute—right in there. I wa to think.

BANJO. Could we get a doctor to s Lorraine has smallpox?

WHITESIDE. Please, Banjo. I've g to think.

BANJO (*opening the library doors* Pardon me, miss, is this t Y.M.C.A.?

(*The doors close.* WHITESIDE *is alo again. He leans back, concentrati intensely. He shakes his head as, o after another, he discards a couple ideas. We hear the outer door op and close, and from the hallw comes* RICHARD. *Immediately behi him is a stalwart-looking* MAN *wi an air of authority.*)

THE MAN (*to* RICHARD, *as he in cates* WHITESIDE). Is this your fathe

ICHARD. No, you idiot. . . . Hello, Ar. Whiteside. I didn't get very far. Any suggestions?

WHITESIDE. I'm very sorry, Richard -very sorry indeed. I wish I were in osition—

TANLEY (*descending the stairs*). Vell, you're *not* in position. . . . 'hank you very much, officer. Here's little something for your trouble.

HE MAN. Thank you, sir. Good day. *He goes.*)

TANLEY. Will you go upstairs please, ichard?

RICHARD *hesitates for a second. ooks at his father, then at* WHITE-IDE; *silently goes up the steps.* MR. TANLEY *follows him, but pauses on ie landing.*)

TANLEY. *Ten* minutes, Mr. Whiteide. (*And he goes.* JOHN *enters from ie dining room, bringing a glass of range juice.*)

OHN. Here you are, Mr. Whiteside. eeling any better?

WHITESIDE. Superb. Any cyanide in his orange juice, John? (*The door-ell rings*) Open the door, John. It's robably some mustard gas from an ld friend.

OHN (*en route to the door*). Yes, r. . . . Say, that crazy fellow made a reat hit with Sarah. He wants to ive her a screen test.

At the outer door we hear LOR-AINE'S *voice: "Good morning! Is Ar. Whiteside up yet?"* JOHN'S *nswer: "Yes, he is, Miss Sheldon— e's right here."* WHITESIDE *groans ; he hears her voice.*)

LORRAINE (*entering, in a very smart Christmas morning costume*). Merry Christmas, darling! Merry Christmas! I've come to have Christmas breakfast with you, my dear. May I? (*She kisses him.*)

WHITESIDE (*nothing matters any more*). Of course, my sprite. John, a tray for Miss Sheldon—better make it one-minute eggs.

LORRAINE. Sherry, it's the most perfect Christmas morning—the snow is absolutely glistening. Too bad you can't get out.

WHITESIDE. Oh, I'll probably see a bit of it. . . . I hear you're off for Lake Placid, my blossom. What time are you going?

LORRAINE. Oh, Sherry, how did you know? Is Bert here?

WHITESIDE. No, he rolled in a little while ago. Worked rather fast, didn't you, dear?

LORRAINE. Darling, I was just swept off my feet by the play—it's fantastically good. Sherry, it's the kind of part that only comes along once in ten years. I'm so grateful to you, darling. Really, Sherry, sometimes I think that you're the only friend I have in the world.

WHITESIDE (*dryly*). Thank you, dear. What time did you say you were leaving—you and Jefferson?

LORRAINE. Oh, I don't know—I think it's four o'clock. You know, quite apart from anything else, Sherry, Bert is really a very attractive man. It makes it rather a pleasure, squaring accounts with little Miss Vitriol. In fact, it's all worked out beautifully.

. . . Sherry lamb, I want to give you the most beautiful Christmas present you've ever had in your life. Now, what do you want? Anything! I'm so deliriously happy that— (*A bellowing laugh comes from the library. She stops, lips compressed*) That sounds like Banjo. Is he here?

WHITESIDE. He is, my dear. Just the family circle gathering at Christmas. (*A look at his watch*) My, how time flies when you're having fun. (BANJO *emerges from the library.*)

BANJO. Why, hello, Sweetie Pants! How are you?

LORRAINE (*not over-cordial*). Very well, thank you. And you, Banjo?

BANJO. I'm fine, fine. How's the mattress business, Lorraine?

LORRAINE. *Very* funny. It's too bad, Banjo, that your pictures aren't as funny as you seem to think *you* are.

BANJO. You've got me there, mama. Say, you look in the pink, Lorraine. . . . Anything in the wind, Whiteside?

WHITESIDE. Not a glimmer.

BANJO. What time does the boat sail?

WHITESIDE. Ten minutes.

LORRAINE. What boat is this?

BANJO. The good ship *Up the Creek*. . . . Oh, well! You feel fine, huh, Lorraine?

LORRAINE. What? Yes, of course I do. . . . Where's that breakfast, Sherry? (MAGGIE *emerges from the library, a sheaf of papers in her hand. She stops imperceptibly as she sees* LORRAINE.)

MAGGIE. I've listed everything exce the New Year's Eve broadcast. Wası there a schedule on that?

WHITESIDE (*uneasily*). I think i on the table there, some place.

MAGGIE. Thank you. (*She turns the papers on the table.*)

LORRAINE (*obviously for* MAGGIE *ears*) New Year's Eve? Oh, Be and I'll hear it in Lake Placid. Yc were at my cottage up there onc weren't you, Sherry? It's lovely, isr it? Away from everything. Just sno and clear, cold nights. (*The doo bell rings*) Oh, that's probably Be I told him to meet me here. (MAGGI *as though she had not heard a wor goes quietly into the library.* LO RAINE *relaxes*) You know, I'm loo ing forward to Lake Placid. Ber the kind of man who will do a winter sports beautifully.

BANJO (*gently*). Will he get tim (*Voices are heard from the hallwa "Whiteside?" "Yes, sir." "America Express."* JOHN *backs into the roon obviously directing a major oper tion.*)

JOHN. All right—come ahead. Ca now—careful—right in here. It's fo you, Mr. Whiteside.

LORRAINE. Why, Sherry, what's this (*Into view come two* EXPRESSMEN *groaning and grunting under th weight of nothing more or less tha an Egyptian mummy case. It seem that* MR. WHITESIDE'S *friends a liable to think of anything.*)

EXPRESSMAN. Where do you war this put?

OHN. Right there.

'HITESIDE. Dear God, if there was ne thing I needed right now it was n Egyptian mummy.

ANJO (*reading from a tag*). "Merry Christmas from the Khedive of Egypt." What did you send *him*? Grant's Tomb?

MR. STANLEY, *drawn by the voices f the* EXPRESSMEN, *has descended he stairs in time to witness this ewest hue and cry.*)

TANLEY (*surveying the scene*). Five inutes, Mr. Whiteside! (*He indiates the mummy case*) Including hat. (*And up the stairs again.*)

ORRAINE. Why, what was all that bout? Who is that man?

'HITESIDE. He announces the time very few minutes. I pay him a small um.

ORRAINE. But what on earth for, herry?

VHITESIDE (*violently*) I lost my vatch!

From the hallway a familiar figure eeps in.)

R. BRADLEY. Oh, excuse me, Mr. Whiteside. Are you busy?

VHITESIDE (*closing his eyes*). Good God!

R. BRADLEY (*coming into the room*). 've written a new chapter on the eft kidney. Suppose I— (*He smiles pologetically at* LORRAINE *and* ANJO) Pardon me. (*Goes into the ibrary.*)

LORRAINE. Is that the plumber again, Sherry? . . . Oh, dear, I wonder where Bert is. . . . Darling, you're not very Christmassy — you're usually bubbling over on Christmas morning. . . . *Who* sent this to you, Sherry—the Khedive of Egypt? You know, I think it's rather beautiful. I must go to Egypt some day—I really must. I know I'd love it. The first time I went to Pompeii I cried all night. All those people—all those lives. Where are they now? Sherry! Don't you ever think about that? I do. Here was a woman—like myself—a woman who once lived and loved, full of the same passions, fears, jealousies, hates. And what remains of any of it now? Just this, and nothing more. (*She opens the case, then, with a sudden impulse, steps into it and folds her arms, mummy-fashion*) A span of four thousand years—a mere atom in the eternity of time—and here am I, another woman living out her life. I want to cry. (*She closes her eyes, and as she stands there, immobilized, the eyes of* BANJO *and* WHITESIDE *meet. The same idea has leaped into their minds.* BANJO, *rising slowly from the couch, starts to approach the mummy case, casually whistling "Dixie." But just before he reaches it* LORRAINE *steps blandly out.*)

LORRAINE. Oh, I mustn't talk this way today. It's Christmas, it's Christmas! (BANJO *puts on a great act of unconcern.*)

WHITESIDE (*rising to the occasion, and dripping pure charm*). Lorraine dear, have you ever played Saint Joan?

LORRAINE. No, I haven't, Sherry. What makes you ask that?

WHITESIDE. There was something about your expression as you stood in that case—there was an absolute halo about you.

LORRAINE. Why, Sherry, how sweet!

WHITESIDE. It transcended any mortal expression I've ever seen. Step into it again, dear.

LORRAINE. Sherry, you're joshing me —aren't you?

WHITESIDE. My dear, I don't make light of these things. I was deeply moved. There was a strange beauty about you, Lorraine—pure da Vinci. Please do it again.

LORRAINE. Well, I don't know exactly what it was that I did, but I'll— (*She starts to step into the case again, then changes her mind*) Oh, I feel too silly, Sherry.
(BANJO's *eyes are fixed somewhere on the ceiling, but he is somewhat less innocent than he seems.*)

WHITESIDE (*returning to the battle*). Lorraine dear, in that single moment you approached the epitome of your art, and you should not be ashamed of it. You asked me a little while ago what I wanted for a Christmas present. All that I want, Lorraine, is the memory of you in that mummy case.

LORRAINE. Why, darling, I'm—all choked up. (*Crossing her arms, she takes a moment or two to throw herself in the mood, then steps reverently into the case*) "Dust thou art, and dust to dust—"
(*Bang!* BANJO *has closed the case and fastened it.* WHITESIDE *leaps out of the chair.*)

WHITESIDE. Eureka!

BANJO. There's service for you!

WHITESIDE. Will she be all right i there?

BANJO. Sure—she can breathe eas I'll let her out as soon as we get o the plane. . . . What are we going t do now? How do we get this out o here?

WHITESIDE. One thing at a time- that's the next step.

BANJO. Think fast, Captain. Thin fast.
(*And* MAGGIE *enters from the li- brary, papers in hand.* WHITESID *scrambles back into his chair;* BANJ *is again the little innocent.*)

MAGGIE. This is everything, Sherr —I'm leaving three carbons. Is ther anything out here? (*She inspects small basket fastened to his chair* What's in this basket?

WHITESIDE (*eager to be rid of her* Nothing at all. Thank you, than you.

MAGGIE. Shall I file these letters Do you want this picture?

WHITESIDE. No—throw everythin away. Wait—give me the picture. want the picture.

MAGGIE. The only thing I haven done is to put all your broadcasts i order. Do you want me to do that?

WHITESIDE (*a flash of recollectio has come to him as he takes* HARRIET *photograph in his hand, but he con trives to smother his excitement* What? . . . Ah—do that, will you Do it right away—it's very important Right away, Maggie.

MAGGIE. I'll see you before I go, Banjo. (*She goes into the library again, closing the doors.*)

WHITESIDE (*watching her out, then jumping up in great excitement*). I've got it!

BANJO. What?

WHITESIDE. I knew I'd seen this face before! I knew it! Now I know how to get this out of here.

BANJO. What face? How?

(*And, at that instant,* MR. STANLEY *comes down the stairs, watch in hand.*)

STANLEY (*vastly enjoying himself*). The time is up, Mr. Whiteside. Fifteen minutes.

WHITESIDE. Ah, yes, Mr. Stanley. Fifteen minutes. But just one favor before I go. I would like you to summon those two officers and ask them to help this gentleman down to the airport with this mummy case. Would you be good enough to do that, Mr. Stanley?

STANLEY. I will do nothing of the kind.

WHITESIDE (*ever so sweetly*). Oh, I think you will, Mr. Stanley. Or shall I inform my radio audience, on my next broadcast, that your sister, Harriet Stanley, is none other than the famous Harriet Sedley, who murdered her mother and father with an axe twenty-five years ago in Gloucester, Massachusetts. . . . (*At which* MR. STANLEY *quietly collapses into a chair*) Come, Mr. Stanley, it's a very small favor. Or would you rather have the good folk of Mesalia repeating at your very doorstep that once-popular little jingle:

"Harriet Sedley took an axe
And gave her mother forty whacks,
And when the job was nicely done,
She gave her father forty-one."

Remember, Mr. Stanley, I too am giving up something. It would make a hell of a broadcast. . . . Well?

STANLEY (*licked at last*). Mr. Whiteside, you are the damnedest person I have ever met.

WHITESIDE. I often think so myself, old fellow. . . . Officers, will you come in here, please?

BANJO. Whiteside, you're a great man. (*He places a reverent kiss on the mummy case.*)

WHITESIDE (*as the* DEPUTIES *enter*). Come right in, officers. Mr. Stanley would like you to help this gentleman down to the airport with this mummy case. He is sending it to a friend in Nova Scotia.

BANJO. Collect.

WHITESIDE. Right, Mr. Stanley?

STANLEY (*weakly*). Yes. . . . Yes.

WHITESIDE. Thank you, gentlemen—handle it carefully. . . . Banjo, my love, you're wonderful and I may write a book about you.

BANJO. Don't bother—I can't read. (*To* MAGGIE, *as she enters from library*) Good-bye, Maggie—love conquers all. . . . Don't drop that case, boys—it contains an antique. (*And out he goes with the mummy case, to say nothing of* MISS LORRAINE SHELDON.)

MAGGIE (*catching on to what has happened*). Sherry! Sherry, was that—?

WHITESIDE. It was indeed. The field is clear and you have my blessing.

MAGGIE. Sherry! Sherry, you old reprobate!

WHITESIDE. Just send me a necktie sometime. My hat and coat, Maggie, and also your railroad ticket. I am leaving for New York.

MAGGIE. You're leaving, Sherry?

WHITESIDE. Don't argue, Rat Girl— Do as you're told.

MAGGIE. Yes, Mr. Whiteside. (*She goes happily into the library, just as* BERT *returns.*)

BERT. Mr. Whiteside, I want to apologize for—

WHITESIDE. Don't give it a thought, Bert. There's been a slight change of plan. Miss Sheldon is off on a world cruise— I am taking your play to Katharine Cornell. Miss Cutler will explain everything. (MAGGIE *brings* WHITESIDE's *coat, hat, cane*) Oh, thank you, Maggie, my darling. (*And just then the* DOCTOR *comes out of the library. Still trying.*)

DR. BRADLEY. Mr. Whiteside, are you very busy?

WHITESIDE. Ah, yes, Doctor. *Ver* busy. But if you ever get to Ne York, Doctor try and find me. (*H takes* MAGGIE *in his arms*) Goo bye, my lamb. I love you very much

MAGGIE. Sherry, you're wonderful.

WHITESIDE. Nonsense. . . . Good-by Jefferson. You'll never know th trouble you've caused.

BERT. Good-bye, Mr. Whiteside.

WHITESIDE. Good-bye, Mr. Stanley I would like to hear, in the near fu ture, that your daughter has marrie her young man and that your son ha been permitted to follow his ow bent. OR ELSE. . . . Merry Christ mas, everybody! (*And out he strolls But the worst is yet to come. Ther is a loud crash on the porch, fo lowed by an anguished yell.* MAGGI *gives a little shriek and rushes ou* BERT *and the* DOCTOR *rush after he Down the stairs come* MRS. STANLEY JUNE *and* RICHARD. *From the dinin room* JOHN *and* SARAH *come running "What's happened?" "What is it? And then we see. Into view com* BERT *and the* DOCTOR, *carrying* MR WHITESIDE *between them. He i screaming his head off.*)

WHITESIDE. Miss Preen! Miss Preen I want Miss Preen back! . . . Mr Stanley, I am suing you for *thre* hundred and fifty thousand dollars (MR. STANLEY *throws up his hand in despair.* MRS. STANLEY *simpl faints away.*)

CURTAIN

The Time of Your Life

BY WILLIAM SAROYAN

TO

GEORGE JEAN NATHAN

In the time of your life, live—so that in that good time there shall be n ugliness or death for yourself or for any life your life touches. Seek goodne everywhere, and when it is found, bring it out of its hiding-place and l it be free and unashamed. Place in matter and in flesh the least of the value for these are the things that hold death and must pass away. Discover in a things that which shines and is beyond corruption. Encourage virtue i whatever heart it may have been driven into secrecy and sorrow by the sham and terror of the world. Ignore the obvious, for it is unworthy of the clea eye and the kindly heart. Be the inferior of no man, nor of any man be th superior. Remember that every man is a variation of yourself. No man guilt is not yours, nor is any man's innocence a thing apart. Despise evil an ungodliness, but not men of ungodliness or evil. These, understand. Hav no shame in being kindly and gentle, but if the time comes in the time c your life to kill, kill and have no regret. In the time of your life, live—s that in that wondrous time you shall not add to the misery and sorrow of th world, but shall smile to the infinite delight and mystery of it.

The Time of Your Life was first produced at the Booth Theatre, New York City, by Eddie Dowling, on October 25, 1939, and closed on October 19, 1940. Following is the original cast:

The Newsboy	Ross Bagdasarian
The Drunkard	John Farrell
Willie	Will Lee
Joe	Eddie Dowling
Nick	Charles de Sheim
Tom	Edward Andrews
Kitty Duval	Julie Haydon
Dudley	Curt Conway
Harry	Gene Kelly
Wesley	Reginald Beane
Lorene	Nene Vibber
Blick	Grover Burgess
Arab	Houseley Stevens, Sr.
Mary L.	Celeste Holme
Krupp	William Bendix
McCarthy	Tom Tully
Kit Carson	Len Doyle
Nick's Ma	Michelette Burani
Sailor	Randolph Wade
Elsie	Cathie Bailey
A Killer	Evelyn Geller
Her Side Kick	Mary Cheffey
A Society Lady	Eva Leonard Boyne
A Society Gentleman	Ainsworth Arnold
First Cop	Randolph Wade
Second Cop	John Farrell

THE PLACE

Nick's Pacific Street Saloon, Restaurant, and Entertainment Palace at th foot of Embarcadero, in San Francisco. A suggestion of room 21 at Th New York Hotel, upstairs, around the corner.

THE TIME

Afternoon and night of a day in October, 1939.

THE TIME OF YOUR LIFE

ACT ONE

NICK'S *is an American place: a San Francisco waterfront honky-tonk.*

At a table, JOE: *always calm, always quiet, always thinking, always eager, always bored, always superior. His expensive clothes are casually and youthfully worn and give him an almost boyish appearance. He is thinking.*

Behind the bar, NICK: *a big red-headed young Italian-American with an enormous naked woman tattooed in red on the inside of his right arm. He is studying* The Racing Form.

The ARAB, *at his place at the end of the bar. He is a lean old man with a rather ferocious old-country mustache, with the ends twisted up. Between the thumb and forefinger of his left hand is the Mohammedan tattoo indicating that he has been to Mecca. He is sipping a glass of beer.*

It is about eleven-thirty in the morning. SAM *is sweeping out. We see only his back. He disappears into the kitchen. The* SAILOR *at the bar finishes his drink and leaves, moving thoughtfully, as though he were trying very hard to discover how to live.*

The NEWSBOY *comes in.*

NEWSBOY (*cheerfully*). Good-morning, everybody. (*No answer. To* NICK) Paper, Mister? (NICK *shakes his head, no. The* NEWSBOY *goes to* JOE) Paper, Mister? (JOE *shakes his head, no. The* NEWSBOY *walks away, counting papers.*)

JOE (*noticing him*). How many you got?

NEWSBOY. Five. (JOE *gives him a quarter, takes all the papers, glances at the headlines with irritation, throws them away. The* NEWSBOY *watches carefully, then goes.*)

ARAB (*picks up paper, looks at headlines, shakes head as if rejecting everything else a man might say about the world*). No foundation. All the way down the line.

(*The* DRUNK *comes in. Walks to the telephone, looks for a nickel in the chute, sits down at* JOE'S *table.* NICK *takes the* DRUNK *out. The* DRUNK *returns.*)

DRUNK (*champion of the Bill of Rights*). This is a free country, ain't it?

(WILLIE, *the marble-game maniac, explodes through the swinging doors and lifts the forefinger of his right hand comically, indicating one beer. He is a very young man, not more than twenty. He is wearing heavy shoes, a pair of old and dirty corduroys, a light green turtle-neck jersey with a large letter "F" on the chest, an oversize two-button tweed coat, and a green hat, with the brim up.* NICK *sets out a glass of beer for him, he drinks it, straightens up vigorously saying "Aaah," makes a solemn face, gives* NICK *a one-finger salute of adieu, and begins to leave, refreshed and restored in spirit. He walks by the marble game, halts suddenly, turns, studies the contraption, gestures as if to say, Oh, no. Turns to go, stops, returns to the machine, studies it, takes a handful of small coins out of his pants pocket, lifts a nickel, indicates with a gesture, One game, no more. Puts the nickel in the slot, pushes in the slide, making an interesting noise.*)

NICK. You can't beat that machine.

WILLIE. Oh, yeah? (*The marbles fall, roll, and take their place. He pushes down the lever, placing one marble in position. Takes a very deep breath, walks in a small circle, excited at the beginning of great drama. Stands straight and pious before the contest. Himself vs. the machine. Willie vs. Destiny. His skill and daring vs. the cunning and trickery of the novelty industry of America, and the whole challenging world. He is the last of the American pioneers, with nothing more to fight but the machine, with no other reward than lights going on and off, and six nickels for one. Before him is the last champion, the machine. He is the last challenger, the young man with nothing to do in the world.* WILLIE *grips the knob delicately, studies the situation carefully, draws the knob back, holds it a moment, and then releases it. The first marble rolls out among the hazards, and the contest is on. At the very beginning of the play "The Missouri Waltz" is coming from the phonograph. The music ends here. This is the signal for the beginning of the play.* JOE *suddenly comes out of his reverie. He whistles the way people do who are calling a cab that's about a block away, only he does it quietly.* WILLIE *turns around, but* JOE *gestures for him to return to his work.* NICK *looks up from The Racing Form.*

JOE (*calling*). Tom. (*To himself.*) Where the hell is he, every time I need him? (*He looks around calmly: the nickel-in-the-slot phonograph in the corner; the open public telephone; the stage; the marble-game; the bar; and so on. He calls again, this time very loud*) Hey, Tom.

NICK (*with morning irritation*). What do you want?

JOE (*without thinking*). I want the boy to get me a watermelon, that's what *I* want. What do *you* want? Money, or love, or fame, or what? You won't get them studying The Racing Form.

NICK. I like to keep abreast of the times.

(TOM *comes hurrying in. He is a great big man of about thirty or so who appears to be much younger because of the childlike expression of his face: handsome, dumb, innocent, troubled, and a little bewildered by everything. He is obviously adult in years, but it seems as if by all rights he should still be a boy. He is defensive as clumsy, self-conscious, overgrown boys are. He is wearing a flashy cheap suit.* JOE *leans back and studies him with casual disapproval.* TOM *slackens his pace and becomes clumsy and embarrassed, waiting for the bawling-out he's pretty sure he's going to get.*)

JOE (*objectively, severely, but a little amused*). Who saved your life?

TOM (*sincerely*). You did, Joe. Thanks.

JOE (*interested*). How'd I do it?

TOM (*confused*). What?

JOE (*even more interested*). How'd I do it?

TOM. Joe, you know how you did it.

JOE (*softly*). I want you to answer me. How'd I save your life? I've forgotten.

TOM (*remembering, with a big sorrowful smile*). You made me eat all that chicken soup three years ago when I was sick and hungry.

JOE (*fascinated*). *Chicken soup?*

TOM (*eagerly*). Yeah.

JOE. Three years? Is it that long?

TOM (*delighted to have the information*). Yeah, sure. 1937. 1938. 1939. This is 1939, Joe.

JOE (*amused*). Never mind what year it is. Tell me the whole story.

TOM. You took me to the doctor. You gave me money for food and clothes, and paid my room rent. Aw, Joe, you know all the different things you did. (JOE *nods, turning away from* TOM *after each question.*)

JOE. You in good health now?

TOM. Yeah, Joe.

JOE. You got clothes?

TOM. Yeah, Joe.

JOE. You eat three times a day. Sometimes four?

TOM. Yeah, Joe. Sometimes five.

JOE. You got a place to sleep?

TOM. Yeah, Joe.
(JOE *nods. Pauses. Studies* TOM *carefully.*)

JOE. Then, where the hell have you been?

TOM (*humbly*). Joe, I was out in the street listening to the boys. They're talking about the trouble down here on the waterfront.

JOE (*sharply*). I want you to be around when I need you.

TOM (*pleased that the bawling-out is over*). I won't do it again. Joe, one guy out there says there's got to be a revolution before anything will ever be all right.

JOE (*impatiently*). I know all about it. Now, here. Take this money. Go up to the Emporium. You know where the Emporium is?

TOM. Yeah, sure, Joe.

JOE. All right. Take the elevator and go up to the fourth floor. Walk around to the back, to the toy department. Buy me a couple of dollars' worth of toys and bring them here.

TOM (*amazed*). Toys? What *kind* of toys, Joe?

JOE. Any kind of toys. Little ones that I can put on this table.

TOM. What do you want toys for, Joe?

JOE (*mildly angry*). *What?*

TOM. All right, all right. You don't have to get sore at *everything*. What'll people think, a big guy like me buying toys?

JOE. *What people?*

TOM. Aw, Joe, you're always making me do crazy things for you, and *I'm* the guy that gets embarrassed. You just sit in this place and make me do all the dirty work.

JOE (*looking away*). Do what I tell you.

TOM. O.K., but I wish I knew why. (*He makes to go.*)

JOE. Wait a minute. Here's a nickel. Put it in the phonograph. Number seven. I want to hear that waltz again.

TOM. Boy, I'm glad *I* don't have to stay and listen to it. Joe, what do you hear in that song anyway? We listen to that song ten times a day. Why can't we hear number six, or two, or nine? There are a lot of other numbers.

JOE (*emphatically*). Put the nickel in the phonograph. (*Pause*) Sit down and wait till the music's over. Then go get me some toys.

TOM. O.K. O.K.

JOE (*loudly*). Never mind being a martyr about it either. The cause isn't worth it.

(TOM *puts the nickel into the machine, with a ritual of impatient and efficient movement which plainly shows his lack of sympathy or enthusiasm. His manner also reveals, however, that his lack of sympathy is spurious and exaggerated. Actually, he is fascinated by the music, but is so confused by it that he pretends he dislikes it. The music begins. It is another variation of "The Missouri Waltz," played dreamily and softly, with perfect orchestral form, and with a theme of weeping in the horns repeated a number of times. At first* TOM *listens with something close to irritation, since he can't understand what is so attractive in the music to* JOE, *and what is so painful and confusing in it to himself. Very soon, however, he is carried away by the melancholy story of grief and nostalgia of the song. He stands, troubled by the poetry and confusion in himself.* JOE, *on the other hand, listens as if he were not listening, indifferent and unmoved. What he's interested in is* TOM. *He turns and glances at* TOM. KITTY DUVAL, *who lives in a room in The New York Hotel, around the corner, comes beyond the swinging doors quietly, and walks slowly to the bar, her reality and rhythm a perfect accompaniment to the sorrowful American music, which is her music, as it is* TOM'S. *Which the world drove out of her, putting in its place brokenness and all manner of spiritually crippled forms. She seems to understand this, and is angry. Angry with herself, full of hate for the poor world, and full of pity and contempt for its tragic, unbelievable, confounded people. She is a small powerful girl, with that kind of delicate and rugged beauty which no circumstance of evil or ugly reality can destroy. This beauty is that element of the immortal which is in the seed of good and common people, and which is kept alive in some of the female of our kind, no matter how accidentally or pointlessly they may have entered the world.* KITTY DUVAL *is somebody. There is an angry purity, and a fierce pride, in her. In her stance, and way of walking, there is grace and arrogance.* JOE *recognizes her as a great person immediately. She goes to the bar.*)

KITTY. Beer.

(NICK *places a glass of beer before her mechanically. She swallows half the drink, and listens to the music again.*

TOM *turns and sees her. He becomes dead to everything in the world but her. He stands like a lump, fascinated and undone by his almost religious adoration for her.* JOE *notices* TOM.)

JOE (*gently*). Tom. (TOM *begins to move toward the bar, where* KITTY *is standing. Loudly*) Tom. (TOM *halts, then turns, and* JOE *motions to him to come over to the table.* TOM *goes over. Quietly*) Have you got everything straight?

TOM (*out of the world*). What?

JOE. What do you mean, what? I just gave you some instructions.

TOM (*pathetically*). What do you want, Joe?

JOE. I want you to come to your senses. (*He stands up quietly and knocks* TOM'S *hat off.* TOM *picks up his hat quickly.*)

TOM. I got it, Joe. I got it. The Emporium. Fourth floor. In the back. The toy department. Two dollars' worth of toys. That you can put on a table.

KITTY (*to herself*). Who the hell is he to push a big man like that around?

JOE. I'll expect you back in a half hour. Don't get side-tracked anywhere. Just do what I tell you.

TOM (*pleading*). Joe? Can't I bet four bits on a horse race? There's a long shot—Precious Time—that's going to win by ten lengths. I got to have money.

(JOE *points to the street.* TOM *goes out.* NICK *is combing his hair, looking in the mirror.*)

NICK. I thought you wanted him to get you a watermelon.

JOE. I forgot. (*He watches* KITTY *a moment. To* KITTY, *clearly, slowly, with great compassion*) What's the dream?

KITTY (*moving to* JOE, *coming to*). What?

JOE (*holding the dream for her*). What's the dream, *now*?

KITTY (*coming still closer*). What dream?

JOE. What dream! The dream you're dreaming.

NICK. Suppose he did bring you a watermelon? What the hell would you do with it?

JOE (*irritated*). I'd put it on this table. I'd look at it. Then I'd eat it. What do you *think* I'd do with it, sell it for a profit?

NICK. How should I know what *you'd* do with *anything*? What I'd like to know is, where do you get your money from? What work do you do?

JOE (*looking at* KITTY). Bring us a bottle of champagne.

KITTY. Champagne?

JOE (*simply*). Would you rather have something else?

KITTY. What's the big idea?

JOE. I thought you might like some champagne. I myself am very fond of it.

KITTY. Yeah, but what's the big idea? You can't push *me* around.

JOE (*gently but severely*). It's not in my nature to be unkind to another human being. I have only contempt for wit. Otherwise I might say something obvious, therefore cruel, and perhaps untrue.

KITTY. You be careful what you think about me.

JOE (*slowly, not looking at her*). I have only the noblest thoughts for both your person and your spirit.

NICK (*having listened carefully and not being able to make it out*). What are you talking about?

KITTY. You shut up. You—

JOE. He owns this place. He's an important man. All kinds of people come to him looking for work. Comedians. Singers. Dancers.

KITTY. I don't care. He can't call me names.

NICK. All right, sister. I know how it is with a two-dollar whore in the morning.

KITTY (*furiously*). Don't you dare call me names. I used to be in burlesque.

NICK. If you were ever in burlesque, I used to be Charlie Chaplin.

KITTY (*angry and a little pathetic*). I *was* in burlesque. I played the burlesque circuit from coast to coast. I've had flowers sent to me by European royalty. I've had dinner with young men of wealth and social position.

NICK. You're dreaming.

KITTY (*to* JOE) *I was in burlesque.* Kitty Duval. That was my name. Life-size photographs of me in costume in front of burlesque theaters all over the country.

JOE (*gently, coaxingly*). I believe you. Have some champagne.

NICK (*going to table, with champagne bottle and glasses*). There he goes again.

JOE. Miss Duval?

KITTY (*sincerely, going over*). That's not my *real* name. That's my *stage* name.

JOE. I'll call you by your stage name.

NICK (*pouring*). All right, sister, make up your mind. Are you going to have champagne with him, or not?

JOE. Pour the lady some wine.

NICK. O.K., Professor. Why you come to this joint instead of one of the high-class dumps uptown is more than I can understand. Why don't you have champagne at the St. Francis? Why don't you drink with a lady?

KITTY (*furiously*). Don't you call me names—you dentist.

JOE. Dentist?

NICK (*amazed, loudly*). What kind of cussing is that? (*Pause. Looking at* KITTY, *then at* JOE, *bewildered*) This guy doesn't belong here. The only reason I've got champagne is because *he* keeps ordering it all the time. (*To* KITTY) Don't think you're the only one he drinks champagne with. He drinks with *all* of them. (*Pause*) He's crazy. Or something.

JOE (*confidentially*). Nick, I think you're going to be all right in a couple of centuries.

NICK. I'm sorry, I don't understand your English.

(JOE *lifts his glass.* KITTY *slowly lifts hers, not quite sure of what's going on.*)

JOE (*sincerely*). To the spirit, Kitty Duval.

KITTY (*beginning to understand, and very grateful, looking at him*). Thank you.

JOE (*calling*). Nick.

NICK. Yeah?

JOE. Would you mind putting a nickel in the machine again? Number—

NICK. Seven. I know. I know. I don't mind at all, Your Highness, although, personally, I'm not a lover of music. (*Going to the machine*) As a matter of fact I think Tchaikowsky was a dope.

JOE. Tchaikowsky? Where'd you ever hear of Tchaikowsky?

NICK. He was a dope.

JOE. Yeah. Why?

NICK. They talked about him on the radio one Sunday morning. He was a sucker. He let a woman drive him crazy.

JOE. I see.

NICK. I stood behind that bar listening to the God-damn stuff and cried like a baby. *None but the lonely heart!* He was a dope.

JOE. What made you cry?

NICK. What?

JOE (*sternly*). What made you cry, Nick?

NICK (*angry with himself*). I don't know.

JOE. I've been underestimating you, Nick. Play number seven.

NICK. They get everybody worked up. They give everybody stuff they shouldn't have. (NICK *puts the nickel into the machine and the Waltz begins again. He listens to the music. Then studies The Racing Form.*)

KITTY (*to herself, dreaming*). I like champagne, and everything that goes with it. Big houses with big porches, and big rooms with big windows, and big lawns, and big trees, and flowers growing everywhere, and big shepherd dogs sleeping in the shade.

NICK. I'm going next door to Frankie's to make a bet. I'll be right back.

JOE. Make one for me.

NICK (*going to* JOE). Who do you like?

JOE (*giving him money*). Precious Time.

NICK. Ten dollars? Across the board?

JOE. No. On the nose.

NICK. O.K. (*He goes.* DUDLEY R. BOSTWICK, *as he calls himself, breaks through the swinging doors, and practically flings himself upon the open telephone beside the phonograph.* DUDLEY *is a young man of about twenty-four or twenty-five, ordinary and yet extraordinary. He is smallish, as the saying is, neatly dressed in bargain clothes, overworked and irritated by the routine and dullness and monotony of his life, apparently nobody and nothing, but in reality a great personality. The swindled young man. Educated, but without the least real understanding. A brave, dumb, salmon-spirit struggling for life in weary, stupefied flesh, dueling ferociously with a banal mind which has been only irritated by what it has been taught. He is a great personality because, against all these handicaps, what he wants is simple and basic: a woman. This urgent and violent need, common yet miraculous enough in itself, considering the unhappy environment of the animal, is the force which elevates him from nothingness to greatness. A ridiculous greatness, but in the nature of things beautiful to behold. All that he has been taught, and everything he believes, is phony, and yet he himself is real, almost superreal, because of this indestructible force in himself. His face is ridiculous. His personal rhythm is tense and jittery. His speech is shrill and violent. His gestures are wild. His ego is disjointed and epileptic. And yet deeply he possesses the same wholeness of spirit, and directness of energy, that is in all species of animals. There is little innate or cultivated spirit in him, but there is no absence of innocent animal force. He is a young man who has been taught that he has a chance, as a person, and believes it. As a matter of fact, he hasn't a chance in the world, and should have been told by somebody, or should not have had his natural and valuable ignorance spoiled by education, ruining an otherwise perfectly good and charming member of the human race. At the telephone he immediately begins to dial furiousl hesitates, changes his mind, stop dialing, hangs up furiously, and suddenly begins again. Not more tha half a minute after the firecracke arrival of* DUDLEY R. BOSTWICK, *occurs the polka-and-waltz arrival o* HARRY. HARRY *is another story. H comes in timidly, turning about uncertainly, awkward, out of plac everywhere, embarrassed and encumbered by the contemporar costume, sick at heart, but determined to fit in somewhere. His arrival constitutes a dance. His clothe don't fit. The pants are a little to large. The coat, which doesn't match is also a little too large, and loose He is a dumb young fellow, but h has ideas. A philosophy, in fact. Hi philosophy is simple and beautifu The world is sorrowful. The worl needs laughter.* HARRY *is funny. Th world needs* HARRY. HARRY *will mak the world laugh. He has probabl had a year or two of high school. H has also listened to the boys at th pool room. He's looking for* NICK *He goes to the* ARAB, *and says, "Ar you Nick?" The* ARAB *shakes hi head. He stands at the bar, waiting He waits very busily.*)

HARRY (*as* NICK *returns*). You Nick

NICK (*very loudly*). *I am Nick.*

HARRY (*acting*). Can you use a grea comedian?

NICK (*behind the bar*). Who, for instance?

HARRY (*almost angry*). Me.

NICK. You? What's funny about you (DUDLEY *at the telephone, is dialing Because of some defect in the apparatus the dialing is very loud.*)

DUDLEY. Hello. Sunset 7349? May I speak to Miss Elsie Mandelspiegel? (*Pause.*)

HARRY (*with spirit and noise, dancing*). I dance and do gags and stuff.

NICK. In costume? Or are you wearing your costume?

DUDLEY. All I need is a cigar.

KITTY (*continuing the dream of grace*). I'd walk out of the house, and stand on the porch, and look at the trees, and smell the flowers, and run across the lawn, and lie down under a tree, and read a book. (*Pause*) A book of poems, maybe.

DUDLEY (*very, very clearly*). Elsie Mandelspiegel. (*Impatiently*) She has a room on the fourth floor. She's a nurse at the Southern Pacific Hospital. Elsie Mandelspiegel. She works at night. Elsie. Yes. (*He begins waiting again.* WESLEY, *a colored boy, comes to the bar and stands near* HARRY, *waiting.*)

NICK. Beer?

WESLEY. No, sir. I'd like to talk to you.

NICK (*to* HARRY). All right. Get funny.

HARRY (*getting funny, an altogether different person, an actor with great energy, both in power of voice, and in force and speed of physical gesture*). Now, I'm standing on the corner of Third and Market. I'm looking around. I'm figuring it out. There it is. Right in front of me. The whole city. The whole world. People going by. They're going somewhere. I don't know where, but they're going. I ain't going *anywhere*. Where the hell can you go? I'm figuring it out. All right, I'm a citizen. A fat guy bumps his stomach into the face of an old lady. They were in a hurry. Fat and old. *They bumped*. Boom. I don't know. It may mean war. *War*. Germany. England. Russia. I don't know for sure. (*Loudly, dramatically, he salutes, about faces, presents arms, aims, and fires*) WAAAAAR. (*He blows a call to arms.* NICK *gets sick of this, indicates with a gesture that* HARRY *should hold it, and goes to* WESLEY.)

NICK. What's on your mind?

WESLEY (*confused*). Well—

NICK. Come on. Speak up. Are you hungry, or what?

WESLEY. Honest to God, I ain't hungry. All I want is a job. I don't want no charity.

NICK. Well, what can you do, and how good are you?

WESLEY. I can run errands, clean up, wash dishes, anything.

DUDLEY (*On the telephone, very eagerly*). Elsie? Elsie, this is Dudley. Elsie, I'll jump in the bay if you don't marry me. Life isn't worth living without you. I can't sleep. I can't think of anything but you. All the time. Day and night and night and day. Elsie, I love you. I love you. What? (*Burning up*) Is this Sunset 7-3-4-9? (*Pause*) 7943? (*Calmly, while* WILLIE *begins making a small racket*) Well, what's your name? *Lorene?* Lorene Smith? I thought you were Elsie Mandelspiegel. What? Dudley. Yeah. Dudley R. Bostwick. Yeah. R. It stands for Raoul, but I never spell it out. I'm pleased to meet *you,* too. What? There's a lot of noise around here. (WILLIE *stops hitting the marble-game*) Where am I? At Nick's, on Pacific Street. I work at the S. P. I told them I was sick and they gave me the afternoon off. Wait a minute. I'll ask them. I'd like to meet *you,* too. Sure. I'll ask them. (*Turns around to* NICK) What's this address?

NICK. Number 3 Pacific Street, you cad.

DUDLEY. Cad? You don't know how I've been suffering on account of Elsie. I take things too ceremoniously. I've got to be more lackadaisical. (*Into telephone*) Hello, Elenore? I mean, Lorene. It's number 3 Pacific Street. Yeah. Sure. I'll wait for you. How'll you know me? You'll *know* me. I'll recognize *you.* Good-by, now. (*He hangs up.*)

HARRY (*continuing his monologue, with gestures, movements, and so on*). I'm standing there. I didn't do anything to anybody. Why should *I* be a soldier? (*Sincerely, insanely*) BOOOOOOOOOM. *WAR!* O.K. War. *I* retreat. *I* hate war. I move to Sacramento.

NICK (*shouting*). All right, Comedian. Lay off a minute.

HARRY (*broken-hearted, going to* WILLIE). Nobody's got a sense of humor any more. The world's dying for comedy like never before, but nobody knows how to *laugh.*

NICK (*to* WESLEY). Do you belong to the union?

WESLEY. What union?

NICK. For the love of Mike, where've you been? Don't you know you can't come into a place and ask for a job and get one and go to work, just like that. You've got to belong to one of the unions.

WESLEY. I didn't know. I got to have a job. Real soon.

NICK. Well, you've got to belong to a union.

WESLEY. I don't want any favors. All I want is a chance to earn a living.

NICK. Go on into the kitchen and tell Sam to give you some lunch.

WESLEY. Honest, I ain't hungry.

DUDLEY (*shouting*). What I've gone through for Elsie.

HARRY. I've got all kinds of funny ideas in my head to help make the world happy again.

NICK (*holding* WESLEY). No, he isn't hungry.

(WESLEY *almost faints from hunger.* NICK *catches him just in time. The* ARAB *and* NICK *go off with* WESLEY *into the kitchen.*)

HARRY (*to* WILLIE). See if you think this is funny. It's my own idea. I created this dance myself. It comes after the monologue. (HARRY *begins to dance.* WILLIE *watches a moment, and then goes back to the game. It's a goofy dance, which* HARRY *does with great sorrow, but much energy.*)

DUDLEY. Elsie. Aw, gee, Elsie. What the hell do I want to see Lorene Smith for? Some girl I don't know.

(JOE *and* KITTY *have been drinking in silence. There is no sound now ex-*

cept the soft-shoe shuffling of HARRY, *the Comedian.*)

JOE. What's the dream now, Kitty Duval?

KITTY (*dreaming the words and pictures*). I dream of home. Christ, I always dream of home. I've no *home*. I've no place. But I always dream of all of us together again. We had a farm in Ohio. There was nothing good about it. It was always sad. There was always trouble. But I always dream about it as if I could go back and Papa would be there and Mamma and Louie and my little brother Stephen and my sister Mary. I'm Polish. Duval! My name isn't Duval, it's Koranovsky. Katerina Koranovsky. We lost everything. The house, the farm, the trees, the horses, the cows, the chickens. Papa died. He was old. He was thirteen years older than Mamma. We moved to Chicago. We tried to work. We tried to stay together. Louie got in trouble. The fellows he was with killed him for something. I don't know what. Stephen ran away from home. Seventeen years old. I don't know where he is. Then Mamma died. (*Pause*) What's the dream? I dream of home. (NICK *comes out of the kitchen with* WESLEY.)

NICK. Here. Sit down here and rest. That'll hold you for a *while*. Why didn't you tell me you were hungry? You all right now?

WESLEY (*sitting down in the chair at the piano*). Yes, I am. Thank you. I didn't know I was *that* hungry.

NICK. Fine. (*To* HARRY *who is dancing*) Hey. What the hell do you think you're doing?

HARRY (*stopping*). That's my own idea. I'm a natural-born dancer and comedian.
(WESLEY *begins slowly, one note, one chord at a time, to play the piano.*)

NICK. You're no good. Why don't you try some other kind of work? Why don't you get a job in a store, selling something? What do you want to be a comedian for?

HARRY. I've got something for the world and they haven't got sense enough to let me give it to them. Nobody knows me.

DUDLEY. Elsie. Now I'm waiting for some dame I've never seen before. Lorene Smith. Never saw her in my life. Just happened to get the wrong number. She turns on the personality, and I'm a cooked Indian. Give me a beer, please.

HARRY. Nick, you've got to see my act. It's the greatest thing of its kind in America. All I want is a chance. No salary to begin. Let me try it out tonight. If I don't wow 'em, O.K., I'll go home. If vaudeville wasn't dead, a guy like me would have a chance.

NICK. You're not funny. You're a sad young punk. What the hell do you want to try to be funny for? You'll break everybody's heart. What's there for you to be funny about? You've been poor all your life, haven't you?

HARRY. I've been poor all right, but don't forget that some things count more than some other things.

NICK. What counts more, for instance, than what else, for instance?

HARRY. Talent, for instance, counts more than money, for instance, that's what, and I've got talent. I get new ideas night and day. Everything comes natural to me. I've got style, but it'll take me a little time to round it out. That's all.

(*By now* WESLEY *is playing something of his own which is very good and out of the world. He plays about half a minute, after which* HARRY *begins to dance.*)

NICK (*watching*). I run the lousiest dive in Frisco, and a guy arrives and makes me stock up with champagne. The whores come in and holler at me that they're ladies. Talent comes in and begs me for a chance to show itself. Even society people come here once in a while. I don't know what for. Maybe it's liquor. Maybe it's the location. Maybe it's my personality. Maybe it's the crazy personality of the joint. The old honky-tonk. (*Pause*) Maybe they can't feel at home anywhere else.

(*By now* WESLEY *is really playing, and* HARRY *is going through a new routine.* DUDLEY *grows sadder and sadder.*)

KITTY. Please dance with me.

JOE (*loudly*). I never learned to dance.

KITTY. Anybody can dance. Just hold me in your arms.

JOE. I'm very fond of you. I'm *sorry*. I *can't* dance. I wish to God I could.

KITTY. Oh, please.

JOE. Forgive me. I'd like to very much.

(KITTY *dances alone.* TOM *comes in with a package. He sees* KITTY *and goes ga-ga again. He comes out of the trance and puts the bundle on the table in front of* JOE.)

JOE (*taking the package*). What'd you get?

TOM. Two dollars' worth of toys. That's what you sent me for. The girl asked me what I wanted with toys. I didn't know what to tell her. (*He stares at* KITTY, *then back at* JOE) Joe? I've got to have some money. After all you've done for me, I'll do anything in the world for you, but, Joe, you got to give me some money once in a while.

JOE. What do you want it for?

(TOM *turns and stares at* KITTY *dancing.*)

JOE (*noticing*). Sure. Here. Here's five. (*Shouting*) Can you dance?

TOM (*proudly*). I got second prize at the Palomar in Sacramento five years ago.

JOE (*loudly, opening package*). O.K., dance with her.

TOM. You mean *her*?

JOE (*loudly*). I mean Kitty Duval, the burlesque queen. I mean the queen of the world burlesque. Dance with her. She wants to dance.

TOM (*worshiping the name Kitty Duval, helplessly*). Joe, can I tell you something?

JOE (*he brings out a toy and winds it*). You don't have to. I know. You love her. You *really* love her. I'm not blind. I know. But take care of yourself. Don't get sick that way again.

NICK (*looking at and listening to* WESLEY *with amazement*). Comes in here and wants to be a dish-washer. Faints from hunger. And then sits down and plays better than Heifetz.

JOE. Heifetz plays the violin.

NICK. All right, don't get careful. He's good, ain't he?

TOM (*to* KITTY). Kitty.

JOE (*he lets the toy go, loudly*). Don't *talk*. Just *dance*.

(TOM *and* KITTY *dance*. NICK *is at the bar, watching everything*. HARRY *is dancing*. DUDLEY *is grieving into his beer*. LORENE SMITH, *about thirty-seven, very overbearing and funny-looking, comes to the bar*.)

NICK. What'll it be, lady?

LORENE (*looking about and scaring all the young men*). I'm looking for the young man I talked to on the telephone. Dudley R. Bostwick.

DUDLEY (*jumping, running to her, stopping, shocked*). Dudley R. (*Slowly*) Bostwick? Oh, yeah. He left here ten minutes ago. You mean Dudley Bostwick, that poor man on crutches?

LORENE. Crutches?

DUDLEY. Yeah. Dudley Bostwick. That's what he *said* his name was. He said to tell you not to wait.

LORENE. Well. (*She begins to go, turns around*) Are you sure *you're* not Dudley Bostwick?

DUDLEY. Who—me? (*Grandly*) My name is Roger Tenefrancia. I'm a French-Canadian. I never saw the poor fellow before.

LORENE. It seems to me your voice is like the voice I heard over the telephone.

DUDLEY. A coincidence. An accident. A quirk of fate. One of those things. Dismiss the thought. That poor cripple hobbled out of here ten minutes ago.

LORENE. He said he was going to commit suicide. I only wanted to be of help. (*She goes*.)

DUDLEY. Be of help? What kind of help could she be of? (DUDLEY *runs to the telephone in the corner*) Gee whiz, Elsie. Gee whiz. I'll never leave you again. (*He turns the pages of a little address book*) Why do I always forget the number? I've tried to get her on the phone a hundred times this week and I still forget the number. She won't come to the phone, but I keep trying anyway. She's out. She's not in. She's working. I get the wrong number. Everything goes haywire. I can't sleep. (*Defiantly*) She'll come to the phone one of these days. If there's anything to true love at all, she'll come to the phone. Sunset 7349. (*He dials the number, as* JOE *goes on studying the toys. They are one big mechanical toy, whistles, and a music box.* JOE *blows into the whistles, quickly, by way of getting casually acquainted with them.* TOM *and* KITTY *stop dancing.* TOM *stares at her*.)

DUDLEY. Hello. Is this Sunset 7349? May I speak to Elsie? Yes. (*Emphatically, and bitterly*) No, this is *not* Dudley Bostwick. This is Roger Tenefrancia of Montreal, Canada. I'm a childhood friend of Miss Mandelspiegel. We went to kindergarten together. (*Hand over phone*) God damn it. (*Into phone*) Yes. I'll wait, thank you.

TOM. I love you.

KITTY. You want to go to my room? (TOM *can't answer*) Have you got two dollars?

TOM (*shaking his head with confusion*). I've got *five* dollars, but I *love* you.

KITTY (*looking at him*). You want to spend *all* that money? (TOM *embraces her. They go.* JOE *watches. Goes back to the toy.*)

JOE. Where's that longshoreman, McCarthy?

NICK. He'll be around.

JOE. What do you think he'll have to say today?

NICK. Plenty, as usual. I'm going next door to see who won that third race at Laurel.

JOE. Precious Time won it.

NICK. That's what you think. (*He goes.*)

JOE (*to himself*). A horse named McCarthy is running in the sixth race today.

DUDLEY (*on the phone*). Hello. Hello, Elsie? Elsie? (*His voice weakens; also his limbs*) My God. She's come to the phone. Elsie, I'm at Nick's on Pacific Street. You've got to come here and talk to me. Hello. Hello, Elsie? (*Amazed*) Did she hang up? Or was I disconnected? (*He hangs up and goes to bar.* WESLEY *is still playing the piano.* HARRY *is still dancing.* JOE *has wound up the big mechanical toy and is watching it work.* NICK *returns.*)

NICK (*watching the toy*). Say. That's some gadget.

JOE. How much did I win?

NICK. How do you know you *won*?

JOE. Don't be silly. He said Precious Time was going to win by ten lengths, didn't he? He's in love, isn't he?

NICK. O.K. I don't know why, but Precious Time won. You got eighty for ten. How do you do it?

JOE (*roaring*). Faith. Faith. How'd he win?

NICK. By a nose. Look him up in The Racing Form. The slowest, the cheapest, the worst horse in the race, and the worst jockey. What's the matter with my luck?

JOE. How much did you lose?

NICK. Fifty cents.

JOE. You should never gamble.

NICK. Why not?

JOE. You always bet fifty cents. You've got no more faith than a flea, that's why.

HARRY (*shouting*). How do you like this, Nick? (*He is really busy now, all legs and arms.*)

NICK (*turning and watching*). Not bad. Hang around. You can wait table. (*To* WESLEY) Hey. Wesley. Can you play that again tonight?

WESLEY (*turning, but still playing the piano*). I don't know for sure, Mr. Nick. I can play *something*.

NICK. Good. *You* hang around, too. (*He goes behind the bar. The atmosphere is now one of warm, natural,*

American ease; every man innocent and good; each doing what he believes he should do, or what he must do. There is deep American naiveté and faith in the behavior of each person. No one is competing with anyone else. No one hates anyone else. Every man is living, and letting live. Each man is following his destiny as he feels it should be followed; or is abandoning it as he feels it must, by now, be abandoned; or is forgetting it for the moment as he feels he should forget it. Although everyone is dead serious, there is unmistakable smiling and humor in the scene; a sense of the human body and spirit emerging from the world-imposed state of stress and fretfulness, fear and awkwardness, to the more natural state of casualness and grace. Each person belongs to the environment, in his own person, as himself: WESLEY *is playing better than ever.* HARRY *is hoofing better than ever.* NICK *is behind the bar shining glasses.* JOE *is smiling at the toy and studying it.* DUDLEY, *although still troubled, is at least calm now and full of melancholy poise.* WILLIE, *at the marble-game, is happy. The* ARAB *is deep in his memories, where he wants to be. Into this scene and atmosphere comes* BLICK. BLICK *is the sort of human being you dislike at sight. He is no different from anybody else physically. His face is an ordinary face. There is nothing obviously wrong with him, and yet you know that it is impossible, even by the most generous expansion of understanding, to accept him as a human being. He is the strong man without strength—strong only among the weak—the weakling who uses force on the weaker.* BLICK *enters casually, as if he were a customer, and immediately* HARRY *begins slowing down.*)

BLICK (*oily, and with mock-friendliness*). Hello, Nick.

NICK (*stopping his work and leaning across the bar*). What do you want to come here for? You're too big a man for a little honky-tonk.

BLICK (*flattered*). Now, Nick.

NICK. Important people never come here. *Here.* Have a drink. (*Whiskey bottle.*)

BLICK. Thanks, I don't drink.

NICK (*drinking the drink himself*). Well, why don't you?

BLICK. I have responsibilities.

NICK. You're head of the lousy Vice Squad. There's no vice here.

BLICK (*sharply*). Street-walkers are working out of this place.

NICK (*angry*). What do you want?

BLICK (*loudly*). I just want you to know that it's got to *stop.*
(*The music stops. The mechanical toy runs down. There is absolute silence, and a strange fearfulness and disharmony in the atmosphere now.* HARRY *doesn't know what to do with his hands or feet.* WESLEY'S *arms hang at his sides.* JOE *quietly pushes the toy to one side of the table, eager to study what is happening.* WILLIE *stops playing the marble-game, turns around and begins to wait.* DUDLEY *straightens up very, very vigorously, as if to say: "Nothing can scare me. I know love is the only thing." The* ARAB *is the same as ever, but watchful.* NICK *is arrogantly aloof. There is a moment of this silence and tension, as though*

BLICK *were waiting for everybody to acknowledge his presence. He is obviously flattered by the acknowledgment of* HARRY, DUDLEY, WESLEY, *and* WILLIE, *but a little irritated by* NICK'S *aloofness and unfriendliness.*)

NICK. Don't look at me. I can't tell a street-walker from a lady. You married?

BLICK. You're not asking *me* questions. *I'm* telling *you.*

NICK (*interrupting*). You're a man of about forty-five or so. You *ought* to know better.

BLICK (*angry*). Street-walkers are working out of this place.

NICK (*beginning to shout*). Now, don't start any trouble with me. People come here to drink and loaf around. I don't care who they are.

BLICK. Well, I do.

NICK. The only way to find out if a lady is a street-walker is to walk the streets with her, go to bed, and make sure. You wouldn't want to do that. *You'd* like to, of course.

BLICK. Any more of it, and I'll have your joint closed.

NICK (*very casually, without ill-will*). Listen. I've got no use for you, or anybody like you. You're out to change the world from something bad to something worse. Something like yourself.

BLICK (*furious pause, and contempt*). I'll be back tonight. (*He begins to go.*)

NICK (*very angry but very calm*). Do yourself a big favor and don't come back tonight. Send somebody else. don't like your personality.

BLICK (*casually, but with contempt*) Don't break any laws. I don't lik yours, either. (*He looks the plac over, and goes. There is a moment o silence. Then* WILLIE *turns and put a new nickel in the slot and starts new game.* WESLEY *turns to the pian and rather falteringly begins to play His heart really isn't in it.* HARR *walks about, unable to dance.* DUD LEY *lapses into his customary melan choly, at a table.* NICK *whistles a lit tle: suddenly stops.* JOE *winds th toy.*)

JOE (*comically*). Nick. You going t kill that man?

NICK. I'm disgusted.

JOE. Yeah? Why?

NICK. Why should I get worked u over a guy like that? Why should hate *him*? He's nothing. He's no body. He's a mouse. But every tim he comes into this place I get burne up. He doesn't want to drink. H doesn't want to sit down. He doesn want to take things easy. Tell me on thing?

JOE. Do my best.

NICK. What's a punk like *that* wan to go out and try to change the worl for?

JOE (*amazed*). Does *he* want t change the world, too?

NICK (*irritated*). You know what mean. What's he want to bother peo ple for? He's *sick*.

JOE (*almost to himself, reflecting o the fact that* BLICK *too wants t change the world*). I guess he wants to change the world at that.

NICK. So I go to work and hate him.

JOE. It's not him, Nick. It's everything.

NICK. Yeah, *I know*. But I've still got no use for him. He's no good. You know what I mean? He hurts little people. (*Confused*) One of the girls tried to commit suicide on account of him. (*Furiously*) I'll break his head if he hurts anybody around here. This is *my* joint. (*Afterthought*) Or anybody's *feelings*, either.

JOE. He may not be so bad, deep down underneath.

NICK. I know all about him. He's no good.

(*During this talk* WESLEY *has really begun to play the piano, the toy is rattling again, and little by little* HARRY *has begun to dance.* NICK *has come around the bar, and now, very much like a child—forgetting all his anger—is watching the toy work. He begins to smile at everything: turns and listens to* WESLEY: *watches* HARRY: *nods at the* ARAB: *shakes his head at* DUDLEY: *and gestures amiably about* WILLIE. *It's his joint all right. It's a good, low-down, honky-tonk American place that lets people alone.*)

NICK. I've got a good joint. There's nothing wrong here. Hey. Comedian. Stick to the dancing tonight. I think you're O.K. Wesley? Do some more of that tonight. That's fine!

HARRY. Thanks, Nick. Gosh, I'm on my way at last. (*On telephone*) Hello, Ma? Is that you, Ma? Harry. I got the job. (*He hangs up and walks around, smiling.*)

NICK (*watching the toy all this time*). Say, that really is something. What is that, anyway?

(MARY L. *comes in.*)

JOE (*holding it toward* NICK, *and* MARY L.). Nick, this is a toy. A contraption devised by the cunning of man to drive boredom, or grief, or anger out of children. A noble gadget. A gadget, I might say, infinitely nobler than any other I can think of at the moment. (*Everybody gathers around* JOE's *table to look at the toy. The toy stops working.* JOE *winds the music box. Lifts a whistle: blows it, making a very strange, funny and sorrowful sound*) Delightful. Tragic, but delightful.

(WESLEY *plays the music-box theme on the piano.* MARY L. *takes a table.*)

NICK. Joe. That girl, Kitty. What's she mean, calling me a dentist? I wouldn't hurt anybody, let alone a tooth.

(NICK *goes to* MARY L.'s *table.* HARRY *imitates the toy. Dances. The piano music comes up, the light dims slowly, while the piano solo continues.*)

CURTAIN

ACT TWO

An hour later. All the people who were at NICK'S *when the curtain came down are still there.* JOE *at his table, quietly shuffling and turning a deck of cards, and at the same time watching the face of the* WOMAN, *and looking at the initials on her handbag, as though they were the symbols of the lost glory of the world. The* WOMAN, *in turn, very casually regards* JOE *occasionally. Or rather senses him; has sensed him in fact the whole hour. She is mildly tight on beer, and* JOE *himself is tight, but as always completely under control; simply sharper. The others are about, at tables, and so on.*

JOE. Is it Madge—Laubowitz?

MARY. Is what *what?*

JOE. Is the name Mabel Lepescu?

MARY. What name?

JOE. The name the initials M. L. stand for. The initials on your bag.

MARY. No.

JOE (*after a long pause, thinking deeply what the name might be, turning a card, looking into the beautiful face of the woman*). Margie Longworthy?

MARY (*all this is very natural and sincere, no comedy on the part of the people involved: they are both solemn, being drunk*). No.

JOE (*his voice higher-pitched, as though he were growing a little alarmed*). Midge Laurie? (MARY *shakes her head*) My initials are J. T.

MARY (*pause*). John?

JOE. No. (*Pause*) Martha Lancaster?

MARY. No. (*Slight pause*) Joseph?

JOE. Well, not exactly. That's my first name, but everybody calls me Joe. The last name is the tough one. I'll help you a little. I'm Irish. (*Pause*) Is it just plain Mary?

MARY. Yes, it is. I'm Irish, too. At least on my father's side. English on my mother's side.

JOE. I'm Irish on both sides. Mary's one of my favorite names. I guess that's why I didn't think of it. I met a girl in Mexico City named Mary once. She was an American from Philadelphia. She got married there. In Mexico City, I mean. While I was *there*. We were in love, too. At least *I* was. You never know about anyone else. They were engaged, you see, and her mother was with her, so they went through with it. Must have been six or seven years ago. She's probably got three or four children by this time.

MARY. Are you still in love with her?

JOE. Well—no. To tell you the truth, I'm not sure. I guess I am. I didn't even know she was engaged until a couple of days before they got married. I thought *I* was going to marry her. I kept thinking all the time about the kind of kids we would be likely to have. My favorite was the third one. The first two were fine. Handsome and fine and intelligent, but that third one was different. Dumb and goofy-looking. I liked *him* a lot. When she told me she was going to be married, I didn't feel so bad about the first two, it was that dumb one.

MARY (*after a pause of some few seconds*). What do you do?

JOE. Do? To tell you the truth, nothing.

MARY. Do you always drink a great deal?

JOE (*scientifically*). Not *always*. Only when I'm awake. I sleep seven or eight hours every night, you know.

MARY. How nice. I mean to drink when you're awake.

JOE (*thoughtfully*). It's a privilege.

MARY. Do you really *like* to drink?

JOE (*positively*). As much as I like to *breathe*.

MARY (*beautifully*). Why?

JOE (*dramatically*). Why do I like to drink? (*Pause*) Because I don't like to be gypped. Because I don't like to be dead most of the time and just a little alive every once in a long while. (*Pause*) If I don't drink, I become fascinated by unimportant things—like everybody else. I get busy. Do things. All kinds of little stupid things, for all kinds of little stupid reasons. Proud, selfish, *ordinary* things. I've done them. Now I don't do anything. *I live all the time.* Then I go to sleep. (*Pause*)

MARY. Do you sleep well?

JOE (*taking it for granted*). Of course.

MARY (*quietly, almost with tenderness*). What are your plans?

JOE (*loudly, but also tenderly*). Plans? I haven't *got* any. *I just get up.*

MARY (*beginning to understand everything*). Oh, yes. Yes, of course. (DUDLEY *puts a nickel in the phonograph.*)

JOE (*thoughtfully*). Why do I drink? (*Pause, while he thinks about it. The thinking appears to be profound and complex, and has the effect of giving his face a very comical and naive expression*) That question calls for a pretty complicated answer. (*He smiles abstractly.*)

MARY. Oh, I didn't mean—

JOE (*swiftly, gallantly*). No. No. I *insist.* I *know* why. It's just a matter of finding words. Little ones.

MARY. It really doesn't matter.

JOE (*seriously*). Oh, yes, it does. (*Clinically*) Now, why do I drink? (*Scientifically*) No. Why does *anybody* drink? (*Working it out*) Every day has twenty-four hours.

MARY (*sadly, but brightly*). Yes, that's true.

JOE. Twenty-four hours. Out of the twenty-four hours at *least* twenty-three and a half are—my God, I don't know why—dull, dead, boring, empty, and murderous. Minutes on the clock, *not time of living*. It doesn't make any difference who you are or what you do, twenty-three and a half hours of the twenty-four are spent *waiting*.

MARY. Waiting?

JOE (*gesturing, loudly*). And the more you wait, the less there is to wait *for*.

MARY (*attentively, beautifully his student*). Oh?

JOE (*continuing*). That goes on for days and days, and weeks and months and years, and years, and the first thing you know *all* the years are dead. All the minutes are dead. You yourself are dead. There's nothing to wait for any more. Nothing except *minutes* on the *clock*. No time of life. Nothing but minutes, and idiocy. Beautiful, bright, intelligent idiocy. (*Pause*) Does that answer your question?

MARY (*earnestly*). I'm afraid it does. Thank you. You shouldn't have gone to all the trouble.

JOE. No trouble at all. (*Pause*) You have children?

MARY. Yes. Two. A son and a daughter.

JOE (*delighted*). How swell. Do they look like you?

MARY. Yes.

JOE. Then why are you sad?

MARY. I was always sad. It's just that after I was married I was allowed to drink.

JOE (*eagerly*). Who are you waiting for?

MARY. No one.

JOE (*smiling*). I'm not waiting for anybody, either.

MARY. My husband, of course.

JOE. Oh, sure.

MARY. He's a lawyer.

JOE (*standing, leaning on the table*). He's a great guy. I like him. I'm very fond of him.

MARY (*listening*). You have responsibilities?

JOE (*loudly*). *One,* and *thousands.* As a matter of fact, I feel responsible to everybody. At least to everybody I meet. I've been trying for three years to find out if it's possible to live what I think is a civilized life. I mean a life that can't hurt any other life.

MARY. You're famous?

JOE. Very. Utterly unknown, but very famous. Would you like to dance?

MARY. All right.

JOE (*loudly*). I'm *sorry*. I don't dance. I didn't think you'd like to.

MARY. To tell you the truth, I don't like to dance at all.

JOE (*proudly—commentator*) I can hardly walk.

MARY. You mean you're tight?

JOE (*smiling*). No. I mean *all* the time.

MARY (*looking at him closely*). Were you ever in Paris?

JOE. In 1929, and again in 1934.

MARY. What month of 1934?

JOE. Most of April, all of May, and a little of June.

MARY. I was there in November and December that year.

JOE. We were there almost at the same time. You were married?

MARY. Engaged. (*They are silent a moment, looking at one another. Quietly and with great charm*) Are you *really* in love with me?

JOE. Yes.

MARY. Is it the champagne?

JOE. Yes. Partly, at least. (*He sits down.*)

MARY. If you don't see me again, will you be very unhappy?

JOE. Very.

MARY (*getting up*). I'm so pleased. (JOE *is deeply grieved that she is going. In fact, he is almost panic-stricken about it, getting up in a way that is full of furious sorrow and regret*) I must go now. Please don't get up. (JOE *is up, staring at her with amazement*) Good-by.

JOE (*simply*). Good-by. (*The* WOMAN *stands looking at him a moment, then turns and goes.* JOE *stands staring after her for a long time. Just as he is slowly sitting down again, the* NEWSBOY *enters, and goes to* JOE'S *table.*)

NEWSBOY. Paper, Mister?

JOE. How many you got this time?

NEWSBOY. Eleven. (JOE *buys them all, looks at the lousy headlines, throws them away. The* NEWSBOY *looks at* JOE, *amazed. He walks over to* NICK *at the bar.*)

NEWSBOY (*troubled*). Hey, Mister, do you own this place?

NICK (*casually but emphatically*). I own this place.

NEWSBOY. Can you use a great lyric tenor?

NICK (*almost to himself*). Great lyric tenor? (*Loudly*) Who?

NEWSBOY (*loud and the least bit angry*). Me. I'm getting too big to sell papers. I don't want to holler headlines all the time. I want to *sing*. You can use a great lyric tenor, can't you?

NICK. What's lyric about you?

NEWSBOY (*voice high-pitched, confused*). My voice.

NICK. Oh. (*Slight pause, giving in*) All right, then—sing! (*The* NEWSBOY *breaks into swift and beautiful song: "When Irish Eyes Are Smiling."* NICK *and* JOE *listen carefully:* NICK *with wonder,* JOE *with amazement and delight.*)

NEWSBOY (*singing*).

When Irish eyes are smiling,
Sure 'tis like a morn in Spring.
In the lilt of Irish laughter,
You can hear the angels sing.
When Irish hearts are happy,
All the world seems bright and gay.
But when Irish eyes are smiling—

NICK (*loudly, swiftly*). Are you Irish?

NEWSBOY (*speaking swiftly, loudly, a little impatient with the irrelevant question*). No. I'm Greek. (*He finishes the song, singing louder than ever*) Sure they steal your heart away. (*He turns to* NICK *dramatically, like a vaudeville singer begging his audience for applause.* NICK *studies the* BOY *eagerly.* JOE *gets to his feet and leans toward the* BOY *and* NICK.)

NICK. Not bad. Let me hear you again about a year from now.

NEWSBOY (*thrilled*). Honest?

NICK. Yeah. Along about November 7th, 1940.

NEWSBOY (*happier than ever before in his life, running over to* JOE). Did you hear it too, Mister?

JOE. Yes, and it's great. What part of Greece?

NEWSBOY. Salonica. Gosh, Mister. Thanks.

JOE. Don't wait a year. Come back with some papers a little later. You're a great singer.

NEWSBOY (*thrilled and excited*). Aw, thanks, Mister. So long. (*Running, to* NICK) Thanks, Mister. (*He runs out.* JOE *and* NICK *look at the swinging doors.* JOE *sits down.* NICK *laughs.*)

NICK. Joe, people are so wonderful. Look at that kid.

JOE. Of course they're wonderful. Every one of them is wonderful.

(MC CARTHY *and* KRUPP *come in, talking.* MC CARTHY *is a big man in work clothes, which make him seem very young. He is wearing black jeans, and a blue workman's shirt. No tie. No hat. He has broad shoulders, a lean intelligent face, thick black hair. In his right back pocket is the longshoreman's hook. His arms are long and hairy. His sleeves are rolled up to just below his elbows. He is a casual man, easy-going in movement, sharp in perception, swift in appreciation of charm or innocence or comedy, and gentle in spirit. His speech is clear and full of warmth. His voice is powerful, but modulated. He enjoys the world, in spite of the mess it is, and he is fond of people, in spite of the mess they are.* KRUPP *is not quite as tall or broad-shouldered as* MC CARTHY. *He is physically encumbered by his uniform, club, pistol, belt, and cap. And he is plainly not at home in the role of policeman. His movement is stiff and unintentionally pompous. He is a naive man, essentially good. His understanding is less than* MC CARTHY'S, *but he is honest and he doesn't try to bluff.*)

KRUPP. You don't understand what I mean. Hi-ya, Joe.

JOE. Hello, Krupp.

MC CARTHY. Hi-ya, Joe.

JOE. Hello, McCarthy.

KRUPP. Two beers, Nick. (*To* MC CARTHY) All I do is carry out orders, carry out orders. I don't know what the idea is behind the order. Who it's for, or who it's against, or why. All I do is carry it out.
(NICK *gives them beer.*)

MC CARTHY. You don't read enough.

KRUPP. I do read. I read The Examiner every morning. The Call-Bulletin every night.

MC CARTHY. And carry out orders. What are the orders now?

KRUPP. To keep the peace down here on the waterfront.

MC CARTHY. Keep it for who? (*To* JOE) Right?

JOE (*sorrowfully*). Right.

KRUPP. How do I know for who? The peace. Just keep it.

MC CARTHY. It's got to be kept for somebody. Who would you suspect it's kept for?

KRUPP. For citizens!

MC CARTHY. I'm a citizen!

KRUPP. All right, I'm keeping it for you.

MC CARTHY. By hitting me over the head with a club? (*To* JOE) Right?

JOE (*melancholy, with remembrance*). I don't know.

KRUPP. Mac, you know I never hit you over the head with a club.

MC CARTHY. But you will if you're on duty at the time and happen to stand on the opposite side of myself, on duty.

KRUPP. We went to Mission High together. We were always good friends. The only time we ever fought was that time over Alma Haggerty. Did *you* marry Alma Haggerty? (*To* JOE) Right?

JOE. Everything's right.

MC CARTHY. No. Did you? (*To* JOE) Joe, are you with me or against me?

JOE. I'm with everybody. One at a time.

KRUPP. No. And that's just what I mean.

MC CARTHY. You mean neither one of us is going to marry the thing we're fighting for?

KRUPP. *I don't even know what it is.*

MC CARTHY. You don't read enough, I tell you.

KRUPP. Mac, you don't know what you're fighting for, either.

MC CARTHY. It's so simple, it's fantastic.

KRUPP. All right, what are you fighting for?

MC CARTHY. For the rights of the inferior. Right?

JOE. Something like that.

KRUPP. The who?

MC CARTHY. The inferior. The world full of Mahoneys who haven't got what it takes to make monkeys out of everybody else, near by. The men who were created equal. Remember?

KRUPP. Mac, you're not inferior.

MC CARTHY. I'm a longshoreman. And an idealist. I'm a man with too much brawn to be an intellectual, exclusively. I married a small, sensitive, cultured woman so that my kids would be sissies instead of suckers. A strong man with any sensibility has no choice in this world but to be a heel, or a *worker*. I haven't the heart to be a heel, so I'm a worker. I've got a son in high school who's already thinking of being a writer.

KRUPP. I wanted to be a writer once.

JOE. Wonderful. (*He puts down the paper, looks at* KRUPP *and* MC CARTHY.)

MC CARTHY. They *all* wanted to be writers. Every maniac in the world that ever brought about the murder of people through war started out in an attic or a basement writing poetry. It stank. So they got even by becoming important heels. And it's still going on.

KRUPP. Is it really, Joe?

JOE. Look at today's paper.

MC CARTHY. Right now on Telegraph Hill is some punk who is trying to be Shakespeare. Ten years from now he'll be a senator. Or a communist.

KRUPP. Somebody ought to do something about it.

MC CARTHY (*mischievously, with laughter in his voice*). The thing to do is to have more magazines. Hundreds of them. *Thousands*. Print everything they write, so they'll believe they're immortal. That way keep them from going haywire.

KRUPP. Mac, you ought to be a writer yourself.

MC CARTHY. I hate the tribe. They're mischief-makers. Right?

JOE (*swiftly*). Everything's right. Right and wrong.

KRUPP. Then why do you read?

MC CARTHY (*laughing*). It's relaxing. It's soothing. (*Pause*) The lousiest people born into the world are writers. Language is all right. It's the people who use language that are lousy. (*The* ARAB *has moved a little closer, and is listening carefully. To the* ARAB) What do you think, Brother?

ARAB (*after making many faces, thinking very deeply*). No foundation. All the way down the line. What. What-not. Nothing. I go walk and look at sky. (*He goes.*)

KRUPP. What? What-not? (*To* JOE) What's that mean?

JOE (*slowly, thinking, remembering*). What? What-not? That means this side, that side. Inhale, exhale. What: birth. What-not: death. The inevitable, the astounding, the magnificent seed of growth and decay in all things. Beginning, and end. That man, in his own way, is a prophet. He is one who, with the help of *beer*, is able to reach that state of deep understanding in which what and what-not, the reasonable and the unreasonable, are *one.*

MC CARTHY. Right.

KRUPP. If you can understand that kind of talk, how can you be a longshoreman?

MC CARTHY. I come from a long line of McCarthys who never married or slept with anything but the most powerful and quarrelsome flesh. (*He drinks beer.*)

KRUPP. I could listen to you two guys for hours, but I'll be damned if I know what the hell you're talking about.

MC CARTHY. The consequence is that all the McCarthys are too great and too strong to be heroes. Only the weak and unsure perform the heroic. They've *got* to. The more heroes you have, the worse the history of the world becomes. Right?

JOE. Go outside and look at it.

KRUPP. You sure can philos—philosoph— Boy, you can talk.

MC CARTHY. I wouldn't talk this way to anyone but a man in uniform, and a man who couldn't understand a word of what I was saying. The party I'm speaking of, my friend, is *YOU.* (*The phone rings.* HARRY *gets up from his table suddenly and begins a new dance.*)

KRUPP (*noticing him, with great authority*). Here. Here. What do you think you're doing?

HARRY (*stopping*). I just got an idea for a new dance. I'm trying it out. Nick. Nick, the phone's ringing.

KRUPP (*to* MC CARTHY). Has he got a right to do that?

MC CARTHY. The living have danced from the beginning of time. I might even say, the dance and the life have moved along together, until now we have— (*To* HARRY) Go into your dance, son, and show us what we have.

HARRY. I haven't got it worked out *completely* yet, but it starts out like this. (*He dances.*)

NICK (*on phone*). Nick's Pacific Street Restaurant, Saloon, and Entertainment Palace. Good afternoon. Nick speaking. (*Listens*) Who? (*Turns around*) Is there a Dudley Bostwick in the joint?
(DUDLEY *jumps to his feet and goes to phone.*)

DUDLEY (*on phone*). Hello. Elsie? (*Listens*) You're coming down? (*Elated. To the saloon*) She's coming down. (*Pause*) No. I won't drink. Aw, gosh, Elsie. (*He hangs up, looks about him strangely, as if he were just born, walks around touching things, putting chairs in place, and so on.*)

MC CARTHY (*to* HARRY). Splendid. Splendid.

HARRY. Then I go into this little routine. (*He demonstrates.*)

KRUPP. Is that good, Mac?

MC CARTHY. It's awful, but it's honest and ambitious, like everything else in this great country.

HARRY. Then I work along into this. (*He demonstrates*) And *this* is where I *really* get going. (*He finishes the dance.*)

MC CARTHY. Excellent. A most satisfying demonstration of the present state of the American body and soul. Son, you're a genius.

HARRY (*delighted, shaking hands with* MC CARTHY). I go on in front of an audience for the first time in my life tonight.

MC CARTHY. They'll be delighted. Where'd you learn to dance?

HARRY. Never took a lesson in my life. I'm a natural-born dancer. And *comedian*, too.

MC CARTHY (*astounded*). You can make people *laugh*?

HARRY (*dumbly*). I can be funny, but they won't laugh.

MC CARTHY. That's odd. Why not?

HARRY. I don't know. They just won't laugh.

MC CARTHY. Would you care to be funny now?

HARRY. I'd like to try out a new monologue I've been thinking about.

MC CARTHY. Please do. I promise you if it's funny I shall *roar* with laughter.

HARRY. This is it. (*Goes into the act, with much energy*) I'm up at Sharkey's on Turk Street. It's a quarter to nine, daylight saving. Wednesday, the eleventh. What I've got is a headache and a 1918 nickel. What I *want* is a cup of coffee. If I buy a cup of coffee with the nickel, I've got to walk home. I've got an eight-ball problem. George the Greek is shooting a game of snooker with Pedro the Filipino. *I'm in rags*. They're wearing thirty-five dollar suits, made to order. I haven't got a cigarette. They're smoking Bobby Burns panatelas. I'm thinking it over, like I always do. George the Greek is in a tough spot. If I buy a cup of coffee, I'll want another cup. What happens? My *ear* aches! My ear. George the Greek takes the cue. Chalks it. Studies the table. Touches the cue-ball delicately. Tick. What happens? He makes the three-ball! What do I do? I get confused. *I go out and buy a morning paper*. What the hell do I want with a morning paper? What I *want* is a cup of coffee, and a good used car. I go out and buy a morning paper. Thursday, the twelfth. Maybe the headline's about *me*. I take a quick look. *No. The headline is not about me.* It's about Hitler. Seven thousand miles away. I'm here. Who the hell is Hitler? Who's behind the eight-ball? I turn around. *Everybody's behind the eight-ball!* (*Pause.* KRUPP *moves toward* HARRY *as if to make an important arrest.* HARRY *moves to the swinging doors.* MC CARTHY *stops* KRUPP.)

MC CARTHY (*to* HARRY). It's the funniest thing I've ever heard. Or *seen*, for that matter.

HARRY (*coming back to* MC CARTHY). Then, why don't you laugh?

MC CARTHY. I don't know, *yet*.

HARRY. I'm always getting funny ideas that nobody will laugh at.

MC CARTHY (*thoughtfully*). It may be that you've stumbled headlong into a new kind of comedy.

HARRY. Well, what good is it if it doesn't make anybody laugh?

MC CARTHY. There are *kinds* of laughter, son. I must say, in all truth, that I *am* laughing, although not *out loud.*

HARRY. I want to *hear* people laugh. *Out loud.* That's why I keep thinking of funny things to say.

MC CARTHY. Well. They may catch on in time. Let's go, Krupp. So long, Joe. (MC CARTHY *and* KRUPP *go.*)

JOE. So long. (*After a moment's pause*) Hey, Nick.

NICK. Yeah.

JOE. Bet McCarthy in the last race.

NICK. You're crazy. That horse is a double-crossing, no-good—

JOE. Bet everything you've got on McCarthy.

NICK. I'm not betting a nickel on him. *You* bet everything you've got on McCarthy.

JOE. I don't need money.

NICK. What makes you think McCarthy's going to win?

JOE. McCarthy's name's McCarthy, isn't it?

NICK. Yeah. So what?

JOE. The *horse* named McCarthy is going to win, *that's all.* Today.

NICK. Why?

JOE. You do what I tell you, and everything will be all right.

NICK. McCarthy likes to talk, that's all. (*Pause*) Where's Tom?

JOE. He'll be around. He'll be miserable, but he'll be around. Five or ten minutes more.

NICK. You don't believe that Kitty, do you? About being in burlesque?

JOE (*very clearly*). I believe dreams sooner than statistics.

NICK (*remembering*). She sure is somebody. Called me a dentist.
(TOM, *turning about, confused, troubled, comes in, and hurries to* JOE'S *table.*)

JOE. What's the matter?

TOM. Here's your five, Joe. I'm in trouble again.

JOE. If it's not organic, it'll cure itself. If it is organic, science will cure it. What is it, organic or non-organic?

TOM. Joe, I don't know— (*He seems to be completely broken down.*)

JOE. What's eating you? I want you to go on an errand for me.

TOM. It's Kitty.

JOE. What about her?

TOM. She's up in her room, crying.

JOE. Crying?

TOM. Yeah, she's been crying for over an hour. I been talking to her all this time, but she won't stop.

JOE. What's she crying about?

TOM. I don't know. I couldn't understand anything. She kept crying and telling me about a big house and collie dogs all around and flowers and one of her brothers dead and the other one lost somewhere. Joe, I can't stand Kitty crying.

JOE. You want to marry the girl?

TOM (*nodding*). Yeah.

JOE (*curious and sincere*). Why?

TOM. I don't know why, exactly, Joe. (*Pause*) Joe, I don't like to think of Kitty out in the streets. I guess I love her, that's all.

JOE. She's a nice girl.

TOM. She's like an angel. She's not like those other street-walkers.

JOE (*swiftly*). Here. Take all this money and run next door to Frankie's and bet it on the nose of McCarthy.

TOM (*swiftly*). All this money, Joe? McCarthy?

JOE. Yeah. Hurry.

TOM (*going*). Ah, Joe. If McCarthy wins we'll be rich.

JOE. Get going, will you?
(TOM *runs out and nearly knocks over the* ARAB *coming back in.* NICK *fills him a beer without a word.*)

ARAB. No foundation, anywhere. Whole world. No foundation. All the way down the line.

NICK (*angry*). McCarthy! Just because you got a little lucky this morning, you have to go to work and throw away eighty bucks.

JOE. He wants to marry her.

NICK. Suppose she doesn't want to marry *him*?

JOE (*amazed*). Oh, yeah. (*Thinking*) Now, why wouldn't she want to marry a nice guy like Tom?

NICK. She's been in burlesque. She's had flowers sent to her by European royalty. She's dined with young men of quality and social position. She's above Tom.
(TOM *comes running in.*)

TOM (*disgusted*). They were running when I got there. Frankie wouldn't take the bet. McCarthy didn't get a call till the stretch. I thought we were going to save all this money. Then McCarthy won by *two* lengths.

JOE. What'd he pay, fifteen to one?

TOM. Better, but Frankie wouldn't take the bet.

NICK (*throwing a dish towel across the room*). Well, for the love of Mike.

JOE. Give me the money.

TOM (*giving back the money*). We would have had about a thousand five hundred dollars.

JOE (*bored, casually, inventing*). Go up to Schwabacher-Frey and get me the biggest Rand-McNally map of the nations of Europe they've got. On your way back stop at one of the pawn shops on Third Street, and buy me a good revolver and some cartridges.

TOM. She's up in her room crying, Joe.

JOE. Go get me those things.

NICK. What are you going to do study the map, and then go out and shoot somebody?

JOE. I want to read the names of some European towns and rivers and valleys and mountains.

NICK. What do you want with the revolver?

JOE. I want to study it. I'm interested in things. Here's twenty dollars, Tom. Now go get them things.

TOM. A big map of Europe. And a revolver.

JOE. Get a good one. Tell the man you don't know anything about firearms and you're trusting him not to fool you. Don't pay more than ten dollars.

TOM. Joe, you got something on your mind. Don't go fool with a revolver.

JOE. Be sure it's a good one.

TOM. Joe.

JOE (*irritated*). What, Tom?

TOM. Joe, what do you send me out for crazy things for all the time?

JOE (*angry*). They're not crazy, Tom. Now, get going.

TOM. What about Kitty, Joe?

JOE. Let her cry. It'll do her good.

TOM. If she comes in here while I'm gone, talk to her, will you, Joe? Tell her about me.

JOE. O.K. Get going. Don't load that gun. Just buy it and bring it here.

TOM (*going*). You won't catch me loading any gun.

JOE. Wait a minute. Take these toys away.

TOM. Where'll I take them?

JOE. Give them to some kid. (*Pause*) No. Take them up to Kitty. Toys stopped me from crying once. That's the reason I had you buy them. I wanted to see if I could find out *why* they stopped me from crying. I remember they seemed awfully stupid at the time.

TOM. Shall I, Joe? Take them up to Kitty? Do you think they'd stop *her* from crying?

JOE. They might. You get curious about the way they work and you forget whatever it is you're remembering that's making you cry. That's what they're for.

TOM. Yeah, Sure. The girl at the store asked me what I wanted with toys. I'll take them up to Kitty. (*Tragically*) She's like a little girl. (*He goes*).

WESLEY. Mr. Nick, can I play the piano again?

NICK. Sure. Practice all you like—until I tell you to stop.

WESLEY. You going to pay me for playing the piano?

NICK. Sure. I'll give you enough to get by on.

WESLEY (*amazed and delighted*). Get money for playing the piano? (*He goes to the piano and begins to play quietly.* HARRY *goes up on the little stage and listens to the music. After a while he begins a soft-shoe dance.*)

NICK. What were you crying about?

JOE. My mother.

NICK. What about her?

JOE. She was dead. I stopped crying when they gave me the toys. (NICK'S MOTHER, *a little old woman of sixty or so, dressed plainly in black, her face shining, comes in briskly, chattering loudly in Italian, gesturing.* NICK *is delighted to see her.*)

NICK'S MOTHER (*in Italian*). Everything all right, Nickie?

NICK (*in Italian*). Sure, Mamma. (NICK'S MOTHER *leaves as gaily and as noisily as she came, after half a minute of loud Italian family talk.*)

JOE. Who was that?

NICK (*to* JOE, *proudly and a little sadly*). My mother. (*Still looking at the swinging doors.*)

JOE. What'd she say?

NICK. Nothing. Just wanted to see me. (*Pause*) What do you want with that gun?

JOE. I study things, Nick. (*An old man who looks as if he might have been Kit Carson at one time walks in importantly, moves about, and finally stands at* JOE'S *table.*)

KIT CARSON. Murphy's the name. Just an old trapper. Mind if I sit down?

JOE. Be delighted. What'll you drink?

KIT CARSON (*sitting down*). Beer. Same as I've been drinking. And thanks.

JOE (*to* NICK). Glass of beer, Nick. (NICK *brings the beer to the table,* KIT CARSON *swallows it in one swig, wipes his big white mustache with the back of his right hand.*)

KIT CARSON (*moving in*). I don't suppose you ever fell in love with a midget weighing thirty-nine pounds?

JOE (*studying the man*). Can't say I have, but have another beer.

KIT CARSON (*intimately*). Thanks, thanks. Down in Gallup, twenty years ago. Fellow by the name of Rufus Jenkins came to town with six white horses and two black ones. Said he wanted a man to break the horses for him because his left leg was wood and he couldn't do it. Had a meeting at Parker's Mercantile Store and finally came to blows, me and Henry Walpal. Bashed his head with a brass cuspidor and ran away to Mexico, but he didn't die.

Couldn't speak a word. Took up with a cattle-breeder named Diego, educated in California. Spoke the language better than you and me. Said, Your job, Murph, is to feed them prize bulls. I said, Fine, what'll I feed them? He said, Hay, lettuce, salt, beer, and aspirin.

Came to blows two days later over an accordion he claimed I stole. I had *borrowed* it. During the fight I busted it over his head; ruined one of the finest accordions I ever saw. Grabbed a horse and rode back across the border. Texas. Got to talking with a fellow who looked honest. Turned out to be a Ranger who was looking for me.

JOE. Yeah. You were saying, a thirty-nine-pound midget.

KIT CARSON. Will I ever forget that lady? Will I ever get over that amazon of small proportions?

JOE. Will you?

KIT CARSON. If I live to be sixty.

JOE. Sixty? You look more than sixty now.

KIT CARSON. That's trouble showing in my face. Trouble and complications. I was fifty-eight three months ago.

JOE. That accounts for it, then. Go ahead, tell me more.

KIT CARSON. Told the Texas Ranger my name was Rothstein, mining engineer from Pennsylvania, looking for something worth while. Mentioned two places in Houston. Nearly lost an eye early one morning, going down the stairs. Ran into a six-footer with an iron claw where his right hand was supposed to be. Said, You broke up my home. Told him I was a stranger in Houston. The girls gathered at the top of the stairs to see a fight. Seven of them. Six feet and an iron claw. That's bad on the nerves. Kicked him in the mouth when he swung for my head with the claw. Would have lost an eye except for quick thinking. He rolled into the gutter and pulled a gun. Fired seven times. I was back upstairs. Left the place an hour later, dressed in silk and feathers, with a hat swung around over my face. Saw him standing on the corner, waiting. Said, Care for a wiggle? Said he didn't. I went on down the street and left town. I don't suppose you ever had to put a dress on to save your skin, did you?

JOE. No, and I never fell in love with a midget weighing thirty-nine pounds. Have another beer?

KIT CARSON. Thanks. (*Swallows glass of beer*) Ever try to herd cattle on a bicycle?

JOE. No. I never got around to that.

KIT CARSON. Left Houston with sixty cents in my pocket, gift of a girl named Lucinda. Walked fourteen miles in fourteen hours. Big house with barb-wire all around, and big dogs. One thing I never could get around. Walked past the gate, anyway, from hunger and thirst. Dogs jumped up and came for me. Walked right into them, growing older every second. Went up to the door and knocked. Big negress opened the door, closed it quick. Said, On your way, white trash.
Knocked again. Said, On your way. Again. On your way. Again. This time the old man himself opened the door, ninety, if he was a day. Sawed-off shotgun, too.
Said, I ain't looking for trouble, Father. I'm hungry and thirsty, name's Cavanaugh.
Took me in and made mint juleps for the two of us.
Said, Living here alone, Father?
Said, Drink and ask no questions. Maybe I am and maybe I ain't. You saw the lady. Draw your own con clusions.
I'd heard of that, but didn't wink out of tact. If I told you that old Southern gentleman was my grandfather, you wouldn't believe me, would you?

JOE. I might.

KIT CARSON. Well, it so happens he wasn't. Would have been romantic if he had been, though.

JOE. Where did you herd cattle on a bicycle?

KIT CARSON. Toledo, Ohio, 1918.

JOE. Toledo, Ohio? They don't herd cattle in Toledo.

KIT CARSON. They don't anymore. They did in 1918. One fellow did, leastaways. Bookkeeper named Sam Gold. Straight from the East Side, New York. Sombrero, lariats, Bull Durham, two head of cattle and two bicycles. Called his place The Gold Bar Ranch, two acres, just outside the city limits.

That was the year of the War, you'll remember.

JOE. Yeah, I remember, but how about herding them two cows on a bicycle? How'd you do it?

KIT CARSON. Easiest thing in the world. Rode no hands. Had to, otherwise couldn't lasso the cows. Worked for Sam Gold till the cows ran away. Bicycles scared them. They went into Toledo. Never saw hide nor hair of them again. Advertised in every paper, but never got them back. Broke his heart. Sold both bikes and returned to New York.

Took four aces from a deck of red cards and walked to town. Poker. Fellow in the game named Chuck Collins, liked to gamble. Told him with a smile I didn't suppose he'd care to bet a hundred dollars I wouldn't hold four aces the next hand. Called it. My cards were red on the blank side. The other cards were blue. Plumb forgot all about it. Showed him four aces. Ace of spades, ace of clubs, ace of diamonds, ace of hearts. I'll remember them four cards if I live to be sixty. Would have been killed on the spot except for the hurricane that year.

JOE. Hurricane?

KIT CARSON. You haven't forgotten the Toledo hurricane of 1918, have you?

JOE. No. There was no hurricane in Toledo in 1918, or any other year.

KIT CARSON. For the love of God, then what do you suppose that commotion was? And how come I came to in Chicago, dream-walking down State Street?

JOE. I guess they scared you.

KIT CARSON. No, that wasn't it. You go back to the papers of November 1918, and I think you'll find there was a hurricane in Toledo. I remember sitting on the roof of a two-story house, floating northwest.

JOE (*seriously*). Northwest?

KIT CARSON. Now, son, don't tell me *you* don't believe me, either?

JOE (*pause. Very seriously, energetically and sharply*). Of course I believe you. Living is an art. It's not bookkeeping. It takes a lot of rehearsing for a man to get to be himself.

KIT CARSON (*thoughtfully, smiling, and amazed*). You're the first man I've ever met who believes me.

JOE (*seriously*). Have another beer. (TOM *comes in with the Rand-McNally book, the revolver, and the box of cartridges.* KIT *goes to bar.*)

JOE (*to* TOM). Did you give her the toys?

TOM. Yeah, I gave them to her.

JOE. Did she stop crying?

TOM. No. She started crying harder than ever.

JOE. That's funny. I wonder why.

TOM. Joe, if I was a minute earlier, Frankie would have taken the bet and now we'd have about a thousand five hundred dollars. How much of it would you have given me, Joe?

JOE. If she'd marry you—*all* of it.

TOM. Would you, Joe?

JOE (*opening packages, examining book first, and revolver next*). Sure. In this realm there's only one subject, and you're it. It's my duty to see that my subject is happy.

TOM. Joe, do you think we'll ever have eighty dollars for a race sometime again when there's a fifteen-to-one shot that we like, weather good, track fast, they get off to a good start, our horse doesn't get a call till the stretch, we think we're going to lose all that money, and then it wins, by a nose?

JOE. I didn't quite get that.

TOM. You know what I mean.

JOE. You mean the impossible. No, Tom, we won't. We were just a little late, that's all.

TOM. We might, Joe.

JOE. It's not likely.

TOM. Then how am I ever going to make enough money to marry her?

JOE. I don't know, Tom. Maybe you aren't.

TOM. Joe, I got to marry Kitty. (*Shaking his head*) You ought to see the crazy room she lives in.

JOE. What kind of a room is it?

TOM. It's little. It crowds you in. It's bad, Joe. Kitty don't belong in a place like that.

JOE. You want to take her away from there?

TOM. Yeah. I want her to live in a house where there's room enough to live. Kitty ought to have a garden, or something.

JOE. You want to take care of her?

TOM. Yeah, sure, Joe. I ought to take care of somebody good that makes me feel like *I'm* somebody.

JOE. That means you'll have to get a job. What can you do?

TOM. I finished high school, but I don't know what I can do.

JOE. Sometimes when you think about it, what do you think you'd like to do?

TOM. Just sit around like you, Joe, and have somebody run errands for me and drink champagne and take things easy and never be broke and never worry about money.

JOE. That's a noble ambition.

NICK (*to* JOE). How do you do it?

JOE. I really don't know, but I think you've got to have the full co-operation of the Good Lord.

NICK. I can't understand the way you talk.

TOM. Joe, shall I go back and see if I can get her to stop crying?

JOE. Give me a hand and I'll go with you.

TOM (*amazed*). What! You're going to get up already?

JOE. She's crying, isn't she?

TOM. She's crying. Worse than ever now.

JOE. I thought the toys would stop her.

TOM. I've seen you sit in one place from four in the morning till two the next morning.

JOE. At my best, Tom, I don't travel by foot. That's all. Come on. Give me a hand. I'll find some way to stop her from crying.

TOM (*helping* JOE). Joe, I never did tell you. You're a different kind of a guy.

JOE (*swiftly, a little angry*). Don't be silly. I don't understand things. I'm trying to understand them.
(JOE *is a little drunk. They go out together. The lights go down slowly, while* WESLEY *plays the piano, and come up slowly on.*)

ACT THREE

A cheap bed in NICK'S *to indicate room 21 of The New York Hotel, upstairs, around the corner from* NICK'S. *The bed can be at the center of* NICK'S, *or up on the little stage. Everything in* NICK'S *is the same, except that all the people are silent, immobile and in darkness, except* WESLEY *who is playing the piano softly and sadly.* KITTY DUVAL, *in a dress she has carried around with her from the early days in Ohio, is seated on the bed, tying a ribbon in her hair. She looks at herself in a hand mirror. She is deeply grieved at the change she sees in herself. She takes off the ribbon, angry and hurt. She lifts a book from the bed and tries to read. She begins to sob again. She picks up an old picture of herself and looks at it. Sobs harder than ever, falling on the bed and burying her face. There is a knock, as if at the door.*

KITTY (*sobbing*). Who is it?

TOM'S VOICE. Kitty, it's me. Tom. Me and Joe.
(JOE, *followed by* TOM, *comes to the bed quietly.* JOE *is holding a rather large toy carousel.* JOE *studies* KITTY *a moment. He sets the toy carousel on the floor, at the foot of* KITTY'S *bed.*)

TOM (*standing over* KITTY *and bending down close to her*). Don't cry any more, Kitty.

KITTY (*not looking, sobbing*). I don't like this life.
(JOE *starts the carousel which makes a strange, sorrowful, tinkling music. The music begins slowly, becomes swift, gradually slows down, and ends.* JOE *himself is interested in the toy, watches and listens to it carefully.*)

TOM (*eagerly*). Kitty. Joe got up from his chair at Nick's just to get you a toy and come here. This one

makes music. We rode all over town in a cab to get it. Listen.
(KITTY *sits up slowly, listening, while* TOM *watches her. Everything happens slowly and somberly.* KITTY *notices the photograph of herself when she was a little girl. Lifts it, and looks at it again.*)

TOM (*looking*). Who's that little girl, Kitty?

KITTY. That's me. When I was seven.

TOM (*looking, smiling*). Gee, you're pretty, Kitty.
(JOE *reaches up for the photograph, which* TOM *hands to him.* TOM *returns to* KITTY *whom he finds as pretty now as she was at seven.* JOE *studies the photograph.* KITTY *looks up at* TOM. *There is no doubt that they really love one another.* JOE *looks up at them.*)

KITTY. Tom?

TOM (*eagerly*). Yeah, Kitty.

KITTY. Tom, when you were a little boy what did you want to be?

TOM (*a little bewildered, but eager to please her*). What, Kitty?

KITTY. Do you remember when you were a little boy?

TOM (*thoughtfully*). Yeah, I remember sometimes, Kitty.

KITTY. What did you want to be?

TOM (*looks at* JOE. JOE *holds* TOM'S *eyes a moment. Then* TOM *is able to speak*). Sometimes I wanted to be a locomotive engineer. Sometimes I wanted to be a policeman.

KITTY. I wanted to be a great actress. (*She looks up into* TOM'S *face*) Tom, didn't you ever want to be a doctor?

TOM (*looks at* JOE. JOE *holds* TOM'S *eyes again, encouraging* TOM *by his serious expression to go on talking*). Yeah, now I remember. Sure, Kitty. I wanted to be a doctor—once.

KITTY (*smiling sadly*). I'm so glad. Because I wanted to be an actress and have a young doctor come to the theater and see me and fall in love with me and send me flowers. (JOE *pantomimes to* TOM, *demanding that he go on talking.*)

TOM. I would do that, Kitty.

KITTY. I wouldn't know who it was, and then one day I'd see him in the street and fall in love with him. I wouldn't know *he* was the one who was in love with me. I'd think about him all the time. I'd dream about him. I'd dream of being near him the rest of my life. I'd dream of having children that looked like him. I wouldn't be an actress all the time. Only until I found him and fell in love with him. After that we'd take a train and go to beautiful cities and see the wonderful people everywhere and give money to the poor and whenever people were sick he'd go to them and make them well again. (TOM *looks at* JOE, *bewildered, confused, and full of sorrow.* KITTY *is deep in memory, almost in a trance.*)

JOE (*gently*). Talk to her, Tom. Be the wonderful young doctor she dreamed about and never found. Go ahead. Correct the errors of the world.

TOM. Joe. (*Pathetically*) I don't know what to say.
(*There is rowdy singing in the hall. A loud young* VOICE *sings: "Sailing, sailing, over the bounding main."*)

VOICE. Kitty. Oh, Kitty! (KITTY *stirs, shocked, coming out of the trance*) Where the hell are you? Oh, Kitty. (TOM *jumps up, furiously.*)

WOMAN'S VOICE (*in the hall*). Who are you looking for, Sailor Boy?

VOICE. The most beautiful lay in the world.

WOMAN'S VOICE. Don't go any further.

VOICE (*with impersonal contempt*). You? No. Not you. Kitty. You stink.

WOMAN'S VOICE (*rasping, angry*). Don't you dare talk to me that way. You pickpocket.

VOICE (*still impersonal, but louder*). Oh, I see. Want to get tough, hey? Close the door. Go hide.

WOMAN'S VOICE. You pickpocket. All of you. (*The door slams.*)

VOICE (*roaring with laughter which is very sad*). Oh—Kitty. Room 21. Where the hell is that room?

TOM (*to* JOE). Joe, I'll kill him.

KITTY (*fully herself again, terribly frightened*). Who is it?
(*She looks long and steadily at* TOM *and* JOE. TOM *is standing, excited and angry.* JOE *is completely at ease, his expression full of pity.* KITTY *buries her face in the bed.*)

JOE (*gently*). Tom. Just take him away.

VOICE. Here it is. Number 21. Three naturals. Heaven. My blue heaven. The west, a nest, and you. Just Molly and me. (*Tragically*) Ah, to hell with everything.
(*A young* SAILOR, *a good-looking boy of no more than twenty or so, who is only drunk and lonely, comes to the bed, singing sadly.*)

SAILOR. Hi-ya, Kitty. (*Pause*) Oh. Visitors. Sorry. A thousand apologies. (*To* KITTY) I'll come back later.

TOM (*taking him by the shoulders, furiously*). If you do, I'll kill you. (JOE *holds* TOM. TOM *pushes the frightened boy away.*)

JOE (*somberly*). Tom. You stay here with Kitty. I'm going down to Union Square to hire an automobile. I'll be back in a few minutes. We'll ride out to the ocean and watch the sun go down. Then we'll ride down the Great Highway to Half Moon Bay. We'll have supper down there, and you and Kitty can dance.

TOM (*stupefied, unable to express his amazement and gratitude*). Joe, you mean you're going to go on an errand for *me*? You mean you're not going to send me?

JOE. That's right. (*He gestures toward* KITTY, *indicating that* TOM *shall talk to her, protect the innocence in her which is in so much danger when* TOM *isn't near, which* TOM *loves so deeply.* JOE *leaves.* TOM *studies* KITTY, *his face becoming childlike and somber. He sets the carousel into motion, listens, watching* KITTY, *who lifts herself slowly, looking only at* TOM. TOM *lifts the turning carousel and moves it slowly toward* KITTY, *as though the toy were his heart. The piano music comes up loudly and the lights go down, while* HARRY *is heard dancing swiftly.*)

BLACKOUT

ACT FOUR

A little later.

WESLEY, *the colored boy, is at the piano.*

HARRY *is on the little stage, dancing.*

NICK *is behind the bar.*

The ARAB *is in his place.*

KIT CARSON *is asleep on his folded arms.*

The DRUNKARD *comes in. Goes to the telephone for the nickel that might be in the return-chute.* NICK *comes to take him out. He gestures for* NICK *to hold on a minute. Then produces a half dollar.* NICK *goes behind the bar to serve the* DRUNKARD *whiskey.*

THE DRUNKARD. To the old, God bless them. (*Another*) To the new, God love them. (*Another*) To—children and small animals, like little dogs that don't bite. (*Another. Loudly*) To reforestation. (*Searches for money. Finds some*) To—President Taft. (*He goes out. The telephone rings.*)

KIT CARSON (*jumping up, fighting*). Come on, *all* of you, if you're looking for trouble. I never asked for quarter and I always gave it.

NICK (*reproachfully*). Hey, Kit Carson.

DUDLEY (*on the phone*). Hello. Who? Nick? Yes. He's here. (*To* NICK) It's for you. I think it's important.

NICK (*going to the phone*). Important! *What's* important?

DUDLEY. He sounded like big-shot.

NICK. Big *what?* (*To* WESLEY *and* HARRY) Hey, you. Quiet. I want to hear this important stuff. (WESLEY *stops playing the piano.* HARRY *stops dancing.* KIT CARSON *comes close to* NICK.)

KIT CARSON. If there's anything I can do, name it. I'll do it for you. I'm fifty-eight years old; been through three wars; married four times; the father of countless children whose *names* I don't even know. I've got no money. I live from hand to mouth. But if there's anything I can do, name it. I'll do it.

NICK (*patiently*). Listen, Pop. For a moment, please sit down and go back to sleep—*for me.*

KIT CARSON. I can do that, too. (*He sits down, folds his arms, and puts his head into them. But not for long. As* NICK *begins to talk, he listens carefully, gets to his feet, and then begins to express in pantomime the moods of each of* NICK'S *remarks.*)

NICK (*on phone*). Yeah? (*Pause*) Who? Oh, I see. (*Listens*) Why don't you leave them alone? (*Listens*) The church-people? Well, to hell with the church-people. I'm a Catholic myself. (*Listens*) All right. I'll send them away. I'll tell them to lay low for a couple of days. Yeah, I know how it is. (NICK's *daughter* ANNA *comes in shyly, looking at her father, and stands unnoticed by the piano.*) What? (*Very angry*) Listen. I don't like that Blick. He was here this morning, and I told him not to come back. I'll keep the girls out of here. You keep Blick out of here. (*Listens*) I know his brother-in-law is important, but I don't want him to come down here. He looks for trouble everywhere, and he always finds it. I don't break any laws. I've got a dive in the lousiest part of town. Five years nobody's been robbed, murdered or gypped. I leave people alone. Your swanky joints uptown make trouble for you every night. (NICK *gestures to* WESLEY—*keeps listening on the phone—puts his hand over the mouthpiece. To* WESLEY *and* HARRY) Start playing again. My ears have got a headache. Go into your dance, son. (WESLEY *begins to play again.* HARRY *begins to dance.* NICK, *into mouthpiece*) Yeah. I'll keep them out. Just see that Blick doesn't come around and start something. (*Pause*) O.K. (*He hangs up.*)

KIT CARSON. Trouble coming?

NICK. That lousy Vice Squad again. It's that gorilla Blick.

KIT CARSON. Anybody at all. You can count on me. What kind of a gorilla is this gorilla Blick?

NICK. Very dignified. Toenails on his fingers.

ANNA (*to* KIT CARSON, *with great, warm, beautiful pride, pointing at* NICK). That's my father.

KIT CARSON (*leaping with amazement at the beautiful voice, the wondrous face, the magnificent event*). Well, bless your heart, child. Bless your lovely heart. I had a little daughter point me out in a crowd once.

NICK (*surprised*). Anna. What the hell are you doing here? Get back home where you belong and help Grandma cook me some supper. (ANNA *smiles at her father, understanding him, knowing that his words are words of love. She turns and goes, looking at him all the way out, as much as to say that she would cook for him the rest of her life.* NICK *stares at the swinging doors.* KIT CARSON *moves toward them, two or three steps.* ANNA *pushes open one of the doors and peeks in, to look at her father again. She waves to him. Turns and runs.* NICK *is very sad. He doesn't know what to do. He gets a glass and a bottle. Pours himself a drink. Swallows some. It isn't enough, so he pours more and swallows the whole drink. To himself*) My beautiful, beautiful baby. Anna, she is you again. (*He brings out a handkerchief, touches his eyes, and blows his nose.* KIT CARSON *moves close to* NICK, *watching* NICK's *face.* NICK *looks at him. Loudly, almost making* KIT *jump*) You're broke, aren't you?

KIT CARSON. Always. Always.

NICK. All right. Go into the kitchen and give Sam a hand. Eat some food and when you come back you can have a couple of beers.

KIT CARSON (*studying* NICK). Anything at all. I know a good man when I see one. (*He goes.* ELSIE MANDELSPIEGEL *comes into* NICK'S. *She is a beautiful, dark girl, with a sorrowful, wise, dreaming face, almost on the verge of tears, and full of pity. There is an aura of dream about her. She moves softly and gently, as if everything around her were unreal and pathetic.* DUDLEY *doesn't notice her for a moment or two. When he does finally see her, he is so amazed, he can barely move or speak. Her presence has the effect of changing him completely. He gets up from his chair, as if in a trance, and walks toward her, smiling sadly.*)

ELSIE (*looking at him*). Hello, Dudley.

DUDLEY (*broken-hearted*). Elsie.

ELSIE. I'm sorry. (*Explaining*) So many people are sick. Last night a little boy died. I love you, but— (*She gestures, trying to indicate how hopeless love is. They sit down.*)

DUDLEY (*staring at her, stunned and quieted*). Elsie. You'll never know how glad I am to see you. Just to see you. (*Pathetically*) I was afraid I'd never see you again. It was driving me crazy. I didn't want to live. Honest. (*He shakes his head mournfully, with dumb and beautiful affection.* TWO STREETWALKERS *come in, and pause near* DUDLEY, *at the bar*) I know. You told me before, but I can't help it, Elsie. I love you.

ELSIE (*quietly, somberly, gently, with great compassion*). I know you love me, and I love you, but don't you see love is impossible in this world?

DUDLEY. Maybe it isn't, Elsie.

ELSIE. Love is for birds. They have wings to fly away on when it's time for flying. For tigers in the jungle because they don't know their end. We know *our* end. Every night I watch over poor, dying men. I hear them breathing, crying, talking in their sleep. Crying for air and water and love, for mother and field and sunlight. We can never know love or greatness. We *should* know both.

DUDLEY (*deeply moved by her words*). Elsie, I love you.

ELSIE. You want to live. *I* want to live, too, but where? Where can we escape our poor world?

DUDLEY. Elsie, we'll find a place.

ELSIE (*smiling at him*). All right. We'll try again. We'll go together to a room in a cheap hotel, and dream that the world is beautiful, and that living is full of love and greatness. But in the morning, can we forget debts, and duties, and the cost of ridiculous things?

DUDLEY (*with blind faith*). Sure, we can, Elsie.

ELSIE. All right, Dudley. Of course. Come on. The time for the new pathetic war has come. Let's hurry, before they dress you, stand you in line, hand you a gun, and have you kill and be killed. (ELSIE *looks at him gently, and takes his hand.* DUDLEY *embraces her shyly, as if he might hurt her. They go, as if they were a couple of young animals. There is a moment of silence. One of the* STREETWALKERS *bursts out laughing.*)

KILLER. Nick, what the hell kind of a joint are you running?

NICK. Well, it's not out of the world. It's on a street in a city, and people come and go. They bring whatever they've got with them and they say what they must say.

THE OTHER STREETWALKER. It's floozies like her that raise hell with our racket.

NICK (*remembering*). Oh, yeah. Finnegan telephoned.

KILLER. That mouse in elephant's body?

THE OTHER STREETWALKER. What the hell does *he* want?

NICK. Spend your time at the movies for the next couple of days.

KILLER. They're all lousy. (*Mocking*) All about love.

NICK. Lousy or not lousy, for a couple of days the flat-foots are going to be romancing you, so stay out of here, and lay low.

KILLER. I always was a pushover for a man in uniform, with a badge, a club and a gun. (KRUPP *comes into the place. The girls put down their drinks.*)

NICK. O.K., get going. (*The* GIRLS *begin to leave and meet* KRUPP.)

THE OTHER STREETWALKER. We was just going.

KILLER. We was formerly models at Magnin's. (*They go.*)

KRUPP (*at the bar*). The strike isn't enough, so they've got to put us on the tails of the girls, too. I don't know. I wish to God I was back in the Sunset holding the hands of kids going home from school, where I belong. I don't like trouble. Give me a beer. (NICK *gives him a beer. He drinks some*) Right now, McCarthy, my best friend, is with sixty strikers who want to stop the finks who are going to try to unload the *Mary Luckenbach* tonight. Why the hell McCarthy ever became a longshoreman instead of a professor of some kind is something I'll never know.

NICK. Cowboys and Indians, cops and robbers, longshoremen and finks.

KRUPP. They're all guys who are trying to be happy; trying to make a living; support a family; bring up children; enjoy sleep. Go to a movie; take a drive on Sunday. They're all good guys, so out of nowhere comes trouble. All they want is a chance to get out of debt and relax in front of a radio while Amos and Andy go through their act. What the hell do they always want to make trouble for? I been thinking everything over, Nick, and you know what I think?

NICK. No. What?

KRUPP. I think we're all crazy. It came to me while I was on my way to Pier 27. All of a sudden it hit me like a ton of bricks. A thing like that never happened to me before. Here we are in this wonderful world, full of all the wonderful things—here we are—all of us, and look at us. Just look at us. We're crazy. We're nuts. We've got everything, but we always feel lousy and dissatisfied just the same.

NICK. Of course we're crazy. Even so, we've got to go on living together. (*He waves at the people in his joint.*)

KRUPP. There's no hope. I don't suppose it's right for an officer of the law to feel the way I feel, but, by God, right or not right, that's how I feel.

Why are we all so lousy? This is a good world. It's wonderful to get up in the morning and go out for a little walk and smell the trees and see the streets and the kids going to school and the clouds in the sky. It's wonderful just to be able to move around and whistle a song if you feel like it, or maybe try to sing one. This is a nice world. So why do they make all the trouble?

NICK. I don't know. Why?

KRUPP. We're crazy, that's why. We're no good any more. All the corruption everywhere. The poor kids selling themselves. A couple of years ago they were in grammar school. Everybody trying to get a lot of money in a hurry. Everybody betting the horses. Nobody going quietly for a little walk to the ocean. Nobody taking things easy and not wanting to make some kind of a killing. Nick, I'm going to quit being a cop. Let somebody else keep law and order. The stuff I hear about at headquarters. I'm thirty-seven years old, and I still can't get used to it. The only trouble is, the wife'll raise hell.

NICK. Ah, the wife.

KRUPP. She's a wonderful woman, Nick. We've got two of the swellest boys in the world. Twelve and seven years old. (*The* ARAB *gets up and moves closer to listen.*)

NICK. I didn't know that.

KRUPP. Sure. But what'll I do? I've wanted to quit for seven years. I wanted to quit the day they began putting me through the school. I didn't quit. What'll I do if I quit? Where's money going to be coming in from?

NICK. That's one of the reasons we're all crazy. We don't know where it's going to be coming in from, except from wherever it happens to be coming in from at the time, which we don't usually like.

KRUPP. Every once in a while I catch myself being mean, hating people just because they're down and out, broke and hungry, sick or drunk. And then when I'm with the stuffed shirts at headquarters, all of a sudden I'm nice to them, trying to make an impression. On who? People I don't like. And I feel disgusted. (*With finality*) I'm going to quit. That's all. Quit. Out. I'm going to give them back the uniform and the gadgets that go with it. I don't want any part of it. This is a good world. What do they want to make all the trouble for all the time?

ARAB (*quietly, gently, with great understanding*). No foundation. All the way down the line.

KRUPP. What?

ARAB. No foundation. No foundation.

KRUPP. I'll say there's no foundation.

ARAB. All the way down the line.

KRUPP (*to* NICK). Is that all he ever says?

NICK. That's all he's been saying *this* week.

KRUPP. What is he, anyway?

NICK. He's an Arab, or something like that.

KRUPP. No, I mean what's he do for a living?

NICK (*to* ARAB). What do you do for a living, brother?

ARAB. Work. Work all my life. All my life, work. From small boy to old man, work. In old country, work. In new country, work. In New York. Pittsburgh. Detroit. Chicago. Imperial Valley. San Francisco. Work. No beg. Work. For what? Nothing. Three boys in old country. Twenty years, not see. Lost. Dead. Who knows? What. What-not. No foundation. All the way down the line.

KRUPP. What'd he say last week?

NICK. Didn't say anything. Played the harmonica.

ARAB. Old country song, I play. (*He brings a harmonica from his back pocket.*)

KRUPP. Seems like a nice guy.

NICK. Nicest guy in the world.

KRUPP (*bitterly*). But crazy. Just like all the rest of us. Stark raving mad. (WESLEY *and* HARRY *long ago stopped playing and dancing. They sat at a table together and talked for a while; then began playing casino or rummy. When the* ARAB *begins his solo on the harmonica, they stop their game to listen.*)

WESLEY. You hear that?

HARRY. That's *something.*

WESLEY. That's crying. That's crying.

HARRY. I want to make people laugh.

WESLEY. That's deep, deep crying. That's crying a long time ago. That's crying a thousand years ago. Some place five thousand miles away.

HARRY. Do you think you can play to that?

WESLEY. I want to *sing* to that, but I can't *sing.*

HARRY. You try and play to that. I'll try to dance. (WESLEY *goes to the piano, and after closer listening, he begins to accompany the harmonica solo.* HARRY *goes to the little stage and after a few efforts begins to dance to the song. This keeps up quietly for some time.* KRUPP *and* NICK *have been silent, and deeply moved.*)

KRUPP (*softly*). Well, anyhow, Nick.

NICK. Hmmmmmmm?

KRUPP. What I said. Forget it.

NICK. Sure.

KRUPP. It gets me down once in a while.

NICK. No harm in talking.

KRUPP (*The* POLICEMAN *again, loudly*). Keep the girls out of here.

NICK (*Loud and friendly*). Take it easy. (*The music and dancing are now at their height.*)

CURTAIN

ACT FIVE

That evening. Fog-horns are heard throughout the scene. A man in evening clothes and a top hat, and his woman, also in evening clothes, are entering.

WILLIE *is still at the marble game.* NICK *is behind the bar.* JOE *is at his table, looking at the book of maps of the countries of Europe. The box containing the revolver and the box containing the cartridges are on the table, beside his glass. He is at peace, his hat tilted back on his head, a calm expression on his face.* TOM *is leaning against the bar, dreaming of love and* KITTY. *The* ARAB *is gone.* WESLEY *and* HARRY *are gone.* KIT CARSON *is watching the boy at the marble game.*

LADY. Oh, come on, please. (*The gentleman follows miserably. The* SOCIETY MAN *and* WIFE *take a table.* NICK *gives them a menu. Outside, in the street, the Salvation Army people are playing a song. Big drum, tambourines, cornet and singing. They are singing "The Blood of the Lamb." The music and words come into the place faintly and comically. This is followed by an old sinner testifying. It is the* DRUNKARD. *His words are not intelligible, but his message is unmistakable. He is saved. He wants to sin no more. And so on.*)

DRUNKARD (*testifying, unmistakably drunk*). Brothers and sisters. I was a sinner. I chewed tobacco and chased women. Oh, I sinned, brothers and sisters. And then I was saved. Saved by the Salvation Army, God forgive me.

JOE. Let's see now. Here's a city. Pribor. Czechoslovakia. Little, lovely, lonely Czechoslovakia. I wonder what kind of a place Pribor was? (*Calling*) Pribor! *Pribor!*
(TOM *leaps.*)

LADY. What's the matter with him?

MAN (*crossing his legs, as if he ought to go to the men's room*). Drunk.

TOM. Who you calling, Joe?

JOE. Pribor.

TOM. Who's Pribor?

JOE. He's a Czech. And a Slav. A Czechoslovakian.

LADY. How interesting.

MAN (*uncrosses legs*). He's drunk.

JOE. Tom, Pribor's a city in Czechoslovakia.

TOM. Oh. (*Pause*) You sure were nice to her, Joe.

JOE. Kitty Duval? She's one of the finest people in the world.

TOM. It sure was nice of you to hire an automobile and take us for a drive along the ocean front and down to Half Moon Bay.

JOE. Those three hours were the most delightful, the most somber, and the most beautiful I have ever known.

TOM. Why, Joe?

JOE. Why? I'm a student. (*Lifting his voice*) Tom. (*Quietly*) I'm a student. I study all things. All. All. And when my study reveals something of beauty in a place or in a person where by all rights only ugliness or death should be revealed, then I know how full of goodness this life is. And that's a good thing to know. That's a truth I shall always seek to verify.

LADY. Are you *sure* he's drunk?

MAN (*crossing his legs*). He's either drunk, or just naturally crazy.

TOM. Joe?

JOE. Yeah.

TOM. You won't get sore or anything?

JOE (*impatiently*). What is it, Tom?

TOM. Joe, where do you get all that money? You paid for the automobile. You paid for supper and the two bottles of champagne at the Half Moon Bay Restaurant. You moved Kitty out of the New York Hotel around the corner to the St. Francis Hotel on Powell Street. I saw you pay her rent. I saw you give her money for new clothes. Where do you get all that money, Joe? Three years now and I've never asked.

JOE (*looking at* TOM *sorrowfully, a little irritated, not so much with* TOM *as with the world and himself, his own superiority. He speaks clearly, slowly and solemnly*). Now don't be a fool, Tom. Listen carefully. If anybody's got any money—to hoard or to throw away—you can be sure he stole it from other people. Not from rich people who can spare it, but from poor people who can't. From their lives and from their dreams. I'm no exception. I *earned* the money I throw away. I stole it like everybody else does. I hurt people to get it. Loafing around this way, I *still* earn money. The money itself earns *more*. I *still* hurt people. I don't know who they are, or where they are. If I did, I'd feel worse than I do. I've got a Christian conscience in a world that's got no conscience at all. The world's trying to get some sort of a *social* conscience, but it's having a devil of a time trying to do *that*. I've got money. I'll always have money, as long as this world stays the way it is. I don't work. I don't make anything. (*He sips*) I drink. I worked when I was a kid. I worked *hard*. I mean hard, Tom. People are supposed to enjoy living. I got tired. (*He lifts the gun and looks at it while he talks*) I decided to get even on the world. Well, you can't enjoy living unless you work. Unless you do something. I don't do anything. I don't *want* to do anything any more. There isn't anything I can do that won't make me feel embarrassed. Because I can't do simple, good things. I haven't the patience. And I'm too smart. Money is the guiltiest thing in the world. It stinks. Now, don't ever bother me about it again.

TOM. I didn't mean to make you feel bad, Joe.

JOE (*Slowly*). Here. Take this gun out in the street and give it to some worthy hold-up man.

LADY. What's he saying?

MAN (*uncrosses legs*). You wanted to visit a honky-tonk. Well, *this* is a honky-tonk. (*To the world*) Married twenty-eight years and she's still looking for adventure.

TOM. How should I know who's a hold-up man?

JOE. Take it away. Give it to somebody.

TOM (*bewildered*). Do I *have* to *give* it to somebody?

JOE. Of course.

TOM. Can't I take it back and get some of our money?

JOE. Don't talk like a business man. Look around and find somebody who appears to be in need of a gun and give it to him. It's a good gun, isn't it?

TOM. The man said it was, but how can I tell who needs a gun?

JOE. Tom, you've seen good people who needed guns, haven't you?

TOM. I don't remember. Joe, I might give it to the wrong kind of guy. He might do something crazy.

JOE. All right. I'll find somebody myself. (TOM *rises*) Here's some money. Go get me this week's *Life, Liberty, Time,* and six or seven packages of chewing gum.

TOM (*swiftly, in order to remember each item*). *Life, Liberty, Time,* and six or seven packages of chewing gum?

JOE. That's right.

TOM. All that chewing gum? What kind?

JOE. Any kind. Mix 'em up. All kinds.

TOM. Licorice, too?

JOE. Licorice, by all means.

TOM. Juicy Fruit?

JOE. Juicy Fruit.

TOM. Tutti-frutti?

JOE. Is there such a gum?

TOM. I think so.

JOE. All right. Tutti-frutti, too. Get *all* the kinds. Get as many kinds as they're selling.

TOM. *Life, Liberty, Time,* and all the different kinds of gum. (*He begins to go.*)

JOE (*calling after him loudly*). Get some jelly beans too. All the different colors.

TOM. All right, Joe.

JOE. And the longest panatela cigar you can find. Six of them.

TOM. Panatela. I got it.

JOE. Give a news-kid a dollar.

TOM. O.K., Joe.

JOE. Give some old man a dollar.

TOM. O.K., Joe.

JOE. Give them Salvation Army people in the street a couple of dollars and ask them to sing that song that goes— (*He sings loudly*)

Let the lower lights be burning, send
a gleam across the wave.

TOM (*swiftly*).

Let the lower lights be burning, send
a gleam across the wave.

JOE. That's it. (*He goes on with the song, very loudly and religiously*)

Some poor, dying, struggling seaman,
you may rescue, you may save.

(*Halts.*)

TOM. O.K., Joe. I got it. *Life, Liberty, Time,* all the kinds of gum they're selling, jelly beans, six panatela cigars, a dollar for a news-kid, a dollar for an old man, two dollars for the Salvation Army. (*Going*)

Let the lower lights be burning, send
a gleam across the wave.

JOE. That's it.

LADY. He's absolutely insane.

MAN (*wearily crossing legs*). You asked me to take you to a honky-tonk, instead of to the Mark Hopkins. You're *here* in a honky-tonk. I can't help it if he's crazy. Do you want to go back to where people *aren't* crazy?

LADY. No, not just yet.

MAN. Well, all right then. Don't be telling me every minute that he's crazy.

LADY. You needn't be huffy about it. (MAN *refuses to answer, uncrosses legs. When* JOE *began to sing,* KIT CARSON *turned away from the marble game and listened. While the man and woman are arguing he comes over to* JOE'*s table.*)

KIT CARSON. Presbyterian?

JOE. I attended a Presbyterian Sunday School.

KIT CARSON. Fond of singing?

JOE. On occasion. Have a drink?

KIT CARSON. Thanks.

JOE. Get a glass and sit down. (KIT CARSON *gets a glass from* NICK, *returns to the table, sits down,* JOE *pours him a drink, they touch glasses just as the Salvation Army people begin to fulfill the request. They sip some champagne, and at the proper moment begin to sing the song together, sipping champagne, raising hell with the tune, swinging it, and so on. The* SOCIETY LADY *joins them, and is stopped by her* HUSBAND) Always was fond of that song. Used to sing it at the top of my voice. Never saved a seaman in my life.

KIT CARSON (*flirting with the* SOCIETY LADY *who loves it*). I saved a seaman once. Well, he wasn't exactly a seaman. He was a darky named Wellington. Heavy-set sort of a fellow. Nice personality, but no friends to speak of. Not until I came along, at any rate. In New Orleans. In the summer of the year 1899. No. Ninety-eight. I was a lot younger of course, and had no mustache, but was regarded by many people as a man of means.

JOE. Know anything about guns?

KIT CARSON (*flirting*). All there is to know. Didn't fight the Ojibways for nothing. Up there in the Lake Takalooca Country, in Michigan. (*Remembering*) Along about in 1881 or two. Fought 'em right up to the shore of the Lake. Made 'em swim for Canada. One fellow in particular, an Indian named Harry Daisy.

JOE (*opening the box containing the revolver*). What sort of a gun would you say this is? Any good?

KIT CARSON (*at sight of gun, leaping*). Yep. That looks like a pretty nice hunk of shooting iron. That's a six-shooter. Shot a man with a six-shooter once. Got him through the palm of his right hand. Lifted his arm to wave to a friend. Thought it was a bird. Fellow named, I believe, Carroway. Larrimore Carroway.

JOE. Know how to work one of these things? (*He offers* KIT CARSON *the revolver, which is old and enormous.*)

KIT CARSON (*laughing at the absurd question*). Know how to work it? Hand me that little gun, son, and I'll show you all about it. (JOE *hands* KIT *the revolver. Importantly*) Let's see now. This is probably a new kind of six-shooter. After my time. Haven't nicked an Indian in years. I believe this here place is supposed to move out. (*He fools around and gets the barrel out for loading*) That's it. There it is.

JOE. Look all right?

KIT CARSON. It's a good gun. You've got a good gun there, son. I'll explain it to you. You see these holes? Well, that's where you put the cartridges.

JOE (*taking some cartridges out of the box*). Here. Show me how it's done.

KIT CARSON (*a little impatiently*). Well, son, you take 'em one by one and put 'em in the holes, like this. There's one. Two. Three. Four. Five. Six. Then you get the barrel back in place. Then cock it. Then all you got to do is aim and fire. (*He points the gun at the* LADY *and* GENTLEMAN *who scream and stand up, scaring* KIT CARSON *into paralysis. The gun is loaded, but uncocked.*)

JOE. It's all set?

KIT CARSON. Ready to kill.

JOE. Let me hold it.
(KIT *hands* JOE *the gun. The* LADY *and* GENTLEMAN *watch, in terror.*)

KIT CARSON. Careful, now, son. Don't cock it. Many a man's lost an eye fooling with a loaded gun. Fellow I used to know named Danny Donovan lost a nose. Ruined his whole life. Hold it firm. Squeeze the trigger. Don't snap it. Spoils your aim.

JOE. Thanks. Let's see if I can unload it. (*He begins to unload it.*)

KIT CARSON. Of course you can.
(JOE *unloads the revolver, looks at it very closely, puts the cartridges back into the box.*)

JOE (*looking at gun*). I'm mighty grateful to you. Always wanted to see one of those things close up. Is it really a good one?

KIT CARSON. It's a beaut, son.

JOE (*aims the empty gun at a bottle on the bar*). Bang!

WILLIE (*at the marble game, as the machine groans*). Oh, Boy! (*Loudly, triumphantly*) There you are, Nick. Thought I couldn't do it, hey? Now, watch. (*The machine begins to make a special kind of noise. Lights go on and off. Some red, some green. A bell rings loudly six times*) One. Two. Three. Four. Five. Six. (*An American flag jumps up.* WILLIE *comes to attention. Salutes*) Oh, boy, what a beautiful country. (*A loud music-box version of the song "America."* JOE, KIT, *and the* LADY *get to their feet. Singing. "My country, 'tis of thee, sweet land of liberty, of thee I sing." Everything quiets down. The flag goes back into the machine.* WILLIE *is thrilled, amazed, delighted.* EVERYBODY *has watched the performance of the defeated machine from wherever he happened to be when the performance began.* WILLIE, *looking around at everybody, as if they had all been on the side of the machine*) O.K. How's that? I knew I could do it. (*To* NICK) Six nickels. (NICK *hands him six nickels.* WILLIE *goes over to* JOE *and* KIT) Took me a little while, but I finally did it. It's scientific, really. With a little skill a man can make a modest living beating the marble games. Not that that's what I want to do. I just don't like the idea of anything getting the best of me. A machine or anything else. Myself, I'm the kind of a guy who makes up his mind to do something, and then goes to work and does it. There's no other way a man can be a success at anything. (*Indicating the letter "F" on his sweater*) See that letter? That don't stand for some little-bitty high school somewhere. That stands for *me*. Faroughli. Willie Faroughli. I'm an Assyrian. We've got a civilization six or seven centuries old, I think. Somewhere along in there. Ever hear of Osman? Harold Osman? He's an Assyrian, too. He's got an orchestra down in Fresno. (*He goes to the* LADY *and* GENTLEMAN) I've never seen you before in my life, but I can tell from the clothes you wear and the company you keep (*Graciously indicating the* LADY) that you're a man who looks every problem straight in the eye, and then goes to work and *solves* it. I'm that way myself. Well. (*He smiles beautifully, takes the* GENTLEMAN'S *hand furiously*) It's been wonderful talking to a nicer type of people for a change. Well. I'll be seeing you. So long. (*He turns, takes two steps, returns to the table. Very politely and seriously*) Good-by, lady. You've got a good man there. Take good care of him. (WILLIE *goes, saluting* JOE *and the world.*)

KIT CARSON (*to* JOE). By God, for a while there I didn't think that young Assyrian was going to do it. That fellow's got something.

(TOM *comes back with the magazines and other stuff.*)

JOE. Get it all?

TOM. Yeah. I had a little trouble finding the jelly beans.

JOE. Let's take a look at them.

TOM. These are the jelly beans.

(JOE *puts his hand into the cellophane bag and takes out a handful of the jelly beans, looks at them, smiles, and tosses a couple into his mouth.*)

JOE. Same as ever. Have some. (*He offers the bag to* KIT.)

KIT CARSON (*flirting*). Thanks! I remember the first time I ever ate jelly beans. I was six, or at the most seven. Must have been in (*Slowly*) eighteen—seventy-seven. Seven or eight. Baltimore.

JOE. Have some, Tom.

(TOM *takes some.*)

TOM. Thanks, Joe.

JOE. Let's have some of that chewing gum. (*He dumps all the packages of gum out of the bag onto the table.*)

KIT CARSON (*flirting*). Me and a boy named Clark. Quinton Clark. Became a Senator.

JOE. Yeah. Tutti-frutti, all right. (*He opens a package and folds all five pieces into his mouth*) Always wanted to see how many I could chew at one time. Tell you what, Tom. I'll bet I can chew more at one time than you can.

TOM (*delighted*). All right. (*They both begin to fold gum into their mouths.*)

KIT CARSON. I'll referee. Now, one at a time. How many you got?

JOE. Six.

KIT CARSON. All right. Let Tom catch up with you.

JOE (*while* TOM'S *catching up*). Did you give a dollar to a news-kid?

TOM. Yeah, sure.

JOE. What'd he say?

TOM. Thanks.

JOE. What sort of a kid was he?

TOM. Little, dark kid. I guess he's Italian.

JOE. Did he seem pleased?

TOM. Yeah.

JOE. That's good. Did you give a dollar to an old man?

TOM. Yeah.

JOE. Was he pleased?

TOM. Yeah.

JOE. Good. How many you got in your mouth?

TOM. Six.

JOE. All right. I got six, too. (*Folds one more in his mouth.* TOM *folds one too.*)

KIT CARSON. Seven. Seven each. (*They each fold one more into their mouths, very solemnly, chewing them into the main hunk of gum*) Eight. Nine. Ten.

JOE (*delighted*). Always wanted to do this. (*He picks up one of the magazines*) Let's see what's going on in the world. (*He turns the pages and keeps folding gum into his mouth and chewing.*)

KIT CARSON. Eleven. Twelve. (KIT *continues to count while* JOE *and* TOM *continue the contest. In spite of what they are doing, each is very serious.*)

TOM. Joe, what'd you want to move Kitty into the St. Francis Hotel for?

JOE. She's a better woman than any of them tramp society dames that hang around that lobby.

TOM. Yeah, but do you think she'll feel at home up there?

JOE. Maybe not at first, but after a couple of days she'll be all right. A nice big room. A bed for sleeping in. Good clothes. Good food. She'll be all right, Tom.

TOM. I hope so. Don't you think she'll get lonely up there with nobody to talk to?

JOE (*looking at* TOM *sharply, almost with admiration, pleased but severe*). There's nobody *anywhere* for *her* to talk to—except *you.*

TOM (*amazed and delighted*). *Me,* Joe?

JOE (*while* TOM *and* KIT CARSON *listen carefully,* KIT *with great appreciation*). Yes, you. By the grace of God, you're the other half of that girl. Not the angry woman that swaggers into this waterfront dive and shouts because the world has kicked her around. *Anybody* can have *her.* You belong to the little kid in Ohio who once dreamed of living. Not with her carcass, for *money,* so she can have food and clothes, and pay rent. With *all* of her. I put her in that hotel, so she can have a chance to gather herself together again. She can't do that in the New York Hotel. You saw what happens there. There's nobody anywhere for her to talk to, except you. They all make her talk like a whore. After a while, she'll *believe* them. Then she won't be able to remember. She'll get lonely. Sure. People can get lonely for *misery,* even. I want her to go on being lonely for *you,* so she can come together again the way she was meant to be from the beginning. Loneliness is good for people. Right now it's the only thing for Kitty. Any more licorice?

TOM (*dazed*). What? Licorice? (*Looking around busily*) I guess we've chewed all the licorice in. We still got Clove, Peppermint, Doublemint, Beechnut, Teaberry, and Juicy Fruit.

JOE. Licorice used to be my favorite. Don't worry about her, Tom, she'll be all right. You really want to marry her, don't you?

TOM (*nodding*). Honest to God, Joe. (*Pathetically*) Only, I haven't got any money.

JOE. Couldn't you be a prize-fighter or something like that?

TOM. Naaaah. I couldn't hit a man if I wasn't sore at him. He'd have to do something that made me hate him.

JOE. You've got to figure out something to do that you won't mind doing very much.

TOM. I wish I could, Joe.

JOE (*thinking deeply, suddenly*). Tom, would you be embarrassed driving a truck?

TOM (*hit by a thunderbolt*). Joe, I never thought of that. I'd like that. Travel. Highways. Little towns. Coffee and hot cakes. Beautiful valleys and mountains and streams and trees and daybreak and sunset.

JOE. There *is* poetry in it, at that.

TOM. Joe, that's just the kind of work I *should* do. Just sit there and travel, and look, and smile, and bust out laughing. Could Kitty go with me, sometimes?

JOE. I don't know. Get me the phone book. Can you drive a truck?

TOM. Joe, you know I can drive a truck, or any kind of thing with a motor and wheels. (TOM *takes* JOE *the phone book.* JOE *turns the pages.*)

JOE (*looking*). Here! Here it is. Tuxedo 7900. Here's a nickel. Get me that number.
(TOM *goes to telephone, dials the number.*)

TOM. Hello.

JOE. Ask for Mr. Keith.

TOM (*mouth and language full of gum*). I'd like to talk to Mr. Keith. (*Pause*) Mr. Keith.

JOE. Take that gum out of your mouth for a minute.
(TOM *removes the gum.*)

TOM. Mr. Keith. Yeah. That's right. Hello, Mr. Keith?

JOE. Tell him to hold the line.

TOM. Hold the line, please.

JOE. Give me a hand, Tom. (TOM *helps* JOE *to the telephone. At phone, wad of gum in fingers delicately*) Keith? Joe. Yeah. Fine. Forget it. (*Pause*) Have you got a place for a good driver? (*Pause*) I don't think so. (*To* TOM) You haven't got a driver's license, have you?

TOM (*worried*). No. But I can get one, Joe.

JOE (*at phone*). No, but he can get one easy enough. To hell with the union. He'll join later. All right, call him a Vice-President and say he drives for relaxation. Sure. What do you mean? Tonight? I don't know why not. San Diego? All right, let him start driving without a license. What the hell's the difference? Yeah. Sure. Look him over. Yeah. I'll send him right over. Right. (*He hangs up*) Thanks. (*To telephone.*)

TOM. Am I going to get the job?

JOE. He wants to take a look at you.

TOM. Do I look all right, Joe?

JOE (*looking at him carefully*). Hold up your head. Stick out your chest. How do you feel?
(TOM *does these things.*)

TOM. Fine.

JOE. You *look* fine, too. (JOE *takes his wad of gum out of his mouth and wraps Liberty magazine around it.*)

JOE. You win, Tom. Now, look. (*He bites off the tip of a very long panatela cigar, lights it, and hands one to* TOM, *and another to* KIT) Have yourselves a pleasant smoke. Here. (*He hands two more to* TOM) Give those slummers one each. (*He indicates the* SOCIETY LADY *and* GENTLEMAN. TOM *goes over and without a word gives a cigar each to the* MAN *and the* LADY. *The* MAN *is offended; he smells and tosses aside his cigar. The* WOMAN *looks at her cigar a moment, then puts the cigar in her mouth.*)

MAN. What do you think you're doing?

LADY. Really, dear. I'd like to.

MAN. Oh, this is too much.

LADY. I'd *really*, really like to, dear. (*She laughs, puts the cigar in her mouth. Turns to* KIT. *He spits out tip. She does the same.*)

MAN (*loudly*). The mother of five grown men, and she's still looking for *romance.* (*Shouts as* KIT *lights her cigar*) No. I forbid it.

JOE (*shouting*). What's the matter with you? Why don't you leave her alone? What are you always pushing your women around for? (*Almost without a pause*) Now, look, Tom. (*The* LADY *puts the lighted cigar in her mouth, and begins to smoke, feeling wonderful*) Here's ten bucks.

TOM. Ten bucks?

JOE. He may want you to get into a truck and begin driving to San Diego tonight.

TOM. Joe, I got to tell Kitty.

JOE. I'll tell her.

TOM. Joe, take care of her.

JOE. She'll be all right. Stop worrying about her. She's at the St. Francis Hotel. Now, look. Take a cab to Townsend and Fourth. You'll see the big sign. Keith Motor Transport Company. He'll be waiting for you.

TOM. O.K., Joe. (*Trying hard*) Thanks, Joe.

JOE. Don't be silly. Get going.
(TOM *goes.* LADY *starts puffing on cigar. As* TOM *goes,* WESLEY *and* HARRY *come in together.*)

NICK. Where the hell have you been? We've got to have some entertainment around here. Can't you see them fine people from uptown? (*He points at the* SOCIETY LADY *and* GENTLEMAN.)

WESLEY. You said to come back at ten for the second show.

NICK. Did I say that?

WESLEY. Yes, sir, Mr. Nick, that's exactly what you said.

HARRY. Was the first show all right?

NICK. That wasn't a show. There was no one here to see it. How can it be a show when no one sees it? People are afraid to come down to the waterfront.

HARRY. Yeah. We were just down to Pier 27. One of the longshoremen and a cop had a fight and the cop hit him over the head with a blackjack. We saw it happen, didn't we?

WESLEY. Yes, sir, we was standing there looking when it happened.

NICK (*a little worried*). Anything else happen?

WESLEY. They was all talking.

HARRY. A man in a big car came up and said there was going to be a meeting right away and they hoped to satisfy everybody and stop the strike.

WESLEY. Right away. *Tonight.*

NICK. Well, it's about time. Them poor cops are liable to get nervous and —shoot somebody. (*To* HARRY, *suddenly*) Come back here. I want you to tend bar for a while. I'm going to take a walk over to the pier.

HARRY. Yes, sir.

NICK (*to the* SOCIETY LADY *and* GENTLEMAN). You society people made up your minds yet?

LADY. Have you champagne?

NICK (*indicating* JOE). What do you think he's pouring out of that bottle, water or something?

LADY. Have you a chill bottle?

NICK. I've got a dozen of them chilled. He's been drinking champagne here all day and all night for a month now.

LADY. May we have a bottle?

NICK. It's six dollars.

LADY. I think we can manage.

MAN. I don't know. I *know* I don't know.
(NICK *takes off his coat and helps* HARRY *into it.* HARRY *takes a bottle of champagne and two glasses to the* LADY *and* GENTLEMAN, *dancing, collects six dollars, and goes back behind the bar, dancing.* NICK *gets his coat and hat.*)

NICK (*to* WESLEY). Rattle the keys a little, son. Rattle the keys.

WESLEY. Yes, sir, Mr. Nick.
(NICK *is on his way out. The* ARAB *enters.*)

NICK. Hi-ya, *Mahmed.*

ARAB. No foundation.

NICK. All the way down the line.
(*He goes.* WESLEY *is at the piano, playing quietly. The* ARAB *swallows a glass of beer, takes out his harmonica, and begins to play.* WESLEY *fits his playing to the Arab's.* KITTY DUVAL, *strangely beautiful, in new clothes, comes in. She walks shyly, as if she were embarrassed by the fine clothes, as if she had no right to wear them. The* LADY *and* GENTLEMAN *are very impressed.* HARRY *looks at her with amazement.* JOE *is reading Time magazine.* KITTY *goes to his table.* JOE *looks up from the magazine, without the least amazement.*)

JOE. Hello, Kitty.

KITTY. Hello, Joe.

JOE. It's nice seeing you again.

KITTY. I came in a cab.

JOE. You been crying again? (KITTY *can't answer. To* HARRY) Bring a glass. (HARRY *comes over with a glass.* JOE *pours* KITTY *a drink.*)

KITTY. I've got to talk to you.

JOE. Have a drink.

KITTY. I've never been in burlesque We were just poor.

JOE. Sit down, Kitty.

KITTY (*sits down*). I tried other things.

JOE. Here's to you, Katerina Koranovsky. Here's to you. And Tom.

KITTY (*sorrowfully*). Where *is* Tom?

JOE. He's getting a job tonight driving a truck. He'll be back in a couple of days.

KITTY (*sadly*). I told him I'd marry him.

JOE. He wanted to see you and say good-by.

KITTY. He's too good for me. He's like a little boy. (*Wearily*) I'm— Too many things have happened to me.

JOE. Kitty Duval, you're one of the few truly innocent people I have ever known. He'll be back in a couple of days. Go back to the hotel and wait for him.

KITTY. That's what I mean. I can't stand being alone. I'm no good. I tried very hard. I don't know what it is. I miss— (*She gestures.*)

JOE (*gently*). Do you really want to come back here, Kitty?

KITTY. I don't know. I'm not sure. Everything *smells* different. I don't know how to feel, or what to think. (*Gesturing pathetically*) I know I don't belong there. It's what I've wanted all my life, but it's too *late*. I try to be happy about it, but all I can do is remember everything and cry.

JOE. I don't know what to tell you, Kitty. I didn't mean to hurt you.

KITTY. You haven't hurt me. You're the only person who's ever been good to me. I've never known anybody like you. I'm not sure about love any more, but I know I love you, and I know I love Tom.

JOE. I love you too, Kitty Duval.

KITTY. He'll want babies. I know he will. I know *I* will, too. Of course I will. I can't— (*She shakes her head.*)

JOE. Tom's a baby himself. You'll be very happy together. He wants you to ride with him in the truck. Tom's good for you. You're good for Tom.

KITTY (*like a child*). Do you want me to go back and wait for him?

JOE. I can't *tell* you what to do. I think it would be a good idea, though.

KITTY. I wish I could tell you how it makes me feel to be alone. It's almost worse.

JOE. It might take a whole week, Kitty. (*He looks at her sharply, at the arrival of an idea*) Didn't you speak of reading a book? A book of poems?

KITTY. I didn't know what I was saying.

JOE (*trying to get up*). Of course you knew. I think you'll like poetry. Wait here a minute, Kitty. I'll go see if I can find some books.

KITTY. All right, Joe.
(*He walks out of the place, trying very hard not to wobble. Fog-horn. Music. The* NEWSBOY *comes in. Looks for* JOE. *Is broken-hearted because* JOE *is gone.*)

NEWSBOY (*to* SOCIETY GENTLEMAN). Paper?

MAN (*angry*). No.
(*The* NEWSBOY *goes to the* ARAB.)

NEWSBOY. Paper, Mister?

ARAB (*irritated*). No foundation.

NEWSBOY. What?

ARAB (*very angry*). No foundation.
(*The* NEWSBOY *starts out, turns, looks at the* ARAB, *shakes head.*)

NEWSBOY. No foundation? How do you figure?
(BLICK *and* TWO COPS *enter.*)

NEWSBOY (*to* BLICK). Paper, Mister?
(BLICK *pushes him aside. The* NEWSBOY *goes.*)

BLICK (*walking authoritatively about the place, to* HARRY). Where's Nick?

HARRY. He went for a walk.

BLICK. Who are you?

HARRY. Harry.

BLICK (*to the* ARAB *and* WESLEY). Hey, you. Shut up.
(*The* ARAB *stops playing the harmonica,* WESLEY *the piano.*)

BLICK (*studies* KITTY). What's your name, sister?

KITTY (*looking at him*). Kitty Duval. What's it to you? (KITTY'S *voice is now like it was at the beginning of the play: tough, independent, bitter and hard.*)

BLICK (*angry*). Don't give me any of your gutter lip. Just answer my questions.

KITTY. You go to hell, you.

BLICK (*coming over, enraged*). Where do you live?

KITTY. The New York Hotel. Room 21.

BLICK. Where do you work?

KITTY. I'm not working just now. I'm looking for work.

BLICK. What kind of work? (KITTY *can't answer*) What kind of work? (KITTY *can't answer. Furiously*) WHAT KIND OF WORK?
(KIT CARSON *comes over.*)

KIT CARSON. You can't talk to a lady that way in *my* presence.
(BLICK *turns and stares at* KIT. *The* COPS *begin to move from the bar.*)

BLICK (*to the* COPS). It's all right, boys. I'll take care of this. (*To* KIT) *What'd you say?*

KIT CARSON. You got no right to hurt people. Who are you?
(BLICK, *without a word, takes* KIT *to the street. Sounds of a blow and a groan.* BLICK *returns, breathing hard.*)

BLICK (*to the* COPS). O.K., boys. You can go now. Take care of him. Put him on his feet and tell him to behave himself from now on. (*To* KITTY *again*) Now answer my question. What kind of work?

KITTY (*quietly*). I'm a whore you son of a bitch. You know what kind of work I do. And I know what kind you do.

MAN (*shocked and really hurt.*) Excuse me, officer, but it seems to me that your attitude—

BLICK. Shut up.

MAN (*quietly*). —is making the poor child say things that are not true.

BLICK. Shut up, I said.

LADY. Well. (*To the* MAN) Are you going to stand for such insolence?

BLICK (*to* MAN, *who is standing*). Are you?

MAN (*taking the* WOMAN'S *arm*). I'll get a divorce. I'll start life all over again. (*Pushing the* WOMAN) Come on. Get the hell out of here! (*The* MAN *hurries his* WOMAN *out of the place,* BLICK *watching them go.*)

BLICK (*to* KITTY). Now. Let's begin again, and see that you tell the truth. What's your name?

KITTY. Kitty Duval.

BLICK. Where do you live?

KITTY. Until this evening I lived at the New York Hotel. Room 21. This evening I moved to the St. Francis Hotel.

BLICK. Oh. To the St. Francis Hotel. Nice place. Where do you work?

KITTY. I'm looking for work.

BLICK. What kind of work do you do?

KITTY. I'm an actress.

BLICK. I see. What movies have I seen you in?

KITTY. I've worked in burlesque.

BLICK. You're a liar.
(WESLEY *stands, worried and full of dumb resentment.*)

KITTY (*pathetically, as at the beginning of the play*). It's the truth.

BLICK. What are you doing here?

KITTY. I came to see if I could get a job here.

BLICK. Doing what?

KITTY. Singing—and—dancing.

BLICK. You can't sing or dance. What are you lying for?

KITTY. I can. I sang and danced in burlesque all over the country.

BLICK. You're a liar.

KITTY. I said lines, too.

BLICK. So you danced in burlesque?

KITTY. Yes.

BLICK. All right. Let's see what you did.

KITTY. I can't. There's no music, and I haven't got the right clothes.

BLICK. There's music. (*To* WESLEY) Put a nickel in that phonograph. (WESLEY *can't move*) Come on. Put a nickel in that phonograph. (WESLEY *does so. To* KITTY) All right. Get up on that stage and do a hot little burlesque number. (KITTY *stands. Walks slowly to the stage, but is unable to move.* JOE *comes in, holding three books*) Get going, now. Let's see you dance the way you did in burlesque, all over the country. (KITTY *tries to do a burlesque dance. It is beautiful in a tragic way.*)

BLICK. All right, start taking them off!
(KITTY *removes her hat and starts to remove her jacket.* JOE *moves closer to the stage, amazed.*)

JOE (*hurrying to* KITTY). Get down from there. (*He takes* KITTY *into his arms. She is crying. To* BLICK) What the hell do you think you're doing?

WESLEY (*like a little boy, very angry*). It's that man, Blick. *He* made her take off her clothes. He beat up the old man, too.
(BLICK *pushes* WESLEY *off, as* TOM *enters.* BLICK *begins beating up* WESLEY.)

TOM. What's the matter, Joe? What's happened?

JOE. Is the truck out there?

TOM. Yeah, but what's happened? Kitty's crying again!

JOE. You driving to San Diego?

TOM. Yeah, Joe. But what's he doing to that poor colored boy?

JOE. Get going. Here's some money. Everything's O.K. (*To* KITTY) Dress in the truck. Take these books.

WESLEY'S VOICE. You can't hurt me. You'll get yours. You wait and see.

TOM. Joe, he's hurting that boy. I'll kill him!

JOE (*pushing* TOM). Get out of here! Get married in San Diego. I'll see you when you get back. (TOM *and* KITTY *go.* NICK *enters and stands at the lower end of bar.* JOE *takes the revolver out of his pocket. Looks at it*) I've always wanted to kill somebody, but I never knew who it should be. (*He cocks the revolver, stands real straight, holds it in front of him firmly and walks to the door. He stands a moment watching* BLICK, *aims very carefully, and pulls trigger. There is no shot.* NICK *runs over and grabs the gun, and takes* JOE *aside.*)

NICK. What the hell do you think you're doing?

JOE (*casually, but angry*). That dumb Tom. Buys a six-shooter that won't even shoot once. (JOE *sits down, dead to the world.* BLICK *comes out, panting for breath.* NICK *looks at him. He speaks slowly.*)

NICK. Blick! I told you to stay out of here! Now get out of here. (*He takes* BLICK *by the collar, tightening his grip as he speaks, and pushing him out*) If you come back again, I'm going to take you in that room where you've been beating up that colored boy, and I'm going to murder you—slowly—with my hands. Beat it! (*He pushes* BLICK *out. To* HARRY) Go take care of the colored boy.
(HARRY *runs out.* WILLIE *returns and doesn't sense that anything is changed.* WILLIE *puts another nickel into the machine, but he does so very violently. The consequence of this violence is that the flag comes up again.* WILLIE, *amazed, stands at attention and salutes. The flag goes down. He shakes his head.*)

WILLIE (*thoughtfully*). As far as I'm concerned, this is the *only* country in the world. If you ask me, *nuts* to Europe! (*He is about to push the slide in again when the flag comes up again. Furiously, to* NICK, *while he salutes and stands at attention, pleadingly*) Hey, Nick. This machine is out of order.

NICK (*somberly*). Give it a whack on the side.
(WILLIE *does so. A hell of a whack. The result is the flag comes up and down, and* WILLIE *keeps saluting.*)

WILLIE (*saluting*). Hey, Nick. Something's wrong. (*The machine quiets down abruptly.* WILLIE *very stealthily slides a new nickel in, and starts a new game. From a distance two pistol shots are heard, each carefully timed.* NICK *runs out. The* NEWSBOY *enters, crosses to* JOE'S *table, senses something is wrong.*)

NEWSBOY (*softly*). Paper, Mister? (JOE *can't hear him. The* NEWSBOY *backs away, studies* JOE, *wishes he could cheer* JOE *up. Notices the phonograph, goes to it, and puts a coin in it, hoping music will make* JOE *happier. The* NEWSBOY *sits down. Watches* JOE. *The music begins. "The Missouri Waltz." The* DRUNKARD *comes in and walks around. Then sits down.* NICK *comes back.*)

NICK (*delighted*). Joe, Blick's dead! Somebody just shot him, and none of the cops are trying to find out who. (JOE *doesn't hear.* NICK *steps back, studying* JOE. *Shouting*) Joe.

JOE (*looking up*). What?

NICK. Blick's dead.

JOE. Blick? Dead? Good! That God-damn gun wouldn't go off. I *told* Tom to get a good one.

NICK (*picking up gun and looking at it*). Joe, you wanted to kill that guy!
(HARRY *returns.* JOE *puts the gun in his coat pocket*) I'm going to buy you a bottle of champagne. (NICK *goes to bar.* JOE *rises, takes hat from rack, puts coat on. The* NEWSBOY *jumps up, helps* JOE *with coat.*)

NICK. What's the matter, Joe?

JOE. Nothing. Nothing.

NICK. How about the champagne?

JOE. Thanks. (*Going.*)

NICK. It's not eleven yet. Where you going, Joe?

JOE. I don't know. Nowhere.

NICK. Will I see you tomorrow?

JOE. I don't know. I don't think so. (KIT CARSON *enters, walks to* JOE. JOE *and* KIT *look at one another knowingly.*)

JOE. Somebody just shot a man. How are you feeling?

KIT. Never felt better in my life. (*Loudly, bragging, but somber*) I shot a man once. In San Francisco. Shot him two times. In 1939, I think it was. In October. Fellow named Blick or Glick or something like that. Couldn't stand the way he talked to ladies. Went up to my room and got my old pearl-handled revolver and waited for him on Pacific Street. Saw him walking, and let him have it, two times. Had to throw the beautiful revolver into the Bay. (HARRY, NICK, *the* ARAB *and the* DRUNKARD *close in around him.* JOE *searches his pockets, brings out the revolver, puts it in* KIT*'s hand, looks at him with great admiration and affection.* JOE *walks slowly to the stairs leading to the street, turns and waves.* KIT, *and then one by one everybody else, waves, and the marble game goes into its beautiful American routine again: flag, lights, and music. The play ends.*)

CURTAIN

Life with Father

BY HOWARD LINDSAY AND
RUSSEL CROUSE

TO

OSCAR SERLIN
WHO STARTED AS OUR PRODUCER AND
REMAINS OUR FRIEND

Life with Father was produced at the Empire Theatre, New York City, by Oscar Serlin, on November 8, 1939. Following is the original cast:

ANNIE	Katherine Bard
VINNIE	Dorothy Stickney
CLARENCE	John Drew Devereaux
JOHN	Richard Simon
WHITNEY	Raymond Roe
HARLAN	Larry Robinson
FATHER	Howard Lindsay
MARGARET	Dorothy Bernard
CORA	Ruth Hammond
MARY	Teresa Wright
THE REVEREND DR. LLOYD	Richard Sterling
DELIA	Portia Morrow
NORA	Nellie Burt
DR. HUMPHREYS	A. H. Van Buren
DR. SOMERS	John C. King
MAGGIE	Timothy Kearse

Staged by Bretaigne Windust

Setting and Costumes by Stewart Chaney

SCENES

The time: late in the 1880's
The entire action takes place in the Morning Room of the Day home on Madison Avenue

ACT ONE

SCENE I

Breakfast time. An early summer morning

SCENE II

Tea time. The same day

ACT TWO

SCENE I

Sunday, after church. A week later

SCENE II

Breakfast time. Two days later
(During Scene II the curtain is lowered to denote a lapse of three hours)

ACT THREE

SCENE I

Mid-afternoon. A month later

SCENE II

Breakfast time. The next morning

LIFE WITH FATHER

ACT ONE

SCENE I

The Morning Room of the Day home at 420 Madison Avenue. In the custom of the Victorian period, this was the room where the family gathered for breakfast, and because it was often the most comfortable room in the house, it served also as a living-room for the family and their intimates.

There is a large arch in the center of the upstage wall of the room, through which we can see the hall and the stairs leading to the second floor, and below them the rail of the stairwell leading to the basement. The room can be closed off from the hall by sliding doors in the archway. The front door of the house, which is stage right, can't be seen, but frequently is heard to slam.

In the Morning Room the sunshine streams through the large window at the right which looks out on Madison Avenue. The room itself is furnished with the somewhat less than comfortable furniture of the period, which is the late 1880's. The general color scheme in drapes and upholstery is green. Below the window is a large comfortable chair where FATHER *generally sits to read his paper. Right of center is the table which serves as a living-room table, with its proper table cover and fruit bowl; but now, expanded by extra leaves, it is doing service as a breakfast table. Against the back wall, either side of the arch, are two console tables which are used by the maid as serving tables. Left of center is a sofa, with a table just above its right end holding a lamp, framed photographs, and other ornaments. In the left wall is a fireplace, its mantel draped with a lambrequin. On the mantel are a clock and other ornaments, and above the mantel is a large mirror in a Victorian frame. The room is cluttered with the minutiæ of the period, including the inevitable rubber plant, and looking down from the walls are the Day ancestors in painted portraits. The room has the warm quality that comes only from having been lived in by a family which enjoys each other's company—a family of considerable means.*

As the curtain rises, ANNIE, *the new maid, a young Irish girl, is finishing setting the table for breakfast. After an uncertain look at the result she crosses over to her tray on the console table.* VINNIE *comes down the stairs and into the room.* VINNIE *is a charming, lovable, and spirited woman of forty. She has a lively mind which darts quickly away from any practical matter. She has red hair.*

ANNIE. Good morning, ma'am.

VINNIE. Good morning, Annie. How are you getting along?

ANNIE. All right, ma'am, I hope.

VINNIE. Now, don't be worried just because this is your first day. Everything's going to be all right—but I do hope nothing goes wrong. (*Goes to the table*) Now, let's see, is the table all set? (ANNIE *follows her*) The cream and the sugar go down at this end.

ANNIE (*placing them where* VINNIE *has indicated*). I thought in the center, ma'am; everyone could reach them easier.

VINNIE. Mr. Day sits here.

ANNIE (*gets a tray of napkins, neatly rolled and in their rings, from the console table*). I didn't know where to place the napkins, ma'am.

VINNIE. You can tell which go where by the rings. (*Takes them from the tray and puts them down as she goes around the table.* ANNIE *follows her*) This one belongs to Whitney—it has his initial on it, "W"; that one with the little dog on it is Harlan's, of course. He's the baby. This "J" is for John and the "C" is for Clarence. This narrow plain one is mine. And this is Mr. Day's. It's just like mine—except that it got bent one morning. And that reminds me—always be sure Mr. Day's coffee is piping hot.

ANNIE. Ah, your man has coffee instead of tea of a morning?

VINNIE. We all have coffee except the two youngest boys. They have their milk. And, Annie, always speak of my husband as Mr. Day.

ANNIE. I will that.

VINNIE (*correcting her*). "Yes, ma'am," Annie.

ANNIE. Yes, ma'am.

VINNIE. And if Mr. Day speaks to you, just say: "Yes, sir." Don't be nervous—you'll get used to him.
(CLARENCE, *the eldest son, about seventeen, comes down the stairs and into the room. He is a manly, serious, good-looking boy. Because he is starting in at Yale next year, he thinks he is grown-up. He is red-headed.*)

CLARENCE. Good morning, Mother. (*He kisses her.*)

VINNIE. Good morning, Clarence.

CLARENCE. Did you sleep well, Mother?

VINNIE. Yes, thank you, dear. (CLARENCE *goes to* FATHER'S *chair and picks up the morning paper. To* ANNIE) We always start with fruit, except the two young boys, who have porridge.
(ANNIE *brings the fruit and porridge to the table.* CLARENCE, *looking at the paper, makes a whistling sound.*)

CLARENCE. Jiminy! Another wreck on the New Haven. That always disturbs the market. Father won't like that.

VINNIE. I do wish that New Haven would stop having wrecks. If they knew how it upset your father—(*Sees that* CLARENCE'S *coat has been torn and mended*) My soul and body,

Clarence, what's happened to your coat?

CLARENCE. I tore it. Margaret mended it for me.

VINNIE. It looks terrible. Why don't you wear your blue suit?

CLARENCE. That looks worse than this one. You know, I burnt that hole in it.

VINNIE. Oh, yes—well, you can't go around looking like that. I'll have to speak to your father. Oh, dear!
(JOHN, *who is about fifteen, comes down the stairs and into the room.* JOHN *is gangly and a little overgrown. He is red-headed.*)

JOHN. Good morning, Mother. (*He kisses her.*)

VINNIE. Good morning, John.

JOHN (*to* CLARENCE). Who won?

CLARENCE. I haven't looked yet.

JOHN. Let me see. (*He tries to take the paper away from* CLARENCE.)

CLARENCE. Be careful!

VINNIE. Boys, don't wrinkle that paper before your father's looked at it.

CLARENCE (*to* JOHN). Yes!
(VINNIE *turns to* ANNIE.)

VINNIE. You'd better get things started. We want everything ready when Mr. Day comes down. (ANNIE *exits*) Clarence, right after breakfast I want you and John to move the small bureau from my room into yours.

CLARENCE. What for? Is somebody coming to visit us?

JOHN. Who's coming?

VINNIE. I haven't said anyone was coming. And don't you say anything about it. I want it to be a surprise.

CLARENCE. Oh! Father doesn't know yet?

VINNIE. No. And I'd better speak to him about a new suit for you before he finds out he's being surprised by visitors.
(ANNIE *enters with a tray on which are two glasses of milk, which she puts at* HARLAN'S *and* WHITNEY'S *places at the table.* WHITNEY *comes down the stairs and rushes into the room. He is about thirteen. Suiting his age, he is a lively active boy. He is red-headed.*)

WHITNEY. Morning. (*He kisses his mother quickly, then runs to* CLARENCE *and* JOHN) Who won?

JOHN. The Giants, 7 to 3. Buck Ewing hit a home run.

WHITNEY. Let me see!
(HARLAN *comes sliding down the banister. He enters the room, runs to his mother, and kisses her.* HARLAN *is a roly-poly, lovable, good-natured youngster of six. He is red-headed.*)

VINNIE. How's your finger, darling?

HARLAN. It itches.

VINNIE (*kissing the finger*). That's a sign it's getting better. Now don't scratch it. Sit down, boys. Get in your chair, darling. (*The boys move to the table and take their places.* CLARENCE *puts the newspaper beside his father's plate.* JOHN *stands waiting to place* VINNIE'S *chair when she sits.)* Now, Annie, watch Mr. Day, and as soon as he finishes his fruit— (*Leaves the admonition hanging in mid-air as the sound of* FATHER'S *voice booms from upstairs.)*

FATHER'S VOICE. Vinnie! Vinnie! (*All eyes turn toward the staircase.* VINNIE *rushes to the foot of the stairs, speaking as she goes.)*

VINNIE. What's the matter, Clare?

FATHER'S VOICE. Where's my necktie?

VINNIE. Which necktie?

FATHER'S VOICE. The one I gave you yesterday.

VINNIE. It isn't pressed yet. I forgot to give it to Margaret.

FATHER'S VOICE. I told you distinctly I wanted to wear that necktie today.

VINNIE. You've got plenty of neckties. Put on another one right away and come down to breakfast.

FATHER'S VOICE. Oh, damn! Damnation! (VINNIE *goes to her place at the table.* JOHN *places her chair for her, then sits.* WHITNEY *has started eating.)*

CLARENCE. Whitney!

VINNIE. Wait for your father, Whitney.

WHITNEY. Oh, and I'm in a hurry! John, can I borrow your glove today? I'm going to pitch.

JOHN. If I don't play myself.

WHITNEY. Look, if you need it, we're playing in that big field at the corner of Fifty-seventh and Madison.

VINNIE. 'Way up there!

WHITNEY. They're building a house on that vacant lot on Fiftieth Street.

VINNIE. My! My! My! Here we move to Forty-eighth Street just to get out of the city!

WHITNEY. Can't I start breakfast, Mother? I promised to be there by eight o'clock.

VINNIE. After breakfast, Whitney, you have to study your catechism.

WHITNEY. Mother, can't I do that this afternoon?

VINNIE. Whitney, you have to learn five questions every morning before you leave the house.

WHITNEY. Aw, Mother—

VINNIE. You weren't very sure of yourself when I heard you last night.

WHITNEY. I know them now.

VINNIE. Let's see. (WHITNEY *rises and faces his mother*) "What is your name?"

WHITNEY. Whitney Benjamin.

VINNIE. "Who gave you this name?"

WHITNEY. "My sponsors in baptism, wherein I was made a member of Christ, the child of God and an inheritor of the Kingdom of Heaven." Mother, if I hadn't been baptized wouldn't I have a name?

VINNIE. Not in the sight of the Church. "What did your sponsors then for you?"

WHITNEY. "They did promise and vow three things in my name—" (FATHER *makes his appearance on the stairway and comes down into the room.* FATHER *is in his forties, distinguished in appearance, with great charm and vitality, extremely well dressed in a conservative way. He is red-headed.*)

FATHER (*heartily*). Good morning, boys. (*They rise and answer him*) Good morning, Vinnie. (*He goes to her and kisses her*) Have a good night?

VINNIE. Yes, thank you, Clare.

FATHER. Good! Sit down, boys. (*The doorbell rings and a postman's whistle is heard.*)

VINNIE. That's the doorbell, Annie. (ANNIE *exits*) Clare, that new suit looks very nice.

FATHER. Too damn tight! (*He sits in his place at the head of the table*) What's the matter with those fellows over in London? I wrote them a year ago they were making my clothes too tight!

VINNIE. You've put on a little weight, Clare.

FATHER. I weigh just the same as I always have. (*Attacks his orange. The boys dive into their breakfasts.* ANNIE *enters with the mail, starts to take it to* VINNIE. FATHER *sees her*) What's that? The mail? That goes to me. (ANNIE *gives the mail to* FATHER *and exits with her tray.*)

VINNIE. Well, Clarence has just managed to tear the only decent suit of clothes he has.

FATHER (*looking through the mail*). Here's one for you, Vinnie. John, hand that to your mother. (*He passes the letter on.*)

VINNIE. Clare dear, I'm sorry, but I'm afraid Clarence is going to have to have a new suit of clothes.

FATHER. Vinnie, Clarence has to learn not to be so hard on his clothes.

CLARENCE. Father, I thought—

FATHER. Clarence, when you start in Yale in the fall, I'm going to set aside a thousand dollars just to outfit you, but you'll get no new clothes this summer.

CLARENCE. Can't I have one of your old suits cut down for me?

FATHER. Every suit I own still has plenty of wear in it. I wear my clothes until they're worn out.

VINNIE. Well, if you want your clothes worn out, Clarence can wear them out much faster than you can.

CLARENCE. Yes, and, Father, you don't get a chance to wear them out. Every time you get a new batch of clothes, Mother sends the old ones to the missionary barrel. I guess I'm just as good as any old missionary. (ANNIE *returns with a platter of bacon and eggs and a pot of coffee.*)

VINNIE. Clarence, before you compare yourself to a missionary, remember the sacrifices they make.

FATHER (*chuckling*). I don't know, Vinnie, I think my clothes would look better on Clarence than on some Hottentot. (*To* CLARENCE) Have that black suit of mine cut down to fit you before your mother gets her hands on it.
(ANNIE *clears the fruit.*)

CLARENCE. Thank you, Father. (*To* JOHN) One of Father's suits! Thank you, sir!

FATHER. Whitney, don't eat so fast.

WHITNEY. Well, Father, I'm going to pitch today and I promised to get there early, but before I go I have to study my catechism.

FATHER. What do you bother with that for?

VINNIE (*with spirit*). Because if he doesn't know his catechism he can't be confirmed!

WHITNEY (*pleading*). But I'm going to pitch today.

FATHER. Vinnie, Whitney's going to pitch today and he can be confirmed any old time.

VINNIE. Clare, sometimes it seems to me that you don't care whether your children get to Heaven or not.

FATHER. Oh, Whitney'll get to Heaven all right. (*To* WHITNEY) I'll be there before you are, Whitney; I'll see that you get in.

VINNIE. What makes you so sure they'll let you in?

FATHER. Well, if they don't I'll certainly raise a devil of a row. (ANNIE *is at* FATHER'S *side with the platter of bacon and eggs, ready to serve him, and draws back at this astounding declaration, raising the platter.*)

VINNIE (*with shocked awe*). Clare, I do hope you'll behave when you get to Heaven.
(FATHER *has turned to serve himself from the platter, but* ANNIE, *not yet recovered from the picture of* FATHER *raising a row at the gates of Heaven, is holding it too high for him.*)

FATHER (*storming*). Vinnie, how many times have I asked you not to engage a maid who doesn't even know how to serve properly?

VINNIE. Clare, can't you see she's new and doing her best?

FATHER. How can I serve myself when she's holding that platter over my head?

VINNIE. Annie, why don't you hold it lower?
(ANNIE *lowers the platter.* FATHER *serves himself, but goes on talking.*)

FATHER. Where'd she come from anyway? What became of the one we had yesterday? I don't see why you can't keep a maid.

VINNIE. Oh, you don't!

FATHER. All I want is service. (ANNIE *serves the others nervously. So far as* FATHER *is concerned, however, the storm has passed, and he turns genially to* WHITNEY) Whitney, when we get to Heaven we'll organize a baseball team of our own. (*The boys laugh.*)

VINNIE. It would be just like you to try to run things up there.

FATHER. Well, from all I've heard about Heaven, it seems to be a pretty unbusinesslike place. They could probably use a good man like me. (*Stamps on the floor three times. It is his traditional signal to summon* MARGARET, *the cook, from the kitchen below.*)

VINNIE. What do you want Margaret for? What's wrong?
(ANNIE *has reached the sideboard and is sniffling audibly.*)

FATHER (*distracted*). What's that damn noise?

VINNIE. Shhh—it's Annie.

FATHER. Annie? Who's Annie?

VINNIE. The maid. (ANNIE, *seeing that she has attracted attention, hurries out into the hall where she can't be seen or heard*) Clare, aren't you ashamed of yourself?

FATHER (*surprised*). What have I done now?

VINNIE. You made her cry—speaking to her the way you did.

FATHER. I never said a word to her—I was addressing myself to you.

VINNIE. I do wish you'd be more careful. It's hard enough to keep a maid—and the uniforms just fit this one.
(MARGARET, *the cook, a small Irishwoman of about fifty, hurries into the room.*)

MARGARET. What's wanting?

FATHER. Margaret, this bacon is good. (MARGARET *beams and gestures deprecatingly*) It's *good*. It's done just right!

MARGARET. Yes, sir! (*She smiles and exits.* ANNIE *returns, recovered, and starts serving the coffee.* VINNIE *has opened her letter and glanced through it.*)

VINNIE. Clare, this letter gives me a good idea. I've decided that next winter I won't give a series of dinners.

FATHER. I should hope not.

VINNIE. I'll give a big musicale instead.

FATHER. You'll give a what?

VINNIE. A musicale.

FATHER (*peremptorily*). Vinnie, I won't have my peaceful home turned into a Roman arena with a lot of hairy fiddlers prancing about.

VINNIE. I didn't say a word about hairy fiddlers. Mrs. Spiller has written me about this lovely young girl who will come for very little.

FATHER. What instrument does this inexpensive paragon play?

VINNIE. She doesn't play, Clare, she whistles.

FATHER. Whistles? Good God!

VINNIE. She whistles sixteen different pieces. All for twenty-five dollars.

FATHER (*stormily*). I won't pay twenty-five dollars to any human peanut stand. (*He tastes his coffee, grimaces, and again stamps three times on the floor.*)

VINNIE. Clare, I can arrange this so it won't cost you a penny. If I invite fifty people and charge them fifty cents apiece, there's the twenty-five dollars right there!

FATHER. You can't invite people to your own house and charge them admission.

VINNIE. I can if the money's for the missionary fund.

FATHER. Then where will you get the twenty-five dollars to pay that poor girl for her whistling?

VINNIE. Now, Clare, let's not cross that bridge until we come to it.

FATHER. And if we do cross it, it will cost me twenty-five dollars. Vinnie, I'm putting my foot down about this musicale, just as I've had to put my foot down about your keeping this house full of visiting relatives. Why can't we live here by ourselves in peace and comfort?
(MARGARET *comes dashing into the room.*)

MARGARET. What's wanting?

FATHER (*sternly*). Margaret, what is this? (*He holds up his coffee cup and points at it.*)

MARGARET. It's coffee, sir.

FATHER. It is not coffee! You couldn't possibly take water and coffee beans and arrive at that! It's slops, that's what it is—slops! Take it away! Take it away, I tell you! (MARGARET *takes* FATHER'S *cup and dashes out.* ANNIE *starts to take* VINNIE'S *cup.*)

VINNIE. Leave my coffee there, Annie! It's perfectly all right!
(ANNIE *leaves the room.*)

FATHER (*angrily*). It is not! I swear I can't imagine how she concocts such an atrocity. I come down to this table every morning hungry—

VINNIE. Well, if you're hungry, Clare, why aren't you eating your breakfast?

FATHER. What?

VINNIE. If you're hungry, why aren't you eating your breakfast?

FATHER (*thrown out of bounds*). I am. (*He takes a mouthful of bacon and munches it happily, his eyes falling on* HARLAN) Harlan, how's that finger? Come over here and let me see it. (HARLAN *goes to his father's side. He shows his finger*) Well, that's healing nicely. Now don't pick that scab or it will leave a scar, and we don't want scars on our fingers, do we? (*He chuckles*) I guess you'll remember after this that cats don't like to be hugged. It's all right to stroke them, but don't squeeze them. Now go back and finish your oatmeal.

HARLAN. I don't like oatmeal.

FATHER (*kindly*). It's good for you. Go back and eat it.

HARLAN. But I don't like it.

FATHER (*quietly, but firmly*). I'll tell you what you like and what you don't like. You're not old enough to know about such things. You've no business not to like oatmeal. It's good.

HARLAN. I hate it.

FATHER (*firmly, but not quietly*). That's enough! We won't discuss it! Eat that oatmeal at once!

(*In contrast to* HARLAN, WHITNEY *has been eating his oatmeal at a terrific rate of speed. He pauses and puts down his spoon.*)

WHITNEY. I've finished *my* oatmeal. May I be excused?

FATHER. Yes, Whitney, you may go. (WHITNEY *slides off his chair and hurries to the stairs*) Pitch a good game.

VINNIE. Whitney!

WHITNEY. I'm going upstairs to study my catechism.

VINNIE. Oh, that's all right. Run along.

WHITNEY (*on the way up*). Harlan, you'd better hurry up and finish your oatmeal if you want to go with me. (*Throughout breakfast* FATHER *has been opening and glancing through his mail. He has just reached one letter, however, that bewilders him.*)

FATHER. I don't understand why I'm always getting damn fool letters like this!

VINNIE. What is it, Clare?

FATHER. "Dear Friend Day: We are assigning you the exclusive rights for Staten Island for selling the Gem Home Popper for popcorn—"

CLARENCE. I think that's for me, Father.

FATHER. Then why isn't it addressed to Clarence Day, Jr.? (*He looks at the envelope*) Oh, it is. Well, I'm sorry. I didn't mean to open your mail.
(MARGARET *returns and slips a cup of coffee to the table beside* FATHER.)

VINNIE. I wouldn't get mixed up in that, Clarence. People like popcorn, but they won't go all the way to Staten Island to buy it.
(FATHER *has picked up the paper and is reading it. He drinks his coffee absentmindedly.*)

FATHER. Chauncey Depew's having another birthday.

VINNIE. How nice.

FATHER. He's always having birthdays. Two or three a year. Damn! Another wreck on the New Haven!

VINNIE. Yes. Oh, that reminds me. Mrs. Bailey dropped in yesterday.

FATHER. Was she in the wreck?

VINNIE. No. But she was born in New Haven. Clarence, you're having tea with Edith Bailey Thursday afternoon.

CLARENCE. Oh, Mother, do I have to?

JOHN (*singing*). "I like coffee, I like tea. I like the girls and the girls like me."

CLARENCE. Well, the girls don't like me and I don't like them.

VINNIE. Edith Bailey's a very nice girl, isn't she, Clare?

FATHER. Edith Bailey? Don't like her. Don't blame Clarence. (FATHER *goes to his chair by the window and sits down with his newspaper and a cigar. The others rise.* HARLAN *runs upstairs.* ANNIE *starts clearing the table and exits with the tray of dishes a little later.* VINNIE *speaks in a guarded tone to the two boys.*)

VINNIE. Clarence, you and John go upstairs and do—what I asked you to.

JOHN. You said the small bureau, Mother?

VINNIE. Shh! Run along.
(*The boys go upstairs, somewhat unwillingly.* MARGARET *enters.*)

MARGARET. If you please, ma'am, there's a package been delivered with a dollar due on it. Some kitchen knives.

VINNIE. Oh, yes, those knives from Lewis & Conger's. (*She gets her purse from the drawer in the console table and gives* MARGARET *a dollar*) Here, give this dollar to the man, Margaret.

FATHER. Make a memorandum of that, Vinnie. One dollar and whatever it was for.

VINNIE (*looking into purse*). Clare, dear, I'm afraid I'm going to need some more money.

FATHER. What for?

VINNIE. You were complaining of the coffee this morning. Well, that nice French drip coffeepot is broken—and you know how it got broken.

FATHER (*taking out his wallet*). Never mind that, Vinnie. As I remember, that coffeepot cost five dollars and something. Here's six dollars. (*He gives her six dollars*) And when you get it, enter the exact amount in the ledger downstairs.

VINNIE. Thank you, Clare.

FATHER. We can't go on month after month having the household accounts in such a mess.

VINNIE (*she sits on the arm of* FATHER'S *chair*). No, and I've thought of a system that will make my bookkeeping perfect.

FATHER. I'm certainly relieved to hear that. What is it?

VINNIE. Well, Clare dear, you never make half the fuss over how much I've spent as you do over my not being able to remember what I've spent it for.

FATHER. Exactly. This house must be run on a business basis. That's why I insist on your keeping books.

VINNIE. That's the whole point, Clare. All we have to do is open charge accounts everywhere and the stores will do my bookkeeping for me.

FATHER. Wait a minute, Vinnie—

VINNIE. Then when the bills come in you'd know exactly where your money had gone.

FATHER. I certainly would. Vinnie, I get enough bills as it is.

VINNIE. Yes, and those bills always help. They show you just where I spent the money. Now if we had charge accounts everywhere—

FATHER. Now, Vinnie, I don't know about that.

VINNIE. Clare dear, don't you hate those arguments we have every month? I certainly do. Not to have those I should think would be worth something to you.

FATHER. Well, I'll open an account at Lewis & Conger's—and one at McCreery's to start with—we'll see how it works out. (*He shakes his head doubtfully. Her victory gained,* VINNIE *moves away.*)

VINNIE. Thank you, Clare. Oh—the rector's coming to tea today.

FATHER. The rector? I'm glad you warned me. I'll go to the club. Don't expect me home until dinner time.

VINNIE. I do wish you'd take a little more interest in the church. (*Goes behind* FATHER'S *chair and looks down at him with concern.*)

FATHER. Vinnie, getting me into Heaven's your job. If there's anything wrong with my ticket when I get there, you can fix it up. Everybody loves you so much—I'm sure God must, too.

VINNIE. I'll do my best, Clare. It wouldn't be Heaven without you.

FATHER. If you're there, Vinnie, I'll manage to get in some way, even if I have to climb the fence.

JOHN (*from upstairs*). Mother, we've moved it. Is there anything else?

FATHER. What's being moved?

VINNIE. Never mind, Clare. I'll come right up, John. (*She goes to the arch, stops. Looks back at* FATHER) Oh, Clare, it's eight-thirty. You don't want to be late at the office.

FATHER. Plenty of time. (VINNIE *looks nervously toward the door, then goes upstairs.* FATHER *returns to his newspaper.* VINNIE *has barely disappeared when something in the paper arouses* FATHER'S *indignation*) Oh, God!

(VINNIE *comes running downstairs.*)

VINNIE. What's the matter, Clare? What's wrong?

FATHER. Why did God make so many damn fools and Democrats?

VINNIE (*relieved*). Oh, politics. (*She goes upstairs again.*)

FATHER (*shouting after her*). Yes, but it's taking the bread out of our mouths. It's robbery, that's what it is, highway robbery! Honest Hugh Grant! Honest! Bah! A fine mayor you've turned out to be. (FATHER *launches into a vigorous denunciation of Mayor Hugh Grant, addressing that gentleman as though he were present in the room, called upon the Day carpet to listen to* FATHER'S *opinion of Tammany's latest attack on his pocketbook*) If you can't run this city without raising taxes every five minutes, you'd better get out and let someone who can. Let me tell you, sir, that the real-estate owners of New York City are not going to tolerate these conditions any longer. Tell me this—are these increased taxes going into public improvements or are they going into graft—answer me that, honestly, if you can, Mr. Honest Hugh Grant. You can't! I thought so. Bah! (ANNIE *enters with her tray. Hearing* FATHER *talking, she curtsies and backs into the hall, as if uncertain whether to intrude on* FATHER *and the Mayor.* VINNIE *comes downstairs*) If you don't stop your plundering of the pocketbooks of the good citizens of New York, we're going to throw you and your boodle Board of Aldermen out of office.

VINNIE. Annie, why aren't you clearing the table?

ANNIE. Mr. Day's got a visitor.

FATHER. I'm warning you for the last time.

VINNIE. Oh, nonsense, he's just reading his paper, Annie. Clear the table. (VINNIE *goes off through the arch.* ANNIE *comes in timidly and starts to clear the table.*)

FATHER (*still lecturing Mayor Grant*). We pay you a good round sum to watch after our interests, and all we get is inefficiency! (ANNIE *looks around trying to see the Mayor and, finding the room empty, assumes* FATHER'S *remarks are directed at her.*) I know you're a nincompoop and I strongly suspect you of being a scalawag. (ANNIE *stands petrified.* WHITNEY *comes downstairs*) It's graft—that's what it is—Tammany graft—and if you're not getting it, somebody else is

WHITNEY (*to* FATHER). Where's John? Do you know where John is?

FATHER. Dick Croker's running this town and you're just his cat's-paw. (VINNIE *comes in from downstairs, and* HARLAN *comes down from upstairs.* FATHER *goes on talking. The others carry on their conversation simultaneously, ignoring* FATHER *and his imaginary visitor.*)

HARLAN. Mother, where's John?

VINNIE. He's upstairs, dear.

FATHER. And as for you, Richard Croker—don't think, just because you're hiding behind these minions you've put in public office, that you're going to escape your legal responsibilities.

WHITNEY (*calling upstairs*). John, I'm going to take your glove!

JOHN (*from upstairs*). Don't you lose it! And don't let anybody else have it either!

VINNIE. Annie, you should have cleared the table long ago. (ANNIE *loads her tray feverishly, eager to escape.*)

FATHER (*rising and slamming down the paper in his chair*). Legal responsibilities—by gad, sir, I mean *criminal* responsibilities. (*The boys start toward the front door.*)

VINNIE (*starting upstairs*). Now you watch Harlan, Whitney. Don't let him be anywhere the ball can hit him. Do what Whitney says, Harlan. And don't be late for lunch. (FATHER *has reached the arch on his way out of the room, where he pauses for a final shot at Mayor Grant.*)

FATHER. Don't forget what happened to William Marcy Tweed—and if you put our taxes up once more, we'll put you in jail! (*He goes out of the archway to the left. A few seconds later he is seen passing the arch toward the outer door wearing his square derby and carrying his stick and gloves. The door is heard to slam loudly.* ANNIE *seizes her tray of dishes and runs out of the arch to the left toward the basement stairs. A second later there is a scream from* ANNIE *and a tremendous crash.* JOHN *and* CLARENCE *come rushing down and look over the rail of the stairs below.* VINNIE *follows them almost immediately.*)

VINNIE. What is it? What happened?

CLARENCE. The maid fell downstairs.

VINNIE. I don't wonder, with your Father getting her so upset. Why couldn't she have finished with the table before she fell downstairs?

JOHN. I don't think she hurt herself.

VINNIE. And today of all days! Boys, will you finish the table? And, Clarence, don't leave the house until I talk to you. (*She goes downstairs. During the following scene* CLARENCE *and* JOHN *remove* VINNIE'S *best breakfast tablecloth and cram it carelessly into the drawer of the console table, then take out the extra leaves from the table, push it together, and replace the living-room table cover and the bowl of fruit.*)

JOHN. What do you suppose Mother wants to talk to you about.

CLARENCE. Oh, probably about Edith Bailey.

JOHN. What do you talk about when you have tea alone with a girl?

CLARENCE. We don't talk about anything. I say: 'Isn't it a nice day?' and she says: "Yes," and I say: "I think it's a little warmer than yesterday," and she says: "Yes, I like warm weather, don't you?" and I say: "Yes," and then we wait for the tea to come in. And then she says: "How many lumps?" and I say: "Two, thank you," and she says: "You must have a sweet tooth," and I can't say: "Yes" and I can't say: "No," so we just sit there and look at each other for half an hour. Then I say: "Well, it's time I was going," and she says: "Must you?" and I say: "I've enjoyed seeing you very much," and she says: "You must come again," and I say: "I will," and get out.

JOHN (*shaking his head*). Some fellows like girls.

CLARENCE. I don't.

JOHN. And did you ever notice fellows, when they get sweet on a girl—the silly things a girl can make them do? And they don't even seem to know they're acting silly.

CLARENCE. Well, not for Yours Truly! (VINNIE *returns from downstairs.*)

VINNIE. I declare I don't see how anyone could be so clumsy.

CLARENCE. Did she hurt herself?

VINNIE. No, she's not hurt—she's just hysterical! She doesn't make sense. Your father may have raised his voice; and if she doesn't know how to hold a platter properly, she deserved it—but I know he didn't threaten to put her in jail. Oh, well! Clarence, I want you to move your things into the front room. You'll have to sleep with the other boys for a night or two.

CLARENCE. You haven't told us who's coming.

VINNIE (*happily*). Cousin Cora. Isn't that nice?

CLARENCE. It's not nice for me. I can't get any sleep in there with those children.

JOHN. Wait'll Father finds out she's here! There'll be a rumpus.

VINNIE. John, don't criticize your father. He's very hospitable after he gets used to the idea. (*The doorbell rings.* JOHN *and* VINNIE *go to the window.*)

JOHN. Yes, it's Cousin Cora. Look, there's somebody with her.

VINNIE (*looking out*). She wrote me she was bringing a friend of hers. They're both going to stay here. (*A limping* ANNIE *passes through the hall*) Finish with the room, boys.

CLARENCE. Do I have to sleep with the other boys and have tea with Edith Bailey all in the same week?

VINNIE. Yes, and you'd better take your father's suit to the tailor's right away, so it will be ready by Thursday.

(VINNIE *goes down the hall to greet* CORA *and* MARY. CLARENCE *hurries off, carrying the table leaves.*)

VINNIE'S VOICE (*in the hall*). Cora dear—

CORA'S VOICE. Cousin Vinnie, I'm so glad to see you! This is Mary Skinner.

VINNIE'S VOICE. Ed Skinner's daughter! I'm so glad to see you. Leave your bags in the hall and come right upstairs.

(VINNIE *enters, going toward the stairs.* CORA *follows her, but, seeing* JOHN, *enters the room and goes to him.* MARY *follows* CORA *in timidly.* CORA *is an attractive country cousin of about thirty.* MARY *is a refreshingly pretty small-town girl of sixteen.*)

CORA (*seeing* JOHN). Well, Clarence, it's so good to see you!

VINNIE (*coming into the room*). Oh, no, that's John.

CORA. John! Why, how you've grown! You'll be a man before your mother! (*She laughs herself at this time-worn quip*) John, this is Mary Skinner. (*They exchange greetings*) Vinnie, I have so much to tell you. We wrote you Aunt Carrie broke her hip. That was the night Robert Ingersoll lectured. Of course she couldn't get there; and it was a good thing for Mr. Ingersoll she didn't. (CLARENCE *enters*) And Grandpa Ebbetts hasn't been at all well.

CLARENCE. How do you do, Cousin Cora? I'm glad to see you.

CORA. This can't be Clarence!

VINNIE. Yes, it is.

CORA. My goodness, every time I see you boys you've grown another foot. Let's see—you're going to St. Paul's now, aren't you?

CLARENCE (*with pained dignity*). St. Paul's! I was through with St. Paul's long ago. I'm starting in Yale this fall.

MARY. Yale!

CORA. Oh, Mary, this is Clarence—Mary Skinner. (MARY *smiles, and* CLARENCE, *the woman-hater, nods politely and walks away*) This is Mary's first trip to New York. She was so excited when she saw a horse car.

VINNIE. We'll have to show Mary around. I'll tell you—I'll have Mr. Day take us all to Delmonico's for dinner tonight.

MARY. Delmonico's!

CORA. Oh, that's marvelous! Think of that, Mary—Delmonico's! And Cousin Clare's such a wonderful host.

VINNIE. I know you girls want to freshen up. So come upstairs. Clarence, I'll let the girls use your room now, and when they've finished you can move, and bring up their bags. They're out in the hall. (*Starts upstairs with* CORA) I've given you girls Clarence's room, but he didn't know about it until this morning and he hasn't moved out yet.

(VINNIE *and* CORA *disappear upstairs.* MARY *follows more slowly and on the second step stops and looks back.* CLARENCE *has gone into the hall with his back toward* MARY *and stares morosely in the direction of their luggage.*)

CLARENCE. John, get their old bags. (JOHN *disappears toward the front door. The voices of* VINNIE *and* CORA *have trailed off into the upper reaches of the house.* CLARENCE *turns to scowl in their direction and finds himself looking full into the face of* MARY.)

MARY. Cora didn't tell me about you. I never met a Yale man before. (*She gives him a devastating smile and with an audible whinny of girlish excitement she runs upstairs.* CLARENCE *stares after her a few seconds, then turns toward the audience with a look of "What happened to me just then?" Suddenly, however, his face breaks into a smile which indicates that, whatever has happened, he likes it.*)

CURTAIN

SCENE II

The same day. Tea time.

VINNIE *and the* RECTOR *are having tea.* THE REVEREND DR. LLOYD *is a plump, bustling man, very good-hearted and pleasant.* VINNIE *and* DR. LLOYD *have one strong point in common: their devotion to the Church and its rituals.* VINNIE'S *devotion comes from her natural piety;* DR. LLOYD'S *is a little more professional.*

At rise, DR. LLOYD *is seated with a cup of tea.* VINNIE *is also seated and* WHITNEY *is standing next to her, stiffly erect in the manner of a boy reciting.* HARLAN *is seated next to his mother, watching* WHITNEY'S *performance.*

WHITNEY (*reciting*). "—to worship Him, to give Him thanks; to put my whole trust in Him, to call upon Him—" (*He hesitates.*)

VINNIE (*prompting*). "—to honor—"

WHITNEY. "—to honor His Holy Name and His word and to serve Him truly all the days of my life."

DR. LLOYD. "What is thy duty toward thy neighbor?"

WHITNEY. Whew! (*He pulls himself together and makes a brave start*) "My duty toward my neighbor is to love him as myself, and to do to all men as I would they should do unto me; to love, honor, and succor my father and my mother; to honor and obey—"

VINNIE. "—civil authorities."

WHITNEY. "—civil authorities. To—to—to—"

VINNIE (*to* DR. LLOYD). He really knows it.

WHITNEY. I know most of the others.

DR. LLOYD. Well, he's done very well for so young a boy. I'm sure if he applies himself between now and Sunday I could hear him again—with the others.

VINNIE. There, Whitney, you'll have to study very hard if you want Dr. Lloyd to send your name in to Bishop Potter next Sunday. I must confess to you, Dr. Lloyd, it's really my fault. Instead of hearing Whitney say his catechism this morning I let him play baseball.

WHITNEY. We won, too; 35 to 27.

DR. LLOYD. That's splendid, my child. I'm glad your side won. But winning over your catechism is a richer and fuller victory.

WHITNEY. Can I go now?

VINNIE. Yes, darling. Thank Dr. Lloyd for hearing you and run along.

WHITNEY. Thank you, Dr. Lloyd.

DR. LLOYD. Not at all, my little man. (WHITNEY *starts out, turns back, takes a piece of cake and runs out.*)

VINNIE. Little Harlan is very apt at learning things by heart.

HARLAN (*scrambling to his feet*). I can spell Constantinople. Want to hear me? (DR. LLOYD *smiles his assent*) *C-o-ennaconny — annaconny* — sissaconny — tan-tan-tee — and a nople and a pople and a Constantinople!

DR. LLOYD. Very well done, my child.

VINNIE (*handing him a cake from the tea tray*). That's nice, darling. This is what you get for saying it so well. (HARLAN *quickly looks at the cake and back to* DR. LLOYD.)

HARLAN. Want me to say it again for you?

VINNIE. No, darling. One cake is enough. You run along and play with Whitney.

HARLAN. I can spell "huckleberry pie."

VINNIE. Run along, dear. (HARLAN *goes out, skipping in rhythm to his recitation.*)

HARLAN. *H-a-huckle — b-a-buckle — h-a-huckle-high. H-a-huckle — b-a-*buckle—huckleberry pie!

DR. LLOYD (*amused*). You and Mr. Day must be very proud of your children. (VINNIE *beams*) I was hoping I'd find Mr. Day at home this afternoon.

VINNIE (*evasively*). Well, he's usually home from the office by this time.

DR. LLOYD. Perhaps he's gone for a gallop in the park—it's such a fine day. He's very fond of horseback riding, I believe.

VINNIE. Oh, yes.

DR. LLOYD. Tell me—has he ever been thrown from a horse?

VINNIE. Oh, no! No horse would throw Mr. Day.

DR. LLOYD. I've wondered. I thought he might have had an accident. I notice he never kneels in church.

VINNIE. Oh, that's no accident! But I don't want you to think he doesn't pray. He does. Why, sometimes you can hear him pray all over the house. But he never kneels.

DR. LLOYD. Never kneels! Dear me! I was hoping to have the opportunity to tell you and Mr. Day about our plans for the new edifice.

VINNIE. I'm so glad we're going to have a new church.

DR. LLOYD. I'm happy to announce that we're now ready to proceed. The only thing left to do is raise the money.

VINNIE. No one should hesitate about contributing to that. (*The front door slams.*)

DR. LLOYD. Perhaps that's Mr. Day now.

VINNIE. Oh, no, I hardly think so. (FATHER *appears in the archway*) Why, it is!

CLARENCE. Oh, damn! I forgot.

VINNIE. Clare, you're just in time. Dr. Lloyd's here for tea.

FATHER. I'll be right in. (*He disappears the other side of the archway.*)

VINNIE. I'll send for some fresh tea. (*She goes to the bellpull and rings for the maid.*)

DR. LLOYD. Now we can tell Mr. Day about our plans for the new edifice.

VINNIE (*knowing her man*). After he's had his tea. (FATHER *comes back into the room.* DR. LLOYD *rises.*)

FATHER. How are you, Dr. Lloyd? (CLARENCE *comes down the stairs and eagerly looks around for* MARY.)

CLARENCE. Oh, it was Father.

DR. LLOYD. Very well, thank you (*They shake hands.*)

CLARENCE (*to* VINNIE). They're not back yet?

VINNIE. No! Clarence, no! (CLARENCE *turns, disappointed, and goes back upstairs.*)

DR. LLOYD. It's a great pleasure to have a visit with you, Mr. Day. Except for a fleeting glimpse on the Sabbath, I don't see much of you. (FATHER *grunts and sits down.* DELIA, *a new maid, enters.*)

DELIA. Yes, ma'am.

VINNIE. Some fresh tea and a cup for Mr. Day. (DELIA *exits and* VINNIE *hurries down to the tea table to start the conversation*) Well, Clare, did you have a busy day at the office?

FATHER. Damn busy.

VINNIE. Clare!

FATHER. Very busy day. Tired out.

VINNIE. I've ordered some fresh tea. (*To* DR. LLOYD) Poor Clare, he must work very hard. He always comes home tired. Although how a man can get tired just sitting at his desk all day, I don't know. I suppose Wall Street is just as much a mystery to you as it is to me, Dr. Lloyd.

DR. LLOYD. No, no, it's all very clear to me. My mind often goes to the business man. The picture I'm most fond of is when I envision him at the close of the day's work. There he sits—this hard-headed man of affairs—surrounded by the ledgers that he has been studying closely and harshly for hours. I see him pausing in his toil—and by chance he raises his eyes and looks out of the window at the light in God's sky and it comes over him that money and ledgers are dross. (FATHER *stares at* DR. LLOYD *with some amazement*) He realizes that all those figures of profit and loss are without importance or consequence—vanity and dust. And I see this troubled man bow his head and with streaming eyes resolve to devote his life to far higher things.

FATHER. Well, I'll be damned! (*At this moment* DELIA *returns with the fresh tea for* FATHER.)

VINNIE. Here's your tea, Clare. (FATHER *notices the new maid.*)

FATHER. Who's this?

VINNIE (*quietly*). The new maid.

FATHER. Where's the one we had this morning?

VINNIE. Never mind, Clare.

FATHER. The one we had this morning was prettier. (DELIA, *with a slight resentment, exits.* FATHER *attacks the tea and cakes with relish*) Vinnie, these cakes are *good*.

DR. LLOYD. Delicious!

VINNIE. Dr. Lloyd wants to tell us about the plans for the new edifice.

FATHER. The new what?

VINNIE. The new church—Clare, you knew we were planning to build a new church.

DR. LLOYD. Of course, we're going to have to raise a large sum of money.

FATHER (*alive to the danger*). Well, personally I'm against the church hop-skipping-and-jumping all over the town. And it so happens that during the last year I've suffered heavy losses in the market—damned heavy losses—

VINNIE. Clare!

FATHER.—so any contribution I make will have to be a small one.

VINNIE. But, Clare, for so worthy a cause!

FATHER.—and if your Finance Committee thinks it's too small they can blame the rascals that are running the New Haven Railroad!

DR. LLOYD. The amount everyone is to subscribe has already been decided.

FATHER (*bristling*). Who decided it?

DR. LLOYD. After considerable thought we've found a formula which we believe is fair and equitable. It apportions the burden lightly on those least able to carry it and justly on those whose shoulders we know are stronger. We've voted that our supporting members should each contribute a sum equal to the cost of their pews. (FATHER's *jaw drops.*)

FATHER. I paid five thousand dollars for my pew!

VINNIE. Yes, Clare. That makes our contribution five thousand dollars.

FATHER. That's robbery! Do you know what that pew is worth today? Three thousand dollars. That's what the last one sold for. I've taken a dead loss of two thousand dollars on that pew already. Frank Baggs sold me that pew when the market was at its peak. He knew when to get out. (*He turns to* VINNIE) And I'm warning you now that if the market ever goes up I'm going to unload that pew.

VINNIE. Clarence Day! How can you speak of the Lord's temple as though it were something to be bought and sold on Wall Street?

FATHER. Vinnie, this is a matter of dollars and cents, and that's something you don't know anything about!

VINNIE. You talking of religion in terms of dollars and cents seems to me pretty close to blasphemy.

DR. LLOYD (*soothingly*). Now, Mrs. Day, your husband is a business man and he has a practical approach toward this problem. We've had to be practical about it too—we have all the facts and figures.

FATHER. Oh, really! What's the new piece of property going to cost you?

DR. LLOYD. I think the figure I've heard mentioned is eighty-five thousand dollars—or was it a hundred and eighty-five thousand dollars?

FATHER. What's the property worth where we are now?

DR. LLOYD. Well, there's quite a difference of opinion about that.

FATHER. How much do you have to raise to build the new church?

DR. LLOYD. Now, I've seen those figures—let me see—I know it depends somewhat upon the amount of the mortgage.

FATHER. Mortgage, eh? What are the terms of the amortization?

DR. LLOYD. Amortization? That's not a word I'm familiar with.

FATHER. It all seems pretty vague and unsound to me. I certainly wouldn't let any customer of mine invest on what I've heard. (*The doorbell rings.*)

DR. LLOYD. We've given it a great deal of thought. I don't see how you can call it vague.
(DELIA *passes along the hall toward the front door.*)

FATHER. Dr. Lloyd, you preach that some day we'll all have to answer to God.

DR. LLOYD. We shall indeed!

FATHER. Well, I hope God doesn't ask you any questions with figures in them.
(CORA'S VOICE *is heard in the hall, thanking* DELIA. VINNIE *goes to the arch just in time to meet* CORA *and*

MARY *as they enter, heavily laden with packages, which they put down.* FATHER *and* DR. LLOYD *rise.*)

CORA, Oh. Vinnie, what a day! We've been to every shop in town and— (*She sees* FATHER) Cousin Clare!

FATHER (*cordially*). Cora, what are you doing in New York?

CORA. We're just passing through on our way to Springfield.

FATHER. We? (CLARENCE *comes downstairs into the room with eyes only for* MARY.)

VINNIE. Oh, Dr. Lloyd, this is my favorite cousin, Miss Cartwright, and her friend, Mary Skinner. (*They exchange mutual how-do-you-do's.*)

DR. LLOYD. This seems to be a family reunion. I'll just run along.

FATHER (*promptly*). Goodbye, Dr. Lloyd.

DR. LLOYD. Goodbye, Miss Cartwright. Goodbye, Miss—er—

VINNIE. Clarence, you haven't said how-do-you-do to Dr. Lloyd.

CLARENCE. Goodbye, Dr. Lloyd.

VINNIE (*to* DR. LLOYD). I'll go to the door with you. (DR. LLOYD *and* VINNIE *go out, talking.*)

FATHER. Cora, you're as welcome as the flowers in May! Have some tea with us. (*To* DELIA) Bring some fresh tea—and some more of those cakes.

CORA. Oh, we've had tea! We were so tired shopping we had tea downtown. (*With a gesture* FATHER *countermands his order to* DELIA, *who removes the tea table and exits.*)

MARY. At the Fifth Avenue Hotel.

FATHER. At the Fifth Avenue Hotel, eh? Who'd you say this pretty little girl was?

CORA. She's Ed Skinner's daughter. Well, Mary, at last you've met Mr. Day. I've told Mary so much about you, Cousin Clare, that she's just been dying to meet you.

FATHER. Well, sit down! Sit down! Even if you have had tea you can stop and visit for a while. As a matter of fact, why don't you both stay to dinner? (VINNIE *enters just in time to hear this and cuts in quickly.*)

VINNIE. That's all arranged, Clare. Cora and Mary are going to have dinner with us.

FATHER. That's fine! That's fine!

CORA. Cousin Clare, I don't know how to thank you and Vinnie for your hospitality.

MARY. Yes, Mr. Day.

FATHER. Well, you'll just have to take pot luck.

CORA. No, I mean—

(VINNIE *speaks quickly to postpone the revelation that* FATHER *has house guests.*)

VINNIE. Clare, did you know the girls are going to visit Aunt Judith in Springfield for a whole month?

FATHER. That's fine. How long are you going to be in New York, Cora?

CORA. All week.

FATHER. Splendid. We'll hope to see something of you, eh, Vinnie? (CORA *looks bewildered and is about to speak.*)

VINNIE. Did you find anything you wanted in the shops?

CORA. Just everything.

VINNIE. I want to see what you got.

CORA. I just can't wait to show you. (*She goes coyly to* FATHER) But I'm afraid some of the packages can't be opened in front of Cousin Clare.

FATHER. Shall I leave the room? (*Laughs at his own joke.*)

CORA. Clarence, do you mind taking the packages up to our room—or should I say your room? (*To* FATHER) Wasn't it nice of Clarence to give up his room to us for a whole week?

FATHER (*with a sudden drop in temperature*). Vinnie!

VINNIE. Come on, Cora, I just can't wait to see what's in those packages. (CORA, MARY, *and* VINNIE *start out.* CLARENCE *is gathering up the packages.*)

FATHER (*ominously*). Vinnie, I wish to speak to you before you go upstairs.

VINNIE. I'll be down in just a minute, Clare.

FATHER. I wish to speak to you now! (*The girls have disappeared upstairs.*)

VINNIE. I'll be up in just a minute, Cora.

(*We hear a faint "All right" from upstairs.*)

FATHER (*his voice is low but stern*). Are those two women encamped in this house?

VINNIE. Now, Clare!

FATHER (*much louder*). Answer me, Vinnie!

VINNIE. Just a minute—control yourself, Clare. (VINNIE, *sensing the coming storm, hurries to the sliding doors.* CLARENCE *has reached the hall with his packages and he, too, has recognized the danger signal and as* VINNIE *closes one door he closes the other, leaving himself out in the hall and* FATHER *and* VINNIE *facing each other in the room.*)

VINNIE (*persuasively*). Now, Clare, you know you've always liked Cora.

FATHER (*exploding*). What has that got to do with her planking herself down in my house and bringing hordes of strangers with her?

VINNIE (*reproachfully*). How can you call that sweet little girl a horde of strangers?

FATHER. Why don't they go to a hotel? New York is full of hotels built for the express purpose of housing such nuisances.

VINNIE. Clare! Two girls alone in a hotel! Who knows what might happen to them?

FATHER. All right. Then put 'em on the next train. If they want to roam —the damned gypsies—lend 'em a hand! Keep 'em roaming!

VINNIE. What have we got a home for if we can't show a little hospitality?

FATHER. I didn't buy this home to show hospitality—I bought it for my own comfort!

VINNIE. Well, how much are they going to interfere with your comfort living in that little room of Clarence's?

FATHER. The trouble is, damn it, they don't live there. They live in the bathroom! Every time I want to take my bath it's full of giggling females—washing their hair. From the time they take, you'd think it was the Seven Sutherland Sisters. I tell you, I won't have it! Send 'em to a hotel. I'll pay the bill gladly, but get them out of here!
(CLARENCE *puts his head through the sliding door.*)

CLARENCE. Father, I'm afraid they can hear you upstairs.

FATHER. Then keep those doors closed!

VINNIE (*with decision*). Clarence, you open those doors—open them all the way! (CLARENCE *does so.*)

VINNIE (*to* FATHER, *lowering her voice, but maintaining her spirit*). Now, Clare, you behave yourself! (FATHER *glares at her angrily*) They're here and they're going to stay here.

FATHER. That enough, Vinnie! I want no more of this argument. (*He goes to his chair by the window, muttering*) Damnation!

CLARENCE (*to* VINNIE). Mother, Cousin Cora's waiting for you.

FATHER. What I don't understand is why this swarm of locusts always descends on us without any warning. (*He sits down.* VINNIE *looks at him; then, convinced of her victory, she goes upstairs*) Damn! Damnation! Damn! (*He follows her upstairs with his eyes; he remembers he is very fond of her*) Vinnie! Dear Vinnie! (*He remembers he is very angry at her*) Damn!

CLARENCE. Father, can't I go along with the rest of you to Delmonico's tonight?

FATHER. What's that? Delmonico's?

CLARENCE. You're taking Mother, Cora, and Mary to Delmonico's for dinner.

FATHER (*exploding*). Oh, God! (*At this sound from* FATHER, VINNIE *comes flying downstairs again*) I won't have it. I won't have it. (FATHER *stamps angrily across the room.*)

VINNIE (*on the way down*). Clarence, the doors!

FATHER. I won't stand it, by God! I won't stand it! (VINNIE *and* CLARENCE *hurriedly close the sliding doors again.*)

VINNIE. Clare! What's the matter now?

FATHER (*with the calm of anger that has turned to ice*). Do I understand that I can't have dinner in my own home?

VINNIE. It'll do us both good to get out of this house. You need a little change. It'll make you feel better.

FATHER. I have a home to have dinner in. Any time I can't have dinner at home this house is for sale!

VINNIE. Well, you can't have dinner here tonight because it isn't ordered.

FATHER. Let me tell you I'm ready to sell this place this very minute if I can't live here in peace. And we can all go and sit under a palm tree and live on breadfruit and pickles.

VINNIE. But, Clare, Cora and Mary want to see something of New York.

FATHER. Oh, that's it! Well, that's no affair of mine! I am not a guide to Chinatown and the Bowery. (*Drawing himself up, he stalks out, throwing open the sliding doors. As he reaches the foot of the stairs,* MARY *comes tripping down.*)

MARY. I love your house, Mr. Day. I could just live here forever. (FATHER *utters a bark of disgust and continues on upstairs.* MARY *comes into the room a little wide-eyed.*) Cora's waiting for you, Mrs. Day.

VINNIE. Oh, yes, I'll run right up. (*She goes upstairs.*)

CLARENCE. I'm glad you like our house.

MARY. Oh, yes, I like it very much. I like green.

CLARENCE. I like green myself. (*She looks up at his red hair.*)

MARY. Red's my favorite color. (*Embarrassed,* CLARENCE *suddenly hears himself talking about something he has never thought about.*)

CLARENCE. It's an interesting thing about colors. Red's a nice color in a house, too; but outside, too much red would be bad. I mean, for instance, if all the trees and the grass were red. Outside, green is the best color.

MARY (*impressed*). That's right! I've never thought of it that way—but when you do think of it, it's quite a thought! I'll bet you'll make your mark at Yale.

CLARENCE (*pleased, but modest*). Oh! (*The outer door is heard to slam.*)

MARY. My mother wants me to go to college. Do you believe in girls going to college?

CLARENCE. I guess it's all right if they want to waste that much time—before they get married, I mean. (JOHN *comes in, bringing* The Youth's Companion.)

JOHN. Oh, hello! Look! A new *Youth's Companion!*
(*They say* "Hello" *to him.*)

CLARENCE (*from a mature height*). John enjoys *The Youth's Companion.* (JOHN *sits right down and starts to read.* CLARENCE *is worried by this*) John! (JOHN *looks at him non-plussed.* CLARENCE *glances toward* MARY. JOHN *remembers his manners and stands.* CLARENCE *speaks formally to* MARY) Won't you sit down?

MARY. Oh, thank you! (*She sits.* JOHN *sits down again quickly and dives back into* The Youth's Companion. CLARENCE *sits beside* MARY.)

CLARENCE. As I was saying—I think it's all right for a girl to go to college if she goes to a girls' college.

MARY. Well, Mother wants me to go to Ohio Wesleyan—because it's Methodist. (*Then almost as a confession*) You see, we're Methodists.

CLARENCE. Oh, that's too bad! I don't mean it's too bad that you're a Methodist. Anybody's got a right to be anything they want. But what I mean is —we're Episcopalians.

MARY. Yes, I know. I've known ever since I saw your minister—and his collar. (*She looks pretty sad for a minute and then her face brightens*) Oh, I just remembered—my father was an Episcopalian. He was baptized an Episcopalian. He was an Episcopalian right up to the time he married my mother. *She* was the Methodist. (MARY'S *tone would have surprised her mother—and even* MARY, *if she had been listening.*)

CLARENCE. I'll bet your father's a nice man.

MARY. Yes, he is. He owns the livery stable.

CLARENCE. He does? Well, then you must like horses.

MARY. Oh, I love horses! (*They are happily united again in their common love of horses.*)

CLARENCE. They're my favorite animal. Father and I both think there's nothing like a horse! (FATHER *comes down the stairs and into the room. The children all stand.*)

MARY. Oh, Mr. Day, I'm having such a lovely time here!

FATHER. Clarence is keeping you entertained, eh?

MARY. Oh, yes, sir. We've been talking about everything—colors and horses and religion.

FATHER. Oh! (*To* JOHN) Has the evening paper come yet?

JOHN. No, sir.

FATHER. What are you reading?

JOHN. *The Youth's Companion*, sir. (WHITNEY *and* HARLAN *enter from the hall,* WHITNEY *carrying a small box.*)

WHITNEY. Look what we've got!

FATHER. What is it?

WHITNEY. Tiddle-dy-winks. We put our money together and bought it.

FATHER. That's a nice game. Do you know how to play it?

WHITNEY. I've played it lots of times.

HARLAN. Show me how to play it.

FATHER. Here, I'll show you. (*Opens the box and arranges the glass and disks.*)

MARY (*hopefully to* CLARENCE). Are you going out to dinner with us tonight?

CLARENCE (*looking at* FATHER). I don't know yet—but it's beginning to look as though I might.

FATHER. It's easy, Harlan. You press down like this and snap the little fellow into the glass. Now watch me —(*He snaps it and it goes off the table*) The table isn't quite large enough. You boys better play it on the floor.

WHITNEY. Come on, Harlan, I'll take the reds, and you take the yellows.

FATHER. John, have you practiced your piano today?

JOHN. I was going to practice this evening.

FATHER. Better do it now. Music is a delight in the home.
(JOHN *exits, passing* CORA *and* VINNIE *as they enter, coming downstairs.*)

VINNIE. Clare, what do you think Cora just told me? She and Clyde are going to be married this fall!

FATHER. Oh, you finally landed him, eh? (*Everybody laughs*) Well, he's a very lucky man. Cora, being married is the only way to live.

CORA. If we can be half as happy as you and Cousin Vinnie—

VINNIE (*who has gone to the children*). Boys, shouldn't you be playing that on the table?

WHITNEY. The table isn't big enough. Father told us to play on the floor.

VINNIE. My soul and body! Look at your hands! Delia will have your supper ready in a few minutes. Go wash your hands right away and come back and show Mother they're clean.
(*The boys pick up the tiddle-dywinks and depart reluctantly. From the next room we hear* JOHN *playing "The Happy Farmer."*)

FATHER (*sitting down on the sofa with* MARY). Vinnie, this young lady looks about the same age you were when I came out to Pleasantville to rescue you.

VINNIE. Rescue me! You came out there to talk me into marrying you.

FATHER. It worked out just the same. I saved you from spending the rest of your life in that one-horse town.

VINNIE. Cora, the other day I came across a tintype of Clare taken in Pleasantville. I want to show it to you. You'll see who needed rescuing. (*She goes to the table and starts to rummage around in its drawer.*)

FATHER. There isn't time for that, Vinnie. If we're going to Delmonico's for dinner hadn't we all better be getting ready? It's after six now.

CORA. Gracious! I'll have to start. If I'm going to dine in public with a prominent citizen like you, Cousin Clare—I'll have to look my best. (*She goes to the arch.*)

MARY. I've changed already.

CORA. Yes, I know, but I'm afraid I'll have to ask you to come along and hook me up, Mary.

MARY. Of course.

CORA. It won't take a minute and then you can come right back.
(FATHER *rises.* MARY *crosses in front of* FATHER *and starts toward the hall, then turns and looks back at him.*)

MARY. Mr. Day, were you always an Episcopalian?

FATHER. What?

MARY. Were you always an Episcopalian?

FATHER. I've always gone to the Episcopal church, yes.

MARY. But you weren't baptized a Methodist or anything, were you? You were baptized an Episcopalian?

FATHER. Come to think of it, I don't believe I was ever baptized at all.

MARY. Oh!

VINNIE. Clare, that's not very funny, joking about a subject like that.

FATHER. I'm not joking—I remember now—I never was baptized.

VINNIE. Clare, that's ridiculous, everyone's baptized.

FATHER (*sitting down complacently*). Well, I'm not.

VINNIE. Why, no one would keep a little baby from being baptized.

FATHER. You know Father and Mother—free-thinkers, both of them—believed their children should decide those things for themselves.

VINNIE. But, Clare—

FATHER. I remember when I was ten or twelve years old, Mother said I ought to give some thought to it. I suppose I thought about it, but I never got around to having it done to me.

(*The shock to* VINNIE *is as great as if* FATHER *had calmly announced himself guilty of murder. She walks to* FATHER *staring at him in horror.* CORA *and* MARY, *sensing the coming battle, withdraw to the neutral shelter of the hall.*)

VINNIE. Clare, do you know what you're saying?

FATHER. I'm saying I've never been baptized.

VINNIE (*in a sudden panic*). Then something has to be done about it right away.

FATHER (*not the least concerned*). Now, Vinnie, don't get excited over nothing.

VINNIE. Nothing! (*Then, as only a woman can ask such a question*) Clare, why haven't you ever told me?

FATHER. What difference does it make?

VINNIE (*the panic returning*). I've never heard of anyone who wasn't baptized. Even the savages in darkest Africa—

FATHER. It's all right for savages and children. But if an oversight was made in my case it's too late to correct it now.

VINNIE. But if you're not baptized you're not a Christian!

FATHER (*rising in wrath*). Why, confound it, of course I'm a Christian! A damn good Christian, too! (FATHER'S *voice tells* CLARENCE *a major engagement has begun. He hurriedly springs to the sliding doors and closes them, removing himself,* MARY, *and* CORA *from the scene of action*) A lot better Christian than those psalm-singing donkeys in church!

VINNIE. You can't be if you won't be baptized.

FATHER. I won't be baptized and I will be a Christian! I beg to inform you I'll be a Christian in my own way.

VINNIE. Clare, don't you want to meet us all in Heaven?

FATHER. Of course! And I'm going to!

VINNIE. But you can't go to Heaven if you're not baptized!

FATHER. That's a lot of folderol!

VINNIE. Clarence Day, don't you blaspheme like that! You're coming to church with me before you go to the office in the morning and be baptized then and there!

FATHER. Vinnie, don't be ridiculous! If you think I'm going to stand there and have some minister splash water on me at my age, you're mistaken!

VINNIE. But, Clare—

FATHER. That's enough of this, Vinnie. I'm hungry. (*Draws himself up and starts for the door. He does not realize that he and* VINNIE *are now engaged in a battle to the death*) I'm dressing for dinner. (*Throws open the doors, revealing* WHITNEY *and* HARLAN, *who obviously have been eavesdropping and have heard the awful revelation of* FATHER'S *paganism.* FATHER *stalks past them upstairs. The two boys come down into the room staring at their mother, who has been standing, too shocked at* FATHER'S *callous impiety to speak or move.*)

WHITNEY. Mother, if Father hasn't been baptized he hasn't any name. In the sight of the Church he hasn't any name.

VINNIE. That's right! (*To herself*) Maybe we're not even married! (*This awful thought takes possession of* VINNIE. *Her eyes turn slowly toward the children and she suddenly realizes their doubtful status. Her hand goes to her mouth to cover a quick gasp of horror as the curtain falls.*)

CURTAIN

ACT TWO

SCENE I

The Same.

The following Sunday. After church.

The stage is empty as the curtain rises. VINNIE *comes into the archway from the street door, dressed in her Sunday best, carrying her prayer book, hymnal, and a cold indignation. As soon as she is in the room,* FATHER *passes across the hall in his Sunday cutaway and silk hat, carrying gloves and cane.* VINNIE *looks over her shoulder at him as he disappears.* CORA, WHITNEY, *and* HARLAN *come into the room,* CORA *glancing after* FATHER *and then toward* VINNIE. *All three walk as though the sound of a footfall might cause an explosion, and speak in subdued tones.*

HARLAN. Cousin Cora, will you play a game of tiddle-dy-winks with me before you go?

CORA. I'm going to be busy packing until it's time to leave.

WHITNEY. We can't play games on Sunday.

(*We hear the door close and* JOHN *enters and looks into the room apprehensively.*)

CORA. John, where are Clarence and Mary?

JOHN. They dropped behind—'way behind! (*He goes upstairs.* WHITNEY *takes* HARLAN'S *hat from him and starts toward the arch.*)

VINNIE. Whitney, don't hang up your hat. I want you to go over to Sherry's for the ice cream for dinner. Tell Mr. Sherry strawberry—if he has it. And take Harlan with you.

WHITNEY. All right, Mother. (*He and* HARLAN, *trained in the good manners of the period, bow and exit.*)

CORA. Oh, Vinnie, I hate to leave. We've had such a lovely week.

VINNIE (*voice quivers in a tone of scandalized apology*). Cora, what must you think of Clare, making such a scene on his way out of church today?

CORA. Cousin Clare probably thinks that you put the rector up to preaching that sermon.

VINNIE (*tone changes from apology to self-defense with overtones of guilt*). Well, I had to go to see Dr. Lloyd to find out whether we were really married. The sermon on baptism was his own idea. If Clare just hadn't *shouted* so—now the whole congregation knows he's never been baptized! But he's going to be, Cora —you mark my words—he's going to be! I just couldn't go to Heaven without Clare. Why, I get lonesome for him when I go to Ohio.

(FATHER *enters holding his watch. He's also holding his temper. He speaks quietly.*)

FATHER. Vinnie, I went to the dining-room and the table isn't set for dinner yet.

VINNIE. We're having dinner late today.

FATHER. Why can't I have my meals on time?

VINNIE. The girls' train leaves at one-thirty. Their cab's coming at one o'clock.

FATHER. Cab? The horse cars go right past our door.

VINNIE. They have those heavy bags.

FATHER. Clarence and John could have gone along to carry their bags. Cabs are just a waste of money. Why didn't we have an early dinner?

VINNIE. There wasn't time for an early dinner and church, too.

FATHER. As far as I'm concerned this would have been a good day to miss church.

VINNIE (*spiritedly*). I wish we had!

FATHER (*flaring*). I'll bet you put him up to preaching that sermon!

VINNIE. I've never been so mortified in all my life! You stamping up the aisle roaring your head off at the top of your voice!

FATHER. That Lloyd needn't preach at me as though I were some damn criminal! I wanted him to know it, and as far as I'm concerned the whole congregation can know it, too!

VINNIE. They certainly know it now!

FATHER. That suits me!

VINNIE (*pleading*). Clare, you don't seem to understand what the church is for.

FATHER (*laying down a new Commandment*). Vinnie, if there's one place the church should leave alone, it's a man's soul!

VINNIE. Clare, dear, don't you believe what it says in the Bible?

FATHER. A man has to use his common sense about the Bible, Vinnie, if he has any. For instance, you'd be in a pretty fix if I gave all my money to the poor.

VINNIE. Well, that's just silly!

FATHER. Speaking of money—where are this month's bills?

VINNIE. Clare, it isn't fair to go over the household accounts while you're hungry.

FATHER. Where are those bills, Vinnie?

VINNIE. They're downstairs on your desk. (FATHER *exits almost eagerly. Figures are something he understands better than he does women*) Of all times! (*To* CORA) It's awfully hard on a woman to love a man like Clare so much.

CORA. Yes, men can be aggravating. Clyde gets me so provoked! We kept company for six years, but the minute he proposed—the moment I said "Yes"—he began to take me for granted.

VINNIE. You have to expect that, Cora. I don't believe Clare has come right out and told me he loves me since we've been married. Of course I know he does, because I keep reminding him of it. You have to keep reminding them, Cora.
(*The door slams.*)

CORA. That must be Mary and Clarence. (*There's a moment's pause. The two women look toward the hall —then at each other with a knowing sort of smile.* CORA *rises, goes up to the arch, peeks out—then faces front and innocently asks:*) Is that you, Mary?

MARY (*dashing in*). Yes!
(CLARENCE *crosses the arch to hang up his hat.*)

CORA. We have to change our clothes and finish our packing. (*Goes upstairs.*)
(CLARENCE *returns as* MARY *starts up the stairs.*)

MARY (*to* CLARENCE). It won't take me long.

CLARENCE. Can I help you pack?

VINNIE (*shocked*). Clarence! (MARY *runs upstairs.* CLARENCE *drifts into the living-room, somewhat abashed.* VINNIE *collects her hat and gloves, starts out, stops to look at* CLARENCE, *then comes down to him*) Clarence, why didn't you kneel in church today?

CLARENCE. What, Mother?

VINNIE. Why didn't you kneel in church today?

CLARENCE (*troubled*). I just couldn't.

VINNIE. Has it anything to do with Mary? I know she's a Methodist.

CLARENCE. Oh, no, Mother! Methodists kneel. Mary told me. They don't get up and down so much, but they stay down longer.

VINNIE. If it's because your father doesn't kneel—you must remember he wasn't brought up to kneel in church. But you were—you always have—and, Clarence, you want to, don't you?

CLARENCE. Oh, yes! I wanted to today! I started to—you saw me start—but I just couldn't.

VINNIE. Is that suit of your father's too tight for you?

CLARENCE. No, it's not too *tight*. It fits fine. But it *is* the suit. Very peculiar things have happened to me since I started to wear it. I haven't been myself since I put it on.

VINNIE. In what way, Clarence? How do you mean?
(CLARENCE *pauses, then blurts out his problem.*)

CLARENCE. Mother, I can't seem to makes these clothes do anything Father wouldn't do!

VINNIE. That's nonsense, Clarence—and not to kneel in church is a sacrilege.

CLARENCE. But making Father's trousers kneel seemed more of a sacrilege.

VINNIE. Clarence!

CLARENCE. No! Remember the first time I wore this? It was at Dora Wakefield's party for Mary. Do you know what happened? We were playing musical chairs and Dora Wakefield sat down suddenly right in my lap. I jumped up so fast she almost got hurt.

VINNIE. But it was all perfectly innocent.

CLARENCE. It wasn't that Dora was sitting on my lap—she was sitting on Father's trousers. Mother, I've got to have a suit of my own. (CLARENCE'S *metaphysical problem is one that* VINNIE *can't cope with at this particular minute.*)

VINNIE. My soul and body! Clarence, you have a talk with your father about it. I'm sure if you approach him the right way—you know—tactfully—he'll see—
(MARY *comes downstairs and hesitates at the arch.*)

MARY. Oh, excuse me.

VINNIE. Gracious! Have you finished your packing?

MARY. Practically. I never put my comb and brush in until I'm ready to close my bag.

VINNIE. I must see Margaret about your box lunch for the train. I'll leave you two together. Remember, it's Sunday. (*She goes downstairs.*)

CLARENCE. I was hoping we could have a few minutes together before you left.

MARY (*not to admit her eagerness*). Cora had so much to do I wanted to get out of her way.

CLARENCE. Well, didn't you want to see me?

MARY (*self-consciously*). I did want to tell you how much I've enjoyed our friendship.

CLARENCE. You're going to write me when you get to Springfield, aren't you?

MARY. Of course, if you write me first.

CLARENCE. But you'll have something to write about—your trip—and Aunt Judith—and how things are in Springfield. You write me as soon as you get there.

MARY. Maybe I'll be too busy. Maybe I won't have time. (*She sits on the sofa.*)

CLARENCE (*with the authority of* FATHER'S *trousers*). You find the time! Let's not have any nonsense about that! You'll write me first—and you'll do it right away, the first day! (*Sits beside her.*)

MARY. How do you know I'll take orders from you?

CLARENCE. I'll show you. (*He takes a quick glance toward the hall*) Give me your hand!

MARY. Why should I?

CLARENCE. Give me your hand, confound it! (MARY *gives it to him.*)

MARY. What do you want with my hand?

CLARENCE. I just wanted it. (*Holding her hand, he melts a little and smiles at her. She melts, too. Their hands, clasped together, are resting on* CLARENCE'S *knee and they relax happily*) What are you thinking about?

MARY. I was just thinking.

CLARENCE. About what?

MARY. Well, when we were talking about writing each other I was hoping you'd write me first because that would mean you liked me.

CLARENCE (*with the logic of the male*). What's writing first got to do with my liking you?

MARY. Oh, you *do* like me?

CLARENCE. Of course I do. I like you better than any girl I ever met.

MARY (*with the logic of the female*). But you don't like me well enough to write first?

CLARENCE. I don't see how one thing's got anything to do with the other.

MARY. But a girl can't write first—because she's a *girl.*

CLARENCE. That doesn't make sense. If a girl has something to write about and a fellow hasn't, there's no reason why she shouldn't write first.

MARY (*starting a flanking movement*). You know, the first few days I was here you'd do anything for me and then you changed. You used to be a lot of fun—and then all of a sudden you turned into an old sober-sides.

CLARENCE. When did I?

MARY. The first time I noticed it was when we walked home from Dora Wakefield's party. My, you were on your dignity! You've been that way ever since. You even dress like an old sober-sides. (CLARENCE'S *face changes as* FATHER'S *pants rise to haunt him. Then he notices that their clasped hands are resting on these very pants, and he lifts them off. Agony obviously is setting in.* MARY *sees the expression on his face*) What's the matter?

CLARENCE. I just happened to remember something.

MARY. What? (CLARENCE *doesn't answer, but his face does*) Oh, I know. This is the last time we'll be together. (*She puts her hand on his shoulder. He draws away.*)

CLARENCE. Mary, please!

MARY. But, Clarence! We'll see each other in a month. And we'll be writing each other, too. I hope we will. (*She gets up*) Oh, Clarence, please write me first, because it will show me how much you like me. Please! I'll show you how much I like you! (*She throws herself on his lap and buries her head on his shoulder.* CLARENCE *stiffens in agony.*)

CLARENCE (*hoarsely*). Get up! Get up! (*She pulls back her head and looks at him, then springs from his lap and runs away, covering her face and sobbing.* CLARENCE *goes to her*) Don't do that, Mary! Please don't do that!

MARY. Now you'll think I'm just a bold and forward girl.

CLARENCE. Oh, no.

MARY. Yes, you will—you'll think I'm bold!

CLARENCE. Oh, no—it's not that.

MARY (*hopefully*). Was it because it's Sunday?

CLARENCE (*in despair*). No, it would be the same any day— (*He is about to explain, but* MARY *flares.*)

MARY. Oh, it's just because you didn't want me sitting on your lap.

CLARENCE. It was nice of you to do it.

MARY. It was nice of me! So you told me to get up! You just couldn't bear to have me sit there. Well, you needn't write me first. You needn't write me any letters at all, because I'll tear them up without opening them! (FATHER *enters the archway, a sheath of bills in his hand and his account book under his arm*) I guess I know now you don't like me! I never want to see you again. I—I— (*She breaks and starts to run toward the stairs. At the sight of* FATHER *she stops, but only for a gasp, then continues on upstairs, unable to control her sobs.* CLARENCE, *who has been standing in unhappy indecision, turns to follow her, but stops short at the sight of* FATHER, *who is standing in the arch looking at him with some amazement.* FATHER *looks from* CLARENCE *toward the vanished* MARY, *then back to* CLARENCE.)

FATHER. Clarence, that young girl is crying—she's in tears. What's the meaning of this?

CLARENCE. I'm sorry, Father, it's all my fault.

FATHER. Nonsense! What's that girl trying to do to you?

CLARENCE. What? No, she wasn't—it was—I—how long have you been here?

FATHER. Well, whatever the quarrel was about, Clarence, I'm glad you held your own. Where's your mother?

CLARENCE (*desperately*). I have to have a new suit of clothes—you've *got* to give me the money for it.
(FATHER'S *account book reaches the table with a sharp bang as he stares at* CLARENCE *in astonishment.*)

FATHER. Young man, do you realize you're addressing your father?
(CLARENCE *wilts miserably and sinks into a chair.*)

CLARENCE. I'm sorry, Father—I apologize—but you don't know how important this is to me. (CLARENCE'S *tone of misery gives* FATHER *pause.*)

FATHER. A suit of clothes is so—? Now, why should a—? (*Something dawns on* FATHER *and he looks up in the direction in which* MARY *has disappeared, then looks back at* CLARENCE) Has your need for a suit of clothes anything to do with that young lady?

CLARENCE. Yes, Father.

FATHER. Why, Clarence! (*Suddenly realizes that women have come into* CLARENCE'S *emotional life and there comes a yearning to protect this inexperienced and defenseless member of his own sex*) This comes as quite a shock to me.

CLARENCE. What does, Father?

FATHER. Your being so grown up! Still, I might have known that if you're going to college this fall—yes, you're at an age when you'll be meeting girls. Clarence, there are things about women that I think you ought to know! (*He goes up and closes the doors, then comes down and sits beside* CLARENCE, *hesitating for a moment before he speaks*) Yes, I think it's better for you to hear this from me than to have to learn it for yourself. Clarence, women aren't the angels that you think they are! Well, now—first, let me explain this to you. You see, Clarence, we men have to run this world and it's not an easy job. It takes work, and it takes thinking. A man has to be sure of his facts and figures. He has to reason things out. Now, you take a woman—a woman thinks—no I'm wrong right there—a woman doesn't think at all! She gets stirred up! And she gets stirred up over the damnedest things! Now, I love my wife just as much as any man, but that doesn't mean I should stand for a lot of folderol! By God! I won't stand for it! (*Looks around toward the spot where he had his last clash with* VINNIE.)

CLARENCE. Stand for what, Father?

FATHER (*to himself*). That's the one thing I will not submit myself to.

(*Has ceased explaining women to* CLARENCE *and is now explaining himself*) Clarence, if a man thinks a certain thing is the wrong thing to do he shouldn't do it. If he thinks a thing is right he should do it. Now that has nothing to do with whether he loves his wife or not.

CLARENCE. Who says it has, Father?

FATHER. They do!

CLARENCE. Who, sir?

FATHER. Women! They get stirred up and then they try to get you stirred up, too. If you can keep reason and logic in the argument, a man can hold his own, of course. But if they can *switch* you—pretty soon the argument's about whether you love them or not. I swear I don't know how they do it! Don't you let 'em, Clarence! Don't you let 'em!

CLARENCE. I see what you mean so far, Father. If you don't watch yourself, love can make you do a lot of things you don't want to do.

FATHER. Exactly!

CLARENCE. But if you do watch out and know just how to handle women—

FATHER. Then you'll be all right. All a man has to do is be firm. You know how sometimes I have to be firm with your mother. Just now about this month's household accounts—

CLARENCE. Yes, but what can you do when they cry?

FATHER (*he gives this a moment's thought*). Well, that's quite a question. You just have to make them understand that what you're doing is for their good.

CLARENCE. I see.

FATHER (*rising*). Now, Clarence, you know all about women. (*Goes to the table and sits down in front of his account book, opening it.* CLARENCE *rises and looks at him.*)

CLARENCE. But, Father—

FATHER. Yes, Clarence.

CLARENCE. I thought you were going to tell me about—

FATHER. About what?

CLARENCE. About women. (FATHER *realizes with some shock that* CLARENCE *expected him to be more specific.*)

FATHER. Clarence, there are some things gentlemen don't discuss! I've told you all you need to know. The thing for you to remember is—be firm! (CLARENCE *turns away. There is a knock at the sliding doors*) Yes, come in.
(MARY *opens the doors.*)

MARY. Excuse me! (MARY *enters.* FATHER *turns his attention to the household accounts.* MARY *goes to the couch and picks up her handkerchief and continues around the couch.* CLARENCE *crosses to meet her above the couch, determined to be firm.* MARY *passes him without a glance.* CLARENCE *wilts, then again assuming firmness, turns up into the arch in an attempt to quail* MARY *with a look.* MARY *marches upstairs ignoring him.* CLARENCE *turns back into the room defeated. He looks down at his clothes unhappily, then decides to be firm with his father. He straightens up and steps toward him. At this moment* FATHER, *staring at a bill, emits his cry of rage.*)

FATHER. Oh, God! (CLARENCE *retreats.* FATHER *rises and holds the bill in question between thumb and forefinger as though it were too repulsive to touch.* VINNIE *comes rushing down the stairs.*)

VINNIE. What's the matter, Clare? What's wrong?

FATHER. I will *not* send this person a check!
(VINNIE *looks at it.*)

VINNIE. Why, Clare, that's the only hat I've bought since March and it was reduced from forty dollars.

FATHER. I don't question your buying the hat or what you paid for it, but the person from whom you bought it—this Mademoiselle Mimi—isn't fit to be in the hat business or any other.

VINNIE. I never went there before, but it's a very nice place and I don't see why you object to it.

FATHER (*exasperated*). I object to it because this confounded person doesn't put her name on her bills! Mimi what? Mimi O'Brien? Mimi Jones? Mimi Weinstein?

VINNIE. How do I know? It's just Mimi.

FATHER. It isn't just Mimi. She must have some other name, damn it! Now, I wouldn't make out a check payable to Charley or to Jimmy, and I won't make out a check payable to Mimi. Find out what her last name is, and I'll pay her the money.

VINNIE. All right. All right. (*She starts out.*)

FATHER. Just a minute, Vinnie, that isn't all.

VINNIE. But Cora will be leaving any minute, Clare, and it isn't polite for me—

FATHER. Never mind Cora. Sit down. (CLARENCE *goes into the hall, looks upstairs, wanders up and down the hall restlessly.* VINNIE *reluctantly sits down opposite* FATHER *at the table*) Vinnie, you know I like to live well, and I want my family to live well. But this house must be run on a business basis. I must know how much money I'm spending and what for. For instance, if you recall, two weeks ago I gave you six dollars to buy a new coffeepot—

VINNIE. Yes, because you broke the old one. You threw it right on the floor.

FATHER. I'm not talking about that. I'm simply endeavoring—

VINNIE. But it was so silly to break that nice coffeepot, Clare, and there was nothing the matter with the coffee that morning. It was made just the same as always.

FATHER. It was not! It was made in a damned barbaric manner!

VINNIE. I couldn't get another imported one. That little shop has stopped selling them. They said the tariff wouldn't let them. And that's your fault, Clare, because you're always voting to raise the tariff.

FATHER. The tariff protects America against cheap foreign labor. (*He sounds as though he is quoting*) Now I find that—

VINNIE. The tariff does nothing but put up the prices and that's hard on everybody, especially the farmer. (*She sounds as though she is quoting back.*)

FATHER (*annoyed*). I wish to God you wouldn't talk about matters you don't know a damn thing about!

VINNIE. I do too know about them. Miss Gulick says every intelligent woman should have some opinion—

FATHER. Who, may I ask, is Miss Gulick?

VINNIE. Why, she's that current-events woman I told you about and the tickets are a dollar every Tuesday.

FATHER. Do you mean to tell me that a pack of idle-minded females pay a dollar apiece to hear another female gabble about the events of the day? Listen to me if you want to know anything about the events of the day!

VINNIE. But you get so excited, Clare, and besides, Miss Gulick says that our President, whom you're always belittling, prays to God for guidance and—

FATHER (*having had enough of Miss Gulick*). Vinnie, what happened to that six dollars?

VINNIE. What six dollars?

FATHER. I gave you six dollars to buy a new coffeepot and now I find that you apparently got one at Lewis & Conger's and charged it. Here's their bill: "One coffeepot—five dollars."

VINNIE. So you owe me a dollar and you can hand it right over. (*She holds out her hand for it.*)

FATHER. I'll do nothing of the kind! What did you do with that six dollars?

VINNIE. Why, Clare, I can't tell you now, dear. Why didn't you ask me at the time?

FATHER. Oh, my God!

VINNIE. Wait a moment! I spent four dollars and a half for that new umbrella I told you I wanted and you said I didn't need, but I did, very much.

(FATHER *takes his pencil and writes in the account book.*)

FATHER. Now we're getting somewhere. One umbrella—four dollars and a half.

VINNIE. And that must have been the week I paid Mrs. Tobin for two extra days' washing.

FATHER (*entering the item*). Mrs. Tobin.

VINNIE. So that was two dollars more.

FATHER. Two dollars.

VINNIE. That makes six dollars and fifty cents. And that's another fifty cents you owe me.

FATHER. I don't owe you anything. (*Stung by* VINNIE'*s tactics into a de-*

termination to pin her butterfly mind down) What you owe me is an explanation of where my money's gone! We're going over this account book item by item. *(Starts to sort the bills for the purposes of cross-examination, but the butterfly takes wing again.)*

VINNIE. I do the very best I can to keep down expenses. And you know yourself that Cousin Phoebe spends twice as much as we do.

FATHER. Damn Cousin Phoebe!—I don't wish to be told how she throws her money around.

VINNIE. Oh, Clare, how can you? And I thought you were so fond of Cousin Phoebe.

FATHER. All right, I am fond of Cousin Phoebe, but I can get along without hearing so much about her.

VINNIE. You talk about your own relatives enough.

FATHER *(hurt)*. That's not fair, Vinnie. When I talk about my relatives I criticize them.

VINNIE. If I can't even speak of Cousin Phoebe—

FATHER. You can speak of her all you want to—but I won't have Cousin Phoebe or anyone else dictating to me how to run my house. Now this month's total—

VINNIE *(righteously)*. I didn't say a word about her dictating, Clare—she isn't that kind!

FATHER *(dazed)*. I don't know what you said, now. You never stick to the point. I endeavor to show you how to run this house on a business basis and you wind up by jibbering and jabbering about everything under the sun. If you'll just explain to me— *(Finally cornered,* VINNIE *realizes the time has come for tears. Quietly she turns them on.)*

VINNIE. I don't know what you expect of me. I tire myself out chasing up and down those stairs all day long —trying to look after your comfort— to bring up our children—I do the mending and the marketing and as if that isn't enough, you want me to be an expert bookkeeper, too.

FATHER *(touched where* VINNIE *has hoped to touch him)*. Vinnie, I want to be reasonable; but can't you understand?—I'm doing all this for your own good. *(*VINNIE *rises with a moan.* FATHER *sighs with resignation)* I suppose I'll have to go ahead just paying the bills and hoping I've got money enough in the bank to meet them. But it's all very discouraging.

VINNIE. I'll try to do better, Clare. *(*FATHER *looks up into her tearful face and melts.)*

FATHER. That's all I'm asking. *(She goes to him and puts her arm around his shoulder)* I'll go down and make out the checks and sign them. *(*VINNIE *doesn't seem entirely consoled, so he attempts a lighter note to cheer her up)* Oh, Vinnie, maybe I haven't any right to sign those checks, since in the sight of the Lord I haven't any name at all. Do you suppose the bank will feel that way about it too —or do you think they'll take a chance? *(He should not have said this.)*

VINNIE. That's right! Clare, to make those checks good you'll have to be baptized right away.

FATHER (*retreating angrily*). Vinnie, the bank doesn't care whether I've been baptized or not!

VINNIE. Well, I care! And no matter what Dr. Lloyd says, I'm not sure we're really married.

FATHER. Damn it, Vinnie, we have four children! If we're not married now we never will be!

VINNIE. Oh, Clare, don't you see how serious this is? You've got to do something about it.

FATHER. Well, just now I've got to do something about these damn bills you've run up. (*Sternly*) I'm going downstairs.

VINNIE. Not before you give me that dollar and a half!

FATHER. What dollar and a half?

VINNIE. The dollar and a half you owe me!

FATHER (*thoroughly enraged*). I don't owe you any dollar and a half! I gave you money to buy a coffeepot for me and somehow it turned into an umbrella for you.

VINNIE. Clarence Day, what kind of a man are you? Quibbling about a dollar and a half when your immortal soul is in danger! And what's more—

FATHER. All right. All right. All right. (*He takes the dollar and a half from his change purse and gives it to her.*)

VINNIE (*smiling*). Thank you, Clare. (VINNIE *turns and leaves the room. Her progress upstairs is a one-woman march of triumph.* FATHER *puts his purse back, gathers up his papers and his dignity, and starts out.* CLARENCE *waylays him in the arch.*)

CLARENCE. Father—you never did tell me—can I have a new suit of clothes?

FATHER. No, Clarence! I'm sorry, but I have to be firm with you, too! (*He stalks off.* JOHN *comes down the stairs carrying a traveling bag, which he takes out toward the front door. He returns empty-handed and starts up the stairs again.*)

CLARENCE. John, come here a minute.

JOHN (*coming into the room*). What do you want?

CLARENCE. John, have you got any money you could lend me?

JOHN. With this week's allowance I'll have about three dollars.

CLARENCE. That's no good. I've got to have enough to buy a new suit of clothes.

JOHN. Why don't you earn some money? That's what I'm going to do. I'm going to buy a bicycle—one of those new low kind, with both wheels the same size—you know, a safety.

CLARENCE. How are you going to earn that much money?

JOHN. I've got a job practically. Look, I found this ad in the paper. (*He hands* CLARENCE *a clipping from his pocket.*)

CLARENCE (*reading*). "Wanted, an energetic young man to handle household necessity that sells on sight. Liberal commissions. Apply 312 West Fourteenth Street, Tuesday from eight to twelve." Listen, John, let me have that job.

JOHN. Why should I give you my job? They're hard to get.

CLARENCE. But I've got to have a new suit of clothes.

JOHN. Maybe I could get a job for both of us. (*The doorbell rings*) I'll tell you what I'll do, I'll ask the man.

FATHER (*hurrying to the foot of the stairs*). Vinnie! Cora! The cab's here. Hurry up! (*Goes through the arch toward the front door.*)

CLARENCE. John, we've both got to get down there early Tuesday—the first thing.

JOHN. Oh, no you don't—I'm going alone. But I'll put in a good word with the boss about you.

FATHER (*off*). They'll be right out. Vinnie! Cora! (*He comes back to the foot of the stairs and calls up*) Are you coming? The cab's waiting!

VINNIE (*from upstairs*). We heard you, Clare. We'll be down in a minute.
(FATHER *comes into the room.*)

FATHER. John, go upstairs and hurry them down. (JOHN *goes upstairs.* FATHER *crosses to the window and looks out, then consults his watch.*)

FATHER. What's the matter with those women? Don't they know cabs cost money? Clarence, go see what's causing this infernal delay!
(CLARENCE *goes out to the hall.*)

CLARENCE. Here they come, Father.
(MARY *comes sedately downstairs. She passes* CLARENCE *without a glance and goes to* FATHER.)

MARY. Goodbye, Mr. Day. I can't tell you how much I appreciate your hospitality.

FATHER. Not at all! Not at all!
(VINNIE *and* CORA *appear at top of stairs and come down.* JOHN *follows with the bags and takes them out.*)

CORA. Goodbye, Clarence. (*She starts into the room.*)

FATHER. Cora, we can say goodbye to you on the sidewalk.

VINNIE. There's no hurry. Their train doesn't go until one-thirty.

FATHER. Cabs cost money. If they have any waiting to do they ought to do it at the Grand Central Depot. They've got a waiting room there just *for* that.

VINNIE (*to* MARY). If there's one thing Mr. Day can't stand it's to keep a cab waiting.

CORA. It's been so nice seeing you again, Clarence. (*She kisses him.* MARGARET *enters with a box of lunch.*)

MARGARET. Here's the lunch.

FATHER. All right. All right. Give it to me. Let's get started. (MARGARET *gives it to him and exits.*)

CORA. Where's John?

FATHER. He's outside. Come on. (*Leads the way.* CORA *and* VINNIE *follow.* MARY *starts.*)

CLARENCE. Mary, aren't you going even to shake hands with me?

MARY. I don't think I'd better. You may remember that when I get too close to you you feel contaminated. (*Starts out.* CLARENCE *follows her.*)

CLARENCE. Mary! (*She stops in the arch. He goes to her*) You're going to write me, aren't you?

MARY. Are you going to write first?

CLARENCE (*resolutely*). No, Mary. There are times when a man has to be firm.
(JOHN *enters.*)

JOHN. Mary, Mother says you'd better hurry out before Father starts yelling. It's Sunday.

MARY. Goodbye, John. I'm very happy to have made *your* acquaintance. (*She walks out. We hear the door close.* JOHN *goes out.* CLARENCE *takes a step toward the door, stops, suffers a moment, then turns to the writing desk, takes paper and pen and ink to the table, and sits down to write a letter.*)

CLARENCE (*writing*). Dear Mary—

CURTAIN

SCENE II

The same.

Two days later. The breakfast table.

HARLAN *and* WHITNEY *are at the table, ready to start breakfast.* CLARENCE *is near the window reading the paper. The places of* JOHN *and* VINNIE *and* FATHER *are empty.* NORA, *a new maid, is serving the fruit and cereal.* NORA *is heavily built and along toward middle age. The doorbell rings and we hear the postman's whistle.* CLARENCE *drops the paper and looks out the window toward the door.* NORA *starts toward the arch.*

CLARENCE. Never mind, Nora. It's the postman. I'll go. (*He runs out through the arch.*)

WHITNEY (*to* NORA). You forgot the sugar. It goes here between me and Father.
(CLARENCE *comes back with three or four letters which he sorts eagerly. Then his face falls in utter dejection.* FATHER *comes down the stairs.*)

FATHER. Good morning, boys! John late? (*He shouts*) John! John! Hurry down to your breakfast.

CLARENCE. John had his breakfast early, Father, and went out to see about something.

FATHER. See about what?

CLARENCE. John and I thought we'd work this summer and earn some money.

FATHER. Good! Sit down boys. (*Goes to his chair.*)

CLARENCE. We saw an ad in the paper and John went down to see about it.

FATHER. Why didn't you go, too?

CLARENCE. I was expecting an answer to a letter I wrote, but it didn't come. Here's the mail. (*He seems depressed.*)

FATHER (*sitting*). What kind of work is this you're planning to do?

CLARENCE. Sort of salesman, the ad said.

FATHER. Um-hum. Well, work never hurt anybody. It's good for them. But if you're going to work, work hard. King Solomon had the right idea about work. "Whatever thy hand findeth to do," Solomon said, "do thy damnedest!" Where's your mother?

NORA. If you please, sir, Mrs. Day doesn't want any breakfast. She isn't feeling well, so she went back upstairs to lie down again.

FATHER (*uneasily*). Now, why does your mother do that to me? She knows it just upsets my day when she doesn't come down to breakfast. Clarence, go tell your mother I'll be up to see her before I start for the office.

CLARENCE. Yes, sir. (*He goes upstairs.*)

HARLAN. What's the matter with Mother?

FATHER. There's nothing the matter with your mother. Perfectly healthy woman. She gets an ache or a twinge and instead of being firm about it, she just gives in to it. (*The postman whistles. Then the doorbell rings.* NORA *answers it*) Boys, after breakfast you find out what your mother wants you to do today. Whitney, you take care of Harlan.

(NORA *comes back with a special delivery letter.*)

NORA. It's a special delivery. (*She hands it to* FATHER, *who tears it open at once.* CLARENCE *comes rushing down the stairs.*)

CLARENCE. Was that the postman again?

WHITNEY. It was a special delivery.

CLARENCE. Yes? Where is it?

WHITNEY. It was for Father.

CLARENCE (*again disappointed*). Oh — (*He sits at the table.* FATHER *has opened the letter and is reading it. Bewildered, he turns it over and looks at the signature.*)

FATHER. I don't understand this at all. Here's a letter from some woman I never even heard of. (FATHER *tackles the letter again.* CLARENCE *sees the envelope, picks it up, looks at the postmark, worried.*)

CLARENCE. Father!

FATHER. Oh, God!

CLARENCE. What is it, Father?

FATHER. This is the damnedest nonsense I ever read! As far as I can make out this woman claims that she sat on my lap and I didn't like it. (CLARENCE *begins to turn red.* FATHER *goes on reading a little further and then holds the letter over in front of* CLARENCE) Can you make out what that word is? (CLARENCE *begins feverishly to read as much as possible, but* FATHER *cuts in*) No, that word right there. (*He points.*)

CLARENCE. It looks like—"curiosity." (FATHER *withdraws the letter,* CLARENCE's *eyes following it hungrily.*)

FATHER (*reads*). "I only opened your letter as a matter of curiosity." (*Breaks off reading aloud as he turns the page.*)

CLARENCE. Yes? Go on.

FATHER. Why, this gets worse and worse! It just turns into a lot of sentimental lovey-dovey mush. (*Crushes the letter, stalks across the room, and throws it into the fireplace,* CLARENCE *watching him with dismay*) Is this someone's idea of a practical joke? Why must I be the butt— (VINNIE *comes hurrying down the stairs. Her hair is down in two braids over her shoulder. She is wearing a lacy combing jacket over her corset cover, and a striped petticoat.*)

VINNIE. What's the matter, Clare? What's wrong?

FATHER (*going to her*). Nothing wrong—just a damn fool letter. How are you, Vinnie?

VINNIE (*weakly*). I don't feel well. I thought you needed me, but if you don't I'll go back to bed.

FATHER. No, now that you're here, sit down with us. (*He moves out her chair*) Get some food in your stomach. Do you good.

VINNIE (*protesting*). I don't feel like eating anything, Clare.
(NORA *enters with a tray of bacon and eggs, stops at the serving table.*)

FATHER (*heartily*). That's all the more reason why you should eat. Build up your strength! (*He forces* VINNIE *into her chair and turns to speak to* NORA, *who has her back to him*) Here— (*Then to* CLARENCE) What's this one's name?

CLARENCE. Nora.

FATHER. Nora! Give Mrs. Day some of the bacon and eggs.

VINNIE. No, Clare! (NORA, *however, has gone to* VINNIE's *side with the platter*) No, take it away, Nora. I don't even want to smell it.
(*The maid retreats, and serves* FATHER; *then* CLARENCE; *then serves coffee and exits.*)

FATHER. Vinnie, it's just weak to give in to an ailment. Any disease can be cured by firmness. What you need is strength of character.

VINNIE. I don't know why you object to my complaining a little. I notice when you have a headache you yell and groan and swear enough.

FATHER. Of course I yell! That's to prove to the headache that I'm stronger than it is. I can usually swear it right out of my system.

VINNIE. This isn't a headache. I think I've caught some kind of a germ. There's a lot of sickness around. Several of my friends have had to send for the doctor. I may have the same thing.

FATHER. I'll bet this is all your imagination, Vinnie. You hear of a lot of other people having some disease and then you get scared and think you have it yourself. So you go to bed and send for the doctor. The doctor —all poppycock!

VINNIE. I didn't say anything about my sending for the doctor.

FATHER. I should hope not. Doctors think they know a damn lot, but they don't.

VINNIE. But Clare, dear, when people are seriously ill you have to do something.

FATHER. Certainly you have to do something! Cheer 'em up—that's the way to cure 'em!

VINNIE (*with slight irony*). How would you go about cheering them up?

FATHER. I? I'd tell 'em—bah! (VINNIE, *out of exasperation and weakness, begins to cry.* FATHER *looks at her amazed*) What have I done now?

VINNIE. Oh, Clare—hush up! (*She moves from the table to the sofa, where she tries to control her crying.* HARLAN *slides out of his chair and runs over to her*) Harlan dear, keep away from Mother. You might catch what she's got. Whitney, if you've finished your breakfast—

WHITNEY (*rising*). Yes, Mother.

VINNIE. I promised Mrs. Whitehead to send over Margaret's recipe for floating-island pudding. Margaret has it all written out. And take Harlan with you.

WHITNEY. All right, Mother. I hope you feel better. (WHITNEY *and* HARLAN *exit.* FATHER *goes over and sits beside* VINNIE *on the sofa.*)

FATHER. Vinnie. (*Contritely*) I didn't mean to upset you. I was just trying to help. (*He pats her hand*) When you take to your bed I have a damned lonely time around here. So when I see you getting it into your head that you're sick, I want to do something about it. (*He continues to pat her hand vigorously with what he thinks is reassurance*) Just because some of your friends have given in to this is no reason why you should imagine you're sick, Vinnie.

VINNIE (*snatching her hand away*). Oh, stop, Clare!—get out of this house and go to your office! (FATHER *is a little bewildered and somewhat indignant at this rebuff to his tenderness. He gets up and goes out into the hall, comes back with his hat and stick, and marches out of the house, slamming the door.* VINNIE *rises and starts toward the stairs.*)

CLARENCE. I'm sorry you're not feeling well, Mother.

VINNIE. Oh, I'll be all right, Clarence. Remember last fall .. had a touch of this and I was all right the next morning.

CLARENCE. Are you sure you don't want the doctor?

VINNIE. Oh, no. I really don't need him—and besides doctors worry your father. I don't want him to be upset.

CLARENCE. Is there anything I can do for you?

VINNIE. Ask Margaret to send me up a cup of tea. I'll try to drink it. I'm going back to bed.

CLARENCE. Do you mind if John and I go out today or will you need us?

VINNIE. You run right along. I just want to be left alone. (*She exits up the stairs.* CLARENCE *starts for the fireplace eager to retrieve* MARY'S *letter.* NORA *enters. He stops.*)

CLARENCE. Oh!—Nora—will you take a cup of tea up to Mrs. Day in her room?

NORA. Yes, sir. (*Exits.* CLARENCE *hurries around the table, gets the crumpled letter, and starts to read it feverishly. He reads quickly to the end, then draws a deep, happy breath. The door slams. He puts the letter in his pocket.* JOHN *enters, carrying two heavy packages.*)

CLARENCE. Did you get the job?

JOHN. Yes, for both of us. Look, I've got it with me.

CLARENCE. What is it?

JOHN. Medicine.

CLARENCE (*dismayed*). Medicine! You took a job for us to go out and sell medicine!

JOHN. But it's wonderful medicine. (*Gets a bottle out of the package and reads from the label*) "Bartlett's Beneficent Balm—A Boon to Mankind." Look what it cures! (*He hands the bottle to* CLARENCE.)

CLARENCE (*reading*). "A sovereign cure for colds, coughs, catarrh, asthma, quinsy, and sore throat; poor digestion, summer complaint, colic, dyspepsia, heartburn, and shortness of breath; lumbago, rheumatism, heart disease, giddiness, and women's complaints; nervous prostration, St. Vitus' dance, jaundice, and la grippe; proud flesh, pink eye, seasickness, and pimples." (*As* CLARENCE *has read off the list he has become more and more impressed.*)

JOHN. See?

CLARENCE. Say, that sounds all right!

JOHN. It's made "from a secret formula known only to Dr. Bartlett."

CLARENCE. He must be quite a doctor!

JOHN (*enthusiastically*). It sells for a dollar a bottle and we get twenty-five cents commission on every bottle.

CLARENCE. Well, where does he want us to sell it?

JOHN. He's given us the territory of all Manhattan Island.

CLARENCE. That's bully! Anybody that's sick at all ought to need a bottle of this. Let's start by calling on friends of Father and Mother.

JOHN. That's a good idea. But wait a minute. Suppose they ask us if we use it at our house?

CLARENCE (*a little worried*). Oh, yes. It would be better if we could say we did.

JOHN. But we can't because we haven't had it here long enough.

(NORA *enters with a tray with a cup of tea. She goes to the table and puts the sugar bowl and cream pitcher on it.*)

CLARENCE. Is that the tea for Mrs. Day?

NORA. Yes.
(*The suspicion of a good idea dawns on* CLARENCE.)

CLARENCE. I'll take it up to her. You needn't bother.

NORA. Thank you. Take it up right away while it's hot. (*She exits.* CLARENCE *watches her out.*)

CLARENCE (*eyeing* JOHN). Mother wasn't feeling well this morning.

JOHN. What was the matter with her?

CLARENCE. I don't know—she was just complaining.

JOHN (*getting the idea immediately and consulting the bottle*). Well, it says here it's good for women's complaints. (*They look at each other.* CLARENCE *opens the bottle and smells its contents.* JOHN *leans over and takes a sniff, too. Then he nods to* CLARENCE, *who quickly reaches for a spoon and measures out a teaspoonful, which he puts into the tea.* JOHN, *wanting to be sure* MOTHER *has enough to cure her, pours still more into the tea from the bottle as the curtain falls. The curtain remains down for a few seconds to denote a lapse of three hours. When the curtain rises again, the breakfast things have been cleared and the room is in order.* HARLAN *is kneeling on* FATHER*'s chair looking out the window as if watching for someone.* MARGARET *comes down from upstairs.*)

MARGARET. Has your father come yet?

HARLAN. Not yet.
(NORA *enters from downstairs with a steaming teakettle and a towel and meets* MARGARET *in the hall.*)

MARGARET. Hurry that upstairs. The doctor's waiting for it. I've got to go out.

NORA. Where are you going?

MARGARET. I have to go and get the minister.
(NORA *goes upstairs.*)

HARLAN. There's a cab coming up the street.

MARGARET. Well, I hope it's him, poor man—but a cab doesn't sound like your father. (*She hurries downstairs.* HARLAN *sees something through the window, then rushes to the stairwell and shouts down to* MARGARET.)

HARLAN. Yes, it's Father. Whitney got him all right. (*Runs back to the window. The front door slams and* FATHER *crosses the arch and hurries upstairs.* WHITNEY *comes into the room*) What took you so long?

WHITNEY. Long? I wasn't long. I went right down on the elevated and got Father right away and we came all the way back in a *cab.*

HARLAN. I thought you were never coming.

WHITNEY. Well, the horse didn't go very fast at first. The cabby whipped him and swore at him and still he wouldn't gallop. Then Father spoke to the horse personally— How is Mother?

HARLAN. I don't know. The doctor's up there now.

WHITNEY. Well, she'd better be good and sick or Father may be mad at me for getting him up here—'specially in a cab.
(FATHER *comes down the stairs muttering to himself.*)

FATHER (*indignantly*). Well, huh! —It seems to me I ought to be shown a little consideration. I guess I've got some feelings, too!

WHITNEY (*hopefully*). Mother's awfully sick, isn't she?

FATHER. How do I know? I wasn't allowed to stay in the same room with her.

WHITNEY. Did the doctor put you out?

FATHER. No, it was your mother, damn it! (*He goes out and hangs up his hat and stick, then returns.* FATHER *may be annoyed, but he is also worried*) You boys keep quiet around here today.

WHITNEY. She must be pretty sick.

FATHER. She must be, Whitney! I don't know! Nobody ever tells me anything in this house. Not a damn thing!
(DR. HUMPHREYS *comes down the stairs. He's the family-doctor type of the period, with just enough whiskers to make him impressive. He carries his satchel.*)

DR. HUMPHREYS. Mrs. Day is quieter now.

FATHER. How sick is she? What's the matter with her?

DR. HUMPHREYS. She's a pretty sick woman, Mr. Day. I had given her a sedative just before you came—and after you left the room I had to give her another. Have you a telephone?

FATHER. A telephone! No—I don't believe in them. Why?

DR. HUMPHREYS. Well, it would only have saved me a few steps. I'll be back in ten minutes. (*He turns to go.*)

FATHER. Wait a minute—I think I'm entitled to know what's the matter with my wife.
(DR. HUMPHREYS *turns back.*)

DR. HUMPHREYS. What did Mrs. Day have for breakfast this morning?

FATHER. She didn't eat anything—not a thing.

DR. HUMPHREYS. Are you sure?

FATHER. I tried to get her to eat something, but she wouldn't.

DR. HUMPHREYS (*almost to himself*). I can't understand it.

FATHER. Understand what?

DR. HUMPHREYS. These violent attacks of nausea. It's almost as though she were poisoned.

FATHER. Poisoned!

DR. HUMPHREYS. I'll try not to be gone more than ten or fifteen minutes. (*He exits.*)

FATHER (*trying to reassure himself*). Damn doctors! They never know what's the matter with anybody. Well, he'd better get your mother well, and damn soon or he'll hear from me.

WHITNEY. Mother's going to get well, isn't she? (FATHER *looks at* WHITNEY *sharply as though he is a little angry at anyone even raising the question.*)

FATHER. Of course she's going to get well!

HARLAN (*running to* FATHER). I hope she gets well soon. When Mamma stays in bed it's lonesome.

FATHER. Yes, it is, Harlan. It's lonesome. (*He looks around the room and finds it pretty empty*) What were you boys supposed to do today?

WHITNEY. I was to learn the rest of my catechism.

FATHER. Well, if that's what your mother wanted you to do, you'd better do it.

WHITNEY. I know it—I think.

FATHER. You'd better be sure.

WHITNEY. I can't be sure unless somebody hears me. Will you hear me?

FATHER (*with sudden willingness to be useful*). All right. I'll hear you, Whitney. (WHITNEY *goes to the mantel and gets* VINNIE'S *prayer book.* FATHER *sits on the sofa.* HARLAN *climbs up beside him.*)

HARLAN. If Mamma's still sick will you read to me tonight?

FATHER. Of course I'll read to you. (WHITNEY *opens the prayer book and hands it to* FATHER.)

WHITNEY. Here it is, Father. Just the end of it. Mother knows I know the rest. Look, start here. (*He points.*)

FATHER. All right. (*Reading*) "How many parts are there in a Sacrament?"

WHITNEY (*reciting*). "Two; the outward visible sign, and the inward spiritual grace."
(FATHER *nods in approval.*)

FATHER. "What is the outward visible sign or form in Baptism?"

WHITNEY. "Water; wherein the person is baptized, in the name of the Father, and of the Son, and of the Holy Ghost." You haven't been baptized, Father, have you?

FATHER (*ignoring it*). "What is the inward and spiritual grace?"

WHITNEY. If you don't have to be baptized, why do I have to be confirmed?

FATHER (*ignoring this even more*). "What is the inward and spiritual grace?"

WHITNEY. "A death unto sin, and a new birth unto righteousness; for being by nature born in sin, and the children of wrath, we are hereby made the children of grace." Is that why you get mad so much, Father—because you're a child of wrath?

FATHER. Whitney, mind your manners! You're not supposed to ask questions of your elders! "What is required of persons to be baptized?"

WHITNEY. "Repentance, whereby—whereby—" (*He pauses.*)

FATHER (*quickly shutting the book and handing it to* WHITNEY). You don't know it well enough, Whitney. You'd better study it some more.

WHITNEY. Now?

FATHER (*softening*). No, you don't have to do it now. Let's see, now, what can we do?

WHITNEY. Well, I was working with my tool chest out in the back yard. (*Edges toward the arch.*)

FATHER. Better not do any hammering with your mother sick upstairs. You'd better stay here.

WHITNEY. I wasn't hammering—I was doing wood-carving.

FATHER. Well, Harlan—how about you? Shall we play some tiddle-dy-winks?

HARLAN (*edging toward* WHITNEY). I was helping Whitney.

FATHER. Oh—all right. (*The boys go out.* FATHER *goes to the stairwell*) Boys, don't do any shouting. We all have to be very quiet around here. (*He stands in the hall and looks up toward* VINNIE, *worried. Then he tiptoes across the room and stares gloomily out of the window. Then he tiptoes back into the hall and goes to the rail of the basement stairs, and calls quietly*) Margaret! (*There is no answer and he raises his voice a little*) Margaret! (*There is still no answer and he lets loose*) Margaret! Why don't you answer when you hear me calling? (*At this moment* MARGARET, *hat on, appears in the arch from the right. having come through the front door.*)

MARGARET. Sh—sh— (FATHER *turns quickly and sees* MARGARET.)

FATHER. Oh, there you are!

MARGARET (*reprovingly*). We must all be quiet, Mr. Day—Mrs. Day is very sick.

FATHER (*testily*). I know she's sick. That's what I wanted you for. You go up and wait outside her door in case she needs anything. (MARGARET *starts upstairs*) And what were you doing out of the house, anyway?

MARGARET. I was sent for the minister.

FATHER (*startled*). The minister!

MARGARET. Yes, he'll be right in. He's paying off the cab. (MARGARET *continues upstairs. The door slams.* THE REVEREND DR. LLOYD *appears in the archway and meets* FATHER *in the hall.*)

DR. LLOYL. I was deeply shocked to hear of Mrs. Day's illness. I hope I can be of some service. Will you take me up to her?

FATHER (*with a trace of hostility*). She's resting now. She can't be disturbed.

DR. LLOYD. But I've been summoned.

FATHER. The doctor will be back in a few minutes and we'll see what he has to say about it. You'd better come in and wait.

DR. LLOYD. Thank you. (*Comes into the room.* FATHER *follows him re-*

luctantly) Mrs. Day has been a tower of strength in the parish. Everyone liked her so much. Yes, she was a fine woman.

FATHER. I wish to God you wouldn't talk about Mrs. Day as if she were dead.

(NORA *comes down the stairs and looks into the room.*)

NORA. Is the doctor back yet?

FATHER. No. Does she need him?

NORA. She's kinda' restless. She's talking in her sleep and twisting and turning. (*She goes downstairs.* FATHER *looks up toward* VINNIE'S *room, worried, then looks angrily toward the front door.*)

FATHER. That doctor said he'd be right back. (*He goes to the window.*)

MARGARET (*coming downstairs*). Here comes the doctor. I was watching for him out the window. (*She goes to the front door. A moment later* DR. HUMPHREYS *enters.*)

FATHER. Well, doctor—seems to me that was a pretty long ten minutes.

DR. HUMPHREYS (*indignantly*). See here, Mr. Day, if I'm to be responsible for Mrs. Day's health, I must be allowed to handle this case in my own way.

FATHER. Well, you can't handle it if you're out of the house.

DR. HUMPHREYS (*flaring*). I left this house because— (DR. SOMERS, *an imposing medical figure, enters and stops at* DR. HUMPHREYS'S *side*) This is Dr. Somers.

DR. SOMERS. How do you do?

DR. HUMPHREYS. I felt that Mrs. Day's condition warranted my getting Dr. Somers here as soon as possible for consultation. I hope that meets with your approval.

FATHER (*a little awed*). Why, yes, of course. Anything that can be done.

DR. HUMPHREYS. Upstairs, doctor! (*The two doctors go upstairs.* FATHER *turns back into the room, obviously shaken.*)

DR. LLOYD. Mrs. Day is in good hands now, Mr. Day. There's nothing you and I can do at the moment to help. (*After a moment's consideration* FATHER *decides there is something that can be done to help. He goes to* DR. LLOYD. FATHER *indicates the seat in front of the table to* DR. LLOYD *and they both sit.*)

FATHER. Dr. Lloyd, there's something that's troubling Mrs. Day's mind. I think you know what I refer to.

DR. LLOYD. Yes—you mean the fact that you've never been baptized.

FATHER. I gathered you knew about it from your sermon last Sunday. (*Looks at him a second with indignant memory*) But let's not get angry. I think something had better be done about it.

DR. LLOYD. Yes, Mr. Day.

FATHER. When the doctors get through up there I want you to talk to Mrs. Day. I want you to tell her something.

DR. LLOYD (*eagerly*). Yes, I'll be glad to.

FATHER. You're just the man to do it! She shouldn't be upset about this –I want you to tell her that my being baptized would just be a lot of damn nonsense.

(*This isn't what* DR. LLOYD *has expected and it is hardly his idea of how to help* MRS. DAY.)

DR. LLOYD. But, Mr. Day!

FATHER. No, she'd take your word on a thing like that--and we've got to do everything we can to help her now.

DR. LLOYD (*rising*). But baptism is one of the sacraments of the Church—

FATHER (*rising*). You're her minister and you're supposed to bring her comfort and peace of mind.

DR. LLOYD. But the solution is so simple. It would take only your consent to be baptized.

FATHER. That's out of the question! And I'm surprised that a grown man like you should suggest such a thing.

DR. LLOYD. If you're really concerned about Mrs. Day's peace of mind, don't you think—

FATHER. Now see here—if you're just going to keep her stirred up about this, I'm not going to let you see her at all. (*He turns away.* DR. LLOYD *follows him.*)

DR. LLOYD. Now, Mr. Day, as you said, we must do everything we can— (*The doctors come downstairs.* FATHER *sees them.*)

FATHER. Well, doctor, how is she? What have you decided?

DR. HUMPHREYS. We've just left Mrs. Day. Is there a room we could use for our consultation?

FATHER. Of course. (MARGARET *starts downstairs*) Margaret, you go back upstairs! I don't want Mrs. Day left alone!

MARGARET. I have to do something for the doctor. I'll go back up as soon as I get it started.

FATHER. Well, hurry. And, Margaret, show these gentlemen downstairs to the billiard room.

MARGARET. Yes, sir. This way, doctor —downstairs. (*Exits, followed by* DR. SOMERS. FATHER *delays* DR. HUMPHREYS.)

FATHER. Dr. Humphreys, you know now, don't you--this isn't serious, is it?

DR. HUMPHREYS. After we've had our consultation we'll talk to you, Mr. Day.

FATHER. But surely you must—

DR. HUMPHREYS. Just rest assured that Dr. Somers will do everything that is humanly possible.

FATHER. Why, you don't mean—

DR. HUMPHREYS. We'll try not to be long. (*Exits.* FATHER *turns and looks at* DR. LLOYD. *He is obviously frightened.*)

FATHER. This Dr. Somers—I've heard his name often—he's very well thought of, isn't he?

DR. LLOYD. Oh, yes indeed.

FATHER. If Vinnie's really—if anyone could help her, he could—don't you think?

DR. LLOYD. A very fine physician. But there's a greater Help, ever present in the hour of need. Let us turn to Him in prayer. Let us kneel and pray. (FATHER *looks at him, straightens, then walks to the other side of the room*) Let us kneel and pray. (FATHER *finally bows his head.* DR. LLOYD *looks at him and, not kneeling himself, raises his head and speaks simply in prayer*) Oh, Lord, look down from Heaven—behold, visit, and relieve this Thy servant who is grieved with sickness, and extend to her Thy accustomed goodness. We know she has sinned against Thee in thought, word, and deed. Have mercy on her, O Lord, have mercy on this miserable sinner. Forgive her—

FATHER. She's not a miserable sinner and you know it! (*Then* FATHER *speaks directly to the Deity*) O God! You know Vinnie's not a miserable sinner. She's a damn fine woman! She shouldn't be made to suffer. It's got to stop, I tell you, it's got to stop! (VINNIE *appears on the stairway in her nightgown.*)

VINNIE. What's the matter, Clare? What's wrong?

FATHER (*not hearing her*). Have mercy, I say, have mercy, damn it!

VINNIE. What's the matter, Clare? What's wrong? (FATHER *turns, sees* VINNIE, *and rushes to her.*)

FATHER. Vinnie, what are you doing down here? You shouldn't be out of bed. You get right back upstairs. (*He now has his arms around her.*)

VINNIE. Oh, Clare, I heard you call. Do you need me?

FATHER (*deeply moved*). Vinnie—I know now how much I need you. Get well, Vinnie. I'll be baptized. I promise. I'll be baptized.

VINNIE. You will? Oh, Clare!

FATHER. I'll do anything. We'll go to Europe, just we two—you won't have to worry about the children or the household accounts— (VINNIE *faints against* FATHER'S *shoulder*) Vinnie! (*He stoops to lift her.*)

DR. LLOYD. I'll get the doctor. But don't worry, Mr. Day—she'll be all right now. (FATHER *lifts* VINNIE *up in his arms*) Bless you for what you've done, Mr. Day.

FATHER. What did I do?

DR. LLOYD. You promised to be baptized!

FATHER (*aghast*). I did? (*With horror* FATHER *realizes he has been betrayed—and by himself*) OH, GOD!

CURTAIN

ACT THREE

SCENE I

The same.

A month later. Mid-afternoon.

VINNIE *is seated on the sofa embroidering petit point.*

MARGARET *enters, as usual uncomfortable at being upstairs.*

MARGARET. You wanted to speak to me, ma'am?

VINNIE. Yes, Margaret, about tomorrow morning's breakfast — we must plan it very carefully.

MARGARET (*puzzled*). Mr. Day hasn't complained to me about his breakfasts lately. As a matter of fact, I've been blessing my luck!

VINNIE. Oh, no, it's not that. But tomorrow morning I'd like something for his breakfast that would surprise him.

MARGARET (*doubtfully*). Surprising Mr. Day is always a bit of a risk, ma'am. My motto with him has always been "Let well enough alone."

VINNIE. But if we think of something he especially likes, Margaret —what would you say to kippers?

MARGARET. Well, I've served him kippers, but I don't recall his ever saying he liked them.

VINNIE. He's never said he didn't like them, has he?

MARGARET. They've never got a stamp on the floor out of him one way or the other.

VINNIE. If Mr. Day doesn't say he doesn't like a thing you can assume that he does. Let's take a chance on kippers, Margaret.

MARGARET. Very well, ma'am. (*She starts out.*)

VINNIE (*innocently*). And, Margaret, you'd better have enough breakfast for two extra places.

MARGARET (*knowingly*). Oh—so that's it! We're going to have company again.

VINNIE. Yes, my cousin, Miss Cartwright, and her friend are coming back from Springfield. I'm afraid they'll get here just about breakfast time.

MARGARET. Well, in that case I'd better make some of my Sunday morning hot biscuits, too.

VINNIE. Yes. We *know* Mr. Day likes those.

MARGARET. I've been getting him to church with them for the last fifteen years. (*The door slams.* MARGARET *goes to the arch and looks*) Oh, it's Mr. Clarence, ma'am. (*Goes off downstairs and* CLARENCE *enters with a large package.*)

CLARENCE. Here it is, Mother. (*He puts it on the table.*)

VINNIE. Oh, it was still in the store! They hadn't sold it! I'm so thrilled. Didn't you admire it, Clarence? (*She hurries over to the table.*)

CLARENCE. Well, it's unusual.

VINNIE (*unwrapping the package*). You know, I saw this down there the day before I got sick. I was walking through the bric-a-brac section and it caught my eye. I was so tempted to buy it! And all the time I lay ill I just couldn't get it out of my head. I can't understand how it could stay in the store all this time without somebody snatching it up. (*She takes it out of the box. It is a large china pug dog*) Isn't that the darlingest thing you ever saw! It does need a ribbon, though. I've got the very thing somewhere. Oh, yes, I know. (*Goes to the side table and gets a red ribbon out of the drawer.*)

CLARENCE. Isn't John home yet?

VINNIE. I haven't seen him. Why?

CLARENCE. Well, you know we've been working, and John went down to collect our money.

VINNIE. That's fine. (*She ties the ribbon around the dog's neck*) Oh, Clarence, I have a secret for just the two of us; who do you think is coming to visit us tomorrow?—Cousin Cora and Mary.

CLARENCE. Yes, I know.

VINNIE. How did you know?

CLARENCE. I happened to get a letter. (JOHN *enters, carrying two packages of medicine.*)

VINNIE. John, did you ever see anything so sweet?

JOHN. What is it?

VINNIE. It's a pug dog. Your father would never let me have a real one, but he can't object to one made of china. This ribbon needs pressing. I'll take it down and have Margaret do it right away. (*Exits with the beribboned pug dog.*)

CLARENCE. What did you bring home more medicine for? (*Then with sudden fright*) Dr. Bartlett paid us off, didn't he?

JOHN. Oh, yes!

CLARENCE (*heaving a great sigh of relief*). You had me scared for a minute. When I went down to McCreery's to get that pug dog for Mother, I ordered the daisiest suit you ever saw. Dr. Bartlett owed us sixteen dollars apiece, and the suit was only fifteen. Wasn't that lucky? Come on, give me my money.

JOHN. Clarence, Dr. Bartlett paid us off in medicine.

CLARENCE. You let him pay us off with that old Beneficent Balm!

JOHN. Well, he thanked us, too, for our services to mankind.

CLARENCE (*in agony*). But my suit!

JOHN. You'll just have to wait for your suit.

CLARENCE. I can't wait! I've got to have it tomorrow—and besides they're making the alterations. I've got to pay for it this afternoon! Fifteen dollars!

JOHN (*helpfully*). Why don't you offer them fifteen bottles of medicine? (CLARENCE *gives it a little desperate thought.*)

CLARENCE. They wouldn't take it. McCreery's don't sell medicine. (JOHN *is by the window and looks out.*)

JOHN. That's too bad. Here comes Father.

CLARENCE. I'll have to brace him for that fifteen dollars. I hate to do it, but I've got to—that's all—I've got to.

JOHN. I'm not going to be here when you do. I'd better hide this somewhere, anyway. (*Takes the packages and hurries upstairs. The door slams.* FATHER *enters and looks into the room.*)

CLARENCE. Good afternoon, sir.

FATHER. How's your mother, Clarence? Where is she?

CLARENCE. She's all right. She's downstairs with Margaret. Oh, Father— (FATHER *goes off down the hall and we hear him calling downstairs.*)

FATHER. Vinnie! Vinnie! I'm home. (*Comes back into the room, carrying his newspaper.*)

CLARENCE. Father, Mother will be well enough to go to church with us next Sunday.

FATHER. That's fine, Clarence. That's fine.

CLARENCE. Father, have you noticed that I haven't been kneeling down in church lately?

FATHER. Clarence, don't let your mother catch you at it.

CLARENCE. Then I've got to have a new suit of clothes right away!

FATHER (*after a puzzled look*). Clarence, you're not even making sense!

CLARENCE. But a fellow doesn't feel right in cut-down clothes—especially your clothes. That's why I can't kneel down in church—I can't do anything in them you wouldn't do.

FATHER. Well, that's a damn good thing! If my old clothes make you behave yourself I don't think you ought to wear anything else.

CLARENCE (*desperately*). *Oh, no!* You're you and I'm me! I want to be myself! Besides, you're older and there are things I've got to do that I wouldn't do at your age.

FATHER. Clarence, you should never do anything I wouldn't do.

CLARENCE. Oh, yes,—look, for instance: Suppose I should want to kneel down in front of a girl?

FATHER. Why in Heaven's name should you want to do a thing like that?

CLARENCE. Well, I've got to get married *sometime*. I've got to propose to a girl *sometime*.

FATHER (*exasperated*). Before you're married, you'll be earning your own clothes, I hope. Don't get the idea into your head I'm going to support you and a wife, too. Besides, at your age, Clarence—

CLARENCE (*hastily*). Oh, I'm not going to be married right away, but for fifteen dollars I can get a good suit of clothes.

FATHER (*bewildered and irritated*). Clarence! (*He stares at him. At this second,* VINNIE *comes through the arch*) Why, you're beginning to talk as crazy as your mother. (*He sees her*) Oh, hello, Vinnie. How're you feeling today?

VINNIE. I'm fine, Clare. (*They kiss*) You don't have to hurry home from the office every day like this.
(CLARENCE *throws himself in the chair by the window, sick with disappointment.*)

FATHER. Business the way it is, no use going to the office at all.

VINNIE. But you haven't been to your club for weeks.

FATHER. Can't stand the damn place. You do look better, Vinnie. What did you do today? (*Drops on the sofa.* VINNIE *stands behind the sofa. Her chatter does not succeed in diverting* FATHER *from his newspaper.*)

VINNIE. I took a long walk and dropped in to call on old Mrs. Whitehead.

FATHER. Well, that's fine.

VINNIE. And, Clare, it was the most fortunate thing that ever happened. I've got wonderful news for you! Who do you think was there? Mr. Morley!

FATHER (*not placing him*). Morley?

VINNIE. You remember—that nice young minister who substituted for Dr. Lloyd one Sunday?

FATHER. Oh, yes! Bright young fellow, preached a good sensible sermon.

VINNIE. It was the only time I ever saw you put five dollars in the plate!

FATHER. Ought to be more ministers like him. I could get along with that young man without any trouble at all.

VINNIE. Well, Clare, his parish is in Audubon—you know, 'way up above Harlem.

FATHER. Is that so?

VINNIE. Isn't that wonderful? Nobody knows you up there. You'll be perfectly safe!

FATHER. Safe? Vinnie, what the devil are you talking about?

VINNIE. I've been all over everything with Mr. Morley and he's agreed to baptize you.

FATHER. Oh, he has—the young whippersnapper! Damn nice of him!

VINNIE. We can go up there any morning, Clare—we don't even have to make an appointment.

FATHER. Vinnie, you're just making a lot of plans for nothing. Who said I was going to be baptized at all?

VINNIE (*aghast*). Why, Clare! *You* did!

FATHER. Now, Vinnie!—

VINNIE. You gave me your promise—your Sacred Promise. You stood right on that spot and said: "I'll be baptized. I promise—I'll be baptized."

FATHER. What if I did?

VINNIE (*amazed, she comes down and faces him*). Aren't you a man of your word?

FATHER (*rising*). Vinnie, that was under entirely different circumstances. We all thought you were dying, so naturally I said that to make you feel better. As a matter of fact, the doctor told me that's what cured you. So it seems to me pretty ungrateful of you to press this matter any further.

VINNIE. Clarence Day, you gave me your Sacred Promise!

FATHER (*getting annoyed*). Vinnie, you were sick when I said that. Now you're well again.

(MARGARET *enters with the pug dog, which now has the freshly pressed ribbon tied around its neck. She puts it on the table.*)

MARGARET. Is that all right, Mrs. Day?

VINNIE (*dismissingly*). That's fine, Margaret, thank you. (MARGARET *exits*) My being well has nothing to do with it. You gave me your word! You gave the Lord your word. If you had seen how eager Mr. Morley was to bring you into the fold! (FATHER, *trying to escape, has been moving toward the arch when suddenly the pug dog catches his eye and he stares at it fascinated*) And you're going to march yourself up to his church some morning before you go to the office and be christened. If you think for one minute that I'm going to—

FATHER. What in the name of Heaven is that?

VINNIE. If you think I'm going to let you add the sin of breaking your Solemn and Sacred Promise—

FATHER. I demand to know what that repulsive object is!

VINNIE (*exasperated in her turn*). It's perfectly plain what it is—it's a pug dog!

FATHER. What's it doing in this house?

VINNIE (*defiantly*). I wanted it and I bought it.

FATHER. You spent good money for that?

VINNIE. Clare, we're not talking about that! We're talking about you. Don't try to change the subject!

FATHER. How much did you pay for that atrocity?

VINNIE. I don't know. I sent Clarence down for it. Listen to me, Clare—

FATHER. Clarence, what did you pay for that?

CLARENCE. I didn't pay anything. I charged it.

FATHER (*looking at* VINNIE). Charged it! I might have known. (*To* CLARENCE) How much was it?

CLARENCE. Fifteen dollars.

FATHER. Fifteen dollars for that eyesore?

VINNIE (*to the rescue of the pug dog*). Don't you call that lovely work of art an eyesore! That will look beautiful sitting on a red cushion by the fireplace in the parlor.

FATHER. If that sits in the parlor, I won't! Furthermore, I don't even want it in the same house with me. Get it out of here! (*He starts for the stairs.*)

VINNIE. You're just using that for an excuse. You're not going to get out of this room until you set a date for your baptism. (FATHER *turns at the foot of the stairs.*)

FATHER. I'll tell you one thing! I'll never be baptized while that hideous monstrosity is in this house. (*He stalks upstairs.*)

VINNIE (*calling after him*). All right! (*She goes to the pug dog*) All right! It goes back this afternoon and he's christened first thing in the morning.

CLARENCE. But, Mother—

VINNIE. Clarence, you heard him say that he'd be baptized as soon as I got this pug dog out of the house. You hurry right back to McCreery's with it—and be sure they credit us with fifteen dollars. (*The fifteen dollars rings a bell in* CLARENCE'S *mind.*)

CLARENCE. Oh, say, Mother, while I was at McCreery's, I happened to see a suit I would like very much and the suit was only fifteen dollars.

VINNIE (*regretfully*). Well, Clarence, I think your suit will have to wait until after I get your father christened.

CLARENCE (*hopefully*) No. I meant that since the suit cost just the same as the pug dog, if I exchanged the pug dog for the suit—

VINNIE. Why, yes! Then your suit wouldn't cost Father anything! Why, how bright of you, Clarence, to think of that!

CLARENCE (*quickly*). I'd better start right away before McCreery's closes. (*They have collected the box, wrapper, and tissue paper.*)

VINNIE. Yes. Let's see. If we're going to take your father all the way up to Audubon— Clarence, you stop at Ryerson & Brown's on your way back and tell them to have a cab here at eight o'clock tomorrow morning.

CLARENCE. Mother, a cab! Do you think you ought to do that?

VINNIE. Well, we can't walk to Audubon.

CLARENCE (*warningly*). But you know what a cab does to Father!

VINNIE. This is an important occasion.

CLARENCE (*with a shrug*). All right! A brougham or a Victoria?

VINNIE. Get one of their best cabs, the kind they use at funerals.

CLARENCE. Those cost two dollars an hour! And if Father gets mad—

VINNIE. Well, if your father starts to argue in the morning, you remember—

CLARENCE (*remembering his suit*). Oh, he agreed to it! We both heard him!
(VINNIE *has removed the ribbon and is about to put the pug dog back in the box.*)

VINNIE (*regretfully*). I did have my heart set on this. (*An idea comes to her*) Still—if they didn't sell him in all that time, he might be safe there for a few more weeks. (*She gives the dog a reassuring pat and puts him in the box. She begins to sing "Sweet Marie" happily.* FATHER *comes down the stairs.* CLARENCE *takes his hat and the box and goes happily and quickly out.* FATHER *watches him*) I hope you notice that Clarence is returning the pug dog.

FATHER. That's a sign you're getting your faculties back. (VINNIE *is singing quietly to herself in a satisfied way*) Good to hear you singing again, Vinnie. (*Suddenly remembering something*) Oh!—on my way uptown I stopped in at Tiffany's and bought you a little something. Thought you might like it. (*He takes out of his pocket a small ring-box and holds it out to her. She takes it.*)

VINNIE. Oh, Clare. (*She opens it eagerly*) What a beautiful ring! (*She takes the ring out, puts it on her finger, and admires it.*)

FATHER. Glad if it pleases you. (*He settles down to his newspaper on the sofa.*)

VINNIE. I don't know how to thank you. (*She kisses him.*)

FATHER. It's thanks enough for me to have you up and around again. When you're sick, Vinnie, this house is like a tomb. There's no excitement.

VINNIE (*sitting beside him*). Clare, this is the loveliest ring you ever bought me. Now that I have this, you needn't buy me any more rings.

FATHER. Well, if you don't want any more.

VINNIE. What I'd really like now is a nice diamond necklace.

FATHER (*alarmed*). Vinnie, do you know how much a diamond necklace costs?

VINNIE. I know, Clare, but don't you see?—your giving me this ring shows that I mean a little something to you. Now, a diamond necklace—

FATHER. Good God, if you don't know by this time how I feel about you! We've been married for twenty years and I've loved you every minute of it.

VINNIE. What did you say? (*Her eyes well with tears at* FATHER'S *definite statement of his love.*)

FATHER. I said we'd been married twenty years and I've loved you every minute of it. But if I have to buy out jewelry stores to prove it—if I haven't shown it to you in my words and actions, I might as well— (*He turns and sees* VINNIE *dabbing her eyes and speaks with resignation*) What have I done now?

VINNIE. It's all right, Clare—I'm just so happy.

FATHER. Happy!

VINNIE. You said you loved me! And this beautiful ring—that's something else I didn't expect. Oh, Clare, I love surprises. (*She nestles against him.*)

FATHER. That's another thing I can't understand about you, Vinnie. Now, *I* like to know what to expect. Then I'm prepared to meet it.

VINNIE (*putting her head on his shoulder*). Yes, I know. But, Clare, life would be pretty dull if we always knew what was coming.

FATHER. Well, it's certainly not dull around here. In this house you never know what's going to hit you tomorrow.

VINNIE (*to herself*). Tomorrow! (*She starts to sing,* FATHER *listening to her happily.*)

"Every daisy in the dell,
Knows my secret, knows it well,
And yet I dare not tell,
Sweet Marie!"

CURTAIN

SCENE II

The same.

The next morning. Breakfast. All the family except JOHN *and* VINNIE *are at the table and in good spirits.*

JOHN (*entering*). Mother says she'll be right down. (*He sits at the table.* MAGGIE, *the new maid, enters with a plate of hot biscuits and serves* FATHER. *As* FATHER *takes a biscuit, he glances up at her and shows some little surprise.*)

FATHER. Who are you? What's your name?

MAGGIE. Margaret, sir.

FATHER. Can't be Margaret. We've got one Margaret in the house.

MAGGIE. At home they call me Maggie, sir.

FATHER (*genially*). All right, Maggie. (MAGGIE *continues serving the biscuits*) Boys, if her name's Margaret, that's a good sign. Maybe she'll stay awhile. You know, boys, your mother used to be just the same about cooks as she is about maids. Never could keep them for some reason. Well, one day about fifteen years ago—yes, it was right after you were born, John—my, you were a homely baby. (*They all laugh at* JOHN's *expense*) I came home that night all tired out and what did I find?—no dinner, because the cook had left. Well, I decided I'd had just about enough of that, so I just marched over to the employment agency on

Sixth Avenue and said to the woman in charge: "Where do you keep the cooks?" She tried to hold me up with a lot of red-tape folderol, but I just walked into the room where the girls were waiting, looked 'em over, saw Margaret, pointed at her, and said: "I'll take that one." I walked her home, she cooked dinner that night, and she's been cooking for us ever since. Damn good cook, too. (*He stamps on the floor three times.* VINNIE *comes down the stairs dressed in white. Somehow she almost has the appearance of a bride going to her wedding.*)

VINNIE. Good morning, Clare. Good morning, boys. (*The boys and* FATHER *rise.* VINNIE *takes her bonnet and gloves and lays them on the chair below the fireplace.* FATHER *goes to* VINNIE'*s chair and holds it out for her, glancing at her holiday appearance.* VINNIE *sits.*)

FATHER. Sit down, boys. (*As* FATHER *returns to his own chair, he notices that all of the boys are dressed in their Sunday best*) Everyone's dressed up this morning. What's on the program for this fine day?
(VINNIE, *who always postpones crises in the hope some miracle will aid her, postpones this one.*)

VINNIE. Well, this afternoon May Lewis's mother is giving a party for everyone in May's dancing class. Harlan's going to that.

HARLAN. I don't want to go, Mamma.

VINNIE. Why, Harlan, don't you want to go to a party and get ice cream and cake?

HARLAN. May Lewis always tries to kiss me. (*This is greeted with family laughter.*)

FATHER (*genially*). When you get a little older, you won't object to girls' wanting to kiss you, will he, Clarence? (MARGARET *comes hurrying in.*)

MARGARET. What's wanting?

FATHER. Margaret, these kippers are *good.* (MARGARET *makes her usual deprecatory gesture toward him*) Haven't had kippers for a long time. I'm glad you remembered I like them.

MARGARET. Yes, sir. (MARGARET *and* VINNIE *exchange knowing looks.* MARGARET *goes out happy.*)

FATHER. What's got into Margaret this morning? Hot biscuits, too!

VINNIE. She knows you're fond of them. (*The doorbell rings.* MAGGIE *goes to answer it.* VINNIE *stirs nervously in her chair*) Who can that be? It can't be the mailman because he's been here.

FATHER (*with sly humor*). Clarence has been getting a good many special deliveries lately. Is that business deal going through, Clarence? (*The family has a laugh at* CLARENCE. MAGGIE *comes back into the arch with a suit box.*)

MAGGIE. This is for you, Mr. Day. Where shall I put it?

CLARENCE (*hastily*). Oh, that's for me, I think. Take it upstairs, Maggie.

FATHER. Wait a minute, Maggie, bring it here. Let's see it.
(CLARENCE *takes the box from* MAGGIE, *who exits. He holds it toward his father.*)

CLARENCE. See, it's for me, Father—Clarence Day, Jr.

FATHER. Let me look. Why, that's from McCreery's and it's marked "Charge." What is it?

VINNIE. It's all right, Clare. It's nothing for you to worry about.

FATHER. Well, at least I think I should know what's being charged to me. What is it?

VINNIE. Now, Clare, stop your fussing. It's a new suit of clothes for Clarence and it's not costing you a penny.

FATHER. It's marked "Charge fifteen dollars"—it's costing me fifteen dollars. And I told Clarence—

VINNIE. Clare, can't you take my word it isn't costing you a penny?

FATHER. I'd like to have you explain why it isn't.

VINNIE (*triumphantly*). Because Clarence took the pug dog back and got the suit instead.

FATHER. Of course, and they'll charge me fifteen dollars for the suit.

VINNIE. Nonsense, Clare. We gave them the pug dog for the suit. Don't you see?

FATHER. Then they'll charge me fifteen dollars for the pug dog.

VINNIE. But, Clare, they can't! We haven't got the pug dog. We sent that back.

FATHER (*bewildered, but not convinced*). Now wait a minute, Vinnie. There's something wrong with your reasoning.

VINNIE. I'm surprised, Clare, and you're supposed to be so good at figures. Why, it's perfectly clear to me.

FATHER. Vinnie! They're going to charge me for one thing or the other.

VINNIE. Don't you let them!
(FATHER *gets up and throws his napkin on the table.*)

FATHER. Well, McCreery's aren't giving away suits and they aren't giving away pug dogs. (*He walks over to the window in his irritation*) Can't you get it through your— (*Looking out the window*) Oh, God!

VINNIE. What is it, Clare? What's wrong?

FATHER. Don't anybody answer the door.

VINNIE. Who is it? Who's coming?

FATHER. Those damn women are back!

WHITNEY. What women?

FATHER. Cora and that little idiot. (CLARENCE *dashes madly up the stairs clutching the box containing his new suit*) They're moving in on us again, bag and baggage! (*The doorbell rings*) Don't let them in!

VINNIE. Clarence Day, as if we could turn our own relatives away!

FATHER. Tell them to get back in that cab and drive right on to Ohio. If they're extravagant enough to take cabs when horse cars run right by our door— (MAGGIE *crosses the hall to answer the doorbell.*)

VINNIE. Now, Clare—you be quiet and behave yourself. They're here and there's nothing you can do about it. (*She starts toward the hall.*)

FATHER (*shouting after her*). Well, why do they always pounce on us without warning?—the damn gypsies!

VINNIE (*from the arch*). Shhh!—Clare! (*Then in her best welcoming tone*) Cora! Mary! It's so nice to have you back again.

CORA. How are you, Vinnie? We've been so worried about you.

VINNIE. Oh, I'm fine now! (CORA *and* MARY *and* VINNIE *enter and* CORA *sweeps right down into the room.*)

CORA. Hello, Harlan! Whitney! Well, Cousin Clare. Here we are again! (*Kisses* FATHER *on the cheek. He draws back sternly.* MARY *looks quickly around the room for* CLARENCE, *then greets and is greeted by the other boys*) And John! Where's Clarence?

MARY. Yes, where is Clarence?

VINNIE. John, go find Clarence and tell him that Cora and Mary are here.

JOHN. Yes, Mother. (*Goes upstairs*).

VINNIE. You got here just in time to have breakfast with us.

CORA. We had breakfast at the depot.

VINNIE. Well, as a matter of fact, we'd just finished.

FATHER (*with cold dignity*). I haven't finished my breakfast!

VINNIE. Well, then sit down, Clare. (*To* CORA *and* MARY) Margaret gave us kippers this morning and Clare's so fond of kippers. Why don't we all sit down? (*Indicates the empty places and the girls sit.* FATHER *resumes his chair and breakfast in stony silence.* MAGGIE *has come into the room to await orders*) Maggie, clear those things away. (*She indicates the dishes in front of the girls, and* MAGGIE *removes them.* FATHER *takes a letter from his stack of morning mail and opens it*) Clare, don't let your kippers get cold. (*To* CORA) Now—tell us all about Springfield.

CORA. We had a wonderful month—but tell us about you, Cousin Vinnie. You must have had a terrible time.

VINNIE. Yes, I was pretty sick, but I'm all right again now.

CORA. What was it?

VINNIE. Well, the doctors don't know exactly, but they did say this—that they'd never seen anything like it before, whatever it was.

CORA. You certainly look well enough now. Doesn't she, Clare? (*Whatever is in the letter* FATHER *has been reading comes to him as a shock.*)

FATHER. Oh, God!

VINNIE. What's the matter, Clare? What's wrong?

FATHER. *John! John!* (JOHN *is seen halfway up the stairs with the girls' bags. He comes running down the stairs, going to* FATHER.)

JOHN. Yes, Father?

FATHER. Have you been going around this town selling medicine?

JOHN (*a little frightened*). Yes, Father.

FATHER. Dog medicine?

JOHN (*indignantly*). No, Father, not dog medicine!

FATHER. It must have been dog medicine!

JOHN. It wasn't dog medicine, Father—

FATHER. This letter from Mrs. Sprague says you sold her a bottle of this medicine and that her little boy gave some of it to their dog and it killed him! Now she wants ten dollars from me for a new dog.

JOHN. Well, he shouldn't have given it to a dog. It's for humans! Why, it's Bartlett's Beneficent Balm—"Made from a secret formula"!

FATHER. Have you been going around among our friends and neighbors selling some damned Dr. Munyon patent nostrum?

JOHN. But it's good medicine, Father. I can prove it by Mother.

FATHER. Vinnie, what do you know about this?

VINNIE. Nothing, Clare, but I'm sure that John—

JOHN. No, I mean that day Mother—

FATHER. That's enough! You're going to every house where you sold a bottle of that concoction and buy it all back.

JOHN (*dismayed*). But it's a dollar a bottle!

FATHER. I don't care how much it is. How many bottles did you sell?

JOHN. A hundred and twenty-eight.

FATHER (*roaring*). A hundred and twenty-eight!

VINNIE. Clare, I always told you John would make a good business man.

FATHER (*calmly*). Young man, I'll give you the money to buy it back—a hundred and twenty-eight dollars. And ten more for Mrs. Sprague. That's a hundred and thirty-eight dollars. But it's coming out of your allowance! That means you'll not get another penny until that hundred and thirty-eight dollars is all paid up. (JOHN *starts toward the hall, counting on his fingers, then turns and addresses his father in dismay.*)

JOHN. I'll be twenty-one years old! (FATHER *glares at him.* JOHN *turns and goes on up the stairs, with the bags.*)

VINNIE (*persuasively*). Clare, you know you've always encouraged the boys to earn their own money.

FATHER. Vinnie, I'll handle this. (*There is a pause. He buries himself in his newspaper.*)

CORA (*breaking through the constraint*). Of course, Aunt Judith sent her love to all of you—

VINNIE. I haven't seen Judith for years. You'd think living so close to

Springfield—maybe I could run up there before the summer's over.

CORA. Oh, she'll be leaving for Pleasantville any day now. Grandpa Ebbetts has been failing very fast and that's why I have to hurry back.

VINNIE. Hurry back? Well, you and Mary can stay with us a few days at least.

CORA. No, I hate to break the news to you, Vinnie, but we can't even stay overnight. We're leaving on the five o'clock train this afternoon.

VINNIE (*disappointed*). Oh, what a pity! (FATHER *lowers the paper.*)

FATHER (*heartily*). Well, Cora, it certainly is good to see you again. (*To* MARY) Young lady, I think you've been enjoying yourself—you look prettier than ever. (MARY *laughs and blushes.*)

WHITNEY. I'll bet Clarence will think so.
(*The doorbell rings.* MAGGIE *crosses to answer it.*)

FATHER. That can't be another special delivery for Clarence. (*To* MARY, *slyly*) While you were in Springfield our postman was kept pretty busy. Sure you girls don't want any breakfast?

MARY. No, thank you. (*Rises and goes to the arch and stands looking upstairs, watching for* CLARENCE.)

CORA. Oh, no, thank you, Cousin Clare, we've had our breakfast.

FATHER. At least you ought to have a cup of coffee with us. Vinnie, you might have thought to order some coffee for the girls.

CORA. No, no, thank you, Cousin Clare. (MAGGIE *appears again in the arch.*)

MAGGIE. It's the cab, ma'am. (*Exits.*)

FATHER. The cab! What cab?

VINNIE. The cab that's to take us to Audubon.

FATHER. Who's going to Audubon?

VINNIE. We all are. Cora, the most wonderful thing has happened!

CORA. What, Cousin Vinnie?

VINNIE (*happily*). Clare's going to be baptized this morning.

FATHER (*not believing his ears*). Vinnie—what are you saying?

VINNIE (*with determination*). I'm saying you're going to be baptized this morning!

FATHER. I am not going to be baptized this morning or any other morning!

VINNIE. You promised yesterday that as soon as I sent that pug dog back you'd be baptized.

FATHER. I promised no such thing!

VINNIE. You certainly did!

FATHER. I never said anything remotely like that!

VINNIE. Clarence was right here and heard it. You ask him!

FATHER. Clarence be damned! I know what I said! I don't remember exactly, but it wasn't that!

VINNIE. Well, I remember. That's why I ordered the cab!

FATHER (*suddenly remembering*). The cab! Oh, my God, that cab! (*He rises and glares out the window at the cab, then turns back and speaks peremptorily*) Vinnie! You send that right back!

VINNIE. I'll do nothing of the kind. I'm going to see that you get to Heaven.

FATHER. I can't go to Heaven in a cab!

VINNIE. Well, you can start in a cab! I'm not sure whether they'll ever let you into Heaven or not, but I know they won't unless you're baptized.

FATHER. They can't keep me out of Heaven on a technicality.

VINNIE. Clare, stop quibbling! You might as well face it—you've got to make your peace with God.

FATHER. I never had any trouble with God until you stirred Him up! (MARY *is tired of waiting for* CLARENCE *and chooses this moment to interrupt.*)

MARY. Mrs. Day?
(VINNIE *answers her quickly, as if expecting* MARY *to supply her with an added argument.*)

VINNIE. Yes, Mary?

MARY. Where do you suppose Clarence is?

FATHER. You keep out of this, young lady! If it hadn't been for you, no one would have known whether I was baptized or not. (MARY *breaks into tears*) Damn! Damnation!

VINNIE. Harlan! Whitney! Get your Sunday hats. (*Calls upstairs*) John! Clarence!
(HARLAN *and* WHITNEY *start out, but stop as* FATHER *speaks.*)

FATHER (*blazing with new fire*). Vinnie, are you mad? Was it your plan that my own children should witness this indignity?

VINNIE. Why, Clare, they'll be proud of you!

FATHER. I suppose Harlan is to be my godfather! (*With determination*) Vinnie, it's no use. I can't go through with this thing and I won't. That's final.

VINNIE. Why, Clare dear, if you feel that way about it—

FATHER. I do!

VINNIE. —the children don't have to go.
(JOHN *enters.*)

JOHN. Yes, Mother?
(FATHER *sees* JOHN *and an avenue of escape opens up.*)

FATHER. Oh, John! Vinnie, I can't do anything like that this morning. I've got to take John down to the office and give him the money to buy back that medicine. (*To* JOHN) When I think of you going around this town selling dog medicine!—

JOHN (*insistently*). It wasn't dog medicine, Father.

FATHER. John, we're starting downtown this minute!

VINNIE. You're doing no such thing! You gave me your Sacred Promise that day I almost died—

JOHN. Yes, and she would have died if we hadn't given her some of that medicine. That proves it's good medicine!

FATHER (*aghast*). You gave your mother some of that dog medicine!

VINNIE. Oh, no, John, you didn't! (*Sinks weakly into the chair below the fireplace.*)

JOHN. Yes, we did, Mother. We put some in your tea that morning.

FATHER. You did what? Without her knowing it? Do you realize you might have killed your mother? You did kill Mrs. Sprague's dog. (*After a solemn pause*) John, you've done a very serious thing. I'll have to give considerable thought as to how you're going to be punished for this.

VINNIE. But, Clare—

FATHER. No, Vinnie. When I think of that day—with the house full of doctors—why, Cora, we even sent for the minister. Why, we might have lost you! (*He goes to* VINNIE, *really moved, and puts his hand on her shoulder*) It's all right now, Vinnie, thank God. You're well again. But what I went through that afternoon —the way I felt—I'll never forget it.

VINNIE. Don't talk that way, Clare. You've forgotten it already.

FATHER. What do you mean?

VINNIE. That was the day you gave me your Sacred Promise.

FATHER. But I wouldn't have promised if I hadn't thought you were dying—and you wouldn't have almost died if John hadn't given you that medicine. Don't you see? The whole thing's illegal!

VINNIE. Suppose I had died! It wouldn't make any difference to you. You don't care whether we meet in Heaven or not—you don't care whether you ever see me and the children again. (*She almost succeeds in crying.* HARLAN *and* WHITNEY *go to her in sympathy, putting their arms around her.*)

FATHER (*distressed*). Now, Vinnie, you're not being fair to me.

VINNIE. It's all right, Clare. If you don't love us enough there's nothing we can do about it.
(*Hurt,* FATHER *walks away to the other side of the room.*)

FATHER. That's got nothing to do with it! I love my family as much as any man. There's nothing within reason I wouldn't do for you, and you know it! All these years I've struggled and worked just to prove— (*He has reached the window and looks out*) There's that damn cab! Vinnie, you're not well enough to go all the way up to Audubon.

VINNIE (*perkily*). I'm well enough if we ride.

FATHER. But that trip would take all morning. And those cabs cost a dollar an hour.

VINNIE (*with smug complacence*). That's one of their best cabs. That costs two dollars an hour.

(FATHER *stares at her a second, horrified—then explodes.*)

FATHER. Then why aren't you ready? Get your hat on! Damn! Damnation! Amen! (*Exits for his hat and stick.* VINNIE *is stunned for a moment by this sudden surrender, then hastily puts on her bonnet.*)

WHITNEY. Let's watch them start! Come on, Cousin Cora, let's watch them start!

CORA. I wouldn't miss it!
(WHITNEY, HARLAN, *and* CORA *hurry out.* VINNIE *starts, but* JOHN *stops her in the arch.*)

JOHN (*contritely*). Mother, I didn't mean to almost kill you.

VINNIE. Now, don't you worry about what your father said. (*Tenderly*) It's all right, dear. (*She kisses him*) It worked out fine! (*She exits.* JOHN *looks upstairs, then at* MARY, *who has gone to the window.*)

JOHN. Mary! Here comes Clarence!
(JOHN *exits.* MARY *sits in* FATHER'S *chair.* CLARENCE *comes down the stairs in his new suit. He goes into the room and right to* MARY. *Without saying a word he kneels in front of her. They both are starry-eyed.* FATHER, *with hat and stick, comes into the arch on his way out. He sees* CLARENCE *kneeling at* MARY'S *feet.*)

FATHER. *Oh, God!*
(CLARENCE *springs up in embarrassment.* VINNIE *re-enters hurriedly.*)

VINNIE. What's the matter? What's wrong?

CLARENCE. Nothing's wrong, Mother — (*Then, for want of something to say*) Going to the office, Father?

FATHER. No! I'm going to be baptized, damn it! (*He slams his hat on angrily and stalks out.* VINNIE *gives a triumphant nod and follows him. The curtain starts down, and as it falls,* CLARENCE *again kneels at* MARY'S *feet.*)

CURTAIN